IF FOUND, please notify and arrange return to owner. This text is important for the owner's preparation for the Uniform Certified Public Accountant Examination.

Name of CPA Candidate _____

Address _____

City, State, Zip _____

Telephone ( ) _____

Additional texts are available from John Wiley and Sons, Inc.

and your local book store.

Order information and form at the back of the book.

This is

Volume II, Problems and Solutions, which is a collection of 2,149 selected objective questions and 196 essay questions and practice problems from recent CPA examinations (including substantially all of the objective questions from the November 1980 exam and May 1981 exam). The questions and problems are organized by topic, e.g., cost, quantitative taxes, etc. paralleling the organization of Volume I. The text contains one-paragraph explanations for each objective question; a solution guide and the AICPA Unofficial Answer for each practice problem; and an essay answer outline and AICPA Unofficial Answer for each essay question. A complete sample examination is included for each of the four parts of the CPA examination.

Also available:

Volume I, Outlines and Study Guides, containing comprehensive outlines of the topics tested on all four sections of the CPA examination. The text consists entirely of review materials including detailed outlines of AICPA pronouncements, e.g., ARBs, APBs, and SASs, as well as FASB pronouncements. Two-way tabulation of the content of 1977 to date examinations provides a detailed topical index of questions and problems available for solution and review. The text also emphasizes "how to answer questions" and "how to take the examination." AICPA grading procedures are explained, including the implications for answering CPA questions and problems. Additionally, explanation and step-by-step examples of the SOLUTIONS APPROACH for practice problems, essay questions, and objective questions are presented.

CPA

EXAMINATION REVIEW

VOLUME II
PROBLEMS and SOLUTIONS

8th EDITION

Irvin N. Gleim, Ph.D., CPA
University of Florida
Gainesville, Florida

&

Patrick R. Delaney, Ph.D., CPA
Northern Illinois University
DeKalb, Illinois

JOHN WILEY & SONS

New York   Chichester   Brisbane   Toronto

Library of Congress Cataloging in Publication Data

Gleim, Irvin N.
  CPA examination review,

  Includes Index.
  Contents: v. 1. Outlines and study guides -- 2.
Problems and solutions.
  1. Accounting--Examinations, questions, etc.
2. Auditing--Examinations, questions, etc. I. Delaney, Patrick R. II. Title.
HF5661.G44 1981   657'.076   81-4488
ISBN 0-471-08905-2 (v. 1)   AACR2
ISBN 0-471-08903-6 (v. 2)

10 9 8 7 6 5 4 3 2 1

PREFACE

The first purpose of Volume II is to provide CPA candidates with recent examination problems organized by topic, e.g., internal control, consolidations, secured transactions, etc. This text includes over 2,100 objective questions (largely 1977 to date). Objective questions are an effective means of studying the material tested on the exam (in contrast to studying the solutions approach). It is also necessary, however, to work with practice problems and essay questions to develop the solutions approach (the ability to solve CPA essay questions and practice problems efficiently).

The second objective of this volume is to explain the AICPA unofficial answers to the examination problems included in this text. The AICPA publishes past CPA examinations and unofficial answers. No explanation is made, however, of the procedures that should have been applied to the examinations problem to obtain the unofficial answers. Relatedly, the unofficial answers to objective questions provide no justification and/or explanation. This text provides explanations of both how to work problems and the unofficial answers to objective questions.

This text is designed to be used in conjunction with Volume I, Outlines and Study Guides. The coverage of topics is in the same sequence as Volume I. Each chapter (and each module within chapters) is a self-contained unit of

1. Objective questions.
2. Practice problems and essay questions.
3. Unofficial answers with explanations for objective questions.
4. Unoffical answers prefaced by answer outlines for essay questions.
5. Unoffical answers prefaced by solution guides for practice problems.

All of the objective questions from the November 1980 and May 1981 examinations have been added to this Eighth Edition. Also many of the essay questions/practice problems from both 1980 exams are included. As new questions and problems are added, older problems are deleted. New problems are not added just for the sake of change. Rather, new problems included in the book emphasize more current topics, pronouncements, etc. New problems also illustrate the most current type and format of problems being used on the examination. The Board of Examiners, their philosophy, and most important, the AICPA examination staff change result in changing types and format of questions and problems.

A Sample Examination for each of the four parts of the exam is included in Appendix A at the end of this volume. The questions and problems for these exams were selected on the basis of a statistical analysis of the last four exams.

In this edition we are including three problems from Kieso and Weygandt, Intermediate Accounting, Third Edition, John Wiley & Sons, Inc. These problems identified by box margin, deal with topics which have not been tested subsequent to the issuance of pronouncements dealing with these topics.

Please carefully read Chapter One "How to Use This Book."

Good Luck on the Exam,

Irvin N. Gleim
Patrick R. Delaney
May 15, 1981

Acknowledgements

The authors are indebted to the American Institute of Certified Public Accountants, Inc. for permission to reproduce unofficial CPA Examination Questions and Answers copyright c 1969, 1971, 1972, 1973, 1974, 1975, 1976, 1977, 1978, 1979, 1980, and 1981. Those which have been adapted are so identified.

Writing an annualized text is always a publishing event and a rejuvenating human experience. The authors are most grateful to the many users of previous editions, both instructors and students who have so generously shared with us their satisfaction with our work and their suggestions for changes and improvements. We hope that this will continue for we have benefited from those communications.

This work continues to be a "community effort." In addition to those colleagues cited as contributors above, we would like to acknowledge and thank those many friends who gave us so many devoted hours to bring this 8th annualized edition to you so quickly after the May 1981 Examination: H. Terri Androff, Duane Abrath, Mary Ann Babich, Elaine Dessouki, Jeanne DeVore, Sandy Donnelly, Patricia L. Finn, Steven E. Garland, Mary Gephart, Patrick Gilliland, Tayea Gilliland, F. Martin Glynn, Gary Hazelton, John Hepp, Christine M. Howard, Debbie Huning, Barbara Huseman, Cooky Ikeler, Mary K. Jester, Kay Kipilo, Paula Krueger, Patricia M. Lambert, Paula A. Lezak, Peter H. London, Rebecca London, Pam Miller, G. Scott Morris, Marcy Secor, Michael Simmons, Les Simms, Laura Spehr, Paul Sullivan, Brian Thornquist, Karen Turnbull, and Karla Tylor.

A special thanks is due to Kevin Williams who skillfully directed the many activities which are an integral part of the timely completion of an annualized version.

ABOUT THE STUDENT CONTRIBUTORS*

Robert H. Barnes, B.S., is a candidate for the MAS degree. Mr. Barnes drafted answer explanations for multiple choice questions in Financial Accounting.

Curtis A. Danekas, B.S., CPA, is a candidate for the MAS degree. He has accepted employment with Ernst & Whinney. Mr. Danekas drafted answer explanations for multiple choice questions in Financial Accounting.

Beverly Hathaway, B.S., CPA, is employed by Peat, Marwick Mitchell & Co. Ms. Hathaway drafted answer explanations for multiple choice questions in Business Law.

Margaret C. Monat, B.S., CPA, is a candidate for the MAS degree. She is employed by Price Waterhouse & Co. Ms. Monat drafted answer explanations for multiple choice questions in Business Law.

Richard Pembrook, B.S., CPA, is a candidate for the MAS degree. Mr. Pembrook drafted answer explanations for multiple choice questions in Business Law.

Paul Sorenson, B.S., is employed by Price Waterhouse & Co. Mr. Sorenson drafted answer explanations for multiple choice questions in Business Law.

Kevin Williams, MAS, CPA, is employed by Price Waterhouse & Co. Mr. Williams drafted answer explanations for multiple choice questions in Income Taxes.

*All students at Northern Illinois University.

ABOUT THE AUTHORS

Irvin N. Gleim is Professor of Accounting at the University of Florida. He received his PhD in Accountancy from the University of Illinois. He is a member of the American Institute of Certified Public Accountants, Florida Institute of Certified Public Accountants, American Accounting Association, American Business Law Association, Institute of Internal Auditors, Institute of Management Accounting, and National Association of Accountants. He has published professional articles in the Journal of Accountancy, the Accounting Review, and The American Business Law Journal. He has developed and taught both proprietary and university CPA review courses. He is author of CIA EXAMINATION REVIEW and CMA EXAMINATION REVIEW, both published by Accounting Publications, Inc.

Patrick R. Delaney is Chair and Associate Professor of Accountancy at Northern Illinois University. He received his PhD in Accountancy from the University of Illinois. He is past president of the Rockford Chapter, National Association of Accountants, is currently vice chairperson of the Illinois CPA Society's Accounting Principles Committee, has served on several other professional committees, and is a member of both the American Accounting Association and the American Institute of CPAs. Professor Delaney has published in The Accounting Review and is a recipient of NIU's Excellence in Teaching Award. He has been involved in NIU's CPA Review Course as director and instructor and has served as an instructor of NASBA's Critique Program.

ABOUT THE FACULTY CONTRIBUTORS

John C. Borke, MAS, CPA, is Assistant Professor of Accounting at the University of Wisconsin-Platteville. He has worked as a staff auditor with Peat, Marwick Mitchell & Company. Professor Borke prepared multiple choice answer explanations and solution guides for the practice problems in Financial Accounting. He also updated the problem material in the Inflation module.

Martin A. Bubley, MBA, CPA, is an Instructor of Accountancy at Northern Illinois University. Mr. Bubley developed a system for categorizing the multiple choice questions.

Edward C. Foth, PhD, CPA, is an Associate Professor and Administrator of the Master of Science in Taxation Program at DePaul University. He has public accounting experience with Arthur Andersen & Co. and teaches in their Basic and Intermediate U.S. Tax Schools. Professor Foth prepared the answer explanations to the multiple choice questions in income taxes and selected the problem material in that area. Professor Foth also selected the problem material in Chapter 8, and modified items in need of change to reflect revisions in the tax law.

Michael Griffin, MAS, CMA, CPA, formerly an Instructor of Accountancy at Northern Illinois University, is employed as a staff accountant by McDonald's Corporation. Mr. Griffin drafted answer explanations for multiple choice questions in income taxes and cost accounting.

Kurt Pany, PhD, CPA is an Associate Professor of Accounting at Arizona State University. He is a member of the American Institute of Certified Public Accountants and the American Accounting Association. Prior to entering academia he worked as a staff auditor for Touche-Ross & Co. Professor Pany prepared the answer explanations for the multiple choice questions and selected the problem material in Chapter 2.

John R. Simon, PhD, CPA, is Associate Professor of Accountancy at Northern Illinois University. He has been a consultant for numerous accounting textbooks and is presently a co-author of an accounting principles supplement, Even Accounting Has Principles, with Richard Lillie. He has taught in NIU's CPA Review Course in each of the last five years. Professor Simon selected and updated the problem material in Chapter 12.

Harold Wright, JD, is Coordinator and Assistant Professor of Business Law at Northern Illinois University. He has taught in NIU's CPA Review Course for the past seven years and has served as an instructor of NASBA's Critique Program. Professor Wright prepared the answer explanations for the multiple choice questions, selected the problem material in Chapter 3, and revised the problem material in need of change to reflect the most recent law.

CHAPTER OUTLINE

CHAPTER ONE

HOW TO USE THIS BOOK

This volume is a collection of recent CPA questions, unofficial answers, answer outlines, solutions guides, and explanations of objective question answers. Note that each chapter or subsection thereof is a self contained unit of

1. Objective questions.
2. Practice problems and essay questions.
3. Unofficial answers with explanations for objective questions.
4. Unofficial answers prefaced by answer outlines for essay questions.
5. Unofficial answers prefaced by solution guides for practice problems.

Also included at the end of this volume is a complete sample CPA examination. It is included to enable candidates to gain experience in taking a "realistic" exam. While studying the modules, the candidate can become accustomed to concentrating on fairly narrow topics. By working through the sample examination near the end of their study program, the candidate will be better prepared for taking the actual examination.

The text is designed and organized to be used in conjunction with Volume I CPA EXAMINATION REVIEW: OUTLINES AND STUDY GUIDES, but may be used with or without any other study source. The chapters and modules within this Volume coincide with the chapters and modules in Volume I.

OUTLINE OF VOLUME II

Module Number	Module Title	Tabulation Abbreviation	Vol. II Page
	Auditing (See Vol. I Chapter 5)		
1	Professional Ethics	ETHI	15
2	Internal Control	IC	46
3	Audit Evidence	EVID	81
4	Audit Reports	REP	134
5	Statistical Sampling	SS	170
6	Auditing EDP	EDP	183
	Business Law (See Vol. 1 Chapter 6)		
7	Contracts	CONT	210
8	Sales	SALE	229
9	Negotiable Instruments	NEGO	246
10	Secured Transactions	SECU	251
11	Bankruptcy	BANK	275
12	Suretyship	SURE	285
13	Agency	AGEN	298

Before you begin working recent CPA problems in this volume, scan through the book and note the chapter organization. Also become familiar with the order of modules in each chapter.

Objective Questions

The objective questions, answers, and explanations to answers can be used in many ways. First, they may be used as a diagnostic evaluation of your knowledge. For example, before beginning to review statistical sampling, you may wish to answer 20 to 30 multiple choice questions to determine your ability to answer CPA questions on statistical sampling. The apparent difficulty of the questions and the correctness of your answers will allow you to determine the necessary breadth and depth of your review. Additionally, exposure to examination questions prior to review and study of the material should provide motivation. You will develop a feel for your level of proficiency and an understanding of the scope and difficulty of past examination questions. Moreover, your review materials will explain concepts encountered in the diagnostic objective questions.

Second, the objective questions can be used as a post-study or post-review evaluation. You should attempt to understand all concepts mentioned (even in incorrect answers) as you answer the questions. In a quantitative methods question, for example, you may know that "regression analysis" is the correct answer, but not be familiar with the alternative answer, "queuing theory." Refer to the explanation of the answer for discussion of alternatives even though you selected the correct response. Thus, unless you completely understand the question and all of the alternative answers, you should read the explanation of the unofficial answer.

Third, you may wish to use the objective questions as a primary study vehicle. This is probably the quickest but least thorough approach. Make a sincere effort to understand the problem and to select the correct reply before referring to the unofficial answer and explanation. In many cases, the explanations will appear inadequate because of your unfamiliarity with the topic. Always refer back to an appropriate study source, such as Volume I, your undergraduate textbooks, AICPA pronouncements, etc.

The objective questions outnumber the essay questions/practice problems by greater than 10 to 1 in this book. This is similar to a typical CPA exam. The May, 1981 exam contained:

	Objective	Essay/ Practice
Auditing	60	4
Business Law	60	4
Practice I	60	2
Practice II	60	2
Theory	60	4
Totals	300	16

The numbers are somewhat misleading in that many essay questions/practice problems contain multiple (and often unrelated) parts.

One difficulty with so many objective questions is that, first, you may overemphasize them. Candidates generally prefer to work objective questions because they are

1. Shorter
2. Require less solution effort
3. Allow educated guessing
4. Are less frustrating than essay questions and practice problems

The over emphasis of objective questions results in an under emphasis of essay questions/practice problems. Remember working essay questions/practice problems from start to finish is just as important as working objective questions.

Another difficulty with the large number of objective questions is that you may tend to become over familiar with the questions. The result may be that you may begin reading the facts and assumptions of previously-studied objective questions into the objective questions on your examination. Guard against this potential problem by reading each objective question with extra care. Ask yourself the following as you work objective question:

1. How is it different (not alike) from previously encountered questions?
2. Where is the catch?
3. What phrase or word could change my interpretation of the question?
4. What assumptions am I making?
5. Did I make a computational or clerical error in my solution?

Although not as critical as for essay questions and practice problems, the solutions approach is relevant to objective questions. The solutions approach is a systematic problem solving methodology. The solutions approach for objective questions consists of the following steps:

1. Analyze the grading explanation, noting any penalty for incorrect answers.
2. Work individual questions in order.
    a. If a question or set of questions appear unduly lengthy or difficult, skip the question(s) until it is evident extra time is available. Put a big question mark in the margin to remind you to return to questions you have skipped or need to review.

3. Cover the answers before reading each question.

   a. The answers are frequently ambiguous in nature which may cause you to misread or misinterpret the question.

4. Read each question carefully.

   a. Study the requirements first so you know what data is important.

   b. If a set of data is the basis for two or more questions, read the requirements of each of the questions before beginning to work the first question (sometimes it is more efficient to work the questions out of order or simultaneously).

5. Anticipate the answer, before looking at the alternative answers.

6. Read the answers and select the <u>best</u> alternative.

7. Mark the correct (or best guess) answer on your examination.

8. After completing all of the individual questions in an overall question, transfer the answers to the machine gradeable answer sheet with extreme care.

   a. Be careful not to fall out of sequence with the answer sheet, because then most of your answers will be wrong.

Your objective question solutions approach should be adjusted to the grading procedure as specified in the instructions to the question (see Chapter 2 of Volume I). If your grade is based on total correct answers, answer all questions to the best of your ability. On the other hand, if there is a penalty for incorrect answers (as there was in Law until November, 1973), you should consider the payoff of omitting some answers.

<u>Essay Questions</u>

Essay questions (in contrast to practice problems) appear on the auditing, business law, and theory sections of the examination. Knowledge of material tested is necessary (but not sufficient) to answer essay questions. Also required is an essay question solutions approach. Even though a candidate knows the material, he or she <u>may not be able to develop a solution to satisfy the grader</u>. You have to practice your solutions approach on past CPA exam essay questions before you sit for the examination. Refer to Chapter 3 of Volume I for extended discussion of the solutions approach. The solutions approach to essay questions consists of the following steps.

1. <u>Glance over the problem</u>. Only scan the problem. Do not read it. Get a feel for the type or category of problem. Before you understand the requirements you cannot discriminate important data from irrelevant data.

2. <u>Study the requirements</u>. "Study" as differentiated from "read." Candidates continually lose points due to misunderstanding the requirements. Underline key phrases and words.

2a. <u>Visualize the solutions format</u>. From the outline and the content of the requirements, determine the expected format of the required solution. Develop an awareness of "schedule and statement format." Put headings on the required statements and schedules.

Often a single requirement will require two or more statements, schedules, etc. A common example is a question followed by "why." Explicitly recognize multiple requirements by numbering or lettering them.

3. <u>Outline the required procedures mentally</u>. Explicitly interrelate the data within the text of the problem to the expected solution format, mentally noting a "to do" list. Determine what it is you are going to do before you get started doing it.

3a. <u>Review applicable principles, knowledge</u>. Before immersing yourself in the details of the problem, quickly (30-60 seconds) review and organize the principles and your knowledge applicable to the problem. Otherwise the details of the problem will confuse and overshadow your previous knowledge of the applicable principles.

4. <u>Study the text of the problem</u>. Read the problem carefully. With the requirements in mind, you now can begin to sort out relevant from irrelevant data. Underline and circle important data. Use a wild-colored pen to mark up your problem. Heavy colored underlining and comments are attention getting and give you confidence.

4a. <u>Prepare a key word outline</u>. Jot down a list of key words (grading concepts) in the margin of the examination. The proximity of the key words to the text of the problem will be more efficient than making notes on a separate sheet of paper which may be misplaced.

4b. <u>Organize the key words into a solution outline</u>. After you have noted all of the grading concepts which bear on the requirements, reorganize the outline for the entire answer. Make sure that you respond to each requirement and do not preempt answers to other requirements.

5. <u>Prepare the solution</u>. You now are in a position to write a neat, complete, organized, labeled solution.

6. <u>Proofread and edit</u>. Do not underestimate the utility of this step. Just recall all of the "silly" mistakes you made on undergraduate examinations. Corrections of errors and completion of oversights during this step can easily be the difference between passing and failing.

7. <u>Review later</u>, time permitting.

The essay questions and unofficial answers may also be used for study purposes without preparation of answers. Before turning to the unofficial answer, study the problem and outline the solution (either mentally or in the margin of the book). As you read the unofficial answers, underline key word and phrases.

Example of Essay Answer Underlining

<u>Problem 1</u>   Review of Internal Control

a.   The objectives of a CPA's review of internal control for an opinion audit are to determine the <u>reliability of the accounting records</u> and from this the <u>extent of the tests to which auditing procedures may be restricted</u>, and to obtain evidence that the <u>financial statements are fairly presented</u>.

It is <u>not possible for a CPA to verify all</u>, or even a major portion, of the large number of transactions comprising a year's operations for most enterprises. In order that he make the most effective and searching investigation possible within practical time limits, he must determine whether the internal controls in force are sufficient to insure the integrity of the accounts. The <u>evaluation of internal control will govern the extent of test checking</u> and will designate those areas requiring the most intensive examination.

The CPA reviews internal control also to assist in evaluating the fairness of the financial statements. Even if the CPA examined all available audit evidence, such an examination would not be conclusive concerning the fair presentation of the financial statements because: (1) <u>transactions may have been omitted</u> from the records, (2) recorded transactions may have been supported by <u>forged documents</u>, or (3) <u>imitation materials</u> may have been substituted for genuine articles. Thus, the CPA relies upon the review of internal control to <u>support the propriety of matters for which evidence is not examined</u> as well as to enhance the reliability of evidence actually examined. Finally, the evaluation of internal control assists the auditor in preparing his <u>letter of recommendations to management</u>.

b.   1.   One advantage of the internal control questionnaire to a CPA is the <u>facility with which it can be completed</u>. If the questions have been predetermined, as is usual, the auditor's responsibility includes the completion of the questionnaire with <u>yes-or-no answers</u>, and written explanations are required only for the "no" or unfavorable answers. Another advantage is that better <u>assurance of complete coverage</u> is provided by the comprehensive list of questions. The questionnaire minimizes the possibility of overlooking important aspects of internal control.

2.   An advantage to the CPA of the memorandum approach in reviewing internal control is that the memorandum is de-signed to explain the precise controls applicable to each examination. In this sense, the memorandum tends to be <u>tailor-made for each engagement</u> and thus offers flexibility in its design and application. A second advantage is that its preparation normally <u>requires a penetrating analysis of the client's system</u> of checks and balances. In requiring a written description of the flow of transactions, records maintained, and the division of responsibilities, the memorandum method minimizes the tendency to perform a perfunctory review.

3.   The use of a flow chart in the study of internal control offers the advantage of a <u>graphic presentation of a system</u> or a series of sequential processes. It shows the steps required and the flow of form or other documents from person to person in carrying out the function depicted. Thus, the <u>tendency to overlook the controls</u> existing between functions or departments is minimized. Another advantage is that the flow chart method <u>avoids the detailed study of written descriptions</u> and procedures without sacrificing the CPA's ability to appraise the effectiveness of internal controls under review. The use of a flow chart is <u>particularly useful</u> in the evaluation of electronic data processing systems.

c.   Even though he may be satisfied that no material weaknesses in the client's internal control system exist, the <u>CPA is required to test transactions</u>. Testing transactions provides <u>direct support for financial statement</u> presentation and is also a means of determining the <u>reliability of the system of internal control</u>.

Control devices are <u>fallible</u>. Even the best of control systems cannot eliminate the <u>possibility of unintentional irregularities</u> resulting from temporary system breakdowns. In addition, there are certain types of actions affecting the reliability of reported data that are <u>not subject to the enterprise control</u> process. Examples include <u>deliberate management irregularities</u>, <u>policy errors by management</u>, and <u>deviations arising from collusion</u>. Through a test of transactions the CPA obtains reasonable assurance that the internal control procedures are in use and are operating as planned, and he may detect material errors of types not susceptible to effective internal control. In addition, such testing enables the CPA to <u>comply with the third standard of field work</u> which calls for obtaining sufficient competent evidential matter to provide a reasonable basis for an opinion.

The underlining should reinforce your study of the answer content and also assist you in learning how to structure your solutions. On the next page, the unofficial answer to an auditing internal control question is underlined to illustrate the technique.

Answer outlines rather than solution guides are provided for essay questions. Preceding each unofficial answer of auditing, business law, and theory essay questions is an outline of the major concepts in the unofficial answer. This will facilitate your study of essay questions.

Finally, recognize that the AICPA does not accept key word outline solutions. The AICPA expects the grading concepts to be explained (integrated) into concise, clear sentences.   The sentence and paragraph format, however, can be organized in outline form per the requirements (as illustrated by the unofficial answer format).

Practice Problems

The solutions approach to practice problems is more critical than for objective and essay questions. Many candidates have trouble with practice due to their inability to "put a handle on" or "gain control of" practice problems. Without an efficient solutions approach, it is easy to spin your wheels and/or be overwhelmed by most practice problems.

To develop a solutions approach for practice problems, you have to work problems from start to finish under examination conditions. Note that the solutions approach for practice problems is almost the same as that for essay questions. The major difference lies in step 4a, the most crucial step for practice problems. Additionally, you should head up required schedules and statements in step 2a and label your solutions in step 5; these will help you organize your solution procedures.

1. Glance over the problem.
2. Study the requirements.
2a. Visualize the solution format (including statement and schedule layout).
3. Outline the required procedures mentally.
3a. Review applicable principles, knowledge.
4. Study the text of the problem.
4a. Prepare intermediary solutions as you study the problem, e.g., calculate goodwill, reconstruct accounts, prepare time diagrams, etc. You will be able to perceive these required intermediary solutions because you already understand the problem requirements. These intermediary

solutions, underlining, and notes in the text of the problem will drastically decrease time spent rereading.

5. Prepare the solution. You now are in a position to write a neat, complete, organized, labeled solution. Label computations, intermediary solutions, assumptions made, etc., on your scratch sheets and turn them in with your solution. (NOTE: but not for objective questions).

6. Proofread and edit.

7. Review later, time permitting.

Little benefit will accrue from consulting the solution guides and unofficial answers before substantially completing the problems. You may use the objective and essay questions, but not the practice problems, to study the material tested, i.e., glancing over the problems, solution guides, and unofficial answers. Misuse of the practice problems by consulting solution guides and unofficial answers prior to substantial completion of solutions will result in unwarranted confidence in your problem-solving ability.

Diagnose Your Weaknesses Prior to the Exam

This volume of problems and solutions provides you with an opportunity to diagnose and correct any exam preparation or exam-taking weaknesses prior to your taking the examination. Rather than perform a post-mortem of your techniques upon failure of the CPA exam, continuously analyze your incorrect problem solutions to determine the cause of the error(s) during preparation for the exam. Treat each incorrect solution as a mistake that will not be repeated (especially on the examination). Also attempt to generalize your weaknesses so that you may change, reinforce, or develop new approaches to exam preparation and exam taking. General categories of candidates' weaknesses include:

1. Failure to understand the requirements.

2. Failure to read the problem.

3. Lack of knowledge of material tested.

4. Inability to apply the solutions approach.

5. Sloppiness, computational errors, etc.

6. Failure to proofread and edit.

7. Failure to implement an examination strategy, e.g., time budgeting, etc.

All of the objective questions appearing on both the November 1980 and the May 1981 examinations have been added to this Eighth Edition. Many of the essay questions/practice problems from both 1980 exams have also been added. Problems deleted were generally older and repetitive problems. The objective is to produce a mixture of problems representative of recent exams and the expectations of future examinations. Some past objective examination questions have been modified to reflect recent changes in law or practice. These are identified by an [†]. The schedule on the next page provides an index to the new problems.

==

NOW IS THE TIME
TO MAKE A COMMITMENT

==

CHAPTER TWO

AUDITING PROBLEMS AND SOLUTIONS

Auditing is tested on Thursday morning from 8:30 to 12:00. The exam traditionally includes 60 multiple choice questions (60% of the auditing grade) and 4 essay questions (each 10% of the auditing grade).

All six categories of auditing questions will probably appear on your exam with slightly heavier emphasis on audit evidence and audit reports. Observe the frequency of occurrence of each topic on the frequency tabulation presented on page 14.

Each question is coded as to month-year, section, problem number, and objective question number. For example, (579, A1, 31) indicates May 1979, audit problem 1, and question number 31. The objective question number is omitted from essay question codes, e.g., (579, A6).

AUDITING PROBLEMS INDEX

	Exam Reference	Number Minutes	Problem Page No.	Answer Page No.
Audit Evidence (EVID)				
114 Multiple Choice				
1. Evidence for Limited Review	1179, A3	15-25	94	117
2. Payroll Input Verification and Examination Procedures	1180, A5	15-25	94	118
3. Procedures for Loss Contingencies	579, A4	15-25	94	119
4. Cutoff Tests	1171, A3	25-30	94	120
5. Balance Sheets--Income Statements	1172, A4	25-30	95	121
6. Client Representation Letters	1172, A5	25-30	95	123
7. Audit Programs	1177, A2	15-25	96	124
8. GAO Audit Standards	1177, A4	15-30	96	125
9. Accounts Receivable Confirmations (Dodge, CPA)	577, A4	15-25	97	126
10. Toyco Bank Reconciliation	577, A5	15-30	97	127
11. Property, Plant, and Equipment	1177, A3	15-25	98	128
12. Physical Count of Securities	573, A4	25-30	99	129
13. Evidential Matter	575, A3	20-25	99	131
14. Inventory Audit Procedures	1176, A4	15-25	99	131
15. Materiality	1178, A3	15-25	100	133
Audit Reports (REP)				
74 Multiple Choice				
1. Materiality	1171, A4	25-30	145	160
2. Report Modifications (Willingham Corp.)	574, A4	20-26	145	161
3. Example Reports	574, A7	20-26	145	163
4. Assurances Given	1180, A3	15-25	146	165
5. Audit Report Deficiencies (Rancho Corp.)	1175, A4	20-25	147	166
6. Write Report (Bale and Booster)	1180, A2	15-25	147	167
7. Rewrite Report (Excelsior Corp.)	1176, A7	15-30	147	168
Statistical Sampling (SS)				
29 Multiple Choice				
1. Statistical Judgment	572, A3	25-30	174	180
2. Statistical Sampling Computations	577, A7	15-25	174	181
Auditing EDP (EDP)				
52 Multiple Choice				

		Exam Reference	Number Minutes	Problem Page No.	Answer Page No.
1.	Computerized Audit Programs	580, A3	15-25	189	199
2.	CPA Knowledge of Computers	578, A4	15-25	189	200
3.	Grandfather-Father-Son Tapes	1171, A7	25-30	189	200
4.	EDP Controls	579, A3	15-25	191	201
5.	Audit of Computerized A/R	1179, A4	15-25	191	202
	Sample Auditing Examination		150-210	1038	1076

Note Regarding References to SASs in Answer Explanations

Beginning with the November 1978 questions, the explanations refer only to the codification para number and not the SAS number. Explanations of earlier questions refer to the SAS number and not the codification number. The Eighth Edition will only contain reference to the codification number.

SAS No.	Codification No.	SAS No.	Codification No.
1*	SAS 1 para nos	20	323
2*	509	21	435
3	321	22	311
4	Superseded by SAS 24	23	318
5	411	24	Superseded by SAS 36
6	335	25	161
7*	315	26	504
8	550	27	553
9	322	28	554
10	Superseded by SAS 24	29	551
11	336	30	642
12	337	31	326
13	Superseded by SAS 24	32	431
14*	621	33*	555
15*	505	34	340
16	327	35	622
17	328	36	722
18	730	37	711
19	333	38	631
		**	350

*Partially superseded. For details, see page 219 of Volume I.

**AICPA is in the process of releasing this SAS.

FREQUENCY OF AUDITING TOPICS
APPEARING ON THE EXAM

EXAM	ETHI	IC	EVID	REP	SS	EDP
May 1977	12 MC	16 MC	21 MC 2	5 MC 1	1	6 MC
Nov 1977	10 MC	14 MC	16 MC 4	10 MC	2 MC	8 MC
May 1978	9 MC 2	12 MC	24 MC 1	11 MC	3 MC	1 MC 1
Nov 1978	7 MC 1	9 MC 1	22 MC 1	14 MC	3 MC	5 MC 1
May 1979*	11 MC	14 MC 1	20 MC 1 1/2	8 MC 1/2	2 MC	5 MC 1
Nov 1979	8 MC	10 MC 1	21 MC 2	11 MC	2 MC	8 MC 1
May 1980	6 MC 1	8 MC 1	26 MC 1	10 MC	3 MC	7 MC 1
Nov 1980	12 MC	8 MC 1	21 MC 1	11 MC 2	4 MC	4 MC
May 1981	9 MC	8 MC 1	22 MC 2	12 MC 1	3 MC	6 MC

*For example, the May 1979 exam contained 60 individual multiple choice (11 ETHI, 14 IC, 20 EVID, 8 REP, 2 SS, 5 EDP) as well as one question on internal control, one and one half questions on evidence, one half question on audit reports, and one question on electronic data processing.

NOTE: Explanation of topic abbreviations appears on page 1.

MULTIPLE CHOICE QUESTIONS (1—72)

1. When a CPA prepares a federal income tax return for an audit client, one would expect
   a. The CPA to take a position of client advocacy.
   b. The CPA to take a position of independent neutrality.
   c. The taxable net income in the audited financial statements to agree with taxable net income in the federal income tax return.
   d. The expenses in the audited financial statements to agree with the deductions in the federal income tax return.

2. Auditing interpretations, which are issued by the staff of the AICPA Auditing Standards Division in order to provide timely guidance on the application of pronouncements of the Auditing Standards Board, are
   a. Less authoritative than a pronouncement of the Auditing Standards Board.
   b. Equally authoritative as a pronouncement of the Auditing Standards Board.
   c. More authoritative than a pronouncement of the Auditing Standards Board.
   d. Nonauthoritative opinions which are issued without consulting members of the Auditing Standards Board.

3. A basic objective of a CPA firm is to provide professional services to conform with professional standards. Reasonable assurance of achieving this basic objective is provided through
   a. Continuing professional education.
   b. A system of quality control.
   c. Compliance with generally accepted reporting standards.
   d. A system of peer review.

4. Cortney has moved to a distant city but desires to continue to retain Blake, CPA, to prepare his personal federal tax return. Blake telephones Cortney after receiving his written list of information to be used in the preparation of the tax return because it appears to contain an understatement of interest expense. Based upon the conversation Blake learns that the interest expense should be double the amount indicated on the written list. Blake, who asked Cortney to send a photocopy of the supporting evidence indicating the correct amount of the interest expense, has not received the correspondence and the filing deadline is five days away. Under the circumstances Blake should
   a. Prepare the return based upon the written information received and **not** sign the preparer's declaration.
   b. Prepare the return based upon the written information received, clearly indicating that an amended return will follow.
   c. Prepare the return based upon the written and oral information received.
   d. Send Cortney a telegram indicating that no tax return will be prepared until all requested data are received.

5. According to the AICPA rules of conduct, contingent fees are permitted by CPAs engaged in tax practice because
   a. This practice establishes fees which are commensurate with the value of the services.
   b. Attorneys in tax practice customarily set contingent fees.
   c. Determinations by taxing authorities are a matter of judicial proceedings which do not involve third parties.
   d. The consequences are based upon findings of judicial proceedings or the findings of tax authorities.

6. A CPA's retention of client records as a means of enforcing payment of an overdue audit fee is an action that is
   a. **Not** addressed by the AICPA Code of Professional Ethics.
   b. Acceptable if sanctioned by the state laws.
   c. Prohibited under the AICPA rules of conduct.
   d. A violation of generally accepted auditing standards.

7. Which of the following is **not** a Management Advisory Service Practice Standard?
   a. In performing management advisory service, a practitioner must act with integrity and objectivity and be independent in mental attitude.
   b. The management advisory services engagement is to be performed by a person or persons having adequate technical training as a management consultant.
   c. Management advisory service engagements are to be performed by practitioners having competence in the analytical approach and process, and in the technical subject matter under consideration.
   d. Before undertaking a management advisory service engagement, a practitioner is to notify the client of any reservations regarding anticipated benefits.

8. Which of the following statements **best** describes the phrase "generally accepted auditing standards?"
   a. They identify the policies and procedures for the conduct of the audit.
   b. They define the nature and extent of the auditor's responsibilities.
   c. They provide guidance to the auditor with respect to planning the audit and writing the audit report.
   d. They set forth a measure of the quality of the performance of audit procedures.

9. The "generally accepted auditing standards" are standards which
   a. Are sufficiently established so that independent auditors generally agree on their existence.
   b. Are generally accepted based upon a pronouncement of the Financial Accounting Standards Board.
   c. Are generally accepted in response to the changing needs of the business community.
   d. Are generally accepted as a consequence of approval of the AICPA membership.

10. Rogers & Co., CPAs, policies require that all members of the audit staff submit weekly time reports to the audit manager, who then prepares a weekly summary work report regarding variance from budget for Rogers' review. This provides written evidence of Rogers & Co.'s professional concern regarding compliance with which of the following generally accepted auditing standards?
    a. Quality control.
    b. Due professional care.
    c. Adequate review.
    d. Adequate planning.

11. It would **not** be appropriate for the auditor to initiate discussion with the audit committee concerning
    a. The extent to which the work of internal auditors will influence the scope of the examination.
    b. Details of the procedures which the auditor intends to apply.
    c. The extent to which change in the company's organization will influence the scope of the examination.
    d. Details of potential problems which the auditor believes might cause a qualified opinion.

12. The SEC has strengthened auditor independence by requiring that management
    a. Engage auditors to report in accordance with the Foreign Corrupt Practices Act.
    b. Report the nature of disagreements with former auditors.
    c. Select auditors through audit committees.
    d. Acknowledge their responsibility for the fairness of the financial statements.

13. In accordance with the AICPA Statements On Responsibilities In Tax Practice, where a question on a federal income tax return has not been answered, the CPA should sign the preparer's declaration only if
    a. The CPA can provide reasonable support for this omission upon examination by IRS.
    b. The **information** requested is not available.
    c. The question is not applicable to the taxpayer.
    d. An explanation of the reason for the omission is provided.

14. In accordance with the AICPA Statements On Responsibilities In Tax Practice, if after having provided tax advice to a client there are legislative changes which affect the advice provided, the CPA
    a. Is obligated to notify the client of the change and the effect thereof.
    b. Is obligated to notify the client of the change and the effect thereof if the client was not advised that the advice was based on existing laws which are subject to change.
    c. Cannot be expected to notify the client of the change unless the obligation is specifically undertaken by agreement.
    d. Cannot be expected to have knowledge of the change.

15. The understanding between the client and the auditor as to the degree of responsibilities to be assumed by each are normally set forth in a (an)
    a. Representation letter.
    b. Engagement letter.
    c. Management letter.
    d. Comfort letter.

16. The concept of materiality would be least important to an auditor in determining the
    a. Transactions that should be reviewed.
    b. Need for disclosure of a particular fact or transactions.
    c. Scope of the CPA's audit program relating to various accounts.
    d. Effects of direct financial interests in the client upon the CPA's independence.

17.   A CPA establishes quality control policies and procedures for deciding whether to accept a new client or continue to perform services for a current client. The primary purpose for establishing such policies and procedures is

   a.   To enable the auditor to attest to the integrity or reliability of a client.

   b.   To comply with the quality control standards established by regulatory bodies.

   c.   To minimize the likelihood of association with clients whose managements lack integrity.

   d.   To lessen the exposure to litigation resulting from failure to detect irregularities in client financial statements.

18.   Operational audits generally have been conducted by internal auditors and governmental audit agencies but may be performed by certified public accountants. A primary purpose of an operational audit is to provide

   a.   A means of assurance that internal accounting controls are functioning as planned.

   b.   Aid to the independent auditor, who is conducting the examination of the financial statements.

   c.   The results of internal examinations of financial and accounting matters to a company's top-level management.

   d.   A measure of management performance in meeting organizational goals.

19.   An auditor who accepts an audit engagement and does not possess the industry expertise of the business entity, should

   a.   Engage financial experts familiar with the nature of the business entity.

   b.   Obtain a knowledge of matters that relate to the nature of the entity's business.

   c.   Refer a substantial portion of the audit to another CPA who will act as the principal auditor.

   d.   First inform management that an unqualified opinion cannot be issued.

20.   A CPA while performing tax services for a client may learn of a material error in a previously filed tax return. In such an instance the CPA should

   a.   Prepare an affidavit with respect to the error.

   b.   Recommend compensating for the prior year's error in the current year's tax return where such action will mitigate the client's cost and inconvenience.

   c.   Advise the client to file a corrected return regardless of whether or not the error resulted in an overstatement or understatement of tax.

   d.   Inform the IRS of the error.

21.   The first general standard requires that a person or persons have adequate technical training and proficiency as an auditor. This standard is met by

   a.   An understanding of the field of business and finance.

   b.   Education and experience in the field of auditing.

   c.   Continuing Professional Education.

   d.   A thorough knowledge of the Statements on Auditing Standards.

22.   The objective of quality control mandates that a public accounting firm should establish policies and procedures for professional development which provide reasonable assurance that all entry-level personnel

   a.   Prepare working papers which are standardized in form and content.

   b.   Have the knowledge required to enable them to fulfill responsibilities assigned.

   c.   Will advance within the organization.

   d.   Develop specialties in specific areas of public accounting.

23.   In pursuing its quality control objectives with respect to assigning personnel to engagements, a CPA firm may use policies and procedures such as

   a.   Rotating employees from assignment to assignment on a random basis to aid in the staff training effort.

   b.   Requiring timely identification of the staffing requirements of specific engagements so that enough qualified personnel can be made available.

   c.   Allowing staff to select the assignments of their choice to promote better client relationships.

   d.   Assigning a number of employees to each engagement in excess of the number required so as not to overburden the staff and interfere with the quality of the audit work performed.

24.   The AICPA Code of Professional Ethics states, in part, that a CPA should maintain integrity and objectivity. Objectivity in the code refers to a CPA's ability

   a.   To maintain an impartial attitude on all matters which come under the CPA's review.

   b.   To independently distinguish between accounting practices that are acceptable and those that are not.

    c.   To be unyielding in all matters dealing with auditing procedures.

    d.   To independently choose between alternate accounting principles and auditing standards.

25.   A publicly-held company that disagrees with the independent auditor on a significant matter affecting its financial statements has several courses of action. Which of the following courses of action would be inappropriate?

    a.   Appeal to the Financial Accounting Standards Board to review the significant matter.

    b.   Modify the financial statements by expressing in the footnotes its viewpoint with regard to the significant matter.

    c.   Ask the auditor to refer in the auditor's opinion to a client footnote which discusses the client point of view with regard to the significant matter.

    d.   Engage another independent auditor.

26.   In pursuing its quality control objectives with respect to acceptance of a client, a CPA firm is not likely to

    a.   Make inquiries of the proposed client's legal counsel.

    b.   Review financial statements of the proposed client.

    c.   Make inquiries of previous auditors.

    d.   Review the personnel practices of the proposed client.

27.   The permanent section of the auditor's working papers generally should include

    a.   Time and expense reports.

    b.   Names and addresses of all audit staff personnel on the engagement.

    c.   A copy of key customer confirmations.

    d.   A copy of the engagement letter.

28.   The independent audit is important to readers of financial statements because it

    a.   Determines the future stewardship of the management of the company whose financial statements are audited.

    b.   Measures and communicates financial and business data included in financial statements.

    c.   Involves the objective examination of and reporting on management-prepared statements.

    d.   Reports on the accuracy of all information in the financial statements.

29.   The first standard of field work recognizes that early appointment of the independent auditor has many advantages to the auditor and the client. Which of the following advantages is least likely to occur as a result of early appointment of the auditor?

    a.   The auditor will be able to plan the audit work so that it may be done expeditiously.

    b.   The auditor will be able to complete the audit work in less time.

    c.   The auditor will be able to better plan for the observation of the physical inventories.

    d.   The auditor will be able to perform the examination more efficiently and will be finished at an early date after the year end.

30.   A CPA should comply with applicable generally accepted auditing standards on every engagement

    a.   Without exception.

    b.   Except in examinations that result in a qualified report.

    c.   Except in engagements where the CPA is associated with unaudited financial statements.

    d.   Except in examinations of interim financial statements.

31.   To emphasize auditor independence from management, many corporations follow the practice of

    a.   Appointing a partner of the CPA firm conducting the examination to the corporation's audit committee.

    b.   Establishing a policy of discouraging social contact between employees of the corporation and the staff of the independent auditor.

    c.   Requesting that a representative of the independent auditor be on hand at the annual stockholders' meeting.

    d.   Having the independent auditor report to an audit committee of outside members of the board of directors.

32.   Which of the following statements best describes why the profession of certified public accountants has deemed it essential to promulgate a code of ethics and to establish a mechanism for enforcing observance of the code?

    a.   A distinguishing mark of a profession is its acceptance of responsibility to the public.

b. A prerequisite to success is the establishment of an ethical code that stresses primarily the professional's responsibility to clients and colleagues.

c. A requirement of most state laws calls for the profession to establish a code of ethics.

d. An essential means of self-protection for the profession is the establishment of flexible ethical standards by the profession.

33. Jones and Barrow, CPAs, are partners in a public accounting firm that has a large tax practice. Jones is a member of the AICPA. Which of the following is the best firm name?

a. Jones & Barrow, members AICPA.

b. Jones & Barrow, Tax Accountants.

c. Jones & Barrow, P.C. (Professional Corporation).

d. Jones & Barrow, Certified Public Accountants.

34. Which of the following actions should be avoided by a CPA?

a. CPA, who is in public practice, agrees to be the committee chairperson for a local fund-raising activity.

b. A CPA, who is an officer of a local bank, arranges a loan for another CPA, who is in public practice.

c. A CPA, who is in public practice, prepares a tax return for a friend without a fee and does not sign the return.

d. A CPA, who is retired from public practice, accepts a finder's fee from a public relations company for introducing a former client to that firm.

35. A CPA, who is a member of the American Institute of Certified Public Accountants, wrote an article for publication in a professional journal. The AICPA Code of Professional Ethics would be violated if the CPA allowed the article to state that the CPA was

a. A member of the American Institute of Certified Public Accountants.

b. A professor at a school of professional accountancy.

c. A partner in a national CPA firm.

d. A practitioner specialized in providing tax services.

36. A CPA examines the financial statements of a local bank. According to the AICPA Code of Professional Ethics, the appearance of independence ordinarily would not be impaired if the CPA

a. Serves on the bank's committee that approves loans.

b. Owns several shares of the bank's common stock.

c. Obtains a short-term loan from the bank.

d. Uses the bank's time-sharing computer service to solve client-related problems.

37. The AICPA Code of Professional Ethics recognizes that the reliance of the public, the government and the business community on sound financial reporting imposes particular obligations on CPAs. The code derives its authority from

a. Public laws enacted over the years.

b. General acceptance of the code by the business community.

c. Requirements of governmental regulatory agencies such as the Securities and Exchange Commission.

d. Bylaws of the American Institute of Certified Public Accountants.

38. The first standard of field work, which states that the work is to be adequately planned, and assistants, if any, are to be properly supervised, recognizes that

a. Early appointment of the auditor is advantageous to the auditor and the client.

b. Acceptance of an audit engagement after the close of the client's fiscal year is generally not permissible.

c. Appointment of the auditor subsequent to the physical count of inventories requires a disclaimer of opinion.

d. Performance of substantial parts of the examination is necessary at interim dates.

39. In pursuing its quality control objectives with respect to independence, a CPA firm may use policies and procedures such as

a. Emphasizing independence of mental attitude in firm training programs and in supervision and review of work.

b. Prohibiting employees from owning shares of the stock of publicly-traded companies.

c. Suggesting that employees conduct their banking transactions with banks that do not maintain accounts with client firms.

d. Assigning employees, who may lack independence, to research positions that do not require participation in field audit work.

40. In connection with the examination of financial statements, an independent auditor could be responsible for failure to detect a material fraud if

   a. Statistical sampling techniques were not used on the audit engagement.

   b. The auditor planned the work in a hasty and inefficient manner.

   c. Accountants performing important parts of the work failed to discover a close relationship between the treasurer and the cashier.

   d. The fraud was perpetrated by one client employee, who circumvented the existing internal controls.

41. A CPA accepts an engagement for a professional service without violating the AICPA Code of Professional Ethics if the service involves

   a. The preparation of cost projections for submission to a governmental agency as an application for a rate increase, and the fee will be paid if there is a rate increase.

   b. Tax preparation, and the fee will be based on whether the CPA signs the tax return prepared.

   c. A litigatory matter, and the fee is not known but is to be determined by a district court.

   d. Tax return preparation, and the fee is to be based on the amount of taxes saved, if any.

42. Richard, CPA, performs accounting services for Norton Corporation. Norton wishes to offer its shares to the public and asks Richard to audit the financial statements prepared for registration purposes. Richard refers Norton to Cruz, CPA, who is more competent in the area of registration statements. Cruz performs the audit of Norton's financial statements and subsequently thanks Richard for the referral by giving Richard a portion of the audit fee collected. Richard accepts the fee. Who, if anyone, has violated professional ethics?

   a. Only Richard.

   b. Both Richard and Cruz.

   c. Only Cruz.

   d. Neither Richard nor Cruz.

43. The AICPA Code of Professional Ethics requires compliance with accounting principles promulgated by the body designated by AICPA Council to establish such principles. The pronouncements comprehended by the code include all of the following except

   a. Opinions issued by the Accounting Principles Board.

   b. AICPA Accounting Research Studies.

   c. Interpretations issued by the Financial Accounting Standards Board.

   d. AICPA Accounting Research Bulletins.

44. An independent auditor must be without bias with respect to the financial statements of a client in order to

   a. Comply with the laws established by governmental agencies.

   b. Maintain the appearance of separate interests on the part of the auditor and the client.

   c. Protect against criticism and possible litigation from stockholders and creditors.

   d. Insure the impartiality necessary for an expression of the auditor's opinion.

45. An independent auditor has the responsibility to plan the audit examinations to search for errors and irregularities that might have a material effect on the financial statements. Which of the following, if material, would be an irregularity as defined in Statements on Auditing Standards?

   a. Misappropriation of an asset or groups of assets.

   b. Clerical mistakes in the accounting data underlying the financial statements.

   c. Mistakes in the application of accounting principles.

   d. Misinterpretation of facts that existed when the financial statements were prepared.

46. A CPA may reduce the audit work on a first-time audit by reviewing the working papers of the predecessor auditor. The predecessor should permit the successor to review working papers relating to matters of continuing accounting significance such as those that relate to

   a. Extent of reliance on the work of specialists.

   b. Fee arrangements and summaries of payments.

   c. Analysis of contingencies.

   d. Staff hours required to complete the engagement.

47. A CPA's retention of client records as a means of enforcing payment of an overdue audit fee is an action that is

   a. Considered acceptable by the AICPA Code of Professional Ethics.

   b. Ill advised since it would impair the CPA's independence with respect to the client.

c.   Considered discreditable to the profession.

d.   A violation of generally accepted auditing standards.

48.   If, during an audit examination, the successor auditor becomes aware of information that may indicate that financial statements reported on by the predecessor auditor may require revision, the successor auditor should

a.   Ask the client to arrange a meeting among the three parties to discuss the information and attempt to resolve the matter.

b.   Notify the client and the predecessor auditor of the matter and ask them to attempt to resolve it.

c.   Notify the predecessor auditor who may be required to revise the previously issued financial statements and auditor's report.

d.   Ask the predecessor auditor to arrange a meeting with the client to discuss and resolve the matter.

49.   Which of the following is not an element of quality control that should be considered by a firm of independent auditors?

a.   Assigning personnel to engagements.

b.   Consultation with appropriate persons.

c.   Keeping records of quality control policies and procedures.

d.   Supervision.

50.   An investor is reading the financial statements of the Stankey Corporation and observes that the statements are accompanied by an auditor's unqualified report. From this the investor may conclude that

a.   Any disputes over significant accounting issues have been settled to the auditor's satisfaction.

b.   The auditor is satisfied that Stankey is financially sound.

c.   The auditor has ascertained that Stankey's financial statements have been prepared accurately.

d.   Informative disclosures in the financial statements but not necessarily in Stankey's footnotes are to be regarded as reasonably adequate.

51.   A major difference of opinion concerning an accounting issue has arisen between an assistant on an audit engagement and the auditor with final responsibility for the engagement. If after consultation the assistant believes it necessary to disassociate himself from the resolution of the matter, both the auditor and his assistant must

a.   Document details of the disagreement and the basis of resolution.

b.   Inform management of the nature of the disagreement.

c.   Inform the company's audit committee of the nature of the disagreement.

d.   Refer the matter to the firm's peer review committee.

52.   The securities of Ralph Corporation are listed on a regional stock exchange and registered with the Securities and Exchange Commission. The management of Ralph engages a CPA to perform an independent audit of Ralph's financial statements. The primary objective of this audit is to provide assurance to the

a.   Regional Stock Exchange.

b.   Board of Directors of Ralph Corporation.

c.   Securities and Exchange Commission.

d.   Investors in Ralph securities.

53.   Which of the following reports is an indication of the changing role of the CPA that calls for an extension of the auditor's attest function?

a.   Report on annual comparative financial statements.

b.   Report on internal control based on an audit.

c.   Report on separate balance sheet of a holding company.

d.   Report on balance sheet and statements of income, retained earnings, and changes in financial position prepared from incomplete financial records.

54.   Which of the following best describes what is meant by generally accepted auditing standards?

a.   Acts to be performed by the auditor.

b.   Measures of the quality of the auditor's performance.

c.   Procedures to be used to gather evidence to support financial statements.

d.   Audit objectives generally determined on audit engagements.

55.   Which of the following underlies the application of generally accepted auditing standards, particularly the standards of field work and reporting?

a.   The elements of materiality and relative risk.

b.   The element of internal control.

c.   The element of corroborating evidence.

d.   The element of reasonable assurance.

56. Which of the following is a conclusion reached by the Commission on Auditors' Responsibilities, the independent commission established by the American Institute of Certified Public Accountants to study the role and responsibilities of independent auditors?
    a.   Different auditing standards should apply to audits of publicly owned and private entities.
    b.   The AICPA Auditing Standards Executive Committee should be replaced by a larger, part-time group.
    c.   The oversight of professional practice should remain with the accounting profession.
    d.   "Safe Harbors" should be made available for all work done by an auditor.

57. The AICPA Committee on Management Services has stated its belief that a CPA should not undertake a management advisory service engagement for implementation of the CPA's recommendations unless
    a.   The client has made a firm decision to proceed with implementation based on a complete understanding and consideration of alternatives.
    b.   The client does not understand the nature and implications of the recommended course of action.
    c.   The client does not have sufficient expertise within its organization to comprehend the significance of the changes being made.
    d.   The CPA withdraws as independent auditor for the client.

58. A firm of CPAs may use policies and procedures such as notifying professional personnel as to the names of audit clients having publicly held securities and confirming periodically with such personnel that prohibited relations do not exist. This is done to achieve effective quality control in which of the following areas?
    a.   Acceptance and continuance of clients.
    b.   Assigning personnel to engagements.
    c.   Independence.
    d.   Inspection.

59. The auditor's judgment concerning the overall fairness of the presentation of financial position, results of operations, and changes in financial position is applied within the framework of
    a.   Quality control.
    b.   Generally accepted auditing standards which include the concept of materiality.
    c.   The auditor's evaluation of the audited company's internal control.
    d.   Generally accepted accounting principles.

60. In pursuing its quality control objectives with respect to assigning personnel to engagements, a firm of independent auditors may use policies and procedures such as
    a.   Designating senior qualified personnel to provide advice on accounting or auditing questions throughout the engagement.
    b.   Requiring timely identification of the staffing requirements of specific engagements so that enough qualified personnel can be made available.
    c.   Establishing at entry levels a policy for recruiting that includes minimum standards of academic preparation and accomplishment.
    d.   Requiring auditing personnel to have current accounting and auditing literature available for research and reference purposes throughout the engagement.

61. Below are the names of four CPA firms and pertinent facts relating to each firm. Unless otherwise indicated, the individuals named are CPAs and partners, and there are no other partners. Which firm name and related facts indicates a violation of the AICPA Code of Professional Ethics?
    a.   Arthur, Barry, and Clark, CPAs (Clark died about five years ago; Arthur and Barry are continuing the firm).
    b.   Dave and Edwards, CPAs (The name of Fredricks, CPA, a third active partner, is omitted from the firm name).
    c.   Jones & Co., CPAs, P.C. (The firm is a professional corporation and has ten other stockholders who are all CPAs).
    d.   George and Howard, CPAs (Howard died three years ago; George is continuing the firm as a sole proprietorship).

62. The primary responsibility for the adequacy of disclosure in the financial statements of a publicly held company rests with the
    a.   Partner assigned to the audit engagement.
    b.   Management of the company.
    c.   Auditor in charge of the field work.
    d.   Securities and Exchange Commission.

63. In which of the following circumstances would a CPA be bound by ethics to refrain from disclosing any confidential information obtained during the course of a professional engagement?
    a.   The CPA is issued a summons enforceable by a court order which orders the CPA to present confidential information.

b. A major stockholder of a client company seeks accounting information from the CPA after management declined to disclose the requested information.

c. Confidential client information is made available as part of a quality review of the CPA's practice by a review team authorized by the AICPA.

d. An inquiry by a disciplinary body of a state CPA society requests confidential client information.

64. The AICPA Code of Professional Ethics would be violated if a CPA accepted a fee for services and the fee was

a. Fixed by a public authority.

b. Based on a price quotation submitted in competitive bidding.

c. Determined, based on the results of judicial proceedings.

d. Payable after a specified finding was obtained.

MAY 1981 QUESTIONS

65. The AICPA Code of Professional Ethics states that a CPA shall not disclose any confidential information obtained in the course of a professional engagement except with the consent of the client. This rule should be understood to preclude a CPA from responding to an inquiry made by

a. The trial board of the AICPA.

b. An investigative body of a state CPA society.

c. A CPA-shareholder of the client corporation.

d. An AICPA voluntary quality review body.

66. Early appointment of the independent auditor will enable

a. A more thorough examination to be performed.

b. A proper study and evaluation of internal control to be performed.

c. Sufficient competent evidential matter to be obtained.

d. A more efficient examination to be planned.

67. In tax practice, which of the following would **not** be considered reasonable support for taking a position contrary to the Internal Revenue Code?

a. Proposed regulations advocated by the IRS.

b. Legal opinions as to the constitutionality of a specific provision.

c. Possible conflicts between two sections of the Internal Revenue Code.

d. Tax court decisions **not** acquiesced to by the IRS.

68. Which of the following statements **best** describes the primary purpose of Statements on Auditing Standards?

a. They are guides intended to set forth auditing procedures which are applicable to a variety of situations.

b. They are procedural outlines which are intended to narrow the areas of inconsistency and divergence of auditor opinion.

c. They are authoritative statements, enforced through the code of professional ethics, and are intended to limit the degree of auditor judgment.

d. They are interpretations which are intended to clarify the meaning of "generally accepted auditing standards."

69. A CPA, while performing an audit, strives to achieve independence in appearance in order to

a. Reduce risk and liability.

b. Maintain public confidence in the profession.

c. Become independent in fact.

d. Comply with the generally accepted standards of fieldwork.

70. The third general standard states that due care is to be exercised in the performance of the examination. This standard should be interpreted to mean that a CPA who undertakes an engagement assumes a duty to perform

a. With reasonable diligence and without fault or error.

b. As a professional who will assume responsibility for losses consequent upon error of judgment.

c. To the satisfaction of the client and third parties who may rely upon it.

d. As a professional possessing the degree of skill commonly possessed by others in the field.

71. Inclusion of which of the following in a promotional brochure published by a CPA firm would be most likely to result in a violation of the AICPA rules of conduct?

a.   Names and addresses, telephone numbers, number of partners, office hours, foreign language competence, and date the firm was established.

b.   Services offered and fees for such services, including hourly rates and fixed fees.

c.   Educational and professional attainments, including date and place of certification, schools attended, dates of graduation, degrees received, and memberships in professional associations.

d.   Names, addresses and telephone numbers of the firm's clients, including the number of years served.

72.   The independent auditor's plan for an examination in accordance with generally accepted auditing standards is influenced by the possibility of material errors. The auditor will therefore conduct the examination with an attitude of

a.   Professional skepticism.
b.   Subjective mistrust.
c.   Objective indifference.
d.   Professional responsiveness.

REPEAT QUESTION

(581,A1,36)   Identical to item 26 above

Problem 1   Audit Committees (1178,A2)

(15 to 25 minutes)

For many years the financial and accounting community has recognized the importance of the use of audit committees and has endorsed their formation.

At this time the use of audit committees has become widespread. Independent auditors have become increasingly involved with audit committees and consequently have become familiar with their nature and function.

Required:

a.   Describe what an audit committee is.

b.   Identify the reasons why audit committees have been formed and are currently in operation.

c.   What are the functions of an audit committee?

Problem 2   Audit Deficiencies (578,A2)

(15 to 25 minutes)

Brown, CPA, received a telephone call from Calhoun, the sole owner and manager of a small corporation. Calhoun asked Brown to prepare the financial statements for the corporation and told Brown that the statements were needed in two weeks for external financing purposes. Calhoun was vague when Brown inquired about the intended use of the statements. Brown was convinced that Calhoun thought Brown's work would constitute an audit. To avoid confusion Brown decided not to explain to Calhoun that the engagement would only be to prepare the financial statements. Brown, with the understanding that a substantial fee would be paid if the work were completed in two weeks, accepted the engagement and started the work at once.

During the course of the work, Brown discovered an accrued expense account labeled "professional fees" and learned that the balance in the account represented an accrual for the cost of Brown's services. Brown suggested to Calhoun's bookkeeper that the account name be changed to "fees for limited audit engagement." Brown also reviewed several invoices to determine whether accounts were being properly classified. Some of the invoices were missing. Brown listed the missing invoice numbers in the working papers with a note indicating that there should be a follow-up on the next en-

gagement. Brown also discovered that the available records included the fixed asset values at estimated current replacement costs. Based on the records available, Brown prepared a balance sheet, income statement and statement of stockholder's equity. In addition, Brown drafted the footnotes but decided that any mention of the replacement costs would only mislead the readers. Brown suggested to Calhoun that readers of the financial statements would be better informed if they received a separate letter from Calhoun explaining the meaning and effect of the estimated replacement costs of the fixed assets. Brown mailed the financial statements and footnotes to Calhoun with the following note included on each page:

"The accompanying financial statements are submitted to you without complete audit verification."

Required:

Identify the inappropriate actions of Brown and indicate what Brown should have done to avoid each inappropriate action.

Organize your answer sheet as follows:

Inappropriate Action	What Brown Should Have Done To Avoid Inappropriate Action

Problem 3   Objectives of Audits (578,A3)

(15 to 25 minutes)

Feiler, the sole owner of a small hardware business, has been told that the business should have financial statements reported on by an independent CPA. Feiler, having some bookkeeping experience, has personally prepared the company's financial statements and does not understand why such statements should be examined by a CPA. Feiler discussed the matter with Farber, a CPA, and asked Farber to explain why an audit is considered important.

Required:

a.   Describe the objectives of an independent audit.

b.   Identify ten ways in which an independent audit may be beneficial to Feiler.

Problem 4   Tax and MAS Ethics Cases (572,A7)

(15 to 20 minutes)

The following cases relate to the CPA's management of his accounting practice. Note: Case 1 has been omitted because it tested old rule 502 which prohibited advertising.

Case 2

Judd Hanlon, CPA, was engaged to prepare the federal income tax return for the Guild Corporation for the year ended December 31, 1971. This is Mr. Hanlon's first engagement of any kind for the Guild Corporation.

In preparing the 1971 return, Mr. Hanlon finds an error on the 1970 return. The 1970 depreciation deduction was overstated significantly——accumulated depreciation brought forward from 1969 to 1970 was understated, and thus the 1970 base for declining balance depreciation was overstated.

Mr. Hanlon reported the error to Guild's controller, the officer responsible for tax returns. The controller stated: "Let the revenue agent find the error." He further instructed Mr. Hanlon to carry forward the material overstatement of the depreciable base to the 1971 depreciation computation. The controller noted that this error also had been made in the financial records for 1970 and 1971 and offered to furnish Mr. Hanlon with a letter assuming full responsibility for this treatment.

Required:

a. Evaluate Mr. Hanlon's handling of this situation.

b. Discuss the additional action that Mr. Hanlon should now undertake.

Case 3

Fred Browning, CPA, has examined the financial statements of the Grimm Company for several years. Grimm's president now has asked Mr. Browning to install an inventory control system for the Company.

Required:

Discuss the factors that Mr. Browning should consider in determining whether to accept this engagement.

Problem 5   Violations of GAAS (1176,A6)

(15 to 25 minutes)

Ray, the owner of a small company, asked Holmes, CPA, to conduct an audit of the company's records. Ray told Holmes that an audit is to be completed in time to submit audited financial statements to a bank as part of a loan application. Holmes immediately accepted the engagement and agreed to provide an auditor's report within three weeks. Ray agreed to pay Holmes a fixed fee plus a bonus if the loan was granted.

Holmes hired two accounting students to conduct the audit and spent several hours telling them exactly what to do. Holmes told the students not to spend time reviewing the controls, but instead to concentrate on proving the mathematical accuracy of the ledger accounts, and summarizing the data in the accounting records that support Ray's financial statements. The students followed Holmes' instructions and after two weeks gave Holmes the financial statements which did not include footnotes. Holmes reviewed the statements and prepared an unqualified auditor's report. The report, however, did not refer to generally accepted accounting principles nor to the year-to-year application of such principles.

Required:

Briefly describe each of the generally accepted auditing standards and indicate how the action(s) of Holmes resulted in a failure to comply with each standard. Organize your answer as follows:

Brief Description of Generally Accepted Auditing Standards	Holmes' Actions Resulting in Failure to Comply with Generally Accepted Auditing Standards

Problem 6   EDP Services (580,A2)

(15 to 25 minutes)

Savage, CPA, has been requested by an audit client to perform a non-recurring engagement involving the implementation of an EDP information and control system. The client requests that in setting up the new system and during the period prior to conversion to the new system, that Savage:

· Counsel on potential expansion of business activity plans.

· Search for and interview new personnel.

· Hire new personnel.

· Train personnel.

In addition, the client requests that during the three months subsequent to the conversion, that Savage:

· Supervise the operation of new system.

· Monitor client-prepared source documents and make changes in basic EDP generated data as Savage may deem necessary without concurrence of the client. Savage responds that he may perform some of the services requested, but not all of them.

Required:

a. Which of these services may Savage perform and which of these services may Savage not perform?

b. Before undertaking this engagement, Savage should inform the client of all significant matters related to the engagement. What are these significant matters?

c. If Savage adds to his staff an individual who specializes in developing computer systems, what degree of knowledge must Savage possess in order to supervise the specialist's activities?

MULTIPLE CHOICE ANSWERS

1.	a	16.	d	31.	d	46.	c	61.	d
2.	a	17.	c	32.	a	47.	c	62.	b
3.	b	18.	d	33.	d	48.	a	63.	b
4.	c	19.	b	34.	c	49.	c	64.	d
5.	d	20.	c	35.	d	50.	a	65.	c
6.	c	21.	b	36.	d	51.	a	66.	d
7.	b	22.	b	37.	d	52.	d	67.	a
8.	d	23.	b	38.	a	53.	b	68.	d
9.	d	24.	a	39.	a	54.	b	69.	b
10.	d	25.	a	40.	b	55.	a	70.	d
11.	b	26.	d	41.	c	56.	c	71.	d
12.	b	27.	d	42.	b	57.	a	72.	a
13.	d	28.	c	43.	b	58.	c		
14.	c	29.	b	44.	d	59.	d		
15.	b	30.	a	45.	a	60.	b		

EXPLANATION OF MULTIPLE CHOICE ANSWERS

1. (1180,A1,4) (a) In tax practice the appearance of independence is not required (ET 52.11) and a member may resolve doubt in favor of his/her client as long as there is reasonable support for the position taken (ET 102). In essence, this allows the CPA to take a position of client advocacy. Answers (c) and (d) are not correct because differences in tax accounting and generally accepted accounting principles may lead to differences between pretax accounting income and taxable income.

2. (1180,A1,5) (a) Section 9000 states that auditing interpretations, issued by the staff of the Auditing Standards Division, are not as authoritative as a pronouncement by the Auditing Standards Board. Note, however, that a member may have to justify a departure from an interpretation if the quality of the member's work is questioned.

3. (1180,A1,10) (b) A system of quality control is necessary to provide a CPA firm with reasonable assurance that it is conforming to generally accepted auditing standards (para161.02). Answers (a) and (d) are both essential elements of a part of a firm's system of quality control. Answer (c) is incorrect because it relates only to reporting.

4. (1180,A1,11) (c) The requirement is the "course of action" the CPA taxpreparer should follow when part of supporting information has been changed by oral communication. The CPA should use both the written and the oral information received (ET 191.07). Answers (a) and (b) are incorrect because a CPA should not prepare a return known to be in error. Answer (d) is incorrect since the CPA made reasonable inquiries and corrected the error.

5. (1180,A1,13) (d) The requirement is the rationale underlying the AICPA rules of conduct allowing contingent fees for CPAs engaged in tax practice. ET 302 indicates that contingent fees are acceptable because they are based on the results of judicial proceedings or the findings of governmental agencies. Answer (a) is incorrect because there is no reason to believe that it is true in all tax practice situations. Answer (b) is incorrect because CPAs do not, in general, base their fees on what other professions charge. Answer (c) is incorrect since judicial proceedings often do involve third parties, and because the existence of a third party is not considered a criterion for permitting contingent fees.

6. (1180,A1,26) (c) The retention of client records as a means of enforcing payment of an overdue audit fee is considered to be an act discreditable to the profession (ET 501.02). Since the Code of Professional Ethics explicitly prohibits the retention of records, answers (a) and (b) are incorrect. Answer (d) is inferior to answer (c) since the issue is addressed only in the Code.

7. (1180,A1,33) (b) The eight Management Advisory Services Practice Standards are included in the Statements on Management Advisory Services (MS 101.04). While answers (a), (c) and (d) are Standards, answer (b) is not.

8. (1180,A1,37) (d) Generally accepted auditing standards (GAAS) deal with measures of the quality of the performance of audit procedures (para 150.01). Answers (a) and (b) are only partially correct since GAAS give limited guidance as to specific policies and procedures and the nature and extent of auditors' responsibilities. Answer (c) is incomplete since it only relates to planning and writing the audit report and not to the other standards.

9. (1180,A1,39) (d) In 1948 the AICPA membership officially approved the ten generally accepted auditing standards. Answers (a) and (c) are inferior answers while answer (b) is totally wrong.

10. (1180,A1,48) (d) The weekly time reports are being used to meet the first standard of field work. The work is to be adequately planned and assistants, if any, are to be properly supervised. Thus, the budget is prepared during the planning stage of the audit and the analysis of variances from budget is used as a part of the supervision process. Answers (a) and (c) are incorrect because quality control and adequate review,

while implicit in the generally accepted auditing standards, are not explicitly a part of them. Answer (b), due professional care, while certainly relevant to the situation described is less complete than adequate planning.

11. (1180,A1,53) (b) While an auditor may reply to audit committee questions concerning the detailed procedures to be applied, initiating the discussion is generally not necessary. Intitiating discussion on the work of internal auditors, answer (a), may be helpful in gaining assistance which will lead to a more efficient audit. Discussing overall effects on audit scope of changes in the company's organization, answer (c), is also acceptable and desirable so as to allow the audit committee to obtain a better understanding of the audit. Answer (d), discussing details of potential problems, is also acceptable since the audit committee as representatives of the stockholders may be able to correct for the problems and, as a minimum, should be aware of them.

12. (1180,A1,55) (b) The SEC strengthened auditor independence by requiring that a Form 8-K disclose any disagreements which have led to a change in auditor; thus the reason for change becomes public information. Answer (a) is incorrect since auditors do not report on whether clients are in conformance with the Foreign Corrupt Practices Act. Answer (c) is incorrect because although audit committees often nominate accounting firms, the decision is generally subject to a vote of the stockholders. Answer (d) is incorrect since there is currently no requirement that management explicitly acknowledge its responsibility for the fairness of the financial statements.

13. (580,A1,2) (d) Statement On Responsibilities In Tax Practice No. 3 requires CPAs to make sure that a reasonable effort has been made to answer all questions on a tax return before the CPA signs the return. If data are not readily available and the question/answer is not significant to the tax liability, the answer may be omitted if the reason for the unanswered question is stated. Answer (a) is incorrect because the explanation of the omission should be provided on the return rather than held for an IRS examination. Answer (b) is incorrect because even if an answer is omitted because the data are not readily available, an explanation of the reason for the omission of an answer should be provided. Answer (c) is incorrect because if a question is not applicable to a taxpayer, the question can be answered "not applicable."

14. (580,A1,22) (c) After providing tax advice to a client, the CPA cannot be expected to notify the client of any subsequent legislative changes which affect the advice previously provided per Statement On Responsibilities In Tax Practice No. 8. If, however, the obligation for the subsequent notification is specifically undertaken by the CPA, the CPA is obviously expected to notify the client of any such changes. Answer (a) is incorrect because the obligation does not exist unless the CPA specifically undertakes the obligation. Answer (b) is incorrect because the CPA is not required to disclaim responsibility for subsequent notification of any changes affecting the advice. Answer (d) is incorrect because the CPA should be expected to have knowledge of all changes if the CPA maintains competence in the area of taxes.

15. (580,A1,32) (b) An engagement letter is used to document the understanding between the client and the auditor regarding the responsibilities of both parties during an audit. Answer (a) is incorrect because a representation letter consists of certain written representations from management as part of an audit made in accordance with GAAS per section 333. Answer (c) is incorrect because a management letter is a letter from the CPA to the client after the conclusion of an engagement which outlines various suggestions for improvements in the accounting system and other client operations that have come to the attention of the CPA. Relatedly, section 323 now requires communication of material weakness in internal accounting control. Formerly these could have been included in a "management letter." Answer (d) is incorrect because a comfort letter is a letter from the CPA to an underwriter assuring the underwriter that all necessary procedures under the Securities Act of 1933 relating to the accountant's work have been complied with per section 630.

16. (580,A1,39) (d) The concept of materiality is not relevant to a CPA's direct financial interest in a client per Ethics Rule 101 which requires an appearance of independence as well as independence in fact. Elsewhere in auditing the concept of materiality is generally inherent (see para 150.04). Answer (a) is incorrect because the materiality of various transactions would help determine which would be reviewed by the auditor. Answer (b) is incorrect because the need for disclosure of particular fact or transaction would be determined by its materiality. Answer (c) is incorrect because the scope of an audit program would be affected by the materiality of the various accounts.

17. (580,A1,58) (c) Policies and procedures should be established for deciding whether to accept or continue a client in order to minimize the likelihood of association with clients whose management lacks integrity per para 7h of Statement on Quality Control Standards No. 1. Answer (a) is incorrect because auditors attest to the fairness of financial statements, not the integrity or reliability of a client. Answer (b) is incorrect because while quality control policies for acceptance of new clients are required by quality control standards, the primary purpose is to avoid clients whose management lack integrity. Answer (d) is incorrect because the primary and immediate purpose of quality control policies over accepting new clients is to avoid clients lacking integrity, even though indirectly this may lessen exposure to litigation.

18. (580,A1,60) (d) The requirement is the primary purpose of an operational audit. Operational auditing is broader than traditional financial auditing or studies of internal control. Operations auditing includes evaluation of controls (both administrative and accounting) as well as evaluation of performance including such things as evaluation of productivity, quality of output, cost of output, efficiency of personnel, and workload assumed by personnel. Thus, operational audits are concerned with management performance in meeting organizational goals. Answers (a), (b), and (c) are concerned with specific controls for accounting matters.

19. (1179,A1,11) (b) An auditor who accepts an audit engagement and does not possess industry expertise of the new client, should obtain the knowledge of matters that relate to the nature of the entity's business organization and its operating characteristics. These include types of products and services, capital structure, related parties, locations, and production, distribution, and compensation methods. Also, the auditor should become acquainted with the economic conditions, government regulations, changes in technology relating to the industry in which the entity operates. See para 311.06-.08. Answer (a) is incorrect because audit expertise rather than financial expertise is required. Presumably the auditor will be able to obtain competence with respect to the industry of the new client. Answer (c) is incorrect because there is no requirement to refer a substantial portion of the audit to another principal auditor. Answer (d) is incorrect because audit opinions are not qualified or disclaimed due to lack of capability of the auditor. If the auditor does not have the competence to undertake the engagement, the auditor should decline the engagement. Rule 201 of the Code of Professional Ethics requires

CPAs to complete all engagements with professional competence, which includes adequate planning and supervision. It is within the planning aspect of an audit that the auditor should obtain a level of knowledge about the client's business that will enable the auditor to plan and perform the examination per GAAS.

20. (1179, A1,20) (c) When a CPA learns of a material error in a previously filed tax return of a tax client, the CPA should advise the client of the error and recommend that the client correct the error in an appropriate manner per AICPA Statement of Responsibilities in Tax Practice No. 6, "Knowledge of Error: Return Preparation." Answer (a) is incorrect because the CPA's responsibility is to advise the client orally or in writing, and an affidavit with respect to the errors is not necessary. Answer (b) is incorrect because the error needs to be corrected per IRS regulations rather than based on mitigation of client cost and inconvenience. Answer (d) is incorrect because the CPA may not inform the IRS without permission per Statement No. 6 and ethics rule 301 prohibiting disclosure of confidential client information without consent of client.

21. (1179,A1,48) (b) The first general standard of GAAS recognizes that a person must obtain proper education and experience in the field of auditing (para 210.02). Answer (a) is incorrect because understanding of the field of business and finance is a necessary but not sufficient condition. Presumably people obtain an understanding of the field of business and finance in the course of obtaining education experience in auditing. Answers (c) and (d) are incorrect because continuing professional education and knowledge of SAS are only parts of the knowledge and experience, i.e., the answers are incomplete.

22. (1179,A1,60) (b) One of the quality control considerations for a firm of independent auditors is that policies and procedures for hiring should be established to provide reasonable assurance that those employees possess the appropriate characteristics to enable them to perform competently (para 160.13). Answers (a), (c), and (d) are more specific objectives than are contemplated in the elements of quality control. The elements of quality control are independence, assigning personnel to the engagements, consultation, supervision, hiring, professional development, advancement, acceptance and continuance of clients, and inspection.

23. (1176,A1,5) (b) The quality control objective with regard to assignment of personnel to engagements should provide reasonable assurance that the work will be performed by those having adequate training and proficiency. Thus,

answers (a), (c), and (d) are incorrect, because they do not provide reasonable assurances that the work will be performed by those having adequate technical training and proficiency. See para 7 of SAS 4.

24. (1176,A2,26)   (a)   Rule 102, Integrity and Objectivity, of the AICPA Professional Code of Ethics states that "A member shall not knowingly misrepresent facts. . ." In the concepts on professional ethics, which precede the rules of conduct, objectivity is described as the "ability to maintain an impartial attitude on all matters." Thus, the concepts of independence, objectivity and integrity refer to a frame of mind rather than specific audit practices, procedures, standards, etc., referred to in answers (b), (c), and (d).

25. (1176,A2,30)   (a)   The FASB does not review or involve itself in specific client-auditor disagreements. Answers (b), (c) and (d) are all possibilities.

26. (1176,A2,32)   (d)   The objective of quality controls with respect to acceptance of a client is to minimize the likelihood of association with a client whose management lacks integrity. SAS 4 (para 20) suggests a review of the financial statements of proposed clients and inquiries of third parties including auditors, attorneys, banks, investment bankers, etc. Answer (d) suggests a narrower and more detailed procedure than is normally undertaken with respect to potential clients.

27. (1176,A2,39)   (d)   Audit working papers are commonly divided into annual files and permanent files. Annual files pertain solely to each year's audit. Permanent files contain more permanent type items such as articles of incorporation, which do not change over time. Thus, the best answer would be a copy of the engagement letter which would probably change less than answers (a), (b), and (c).

28. (1176,A3,56)   (c)   The independent audit consists of the examination of and reporting on management prepared statements. Answer (a) is incorrect because the audit does not determine future management activities. Answer (b) is incorrect because the audit and audit report do not measure and communicate the financial and business data in the statements. Rather the accounting system measures and communicates this financial and business data. Answer (d) is incorrect, because it is fairness rather than accuracy which is reported upon (para 110.01, SAS 1).

29. (1176,A3,60) (b) See para 310.03 of SAS 1. Answers (a), (c), and (d) are explicitly stated as advantages of early appointment of the independent auditor. Additionally, early appointment will allow early correction of accounting problems and thus increased service to the client. Thus, while the auditor can do a better job as a result of early appointment, there are probably little efficiencies in terms of time expended.

30. (577,A1,3)   (a)   Note that the requirement states applicable GAAS. Ethics Rule 202 requires compliance with applicable GAAS when a CPA is associated with financial statements. Answers (b), (c), and (d) all imply association with financial statements and thus require compliance with applicable GAAS.

31. (577,A1,14)   (d)   The requirement is a method to emphasize auditor independence from management. Having the independent auditor report to an audit committee made up of nonmanagement members of the board of directors emphasizes the auditor's independence from management. Corporate audit committees made up of outside board members also helps overcome the internal control limitation whereby top management may be able to circumvent or ignore internal controls. For example, if the CPA reports to the chief operating officer and the chief operating officer has been using the corporate plane for personal business, internal control is inoperative. Answer (a) is incorrect because the CPA firm's independence would be impaired if a partner served on the corporation's audit committee (specifically prohibited per Ethics Rule 101). Answer (b) is incorrect because discouraging social contact between corporate employees and the independent auditor does not relate to the auditor's independence from management. Answer (c) is incorrect because the CPA on hand for the stockholders' meeting usually sits with corporate management, and thus does not emphasize independence.

32. (577,A1,18)   (a)   The requirement is the best answer describing why the CPA profession promulgates and enforces a code of ethics. The first sentence of the AICPA Code of Professional Ethics states, "A distinguishing mark of a professional is his acceptance of responsibility to the public." Answer (b) is incorrect because the code of ethics emphasizes professional responsibilities in addition to responsibilities to clients and colleagues such as competence, compliance with technical standards, independence, integrity, objectivity, etc. Answer (c) is incorrect, because while state statutes may call for

ethical codes, the CPA profession's responsibility to the public requires an ethical code irrespective of state laws. Answer (d) is incorrect because the ethical code contains rules of conduct which set forth the minimum levels of acceptable conduct which are both mandatory and enforceable.

33.   (577,A3,41)   (d) Ethics Rule 505 specifies that members cannot practice under a firm name that indicates specialization, i.e., answer (b); indicates membership in the AICPA, unless all partners are members i.e. answer (a); or is misleading as to the type of organization, i.e., answer (c). The problem did not indicate that Jones and Barrow were practicing as a professional corporation.

34.   (577,A3,52)   (c) Statements on Responsibilities in Tax Practice No. 1 requires CPAs to sign tax returns as preparer whether or not compensation is received for preparing the return. The ethical rules of conduct only apply to CPAs engaged in the practice of public accounting, with the exception of Rule 102, Integrity and Objectivity, and Rule 501, Acts Discreditable. Thus, answers (b) and (d) do not present a problem. Answer (a), fund raising, is a typical public service activity of CPAs.

35.   (1177,A1,2)   (d) Answer (d) was correct before Ethics Rule 502 was twice modified to only prohibit false or deceptive advertising. Indicating a specialization used to be prohibited. The interpretation also indicates that the author description should not refer to a specialization, such as tax services. Answers (a), (b), and (c) are common descriptions of author CPAs in professional accounting periodicals. Practicing under a firm name indicating a specialization is still prohibited by Ethics Rule 505.

36.   (1177,A1,4)   (d) The requirement is to determine the situation which would not appear to impair the independence of the CPA. Answer (a) is incorrect because if the CPA approved loans to clients, the CPA would not be independent with respect to determining the collectibility of the loans. Answer (b) is incorrect because ownership of stock is a direct violation of ethics rule 101 (independence) which prohibits any direct financial interest in the client. Answer (c) is incorrect because a loan to the bank (unless a fully secured mortgage loan from a savings and loan) would impair the CPA's independence with regard to the client. Answer (d), use of a bank's time-sharing computer service, would not impair the CPA's independence, but rather be a normal business transaction between client and CPA.

37.   (1177,A1,9)   (d) The AICPA code of ethics has been adopted by the membership of the AICPA. Relatedly, the bylaws of the AICPA provide that the trial board may admonish, suspend, or expel a member who is found guilty of infringing on the bylaws or the code of ethics. Thus, there are no public laws which enforce the AICPA's code of ethics. It should be noted that many state public accountancy statutes incorporate various aspects of the AICPA's code of ethics. The general acceptance of the AICPA's code of ethics by the business community does not give authority to the code. Finally, while the SEC has provided impetus to the development of professional ethics, particularly in the area of independence, the SEC does not provide authority for the AICPA's code of ethics.

38.   (1177,A1,26)   (a) Early appointment permits better planning by the auditor as well as other preliminary work (para 310.03, SAS 1). Answer (b) is incorrect because acceptance of an audit engagement after the end of the client's fiscal year is acceptable. The auditor, however, may be forced to express a qualified or disclaimer of opinion (para 310.04, SAS 1). Answer (c) is incorrect because while the auditor is generally required to be present at physical inventories (if quantities are determined solely by count), the physical inventory can be postponed or another physical inventory can be taken under observation of the auditor when the auditor is appointed after year end (para 310.04, .09, SAS 1). Answer (d) is incorrect because there is no requirement that substantial parts of examinations be made before year end (para 310.05—.09, SAS 1).

39.   (1177,A1,27)   (a) The objective of firm policies and procedures to maintain firm independence is to provide reasonable assurance that all persons at all organizational levels maintain independence in fact and in appearance. See ethics rule 101 and para 5 and 6 of SAS 4. Answers (b), (c), and (d) are answers which are overly restrictive and/or do not maintain independence.

40.   (1177,A1,28)   (b) Answer (a) is incorrect because statistical sampling techniques are not a required audit procedure. Statistical sampling is compatible with, but not required by, GAAS (para 320b.01, SAS 1). Answer (c) is incorrect because auditors do not attempt to gauge the personal relationships of client employees. Related party transactions (SAS 6) have to do with transactions between the client and third parties, not internal employee relations. Answer (d) is incorrect because there are limitations of internal control (para 320.34, SAS 1) due to the concept of reasonable assurance,

i.e., cost benefit analysis (para 320.32, SAS 1). Answer (b), planning the audit in a hasty and inefficient manner, is not in compliance with the first standard of field work requiring adequate planning and supervision.

Also see para 110.05—.08, SAS 1. The auditor's responsibility with regard to detection of fraud generally is to conduct the examination with due professional skill in accordance with GAAS.

41.   (1177,A1,36) (c) Ethics rule 302 prohibits CPAs from offering services on a basis contingent with findings. Fees, however, may vary with complexity of services rendered, or be fixed by courts, or in tax matters, findings of government agencies may determine fees. Thus, answer (c) is correct. Answer (d) is incorrect because in tax return preparation, the fee would be determined by the accountant's findings, not by the government agency. Answers (a) and (b) similarly are contingent upon the accountant's findings.

42.   (1177,A1,37) (b) Ethics rule 503 prohibits CPAs from paying or accepting commissions to obtain or to refer clients. This rule, of course, does not apply to the purchase and sale of professional accounting practices or prohibit payment for services rendered. In this case, however, the referring CPA did not perform any professional services, but was given, and subsequently accepted, a portion of the audit fees. Thus, both the CPAs have violated rule 503.

43.   (578,A1,14) (b)   Rule 203 of the Code of Professional Ethics requires compliance with accounting rules promulgated by the FASB which include

1.   Statements of Financial Accounting Standards
2.   FASB Interpretations
3.   Accounting Research Bulletins and APB Opinions not modified by the FASB.

Alternative presentation is permitted if the statements would have otherwise been misleading. All other accounting pronouncements are not contemplated by this rule, including AICPA Accounting Research Studies.

44.   (578,A1,19) (d)   Rule 101 of the Code of Professional Ethics prohibits CPAs from expressing an opinion on financial statements unless the CPA is independent with respect to the client. Independence is the ability to act with integrity and objectivity, i.e., to be without bias with respect to

the financial statements. Answer (a) is incorrect because there are no laws which require CPAs to be independent. Answer (b) is incorrect because CPAs need to be impartial rather than merely maintaining the appearance of separate interest. Answer (c) is incorrect because independence, by itself, provides little protection against criticism and litigation.

45.   (578,A1,28) (a)   The requirement is an example of an irregularity as defined in the SASs. Irregularities are defined in para 3 of SAS 16 to be intentional distortions of financial statements including management fraud and misappropriation of assets. The term "errors" refers to unintentional mistakes which is contemplated by answers (b), (c), and (d).

46.   (578,A1,33) (c)   Para 9 of SAS 7 provides two examples of matters of continuing accounting significance which are usually provided to successor auditors by predecessor auditors. The two examples are working paper analysis of balance sheet accounts and matters surrounding contingencies. These are items which would facilitate the predecessor's audit. Answers (a), (b), and (d) relate to the predecessor firm's auditing philosophy rather than to data underlying the client's financial statements as indicated in answer (c), i.e., analysis of contingencies.

47.   (578,A1,38) (c)   A CPA's retention of client records in attempt to force payment of an overdue audit fee is unprofessional and discreditable to the profession. This was a recent AICPA ethics ruling. Thus answer (a) is incorrect. Answer (d) is incorrect because GAAS are directed toward the auditor's judgment and professional performance rather than ethical problems. Answer (b) is incorrect because retention of client records would probably aggravate a CPA-client relationship rather than impair independence.

48.   (578,A1,44) (a)   When a successor auditor becomes aware of information indicating a predecessor auditor may have to take steps to have prior financial statements revised, the successor auditor cannot contact the predecessor auditor directly due to the confidential relationship to the client. Accordingly, the CPA should request that the client arrange a meeting among the three parties to discuss the potential problems and seek their resolution. See para 10 of SAS 7. Answers (b), (c), and (d) are incorrect because the CPA must have the client's permission before discussing the matter with the predecessor auditor.

49.   (578,A1,47)   (c)   SAS 4 suggests 9 considerations in establishing policies to provide assurance that CPA firms will comply with GAAS. The 9 considerations include those concerned with assigning personnel to engagements, consultations with appropriate persons, and supervision. Para 4 of SAS 4 specifically points out that keeping records concerning quality control policies and procedures may be convenient, but is not in itself an element of quality control.

50.   (578,A1,48)   (a)   An unqualified audit report indicates that disputes over significant accounting issues have been settled to the auditor's satisfaction. If any such disputes have not been settled, the auditor will be obligated to render an opinion other than unqualified. Answer (b) is incorrect because a CPA may issue an unqualified opinion on a company which is losing money and has other types of problems. Answer (c) is incorrect because there is no assertion as to accuracy by CPAs. Rather, CPAs assert that financial statements are fairly presented per GAAP. Answer (d) is incorrect because the financial statement footnotes are regarded as an integral part of the financial statements and must contain adequate informative disclosures per the third standard of reporting.

51.   (579,A1,4)   (a)   If differences of opinion concerning accounting or auditing issues develop among personnel during an examination, audit assistants should document their disagreement. The basis of resolution of the disagreement should also be documented per para 311.12. Answers (b) and (c) are incorrect because the resolution of the disagreement between accounting staff members is a matter internal to the auditing firm and should not be brought to the attention of either client management or the client's audit committee. Answer (d) is incorrect because the firm's peer review committee is concerned with the adequacy of the systems of quality controls rather than resolving conflicts between auditing staff.

52.   (579,A1,9)   (d)   The primary objective of an audit of any company is to express an opinion on the fairness of the financial statements per para 110.01. The primary or motivating benefit is to the investors in a public company rather than the associated stock exchange, board of directors, or SEC. These latter three institutions themselves exist for the benefit of investors.

53.   (579,A1,22)   (b)   A report on internal control is an extension of the auditor's traditional attest function which expresses an opinion on the fairness of financial statements. Answers (a) annual comparative statements, (c) separate balance sheets, and (d) financial statements prepared from incomplete data, are incorrect because they describe reports on traditional financial data. See section 640, "Reports on Internal Control."

54.   (579,A1,25)   (b)   Generally accepted auditing standards deal with the qualifications of the auditor and with measures of the quality of performance of auditors, whereas audit procedures relate to acts to be performed during the audit (paras 150.01 and 201.01). Thus answers (a), acts to be performed, and (c), procedures to be used, are not auditing standards but are auditing procedures. Answer (d) is incorrect because audit objectives do not provide measures of the qualifications of the auditor or the quality of his performance.

55.   (579,A1,27)   (a)   The elements of materiality and relative risk underlie the application of all the standards, particularly the standards of field work and reporting (para 150.03). Answers (b), internal control, and (c), corroborating evidence, are incorrect because GAAS are concerned with measures of quality of performance rather than with elements of audit evidence. Answer (d) is incorrect because reasonable assurance is a basic concept of internal control, which recognizes that the cost of internal control should not exceed the benefits expected to be derived (para 320.32).

56.   (579,A1,28)   (c)   The Commission on Auditor's Responsibilities developed conclusions and made recommendations concerning appropriate responsibilities of independent auditors. The Commission concluded that although the accounting profession could make changes to improve its efficiency, in general it was working well and should remain in the private sector. Answer (a) is incorrect because the Commission specifically concluded that auditing standards should be the same for all publicly owned and privately held corporations. Answer (b) is incorrect because the recommendation was that the Auditing Standards Executive Committee should be replaced by a smaller full-time group. Answer (d) is incorrect because "safe harbors" means an exclusion of liability under the SEC acts. While the Commission did recognize the need for some form of statutory limitation on monetary damages, the Commission did not attempt to rule out all liability for auditors.

57.   (579,A1,35)   (a)   Statement on Management Advisory Services No. 3 states that a CPA should not undertake an MAS engagement which includes implementation unless the client

a. Understands the implications.
b. Makes a firm decision to proceed with implementation.
c. Accepts overall responsibility.
d. Has expertise to handle the implementation.
e. Has ability to maintain and operate the system.

Thus, answers (b) and (c) are incorrect because the client must understand the implications of the new system. Answer (d) is incorrect because a CPA is allowed to provide both management services and act as independent auditor. Ethics rule 101 does not contemplate management services impairing an auditor's independence.

58. (579,A1,50) (c) The requirement is the area in which effective quality control policies and procedures will be achieved by periodically notifying professional personnel of the names of clients that have publicly held securities. Section 160 provides quality control considerations for firms of independent auditors to assure that firms, as well as individuals, comply with GAAS. The basic element of quality control for independence requires that policies and procedures be established to provide reasonable assurance that persons at all organizational levels maintain independence in fact and in appearance (para 160.05). Answers (a), acceptance and continuation of client's independence, (b) assigning personnel to engagements, and (d) inspection, are other elements of quality control but are not enhanced by notification of securities for which prohibited relationships exist.

59. (579,A1,60) (d) The auditor's judgment concerning the fairness of financial statements should be applied within the framework of generally accepted accounting principles per para 411.03. Answer (a) is incorrect because quality control has to do with assurance that a CPA firm complies with GAAS (per section 160). Answer (b) is incorrect because GAAS have to do with the adequacy of an audit rather than the fairness of financial statement presentation. Answer (c) is also incorrect because the auditor's evaluation of internal control is less relevant to the overall fairness of financial statements than the framework of GAAP.

60. (1178,A1,7) (b) With respect to the objective of quality control regarding personnel assignment to engagements, timely identification of staffing requirements so that enough qualified personnel can be available is required (SAS 4, para 7-8). Answer

(a) is incorrect because designating senior qualified personnel to provide advice on accounting and auditing questions throughout the engagement is a consultation quality control objective (SAS 4, para 9-10). Answer (c) is incorrect because establishing minimum standards for recruiting is a hiring quality control objective (para 13-14). Answer (d) is incorrect because requiring current accounting and auditing literature availability is a consultation control objective (para 9-10).

61. (1178,A1,27) (d) The requirement is to identify the CPA firm name which is in violation of Rule 505 of the Code of Professional Ethics. CPAs are not permitted to practice under a firm name that is misleading about form of organization. Here, an individual is practicing as a sole proprietor in the name of a partnership. Note that Rule 505 does permit an individual to practice in the name of the former partnership for up to two years. Here the former partner died three years ago. Answer (a) does not constitute an ethics violation as the partnership name does not contain any fictitious names and is not misleading about the form of organization. Answers (b) and (c) are not violations of the code of ethics as all partners or stockholders do not have to have their names in the partnership name. Answer (c) is not a violation of ethics as the result of being a professional corporation, as it conforms to the professional corporation characteristics per AICPA Council.

62. (1178,A1,28) (b) Financial statements are the representations of management, and management has responsibility for producing proper financial statements (para 110.02 of SAS 1). The partner assigned to the audit engagement (answer (a)) has responsibility for expressing an opinion as to fairness of the financial statements. The auditor in charge of field work (answer (c)) has the responsibility to gather audit evidence regarding the fairness of the financial statements. The SEC (answer (d)) has the responsibility for enforcing the Securities Acts which does not include primary responsibility for disclosure in the financial statements of particular companies.

63. (1178,A1,30) (b) Ethics rule 301 precludes CPAs from disclosing confidential client data without the consent of the client. Rule 301, however, shall not preclude compliance with Rule 202 (Compliance with GAAS) and Rule 203 (Compliance with GAAP), compliance with an enforceable subpoena, and disclosure to AICPA-authorized voluntary quality review programs and AICPA trial board actions. Answer (b)

is correct because the major stockholder is not the client. Answers (a), (c), and (d) are incorrect because Rule 301 specifically permits compliance with validly issued subpoenas and disclosure to quality-control review boards and disciplinary bodies of state CPA societies.

64.   (1178,A1,40)   (d)   Rule 302 of the Code of Professional Ethics precludes CPAs from offering their services for a fee that is contingent upon their findings. Answer (a) is incorrect because fees fixed by a public authority are not contingent. Answer (b) is incorrect because CPAs are now permitted by the AICPA to obtain work by competitive bidding. Answer (c) is incorrect because fees determined by judicial proceedings are not contingent.

MAY 1981 ANSWERS

65.   (581,A1,1)   (c)   The requirement is to determine the circumstance under which a CPA is not allowed to disclose confidential information. Disclosure to an individual CPA-shareholder is not allowed without the consent of the client (i.e., the board of directors and/or management). ET 301.01 requires a CPA to respond to the trial board of the AICPA [answer (a)], an investigative body of a state CPA society [answer (b)] and allows responses for voluntary quality reviews [answer (d)].

66.   (581,A1,15)   (d)   The requirement is to determine an advantage of early appointment of the auditor. The early appointment of the independent auditor enables the auditor to plan his/her work so that it may be done expeditiously and to determine the extent to which it can be done before the balance sheet date. Such preliminary work by the auditor permits the examination to be performed in a more efficient manner and to be completed at an early date after the year end (para 310.03). Answer (a) is incorrect because the overall scope of the examination must remain the same regardless of appointment date. Answer (b) is incorrect because a proper study and evaluation of internal control may be performed even without early appointment. Answer (c) similarly is incorrect because sufficient competent evidential matter must be obtained regardless of the appointment date.

67.   (581,A1,38)   (a)   The requirement is to determine a circumstance which would not be considered to be reasonable support for taking a position contrary to the Internal Revenue Code. The existence of proposed regulations is not sufficient support. Answers (b), (c), and (d) are all considered adequate (TX 201).

68.   (581,A1,41)   (d)   The requirement is to determine the primary purpose of Statements on Auditing

Standards. Statements on Auditing Standards are interpretations of generally accepted auditing standards (Section 100). While answers (a), (b), and (c) may all, to some extent, be the result of Statements on Auditing Standards, none of them can be considered to be the primary purpose.

69.   (581,A1,47)   (b)   The requirement is to determine the reason for CPA concern with independence in appearance. To maintain public confidence in the profession the appearance of independence is necessary. The profession uses the criterion of whether reasonable men, having knowledge of all the facts and taking into consideration normal strength of character and normal behavior under the circumstances, would conclude that a specified relationship between a CPA and a client poses an unacceptable threat to the CPA's integrity or objectivity (ET 52.09). Answer (a) is incorrect because, while it may be a side benefit of perceived independence, reducing risk and liability is not the primary reason for the standard. Answer (c) is incorrect because independence in appearance does not imply independence in fact. Answer (d) is incorrect since the independence standard is a general standard.

70.   (581,A1,48)   (d)   The requirement is to interpret the meaning of the third general standard which pertains to due care. A CPA is to perform with the degree of skill commonly possessed by others in the field. (para 230.03). Answer (a) is incorrect since it is probably impossible for anyone to perform without error. Answer (b) is incorrect since a professional will not in general be responsible for pure errors of judgment (para 230.03). Answer (c) is incorrect since both the client and third parties may well be dissatisfied by the results of an audit (e.g., a qualified opinion).

71.   (581,A1,49)   (d)   The requirement is to determine which information in a recruiting brochure might result in a code of ethics violation. Answers (a), (b), and (c) are presented in the code of ethics as acceptable forms of advertising (ET 502.02). Answer (d) is questionable. For example, the mere engagement of a CPA firm is often confidential and thus its disclosure might violate the code of ethics (ET 391.014).

72.   (581,A1,58)   (a)   The requirement is to determine the auditor's attitude when conducting an examination. The auditor should plan and perform his/her examination with an attitude of professional skepticism, recognizing that the application of his/her auditing procedures may produce evidential matter indicating the possibility of errors or irregularities (para 327.06). Answers (b) and (c) are incorrect because the auditor does not approach an audit with mistrust or indifference. Answer (d) is less accurate than answer (a) when an auditor is considering material errors.

ANSWER OUTLINE

Problem 1   Audit Committees

a. Audit committee is part of company organizational structure

Special committee formed by board of directors
Ideally a group of outside directors
Provides liaison between the CPA and board of directors
Helps fulfill public financial reporting responsibility

b. Audit committee helps board of directors exercise due care

Improves responsiveness to financial reporting duty
Recognizes reporting responsibility to the public investor
Reinforces auditor independence from management

c. Audit committee functions may include:

1. Select auditor and review audit fee and engagement letter
2. Review auditor's overall audit plan
3. Review preliminary annual financial statements
4. Review results of audit, e.g.,
   Restrictions
   Cooperation received
   Audit findings
   Audit recommendations
5. Review auditor's evaluation of internal control
6. Review company's accounting, financial, and operating controls
7. Review internal audit reports
8. Review preliminary interim financial reports
9. Review policies on unethical and illegal procedures
10. Review financial statements for regulatory agencies
11. Review auditor's observations of company personnel
12. Participate in the selection of accounting policies
13. Review impact of proposed accounting pronouncements
14. Review company's insurance program
15. Review auditor's management letter

UNOFFICIAL ANSWER

Problem 1   Audit Committees

a.   An audit committee is an important part of a company's organizational structure. It is a special committee formed by the board of directors. It is ideally a group of outside directors who have no active day-to-day operations role and who are a liaison between the independent auditor and the board of directors. The audit committee assists and advises the full board of directors, and, as such, aids the board in fulfilling its responsibility for public financial reporting.

b.   Audit committees have been formed to satisfy the shareholders' need for assurance that directors are exercising due care in the performance of their duties. They were formed so that a company can be more responsive to the needs of those interested in financial reporting. Their formation, itself, is a recognition of the responsibilities of both the corporation and its auditor to the public investor. Also, they have been formed to reinforce auditor independence, particularly the appearance of independence, from the management of a company whose financial statements are being examined by the auditor.

c.   The functions of an audit committee may include the following:

· Select the independent auditor; discuss audit fee with the auditor; review auditor's engagement letter.
· Review the independent auditor's overall audit plan (scope, purpose, and general audit procedures).
· Review the annual financial statements before submission to the full board of directors for approval.
· Review the results of the auditor's examination including experiences, restrictions, cooperation received, findings, and recommendations. Consider matters that the auditor believes should be brought to the attention of the directors or shareholders.
· Review the independent auditor's evaluation of the company's internal control systems.
· Review the company's accounting, financial, and operating controls.
· Review the reports of internal audit staff.
· Review interim financial reports to shareholders before they are approved by the board of directors.
· Review company policies concerning political contributions, conflicts of interest, and compliance with federal, state, and local laws and regulations, and investigate compliance with those policies.
· Review financial statements that are part of prospectuses or offering circulars; review reports before they are submitted to regulatory agencies.
· Review independent auditor's observations of financial and accounting personnel.
· Participate in the selection and establishment of accounting policies; review the accounting for specific items or transactions as well as alternative treatments and their effects.

· Review the impact of new or proposed pronounce-ments by the accounting profession or regulatory bodies.
· Review the company's insurance program.
· Review and discuss the independent auditor's management letter.

ANSWER OUTLINE

Problem 2   Audit Deficiencies

1. Accepted engagement without determining in-tended use of statements
   Discuss the intended statement use with client
   Indicate alternative services available
2. Allowed client confusion about type of services to be provided
   Explain preparation of statements in contrast to audit
3. Accepted client without investigation of client
   Make inquiry of client to insure client in-tegrity
4. Accepted engagement without confirming in writing
   Prepare an engagement letter and send to client
5. Performed work on a contingent fee basis
   Accept fee based upon work to be performed

6. Used account name "Fees for Limited Audit Engagement"
   Do not use word "audit" in nonaudit en-gagements
   Use the term "accounting services"
7. Ignored missing invoices
   Advise client of missing invoices
   Encourage investigation of missing invoices
8. Prepared incomplete set of financial statements
   Prepare a statement of changes in financial position
   If not presented, disclose in disclaimer of opinion
9. Failed to disclose noncompliance with GAAP in footnotes
   Insist on appropriate revision of statements
   If not revised, disclose noncompliance in disclaimer of opinion
10. Failed to indicate clearly that statements were unaudited
    "Without complete audit verification" implies some audit
    Indicate statements are not audited and no opinion is expressed
    Mark each page "unaudited"

UNOFFICIAL ANSWER

Problem 2   Audit Deficiencies

Inappropriate Action	What Brown Should Have Done to Avoid Inappropriate Action
· Brown should not have accepted the assignment without determining the intended use of the finan-cial statements.	· Brown should have discussed with Calhoun the intended use of the statements.
	· Brown should have appraised Calhoun's needs and expectations and should have advised Calhoun about the types of professional services appropri-ate in light of Calhoun's objectives.
· Brown should not have ignored Calhoun's con-fusion about the services provided.	· Brown should have explained to Calhoun that preparation of financial statements is normally an engagement for accounting services and not an audit of financial statements.
· There is no indication that Brown considered poli-cies and procedures with regard to acceptance of this new client.	· Brown should have made appropriate inquiries to minimize any likelihood of association with a client whose management lacks integrity.
· Brown should not have accepted a verbal engage-ment without confirming it in writing.	· The verbal commitment should have been followed up with an engagement letter that included a de-scription, as specific as possible, of the nature and extent of the accounting service to be performed.

Inappropriate Action	What Brown Should Have Done to Avoid Inappropriate Action
· Brown should not have accepted the contingent fee arrangement.	· Brown should have accepted a fee arrangement that was based on the work to be performed, not on a contingency such as finishing within a certain time period.
· Brown should not have suggested that the account name be changed to "fees for limited audit engagement."	· The word "audit" should not be used on non-audit engagements. Brown should not have suggested any change or should have persuaded Calhoun to use the words "accounting services" and should have made certain that Calhoun understood the difference between an accounting service and an audit examination of the financial statements in accordance with generally accepted auditing standards.
· Brown should not have ignored the missing invoices.	· Brown should have advised Calhoun of the missing invoices. · Brown should have suggested that Calhoun expedite an investigation of the missing invoices, or, if Calhoun so desired, Brown could have investigated the matter as an additional accounting service.
· Brown should not have prepared an incomplete set of financial statements.	· Brown should have prepared a statement of changes in financial position, which APB Opinion no. 19 requires to be presented whenever a balance sheet and income statement are presented. · If Calhoun did not wish to include a statement of changes in financial position with the other basic statements, Brown should have appropriately referred to the incomplete presentation in the disclaimer of opinion.
· Brown should not have prepared a footnote that failed to disclose lack of conformity with generally accepted accounting principles.	· Brown should have insisted on appropriate revision of the unaudited statements so that they no longer reflect assets at replacement costs. · If Calhoun did not wish to make revisions, Brown should set forth reservations in the disclaimer of opinion with respect to the unacceptable accounting and lack of disclosure and the dollar effect.
Brown's attempt at a disclaimer did not clearly indicate that the statements had not been audited.	· Brown should have avoided using the words "without complete audit verification." These words imply that some type of audit was performed, and, because of them, Brown may be assuming more responsibility than originally intended.

· Brown's disclaimer of opinion should have stated
  that the financial statements "were not audited
  by me and accordingly I do not express an
  opinion on them."

· In addition each page of the financial statements
  should have been clearly and conspicuously marked
  as "unaudited."

ANSWER OUTLINE

Problem 3   Objectives of Audits

a. Objectives of an independent audit
   An examination of the statements per GAAS
   Assesses fairness of the statements per GAAP
      Including consistency
   Auditor as independent expert adds credibility
      to statements
      Insiders do not have objectivity to report
         on own company

b. Independent audits are beneficial to clients
   1. Basis for extension of credit
   2. Provides credit rating agencies with credit infor-
      mation
   3. Assists in preparation of tax returns
   4. Establishes losses from fire, theft, etc.
   5. Determines amounts due per various contracts
         E.g., bonuses, cost-plus contracts, etc.
   6. Provides data for proposed sales, mergers, etc.
   7. Provides basis for changes in accounting practices
   8. Basis for action in bankruptcy and insolvency
   9. Determines proper execution of trust agreements
   10. Furnishes estates with data to obtain proper
       settlements
   11. Provides review of client organization, procedures,
       etc.
   12. Establishes, improves systems of internal control
   13. Provides an important aid in tax audits, court
       actions
   14. Discourages employees from planning errors,
       irregularities
   15. Provides industry-wide comparisons
   16. Provides a realistic look at inventories
   17. Reviews adequacy of insurance coverage
   18. Makes professional knowledge of auditor avail-
       able to client

UNOFFICIAL ANSWER

Problem 3   Objectives of Audits

a.   Farber should explain to Feiler that an independent audit is an examination of the financial
statements in accordance with certain generally accepted auditing standards. The objective of an
ordinary examination is to render an opinion on
the fairness with which the financial statements
present financial position, results of operations, and
changes in financial position in conformity with
generally accepted accounting principles applied on
a consistent basis. The auditor, after an objective
evidence-gathering examination, expresses an opinion
and "bears witness" to the fair presentation of
financial statements. An independent expert is
needed to lend credibility to the financial statements. It would not be meaningful for a company to report on itself without the attestation
of an independent party because the company,
itself, might not be objective.

b.   Farber should inform Feiler of the following
ways in which an independent audit can be beneficial:

   1.   To serve as a basis for the extension of
         credit.
   2.   To supply credit rating agencies with re-
         quired information.
   3.   To serve as a basis for preparation of tax
         returns.
   4.   To establish amounts of losses from fire,
         theft, burglary, and so forth.
   5.   To determine amounts receivable or pay-
         able under
         a. agreements for bonuses based on profits.
         b. contracts for sharing expenses.
         c. cost-plus contracts.
   6.   To provide data for proposed changes in
         financial structure or to supply proper fin-

ancial data in the event of a proposed sale or merger.

7. To serve as a basis for changes in accounting or recording practices.

8. To serve as a basis for action in bankruptcy and insolvency cases.

9. To determine proper execution of trust agreements.

10. To furnish estates with information in order to obtain proper settlements and avoid costly litigation.

11. To provide a review of many aspects of the organization's activities and procedures.

12. To establish and/or improve systems of internal control.

13. To provide important aid in case of tax audits, court actions, and so forth.

14. To discourage employees from planning errors, irregularities, and so forth, by making them aware of auditor presence.

15. To provide industry-wide comparisons.

16. To provide a realistic look at inventories.

17. To review adequacy of insurance coverage.

18. To provide the professional knowledge of an external auditor, which is generally superior to the client's bookkeeping experience.

ANSWER OUTLINE

Problem 4   Tax and MAS Ethics Cases

2a.   The error was properly pointed out to the client
       Client should file an amended tax return
       CPA had no obligation to report the error to the IRS
           CPA was prohibited by confidential relationship

2b.   Hanlon should discuss the error with client executives
       Impressing the seriousness of the situation
       Including possible consequences
       Hanlon should consider withdrawal if client fails to amend the return
       CPA cannot prepare the 1971 return carrying forward the error
       The CPA, not the controller, must sign the preparer's declaration

3.   Browning must consider his competence to undertake the assignment
           Is he capable of obtaining the necessary training
           Or arranging for adequate assistance
       Lacking competence, he must refuse the engagement
       Relationship of the engagement to audit independence
           CPA must avoid active participation in management

Management should take final responsibility for the system
Client should participate in the MAS study

UNOFFICIAL ANSWER

Problem 4   Tax and MAS Ethics Cases

Note: Case 1 has been omitted because it tested old rule 502 which prohibited advertising.

Case 2

a. When Mr. Hanlon discovered the error, he properly referred it to the responsible Corporation officer. He also should have recommended proper remedial action: the filing of an amended 1970 return and correction of Guild's financial records. Mr. Hanlon had no obligation to report the error to the Internal Revenue Service; in fact, he was prohibited from doing this by his confidential relationship with his client.

b. In view of the controller's reaction to the error, Mr. Hanlon should consider discussions with one or more higher level officers of the Corporation and should put his recommendations in writing. He must impress upon the client the seriousness of this situation and the potential consequences and urge compliance with the tax law, which requires an amended return. He should consider withdrawal from the engagement if the client is unwilling to file the amended return.

Mr. Hanlon should refuse absolutely to prepare the 1971 tax return using the erroneous balance of accumulated undepreciated cost. If he prepares the return, he must sign the preparer's declaration and affirm that the return is true and correct to the best of his knowledge. The controller's letter cannot relieve him of his obligation.

Case 3

Two factors that Mr. Browning must consider in determining whether to accept this engagement are (1) his competence to undertake the assignment and (2) the effects of the engagement upon his independence as Grimm's auditor.

Mr. Browning is professionally responsible for evaluating his competence to provide service in any specific area. If he lacks experience, he must decide if he has or can obtain the necessary training or else arrange for adequate assistance. If he decides that he lacks **competence**, he must refuse the engagement, and, if possible, assist the client in finding a consultant who is competent to undertake the inventory control study.

The effect upon Mr. Browning's independence as auditor of Grimm's financial statements is a separate consideration. It is proper for an auditor to suggest improvements in internal control as a by-product of his examination or to undertake a special review for the purpose of recommending action. But he should avoid active participation in management and should not take final responsibility for installing the system. He should act only in an advisory capacity——decision should be made by Grimm's management. If Mr. Browning becomes too closely identified with management, the new system or its results, he may be unable to maintain an impartial mental attitude in his examination of the financial statements.

Client participation in the inventory control study is desirable even if there is no threat to audit independence. The CPA cannot be involved in continuing operations, and the client can better assume full responsibility for operating a new system if he has been involved in planning and operating it. Client participation also will result in procedures that better recognize his particular needs.

ANSWER OUTLINE

Problem **5**   Violations of GAAS

1. Adequate technical training and auditing proficiency
   Students had neither
2. Independence
   Contingent fee nullifies
3. Due professional care
   Lack of review and supervision
   Failure to comply with GAAS
4. Adequate planning and supervision
   Inadequate planning and no supervision
5. Proper study and evaluation of internal control
   None undertaken
6. Sufficient competent evidential matter
   None obtained
7. In accordance with GAAP
   No reference in report
   No basis for assertion
8. GAAP consistently applied
   No reference in report
   No basis for assertion
9. Adequate informative disclosure
   No statement footnotes
   No exception in report
10. Expression of opinion on statements as a whole
    Given but not on basis of proper audit

Problem **5**   Violations of GAAS   UNOFFICIAL ANSWER

Brief Description of Generally Accepted Auditing Standards	Holmes's Actions Resulting in Failure to Comply With Generally Accepted Auditing Standards
General Standards	
(1) The examination is to be performed by a person or persons having adequate technical training and proficiency as an auditor.	(1) It was inappropriate for Holmes to hire two students to conduct the audit. The examination must be conducted by persons with proper education and experience in the field of auditing. Although a junior assistant has not completed his formal education he may help in the conduct of the examination as long as there is proper supervision and review.
(2) In all matters relating to the assignment, an independence in mental attitude is to be maintained by the auditor or auditors.	(2) To satisfy the second general standard, Holmes must be without bias with respect to the client under audit. Holmes has an obligation for fairness to the owners, management, and creditors who may rely on the report. Because of the

Brief Description of Generally Accepted Auditing Standards	Holmes's Actions Resulting in Failure to Comply With Generally Accepted Auditing Standards
	financial interest in whether the bank loan is granted to Ray, Holmes is independent in neither fact nor appearance with respect to the assignment undertaken.
(3) Due professional care is to be exercised in the performance of the examination and the preparation of the report.	(3) This standard requires Holmes to perform the audit with due care, which imposes on Holmes and everyone in Holmes's organization a responsibility to observe the standards of field work and reporting. Exercise of due care requires critical review at every level of supervision of the work done and the judgments exercised by those assisting in the examination. Holmes did not review the work or the judgments of the assistants and clearly failed to adhere to this standard.

Standards of Field Work

(1) The work is to be adequately planned and assistants, if any, are to be properly supervised.	(1) This standard recognizes that early appointment of the auditor has advantages for the auditor and the client. Holmes accepted the engagement without considering the availability of competent staff. In addition, Holmes failed to supervise the assistants. The work performed was not adequately planned.
(2) There is to be a proper study and evaluation of the existing internal control as a basis for reliance thereon and for the determination of the resultant extent of the tests to which auditing procedures are to be restricted.	(2) Holmes did not study the system of internal control nor did the assistants conduct such a study. There appears to have been no audit examination at all. The work performed was more an accounting service than it was an auditing service.
(3) Sufficient, competent evidential matter is to be obtained through inspection, observation, inquiries, and confirmations to afford a reasonable basis for an opinion regarding the financial statements under examination.	(3) Holmes acquired no evidence that would support the financial statements. Holmes merely checked the mathematical accuracy of the records and summarized the accounts. Standard audit procedures and techniques were not performed.

Standards of Reporting

| (1) The report shall state whether the financial statements are presented in accordance with generally accepted accounting principles. | (1) Holmes's report made no reference to generally accepted accounting principles. Because Holmes did not conduct a proper examination, the report should state that no opinion can be expressed as to the fair presentation of the financial statements in accordance with generally accepted accounting principles. |

Brief Description of Generally Accepted Auditing Standards	Holmes's Actions Resulting in Failure to Comply With Generally Accepted Auditing Standards
(2) The report shall state whether such principles have been consistently observed in the current period in relation to the preceding period.	(2) Holmes's report makes no reference to the consistent application of accounting principles. Holmes's improper examination would not enable such an expression on consistency.
(3) Informative disclosures in the financial statements are to be regarded as reasonably adequate unless otherwise stated in the report.	(3) Management is primarily responsible for adequate disclosure in the financial statements, but when the statements do not contain adequate disclosures the auditor should make such disclosures in the auditor's report. In this case both the statements and the auditor's report lack adequate disclosures.
(4) The report shall either contain an expression of opinion regarding the financial statements taken as a whole or an assertion to the effect that an opinion cannot be expressed. When an overall opinion cannot be expressed, the reasons therefor should be stated. In all cases where an auditor's name is associated with financial statements, the report should contain a clear-cut indication of the character of the auditor's examination, if any, and the degree of responsibility he is taking.	(4) Although the Holmes report contains an expression of opinion, such opinion is not based on the results of a proper audit examination. Holmes should disclaim an opinion because he failed to conduct an examination in accordance with generally accepted auditing standards.

ANSWER OUTLINE

Problem 6   EDP Services

a.   Services that Savage may perform
 1.   Counsel on potential expansion plans
 2.   Search for and interview new personnel
 3.   Train personnel

Services that Savage may not perform
 1.   Hire new personnel
 2.   Instruct and train new personnel
 3.   Supervise operation of system
 4.   Monitor client's source documents and make changes in EDP generated data without client concurrence

b.   Significant matters of which client should be informed
 1.   Engagement objectives
 2.   Scope
 3.   Approach
 4.   Role of personnel

 5.   Manner in which results are to be communicated
 6.   Timetable
 7.   Fee

c.   Degree of knowledge necessary to supervise specialist
 Ability to define tasks
 Ability to evaluate end product

UNOFFICIAL ANSWER

Problem 6   EDP Services

a.

Services That Savage May Perform	Services That Savage May Not Perform
· Counsel on potential expansion plans.	· Hire new personnel.
· Search for and interview new personnel.	· Supervise the operation of the system.
· Train personnel.	· Monitor client-prepared source documents and make

> changes in basic EDP
> generated data with-
> out concurrence of
> the client.

b. The significant matters related to an engagement
    generally include (a) the engagement's objectives,
    (b) the scope, (c) the approach, (d) the role of all
    personnel, (e) the manner in which results are
    to be communicated, (f) the timetable, and (g) the
    fee.

c. Savage must be qualified to supervise and evaluate
    the work of specialist employees. Although super-
    vision does not require that Savage be qualified to
    perform each of the specialist's tasks, Savage
    should be able to define the tasks and evaluate the
    end product.

MULTIPLE CHOICE QUESTIONS (1—66)

1. Which of the following would be **least** likely to be included in an auditor's tests of compliance?
   a. Inspection.
   b. Observation.
   c. Inquiry.
   d. Confirmation.

2. Tests of compliance are concerned primarily with each of the following questions **except**
   a. How were the procedures performed?
   b. Why were the procedures performed?
   c. Were the necessary procedures performed?
   d. By whom were the procedures performed?

3. A decision table is most closely associated with which of the following auditor functions?
   a. Preparation of a generalized EDP computer audit program.
   b. Preliminary review of the client's system of internal control.
   c. Performance of tests of balances and transactions.
   d. Preparation of an audit program.

4. The sequence of steps in gathering evidence as the basis of the auditor's opinion is:
   a. Substantive tests, internal control review and compliance tests.
   b. Internal control review, substantive tests and compliance tests.
   c. Internal control review, compliance tests and substantive tests.
   d. Compliance tests, internal control review and substantive tests.

5. With respect to an internal control measure that will assure accountability for fixed asset retirements, management should implement a system that includes
   a. Continuous analysis of miscellaneous revenue to locate any cash proceeds from sale of plant assets.
   b. Periodic inquiry of plant executives by internal auditors as to whether any plant assets have been retired.
   c. Continuous utilization of serially numbered retirement work orders.
   d. Periodic observation of plant assets by the internal auditors.

6. Which of the following is a primary function of the purchasing department?
   a. Authorizing the acquisition of goods.
   b. Ensuring the acquisition of goods of a specified quality.
   c. Verifying the propriety of goods acquired.
   d. Reducing expenditures for goods acquired.

7. An auditor evaluates the existing system of internal control in order to
   a. Determine the extent of compliance tests which must be performed.
   b. Determine the extent of substantive tests which must be performed.
   c. Ascertain whether irregularities are probable.
   d. Ascertain whether any employees have incompatible functions.

8. Which of the following precedures would best detect the theft of valuable items from an inventory that consists of hundreds of different items selling for $1 to $10 and a few items selling for hundreds of dollars?
   a. Maintain a perpetual inventory of only the more valuable items with frequent periodic verification of the validity of the perpetual inventory record.
   b. Have an independent CPA firm prepare an internal control report on the effectiveness of the administrative and accounting controls over inventory.
   c. Have separate warehouse space for the more valuable items with sequentially numbered tags.
   d. Require an authorized officer's signature on all requisitions for the more valuable items.

9. Proper segregation of functional responsibilities calls for separation of the
   a. Authorization, approval, and execution functions.
   b. Authorization, execution, and payment functions.
   c. Receiving, shipping, and custodial functions.
   d. Authorization, recording, and custodial functions.

10. Jackson, the purchasing agent of Judd Hardware Wholesalers, has a relative who owns a retail hardware store. Jackson arranged for hardware to be delivered by manufacturers to the retail store on a C.O.D. basis thereby enabling his relative to buy at Judd's wholesale prices. Jackson was probably able to accomplish this because of Judd's poor internal control over
   a. Purchase orders.
   b. Purchase requisitions.
   c. Cash receipts.
   d. Perpetual inventory records.

11. The auditor's review of the client's system of

internal control is documented in order to substantiate
   a.   Conformity of the accounting records with generally accepted accounting principles.
   b.   Representation as to adherence to requirements of management.
   c.   Representation as to compliance with generally accepted auditing standards.
   d.   The fairness of the financial statement presentation.

12.   It is important for the CPA to consider the competence of the audit clients' employees because their competence bears directly and importantly upon the
   a.   Cost/benefit relationship of the system of internal control.
   b.   Achievement of the objectives of the system of internal control.
   c.   Comparison of recorded accountability with assets.
   d.   Timing of the tests to be performed.

13.   Which of the following audit tests would be regarded as a test of "compliance?"
   a.   Tests of the specific items making up the balance in a given general ledger account.
   b.   Tests of the inventory pricing to vendors' invoices.
   c.   Tests of the signatures on cancelled checks to board of director's authorizations.
   d.   Tests of the additions to property, plant, and equipment by physical inspections.

14.   Which of the following is essential to determine whether the necessary internal control procedures were prescribed and are being followed?
   a.   Developing questionnaires and checklists.
   b.   Studying and evaluating administrative control policies.
   c.   Reviewing the system and testing compliance.
   d.   Observing employee functions and making inquiries.

15.   In general, a material internal control weakness may be defined as a condition in which material errors or irregularities would ordinarily not be detected within a timely period by
   a.   An auditor during the normal study and evaluation of the system of internal control.
   b.   A controller when reconciling accounts in the general ledger.
   c.   Employees in the normal course of performing their assigned functions.
   d.   The chief financial officer when reviewing interim financial statements.

16.   Propex Corporation uses a voucher register and does not record invoices in a subsidiary ledger. Propex will probably benefit most from the additional cost of maintaining an accounts payable subsidiary ledger if
   a.   There are usually invoices in an unmatched invoice file.
   b.   Vendors' requests for confirmation of receivables often go unanswered for several months until paid invoices can be reviewed.
   c.   Partial payments to vendors are continuously made in the ordinary course of business.
   d.   It is difficult to reconcile vendors' monthly statements.

17.   For internal control purposes, which of the following individuals should preferably be responsible for the distribution of payroll checks?
   a.   Bookkeeper.
   b.   Payroll clerk.
   c.   Cashier.
   d.   Receptionist.

18.   For the purpose of proper accounting control, postdated checks remitted by customers should be
   a.   Restrictively endorsed.
   b.   Returned to customer.
   c.   Recorded as a cash sale.
   d.   Placed in the joint custody of two officers.

19.   The primary purpose of performing compliance tests is to provide reasonable assurance that
   a.   Accounting control procedures are being applied as prescribed.
   b.   The flow of transactions through the accounting system is understood.
   c.   Transactions are recorded at the amounts executed.
   d.   All accounting control procedures leave visible evidence.

20.   In order to safeguard the assets through proper internal control, accounts receivable that are written off are transferred to a (an)
   a.   Separate ledger.
   b.   Attorney for evidence in collection proceedings.
   c.   Tax deductions file.
   d.   Credit manager since customers may seek to reestablish credit by paying.

21.   Where no independent stock transfer agents are employed and the corporation issues its own stocks and maintains stock records, cancelled stock certificates should
   a.   Be defaced to prevent reissuance and attached to their corresponding stubs.

b. Not be defaced, but segregated from other stock certificates and retained in a cancelled certificates file.

c. Be destroyed to prevent fraudulent reissuance.

d. Be defaced and sent to the secretary of state.

22. Which of the following is an internal accounting control weakness related to factory equipment?

a. Checks issued in payment of purchases of equipment are not signed by the controller.

b. All purchases of factory equipment are required to be made by the department in need of the equipment.

c. Factory equipment replacements are generally made when estimated useful lives, as indicated in depreciation schedules, have expired.

d. Proceeds from sales of fully depreciated equipment are credited to other income.

23. A management information system is designed to ensure that management possesses the information it needs to carry out its functions through the integrated actions of

a. Data-gathering, analysis and reporting functions.

b. A computerized information retrieval and decision-making system.

c. Statistical and analytical review functions.

d. Production-budgeting and sales-forecasting activities.

24. Proper internal control over the cash payroll function would mandate which of the following?

a. The payroll clerk should fill the envelopes with cash and a computation of the net wages.

b. Unclaimed pay envelopes should be retained by the paymaster.

c. Each employee should be asked to sign a receipt.

d. A separate checking account for payroll be maintained.

25. A company policy should clearly indicate that defective merchandise returned by customers is to be delivered to the

a. Sales clerk.

b. Receiving clerk.

c. Inventory control clerk.

d. Accounts receivable clerk.

26. A CPA reviews a client's payroll procedures.

The CPA would consider internal control to be less than effective if a payroll department supervisor was assigned the responsibility for

a. Reviewing and approving time reports for subordinate employees.

b. Distributing payroll checks to employees.

c. Hiring subordinate employees.

d. Initiating requests for salary adjustments for subordinate employees.

27. Which of the following is the most important internal control procedure over acquisitions of property, plant and equipment?

a. Establishing a written company policy distinguishing between capital and revenue expenditures.

b. Using a budget to forecast and control acquisitions and retirements.

c. Analyzing monthly variances between authorized expenditures and actual costs.

d. Requiring acquisitions to be made by user departments.

28. Which of the following would be the best protection for a company that wishes to prevent the "lapping" of trade accounts receivable?

a. Segregate duties so that the bookkeeper in charge of the general ledger has no access to incoming mail.

b. Segregate duties so that no employee has access to both checks from customers and currency from daily cash receipts.

c. Have customers send payments directly to the company's depository bank.

d. Request that customers' payment checks be made payable to the company and addressed to the treasurer.

29. One reason why an auditor uses a flowchart is to aid in the

a. Evaluation of a series of sequential processes.

b. Study of the system of responsibility accounting.

c. Performance of important, required, dual-purpose tests.

d. Understanding of a client's organizational structure.

30. Which of the following is an internal control weakness for a company whose inventory of supplies consists of a large number of individual items?

a. Supplies of relatively little value are expensed when purchased.

b. The cycle basis is used for physical counts.

c. The storekeeper is responsible for maintenance of perpetual inventory records.

d. Perpetual inventory records are maintained only for items of significant value.

31. In order to avoid the misappropriation of company-owned marketable securities, which of the following is the best course of action that can be taken by the management of a company with a large portfolio of marketable securities?

a. Require that one trustworthy and bonded employee be responsible for access to the safekeeping area, where securities are kept.

b. Require that employees who enter and leave the safekeeping area sign and record in a log the exact reason for their access.

c. Require that employees involved in the safekeeping function maintain a subsidiary control ledger for securities on a current basis.

d. Require that the safekeeping function for securities be assigned to a bank that will act as a custodial agent.

32. Which of the following internal control procedures will most likely prevent the concealment of a cash shortage resulting from the improper write-off of a trade account receivable?

a. Write-offs must be approved by a responsible officer after review of credit department recommendations and supporting evidence.

b. Write-offs must be supported by an aging schedule showing that only receivables overdue several months have been written-off.

c. Write-offs must be approved by the cashier who is in a position to know if the receivables have, in fact, been collected.

d. Write-offs must be authorized by company field sales employees who are in a position to determine the financial standing of the customers.

33. A secondary objective of the auditor's study and evaluation of internal control is that the study and evaluation provide

a. A basis for constructive suggestions concerning improvements in internal control.

b. A basis for reliance on the system of internal accounting control.

c. An assurance that the records and documents have been maintained in accordance with existing company policies and procedures.

d. A basis for the determination of the resultant extent of the tests to which auditing procedures are to be restricted.

34. Effective internal accounting control over the payroll function should include procedures that segregate the duties of making salary payments to employees and

a. Controlling unemployment insurance claims.

b. Maintaining employee personnel records.

c. Approving employee fringe benefits.

d. Hiring new employees.

35. Effective internal control over the payroll function would include which of the following?

a. Total time recorded on time-clock punch cards should be reconciled to job reports by employees responsible for those specific jobs.

b. Payroll department employees should be supervised by the management of the personnel department.

c. Payroll department employees should be responsible for maintaining employee personnel records.

d. Total time spent on jobs should be compared with total time indicated on time-clock punch cards.

36. Effective internal control requires organizational independence of departments. Organizational independence would be impaired in which of the following situations?

a. The internal auditors report to the audit committee of the board of directors.

b. The controller reports to the vice president of production.

c. The payroll accounting department reports to the chief accountant.

d. The cashier reports to the treasurer.

37. Effective internal control over the purchasing of raw materials should usually include all of the following procedures except

a. Systematic reporting of product changes which will affect raw materials.

b. Determining the need for the raw materials prior to preparing the purchase order.

c. Obtaining third-party written quality and quantity reports prior to payment for the raw materials.

d. Obtaining financial approval prior to making a commitment.

38. Which of the following best describes why publicly-traded corporations follow the practice of having the outside auditor appointed by the board

of directors or elected by the stockholders?

    a.   To comply with the regulations of the Financial Accounting Standards Board.

    b.   To emphasize auditor independence from the management of the corporation.

    c.   To encourage a policy of rotation of the independent auditors.

    d.   To provide the corporate owners with an opportunity to voice their opinion concerning the quality of the auditing firm selected by the directors.

39. To achieve effective internal accounting control over fixed-asset additions, a company should establish procedures that require

    a.   Capitalization of the cost of fixed-asset additions in excess of a specific dollar amount.

    b.   Performance of recurring fixed-asset maintenance work solely by maintenance department employees.

    c.   Classification as investments, those fixed-asset additions that are not used in the business.

    d.   Authorization and approval of major fixed-asset additions.

40. Which of the following is an effective internal accounting control measure that encourages receiving department personnel to count and inspect all merchandise received?

    a.   Quantities ordered are excluded from the receiving department copy of the purchase order.

    b.   Vouchers are prepared by accounts payable department personnel only after they match item counts on the receiving report with the purchase order.

    c.   Receiving department personnel are expected to match and reconcile the receiving report with the purchase order.

    d.   Internal auditors periodically examine, on a surprise basis, the receiving department copies of receiving reports.

41. To strengthen the system of internal accounting control over the purchase of merchandise, a company's receiving department should

    a.   Accept merchandise only if a purchase order or approval granted by the purchasing department is on hand.

    b.   Accept and count all merchandise received from the usual company vendors.

    c.   Rely on shipping documents for the preparation of receiving reports.

    d.   Be responsible for the physical handling of merchandise but not the preparation of receiving reports.

42. A client's materials-purchasing cycle begins with requisitions from user departments and ends with the receipt of materials and the recognition of a liability. An auditor's primary objective in reviewing this cycle is to

    a.   Evaluate the reliability of information generated as a result of the purchasing process.

    b.   Investigate the physical handling and recording of unusual acquisitions of materials.

    c.   Consider the need to be on hand for the annual physical count if this system is not functioning properly.

    d.   Ascertain that materials said to be ordered, received, and paid for are on hand.

43. The two phases of the auditor's study of internal accounting control are referred to as "review of the system" and "tests of compliance." In the tests of compliance phase the auditor attempts to

    a.   Obtain a reasonable degree of assurance that the client's system of controls is in use and is operating as planned.

    b.   Obtain sufficient, competent evidential matter to afford a reasonable basis for the auditor's opinion.

    c.   Obtain assurances that informative disclosures in the financial statements are reasonably adequate.

    d.   Obtain knowledge and understanding of the client's prescribed procedures and methods.

44. Which of the following is an effective internal accounting control over accounts receivable?

    a.   Only persons who handle cash receipts should be responsible for the preparation of documents that reduce accounts receivable balances.

    b.   Responsibility for approval of the write-off of uncollectible accounts receivable should be assigned to the cashier.

    c.   Balances in the subsidiary accounts receivable ledger should be reconciled to the general ledger control account once a year, preferably at year-end.

    d.   The billing function should be assigned to persons other than those responsible for maintaining accounts receivable subsidiary records.

45. Effective internal accounting control over unclaimed payroll checks that are kept by the treasury department would include accounting department procedures that require

a. Effective cancelation and stop payment orders for checks representing unclaimed wages.

b. Preparation of a list of unclaimed wages on a periodic basis.

c. Accounting for all unclaimed wages in a current liability account.

d. Periodic accounting for the actual checks representing unclaimed wages.

46. At interim dates an auditor evaluates a client's internal accounting control procedures and finds them to be effective. The auditor then performs a substantial part of the audit engagement on a continuous basis throughout the year. At a minimum, the auditor's year-end audit procedures must include

a. Determination that the client's internal accounting control procedures are still effective at year-end.

b. Confirmation of those year-end accounts that were examined at interim dates.

c. Tests of compliance with internal control in the same manner as those tests made at the interim dates.

d. Comparison of the responses to the auditor's internal control questionnaire with a detailed flowchart at year-end.

47. The ultimate risk against which the auditor requires reasonable protection is a combination of two separate risks. The first of these is that material errors will occur in the accounting process by which the financial statements are developed, and the second is that

a. A company's system of internal control is not adequate to detect errors and irregularities.

b. Those errors that occur will not be detected in the auditor's examination.

c. Management may possess an attitude that lacks integrity.

d. Evidential matter is not competent enough for the auditor to form an opinion based on reasonable assurance.

48. One important reason why a CPA, during the course of an audit engagement, prepares systems flowcharts is to

a. Reduce the need for inquiries of client personnel concerning the operations of the system of internal accounting control.

b. Depict the organizational structure and document flow in a single chart for review and reference purposes.

c. Assemble the internal control findings into a comprehensible format suitable for analysis.

d. Prepare documentation that would be useful in the event of a future consulting engagement.

49. Which of the following best describes the inherent limitations that should be recognized by an auditor when considering the potential effectiveness of a system of internal accounting control?

a. Procedures whose effectiveness depends on segregation of duties can be circumvented by collusion.

b. The competence and integrity of client personnel provides an environment conducive to accounting control and provides assurance that effective control will be achieved.

c. Procedures designed to assure the execution and recording of transactions in accordance with proper authorizations are effective against irregularities perpetrated by management.

d. The benefits expected to be derived from effective internal accounting control usually do not exceed the costs of such control.

50. Which of the following is an effective internal accounting control over cash payments?

a. Signed checks should be mailed under the supervision of the check signer.

b. Spoiled checks which have been voided should be disposed of immediately.

c. Checks should be prepared only by persons responsible for cash receipts and cash disbursements.

d. A check-signing machine with two signatures should be utilized.

51. When considering internal control, an auditor must be aware of the concept of reasonable assurance which recognizes that

a. The employment of competent personnel provides assurance that the objectives of internal control will be achieved.

b. The establishment and maintenance of a system of internal control is an important responsibility of the management and not of the auditor.

c. The cost of internal control should not exceed the benefits expected to be derived from internal control.

d. The segregation of incompatible functions is necessary to obtain assurance that the internal control is effective.

52. With respect to a small company's system of purchasing supplies, an auditor's primary concern should be to obtain satisfaction that supplies ordered and paid for have been
   a. Requested by and approved by authorized individuals who have no incompatible duties.
   b. Received, counted, and checked to quantities and amounts on purchase orders and invoices.
   c. Properly recorded as assets and systematically amortized over the estimated useful life of the supplies.
   d. Used in the course of business and solely for business purposes during the year under audit.

53. Which of the following best describes the primary reason for the auditor's use of flowcharts during an audit engagement?
   a. To comply with the requirements of generally accepted auditing standards.
   b. To classify the client's documents and transactions by major operating functions, e.g., cash receipts, cash disbursements, etc.
   c. To record the auditor's understanding of the client's system of internal accounting control.
   d. To interpret the operational effectiveness of the client's existing organizational structure.

54. When considering the effectiveness of a system of internal accounting control, the auditor should recognize that inherent limitations do exist. Which of the following is an example of an inherent limitation in a system of internal accounting control?
   a. The effectiveness of procedures depends on the segregation of employee duties.
   b. Procedures are designed to assure the execution and recording of transactions in accordance with management's authorization.
   c. In the performance of most control procedures, there are possibilities of errors arising from mistakes in judgment.
   d. Procedures for handling large numbers of transactions are processed by electronic data processing equipment.

55. A system of internal accounting control normally would include procedures that are designed to provide reasonable assurance that
   a. Employees act with integrity when performing their assigned tasks.
   b. Transactions are executed in accordance with management's general or specific authorization.
   c. Decision processes leading to management's authorization of transactions are sound.
   d. Collusive activities would be detected by segregation of employee duties.

56. A company has additional temporary funds to invest. The board of directors decided to purchase marketable securities and assigned the future purchase and sale decisions to a responsible financial executive. The best person(s) to make periodic reviews of the investment activity should be
   a. The investment committee of the board of directors.
   b. The treasurer.
   c. The corporate controller.
   d. The chief operating officer.

57. An independent auditor has concluded that the client's records, procedures, and representations can be relied upon based on tests made during the year when internal control was found to be effective. The auditor should test the records, procedures, and representations again at year-end if
   a. Inquiries and observations lead the auditor to believe that conditions have changed significantly.
   b. Comparisons of year-end balances with like balances at prior dates revealed significant fluctuations.
   c. Unusual transactions occurred subsequent to the completion of the interim audit work.
   d. Client records are in a condition that facilitate effective and efficient testing.

58. Internal control is a function of management, and effective control is based upon the concept of charge and discharge of responsibility and duty. Which of the following is one of the overriding principles of internal control?
   a. Responsibility for accounting and financial duties should be assigned to one responsible officer.
   b. Responsibility for the performance of each duty must be fixed.
   c. Responsibility for the accounting duties must be borne by the auditing committee of the company.
   d. Responsibility for accounting activities and duties must be assigned only to employees who are bonded.

MAY 1981 QUESTIONS

59.   The primary purpose of the auditor's study and evaluation of internal control is to provide a basis for

    a.   Determining whether procedures and records that are concerned with the safeguarding of assets are reliable.

    b.   Constructive suggestions to clients concerning improvements in internal control.

    c.   Determining the nature, extent, and timing of audit tests to be applied.

    d.   The expression of an opinion.

60.   The purpose of tests of compliance is to provide reasonable assurance that the

    a.   Accounting treatment of transactions and balances is valid and proper.

    b.   Accounting control procedures are functioning as intended.

    c.   Entity has complied with disclosure requirements of generally accepted accounting principles.

    d.   Entity has complied with requirements of quality control.

61.   During the review of an EDP internal control system an auditor may review decision tables prepared by the client. A decision table is usually prepared by a client to supplement or replace the preparation of

    a.   An internal control questionnaire when the number of alternative responses is large.

    b.   A narrative description of a system where transactions are not processed in batches.

    c.   Flowcharts when the number of alternatives is large.

    d.   An internal control questionnaire not specifically designed for an EDP installation.

62.   A CPA examines a sample of copies of December and January sales invoices for the initials of the person who verified the quantitative data. This is an example of a

    a.   Compliance test.

    b.   Substantive test.

    c.   Cutoff test.

    d.   Statistical test.

63.   An auditor's flowchart of a client's internal control system is a diagrammatic representation which depicts the auditor's

    a.   Understanding of the system.

    b.   Program for compliance tests.

    c.   Documentation of the study and evaluation of the system.

    d.   Understanding of the types of irregularities which are probable, given the present system.

64.   In the audit of which of the following types of profit-oriented enterprises would the auditor be most likely to place special emphasis on testing the internal controls over proper classification of payroll transactions?

    a.   A manufacturing organization.

    b.   A retailing organization.

    c.   A wholesaling organization.

    d.   A service organization.

65.   When evaluating inventory controls with respect to segregation of duties, a CPA would be **least** likely to

    a.   Inspect documents.

    b.   Make inquiries.

    c.   Observe procedures.

    d.   Consider policy and procedure manuals.

66.   The objective of precision in sampling for compliance testing on an internal control system is to

    a.   Determine the probability of the auditor's conclusion based upon reliance factors.

    b.   Determine that financial statements taken as a whole are not materially in error.

    c.   Estimate the reliability of substantive tests.

    d.   Estimate the range of procedural deviations in the population.

PROBLEMS

Problem 1   Evaluation of Internal Control (1179,A5)

(15 to 25 minutes)

Internal control comprises the plan of organization and all of the coordinate methods and measures adopted within a business to safeguard its assets, check the accuracy and reliability of its accounting data, promote operational efficiency, and encourage adherence to prescribed managerial policies.

Required:

a.   What is the purpose of the auditor's study and evaluation of internal control?

b.   What are the objectives of a preliminary evaluation of internal control?

c.   How is the auditor's understanding of the system of internal control documented?

d.   What is the purpose of tests of compliance?

Problem 2   Material Purchase IC Weaknesses (1173,A6)

(25 to 30 minutes)

You have been engaged by the management of Alden, Inc., to review its internal control over the purchase, receipt, storage, and issue of raw materials. You have prepared the following comments which describe Alden's procedures.

Raw materials, which consist mainly of high-cost electronic components, are kept in a locked storeroom. Storeroom personnel include a supervisor and four clerks. All are well trained, competent, and adequately bonded. Raw materials are removed from the storeroom only upon written or oral authorization of one of the production foremen.

There are no perpetual-inventory records; hence, the storeroom clerks do not keep records of goods received or issued. To compensate for the lack of perpetual records, a physical-inventory count is taken monthly by the storeroom clerks who are well supervised. Appropriate procedures are followed in making the inventory count.

After the physical count, the storeroom supervisor matches quantities counted against predetermined reorder level. If the count for a given part is below the reorder level, the supervisor enters the part number on a materials-requisition list and sends this list to the accounts-payable clerk. The accounts-payable clerk prepares a purchase order for a predetermined reorder quantity for each part and mails the purchase order to the vendor from whom the part was last purchased.

When ordered materials arrive at Alden, they are received by the storeroom clerks. The clerks count the merchandise and agree the counts to the shipper's bill of lading. All vendors' bills of lading are initialed, dated, and filed in the storeroom to serve as receiving reports.

Required:

Describe the weaknesses in internal control and recommend improvements of Alden's procedures for the purchase, receipt, storage, and issue of raw materials. Organize your answer sheet as follows:

Weaknesses	Recommended Improvements

Problem 3   Customer Invoice IC Weaknesses (572,A6)

(25 to 30 minutes)

George Beemster, CPA, is examining the financial statements of the Louisville Sales Corporation, which recently installed an off-line electronic computer. The following comments have been extracted from Mr. Beemster's notes on computer operations and the processing and control of shipping notices and customer invoices:

To minimize inconvenience Louisville converted without change its existing data processing system, which utilized tabulating equipment. The computer company supervised the conversion and has provided training to all computer department employees (except key punch operators) in systems design, operations and programming.

Each computer run is assigned to a specific employee, who is responsible for making program changes, running the program and answering questions. This procedure has the advantage of eliminating the need for records of computer operations because each employee is responsible for his own computer runs.

At least one computer department employee remains in the computer room during office hours, and only computer department employees have keys to the computer room.

System documentation consists of those materials furnished by the computer company — a set of record formats and program listings. These and the tape library are kept in a corner of the computer department.

The company considered the desirability of programmed controls but decided to retain the manual controls from its existing system.

Company products are shipped directly from public warehouses which forward shipping notices to general accounting. There a billing clerk enters the price of the item and accounts for the numerical sequence of shipping notices from each warehouse. The billing clerk also prepares daily adding machine tapes ("control tapes") of the units shipped and the unit prices.

Shipping notices and control tapes are forwarded to the computer department for key punching and processing. Extensions are made on the computer. Output consists of invoices (in six copies) and a daily sales register. The daily sales register shows the aggregate totals of units shipped and unit prices which the computer operator compares to the control tapes.

All copies of the invoice are returned to the billing clerk. The clerk mails three copies to the customer, forwards one copy to the warehouse, maintains one copy in a numerical file and retains one copy in an open invoice file that serves as a detailed accounts receivable record.

Required:

Describe weaknesses in internal control over information and data flows and the procedures for processing shipping notices and customer invoices and recommend improvements in these controls and processing procedures. Organize your answer sheets as follows:

Weaknesses	Recommended Improvements

Problem 4   Payroll IC Weakness (580,A5)

(15 to 25 minutes)

A CPA's audit working papers contain a narrative description of a **segment** of the Croyden Factory, Inc., payroll system and an accompanying flowchart as follows:

NARRATIVE

The internal control system with respect to the personnel department is well-functioning and is **not** included in the accompanying flowchart.

At the beginning of each work week payroll clerk No. 1 reviews the payroll department files to determine the employment status of factory employees and then prepares time cards and distributes them as each individual arrives at work. This payroll clerk, who is also responsible for custody of the signature stamp machine, verifies the identity of each payee before delivering signed checks to the foreman.

At the end of each work week the foreman distributes payroll checks for the preceding work week. Concurrent with this activity, the foreman reviews the current week's employee time cards, notes the regular and overtime hours worked on a summary form, and initials the aforementioned time cards. The foreman then delivers all time cards and unclaimed payroll checks to payroll clerk No. 2.

Required:
a. Based upon the narrative and accompanying flowchart, what are the weaknesses in the system of internal control?
b. Based upon the narrative and accompanying flowchart, what inquiries should be made with respect to clarifying the existence of **possible additional weaknesses** in the system of internal control?

Note: Do not discuss the internal control system of the personnel department.

Flow chart appears
on next page

CROYDEN INC., FACTORY PAYROLL SYSTEM

FACTORY EMPLOYEES	FACTORY FOREMAN	PERSONNEL	PAYROLL CLERK NO. 1	PAYROLL CLERK NO. 2	BOOKKEEPING

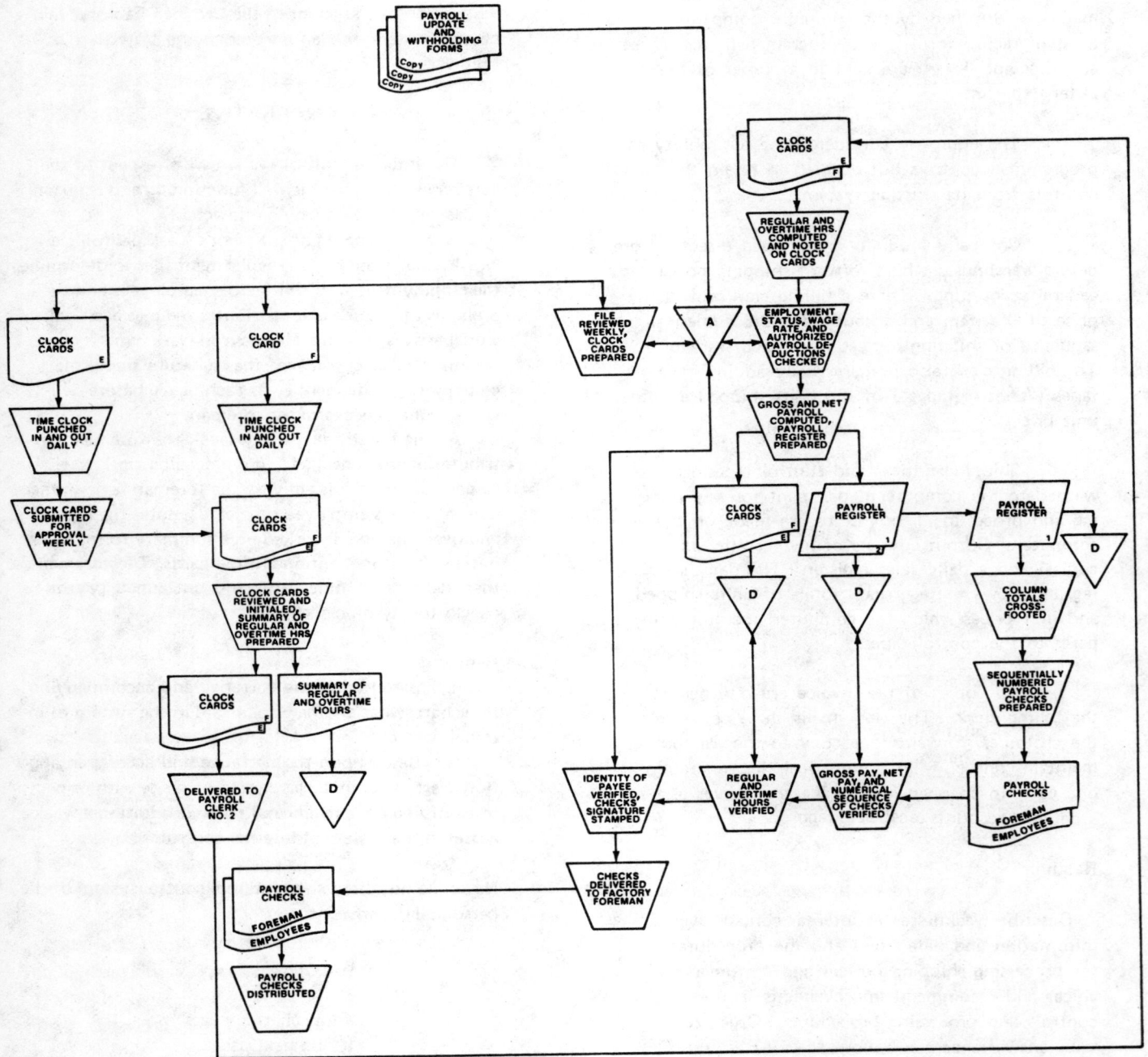

PAYROLL UPDATE AND WITHHOLDING FORMS — Copy / Copy / Copy

CLOCK CARDS — F

REGULAR AND OVERTIME HRS. COMPUTED AND NOTED ON CLOCK CARDS

FILE REVIEWED WEEKLY, CLOCK CARDS PREPARED

A

EMPLOYMENT STATUS, WAGE RATE, AND AUTHORIZED PAYROLL DEDUCTIONS CHECKED

GROSS AND NET PAYROLL COMPUTED, PAYROLL REGISTER PREPARED

CLOCK CARDS — E

CLOCK CARD — F

TIME CLOCK PUNCHED IN AND OUT DAILY

TIME CLOCK PUNCHED IN AND OUT DAILY

CLOCK CARDS SUBMITTED FOR APPROVAL WEEKLY

CLOCK CARDS — F

CLOCK CARDS REVIEWED AND INITIALED, SUMMARY OF REGULAR AND OVERTIME HRS PREPARED

CLOCK CARDS — F

CLOCK CARDS — E

PAYROLL REGISTER — 1

PAYROLL REGISTER — 1

D

COLUMN TOTALS CROSS-FOOTED

SEQUENTIALLY NUMBERED PAYROLL CHECKS PREPARED

CLOCK CARDS — E

SUMMARY OF REGULAR AND OVERTIME HOURS

DELIVERED TO PAYROLL CLERK NO. 2

D

D

D

IDENTITY OF PAYEE VERIFIED, CHECKS SIGNATURE STAMPED

REGULAR AND OVERTIME HOURS VERIFIED

GROSS PAY, NET PAY, AND NUMERICAL SEQUENCE OF CHECKS VERIFIED

PAYROLL CHECKS — FOREMAN — EMPLOYEES

CHECKS DELIVERED TO FACTORY FOREMAN

PAYROLL CHECKS — FOREMAN — EMPLOYEES

PAYROLL CHECKS DISTRIBUTED

Problem 5   Internal Control Limitations (1172,A6)

(25 to 30 minutes)

The financial statements of the Tiber Company have never been audited by an independent CPA. Recently Tiber's management asked Anthony Burns, CPA, to conduct a special study of Tiber's internal control; this study will not include an examination of Tiber's financial statements. Following completion of his special study, Mr. Burns plans to prepare a report that is consistent with the requirements of Statement on Auditing Procedure No. 49, "Reports on Internal Control."

Required:

a. Describe the inherent limitations that should be recognized in considering the potential effectiveness of any system of internal control.

b. Explain and contrast the review of internal control that Mr. Burns might make as part of an examination of financial statements with his special study of Tiber's internal control, covering each of the following:

1.   Objectives of review or study.

2.   Scope of review or study

3.   Nature and content of reports.

Organize your answer for part b as follows:

Examination of Financial Statements	Special Study
1. Objective	1. Objective
2. Scope	2. Scope
3. Report	3. Report

c. In connection with a loan application, Tiber plans to submit the CPA's report on his special study of internal control, together with its latest unaudited financial statements, to the Fourth National Bank.

Discuss the propriety of this use of the CPA's report on internal control.

Problem 6   Purchasing Function Flowchart (1175,A6)

(20 to 25 minutes)

Anthony, CPA, prepared the flowchart on the following page which portrays the raw materials purchasing function of one of Anthony's clients, a medium-sized manufacturing company, from the preparation of initial documents through the vouching of invoices for payment in accounts payable. The flowchart was a portion of the work performed on the audit engagement to evaluate internal control.

Required:

Identify and explain the systems and control weaknesses evident from the flowchart on the following page. Include the internal control weaknesses resulting from activities performed or not performed. All documents are prenumbered.

Flowchart appears on next page.

Problem 7   Purchasing Department Controls (1178,A4)

(15 to 25 minutes)

Long, CPA, has been engaged to examine and report on the financial statements of Maylou Corporation. During the review phase of the study of Maylou's system of internal accounting control over purchases, Long was given the following document flowchart for purchases.

Required:
a. Identify the procedures, relating to purchase requisitions and purchase orders, that Long would expect to find if Maylou's system of internal control over purchases is effective. For example, purchase orders are prepared only after giving proper consideration to the time to order, and quantity to order. Do not comment on the effectiveness of the flow of documents as presented in the flowchart or on separation of duties.

b. What are the factors to consider in determining—
1.   The time to order?
2.   The quantity to order?

MEDIUM-SIZED MANUFACTURING COMPANY
FLOWCHART OF RAW MATERIALS PURCHASING FUNCTION

Date _____
Prepared By _____
Approved By _____

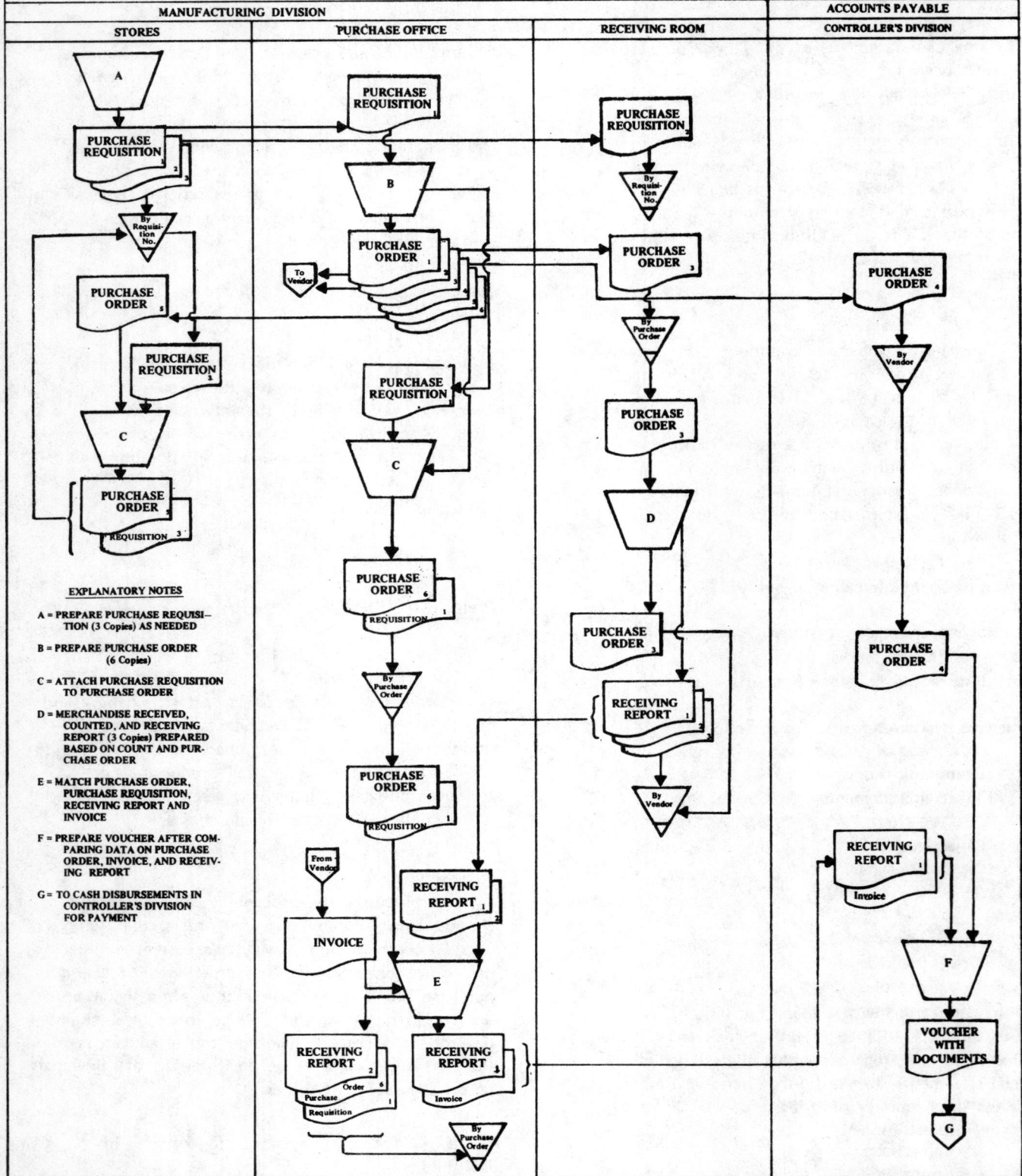

MANUFACTURING DIVISION			ACCOUNTS PAYABLE
STORES	PURCHASE OFFICE	RECEIVING ROOM	CONTROLLER'S DIVISION

A

PURCHASE REQUISITION 2

By Requisition No.

PURCHASE ORDER 5

PURCHASE REQUISITION 1

C

PURCHASE ORDER 5
REQUISITION 3

PURCHASE REQUISITION 1

B

PURCHASE ORDER 1
2 3 4 5 6

To Vendor

PURCHASE REQUISITION 1

C

PURCHASE ORDER 6
REQUISITION 1

By Purchase Order

PURCHASE ORDER 6
REQUISITION 1

From Vendor

INVOICE

RECEIVING REPORT 1 2

E

RECEIVING REPORT 2
Order 6
Purchase
Requisition 1

RECEIVING REPORT 3
Invoice

By Purchase Order

PURCHASE REQUISITION 3

By Requisition No.

PURCHASE ORDER 3

By Purchase Order

PURCHASE ORDER 3

D

PURCHASE ORDER 3

RECEIVING REPORT 1 2 3

By Vendor

PURCHASE ORDER 4

By Vendor

PURCHASE ORDER 4

RECEIVING REPORT 1
Invoice

F

VOUCHER WITH DOCUMENTS

G

EXPLANATORY NOTES

A = PREPARE PURCHASE REQUISITION (3 Copies) AS NEEDED

B = PREPARE PURCHASE ORDER (6 Copies)

C = ATTACH PURCHASE REQUISITION TO PURCHASE ORDER

D = MERCHANDISE RECEIVED, COUNTED, AND RECEIVING REPORT (3 Copies) PREPARED BASED ON COUNT AND PURCHASE ORDER

E = MATCH PURCHASE ORDER, PURCHASE REQUISITION, RECEIVING REPORT AND INVOICE

F = PREPARE VOUCHER AFTER COMPARING DATA ON PURCHASE ORDER, INVOICE, AND RECEIVING REPORT

G = TO CASH DISBURSEMENTS IN CONTROLLER'S DIVISION FOR PAYMENT

Maylou Corporation
DOCUMENT FLOWCHART FOR PURCHASES

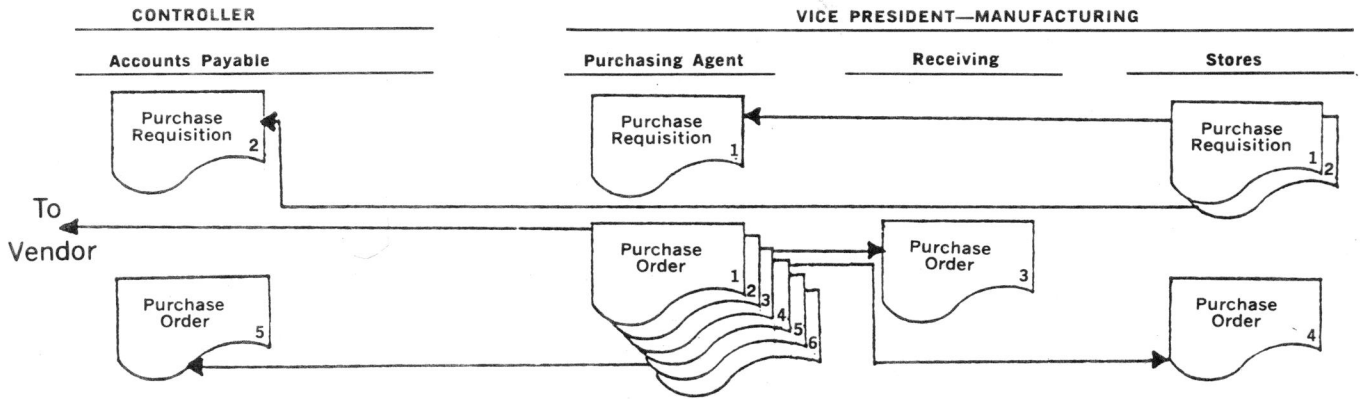

Problem 8 Cash Receipts IC Weaknesses
(1180,A4)

(15 to 25 minutes)

The Art Appreciation Society operates a museum for the benefit and enjoyment of the community. During hours when the museum is open to the public, two clerks who are positioned at the entrance collect a five dollar admission fee from each nonmember patron. Members of the Art Appreciation Society are permitted to enter free of charge upon presentation of their membership cards.

At the end of each day one of the clerks delivers the proceeds to the treasurer. The treasurer counts the cash in the presence of the clerk and places it in a safe. Each Friday afternoon the treasurer and one of the clerks deliver all cash held in the safe to the bank, and receive an authenticated deposit slip which provides the basis for the weekly entry in the cash receipts journal.

The board of directors of the Art Appreciation Society has identified a need to improve their system of internal control over cash admission fees. The board has determined that the cost of installing turnstiles, sales booths or otherwise altering the physical layout of the museum will greatly exceed any benefits which may be derived. However, the board has agreed that the sale of admission tickets must be an integral part of its improvement efforts.

Smith has been asked by the board of directors of the Art Appreciation Society to review the internal control over cash admission fees and provide suggestions for improvement.

Required:

Indicate weakness in the existing system of internal control over cash admission fees, which Smith should identify, and recommend one improvement for each of the weaknesses identified.

Organize the answer as indicated in the following illustrative example:

Weakness	Recommendation
1. There is no basis for establishing the documentation of the number of paying patrons.	*1. Prenumbered admission tickets should be issued upon payment of the admission fee.*

MULTIPLE CHOICE ANSWERS

1.	d	15.	c	29.	a	43.	a	57.	a
2.	b	16.	c	30.	c	44.	d	58.	b
3.	b	17.	d	31.	d	45.	d	59.	c
4.	c	18.	a	32.	a	46.	a	60.	b
5.	c	19.	a	33.	a	47.	b	61.	c
6.	b	20.	a	34.	d	48.	c	62.	a
7.	b	21.	a	35.	d	49.	a	63.	a
8.	a	22.	b	36.	b	50.	a	64.	a
9.	d	23.	a	37.	c	51.	c	65.	a
10.	a	24.	c	38.	b	52.	b	66.	d
11.	c	25.	b	39.	d	53.	c		
12.	b	26.	b	40.	a	54.	c		
13.	c	27.	b	41.	a	55.	b		
14.	c	28.	c	42.	a	56.	a		

EXPLANATION OF MULTIPLE CHOICE ANSWERS

1. (1180,A1,2)   (d)   Auditors perform compliance tests to provide reasonable assurance that prescribed accounting control procedures are being followed. Inspection procedures (answer (a)) are used to test whether and by whom control procedures were performed and to permit an evaluation of the propriety of their performance (para 320.58). Observation (answer (b)) and inquiry (answer (c)) may be used, for example, to test controls which leave no audit trail (para 320.59). Confirmation (answer (d)) is used primarily to enable the auditor to substantiate the existence of an account balance; it is, therefore, considered a substantive test.

2. (1180,A1,8)   (b)   Compliance tests are primarily concerned with testing internal accounting controls which relate to the tests specified in answers (a), (c), and (d), see para 320.57. Answer (b) is the answer since the "why" pertains more directly to administrative controls.

3. (1180,A1,14)   (b)   CPAs use questionnaires, narrative memoranda, flowcharts and <u>decision tables</u> to record information during the preliminary review of the client's system of internal control (para 320.53). Answer (a) is incorrect since a decision table probably would not be necessary for the preparation of a generalized EDP computer audit program. Answer (c) is incorrect since decision tables have rarely been associated with tests of balances and transactions. Answer (d) is also incorrect since auditors generally have not used decision tables to prepare audit programs.

4. (1180,A1,30)   (c)   Auditors first review internal control to gain knowledge and understanding as to the procedures and methods prescribed. Compliance tests are then performed for areas in which the auditor decides to rely on these procedures and methods (para 320.50). Subsequently, substantive tests, the scope of which is determined by the internal control review and the compliance tests, are performed.

5. (1180,A1,35)   (c)   All four answers may, in certain circumstances, assure accountability for fixed assets retirements. Answer (c) is best because continuous utilization of serially numbered retirement orders will assist in control of all retirements (possibly limited by a materiality factor) since, if used properly, they will help assure that only properly authorized retirements will be made. Answer (a) is less complete since it will only help for assets which are sold. The unsystematic nature of the controls in answers (b) and (d) is likely to limit their effectiveness.

6. (1180,A1,40)   (b)   Purchasing departments ensure the acquisition of goods of a specified quality. Answer (a) is incorrect since authorization of acquisition comes from the department needing the goods. Answer (c) is incorrect since the verification of the propriety of the goods acquired is done by receiving and possibly stores. Answer (d) is incomplete since purchasing is much more involved with acquiring goods than is encompassed by selecting the cheapest goods available.

7. (1180,A1,44)   (b)   The auditor's evaluation of internal control allows him/her to determine the nature, timing, and extent of substantive tests which must be performed (para 320.55). Answer (a) is inaccurate because the auditor used compliance tests to evaluate internal control (para 320.55). Answer (c) is incomplete since irregularities are only one of several types of internal control problems which may lead to financial statement errors. Answer (d) is incorrect because although the auditor is certainly concerned about incompatible functions, this is not in and of itself the primary reason for internal control evaluation.

8. (1180,A1,52)   (a)   To detect the theft of valuable items a perpetual inventory system with periodic verification will be most helpful because differences between the quantity counted and the quantity in inventory are identified. Answer (b) is incorrect because while a CPA's internal control report might assist management in developing controls to <u>prevent</u> thefts, <u>detection</u> would not necessarily occur. Answer (c) is incomplete since sequentially numbered tag and separate

warehouse space alone will have a limited effect. Answer (d) is also incomplete since an officer's signature alone will not detect thefts.

9.   (580,A1,7) (d) Proper segregation of the functional responsibilities requires separation of (1) authorization, (2) recording, and (3) custodial functions. Per para 320.36 incompatible functions are those that place any person in a position both to perpetrate and to conceal errors and irregularities. Thus, those that authorize transactions must be separated from those who account for the transactions and from those who have custody of any related assets. Answers (a), (b), and (c) are incorrect because they do not include the required accounting (or recording) function.

10.   (580,A1,16) (a) The requirement is the internal control weakness which permits the purchasing agent of Judd Hardware Wholesalers to divert incoming C.O.D. shipments to a relative's retail store. If purchase orders are issued by Judd Hardware and the purchase orders are never received, there is an internal control weakness over the purchase orders. All purchase orders should be accounted for and followed up to assure receipt of orders that are issued. Answer (b) is incorrect because purchase requisitions are internal documents which are prepared by user departments and sent to the purchasing department for action. Answer (c) is incorrect because the failure to detect purchase orders that were not received has nothing to do with cash receipts. Answer (d) is incorrect because perpetual inventory records cannot be relied upon to detect the nonreceipt of purchase orders, i.e., perpetual inventory records are only activated once the goods are received.

11.   (580,A1,33) (c) The auditor documents the review of the client's system of internal control to comply with generally accepted auditing standards per Section 338 and per para 320.53. Answer (a) is incorrect because the auditor's review of a system of internal control does not evaluate the conformity of accounting records with GAAP. Answer (b) is incorrect because a review of the system of internal control only provides information about the prescribed internal control system. The compliance tests rather than the review determine whether the prescribed system is in effect. Answer (d) is incorrect because the review of the internal control system can only indirectly reflect on the fairness of the financial statements.

12.   (580,A1,41) (b) Per para 320.35, reasonable assurance that the objectives of accounting control are achieved depends on the competence and integrity of

personnel, the independence of their assigned functions, and their understanding of the prescribed procedures. Answer (a) is incorrect because the cost/benefit relationship of internal control is a basic concept of internal control rather than an essential characteristic of internal accounting control per para 320.30. Answer (c) is incorrect because comparison of recorded accountability with assets is a required element of internal control irrespective of employee competence. Answer (d) is incorrect because the timing of the tests to be performed is not largely affected by the competence of client employees (see para 310.05-310.09).

13.   (580,A1,47) (c) The requirement is the audit test which would be considered a test of compliance. Tests of compliance are primarily concerned with "were the necessary procedures performed, how were they performed, and by whom were they performed?" per para 320.57. Tests of signatures on cancelled checks will determine whether the checks were signed by those authorized by the board of directors. Answer (a) is incorrect because tests of specific items making up a balance in a ledger account would be a transactions test. Answer (b) is incorrect because tests of inventory pricing to vendors' invoices also is a transactions test. Answer (d) is incorrect because tests of additions of property, plant, and equipment would also be a transactions test.

14.   (580,A1,50) (c) The requirement is the procedures necessary to determine whether internal control procedures were prescribed and are being followed. The review of the system of internal control results in a knowledge and understanding of the procedures and methods prescribed, and the tests of compliance result in a reasonable degree of assurance that the controls are in use and are operating as planned. Answer (a) is incorrect because developing questionnaires and checklists determines control procedures that are prescribed but does not determine whether they are being followed. Answer (b) is incorrect because the auditor's study and evaluation of internal control is concerned with studying and evaluating accounting controls rather than administrative controls. Answer (d) is incorrect because observing employee functions determines whether control procedures are being followed but not if they were prescribed.

15.   (580,A1,51) (c) A material internal control weakness is a procedure or lack thereof that does not provide reasonable assurance that errors or irregularities materially affecting the financial statements would be prevented or detected within a timely period by employees performing their normal functions. See para 320.68. Answers (a), (b), and (d) base detection

on action of an auditor, a controller, and a chief financial officer which are all incorrect because material weaknesses in internal control are precluded by the system as a whole rather than by one person.

16.   (580,A1,56)   (c) Answer (a) is incorrect because the function of an unmatched invoice file is to hold off paying invoices until the receiving report and purchase order are received. There would be invoices in an unmatched invoice file even with the accounts payable sub ledger. Answer (b) is incorrect because the corporation receives no benefit from confirming vendors' requests for confirmations. Answer (d), although correct, is not as beneficial as answer (c). Answer (c) is the best answer because it carries the *most* benefit. The sub ledger would be used to keep track of the amounts still payable after partial payments. Otherwise, the partial payments would have to be written on the voucher register in order to keep track of the amount still due.

17.   (1179,A1,5)   (d) From an internal control viewpoint, the person to distribute payroll checks should follow the dictum of separation of functional responsibilities: record keeping, custodianship, authorization, and operations. The receptionist would be independent of those keeping payroll records (answer a), preparing the payroll (answer b), and those with custodianship over cash (answer c).

18.   (1179,A1,10)   (a) The requirement is the best internal accounting control over postdated checks when received from customers. Internal accounting control concerns transaction execution per proper authorization, proper recording of transactions, restricted access to assets, and comparison of accountability with existing assets. Restrictively endorsing postdated checks will restrict the checks to the client company which is desired. Answer (b) is incorrect because the checks should be held and deposited rather than returned to the customer. Returning checks to customers will not establish a control over the checks. Answer (c) is incorrect because postdated checks do not necessarily arise from a cash sale in that they may well be payment of receivables. Also, they are not cash (until the date of the checks). Answer (d) is incorrect because placing postdated checks in the custody of 2 officers would be unnecessary control where the cost of internal control exceeded the benefits expected to be derived (see para 320.32).

19.   (1179,A1,21)   (a) The purpose of tests of compliance is to provide reasonable assurance that accounting control procedures are being applied as prescribed per para 320.55. Answer (b) is incorrect because understanding the flow of transactions through the accounting system is part of the review of the accounting system to gain knowledge and understanding of the procedures and methods prescribed. Answer (c) is incorrect because providing assurance that transactions are recorded at the amounts executed is only one of the four objectives of accounting control per para 320.28. Presumably, compliance tests are concerned with all four objectives of internal control. Answer (d) is incorrect because certain aspects of accounting control require segregation of duties which do not leave an audit trail as recognized in para 320.59, .61, and .63.

20.   (1179,A1,28)   (a) Once accounts receivable are written off they should be controlled for possible future collection. Accordingly, they should be recorded to maintain accountability (para 320.28b) as in a separate ledger. If they were simply written off and forgotten, there would be no means of maintaining accountability over these contingent assets. Answer (b) is incorrect because accounts transferred to an attorney for collection would not be written off, i.e., if they were bad debts, there would be no basis for collection proceedings. Answer (c) is incorrect because the requirement is for proper internal control over the receivables rather than information to prepare tax returns. Answer (d) is incorrect because credit managers should not have control over accounts that have been written off because there is not sufficient separation of functional responsibilities.

21.   (1179,A1,42)   (a) Cancelled stock certificates should be defaced and attached to corresponding stubs as is done with voided checks. The objective of the control is to prevent reissuance. Answer (b) is incorrect because failure to deface permits reissuance. Answer (c) is incorrect because destruction of the certificates would preclude their control, i.e., their existence after defacing provides assurance that they cannot be reissued. If the certificates were destroyed, one or more might be reissued without any proof that such occurred. Answer (d) is incorrect because the Secretary of State has no interest in receiving defaced and cancelled stock certificates.

22.   (1179,A1,45)   (b) The requirement is an internal control weakness related to factory equipment. All purchases of factory equipment should be made by a purchasing department rather than a department in need of the equipment. A purchasing department should be utilized to maintain proper control over the authorization and execution of purchasing. Answer (a) is incorrect because controllers should not sign checks as they have recordkeeping responsibility over cash. Check signing includes the authorization function which should not be combined with the recordkeeping function. Answer (c) is incorrect because when purchases are made does not change the need for a purchasing department. Answer (d) is incorrect because the method of accounting for sale of fully depreciated equipment has nothing to do with purchasing procedures.

23. (1179,A1,52) (a) Management information systems consist of data gathering, data analysis, and reporting functions. It is an integrated process to insure that management possesses the information it needs to carry-out its functions. Answer (a) is correct because it is a broader, more comprehensive definition than answers (b), (c), and (d). Answer (b) is incorrect because management information systems may include a computerized information retrieval and decision making system but it is not required. Answer (c) is incorrect because while a management information system may include statistical and analytical review functions, they are not required. Answer (d) is incorrect because production budgeting and sales forecasting activities are not mandatory in a management information system.

24. (1179,A1,54) (c) If payment of wages were to be in cash, each employee receiving payment should be required to sign a receipt for the amount of pay received. Thus, there would be control over the total a-mount disbursed as well as amounts disbursed to each individual employee. Answer (a) is incorrect because if a signed receipt is not received from each employee paid, there would be no proof of payment. Even though the pay envelopes include both cash and a computation of net wages, the employees should have the opportunity to count the cash received before signing a payroll receipt. Answer (b) is incorrect because unclaimed pay envelopes should not be retained by the paymaster, but rather deposited in a bank account by the cashier. Answer (d) is incorrect because the wage payment will be made in cash and not by check. Accordingly, a receipt must be obtained for each cash payment.

25. (1179,A1,55) (b) All of the company's incoming merchandise should be delivered to the receiving clerk. The receiving clerk can then prepare a receiving report for defective items returned by customers. Answer (a) is incorrect because in most cases other than retail outlets, sales clerks are unequipped to receive merchandise or prepare the necessary paperwork. Answer (c) is in-

correct because an inventory control clerk would have a control function over inventory. Since this title does not have well-defined uniform meaning, the control clerk could have an internal control function or an accounting function depending on the circumstances. Either way, such a clerk would generally not be in the position to perform the receiving function. Answer (d) is incorrect because the accounts receivable should be separated from the sales returns function and inventory control function.

26. (1179,A1,59) (b) The payroll department supervisor should not distribute payroll checks to employees, because the payroll supervisor would be in a position to prepare checks to ficticious employees and keep the checks. Answer (a) is incorrect because the payroll department supervisor should review approved time reports for those employees in the payroll department under the supervisor's supervision. Answer (c) is incorrect because as supervisor, the supervisor should hire subordinate employees. Answer (d) is incorrect because the supervisor should initiate requests for salary adjustments for subordinate employees.

27. (578,A1,5) (b) Note that the requirement is the most important internal control procedure over acquisitions of property. Answer (b) is correct, because using budgets to control acquisitions implies a follow-up analysis of budget variances as suggested by answer (c). The use of budgets also permits the level of authorized expenditures to be controlled which does not occur with answer (c). Thus answer (b) is better than (c). Answer (a) is incorrect because a written policy distinguishing capital and revenue expenditures will not provide a control over acquisitions of property. Answer (d) is incorrect because further delegation of acquisitions to user departments will weaken controls over property acquisitions rather than strengthen them.

28. (578,A1,9) (c) Lapping of trade accounts receivable is an abstraction of funds and subsequent delay in crediting receipts to accounts receivable. If the customers sent payments directly to a depository bank, there is no opportunity for abstractions or subsequent misapplication. Answer (a) is incorrect because lapping involves incorrect entries in the subsidiary ledgers, not the general ledger. Answers (b) and (d) are incorrect because lapping can occur by forging checks, i.e., there is no requirement that abstraction be made directly from cash.

29. (578,A1,17) (a) Flowcharts assist auditors in evaluating client internal control procedures which are a series of sequential processes, e.g., approval of a voucher or payment. Answer (b) is incorrect because CPAs study the system of internal control, not systems of responsibility accounting. Answer (c) is incorrect because dual-purpose tests are not required and they cannot be performed with flowcharts (see para 320B.37 of SAS 1). Answer (d) is incorrect because auditors prepare and use systems flowcharts, not client organizational charts.

30. (578,A1,21) (c) If the storekeeper, who is involved in physical control, is also allowed to keep inventory records, there is an internal control weakness. One of the basic concepts of internal control is segregation of functional responsibilities. See para 320.36 of SAS 1. Answers (a), (b), and (d) describe normal operating procedures.

31. (578,A1,26) (d) The best control against misappropriation of marketable securities is to assign the custodial responsibilities to a bank. If securities are lost or missing, the bank will be responsible, i.e., the client will not have to be concerned with misappropriation of securities. Answer (a) is incorrect because even trustworthy bonded employees may misappropriate assets. Answer (b) is incorrect because employees who enter the safekeeping area can still misappropriate securities even though they are required to record the reason for their entry in a log. Answer (c) is incorrect because requiring persons with custodial responsibilities also to keep records does not provide much additional control. Remember that the functional responsibilities of custodianship and record-keeping are to be separated.

32. (578,A1,32) (a) If A/R write-offs must be approved by an officer on the basis of credit department recommendations including supporting evidence, there is very little likelihood of improper write-offs to conceal cash shortages. Answer (b) is incorrect because receivables overdue by several months is not a basis for write-off; uncollectibility is. Answer (c) is incorrect because the cashier could conceal cash shortages by approving A/R write-offs. Answer (d) is incorrect because sales employees could accept payments from customers and then authorize the accounts to be written off.

33. (578,A1,40) (a) A secondary objective of the study and evaluation of internal control is to provide a basis for constructive suggestions concerning improvements in internal control (para 320.07, SAS 1).

The primary purpose of the study and evaluation of internal control is to comply with the second standard of field work which requires proper study and evaluation of internal control as a basis for reliance on internal control and to determine the extent of additional required auditing tests and procedures. This primary objective includes answers (b), (c), and (d).

34. (578,A1,41) (d) The payroll function should be separated from the hiring function. Hiring new employees effectively authorizes pay. The functional responsibilities of payroll authorization and payroll payment should be separated. Payroll functions commonly include controlling unemployment claims, maintaining personnel records, and approving fringe benefits (answers (a), (b), and (c)).

35. (579,A1,37) (d) The requirement is an effective internal control technique over the payroll function. Note that you are looking for the best answer of the four alternatives. Total time spent on individual jobs should be compared with total time per the time clock. This will insure that all time is properly allocated to individual jobs, and excess time was not incurred that was not chargeable to specific jobs. Answer (a) is incorrect because employees should not be permitted to reconcile or check their own job reports, i.e., there should be a separate review. Answers (b) and (c) are incorrect because the payroll department and the personnel department should be separate, as they have separate functional responsibilities. The personnel department authorizes the hiring and pay levels of employees whereas the payroll department expends funds. These functional responsibilities should be separate, and neither department should supervise the other department.

36. (579,A1,42) (b) The requirement is a situation causing the impairment of organizational independence. The controller, who is in charge of accounting, should be independent of the production function. Since the accounting function reports on the production function, there would be a conflict of interest if the controller reported to the vice president of production. Answer (a) is incorrect because internal auditors typically report to the audit committee of the board of directors. Answer (c) is incorrect because the payroll department should report to the chief accountant, as the chief accountant has responsibility for the payroll accounting function. Answer (d) is incorrect because cashiers typically account and report to the treasurer because the treasurer has responsibility for cash custodianship.

37. (579,A1,48) (c) The requirement is a procedure that is not normally used in internal control over purchasing raw materials. Normally, third-party (i.e., non-client) reports regarding quality and quantity, as in answer (c), are not required. Answer (a) is incorrect because reporting product changes affecting types of needed raw materials is required to achieve efficient purchasing of raw materials. Answer (b) is incorrect because determining the need for raw materials is essential prior to purchasing. Answer (d) is incorrect because purchase commitments should not be entered into prior to obtaining financial approval.

38. (579,A1,49) (b) Independent auditors are elected by the stockholders or appointed by the board of directors to emphasize auditor independence from client management. Since the financial statements on which the auditor is to express an opinion as to fairness are the presentation of management, auditors need to be independent of management. Answer (a) is incorrect because the FASB has not issued regulations regarding appointment of auditors. The FASB is concerned with promulgating GAAP, not GAAS. Answer (c) is incorrect because rotation of independent auditors is not encouraged due to the expenses which would be incurred. Answer (d) is incorrect because corporate owners are not in a position to evaluate the quality of auditing firms.

39. (577,A1,1) (d) The requirement is effective internal control procedures over fixed asset additions. Internal accounting controls consist of the plan of organization and procedures to assure transactions are executed per proper authorization, transactions are properly recorded, access to assets is limited, and recorded accountability is periodically compared with existing assets. Thus, both answers (a) and (d) support internal accounting control over additions to fixed assets. Answer (d) appears to be a better answer because the question is concerned with additions to fixed assets, i.e., procuring fixed assets.

40. (577,A1,7) (a) The requirement is the internal control measure to encourage receiving department personnel to count and inspect all merchandise received. If the quantities ordered are not known to the receiving department personnel, they will have to count and inspect the incoming merchandise without prejudice. In other words, they will not count to an expected number. Answer (b) is incorrect because it does not relate to the requirement, i.e., counting and inspecting. Answer (c) is incorrect because receiving department personnel should only count and inspect and not per-

form reconciliations. Answer (d) is incorrect because an examination of the receiving report will not indicate whether counts were made by receiving department personnel. It will only indicate that numbers were recorded by receiving department personnel.

41. (577,A1,17) (a) The requirement is the best procedure to strengthen internal control over purchases that can be carried out by the receiving department. The receiving department should not accept merchandise unless the purchase of merchandise has been properly approved. Answer (b) is incorrect because the receiving department should accept only merchandise properly ordered from the usual company vendors. Answer (c) is incorrect because receiving personnel should physically count and inspect incoming merchandise before preparing receiving reports. Answer (d) is incorrect because the receiving department can both physically handle the incoming items and prepare receiving reports.

42. (577,A2,22) (a) The CPA's primary objective in reviewing the materials purchasing cycle is to evaluate the reliability of the information generated as a result of the purchasing process. This is in accordance with the second standard of field work which requires there to be a "proper study and evaluation of existing internal control as a basis for reliance thereon. . ." Thus, answer (a) also encompasses answers (b), (c), and (d).

43. (577,A2,23) (a) The objective of compliance tests is to obtain a reasonable degree of assurance that a client's prescribed system of internal control is in use and effective (SAS 1, para 320.55.) The study of internal control is required by the second standard of field work. The third standard of field work concerns sufficient, competent, evidential matter, which is answer (b). The third standard of reporting requires adequate informative disclosure, which is answer (c). Answer (d) describes the review of the system of internal control, which involves obtaining knowledge and understanding of the prescribed procedures and methods (SAS 1, para 320.51).

44. (577,A2,26) (d) The billing function is an authorization function which quite correctly needs to be separated from the recordkeeping function. Answer (a) is not an effective control because custodianship responsibilities are not separated from recordkeeping responsibilities. Answer (b) is incorrect because authorization responsibilities are not separated from custodianship responsibilities. Answer (c) is incorrect because the reconciliation of the subsidiary ledger to the general ledger should be done more than once a year.

45. (577,A2,31) (d) The requirement is an accounting department procedure over unclaimed payroll checks kept by the treasury department. Answers (a) and (b) would be undertaken by the treasury department. Answer (c) is incorrect because if the unclaimed wages are in a current liability account, they would be cancelled, not held by the treasury department.

46. (577,A2,32) (a) Para 310.06 of SAS 1 indicates that the auditor must be satisfied that internal control continues to be effective at year end even if the internal control was satisfactory per interim audit tests. Also see para 320.61. Answers (b), (c), and (d) all represent possible audit procedures, but are not prescribed as a minimum.

47. (577,A2,35) (b) See para 320.72 of SAS 1. Financial statements may be misleading as a result of first, material errors occurring in the accounting process, and second, no detection of the material errors by the auditor. The auditor relies on internal control to reduce the first risk, and relies on audit procedures to reduce the second risk.

48. (577,A2,38) (c) Systems flowcharts are prepared as part of the review of the system of internal control (para 320.52, SAS1). Answer (b) is incorrect because the entire organizational structure and document flow of a large company usually cannot be depicted in a single flow chart. Answers (a) and (d) are only tangential to the preparation of systems flowcharts by auditors.

49. (577,A3,42) (a) The requirement is the best description of the inherent limitations concerning a system of internal control. Para 320.34 of SAS 1 describes inherent limitations that can render a system of internal control ineffective. Included are the possibilities of misunderstanding instructions, mistakes of judgment, personal carelessness, distraction, fatigue, collusion among employees whose duties are segregated, and perpetrations by management. Answers (b), (c), and (d) describe basic concepts of internal control and are found in para 320.35, 320.37, and 320.32 respectively.

50. (1178,A1,2) (a) The requirement is the effective internal accounting control over cash payments. The person signing checks should supervise or control the mailing of the checks. The check signer reviews the supporting documentation and authorizes the requested disbursement. By controlling the mailing of the checks, there is reasonable assurance that the payee will receive the payment. If the payee is not due the money, presumably the payee will contact the payor. If the signed checks were returned to the person preparing the checks, that person could prepare checks to false payees or abscond with checks to bona fide payees without collusion with others. Answer (b) is incorrect because voided checks should be retained as proof that they have not been (or will not be) issued. Answer (c) is incorrect because persons preparing checks should not have access to cash receipts and disbursements, e.g., to eliminate opportunities for kiting. Answer (d) is incorrect because a check signing machine with two signatures provides little control unless separate persons, responsible for authorizing individual payments, control the signature plates.

51. (1178,A1,4) (c) The system of internal accounting controls provides reasonable, not absolute, assurance of safeguarding assets and the reliability of financial records (para 320.32 of SAS 1), i.e., cost of internal control should not exceed the benefits. Reasonable assurance is one of the basic concepts of internal control. Answer (b) is incorrect because management responsibility for the system of internal control is a different basic concept of internal control (para 320.31). Answer (a), employment of competent personnel, and answer (d), segregation of incompatible functions, are essential characteristics of internal control (para 320.35-.36).

52. (1178,A1,36) (b) The auditor's primary concern over purchasing supplies in a small company is with respect to proper recording and expensing as used. Internal accounting control is primarily concerned with the safeguarding of assets and the reliability of financial records. Note that the requirement concerns internal control once the supplies have been ordered and paid for. Thus answer (b) is correct because receiving, counting and checking the quantities on purchase orders provides control over supplies already purchased and paid for. Answer (a) is incorrect because in a small company there may not be any authorized individual with no incompatible duties. Answer (c) is incorrect because supplies are expensed as used, not over their useful life. Answer (d) is incorrect because the supplies may remain unused as of the end of the period under audit.

53. (1178,A1,42) (c) The two phases of the study of a system of internal accounting control are review of the system and tests of compliance. The review of the system of internal accounting control obtains information about the system of organization and prescribed procedures and is the basis for the tests of compliance and evaluation of the system. Based on an understanding of the system of internal accounting control, the information is recorded by auditors as answers to questionnaires, narrative memoranda, flowcharts, and decision tables. Answer (a) is incorrect because GAAS do not require the use of flowcharts even though a study and evaluation of the system of internal control is required. Answer (b) is incorrect because flowcharts do not classify; rather, they graphically depict documentation flows. Answer (d) is incorrect because audit engagements are not directed toward interpreting the operational effectiveness of a client's organizational structure.

54. (1178,A1,49) (c) The requirement is an example of an inherent limitation in a system of internal control. See para 320.34 of SAS 1. Errors arising from misunderstanding of instructions, mistakes of judgment, personal carelessness, and fatigue are inherent limitations. Answer (a) is incorrect because segregation of functions is an essential characteristic, not an inherent limitation, of internal control. Answer (b) is incorrect because assuring the execution and recording of transactions in accordance with management authorization is one of the two primary objectives of internal accounting control. Answer (d) is incorrect because systems of internal control have been developed to enable large numbers of transactions to be processed efficiently with reasonable assurance that material errors or irregularities are prevented or detected within a timely period.

55. (1178,A1,58) (b) Internal accounting control has two major objectives: safeguarding assets and promoting reliability of financial records. As a result, a system of internal accounting control provides reasonable assurances that 1) transactions are recorded per management's authorization, 2) transactions are recorded as necessary, 3) access to assets is permitted only with management's authorization, 4) recorded accountability of assets is compared with physical assets periodically (para 320.28 of SAS 1). Answer (a) is incorrect because an internal control system assumes that employees act with integrity and determines the contrary when irregularities occur. Answer (c) is incorrect because the decision processes leading to management's

authorization concern internal administrative control rather than internal accounting control (para 320.27). Answer (d) is incorrect because one of the limitations of internal control systems is that they may be circumvented by collusion (para 320.34).

56. (579,A1,10) (a) The requirement is the person(s) to make periodic reviews of investment activity delegated by the board of directors to a financial executive. The review should be made by an investment committee of the board of directors, as the authority was delegated by the board of directors. Answers (b), treasurer, (c), corporate controller, and (d), chief operating officer, are incorrect because they did not make the delegation and therefore should not make the periodic reviews. Also the treasurer has custodial functional responsibility and the controller has accounting functional responsibility, which would further preclude them from authorization functional responsibility.

57. (579,A1,16) (a) The requirement is the situation in which auditors should retest records and procedures as well as apply new compliance tests at year end, when these tests have already been done during the year and internal control has been found to be effective. Auditors should retest records and transactions if year-end inquiries and observations lead the auditor to believe conditions have changed significantly (para 310.06). Answer (b) is incorrect because significant fluctuations in account balances are acceptable if they can be explained by a change in business conditions. If, however, the conditions of the records and internal control systems have changed, additional year-end work is required. Answer (c) is incorrect because unusual transactions subsequent to the interim audit work should be examined on an individual basis (para 310.06). Answer (d) is incorrect because significantly changed conditions would require retesting whether or not client records are in a condition to facilitate the retesting.

58. (579,A1,20) (b) The requirement is an overriding principle of internal control regarding the concept of charge and discharge of responsibility and duties. Answer (b) is correct because if there is to be a concept of charge and discharge of responsibility, responsibility for performance of each duty must be fixed. Answers (a) and (c) are incorrect because they are concerned with assigning accounting duties to either a responsible officer or an audit committee, either of which may or may not be appropriate within the environmental setting of a particular entity. Answer (d) is incorrect be-

cause employees carrying on accounting activities do not necessarily need to be bonded. Generally, employees having access to monies are bonded. The concept of bonding is not related to the concept of charge and discharge of responsibility and duties.

MAY 1981 ANSWERS

59.   (581,A1,7)   (c)   The requirement is to determine the primary purpose of the auditor's study and evaluation of internal control. The purpose of the auditor's study and evaluation of internal control is to establish a basis for reliance thereon in determining the nature, extent, and timing of audit tests to be applied in the examination of the financial statements (para. 320.06). Answer (a) is incorrect because the safeguarding of assets is only a portion of the definition of accounting controls; the reliability of financial records for reporting purposes is also included. Providing constructive suggestions (answer b) is a secondary objective of the evaluation of internal control. Answer (d) is incorrect because in the normal financial statement audit the expression of an opinion is based only in part on the results of the evaluation of internal control.

60.   (581,A1,8)   (b)   The requirement is to determine the purpose of tests of compliance. Tests of compliance are performed to provide reasonable assurance that the accounting control procedures are being applied as prescribed (para. 320.55). Answer (a), while partially correct, is incorrect since compliance tests do not, in general, consider whether balances are valid and proper. Answer (c) is incorrect because substantive tests primarily test adequacy of disclosure. Answer (d) is incorrect because most compliance tests do not test entity quality control procedures.

61.   (581,A1,22)   (c)   The requirement is to determine why a client would prepare a decision table. A decision table is frequently prepared as an alternative or as a supplement to a flowchart (especially a program flowchart). Flowcharts emphasize the sequence of operations while decision tables emphasize the alternative logic relationships among the data being processed. While answers (a) and (d) are partially correct, the combinations they represent do not occur as frequently as those outlined in flowcharts, answer (c). Answer (b) is incorrect, as decision tables are most frequently used with batched transactions.

62.   (581,A1,39)   (a)   The requirement is to determine what type of test an auditor applies in examining initials on sales invoices. Tests of compliance provide reasonable assurance that accounting control procedures are being applied as prescribed (para. 320.55). Examin-

ing the initials of the individual who verified the quantitative data on the sales invoices tests firm compliance with the prescribed control. Answer (b) is incorrect because the test does not substantiate the validity and propriety of accounting treatment of transactions and balances. Answer (c) is incorrect since cutoff tests relate to testing dates on such invoices at year-end to determine whether they have been recorded in the proper period. Answer (d) is incorrect since the test may or may not be performed using statistical sampling.

63.   (581,A1,50)   (a)   The requirement is to determine the purpose of a flowchart to an auditor. Auditors frequently use flowcharts to document their understanding of their clients' systems of internal control. Answer (b) is incorrect since a flowchart is certainly not synonymous with a compliance audit program. Answer (c) is incomplete because, while the flowchart documents the study of internal control, it does not evaluate the system; compliance tests are also used to assist in evaluating whether the system is working as purported. Although a flowchart [answer (d)] may assist the auditor in determining possible types of irregularities, it does not in and of itself provide such understanding.

64.   (581,A1,51)   (a)   The requirement is to determine the type of firm for which payroll classification is most important. Payroll classification is most important for a manufacturing firm because a portion of salaries is inventoried in the manufactured product. Answers (b), (c), and (d) are incorrect because all salaries will typically be directly expensed.

65.   (581,A1,59)   (a)   The requirement is to determine the least likely inventory audit procedure relating to segregation of duties. Because many aspects of the segregation of duties leave no audit trail of documentary evidence, inspecting documents is least likely (para 320.59). The auditor will make inquiries [answer (b)], observe procedures [answer (c)], and consider policy and procedure manuals [answer (d)] to determine both how the duties are purported to be and actually segregated.

66.   (581,A1,60)   (d)   The requirement is to determine the objective of precision in sampling. Precision is calculated to determine the range of procedural deviations in the population (para 320B.17). Answer (a) is incorrect because probabilities relate more directly to reliability. Answer (b) is incorrect because errors on financial statements in materiality terms relate to variables sampling. Answer (c) is incorrect because it does not accurately indicate the relationship between reliability and precision.

ANSWER OUTLINE

Problem 1   Evaluation of Internal Control

a.   GAAS requires internal control study and evaluation to
        Determine nature of audit tests
           Extent of audit tests
           Timing of audit tests
        Provide constructive suggestions to client

b.   Preliminary evaluation of internal control
        Considers types of errors and irregularities that could occur
        Determines the necessary prescribed controls
        Determines whether necessary controls are prescribed
        Allows an initial opinion on the prescribed procedures

c.   Auditor documentation of internal control understanding
        Questionnaires
        Memoranda
        Decision tables
        Flow charts

d.   Compliance tests provide reasonable assurance that accounting control procedures are followed

UNOFFICIAL ANSWER

Problem 1   Evaluation of Internal Control

a.   Generally accepted auditing standards require that the auditor study and evaluate the existing internal controls as a basis for reliance thereon in determining the nature, extent, and timing of audit tests to be applied. This frequently provides a basis for constructive suggestions to clients concerning improvements in internal control.

b.   The purpose of a preliminary evaluation is to afford the auditor an opportunity to (1) consider the types of errors and irregularities that could occur, (2) determine the accounting control procedures that should prevent or detect such errors and irregularities, (3) determine whether the necessary procedures are prescribed, and (4) form an initial opinion as to whether the prescribed procedures are being followed satisfactorily.

c.   Documentation may be in the form of questionnaires, narrative memorandums, decision tables, flow charts, and so forth.

d.   The purpose of tests of compliance is to provide reasonable assurance that the accounting control procedures are being applied as prescribed.

ANSWER OUTLINE

Problem 2   Material Purchase IC Weaknesses

1.   Raw materials may be obtained by oral authorization
        Proper written authorization should be required

2.   Perpetual inventory system does not exist
        Periodic method may allow stockouts or overstocks
           Establish adequate perpetual inventory system

3.   Raw material purchases do not vary with production demands
        Purchases should be based upon production schedules

4.   Purchasing function and invoice payment are combined
        Require centralized purchasing with prenumbered purchase orders
        Separate purchasing and payment functions

5.   The same vendor is always used
        Use competitive bids

6.   There is no receiving department
        Establish receiving department

7.   There is no inspection of goods upon receipt
        Establish inspection department with inspection reports

UNOFFICIAL ANSWER

Problem 2   Material Purchase IC Weaknesses

Weaknesses	Recommended Improvements
1. Raw materials may be removed from the storeroom upon oral authorization from one of the production foremen.	1. Raw materials should be removed from the storeroom only upon written authorization from an authorized production foreman. The authorization forms should be prenumbered and accounted for, list quantities and job or production number, and be signed and dated.

Weaknesses	Recommended Improvements
2. Alden's practice of monthly physical-inventory counts does not compensate for the lack of a perpetual-inventory system. Quantities on hand at the end of one month may not be sufficient to last until the next month's count. If the company has taken this into account in establishing reorder levels, then it is carrying too large an investment in inventory.	2. A perpetual-inventory system should be established under the control of someone other than the storekeepers. The system should include quantities and values for each item of raw material. Total inventory value per the perpetual records should be agreed to the general ledger at reasonable intervals. When physical counts are taken they should be compared to the perpetual records. Where differences occur they should be investigated, and if the perpetual records are in error they should be adjusted. Also, controls should be established over obsolescence of stored materials.
3. Raw materials are purchased at a predetermined reorder level and in predetermined quantities. Since production levels may often vary during the year, quantities ordered may be either too small or too great for the current production demands.	3. Requests for purchases of raw materials should come from the production-department management and be based on production schedules and quantities on hand per the perpetual records.
4. The accounts-payable clerk handles both the purchasing function and payment of invoices. This is not a satisfactory separation of duties.	4. The purchasing function should be centralized in a separate department. Prenumbered purchase orders should originate from and be controlled by this department. A copy of the purchase order should be sent to the accounting and receiving departments. Consideration should be given to whether the receiving copy should show quantities.
5. Raw materials are always purchased from the same vendor.	5. The purchasing department should be required to obtain competitive bids on all purchases over a specified amount.
6. There is no receiving department or receiving report. For proper separation of duties, the individuals responsible for receiving should be separate from the storeroom clerks.	6. A receiving department should be established. Personnel in this department should count or weigh all goods received and prepare a prenumbered receiving report. These reports should be signed, dated, and controlled. A copy should be sent to the accounting department, purchasing department, and storeroom.
7. There is no inspection department. Since high-cost electronic components are usually required to meet certain specifications, they should be tested for these requirements when received.	7. An inspection department should be established to inspect goods as they are received. Prenumbered inspection reports should be prepared and accounted for. A copy of these reports should be sent to the accounting department.

ANSWER OUTLINE

Problem 3   Customer Invoice IC Weaknesses

1. Inadequate separation of computer department
   functions
   Systems analysis and design
   Programming
   Machine operation

Control

2. No record of computer operations
   Establish usage log to be reconciled by supervisor

3. Inadequate physical control over computer
   Restrict access to computer room
   Restrict programmers usage also

4. Inadequate documentation of systems
      Establish flowcharts
      Record layouts
      Program listings
      Operator instructions

5. Inadequate physical control over tape files, etc.
      Establish program and tape library under separate
      control

6. Inadequate use of program controls
      Implement program controls to supplement existing
      manual controls

7. Billing clerk insertion of prices is subject to error
      Pricing of shipping notices should be computerized

8. Manually reviewing numerical sequence is inefficient
      Computerize check for missing shipping notices

9. Computer input control ineffective
      Control tapes should be checked against the daily
      sales register

10. Billing clerk should not maintain AR
      Receivable clerk should be independent of billing
      and cash collections

11. Manual AR records inefficient
      Computerize on magnetic tape

12. Billing clerk should not receive or mail invoices
      Mail invoices directly from computer department

13. Chronological file of invoices unnecessary
      Already provided by daily sales register

14. Duplicate warehouse invoices unnecessary
      Computer can print listing of invoices for each
      warehouse

UNOFFICIAL ANSWER

Problem 3   Customer Invoice IC Weaknesses

Weakness	Recommended Improvements
1. Computer department functions have not been properly separated. Under existing procedures one employee completely controls programming and operations.	1. The functions of systems analysis and design, programming, machine operation and control should be assigned to different employees. This also should improve efficiency since different levels of skill are involved.
2. Records of computer operations have not been maintained.	2. In order to properly control usage of the computer, a usage log should be kept and reconciled with running times by the supervisor. The system also should provide for preparation of error lists on the console typewriter. These should be removable only by the supervisor or a control clerk independent of the computer operators.
3. Physical control over computer operations is not adequate. All computer department employees have access to the computer.	3. Only operating employees should have access to the computer room. Programmers' usage should be limited to program testing and debugging.
4. System operations have not been adequately documented. No record has been kept of adaptations made by the programmer or new programs.	4. The company should maintain up-to-date system and program flow charts, record layouts program listings and operator instructions. All changes in the system should be documented.
5. Physical control over tape files and systems documentation is not adequate. Materials are unguarded and readily available in the computer department. Environmental control may not be satisfactory.	5. Programs and tape libraries should be carefully controlled in a separate location. Preferably a librarian who does not have access to the computer should control these materials and keep a record of usage. The Company should consult with the computer company about necessary environmental controls.

Weaknesses	Recommended Improvements
6. The Company has not made use of programmed controls. Some of the procedures and controls used in the tabulating system may be unnecessary or ineffective in the computerized system.	6. Programmed controls should be used to supplement existing manual controls, and an independent review should be made of manual controls and tabulating system procedures to determine their applicability. Examples of computer checks that might be programmed include data validity tests, check digits, limit and reasonableness tests, sequence checks and error routines for unmatched items, erroneous data and violations of limits.
7. Insertion of prices on shipping notices by the billing clerk is inefficient and subject to error.	7. The Company's price list should be placed on a master file in the computer and matched with product numbers on the shipping notices to obtain appropriate prices.
8. Manual checking of the numerical sequence of shipping notices also is inefficient.	8. The computer should be programmed to check the numerical sequence of shipping notices and list missing numbers.
9. Control over computer input is not effective. The computer operator has been given responsibility for checking agreement of output with the control tapes. This is not an independent check.	9. The billing clerk (or another designated control clerk) should retain the control tapes and check them against the daily sales register. This independent check should be supplemented by programming the computer to check control totals and print error messages where appropriate.
10. The billing clerk should not maintain accounts-receivable detail records.	10. If receivable records are to be maintained manually, a receivable clerk who is independent of billing and cash collections should be designated. If the records are updated by the computer department, as recommended below, there still should be an independent check by the general accounting department.
11. Accounts-receivable records are maintained manually in an open invoice file.	11. These records could be maintained more efficiently on magnetic tape.
12. The billing clerk should not receive or mail invoices.	12. Copies of invoices should be forwarded by the computer department to the customer (or to the mailroom) and distributed to other recipients in accordance with established procedures.
13. Maintaining a chronological file of invoices appears to be unnecessary.	13. This file's purpose may be fulfilled by the daily sales register.
14. Sending duplicate copies of invoices to the warehouse is inefficient.	14. The computer can be programmed to print a daily listing of invoices applicable to individual warehouses. This will eliminate the sorting of invoices.

ANSWER OUTLINE

Problem 4   Payroll IC Weaknesses

a.   Weaknesses in system of internal control
a1.   Lack of approval of foreman's clock card
a2.   Computation of regular and overtime hours by payroll clerk no. 2 not compared with foreman's summary
a3.   Computations and rates of pay not checked by independent person
a4.   Payroll checks not reconciled to payroll register
a5.   Payroll clerk should not have custody of signature-stamp machine and blank checks
a6.   Payroll not approved by officer
a7.   Payroll checks should not be distributed by foreman
a8.   Unclaimed checks not held by independent employee
a9.   Comparison of hours on check with hours on clock card should not be done by clerk who did original computation
a10.   Comparison of payroll on check with register should not be done by clerk who prepared register

b.   Inquiries concerning possible additional weaknesses
b1.   Are clock cards checked for foreman's approval?
b2.   Is overtime on clock cards approved?
b3.   Is data in payroll files checked with personnel files?
b4.   Is clock card punching observed by timekeeper?
b5.   Are other mitigating internal controls in existence? e.g., bonding, required vacations

UNOFFICIAL ANSWER

Problem 4   Payroll IC Weaknesses

a.   Weaknesses in the system of internal control are the following:

1.   Lack of approval of the foreman's clock card by an appropriate supervisor is an unsound practice. Employees should not be permitted to maintain their own time records and submit them without approval.

2.   The computation of regular and overtime hours prepared by payroll clerk no. 2 that is used in the preparation of the payroll register is not compared with the summary of regular and overtime hours prepared by the foreman.

3.   Arithmetic computations and rates of pay used in the preparation of the payroll register are not checked by a person who is independent of their preparation and payroll register columns are not verified (re-added) by a person other than the preparer of the payroll register.

4.   Payroll checks are not reconciled to the payroll register in order to prevent improper disbursements.

5.   A signature-stamp machine should not be in the custody of any payroll clerk who has access to unsigned checks.

6.   Payroll is not approved by an officer of the company.

7.   Since the paymaster should be independent of the payroll process, signed payroll checks should not be distributed by the foreman.

8.   Unclaimed payroll checks should be in the custody of an employee who is independent of the payroll process.

9.   The comparison of (regular and overtime) hours indicated on payroll check (or attachments) with (regular and overtime) hours indicated on clock cards should not be performed by the clerk who is responsible for the original computation of (regular and overtime) hours indicated on clock cards.

10.   The comparison of gross and net payroll indicated on payroll check (or attachments) with gross and net payroll indicated in the payroll register should not be performed by the clerk who is responsible for preparing the payroll register.

b.   One should inquire whether:

1.   Payroll clerk no. 2 checks clock cards for the foreman's written approval.

2.   Approved overtime is indicated on clock cards.

3.   Employment, wage, and related data in payroll files are periodically crosschecked with personnel files for agreement.

4.   The punching of clock cards is observed by a timekeeper.

5.   Other mitigating internal control measure (for example, bonding, required vacations, and so forth) are in existence.

ANSWER OUTLINE

Problem 5   Internal Control Limitations

a. Inherent IC limitations
   Misunderstanding of instructions, mistakes, etc.
   Circumvented by collusion
   Circumvented by management
      Execution and recording of transactions
      Estimates and judgments
   Projection of current internal control impossible
   IC system provides reasonable but not absolute assurance

b. Examination of financial statements
   1. To rely on internal control in audit
      Intermediary step for opinion on statements
   2. Per standard internal control evaluation per GAAS
      Includes some testing
   3. No specific reference in audit report
   Special study of internal control
   1. To form conclusions on IC effectiveness
      No opinion on statements
   2. Scope varies by engagement
      Generally wider than audit review
      Does not have to include testing
   3. IC report is end product of special study

c. IC reports probably not useful to third parties
   They are not directly concerned with IC
      Cannot take direct action
   IC reports cannot be issued with unauditeds
   May indicate statements are audited
   Tiber should inform bank that statements are
      unaudited
      Unaudited statements should be accompanied
      by disclaimer of opinion

UNOFFICIAL ANSWER

Problem 5   Internal Control Limitations

a.   Inherent limitations that should be recognized in considering the effectiveness of any system of internal control follows:

   1.   In the performance of most control procedures errors can result from misunderstanding of instructions, mistakes of judgment, carelessness, or other personal factors.

2.   Control procedures, the effectiveness of which depends upon segregation of duties, can be circumvented by collusion.

3.   Control procedures can be circumvented intentionally by management with respect to
   (a)   The execution and recording of transactions.
   (b)   The estimates and judgments required in the preparation of financial statements.

4.   Projection of a current evaluation of internal control to future periods is subject to the risks that
   (a)   Procedures may become inadequate because of changes in conditions.
   (b)   The degree of compliance with procedures may deteriorate.

   A satisfactory system of internal control can be expected to provide reasonable, but not absolute assurance that its objectives will be accomplished. Conversely, weaknesses in a system do not necessarily mean that errors and irregularities will occur.

b. Examination of Financial Statements	Special Study
I. Objective:	**1. Objectives:**
(a) Purpose of review is to establish a basis for relying upon internal control in determining nature, timing, and extent of tests to be applied in the examination of financial statements.	(a) Purpose of review is to form conclusions concerning the functioning of the Company's system of internal control.
(b) CPA performs his review of internal control as an intermediate step in formulation of his opinion on financial statements.	(b) CPA cannot form an opinion on financial-statement presentation because he does not perform the additional auditing procedures necessary for an opinion.
2. Scope:	**2. Scope:**
(a) Review includes the procedures required for auditor's examination of financial statements.	(a) Scope of review will vary among engagements according to the specific objectives and arrangements of each engagement.
(b) Review always includes some testing of internal control.	(b) Breadth of review is usually wider; e.g., it may include review of administrative controls as well as internal accounting controls.
	(c) Study may or may not include testing of client's system.
3. Report:	**3. Report:**
(a) CPA makes no specific reference to internal control in his short-form report on financial statements, but the adequacy of his review is subsumed in his statement that he has conducted his examination in accordance with generally accepted auditing standards and accordingly has included such tests of the accounting records and such other auditing procedures as he considered necessary in the circumstances. Weaknesses in internal control are disclosed where this is appropriate.	(a) Report is end product of CPA's review.
(b) The CPA may comment on weaknesses in internal control and suggestions for improvement in a supplemental memorandum to his client.	(b) CPA includes in his report: (1) A description of purpose and scope of study. (2) An indication of whether scope of study included testing of system. (3) Objectives of internal control and relationship of costs and benefits. (4) Limitations of study. (5) Weaknesses disclosed by study.

c. The principal issues here are (1) the usefulness of the report on internal control to a third party such as the fourth National Bank and (2) the potentially misleading effect of such a report when it is associated with unaudited financial statements.

While it is evident that reports on internal control can serve a useful purpose for management, regulatory agencies, and other independent auditors, the usefulness of such reports to the general public is questionable. Members of the latter group are not directly concerned with internal control and rarely are in a position to take direct action as a result of reports thereon. However, such a report could be useful in making decisions about the quality of management. Further, the effectiveness of internal control affects the reliance that may be placed upon unaudited financial statements. The danger in both of these uses is that unwarranted conclusions may be based upon the evaluation expressed in the report.

Management generally has the responsibility of determining the usefulness of a report on internal control to the general public, but a CPA in no event should authorize this report to be issued to the general public in a document that includes unaudited financial statements because the CPA's description of his review might cause readers to believe that the financial statements have been audited. (For this reason the CPA does not report in his disclaimer the auditing procedures that he may have performed in connection with unaudited financial statements.)

Tiber should appropriately inform the bank that the financial statements are unaudited and that the report on internal control is presented only as a source of general information about the Company and its management. The risk of misunderstanding will be reduced if Mr. Burns adopts a form of report on internal control that describes in reasonable detail the objectives and limitations of his review. If the unaudited financial statements are identified in any way with Mr. Burns, they should be accompanied by his disclaimer of opinion.

ANSWER OUTLINE

Problem 6   Purchasing Function Flowchart

Question requires identification and explanation of control problems. Only improvements are listed below.
  Require proper approval of purchase requisitions
  Delete purchase requisition copy sent to receiving room
  Compare purchase requisitions and purchase orders
  Separate file for unmatched purchase requisitions
  Review need prior to preparing purchase order
  Negotiate with different vendors for best price
  Purchase office to review invoice prior to approving for payment
  Do not show quantities on purchase orders sent to receiving room
  Establish procedures for vendors' misshipments
  Send copy of receiving report to stores department
  Establish control over number of vouchers submitted for payment
  Establish control over dollars of vouchers submitted for payment
  Examine documents prior to voucher preparation
  Treasurer, not controller, should be responsible for cash disbursements
  Establish procedures for purchase returns
  Establish procedures for reconciling discrepancies
  Establish control over prenumbered forms

UNOFFICIAL ANSWER

Problem 6   Purchasing Function Flowchart

The identification and explanation of the systems and control problems are as follows:

1.   The purchase requisition is not approved. The purchase requisition should be approved by a responsible person in the stores department. The approval should be indicated on the purchase requisition after the approver is satisfied that it was properly prepared based on a need to replace stores or the proper request from a user department.

2.   Purchase requisition number two is not required. Purchase requisitions are unnecessarily sent from the stores department to the receiving room. The receiving room does not make any use of the purchase requisitions and no purpose seems to exist for the receiving room to obtain a copy. A copy of the requisition might be sent from stores directly to accounts payable where it can be compared to the purchase order to verify that the merchandise requisitioned by an authorized employee has been properly ordered.

3.   Purchase requisitions and purchase orders are not compared in the stores department. Although purchase orders are attached to purchase requisitions in the stores department, there is no indication that any comparison is made of the two documents. Prior to attaching the purchase order to the purchase requisition the requisitioner's function should include a check that—
a.   Prices are reasonable.
b.   The quality of the materials ordered is acceptable.
c.   Delivery dates are in accordance with company needs.
d.   All pertinent data on the purchase order and purchase requisition (e.g.,

quantities, specifications, delivery dates, etc.) are in agreement. Since the requisitioner will be charged for the materials ordered, the requisitioner is the logical person to perform the steps.

4. Purchase orders and purchase requisitions should not be combined and filed with the unmatched purchase requisitions, in the stores department. A separate file should be maintained for the combined and matched documents. The unmatched purchase requisitions file can serve as a control over merchandise requisitioned but not yet ordered.

5. Preliminary review should be made before preparing purchase orders. Prior to preparation of the purchase order the purchase office should review the company's need for the specific materials requisitioned and approve the request.

6. The purchase office should attempt to obtain the highest quality merchandise at the lowest possible price, and the procedures that are followed to achieve this should be included on the flowchart. There is no indication that the purchase office submits purchase orders to competitive bidding when appropriate. That office should be directly involved with vendors in determining the cost of materials ordered and should be primarily responsible for deciding at what price materials should be ordered and which vendor should be used.

7. The purchase office does not review the invoice prior to processing approval. The purchase office should review the vendor's invoice for overall accuracy and completeness, verifying quantity, prices, specifications, terms, dates, etc., and if the invoice is in agreement with the purchase order, receiving report, and purchase requisition, the purchase office should clearly indicate on the invoice that it is approved for payment processing. The approval invoice should be sent to the accounts payable department.

8. The copy of the purchase order sent to the receiving room generally should not show quantities ordered, thus forcing the department to count goods received. In addition to counting the merchandise received from the vendor, the receiving department personnel should examine the condition and quality of the merchandise upon receipt.

9. There is no indication of the procedures in effect when the quantity of merchandise received differs from what was ordered. Procedures for handling over-shipments and short-shipments should be clearly outlined and included on the flowchart.

10. The receiving report is not sent to the stores department. A copy of the receiving report should be sent from the receiving room directly to the stores department with the materials received. The stores department, after verifying the accuracy of the receiving report, should indicate approval on that copy and send it to the accounts payable department. The copy sent to accounts payable will serve as proof that the materials ordered were received by the company and are in the user department.

11. There is no indication of control over vouchers in the accounts payable department. In the accounts payable department a record of all vouchers submitted to the cashier should be maintained, and a copy of the vouchers should be filed in an alphabetical vendor reference file.

12. There is no indication of control over dollar amounts on vouchers. Accounts payable personnel should prepare and maintain control sheets on the dollar amounts of vouchers. Such sheets should be sent to departments posting transactions to general and subsidiary ledgers.

13. There is no examination of documents prior to voucher preparation. In addition to the matching procedure, the mathematical accuracy of all documents should be verified prior to preparation of vouchers.

14. The controller should not be responsible for cash disbursements. The cash disbursement function should be the responsibility of the treasurer, not the controller, so as to provide proper division of responsibility between the custody of assets and the recording of transactions.

15. There is no indication of the company's procedures for handling purchase returns. Although separate return procedures may be in effect and included on a separate flowchart, some indications of this should be included as part of the purchases flowchart.

16. Discrepancy procedures are not indicated. The flowchart should indicate what procedures are followed whenever matching reveals a difference between the information on the documents compared.

17. There is no indication of any control over prenumbered forms. All prenumbered documents should be accounted for.

ANSWER OUTLINE

Problem 7   Purchasing Department Controls

a. Effective internal accounting control procedures
   1. Purchase requisition prepared when goods needed
   2. Purchase requisition copy on file in stores department
   3. Responsible person in stores dept. approves requisitions
        Based on need for goods
        Clearly indicates approval on requisition
   4. Purchase orders can be issued only after proper approval
   5. Vendors are requested to confirm purchase orders
   6. Purchase requisitions are filed with purchase orders
   7. Copies of purchase orders sent to receiving department
        But do not include quantities ordered
   8. Purchase orders are numbered and all numbers accounted for
   9. Receiving dept. only accepts goods per purchase orders

b. 1. The time to order is determined by
        Quantities on hand
        Expected rate of use
        Time it takes to receive goods (lead time)
        Cost of owning versus cost of stock-out
   2. The order quantity of supplies, etc., is based on
        Expected use
        Order costs
        Ability to receive goods
        Ability to pay for goods
        Set-up costs
        Storage costs
        Interest on investment
        Risk of obsolescence

        Quantity discounts
        Shipping costs
        Calculated by economic order quantity

UNOFFICIAL ANSWER

Problem 7   Purchasing Department Controls

a.   Those internal accounting control procedures that Long would expect to find if Maylou's system of internal accounting control over purchases is effective are as follows:

·   Purchase requisitions are prepared and/or approved only after there has been a proper determination of the need for the goods requested.

·   One copy of the purchase requisition is maintained on file in the stores department.

·   Purchase requisitions are approved by a responsible person in the stores department. Approval is given only after that person is satisfied that a need exists and that the requisition is properly prepared. Approval is clearly indicated on requisitions.

·   Purchase orders are issued only after they are approved by persons given the specific responsibility to make such approval.

·   Vendors are requested to confirm purchase orders. This indicates acceptance and constitutes a contractual commitment.

·   Purchase requisitions are filed with purchase orders, and both are maintained in an orderly file in the purchase office.

·   Copies of purchase orders sent to the receiving department do not include the quantities of merchandise ordered.

·   All purchase orders are numbered, and all numbers are accounted for. This allows control over purchase orders canceled or rejected by vendors.

·   Receiving department accepts only those goods for which a purchase order is on hand.

b.
1.   The question when to order depends primarily on quantities on hand, rate of use, and the lead

time between order placement and receipt of goods. Other factors include the trade-off between the cost of owning and storing merchandise versus the risk of being out of stock.

2.   Factors considered in determining how much to order include expected use, costs of placing an order, receiving and paying for what has been purchased, set-up costs, storage costs, interest on investment, risk of obsolescence or deterioration, quantity discounts, and shipping costs. The determination is made judgmentally or mathematically by arriving at an economic order quantity.

ANSWER OUTLINE

Problem 8   Cash Receipts IC Weaknesses

Weaknesses in and Recommended Improvements for Internal Control

a.   No segregation of duties between persons collecting admission fees and persons authorizing admission
> One clerk (collection clerk) should collect admission fees and issue prenumbered tickets
> Another clerk (admission clerk) should authorize admission upon receipt of ticket or proof of membership

b.   No independent count made of paying patrons
> Admission clerk should retain a portion of the prenumbered admission ticket

c.   No proof of accuracy of amounts collected by the clerks
> Each day treasurer should reconcile admission ticket stubs with cash collected by treasurer

d.   Cash receipts records not promptly prepared
> Collection clerk should record cash collections daily
> Recording should be a permanent record to serve as first record of accountability

e.   Cash receipts are not promptly deposited
> Deposit cash at least once a day

f.   No proof of accuracy of amounts deposited
> Compare authenticated deposit slips with daily cash collections
> Investigate and resolve discrepancies promptly
> Treasurer should establish policy including analytical review of cash collections

g.   No record of internal accountability for cash
> Treasurer should issue signed receipt for all proceeds received from collection clerk
> Maintain receipts and periodically check against cash collection and deposit records

UNOFFICIAL ANSWER

Problem 8   Cash Receipts IC Weaknesses

Weakness	Recommendation
1. There is no segregation of duties between persons responsible for collecting admission fees and persons responsible for authorizing admission.	1. One clerk (hereafter referred to as the collection clerk) should collect admission fees and issue prenumbered tickets. The other clerk (hereafter referred to as the admission clerk) should authorize admission upon receipt of the ticket or proof of membership.
2. An independent count of paying patrons is not made.	2. The admission clerk should retain a portion of the prenumbered admission ticket (admission ticket stub).
3. There is no proof of accuracy of amounts collected by the clerks.	3. Admission ticket stubs should be reconciled with cash collected by the treasurer each day.
4. Cash receipts records are not promptly prepared.	4. The cash collections should be recorded by the collection clerk daily on a permanent record that will serve as the first record of accountability.
5. Cash receipts are not promptly deposited. Cash should not be left undeposited for a week.	5. Cash should be deposited at least once each day.
6. There is no proof of accuracy of amounts deposited.	6. Authenticated deposit slips should be compared with daily cash collection records. Discrepancies should be promptly investigated and resolved. In addition, the treasurer should establish policy that includes an analytical review of cash collections.
7. There is no record of the internal accountability for cash.	7. The treasurer should issue a signed receipt for all proceeds received from the collection clerk. These receipts should be maintained and should be periodically checked against cash collection and deposit records.

MULTIPLE CHOICE QUESTIONS (1—114)

1.   Which of the following is **not** a typical analytical review procedure?
- a.   Study of relationships of the financial information with relevant nonfinancial information.
- b.   Comparison of the financial information with similar information regarding the industry in which the entity operates.
- c.   Comparison of recorded amounts of major disbursements with appropriate invoices.
- d.   Comparison of the financial information with budgeted amounts.

2.   When outside firms of nonaccountants specializing in the taking of physical inventories are used to count, list, price and subsequently compute the total dollar amount of inventory on hand at the date of the physical count, the auditor will ordinarily
- a.   Consider the report of the outside inventory-taking firm to be an acceptable alternative procedure to the observation of physical inventories.
- b.   Make or observe some physical counts of the inventory, recompute certain inventory calculations and test certain inventory transactions.
- c.   **Not** reduce the extent of work on the physical count of inventory.
- d.   Consider the reduced audit effort with respect to the physical count of inventory as a scope limitation.

3.   All corporate capital stock transactions should ultimately be traced to the
- a.   Minutes of the Board of Directors.
- b.   Cash receipts journal.
- c.   Cash disbursements journal.
- d.   Numbered stock certificates.

4.   In order to efficiently establish the correctness of the accounts payable cutoff, an auditor will be most likely to
- a.   Coordinate cutoff tests with physical inventory observation.
- b.   Compare cutoff reports with purchase orders.
- c.   Compare vendors' invoices with vendors' statements.
- d.   Coordinate mailing of confirmations with cutoff tests.

5.   The auditor is **most** likely to verify accrued commissions payable in conjunction with the
- a.   Sales cutoff review.
- b.   Verification of contingent liabilities.
- c.   Review of post balance sheet date disbursements.
- d.   Examination of trade acccounts payable.

6.   Auditors often request that the audit client send a letter of inquiry to those attorneys who have been consulted with respect to litigation, claims, or assessments. The primary reason for this request is to provide the auditor with
- a.   An estimate of the dollar amount of the probable loss.
- b.   An expert opinion as to whether a loss is possible, probable or remote.
- c.   Information concerning the progress of cases to date.
- d.   Corroborative evidential matter.

7.   Which of the following **best** describes how the detailed audit program of the CPA who is engaged to audit the financial statements of a large publicly held company compares with the audit client's comprehensive internal audit program?
- a.   The comprehensive internal audit program is more detailed and covers areas that would normally **not** be reviewed by the CPA.
- b.   The comprehensive internal audit program is more detailed although it covers less areas than would normally be covered by the CPA.
- c.   The comprehensive internal audit program is substantially identical to the audit program used by the CPA because both review substantially identical areas.
- d.   The comprehensive internal audit program is less detailed and covers less areas than would normally be reviewed by the CPA.

8.   An auditor would be **least** likely to use confirmations in connection with the examination of
- a.   Inventories.
- b.   Long-term debt.
- c.   Property, plant, and equipment.
- d.   Stockholders' equity.

9.   The auditor's count of the client's cash should be coordinated to coincide with the
    a.   Study of the system of internal controls with respect to cash.
    b.   Close of business on the balance sheet date.
    c.   Count of marketable securities.
    d.   Count of inventories.

10.   Which of the following procedures is **least** likely to be performed before the balance sheet date?
    a.   Observation of inventory.
    b.   Review of internal control over cash disbursements.
    c.   Search for unrecorded liabilities.
    d.   Confirmation of receivables.

11.   An auditor would be **most** likely to learn of slow-moving inventory through
    a.   Inquiry of sales personnel.
    b.   Inquiry of stores personnel.
    c.   Physical observation of inventory.
    d.   Review of perpetual inventory records.

12.   Which of the following is **not** one of the auditor's primary objectives in an examination of marketable securities?
    a.   To determine whether securities are authentic.
    b.   To determine whether securities are the property of the client.
    c.   To determine whether securities actually exist.
    d.   To determine whether securities are properly classified on the balance sheet.

13.   Several years ago Conway, Inc., secured a conventional real estate mortgage loan. Which of the following audit procedures would be **least** likely to be performed by an auditor examining the mortgage balance?
    a.   Examine the current years' cancelled checks.
    b.   Review the mortgage amortization schedule.
    c.   Inspect public records of lien balances.
    d.   Recompute mortgage interest expense.

14.   Which of the following eliminates voluminous details from the auditor's working trial balance by classifying and summarizing similar or related items?
    a.   Account analyses.
    b.   Supporting schedules.
    c.   Control accounts.
    d.   Lead schedules.

15.   In the examination of which of the following general ledger accounts will tests of procedures be particularly appropriate?
    a.   Equipment.
    b.   Bonds payable.
    c.   Bank charges.
    d.   Sales.

16.   Which of the following analytical review procedures should be applied to the income statement?
    a.   Select sales and expense items and trace amounts to related supporting documents.
    b.   Ascertain that the net income amount in the statement of changes in financial position agrees with the net income amount in the income statement.
    c.   Obtain from the proper client representatives, the beginning and ending inventory amounts that were used to determine costs of sales.
    d.   Compare the actual revenues and expenses with the corresponding figures of the previous year and investigate significant differences.

17.   Which of the following is the **best** audit procedure for determining the existence of unrecorded liabilities?
    a.   Examine confirmation requests returned by creditors whose accounts appear on a subsidiary trial balance of accounts payable.
    b.   Examine unusual relationships between monthly accounts payable balances and recorded purchases.
    c.   Examine a sample of invoices a few days prior to and subsequent to year-end to ascertain whether they have been properly recorded.
    d.   Examine a sample of cash disbursements in the period subsequent to year-end.

18.   When examining a client's statement of changes in financial position, for audit evidence, an auditor will rely primarily upon
    a.   Determination of the amount of working capital at year-end.
    b.   Cross-referencing to balances and transactions reviewed in connection with the examination of the other financial statements.
    c.   Analysis of significant ratios of prior years as compared to the current year.
    d.   The guidance provided by the APB Opinion on the statement of changes in financial position.

19. In determining the adequacy of the allowance for uncollectible accounts, the **least** reliance should be placed upon which of the following?
   a. The credit manager's opinion.
   b. An aging schedule of past due accounts.
   c. Collection experience of the client's collection agency.
   d. Ratios calculated showing the past relationship of the valuation allowance to net credit sales.

20. When title to merchandise in transit has passed to the audit client, the auditor engaged in the performance of a purchase cutoff will encounter the greatest difficulty in gaining assurance with respect to the
   a. Quantity.
   b. Quality.
   c. Price.
   d. Terms.

21. A corporate balance sheet indicates that one of the corporate assets is a patent. An auditor will **most** likely obtain evidence regarding the continuing validity and existence of this patent by obtaining a written representation from
   a. A patent attorney.
   b. A regional State Patent Office.
   c. The patent inventor.
   d. The patent owner.

22. To be competent, evidence must be both
   a. Timely and substantial.
   b. Reliable and documented.
   c. Valid and relevant.
   d. Useful and objective.

23. During the first part of the current fiscal year, the client company began dealing with certain customers on a consignment basis. Which of the following audit procedures is least likely to bring this new fact to the auditor's attention?
   a. Tracing of shipping documents to the sales journal.
   b. Test of cash receipts transactions.
   c. Confirmation of accounts receivable.
   d. Observation of physical inventory.

24. Which of the following audit procedures would be least likely to lead the auditor to find unrecorded fixed asset disposals?
   a. Examination of insurance policies.
   b. Review of repairs and maintenance expense.
   c. Review of property tax files.
   d. Scanning of invoices for fixed asset additions.

25. Most of the independent auditor's work in formulating an opinion on financial statements consists of
   a. Studying and evaluating internal control.
   b. Obtaining and examining evidential matter.
   c. Examining cash transactions.
   d. Comparing recorded accountability with assets.

26. A CPA has received an attorney's letter in which no significant disagreements with the client's assessments of contingent liabilities were noted. The resignation of the client's lawyer shortly after receipt of the letter should alert the auditor that
   a. Undisclosed unasserted claims may have arisen.
   b. The attorney was unable to form a conclusion with respect to the significance of litigation, claims and assessments.
   c. The auditor must begin a completely new examination of contingent liabilities.
   d. An adverse opinion will be necessary.

27. In the audit of a medium-sized manufacturing concern, which one of the following areas would be expected to require the least amount of audit time?
   a. Owners' equity.
   b. Revenue.
   c. Assets.
   d. Liabilities.

28. Which of the following procedures is not included in a review engagement of a nonpublic entity?
   a. Inquiries of management.
   b. Inquiries regarding events subsequent to the balance sheet date.
   c. Any procedures designed to identify relationships among data that appear to be unusual.
   d. A study and evaluation of internal control.

29. Those procedures specifically outlined in an audit program are primarily designed to
   a. Gather evidence.
   b. Detect errors or irregularities.
   c. Test internal systems.
   d. Protect the auditor in the event of litigation.

30. An auditor will usually trace the details of the test counts made during the observation of the physical inventory taking to a final inventory schedule. This audit procedure is undertaken to provide evidence that items physically present and observed by the audi-

tor at the time of the physical inventory count are
   a.   Owned by the client.
   b.   Not obsolete.
   c.   Physically present at the time of the preparation of the final inventory schedule.
   d.   Included in the final inventory schedule.

31.   The auditor can best verify a client's bond sinking fund transactions and year-end balance by
   a.   Confirmation with the bond trustee.
   b.   Confirmation with individual holders of retired bonds.
   c.   Recomputation of interest expense, interest payable, and amortization of bond discount or premium.
   d.   Examination and count of the bonds retired during the year.

32.   The physical count of inventory of a retailer was higher than shown by the perpetual records. Which of the following could explain the difference?
   a.   Inventory items had been counted but the tags placed on the items had not been taken off the items and added to the inventory accumulation sheets.
   b.   Credit memos for several items returned by customers had not been prepared.
   c.   No journal entry had been made on the re-
tailer's books for several items returned to its suppliers.
   d.   An item purchased "FOB shipping point" had not arrived at the date of the inventory count and had not been reflected in the perpetual records.

33.   Treetop Corporation acquired a building and ar-
ranged mortgage financing during the year. Verification of the related mortgage acquisition costs would be least likely to include an examination of the related
   a.   Deed.
   b.   Cancelled checks
   c.   Closing statement.
   d.   Interest expense.

34.   Johnson is engaged in the audit of a utility which supplies power to a residential community. All accounts receivable balances are small and internal control is effective. Customers are billed bi-monthly. In order to determine the validity of the accounts receivable bal-
ances at the balance sheet date, Johnson would most likely
   a.   Examine evidence of subsequent cash receipts instead of sending confirmation requests.
   b.   Send positive confirmation requests.

   c.   Send negative confirmation requests.
   d.   Use statistical sampling instead of sending confirmation requests.

35.   The auditor may conclude that depreciation charges are insufficient by noting
   a.   Insured values greatly in excess of book values.
   b.   Large amounts of fully depreciated assets.
   c.   Continuous trade-ins of relatively new assets.
   d.   Excessive recurring losses on assets retired.

36.   The auditor is least likely to learn of retirements of equipment through which of the following?
   a.   Review of the purchase return and allow-
ance account.
   b.   Review of depreciation.
   c.   Analysis of the debits to the accumulated depreciation account.
   d.   Review of insurance policy riders.

37.   How does the extent of substantive tests required to constitute sufficient evidential matter vary with the auditor's reliance on internal control?
   a.   Randomly.
   b.   Disproportionately.
   c.   Directly.
   d.   Inversely.

38.   To check the accuracy of hours worked, an auditor would ordinarily compare clock cards with
   a.   Personnel records.
   b.   Shop job time tickets.
   c.   Labor variance reports.
   d.   Time recorded in the payroll register.

39.   Once satisfied that the balance sheet and income statement are fairly presented in accordance with gen-
erally accepted accounting principles, an auditor who is examining the statement of changes in financial position would be most concerned with details of transactions in
   a.   Cash.
   b.   Trade receivables.
   c.   Notes payable.
   d.   Dividends payable.

40.   When an examination is made in accordance with generally accepted auditing standards, the independent auditor must
   a.   Utilize statistical sampling.
   b.   Employ analytical review procedures.
   c.   Obtain certain written representations from management.
   d.   Observe the taking of physical inventory on the balance sheet date.

41.   In verifying debits to perpetual inventory records of a non-manufacturing firm, the auditor would be most interested in examining the purchase
    a.   Journal.
    b.   Requisitions.
    c.   Orders.
    d.   Invoices.

42.   Auditor confirmation of accounts payable balances at the balance sheet date may be unnecessary because
    a.   This is a duplication of cutoff tests.
    b.   Accounts payable balances at the balance sheet date may not be paid before the audit is completed.
    c.   Correspondence with the audit client's attorney will reveal all legal action by vendors for nonpayment.
    d.   There is likely to be other reliable external evidence to support the balances.

43.   The third standard of fieldwork states that sufficient competent evidential matter may in part be obtained through inspection, observation, inquiries, and confirmations to afford a reasonable basis for an opinion regarding the financial statements under examination. The evidential matter required by this standard may in part be obtained through
    a.   Auditor working papers.
    b.   Proper planning of the audit engagement.
    c.   Analytical review procedures.
    d.   Review of the system of internal control.

44.   The primary difference between an audit of the balance sheet and an audit of the income statement lies in the fact that the audit of the income statement deals with the verification of
    a.   Transactions.
    b.   Authorizations.
    c.   Costs.
    d.   Cutoffs.

45.   In connection with a review of the prepaid insurance account, which of the following procedures would generally not be performed by the auditor?
    a.   Recompute the portion of the premium that expired during the year.
    b.   Prepare excerpts of insurance policies for audit working papers.
    c.   Confirm premium rates with an independent insurance broker.
    d.   Examine support for premium payments.

46.   The auditor tests the quantity of materials charged to work-in-process by tracing these quantities to
    a.   Cost ledgers.
    b.   Perpetual inventory records.
    c.   Receiving reports.
    d.   Material requisitions.

47.   Which of the following is the best evidence of real estate ownership at the balance sheet date?
    a.   Title insurance policy.
    b.   Original deed held in the client's safe.
    c.   Paid real estate tax bills.
    d.   Closing statement.

48.   With respect to contingent liabilities, the Standard Bank Confirmation Inquiry form approved jointly by the AICPA and the Bank Administration Institute requests information regarding notes receivable
    a.   Held by the bank in a custodial account.
    b.   Held by the bank for collection.
    c.   Collected by the bank.
    d.   Discounted by the bank.

49   The auditor should insist that a representative of the client be present during the physical examination of securities in order to
    a.   Lend authority to the auditor's directives.
    b.   Detect forged securities.
    c.   Coordinate the return of all securities to proper locations.
    d.   Acknowledge the receipt of securities returned.

50.   An inventory turnover analysis is useful to the auditor because it may detect
    a.   Inadequacies in inventory pricing.
    b.   Methods of avoiding cyclical holding costs.
    c.   The optimum automatic reorder points.
    d.   The existence of obsolete merchandise.

51.   Which of the following ultimately determines the specific audit procedures necessary to provide an independent auditor with a reasonable basis for the expression of an opinion?
    a.   The audit program.
    b.   The auditor's judgment.
    c.   Generally accepted auditing standards.
    d.   The auditor's working papers.

52.   An auditor's examination performed in accordance with generally accepted auditing standards generally should

a. Be expected to provide assurance that illegal acts will be detected where internal control is effective.

b. Be relied upon to disclose violations of truth in lending laws.

c. Encompass a plan to actively search for illegalities which relate to operating aspects.

d. Not be relied upon to provide assurance that illegal acts will be detected.

53. One reason why the independent auditor makes an analytical review of the client's operations is to identify probable

a. Weaknesses of a material nature in the system of internal control.

b. Unusual transactions.

c. Non-compliance with prescribed control procedures.

d. Improper separation of accounting and other financial duties.

54. Significant unexpected fluctuations identified by analytical review procedures will usually necessitate a (an)

a. Consistency qualification.

b. Review of internal control.

c. Explanation in the representation letter.

d. Auditor investigation.

55. Which of the following statements best describes the auditor's responsibility regarding the detection of fraud?

a. The auditor is responsible for the failure to detect fraud only when such failure clearly results from nonperformance of audit procedures specifically described in the engagement letter.

b. The auditor must extend auditing procedures to actively search for evidence of fraud in all situations.

c. The auditor must extend auditing procedures to actively search for evidence of fraud where the examination indicates that fraud may exist.

d. The auditor is responsible for the failure to detect fraud only when an unqualified opinion is issued.

56. The date of the management representation letter should coincide with the

a. Date of the auditor's report.

b. Balance sheet date.

c. Date of the latest subsequent event referred to in the notes to the financial statements.

d. Date of the engagement agreement.

57. Failure to detect material dollar errors in the financial statements is a risk which the auditor primarily mitigates by

a. Performing substantive tests.

b. Performing compliance tests.

c. Evaluating internal control.

d. Obtaining a client representation letter.

58. During an examination Wicks learns that the audit client was granted a three month waiver of the repayment of principal on the installment loan with Blank Bank without an extension of the maturity date. With respect to this loan, the audit program used by Wicks would be least likely to include a verification of the

a. Interest expense for the year.

b. Balloon payment.

c. Total liability at year end.

d. Installment loan payments.

59. During 1979, a bookkeeper perpetrated a theft by preparing erroneous W-2 forms. The bookkeeper's FICA withheld was overstated by $500.00 and the FICA withheld from all other employees was understated. Which of the following is an audit procedure which would detect such a fraud?

a. Multiplication of the applicable rate by the individual gross taxable earnings.

b. Utilizing form W-4 and withholding charts to determine whether deductions authorized per pay period agree with amounts deducted per pay period.

c. Footing and crossfooting of the payroll register followed by tracing postings to the general ledger.

d. Vouching cancelled checks to federal tax forms 941.

60. Analytical review procedures are

a. Statistical tests of financial information designed to identify areas requiring intensive investigation.

b. Analytical tests of financial information made by a computer.

c. Substantive tests of financial information made by a study and comparison of relationships among data.

d. Diagnostic tests of financial information which may not be classified as evidential matter.

61. When auditing a public warehouse, which of the following is the most important audit procedure with respect to disclosing unrecorded liabilities?
   a. Confirmation of negotiable receipts with holders.
   b. Review of outstanding receipts.
   c. Inspection of receiving and issuing procedures.
   d. Observation of inventory.

62. Some firms which dispose of only a small part of their total output by consignment shipments fail to make any distinction between consignment shipments and regular sales. Which of the following would suggest that goods have been shipped on consignment?
   a. Numerous shipments of small quantities.
   b. Numerous shipments of large quantities and few returns.
   c. Large debits to accounts receivable and small periodic credits.
   d. Large debits to accounts receivable and large periodic credits.

63. An audit program provides proof that
   a. Sufficient competent evidential matter was obtained.
   b. The work was adequately planned.
   c. There was compliance with generally accepted standards of reporting.
   d. There was a proper study and evaluation of internal control.

64. A client's procurement system ends with the assumption of a liability and the eventual payment of the liability. Which of the following best describes the auditor's primary concern with respect to liabilities resulting from the procurement system?
   a. Accounts payable are not materially understated.
   b. Authority to incur liabilities is restricted to one designated person.
   c. Acquisition of materials is not made from one vendor or one group of vendors.
   d. Commitments for all purchases are made only after established competitive bidding procedures are followed.

65. Which of the following is the best way for an auditor to determine that every name on a company's payroll is that of a bona fide employee presently on the job?
   a. Examine personnel records for accuracy and completeness.
   b. Examine employees' names listed on payroll tax returns for agreement with payroll accounting records.

   c. Make a surprise observation of the company's regular distribution of paychecks.
   d. Visit the working areas and confirm with employees their badge or identification numbers.

66. Governmental auditing often extends beyond examinations leading to the expression of opinion on the fairness of financial presentation and includes audits of efficiency, economy, effectiveness, and also
   a. Accuracy.
   b. Evaluation.
   c. Compliance.
   d. Internal control.

67. Confirmation of individual accounts receivable balances directly with debtors will, of itself, normally provide evidence concerning the
   a. Collectibility of the balances confirmed.
   b. Ownership of the balances confirmed.
   c. Validity of the balances confirmed.
   d. Internal control over balances confirmed.

68. In connection with the audit of a current issue of long-term bonds payable, the auditor should
   a. Determine whether bondholders are persons other than owners, directors, or officers of the company issuing the bond.
   b. Calculate the effective interest rate to see if it is substantially the same as the rates for similar issues.
   c. Decide whether the bond issue was made without violating state or local law.
   d. Ascertain that the client has obtained the opinion of counsel on the legality of the issue.

69. In connection with the third generally accepted auditing standard of field work, an auditor examines corroborating evidential matter which includes all of the following except
   a. Client accounting manuals.
   b. Written client representations.
   c. Vendor invoices.
   d. Minutes of board meetings.

70. Subsequent events affecting the realization of assets ordinarily will require adjustment of the financial statements under examination because such events typically represent
   a. The culmination of conditions that existed at the balance sheet date.
   b. The final estimates of losses relating to casualties occurring in the subsequent events period.

c.   The discovery of new conditions occurring in the subsequent events period.

d.   The preliminary estimate of losses relating to the balance sheet date.

71.   The auditor can best verify a client's bond sinking fund transactions and year-end balance by

a.   Recomputation of interest expense, interest payable, and amortization of bond discount or premium.

b.   Confirmation with individual holders of retired bonds.

c.   Confirmation with the bond trustee.

d.   Examination and count of the bonds retired during the year.

72.   An auditor must obtain written client representations that normally should be signed by

a.   The president and the chairperson of the board.

b.   The treasurer and the internal auditor.

c.   The chief executive officer and the chief financial officer.

d.   The corporate counsel and the audit committee chairperson.

73.   Which of the following is the most important consideration of an auditor when examining the stockholders' equity section of a client's balance sheet?

a.   Changes in the capital stock account are verified by an independent stock transfer agent.

b.   Stock dividends and/or stock splits during the year under audit were approved by the stockholders.

c.   Stock dividends are capitalized at par or stated value on the dividend declaration date.

d.   Entries in the capital stock account can be traced to a resolution in the minutes of the board of directors' meetings.

74.   Which of the following is generally included or shown in the auditor's working papers?

a.   The procedures used by the auditor to verify the personal financial status of members of the client's management team.

b.   Analyses that are designed to be a part of, or a substitute for, the client's accounting records.

c.   Excerpts from authoritative pronouncements that support the underlying generally accepted accounting principles used in preparing the financial statements.

d.   The manner in which exceptions and unusual matters disclosed by the auditor's procedures were resolved or treated.

75.   If the independent auditor decides that the work performed by internal auditors may have a bearing on the independent auditor's own procedures, the independent auditor should consider the objectivity of the internal auditors. One method of judging objectivity is to

a.   Review the recommendations made in the reports of internal auditors.

b.   Examine, on a test basis, documentary evidence of the work performed by internal auditors.

c.   Inquire of management about the qualifications of the internal audit staff.

d.   Consider the client's practices for hiring, training, and supervising the internal audit staff.

76.   The independent auditor should acquire an understanding of the internal audit function as it relates to the independent auditor's study and evaluation of internal accounting control because

a.   The audit programs, working papers, and reports of internal auditors can often be used as a substitute for the work of the independent auditor's staff.

b.   The procedures performed by the internal audit staff may eliminate the independent auditor's need for an extensive study and evaluation of internal control.

c.   The work performed by internal auditors may be a factor in determining the nature, timing, and extent of the independent auditor's procedures.

d.   The understanding of the internal audit function is an important substantive test to be performed by the independent auditor.

77.   During the course of an audit engagement an auditor prepares and accumulates audit working papers. The primary purpose of the audit working papers is to

a.   Aid the auditor in adequately planning his work.

b.   Provide a point of reference for future audit engagements.

c.   Support the underlying concepts included in the preparation of the basic financial statements.

d.   Support the auditor's opinion.

78.   The sufficiency and competency of evidential matter ultimately is based on the

a.   Availability of corroborating data.

b.   Generally accepted auditing standards.

c.   Pertinence of the evidence.

d.   Judgment of the auditor.

79. When an auditor tests a client's cost accounting system, the auditor's tests are primarily designed to determine that
   a. Quantities on hand have been computed based on acceptable cost accounting techniques that reasonably approximate actual quantities on hand.
   b. Physical inventories are in substantial agreement with book inventories.
   c. The system is in accordance with generally accepted accounting principles and is functioning as planned.
   d. Costs have been properly assigned to finished goods, work-in-process and cost of goods sold.

80. Auditors sometimes use comparison of ratios as audit evidence. For example, an unexplained decrease in the ratio of gross profit to sales may suggest which of the following possibilities?
   a. Unrecorded purchases.
   b. Unrecorded sales.
   c. Merchandise purchases being charged to selling and general expense.
   d. Fictitious sales.

81. Which of the following might be detected by an auditor's cut-off review and examination of sales journal entries for several days prior to and subsequent to the balance sheet date?
   a. Lapping year-end accounts receivable.
   b. Inflating sales for the year.
   c. Kiting bank balances.
   d. Misappropriating merchandise.

82. An auditor is testing sales transactions. One step is to trace a sample of debit entries from the accounts receivable subsidiary ledger back to the supporting sales invoices. What would the auditor intend to establish by this step?
   a. Sales invoices represent bona fide sales.
   b. All sales have been recorded.
   c. All sales invoices have been properly posted to customer accounts.
   d. Debit entries in the accounts receivable subsidiary ledger are properly supported by sales invoices.

83. One of the auditor's objectives in observing the actual distribution of payroll checks is to determine that every name on the payroll is that of a bona fide employee. The payroll observation is an auditing procedure that is generally performed for which of the following reasons?

   a. The professional standards that are generally accepted require the auditor to perform the payroll observation.
   b. The various phases of payroll work are not sufficiently segregated to afford effective internal accounting control.
   c. The independent auditor uses personal judgment and decides to observe the payroll distribution on a particular audit.
   d. The standards that are generally accepted by the profession are interpreted to mean that payroll observation is expected on an audit unless circumstances dictate otherwise.

84. Which of the following would detect an understatement of a purchase discount?
   a. Verify footings and crossfootings of purchases and disbursement records.
   b. Compare purchase invoice terms with disbursement records and checks.
   c. Compare approved purchase orders to receiving reports.
   d. Verify the receipt of items ordered and invoiced.

85. Which of the following is not a procedure performed primarily for the purpose of expressing an opinion on the financial statements, but may bring possible illegal acts to the auditor's attention?
   a. Study and evaluation of internal accounting control.
   b. Review of internal administrative control.
   c. Tests of transactions.
   d. Tests of balances.

86. Audit evidence can come in different forms with different degrees of persuasiveness. Which of the following is the least persuasive type of evidence?
   a. Documents mailed by outsiders to the auditor.
   b. Correspondence between auditor and vendors.
   c. Sales invoices inspected by the auditor.
   d. Computations made by the auditor.

87. Which of the following best describes the independent auditor's approach to obtaining satisfaction concerning depreciation expense in the income statement?
   a. Verify the mathematical accuracy of the amounts charged to income as a result of depreciation expense.

b. Determine the method for computing depreciation expense and ascertain that it is in accordance with generally accepted accounting principles.

c. Reconcile the amount of depreciation expense to those amounts credited to accumulated depreciation accounts.

d. Establish the basis for depreciable assets and verify the depreciation expense.

88. A lawyer's response to a letter of audit inquiry may be limited to matters that are considered individually or collectively material to the financial statements if

    a. The auditor has instructed the lawyer regarding the limits of materiality in financial statements.

    b. The client and the auditor have agreed on the limits of materiality and the lawyer has been notified.

    c. The lawyer and auditor have reached an understanding on the limits of materiality for this purpose.

    d. The lawyer's response to the inquiry explains the legal meaning of materiality limits and establishes quantitative parameters.

89. During the year under audit, a company has completed a private placement of a substantial amount of bonds. Which of the following is the most important step in the auditor's program for the examination of bonds payable?

    a. Confirming the amount issued with the bond trustee.

    b. Tracing the cash received from the issue to the accounting records.

    c. Examining the bond records maintained by the transfer agent.

    d. Recomputing the annual interest cost and the effective yield.

90. If as a result of auditing procedures an auditor believes that the client may have committed illegal acts, which of the following actions should be taken immediately by the auditor?

    a. Consult with the client's counsel and the auditor's counsel to determine how the suspected illegal acts will be communicated to the stockholders.

    b. Extend normal auditing procedures to ascertain whether the suspected illegal acts may have a material effect on the financial statements.

    c. Inquire of the client's management and consult with the client's legal counsel or

other specialists, as necessary, to obtain an understanding of the nature of the acts and their possible effects on the financial statements.

d. Notify each member of the audit committee of the board of directors of the nature of the acts and request that they give guidance with respect to the approach to be taken by the auditor.

91. When a CPA is approached to perform an audit for the first time, the CPA should make inquiries of the predecessor auditor. This is a necessary procedure because the predecessor may be able to provide the successor with information that will assist the successor in determining

    a. Whether the predecessor's work should be utilized.

    b. Whether the company follows the policy of rotating its auditors.

    c. Whether in the predecessor's opinion internal control of the company has been satisfactory.

    d. Whether the engagement should be accepted.

92. The audit working papers often include a client-prepared aged trial balance of accounts receivable as of the balance sheet date. This aging is best used by the auditor to

    a. Evaluate internal control over credit sales.

    b. Test the accuracy of recorded charge sales.

    c. Estimate credit losses.

    d. Verify the validity of the recorded receivables.

93. Which of the following is not a principal objective of the auditor in the examination of revenues?

    a. To verify cash deposited during the year.

    b. To study and evaluate internal control, with particular emphasis on the use of accrual accounting to record revenue.

    c. To verify that earned revenue has been recorded, and recorded revenue has been earned.

    d. To identify and interpret significant trends and variations in the amounts of various categories of revenue.

MAY 1981 QUESTIONS

94. Which of the following is **not** a primary objective of the auditor in the examination of accounts receivable?

a. Determine the approximate realizable value.

b. Determine the adequacy of internal controls.

c. Establish validity of the receivables.

d. Determine the approximate time of collectibility of the receivables.

95. In general, material irregularities perpetrated by which of the following are **most** difficult to detect?

a. Cashier.

b. Controller.

c. Internal auditor.

d. Key-punch operator.

96. A sales cutoff test of billings complements the verification of

a. Sales return.

b. Cash.

c. Accounts receivable.

d. Sales allowances.

97. During an examination of a publicly-held company, the auditor should obtain written confirmation regarding debenture transactions from the

a. Debenture holders.

b. Client's attorney.

c. Internal auditors.

d. Trustee.

98. An audit program for the examination of the retained earnings account should include a step that requires verification of the

a. Market value used to charge retained earnings to account for a two-for-one stock split.

b. Approval of the adjustment to the beginning balance as a result of a write-down of an account receivable.

c. Authorization for both cash and stock dividends.

d. Gain or loss resulting from disposition of treasury shares.

99. The accuracy of perpetual inventory records may be established, in part, by comparing perpetual inventory records with

a. Purchase requisitions.

b. Receiving reports.

c. Purchase orders.

d. Vendor payments.

100. The auditor should ordinarily mail confirmation requests to all banks with which the client has conducted any business during the year, regardless of the year-end balance, since

a. The confirmation form also seeks information about indebtedness to the bank.

b. This procedure will detect kiting activities which would otherwise not be detected.

c. The mailing confirmation forms to all such banks is required by generally accepted auditing standards.

d. This procedure relieves the auditor of any responsibility with respect to nondetection of forged checks.

101. Which of the following analyses appearing in a predecessor's working papers is the successor auditor **least** likely to be interested in reviewing?

a. Analysis of noncurrent balance sheet accounts.

b. Analysis of current balance sheet accounts.

c. Analysis of contingencies.

d. Analysis of income statement accounts.

102. Which of the audit procedures listed below would be **least** likely to disclose the existence of related party transactions of a client during the period under audit?

a. Reading "conflict-of-interest" statements obtained by the client from its management.

b. Scanning accounting records for large transactions at or just prior to the end of the period under audit.

c. Inspecting invoices from law firms.

d. Confirming large purchase and sales transactions with the vendors and/or customers involved.

103. In which of the following instances would it be appropriate for the auditor to refer to the work of an appraiser in the auditor's report?

a. An unqualified opinion is expressed and the auditor wishes to place emphasis on the use of a specialist.

b. A qualified opinion is expressed because of a major uncertainty unrelated to the work of the appraiser.

c. An adverse opinion is expressed based on a difference of opinion between the client and the outside appraiser as to the value of certain assets.

d. A disclaimer of opinion is expressed due to a scope limitation imposed on the auditor by the appraiser.

104. An example of a transaction which may be indicative of the existence of related parties is

a. Borrowing or lending at a rate of interest which equals the current market rate.

b. Selling real estate at a price that is comparable to its appraised value.

c. Making large loans with specified terms as to when or how the funds will be repaid.

d. Exchanging property for similar property in a nonmonetary transaction.

105. A common audit procedure in the audit of payroll transactions involves tracing selected items from the payroll journal to employee time cards that have been approved by supervisory personnel. This procedure is designed to provide evidence in support of the audit proposition that

a. Only bona fide employees worked and their pay was properly computed.

b. Jobs on which employees worked were charged with the appropriate labor cost.

c. Internal controls relating to payroll disbursements are operating effectively.

d. All employees worked the number of hours for which their pay was computed.

106. Analytical review procedures may be classified as being primarily

a. Compliance tests.

b. Substantive tests.

c. Tests of ratios.

d. Detailed tests of balances.

107. Patentex developed a new secret formula which is of great value because it resulted in a virtual monopoly. Patentex has capitalized all research and development costs associated with this formula. Greene, CPA, who is examining this account, will probably

a. Confer with management regarding transfer of the amount from the balance sheet to the income statement.

b. Confirm that the secret formula is registered and on file with the county clerk's office.

c. Confer with management regarding a change in the title of the account to "goodwill."

d. Confer with management regarding ownership of the secret formula.

108. The auditor's program for the examination of long-term debt should include steps that require the

a. Verification of the existence of the bondholders.

b. Examination of any bond trust indenture.

c. Inspection of the accounts payable subsidiary ledger.

d. Investigation of credits to the bond interest income account.

109. When an independent auditor decides that the work performed by internal auditors may have a bearing on the nature, timing, and extent of contemplated audit procedures, the independent auditor should plan to evaluate the objectivity of the internal auditors. Relative to objectivity, the independent auditor should

a. Consider the organizational level to which internal auditors report the results of their work.

b. Review the quality control program in effect for the internal audit staff.

c. Examine the quality of the internal audit reports.

d. Consider the qualifications of the internal audit staff.

110. Which of the following explanations might satisfy an auditor who discovers significant debits to an accumulated depreciation account?

a. Extraordinary repairs have lengthened the life of an asset.

b. Prior years' depreciation charges were erroneously understated.

c. A reserve for possible loss on retirement has been recorded.

d. An asset has been recorded at its fair value.

111. To conceal defalcations involving receivables, the auditor would expect an experienced bookkeeper to charge which of the following accounts?

a. Miscellaneous income.

b. Petty cash.

c. Miscellaneous expense.

d. Sales returns.

112. Once a CPA has determined that accounts receivable have increased due to slow collections in a "tight money" environment, the CPA would be likely to

a. Increase the balance in the allowance for bad debts account.

b. Review the going concern ramifications.

c. Review the credit and collection policy.

d. Expand tests of collectibility.

113. To establish illegal "slush funds," corporations may divert cash received in normal business operations. An auditor would encounter the greatest difficulty in detecting the diversion of proceeds from

a. Scrap sales.

b. Dividends.

c. Purchase returns.

d. C.O.D. sales.

114. Which of the following statements best describes the auditor's responsibility with respect to illegal acts that do **not** have a material effect on the client's financial statements?

    a.   Generally, the auditor is under no obligation to notify parties other than personnel within the client's organization.

    b.   Generally, the auditor is under an obligation to see that stockholders are notified.

    c.   Generally, the auditor is obligated to disclose the relevant facts in the auditor's report.

    d.   Generally, the auditor is expected to compel the client to adhere to requirements of the Foreign Corrupt Practices Act.

REPEAT QUESTION

(581,A1,32)   Identical to item **50** above

PROBLEMS

Problem **1**   Evidence for Limited Review (1179,A3)

(15 to 25 minutes)

Loman, CPA, who has examined the financial statements of the Broadwall Corporation, a publicly held company, for the year ended December 31, 1979, was asked to perform a limited review of the financial statements of Broadwall Corporation for the period ending March 31, 1980. The engagement letter stated that a limited review does not provide a basis for the expression of an opinion.

Required:

    a.   Explain why Loman's limited review will **not** provide a basis for the expression of an opinion

    b.   What are the review procedures which Loman should perform, and what is the purpose of each procedure? Structure your response as follows:

Procedure	Purpose of Procedure

Problem 2   Payroll Input Verification and
                Examination Procedures (1180,A5)

(15 to 25 minutes)

James, who was engaged to examine the financial statements of Talbert Corporation, is about to audit payroll. Talbert uses a computer service center to process weekly payroll as follows:

Each Monday Talbert's payroll clerk inserts data in appropriate spaces on the preprinted service center prepared input form, and sends it to the service center via messenger. The service center extracts new permanent data from the input form and updates master files. The weekly payroll data are then processed. The weekly payroll register and payroll checks are printed and delivered by messenger to Talbert on Thursday.

Part of the sample selected for audit by James includes the following input form and payroll register:

See following page

Required:

    a.   Describe how James should verify the information in the payroll input form shown on the following page.

    b.   Describe (but do **not** perform) the procedures that James should follow in the examination of the November 12, 1979, payroll register shown on the following page.

Problem **3**   Procedures for Loss Contingencies
             (579,A4)

(15 to 25 minutes)

During an audit engagement Harper, CPA, has satisfactorily completed an examination of accounts payable and other liabilities and now plans to determine whether there are any loss contingencies arising from litigation, claims, or assessments.

Required:

What are the audit procedures that Harper should follow with respect to the existence of loss contingencies arising from litigation, claims, and assessments? Do not discuss reporting requirements.

Problem **4**   Cutoff Tests (1171,A3)

(25 to 30 minutes)

In connection with his examination of the financial statements of Houston Wholesalers, Inc. for the year ended June 30, 1971, a CPA performs several cutoff tests.

Required:

    a. 1. What is a cutoff test?
        2. Why must cutoff tests be performed for both the beginning and the end of the audit period?

    b.   The CPA wishes to test Houston's sales cutoff at June 30, 1971. Describe the steps he should include in this test.

    c.   The CPA obtains a July 10, 1971, bank statement directly from the bank. Explain how he will use this cutoff bank statement:
        1. In his review of the June 30, 1971, bank reconciliation.
        2. To obtain other audit information.

(Problem 2 continued)

Talbert Corporation Payroll Input — Week Ending Friday, Nov. 23, 1979

Name	Social Security	W-4 Information	Hourly Rate	Reg	OT	Bonds	Union	Other
				Hours		*Special Deductions*		
A. Bell	999-99-9991	M-1	10.00	35	5	18.75		
B. Carr	999-99-9992	M-2	10.00	35	4			
C. Dawn	999-99-9993	S-1	10.00	35	6	18.75	4.00	
D. Ellis	999-99-9994	S-1	10.00	35	2		4.00	50.00
E. Frank	999-99-9995	M-4	10.00	35	1		4.00	
F. Gillis	999-99-9996	M-4	10.00	35			4.00	
G. Hugh	999-99-9997	M-1	7.00	35	2	18.75	4.00	
H. Jones	999-99-9998	M-2	7.00	35			4.00	25.00
J. King	999-99-9999	S-1	7.00	35	4		4.00	
New Employee								
J. Smith	999-99-9990	M-3	7.00	35				

— Employee Data -- Permanent File — / —Current Week's Payroll Data —

Talbert Corporation Payroll Register — Nov. 23, 1979

Employee	Social Security	Reg	OT	Reg	OT	Gross Payroll	FICA	Fed	State	Other Withheld	Net Pay	Check No.
		Hours		*Payroll*			*Taxes Withheld*					
A. Bell	999-99-9991	35	5	350.00	75.00	425.00	26.05	76.00	27.40	18.75	276.80	1499
B. Carr	999-99-9992	35	4	350.00	60.00	410.00	25.13	65.00	23.60		296.27	1500
C. Dawn	999-99-9993	35	6	350.00	90.00	440.00	26.97	100.90	28.60	22.75	260.78	1501
D. Ellis	999-99-9994	35	2	350.00	30.00	380.00	23.29	80.50	21.70	54.00	200.51	1502
E. Frank	999-99-9995	35	1	350.00	15.00	365.00	22.37	43.50	15.90	4.00	279.23	1503
F. Gillis	999-99-9996	35		350.00		350.00	21.46	41.40	15.00	4.00	268.14	1504
G. Hugh	999-99-9997	35	2	245.00	21.00	266.00	16.31	34.80	10.90	22.75	181.24	1505
H. Jones	999-99-9998	35		245.00		245.00	15.02	26.40	8.70	29.00	165.88	1506
J. King	999-99-9999	35	4	245.00	42.00	287.00	17.59	49.40	12.20	4.00	203.81	1507
J. Smith	999-99-9990	35		245.00		245.00	15.02	23.00	7.80		199.18	1508
Totals		350	24	3,080.00	333.00	3,413.00	209.21	540.90	171.80	159.25	2,331.84	

Problem 5   Balance Sheet--Income Statement (1172,A4)

(25 to 30 minutes)

Part a. In a properly planned examination of financial statements, the auditor coordinates his reviews of specific balance-sheet and income-statement accounts.

Required:

Why should the auditor coordinate his examination of balance-sheet accounts and income-statement accounts? Discuss and illustrate by examples.

Part b. A properly designed audit program enables the auditor to determine conditions or establish relationships in more than one way.

Required:

Cite various procedures that the auditor employs that might lead to detection of each of the following two conditions:

1. Inadequate allowance for doubtful accounts receivable.
2. Unrecorded retirements of property, plant, and equipment.

Problem 6   Client Representation Letters (1172,A5)

(25 to 30 minutes)

The major written understandings between a CPA and his client, in connection with an examination of financial statements, are the engagement (arrangements) letter and the client's representation letters.

Required:

a. 1. What are the objectives of the engagement (arrangements) letter?
   2. Who should prepare and sign the engagement letter?
   3. When should the engagement letter be sent?
   4. Why should the engagement letter be renewed periodically?

b. 1. What are the objectives of the client's representation letters?
   2. Who should prepare and sign the client's representation letters?
   3. When should the client's representation letters be obtained?
   4. Why should the client's representation letters be prepared for each examination?

c. A CPA's responsibilities for providing accounting services sometimes involve his association with unaudited financial statements. Discuss the need in this circumstance for:
   1. An engagement letter.
   2. Client's representation letters.

Problem 7   Audit Programs (1177,A2)

(15 to 25 minutes)

Part a.   The first generally accepted auditing standard of field work requires, in part, that "the work is to be adequately planned." An effective tool that aids the auditor in adequately planning the work is an audit program.

Required:

What is an audit program, and what purposes does it serve?

Part b.   Auditors frequently refer to the terms "Standards" and "Procedures." Standards deal with measures of the quality of the auditor's performance. Standards specifically refer to the ten generally accepted auditing standards. Procedures relate to those acts that are performed by the auditor while trying to gather evidence. Procedures specifically refer to the methods or techniques used by the auditor in the conduct of the examination.

Required:

List at least eight different types of procedures that an auditor would use during an examination of financial statements. For example, a type of procedure that an auditor would frequently use is the observation of activities and conditions. Do not discuss specific accounts.

Problem 8   GAO Audit Standards (1177,A4)

(15 to 30 minutes)

Jones and Todd, a local CPA firm, received an invitation to bid for the audit of a local, federally-assisted program. The audit is to be conducted in accordance with the audit standards published by the General Accounting Office (GAO), a federal auditing agency. Jones and Todd has become familiar with the GAO standards and recognizes that the GAO standards are not inconsistent with generally accepted auditing standards (GAAS). The GAO standards, unlike GAAS, are concerned with more than the financial aspects of an entity's operations. The GAO standards broaden the definition of auditing by establishing that the full scope of an audit should encompass the following elements:

1. An examination of financial transactions, accounts, and reports, including an evaluation of compliance with applicable laws and regulations.
2. A review of efficiency and economy in the use of resources, such as personnel and equipment.
3. A review to determine whether desired results are effectively achieved (program results).

Jones and Todd has been engaged to perform the audit of the program and the audit is to encompass all three elements.

Required:

a. Jones and Todd should perform sufficient audit work to satisfy the financial and compliance element of the GAO standards. What should such audit work determine?

b. After making appropriate review and inquiries, what uneconomical practices or inefficiencies should Jones and Todd be alert to, in satisfying the efficiency and economy element encompassed by the GAO standards?

c. After making appropriate review and inquiries, what should Jones and Todd consider to satisfy the program results element encompassed by the GAO standards?

Problem 9   Accounts-Receivable Confirmations
(577,A4)

(15 to 25 minutes)

Dodge, CPA, is examining the financial statements of a manufacturing company with a significant amount of trade accounts receivable. Dodge is satisfied that the accounts are properly summarized and classified and that allocations, reclassifications, and valuations are made in accordance with generally accepted accounting principles. Dodge is planning to use accounts-receivable confirmation requests to satisfy the third standard of field work as to trade accounts receivable.

Required:

a.   Identify and describe the two forms of accounts-receivable confirmation requests and indicate what factors Dodge will consider in determining when to use each.

b.   Assume Dodge has received a satisfactory response to the confirmation requests. Describe how Dodge could evaluate collectibility of the trade accounts receivable.

Problem 10   Toyco Bank Reconciliation (577,A5)

(15 to 30 minutes)

Toyco, a retail toy chain, honors two bank credit cards and makes daily deposits of credit card sales in two credit card bank accounts (Bank A and Bank B). Each day Toyco batches its credit card sales slips, bank deposit slips, and authorized sales return documents, and keypunches cards for processing by its electronic data processing department. Each week detailed computer printouts of the general ledger credit card cash accounts are prepared. Credit card banks have been instructed to make an automatic weekly transfer of cash to Toyco's general bank account. The credit card banks charge back deposits that include sales to holders of stolen or expired cards.

The auditor conducting the examination of the 1976 Toyco financial statements has obtained the following copies of the detailed general ledger cash account printouts, a summary of the bank statements and the manually prepared bank reconciliations, all for the week ended December 31, 1976.

Toyco
DETAILED GENERAL LEDGER CREDIT CARD CASH ACCOUNT PRINTOUTS
For the Week Ended December 31, 1976

	Bank A	Bank B
	Dr. or (Cr.)	Dr. or (Cr.)
Beginning Balance		
- December 24, 1976	$12,100	$ 4,200
Deposits		
- December 27, 1976	2,500	5,000
- December 28, 1976	3,000	7,000
- December 29, 1976	0	5,400
- December 30, 1976	1,900	4,000
- December 31, 1976	2,200	6,000
Cash Transfer		
- December 27, 1976	(10,700)	0
Chargebacks		
- Expired cards	(300)	(1,600)
Invalid deposits (physically deposited in wrong account)	(1,400)	(1,000)
Redeposit of invalid deposits	1,000	1,400
Sales returns for week ending December 31, 1976	(600)	(1,200)
Ending Balance		
- December 31, 1976	$ 9,700	$29,200

Toyco
SUMMARY OF THE BANK STATEMENTS
For the Week Ended December 31, 1976

	Bank A	Bank B
	(Charges) or Credits	
Beginning Balance		
- December 24, 1976	$10,000	$ 0
Deposits dated		
- December 24, 1976	2,100	4,200
- December 27, 1976	2,500	5,000
- December 28, 1976	3,000	7,000
- December 29, 1976	2,000	5,500
- December 30, 1976	1,900	4,000
Cash transfers to general bank account		
- December 27, 1976	(10,700)	0
- December 31, 1976	0	(22,600)
Chargebacks		
- Stolen cards	(100)	0
- Expired cards	(300)	(1,600)
Invalid deposits	(1,400)	(1,000)
Bank service charges	0	(500)
Bank charge (unexplained)	(400)	0
Ending Balance		
- December 31, 1976	$ 8,600	$ 0

Toyco
BANK RECONCILIATIONS
For the Week Ended December 31, 1976

Code No.		Bank A	Bank B
		Add or (Deduct)	
1.	Balance per bank statement - December 31, 1976	$8,600	$ 0
2.	Deposits in transit - December 31, 1976	2,200	6,000
3.	Redeposit of invalid deposits - (physically deposited in wrong account)	1,000	1,400
4.	Difference in deposits of December 29, 1976	(2,000)	(100)
5.	Unexplained bank charge	400	0
6.	Bank cash transfer not yet recorded	0	22,600
7.	Bank service charges	0	500
8.	Chargebacks not recorded - Stolen cards	100	0
9.	Sales returns recorded but not reported to the bank	(600)	(1,200)
10.	Balance per general ledger - December 31, 1976	$9,700	$29,200

Required:

Based on a review of the December 31, 1976, bank reconciliations and the related information available in the printouts and the summary of bank statements, describe what action(s) the auditor should take to obtain audit satisfaction for each item on the bank reconciliations.

Assume that all amounts are material and all computations are accurate.

Organize your answer sheet as follows using the appropriate code number for each item on the bank reconciliations:

Code No.	Action(s) to be taken by the auditor to obtain audit satisfaction
1.	

Problem 11   Property, Plant & Equipment (1177,A3)

(15 to 25 minutes)

Rivers, CPA, is the auditor for a manufacturing company with a balance sheet that includes the caption "Property, Plant and Equipment." Rivers has been asked by the company's management if audit adjustments or reclassifications are required for the following material items that have been included or excluded from "Property, Plant & Equipment."

1.   A tract of land was acquired during the year. The land is the future site of the client's new headquarters which will be constructed in the following year. Commissions were paid to the real estate agent used to acquire the land, and expenditures were made to relocate the previous owner's equipment. These commissions and expenditures were expensed and are excluded from "Property, Plant & Equipment."

2.   Clearing costs were incurred to make the land ready for construction. These costs were included in "Property, Plant & Equipment."

3.   During the land clearing process, timber and gravel were recovered and sold. The proceeds from the sale were recorded as other income and are excluded from "Property, Plant & Equipment."

4.   A group of machines was purchased under a royalty agreement which provides royalty payments based on units of production from the machines. The cost of the machines, freight costs, unloading charges, and royalty payments were capitalized and are included in "Property, Plant & Equipment."

Required:

a.   Describe the general characteristics of assets, such as land, buildings, improvements, machinery, equipment, fixtures, etc., that should normally be classified as "Property, Plant & Equipment," and identify audit objectives (i.e., how an auditor can obtain audit satisfaction) in connection with the examination of "Property, Plant & Equipment." Do not discuss specific audit procedures.

b.   Indicate whether each of the above items numbered 1 to 4 requires one or more audit adjustments or reclassifications, and explain why such adjustments or reclassifications are required or not required.

Organize your answer as follows:

Item Number	Is Audit Adjustment or Reclassification Required? Yes or No	Reasons Why Audit Adjustment or Reclassification is Required or Not Required

Problem 12   Physical Count of Securities (573,A4)

(25 to 30 minutes)

In connection with his examination of the financial statements of Belasco Chemicals, Inc., Kenneth Mack, CPA, is considering the necessity of inspecting marketable securities on the balance-sheet date, May 31, 1973, or at some other date. The marketable securities held by Belasco include negotiable bearer bonds, which are kept in a safe in the treasurer's office, and miscellaneous stocks and bonds kept in a safe deposit box at The Merchants Bank. Both the negotiable bearer bonds and the miscellaneous stocks and bonds are material to proper presentation of Belasco's financial position.

Required:

a. What are the factors that Mr. Mack should consider in determining the necessity for inspecting these securities on May 31, 1973, as opposed to other dates?

b. Assume that Mr. Mack plans to send a member of his staff to Belasco's offices and The Merchants Bank on May 31, 1973, to make the security inspection. What instructions should he give to this staff member as to the conduct of the inspection and the evidence to be included in the audit working papers? (Note: Do not discuss the valuation of securities; the income from securities; or the examination of information contained in the books and records of the Company.)

c. Assume that Mr. Mack finds it impracticable to send a member of his staff to Belasco's offices and The Merchants Bank on May 31, 1973. What alternative procedures may he employ to assure himself that the Company had physical possession of its marketable securities on May 31, 1973, if the securities are inspected (1) May 28, 1973? (2) June 5, 1973?

Problem 13   Evidential Matter (575,A3)

(20 to 25 minutes)

The third generally accepted auditing standard of field work requires that the auditor obtain sufficient competent evidential matter to afford a reasonable basis for an opinion regarding the financial statements under examination. In considering what constitutes sufficient competent evi-

dential matter, a distinction should be made between underlying accounting data and all corroborating information available to the auditor.

Required:

a. Discuss the nature of evidential matter to be considered by the auditor in terms of the underlying accounting data, all corroborating information available to the auditor, and the methods by which the auditor tests or gathers competent evidential matter.

b. State the three general presumptions that can be made about the validity of evidential matter with respect to comparative assurance, persuasiveness, and reliability.

Problem 14   Inventory Audit Procedures (1176,A4)

(15 to 25 minutes)

Ace Corporation does not conduct a complete annual physical count of purchased parts and supplies in its principal warehouse but uses statistical sampling instead to estimate the year-end inventory. Ace maintains a perpetual inventory record of parts and supplies and believes that statistical sampling is highly effective in determining inventory values and is sufficiently reliable to make a physical count of each item of inventory unnecessary.

Required:

a. Identify the audit procedures that should be used by the independent auditor that change or are in addition to normal required audit procedures when a client utilizes statistical sampling to determine inventory value and does not conduct a 100 percent annual physical count of inventory items.

b. List at least ten normal audit procedures that should be performed to verify physical quantities whenever a client conducts a periodic physical count of all or part of its inventory.

Problem 15   Materiality (1178,A3)

(15 to 25 minutes)

During the course of an audit engagement an
independent auditor gives serious consideration
to the concepts of materiality. This concept of
materiality is inherent in the work of the independent auditor and is important for planning, preparing, and modifying audit programs. The concept
of materiality underlies the application of all the
generally accepted auditing standards, particularly
the standards of field work and reporting.

Required:
   a.   Briefly describe what is meant by the
independent auditor's concept of materiality.
   b.   What are some common relationships
and other considerations used by the auditor in
judging materiality?
   c.   Identify how the planning and execution of an audit program might be affected by
the independent auditor's concept of materiality.

MULTIPLE CHOICE ANSWERS

1.	c	24.	b	47.	c	70.	a	93.	a
2.	b	25.	b	48.	d	71.	c	94.	d
3.	a	26.	a	49.	d	72.	c	95.	b
4.	a	27.	a	50.	d	73.	d	96.	c
5.	a	28.	d	51.	b	74.	d	97.	d
6.	d	29.	a	52.	d	75.	a	98.	c
7.	a	30.	d	53.	b	76.	c	99.	b
8.	c	31.	a	54.	d	77.	d	100.	a
9.	c	32.	b	55.	c	78.	d	101.	d
10.	c	33.	a	56.	a	79.	d	102.	d
11.	d	34.	c	57.	a	80.	b	103.	c
12.	a	35.	d	58.	b	81.	b	104.	d
13.	c	36.	a	59.	a	82.	d	105.	d
14.	d	37.	d	60.	c	83.	b	106.	b
15.	d	38.	b	61.	c	84.	b	107.	a
16.	d	39.	c	62.	c	85.	b	108.	b
17.	d	40.	c	63.	b	86.	c	109.	a
18.	b	41.	d	64.	a	87.	d	110.	a
19.	a	42.	d	65.	c	88.	c	111.	d
20.	b	43.	c	66.	c	89.	b	112.	d
21.	a	44.	a	67.	c	90.	c	113.	a
22.	c	45.	c	68.	d	91.	d	114.	a
23.	d	46.	d	69.	a	92.	c		

EXPLANATION OF MULTIPLE CHOICE ANSWERS

1.   (1180,A1,1)   (c)   Analytical review procedures are used to gather evidence with respect to relationships among various accounting and non-accounting data, para 318.06. Answers (a), (b), and (d) are specifically identified as analytical review procedures in para 318.06. Answer (c) is an example of a test of details of transactions and balances.

2.   (1180,A1,6)   (b)   The auditor ordinarily may reduce the extent of his/her work when outside firms are involved (para 9509.06), thus answer (b) is accurate. Answer (a) is incorrect since some procedures are required. The reduction of work makes answer (c) incorrect. Answer (d) is incorrect since the auditor's scope has not been limited by either the client or by the circumstances (para 509.10—.13).

3.   (1180,A1,7)   (a)   Answer (a) is correct since only the Minutes will show whether the stock issuance or retirement has been properly authorized. Although the auditor may examine cash receipts (for issuances) and cash disbursements (retirements), the requirement specifies "ultimately traced to" thus, neither answers (b) and (c) meet the requirement. Answer (d) is incorrect; once the stock is issued, the stockholders possess the stock certificates.

4.   (1180,A1,18)   (a)   The auditor seeks to determine that both sides of the purchase transaction, inventory acquisition and accounts payable, are treated in the proper period. Thus, payables should exist for items received before year-end and for other goods for which title has passed. Answer (b) is incorrect since the purchase order, generally an internal document, is of limited assistance, if any, in determining when title has passed. Answer (c) is incorrect because the evidence obtained by comparing invoices with statements does not answer the question of when title passed. Answer (d) is incorrect; although cutoff tests and accounts payable both relate to year-end balances, coordinating the mailing of confirmations is not necessary.

5.   (1180,A1,19)   (a)   Commissions are directly related to sales in verifying accrued commission payable, the auditor seeks to determine that both are recorded in the proper period. Answer (b) is incorrect because contingent liabilities generally have little to do with commissions; in most cases, the liability exists when the sale occurs. Answer (c) is incorrect because the overall general nature of the post balance sheet review makes discovery difficult, although certainly possible. Answer (d) is incorrect because the examination trade accounts payable will be of assistance in verifying accrued commissions only in those cases in which there are classification errors.

6.   (1180,A1,21)   (d)   CPAs use a letter of audit inquiry to the client's lawyer as the primary means of corroborating information outlined by the client concerning litigations, claims and assessments (para 337.08). While answers (a), (b), and (c) are all partially correct, since such information may be provided by the lawyer, they are all more limited and incomplete than is (d) which includes all of them.

7.   (1180,A1,27)   (a)   Internal auditors perform a number of detailed tests by reviewing operating practices related to efficiency and economy; they also make special inquiries for their management which are not typically performed by CPAs (para 322.02). Thus answers (b), (c), and (d) are all incorrect since they suggest either an equal or more limited scope of internal auditor involvement as compared to the external auditor.

8.   (1180,A1,29)   (c)   To be effective confirmation must be sent to parties who are likely to be able to respond meaningfully. Confirmations may be used effectively for inventories (answer (a)) which are, for example, consigned. Long-term creditors (answer (b)) will generally keep current records of amounts owed them and this will make confirmations possible. Stock-

holders (answer (d)) can generally reply as to the amount of stock they hold. In the case of property, plant, and equipment, however, those who have sold the equipment will not generally be able to provide assistance since they will not have conveniently available records on historic sales to each customer. That is, many of these sales will have been made many years ago and the related records will not be conveniently available.

9. (1180,A1,31)   (c)   Coordination of the performance of auditing procedures for readily negotiable assets and liabilities (e.g., cash on hand and in banks, securities owned, bank loans and other related items) is important since their form may be easily and quickly altered (para 310.08). Answer (a) is incorrect since the study of cash internal controls is performed early in the audit to determine scope of subsequent tests. Answer (b) is incorrect since, despite the fact that the cash count is frequently performed at the balance sheet date, it is not necessary. Answer (d) is inferior to answer (c) because inventories are not as readily negotiable as marketable securities.

10. (1180,A1,34)   (c)   The search for unrecorded liabilities is performed near the completion of the audit to determine that proper cutoffs have been made and to give the auditor additional information in his evaluations of accounts as of the balance sheet date. While the observation of inventory (answer (a)) and the confirmation of receivables (answer (d)) are frequently done at the date of the balance sheet, strong internal controls may allow the auditor to perform both of these procedures earlier. The review of internal controls over cash receipts (answer (b)) is frequently performed prior to year-end.

11. (1180,A1,36)   (d)   The auditor may learn of slow-moving inventory through any of these methods. However, answer (d) is better than answers (a) and (b) because direct personal knowledge obtained through physical examination, observation, computation, and inspection is more persuasive than information obtained indirectly (para 330.08). Answer (c) will only be effective for items which the auditor knows to be obsolete (either by observation of the items' condition or by personal knowledge concerning the items). Answer (d) will allow the auditor to evaluate turnover rates for all important inventory items.

12. (1180,A1,38)   (a)   In an examination of investments auditors must establish existence (answer (c)), ownership (answer (b)), cost, carrying amount, and any related disclosures required (e.g., balance

sheet classification (answer (d)). Authenticity, answer (a) is not a primary objective.

13. (1180,A1,42)   (c)   It is unlikely that public records will have the required current mortgage balance. Answer (a) describes a procedure, the examination of cancelled checks, that provides evidence that the payments have been made. Answers (b) and (d), reviewing the amortization schedule and recomputing interest expense, gives the portions of the payments representing principle (reduction of mortgage balance) and interest.

14. (1180,A1,46)   (d)   Lead schedules serve to accumulate similar or related information before it is transferred to the working trial balance. Answer (a) is incorrect because account analyses show the changes in accounts during the year which normally would not appear on a working trial balance. Answer (b) is incorrect since supporting schedules are normally included in account analyses. Answer (c), control accounts, eliminate details from the clients' general ledger.

15. (1180,A1,49)   (d)   Tests of procedures are appropriate when the cost of testing and relying on an effective control is less than the cost of increased substantive tests which are necessary if the control is not tested (see para 320.55 for more on this relationship). This cost relationship is believed to occur most frequently in accounts with numerous transactions such as sales since the audit cost of directly substantiating the account is high. Answers (a) and (b) are incorrect since equipment and bonds payable represent accounts with fewer annual transactions than sales resulting in a low cost to substantiate the balances. Answer (c) is incorrect because bank charges will generally be low in both number of charges and dollar terms. If significant in dollar terms, they would certainly be of concern to the auditor who would wish to substantiate them.

16. (1180,A1,50)   (d)   Analytical review procedures are used to gather evidence relative to relationships among various accounting and non-accounting data. The procedure of comparison of the financial information with information of prior periods [answer (d)] is a suggested analytical review procedure per para 318.06a. Answer (a) is incorrect since it is an example of a test of details of transactions and balances. Answer (b), while desirable, is not a required analytical review procedure for the income statement. Answer (c) is incorrect since the inventory information suggested is available through balance sheet review procedures.

17. (1180,A1,51) (d) The search for unrecorded liabilities is performed near the completion of the audit to determine that proper cutoffs have been made and to give the auditor additional information in his/her evaluations of account balances as of the balance sheet date. One of the principal procedures used to accomplish this objective is the examination of a sample of cash disbursements in the period subsequent to year-end [answer (d)]. Answer (a) is incorrect since it will only be effective for creditors already recorded in the accounts payable ledger. Answer (b) is incorrect since for unrecorded items it is likely that both the purchases account and the accounts payable account will be understated. Answer (c) is of limited assistance because of the few days involved.

18. (1180,A1,54) (b) Because audit tests have been performed on balance sheet and income statement accounts the auditor ordinarily will be able to cross-reference balances on the statement of changes in financial position to these other statements. Answer (a) is incorrect because determination of the amount of working capital is only one check needed in cases in which the statement is prepared on that basis. Answer (c) is incorrect since the pertinent ratios have already been calculated in auditing the balance sheet and income statement. Answer (d) is incorrect since no <u>auditing</u> guidance is provided in APB 19 on the statement of changes in financial position.

19. (1180,A1,57) (a) The credit manager's opinion generally will receive the least reliance since it is she/he who made the credit decisions and since evidence obtained directly (evidence described in answers (b), (c), and (d)) is more credible than that received indirectly.

20. (1180,A1,58) (b) The vendor's invoice may be used in a purchase cutoff. The invoice will assist the auditor in obtaining information on quantity (answer (a)), price (answer (b)) and terms (answer (d)). It will give limited assistance on the quality of the item which is in transit and is thus not available.

21. (1180,A1,60) (a) Questions on the <u>continuing</u> validity and existence of a patent may be answered by a patent attorney. Answer (b) is incorrect since regional State Patent Offices do not exist. Answer (c) is incorrect since the patent inventor may not have current information on the validity and existence of the patent. Answer (d) is incorrect since the patent owner which may be the firm you are auditing is not as independent as a patent attorney and does not have the legal expertise to credibly reply on validity and existence questions.

22. (580,A1,1) (c) Per para 330.08, evidence must be both valid and relevant to be competent. Validity relates to the circumstances under which it was obtained. For example, evidential matter obtained from independent sources outside the client enterprise is superior to evidential matter obtained from sources within the client enterprise. Answers (a), (b), and (d) are incorrect because while evidence should be timely, substantial, reliable, documented, useful, and objective, these terms do not constitute the definition of competence of evidential matter per section 330 of the SASs.

23. (580,A1,4) (d) The requirement is the audit procedure least likely to disclose that certain customers are being dealt with on a consignment basis. Observation of physical inventory would not indicate that shipments have been made on a consignment basis. Irrespective of whether sales are on a regular basis or a consignment basis, the inventory would not be in the client's possession. Answer (a) is incorrect because tracing the shipping documents to the sales journal would disclose the consignment arrangement if the sales journal indicated sale terms. Answer (b) is incorrect because testing cash receipts transactions and the relating documentation would probably provide an indication of consignment sales. Answer (c) is incorrect because confirmation of accounts receivable would provide consignees with the opportunity of indicating that no receivable existed because they were holding the goods on consignment.

24. (580,A1,8) (b) The requirement is the audit procedure which would be least likely to detect unrecorded fixed asset disposals. Review of repair and maintenance expense would only point out unrecorded fixed asset disposals if repair and maintenance expense decreased drastically and there were no recorded fixed asset disposals. Answer (a) is incorrect because examination of insurance policies would point out acquisitions of new assets as they became insured and raise the question of related asset disposals. Answer (c) is incorrect because review of property tax files and changes therein would indicate possible asset disposals. Answer (d) is incorrect because fixed asset additions are frequently accompanied by disposals of assets that are being replaced.

25. (580,A1,9) (b) The requirement is where CPAs incur most of their work in forming an opinion on financial statements. The auditor's report is based upon evidential matter which is obtained through the application of audit procedures to the financial statements and underlying accounting records. Since obtaining and examining evidential matter (required by the third standard of fieldwork) encompasses the study and eval-

uation of internal control (required by the second standard of fieldwork), answer (b) is better than (a). Para 320.70 points out that the tests of transactions envisioned in substantive tests often are accomplished concurrently with compliance tests. Answers (c), examining cash transactions, and (d), comparing recorded accountability with assets, are much more specific answers and thus require less time.

26.   (580,A1,11)   (a)   If a client's lawyer resigned shortly after the receipt of an attorney's letter which indicated no significant disagreements with the client's assessment of contingent liabilities, the auditor should inquire why the attorney resigned. The auditor's concern is whether any undisclosed unasserted claims have arisen. Per para 337.11 a lawyer may be required to resign if his advice concerning reporting for litigation, claims, and assessments is disregarded by the client. Accordingly, the resignation shortly after issuance of an attorney's letter may indicate a problem. Answer (b) is incorrect because the attorney issued a letter indicating no significant disagreement with the client's assessment of contingent liabilities. Answers (c) and (d) are incorrect because para 337.11 only suggests that the auditor should consider the need for inquiries, i.e., para 337.11 does not require a complete new exam of contingent liabilities or an adverse opinion.

27.   (580,A1,12)   (a)   The requirement is the area which would require the least amount of time in an audit of a medium-sized manufacturing concern. The number of transactions affecting owners' equity are few in number relative to transactions affecting revenue, assets, and liabilities. Generally only dividend payments, sales of stock, treasury stock transactions, and stock dividends affect owners' equity. Thus all owners' equity transactions can be verified in relatively little time.

28.   (580,A1,13)   (d)   The requirement is the procedure that is not part of a review engagement of a non-public entity. The nature, timing, and extent of limited review procedures are set forth in section 721 (SAS 24) but do not apply to interim financial information included in documents filed with the SEC per para 721.02. The objective of a review of interim financial information is to develop a professional conclusion concerning statement compliance with GAAP through only inquiry and analytical review procedures. Accordingly, other auditing procedures such as the study and evaluation of internal control, tests of accounting records, inspection, observation and confirmation, and other auditing procedures are not performed. Specifically included as analytical review procedures

per para 721.06 are answer (a), inquiries of management, answer (b), inquiry concerning subsequent events, and answer (c), procedures to identify unusual relationships among data.

29.   (580,A1,14)   (a)   The requirement is the primary purpose of the procedures listed in an audit program. Audit procedures are *primarily* designed to gather audit evidence which becomes the basis of the auditor's report. Audit programs are required per para 311.05. Completion of the audit program and any additional audit procedures should provide sufficient competent evidential matter for an opinion on the financial statements as required by the third standard of fieldwork. Answer (b), detection of errors and irregularities, answer (c), tests of internal systems, and answer (d) protection in the event of litigation are all benefits of completing an audit program but are not the primary objective.

30.   (580,A1,15)   (d)   Tracing the test counts from the observation of physical inventory to the final inventory schedule determines that items observed by the auditor are included in the final inventory schedule. Answers (a) and (b) are incorrect because tracing the test count data to the final inventory schedule provides no evidence of the ownership or the obsolescence of the inventory. Answer (c) is incorrect because while the inventory was present for the auditor's observation and test count, it may have been shipped prior to the auditor's tracing the test count data to the final inventory schedule.

31.   (580,A1,19)   (a)   The best verification of a client's bond sinking fund transactions and year-end balance is confirmation with the bond trustee. The bond trustee is an independent party and accordingly can provide valid evidence. Answer (b) is incorrect because the individual holders of the retired bonds would not even collectively have knowledge of all possible bond sinking fund transactions, much less the year-end balance. Answer (c) is incorrect because amortization of bond discount or premium would have no effect on bond sinking fund transactions even if bond interest were being paid by the sinking fund (which is usually not the case). Answer (d) is incorrect because an examination and count of the bonds retired during the year would not verify the transactions (e.g., how much was paid for the bond) and give no indication of the year-end balance in the fund. The year-end balance is cumulative over all the transactions from the inception of the fund.

32. (580,A1,23) (b) The requirement is the situation which would result in a physical inventory in excess of the perpetual book inventory. If credit memos for items returned by customers to the client had not been prepared, the perpetual records would not be adjusted to reflect the returned items. Thus, the physical inventory would be greater than the perpetual records indicated. Answer (a) is incorrect because if the inventory count tags had not been pulled from the inventory, they would not be reflected on the physical inventory sheets and thus the physical inventory accumulation would be understated. Answer (c) is incorrect because if a general entry had not been made to reflect items returned to the client's suppliers, the perpetual records would be overstated. Answer (d) is incorrect because an item shipped FOB shipping point was both not included in the inventory count and not included in the perpetual records which will not create a difference in either (note that the items should be included in both the inventory count and the perpetual records).

33 (580,A1,28) (a) The requirement is the document least likely to provide evidence regarding mortgage acquisition costs. Deeds generally consist of a legal conveyance of rights to use real property. Frequently the sales price is not even specified and the related mortgage acquisition costs are much less likely to be stated in a deed. Answer (b) is incorrect because cancelled checks would provide verification of mortgage acquisition costs. Answer (c) is incorrect because the closing statement would provide a detailed listing of the costs of acquiring the real property, including possible mortgage acquisition costs. Answer (d) is incorrect because examination of interest expense would also relate to the mortgage acquisition costs.

34. (580,A1,29) (c) The requirement is the verification technique for accounts receivable from residential customers during the audit of an electric utility. Per para 331.05 negative confirmations are particularly useful when internal control is effective and there is a large number of small balances. Additionally they are used when the auditor believes the recipients are not likely to give them much consideration which is probably the case with confirmation of utility bills. Answer (a) is incorrect because confirmation requests should be sent per para 331.01. Answer (b) is incorrect because para 331.05 indicates that negative rather than positive confirmation requests are more appropriate in this case. Answer (d) is incorrect because if statistical sampling were used, it would only be used to select the accounts to confirm and evaluate the results of the confirmation, i.e., would help implement the confirmation plan but not be a substitute.

35. (580,A1,30) (d) An indicator that depreciation charges are insufficient would be excessive recurring losses on assets being retired, i.e., insufficient depreciation was taken on those assets. Answer (a) is incorrect because insured values should be based on market values which are normally expected to be in excess of book values in periods of inflation. Answer (b) is incorrect because large amounts of fully depreciated assets would indicate the opposite of insufficient depreciation charges. Answer (c) is incorrect because continuous trade-ins of relatively new assets provide no indication of the adequacy of depreciation charges (the related gain or loss on disposal does).

36. (580,A1,31) (a) The requirement is the least likely means to learn of retirements of equipment. The purchase return and allowance account is credited upon the return of merchandise purchased by the client. Since there is no relationship between merchandise returned and equipment and there are no entries related to purchase returns upon retirement of equipment, review of the purchase return and allowance account would provide no evidence of the equipment retirements. Answer (b) is incorrect because equipment retirements will reduce depreciation. Answer (c) is incorrect because debits to the accumulated depreciation account arise when equipment is retired. Answer (d) is incorrect because insurance policy riders are often added for new equipment, and new equipment often replaces old equipment which has been retired.

37. (580,A1,37) (d) As the auditor's reliance on internal control increases, the extent of substantive tests required decreases. Conversely, when the auditor's reliance on internal control decreases (i.e., is weak), the extent of substantive tests required increases. See section 320B, and especially para 320B.28 through 320B.36.

38. (580,A1,40) (b) The requirement is the method of checking the accuracy of hours worked. Comparison of shop job time tickets with time clock cards would provide a means of determining the accuracy of the time clock cards, i.e., if the time reported on shop time tickets varied significantly from the time clock data, additional procedures would have to be applied to satisfy the auditor as to the accuracy of hours worked. Answer (a) is incorrect because personnel records would not provide information as to the number of hours worked. Answer (c) is incorrect because labor variance reports would be primarily concerned with differences between standard and actual hours incurred in aggregate rather than the hours worked by individuals. Answer (d) is incorrect because the time recorded on the payroll register is usually based upon the hours recorded

on the time cards, i.e., the payroll register would not provide an independent verification of the clock card time.

39.   (580,A1,44) (c)   The requirement is the account that the auditor would be concerned with in the examination of the statement of changes in financial position after the auditor is satisfied with the balance sheet and income statement. The auditor would examine notes payable (a noncurrent account) to determine financing and investing activities that occurred, i.e., changes in noncurrent accounts. If the statement of changes in financial position is based upon the cash format, the net change in trade receivables and the net change in dividend payables (both current items) are each included as an item affecting operations. Each transaction involving notes payable, however, is generally considered a financing and investing activity which is generally disclosed. The auditor's interest in notes payable is equally true when the statement of changes in financial position is based on a working capital approach. Answer (a) is incorrect because the auditor analyzes the changes in the noncurrent accounts rather than the cash account if a working capital format is used. If a cash format is used, the auditor also analyzes the individual changes in the noncurrent accounts and additionally the gross changes in the current accounts.

40.   (580,A1,45) (c)   Audits per GAAS require the auditor to obtain certain written representations for management per para 333.01. Answer (a) is incorrect because the use of statistical sampling is permissive rather than mandatory under GAAS per para 320A.05. Answer (b) is incorrect because analytical review procedures are not required per para 318.01. Answer (d) is incorrect because inventory observation on the balance sheet date is not required per para 331.09 through para 331.13.

41.   (580,A1,49)   (d)   The requirement is the source to verify debits to perpetual inventory records of a non-manufacturing firm. The purchase invoices prepared by the vendor provide an excellent means of verifying debits to perpetual inventory records. Answer (a) is incorrect because the purchases journal is a client-prepared document which is a less valid form of audit evidence than a document prepared by independent third parties, e.g., a vendor invoice. Answer (b) is incorrect because the purchase requisitions are internal requests within the client's firm to the client's purchasing department and would not be a basis for debiting perpetual inventory records. Answer (c) is incorrect because purchase orders issued by the client's purchasing department would not be a basis for debiting perpetual inventory records as the purchase orders may go unfiled by suppliers.

42.   (580,A1,52) (d)   The requirement is why is confirmation of accounts payable unnecessary. Accounts payable are usually not confirmed because there is better evidence available to the auditor, i.e., examination of cash payments subsequent to the balance sheet date. If the auditor reviews all cash payments for a sufficient time after the balance sheet date for items pertaining to the period under audit and finds no such payments which were not recorded as liabilities at year end, the auditor is reasonably assured that accounts payable were not understated.

43.   (580,A1,55) (c)   The requirement is the means of obtaining audit evidence to comply with the third standard of fieldwork. Per para 320.70, the evidential matter required by the third standard of fieldwork is obtained by (1) tests of details of transactions and balances and (2) analytical review procedures. Answer (a) is incorrect because the evidential matter obtained is documented in audit work papers, not obtained through the work papers. Answer (b) is incorrect because planning of the audit engagement provides a means for efficiently obtaining the evidential matter that is required rather than the actual obtaining of the evidence. Answer (d) is incorrect because the review of the system of internal control only determines what control procedures are prescribed. In contrast, the tests of compliance provide evidential matter which concurrently functions as tests of details (para 320.70).

44.   (580,A1,57) (a)   Generally the audit of a balance sheet is considered a test or verification of balances and the audit of an income statement is considered a test of transactions. Answer (b) is incorrect because all activities affecting accounts are executed in accordance with management's general or specific authorization per para 320.28a. Answer (c) is incorrect because the auditor is equally concerned with the cost of assets in the audit of a balance sheet as the costs of producing revenue in the audit of an income. Answer (d) is incorrect because the auditor is concerned with cutoffs in auditing the balance sheet, e.g., cash cutoff, as well as cutoffs in the income statement. Cutoff simply refers to verifying that only transactions of the current period are reflected in the current financial statements.

45.   (1179,A1,3)   (c)   Auditors generally do not confirm insurance premium rates with independent brokers because the insurance company's statements and invoices provide adequate evidence of the cost of the insurance policies. Answer (a) is incorrect because the computation of the insurance premium that is expired helps determine the amount of insurance that remains unexpired at the end of the period.

Answer (d) is incorrect because verification of premium payment is essential evidence to support prepaid insurance. Answer (b) is incorrect because auditors usually do take excerpts of insurance policies into the auditing workpapers in conjunction with review of the prepaid insurance account, e.g., expiration dates, coverage limits, etc.

46.   (1179,A1,4)   (d)   The requirement is supporting documentation for quantities of materials charged to work-in-process. Material requisitions by production departments would be the basis for charging materials to work-in-process. Answer (a) is incorrect because cost ledgers include the work-in-process account, and therefore are not a source of supporting information to initiate transactions which would be recorded later in the cost ledgers. Answer (b) is incorrect because perpetual inventory records are maintained based upon supporting or initiating documentation such as material requisitions. Answer (c) is incorrect because receiving reports are generally prepared by the receiving department when received from third parties at the plant itself. Generally, receiving reports are not prepared in addition to the material requisitions for movement.

47.   (1179,A1,14)   (c)   The best evidence of real estate ownership is paid real estate tax bills. This is true even though in many jurisdictions real estate tax bills are sent to the seller in the year that real estate is sold. In subsequent years the tax collector sends bills to the new owner. Answer (a) is incorrect because title insurance policies once issued can be retained by the insuree long after the property is sold. Answer (b) is incorrect because the real estate deed transferring property to the client can also be held long after the client issues a new deed transferring ownership to someone else. Answer (d) is incorrect because the closing statement for the purchase of the property can be retained long after the property is sold to a third party.

48.   (1179,A1,15)   (d)   The standard bank confirmation form requests:
   a.   Balances to the credit of the client
   b.   Direct liabilities for client's loans
   c.   Client contingent liability on endorsed or discounted notes
   d.   Other direct or contingent liabilities, open letters of credit, etc.
   e.   Security agreements under the UCC

Thus with respect to contingent liabilities, concern regarding notes receivable is on those discounted by the bank. Answers (a), (b), and (c) are incorrect because they are not contingent liabilities of the client.

49.   (1179,A1,17)   (d)   Client presence during the physical examination of securities is for the auditor's protection. Generally, the auditor obtains a written receipt for the return of all of the securities, so if in fact there is a shortage, the auditor cannot be suspected. Answer (a) is incorrect because any directive the auditor would give in the absence of a client representative would be to the auditor's own staff. Answer (b) is incorrect because if there was a need for an expert to detect the possibility of fraudulent securities, the auditor would not rely on a client representative. The auditor would have to engage a specialist per section 336. Answer (c) is incorrect because the client returns all securities to proper locations rather than the auditor. Also, the auditor would probably make arrangements to examine and count securities at the client's facilities to safeguard the securities.

50.   (1179,A1,22)   (d)   Inventory turnover analysis may be useful to the auditor in detecting existence of obsolete merchandise. As the proportion of obsolete merchandise to total inventory grows, the inventory turnover would decrease. Answer (a) is incorrect because the mispricing of inventory would have to be very material to effect the inventory turnover ratio. Recall that the inventory turnover ratio is cost of goods sold divided by the average inventory. Thus, the inventory would have to be substantially incorrect to effect the turnover ratio to a noticeable degree. Answers (b) and (c) are incorrect because the auditor's first concern is with the fairness of presentation of the financial statements rather than control over inventory holding and inventory order costs.

51.   (1179,A1,24)   (b)   The auditor must exercise his professional judgment in determining which audit procedures are necessary to afford a reasonable basis for an opinion per para 110.04. Answer (a) is incorrect because the audit program is simply a listing of audit procedures which is prepared by the auditor to guide the audit. During the audit, the audit program must be revised to accomodate the auditor's findings throughout, i.e., it is dynamic rather than static. Answer (c) is incorrect because GAAS are measures of quality of the performance of the acts and objectives to be obtained from audit procedures. They concern themselves with the auditor's professional qualities and judgment in the performance of an audit engagement (150.01). Answer (d) is incorrect because audit workpapers aid the auditor in the conduct of the examination and provide support for the auditor's opinion but do not determine the specific procedures to be performed (338.02).

52. (1179,A1,25) (d)   An examination per GAAS cannot be expected to provide assurance that illegal acts will be detected per para 328.03. Auditors are proficient in accounting and auditing but not in determination of the legality of various acts. Thus, answer (a) is incorrect because audits do not assure the detection of illegal acts. Answer (b) is incorrect because there is no assurance that illegal acts which specifically violate the truth in lending laws will be disclosed. Answer (c) is incorrect because auditors do not plan to actively search for illegalities in the course of an audit for GAAS. Rather, auditors are aware of the possibility of illegal acts having a material effect on the statements. Accordingly, auditors should take action once they believe illegal acts may have occurred. At this point, the auditor must first gain an understanding of the possible illegal act and then whether it occurred and its effect on the financial statements. This can be done in conjunction with the help of the client and other specialists.

53. (1179,A1,27) (b)   A major reason for an analytical review of client operations is to identify unexpected fluctuations or transactions per para 318.04. Analytical review procedures are substantive tests of financial information made by study and comparison of relationships among the data per para 318.02. Thus, they are not tests of internal control, and therefore would not identify major weaknesses in internal control (answer a), noncompliance with control procedures (answer c), or improper separation of functional responsibilities (answer d).

54. (1179,A1,30) (d)   The auditor should investigate unexpected fluctuations identified by analytical review procedures if the auditor believes they are indicative of matters that may have a significant effect on the examination per para 318.04 and .08. If management is unable to provide an acceptable explanation, the auditor should extend the audit procedures. Answer (a) is incorrect because unexpected fluctuations may have a reasonable explanation which would not create the need for a consistency qualification. Answer (b) is incorrect because the review of internal control is undertaken to understand the prescribed system of internal control. Answer (c) is incorrect because unexpected fluctuations can normally be investigated without requiring the explanation in the client representation letter. While explanations in the client representation letter may sometimes be necessary, they are not normally or usually necessary.

55. (1179,A1,33) (c)   Auditors should extend audit procedures to detect fraud when the examination indicates that fraud may exist per para 327.14. Answer (a) is incorrect because engagement letters do not specify audit procedures. Answer (b) is incorrect because while the auditor plans the examination with the attitude of skepticism, special audit procedures to detect fraud are not routinely made unless the examination indicates that material errors or irregularities may exist (para 327.05 and .14). Answer (d) is incorrect because issuance of an opinion other than an unqualified opinion does not relieve the auditor of his responsibility to detect fraud if it should be detected in complying with GAAS.

56. (1179,A1,34) (a)   Section 333 requires auditors to obtain written representations from management to be in compliance with GAAS. The specific representations depend on the circumstances of the engagement and nature of the financial statements. The written representation should include managerial acknowledgement of its responsibility for the statements, availability of all financial records and related data, subsequent events, etc., para 333.09 indicates that the written representation letter should be dated as of the date of the auditor's report due to the auditor's concern with subsequent events. Answers (b), (c), and (d) are all incorrect because the management representation letter should be dated as of the date of the auditor's report.

57. (1179,A1,37)   (a) The auditor faces two separate risks. The first risk is that material errors may occur in the accounting process, and the second risk is that material errors that have occurred will not be detected in the auditor's examination. The auditor relies on internal control to reduce the first risk and substantive tests to reduce the second risk. See para 320.70-.73 and 320A.14-.15.

58. (1179,A1,43) (b)   The requirement is the least likely item to be verified with respect to an installment loan. The balloon payment due at the end of the note (because the principle was waived for 3 months without extending the maturity date) is not of concern to the presentation of the current period's financial statements. Answer (a) is incorrect because the auditor will need to verify interest expense for the current period on the installment note. Answer (c) is incorrect because the auditor is very concerned with the proper statement of the year-end liability in the balance sheet. Answer (d) is incorrect because the current year's installment loan payments consist of interest expense for the year and reduction of the liability.

59. (1179,A1,44) (a)   The requirement is the audit procedure to detect a bookkeeper overstating one person's W-2 by $500 and deducting it from another person's W-2. Multiplying the applicable FICA rate by the individual gross taxable earnings of each individual would detect that some FICA withholdings were understated and others were overstated. Answer (b) is incorrect because the error occurred in preparation of W-2 forms rather than the amount withheld per pay period. Answer (c) is incorrect because footing and cross-footing the payroll register and tracing postings to the general ledger would not detect W-2 forms completed in error. Answer (d) is incorrect because the total amount contributed per federal tax form 941 was correct. The error was made in preparation of individual W-2 forms.

60. (1179,A1,50) (c)   Per para 318.02, analytical review procedures are substantive tests of financial information made by a study and comparison of relationships among data. Other substantive tests include the tests of transactions and tests of balances. Answer (a) is incorrect because analytical review procedures may be applied on either a statistical or subjective basis. Note that statistical sampling is not a fundamentally different audit approach, and its use is permitted rather than required per GAAS (see para 320A.05). Answer (b) is incorrect because analytical review procedures may be done either manually or by a computer. There is no requirement that a computer be utilized. Answer (d) is incorrect because analytical review procedures clearly result in evidential matter required by the third standard of field work (see para 320.70).

61. (1179,A1,51) (c)   The requirement is the most important audit procedure for disclosing unrecorded liabilities of a public warehouse. Warehouse receipts are issued upon storage of goods. They may be negotiable or non-negotiable and are regulated by either the UCC or the Uniform Warehouse Receipts Act. Goods represented by negotiable warehouse receipts can be released only by surrender of the receipt, but goods represented by non-negotiable receipt may be released upon valid instructions of the holder of the receipt. Inspection of receiving and issuing procedures will permit the auditor to thoroughly evaluate the internal control system over the custodial responsibilities of the warehousemen. If the custodial responsibilities are not properly discharged, there may be significant unrecorded liabilities (para 901.18). Answer (a) is incorrect because confirmation of negotiable instruments may be impractical due to nonidentifiability of the holder of the negotiable receipt. Answer (b) is incorrect because a review of outstanding receipts cannot be made because the auditor has no knowledge of who may hold "unrecorded" receipts. Answer (d) is incorrect because an observation of inventory will

only determine what is on hand. The amount of inventories on hand must be coupled with a review of outstanding warehouse receipts to determine any unrecorded liabilities.

62. (1179,A1,57) (c)   The requirement is the type of conditions suggesting consignment sales may have been recorded as regular sales. When consignment sales are shipped as regular sales, accounts receivable are credited. Because the consignee is under no obligation to pay for the goods until they are sold, accounts receivable would increase as in answer (c). Answers (a) and (b) are incorrect because the change in accounts receivable is of concern rather than the number and size of shipments. Answer (d) is incorrect because the presumption would be that it would take longer for the consignee to sell the goods than for the company to collect on regular credit sales.

63. (1179,A1,58) (b)   An audit program provides proof that an audit was adequately planned and is required per para 311.05. The audit program should contain reasonable detail of the audit procedures which the auditor believes are required to accomplish the objectives of the examination. Note that as the examination progresses, it may be necessary to modify the audit program. See section 338. Answers (a) and (d) are incorrect because an audit program is only a list of procedures to obtain audit evidence. Unless the audit program is undertaken and adequately documented, there is no proof of sufficient competent evidencial matter or a proper study. Answer (c) is incorrect because audit programs largely affect field work whereas GAAS include general standards and reporting standards as well as field standards.

64. (1178,A1,12) (a)   The primary concern with respect to liabilities arising from procurement of goods and services is possible understatement of the related liabilities. By their nature, accounts payable may be understated because of nonrecording. A much lesser concern is overstatement of liabilities. Answer (b), restriction of authority to incur liability, answer (c), acquisition made from more than one vendor, and answer (d), established competitive bidding procedures, are incorrect because they only concern specific aspects of the procurement system rather than the auditor's primary concern with the liabilities arising from the procurement system.

65. (1178,A1,17) (c)   The requirement is the best way to determine that all people listed on a company's payroll are bona fide employees presently on the job. A surprise observation of the regular distribution of

paychecks would identify any paychecks for which there were not employees. These could be followed up to determine that the employees are currently working, but were sick, etc. Answer (a) is incorrect because personnel records could be accurate and complete but some purported employees still not be currently working for the company. Answer (b) is incorrect because agreement between payroll tax returns and payroll accounting records does not guarantee current employment of the employees. Answer (d) is incorrect because confirmation of badge and identification numbers with employees in the work areas will not identify employees on the payroll who are not working unless all employees are confirmed. In contrast, answer (c) provides a test check.

66.   (1178,A1,18) (c)   In addition to the expression of an opinion on the fairness of financial statements, governmental audits often require audits of compliance with regulations. Answers (a), accuracy, and (d), internal control, are incorrect because they refer to aspects of the examination leading to the expression of an opinion on the fairness of financial presentation. Answer (b) is nonsensical. It is not possible for an auditor to audit evaluation.

67.   (1178,A1,19) (c)   Confirming accounts receivable directly with debtors indicates the validity of the amounts receivable. Accounts receivable confirmation does not confirm collectibility (answer (a)), ownership (answer (b)), or internal control thereover (answer (d)).

68.   (1178,A1,24) (d)   The requirement is an audit procedure with respect to long-term bonds payable. As the auditor is concerned with the legality of an issue of bonds, the auditor must rely on an opinion of counsel, rather than decide on the legality himself as suggested in answer (c). Answer (a) is incorrect because long-term bonds payable may be, and often are, held by owners, directors, or officers of the issuing company. Answer (b) is incorrect because the auditor would calculate the effective rate of interest only to see that the proper amount of interest had been expensed during the period.

69.   (1178,A1,26) (a)   The requirement is which of the answers does not represent corroborating evidential matter. There are two categories of evidential matter: underlying accounting data and all corroborating information (para 330.03, SAS 1). Client accounting manuals constitute the underlying accounting data (para 330.04). Written client representations (answer

(b)), vendor invoices (answer (c)), and minutes of board meetings (answer (d)) constitute corroborating evidential matter (para 330.05).

70.   (1178,A1,29) (a)   The requirement is the type of subsequent event that ordinarily requires adjustment of the financial statements. Per para 560.03 of SAS 1, subsequent events that provide additional evidence as to conditions at the date of the balance sheet result in adjustments of the financial statements at that date. The second type of subsequent event (para 560.05) is that which reflects on conditions that did not exist at the date of the balance sheet and thus does not require the financial statements to be adjusted. Answers (b), (c), and (d) are incorrect because the possible impairments to assets occurred as a result of conditions developing during the subsequent events period, which is after year-end.

71.   (1178,A1,31) (c)   The requirement is the best verification technique for a client's bond sinking fund transactions. The trustee who administers the sinking fund is usually an independent third party with whom the auditor can confirm the sinking fund transactions. Answer (a) is incorrect because interest expense and interest payable have to do with the bond liability, not the sinking fund. Answer (b) is incorrect because individual holders of retired bonds are not privy to all the transactions of a bond sinking fund. Answer (d) is incorrect because bond retirements are not the only transactions occurring in a bond sinking fund.

72.   (1178,A1,38) (c)   The written client representation letter should normally be signed by the chief executive officer and the chief financial officer (para 9, SAS 19). The representations are those of management with respect to the fair presentation of the financial statements. Accordingly it is important that the chief financial officer in addition to the chief executive officer sign the report. Thus only answer (c) is the logical, as well as the correct, answer per SAS 19.

73.   (1178,A1,43) (d)   Note that the problem requires you to select the best answer. Answer (d) is the best answer among the alternatives. A primary concern in the examination of the stockholders' equity section of the balance sheet is proper authorization of transactions affecting the capital stock account. Answer (a) is not the best answer because the independent stock transfer agent does not verify changes in the capital stock account; the transfer agent maintains the capital stock subsidiary ledger which keeps track of who owns how much stock. Also, in nonpublic companies,

the client company probably maintains the stockholder records manually. Answer (b) is incorrect because stock dividends and/or stock splits may not require approval by the stockholders. Answer (c) is incorrect because stock dividends are normally capitalized at the market value on the dividend declaration date (para 10 of Chapter 7b, ARB 43). Note an exception exists for closely-held companies where par or stated value may be capitalized per para 12.

74. (1178,A1,45) (d)   Audit workpapers aid the auditor in the conduct of his work and provide important support for the auditor's opinion including compliance with GAAS. Per para 338.05e of SAS 1, audit workpapers generally include how exceptions and unusual matters are resolved or treated. Answer (a) is incorrect because the personal financial status of the client's management team is not relevant to the fairness of the client company's financial statements. Answer (b) is incorrect because para 338.07 specifically precludes audit workpapers from being a part of or a substitute for a client's accounting records, i.e., client accounting records should stand on their own. Answer (c) is incorrect because reference to pertinent authoritative pronouncements in the audit workpapers is sufficient and even these citations may not be necessary to comply with GAAS.

75. (1178,A1,50) (a)   The requirement is a method of judging the objectivity of the internal auditors of an audit client (para 7, SAS 9). Regarding objectivity of internal auditors, the organizational level to which internal auditors report is important. Another method of judging internal auditor's objectivity is to review the recommendations made in their reports. Answers (b), (c), and (d), the work performed by internal auditors, qualifications of internal auditors, and client practices for hiring, training, etc., reflect on the competence rather than the objectivity of internal auditors.

76. (1178,A1,51) (c)   The work of the internal auditor may affect the nature, timing, and extent of the substantive tests. See para 1 of SAS 9. Answer (a) is incorrect because the work of internal auditors may not be substituted for the work of the CPA. Answer (b) is incorrect because the second standard of field work requires a study and evaluation of internal control by the independent auditor. Answer (d) is incorrect because understanding the internal audit function is not a substantive test. Substantive tests include two general classes of audit procedures: 1) tests of details of transactions and balances, and 2) analytical review procedures applied to financial information (para 320.70 of SAS 1 as amended by ftn 1 of SAS 23).

77. (1178,A1,56) (d)   Note the requirement is the primary purpose of audit workpapers. While workpapers serve mainly to both aid the auditor in his work and provide important support for the auditor's opinion (para 338.02, SAS 1), the primary purpose is certainly to support the auditor's opinion. Answers (a) and (b) aid the auditor in providing a reference point for future audits and aid the auditor in his work, but these are not the primary purposes of audit workpapers. Answer (c) is incorrect because, while the auditor is concerned with the underlying concepts in preparing basic financial statements, the primary concern is with the fairness of the financial statements in terms of GAAP rather than their underlying concepts.

78. (1178,A1,57) (d)   The auditor must evaluate all evidential matter to determine its competence and sufficiency. The evaluation is based on the judgment of the auditor (para 330.08-.09, SAS 1). Answer (a) is incorrect because corroborating data is one of the two types of evidential matter; the other is underlying accounting data (para 330.03-.05). Answer (b) is incorrect because GAAS do not define competency and sufficiency of evidential matter; this is a matter for the auditor's judgment. Answer (c) is incorrect because pertinence or relevance is only one of the criteria that determine competence; the other is validity (para 330.08).

79. (579,A1,6) (d)   The major objective in testing a client's cost accounting system is to ensure that costs have been properly assigned to finished goods, work-in-process, and cost of goods sold. Answers (a) and (b) are incorrect because they are only concerned with physical quantities rather than with total costs. Answer (c) is incorrect because generally accepted accounting principles do not apply to cost accounting systems.

80. (579,A1,8) (b)   The requirement is to identify the type of transaction which would decrease the ratio of gross profit to sales. The solutions approach is to set up a diagram and analyze each of the alternatives as illustrated below. Unrecorded purchases would increase gross profit and increase the ratio. Unrecorded sales would decrease both sales and gross profit by equal amounts and thus decrease the ratio. Note that the ratio is less than 1/1. Merchandise being expensed to general expense would increase gross profit and increase the ratio. Fictitious sales would increase sales and gross profit by equal amounts. The ratio would increase because the ratio is less than 1/1.

	a.	b.	c.	d.
Gross profit	+	−	+	+
Sales	0	−	0	+

81. (579,A1,13) (b) The requirement is the irregularity to be detected by doing a cutoff analysis of the sales journal. Holding sales journal open,
i.e., recording sales of the next period in this period,
inflates sales in the current period. Answer (a) is incorrect because lapping year-end accounts receivable
is a defalcation process of holding cash and delay-
ing recording of the receipts, i.e., a permanent float.
Answer (c) is incorrect because kiting involves drawing an unrecorded check on one bank and deposit-
ing it in another bank at year-end (the monies are
recorded as being in both banks). Answer (d) is
incorrect because misappropriating merchandise would
not be apparent from examining the sales journal.

82. (579,A1,15) (d) The requirement is the objective of tracing sample entries from the accounts
receivable subsidiary ledger to supporting sales invoices. Thus the auditor would determine that entries in the accounts receivable subsidiary ledger are
properly supported by sales invoices. Answer (a)
is incorrect because the audit procedure did not
verify that sales invoices represent bona fide sales.
Answer (b) is incorrect because sales invoices have
not been traced to the sales journal. Answer (c) is
incorrect because sales invoices were not traced to
customer accounts.

83. (579,A1,19) (b) Payroll observation would
be performed if adequate internal control did not
exist over the payroll function. A typical problem
in the payroll area is fictitious employees, which
would be detected by a payroll distribution observation. Answers (a) and (d) are incorrect because
GAAS do not specify that payroll observation be
generally performed. Answer (c) is incorrect because the personal judgment leading to the payroll observation decision would probably be based
on weak internal control. Also the auditor always
uses personal judgment.

84. (579,A1,23) (b) The requirement is a procedure to detect understatement of purchase discounts. Such understatement would be determined
by comparing purchase invoice terms with disbursement records and checks. Answer (a) is incorrect
because verification of purchases and disbursement
records would not indicate unrecorded purchase discounts or discounts not taken. Answer (c) is incorrect because comparison of purchase orders to receiving reports does not relate to purchase discounts.
Answer (d) is incorrect because verification of items
received and related invoices ignores the payment
portion of the transaction.

85. (579,A1,29) (b) Review of internal administrative control is not a procedure performed primarily
for the purpose of expressing an opinion on financial
statements. Rather, accountants review internal accounting control. See para 320.27. Answers (a), study of internal accounting control, (c), tests of transactions, and
(d), tests of balances, are all performed for the purpose
of expressing an opinion on the financial statements.

86. (579,A1,31) (c) The requirement is the least
persuasive type of evidence. To be competent, evidence must be both valid and relevant. See para
330.08. The validity of evidence is determined by
how it was obtained. Evidence obtained from independent sources is better than evidence obtained from
the client. Evidence generated under good internal
control is better than evidence generated under weak
internal control. Direct personal knowledge through
computations, etc., is better evidence than evidence
obtained from the client. Here the sales invoices,
prepared by the client, are less persuasive than computations made by the auditor (d), correspondence
with outside vendors (b), and other documents mailed
by outsiders to the auditor (a).

87. (579,A1,32) (d) The requirement is the best
approach to obtain satisfactory evidence concerning
depreciation expense in the income statement. Answer
(d) is concerned with both the basis for depreciating
assets and verification of the depreciation expense
computed. Answer (a) is incorrect because it is only
concerned with the mathematical accuracy of the
computations. Answer (b) is incorrect because it is
only concerned with the method of computing depreciation expense. Answer (c) is incorrect because
it only verifies the proper posting of depreciation
expense to the accumulated depreciation account.

88. (579,A1,33) (c) A lawyer's response to a
letter of audit inquiry may be limited to material
matters if the lawyer and auditor have reached an
understanding on what materiality means (para
337.12). Note that the lawyer responds to the auditor as a result of the letter of audit inquiry sent by
the client to the lawyer. Answer (a) is incorrect because the auditor is not in a position to instruct
the client's lawyer. Answer (b) is incorrect because
the auditor and lawyer agree on the materiality, not
the client and the auditor. Answer (d) is incorrect
because the legal meaning of materiality is not a
major concern to the auditor.

89. (579,A1,58) (b) The requirement is the most important procedure in the examination of bonds payable when bonds were issued during the period. The most important procedure is to trace the amount of cash received to the accounting records. The auditor's concern is that all of the cash that was supposed to be received was received and accounted for. Answer (a) is incorrect because there would not be a bond trustee if there was a private placement. Answer (c) is incorrect because it is not so much who owns the bonds but how many bonds are outstanding. Answer (d) is incorrect because the requirement concerns the amount of bonds payable rather than the annual interest cost.

90. (579,A1,38) (c) When the auditor believes the client may have committed illegal acts, the auditor should discuss the matter with client management and client's legal counsel to obtain an understanding of the nature of the acts and their possible effect on the statements. The auditor may also perform additional audit procedures (para 328.04). Note that the requirement in this question concerns an auditor who believes a client may have committed an illegal act, not that an illegal act was committed. Once an illegal act is identified, it must be evaluated as to the effect on the financial statements, including any contingent monetary effects. Additionally, the adequacy of disclosure should be evaluated. Answers (a) and (d) are incorrect because they assume illegal acts have occurred. Answer (b) is incorrect because the auditor should consult with the client concerning the possible illegal acts before extending audit procedures (para 328.04).

91. (579,A1,44) (d) The successor auditor is required to communicate with the predecessor auditor to obtain information concerning the client to help determine whether the engagement should be accepted (para 315.04). Answer (a) is incorrect because the auditor will review the predecessor auditor's work papers only to help determine whether accounting principles have been applied consistently. Answer (b) is incorrect because the requirement of successor auditors communicating with predecessor auditors discourages the process of rotating auditors, especially due to client-auditor disagreements about accounting principles and audit procedures. Answer (c) is incorrect because the successor auditor does not need to determine whether or not, in the predecessor's opinion, internal control was satisfactory.

92. (579,A1,54) (c) The requirement is the best use of an aged trial balance of accounts receivable. Accounts receivable are aged to evaluated the adequacy of the allowance for doubtful accounts, i.e.,

estimate credit losses. Answer (a) is incorrect because aging accounts receivable does not evaluate internal control over credit sales. Answer (b) is incorrect because aging accounts receivable does not test the accuracy of recorded charge sales. Answer (d) is incorrect because aging accounts receivable does not verify the validity of recorded receivables.

93. (579,A1,55) (a) When examining revenues, verification of cash deposited during the year is not a principal objective. Cash receipts is a different transaction cycle than the revenue cycle. The auditor breaks the client's businesss operations down into cycles that are evaluated separately. During the examination of revenues, the auditor must study and evaluate internal control (b), verify that earned revenue has been recorded and recorded revenue has been earned (c), and identify and analyze significant trends and variations in various categories of revenue (d).

MAY 1981 ANSWERS

94. (581,A1,4) (d) The requirement is to determine which is not a primary objective in the examination of accounts receivable. Determining the approximate time of collection is not a primary objective; it is a method for determining whether the accounts are properly valued. Answers (a), (b), and (c) all represent primary objectives of the auditor in the examination of accounts receivable.

95. (581,A1,5) (b) The requirement is to determine which irregularity is most difficult to detect. The controller will generally have recordkeeping authority as well as some authorization authority (various adjustments, etc.). This combination makes it possible for the controller to perpetrate and conceal irregularities which are difficult to detect. Answer (a), irregularities perpetrated by the cashier, will often be detected since is is doubtful that the cashier will have the recordkeeping responsibilities necessary to conceal the irregularity. Answer (c) is incorrect because the internal auditor will typically have neither custody nor recordkeeping responsibility. Answer (d) is incorrect because the key-punch operator's irregularities will be limited due to lack of access to assets. Also, the recordkeeping controls in a system designed to detect key-punching errors limits the key-punch operator's ability to perpetrate irregularities.

96. (581,A1,9) (c) The requirement is to determine which type of account analysis most directly complements the sales cutoff test. The primary pur-

pose of a sales cutoff test is to obtain reasonable assurance that sales and accounts receivable are recorded in the accounting period during which title has passed. Answers (a) and (d) are incorrect because returns and allowances on cutoff sales will typically occur subsequent to the cutoff period. Similarly, answer (b), cash, is incorrect since the cash for cutoff sales will not be received until some time after billing.

97. (581,A1,10) (d) The requirement is to determine from whom the auditor should obtain written confirmation for debenture transactions of a publicly-held company. Firms will almost always utilize the services of an independent trustee when debentures are outstanding. The trustee will maintain records on the bond transactions during the year. Answer (a) is incorrect because debenture holders will generally be able to confirm only balances (as opposed to transactions) at any one point in time. The client's attorney, answer (b), does not generally maintain detailed transaction records pertaining to debentures. Internal auditors, answer (c), will in general have no more detailed information on the debentures than that already available to the auditor from the firm being audited. Also, internal auditors provide internally generated evidence which is not in general considered as reliable as externally generated evidence.

98. (581,A1,14) (c) The requirement is to determine a likely step in the audit program for retained earnings. The legality of a dividend depends in part on whether it has been properly authorized (state laws differ on specific requirements). Thus, the auditor must determine that proper authorization exists, as both cash and stock dividends affect retained earnings. Answer (a) is incorrect since only a memo entry is required for a stock split. Answer (b) is incorrect because the write-down of an account receivable will not, in general, be recorded in retained earnings. Answer (d) is incorrect because gains from the disposition of treasury shares are recorded in paid-in capital accounts.

99. (581,A1,16) (b) The requirement is to determine an audit step to establish the accuracy of perpetual inventory records. The receiving report will indicate the quantity actually received. Answers (a) and (c) are incorrect because they deal with the quantity ordered; this may differ from the quantity received. The actual payment to the vendor, answer (d), will not be as helpful as the receiving report because it will be difficult to convert the amount of the payment to individual items received. In addition to the payment, the vendor's invoice and/or the receiving report will be needed.

100. (581,A1,17) (a) The requirement is to determine why an auditor should normally mail confirmations to all banks with which the client has conducted business during the year. The standard bank confirmation form elicits information on actual liabilities, contingent liabilities, and security agreements under the Uniform Commercial Code in addition to year-end cash balance information. The confirmation is therefore helpful in detecting unrecorded and contingent liabilities. Answer (b) is incorrect because the confirmation is of limited assistance in detecting kiting since only the bank's year end balance for cash is included (an inter-bank transfer schedule is more helpful for detecting kiting). Answer (c) is incorrect because generally accepted auditing standards do not explicitly require the confirmation of all accounts. Answer (d) is incorrect because the procedure will not, in and of itself, relieve the auditor of responsibility for forged checks.

101. (581,A1,19) (d) The requirement is to determine the account analysis of a predecessor auditor which the successor auditor is least likely to be interested in reviewing. The predecessor will normally review working papers of continuing accounting significance. Prior income statement accounts are less likely to have continuing significance than are answers (a), (b), and (c) (see para 315.09 which explicitly outlines (a), (b), and (c) as areas of interest).

102. (581,A1,25) (d) The requirement is to determine the audit procedure least likely to disclose related party transactions. The confirmation of large purchase and sales transactions by itself will generally not disclose related party transactions. Answers (a), (b), and (c) are all recommended procedures in para 335.13 for identifying material transactions with related parties.

103. (581,A1,26) (c) The requirement is to determine the circumstance in which it is appropriate for an auditor to refer to the work of a specialist. When an auditor decides to modify his/her opinion as a result of the findings of a specialist, reference to the specialist may be made in the auditor's report (para 336.12). When an unqualified opinion is given, as in answer (a), the auditor should not refer to the work of the specialist (para 336.11). Answer (b) is incorrect because the qualification is unrelated to the work of the appraiser. Answer (d) is incorrect because the appraiser will not, in general, be imposing scope limitations on the auditor.

104. (581,A1,27) (d) The requirement is to determine the transaction which may be indicative of the existence of related parties. Exchanging property for similar property in a nonmonetary transaction may

indicate the existence of related parties (the exchange may or may not approximate what would occur in an arms-length transaction). Answers (a), (b), and (c) all represent attributes of normal arms-length transactions.

105. (581,A1,28)   (d)   The requirement is to determine the purpose of tracing selected items from the payroll journal to employee time cards during the audit of payroll. The employee time card will generally include information such as the employee's name, number, and hours worked. A properly approved time card will thus provide evidence that the number of hours paid was the number of hours worked. Answer (a) is incorrect because the auditor will generally need sources other than the time card to determine the pay rate. Answer (b) is incorrect because the individual product job card is not being examined. Answer (c) is incorrect, because simply examining the time card will not directly test the payroll disbursements.

106. (581,A1,37)   (b)   The requirement is to determine which type of test analytical review procedures are. Analytical review procedures are substantive tests of financial information made by a study and comparison of relationships among data (para 318.02). Answer (a) is incorrect because compliance tests are used to directly test controls. Answer (c) is incorrect because tests of ratios are only one of many possible analytical review procedures. Answer (d) is incorrect because detailed tests of balances are a separate type of substantive test.

107. (581,A1,40)   (a)   The requirement is to determine proper procedures relating to research and development costs. The proper accounting for research and development costs is to expense them in the period incurred. Therefore, the firm's capitalization of the expenditures [answer (a)] is likely to be of concern to the auditor. Answer (b) is incorrect since the county clerk will probably not have registered the secret formula. Answer (c) is incorrect since the costs do not qualify as goodwill. Answer (d) is incomplete since the fact that Patentex developed the formula would indicate that ownership is not the primary topic of concern here.

108. (581,A1,43)   (b)   The requirement is to identify a procedure which would be used in examining long-term debt. The auditor will examine the bond trust indenture to obtain an understanding of the material aspects of the debt. Due to the existence of a trustee for bond transactions, the confirmation and verification [answer (a)] of the existence of the bondholders will not be necessary in most circumstances. Answer (c) is incorrect because accounts payable will

frequently be associated with normal current trade accounts. Answer (d) is incorrect because long-term debt is not related to bond interest income.

109. (581,A1,44)   (a)   The requirement is to determine how an independent auditor should evaluate the objectivity of internal auditors. When considering the objectivity of internal auditors, the independent auditor should consider the organizational level to which internal auditors report the results of their work and the organizational level to which they report administratively (para 322.07). Answers (b), (c), and (d) all could be used as procedures to test the competence of internal auditors.

110. (581,A1,45)   (a)   The requirement is to determine an explanation for significant debits to accumulated depreciation. Extraordinary repairs which lengthen the life of an asset are properly accounted for by debiting the accumulated depreciation account. Answer (b) is incorrect because understated past depreciation would require a credit in accumulated depreciation. Answer (c) is incorrect because a reserve for a possible loss would not decrease past depreciation. Answer (d) is incorrect because an auditor would not be satisfied with an increase in the asset's book value to its fair value.

111. (581,A1,46)   (d)   The requirement is to determine the most likely method an experienced bookkeeper would use to conceal a defalcation in accounts receivable. A debit to sales returns with a credit to accounts receivable is a normal entry for returns and is one which would not appear questionable. Answer (a) is incorrect because the write-off of the receivable would require a debit to miscellaneous income, an extremely unusual and noticeable entry. Answer (b) is incorrect because petty cash will be limited to small entries and because the entry would appear unusual. Answer (c) is incorrect because a debit to a miscellaneous expense and a credit to accounts receivable would also be unusual and noticeable.

112. (581,A1,55)   (d)   The requirement is to determine likely audit procedures for accounts receivable during a period of slow collections caused by "tight money." The primary problem in such a period of time is to determine whether the account is properly valued; that is, are the accounts collectable? Answer (a) is incorrect since the auditor does not increase (or decrease) balances, although collectability tests may result in a proposed adjustment. Answer (b) is incorrect because any going concern ramifications will be considered subsequent to collectability tests, if at all. Answer (c), while possibly a part of the collectability tests, is less complete than answer (d).

113. (581,A1,56)   (a)   The requirement is to determine the area in which an auditor will have the most difficult time detecting an illegal diversion of proceeds. Because scrap sales are generally irregular in nature, they often are inadequately controlled by the internal control system. Answers (b), (c), and (d) are all typical, frequently recurring business transactions which are under the internal control system.

114. (581,A1,57)   (a)   The requirement is to determine the auditor's responsibility with respect to immaterial illegal acts. The auditor will typically only notify personnel in the client's organization (para 328.19). Answer (b) is incorrect because Statements on Auditing Standards suggest that the need to notify additional parties of an illegal act is the responsibility of management (para 328.19). Answer (c) is incorrect because the auditor need not disclose immaterial acts in the report. Answer (d) is incorrect because the auditor is not in a position to force anyone to comply with the Foreign Corrupt Practices Act.

ANSWER OUTLINE

Problem 1   Evidence for Limited Review

a.   A limited review does not provide a basis for an opinion
      It is not based on an audit per GAAS, i.e., no
      1.   Study an evaluation of internal control
      2.   Tests of accounting records
      3.   Inspection, observation, and confirmation
      4.   Other auditing procedures

b.   Normal limited review procedures include:
      1.   Inquiry of the accounting system for interim statements
            To understand the recording, classification, and summarizing of interim transactions
      2.   Inquiry of significant changes in internal control
            To ascertain possible effect on the statements
      3.   Analytical review of the statements
            To identify and inquire about unusual items, relationships
      4.   Read minutes of stockholder, director, etc., meetings
            To identify actions affecting the statements
      5.   Read the statements
            To see if they are per GAAP
      6.   Consider items that have previously required adjustments
            To adjust again if necessary
      7.   Obtain limited review reports from other auditors
            To contribute to basis for limited review report
      8.   Inquire if statements are per GAAP, about changes in business activities, subsequent events, other questions
            to become aware of significant matters
      9.   Obtain written management representation about management responsibility for the statements, their completeness, etc.
            To reduce possibility of misunderstandings

UNOFFICIAL ANSWER

Problem 1   Evidence for Limited Review

a.   A limited review of interim financial statements does not provide a basis for the expression of an opinion because a limited review is not an examination performed in accordance with generally accepted auditing standards — that is, it does not contemplate a study and evaluation of internal accounting control, tests of accounting records and of responses to inquiries by obtaining corroborating evidential matter through inspection, observation, or confirmation, and certain other procedures ordinarily performed during an audit.

b.   The procedures that Loman must perform consist primarily of inquiries and analytical procedures concerning significant accounting matters relating to the financial information to be reported. The procedures that Loman should apply ordinarily may be limited to the following:

Procedure	*Purpose of Procedure*
• Inquiry concerning the accounting system with respect to the preparation of interim financial statements.	To obtain an understanding of the manner in which transactions are recorded, classified, and summarized in the preparation of interim financial statements.
• Inquiry concerning any significant changes in the system of internal accounting control.	To ascertain their potential effect on the preparation of interim financial statements.
• Analytical review of interim financial statements.	To identify and inquire about relationships and individual items that appear to be unusual.
• Reading the minutes of meetings of stockholders, board of directors, and committees of the board of directors.	To identify actions that may affect the interim financial statements.
• Reading the interim financial statements.	To consider, on the basis of information coming to the accountant's attention, whether the information to be reported conforms with generally accepted accounting principles.
• Considering the types of matters that have previously required adjustments.	To give adequate consideration to matters that historically warrant consideration.

Procedure	Purpose of Procedure
• Obtaining reports from other accountants who may have been engaged to make a limited review of the interim financial information of significant segments of the reporting entity, its subsidiaries, or other investees.	As a basis, in part, for the report.
• Inquiry of officers and other executives having responsibility for financial and accounting matters concerning — (a) Whether the interim financial statements have been prepared in conformity with generally accepted accounting principles consistently applied. (b) Changes in the entity's business activities or accounting practices. (c) Matters about which questions have arisen in applying the foregoing procedures. (d) Events subsequent to the date of the interim financial statements that would have a material effect on the presentation of such statements.	In order to become aware of significant matters affecting the interim financial statements.
• Obtain a written representation from management concerning its responsibility for the financial information, completeness of minutes, subsequent events, and other matters for which Loman believes written representations are appropriate.	In order to reduce the possibility of misunderstandings.

ANSWER OUTLINE

Problem 2   Payroll Input Verification and Examination Procedures

a.   To verify the information in the input form James should

a1.   Compare name, social security number, and withholding data on input form with W-4 forms

a2.   Compare names with employment authorizations

a3.   Compare pay rates with wage authorizations and union contracts

a4.   Compare number of hours worked (regular and overtime) with approved time sheets or other supportive records:
Recompute regular and overtime hours

a5.   Inspect employee authorization forms for "special deductions."

b.   Procedures to be performed examining the November 12, 1979 payroll register

b1.   Compare input information with information in payroll register and information on issued payroll checks
e.g., spelling of names, correctness of social security numbers, hours, rates and deductions

b2.   Test payroll deductions using withholding tax tables to recompute social security and withholding taxes

b3.   Manually compute gross and net pays and compare with computer printed figures

b4.   Compare payroll summary totals with other pay periods; investigate unusual variations among periods

b5.   Check footings and crossfooting in payroll register

b6.   Perform other related auditing procedures deemed necessary in circumstances

UNOFFICIAL ANSWER

Problem 2   Payroll Input Verification and Examination Procedures

a.   In order to verify the information in the input form James should—

·   Compare name, social security number, and withholding data on the input form with W-4 forms.

·   Compare names with employment authorizations.

·   Compare pay rates with wage authorizations and union contracts.

- Compare number of hours worked (regular and overtime) with approved time sheets or other supportive reports; recompute regular and overtime hours.
- Inspect employee authorization forms for "special deductions."

b.   James should perform the following procedures in the examination of the November 23, 1979, payroll register:
- Compare information on the input form with information in the payroll register and information on issued payroll checks (for example, spelling of names, correctness of social security numbers, hours, rates, and deductions).
- Test payroll deductions by using withholding tax tables to recompute social security and withholding taxes.
- Manually compute gross and net pays and compare with computer printed figures.
- Compare payroll summary totals with other pay periods; investigate any unusual variations among periods.
- Check footings and crossfootings in the payroll register.
- Perform other related basic auditing procedures that may be deemed necessary in accordance with the circumstances.

ANSWER OUTLINE

Problem 3   Procedures for Loss Contingencies

Procedures for loss contingencies from litigation, claims, etc.
1.   Discuss with client the client policies and procedures to
            Identify, evaluate, and account
            For litigation, claims, and assessments
2.   Obtain client description and evaluation of litigations, claims, etc.
            As of balance sheet date
            From balance sheet date to time information received
            Also matters referred to counsel
            Management assurance of disclosure per SFAS 5
                Usually in representation letter
3.   Examine client documents re litigations, claims, etc.
            Including correspondence and invoices from attorneys

4.   Obtain written client representation that
            All unasserted claims probable of assertion
                Have been disclosed per GAAP
                After consultation with attorneys
5.   With client's permission, inform attorney of the assurance
6.   Have client send letter of inquiry to attorneys
7.   Other sources of information re claims, assessments, etc.
            Minutes of appropriate committees
            Contracts, loan agreements, leases, etc.
            Correspondence from governmental agencies
            Bank confirmation forms for client guarantees

UNOFFICIAL ANSWER

Problem 3   Procedures for Loss Contingencies

Since the events or conditions that should be considered in the financial accounting for and reporting of litigation, claims, and assessments are matters within the direct knowledge, and often, control of management of an entity, management is the primary source of information about such matters. Accordingly, the independent auditor's procedures with respect to the existence of loss contingencies arising from litigation, claims, and assessments should include the following:

1.   Inquire of and discuss with management the policies and procedures adopted for identifying, evaluating, and accounting for litigation, claims, and assessments.

2.   Obtain from management a description and evaluation of litigation, claims, and assessments that existed at the date of the balance sheet being reported on, and during the period from the balance sheet date to the date the information is furnished, including an identification of those matters referred to legal counsel, and obtain assurances from management, ordinarily in the form of representation letters that they have disclosed all such matters required to be disclosed by generally accepted accounting principles (Statement of Financial Accounting Standards no. 5).

3.   Examine documents in the client's possession concerning litigation, claims, and assessments, including correspondence and invoices from lawyers.

4. Obtain assurance from management, ordinarily in the form of a client representation letter, that they have disclosed all unasserted claims that the lawyer has advised them are probable of assertion and must be disclosed in accordance with generally accepted accounting principles (Statement of Financial Accounting Standards no. 5).

In addition, the auditor, with the client's permission, should inform the lawyer that the client has given the auditor this assurance. This client representation may be communicated by the client in the inquiry letter or by the auditor in a separate letter. The auditor should request the client's management to send a letter of inquiry to those lawyers with whom they consulted concerning litigation, claims, and assessments.

Examples of other procedures undertaken for different purposes that might also disclose litigation, claims, and assessments are the following:

Reading minutes of stockholders, directors, and appropriate committee meetings held during and subsequent to the period being examined.

Reading contracts, loan agreements, leases, and correspondence from taxing or other governmental agencies, and similar documents.

Obtaining information concerning guarantees from bank confirmation forms.

Inspecting other documents for possible guarantees by the client.

ANSWER OUTLINE

Problem 4   Cutoff Tests

a1. Cutoff date is last day of reporting period
Cutoff test assures proper application of cutoff date

a2. Cutoff tests at beginning and end of period
Assure proper reporting of expense and revenue
On continuing engagements, no retest of beginning cutoff

b. Sales cutoff test should
Determine cutoff policy and reasonableness
Select a sample of sales invoices around cutoff date
Trace invoices to shipping documents to verify proper treatment
Determine proper costing of sales
Select a sample of shipping documents
Trace to the sales invoice
Insure proper recording
Review cutoff for sales returns and allowances

c1. The bank cutoff statement is used to determine if
Opening balance agrees with prior "balance per bank"
Returned checks dated prior to July 1 were outstanding on reconciliation
Deposits in transit cleared
Interbank transfers were properly reported
Other reconciling items are cleared up

c2. Other audit procedures include
Investigating unusual entries on cutoff statement
Examining canceled checks
Reviewing other documents received with bank statement
These procedures might point out
Irregular payments or other items
Unrecorded transactions near year-end
Abnormal sales returns in new year
NSF checks applicable to old year
Material expenditures during cutoff period

UNOFFICIAL ANSWER

Problem 4   Cutoff Tests

a. 1. The cutoff date is the date that a company stops transaction flow for purposes of financial closing. Most often this will coincide with the balance sheet date, but it may be a few days before or after. The period between cutoff and the balance sheet date should not include abnormal activity. A company may not use the same cutoff date for all transactions, but it should be consistent between accounting periods. A cutoff test generally involves the examination (on a test basis) of underlying support for transactions recorded during short periods before and after the balance sheet date (or other cutoff date). The auditor performs a cutoff test to determine whether transactions are recorded in the proper accounting period, establish that cutoff was consistent between periods and determine that activity was normal between cutoff and the balance sheet date.

2. The auditor must perform cutoff tests at the beginning and end of the audit period in order to assure himself that cutoff was consistent at the two dates and that a single period's revenues and expenses have

been recorded within the period. If the auditor examined the prior year's statements, he would not repeat his beginning cutoff tests.

b. The CPA's test of the sales cutoff at June 30, 1971, should include the following steps:

   1. Determine what Houston's cutoff policy is, review the policy for reasonableness and compare it to the prior year for consistency.
   2. Select a sample of sales invoices (including the last serial invoice number) from those recorded in the last few days of June and the first few days of July.
   3. Trace these sales invoices to shipping documents and determine that sales have been recorded in the proper period in accordance with company cutoff policy.
   4. Determine that the cost of the goods sold has been recorded in the period of sale.
   5. Select a sample of shipping documents for the same period and trace these to the sales invoice. Determine that the sale and the cost of goods sold have been recorded in the proper period.
   6. Review the cutoff for sales returns and allowances, determine that it has been based upon a consistent policy and that there have not been abnormal sales returns and allowances in July; this might indicate either an overstatement of sales during the audit period or the need for a valuation account at June 30, 1971, to provide for future returns and allowances.

c. 1. The CPA will use the July 10, 1971, cutoff bank statement in his review of the June 30, 1971, bank reconciliation to determine whether:

   a. The opening balance on the cutoff bank statement agrees with the "balance per bank" on the June 30, 1971, reconciliation.
   b. The June 30, 1971, bank reconciliation includes those canceled checks that were returned with the cutoff bank statement and are dated or bear bank endorsements prior to July 1.
   c. Deposits in transit cleared within a reasonable time.

   d. Interbank transfers have been considered properly in determining the June 30, 1971, adjusted bank balance.
   e. Other reconciling items which had not cleared the bank at June 30, 1971, (such as bank errors) clear during the cutoff period.

   2. The CPA may obtain other audit information by:

   a. Investigating unusual entries on the cutoff bank statement.
   b. Examining canceled checks, particularly noting unusual payees or endorsements.
   c. Reviewing other documentation supporting the cutoff bank statement.

   Among the transactions or circumstances which these procedures might disclose are:

   a. Irregular payments or payments related to matters which the CPA should investigate. For example, he would want to learn the reason for an unusual legal fee or a payment to a company officer.
   b. Borrowings in the new fiscal year or repayment of recorded or unrecorded loans outstanding at year-end.
   c. Abnormal sales returns during the new fiscal year.
   d. NSF checks applicable to the year ended June 30, 1971.
   e. Material expenditures during the cut-off period.

ANSWER OUTLINE

Problem 5   Balance Sheet—Income Statement

a. Real and nominal accounts are interrelated
   Audit tests can verify both accounts
   Proper planning is necessary

b1. Allowance for doubtful accounts procedures
   Compare current accounts and ratios with prior years
   Review aging schedule
   Discuss collection problems with management
   Follow up on confirmation exceptions, non-responses
   Evaluate cash collections of subsequent period

b2.   Procedures to detect unrecorded property retirements
      Tour the physical facilities
  -   Inquire about retirements
      Inquire about discontinued operations, etc.
      Investigate retirements related to new acquisitions
      Investigate salvage credits or miscellaneous incomes
      Inquire about major property acquisitions
      Investigate discrepancies in client's physical inventory of plant
      Investigate reduced insurance or property taxes
      Review depreciation schedules and tax returns

UNOFFICIAL ANSWER

Problem 5   Balance Sheet——Income Statement

a.   Coordination of the examination of balance-sheet accounts and income-statement accounts recognizes the interrelationships among these accounts and the normal transaction flow from asset to expense. Nearly all income account transactions involve an offsetting entry to a balance-sheet account. Thus the procedural tests that the auditor performs to test internal control (tests of cash, disbursements, payroll, materials, and sales) provide him with substantiation for both balance-sheet and income-statement accounts. Similarly, his cutoff tests help him to evaluate the propriety of revenue recognition (which simultaneously creates an asset) and to identify the incurrence of expense and its corollary, liability creation or asset diminution. Because these accounts are related, failure to properly plan and coordinate the examination could lead to duplication of effort or to omission of procedures.

b.   1.   In evaluating the Allowance for Doubtful Accounts Receivable, the auditor will perform the following:

(a)   Compare the allowance as a percentage of receivables and the year's provision as a percentage of credit sales to prior years' percentages and evaluate reasonableness in terms of current economic conditions and credit policies.

(b)   Review an aging of accounts receivable and investigate the collectibility of overdue accounts.

(c)   Discuss collection problems and the adequacy of the Allowance for Doubtful Accounts Receivable with the **credit** manager or other responsible employee. (It may be necessary to extend this discussion to the company attorney or collection agent.)

(d)   Follow up on confirmation responses and non-responses that indicate collection problems.

(e)   Evaluate the reasonableness of cash collections of accounts receivable during the subsequent period.

2.   The auditor may detect unrecorded retirements of plant, property, and equipment from the following procedures:

(a)   His tour of the company plant noting inactive or obsolete equipment.

(b)   Inquiry about retirement and replacements during interviews with operating personnel.

(c)   Inquiry about retirements related to operations that have been discontinued, curtailed, or modified during the year. (Such evidence may arise from review of the minutes or a variety of other sources.)

(d)   Determination of whether related retirements have been recorded in connection with his examination of construction work orders and other plant additions.

(e)   Follow-up on salvage credits or gains and losses from property disposal by reviewing miscellaneous income accounts, miscellaneous cash receipts, etc.

(f)   Inquiry about or visits to major property additions from prior years. (The extent of the auditor's inventory of physical plant depends upon his assessment of the effectiveness of client procedures for recording additions and retirements.)

(g)   Follow-up on discrepancies noted in the client's last physical inventory of plant.

(h)   Investigation of instances of reduced insurance coverage or property tax assessment.

(i)   Review of depreciation schedules and income tax returns.

ANSWER OUTLINE

Problem 6   Client Representation Letter

a1.   Objectives of the client engagement letter
Assure agreement between client and CPA
Inform client about CPA's work and expected
results
Written record of CPA's responsibilities

a2.   Engagement letters follow up verbal understandings
Client should endorse a copy and return to the CPA

a3.   Engagement letter is appropriate at the beginning of
the engagement

a4.   Engagement letter is most useful on first engagements
But should be used in subsequent engagements
May be changes in circumstances

b1.   Objectives of client's representation letter
Written documentation of client's replies to inquiries
Avoid misunderstandings about client representations
Reminder that client has primary responsibility for
statements
Complements CPA's examination of statements

b2.   Representation letters should be on client's stationery
and signed by client
CPA usually drafts letter

b3.   All representations should be obtained before concluding field work
Subsequent event letter as of last day of field work

b4.   Client letters are important evidence
Should be prepared for each examination

c1.   Engagement letter is very important for unaudited
engagements
Due to potential client misunderstanding

c2.   Client representations complement, not substitute,
audit procedures
Thus limit usefulness on unaudited engagements

UNOFFICIAL ANSWER

Problem 6   Client Representation Letter

a.   1.   The objectives of the engagement letter are
to
(a)   Make sure that the CPA and his
client are in agreement as to the
nature of the engagement.
(b)   Inform the client about the scope
of the CPA's work and what may be
expected to result.

(c)   Provide a written record of the responsibilities assumed by the CPA
and those retained by the client.
(This understanding protects both
the CPA and his client.)

2.   The CPA usually prepares the engagement
letter as a follow-up to a verbal understanding that he and his client have reached. It
is desirable that the client endorse and
return an approved copy of the engagement letter to the CPA. It also is acceptable for the client to prepare his own letter summarizing his understanding of the
nature of the engagement.

3.   Preferably the engagement letter should be
sent at the beginning of the engagement so
that misunderstandings, if any, can be
remedied.

4.   Obviously, the engagement letter will be
most useful in clarifying misunderstandings
on a first engagement. But it is desirable
that the letter be renewed periodically.
Client personnel or the nature of the engagement may change, and the resubmis-
sion of the letter gives both parties an
opportunity to review the circumstances.
Accordingly, for recurring examinations of
financial statements, it is appropriate to
prepare an engagement letter at the start
of each examination. For other continuing
engagements, the engagement letter also
should be updated periodically — probably
on a yearly basis.

b.   1.   The objectives of the client's representation letter are to
(a)   Provide written documentation for
the client's replies to inquiries made
by the CPA in the course of his
examination of the client's financial statements. This is particularly
important for information that is
not shown in the accounting records
or might not otherwise be discovered.
(b)   Avoid misunderstandings as to client
representations and force the client
to consider the correctness of his
representations.
(c)   Remind the client of his primary
responsibility for the financial statements.
(d)   Complement (rather than substitute

for) the CPA's examination of the financial statements.

2. Representation letters should be prepared on the client's stationery and signed by appropriate officers and employees. In most cases the CPA will draft the representation letter, but the officer or employee must accept the statements in the letter as his own representations.

It is important that the representation letter be signed by one or more officers or responsible employees who are knowledgeable about the particular area or activity reported upon. For example (and depending on the circumstances), the company secretary might prepare the presentation concerning minutes of the board of directors, the controller might affirm the fair presentation of the financial statements and recording of liabilities, and the purchasing agent might report on purchase commitments.

3. All client representations should be obtained before the end of field work. If the representation letter refers to events occurring in the subsequent period, it is appropriate that the letter be signed, dated, and delivered to the auditor on the last day of field work.

4. Client representation letters are evidential matter supporting the auditor's opinion. Accordingly, they should be prepared for each succeeding examination of financial statements. If the auditor's report is updated, he should obtain from the client an additional representation as to events occurring subsequent to the date of his previous report.

c. 1. The CPA definitely should prepare an engagement letter if his responsibilities involve unaudited financial statements. Many individuals do not understand the varied nature of the CPA's work and misinterpret any rendering of accounting services as implying that an audit has been performed. The engagement letter will provide additional clarification at a propitious time, before the work is done. Also, the engagement letter protects the CPA against later claims that he agreed to perform an audit.

2. Client representations are intended only to complement the auditor's procedures, not to substitute for them. Accordingly, there usually will be little advantage in obtaining them in connection with unaudited financial statements. In certain cases, however, it may be advisable to obtain client representations, but if the CPA has reservations about unaudited financial statements with which he is associated, he cannot rely upon a client's representation to relieve him of responsibility for describing these reservations in his disclaimer of opinion.

ANSWER OUTLINE

Problem 7   Audit Programs

a. Audit program — list of audit procedures
   Record of work performed
   Proof of compliance with GAAS
   Outline of evidence gathering procedures
      Of actual transactions
      Of account balances

b. Types of audit procedures
      Observation of activity
      Physical (test) counts
      Confirmation
      Inspection of documents
      Recomputation
      Retracing bookkeeping procedures, etc.
      Scanning
      Inquiry of client personnel (including review of
        minutes)
      Examination and corroboration of subsidiary records
      Correlation with related information
        I.e., reasonableness
        Ratio and trend analysis
      Use of sampling to test transactions
      Review of subsequent events
      Attorney's letter and other legal representations
      Reliance on outside experts

UNOFFICIAL ANSWER

Problem 7   Audit Programs

a. An audit program is a set of the auditor's logically planned examination procedures. The audit program is the auditor's plan of action. It serves as an outline of those evidence-gathering procedures that the auditor will follow during the examination. An audit program serves as a record of the work performed during the examination. It represents evidence that the examination was conducted in accordance with generally accepted auditing standards. It is a list of the detailed procedures or techniques that the auditor will follow in connection with authentication work. Since an audit program typically includes steps to gain corroborative evidence, it serves as a list of procedures necessary to test actual transactions and resulting balances. A typical audit program would include steps that require the auditor to perform certain techniques.

b. Types of procedures that would be used by the auditor during an examination of financial statements are the following:

(1) Observation of activities and conditions.

(2) Physical examination and count.

(3) Confirmation.

(4) Inspection of authoritative documents.

(5) Recomputation (including footings, cross-footings, extensions, recalculations, etc.).

(6) Retracing (including tracing bookkeeping procedures, walking through the system, checking data processing flow, agreeing evidence to accounting records, flow-charting, checking audit trail, vouching, etc.).

(7) Scanning (including skimming).

(8) Inquiry (including discussion, questioning, etc.).

(9) Examination and corroboration of subsidiary records (including reconciliation or tie-in to control accounts).

(10) Correlation with related information (including ratio and trend analysis, analytic review, analytic comparisons of actual data with expected results or norms, etc.).

(11) Testing (including sampling, tests of transactions).

(12) Review of subsequent events (including cutoff examination of cash receipts and disbursements in subsequent events period).

(13) Reliance on outside experts.

(14) Examination of legal letters (including obtaining legal representations).

ANSWER OUTLINE

Problem 8   GAO Audit Standards

a. Audit objectives
Effective control over revenues, expenditures, assets, and liabilities
Proper accounting per GAO standards
Financial reports are accurate, reliable, etc.
Compliance with applicable laws and regulations

b. Procedures which are ineffective or without cost justification
Overstaffing, duplication of effort, etc.
Work serving no useful purpose, i.e., ineffective
Inefficient use of equipment
Faulty buying practices, etc.
Wasteful use of resources, e.g., utilities, space

c. Evaluation of program results
Relevance and validity of client's criteria
Appropriateness of client's evaluation methods
Review accuracy of data accumulated
Review reliability of results obtained

UNOFFICIAL ANSWER

Problem 8   GAO Audit Standards

a. Examinations of financial transactions, accounts, and reports and compliance with applicable laws and regulations shall include sufficient audit work to determine whether:

(1) The audited entity is maintaining effective control over revenues, expenditures, assets, and liabilities.

(2) The audited entity is properly accounting for resources, liabilities, and operations.

(3) The financial reports contain accurate, reliable, and useful financial data and are fairly presented.

(4) The entity is complying with the requirements of applicable laws and regulations.

b. A review of efficiency and economy shall include inquiry into whether, in carrying out its responsibilities, the audited entity is giving due consideration to conservation of its resources and minimum expenditure of effort. Examples of uneconomical practices or inefficiencies the auditor should be alert to include the following:

(1) Procedures, whether officially prescribed or merely followed, which are ineffective or

(2) Duplication of effort by employees or between organizational units.

(3) Performance of work which serves little or no useful purpose.

(4) Inefficient or uneconomical use of equipment.

(5) Overstaffing in relation to work to be done.

(6) Faulty buying practices and accumulation of unneeded or excess quantities of property, materials, or supplies.

(7) Wasteful use of resources.

c. A review of the results of programs or activities shall include inquiry into the results or benefits achieved and whether the programs or activities are meeting established objectives. The auditor should consider the following:

(1) The relevance and validity of the criteria used by the audited entity to judge effectiveness in achieving program results.

(2) The appropriateness of the methods followed by the entity to evaluate effectiveness in achieving program results.

(3) The accuracy of the data accumulated.

(4) The reliability of the results obtained.

ANSWER OUTLINE

Problem 9   Accounts-Receivable Confirmations

a. There are positive and negative confirmations
All positive confirmations require response
    Use when account balances are large
    Also when disputed, inaccurate, irregular
    Or when consideration of negative confirmation
      is unlikely
Negative confirmation requires response only when
  balance is incorrect
    Use when internal control is effective
    Use when balances are small, numerous
    When consideration by recipient is expected
Negative form requires practicable alternative procedures to follow up

b. Debtor's acknowledgement of debt does not indicate collectibility
Aging schedule indicates collectibility
    Old accounts most likely uncollectible
    Prepared by date of sale or maturity
    Separates past due and current
    Aging schedule supports allowance account
    Discuss collectibility with client
    Review external credit reports
    Compare current year's bad debts with prior periods
    Review accounts currently written off
    Examine subsequent collections
    Adjust allowance account

UNOFFICIAL ANSWER

Problem 9   Accounts-Receivable Confirmations

a. There are two forms of accounts receivable confirmation requests; the "positive" form and the "negative" form.

A positive form asks the debtor to respond whether or not the debtor is in agreement with the information on the confirmation request. A negative form asks the debtor to respond only if the debtor disagrees with the information on the confirmation request. The negative form generally requires follow-up by the auditor in the form of practicable alternative procedures that are used to obtain necessary evidence.

The use of the positive form is preferable when individual account balances are relatively large, when there is reason to believe that there may be a substantial number of accounts in dispute, or with inaccuracies or irregularities.

The negative form is useful when internal control surrounding accounts receivable is considered to be effective, and a large number of small balances is involved, and the auditor has no reason to believe that persons receiving the requests are unlikely to give them consideration.

b. A debtor's acknowledgement of indebtedness does not indicate whether the indebtedness is collectible. A good indicator of collectibility is an aging schedule. Generally, the older an account is, the less likely it will be collected. An aging schedule should age accounts according to date of sale (billing date) or according to date of maturity (payment date). The aging schedule should segregate past-due and current accounts.

Dodge should review, analyze, and interpret the aging schedule to determine whether the client's allowance for doubtful accounts is adequate. Material differences, if any, should be adjusted by the client.

In connection with the aging review and interpretation, Dodge should investigate all accounts receivable losses of preceding periods and the amounts of uncollectible accounts charged off in the current period to determine if the bad debt rate is increasing, and if charge-offs because of uncollectibility are properly approved. After a review of correspondence, minutes, and collection procedures and after discussion with the appropriate client credit and collection officials, Dodge should prepare an estimate of the possible collection losses and compare the estimate to the amount of the recorded allowance. Where necessary Dodge should review client credit files as well as reports of external credit agencies. Dodge should also examine subsequent cash receipts to ascertain what portion of amounts owing at the balance sheet date have actually been collected in the subsequent period.

ANSWER OUTLINE

Problem 10   Toyco Bank Reconciliation

1. Confirm with standard bank confirmation
   Compare balance to confirmation and bank statement
   Obtain bank cutoff statement directly from bank
   Inquire about the weekly transfer from Bank "A"

2. Examine cutoff statement for deposits

3. Examine cutoff bank statement for redeposit
   Recommend strengthened internal control over deposits

4. Examine 12-29 sales and deposit slips
   No deposit on books for Bank "A"
   If a misposting, adjust
   If books are correct, notify bank
   Explain $100 difference per bank and per book

5. Client should contact bank about bank charge
   Discuss nature of unexplained bank charge with client
   Determine if the charge was proper
   If incorrect, look at subsequent cutoff for credit
   Make necessary adjustments

6. Determine why Bank "B" transfer is not recorded

7. Determine if the charge was proper
   If incorrect, look at subsequent statement for credit
   Make necessary adjustments

8. Why were the credit card chargebacks not recorded
   Examine IC over credit card acceptance

Count all documents on hand and verify chargeback total
All chargebacks should be properly recorded
   To properly reflect sales and cash balances

9. Examine subsequent weeks' statements for proper recording of sales returns
   Why have sales returns not been reported to bank

10. Trace reconciliation balance to general ledger

UNOFFICIAL ANSWER

Problem 10   Toyco Bank Reconciliation

Code Number	Actions to Be Taken by Auditor
1.	The auditor should use the standard bank cash confirmation form to confirm both bank balances. The auditor should compare the bank balances to the amounts on the confirmations returned by the banks and to the bank statements. Differences should be investigated. The auditor should ascertain why Bank A has a cash balance that was not transferred to the general account. The auditor should arrange to obtain directly from each bank copies of the bank statements and related documents for subsequent weeks through the auditor's cutoff date.
2.	The auditor should examine the bank statements of the subsequent week to ascertain whether these deposits have been properly credited to the account of Toyco. Discrepancies should be investigated.
3.	The auditor should review the status of these deposits by examining the bank statements of the subsequent week to ascertain whether these deposits were properly resubmitted and credited to the proper bank account. The auditor should review the frequency of such invalid deposits and recommend that the company strengthen control in this area.
4.	The auditor should examine all sales and deposit documents that were prepared on December 29, 1976. Since no journal entry was made on that date for Bank A, the auditor should trace postings of the

Code Number	Actions to Be Taken by Auditor
	day's sales, and if there was a misposting, the auditor should recommend that the client adjust the accounts. If there were no Bank A credit card sales on December 29, 1976 (which is unlikely), the $2,000 bank deposit should not have been credited to the Toyco bank account. If so, the auditor should suggest that Toyco contact the bank to adjust the bank error. The auditor should compare the documents that support the Bank B ledger debit of $5,400 to those that support the $5,500 deposit to the bank account. Differences should be accounted for and adjustments should be made where necessary.
5.	The bank charge should be explained. The auditor should discuss the item with the client and, if necessary, the client should contact the bank for an explanation. If the item is incorrectly charged by the bank the auditor should examine the bank statement of the subsequent week to see if the item was properly adjusted. If the charge is correct the auditor should suggest that the client adjust the accounts to properly reflect the charge.
6.	The auditor should examine the client's accounting records to determine why the cash transfer from Bank B to the depository bank account was not recorded in the company's books of account.
7.	The auditor should verify the Bank B service charge by referring to the original agreement between Toyco and the bank when the account was opened. The auditor should also verify why there is no charge for Bank A and, if necessary, suggest that an adjustment be made to record the charge.
8.	The auditor should obtain reasons why chargebacks for stolen cards have not been recorded and should examine the internal control over the acceptance of credit cards. A count of all documents on hand should be conducted and the total amount of the chargebacks should be verified. All chargebacks should be recorded so that adjusted sales and cash balances can be properly reflected in the financial statements.

Code Number	Actions to Be Taken by Auditor
9.	The auditor should examine the bank statements of the subsequent week to ascertain whether all sales returns for the preceding week have been recorded by the banks. The auditor should ascertain why these documents have not been sent to the bank for processing.
10.	The auditor should ascertain that these unadjusted amounts agree with the general ledger account balances.

ANSWER OUTLINE

Problem 11   Property, Plant & Equipment

a.   Characteristics of property, plant and equipment
        Only fixed tangible capital assets
        Useful lives in excess of one year
        Used in operations
            I.e., not purchased for resale
    Audit objectives of property, plant and equipment
        IC is adequate
        Assets exist
        Assets are owned by the client
        Proper disclosure of liens
        Depreciation method is acceptable
        Dollar amounts are supported by records, invoices, etc.
        Proper accounting for additions, disposals, retirements
        Non-capital items charged to maintenance accounts
        Assets are valued per GAAP
        Adequate informative disclosure of the assets

b1. Yes, commissions and equipment relocation expenditures are land costs

b2. No, clearing costs are land costs

b3. Yes, sale of timber and gravel reduce the cost of land

b4. Yes, all costs relating to equipment are capitalized
        Royalty payments are expensed

UNOFFICIAL ANSWER

Problem 11 Property, Plant & Equipment

a.   "Property, Plant & Equipment" normally includes only fixed tangible assets. Fixed tangible assets are capital assets with useful lives generally in excess of one year that are used in the operation of the business and that are not purchased for resale purposes. In connection with the examination of property, plant, and equipment (PP&E) the auditor must be satisfied that—

(1) Internal controls over PP&E and PP&E acquisitions are adequate.

(2) Assets included in PP&E exist and are being used in the normal operations of the business.

(3) Assets included in PP&E are owned by the company whose financial statements are being examined.

(4) Assets included in PP&E are not encumbered by liens or, if so, the facts are properly disclosed in the footnotes to the financial statements.

(5) Depreciation and/or amortization methods

are proper.

(6) Amounts in the financial statements are in substantial agreement with the supporting records.

(7) Accounting for additions, disposals, and retirements is proper.

(8) Maintenance accounts do not include items that should be capitalized.

(9) The valuation and the disclosure of the method of evaluation are acceptable.

(10) Important information relating to the assets is properly disclosed.

b.

Item No.	Is Audit Adjustment or Reclassification Required? Yes or No	Reasons Why Audit Adjustment or Reclassification Is Required or Not Required
1.	Yes	Commissions paid to real estate agents are costs directly related to the acquisition of the property and should be included in the land cost. Costs of removing, relocating, or reconstructing property of others to acquire possession are costs that are directly attributable to conditioning the property for use and should be included in land costs. An adjustment is required for these items so that total land costs can properly be included in "Property, Plant & Equipment."
2.	No	No adjustment is required because clearing costs are costs that are directly attributable to conditioning the property for use and should be included in land costs which are part of "Property, Plant & Equipment."
3.	Yes	Since clearing costs are costs of the land, amounts realized from the sale of materials recovered, such as timber and gravel, should be a reduction of the cost of the land and should not be recorded as other income.
4.	Yes	All costs relating to the purchase of machinery and equipment should be capitalized. For purchased items such costs would include invoice price, freight costs, and unloading charges. Royalty payments, however, should not be included in the cost of the machinery. Such payments should be charged to expenses as they accrue. The machinery costs, other than royalty payments, should be included in "Property, Plant & Equipment."

ANSWER OUTLINE

Problem 12 Physical Count of Securities

a.   Necessity of 5-31-73 security count
        Number of transactions in June
        Company control over securities
        Whether custodian also has access to cash, etc.
    Confirmation is permissible if from independent custodian
        Otherwise examination is necessary

b.   Instructions for the inspection of securities
        Inspect in presence of custodian
            Obtain written representation from custodian
        Make count at close of business
        Coordinate count with examination of cash, etc.
        Client representative to accompany custodian and be present during safe deposit box count
        Note last date of access to safe deposit box
        List all contents of safe deposit box
        Include all data concerning securities

c.   If client does not need access to securities
          Count on 5-28-73 and seal
          Break seal after year-end
       If client needs access to securities
          Verify support for all intervening transactions
          Including examination of cash and negotiable
             instruments at 5-31-73

UNOFFICIAL ANSWER

Problem 12   Physical Count of Securities

a.   Besides materiality, the principal factors to be considered in determining the necessity for a security count on May 31, 1973, are the expected number of transactions and the company's control over the securities. Of particular importance is whether the custodian of the securities has access to cash and other negotiable instruments. In this case the auditor must be alert to the possibility of substitution.

Only if the securities are in safekeeping with an independent reputable custodian may the auditor rely on confirmation. Otherwise, unless the value of the securities is immaterial, he generally will examine the securities at some point in his audit, preferably but not necessarily at the balance-sheet date. The fewer the number of transactions, the easier it is to count and reconcile at some other date. If physical control is good, it may be possible to provide safeguards against accessibility between the time of the count and the balance-sheet date.

b.   1.   The securities must be inspected in the presence of the custodian(s) and subject to the custodian's control and the staff member should obtain a written statement confirming that this was done and that the securities remained under the custodian's control throughout the inspection.

      2.   The count should be made as near to the close of business as possible.

      3.   The count should be coordinated with any examination of cash, notes receivable, or other negotiable instruments so as to avoid substitution and duplicate counts.

      4.   The officials responsible for the safe deposit box should accompany the staffman to the bank and be present during his count.

5.   The staffman should note the last date of access to the safe deposit box.

6.   The staffman should list all contents of the safe deposit box and inquire as to the nature of unusual items included in the box, e.g., securities in the name of officers.

7.   The staffman should list (or compare to a previously prepared list) the following data (to the extent applicable) for later comparison to company records and the auditor's working papers for the prior year:
      (1)   Serial number.
      (2)   Name of issuer.
      (3)   Face value or par value.
      (4)   Number of shares.
      (5)   Name of registration.
      (6)   Maturity dates.
      (7)   Interest and dividend rates and dates.
      (8)   Maturity date for next succeeding coupon attached to bearer bond. (The staffman should note that all coupons are attached).

c.   The key consideration here is whether the company must have access to the securities between the date of the count and the balance-sheet date.

If not, then Mr. Mack can proceed as follows:
1.   Examine the negotiable bearer bonds on May 28, 1973; seal them in an envelope or container for retention in the client's safe; and examine and break the seal subsequent to the year end.

          Visit the safe deposit box on May 28 1973. Arrange for direct confirmation from the bank as to access to the safe deposit box between May 28, 1973, and May 31, 1973.

2.   Prior to May 31, 1973, seal the negotiable bearer bonds into an envelope. At June 5 1973, examine and break the seal, and examine the negotiable bearer bonds.

          After inspecting the safe deposit box on June 5, 1973, examine the bank records to verify that no one had access to the box since May 31, 1973.

If Belasco must have access to the securities

between the balance-sheet date and the count, then Mr. Mack should examine support for intervening transactions. This review would be reinforced by his examination of cash balances and other negotiable instruments at May 31 to insure that there was no substitution or duplicate counting.

ANSWER OUTLINE

Problem 13 Evidential Matter

a.   Books of original entry are primary evidence source
     Auditor tests data by analysis and review, retracing procedural steps, recalculation, and reconciliation
   Underlying accounting data not sufficient by itself
     Support underlying accounting data with corroborating evidence
     Includes checks, invoices, contracts, minutes, confirmations, etc.
     Statistical sampling techniques may be appropriate
   Evidence must be relevant and valid

b1.   Evidence from independent sources is better than that from client sources

b2.   Accounting data developed under good IC is better than that under poor IC

b3.   Direct personal knowledge is more persuasive than indirect knowledge

UNOFFICIAL ANSWER

Problem 13   Evidential Matter

a.   The books of original entry, general and subsidiary ledgers, related accounting manuals, and less formal accounting records such as worksheets are the primary source of evidence supporting the financial statements. The auditor tests this data by analysis and review, by retracing the procedural steps followed in the accounting process and in developing the worksheets, by recalculation, and by reconciling related types and applications of the same information.

While the underlying accounting data is absolutely necessary to form an opinion on the financial statements, it is not, by itself, sufficient support. The auditor must gather and examine corroborating evidence to support the underlying accounting data and representations in the financial statements. This corroborating evidence includes documentary material such as checks, invoices, contracts, and minutes of meetings; confirmations and other written representations by knowledgeable people; information obtained by the auditor by inquiry, observation, inspection, and physical examination; and other information developed by, or available to, the auditor which permits him to reach conclusions through valid reasoning.

In determining how to gather sufficient competent evidential matter the auditor might consider using statistical sampling techniques which have been found to be advantageous in certain instances. The use of statistical sampling, however, does not reduce the use of judgement by the auditor.

To be of any value in forming an opinion on the financial statements, the evidence must be relevant to the situation and it must be valid. The validity of audit evidence is primarily dependent upon the circumstances under which it is obtained.

b.   1.   Evidential matter obtained from independent sources outside an enterprise provides greater assurance of reliability than that which is secured solely within the enterprise.

      2.   Accounting data and financial statements developed under satisfactory conditions of internal control are more reliable than those which are developed under unsatisfactory conditions of internal control.

      3.   Direct personal knowledge obtained by the independent auditor through physical examination, observation, computation, and inspection is more persuasive than information obtained indirectly.

ANSWER OUTLINE

Problem 14   Inventory Audit Procedures

a. Audit procedures peculiar to statistical sampling
     Review client procedures to ascertain reliability
     Become satisfied that the sampling plan has statistical validity
       It will be properly applied
       Precision and reliability are reasonable
     Ensure all parts are included in the perpetual inventory record
     Observe drawing of sample
     Observe actual physical counts and client counting procedures
     Review the statistical evaluation

b. Audit procedures for physical inventory count

    Review client inventory procedures

    Observe physical count

    Make test counts

    Trace count data to inventory records

    Trace items from inventory records to count data

    Trace random items from the warehouse to perpetual records

    Verify footings of inventory records

    Compare physical inventory records with subsidiary ledger records

    Ascertain proper purchase and sales cutoff

    Review merchandise in transit and consigned goods

    Confirm inventory in warehouses

    Perform overall analytical review of inventories

    Account for all inventory count sheets

    Review classification of inventory items

    Review for obsolete merchandise

UNOFFICIAL ANSWER

Problem 14   Inventory Audit Procedures

a.   When a client uses statistical sampling to estimate inventories, the auditor should perform procedures similar to the following:

(1)   The auditor should review the client's procedures and methods for determining inventories to ascertain that they are sufficiently reliable to produce results substantially the same as those that would be obtained by a 100% inventory count.

(2)   The auditor should be satisfied that the statistical sampling plan to be used by the client has statistical validity, that it will be properly applied, and the planned precision and reliability, as defined statistically, will be reasonable in the circumstance.

(3)   The auditor should ascertain that proper steps have been taken to ensure that all parts and supplies in the warehouse are included in the perpetual inventory record. This would normally be checked in advance of the physical count.

(4)   The auditor should be present when the sample is drawn to make sure that the requirements for random selection are properly observed and that all items in the inventory have an equal or determinable probability of selection.

(5)   The auditor must be present to observe counts and must be satisfied with the client's counting procedures. The inventory observation can be made either during or after the year end of the period under audit if well-kept perpetual records are maintained and the client makes periodic comparisons of physical counts with such records.

(6)   The auditor should review the statistical evaluation and be satisfied that the estimated value of the precision at a given level of reliability meets the materiality requirements set for the audit.

b.   In addition to the above, the following standard audit procedures for verification of physical quantities should be performed whether the client conducts a periodic physical count for all or part of its inventory:

(1)   Review and be satisfied with the client's physical inventory-taking procedures.

(2)   Observe the physical count.

(3)   Make test counts where appropriate.

(4)   Trace selected count data to the inventory compilation.

(5)   Select items from compilation and trace them to original count data.

(6)   Select items from the warehouse at random and trace these items to the perpetual inventory record.

(7)   Verify footings.

(8)   Compare inventory compilation amounts to the subsidiary ledger control and investigate significant differences.

(9)   Ascertain that there was a proper purchases and sales cutoff.

(10)   Review the treatment of merchandise in transit and consigned merchandise.

(11)   Confirm merchandise in warehouses.

(12)   Perform an overall analytic review of inventories.

(13) Account for all client inventory count sheets.

(14) Be sure inventory items are properly classified, in good condition, and of proper quality.

ANSWER OUTLINE

Problem 15   Materiality

a. Materiality in auditing means importance
   Relative or absolute
   May be dependent on item's nature and/or its size
   Not uniformly quantifiable concept
   Requires professional judgment in each individual case
      Based on quantitative or qualitative characteristics
      Based on what would influence decisions of those reading financial statements
      In the context of fairly presented statements
      Based on relative effect singly or cumulatively

b. Common considerations in judging materiality
   1. Net income
   2. Gross margin
   3. Sales
   4. Total assets
   5. Total current assets
   6. Total current liabilities
   7. Nature of item(s)
   8. Potential litigation
   9. Future impact on statements
   10. Changes in net income
   11. Trends in net income

c. Audit programs are affected by the concept of materiality
   Emphasis on items which are relatively more important
      I.e., where possibility of material error is greater
   In audit planning, materiality determines items to receive limited attention
   Materiality is also used to evaluate errors discovered

UNOFFICIAL ANSWER

Problem 15   Materiality

a.   The element of materiality implies importance—relative or absolute—and the materiality of an item may be dependent upon its nature or its size, or both. Materiality is not a universally quantifiable concept; it must be determined in light of professional judgment on a case-by-case basis. There is some general agreement, however, that materiality should be based on what would influence decisions of the reader of the financial statements. Materiality may depend on either quantitative or qualitative characteristics, often on a combination of both. Auditors generally view materiality in terms of its importance in the context of presenting fairly, primarily in quantitative terms, the financial position for an enterprise, in conformity with generally accepted accounting principles. In assessing a matter's importance, auditors consider its nature as well as its relative magnitude and relative financial effect either singly or cumulatively in light of the surrounding circumstances.

b.   Some usual common relationships and other considerations used by the auditor in judging materiality are these:
   1. net income
   2. gross margin
   3. sales
   4. total assets
   5. total current assets
   6. total current liabilities
   7. nature of items or an item
   8. potential litigation
   9. future impact on financial statements
   10. changes in net income
   11. trends of net income

c.   An auditor's program will be affected by materiality because there should be stronger grounds to sustain an opinion with respect to both items that are relatively more important and items in which the possibilities of material error are greater than with respect to items of lesser importance or items in which the possibility of material error is remote.

   In planning the audit program, materiality is used as a criterion for determining the items that are to receive limited attention in terms of either the conclusiveness of evidence gathered or the extent of items examined.

   In the execution of the program, materiality is used to evaluate any errors discovered.

MULTIPLE CHOICE QUESTIONS (1-74)

1. Stone was asked to perform the first audit of a wholesale business that does **not** maintain perpetual inventory records. Stone has observed the current inventory but has **not** observed the physical inventory at the previous year-end date and concludes that the opening inventory balance, which is **not** auditable, is a material factor in the determination of cost of goods sold for the current year. Stone will probably
   a. Decline the engagement.
   b. Express an unqualified opinion on the balance sheet and income statement except for inventory.
   c. Express an unqualified opinion on the balance sheet and disclaim an opinion on the income statement.
   d. Disclaim an opinion on the balance sheet and income statement.

2. The annual report of a publicly held company presents the prior year's financial statements which are clearly marked "unaudited" in comparative form with current year audited financial statements. The auditor's report should
   a. Express an opinion on the audited financial statements and contain a separate paragraph describing the responsibility assumed for the financial statements of the prior period.
   b. Disclaim an opinion on the unaudited financial statements, modify the consistency phrase, and express an opinion on the current year's financial statements.
   c. State that the unaudited financial statements are presented solely for comparative purposes and express an opinion only on the current year's financial statements.
   d. Express an opinion on the audited financial statements and state whether the unaudited financial statements were compiled or reviewed.

3. Under which of the following circumstances may audited financial statements contain a note disclosing a subsequent event which is labeled unaudited?
   a. When the subsequent event does **not** require adjustment of the financial statements.
   b. When the event occurs after completion of fieldwork and before issuance of the auditor's report.
   c. When audit procedures with respect to the subsequent event were **not** performed by the auditor.
   d. When the event occurs between the date of the auditor's original report and the date of the reissuance of the report.

4. When an independent CPA is associated with the financial statements of a publicly held entity, but has **not** audited or reviewed such statements, the appropriate form of report to be issued must include a (an)
   a. Negative assurance.
   b. Compilation opinion.
   c. Disclaimer of opinion.
   d. Explanatory paragraph.

5. A note to the financial statements of the First Security Bank indicates that all of the records relating to the bank's business operations are stored on magnetic discs, and that there are no emergency back-up systems or duplicate discs stored since the First Security Bank and their auditors consider the occurrence of a catastrophe to be remote. Based upon this, one would expect the auditor's report to express
   a. A "subject to" opinion.
   b. An "except for" opinion.
   c. An unqualified opinion.
   d. A qualified opinion.

6. For a reporting entity that has participated in related party transactions that are material, disclosure in the financial statements should include
   a. The nature of the relationship and the terms and manner of settlement.
   b. Details of the transactions within major classifications.
   c. A statement to the effect that a transaction was consummated on terms no less favorable than those that would have been obtained if the transaction had been with an unrelated party.
   d. A reference to deficiencies in the entity's system of internal accounting control.

7. Which of the following should be recognized in the auditor's report, whether or **not** the item is fully disclosed in the financial statements?
   a. A change in accounting estimate.
   b. Correction of an error not involving a change in accounting principle.
   c. A change from a nonaccepted accounting principle to a generally accepted one.
   d. A change in classification.

8. Which of the following statements with respect to an auditor's report expressing an opinion on a specific item on a financial statement is correct?

    a. Materiality must be related to the specified item rather than to the financial statements taken as a whole.

    b. Such a report can only be expressed if the auditor is also engaged to audit the entire set of financial statements.

    c. The attention devoted to the specified item is usually less than it would be if the financial statements taken as a whole were being audited.

    d. The auditor who has issued an adverse opinion on the financial statements taken as a whole can never express an opinion on a specified item in these financial statements.

9. The objective of a review of the interim financial information of a publicly held company is to

    a. Provide the accountant with a basis for the expression of an opinion.

    b. Estimate the accuracy of financial statements based upon limited tests of accounting records.

    c. Provide the accountant with a basis for reporting to the board of directors or stockholders.

    d. Obtain corroborating evidential matter through inspection, observation and confirmation.

10. A CPA has audited financial statements and issued an unqualified opinion on them. Subsequently the CPA was requested to compile financial statements for the same period that omit substantially all disclosures and are to be used for comparative purposes. In these circumstances the CPA may report on comparative compiled financial statements that omit such disclosures provided the

    a. Missing disclosures are immaterial in amount.

    b. Financial statements and notes appended thereto are not misleading.

    c. Accountant's report indicates the previous audit and the date of the previous report.

    d. Previous auditor's report accompanies the comparative financial statement.

11. A company issues audited financial statements under circumstances which require the presentation of a statement of changes in financial position. If the company refuses to present a statement of changes in financial position, the independent auditor should

    a. Disclaim an opinion.

    b. Prepare a statement of changes in financial position and note in a middle paragraph of the report that this statement is auditor-prepared.

    c. Prepare a statement of changes in financial position and disclose in a footnote that this statement is auditor-prepared.

    d. Qualify his opinion with an "except for" qualification and a description of the omission in a middle paragraph of the report.

12. Which of the following, when materially affecting comparability, would ordinarily be referred to by an independent auditor reporting on the statement of changes in financial position?

    a. Changing from a balanced to an unbalanced form of presentation.

    b. Changes in terminology.

    c. Changing from a cash to working capital form of presentation.

    d. Changes in the content of working capital.

13. An auditor is reporting on cash-basis financial statements. These statements are best referred to in his opinion by which one of the following descriptions?

    a. Financial position and results of operations arising from cash transactions.

    b. Assets and liabilities arising from cash transactions, and revenue collected and expenses paid.

    c. Balance sheet and income statement resulting from cash transactions.

    d. Cash balance sheet and the source and application of funds.

14. The fourth reporting standard requires the auditor's report to either contain an expression of opinion regarding the financial statements, taken as a whole, or an assertion to the effect that an opinion cannot be expressed. The objective of the fourth standard is to prevent

    a. The CPA from reporting on one basic financial statement and not the others.

    b. The CPA from expressing different opinions on each of the basic financial statements.

    c. Misinterpretations regarding the degree of responsibility the auditor is assuming.

    d. Management from reducing its final responsibility for the basic financial statements.

15.   A CPA's client has changed from straight-line depreciation to sum-of-the-years-digits depreciation. The effect on this year's income is immaterial but in the future the change, which is adequately disclosed in the notes to the financial statements, may be expected to result in materially different results. Based upon this fact, the auditor should express

- a.   An unqualified opinion.
- b.   A consistency exception.
- c.   A "subject to" opinion.
- d.   An "except for" opinion.

16.   In a first audit of a new company the auditor's report will

- a.   Remain silent with respect to consistency.
- b.   State that the accounting principles have been applied on a consistent basis.
- c.   State that accounting principles have been applied consistently during the period.
- d.   State that the consistency standard does not apply because the current year is the first year of audit.

17.   Jones, CPA, is the principal auditor who is auditing the consolidated financial statements of his client. Jones plans to refer to another CPA's examination of the financial statements of a subsidiary company but does not wish to present the other CPA's audit report. Both Jones and the other CPA's audit reports have noted no exceptions to generally accepted accounting principles. Under these circumstances the opinion paragraph of Jones' consolidated audit report should express

- a.   An unqualified opinion.
- b.   A "subject to" opinion.
- c.   An "except for" opinion.
- d.   A principal opinion.

18.   Which of the following requires recognition in the auditor's opinion as to consistency?

- a.   Changing the salvage value of an asset.
- b.   Changing the presentation of prepaid insurance from inclusion in "other assets" to disclosing it as a separate line item.
- c.   Division of the consolidated subsidiary into two subsidiaries which are both consolidated.
- d.   Changing from consolidating a subsidiary to carrying it on the equity basis.

19.   Whenever special reports, filed on a printed form designed by authorities, call upon the independent auditor to make an assertion that the auditor believes is not justified, the auditor should

- a.   Submit a short-form report with explanations.
- b.   Reword the form or attach a separate report.
- c.   Submit the form with questionable items clearly omitted.
- d.   Withdraw from the engagement.

20.   When an adverse opinion is expressed, the opinion paragraph should include a direct reference to

- a.   A footnote to the financial statements which discusses the basis for the opinion.
- b.   The scope paragraph which discusses the basis for the opinion rendered.
- c.   A separate paragraph which discusses the basis for the opinion rendered.
- d.   The consistency or lack of consistency in the application of generally accepted accounting principles.

21.   An auditor need not mention consistency in the audit report if

- a.   The client has acquired another company through a "pooling of interests."
- b.   An adverse opinion is issued.
- c.   This is the first year the client has had an audit.
- d.   Comparative financial statements are issued.

22.   A CPA's report on a client's balance sheet, income statement, and statement of changes in financial position was sent to the stockholders. The client now wishes to present only the balance sheet along with an appropriately modified auditor's report in a newspaper advertisement. The auditor may

- a.   Permit the publication as requested.
- b.   Permit only the publication of the originally issued auditor's report and accompanying financial statements.
- c.   Not permit publication of a modified auditor's report.
- d.   Not permit publication of any auditor's report in connection with a newspaper advertisement.

23. After performing all necessary procedures a predecessor auditor reissues a prior-period report on financial statements at the request of the client without revising the original wording. The predecessor auditor should

    a. Delete the date of the report.
    b. Dual-date the report.
    c. Use the reissue date.
    d. Use the date of the previous report.

24. A limitation on the scope of the auditor's examination sufficient to preclude an unqualified opinion will always result when management

    a. Engages an auditor after the year-end physical inventory count.
    b. Refuses to furnish a representation letter.
    c. Knows that direct confirmation of accounts receivable with debtors is not feasible.
    d. Engages an auditor to examine only the balance sheet.

25. If the auditor believes that financial statements which are prepared on a comprehensive basis of accounting other than generally accepted acounting principles are not suitably titled, the auditor should

    a. Modify the auditor's report to disclose any reservations.
    b. Consider the effects of the titles on the financial statements taken as a whole.
    c. Issue a disclaimer of opinion.
    d. Add a footnote to the financial statements. which explains alternative terminology.

26. When asked to perform an examination in order to express an opinion on one or more specified elements, accounts or items of a financial statement, the auditor

    a. May not describe auditing procedures applied.
    b. Should advise the client that the opinion will result in a piecemeal opinion.
    c. May assume that the first standard of reporting with respect to generally accepted accounting principles does not apply.
    d. Should comply with the request only if they constitute a major portion of the financial statements on which an auditor has disclaimed an opinion based on an audit.

27. With respect to issuance of an audit report which is dual dated for a subsequent event occurring after the completion of fieldwork but before issuance of the auditor's report, the auditor's responsibility for events occurring subsequent to the completion of fieldwork is

    a. Extended to include all events occurring until the date of the last subsequent event referred to.
    b. Limited to the specific event referred to.
    c. Limited to all events occurring through the date of issuance of the report.
    d. Extended to include all events occurring through the date of submission of the report to the client.

28. Jerome has completed an examination of the financial statements of Bold, Inc. Last year's financial statements were examined by Smith, CPA. Since last year's financial statements will be presented for comparative purposes without Smith's report, Jerome's report should

    a. State that the prior year's financial statements were examined by another auditor.
    b. State that the prior year's financial statements were examined by Smith.
    c. Not refer to the prior year's examination.
    d. Refer to Smith's report only if the opinion was other than unqualified.

29. Which of the following would not be included in a CPA's report based upon a review of the financial statements of a non-public entity?

    a. A statement that the review was in accordance with generally accepted auditing standards.
    b. A statement that all information included in the financial statements are the representations of management.
    c. A statement describing the principal procedures performed.
    d. A statement describing the auditor's conclusions based upon the results of the review.

30. The auditor who intends to express a qualified opinion should disclose all the substantive reasons in a separate explanatory paragraph of the report, except when the opinion paragraph

    a. Makes reference to a note in the financial statements which discloses the pertinent facts.
    b. Describes a limitation on the scope of the examination.
    c. Describes an insufficiency in evidential matter.
    d. Has been modified because of a change in accounting principle.

31.   When financial statements are prepared on the basis of a going concern and the auditor believes that the client may not continue as a going concern, the auditor should issue
    a.   A "subject to" opinion.
    b.   An unqualified opinion with an explanatory middle paragraph.
    c.   An "except for" opinion.
    d.   An adverse opinion.

32.   The principal auditor is satisfied with the independence and professional reputation of the other auditor who has audited a subsidiary but wants to indicate the division of responsibility. The principal auditor should
    a.   Modify the scope paragraph of the report.
    b.   Modify the scope and opinion paragraphs of the report.
    c.   Not modify the report except for inclusion of an explanatory middle paragraph.
    d.   Modify the opinion paragraph of the report.

33.   When a contingency is resolved immediately subsequent to the issuance of a report which was qualified with respect to the contingency, the auditor should
    a.   Insist that the client issue revised financial statements.
    b.   Inform the audit committee that the report cannot be relied upon.
    c.   Take no action regarding the event.
    d.   Inform the appropriate authorities that the report cannot be relied upon.

34.   An auditor's report must state whether financial statements are presented in accordance with generally accepted accounting principles in each of the following situations except on an engagement involving
    a.   A development-stage enterprise.
    b.   A corporation in liquidation.
    c.   A not-for-profit entity.
    d.   A regulated company.

35.   The auditor's opinion makes reference to generally accepted accounting principles (GAAP). Which of the following best describes GAAP?
    a.   The interpretations of accounting rules and procedures by certified public accountants on audit engagements.
    b.   The pronouncements made by the Financial Accounting Standards Board and its predecessor, the Accounting Principles Board.
    c.   The guidelines set forth by various governmental agencies that derive their authority from Congress.
    d.   The conventions, rules, and procedures which are necessary to define the accepted accounting practices at a particular time.

36.   On January 28, 1977, a customer of Tom Corporation suffered a total loss as a result of a major casualty. On March 1, 1977, Tom wrote off as uncollectible a large receivable from this customer. The auditor's report on Tom's financial statements for the year ended December 31, 1976, has not yet been issued. The write-off in the subsequent period requires
    a.   Disclosure in the 1976 financial statements.
    b.   Adjustment to the 1976 financial statement.
    c.   Presentation of the 1976 financial statements with a prior period adjustment.
    d.   No adjustment or disclosure in the 1976 financial statements but disclosure in the 1977 financial statements.

37.   The fourth generally accepted auditing standard of reporting requires an auditor to render a report whenever an auditor's name is associated with financial statements. The overall purpose of the fourth standard of reporting is to require that reports
    a.   State that the examination of financial statements has been conducted in accordance with generally accepted auditing standards.
    b.   Indicate the character of the auditor's examination and the degree of responsibility assumed by the auditor.
    c.   Imply that the auditor is independent in fact as well as in appearance with respect to the financial statements under examination.
    d.   Express whether the accounting principles used in preparing the financial statements have been applied consistently in the period under examination.

38. The auditor's report makes reference to the basic financial statements, which are customarily considered to be the balance sheet and the statements of
   a. Income and changes in financial position.
   b. Income, changes in retained earnings, and changes in financial position.
   c. Income, retained earnings, and changes in financial position.
   d. Income and retained earnings.

39. In which of the following circumstances would an auditor be required to issue a qualified report with a separate explanatory paragraph?
   a. The auditor satisfactorily performed alternative accounts receivable procedures because scope limitations prevented performance of normal procedures.
   b. The financial statements reflect the effects of a change in accounting principles from one period to the next.
   c. A particular note to the financial statements discloses a company accounting method which deviates from generally accepted accounting principles.
   d. The financial statements of a significant subsidiary were examined by another auditor, and reference to the other auditor's report is to be made in the principal auditor's report.

40. An auditor should not render a report on
   a. The achievability of forecasts.
   b. Client internal control.
   c. Management performance.
   d. Quarterly financial information.

41. Which of the following material asset accounts would an auditor take exception to in the auditor's report?
   a. Franchise fees paid.
   b. Goodwill resulting from revaluation based on an objective appraisal by an expert.
   c. Excess cost over the fair value of the assets of a significant subsidiary.
   d. Research and development costs that will be billed to a customer at a subsequent date.

42. The term "special reports" may include all of the following except reports on financial statements
   a. Of an organization that has limited the scope of the auditor's examination.
   b. Prepared for limited purposes such as a report that relates to only certain aspects of financial statements.

   c. Of a not-for-profit organization which follows accounting practices differing in some respects from those followed by business enterprises organized for profit.
   d. Prepared in accordance with a cash basis of accounting.

43. On February 13, 1978, Fox, CPA, met with the audit committee of the Gem Corporation to review the draft of Fox's report on the company's financial statements as of and for the year ended December 31, 1977. On February 16, 1978, Fox completed all remaining field work at the Gem Corporation's headquarters. On February 17, 1978, Fox typed and signed the final version of the auditor's report. On February 18, 1978, the final report was mailed to Gem's audit committee. What date should have been used on Fox's report?
   a. February 13, 1978.
   b. February 16, 1978.
   c. February 17, 1978.
   d. February 18, 1978.

44. The consistency standard does not apply to an accounting change that results from a change in
   a. An accounting principle that is not generally accepted.
   b. An accounting estimate.
   c. The reporting entity.
   d. An accounting principle inseparable from a change in accounting estimate.

45. When comparative financial statements are presented, the fourth standard of reporting, which refers to financial statements "taken as a whole," should be considered to apply to the financial statements of the
   a. Periods presented plus the one preceding period.
   b. Current period only.
   c. Current period and those of the other periods presented.
   d. Current and immediately preceding period only.

46. With respect to consistency, which of the following should be done by an independent auditor, who has not examined a company's financial statements for the preceding year but is doing so in the current year?

a. Report on the financial statements of the current year without referring to consistency.

b. Consider the consistent application of principles within the year under examination but not between the current and preceding year.

c. Adopt procedures, that are practicable and reasonable in the circumstances to obtain assurance that the principles employed are consistent between the current and preceding year.

d. Rely on the report of the prior year's auditors if such a report does not take exception as to consistency.

47. If, as a result of a limited review of interim financial information, a CPA concludes that such information does not conform with generally accepted accounting principles, the CPA should

a. Insist that the management conform the information with generally accepted accounting principles and if this is not done, resign from the engagement.

b. Adjust the financial information so that it conforms with generally accepted accounting principles.

c. Prepare a qualified report that makes reference to the lack of conformity with generally accepted accounting principles.

d. Advise the board of directors of the respects in which the information does not conform with generally accepted accounting principles.

48. If the auditor believes that required disclosures of a significant nature are omitted from the financial statements under examination, the auditor should decide between issuing

a. A qualified opinion or an adverse opinion.

b. A disclaimer of opinion or a qualified opinion.

c. An adverse opinion or a disclaimer of opinion.

d. An unqualified opinion or a qualified opinion.

49. A CPA is associated with client-prepared financial statements, but is not independent. With respect to the CPA's lack of independence, which of the following actions by the CPA might confuse a reader of such financial statements?

a. Stamping the word "unaudited" on each page of the financial statements.

b. Disclaiming an opinion and stating that independence is lacking.

c. Issuing a qualified auditor's report explaining the reason for the auditor's lack of independence.

d. Preparing an auditor's report that included essential data that was not disclosed in the financial statements.

50. Morgan, CPA, is the principal auditor for a multinational corporation. Another CPA has examined and reported on the financial statements of a significant subsidiary of the corporation. Morgan is satisfied with the independence and professional reputation of the other auditor, as well as the quality of the other auditor's examination. With respect to Morgan's report on the financial statements, taken as a whole, Morgan

a. Must not refer to the examination of the other auditor.

b. Must refer to the examination of the other auditor.

c. May refer to the examination of the other auditor.

d. May refer to the examination of the other auditor, in which case Morgan must include in the auditor's report on the consolidated financial statements, a qualified opinion with respect to the examination of the other auditor.

51. Nonaccounting data included in a long-form report have been subjected to auditing procedures. The auditor's report should state this fact and should explain that the nonaccounting data are presented for analysis purposes. In addition, the auditor's report should state whether the nonaccounting data are

a. Beyond the scope of the normal engagement and, therefore, not covered by the opinion on the financial statements.

b. Within the framework of generally accepted auditing standards, which apply to the financial statements, taken as a whole.

c. Audited, unaudited, or reviewed on a limited basis.

d. Fairly stated in all material respects in relation to the basic financial statements, taken as a whole.

52. When a client declines to make essential disclosures in the financial statements or in the footnotes, the independent auditor should
   a. Provide the necessary disclosures in the auditor's report and appropriately modify the opinion.
   b. Explain to the client that an adverse opinion must be issued.
   c. Issue an unqualified report and inform the stockholders of the improper disclosure in an "unaudited" footnote.
   d. Issue an opinion "subject to" the client's lack of disclosure of supplementary information as explained in a middle paragraph of the report.

53. A CPA has a financial interest in a corporation and is associated with that corporation's unaudited financial statements. Under such circumstances the CPA's report should state that the CPA is not independent with respect to the corporation and should include
   a. A statement that the financial statements were unaudited and accordingly the CPA does not express an opinion on the financial statements.
   b. A description of the reasons for the CPA's lack of independence and a disclaimer of opinion on the financial statements.
   c. A statement that each page of the financial statements is "unaudited" and a qualified opinion on the financial statements.
   d. A description of the reasons for the CPA's lack of independence and a qualified opinion on the financial statements.

54. When a principal auditor decides to make reference to the examination of another auditor, the principal auditor's report should clearly indicate the
   a. Principal auditor's qualification on the overall fairness of the financial statements, taken as a whole, "subject to" the work and report of the other auditor.
   b. Procedures that were performed by the other auditor in connection with the other auditor's examination.
   c. Division of responsibility between that portion of the financial statements covered by the examination of the principal auditor and that covered by the examination of the other auditor.
   d. Procedures that were performed by the principal auditor to obtain satisfaction as to the reasonableness of the examination of the other auditor.

55. When the report of a principal auditor makes reference to the examination made by another auditor, the other auditor may be named if express permission to do so is given and
   a. The report of the principal auditor names the other auditor in both the scope and opinion paragraphs.
   b. The principal auditor accepts responsibility for the work of the other auditor.
   c. The report of the other auditor is presented together with the report of the principal auditor.
   d. The other auditor is not an associate or correspondent firm whose work is done at the request of the principal auditor.

56. Which of the following best describes the reference to the expression "taken as a whole" in the fourth generally accepted auditing standard of reporting?
   a. It applies equally to a complete set of financial statements and to each individual financial statement.
   b. It applies only to a complete set of financial statements.
   c. It applies equally to each item in each financial statement.
   d. It applies equally to each material item in each financial statement.

57. A company includes selected interim financial information in a note to its annual financial statements. The independent auditor has made a limited review of the information and is satisfied with its presentation. Under these circumstances, the auditor's report on the annual financial statements
   a. Should be modified to make reference to the limited review and the selected interim financial information.
   b. Need not be modified to make reference to the limited review but should be modified to make reference to the selected financial information.
   c. Should be modified to make reference to the limited review but not the selected interim financial information.
   d. Need not be modified to make reference to the limited review or the selected interim financial information.

58.   If an auditor wishes to issue a qualified opinion because the financial statements include a departure from generally accepted accounting principles, the auditor's report should have an explanatory paragraph referring to a footnote that discloses the principal effects of the subject matter of the qualification. The qualification should be referred to in the opinion paragraph by using language such as

   a.   "With the exception of."
   b.   "When read in conjunction with the footnotes."
   c.   "With the foregoing explanation."
   d.   "Subject to the departure explained in the footnotes."

59.   If the auditor discovers that the carrying amount of a client's investments is overstated because of a loss in value which is other than a temporary decline in market value, the auditor should insist that

   a.   The approximate market value of the investments be shown on the face of the balance sheet.
   b.   The investments be classified as long term for balance sheet purposes with full disclosure in the footnotes.
   c.   The loss in value be recognized in the financial statements of the client.
   d.   The equity section of the balance sheet separately show a charge equal to the amount of the loss.

60.   Which event that occurred after the end of the fiscal year under audit but prior to issuance of the auditor's report would not require disclosure in the financial statements?

   a.   Sale of a bond or capital stock issue.
   b.   Loss of plant or inventories as a result of fire or flood.
   c.   A major drop in the quoted market price of the stock of the corporation.
   d.   Settlement of litigation when the event giving rise to the claim took place after the balance-sheet date.

61.   A footnote to a company's financial statements includes an indication that the company's auditor performed certain procedures regarding the company's unaudited replacement cost information. The footnote does not indicate whether the auditor expresses an opinion on the replacement cost information. Which of the following is appropriate in these circumstances?

   a.   The auditor's report on the audited financial statements should be expanded to include a disclaimer of opinion on the replacement cost information.

   b.   A separate report on the unaudited replacement cost information should be rendered and should include a disclaimer of opinion on the replacement cost information.
   c.   The auditor's report on the audited financial statements should be qualified because of the replacement cost information.
   d.   A separate report on the replacement cost information should be rendered and should indicate whether the information is fairly presented in relation to the basic financial statements.

62.   An auditor is unable to determine the amounts associated with certain illegal acts committed by a client. In these circumstances the auditor would most likely

   a.   Issue either a qualified opinion or a disclaimer of opinion.
   b.   Issue only an adverse opinion.
   c.   Issue either a qualified opinion or an adverse opinion.
   d.   Issue only a disclaimer of opinion.

63.   Which of the following circumstances would not be considered a departure from the auditor's standard report?

   a.   The auditor wishes to emphasize a particular matter regarding the financial statements.
   b.   The auditor's opinion is based in part on the report of another auditor.
   c.   The financial statements are affected by a departure from a generally accepted accounting principle.
   d.   The auditor is asked to report only on the balance sheet but has unlimited access to information underlying all the basic financial statements.

64.   An auditor's report would be designated as a special report when it is issued in connection with which of the following?

   a.   Financial statements for an interim period which are subjected to a limited review.
   b.   Financial statements which are prepared in accordance with a comprehensive basis of accounting other than generally accepted accounting principles.

c. Financial statements which purport to be in accordance with generally accepted accounting principles but do not include a presentation of the statement of changes in financial position.

d. Financial statements which are unaudited and are prepared from a client's accounting records.

MAY 1981 QUESTIONS

65. Once the initial audit of a newly constructed industrial plant has been performed, with respect to consistency, which of the following is of **least** concern to the continuing auditor in the following year?
   a. Prior years' capitalization policy.
   b. Prior years' capitalized costs.
   c. Prior years' depreciation methods.
   d. Prior years' depreciable life.

66. Karr has examined the financial statements of Lurch Corporation for the year ended December 31, 1980. Although Karr's field work was completed on February 27, 1981, Karr's auditor's report was dated February 28, 1981, and was received by the management of Lurch on March 5, 1981. On April 4, 1981, the management of Lurch asked that Karr approve inclusion of this report in their annual report to stockholders which will include unaudited financial statements for the first quarter ended March 31, 1981. Karr approved of the inclusion of this auditor's report in the annual report to stockholders. Under the circumstances Karr is responsible for inquiring as to subsequent events occuring through
   a. February 27, 1981.
   b. February 28, 1981.
   c. March 31, 1981.
   d. April 4, 1981.

67. Which of the following consistency phrases would be contained in a continuing auditor's standard report on comparative financial statements?
   a. Applied on a consistent basis.
   b. Applied on a basis consistent with that of the preceding year.
   c. Applied consistently during interim periods.
   d. Applied consistently with previous years audited.

68. Which of the following would **not** be required for the statements to be "presented fairly" in conformity with generally accepted accounting principles?

a. That generally accepted accounting principles be followed in presenting all material items in the statements.
   b. That the generally accepted accounting principles selected from alternatives be appropriate for the circumstances of the particular company.
   c. That generally accepted accounting principles be applied on a basis consistent with those followed in the prior year.
   d. That generally accepted accounting principles selected from alternatives reflect transactions in accordance with their substance.

69. An auditor is confronted with an exception considered sufficiently material as to warrant some deviation from the standard unqualified auditor's report. If the exception relates to a departure from generally accepted accounting principles, the auditor must decide between expressing a (an)
   a. Adverse opinion and a "subject to" opinion.
   b. Adverse opinion and an "except for" opinion.
   c. Adverse opinion and a disclaimer of opinion.
   d. Disclaimer of opinion and a "subject to" opinion.

70. A continuing auditor would update his opinion on prior financial statements by issuing a "subject to" opinion for the
   a. Subsequent resolution of an uncertainty in the current period.
   b. Discovery of an uncertainty in the current period.
   c. Discovery of an uncertainty in the current period that relates to the prior-period statements being reported on.
   d. Restatement of prior-period statements in conformity with generally accepted accounting principles.

71. In which of the following circumstances would an adverse opinion be appropriate?
   a. The auditor is not independent with respect to the enterprise being audited.
   b. An uncertainty prevents the issuance of an unqualified opinion.
   c. The statements are **not** in conformity with APB Opinion No. 8 regarding pension plans.
   d. A client-imposed scope limitation prevents the auditor from complying with generally accepted auditing standards.

7 2. Before reissuing a report which was previously issued on the financial statements of a prior period, a predecessor auditor should

  a. Review the successor auditor's working papers.
  b. Examine significant transactions or events since the date of previous issuance.
  c. Obtain a signed engagement letter from the client.
  d. Obtain a letter of representation from the successor auditor.

73. A modification of the CPA's report on a review of the interim financial statements of a publicly-held company would be necessitated by which of the following?

  a. An uncertainty.
  b. Lack of consistency.
  c. Reference to another accountant.
  d. Inadequate disclosure.

74. Thomas, CPA, has examined the consolidated financial statements of Kass Corporation. Jones, CPA, has examined the financial statements of the sole subsidiary which is material in relation to the total examined by Thomas. It would be appropriate for Thomas to serve as the principal auditor, but it is impractical for Thomas to review the work of Jones. Assuming an unqualified opinion is expressed by Jones, one would expect Thomas to

  a. Refuse to express an opinion on the consolidated financial statements.
  b. Express an unqualified opinion on the consolidated financial statements and not refer to the work of Jones.
  c. Express an unqualified opinion on the consolidated financial statements and refer to the work of Jones.
  d. Express an "except for" opinion on the consolidated financial statements and refer to the work of Jones.

REPEAT QUESTIONS

(581,A1,13)   Identical to item 37 above
(581,A2,42)   Identical to item 64 above

PROBLEMS

Problem 1 Materiality (1171,A4)

(25 to 30 minutes)

The concept of materiality is important to the CPA in his examination of financial statements and expression of opinion upon these statements.

Required:

Discuss the following:

a. How are materiality (and immateriality) related to the proper presentation of financial statements?

b. In what ways will considerations of materiality affect the CPA in
1. Developing his audit program?
2. Performance of his auditing procedures?

c. What factors and measures should the CPA consider in assessing the materiality of an exception to financial statement presentation?

d. How will the materiality of a CPA's exceptions to financial statements influence the type of opinion he expresses? (The relationship of materiality to each type of auditor's opinion should be considered).

Problem 2 Report Modifications (574,A4)

(20 to 26 minutes)

Charles Burke, CPA, has completed field work for his examination of the Willingham Corporation for the year ended December 31, 1973, and now is in the process of determining whether to modify his report. Presented below are two, independent, unrelated situations which have arisen.

Situation I

In September 1973, a lawsuit was filed against Willingham to have the court order it to install pollution control equipment in one of its older plants. Willingham's legal counsel has informed Burke that it is not possible to forecast the outcome of this litigation; however, Willingham's management has informed Burke that the cost of the pollution-control equipment is not economically feasible and that the plant will be closed if the case if lost. In addition,

Burke has been told by management that the plant and its production equipment would have only minimal resale values and that the production that would be lost could not be recovered at other plants.

Situation II

During 1973, Willingham purchased a franchise amounting to 20% of its assets for the exclusive right to produce and sell a newly patented product in the northeastern United States. There has been no production in marketable quantities of the product anywhere to date. Neither the franchisor nor any franchisee has conducted any market research with respect to the product.

Required:

In deciding the type-of-report modification, if any, Burke should take into account such considerations as follows:

> Relative magnitude
> Uncertainty of outcome
> Likelihood of error
> Expertise of the auditor
> Pervasive impact on the financial statement
> Inherent importance of the item

Discuss Burke's type-of-report decision for each situation in terms of the above and other appropriate considerations. Assume each situation is adequately disclosed in the notes to the financial statements. Each situation should be considered independently. In discussing each situation, ignore the other. It is not necessary for you to decide the type of report which should be issued.

Problem 3 Example Reports (574,A7)

(Note: This problem does not reflect SAS 15 which requires auditors to report on comparative financial statements)
(20 to 26 minutes)

Presented below are three independent, unrelated auditor's reports. The corporation being reported on in each case, is profit oriented and publishes general-purpose financial statements for distribution to owners, creditors, potential investors, and the general public. Each of the following reports contains deficiencies.

Auditor's Report I

We have examined the consolidated balance sheet of Belasco Corporation and subsidiaries as of December 31, 1973, and the related consolidated statements of income and retained earnings and changes in financial position for the year then ended. Our examination was made in accordance with generally accepted auditing standards and accordingly included such tests of the accounting records and such other auditing procedures as we considered necessary in the circumstances. We did not examine the financial statements of Seidel Company, a major consolidated subsidiary. These statements were examined by other auditors whose report thereon has been furnished to us, and our opinion expressed herein, insofar as it relates to Seidel Company, is based solely upon the report of the other auditors.

In our opinion, except for the report of the other auditors, the accompanying consolidated balance sheet and consolidated statements of income and retained earnings and changes in financial position present fairly the financial position of Belasco Corporation and subsidiaries at December 31, 1973, and the results of its operations and the changes in its financial position for the year then ended, in conformity with generally accepted accounting principles applied on a basis consistent with that of the preceding year.

Auditor's Report II

The accompanying balance sheet of Jones Corporation as of December 31, 1973, and the related statements of income and retained earnings and changes in financial position for the year then ended were not audited by us; however, we confirmed cash in the bank and performed a general review of the statements.

During our engagement, nothing came to our attention to indicate that the aforementioned financial statements do not present fairly the financial position of Jones Corporation at December 31, 1973, and the results of its operations and the changes in its financial position for the year then ended, in conformity with generally accepted accounting principles applied on a basis consistent with that of the preceding year; however, we do not express an opinion on them.

Auditor's Report III

I made my examination in accordance with generally accepted auditing standards. However, I am not independent with respect to Mavis Corporation be-cause my wife owns 5% of the outstanding common stock of the company. The accompanying balance sheet as of December 31, 1973, and the related statements of income and retained earnings and changes in financial position for the year then ended were not audited by me; accordingly, I do not express an opinion on them.

Required:

For each auditor's report describe the reporting deficiencies, explain the reasons therefore, and briefly discuss how the report should be corrected. Each report should be considered separately. When discussing one report, ignore the other two. Do not discuss the addressee, signatures, and date. Also, do not rewrite any of the auditor's reports. Organize your answer sheet as follows:

Report No.	Deficiency	Reason	Correction

Problem 4   Assurances Given (1180,A3)

(15 to 25 minutes)

The auditor should obtain a level of knowledge of the entity's business, including events, transactions, and practices, that will enable the planning and performance of an examination in accordance with generally accepted auditing standards. Adhering to these standards enables the auditor's report to lend credibility to financial statements by providing the public with certain assurances.

Required:

a. How does knowledge of the entity's business help the auditor in the planning and performance of an examination in accordance with generally accepted auditing standards?

b. What assurances are provided to the public when the auditor states that the financial statements "present fairly . . . in conformity with generally accepted accounting principles applied on a consistent basis?"

Problem 5   Audit Report Deficiencies (1175,A4)

(Note: This problem does not reflect SAS 15 which requires auditors to report on comparative financial statements)
(20 to 25 minutes)

Upon completion of all field work on September 23, 1975, the following "short-term" report was rendered by Timothy Ross to the Directors of The Rancho Corporation.

To the Directors of
The Rancho Corporation:

We have examined the balance sheet and the related statement of income and retained earnings of The Rancho Corporation as of July 31, 1975. In accordance with your instructions, a complete audit was conducted.

In many respects, this was an unusual year for The Rancho Corporation. The weakening of the economy in the early part of the year and the strike of plant employees in the summer of 1975 led to a decline in sales and net income. After making several tests of sales records, nothing came to our attention that would indicate that sales have not been properly recorded.

In our opinion, with the explanation given above, and with the exception of some minor errors that are considered immaterial, the afore-mentioned financial statements present fairly the financial position of The Rancho Corporation at July 31, 1975, and the results of its operations for the year then ended, in conformity with pronouncements of the Accounting Principles Board and the Financial Accounting Standards Board applied consistently throughout the period.

Timothy Ross, CPA
September 23, 1975

Required:

List and explain deficiencies and omissions in the auditor's report. The type of opinion (unqualified, qualified, adverse, or disclaimer) is of no consequence and need not be discussed.

Organize your answer sheet by paragraph (scope, explanatory, and opinion) of the auditor's report.

Problem 6   Write Report (1180,A2)

(15 to 25 minutes)

Rose & Co., CPAs, has satisfactorily completed the examination of the financial statements of Bale & Booster, a partnership, for the year ended December 31, 1979. The financial statements which were prepared on the entity's income tax (cash) basis include footnotes which indicate that the partnership was involved in continuing litigation of material amounts relating to alleged infringement of a competitor's patent. The amount of damages, if any, resulting from this litigation could not be determined at the time of completion of the engagement. The prior years' financial statements were not presented.

Required:
Based upon the information presented, prepare an auditor's report which includes appropriate explanatory disclosure of significant facts.

Problem 7   Rewrite Report (1176,A7)

(15 to 30 minutes)

Roscoe, CPA, has completed the examination of the financial statements of Excelsior Corporation as of and for the year ended December 31, 1975. Roscoe also examined and reported on the Excelsior financial statements for the prior year. Roscoe drafted the following report for 1975.

March 15, 1976

We have examined the balance sheet and statements of income and retained earnings of Excelsior Corporation as of December 31, 1975. Our examination was made in accordance with generally accepted accounting standards and accordingly included such tests of the accounting records as we considered necessary in the circumstances.

In our opinion, the above mentioned financial statements are accurately prepared and fairly presented in accordance with generally accepted accounting principles in effect at December 31, 1975.

Roscoe, CPA
(Signed)

Other Information:

    •   Excelsior is presenting comparative
financial statements.

    •   Excelsior does not wish to present
a statement of changes in financial position
for either year.

    •   During 1975 Excelsior changed its
method of accounting for long-term construction contracts and properly reflected the effect
of the change in the current year's financial
statements. Roscoe is satisfied with Excelsior's
justification for making the change. The change
is discussed in footnote number 12.

    •   Roscoe was unable to perform nor-
mal accounts receivable confirmation procedures
but alternate procedures were used to satisfy
Roscoe as to the validity of the receivables.

    •   Excelsior Corporation is the defendant in
a litigation, the outcome of which is highly uncertain. If the case is settled in favor of the plaintiff,
Excelsior will be required to pay a substantial
amount of cash which might require the sale of
certain fixed assets. The litigation and the possible
effects have been properly disclosed in footnote
number 11.

    •   Excelsior issued debentures on January 31,
1974, in the amount of $10,000,000. The funds
obtained from the issuance were used to finance
the expansion of plant facilities.   The debenture
agreement restricts the payment of future cash
dividends to earnings after December 31, 1980.
Excelsior declined to disclose this essential data
in the footnotes to the financial statements.

Required:

    Consider all facts given and rewrite the audi-
tor's report in acceptable and complete format incorporating any necessary departures from the standard (short form) report.

    Do not discuss the draft of Roscoe's report
but identify and explain any items included in
"Other Information" that need not be part of
the auditor's report.

MULTIPLE CHOICE ANSWERS

1.	c	16.	a	31.	a	46.	c	61.	a
2.	a	17.	a	32.	b	47.	d	62.	a
3.	d	18.	d	33.	c	48.	a	63.	d
4.	c	19.	b	34.	b	49.	c	64.	b
5.	c	20.	c	35.	d	50.	c	65.	b
6.	a	21.	b	36.	a	51.	d	66.	b
7.	c	22.	a	37.	b	52.	a	67.	a
8.	a	23.	d	38.	c	53.	a	68.	c
9.	c	24.	b	39.	c	54.	c	69.	b
10.	c	25.	a	40.	a	55.	c	70.	c
11.	d	26.	c	41.	b	56.	a	71.	c
12.	c	27.	b	42.	a	57.	d	72.	d
13.	b	28.	a	43.	b	58.	a	73.	d
14.	c	29.	a	44.	b	59.	c	74.	c
15.	a	30.	d	45.	c	60.	c		

EXPLANATION OF MULTIPLE CHOICE ANSWERS

1. (1180,A1,9) (c) For the case described in this question, the auditor will be able to gather evidence on all year-end balances. However, evidence with respect to the beginning inventory is lacking making the verification of Cost of Goods Sold, an income statement element, impossible. If no other problems arise, the auditor will be able to issue an unqualified opinion on the balance sheet and a disclaimer on the income statement (para 509.05). Answer (a) is incorrect since no reason is given for declining the engagement. Answer (b) is incorrect since it describes a form of audit report not permitted under GAAS. Answer (d) is incorrect since the auditor may render an opinion on the year-end balance sheet.

2. (1180,A1,15) (a) A separate paragraph decribing the responsibility taken is required (para 504.15). Answer (b) is incorrect since there is no indication that the accounting principles have not been consistently applied. Answer (c) is incorrect because the auditor may not restrict the use of the financial statements to comparative analysis. Answer (d) is incorrect since the statements were not compiled or reviewed; these forms of auditor association are for non-public firms.

3. (1180,A1,16) (d) The type of events in answers (a), (b) and (c) need to be audited (para 509.10—.13). However, when a report is being reissued the subsequent event may be labeled unaudited (para 530.08 and para 9509.24).

4. (1180,A1,17) (c) In this situation, the requirement is the proper form of the auditor's report

to be issued when an independent CPA is associated with a public entity's financial statements that he has not audited or reviewed. A disclaimer is issued in this situation per para 504.05. Answer (a) is incorrect since the required disclaimer should include no assurance, positive or negative. Answer (b) is incorrect since compilations are limited to non-public firms (AR 100). Answer (d) is incorrect since no explanatory paragraph is added.

5. (1180,A1,22) (c) Because the likelihood of loss is remote, there is no need to modify the audit report (para 509.21). Answer (a) is only appropriate when there is significant uncertainty involved. Answer (b) is incorrect since there is no departure from generally accepted accounting principles. Answer (d) is incorrect since the use of both types of qualifications, subject to and except for, are not permitted per GAAS.

6. (1180,A1,23) (a) This is the disclosure specified in para 335.17. Answers (b) and (c) are not, in general, required. Answer (d) is not germane to the requirement.

7. (1180,A1,24) (c) A change from a non-accepted accounting principle to a generally accepted one should be treated as a correction of an error and the auditor's report should contain a consistency exception (para 420.10). Answers (a), (b) and (d), unless other complications arise, do not affect the audit report; that is, an unqualified report may be issued.

8. (1180,A1,28) (a) When issuing a special report on a specific financial statement item, the measurement of materiality must be related to that item (para 621.11). Answer (b) is incorrect since an auditor may report on a single item without performing a complete financial statement audit (para 621.09). Answer (c) is incorrect; the materiality threshhold is lower for a single item than it would be for an overall audit causing the examination for a single item to be more extensive (para 621.11). Answer (d) is correct only in cases in which such reporting would be tantamount to expressing a piecemeal opinion (para 621.12).

9. (1180,A1,32) (c) The objective of a review of interim information is to provide the accountant with a basis for reporting to the board of directors or stockholders on whether material modifications should be made to financial information to make it conform with generally accepted accounting principles (para 721.03). Answer (a) is incorrect since it states the objective of an audit, not a review (para 721.03). Answer (b) is correct in that reviews do include limited tests of accounting records but it is incorrect in that they do

not provide an "estimate of the accuracy of financial statements." Answer (d) is incorrect since the reviews consist primarily of inquiry and analytical review procedures (para 721.06) as opposed to inspection, observation, and confirmation procedures.

10. (1180,A1,45)   (c)   A CPA may report on comparative compiled statements which omit substantially all disclosures, to financial statements which were previously audited if an additional paragraph indicating the previous audit and the date of the previous report is included (AR 200.29). Answer (a) is incorrect because there is no requirement that the missing disclosures be immaterial. Answer (b) is correct only in circumstances in which the CPA has knowledge that the omission of disclosures is undertaken with the intention of misleading users (AR 100.19). Answer (d) is incorrect since there is no requirement that the previous auditor's report accompany the comparative statements.

11. (1180,A1,56)   (d)   Omission of a statement of changes in financial position results in an "except for" qualified report with a middle paragraph describing the omission (para 545.04—.05). Neither a disclaimer (answer (a)) or the preparation of a statement of changes in financial position (answer (b) and (c)) is necessary.

12.   (580,A1,6) (c)   The requirement is the type of change in the statement of changes in financial position that should be referred to by the CPA in the audit report. Changing from the cash to the working capital form of presentation constitutes a change in the application of accounting principles and involves the consistency standard per para 420.16. Thus, the auditor should express an exception as to consistency in the audit opinion. Answer (a) is incorrect because a change from the balanced to an unbalanced form of presentation is considered a reclassification per para 420.15 and does not require mention in the audit report. Answer (b) is incorrect because changes in terminology are not a material change per para 9 of APB 19, as the APB recognized "the need for flexibility in form, content, and terminology." Answer (d) is incorrect because changes in the content of working capital are expected from period to period and do not involve the consistency standard per para 420.17.

13.   (580,A1,20) (b)   The preferable titles when reporting on cash basis financial statements are assets and liabilities arising from cash transactions, and revenue collected and expenses paid. See para 621.07. Terms such as balance sheet, statement of financial position, statement of income, statement of operations, and statement of changes in financial position should be avoided. Accordingly, answers (a), (c), and (d) are incorrect.

14.   (580,A1,24) (c)   The objective of the fourth standard of reporting (requiring an expression of opinion on the financial statements as a whole) is to prevent misinterpretation of the degree of responsibility the auditor is assuming when the auditor is associated with financial statements per para 509.05. Answer (a) is incorrect because the auditor may report on one basic statement and not the other statements which is not a scope limitation, as long as the auditor has access to information underlying all the statements per para 509.13. Answer (b) is incorrect because the auditor may express an unqualified opinion on one of the statements and express a qualified, adverse, or disclaimer on another if circumstances call for this treatment per para 509.05. Answer (d) is incorrect because the auditor's standard report consists of two paragraphs. The first is the scope paragraph which describes statements being audited and compliance with GAAS. The second is the opinion paragraph which states the auditor's opinion on the financial statements in terms of compliance with GAAP. There is no mention in the auditor's report of management's final responsibility for the financial statements.

15.   (580,A1,25) (a)   If there is a change from straight-line to SYD depreciation and the effect on this year's income is immaterial, the auditor need not express an exception as to consistency in the current period if the change is disclosed in the notes to the financial statements per para 420.18. Thus, the fact that the change in accounting principle has no material effect on this period precludes the need for a consistency exception which is answer (b). Answer (c) is incorrect because a "subject to" opinion is only issued when the financial statements are subject to an uncertainty per para 509.35. Answer (d) is incorrect because an "except for" opinion is a qualified opinion, i.e., a contingency exception.

16.   (580,A1,26) (a)   In the first audit of a new company, the auditor's report should remain silent with respect to consistency because no previous period exists with which to make a comparison. See para 420.21. Answer (b) is incorrect because there is no basis to state that accounting principles have been applied on a consistent basis. Answer (c) is incorrect because there is an implication that accounting principles have been applied consistently during a period unless so stated. Answer (d) is incorrect because the consistency standard applies within the current year (no mention is necessary) even though the current year is the first year of operations.

17. (580,A1,36) (a) When a principal CPA refers to another CPA's examination, the CPA's audit report is considered an unqualified opinion per para 509.14 and para 543.08. The report of the other auditor is only required to be presented if the other auditor is named per para 543.07 (note that the other auditor does not have to be and is usually not named). Answers (b) and (c) are incorrect because "subject to" and "except for" opinions are qualified opinions. Answer (d) is incorrect because a principal opinion is a nonsense term.

18. (580,A1,42) (d) The requirement is the accounting change which requires recognition in the auditor's opinion as to consistency. Changing from consolidating a subsidiary to carrying on the equity basis is a change in reporting entity per para 420.07. Changes in reporting entities, changes in accounting principles, correction of errors, and changes in principles inseparable from changes in estimates all affect consistency and must be referred to in the auditor's opinion. Answer (a) is incorrect because changing the salvage value of an asset is considered a change in an accounting estimate which does not affect consistency per para 420.12. Answer (b) is incorrect because changing the presentation of prepaid insurance from inclusion in other assets to a separate item is a change in classification which does not affect consistency per para 420.14. Answer (c) is incorrect because division of a consolidated subsidiary into two consolidated subsidiaries is a change in classification not affecting consistency per para 420.14.

19. (580,A1,46) (b) If printed forms or schedules include wording which is unacceptable to the auditor, the auditor should reword the forms or attach a separate report per para 621.21. Answer (a) is incorrect because a short-form report is not required and may not be appropriate, e.g., a report on a comprehensive basis of accounting other than GAAP. Answer (c) is incorrect because the form should be reworded or a separate report should be issued. Answer (d) is incorrect because the auditor would only withdraw from the engagement if the rewording or separate report were unacceptable to the client.

20. (580,A1,48) (c) The opinion paragraph of an adverse opinion should refer to a separate paragraph which discusses the basis for the opinion rendered per para 509.43. Answer (a) is incorrect because the auditor (not the client) should disclose all the substantive reasons for the adverse opinion and the principal effects on the financial position and results of operation per para 509.42. Answer (b) is incorrect because no mention of the nonconformity with GAAP is made in the scope paragraph. Answer (d) is incorrect because adverse opinions are only issued when the financial statements taken as a whole do not present fairly per GAAP. Generally there is no reference to consistency unless the auditor has specific exceptions as to consistency (para 509.44).

21. (580,A1,53) (b) The requirement is when does an auditor need not mention consistency. Per para 509.44 auditors should not refer to consistency when an adverse opinion is issued because consistency implies the application of GAAP. Answer (a) is incorrect because if a pooling of interests is not applied retroactively to comparative financial statements, the financial statements are not per GAAP (see APB 16 and para 546.12). Answer (c) is incorrect because in the first year of an audit the auditor can compare the accounting principles used in the current period to those applied in the prior period. Only when the client is in the first year of operations, there is no mention of consistency per para 420.21. Answer (d) is incorrect because the second standard of reporting requires that the audit opinion state whether GAAP have been applied consistently.

22. (1179,A1,8) (a) The issue is whether a client may utilize only a balance sheet and an appropriately modified auditor's report in a newspaper advertisement when the auditor originally issued an audit report on all the financial statements. First, ethics ruling 86 on "other responsibilities" permits a CPA to be engaged to verify financial data used in a client's advertising and the CPA's name be used in such advertising. Thus, presentation of the modified auditor's report in a newspaper advertisement is not an ethics problem. Second, auditor reissuance of a report on only a balance sheet would be permissable per para 509.13 which indicates that reporting on one basic financial statement and not the others involves limited reporting objectives rather than a limitation in scope. Here, there apparently was no limitation in scope as a complete audit was done in all the statements. Thus, answer (b) is incorrect because an appropriately modified report can be issued per para 509.13. Answers (c) and (d) are incorrect because there is no ethics violation.

23. (1179,A1,9) (d) When a predecessor auditor reissues an audit report, without revising the original wording, the auditor should use the date of the previous report per para 505.11. This avoids any implications that the auditor has re-examined any records, transactions, or events after the date of the original report. If however the auditor revises his report or the financial statements are restated, the report should be dual dated per para 530.05. Answers (a), (b), and

(c) are all incorrect because the date of the previous report should be used.

24. (1179,A1,12) (b) When management refuses to furnish a representation letter, the scope of the auditor's examination has been limited sufficiently to preclude an unqualified opinion per para 333.11. Answer (a) is incorrect because para 310.04 indicates that a CPA may accept an audit engagement after year-end and still issue an unqualified opinion. Answer (c) is incorrect because if direct confirmation of accounts receivable is not feasible, alternative procedures should be employed to obtain adequate evidence necessary to satisfy the auditor as to the receivables. The availability of alternative procedures to obtain adequate evidence determines whether a limitation of scope exists (see sections 330 and 331). Answer (d) is incorrect because an engagement where the auditor reports only on the balance sheet is limitation of reporting objectives rather than limitation of scope as long as there is no restriction on the auditor's access to information (para 509.13).

25. (1179,A1,13) (a) If the auditor believes that financial statements prepared per a comprehensive basis other than GAAP are not suitably titled, he should modify his report to disclose any reservations per para 621.07. Titles such as balance sheet, income statement, etc., generally only apply to financial statements per GAAP. Financial statements per the cash basis or income tax basis should be suitably described. Answer (b) is incorrect because the auditor has determined the effects of the titles as being not suitable per the problem. Answer (c) is incorrect because a disclaimer should only be issued when the auditor is not expressing an opinion on the financial statements. Here, the titles were found to be not suitable, and thus the CPA must express his reservations in an unqualified or adverse opinion. Answer (d) is incorrect because the financial statements and related footnotes are the representations of management rather than the auditor. Thus, the auditor's reservations belong in the audit report rather than in the statements.

26. (1179,A1,18) (c) Reports on specified elements or accounts of a financial statement are special reports. The standards for special reports are outlined in para 621.09-.14. The general standards, the standards of field work, and the third and fourth standards of reporting are applicable. Since specified elements are not statements, the first standard of reporting regarding GAAP is not applicable. The second standard of reporting (consistency) is applicable if the elements of accounts, etc., are prepared per GAAP. Answer (a) is incorrect because the special report on specified elements may

describe the results of applying agreed upon procedures to one or more elements per para 621.09b. Answer (b) is incorrect because piecemeal opinions are inappropriate and should not be issued in any situation per para 509.48. Answer (d) is incorrect because reporting on an element which constitutes a major portion of the financial statements on which an auditor has disclaimed an opinion based on an audit is a piecemeal opinion which is prohibited.

27. (1179,A1,26) (b) When an audit report is dual dated for a subsequent event occurring after completion of field work, the auditor's responsibility for events occurring subsequent to the completion of the field work is limited to the specific event for which the report is dual dated, per para 530.05. If the auditor dates the report as of the subsequent event occurring after the completion of field work, the auditor's responsibility is extended to all events occurring to the date of the last subsequent event, as in answer (a). Answers (c) and (d) are incorrect because the auditor's responsibility for subsequent events is to the date of the auditor's report which is generally the date of completion of field work rather than the date of issuance (submission to the client) of the report.

28. (1179,A1,36) (a) When the financial statements of prior periods are presented as comparative statements in the current year and were examined by a predecessor auditor, the successor auditor should indicate in the scope paragraph (1) that the financial statements of the prior period were examined by other auditors, (2) date of the report, (3) type of opinion, and (4) substantive reasons if other than unqualified. See para 505.12. Answer (b) is incorrect because the other CPA should not be named by the successor auditor if the predecessor auditor's report is not presented. Answer (c) is incorrect because para 505.12 requires reference to the prior year's examination. Answer (d) is incorrect because reference to the predecessor's examination is required in all cases. Also, further explanation is required if the predecessor's report is other than unqualified.

29. (1179,A1,39) (a) Reviews, in contrast to audits of financial statements, are not made in accordance with GAAS. Reviews are made in accordance with standards established by the AICPA which are Statements on Standards for Accounting and Review of Services. SSARS 1, Compilation and Review of Financial Statements, provides standards for performing reviews and compilations and issuing reports thereon. Answer (b) is incorrect because reports on reviews do state that the financial statements are representations of management. Answer (c) is incorrect because a report on a review does indicate that the review consists principally of inquiries of company personnel and analytical procedures applied to the financial data. Answer (d) is incorrect because a report on a review does describe the accountant's conclusions based upon the results of the review.

30. (1179,A1,41) (d) Para 509.32 indicates that a separate explanatory paragraph is required in qualified reports except when the qualification is with respect to a change in accounting principle. Answer (a) is incorrect because a reference note to the financial statement would probably be with respect to significant uncertainties and be the reason for qualification, and therefore require a separate explanatory paragraph. Answers (b) and (c) are incorrect because limitations of the scope of the audit require a separate explanatory paragraph as well as reference to in both the scope and opinion paragraphs (para 509.34).

31. (1179,A1,46) (a) When an auditor believes that the client may not continue as a going concern, he should express a qualified "subject to" opinion. See para 509.35. Answer (b) is incorrect because a significant uncertainty with respect to the going concern assumption requires a qualified opinion. See para 509.23. Answer (c) is incorrect because an "except for" opinion is used in all qualified opinions except for those being qualified due to an uncertainty (para 509.35). Answer (d) is incorrect because an adverse opinion is to be expressed if the financial statements do not fairly represent. Here the problem specified that there may be a going concern problem, not that there is one.

32. (1179,A1,49) (b) When a principal auditor wants to indicate division of responsibility with another auditor, the principal auditor should refer to the examination of the other auditor in the scope and opinion paragraphs of the audit report per para 509.14. Also, see para 543.06-.09. Answers (a), (c), and (d) are incorrect because the auditor should modify both the scope and opinion paragraphs of the audit report.

33. (1179,A1,56) (c) When a contingency is resolved immediately subsequent to the issuance of a report which was qualified with respect to the contingency, the auditor is not required to take any action regarding the event. Resolution of the contingency after the issuance of the report is not subsequent discovery of facts existing at the date of the auditor's report (section 561). Because the contingency did result in a qualified report, the auditor was aware of the facts existing at the date of the auditor's report. Also, the auditor's responsibility for continuing inquiry is precluded by para 561.03.

Also, see para 509.26 and 505.06-.07. Answers (a), (b), and (d) are incorrect because the contingency has been disclosed in the financial statements and audit report, i.e., the statements were not misleading at the time of issuance.

34. (577,A1,11) (b) Per section 620 of SAS 1 (now superseded by section 621), the first standard of reporting (GAAP) does not apply to statements that do not purport to present financial position and results of operations, e.g., cash basis accounting, liquidation accounting, etc. (para 620.04). Reports on development stage enterprises, not-for-profit entities and regulated companies require statements concerning compliance per GAAP (para 544.02, para 620.08, and SFAS 7).

Note section 620 has been superseded by section 621. Under section 621, the auditor must disclose noncompliance with GAAP when a comprehensive basis of accounting other than GAAP is used. Thus there is no correct answer to this question per section 621.

35. (577,A1,16) (d) The requirement is the definition of GAAP. GAAP are the "conventions, rules, and procedures necessary to define accepted accounting practice at a particular time" (para 2, SAS 5). There is no single source of reference for all established accounting principles. The AICPA Code of Ethics requires compliance with FASB statements and interpretations, APB opinions, and AICPA account research bulletins (ARBs). Additional sources of GAAP are AICPA accounting interpretations, AICPA industry audit and accounting guides, industry accounting practices, textbooks, professional articles, AICPA statements of position, etc.

36. (577,A2,21) (a) The requirement is the treatment of a material bad debt occurring after year end but before issuance of the audit report. There are two types of subsequent events that require consideration by the auditor. The first type of subsequent event affects the accounts as of year end and thus requires adjustment of such accounts. The second type of subsequent event is one which does not affect the year-end accounts, because it occurs after year end, but which may be so material as to require disclosure to keep the statements from being misleading. See para 560.03 and 560.05 of SAS 1. In this case the bad debt should be disclosed in the 1976 financial statements. Pro forma financial data may be an appropriate method of disclosure if the subsequent event has a significant impact on the statements. Additionally the auditor could discuss the matter in an explanatory

paragraph in the audit report if the subsequent event had a tremendously material impact on the financial statements (para 560.09).

37. (1177,A1,11) (b) The fourth standard of reporting states, "the report shall contain an expression of opinion regarding the financial statements taken as a whole, or an assertion to the effect that an opinion cannot be expressed. When an over-all opinion cannot be expressed, the reasons therefor should be stated. In all cases when an auditor's name is associated with financial statements, the report should contain a clear-cut indication of the character of the auditor's examination, if any, and the degree of the responsibility he is taking."

Answer (a) is incorrect because the scope paragraph, not the opinion paragraph, of the report indicates that the examination is per GAAS. Answer (c) is incorrect because the second general standard refers to independence. Answer (d) is incorrect because the first standard of reporting refers to compliance with GAAP.

38. (1177,A1,12) (c) The basic financial statements are the:
1. Balance sheet
2. Statement of income
3. Statement of retained earnings
4. Statement of changes in financial position.
See para 6 of SAS 2 and note that answer (b) is incorrect because reference is made to the statement of changes in retained earnings. The correct title of the statement is the statement of retained earnings (even though the statement is merely a reconciliation of the beginning and ending balances of retained earnings).

39. (1177,A1,21) (c) When auditors express a qualified opinion, they must disclose all substantial reasons in a separate explanatory paragraph. The requirements for an explanatory paragraph, however, do not exist when the opinion paragraph is modified due to a change in accounting principle (para 32 of SAS 2). Thus answer (b) is incorrect. Answer (a) is incorrect because a qualified opinion is not required if the auditor conducts the examination per GAAS and applies all procedures necessary in the circumstances (para 10, SAS 2). Here the auditor has satisfied himself with alternative procedures. Answer (d) is incorrect because reference to another auditor's report by a principal auditor only requires disclosure in the scope paragraph and reference to the report of the other auditor in the opinion paragraph. It is not considered a qualified opinion (para 14, SAS 2).

40. (1177,A1,40) (a) Ethics rule **201** prohibits CPAs from being associated with a forecast in such a manner that it appears that the CPA is vouching for the accuracy of a forecast. Thus the CPA cannot render a report on the achievability of forecast. Answer (b) is incorrect because reports on internal control are permitted or required per sections 640 and 641 of SAS 1 and SAS 20. Answer (c) is incorrect because CPAs' reports generally cover management performance, i.e., review of internal control which includes the safeguarding of assets. The financial statements report on management's performance on which CPAs issue an opinion. Answer (d) is incorrect because SAS 24 prescribes reporting on interim financial statements.

41. (578,A1,1) (b) Goodwill resulting from asset appraisals is not permitted per GAAP, i.e., appraisal revaluations of assets are not permitted per para 17 of APB 6. Answer (a) is incorrect because franchise fees are an intangible asset which should be recorded at cost per para 11 of APB 17. Answer (c) is incorrect because the excess of cost over fair value of a subsidiary should be recorded as an asset per para 87 of APB 16. Answer (d), R&D performed for others under contract, is incorrect because these costs should be deferred and matched with the associated revenues (see para 2 of SFAS 2).

42. (578,A1,10) (a) See SAS 14, Special Reports. Special reports are appropriate for:

a. Financial statements per a comprehensive basis of accounting other than GAAP;
b. Specified elements or aspects of a financial statement;
c. Compliance with contractual agreements, regulatory requirements, etc.;
d. Financial information presented in prescribed forms.

GAAS are generally applicable when an auditor examines and reports on any financial statements. Accordingly if there is a limitation in scope, the auditor must qualify or disclaim, rather than issue a special report. Answers (b), (c), and (d) provide examples of applications of special reports. Answers (c) and (d) are examples of a comprehensive basis of accounting other than GAAP.

43. (578,A1,13) (b) Audit reports are generally dated as of the completion of field work. See para 530.01 of SAS 1. In this case the field work

was completed on February 16 and should be so dated, even though the report was typed on February 17 and delivered on February 18. If subsequent events occurring after completion of field work are disclosed in the statements, the report is either dated as of the subsequent event or dual-dated, i.e., dated as of completion of field work except for the footnote describing the subsequent event.

44. (578,A1,18) (b) Accounting changes that affect consistency include:

a.   Change in accounting principle;
b.   Change in reporting entity;
c.   Correction of an error in principle (including one that is not per GAAP);
d.   Change in principle inseparable from change in estimate.

See para 420.06—.11 of SAS 1. Changes which do not affect consistency and do not need to be mentioned in the report (if they are disclosed in the footnotes) include:

a.   Change in accounting estimate;
b.   Error correction not involving an accounting principle;
c.   Changes in classification or reclassification;
d.   Variations in format of statement of changes;
e.   Substantially different transactions or events;
f.   Changes expected to have material future effect.

See para 420.12—.19, SAS 1. Thus, answers (a), (c), and (d) all affect consistency and the consistency standard requires recognition in the auditor's report. Answer (b), a change in accounting estimate does not affect consistency.

45. (578,A1,25) (c) SAS 15, Reports on Comparative Financial Statements, extends the fourth standard of reporting to the financial statements of prior periods that are presented on a comparative basis with those of the current period (para 2). Normally the auditor's report will be dated as of the completion of the most recent examination. Answer (a) is incorrect because the auditor only reports on the statements being presented.

46. (578,A1,31) (c) On the first examination, the CPA should adopt procedures that are practical and reasonable to assure that accounting principles are consistent between the current and the preceding year. See para 546.14 of SAS 1. Answer (a) is incorrect because auditors only report on the current year with-

out referring to consistency when it is the first year of client operations. Answer (b) is incorrect because consistency refers to consistency between periods, not within periods. Answer (d) is incorrect because the prior year's audit report does not indicate the accounting principles used in the prior year. Also an exception in the prior year's audit report as to consistency would only indicate an inconsistency between the year prior to the prior period, and not between the current and the prior period.

47. (578,A1,37) (d) When a limited review of interim financial statements indicates noncompliance with GAAP, the CPA should inform management and the audit committee of the board of directors of the nature of the noncompliance with GAAP. If after informing the management and board of directors the financial statements are not restated per GAAP, the auditor should modify the report on the interim statements per para 721.21. Answer (b) is incorrect because the client, not the CPA, should adjust the statements to conform with GAAP. Answer (c) is incorrect because an audit has not been performed. Answer (a) is incorrect because CPAs withdraw from engagements when a modified report is not accepted by the client.

48. (578,A1,42) (a) If material required disclosures are omitted from financial statements, the CPA is aware that the statements are not per GAAP and a qualified or adverse opinion is required. See para 17 of SAS 2 as well as para 430.01—.06 and 545.01—.05 of SAS 1. The matter is also discussed in footnote 6 of SAS 21. Answers (b), (c), and (d) are incorrect because neither a disclaimer nor an unqualified opinion is appropriate when there is noncompliance with GAAP.

49. (578,A1,54) (c) Auditors who are not independent should disclaim and disclose that there is a lack of independence. There should be no discussion of the reason for lack of independence, because such discussion may confuse the reader concerning the importance of the impairment of independence. See section 517 in SAS 1. Answer (a) is incorrect because the word "unaudited" should appear on each page of unaudited statements (para 517.03). Answer (b) is incorrect because disclaiming an opinion for non-independence without explanation is the correct procedure. Answer (d) is incorrect because even though the CPA is not independent and disclaims an opinion, the auditor is obligated to set forth any reservations concerning the financial statements (para 517.06). As of 7/1/79, SSARS 1, "Compilation and Review of Financial Statements," will set standards for unaudited engagements.

50. (1178,A1,1)   (c)   The requirement is whether the principal auditor should refer to the examination of another auditor. The principal auditor may or may not refer to the examination of the other auditor depending on whether the principal auditor is satisfied with respect to the independence and professional reputation of the other auditor (para 543.04 of SAS 1). If the principal auditor does not refer to the examination of the other auditor, the principal auditor takes responsibility for the work of the other auditor (para 543.03). When the principal auditor refers to the examination of the other auditor, responsibility is divided between the principal auditor and the other auditor. Reference to the other auditor is not considered a qualification.

If the principal auditor decides to take responsibility for the work of the other auditor, the principal auditor should consider visiting the other auditor to discuss audit procedures applied, to review the audit programs of the other auditor, and to review the working papers of the other auditor (para 543.12). Answers (a) and (b) are incorrect because the principal auditor has a choice in deciding whether or not to refer to the other auditor. Answer (d) is incorrect because reference to the other auditor's report is not a qualification, but is a clarification of the responsibility assumed by the principal auditor (para 543.08).

51. (1178,A1,5)   (d)   If nonaccounting data are included in a long-form report and have been subjected to auditing procedures, the audit report should indicate if they are fairly stated in all material respects in relation to the basic financial statements taken as a whole (para 610.02b of SAS 1). Answer (a) is incorrect because audit opinions must be based upon all audit work done, not just audit work common to a normal engagement. Answer (b) is incorrect because data are presented with respect to generally accepted accounting principles, not generally accepted auditing standards. Answer (c) is incorrect because the problem stated that the nonaccounting data had been subjected to auditing procedures.

52. (1178,A1,9)   (a)   When a client declines to make essential disclosures, the independent auditor should provide the disclosures where practicable, and modify the audit opinion. See para 430.04 and 545.01 and .05 of SAS 1 and para 17 of SAS 2. Answer (b) is incorrect because a qualified opinion may be appropriate rather than an adverse opinion. Answer (c) is incorrect because improper disclosures result in financial statements not per GAAP (para 430.02, SAS 1), and an unaudited footnote would not be

appropriate in view of the audit. Answer (d) is incorrect because a "subject to" opinion is appropriate only when a qualified opinion is issued due to an uncertainty (para 35, SAS 2).

53. (1178,A1,13)   (a)   When CPAs are not independent, a disclaimer should be issued indicating non-independence (para 517.02, SAS 1). Answer (b) is incorrect because the reason for lack of independence should not be described as such reasons might confuse the reader concerning the importance of the independence impairment. Answer (c) is incorrect because while each page of the financial statements should be marked "unaudited," a disclaimer, rather than a qualified opinion, should be issued. Answer (d) is incorrect because neither the reasons for the CPA's lack of independence nor a qualified opinion should be presented on statements where independence is lacking. As of 7/1/79, SSARS 1, "Compilation and Review of Financial Statements," will set standards for unaudited engagements.

54. (1178,A1,15)   (c)   When the principal auditor refers to the examination of another auditor, the principal auditor's report should indicate the divided responsibility (para 543.03, SAS 1). The reference to the other auditor is not a qualification of the opinion, but rather an indication of divided responsibility (para 543.08). The divided responsibility should be indicated in both the scope and opinion paragraphs. Also the magnitude of the portion of the financial statements examined by the other auditor (in dollars or percentages of total assets, revenues, etc.) should be disclosed (para 543.07). Answer (a) is incorrect because the principal auditor does not qualify his report, and the "subject to" qualification is issued only when uncertainties exist. Answers (b) and (d) are incorrect because audit procedures are not listed in the auditor's report.

55. (1178,A1,16)   (c)   When the other auditor is named, the report of the other auditor must be presented (para 543.07, SAS 1). Answer (a) is incorrect because there is no requirement that the other auditor be named in both the scope and opinion paragraphs. Answer (b) is incorrect because if the principal auditor accepted the responsibility for the other auditor's work, there would be no reference to the other auditor. Answer (d) is incorrect because there is no differentiation between other auditors who are associates or correspondence firms and those who are not.

56. (1178,A1,23) (a)   "Taken as a whole" in the fourth standard of reporting in context is "the report shall either contain an expression of opinion regarding the financial statements, taken as a whole, or an assertion to the effect that an opinion cannot be expressed." The expression applies equally to a complete set of financial statements and to each individual statement. For example, an unqualified opinion may be expressed on one of the financial statements, and a qualified, adverse, or disclaimer on another (para 5, SAS 2). Answer (b) is incorrect because the expression applies to individual statements as well as complete sets of statements. Answers (c) and (d) are incorrect because "taken as a whole" does not refer to individual items in each financial statement.

57. (1178,A1,47)   (d)   Per para 26 of SAS 24, an audit report need not be modified if selected interim financial information is included in a footnote to the annual financial statements. The footnote should be headed "unaudited interim financial information." If the footnote is not properly marked as unaudited, the audit report should indicate that a limited review was made and no opinion is expressed on the data presented. If the scope of the limited review was restricted or there is nonconformity with GAAP, the audit report should be expanded to so state. Answers (a), (b), and (c) are incorrect because no reference is needed to either the limited review or to the selected interim financial information unless the scope of the limited review was restricted or there was nonconformity with GAAP.

58. (1178,A1,48) (a)   Para 35 of SAS 2 requires the word "except" or "exception" in a qualified opinion unless the qualification arises from an uncertainty, and then the language "subject to" is to be used. Answers (b) and (c) are phrases which are not clear and/or forceful enough and should not be used. Answer (d), "subject to," should only be used to qualify as to an uncertainty.

59. (1178,A1,53) (c)   When there is a decline in market value of investments which is not temporary, i.e., permanent, the loss in value should be recognized in the client's financial statements. Per para 9 of SFAS 12, any loss in value of investments in marketable equity securities in a current portfolio is recognized in the period of declining value. Per para 21, decline in market value of noncurrent marketable equity securities is also recognized as a loss. The same rules apply to all investments based on the doctrine of conservatism. Answer (a) is incorrect because writedown is required. Answer (b) is incorrect because a loss in value which is other than temporary does not necessarily change the classification from current to long-term, e.g., the investments may be sold shortly thereafter. Answer (d) is incorrect because deferred charges shown in the equity section of the balance sheet are only for temporary losses on investments in equity securities per SFAS 12.

60. (579,A1,1)   (c)   The requirement is the type of subsequent event that would not require disclosure in financial statements. Para 560.06 provides examples of items requiring disclosure in statements that include answers (a), (b), and (d). If any of these items had occurred in the period under audit, they would be reflected in the financial statements. If any of these items occurred in the subsequent period before the last day of field work, they should be disclosed in the footnotes to the financial statements. Answer (c) however, a major drop in the quoted market price of the corporation stock, would not have affected the financial statements and accordingly would not have to be disclosed as a subsequent event.

61. (579,A1,17)   (a)   Specified replacement cost information required by the SEC is normally presented in an unaudited footnote to the financial statements. The auditor should read the footnote information and make inquiries of client management to determine whether the replacement cost information is prepared per SEC regulation S-X, and the disclosures are consistent with management's response to audit inquiries (para 730.04). Normally no reference is made in the auditor's report unless the auditor takes exception to the replacement cost data or has been unable to apply the limited procedures recommended in section 730. If, however, the replacement cost information is not clearly marked unaudited or indicates that audit procedures were performed with respect to the information, without also disclaiming an opinion on the information, the auditor's report should be expanded to include a disclaimer of opinion on the replacement cost information. Answers (b) and (d) are incorrect because separate reports on replacement cost data are not necessary. Answer (c) is incorrect because the auditor wishes to disclaim responsibility for the replacement cost information rather than qualify the audit report.

62. (579,A1,36)   (a)   If an auditor is unable to determine the amounts associated with the illegal acts committed by a client, the auditor should consider the need to qualify or disclaim due to a scope limitation. Since it is a scope limitation, an

adverse opinion, answers (b) and (c) would not be appropriate. Answer (d) is incorrect because a qualified opinion may be appropriate depending upon the materiality of the act.

63.   (579,A1,52)   (d)   Reporting on only a balance sheet does not otherwise involve a scope limitation, i.e., the audit procedures are the same as if all basic statements were going to be reported on. If there are no scope restrictions, it is considered a reporting restriction. See para 509.13. Per para 509.09, circumstances resulting in the departure from the standard report are:

a.   Scope is restricted as to audit procedures.
b.   Opinion is based in part on report of another auditor.
c.   Statements depart from GAAP.
c.   Statements depart from accounting principles promulgated by FASB.
e.   Accounting principles are inconsistently applied.
f.   Statements are affected by uncertainty.
g.   Auditor wishes to emphasize a matter regarding the statements.

64.   (579,A1,56)   (b)   The requirement is the type of report to be designated as a special report. Section 621, "Special Reports," applies to reports on:

a.   Financial statements prepared per a comprehensive basis of accounting other than GAAP
b.   Specified elements, accounts, etc. of financial statements
c.   Compliance with aspects of contractual regulations or regulatory requirements
d.   Financial information in prescribed forms

Answer (a) is incorrect because financial statements subjected to a limited review are accompanied by an accountant's report (not auditor's) on interim financial information (section 721). Answer (c) is incorrect because financial statements per GAAP that do not include a statement of changes in financial position will require a qualified report, per para 545.04. Answer (d) is incorrect because financial statements which are unaudited are either accompanied by an accountant's compilation report or an accountant's review report, per "Compilation and Review of Financial Statements," which is SSARS No. 1.

MAY 1981 ANSWERS

65.   (581,A1,2)   (b)   The requirement is to determine the matter which will not affect the CPA's report as to consistency. The prior years' capitalized costs are not of concern to the auditor in subsequent periods

in so far as consistency is concerned, because once these costs have been capitalized there will be no change in their treatment. If the prior years' capitalization policy [answer (a)] and/or prior years' depreciation methods [answer (c)] are changes as of the beginning of the current period, a consistency exception would result. A consistency exception could also arise in connection with a change in the prior years' depreciable life [answer (d)] if the depreciation method were changed at the same time resulting in an inseparable estimate and principle change.

66.   (581,A1,12)   (b)   The requirement is to determine the proper dating of an audit report included in documents containing audited financial statements. The auditor is required to perform audit procedures relating to subsequent events through the date of the audit report (February 28 in this question). Answer (a) is incorrect because the report is outstanding and, for some reason, the auditor chose not to date it the last day of field work (e.g., possibly due to the existence of a subsequent event). Answers (c) and (d) are incorrect because the auditor's responsibility with respect to information in documents containing audited financial statements does not extend beyond the financial information identified in his/her report and the auditor has no obligation to perform any procedures to corroborate the other information contained in the annual report. The auditor need only read the other information and consider whether it appears inconsistently or incorrectly, see para 550.04.

67.   (581,A1,23)   (a)   The requirement is to determine the standard consistency statement in an audit report. Para 505.03 prescribes the wording: "applied on a consistent basis."

68.   (581,A1,29)   (c)   The requirement is to determine an attribute which is unnecessary for items to be "presented fairly" in conformity with generally accepted accounting principles. Financial statements may "present fairly" despite the fact that there is a lack of consistency. Answers (a), (b), and (d) are all necessary for fair presentation (para 411.04).

69.   (581,A1,30)   (b)   The requirement is to determine the type of audit report issued when there is a departure from generally accepted accounting principles. When financial statements are materially affected by a departure from generally accepted accounting principles, the auditor should express an "except for" qualified opinion or an adverse opinion (para 509.15-.17, 509.35-.36, 509.41-.44). Answer (a) is incorrect because a "subject to" qualified opinion is used in cases of future uncertainty. Answer (c) is incorrect be-

cause a disclaimer is issued when an auditor does not have an opinion on the financial statements. Likewise, answer (d), a disclaimer and a "subject to" qualified report, is incorrect for the above reasons.

70. (581,A1,31)   (c)   The requirement is for a circumstance in which an updated "subject to" opinion should be issued. The discovery of an uncertainty in a subsequent period will lead either to a "subject to" qualified opinion or a disclaimer (para 505.06-.07). Answer (a) is incorrect because it eliminates the need for a "subject to" qualified report. Answer (b) is incorrect because the discovery of an uncertainty in the current period does not affect the prior-period statements. Answer (d) is incorrect because the restatement of prior-period statements will typically result in an unqualified opinion.

71. (581,A1,33)   (c)   The requirement is for a circumstance in which an adverse opinion would be appropriate. An adverse opinion may be necessary in cases in which financial statements depart from generally accepted accounting principles, in this case, pension plan accounting. Answer (a) is incorrect because a lack of independence will lead to a disclaimer. Answer (b) is incorrect because uncertainties lead to "subject to" qualifications or disclaimers. Answer (d) is incorrect because an auditor will generally disclaim an opinion in cases in which significant client-imposed scope restrictions exist.

72. (581,A1,52)   (d)   The requirement is to determine what a predecessor auditor must do before an audit report is re-issued. Answer (d), obtaining a letter of representation, is correct; the auditor must also read the current financial statements and compare them to the prior-period statements (para 505.09). Answer (a) is incorrect since the various Statements on Auditing Standards contain no requirement that the predecessor review the successor's working papers. Answers (b) and (c) are incorrect since they relate to procedures which the successor auditor will perform.

73. (581,A1,53)   (d)   The requirement is to determine the circumstance which will lead to a modification of an interim report. Departures from generally accepted accounting principles, which include adequate disclosure, require modification of the accountant's report (para 721.20). Normally neither an uncertainty [answer (a)] nor a lack of consistency [answer (b)] would cause a report modification (para 721.20). Reference to another accountant [answer (c)] is not considered a modification (para 721.19).

74. (581,A1,54)   (c)   The requirement is to determine principal auditor reporting responsibility when s/he finds it impractical to review the work of another auditor. In such cases, the principal auditor will make reference to the examination of the other auditor and issue an unqualified report (para 543.06). Answer (a) is incorrect because if it is appropriate for Thomas to be the principal auditor, and if Jones has issued an unqualified report, there is no reason to refuse to express an opinion. Answer (b) is incorrect because additional procedures are required when a decision is made not to make reference to the other auditor (para 543.12-.13). Answer (d) is incorrect because the division of responsibility within an audit report is not considered an "except for" qualified opinion.

ANSWER OUTLINE

Problem 1   Materiality

a1. Materiality is the relative significance of an account,
       item, activity, etc.
         Informative disclosure
         Proper presentation of financial statements
         Qualitatively: nature of the item
         Quantitatively: relative size
       A misstatement is material if it affects a decision
       of the user

b1. Materiality and review of IC determine scope of
       examination
         Thus emphasis will vary among engagements

b2. Auditor emphasizes larger and more sensitive trans-
       actions
         Lower sampling rate is used on smaller amounts
       Errors must be evaluated for degree of significance

c.   Criteria for assessing materiality depends on circum-
       stances
         E.g., effect on key ratios and earnings
         Materiality is estimated to be 5% to 20% of net
           income
         Sensitive items are material even in minor amounts
         Relative size is more important than absolute size
         Cumulative effect of exceptions is also important

d1. Unqualified when misstatements are immaterial

d2. Qualified when misstatements are material
         But overall opinions still may be rendered
         Or if uncertainty, then a "subject to" opinion

d3. Adverse if auditor's exceptions are so material
         I.e., statements are not presented fairly

d4. Disclaimer if scope limitations prevent forming an
       opinion

d5. Piecemeal opinions have been precluded by para 48,
       SAS 2

UNOFFICIAL ANSWER

Problem 1   Materiality

a. The concept of materiality refers to the relative
significance of an account, activity or item to informative disclosure and a proper presentation of financial position and the results of operations. Materiality has qualitative and quantitative aspects; both the
nature of the item and its relative size enter into its
evaluation.

An accounting misstatement is said to be
material if knowledge of the misstatement will affect
the decisions of the average intelligent reader of the
financial statements. Financial statements are misleading if they omit a material fact or include so
many immaterial matters as to be confusing. In his
examination, the auditor concentrates his efforts in
proportion to degrees of materiality and relative
risk and disregards immaterial items.

b.   1.   The materiality of an account or activity
          and the results of the review of internal
          control determine the scope of the audi-
          tor's examination. Emphasis will not be
          uniform among engagements; for example,
          more attention will be paid to inventories
          in a manufacturing company than in a ser-
          vice company. In the former, inventories
          normally constitute a large portion of
          assets, and misstatement vitally affects
          net income. In contrast, the quantities
          of supplies on hand at a service company
          usually are minor.

     2.   In executing his audit program the auditor
          will stress review of the larger and more
          sensitive transactions. He cannot ignore
          the transactions which are immaterial by
          themselves and material cumulatively, but
          a lower sampling rate may be used.

          When he finds errors, the auditor
          must assess the degree of significance. In
          doing this his concept of materiality will
          not be based solely upon the size of the
          error, particularly if the error was noted
          in a test rather than a 100% review. When
          critical (or significant) errors are discovered
          in tests, the auditor will generally extend
          the scope of his examination to confirm
          his finding. Once he has established an
          estimate of the degree of error present in
          the financial statements, he may then dis-
          cuss with the client the necessity for ad-
          justment.

c. The relevant criteria for assessing materiality will
depend upon the circumstances and the nature of the
item and will vary greatly among companies. For
example, an error in current assets or current liabilities will be more important for a company with a
flow of funds problem than for one with adequate
working capital.

The effect upon net income (or earnings per
share) is the most commonly used measure of materi-

ality. This reflects the prime importance attached to net income by investors and other users of the statements. The effects upon assets and equities are also important as are misstatements of individual accounts and subtotals included in the financial statements. The auditor will note the effects of misstatements on key ratios such as gross margin, the current ratio or the debt-equity ratio and will consider such special circumstances as the effects on debt agreement covenants and the legality of dividend payments.

There are no rigidly accepted standards or guidelines for assessing materiality. The lower bound of materiality has been variously estimated at 5% to 20% of net income, but the determination will vary based upon the individual case and might not fall within these limits. Certain items, such as a questionable loan to a company officer, may be considered material even when minor amounts are involved. In contrast a large misclassification among expense accounts may not be deemed material if there is no misstatement of net income.

The CPA will be more concerned with the relative size of the item (in terms of the particular company's financial position and results of operations) than its absolute size. Usually he will base decisions upon the normal level of an account or activity— thus, if reported net income this year is $100,000, but based upon past experience and future expectations, normal net income is $1,000,000, an adjustment with an income effect of $20,000 probably will not be considered material unless unusual circumstances are involved. The income tax effect of errors also should be considered.

The auditor should determine and assess the effects of exceptions not only individually but also cumulatively. Adjustments passed in prior years because of immateriality should be included in this cumulative assessment to the extent that they affect the current year.

d. The CPA's assessment of the materiality of his exceptions to financial statements will influence his selection of the type of auditor's opinion as follows:

1. Unqualified Opinion
    If the effects of a misstatement are immaterial, the auditor will make no opinion qualification.

2. Qualified Opinion
    a. If the effects of a misstatement are material, but the auditor can still render an overall opinion as to financial position and the results of operations, he will qualify his opinion, generally by the use of phrases including the terms "except" or "exception."

    b. If his qualification is based upon an uncertain situation, but he can still render an overall opinion, the auditor will qualify his opinion by the use of a phrase including the term "subject to."

3. Adverse Opinion
    If an auditor's exceptions are so material that he feels the overall financial position or results of operations are not presented fairly, he will issue an adverse opinion. He will state that the financial statements do not present fairly the financial position or results of operations in conformity with generally accepted accounting principles. A disclaimer of opinion would not be appropriate in these circumstances.

4. Disclaimer of Opinion
    If the scope of his examination has been so limited, or such unusual uncertainties exist, that he does not have sufficient evidence to form an opinion upon the fairness of presentation of the financial statements as a whole, the auditor will disclaim any opinion on the financial statements.

5. Piecemeal Opinion
    Discussion omitted here.

ANSWER OUTLINE

Problem 2   Report Modifications

Audit report is a one-way communication
    It must fairly communicate auditor's opinion to report reader
Situation I hinges on losing a law suit
    And impact on financial statements
    Based on relative magnitude of dollar effect
Confirm uncertainty of outcome with client lawyer
Magnitude of a loss may require disclaimer of opinion
    Also the effect of a loss must be verified
    I.e., client may be overstating effects of loss
    Also length of time of impact of decision is necessary

In Situation II relative magnitude is important
   The franchise amounts to 20% of assets
   Can client recover franchise cost from future sales
Evaluate client's past performance in similar products
Consider auditor's expertise to evaluate cost recovery
  probability
Base decision on documentation and thoroughness of client
   Including minutes of negotiations
   Possibly outside expert's opinion
   Determine effect of franchise failure on going concern

UNOFFICIAL ANSWER

Problem 2   Report Modifications

In deciding the type of auditor's report to issue, Burke must always keep in mind that his report is a one-way communication which must fairly communicate his opinion to the report reader. He has a clear responsibility to guard against misleading the report reader.

Situation I

In situation I, Burke must consider the probability of Willingham losing the lawsuit and what impact this will have on the fair presentation of the financial statements. The impact would first be measured by the relative magnitude of the dollar effect in relation to other items in the financial statements such as net income, total fixed assets, or total net assets.

In gathering his evidence Burke would have confirmed the uncertainty of the outcome of the lawsuit with Willingham's independent legal counsel. With Willingham's consent Burke might want to get an opinion of another independent legal counsel such as his own. If legal counsel cannot give an opinion on the outcome of the lawsuit it would be unreasonable to assume Burke will have the expertise necessary to make this decision. But he should have the expertise to evaluate the effect on the financial statements if the lawsuit is lost. In this evaluation he should consider the impact of other ramifications such as existing commitments and union contracts at that plant.

His evaluation of the aggregate effect of an adverse decision will determine the type of report he will issue. If he concludes that the consequences of losing the lawsuit are of such a widespread nature as to have a pervasive impact on the financial statements and that the company cannot continue as a going concern, he will most likely issue a disclaimer of opinion because he does not have the expertise to evaluate the outcome of the case.

In reaching his decision, Burke must consider the validity of the statements made by management—namely, that the purchase of the required equipment is not economically feasible, that the plant would have to be closed, that the plant and its production equipment would have only minimal resale value, and that the production could not be recovered at other plants. In this respect, Burke should consider any past experience of Willingham or other similar companies. For example, if Willingham had been required to install pollution-control equipment in other plants and had done so economically, Burke may consider Willingham's statement on the current situation as overreacting. If this were the case, Burke may need to reevaluate the relative magnitude of the dollar impact of closing the plant in relation to an independent evaluation of the economic feasibility of installing the pollution-control equipment.

Burke must also consider how long it will take before there is an impact on the financial statements. There may be evidence that the case will be litigated for a number of years; or, if the case is lost, that the court may allow Willingham an extended period of time to install pollution-control equipment. Under these circumstances Burke may consider the possible outcome to have little effect on decisions applicable to the current financial statements because the postponement would lower the expected relative magnitude in relation to the current financial statements and would also give the company time to increase its ability to absorb the impact of an adverse decision. Thus, this exception may not be relevant to the current year's report.

Situation II

In situation II, Burke must again consider the relative magnitude of the dollar effect in relation to other items in the financial statements. Since the franchise amounts to 20% of Willingham's assets, Burke should be most concerned over the probability and timing of Willingham's recovering the franchise cost from future sales. His measure of this would most likely be based on two other considerations.

First would be the past experience, if any, of Willingham in similar ventures. If Willingham has a good record of past performance in developing similar products, Burke may be satisfied that the probability of the recovery is high.

Second, Burke should consider if he, as an auditor, has the expertise to determine the probability of the recovery of the franchise cost. This consideration is necessary for Burke to determine if he can accept the responsibility for the evaluation of the item relative to fair presentation in the financial statements.

In reaching a decision, Burke must evaluate the underlying documentation and especially the thoroughness and objectivity with which Willingham's management investigated the franchise and possibility of success before entering into the agreement. Burke should have studied minutes and notes of the negotiations leading to the purchase and financial projections of the overall effect on Willingham's operations of adding the franchise. In addition, while gathering evidence

for reaching this decision, Burke might want to obtain, with Willingham's consent, an independent expert's opinion on the marketing prospects of the newly patented product.

Burke should also consider the nature of the item—whether it relates to a specific matter or a general condition. Is the exception only a matter of realization of a specific asset or is there a question of whether Willingham can continue as a going concern if it cannot recover the cost of the franchise? In the latter case the exception could permeate the financial statements and make a reader's appraisal of them virtually impossible.

ANSWER OUTLINE
NOTE: The outline format of the Unofficial Answer precludes the necessity for an Answer Outline
Problem 3   Example Reports

UNOFFICIAL ANSWER

Problem 3   Example Reports

Report No.	Deficiency	Reason	Correction
1	(1) There is not a clear indication of the division of responsibility between the principal auditor and the other auditors.	Since the principal auditor has decided to make reference in his report to the examination made by other auditors and not assume responsibility for their work, he should indicate clearly the division of responsibility between himself and the other auditors in expressing his opinion on the financial statements.	To indicate the division of responsibility between the auditors, the report should disclose the magnitude of the portion of the financial statements examined by the other auditors. This is usually done by stating in the scope paragraph the dollar amount or percentages of one or more of the following: total assets, total revenues, or other appropriate criteria, whichever most clearly reveals the portion of the financial statements examined by the other auditors.
	(2) The opinion is qualified by use of the phrase "except for the report of the other auditors."	Reference in the report of the principal auditor to the fact that part of the examination was performed by other auditors should not be construed as a qualification of the opinion or as being inferior in professional standing to a report in which no reference is made.	This error could be corrected by the principal auditor reporting that his opinion is based upon his examination and the report of other auditors.

Report No.	Deficiency	Reason	Correction
II	(1) Even though the financial statements are unaudited, the auditor's report refers to certain audit procedures that he performed.	When financial statements are unaudited, the mention of any auditing procedures that may have been performed may cause the reader to believe that the financial statements were audited; therefore, he may place undue reliance on them. The auditor is responsible for giving a clear-cut indication of the character of his examination, if any, and the degree of responsibility he is taking.	Delete reference to any auditing procedures and report only that the statements are unaudited and that he expresses no opinion on them
	(2) The auditor's report provides negative assurance that the financial statements are fairly presented in conformity with generally accepted accounting principles applied on a consistent basis.	When financial statements are unaudited, any reference to generally accepted accounting principles applied on a consistent basis may temper the disclaimer of opinion and cause the reader to believe they were, in fact, audited. Negative assurance is permissible in special situations, (e.g., letters to underwriters) but never to cover data which purports to present financial position, results of operations, or changes in financial position.	Delete the negative assurance phrase and any reference to generally accepted accounting principles applied on a consistent basis.
III*	(1) The first sentence of the report states that the examination was made in accordance with generally accepted auditing standards.	The examination has not been made in accordance with generally accepted auditing standards because the second general standard requires that the auditor be independent. This sentence is also inconsistent with the final sentence of the report which states that the financial statements were not audited.	Delete the first sentence.

Report No.	Deficiency	Reason	Correction
	(2) The auditor disclosed the reason for lack of independence—his wife owns 5% of the stock of the company.	This disclosure might confuse the reader; i.e., the reader may not believe that this investment prevents the auditor from being independent and he may, therefore, place undue reliance on the auditor's report and the financial statements. Since independence is a matter of professional judgment, the reader should not be called upon to make this judgment.	Delete the reason for lack of independence.

*   The following comments are not addressed to the deficiencies in Auditor's Report II and, as such, are not responsive to the question: Notwithstanding, given the purposes for which the financial statements were to be used, at least a moral, if not an ethical, question is raised as to whether the CPA should have accepted this engagement knowing he was not independent and would thus have to disclaim an opinion on the financial statements. A CPA's report based on lack of independence adds nothing to the credibility of the financial statements on which the CPA reports. The attest function is unique to the CPA. Independence, in turn, is a critical element of the attest function. Take the attest function away, and the public loses the benefit of a process and service which, by law, it has assigned to CPAs.

We have found no official pronouncement which would preclude a CPA from accepting an engagement when he lacks independence. However, the spirit, if not the letter, of the AICPA Code of Professional Ethics would seem to require a CPA to consider the relevant facts and exercise his professional judgment in deciding whether to accept an engagement when he knows he is not independent.

ANSWER OUTLINE

Problem 4   Assurances Given

a.   Knowledge of an entity's business assists the auditor in

a1.   Identifying areas of special consideration

a2.   Assessing conditions under which accounting data are produced, processed, reviewed, and accumulated within the organization

a3.   Evaluating the reasonableness of estimates, e.g., valuation of inventories, depreciation, allowances for doubtful accounts, and percentage of completion of long-term contracts

a4.   Evaluating reasonableness of management representations

a5.   Making judgments about appropriateness of accounting principles applied and adequacy of disclosures

a6.   Perceiving conflicts of interest and planning of internal control evaluations

b.   Assurances provided by the statement that financial statements are presented "fairly . . . in conformity with generally accepted accounting principles applied on a consistent basis." include

b1.   Accounting principles selected and applied have general acceptance

b2.   Accounting principles are appropriate in the circumstances

b3.   Financial statements, including the related notes, are informative of matters that may affect their use, understanding and interpretation

b4.   Information presented in financial statements is classified and summarized in a reasonable manner (neither too detailed nor too condensed)

b5.   Financial statements reflect underlying events and transactions within a range of acceptable limits

b6.   Comparability of financial statements between periods has not been materially affected by changes in accounting principles

UNOFFICIAL ANSWER

Problem 4   Assurance Given

a.   Knowledge of the entity's business helps the auditor in—

· Identifying areas that may need special consideration.

· Assessing conditions under which accounting data are produced, processed, reviewed, and accumulated within the organization.

· Evaluating the reasonableness of estimates, such as valuation of inventories, depreciation, allowances for doubtful accounts, and percentage of completion of long-term contracts.

· Evaluating the reasonableness of management representations.

· Making judgments about the appropriateness of the accounting principles applied and the adequacy of disclosures.

· Perceiving conflicts of interest and planning internal control evaluations.

b.   When the auditor states that the financial statements are presented "fairly . . . in conformity with generally accepted accounting principles applied on a consistent basis," the public is assured that in the auditor's judgment—

· The accounting principles selected and applied have general acceptance.

· The accounting principles are appropriate in the circumstances.

· The financial statements, including the related notes, are informative of matters that may affect their use, understanding, and interpretation.

· The information presented in the financial statements is classified and summarized in a reasonable manner (neither too detailed nor too condensed).

· The financial statements reflect the underlying events and transactions within a range of acceptable limits.

· The comparability of financial statements between periods has not been materially affected by changes in accounting principles.

ANSWER OUTLINE

Problem 5   Audit Report Deficiencies

1. Balance sheet is as of a certain date and income statement for period of time

2. Reference to GAAS omitted

3. Reference to tests of accounting records omitted

4. Reference to client instructions is misleading

5. Reference to "complete" audit is misleading

6. No reference to statement of changes in financial position

7. Explanatory paragraph is improper

8. Negative assurance is not permissible

9. Reference to the "above explanation" is unclear

10. Minor errors should not be mentioned

11. Reference is needed to GAAP

12. Reference to consistency is inadequate

UNOFFICIAL ANSWER

Problem 5   Audit Report Deficiencies

Scope Paragraph

1. The scope section reference to the financial statements is inaccurate. The balance sheet examination is made as of a certain date, while the statement of income and retained earnings examination is made for the period ending on a certain date.

2. The standard reference to adherence to generally accepted auditing standards is omitted. All examinations of financial statements should be conducted in accordance with these standards, and this should be noted in the scope paragraph.

3. The standard reference to tests of accounting records and other procedures considered necessary in the circumstances is omitted. Such reference is necessary for a clear understanding of the scope of the work performed.

4. The reference to instructions from the client should be omitted because such reference might mislead readers into concluding that the client determined the adequacy of audit scope or that there was some limitation on the procedures.

5. The reference to a "complete" audit is unclear and should be omitted. It implies a detailed audit of all transactions, which is unnecessary and apparently was not performed. The auditor has already indicated in the first sentence that an audit was performed, and the remainder of the standard scope

paragraph would adequately describe the nature of the examination, assuming that all necessary procedures were applied.

6. There is no reference to the statement of changes in financial position. This statement is one of the basic statements that must be presented by the company and should be examined by the auditor and included in the audit report. If the company does not wish to present this statement, the middle paragraph should state that the company declined to present a statement of changes in financial position for the year ended July 31, 1975, and that presentation of such statement summarizing the company's financing and investing activities and other changes in financial position is required by Opinion No. 19 of the Accounting Principles Board. In such a case the auditor should qualify the auditor's report because the omission results in an incomplete presentation because it is a departure from an opinion of the Accounting Principles Board.

Explanatory (Middle) Paragraph

7. An auditor may decide against an opinion qualification but still wish to emphasize explanatory material regarding the financial statements. That apparently was the intent here, but the subject matter of this paragraph is considered inappropriate for such treatment. It is not directed toward clarification of the statements or disclosure of a subsequent event that actually has occurred. Rather, it may be typified as financial analysis and interpretation.

8. The last sentence is inappropriate because it might leave the readers with the impression that the scope of the examination was limited. In such circumstances, reports should not be issued which temper the qualification or disclaimer of opinion by the inclusions of expressions such as "nothing came to our attention that would indicate that sales have not been properly recorded." Such negative assurance is not permissible.

Opinion Paragraph

9. The phrase "with the explanation given above" is not clear, does not denote an

opinion exception, and should not be used in the opinion paragraph. If the auditor intends to provide additional explanatory material in the report without qualifying the opinion, the auditor should not refer to this material in the opinion paragraph.

10. If minor errors are immaterial individually and cumulatively, no reference to them should be made in the auditor's report. Inserting such a comment might produce unwarranted doubts about the accuracy of the statements.

11. The auditor's criteria for evaluating fairness are generally accepted accounting principles, and the report should make reference to them. Pronouncements of the Accounting Principles Board and Financial Accounting Standards Board, which are cited as criteria in this report, constitute authoritative support for some generally accepted accounting principles, but they do not cover all aspects of financial accounting and reporting. Other sources of support must be sought in areas where these opinions are inapplicable or lacking in coverage.

12. The reference to consistency is inadequate. The auditor's responsibility is to indicate whether accounting principles have been consistently applied in the current period in relation to the preceding period. Since only one year's statements are provided, this requirement is not satisfied by noting that accounting principles were applied consistently throughout the period. The responsibility to express an opinion as to consistency is not affected by the circumstance that this is the auditor's first audit or that only one year's statements are provided. If the auditor cannot form an opinion as to consistency, he must disclaim an opinion.

ANSWER OUTLINE

Problem 6   Write Report

a. Address to partnership (Bale & Booster)

b. Financial statements examined
b1. Statement of assets, liabilities, and capital: income tax (cash) basis as of 12-31
b2. Statement of revenues and expenses and changes in partners' capital accounts: income tax (cash) basis for year ended 12-31

c.   Reference to GAAS

d.   Reference to tests of accounting records

e.   Reference to other auditing procedures as considered necessary

f.   Explanation of income tax (cash basis)

f1.   Certain revenue and related assets recognized when cash received

f2.   Certain expenses recognized when paid

g.   Financial statements not in accordance with GAAP

h.   Separate paragraph disclosing patent infringement litigation

h1.   Damage not subject to estimate

i.   Opinion refers to fair presentation of statements on income tax (cash) basis

i1.   Statement of assets, liabilities, and capital as of 12-31

i2.   Statement of revenues and expenditures and changes in partners' capital accounts for year ended 12-31

j.   Auditor should refer to footnote describing income tax (cash) basis

k.   Opinion should refer to consistency

UNOFFICIAL ANSWER

Problem 6 Write Report

Addressee:

We have examined the statement of assets, liabilities, and capital (income tax (cash) basis) of Bale & Booster, a partnership, as of December 31, 1979, and the related statement of revenue and expenses (income tax (cash) basis) and the statement of changes in partners' capital accounts (income tax (cash) basis) for the year then ended. Our examination was made in accordance with generally accepted auditing standards and, accordingly, included such tests of the accounting records and such other auditing procedures as we considered necessary in the circumstances.

As described in note X, the partnership's policy is to prepare its financial statements on the accounting basis used for income tax purposes; consequently, certain revenue and related assets are recognized when

received rather than when earned, and certain expenses are recognized when paid rather than when the obligation is incurred. Accordingly, the accompanying financial statements are not intended to present financial position and results of operations in conformity with generally accepted accounting principles.

In addition, the company is involved in continuing litigation relating to patent infringement. The amount of damages, if any, resulting from this litigation cannot be determined at this time.

In our opinion, the financial statements referred to above present fairly the assets, liabilities, and capital of the Bale & Booster partnership as of December 31, 1979, and its revenue and expenses and changes in its partners' capital accounts for the year then ended, on the income tax (cash) basis of accounting as described in note X, which basis has been applied in a manner consistent with that of the preceding year.

Date   *Firm Name*

ANSWER OUTLINE

Problem 7   Rewrite Report

1.   Address to company directors or stockholders

2.   Balance sheets as of 12-31 and other statements for years ending

3.   Reference to GAAS

4.   Reference to tests of accounting records

5.   Reference to other auditing procedures as considered necessary

6.   Auditor should report on comparative statements

7.   Separate paragraph disclosing debentures restrictions

8.   Separate paragraph disclosing omission of statement of changes

9.   Separate paragraph disclosing litigation

10.   Opinion qualified for omission of debentures data

11.   Opinion qualified for omission of statement of changes

12.   Opinion subject to results of litigation

13.   Opinion refers to fair presentation of financial position

14.   Opinion refers to fair presentation of results of operations

15. Opinion should refer to consistency (no qualification)

16. Auditor should concur with the change

17. Auditor should refer to footnote describing change

18. No mention necessary of accounts receivable confirmations

UNOFFICIAL ANSWER

Problem 7   Rewrite Report

To the Board of Directors of
The Excelsior Corporation

We have examined the balance sheets of the Excelsior Corporation at December 31, 1975, and December 31, 1974, and the related statements of income and retained earnings for the years then ended. Our examinations were made in accordance with generally accepted auditing standards and, accordingly, included such tests of the accounting records and such other auditing procedures as we considered necessary in the circumstances.

On January 15, 1974, the corporation issued debentures in the amount of $10,000,000 for the purpose of financing expansion of plant facilities. The debenture agreement restricts the payment of future cash dividends to earnings after December 31, 1980.

The corporation declined to present statements of changes in financial position for the years ended December 31, 1975, and December 31, 1974. Presentation of such statements summarizing the corporation's financing and investing activities and other changes in its financial position is required by Opinion No. 19 of the Accounting Principles Board.

As discussed in footnote 11 of the financial statements, the corporation is the defendant in a lawsuit relating to (state type of litigation). The ultimate outcome of the lawsuit cannot presently be determined, and no provision for any liability that may result has been made in the financial statements.

In our opinion, except for the omission of the debenture information discussed in the second paragraph and except that the omission of statements of changes in financial position results in an incomplete presentation as explained in the third paragraph and subject to the effects, if any, on the financial statements of the ultimate resolution of the litigation discussed in the preceding paragraph, the aforementioned financial statements present fairly the financial position of Excelsior Corporation at December 31, 1975, and December 31, 1974, and the results of its operations for the years then ended in conformity with generally accepted accounting principles applied on a consistent basis after restatement for the change, with which we concur, in the method of accounting for long-term construction contracts as described in footnote 12 of the financial statements.

Roscoe, CPA
(Signed)
March 15, 1976

Item that need not be part of the auditor's report

The only item in "other information" that is not part of the above auditor's report is Roscoe's failure to perform normal accounts receivable audit confirmation procedures. Such procedures are required, but if circumstances such as the timing of the auditor's work make it impracticable or impossible to perform them, the auditor can use alternate procedures to obtain satisfaction concerning the validity of the accounts receivable. If alternate procedures are used, the auditor need not make reference in the report to them or to the omission of normal procedures.

MULTIPLE CHOICE QUESTIONS (1—29)

1. When using a statistical sampling plan, the auditor would probably require a smaller sample if the
    a.   Population increases.
    b.   Desired precision interval narrows.
    c.   Desired reliability decreases.
    d.   Expected error occurrence rate increases.

2. Use of the ratio estimation sampling technique to estimated dollar amounts is **inappropriate** when
    a.   The total book value is known and corresponds to the sum of all the individual book values.
    b.   A book value for each sample item is unknown.
    c.   There are some observed differences between audited values and book values.
    d.   The audited values are nearly proportional to the book values.

3. Jones, CPA, believes the industry-wide occurrence of client billing errors is 3% and has established a maximum acceptable occurrence rate of 5%. In the review of client invoices Jones should use
    a.   Discovery sampling.
    b.   Attribute sampling.
    c.   Stratified sampling.
    d.   Variable sampling.

4. A CPA examining inventory may appropriately apply sampling for attributes in order to estimate the
    a.   Average price of inventory items.
    b.   Percentage of slow-moving inventory items.
    c.   Dollar value of inventory.
    d.   Physical quantity of inventory items.

5. If certain forms are not consecutively numbered
    a.   Selection of a random sample probably is not possible.
    b.   Systematic sampling may be appropriate.
    c.   Stratified sampling should be used.
    d.   Random number tables cannot be used.

6. The objective of precision in sampling for compliance testing on an internal control system is to
    a.   Determine the probability of the auditor's conclusion based upon reliance factors.
    b.   Determine that financial statements taken as a whole are not materially in error.
    c.   Estimate the reliability of substantive tests.
    d.   Estimate the range of procedural deviations in the population.

7. The major reason that the difference and ratio estimation methods would be expected to produce audit efficiency is that the
    a.   Number of members of the populations of differences or ratios is smaller than the number of members of the population of book values.
    b.   Beta risk may be completely ignored.
    c.   Calculations required in using difference or ratio estimation are less arduous and fewer than those required when using direct estimation.
    d.   Variability of the populations of differences or ratios is less than that of the populations of book values or audited values.

8. Auditors who prefer statistical to judgmental sampling believe that the principal advantage of statistical sampling flows from its unique ability to
    a.   Define the precision required to provide audit satisfaction.
    b.   Provide a mathematical measurement of uncertainty.
    c.   Establish conclusive audit evidence with decreased audit effort.
    d.   Promote a more legally defensible procedural approach.

9. An auditor selects a preliminary sample of 100 items out of a population of 1,000 items. The sample statistics generate an arithmetic mean of $60, a standard deviation of $6 and a standard error of the mean of $.60. If the sample was adequate for the auditor's purposes and the auditor's desired precision was plus or minus $1,000, the minimum acceptable dollar value of the population would be
    a. $61,000.
    b. $60,000.
    c. $59,000.
    d. $58,800.

10. Which of the following sampling plans would be designed to estimate a numerical measurement of a population, such as a dollar value?
    a.   Numerical sampling.
    b.   Discovery sampling.
    c.   Sampling for attributes.
    d.   Sampling for variables.

11.   An auditor selects a preliminary sample of 100 items out of a population of 1,000 items. The sample statistics generate an arithmetic mean of $120, a standard deviation of $12 and a standard error of the mean of $1.20. If the sample was adequate for the auditor's purposes and the auditor's desired precision was plus or minus $2,000, the minimum acceptable dollar value of the population would be

    a. $122,000.
    b. $120,000.
    c. $118,000.
    d. $117,600.

12.   Auditors often utilize sampling methods when performing tests of compliance. Which of the following sampling methods is most useful when testing for compliance?

    a.   Attribute sampling.
    b.   Variable sampling.
    c.   Unrestricted random sampling with replacement.
    d.   Stratified random sampling.

13.   Which of the following best describes the distinguishing feature of statistical sampling?

    a.   It requires the examination of a smaller number of supporting documents.
    b.   It provides a means for measuring mathematically the degree of uncertainty that results from examining only part of a population.
    c.   It reduces the problems associated with the auditor's judgment concerning materiality.
    d.   It is evaluated in terms of two parameters: statistical mean and random selection.

14.   When using statistical sampling for tests of compliance an auditor's evaluation of compliance would include a statistical conclusion concerning whether

    a.   Procedural deviations in the population were within an acceptable range.
    b.   Monetary precision is in excess of a certain predetermined amount.
    c.   The population total is not in error by more than a fixed amount.
    d.   Population characteristics occur at least once in the population.

15.   In performing a review of his client's cash disbursements, a CPA uses systematic sampling with a random start. The primary disadvantage of systematic sampling is that population items

    a.   Must be reordered in a systematic pattern before the sample can be drawn.
    b.   May occur in a systematic pattern, thus negating the randomness of the sample.
    c.   May occur twice in the sample.
    d.   Must be replaced in the population after sampling to permit valid statistical inference.

16.   From prior experience, a CPA is aware of the fact that cash disbursements contain a few unusually large disbursements. In using statistical sampling, the CPA's best course of action is to

    a.   Eliminate any unusually large disbursements which appear in the sample.
    b.   Continue to draw new samples until no unusually large disbursements appear in the sample.
    c.   Stratify the cash-disbursements population so that the unusually large disbursements are reviewed separately.
    d.   Increase the sample size to lessen the effect of the unusually large disbursements.

17.   In connection with his test of the accuracy of inventory counts, a CPA decides to use discovery sampling. Discovery sampling may be considered a special case of

    a.   Judgemental sampling.
    b.   Sampling for variables.
    c.   Stratified sampling.
    d.   Sampling for attributes.

18.   Precision is a statistical measure of the maximum likely difference between the sample estimate and the true but unknown population total, and is directly related to

    a.   Reliability of evidence.
    b.   Relative risk.
    c.   Materiality.
    d.   Cost benefit analysis.

19.   An important statistic to consider when using a statistical sampling audit plan is the population variability. The population variability is measured by the

    a.   Sample mean.
    b.   Standard deviation.
    c.   Standard error of the sample mean.
    d.   Estimated population total minus the actual population total.

20.   What is the primary objective of using stratification as a sampling method in auditing?

    a.   To increase the confidence level at which a decision will be reached from the results of the sample selected.
    b.   To determine the occurrence rate for a given characteristic in the population being studied.

c.   To decrease the effect of variance in the total population.

d.   To determine the precision range of the sample selected.

21.   For a large population of cash disbursement transactions, Smith, CPA, is testing compliance with internal control by using attribute sampling techniques.   Anticipating an occurrence rate of 3 percent Smith found from a table that the required sample size is 400 with a desired upper precision limit of 5 percent and reliability of 95 percent.   If Smith anticipated an occurrence rate of only 2 percent but wanted to maintain the same desired upper precision limit and reliability the sample size would be closest to

a.   200.
b.   400.
c.   533.
d.   800.

22.   To satisfy the auditing standard to make a proper study and evaluation of internal control, Harvey Jones, CPA, uses statistical sampling to test compliance with internal control procedures. Why does Jones use this statistical-sampling technique?

a.   It provides a means of measuring mathematically the degree of reliability that results from examining only a part of the data.

b.   It reduces the use of judgment required of Jones because the AICPA has established numerical criteria for this type of testing.

c.   It increases Jones' knowledge of the client's prescribed procedures and their limitations.

d.   It is specified by generally accepted auditing standards.

23.   There are many kinds of statistical estimates that an auditor may find useful, but basically every accounting estimate is either of a quantity or of an error rate.   The statistical terms that roughly correspond to "quantities" and "error rate", respectively, are

a.   Attributes and variables.
b.   Variables and attributes.
c.   Constants and attributes.
d.   Constants and variables.

24.   How should an auditor determine the precision required in establishing a statistical sampling plan?

a.   By the materiality of an allowable margin of error the auditor is willing to accept.

b.   By the amount of reliance the auditor will place on the results of the sample.

c.   By reliance on a table of random numbers.

d.   By the amount of risk the auditor is willing to take that material errors will occur in the accounting process.

25.   Which of the following is an advantage of systematic sampling over random number sampling?

a.   It provides a stronger basis for statistical conclusions.

b.   It enables the auditor to use the more efficient " sampling with replacement" tables.

c.   There may be correlation between the location of items in the population, the feature of sampling interest, and the sampling interval.

d.   It does not require establishment of correspondence between random numbers and items in the population.

26.   An auditor makes separate compliance and substantive tests in the accounts payable area which has good internal control.   If the auditor uses statistical sampling for both of these tests, the confidence level established for the substantive test is normally

a.   The same as that for tests of compliance.

b.   Greater than that for tests of compliance.

c.   Less than that for tests of compliance.

d.   Totally independent of that for tests of compliance.

MAY 1981 QUESTIONS

27.   An advantage of using statistical sampling techniques is that such techniques

a.   Mathematically measure risk.

b.   Eliminate the need for judgmental decisions.

c.   Define the values of precision and reliability required to provide audit satisfaction.

d.   Have been established in the courts to be superior to judgmental sampling.

28.   In estimation sampling for attributes, which one of the following must be known in order to appraise the results of the auditor's sample?

    a.   Estimated dollar value of the population.

    b.   Standard deviation of the values in the population.

    c.   Actual occurrence rate of the attribute in the population.

    d.   Sample size.

29.   The auditor faces a risk that the examination will not detect material errors which occur in the accounting process. In regard to minimizing this risk, the auditor primarily relies on

    a.   Substantive tests.

    b.   Compliance tests.

    c.   Internal control.

    d.   Statistical analysis.

PROBLEMS

Problem 1 Statistical Judgment (572,A3)
        (25 to 30 minutes)

   The use of statistical sampling techniques in an examination of financial statements does not eliminate judgmental decisions.

Required:

  a. Identify and explain four areas where judgment may be exercised by a CPA in planning a statistical sampling test.

  b. Assume that a CPA's sample shows an unacceptable error rate. Describe the various actions that he may take based upon this finding.

  c. A nonstratified sample of 80 accounts payable vouchers is to be selected from a population of 3,200. The vouchers are numbered consecutively from 1 to 3,200 and are listed, 40 to a page, in the voucher register. Describe four different techniques for selecting a random sample of vouchers for review.

Problem 2 Statistical Sampling Computations (577,A7)

       (15 to 25 minutes)

   During the course of an audit engagement, a CPA attempts to obtain satisfaction that there are no material misstatements in the accounts receivable of a client. Statistical sampling is a tool that the auditor often uses to obtain representative evidence to achieve the desired satisfaction. On a particular engagement an auditor determined that a material misstatement in a population of accounts would be $35,000. To obtain satisfaction the auditor had to be 95% confident that the population of accounts was not in error by $35,000. The auditor decided to use unrestricted random sampling with replacement and took a preliminary random sample of 100 items (n) from a population of 1,000 items (N). The sample produced the following data:

  Arithmetic mean of sample items ($\bar{x}$) $4,000
  Standard deviation of sample items (SD) $ 200

The auditor also has available the following information:

  Standard error of the mean (SE) = SD ÷ $\sqrt{n}$
  Population precision (P) = N x R x SE

Partial List of Reliability Coefficients

If Reliability Coefficient (r) is	Then Reliability is
1.70	91.086%
1.75	91.988
1.80	92.814
1.85	93.568
1.90	94.256
1.95	94.882
1.96	95.000
2.00	95.450
2.05	95.964
2.10	96.428
2.15	96.844

Required:

  a. Define the statistical terms "reliability" and "precision" as applied to auditing.

  b. If all necessary audit work is performed on the preliminary sample items and no errors are detected,

   (1) What can the auditor say about the total amount of accounts receivable at the 95% reliability level?

   (2) At what confidence level can the auditor say that the population is not in error by $35,000?

  c. Assume that the preliminary sample was sufficient,

   (1) Compute the auditor's estimate of the population total.

   (2) Indicate how the auditor should relate this estimate to the client's recorded amount.

MULTIPLE CHOICE ANSWERS

1.	c	7.	d	13.	b	19.	b	25.	d
2.	b	8.	b	14.	a	20.	c	26.	c
3.	b	9.	c	15.	b	21.	a	27.	a
4.	b	10.	d	16.	c	22.	a	28.	d
5.	b	11.	c	17.	d	23.	b	29.	a
6.	d	12.	a	18.	c	24.	a		

EXPLANATION OF MULTIPLE CHOICE ANSWERS

1. (1180,A1,20)   (c)   The requirement is to identify the situation which would result in a smaller sample. A lower reliability (i.e., a higher chance of error) decreases the required sample size. A larger population (answer (a)), a narrower precision interval (answer (b)) or an increase in the expected error occurrence rate (answer (d)) all result in a larger sample.

2. (1180,A1,41)   (b)   The ratio estimation sampling technique is based on comparing the ratio of the book value to the audited value of the sampled items. Answer (b) is the answer because the method cannot be used when there is no book value to make the comparison. The circumstances described in answers (a) and (c) are necessary for ratio point and interval estimation. Answer (d) describes the circumstances in which the use of ratio estimation will be efficient in terms of required sample size.

3. (1180,A1,43)   (b)   A typical application of attribute sampling in auditing is to estimate error rates in areas such as billing customers. Answer (a), discovery sampling, is incorrect since it can only be used effectively in situations in which expected error rates are very low (e.g., less than 1 percent). Answer (c) is incorrect since stratification is most frequently utilized in variables sampling. Answer (d) variable sampling is used in situations in which the auditor wishes to estimate dollar or quantity errors, not error rates.

4. (1180,A1,59)   (b)   Attribute sampling may be used to estimate the percentage of slow-moving inventory items by defining the attribute of interest as items which are either (1) slow-moving or (2) not slow-moving. Answers (a), (c), and (d) all represent examples of variables sampling since either a dollar value or a quantity is being estimated.

5. (580,A1,5) (b)   The requirement is the correct statement concerning a statistical sampling application where the population consists of forms which are not consecutively numbered. Answer (b) is correct because it is not incorrect, i.e., all the other answers are incorrect. Systematic sampling is a procedure where a ran-

dom start is obtained and then every n^{th} item is selected. For example, a sample of forty from a population of a thousand would require selecting every 25th item after obtaining a random start between items 1 through 25.

Answer (a) is incorrect because selection of a random sample is possible even though the population is not consecutively numbered. Answer (c) is incorrect because there is no special reason for using stratified sampling. Stratified sampling breaks down the population into subpopulations and applies different selection methods to each subpopulation. This selection method is used when the population consists of different types of items, e.g., large balances and small balances. Answer (d) is incorrect because random number tables can be used even though the forms are not consecutively numbered. If random numbers are selected for which there are no forms, they are ignored. This is the same as if there were 86,000 items in a consecutively numbered population and random numbers selected between 86,000 and 99,999 are ignored.

6.   (580,A1,27) (d) Precision in sampling for compliance testing is the plus or minus (range) in the error rate (procedural deviations). Answer (a) is incorrect because "the auditor's conclusion based upon reliance factors" is a nonsense concept. Answer (b) is incorrect because compliance testing relates to the system of internal control and the system of internal control of and by itself does not provide assurance that the financial statements taken as a whole are not materially in error. In addition to an effective system of internal control, substantive tests including analytical review procedures and tests of transactions and balances are required. Answer (c) is incorrect because the reliability of substantive tests is independent of compliance testing.

7.   (580,A1,43) (d)   Difference and ratio estimation methods are statistical sampling methods. They measure the difference between audit and book values or the ratio of audit to book values. As these differences should not be great, the population of these differences will have little variance. In statistical sampling the less variation in a population, the smaller the required sample to provide an estimate of the population. In other words, difference and ratio estimation methods are more efficient because the differences between audit and book values are expected to vary less than the actual items in the population.

Answer (a) is incorrect because the number of members in the population for differences or ratio methods would be the same as the number of items in the population for a direct estimation method. In difference sampling, many items would be zero because audit and book are the same, and in ratio sampling, many of the members would be 1 for the same reason. Answer (b) is incorrect because beta risk can never be ignored, as beta risk is the risk of accepting an incorrect (unacceptable) population. Alpha risk is the risk of rejecting a correct (acceptable) population. Answer (c) is incorrect because the calculations required in difference and ratio sampling are similar to those used in direct estimation sampling.

8. (1179,A1,6) (b) Statistical sampling permits quantitative or mathematical assessment of the precision of the sample (how close the sample represents the population) and the reliability of the sample (the percentage of times the sample accurately represents the population). Thus, statistical sampling provides a measurement of the uncertainty of the sample. See para 320b.06-.10. Answer (a) is incorrect because auditors must use their judgment to determine the desired precision before implementing statistical sampling tests. Answer (c) is incorrect because conclusive audit evidence is not possible, i.e., a little risk always exists without 100% verification. Answer (d) is incorrect because existing statutes or case laws do not provide a basis for determining whether statistical sampling is a more legally defensible approach than judgmental sampling.

9. 1179,A1,38) (c) The requirement is the minimum acceptable dollar value of the population. Given desired precision of ± $1,000, 1,000 items, and a mean of $60, the auditor's estimated population value is $60,000 ± $1,000, i.e., $59,000 to $61,000.

10. 579,A1,18) (d) The requirement is the sampling plan which would estimate a numerical measurement of a population, such as a dollar value. Sampling for variables or estimation of variables sampling is designed to estimate the mean item in the population from which the total value of the population can be estimated. Answer (a) is incorrect because numerical sampling is a nonsense term. All quantitative sampling must be numerical. Answers (b) and (c) are incorrect because discovery sampling is a special case of sampling for attributes. Sampling for attributes samples binary data, i.e., right or wrong, error or nonerror, good or bad, etc.

11. (1177,A1,44) (c) The requirement is the minimum acceptable dollar value of the population. The auditor has specified a precision of $2,000, i.e., plus or minus limits about the sample estimate. Here the means of the sample is $120 and the population size is 1,000. Thus, based on the sample, the population is estimated to be $120,000. Since the pre-

cision limits are $2,000, the minimum acceptable dollar value would be $118,000. The standard deviation (here $12) is a statistical index of variation within the population. The standard error of the mean is the standard deviation of the distribution of sample means. The relation of the $12 standard deviation to the standard error of the mean of $1.20 exists, because the standard error of the mean is the standard deviation of the population divided by the square root of the sample size, i.e., $12/\sqrt{100} = 1.20.

12. (578,A1,2) (a) Compliance tests utilize attribute sampling. Attribute sampling is based on the binomial distribution which describes yes/no decisions, and error/nonerror situations. Answer (b) is incorrect because variables sampling utilizes the normal distribution which is continuous, i.e., elements of the population can take on a continuum of the variables, such as receivables and inventories. Answers (c) and (d) are incorrect because they are sample selection methods rather than sampling methods. Unrestricted random sampling with replacement is a sampling method where population items can be reselected. The advantage of unrestricted random sampling with replacement is ease of underlying statistical calculations. Stratified random sampling is the stratification of the population, and then application of random sampling to each strata.

13. (578,A1,30) (b) Statistical sampling provides a means of quantifying sample precision and sampling risk. Sample precision is the expected closeness of sample results to the actual population true values. Risk of accepting a sample is the percentage of times the sample will not be representative of the population (it is calculated as one minus the confidence level). Answer (a) is incorrect because statistical sampling, in contrast to judgmental sampling, may require a larger or smaller sample, i.e., there is no specified relationship. Answer (c) is incorrect because the auditor has the same materiality judgments with judgmental as with statistical sampling. Answer (d) is incorrect because there are many parameters with which to evaluate statistical sampling, e.g., ease of use, quantifiability, confidence level, precision, cost, etc.

14. (578,A1,56) (a) In compliance tests the auditor is concerned with the population error rate. Thus the auditor wishes to determine that the error rate is within an acceptable range. Answer (b) is incorrect because compliance tests are not concerned with monetary amounts but rather with error rates. Answer (c) is incorrect because auditor concern is with the error rate, not the absolute

number of error rates in a given population. Answer (d) is a nonsense answer—"population characteristics occur at lease once in the population."

15. (573,A2,17) (b) Systematic sampling is a sample selection method wherein every *nth* item is selected for observation. Thus, if a sample of one hundred were to be taken from 1,000, one might select every 10th item in the population after beginning with a random number between one and ten. The problem with systematic sampling is that population items may occur in a systematic fashion, e.g., large items may be coded with a nine in the units digit.

16. (573,A2,18) (c) The few unusually large cash disbursements will significantly increase the variance in the population of all cash receipts which will in turn increase the required sample size. An alternative is to **use** two homogeneous populations. One population would contain the unusually large disbursements, and the other population would contain the rest of the cash disbursements. This methodology is known as stratified sampling and will reduce the required sample size.

17. (573,A2,19) (d) Both discovery sampling and acceptance sampling are special cases of sampling for attributes. Discovery sampling is a special case of acceptance sampling. In discovery sampling there should be no opportunity to observe more than one occurrence, because it is designed to sample for serious or critical errors. Once a critical or serious error is discovered, the sampling plan will probably be abandoned and a more comprehensive examination undertaken.

18. (1176,A1,7) (c) Precision and reliability are statistical terms. Precision relates to materiality and reliability relates to the reasonableness of the opinion. Precision is the plus or minus limits around the sample result, i.e., the range in which the actual population parameter will be acceptable to the auditor. Reliability (or confidence level) indicates the number of times out of one hundred that the conclusions drawn, based upon the sample, will be correct (SAS 1, para 320A.03 and 320A.10). Relative risk refers to the requirement that additional audit work be undertaken in areas more susceptible to irregularities, e.g., where internal control would be weak (para 150.05 of SAS 1). Cost-benefit analysis refers to the need for a rational relationship between the cost of ob-

taining evidence and the usefulness of the evidence obtained (para 330.13 of SAS 1).

19. 1176,A2,33) (b) The size or value of a group of items can be described in terms of a measure of variability. The common measures of central tendency are the mean (average), mode, and median. The common measures of dispersion are range, standard deviation, variance (which is the standard deviation squared), and quartile deviations.

The requirement here is to identify an index of population variability. The standard deviation is a measure of population variability. The standard error of the sample mean is the standard deviation of the distribution of sample means (hypothetical distribution of many means of a constant sample size from the same population). The sample mean is the average of a sample.

Answer (d), the estimated population total minus the actual population total is sampling error if the estimated population was based upon a proper sampling method. It illustrates the concept of precision, i.e., the range about the sample size that would include the actual population perimeter. See para 320A.03 of SAS 1.

20. (575,A1,18) (c) Stratified sampling is a technique of breaking the population down into subpopulations and applying different sample selection methods to the subpopulations. Stratified sampling is used to minimize the variance within the overall population. Recall that as variance increases, so does the required sample size (because of the extreme values). Thus stratification allows the selection of subpopulations to reduce the effect of dispersion in the population.

21. ʻ(575,A2,31) (a) If the anticipated occurrence rate is reduced from .03 to .02 and the upper precision limit remains constant at .05, the precision is increased from .02 to .03. The effect of increasing or widening precision limits is to require less precision of the sample, and thus require a smaller sample size. Additionally, as the expected occurrence rate in attribute sampling (the mean of the binomial distribution) becomes smaller in size, the distribution of sample means become tighter, i.e., less dispersion, and a smaller sample size is required. Thus the sample size has to be reduced from 400 and the only alternative answer is (a). Using the formulas

for attribute sampling, however, the required sample size with an expected occurrence rate of 3% would be 291, given an infinite population as computed in the first formulation below. Changing the formula to an expected occurrence rate of .02 and precision .03 (.05 minus .02) results in a sample size of about 88 as computed below.

$$n = \frac{C^2 \cdot pq}{pre^2} = \frac{2^2 \cdot .97 \quad .03}{.02^2} = \frac{4 \cdot .0291}{.0004} = 291$$

$$n = \frac{2^2 \cdot .98 \cdot .02}{.03^2} = \frac{4 \cdot .0196}{.0009} = 88$$

22. (575,A2,38) (a) Statistical sampling provides a means of measuring mathematically the degree of reliability that results from examining only a sample of the population. See para 320B.06 of SAS 1. Answer (b) is incorrect because statistical sampling does not reduce the use of judgment by the CPA. Among other things the CPA must establish the confidence level, precision level, sampling method, and selection method, all of which require the auditor's judgment. Answer (c) is incorrect because statistical sampling has only to do with the selection of items or procedures to be examined by the auditor and the evaluation of the results of the auditor's examination. It does not have to do with the actual examination of items or procedures by the auditor. Answer (d) is incorrect as GAAS does not require statistical sampling for compliance tests. See para 320.62 of SAS 1.

23. (575,A2,39) (b) Statistical sampling accounting applications are either based on variables sampling or attribute sampling. Variables sampling is measurement of a continuous variable, i.e., a variable such as number of items in inventory or amount of accounts receivable. The variable being estimated can take on a continuum of values, e.g., zero to infinity. Variable sampling is based upon the normal distribution. Attribute sampling is based on the binomial distribution and sample items must be binary in nature, i.e., right or wrong, correct or incorrect etc. Attribute sampling is most applicable to tests of compliance and variables sampling is most applicable to substantive tests.

24. (1175,A2,27) (a) Precision is the plus or minus limits, or range, set by the auditor. The auditor must determine an acceptable range of an error rate for attribute sampling, or an acceptable range of the amount of inventory,

accounts receivable, etc. in variables sampling. Answer (b) is wrong because the amount of reliance refers to the confidence level of the sample. Answer (c) is a nonsense answer as the concept of reliance does not apply to a table of random numbers. Answer (d) is incorrect because the amount of risk is the complement of the level of confidence, e.g., a 95% confidence level results in a 5% level of risk.

25. (1175,A2,29) (d) Systematic sampling is a method of selecting sample items by beginning with one random item and then taking every *nth* item in the population. Divide the number of items in the population by the required sample size to determine n. Thus answer (d) is correct because one does not have to match items in the population with random numbers. Answer (a) is incorrect because systematic sampling when properly used is as good as any other sample selection method. Answer (b) is incorrect because systematic sampling does not require the use of random number tables beyond the selection of the first item. Answer (c) is incorrect because systematic sampling should not be used when there is a correlation between the location of items in the population, e.g., large balances, and their part or item number (for example, a system where large items have part numbers ending with the digit nine).

26. (1175,A2,30) (c) Discussion in Appendix B of Section 320 of SAS 1 assumes that reliability of confidence levels of compliance tests will be greater (usually 95% or 90%) than substantive test confidence levels. See para 320B.23 for discussion of reliability of compliance tests and para 320B.28 for reliability of substantive tests. Also see para 320B.35 for examples of related confidence levels of compliance tests and substantive tests. The basis for this assumption is the conclusion drawn in Appendix A that the reliance on compliance and substantive tests are combined. Also, in discussing substantive tests, para 320A.19 states "specifying (substantive) reliability levels that vary inversely with the subjective reliance assigned to internal control. . ."

Given a relatively high confidence level for compliance tests and a high compliance-substantive combined confidence level, the required confidence level for substantive tests will be less than the compliance confidence level.

MAY 1981 ANSWERS

27. (581,A1,11) (a) The requirement is to determine an advantage of statistical sampling. The distinguishing feature of statistical sampling is that it provides a means for measuring mathematically the degree of uncertainty that results from examining only a part of the data (para 320B.08). Answer (b) is incorrect since statistical sampling still requires the auditor to make judgmental decisions (e.g., set appropriate precision and reliability levels). While answer (c) is a correct statement insofar as it relates to auditor responsibility, it cannot be considered an advantage of statistical sampling. The courts have not definitively ruled on the merits of statistical vs. judgmental sampling, thus, answer (d) is incorrect.

28. (581,A1,18) (d) The requirement is to determine the information necessary to appraise the results of an attribute sample. Sample size is needed to evaluate the results. Answer (a) is incorrect because the estimated dollar value of the population is used only in variables sampling. Answer (b), the standard deviation of the values in the population, also deals with variables sampling. Answer (c) is incorrect since the auditor will not know the actual occurrence rate of the attribute in the population unless she/he audits the entire population.

29. (581,A1,24) (a) The requirement is to determine how auditors minimize the risk of not detecting material errors which occur in the accounting process. The purpose of substantive tests is to obtain evidence as to the validity and the propriety of accounting treatment of transactions and balances or, conversely, of errors or irregularities (para 320.70). Answer (b) is incorrect because compliance tests provide assurance that the accounting control procedures are being applied as prescribed. Answer (c) is incorrect since the question presumes the existence of a breakdown in internal control. Answer (d) is incorrect because the auditor may or may not choose to use a statistical approach in the substantive tests she/he performs.

ANSWER OUTLINE

Problem 1   Statistical Judgment

a. Sampling decisions requiring auditor judgment
  Sample design
  Sample method
  Sample selection technique
  Specified precision (confidence interval)
  Specified reliability (confidence level)

b. Alternatives available to an unacceptable error rate
  Enlarge sample
  Isolate type of error
  Have client reprocess the data
  Qualify opinion

c. Nonstratified random sample selection techniques
  Random sample
    Table of random numbers
    Terminal digits
    Random number generator
  Systematic sample
    Every *n*th item
    Randomly varying sample interval
    Every random *n*th item
  Cluster sample

UNOFFICIAL ANSWER

Problem 1   Statistical Judgment

a. Areas where judgment may be exercised by a CPA in planning a statistical sampling test include:

1. The sample design—the CPA must define the population in terms of its size, the characteristics of significance to the audit and what constitutes an error.

2. Sampling method—the CPA must determine the type of sampling method to be used (e.g., sampling for attributes, discovery sampling, acceptance sampling) and the most efficient means of selecting the sample.

3. Selection technique—the CPA must decide which sampling selection process is to be used (e.g., stratified sampling, cluster sampling, systematic sampling.)

4. Specified precision (confidence interval)—this is the range within which the sample statistic (e.g., error rate) may fall and still be acceptable to the CPA. It will be based upon the materiality of the account or activity being examined and the nature of the error or other characteristic.

5. Specified reliability (confidence level)—this is the probability that the sample statistic will fall with the specified precision limits if the population error rate is acceptable. It will be based upon the materiality of the account or activity being examined, the nature of the error and the reliance placed upon internal control.

b. If the CPA's sample shows an unacceptable error rate, he may take the following actions:

1. He may enlarge his sample or select another sample. If his sample design has been sound, additional sampling will confirm his original findings in most cases. But the auditor may wish to have greater statistical accuracy if the sample is to be the basis of a recommended adjustment.

2. He may isolate the type of error and expand his examination as it relates to the transactions that give rise to that type of error.

3. He may ask the client to reprocess the data and prepare an adjusting journal entry and then make an appropriate review of the client's work. In some cases it may be satisfactory to prepare the adjusting journal entry based upon the auditor's sample—this approach is most applicable when stratified sampling was used or both the specified precision and specified reliability were high.

4. If the client refuses to accept or investigate the auditor's finding or error, or if it is impracticable to determine the overall degree of error with acceptable precision, the CPA should evaluate the necessity of opinion qualification. This determination will depend upon materiality—the nature of the error and its effects upon financial statement presentation. Based upon the degree of materiality, the CPA may render an unqualified, a qualified ("except for") or adverse opinion; a "subject to" opinion is not justified. The CPA will disclaim an opinion if his scope is so limited that he cannot form an opinion on the fairness of presentation of the financial statements as a whole.

c. Techniques for selecting a nonstratified random sample of accounts-payable vouchers include the following:

Random Sample. A random sample is a sample of a given size drawn from a population in a manner such that every possible sample of that size is equally likely to be drawn. Items may be selected randomly by:

1. Table of Random Numbers. Use one of a number of published tables. Using four columns in the table, select the first 80 numbers which fall within the range 1 to 3,200. The starting point in the table should be selected randomly and the path to be followed through the table should be set in advance and followed consistently.

2. Terminal Digits. Select two two-digit numbers randomly and examine all vouchers ending in this number. Select one more two-digit number randomly and examine every other voucher ending in this number, making the initial selection (from the first hundred or second hundred vouchers) on a random basis.

3. Random Number Generator. Using a utility computer program, generate a list of 80 random numbers.

Systematic Sample. A systematic sample is drawn by selecting every *nth* item beginning with a random start.

1. Every nth Item. Select every 40th voucher after selecting the initial voucher (from 1 to 40) randomly.

2. Randomly Varying Sample Interval. Select an initial item randomly and after the selection of each sample item obtain a random number between 1 and 80 and add it to the number of the previously selected item to obtain the number of the next item.

3. Every Random *nth* Item. Select a number from a random number table between 1 and 40 and select that item from among the first 40 items. A second random number between 1 and 40 (plus 40) would be used to select the item within the second group of 40 items, etc.

Cluster Sample. Instead of drawing individual sample items, select groups of contiguous sample items. For example, using a random number table, select two pages within the voucher register and review all vouchers on those pages. (A disadvantage of this method is that consecutive vouchers may be for similar expenditures and the sample may not provide adequate coverage of the range of expenditures.)

ANSWER OUTLINE

Problem 2   Statistical Sampling Computations

a.   Precision and reliability are interdependent and inseparable
Reliability is percentage of times range will include actual population value
Reliability relates to the reasonableness of data
  Mathematical probability that sample value will not differ from population value by more than the stated precision
Precision is range of values about the sample result
Precision limits are highest and lowest values of the range
Precision relates to materiality

b1. $P = N \times R \times SE$

$$= 1{,}000 \times 1.96 \times \left(\frac{\$200}{\sqrt{100}} \right)$$

$$= \$39{,}200$$

where   N = items in population
R = reliability
SE = standard error

b2. $P = N \times R \times SE$

$$R = \frac{P}{N \times SE}$$

$$= \frac{\$35{,}000}{1{,}000 \times \$20}$$

$= 1.75$ which is 91.9% reliability

c1.   Population total is mean ($4,000) x items in population (1,000) = $4,000,000

c2.   Precision limits are $4,000,000 ± $35,000
If client's balance is outside acceptable range, extend sample

UNOFFICIAL ANSWER

Problem 2   Statistical Sampling Computations

a.   Reliability and precision are statistical terms that are interdependent and inseparable. Precision is expressed as a range of values, plus or minus, around the sample result, and "reliability," or confidence, is expressed as the proportion of such ranges from all possible similar samples of the same size that would include the actual population value. Stated in another way, precision expresses the range of limits within which the sample result is expected to be accurate, while reliability expresses the mathematical probability of achieving that degree of accuracy.

The terms are usefully adapted to the auditor's purposes by relating precision to materiality and reliability to the reasonableness of the basis for the auditor's opinion.

b. (1) At the 95% confidence level the auditor can be assured that the estimated population total is not in error by more than or less than $39,200.

$$P = N \times R \times SE$$
$$P = 1,000 \times 1.96 \times \frac{200}{\sqrt{100}} = 1,000 \times$$
$$1.96 \times \frac{200}{10} = 1,000 \times 1.96 \times 20 = \$39,200$$

(2) The auditor can be 91.988% confident that the estimated population total is not in error by more than or less than $35,000.

$$P = N \times R \times SE$$
$$R = \frac{P}{N \times SE} = \frac{\$35,000}{1,000 \times 20} = 1.75$$

R = 91.988%

c. (1) The estimated population total, or point estimate, based on the preliminary sample data would be equal to the arithmetic mean multiplied by the number of items in the population or $4,000 × 1,000 = $4,000,000.

(2) If the original sample is sufficient, the auditor would be willing to accept an accounts receivable balance that is within plus or minus $35,000 from this amount. The auditor would be willing to accept an accounts receivable balance anywhere between $3,965,000 ($4,000,000 − $35,000) and $4,035,000 ($4,000,000 + $35,000). If the client's accounts receivable balance is not within this range, the auditor could not accept the client's balance based on the work performed on the preliminary sample items. The auditor would likely extend the sample by selecting additional items until the recorded amount fell within the precision limits. The additional sample items would have to change the sample mean by an amount sufficient enough to make the point estimate acceptable.

MULTIPLE CHOICE QUESTIONS (1—52)

1.   When erroneous data are detected by computer program controls, such data may be excluded from processing and printed on an error report. The error report should most probably be reviewed and followed up by the
- a.   EDP control group.
- b.   System analyst.
- c.   Supervisor of computer operations.
- d.   Computer programmer.

2.   The auditor's preliminary understanding of the client's EDP system is primarily obtained by
- a.   Inspection.
- b.   Observation.
- c.   Inquiry.
- d.   Evaluation.

3.   An auditor will use the EDP test data method in order to gain certain assurances with respect to the
- a.   Input data.
- b.   Machine capacity.
- c.   Procedures contained within the program.
- d.   Degree of keypunching accuracy.

4.   To replace the human element of error detection associated with manual processing, a well-designed automated system will introduce
- a.   Dual circuitry.
- b.   Programmed limits.
- c.   Echo checks.
- d.   Read after write.

5.   The program flowcharting symbol representing a decision is a
- a.   Triangle.
- b.   Circle.
- c.   Rectangle.
- d.   Diamond.

6.   The client's EDP exception reporting system helps an auditor to conduct a more efficient audit because it
- a.   Condenses data significantly.
- b.   Highlights abnormal conditions.
- c.   Decreases the EDP compliance testing.
- d.   Is an efficient EDP input control.

7.   Which of the following is an advantage of generalized computer audit packages?
- a.   They are all written in one identical computer language.
- b.   They can be used for audits of clients that use differing EDP equipment and file formats.
- c.   They have reduced the need for the auditor to study input controls for EDP-related procedures.
- d.   Their use can be substituted for a relatively large part of the required compliance testing.

8.   In a daily computer run to update checking account balances and print-out basic details on any customer's account that was overdrawn, the overdrawn account of the computer programmer was never printed. Which of the following control procedures would have been most effective in detecting this irregularity?
- a.   Use of the test-deck approach by the auditor in testing the client's program and verification of the subsidiary file.
- b.   Use of a running control total for the master file of checking account balances and comparison with the printout.
- c.   A program check for valid customer code.
- d.   Periodic recompiling of programs from documented source decks, and comparison with programs currently in use.

9.   If a control total were to be computed on each of the following data items, which would best be identified as a hash total for a payroll EDP application?
- a.   Gross pay.
- b.   Hours worked.
- c.   Department number.
- d.   Number of employees.

10.   After a preliminary phase of the review of a client's EDP controls, an auditor may decide not to perform compliance tests related to the control procedures within the EDP portion of the client's internal control system. Which of the following would not be a valid reason for choosing to omit compliance tests?
- a.   The controls appear adequate.
- b.   The controls duplicate operative controls existing elsewhere in the system.
- c.   There appear to be major weaknesses that would preclude reliance on the stated procedure.
- d.   The time and dollar costs of testing exceed the time and dollar savings in substantive testing if the compliance tests show the controls to be operative.

11. In updating a computerized accounts receivable file, which one of the following would be used as a batch control to verify the accuracy of the posting of cash receipts remittances?
    a. The sum of the cash deposits plus the discounts less the sales returns.
    b. The sum of the cash deposits.
    c. The sum of the cash deposits less the discounts taken by customers
    d. The sum of the cash deposits plus the discounts taken by customers

12. Which of the following is a computer test made to ascertain whether a given characteristic belongs to the group?
    a. Parity check.
    b. Validity check.
    c. Echo check.
    d. Limit check.

13. Which of the following is necessary to audit balances in an on-line EDP system in an environment of destructive updating?
    a. Periodic dumping of transaction files.
    b. Year-end utilization of audit hooks.
    c. An integrated test facility.
    d. A well documented audit trail.

14. Accounting control procedures within the EDP activity may leave no visible evidence indicating that the procedures were performed. In such instances, the auditor should test these accounting controls by
    a. Making corroborative inquiries.
    b. Observing the separation of duties of personnel.
    c. Reviewing transactions submitted for processing and comparing them to related output.
    d. Reviewing the run manual.

15. The most efficient and least costly method of dumping information for purposes of maintaining a backup file is from disk to
    a. Dump.
    b. Printout.
    c. Cards.
    d. Tape.

16. A primary advantage of using generalized audit packages in the audit of an advanced EDP system is that it enables the auditor to
    a. Substantiate the accuracy of data through self-checking digits and hash totals.
    b. Utilize the speed and accuracy of the computer.
    c. Verify the performance of machine operations which leave visible evidence of occurrence.
    d. Gather and store large quantities of supportive evidential matter in machine readable form.

17. Compliance testing of an advanced EDP system
    a. Can be performed using only actual transactions since testing of simulated transactions is of no consequence.
    b. Can be performed using actual transactions or simulated transactions.
    c. Is impractical since many procedures within the EDP activity leave no visible evidence of having been performed.
    d. Is inadvisable because it may distort the evidence in master files.

18. Any assessment of the operational capabilities of a computer system must consider downtime. Even in a fully-protected system, downtime will exist because of
    a. Electrical power losses.
    b. Unscheduled maintenance.
    c. Unauthorized entry.
    d. Keypunching errors.

19. The normal sequence of documents and operations on a well-prepared systems flowchart is
    a. Top to bottom and left to right.
    b. Bottom to top and left to right.
    c. Top to bottom and right to left.
    d. Bottom to top and right to left.

20. So that the essential accounting control features of a client's electronic data processing system can be identified and evaluated, the auditor must, at a minimum, have
    a. A basic familiarity with the computer's internal supervisory system.
    b. A sufficient understanding of the entire computer system.
    c. An expertise in computer systems analysis.
    d. A background in programming procedures.

21. Program controls, in an electronic data processing system, are used as substitutes for human controls in a manual system. Which of the following is an example of a program control?

    a.   Dual read.
    b.   Echo check.
    c.   Validity check.
    d.   Limit and reasonableness test.

22. Some electronic data processing accounting control procedures relate to all electronic data processing activities (general controls) and some relate to specific tasks (application controls). General controls include

    a.   Controls designed to ascertain that all data submitted to electronic data processing for processing have been properly authorized.
    b.   Controls that relate to the correction and resubmission of data that was initially incorrect.
    c.   Controls for documenting and approving programs and changes to programs.
    d.   Controls designed to assure the accuracy of the processing results.

23. An auditor obtains a magnetic tape that contains the dollar amounts of all client inventory items by style number. The information on the tape is in no particular sequence. The auditor can best ascertain that no consigned merchandise is included on the tape by using a computer program that

    a.   Statistically selects samples of all amounts.
    b.   Excludes all amounts for items with particular style numbers that indicate consigned merchandise.
    c.   Mathematically calculates the extension of each style quantity by the unit price.
    d.   Prints on paper the information that is on the magnetic tape.

24. An internal **administrative control** that is sometimes used in connection with procedures to detect unauthorized or unexplained computer usage is

    a.   Maintenance of a computer tape library.
    b.   Use of file controls.
    c.   Maintenance of a computer console log.
    d.   Control over program tapes.

25. Auditors often make use of computer programs that perform routine processing functions such as sorting and merging. These programs are made available by electronic data processing companies and others and are specifically referred to as

    a.   User programs.
    b.   Compiler programs.
    c.   Supervisory programs.
    d.   Utility programs.

26. Parity checks, read-after-write checks, and duplicate circuitry are electronic data processing controls that are designed to detect

    a.   Erroneous internal handling of data.
    b.   Lack of sufficient documentation for computer processes.
    c.   Illogical programming commands.
    d.   Illogical uses of hardware.

27. Where computers are used, the effectiveness of internal accounting control depends, in part, upon whether the organizational structure includes any incompatible combinations. Such a combination would exist when there is no separation of the duties between

    a.   Documentation librarian and manager of programming.
    b.   Programmer and console operator.
    c.   Systems analyst and programmer.
    d.   Processing control clerk and keypunch supervisor.

28. Accounting functions that are normally considered incompatible in a manual system are often combined in an electronic data processing system by using an electronic data processing program, or a series of programs. This necessitates an accounting control that prevents unapproved

    a.   Access to the magnetic tape library.
    b.   Revisions to existing computer programs.
    c.   Usage of computer program tapes.
    d.   Testing of modified computer programs.

29. Which of the following is a characteristic of an integrated system for data processing?

    a.   An integrated system is a real-time system where files for different functions with similar information are separated.
    b.   A single input record describing a transaction initiates the updating of all files associated with the transaction.
    c.   Parallel operations strengthen internal control over the computer processing function.
    d.   Files are maintained according to organizational functions such as purchasing, accounts payable, sales, etc.

30. The primary purpose of a generalized computer audit program is to allow the auditor to
   a. Use the client's employees to perform routine audit checks of the electronic data processing records that otherwise would be done by the auditor's staff accountants.
   b. Test the logic of computer programs used in the client's electronic data processing systems.
   c. Select larger samples from the client's electronic data processing records than would otherwise be selected without the generalized program.
   d. Independently process client electronic data processing records.

31. Which of the following employees normally would be assigned the operating responsibility for designing an electronic data processing installation, including flowcharts of data processing routines?
   a. Computer programmer.
   b. Data processing manager.
   c. Systems analyst.
   d. Internal auditor.

32. An auditor should be familiar with a client's electronic data processing hardware and software. An important element of the client's software is the program. Another element of software is the
   a. Cathode ray tube (CRT).
   b. Central processing unit (CPU).
   c. Magnetic tape drive.
   d. Compiler.

33. When an on-line, real-time (OLRT) electronic data processing system is in use, internal control can be strengthened by
   a. Providing for the separation of duties between keypunching and error listing operations.
   b. Attaching plastic file protection rings to reels of magnetic tape before new data can be entered on the file.
   c. Preparing batch totals to provide assurance that file updates are made for the entire input.
   d. Making a validity check of an identification number before a user can obtain access to the computer files.

34. Which of the following would lessen internal control in an electronic data processing system?
   a. The computer librarian maintains custody of computer program instructions and detailed listings.
   b. Computer operators have access to operator instructions and detailed program listings.
   c. The control group is solely responsible for the distribution of all computer output.
   d. Computer programmers write and debug programs which perform routines designed by the systems analyst.

35. The machine-language program that results when a symbolic-language program is translated is called a (an)
   a. Processor program.
   b. Object program.
   c. Source program.
   d. Wired program.

36. In connection with the study of internal control, an auditor encounters the following flowcharting symbols:

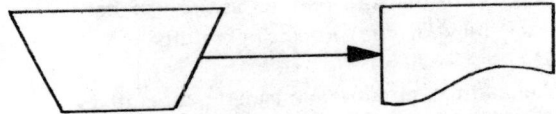

The auditor would conclude that
   a. A master file has been created by a manual operation.
   b. A master file has been created by a computer operation.
   c. A document has been generated by a computer operation.
   d. A document has been generated by a manual operation.

37. Automated equipment controls in an electronic data processing system are designed to detect errors arising from
   a. Operation of the electronic data processing equipment.
   b. Lack of human alertness.
   c. Incorrect input and output data.
   d. Poor management of the electronic data processing installation.

38. A control feature in an electronic data processing system requires the central processing unit (CPU) to send signals to the printer to activate the print mechanism for each character. The print mechanism, just prior to printing, sends a signal back to the

CPU verifying that the proper print position has been activated. This type of hardware control is referred to as

    a.   Echo control.

    b.   Validity control.

    c.   Signal control.

    d.   Check digit control.

39. An electronic data processing technique, which collects data into groups to permit convenient and efficient processing, is known as

    a.   Document-count processing.

    b.   Multi-programming.

    c.   Batch processing.

    d.   Generalized-audit processing.

40. Which of the following employees in a company's electronic data processing department should be responsible for designing new or improved data processing procedures?

    a.   Flowchart editor.

    b.   Programmer.

    c.   Systems analyst.

    d.   Control-group supervisor.

41. A computer service center processes, for an auditor's client, financial data that has a material effect on that client's financial statements. The independent auditor need not consider a review of the service center controls if

    a.   The service center controls have already been reviewed by the internal audit team of the client.

    b.   The service center processes data exclusively for the audit client and its subsidiaries.

    c.   The user controls relied upon, which are external to the service center, are adequate to provide assurance that errors and irregularities may be discovered with reasonable promptness.

    d.   The service center is a partially-owned subsidiary of the client company, whose financial statements are examined by another CPA.

42. An independent auditor studies and evaluates a client's electronic data processing system. The auditor's study portion includes two phases: (1) a review or investigation of the system and (2) tests of compliance. The latter phase might include which of the following?

    a.   Examination of systems flowcharts to determine whether they reflect the current status of the system.

    b.   Examination of the systems manuals to determine whether existing procedures are satisfactory.

    c.   Examination of the machine room log book to determine whether control information is properly recorded.

    d.   Examination of organization charts to determine whether electronic data processing department responsibilities are properly separated to afford effective control.

43. An auditor can use a generalized computer audit program to verify the accuracy of

    a.   Data processing controls.

    b.   Accounting estimates.

    c.   Totals and sub-totals.

    d.   Account classifications.

44. The purpose of using generalized computer programs is to test and analyze a client's computer

    a.   Systems.

    b.   Equipment.

    c.   Records.

    d.   Processing logic.

45. In an electronic data processing system, automated equipment controls or hardware controls are designed to

    a.   Arrange data in a logical sequential manner for processing purposes.

    b.   Correct errors in the computer programs.

    c.   Monitor and detect errors in source documents.

    d.   Detect and control errors arising from use of equipment.

46. Which of the following client electronic data processing (EDP) systems generally can be audited without examining or directly testing the EDP computer programs of the system?

    a.   A system that performs relatively uncomplicated processes and produces detailed output.

    b.   A system that affects a number of essential master files and produces a limited output.

    c.   A system that updates a few essential master files and produces no printed output other than final balances.

    d.   A system that performs relatively complicated processing and produces very little detailed output.

47. What is the computer process called when data processing is performed concurrently with a particular activity and the results are available soon enough to influence the particular course of action being taken or the decision being made?

    a. Batch processing.
    b. Realtime processing.
    c. Integrated data processing.
    d. Random access processing.

MAY 1981 QUESTIONS

48. The computer system **most** likely to be used by a large savings bank for customers' accounts would be

    a. An on-line, real time system.
    b. A batch processing system.
    c. A generalized utility system.
    d. A direct access data base system.

49. In the study and review of a client's EDP internal control system, the auditor will encounter general controls and application controls. Which of the following is an application control?

    a. Dual read.
    b. Hash total.
    c. Systems flowchart.
    d. Control over program changes.

50. Assume that an auditor estimates that 10,000 checks were issued during the accounting period. If an EDP application control which performs a limit check for each check request is to be subjected to the auditor's test-data approach, the sample should include

    a. Approximately 1,000 test items.
    b. A number of test items determined by the auditor to be sufficient under the circumstances.
    c. A number of test items determined by the auditor's reference to the appropriate sampling tables.
    d. One transaction.

51. A procedural control used in the management of a computer center to minimize the possibility of data or program file destruction through operator error includes

    a. Control figures.
    b. Crossfooting tests.
    c. Limit checks.
    d. External labels.

52. The use of a header label in conjunction with magnetic tape is **most** likely to prevent errors by the

    a. Computer operator.
    b. Keypunch operator.
    c. Computer programmer.
    d. Maintenance technician.

REPEAT QUESTION

(581,A1,3)   Identical to item **32** above

<u>Problem 1</u>   Computerized Audit Programs
(580,A3)

(15 to 25 minutes)

After determining that computer controls are valid, Hastings is reviewing the sales system of Rosco Corporation in order to determine how a computerized audit program may be used to assist in performing tests of Rosco's sales records.

Rosco sells crude oil from one central location. All orders are received by mail and indicate the pre-assigned customer identification number, desired quantity, proposed delivery date, method of payment and shipping terms. Since price fluctuates daily, orders do not indicate a price. Price sheets are printed daily and details are stored in a permanent disc file. The details of orders are also maintained in a permanent disc file.

Each morning the shipping clerk receives a computer printout which indicates details of customers' orders to be shipped that day. After the orders have been shipped, the shipping details are inputted in the computer which simultaneously updates the sales journal, perpetual inventory records, accounts receivable, and sales accounts.

The details of all transactions, as well as daily updates, are maintained on discs which are available for use by Hastings in the performance of the audit.

Required:
a.   How may a computerized audit program be used by Hastings to perform substantive tests of Rosco's sales records in their machine readable form? **Do not discuss accounts receivable and inventory.**
b.   After having performed these tests with the assistance of the computer, what other auditing procedures should Hastings perform in order to complete the examination of Rosco's sales records?

<u>Problem 2</u>   CPA Knowledge of Computers (578,A4)

(15 to 25 minutes)

The following five topics are part of the relevant body of knowledge for CPAs having field work or immediate supervisory responsibility in audits involving a computer:

1. Electronic data processing (EDP) equipment and its capabilities.
2. Organization and management of the data processing function.
3. Characteristics of computer based systems.
4. Fundamentals of computer programming.
5. Computer center operations.

CPAs who are responsible for computer audits should possess certain general knowledge with respect to each of these five topics. For example, on the subject of EDP equipment and its capabilities, the auditor should have a general understanding of computer equipment and should be familiar with the uses and capabilities of the central processor and the peripheral equipment.

Required:
For each of the topics numbered 2 through 5 above, describe the general knowledge that should be possessed by those CPAs who are responsible for computer audits.

<u>Problem 3</u>   Grandfather-Father-Son Tapes (1171,A7)

(25 to 30 minutes)

Roger Peters, CPA, has examined the financial statements of the Solt Manufacturing Company for several years and is making preliminary plans for the audit for the year ended June 30, 1972. During this examination Mr. Peters plans to use a set of generalized computer audit programs. Solt's EDP manager has agreed to prepare special tapes of data from Company records for the CPA's use with the generalized programs.

The following information is applicable to Mr. Peters' examination of Solt's accounts payable and related procedures:

1.   The formats of pertinent tapes are on the following page.
2.   The following monthly runs are prepared:
a.   Cash disbursements by check number.
b.   Outstanding payables.
c.   Purchase journals arranged (1) account charged and (2) by vendor.

3.   Vouchers and supporting invoices, receiving reports and purchase order copies are filed by vendor code. Purchase orders and checks are filed numerically.

4. Company records are maintained on magnetic tapes. All tapes are stored in a restricted area within the computer room. A grandfather-father-son policy is followed for retaining and safeguarding tape files.

Required:

a. Explain the grandfather-father-son policy. Describe how files could be reconstructed when this policy is used.

b. Discuss whether Company policies for retaining and safeguarding the tape files provide adequate protection against losses of data.

c. Describe the controls that the CPA should maintain over:
1. Preparing the special tape.
2. Processing the special tape with the generalized computer audit programs.

d. Prepare a schedule for the EDP manager outlining the data that should be included on the special tape for the CPA's examination of accounts payable and related procedures. This schedule should show the:
1. Client tape from which the item should be extracted.
2. Name of the item of data.

Master File—Vendor Name

Vendor Code	Recd Type	Space	Blank	Vendor Name	Blank	Card Code 100

Master File—Vendor Address

Vendor Code	Recd Type	Space	Blank	Address—Line 1	Address—Line 2	Address—Line 3	Blank	Card Code 120

Transaction File—Expense Detail

Vendor Code	Recd Type	Voucher Number	Blank	Batch	Voucher Number	Voucher Date	Vendor Code	Invoice Date	Due Date	Invoice Number	Purchase Order Number	Debit Account	Prd Type	Product Code	Blank	Amount	Quantity	Card Code 160

Transaction File—Payment Detail

Vendor Code	Recd Type	Voucher Number	Blank	Batch	Voucher Number	Voucher Date	Vendor Code	Invoice Date	Due Date	Invoice Number	Purchase Order Number	Check Number	Check Date	Blank	Amount	Blank	Card Code 170

Problem 4 EDP Controls (579,A3)

(15 to 25 minutes)

When auditing an electronic data processing (EDP) accounting system, the independent auditor should have a general familiarity with the effects of the use of EDP on the various characteristics of accounting control and on the auditor's study and evaluation of such control. The independent auditor must be aware of those control procedures that are commonly referred to as "general" controls and those that are commonly referred to as "application" controls. General controls relate to all EDP activities and application controls relate to specific accounting tasks.

Required:

a. What are the general controls that should exist in EDP-based accounting systems?

b. What are the purposes of each of the following categories of application controls?

1. Input controls
2. Processing controls
3. Output controls

Problem 5 Audit of Computerized A/R (1179,A4)

(15 to 25 minutes)

In the past, the records to be evaluated in an audit have been printed reports, listings, documents and written papers, all of which are visible output. However, in fully computerized systems which employ daily updating of transaction files, output and files are frequently in machine-readable forms such as cards, tapes, or disks. Thus, they often present the auditor with an opportunity to use the computer in performing an audit.

Required:

Discuss how the computer can be used to aid the auditor in examining accounts receivable in such a fully computerized system.

MULTIPLE CHOICE ANSWERS

1.	a	12.	b	23.	b	34.	c	45.	d
2.	c	13.	d	24.	c	35.	c	46.	a
3.	c	14.	c	25.	d	36.	d	47.	b
4.	b	15.	d	26.	a	37.	a	48.	a
5.	d	16.	b	27.	b	38.	a	49.	b
6.	b	17.	b	28.	b	39.	c	50.	d
7.	b	18.	b	29.	b	40.	c	51.	d
8.	d	19.	a	30.	d	41.	c	52.	a
9.	c	20.	b	31.	c	42.	c		
10.	a	21.	d	32.	d	43.	c		
11.	d	22.	c	33.	d	44.	c		

EXPLANATION OF MULTIPLE CHOICE ANSWERS

1.   (1180,A1,3)   (a)   An error report should be reviewed and followed up by the EDP control group whose responsibility it is to supervise and monitor the input, operations, and distribution of output. Answer (b) is incorrect because the systems analyst is responsible for designing the system. Answer (c) s incorrect since the supervisor of computer operations is responsible for determining that programs are properly run (i.e., operations should be separate from error correction). Answer (d) is incorrect since the programmer should be limited to writing programs and the initial debugging thereof.

2. (1180,A1,12)   (c)   The requirement is the means by which an auditor obtains a "preliminary understanding" of the client's EDP system. As indicated in para 321.25, the auditor's preliminary understanding is ordinarily obtained by inquiry. Inspection (answer (a)), observation (answer (b)), and evaluation (answer (d)), are procedures performed in subsequent compliance testing (para 320.58—.59).

3. (1180,A1,25)   (c)   When using the test data approach the auditor processes dummy transactions through the client's computer program to test the controls within the program. Answer (a) s incorrect because the auditor is not attempting to gain assurance as to the inputted test data itself; this data consists of dummy transactions. Answers (b) and (d) are wrong since neither machine capacity nor keypunching accuracy are tested by these dummy transactions prepared by the auditor.

4. (1180,A1,47)   (b) Programmed limits in a computer program replace the human element of error detection by having the computer test inputs for reasonableness (e.g., no hourly employee's input hourly

wage rate should be higher than some established, known limit). Answer (a) is incorrect since dual circuitry is a double-wiring of the equipment to assure no malfunctioning. Answer (c) is incorrect since echo checks are a hardware control which involve transmitting data received by an output unit back to the source unit (e.g., to test whether the printer is operating). Answer (d) is incorrect; read after write does not take the place of human error detection since it is a procedure in which information is returned to the sending unit for review of its accuracy.

5.   (580,A1,10) (d) The flowcharting symbol which represents a decision is a diamond. On a flow chart it indicates which alternative path is to be followed. Answer (a) is incorrect because a triangle represents off-line storage. Answer (b) is incorrect because a circle with a straight line pointing to the right at the bottom of the circle represents a magnetic tape. Answer (c) is incorrect because a rectangle represents an operation which is a process resulting in a change in the information or in the flow direction.

6.   (580,A1,17) (b) The requirement is the function of an EDP exception reporting system. An exception reporting system highlights abnormal or unusual conditions. Answer (a) is incorrect because an exception reporting system only reports exceptions and does not condense data. Answer (c) is incorrect because an exception reporting system provides assistance to the analytical review segment of an audit rather than the compliance testing segment of an audit. Answer (d) is incorrect because an exception reporting system would report all exceptions, i.e., input, processing, and output exceptions.

7.   (580,A1,18) (b) The requirement is an advantage of generalized computer audit packages. As the term "generalized" implies, generalized computer audit packages can be used for audits of clients that use different EDP equipment and file formats. They are simply a very generalized input-output program. Answer (a) is incorrect because generalized computer audit packages are written in many computer languages. In fact, they must be written in the same language or a compatible language to the computer language used in the client's system. Answers (c) and (d) are incorrect because generalized computer audit packages may be used to assist the auditor in studying input controls and related compliance testing, but they are not a substitute for either.

8.   (580,A1,21) (d) The requirement is the EDP control procedure to detect an irregularity whereby a computer programmer who modified a program not to

print out his own personal overdrawn account. Answer (d), periodic recompiling of the program from the original source deck and comparison with the program currently in use would detect the modification. Answer (a) is incorrect because use of a test-deck approach by the auditor would only detect the problem if the test data overdrew the programmer's account. Answer (b) is incorrect because using a running control total of all checking account balances could not be meaningfully compared with a printout of overdrawn accounts. This would have been a very good answer if it had been a running control totals of all overdrawn account balances. Answer (c) is incorrect because a program check for a valid customer code would only detect those transactions for which the customer code was incorrectly inputted or no such customer existed.

9. (580,A1,38) (c) The requirement is which data item would be best identified as a hash total. A hash total is a meaningless control total such as total of all invoice numbers in a batch of sales invoices. Hash totals are utilized to determine if any data items are lost. Here the department numbers of all employees added together would provide such a "meaningless" total which would indicate whether anyone's data items were omitted. Answers (a), (b), and (d) are incorrect because totals of gross pay, hours worked and number of employees are all meaningful totals.

10. (580,A1,54) (a) The requirement is an invalid reason for choosing to omit compliance tests of EDP controls after a review of the system had been completed. If the controls appear adequate, the auditor tests compliance unless (1) the costs of compliance testing are expected to exceed the savings in substantive tests, which is answer (d), or (2) the EDP controls are redundant to other internal control procedures, which is answer (b); see para 321.26. Answer (c) is incorrect because the auditor should not expend the effort on the tests of compliance if the review of the system indicates that there are major weaknesses which would preclude reliance on the system irrespective of the outcome of the tests of compliance.

11. (580,A1,59) (d) The requirement is the batch control to verify the accuracy of a cash receipts posting. Since the accounts receivable will be credited for the amount of cash received plus discounts taken by the customers, the control total should be the sum of the cash deposits plus the discounts taken by the customers. Answer (a) is incorrect because cash receipts are being posted, not sales returns. Answer (b) is incorrect because the accounts receivable will be credited for discounts taken in addition to cash deposits. Answer (c) is incorrect because the credits are to accounts receivable for the sum of cash deposits plus, not less, the discounts taken.

12. (1179,A1,2) (b) A validity check determines whether a character is legitimate per the given character set. Note the validity check determines whether a given character is within the desired group. Answer (a) is incorrect because a parity check is a summation check in which the binary digits of a character are added to determine whether the sum is odd or even. Another bit, the parity bit, is turned on or off so the total number of bits will be odd or even as required. Answer (c) is incorrect because an echo check is a hardware control wherein data is transmitted back to its source and compared to the original data to verify the transmission correctness. Answer (d) is incorrect because a limit or reasonableness check is a programmed control based on specified limits. For example, a calendar month cannot be numbered higher than 12, or a week cannot have more than 168 hours.

13. (1179,A1,19) (d) Destructive updating in an on-line EDP system is destruction of transaction files. Accordingly, auditing of the balances in accounts where transactions are periodically destroyed requires a well documented audit trail for the auditor. Answer (a) is incorrect because the auditor needs more than periodic dumping of files, even though periodic dumping of files may be a part of a well documented audit trail. Answer (b) is incorrect because year-end utilization of audit hooks would not be feasible as transaction files would have been destroyed during the year. Audit hooks describe a method of retaining selected or all transaction files for the auditor. Audit hooks have to be utilized during the year, i.e., prior to destruction of the transaction files to be feasible. Answer (c) is incorrect because an integrated test facility describes compliance testing through utilization of actual or dummy transactions, i.e., it is not a test of balances.

14. (1179,A1,23) (c) The requirement is the method of testing accounting controls for an EDP activity that leaves no visible evidence that the control procedures were performed. When EDP control procedures leave no visible evidence indicating the procedures have been performed, the auditor should test these controls by reviewing transactions submitted for processing and by comparing them with the related output. The objective is to determine that no transactions tested with unacceptable conditions went unreported and without appropriate resolution. This procedure can be undertaken by submitting for comparison actual client live data or dummy trans-

actions (see para 321.29). Answer (a) is incorrect because corroborative inquiries will not test the accounting controls per se. Answer (b) is incorrect because observing the separation of functional responsibilities is less applicable to an EDP activity because frequently many previously separated functions are combined in an EDP activity as discussed in para 321.12. Answer (d) is incorrect because the run manual consists of program documentation including the problem statement, system flowchart, operating instructions, record layouts, program flowcharts, program listing, test data, and an approval and change sheet. Reviewing the run manual would be part of the review of the system's controls and not part of the test of the system.

15. (1179,A1,31) (d)   The requirement is the most efficient and least costly method of dumping information from disks. Answer (a) is incorrect because dump is a nonsense term in the sense that it does not describe a form of storage. Answers (b) and (c) are incorrect because magnetic tapes are a much more efficient and thus less costly form of storage than printouts and punched cards.

16. (1179,A1,32) (b)   Generalized audit packages provide a means of converting machine readable data into auditor readable data with added data manipulation routines including various sort and arithmetic functions. Thus, generalized audit packages utilize the speed and accuracy of the computer. Answer (a) is incorrect because audit packages do not substantiate data through self-checking digits and hash totals. While this may be feasible through general audit packages, it is not practical in that self-checking digits and hash totals should be controls found in client software. Answer (c) is incorrect because the performance of machine operations which leaves visible evidence of occurrence can be checked manually by the auditor. Answer (d) is incorrect because general audit packages generally convert machine readable data into auditor readable form rather than gather and store data in machine readable form.

17. (1179,A1,35) (b)   Compliance testing is concerned with determining that the necessary control procedures are being performed as planned. EDP system program controls are relied on heavily to detect errors or invalid data, but the control generally leaves no visible evidence that the procedures have been performed. Accordingly, the auditor's approach is to review transactions submitted for processing to determine that no unacceptable transactions are accepted when they should be rejected. The auditor may use actual client transactions or simulated transactions. In either case, the transactions that are recorded in the system will usually have to be reversed.

Answer (a) is incorrect because the auditor has the option of using either actual transactions or simulated transactions. In fact, simulated transactions give the auditor a better opportunity of designing erroneous types of transactions. Answer (c) is incorrect because compliance testing of EDP systems is very important in that relatively more concern is placed on internal control in EDP systems due to the lack of an audit trail. Answer (d) is incorrect because compliance testing is necessary even though there is a small chance that evidence in master files may be distorted. Recall that all test transactions must be reversed out of the system so as not to distort evidence in master files.

18.   (1179,A1,47) (b)   A fully protected EDP system has adequate internal controls including processing controls, external controls including proper separation of duties, physical controls including environmental controls, insurance, alternative power sources, scheduled maintenance, etc. Thus, downtime only arises due to unscheduled maintenance. Answer (a) electrical power losses, answer (c) unauthorized entry, and answer (d) keypunching errors would all be provided for in a fully protected system.

19. (1176,A1,13) (a)   As a convention, flowcharts flow from top to bottom and left to right. This is a convention just as we read textual material from left to right and top to bottom.

20.(1176,A1,16) (b)   The audit standard requiring adequate technical training and proficiency as an auditor implies a sufficient understanding of an entire computer system in order to evaluate its control features. See para 4 of SAS 3. Answers (a), (c), and (d) refer to EDP specialties which may be desirable, but are not by themselves sufficient to evaluate the control features of an EDP system.

21.(1176,A1,17) (d)   The limit (reasonableness) test is a control based on established limits. For example, a calendar month may not be numbered higher than twelve. A week cannot have more than 168 hours. Additionally, a reasonableness test on payroll might require an exception report for any employee getting paid for over 60 hours. The validity check is a hardware control to determine whether a character belongs within a character set, e.g., numeric. An echo check is a hardware control upon the transmission of data accomplished by the receiving unit returning the data to the sending unit for comparison to the original data. The dual read, another hardware control, provides for two independent readings and comparisons of data.

22. (1176,A2,21) (c) Answers (a) and (b) refer to input controls. Answer (d) refers to processing controls. This is based upon a dichotomy of general controls and application controls with a further breakdown of application controls into input controls, processing controls, and output controls. See para 7 and 8 SAS 3.

23. (1176,A2,29) (b) Since the objective is to exclude consigned merchandise, the auditor should request a listing of all items on the magnetic type that have a style number indicating consigned merchandise, i.e., an exception report. Answers (a), (c) and (d) do nothing to differentiate client inventory from consigned merchandise.

24. (1176,A2,52) (c) A computer console log provides a record of all operator intervention, i.e., instructions, to the CPU. Thus, activation of unauthorized programs or intervention in existing programs, e.g., adjustment of payroll records, would be recorded on the console log. Answers (a), (b), and (d) all refer to library type controls. Maintenance of a computer tape library would provide physical control over computer tapes, as also is implied in answer (d). Answer (b), file controls, refers to a general group of controls restricting access to files such as header labels.

25. (577,A1,10) (d) The requirement is the name for a routine processing function for which computer programs have been previously written. Examples of some of these programs are sorting and merging, computing square roots, random number generators, etc. These programs are known as utility programs. User programs are those that are prepared for, or by, a user for a specific purpose. Compiler programs convert compiler languages, such as FORTRAN and COBOL, to machine language. Supervisory programs are used in complicated EDP systems to direct the CPU in simultaneous processing of multiple programs.

26. (577,A2,25) (a) The requirement is to determine the function of parity checks, read after write checks, and duplicate circuitry, which are all hardware controls. These hardware controls have been developed to detect and control mishandling of data within the computer, i.e., they detect electronic or mechanical problems in the movement and storage of data. Thus they are not relevant to the detection and control of the problems set forth in answers (b), (c), and (d), which

were lack of sufficient documentation, illogical programming commands, and illogical uses of hardware.

27. (577,A2,34) (b) The requirement is to identify the two EDP functions which, when combined, pose a serious internal accounting control weakness in the organizational structure. Generally the systems analysis, programming, and computer operating functions are separated. The major problem occurs when the programming and operating functions are combined. Often in small organizations the systems analyst and programmer are one and the same person. If the programmer has access to the CPU, the programmer is in a position to perpetrate and conceal errors and irregularities.

28. (577,A2,36) (b) The requirement is the accounting control relevant to the use of a program or series of programs. It is important not to revise existing computer programs without proper approval so that changes in one program can be related to changes in the other programs.

29. (577,A3,45) (b) An integrated data processing system is one in which the design minimizes processing duplication of a given transaction. Fully integrated systems update all files affected by a transaction. The files may be physically or logically separated or extensively interconnected as in data-base oriented systems. Thus answer (a) is not always true in integrated systems.

30. (577,A3,47) (d) Generalized computer audit programs permit the CPA to independently process client EDP records. Answer (a) is incorrect because the auditor should oversee the use of the computer to perform the routine audit checks of the EDP records. Answer (b) is incorrect because the test deck approach, rather than generalized audit program approach, is used to test the logic of client programs. Answer (c) is incorrect because while larger samples are possible with the use of generalized programs, it is not the primary purpose.

31. (1178,A1,6) (c) The systems analyst is responsible for designing the EDP system, including the goals and means of achieving the goals, based upon the nature of the business and its information needs. The systems analyst outlines the data processing system for the computer programmer with systems flowcharts. Answer (a) is incorrect because computer programmers write the program based upon the work of the systems analyst. Answer (b) is incorrect because the data processing manager has responsibility for overall EDP function (systems design, programming, operating, library, etc.). Answer (d) is incorrect because the internal auditor may review the systems design and program flowcharts, but does not initially design them.

32. (1178,A1,8)   (d)   The requirement is an element of software. Compilers are software. The compiler program translates a source program (written in FORTRAN, COBOL, etc.) into an object program which is machine-readable, i.e., instructions to be followed by the CPU. Answer (a) is incorrect because a cathode ray tube is a television-like device (hardware) to display input or output data. Answer (b) is incorrect because the CPU (central processing unit, mainframe) is the principal hardware component of a computer containing the mathematic unit, primary storage, and a control unit. Answer (c) is incorrect because a magnetic tape drive is a hardware unit which reads and writes on magnetic tape, i.e., a storage device, as well as an input and output device.

33. (1178,A1,11)   (d)   The requirement is an internal control procedure relevant to on-line, real-time systems (OLRT). On-line refers to a terminal or input device that is in direct communication with the CPU. Real-time refers to the immediate, timely response by the CPU to the process being monitored. Only on real-time systems can a validity check be processed to determine whether a user is authorized to have access to computer files. Answers (a), (b), and (c) do not apply to OLRT as they imply lack of direct communication with the CPU. Answer (a) is concerned with the separation of keypunching and error listing operations. Answer (b) is concerned with file protection rings on magnetic tapes. Answer (c) concerns batch totals. These are appropriate control measures for a batch processing system.

34. (1178,A1,46)   (b)   The requirement is the situation which would lessen internal control over an EDP system. Computer operators who have access to detailed program listings have the opportunity to modify the programs. Answers (a), (c), and (d) all represent standard operating procedures to strengthen internal control within an EDP system.

35. (579,A1,14)   (b)   Symbolic languages are those that are in symbols, words, etc., that can be read by people, e.g., FORTRAN and COBOL. When a symbolic-language (source) program is translated, it is translated into an object program that is machine readable. Thus answer (c) is incorrect because the source program is a symbolic-language program. Answer (a) is incorrect

because processor program is a nonsense term. Answer (d) is incorrect because a wired program refers to first-generation computers, which require manual wiring of the CPU to perform desired operations.

36. (579,A1,34)   (d)   The requirement is an interpretation of two flowcharting symbols. A trapezoid with a shorter bottom than top refers to a manual operation which is an off-line process. An otherwise rectangular symbol with a curved bottom line indicates a document. Accordingly the symbols indicate that a document has been prepared by a manual operation. Answers (a) and (b) are incorrect because neither symbol indicates a master file has been prepared. Answers (b) and (c) are incorrect because there has not been a computer operation, i.e., it has been manual.

37. (1177,A1,1)   (a)   Automated equipment controls (hardware controls) are designed to detect, report, or prevent operational errors within the computer. For example, misreading of magnetic tapes by a tape reader or storage of erroneous data are detected or prevented by the dual-gap heads and parity checks. Other hardware controls are the echo check, dual circuitry, boundary protection, interlock, file protection rings, etc. Answers (b), (c), and (d) all relate to human error which the computer hardware cannot generally detect.

38. (1177,A1,18) (a)   An echo check or control consists of transmitting data back to the source unit for comparison with the original data that were transmitted. In this case, the print command is sent to the printer and then returned to the CPU to verify that the proper command was received. A validity check consists of the examination of a bit pattern to determine that the combination is legitimate for the system character set, i.e., that the character represented by the bit combination is valid per the system. Answer (c), a signal control or signal check, appears to be a nonsense term. Answer (d), check digit control, is a programmed control wherein the last character or digit can be calculated from the previous digits.

39. (1177,A1,23)   (c)   Batch processing groups transactions together until a sufficient number is accumulated to permit efficient processing. Multiprogramming is a systems configuration which permits more than one program to be worked on by a given computer at one time. Answers (a), document count processing, and (d), generalized-audit processing, appear to be nonsense terms.

40.   (1177,A1,34) (c)   Systems analysts are responsible for designing new data processing procedures. Answer (a) is incorrect because flowchart editor appears to be a nonsense term. Answer (b) is incorrect because programmers are in charge of coding those procedures, i.e., writing the program to instruct the computer to carry out the new procedures. Answer (d) is incorrect because the control-group supervisor is the individual in charge of those personnel assigned the responsibility of implementing internal control.

41.   (1177,A1,38) (c)   Answer (a) is incorrect because the auditor would have to review the service center controls, even though the internal audit team of the client reviewed the controls (para 1, SAS 9). Answer (b) is incorrect because a service center serving only the client would be the same as an in-house system and would require full review of the controls per SAS 3, para 3. Answer (d) is incorrect because only the financial statements of the service center were reviewed by another CPA, not the controls. Answer (c) is correct because the user controls, i.e., those outside of the service center, are adequate to detect errors and irregularities with reasonable promptness (para 9, SAS 3).

42.   (1177,A1,39) (c)   Answers (a), (b), and (d) all refer to review or investigation of the system. The review of the system indicates the controls that are supposed to be in effect. The second phase, tests of compliance, is designed to determine if the purported controls are in effect, e.g., examination of log books to determine whether information is properly recorded.

43.   (1177,A1,51) (c)   Generalized computer audit programs are those which are used to handle the general-clerical type procedures involved in audit, i.e., those tasks best handled by computers, such as determining totals and subtotals. Answers (a), (b), and (d) require auditor judgment rather than simple clerical skills, as in answer (c).

44.   (1177,A1,53) (c)   Generalized computer programs test client computer records. Testing and analysis of systems, equipment, and processing logic are undertaken by the auditor, as these require auditor judgment. Generalized computer audit programs are commonly used to evaluate the records produced by clients' systems. Evaluation of client systems, equipment, and processing logic is part of the evaluation of internal control for which generalized computer audit programs are not used.

45.   (578,A1,20)   (d)   Hardware controls are part of the computer's equipment and circuitry and are designed to prevent and/or detect equipment malfunctions. Answers (a), (b), and (c) are handled by procedural controls, i.e., steps taken by personnel to improve the efficiency of processing, to assure the accuracy of programs and data (including completeness of input data).

46.   (579,A1,46)   (a)   The requirement is the type of EDP system that can be audited without examining or directly testing EDP computer programs, i.e., auditing around the system. Auditing around the system is possible if the system performs uncomplicated processes and produces detailed output, i.e., is a fancy bookkeeping machine. Answers (b), (c), and (d) all describe more complicated EDP systems that produce only limited output. In these more complicated systems, the data and related controls are within the system, and thus the auditor must examine the system itself.

Per para 321.04, auditors must identify and evaluate the accounting controls in all EDP systems. Further, complex EDP systems require auditor specialized expertise to perform the necessary procedures.

47.   (579,A1,51)   (b)   On-line, realtime systems are those in which processing is performed as data is inputted and the results are immediately outputted to influence operations or decisions. Answer (a) is incorrect because batch processing describes systems in which records are collected into groups (batches) before processing. Then entire groups of records are processed on a regular basis. Answer (c) is incorrect because integrated data processing refers to a system, batch or realtime, in which duplicate records and duplicate operations are minimized. Answer (d), random access processing, is incorrect because it is a method of data access, e.g., random versus sequential, not a method of processing.

MAY 1981 ANSWERS

48.   (581,A1,6)   (a)   The requirement is to determine the most likely computer system for a large savings bank's customers' accounts. An on-line, real time system implies the existence of on-line inquiry ability for customers' accounts. Answer (b) is incorrect because of the need for on-line inquiry. Answer (c) is not a computer system. Answer (d), while possible, is less likely than answer (a) and may not have the necessary on-line inquiry capability.

49. (581,A1,20)   (b)   The requirement is to determine an example of an application control in an EDP system. General controls pertain to the EDP environment and all EDP activities. Application controls relate to specific tasks performed by EDP (para 321.06-.09). A hash total (e.g., an accumulation of all employees' social security numbers to help determine that the correct employees have been run on the payroll program) relates to a specific task. Answers (a), (c), and (d) are all general controls which will apply to all EDP activities.

50. (581,A1,21)   (d)   The requirement is the sample size which is necessary when an EDP application control which performs a limit check for each check request is to be subjected to the auditor's test-data. Since the objective of this test is to determine if the limit check control is working, all that is necessary is to input one request in excess of the limit.

51. (581,A1,34)   (d)   The requirement is to determine an EDP control to prevent file destruction by the operator. External labels will prevent file destruction by properly identifying the file. Answers (a), (b), and (c) are all incorrect because they address the accuracy of information on a file, not the physical security of a program file.

52. (581,A1,35)   (a)   The requirement is to determine whose errors a header label on a header tape is likely to prevent. Since the header label is actually on the magnetic tape, it is the computer operator whose errors will be prevented. Answer (b) is incorrect because the keypunch operator deals with punch cards. Answer (c) is incorrect because the programmer will write the programs and not run them under a good system of internal control. Answer (d) is incorrect because the maintenance technician will not run the magnetic tape.

ANSWER OUTLINE

Problem 1   Computerized Audit Programs

a.   Use of computer to perform substantive tests of sales records
1. Test extensions and footings
2. Verify accuracy of postings
3. Determine that all documents are accounted for
4. Select sales transactions for review
5. Print a list of items selected and relevant data
6. Select all debits to sales account and postings to sales account not from sales journal
7. Analytical review
8. Compare duplicate data in separate files
9. Examine records for quality

b.   Other procedures to complete audit of sales records
1. Trace postings from journal to invoices
2. Trace data from invoices to journal
3. Compare dates of recorded transactions with shipping records
4. Determine that all shipping documents are accounted for
5. Examine documents for approval
6. Determine extent and nature of transactions with major customers
7. Verify sales cutoffs
8. Compare invoices to daily price list

UNOFFICIAL ANSWER

Problem 1   Computerized Audit Programs

a.   Based upon the information given the computer may be used by Hastings to do the following:
- Test extensions and footings of computerized sales records that serve as a basis for the preparation of the invoices and sales journal.
- Verify the mathematical accuracy of postings from the sales journal to appropriate ledger accounts.
- Determine that all sales invoices and other related documents have been accounted for (for example, by accounting for the integrity of the numerical sequence).
- Select sales transactions for review (based upon predetermined criteria) through a review of the sales journal or the accounts receivable subsidiary ledger.
- Print a workpaper that lists each item selected, with relevant data inserted in applicable columns.

- Select all debits posted to the sales account and all postings to the sales account from a source other than the sales journal.
- Analytically review recorded sales by use of predetermined criteria (percentage relationships, gross margin, trends, and so forth, on a periodic or annual basis).
- Compare duplicate data maintained in separate files for correctness. For example, the computer may be used to compare the client's records of quantities sold with the client's records of quantities shipped.
- Examine records for quality (completeness, consistency, and so forth). [The quality of visible records is readily apparent to the auditor. Sloppy record-keeping, lack of completeness, and so on, are observed by the auditor in the normal course of the audit. If machine-readable records are evaluated manually, a complete printout is needed to examine their quality. Hastings may choose to use the computer to examine these records for quality].

b.   In addition to the procedures outlined above, Hastings should do the following:
- Trace postings from the sales journal to invoice copies.
- Trace data from sales invoices to the sales journal.
- Compare dates of recorded sales transactions with dates on shipping records.
- Determine that all shipping documents have been accounted for (for example, by accounting for the integrity of the numerical sequence).
- Examine documents for appropriate approval (for example, grant of credit, shipment of goods, and determination of price and billing).
- Determine the extent and nature of business transacted with major customers (for indications of previously undisclosed relationships — related parties — and for determination of applicability of disclosure requirements required by generally accepted accounting principles).
- Verify the sales cutoff at the beginning and end of the period to determine whether the recorded sales represent revenues of the period.
- Test pricing by comparing invoices to daily price list.

ANSWER OUTLINE

Problem 2   CPA Knowledge of Computer

The auditor should understand

2. EDP organization and management
   Arrangements of EDP duties including
      Organization
      Supervision
      Division of Duties
   Application of management principles to EDP

3. Characteristics of computer-based systems
   File organization, process flow, and system design
   Methods of safeguarding computer files
   Audit trails
   Analysis and design of a modestly complex system
   Accounting control procedures
      General controls and application controls

4. Fundamentals of programming
   Preparation of specifications for programs
   Supervision of program preparation

5. Computer center operations
   Use of software in computer operations
   Role of computer operator
   Supervision of running computer audit programs

UNOFFICIAL ANSWER

Problem 2   CPA Knowledge of Computer

2. Organization and management of the data processing function

   The auditor should understand the typical duties and different structural arrangements of organization, supervision, and division of EDP duties. The auditor should understand the application of management principles to the data processing function.

3. Characteristics of computer based systems

   The auditor should have a broad knowledge of file organization, process flow, and system design and should also understand the various methods for safeguarding computer files and the problems of including audit trails. The auditor should have the ability to analyze and design an information system of modest complexity. The auditor should be familiar with accounting control procedures that relate to all EDP activities (general controls) and those that relate to specific accounting tasks (application controls).

4. Fundamentals of computer programming

   The auditor should understand what programming entails and should have the ability to prepare specifications for and supervise preparation of a computer program.

5. Computer center operations

   The auditor should understand the use of software in the operation of the computer. The auditor should understand the role of the computer operator and should be able to supervise the running of the computer audit programs.

ANSWER OUTLINE

Problem 3   Grandfather-Father-Son Tapes

a.   Grandfather-father-son describes successive updating
     Provides method of reconstructing a current tape
     Old son tape becomes new father tape, etc.

b.   Two generations of backup provide adequate protection
     Different storage areas should be used
        Each with limited access

c1. CPA participation is based upon EDP control
        E.g., separation of EDP from purchasing, AP, disbursements
     CPA should specify tape format
        Be satisfied that all items are on special tape

c2. Maintain physical control over special tape and other materials

d.   Data on the special tape are listed in the Unofficial Answer below

UNOFFICIAL ANSWER

Problem 3   Grandfather-Father-Son Tapes

a.   A grandfather-father-son tape retention policy is one under which two predecessor tape files are held as back-up for the current file. This provides a method for reconstruction of the tape files in the event of accidental destruction of a tape used during processing. The use of this concept is illustrated as follows: At the end of period 3, a company holds master tapes as of the ends of periods 1 (grandfather) and 2 (father) and transaction tapes for periods 2 and 3. Transactions for period 3 are then processed with the father tape to form a son tape. Following the processing of period 3 transactions, the company holds master tapes as of the end of periods 1 (grandfather), 2 (father) and 3 (son) and transaction tapes for periods 2 and 3. The father tape can be replicated by processing the grandfather tape with period 2 transactions, and the son tape can be replicated by processing the father tape with period 3 transactions. Period 4 transactions are processed at the end of period 4 with the son tape (master file at the end of period 3) to form a new son file. The old son tape becomes the new father tape, the old father tape becomes the new grandfather tape and the old grandfather tape (end of period I) together with the transaction tape for period 2 may be released. Should anything happen to the old son tape during the updating with period 4 transactions, it may be replicated from the father tape and the period 3 transactions.

b. Holding two generations of backup tapes generally provides adequate protection. An additional generation might be maintained if the tape file is crucial or if there is a high rate of tape destruction. Since all tapes are stored together, they are vulnerable to loss through a common catastrophe——fire, theft or malicious act. Reconstruction from predecessor tapes can only be effected if the predecessor tapes are in existence. For this reason it is desirable that at least one generation of backup tapes be maintained in a separate location that is well protected from environmental hazards such as fires or magnetic interference. Access to both storage areas should be limited, and the librarianship function should be specifically assigned.

c. I. The extent of the CPA's participation in preparation of the special tape and of his review of the tape will depend upon his assessment of computer department capabilities and his evaluation of EDP controls, particularly the separation of data processing from the purchasing, accounts payable and disbursement functions. As a minimum, he should clearly indicate tape format and the data that he requires and must perform some testing to satisfy himself that all items have been included on the special tape. He may accomplish this by tracing items on a test basis from Company records to a print-out of the special tape and comparing print-out totals to Company records.

   2. The CPA should maintain physical control over the special tape, the general computer audit programs and any printouts prepared for him. He should take his programs and data directly to the machine operators and be present during the processing. He should keep confidential the transactions selected for review and the method for selecting them.

d.   Solt Manufacturing Company

       Schedule of Data to be Retained on the Special Tape

Source—Client Tape	Item of Data
Master file—vendor name	Vendor code Vendor name
Transaction file—expense detail	Voucher number Voucher date Invoice date Invoice number Purchase order number Debit account Amount
Transaction file—payment detail	Check number Check date

If the auditor plans to circularize vendors, he may also request addresses, either on this tape or in another listing.

ANSWER OUTLINE

Problem 4   EDP Controls

a.   General EDP controls
   1. Plan of organization and operation
   2. Procedures for documenting, reviewing, testing, and approving new programs and program changes
   3. Hardware controls
   4. Access controls to equipment and data files
   5. Other data and procedural controls

b1. Input controls provide reasonable assurance that inputted data
     Have been properly authorized
     Are converted into machine sensible form
     Have not been lost, suppressed, added, duplicated, or altered

b2. Processing controls provide reasonable assurance EDP has been performed as intended, E.G.,
     All transactions processed as authorized
     No authorized transactions are omitted
     No unauthorized transactions are added

b3.   Output controls provide reasonable assurance
          Of the accuracy of processing results
                  E.G., account listings, reports, mag-
                  netic files, etc.
          That only authorized personnel receive the
          output

UNOFFICIAL ANSWER

Problem 4   EDP Controls

a.   General control features in most EDP-based
accounting systems are classified in Statement on
Auditing Standards no. 3 as follows:
1.   The plan or organization and operation
     of the EDP activity.
2.   The procedures for documenting, re-
     viewing, testing, and approving systems
     or programs and changes thereto.
3.   Controls built into the equipment (i.e.,
     hardware controls).
4.   Controls over access to equipment and
     data files.
5.   Other data and procedural controls af-
     fecting overall EDP operations.

b 1.   Input controls are designed to provide reason-
       able assurance that data received for proces-
       sing by EDP have been properly authorized and
       converted into machine-sensible form and
       identified and that data (including data trans-
       mitted over communication lines) have not
       been lost, suppressed, added, duplicated, or
       otherwise improperly changed.
2.   Processing controls are designed to provide
     reasonable assurance that electronic data pro-
     cessing has been performed as intended for the
     particular application (i.e., that all transac-
     tions are processed as authorized, that no
     authorized transactions are omitted, and that
     no unauthorized transactions are added).
3.   Output controls are designed to assure the accu-
     racy of the processing result (such as account
     listings or displays, reports, magnetic files,
     invoices, or disbursement checks) and to
     assure that only authorized personnel receive
     the output.

ANSWER OUTLINE

Problem 5   Audit of Computerized A/R

Computer uses in auditing accounts receivable

1.   Recomputing extensions and footings to
     test for accuracy
2.   Selecting and printing confirmation
     requests
3.   Examining records for completeness,
     consistency, validity
4.   Summarizing data and analyses useful to
     the auditor
5.   Selecting and printing audit samples
6.   Comparing duplicate data for correctness
     and consistency
7.   Comparing confirmation information with
     company records
8.   Listing accounts confirmed with relevant
     data
9.   Comparing account balances to credit
     limits

UNOFFICIAL ANSWER

Problem 5   Audit of Computerized A/R

● Testing Extensions and Footings.
The computer can be used to perform simple summa-
tions and other computations to test the correctness
of extensions and footings. The auditor may choose
to perform tests on all records instead of just on
samples, since the speed and low cost per computation of the computer enable this at only a small extra
amount of time and expense.

● Selecting and Printing Confirmation Requests.
The computer can select and print out confirmation
requests on the basis of quantifiable selection criteria.
The program can be written to select the accounts according to any set of criteria desired and using any
sampling plan.

● Examining Records for Quality (Completeness,
Consistency, Valid Conditions, etc.).
The quality of visible records is readily apparent
to the auditor. Sloppy record-keeping, lack of completeness, and so on, are observed by the auditor in
the normal course of the audit. If machine-readable
records are evaluated manually, however, a complete
printout is needed to examine their quality. The
auditor may choose to use the computer for examining these records for quality.

If the computer is to be used for the examination, a program is written to examine the record for completeness, consistency among different items, valid conditions, reasonable amounts, and so forth. For instance, customer file records might be examined to determine those for which no credit limit is specified, those for which account balances exceed credit limit, and those for which credit limits exceed a stipulated amount.

- Summarizing Data and Performing Analyses Useful to the Auditor.
  The auditor frequently needs to have the client's data analyzed and/or summarized. Such procedures as aging accounts receivable or listing all credit balances in accounts receivable can be accomplished with a computer program.

- Selecting and Printing Audit Samples.
  The computer may be programmed to select audit samples by the use of random numbers or by systematic selection techniques. The sample selection procedure may be programmed to use multiple criteria, such as the selection of a random sample of items under a certain dollar amount plus the selection of all items over a certain dollar amount. Other considerations can be included, such as unusual transactions, dormant accounts, and so forth.

- Comparing Duplicate Data (Maintained in Separate Files) for Correctness and Consistency.
  Where there are two or more separate records having identical data fields, the computer can be used to test for consistency—for instance, to compare catalogue prices with invoice prices.

- Comparing Confirmation Information with Company Records.
  For example, the computer can be used to compare payment dates indicated on customer confirmations with client cash receipts records.

- The computer may be programmed to print a workpaper listing of each account selected, with relevant data inserted in applicable columns.

- The computer may be programmed to compare the customer's account balance with the customer's history of purchases or to determine whether credit limits have been exceeded.

CHAPTER THREE
BUSINESS LAW PROBLEMS AND SOLUTIONS

Business law is tested on Friday morning from 8:30 to 12:00. Recent business law exams have consisted of 60 multiple choice questions and 4 essay questions. The 60 multiple choice questions have comprised 60% of the business law grade and the 4 essay questions have comprised 40% of the grade. Essay questions generally contain 2 to 4 parts, and frequently the parts are unrelated even to the point of testing unrelated topics, e.g., part "a" tests anti-trust and part "b" tests bankruptcy.

Recent business law exams have covered almost all of the 16 business law topics (May 1980 did cover all 16 topics). Study the frequency of occurrence of each of the 16 topics on the frequency tabulation presented on page 209.

Even more so than in other sections of the examination, CPA candidates tend to overemphasize multiple choice questions due to the candidates' unfamiliarity with business law topics relative to accounting topics. Law essay questions, however, require special attention because they generally require yes-no type conclusions at the beginnings of their answers (which are generally not required in the other exam sections).

A recent development is the testing of tax theory concepts on the law section. The November 1977, May 1978, and May 1979 exams contained a question with one of the requirements asking for the tax implications of an action, e.g., what are the tax consequences of issuing preferred stock instead of debt?

Each question is coded as to month-year, section, problem number, and objective question number, e.g., (1179,L1,43): where 1179 is November 1979; L1 is law problem 1; and 43 is the multiple choice question number. Some questions were altered to make them applicable due to changes in the law (bankruptcy). The altered questions are designated by the symbol [†].

BUSINESS LAW INDEX	Exam Reference	Number Minutes	Problem Page No.	Answer Page No.
Contracts (CONT)				
42 Multiple Choice				
1. Contract Validity	576,L5b	12-15	218	226
2. Offer and Acceptance; Revocation; Rejection	1180,L5	15-20	218	226
3. Substantial Performance; Effectiveness of Acceptance	580,L3a&b	15-20	219	227

	Exam Reference	Number Minutes	Problem Page No.	Answer Page No.
Sales (SALE)				
32 Multiple Choice				
1. Breach of Warranty; Warranty of Title	1177, L7a&b	15-20	235	243
2. Option Contract; Risk of Loss; Pre-Existing Duty; Contract Interference	1178, L5	20-25	235	244
3. Consignments	580, L4a	7-10	237	245
Negotiable Instruments (NEGO)				
29 Multiple Choice				
1. Bank as Holder in Due Course; Material Alteration; Non-negotiable Instrument	1179, L3	20-25	252	258
2. Negotiability of Instrument; Types of Indorsements	578, L2	25-30	253	259
Secured Transactions (SECU)				
25 Multiple Choice				
1. Perfection and Priorities	573, L5	15-20	266	272
2. Perfection and Priorities	1178, L2a	10-15	266	272
3. Field Warehousing; Security Interest in Negotiable Document of Title	580, L4b	7-10	266	273
Bankruptcy (BANK)				
23 Multiple Choice				
1. Priority of Claimants	577, L7a	15-20	279	283
2. Security Interest as a Voidable Preference	1180, L3b	7-10	279	284
Suretyship (SURE)				
30 Multiple Choice				
1. Modification of Surety's Contract; Surety's Right of Reimbursement	1179, L4	20-25	290	296
2. Effect of Contract Changes	1173, L7b&c	10-15	290	296
3. Surety's Consideration; Surety's Liability upon Default	1180, L3a	7-10	290	297
Agency (AGEN)				
33 Multiple Choice				
1. Ratification; Agency Coupled with an Interest	580, L5a&b	10-15	304	311
2. Vicarious Liability	1178, L3a&b	10-15	304	311

	Exam Reference	Number Minutes	Problem Page No.	Answer Page No.
Partnerships (PART)				
30 Multiple Choice				
1. Assumed and Name Statute; Fiduciary Responsibility; Dissolution; Assignment of Partnership Interest	579, L4	20-25	319	325
2. Wrongful Dissolution; Limited Partnership	580, L5c&d	10	319	326
3. Criteria for Partnership; Liability of Partners	578, L5	15-20	320	327
Corporations (CORP)				
40 Multiple Choice				
1. Dividends; Contracts with Director; Director Fiduciary Responsibility	579, L3	25-30	337	345
2. Pre-Incorporation Contracts; Director Fiduciary Responsibility	578, L4	25-30	337	346
3. Declaration of Dividends	1180, L2a	7-10	338	348
Antitrust (ANTI)				
25 Multiple Choice				
1. Price Fixing and Discrimination	577, L6b&c	15-20	354	360
2. Price Discrimination	1180, L2b	10-12	354	360
Federal Securities Law (FEDE)				
22 Multiple Choice				
1. Registration; Receptive Devices; Insider Information	1176, L7	20-25	366	371
2. Reg. A and Rule 10b-5	1178, L4	20-25	366	372
Accountant's Legal Liability (ACCO)				
25 Multiple Choice				
1. Effect of Disclaimer on Liability; Partnership Liability; Third Party Liability	577, L4	20-25	379	385
2. Antifraud Section of Security Act of 1934; Liability and Defenses Under Sec. 11(A) of 1933 Act	1180, L4	15-20	379	386
3. Liability Under Tax Reform Act of 1976 and Securities Act of 1933	580, L2	20-25	380	387
Employer-Employee Relations (EREE)				
26 Multiple Choice				
1. Workmen's Compensation	1178, L3c	5-10	395	399

	Exam Reference	Number Minutes	Problem Page No.	Answer Page No.
Property (PROP)				
31 Multiple Choice				
1. Assignment of Lease; Fixture; Real vs. Personal Property	579, L5	15-20	406	412
2. Landlord-Tenant Problems	574, L4b	10-15	406	413
3. Purchase Subject to Mortgage	580, L4c	7-10	407	413
Insurance (INSU)				
27 Multiple Choice				
1. Insurable Interest	1176, L6b&c	15-20	421	426
2. Insurable Interest	1174, L7c	5-10	421	426
Trusts and Estates (TRUS)				
26 Multiple Choice				
1. Trust Principal and Income	576, L7b	7-10	431	436
Sample Business Law Examination		175-210	1047	1082

FREQUENCY OF BUSINESS LAW TOPICS APPEARING ON THE EXAM

EXAM	CONT	SALE	NEGO	SECU	BANK	SURE	AGEN	PART	CORP	ANTI	FEDE	ACCO	EREE	PROP	INSU	TRUS
May 1977	5 MC	5 MC	7 MC	1/2	1/2	3 MC	4 MC		4 MC		4 MC		3 MC	7 MC	5 MC	1 MC
Nov 1977	1	1	9 MC	5 MC	5 MC	4 MC	1	5 MC	1	1		1	4 MC	2 MC	3 MC	2 MC
May 1978	11 MC	5 MC		3 MC	4 MC	2 MC	6 MC	5 MC	1	4 MC	2 MC	5 MC	2 MC	4 MC	3 MC	4 MC
Nov 1978	4 MC, 4/5	3 MC, 1/5	7 MC, 1	1		4 MC	1	1	6 MC	4 MC	1 MC, 1	1		3 MC	3 MC	5 MC
May 1979	10 MC	4 MC	8 MC	6 MC	5 MC	3 MC	2 MC	1	1	4 MC	3 MC	5 MC	2 MC	1	3 MC	
Nov 1979	8 MC	2 MC	1	5 MC		1	3 MC	7 MC	1	7 MC	4 MC	1	2 MC	5 MC	3 MC	4 MC
May 1980	2 MC	7 MC, 1	8 MC	1/2	5 MC	4 MC	1/2	1/2	8 MC	4 MC		1	2 MC	2 MC, 1/2	3 MC	5 MC
Nov 1980	4 MC, 1	3 MC	10 MC		1/2	1/2, 1/2	6 MC	6 MC	1 MC	1 MC, 1/2	6 MC, 1/2	1	3 MC	3 MC	5 MC	4 MC
May 1981	7 MC	7 MC	1	1	5 MC	5 MC	6 MC	1	8 MC	3 MC	1	6 MC	3 MC	3 MC	4 MC	3 MC

NOTE: See page 14 for a complete explanation of the above coding. Explanation of topic abbreviations appears below.

CONT (Mod. 7) Contracts

SALE (Mod. 8) Sales
NEGO (Mod. 9) Negotiable Instruments
SECU (Mod.10) Secured Transactions

BANK (Mod.11) Bankruptcy

SURE (Mod.12) Suretyship
AGEN (Mod.13) Agency

PART (Mod.14) Partnerships

CORP (Mod.15) Corporations

ANTI (Mod.16) Antitrust
FEDE (Mod.17) Federal Securities Law

ACCO (Mod.18) Accountant's Legal Liability

EREE (Mod.19) Employer-Employee Relations

PROP (Mod.20) Property
INSU (Mod.21) Insurance

TRUS (Mod.22) Trusts and Estates

MULTIPLE CHOICE QUESTIONS (1—42)

1. Base Electric Co. has entered an agreement to buy its actual requirements of copper wiring for six months from the Seymour Metal Wire Company and Seymour Metal has agreed to sell all the copper wiring Base will require for six months. The agreement between the two companies is

   a. Unenforceable because it is too indefinite.
   b. Unenforceable because it lacks mutuality of obligation.
   c. Unenforceable because of lack of consideration.
   d. Valid and enforceable.

2. The Balboa Custom Furniture Company sells fine custom furniture. It has been encountering difficulties lately with some customers who have breached their contracts after the furniture they have selected has been customized to their order or the fabric they have selected has been cut or actually installed on the piece of furniture purchased. The company therefore wishes to resort to a liquidated damages clause in its sales contract to encourage performance or provide an acceptable amount of damages. Regarding Balboa's contemplated resort to a liquidated damages clause, which of the following is correct?

   a. Balboa may not use a liquidated damages clause since it is a merchant and is the preparer of the contract.
   b. Balboa can simply take a very large deposit which will be forfeited if performance by a customer is not made for any reason.
   c. The amount of the liquidated damages stipulated in the contract must be reasonable in light of the anticipated or actual harm caused by the breach.
   d. Even if Balboa uses a liquidated damages clause in its sales contract, it will nevertheless have to establish that the liquidated damages claimed did not exceed actual damages by more than 10%.

3. Fernandez is planning to attend an auction of the assets of Cross & Black, one of his major competitors who is liquidating. In the conduct of the auction, which of the following rules applies?

   a. Such a sale is without reserve unless the goods are explicitly put up with reserve.
   b. A bidder may retract his bid at any time until the falling of the hammer.
   c. The retraction of a bid by a bidder revives the previous bid.
   d. If the auction is without reserve, the auctioneer can withdraw the article at any time prior to the fall of the hammer.

4. Joseph Manufacturing, Inc., received an order from Raulings Supply Company for certain valves it manufactured. The order called for prompt shipment. In respect to Joseph's options as to the manner of acceptance, which of the following is **incorrect?**

   a. Joseph can accept only by prompt shipment since this was the manner indicated in the order.
   b. The order is construed as an offer to enter into either a unilateral or bilateral contract and Joseph may accept by a promise of or prompt shipment.
   c. If Joseph promptly ships the goods, Raulings must be notified within a reasonable time.
   d. Joseph may accept by mail, but he must make prompt shipment.

5. Monrad is contemplating making a contract for the purchase of certain real property. Which of the following is incorrect insofar as such a contract is concerned?

   a. It must meet the requirements of the statute of frauds.
   b. If the agreement is legally consummated, Monrad could obtain specific performance.
   c. The contract is nonassignable as a matter of law.
   d. An implied covenant of marketability applies to the contract.

6. Marblehead Manufacturing, Inc., contracted with Wellfleet Oil Company in June to provide its regular supply of fuel oil from November 1 through March 31. The written contract required Marblehead to take all of its oil requirements exclusively from Wellfleet at a fixed price subject to an additional amount not to exceed 10% of the contract price and only if the market price increases during the term of the contract. By the time performance was due on the contract, the market price had already risen 20%. Wellfleet seeks to avoid performance. Which of the following will be Wellfleet's best argument?

   a. There is no contract since Marblehead was not required to take any oil.
   b. The contract fails because of lack of definiteness and certainty.
   c. The contract is unconscionable.
   d. Marblehead has ordered amounts of oil unreasonably disproportionate to its normal requirements.

7. In the process of negotiating the sale of his manufacturing business to Grand, Sterling made certain untrue statements which Grand relied upon.

Grand was induced to purchase the business for $10,000 more than its true value. Grand is not sure whether he should seek relief based upon misrepresentation or fraud. Which of the following is a correct statement?

    a.   If Grand merely wishes to rescind the contract and get his money back, misrepresentation is his best recourse.

    b.   In order to prevail under the fraud theory, Grand must show that Sterling intended for him to rely on the untrue statements; whereas he need not do so if he bases his action on misrepresentation.

    c.   Both fraud and misrepresentation require Grand to prove that Sterling knew the statements were false.

    d.   If Grand chooses fraud as his basis for relief, the statute of fraud applies.

8. Which of the following will not be sufficient to satisfy the consideration requirements for a contract?

    a.   The offeree expends both time and money in studying and analyzing the offer.

    b.   The offeree makes a promise which is a legal detriment to him.

    c.   The offeree performs the act requested by the offeror.

    d.   The offeree makes a promise which benefits the offeror.

9. Marsh and Lennon entered into an all inclusive written contract involving the purchase of a tract of land. Lennon claims that there was a contemporaneous oral agreement between the parties which called for the removal by Marsh of several large rocks on the land. Marsh relies upon the parol evidence rule to avoid having to remove the rocks. Which of the following is correct?

    a.   The parol evidence rule does not apply to contemporaneous oral agreements.

    b.   Since the statute of frauds was satisfied in respect to the contract for the purchase of the land, the parol evidence rule does not apply.

    c.   Since the oral agreement does not contradict the terms of the written contract, the oral agreement is valid despite the parol evidence rule.

    d.   The parol evidence rule applies and Lennon will be precluded from proving the oral promise in the absence of fraud.

10. Master Corporation, a radio and television manufacturer, invited Darling Discount Chain to examine several odd lots of discontinued models and make an offer for the entire lot. The odd lots were segregated from the regular inventory but inadvertently included 15 current models. Darling was unaware that Master did not intend to include the 15 current models in the group. Darling made Master an offer of $9,000 for the entire lot, which represented a large discount from the normal sales price. Unaware of the error, Master accepted the offer. Master would not have accepted had it known of the inclusion of the 15 current models. Upon learning of the error, Master alleged mistake as a defense and refused to perform. Darling sued for breach of contract. Under the circumstances, what is the status of·the contract?

    a.   There is no contract since Master did not intend to include the 15 current models in the group of radios to be sold.

    b.   The contract is voidable because of a unilateral mistake.

    c.   The contract is voidable because of a mutual mistake.

    d.   There is a valid and binding contract which includes the 15 current-model radios.

11. A salesman for A & C Company called upon the purchasing agent for Major Enterprises, Inc., and offered to sell Major 1,500 screwdriver sets at $1.60 each. Major's purchasing agent accepted and the following day sent A & C a purchase order which bore Major's name and address at the top and also had the purchasing agent's name and title stamped at the bottom with his initials. The purchase order recited the agreement reached orally the prior day. Subsequently, Major decided it did not want the screwdriver sets since it was overstocked in that item. Major thereupon repudiated the contract and asserted the statute of frauds as a defense. Under the.circumstances, which of the following is correct?

    a.   The statute of frauds does not apply to this transaction since performance is to be completed within one year from the date of the making of the contract.

    b.   Major will lose but only if its purchasing agent's authority to make the contract was in writing.

    c.   The fact that an authorized agent of A & C did not sign the purchase order prevents its use by A & C against Major to satisfy the statute of frauds.

    d.   The purchase order is sufficient to satisfy the statute of frauds even though the purchasing agent never signed it in full.

12. Lally sent Queen Supply Company, Inc., a telegram ordering $700 of general merchandise. Lally's telegram indicated that immediate shipment was necessary. That same day Queen delivered the goods to the Red Freight Company. The shipment was delayed due to a breakdown of the truck which was transporting the goods. When the merchandise did not arrive as promptly as expected, Lally notified Queen that it revoked the offer and was purchasing the goods elsewhere. Queen indicated to Lally that the merchandise had been shipped the same day Lally had ordered it and Lally's revocation was not good. Which of the following statements best describes the transaction?

    a.   The statute of frauds will be a defense on any action by Queen to enforce the contract.

    b.   Prompt shipment of the merchandise by Queen constituted an acceptance.

    c.   Lally's revocation of the offer was effective since Lally had not received a notice of acceptance.

    d.   Lally's order was an offer to Queen to enter into a bilateral contract which could be accepted only by a promise.

13. Which of the following omissions will prevent a writing from satisfying the statute of frauds with respect to the sale of goods?

    a.   It does not indicate that a sale has occurred.

    b.   It is not signed by both the buyer and seller.

    c.   The time and place of delivery are not indicated.

    d.   The payment terms are not contained in the writing.

14. Under what conditions will the statute of frauds be a defense under the Uniform Commercial Code where there is a contract for the sale of goods worth more than $500?

    a.   The seller has completed goods specially manufactured for the buyer which are not salable in the ordinary course of the seller's business.

    b.   The written memorandum omits several important terms but states the quantity, and it is signed by the party to be charged.

    c.   The party asserting the statute of frauds admits under oath to having made the contract.

    d.   The goods in question are fungible and actively traded by merchants in the business community.

15. Walker and White entered into a written contract involving the purchase of certain used equipment by White. White claims that there were oral understandings between the parties which are included as a part of the contract. Walker pleads the parol evidence rule. This rule applies to

    a.   Subsequent oral modifications of the written contract by the parties.

    b.   Additional consistent terms even if the contract was not intended as a complete and exclusive listing of all terms of the agreement.

    c.   A contemporaneous oral understanding of the parties which contradicts the terms of a written contract intended as the final expression of the agreement between the parties.

    d.   Evidence in support of the oral modification based upon the performance by Walker.

16. On March 15, 1977, Smith received an oral offer to work as an account executive for Wonder Stock Brokerage Company. Smith orally accepted the offer on April 1, 1977, and agreed to begin work on May 1, 1977. The duration of the contract was one year from May 1, 1977, and provided a $20,000 salary plus a bonus based on commissions earned. Under these circumstances, which of the following is true?

    a.   Smith has an agency coupled with an interest.

    b.   The contract in question is not subject to the statute of frauds.

    c.   Smith would be permitted to delegate his performance to another equally competent person.

    d.   Although Smith's contract is silent on the point, Smith has an implied right to reimbursement for the reasonable and necessary expenses incurred on behalf of Wonder.

17. A contract was created by a false representation of a material fact. The fact was known to be false by the person making the representation, and there was an intent to deceive the party who relied on the representation to his detriment. The contract is voidable on the basis of

    a.   Undue influence.

    b.   Fraud.

    c.   Duress.

    d.   Negligence.

18. A contract effecting an unreasonable restraint of trade is invalid or void as against public policy, but a contract containing a covenant not to compete is valid if it is

    a.   In writing.

    b.   Filed with the Attorney General.

    c.   Reasonable as to area and time.

    d.   For services.

19. Martin Stores, Inc., decided to sell a portion of its eight-acre property. Consequently, the president of Martin wrote several prospective buyers the following letter:

Dear Sir: We are sending this notice to several prospective buyers because we are interested in selling four acres of our property located in downtown Metropolis. If you are interested, please communicate with me at the above address. Don't bother to reply unless you are thinking in terms of at least $100,000.

                    James Martin, President

Under the circumstances, which of the following is correct?

    a.   The statute of frauds does not apply because the real property being sold is the division of an existing tract which had been properly recorded.

    b.   Markus, a prospective buyer, who telegraphed Martin that he would buy at $100,000 and forwarded a $100,000 surety bond to guarantee his performance, has validly accepted.

    c.   Martin must sell to the highest bidder.

    d.   Martin's communication did not constitute an offer to sell.

20. Fashion Swimming Pools, Inc., mailed a letter to Direct Distributors offering a three-year franchise dealership. The offer stated the terms in detail and at the bottom stated that "the offer would not be withdrawn prior to October 1, 1978." Under the circumstances, which of the following is correct?

    a.   The offer is an irrevocable option which can not be withdrawn prior to October 1, 1978.

    b.   A letter of acceptance from Direct to Fashion sent on October 1, 1978, but not received until October 2, 1978, would not create a valid contract.

    c.   The statute of frauds would not apply to the proposed contract.

    d.   The offer can not be assigned to another party if Direct chooses not to accept.

21. Mayer wrote Jackson and offered to sell Jackson a building for $50,000. The offer stated it would expire 30 days from July 1, 1978. Mayer changed his mind and does not wish to be bound by his offer. If a legal dispute arises between the parties regarding whether there has been a valid acceptance of the offer, which of the following is correct?

    a.   The offer can not be legally withdrawn for the stated period of time.

    b.   The offer will not expire prior to the 30 days even if Mayer sells the property to a third person and notifies Jackson.

    c.   If Jackson phoned Mayer on August 1 and unequivocally accepted the offer, it would create a contract, provided he had no notice of withdrawal of the offer.

    d.   If Jackson categorically rejects the offer on July 10th, Jackson can not validly accept within the remaining stated period of time.

22. Exeter Industries, Inc., orally engaged Werglow as one of its district sales managers for an 18-month period commencing April 1, 1978. Werglow commenced work on that date and performed his duties in a highly competent manner for several months. On October 1, 1978, the company gave Werglow a notice of termination as of November 1, 1978, citing a downturn in the market for its products. Werglow sues seeking either specific performance or damages for breach of contract. Exeter pleads the statute of frauds and/or a justified dismissal due to the economic situation. What is the probable outcome of the lawsuit?

    a.   Werglow will prevail because the statute of frauds does not apply to contracts such as his.

    b.   Werglow will prevail because he has partially performed under the terms of the contract.

    c.   Werglow will lose because the reason for his termination was caused by economic factors beyond Exeter's control.

    d.   Werglow will lose because such a contract must be in writing and signed by a proper agent of Exeter.

23. Arthur sold his house to Michael. Michael agreed to pay the existing mortgage on the house. The Safety Bank, which held the mortgage, released Arthur from liability on the debt. The above declared transaction (relating to the mortgage debt) is

a. A delegation.
b. A novation.
c. Invalid in that bank did not receive any additional consideration from Arthur.
d. Not a release of Arthur if Michael defaults, and the proceeds from the sale of the mortgaged house are insufficient to satisfy the debt.

24. Williams purchased a heating system from Radiant Heating, Inc., for his factory. Williams insisted that a clause be included in the contract calling for service on the heating system to begin not later than the next business day after Williams informed Radiant of a problem. This service was to be rendered free of charge during the first year of the contract and for a flat fee of $200 per year for the next two years thereafter. During the winter of the second year, the heating system broke down and Williams promptly notified Radiant of the situation. Due to other commitments, Radiant did not send a man over the next day. Williams phoned Radiant and was told that the $200 per year service charge was uneconomical and they could not get a man over there for several days. Williams in desperation promised to pay an additional $100 if Radiant would send a man over that day. Radiant did so and sent a bill for $100 to Williams. Is Williams legally required to pay this bill and why?

a. No, because the pre-existing legal duty rule applies to this situation.
b. No, because the statute of frauds will defeat Radiant's claim.
c. Yes, because Williams made the offer to pay the additional amount
d. Yes, because the fact that it was uneconomical for Radiant to perform constitutes economic duress which freed Radiant from its obligation to provide the agreed-upon service.

25. Montbanks' son, Charles, was seeking an account executive position with Dobbs, Smith, and Fogarty, Inc., the largest brokerage firm in the United States. Charles was very independent and wished no interference by his father. The firm, after several weeks deliberation, decided to hire Charles. They made him an offer on April 12, 1979, and Charles readily accepted. Montbanks feared that his son would not be hired. Being unaware of the fact that his son had been hired, Montbanks mailed a letter to Dobbs on April 13 in which he promised to give the brokerage firm $50,000 in commission business if the firm would hire his son. The letter was duly received by Dobbs and they wish to enforce it against Montbanks. Which of the following statements is correct?

a. Past consideration is no consideration, hence there is no contract.
b. The pre-existing legal duty rule applies and makes the promise unenforceable.
c. Dobbs will prevail since the promise is contained in a signed writing.
d. Dobbs will prevail based upon promissory estoppel.

26. Abacus Corporation sent Frame Company an offer by a telegram to buy its patent on a calculator. The Abacus telegram indicated that the offer would expire in ten days. The telegram was sent on February 1, 1979, and received on February 2, 1979, by Frame. On February 8, 1979, Abacus telephoned Frame and indicated they were withdrawing the offer. Frame telegraphed an acceptance on the 11th of February. Which of the following is correct?

a. The offer was an irrevocable offer, but Frame's acceptance was too late.
b. Abacus' withdrawal of the offer was ineffective because it was not in writing.
c. Since Frame used the same means of communication, acceptance was both timely and effective.
d. No contract arose since Abacus effectively revoked the offer on February 8, 1979.

27. Strattford Theaters made a contract with Avon, Inc., for the purchase of $450 worth of theater supplies. Delivery was to take place in one month. One week after accepting the order, the price of materials and labor increased sharply. In fact, to break even on the contract, Avon would have to charge an additional $600. Avon phoned Strattford and informed them of the situation. Strattford was sympathetic and said they were sorry to hear about the situation but that the best they would be willing to do was split the rise in price with Avon. Avon accepted the modification on Strattford's terms. As a result of the above modification, which of the following is correct?

a. Avon's continuing to perform the contract after informing Strattford of the price difficulty constitutes consideration for the modification of the price.
b. The oral modification is not effective since there was no consideration.
c. The statute of frauds applies to the contract as modified.
d. The contract contained an implied promise that it was subject to price rises.

28. Mara Oil, Inc., had a contract with Gotham Apartments to supply it with its fuel oil needs for

the year, approximately **10,000** gallons. The price was fixed at ten cents above the price per gallon that Mara paid for its oil. Due to an exceptionally cold winter, Mara found that its capacity to fulfill this contract was doubtful. Therefore, it contacted Sands Oil Company and offered to assign the contract to it for $100. Sands agreed. Which of the following is correct as a result of the above assignment?

    a.   The contract with Gotham was neither assignable nor delegable.

    b.   Mara is now released from any further obligation to perform the Gotham contract.

    c.   Mara has effectively assigned to Sands its rights and delegated its duties under the terms of the contract with Gotham.

    d.   In the event Sands breaches the contract with Gotham, Mara has no liability.

29. Higgins orally contracted to pay $3,500 to Clark for $4,000 of thirty-day accounts receivable that arose in the course of Clark's office equipment leasing business. Higgins subsequently paid the $3,500. What is the legal status of this contract?

    a.   The contract is unenforceable by Higgins since the statute of frauds requirement has not been satisfied.

    b.   If Higgins failed to notify the debtors whose accounts were purchased, they will, upon payment in good faith to Clark, have no liability to Higgins.

    c.   The contract in question is illegal because it violates the usury laws.

    d.   Higgins will be able to collect against the debtors free of the usual defenses which would be assertable against Clark.

30. Ames and Bates have agreed that Bates will sell a parcel of land to Ames for $10,000 if the land is rezoned from residential to industrial use within six months of the agreement. Bates agreed to use his best efforts to obtain the rezoning, and Ames agreed to make a $2,000 good-faith deposit with Bates two weeks after the date of the agreement. What is the status of this agreement?

    a.   No contract results because the event is contingent.

    b.   The agreement is probably unenforceable because Bates would be required to attempt to influence governmental action.

    c.   The parties have entered into a bilateral contract subject to a condition.

    d.   Ames is not obligated to make the deposit at the agreed time even though Bates has by then made an effort to procure a rezoning.

31. The Johnson Corporation sent its only pump to the manufacturer to be repaired. It engaged Travis, a local trucking company, both to deliver the equipment to the manufacturer and to redeliver it to Johnson promptly upon completion of the repair. Johnson's entire plant was inoperative without this pump, but the trucking company did not know this. The trucking company delayed several days in its delivery of the repaired pump to Johnson. During the time it expected to be without the pump, Johnson incurred $5,000 in lost profits. At the end of that time Johnson rented a replacement pump at a cost of $200 per day. As a result of these facts, what is Johnson entitled to recover from Travis?

    a.   The $200 a day cost incurred in renting the pump.

    b.   The $200 a day cost incurred in renting the pump plus the lost profits.

    c.   Actual damages plus punitive damages.

    d.   Nothing because Travis is not liable for damages.

32. Cutler sent Foster the following offer by mail:

"I offer you 150 Rex portable electric typewriters, model J-1, at $65 per typewriter, F.O.B. your truck at my warehouse, terms 2/10, net/30. I am closing out this model, hence the substantial discount. Accept all or none. (signed) Cutler"

Foster immediately wired back:

"I accept your offer re the Rex electric typewriters, but will use Blue Express Company for the pickup, at my expense of course. In addition, if possible, could you have the shipment ready by Tuesday at 10:00 AM because of the holidays? (signed) Foster"

Based on the above correspondence, what is the status of Foster's acceptance?

    a.   It is not valid because it states both additional and different terms than those contained in the offer.

    b.   It represents a counteroffer which will become a valid acceptance if not negated by Cutler within 10 days.

    c.   It is valid but will not be effective until received by Cutler.

    d.   It is valid upon dispatch despite the fact it states both additional and different terms than those contained in the offer.

33. Bonnie Brook Wholesalers ordered 10,000 five-pound bags of standard granulated household sugar from Crane Sugar Plantations, Inc., for delivery within two months. Crane underestimated its existing backlog of orders and overestimated its inventory. As a result Crane found that it would be either unable or extremely hard-pressed to fill the order on time. Consequently, Crane assigned the contract to Devon Sugars, Inc., a smaller local producer and jobber, and paid Devon $200. Midway through the performance Devon defaulted because one of its suppliers' warehouses was destroyed by fire. Bonnie seeks to recover damages for breach of contract from both Crane and Devon. In the event of litigation, which of the following statements is correct?

    a. The unforeseen fire which destroyed the supplier's warehouse negates any liability on Devon's part.

    b. Devon will prevail because Devon has no contractual duty to Bonnie.

    c. Bonnie will not prevail against either Crane or Devon unless Bonnie first exhausts its rights against the supplier whose warehouse was destroyed.

    d. Bonnie will prevail against either Crane or Devon but will be entitled to only one recovery.

34. Unless the offer specifies otherwise, an acceptance is generally effective when it is

    a. Signed by the offeree.

    b. Received by the offeror.

    c. Delivered by the communicating agency.

    d. Dispatched by the offeree.

35. Martinson Services, Inc., agreed to rent two floors of office space in Jason's building for five years. An escalation clause in the lease provided for a $200 per month increase in rental in the fifth year of occupancy by Martinson. Near the end of the fourth year, during a serious economic recession, Martinson's business was doing very poorly. Martinson called upon Jason to inform him that Martinson could not honor the lease if the rent was increased in the fifth year. Jason agreed in a signed writing to allow Martinson to remain at the prior rental, and Martinson did so. At the end of the fifth year Martinson moved to another office building. Then, Jason demanded payment of $2,400 from Martinson.

What is the legal standing of the parties involved?

    a. A binding accord and satisfaction has resulted between the parties.

    b. The agreed upon rent reduction is valid due to the increased burden of performance as a result of events beyond Martinson's control.

    c. Martinson's relinquishment of the legal right to breach the contract provides the consideration for the reduction in rent.

    d. The writing signed by Jason does not bind him to the agreed reduction in rent.

36. In the event the purchaser seeks to rescind a contract for the purchase of land because of the seller's misrepresentation (as contrasted with seeking damages for the tort of fraud), the plaintiff (purchaser)

    a. Need not show knowledge of falsity on the defendant's part (seller) in order to recover.

    b. Need not show reliance upon the misrepresentation on his part in order to recover.

    c. Can resort to the Statute of Frauds in order to obtain a rescission on the contract.

    d. Will prevail only if there was misrepresentation in the execution which renders the contract void.

MAY 1981 QUESTIONS

37. Smith contracted to perform for $500 certain services for Jones. Jones claimed that the services had been performed poorly. Because of this, Jones sent Smith a check for only $425. Marked clearly on the check was "payment in full". Smith crossed out the words "payment in full" and cashed the check. Assuming that there was a bona fide dispute as to whether Smith had in fact performed the services poorly, the majority of courts would hold that

    a. The debt is liquidated, and Smith can collect the remaining $75.

    b. The debt is liquidated, but Jones by adding the words "payment in full" cancelled the balance of the debt owed.

    c. The debt is unliquidated and the cashing of the check by Smith completely discharged the debt.

    d. The debt is unliquidated, but the crossing out of the words "payment in full" by Smith revives the balance of $75 owed.

38. Harper is opening a small retailing business in Hometown, U.S.A. To announce her grand opening, Harper places an advertisement in the newspaper

quoting sales prices on certain items in stock. Many local residents come in and make purchases. Harper's grand opening is such a huge success that she is unable to totally satisfy the demand of the customers. Which of the following correctly applies to the situation?

    a.   Harper has made an offer to the people reading the advertisement.

    b.   Harper has made a contract with the people reading the advertisement.

    c.   Harper has made an invitation seeking offers.

    d.   Any customer who demands the goods advertised and tenders the money is entitled to them.

39.   On March 1, Wilkins wrote Conner a letter and offered to sell him his factory for $150,000. The offer stated that the acceptance must be received by him by April 1. Under the circumstances, Wilkins' offer

    a.   Will be validly accepted if Conner posts an acceptance on April 1.

    b.   May be withdrawn at any time prior to acceptance.

    c.   May **not** be withdrawn prior to April 1.

    d.   Could **not** be validly accepted since Wilkins could assert the Statute of Frauds.

40.   Maurice sent Schmit Company a telegram offering to sell him a one-acre tract of commercial property located adjacent to Schmit's warehouse for $8,000. Maurice stated that Schmit had three days to consider the offer and in the meantime the offer would be irrevocable. The next day Maurice received a better offer from another party, and he telephoned Schmit informing him that he was revoking the offer. The offer was

    a.   Irrevocable for three days upon receipt by Schmit.

    b.   Effectively revoked by telephone.

    c.   Never valid, since the Statute of Frauds applies.

    d.   Not effectively revoked because Maurice did **not** use the same means of communication.

41.   Martin agreed to purchase a two-acre home site from Foxworth. The contract was drafted with great care and meticulously set forth the alleged agreement between the parties. It was signed by both parties. Subsequently, Martin claimed that the contract did not embody all of the agreements that the parties had reached in the course of their negotiations. Foxworth has asserted that the parol evidence rule applies. As such, the rule

    a.   Applies to both written and oral agreements relating to the contract made prior to the signing of the contract.

    b.   Does **not** apply to oral agreements made at the time of the signing of the contract.

    c.   Applies exclusively to written contracts signed by both parties.

    d.   Is **not** applicable if the Statute of Frauds applies.

42.   Wilcox mailed Norriss an unsigned contract for the purchase of a tract of real property. The contract represented the oral understanding of the parties as to the purchase price, closing date, type of deed, and other details. It called for payment in full in cash or certified check at the closing. Norriss signed the contract, but added above his signature the following:

> This contract is subject to my (Norriss) being able to obtain conventional mortgage financing of $100,000 at 13% or less interest for a period of not less than 25 years.

Which of the following is correct?

    a.   The parties had already made an enforceable contract prior to Wilcox's mailing of the formalized contract.

    b.   Norriss would **not** be liable on the contract under the circumstances even if he had **not** added the "conventional mortgage" language since Wilcox had **not** signed it.

    c.   By adding the "conventional mortgage" language above his signature, Norriss created a condition precedent to his contractual obligation and made a counteroffer.

    d.   The addition of the "conventional mortgage" language has **no** legal effect upon the contractual relationship of the parties since it was an implied condition in any event.

REPEAT QUESTION

(581,L1,9)   Identical to item 32 above

PROBLEMS

Problem 1　　Contract Validity (576,L5b)

(12 to 15 minutes)

Part b.　　　Mark Candy Wholesalers, Inc. entered into a contract with Brown & Sons, a family partnership, which owned three small candy stores. Mark agreed to supply Brown & Sons with "its entire requirements of candy for its stores for one year" at fixed prices. Brown agreed to purchase its requirements exclusively from Mark. The price of sugar increased drastically shortly after the first month of performance. Mark breached the contract because the prices at which it was required to deliver imposed a severe financial hardship which would be ruinous. Mark asserts the following legal justifications for its actions:

1.　　The contract is unenforceable for want of consideration in that Brown & Sons did not agree to take any candy at all. That is, Brown & Sons was not specifically required to purchase candy if it did not require any.

2.　　The contract is too indefinite and uncertain as to the quantity which might be ordered and hence is unenforceable.

3.　　Performance is excused or the ground of legal impossibility because of the severe financial hardship imposed upon Mark as a result of the drastic rise in the price of sugar. This unforeseen event falls within the rule of implied conditions and makes the contract voidable.

Required:

Discuss the validity of each of the legal justifications asserted by Mark.

Problem 2　　Offer and Acceptance; Revocation; Rejection (1180,L5)

(15 to 20 minutes)

Part a. Fennimore owned a ranch which was encumbered by a seven percent (7%) mortgage held by the Orange County Bank. As of July 31, 1980, the outstanding mortgage amount was $83,694. Fennimore decided to sell the ranch and engage in the grain storage business. During the time that he was negotiating the sale of the ranch, the bank sent out an offer to several mortgagors indicating a five percent (5%) discount on the mortgage if the mortgagors would pay the entire mortgage in cash or by certified check by July 31, 1980. The bank was doing this in order to liquidate older unprofitable mortgages which it had on the books. Anyone seeking to avail himself of the offer was required to present his payment at the Second Street branch on July 31, 1980. Fennimore, having obtained a buyer for his property, decided to take advantage of the offer since his buyer was arranging his own financing and was not interested in assuming the mortgage. Therefore, on July 15th he wrote the bank a letter which stated: "I accept your offer on my mortgage, see you on July 31, 1980, I"ll have a certified check." Fennimore did not indicate that he was selling the ranch and would have to pay off the full amount in any event. On July 28, the bank sent Fennimore a letter by certified mail which was received by Fennimore on the 30th of July which stated: "We withdraw our offer. We are over subscribed. Furthermore, we have learned that you are selling your property and the mortgage is not being assumed." Nevertheless, on July 31 at 9:05 in the morning when Fennimore walked in the door of the bank holding his certified check, Vogelspiel, a bank mortgage officer, approached him and stated firmly and clearly that the bank's offer had been revoked and that the bank would refuse to accept tender of payment. Dumbfounded by all this, Fennimore nevertheless tendered the check, which was refused.

Required:

Answer the following, setting forth reasons for any conclusions stated.

In the eventual lawsuit that ensued, who will prevail?

Part b. Austin wrote a letter and mailed it to Hernandez offering to sell Hernandez his tuna canning business for $125,000. Hernandez promptly mailed a reply acknowledging receipt of Austin's letter and expressing an interest in purchasing the cannery. However, Hernandez offered Austin only $110,000. Later Hernandez decided that the business was in fact worth at least the $125,000 that Austin was asking. He therefore decided to accept the original offer tendered to him at $125,000 and telegraphed Austin an unconditional acceptance at $125,000. The telegram reached Austin before Hernandez' prior letter, although the letter arrived later that day. Austin upon receipt of the telegram telegraphed Hernandez that as a result of further analysis as to the worth of the business, he was not willing to sell at less than $150,000. Hernandez claims a contract at $125,000 resulted from his telegram. Austin asserts either that there is no contract or that the purchase price is $150,000.

Required:

Answer the following, setting forth reasons for any conclusions stated.

If the dispute goes to court, who will prevail?

Problem 3   Substantial Performance; Effectiveness of Acceptance (580,L3a & b)

(15 to 20 minutes)

Part a. Smithers contracted with the Silverwater Construction Corporation to build a home. The contract contained a detailed set of specifications including the type, quality, and manufacturers' names of the building materials that were to be used. After construction was completed, a rigid inspection was made of the house and the following defects were discovered.

1.   Some of the roofing shingles were improperly laid.

2.   The ceramic tile in the kitchen and three bathrooms was not manufactured by Disco Tile Company as called for in the specifications. The price of the alternate tile was $325 less than the Disco but was of approximately equal quality.

3.   The sewerage pipes that were imbedded in concrete in the basement were also not manufactured by the specified manufacturer. It could not be shown that there was any difference in quality and the price was the same.

4.   Various minor defects such as improperly hung doors.

Silverwater has corrected defects 1 and 4 but has refused to correct defects 2 and 3 because the cost would be substantial. Silverwater claims it is entitled to recover under the contract and demands full payment. Smithers is adamant and is demanding literal performance of the contract or he will not pay.

Required: Answer the following, setting forth reasons for any conclusions stated.

1.   If the dispute goes to court, who will prevail, assuming Silverwater's breach of contract was intentional?

2.   If the dispute goes to court, who will prevail, assuming Silverwater's breach of contract was unintentional?

Part b. Jane Anderson offered to sell Richard Heinz a ten acre tract of commercial property. Anderson's letter indicated the offer would expire on March 1, 1980, at 3:00 p.m. and that any acceptance must be received in her office by that time. On Febru-

ary 29, 1980, Heinz decided to accept the offer and posted an acceptance at 4:00 p.m. Heinz indicated that in the event the acceptance did not arrive on time, he would assume there was a contract if he did not hear anything from Anderson in five days. The letter arrived on March 2, 1980. Anderson never responded to Heinz's letter. Heinz claims a contract was entered into and is suing thereon.

Required: Answer the following, setting forth reasons for any conclusions stated.

Is there a contract?

MULTIPLE CHOICE ANSWERS

1.	d	10.	d	19.	d	28.	c	37.	c
2.	c	11.	d	20.	d	29.	b	38.	c
3.	b	12.	b	21.	d	30.	c	39.	b
4.	a	13.	a	22.	d	31.	a	40.	b
5.	c	14.	d	23.	b	32.	d	41.	a
6.	d	15.	c	24.	a	33.	d	42.	c
7.	a	16.	d	25.	a	34.	d		
8.	a	17.	b	26.	d	35.	d		
9.	d	18.	c	27.	c	36.	a		

EXPLANATION OF MULTIPLE CHOICE QUESTIONS

1. (1180,L1,11)   (d)   This agreement is a requirements contract and is both valid and enforceable if executed in good faith. Answers (a), (b) and (c) are therefore incorrect.

2. (1180,L1,13)   (c)   A liquidated damage provision is a contractual provision which states the amount of damages that will occur if either party breaches the contract. If the amount is reasonable in light of the anticipated or actual harm caused by the breach, it is enforceable. Answer (c) is correct. Answer (a) is incorrect because the fact that the preparer of the contract is a merchant has no bearing on the use of a liquidated damage clause. Answer (b) is incorrect because retaining a large deposit could be considered unconscionable and unenforceable. The reasonableness of a liquidated damage clause is judged in light of anticipated harm, not by a set percentage by which the liquidated damages exceed the actual damages.

3. (1180,L1,14)   (b)   The correct answer is (b). In an auction, the offer is accepted when the hammer goes down and the bidder can retract his bid until this time. The law presumes the sale is with reserve unless the owner announces the auction is without reserve, making answer (a) incorrect. Answer (d) is incorrect because an auction without reserve implies that the owner must sell to the highest bidder. Answer (d) describes an auction with reserve. Answer (c) is incorrect since the retraction of a bid does not revive the previous bid.

4. (1180,L1,15)   (a)   When possible, an offer is interpreted to permit acceptance by either an act or a promise to perform the act. Answer (a) is correct because the offer in question can be interpreted to permit either prompt shipment of the goods or the promise to do so. However, if Joseph accepts by a promise, shortly thereafter he must make prompt shipment.

5. (580,L1,20)   (c)   Real property contracts are assignable; thus, the statement in answer (c) is incorrect making answer (c) the correct answer. The Statute of Frauds demands the sale of an interest in real property to be in writing, thus answer (a) is incorrect. Answer (b) is incorrect because specific performance is an available remedy for breach of a real property contract. The seller impliedly covenants that the title being transferred is marketable (reasonably free from doubt).

6. (580,L1,29)   (d)   The agreement involved is a requirements contract; thus Marblehead's ordering of unreasonably disproportionate amounts of oil would be a breach by them. A requirements contract is considered definite and both parties are viewed as having provided consideration, thus answers (a), (b), and (c) are incorrect.

7. (1179,L1,2)   (a)   A party to a contract who wishes to rescind the agreement and obtain a refund should seek the refund on the basis of misrepresentation rather than fraud. Misrepresentation does not require the plaintiff to prove actual intent on the part of the defendant but fraud does. Answer (b) is incorrect because the fraud theory requires that the defendant knowingly intended to commit fraud. Showing the defendant intended for the plaintiff to rely on a statement which later proved untrue is insufficient to establish an action in fraud. Answer (c) is incorrect because only in a fraud case would the plaintiff be required to prove the defendant knew the statements were false. In misrepresentation, proof is limited to establishing the statements were false. Answer (d) is incorrect since the statute of frauds applies to the written requirements of contracts and has nothing to do with the tort of fraud.

8. (1179,L1,3)   (a)   The recipient of an offer who expends his time and money in studying and analyzing an offer would not satisfy the requirements of consideration to form a contract, because such efforts are not at the request of the offeror. Answer (b) is incorrect because where the offeree makes a promise which is a legal detriment to him or a benefit to the offeror, such promise is legal consideration. Answer (c) is also incorrect because if the offeree performs an act requested by the offeror, the consideration requirement has been satisfied. Similarly, answer (d) is incorrect because it is an example of the offeree making a promise which benefits the offeror, and again the requirement of consideration is satisfied. Note that answers (b) and (d) each assume that the act or promise was solicited by the offeror.

9. (1179,L1,4)   (d)   The parol evidence rule does apply to the stated facts because the evidence introduced is a contemporaneous oral agreement in the face of a

comprehensive written agreement. Answer (a) is incorrect because the parol evidence rule does apply to contemporaneous oral agreements. The rule is based on the presumption that the parties have incorporated every material item into the written agreement. However, the parol evidence rule does not exclude subsequent agreements although an "entirety" clause will. An "entirety" clause allows only written changes to be enforced. Answer (b) is incorrect because the parol evidence rule is designed to protect a written contract from change or contradiction. Complying with the statute of frauds in no way effects whether the parol evidence rule applies or not in a written contract. Answer (c) is incorrect because in substance, the oral agreement does contradict the written contract. As the contract is written, the seller's obligation would be to deliver a title along with proof of marketable title. Under the oral agreement an additional legal duty of the seller, Marsh, would be to remove several large rocks on the land which is in conflict with the written contract.

10.   (1179,L1,7)   (d)   There is a valid and binding contract which includes the 15 current model radios. The mistake alleged by Masters is a unilateral mistake and the general rule is that one party to a contract cannot avoid the agreement on the grounds that a mistake was made when the other party has no notice of the mistake and acts in good faith. This seems to be the case here. Answers (a) and (b) are incorrect because of the general rule stated above that agreements are not voidable on the basis of a unilateral mistake. Answer (c) is incorrect because the contract was not entered into as a result of a mutual mistake but rather as a result of a unilateral mistake. Darling Discount did not make a mistake, and they made a good faith bid based on the entire lot of radios that they were shown by Master.

11.   (1179,L1,8)   (d)   The purchase order which recited the oral agreement of the prior day is known under the UCC as a confirmation. For UCC cases, written confirmations satisfy the provision of the statute of frauds. The stamped name, title, and initials of the agent at the bottom of the purchase order would constitute a sufficient "signature" and therefore would indicate that Major Corporation's agent intended to authenticate the document. Answer (a) is incorrect because the statute of frauds does apply to this transaction since it involves the sale of goods in excess of $500. Answer (b) is incorrect because the purchasing agent's authority to make this particular contract need not be in writing but may be considered to be implied or apparent from his position. In general, there is no requirement that the authority of agents be in writing. Answer (c) is incorrect because the statute of frauds is satisfied if the party against whom the action is brought has signed. Thus,

the absence of a signature by A & C is of no importance in so far as enforcement against Major is concerned. In any event, a confirmation which is binding on the sender is also binding on the receiver unless objected to by the receiver. Hence the confirmation satisfies the statute of frauds for both parties.

12.   (1179,L1,9)   (b)   An offer which is ambiguous as to whether or not the offeror is bargaining for shipment of merchandise or the promise to ship can be accepted by the offeree doing either. Thus, the prompt shipment of the merchandise by Queen constitutes an acceptance and also passes the risk of loss (or delay as here) to the buyer, Lally. Answer (a) is incorrect because the statute of frauds has been satisfied by the telegram and by the fact that due to ambiguity the nature of the contract is unilateral requiring only that Queen ship the goods. Answer (c) is incorrect because Lally's revocation was not effective because it was received after acceptance. The absence of a notice of acceptance was a risk that Lally assumed in making a unilateral offer. Answer (d) is incorrect because Lally's order was an offer to enter into a unilateral contract since a reasonable reading of Lally's telegram was that they were bargaining for the act of immediate shipment and not a promise to ship.

13.   (1179,L1,11) (a)   In order for a writing to satisfy the statute of frauds with respect to the sale of goods, it must indicate that a sale has occurred. Otherwise, the writing is not sufficient proof that a sales contract has been entered into. Answer (b) is incorrect because a writing which otherwise satisfies the statute of frauds need not be signed by both buyer and seller. It is enforceable against the party who has signed, and in cases of valid written confirmation it is enforceable against both parties even though one party has not signed. Answer (c) is incorrect because under the Uniform Commercial Code, which regulates the sale of goods, any writing establishing an agreement which omits the time and place of delivery shall have these supplied by the code itself. In the absence of prior dealings or some strong established custom, time is always deemed to be a reasonable time, and the place of delivery is generally the seller's place of business. Answer (d) is incorrect because the absence of payment terms are not fatal in a writing which otherwise satisfies the statute of frauds since the code will infer that cash is the form of payment unless there are prior dealings or an industry custom or practice which overrides this inference.

14.   (1176,L1,5)   (d)   The general rule is an agreement for the sale of goods for $500 or more is required to be in writing. Fungible

goods actively traded by merchants comes within this rule as would other goods. A contract for specially manufactured goods not suitable for sale in the ordinary course of the seller's business is an exception to the general rule if the seller has made a substantial start in their manufacture. No special form is required for the writing except that it must be signed by the party sought to be charged and quantity is the one term that cannot be left out under the UCC. As a practical matter, the other important terms, e.g., price, should be included. Another exception to the statute of frauds is if the party asserting the statute admits the contract in court.

15. (1176,L1,6) (c) The parol evidence rule prohibits contradiction of a written contract, intended as the complete and final expression of an agreement between contracting parties, by prior or contemporaneous oral evidence. It does not prohibit subsequent oral modifications, nor does it prohibit evidence of consistent (or inconsistent) terms where the written contract was not intended as a complete and final expression of the agreement. Evidence based upon performance could imply a subsequent modification which is not prohibited by the parol evidence rule. Thus (c) is a better answer than (d).

16. (577,L2,28) (d) As an executive employee of Wonder, Smith is entitled to reimbursement for the reasonable and necessary expenses incurred on behalf of Wonder. Smith is an agent but has no other interest in the agency, i.e., no ownership interest. The statute of frauds is applicable to this contract. The contract by its terms cannot be performed within one year from the date of the contract (April 1, 1977, to May 1, 1978). He cannot delegate his performance because he was hired for his personal qualities, not just to perform mechanical duties.

17. (577,L3,34) (b) The essential elements of fraud are misrepresentation of a material fact, intent to mislead, reasonable reliance by the other party, and injury to others. Duress involves the use of force or severe economic pressure to cause an individual to do what he would not have done of his own free will. Undue influence, although similar to duress, involves the use of mental coercion, e.g., son's influence over senile old mother. Negligence in words or actions may result in an unintended misrepresentation of a material fact and would establish a voidable contract.

18. (577,L3,35) (c) A covenant not to compete is enforceable if under all the facts and circumstances of the particular case the restraint is necessary and the duration and the area encompassed are reasonable. For example, if "A" sold his small local grocery store to "B", "B" could reasonably ask for a covenant from "A" that "A" would not engage in the grocery business for one year within two square miles and deprive "B" of the goodwill of the business he has purchased. It need not be in writing unless it extends over more than one year. There is no need to file any such contract with the Attorney General. The consideration may be money, property, services, or another promise.

19. (1178,L1,27) (d) The communication by James Martin, President of Martin Stores, Inc., did not constitute an offer to sell, but instead was an invitation to negotiate. The Statute of Frauds applies to the sales of interests in real property whether or not recorded, and thus answer (a) is incorrect. Answer (b) is incorrect because Markus has only made an offer and not an acceptance since no offer had been made to Markus. Answer (c) is incorrect because Martin need not sell to anyone. Martin has simply made an invitation to negotiate and may accept or reject any offers.

20. (1178,L1,28) (d) Offers to contract may only be accepted by the person to whom they were made. They are not assignable to another party unless the offeror chooses to accept the assignment. Answer (a) is incorrect because no option is created since no consideration was paid. Also it is not a firm offer under the UCC because the subject matter is a service arrangement and not goods. Answer (b) is incorrect because under the facts, if an acceptance from Direct to Fashion had been sent on October 1, 1978, it would create a valid acceptance, and thus a contract. The acceptance is deemed made on the day transmitted. Answer (c) is incorrect because the Statute of Frauds would apply to the subject arrangement as it involves a contract that cannot be performed by its terms within one year.

21. (1178,L1,29) (d) A rejection effectively terminates an offer, and thus the offeree cannot validly accept later, even though he purports to do so within the remaining stated period of the offer. Answer (a) is incorrect because the offer as stated can be withdrawn at any time prior to acceptance. Answer (b) is incorrect because the offer would be terminated if the offeror sells the property to a third person and notifies a prior offeree. Answer (c) is incorrect because the subject matter is real estate and an oral acceptance would be unenforceable due to the lack of a writing.

22. (1178,L1,30) (d) The Statute of Frauds requires contracts that cannot be performed within a period of one year to be in writing to be enforceable. This contract of employment is for 18 months, and thus Werglow will not prevail because such a contract must be in writing and signed by an agent of the employer corporation. Thus, answer (a) is incorrect because the Statute of Frauds does apply to employment contracts such as Werglow's. The fact that partial performance has occurred as in answer (b) does not displace the Statute of Frauds. Answer (c) is incorrect because economic factors are not accepted as cause for terminating an otherwise valid contract. The general rule is that impossibility or hardship do not justify breach of an otherwise valid contract.

23. (579,L1,8) (b) When the creditor agrees to substitute a new debtor for the original debtor, a novation has occurred. Answer (a) is incorrect because in a delegation the original debtor remains liable to the creditor. Answer (c) is incorrect because the bank did receive consideration: Michael agreed to pay the mortgage in exchange for Arthur's being released. Answer (d) is incorrect since Arthur was released.

24. (579,L1,9) (a) As part of the original contract Radiant agreed to service the heating system purchased by Williams for a flat rate of $200 per year. Thus, Radiant was under a pre-existing legal duty to perform the maintenance work and any subsequent promise to pay for such services is without consideration and unenforceable. Answer (b) is incorrect because the Statute of Frauds is not applicable to this problem. The dispute is over a service arrangement and not the sale of goods. Answer (c) is incorrect because the offer to pay the additional amount makes no difference with respect to the requirement of consideration. Answer (d) is incorrect because an uneconomical contract does not free a party from a contract unless significant unforeseen difficulties are encountered.

25. (579,L1,11) (a) Montbanks promised to give Dobbs $50,000 in commission business if the firm would hire Charles. However Dobbs already had hired him. Therefore a promise by Dobbs to hire Charles is past consideration which does not create a contract. Answer (b) is incorrect because Dobbs already hired Charles. Therefore the legal duty to hire him was complete. Answer (c) is incorrect because a signed writing will not cure a lack of consideration. Answer (d) is incorrect because Dobbs did not hire Charles while relying on Montbanks' promise.

26. (579,L1,17) (d) No contract arose since Abacus effectively revoked its offer on 2/8/79 prior to Frame's acceptance by telephoning Frame and withdrawing the offer. Although the original offer indicated that it would expire in ten days, it did not contain a promise that it would not be withdrawn or was irrevocable. Answer (a) is incorrect since it was not an irrevocable offer and in any event, Frame's acceptance would have been timely had the offer not been revoked. Answer (b) is incorrect because the withdrawal of an offer need not be in writing to be effective. It may be communicated in any manner. Answer (c) is incorrect because the offer was revoked before Frame sent its acceptance. However, had the offer not been revoked, Frame's acceptance would have been effective when sent.

27. (579,L1,33) (c) Theater supplies constitute goods under the Uniform Commercial Code. Under the Statute of Frauds an agreement for the sale of goods in the amount of $500 or more must be in writing to be enforceable. Although the original contract was for $450, the contract as modified exceeds $500, and therefore the Statute of Frauds must be complied with. Answer (a) is incorrect because Avon's performance of the contract after the price increase did not constitute consideration for the modification of the price. Avon had a pre-existing legal duty to perform without regard to price increases. Answer (b) is incorrect because under the UCC a modification of a contract does not require consideration. Answer (d) is incorrect because contracts do not contain an implied promise that they are subject to price increases.

28. (579,L1,34) (c) Mara Oil has effectively assigned all its rights under the contract with the Gotham Apartments to the Sands Oil Company and has effectively delegated its duties under that contract. This is permissible because a contract to supply the annual requirement of fuel oil to apartment houses would not be considered a personal contract, and in the absence of a provision in the contract prohibiting assignment or delegation, it would be effective. Thus, answer (a) is incorrect. However, Mara, the original contracting party, is not released, as suggested by answer (b) nor relieved of potential liability, as in answer (d), in the event that Sands should not fully perform the contract with Gotham Apartments. Mara remains liable unless expressly released by Gotham Apartments.

29. (578,L1,16) (b) Higgins has received an assignment of the accounts receivable. An assignee must give notice to the debtors of the assignment; otherwise, the debtors have no liability to the assignee. Answer (a) is incorrect because the Statute of Frauds applies to sales of intangibles in excess of $5,000. Also under the UCC, oral contracts are enforceable to the extent that payment has been made and accepted. Answer (c) is incorrect because the transaction is not a loan of money, but rather a sale of accounts receivable. Answer (d) is incorrect because an assignee normally stands in the shoes of the assignor and is subject to any defenses the debtor could assert against the assignor.

30. (578,L1,21) (c) The parties have entered into a bilateral contract, i.e., a promise for a promise, which is subject to a condition of obtaining rezoning. Answer (a) is incorrect because a contract may be contingent or conditioned as long as it is sufficiently definite that the court can ascertain the intent of the parties. Answer (b) is incorrect because an attempt to obtain rezoning is not illegal or contrary to public policy. Answer (d) is incorrect because Ames is obligated to make the deposit even if Bates has not yet made an effort to procure a rezoning.

31. (578,L1,22) (a) The trucking company was engaged to redeliver the pump promptly upon completion of the repair. The delay in returning the pump was a breach of contract. The $200/day pump rental is Johnson Corporation's actual damages which are recoverable. Answer (b) is incorrect because the lost profits are not recoverable. The lost profits were not foreseeable, i.e., the trucking company did not know the special circumstances of Johnson's plant. Answer (c) is incorrect because punitive damages are not normally allowed for breach of contract. Answer (d) is incorrect because in any breach of contract, the nonbreaching party is liable for a minimum of nominal damages.

32. (578,L1,36) (d) Foster's acceptance is valid upon dispatch under the rules of constructive communication, even though it stated both additional and different terms than those contained in the offer. Overall, Foster's communication manifested an intent to accept and enter into a contract. The additional and different terms are neither material nor contrary to the terms of the original offer. Answer (a) is incorrect because additional or different terms in offers between merchants will not destroy the nature of the communication as being an acceptance per the UCC. Answer (b) is incorrect because the subject communication should be understood to be an acceptance and not a counteroffer. Additionally no UCC rule provides that a counteroffer becomes valid if not negated or rejected by the party receiving it. Answer (c) s incorrect because

Foster's acceptance was effective when sent. It was a reasonable means of acceptance and placed in an independent agency's control.

33. (578,L1,44) (d) An assignment of a contract means both an assignment of rights and a delegation of duties. The assignor also remains liable if the assignee does not perform the duties. Therefore Bonnie will prevail against either Crane (assignor) or Devon (assignee). As in any recovery of damages, the injured party may only make one recovery no matter how many parties are liable. The burning of the warehouse does not negate Devon's liability since the contract was not conditioned on the existence of a supplier. Answer (b) is incorrect because Devon's contractual duty arose from the delegation of duties that went with the assignment of the contract. Answer (c) is incorrect because Bonnie did not contract with the supplier and has no rights against him. Bonnie may sue either Crane or Devon immediately.

34. (576,L1,4) (d) An acceptance is generally effective when it is dispatched by the offeree through an independent agency for transmission (constructive communication). If it is not sent by an independent agency, it is not effective until actually received by the offeror. The offeror may specify when the acceptance is effective irrespective of the manner of transmission, but that is not the case here. An offer need not be signed, i.e., it may be oral or written without a signature.

35. (575,L1,7) (d) In the absence of a controlling statute Jason is not bound by the writing because he received no consideration to support it. Martinson did not have the legal right to breach, and thus refraining from the breach is not legal forbearance. Neither is the promise to remain and pay the reduced rent for the fifth year consideration, because this was an obligation of the original contract and is therefore a pre-existing duty. A change in economic conditions is not an excuse for non-performance nor for a rent reduction.

36. (575,L1,1) (a) The purchaser need not show knowledge of falsity by the seller, because reckless mistakes or utter disregard for truth can be a substitute for intentional deception. Reliance upon misrepresentation is a necessary element of fraud. Noncompliance with the Statute of Frauds merely makes the contract unenforceable. Misrepresentation can be made prior to execution, i.e., inducing the purchaser to purchase.

MAY 1981 ANSWERS

37.   (581,L1,7)   (c)   At the time the contract was made, the debt was liquidated since the amount was certain ($500). However, the bona fide dispute changed the debt to an unliquidated debt. Payment of a lesser sum to discharge an unliquidated debt will be effective if accepted as payment in full since each party gives consideration in the form of forfeiting a claim to dispute the amount of the debt. Smith's cashing of the check was acceptance of a settlement for the full amount of the debt. Answers (a) and (b) are incorrect since they refer to liquidated debts and this debt is un-liquidated. Answer (d) is incorrect since the fact that Smith crossed out the words "paid in full" has no effect. The check must be accepted in the manner offered and Smith's cashing of the check discharges the entire unliquidated debt.

38.   (581,L1,8)   (c)   Advertisements or other offers to trade such as price lists are usually consider-ed proposals for negotiation or invitations seeking offers. In some cases, such an advertisement could be considered to be an offer if its terms were so specific as to single out a particular person or group as offer-ees (e.g., an ad offers a sale price to the first person to arrive at the store the next day). Usually, however, as in this case, such promotions are not considered to be offers. Since Harper's advertisement merely quotes prices on items in stock, it would not be construed as an offer (a), and if no offer is made, there can be no valid acceptance or contract formed as a result of such an ad [(b) and (d)].

39.   (581,L1,10)   (b)   This question deals with an offer to sell real property, thus the UCC, hence, the firm offer rule, does not apply. Since this offer does not fall under the UCC or contain a provision for con-sideration to be paid to hold open the offer (an option), the offer may be withdrawn anytime prior to accept-ance. Answer (a) is untrue since a valid acceptance would have to be received, not posted, by April 1 in order to comply with the offer. Answer (c) is incorrect because an offer not supported by consideration and not subject to UCC rules may be withdrawn at any time. Answer (d) is incorrect since the Statute of Frauds requires only the contract for the sale of real property (not the offer) to be in writing.

40.   (581,L1,11)   (b)   This question deals with an offer to sell real property; the UCC — and thus, the firm offer rule — do not apply. Since Schmit gave no consideration for the option to buy the property, Maurice may revoke the offer any time before Schmit accepts. Answer (a) is incorrect since only a merchant

offeror making an offer for the sale of goods under the UCC would be bound to hold open an offer without consideration for a stated period of time. Answer (c) is incorrect since the Statute of Frauds applies only to the contract for sale of real property, and not an offer to buy; thus, the offer need not be in writing. Answer (d) is incorrect, since a nonmerchant may revoke an offer not supported by consideration any time before acceptance by the offeree. There is no restriction on how this revocation may be communicated.

41.   (581,1L1,12)   (a)   The parol evidence rule ap-plies to all written contracts and states that once an agreement is reduced to writing, the parties may not introduce oral or written agreements made prior to the written agreement in an attempt to alter or contradict the terms of the written agreement. This is true when the parties intended that the writing constitute their complete contract. Answer (b) is incorrect because the parol evidence rule would apply to all oral agreements made contemporaneously with the written contract. Answer (c) is incorrect since there is no requirement that both parties sign the contract in order for this rule to apply. Answer (d) is incorrect because the parol evi-dence rule is applied whether or not the Statute of Frauds requires a particular contract to be in writing.

42.   (581,L1,13)   (c)   The acceptance of an offer must conform exactly to the terms of the offer. If a party intends to accept an offer, but includes additional or different terms which are intended to become part of the contract, this constitutes a counteroffer and not an acceptance (a possible exception to this exists with contracts made between two merchants concerning the sale of goods). Norriss' additional term is a condition precedent and constitutes a counteroffer. Answer (a) is incorrect because a contract for the sale of real property must be in writing (under the Statute of Frauds) to be enforceable unless the doctrine of partial performance applies. Answer (b) is incorrect since a valid contract need only be signed by the party to be charged with performance. Answer (d) is untrue because the addition of a condition precedent has a significant effect on the contractual relationship since it prevents a contract from being formed unless Wilcox accepts the new term.

ANSWER OUTLINE

Problem 1   Contract Validity

b1.   Invalid: Brown gave consideration
        Brown was to purchase entire requirements
        Buyer expected to act in good faith

b2.   Invalid: Quantity not too indefinite
        Expected to purchase requirements in good faith
        Prior requirements used to measure
        An open term contract does not fail where parties
          intended contract

b3.   Invalid: No legal impossibility exists
        Not physically or objectively impossible
        Additional financial burden not an excuse
        To excuse performance here would impair validity
          of many contracts

UNOFFICIAL ANSWER

Problem 1   Contract Validity

b.   1.   This asserted legal justification is in-
            valid. First, Brown & Sons did give
            consideration in that they promised
            to purchase their candy needs exclu-
            sively from Mark. Second, the courts
            have sustained the validity of such
            requirement contracts based upon a
            logical interpretation of the agreement
            on the buyer's part to act in good
            faith and to take his usual or normal
            amount of the product involved.

      2.   This asserted legal justification is also
            invalid. Although some limited indefinite-
            ness and uncertainty is present, this will
            not invalidate the agreement. The Uniform
            Commercial Code provides that a contract
            of sale does not fail for indefiniteness even
            though one or more terms are left **open**
            if the parties have intended to make a
            contract and there is a reasonably cer-
            tain basis for giving an appropriate reme-
            dy. Furthermore, the code provides that
            when a contract measures the quantity in
            terms of output of the seller or require-
            ments of the buyer, it means such actual
            output or requirements as may occur in
            good faith. Mark's good faith is presumed,
            and prior requirements may be used to
            ascertain the quantities.

3.   The asserted legal justification based upon
      a drastic change in price is invalid. The
      courts will not recognize a subsequent
      implied condition of this nature to per-
      mit a party to avoid his obligation under
      a contract. Moreover, while the modern
      trend of the courts may be somewhat
      more lenient in finding the existence of
      impossibility, they will not excuse per-
      formance unless the performance is ren-
      dered physically and objectively impossi-
      ble.

      The development of an additional
      financial burden or hardship upon a
      party to a contract is not sufficient to
      provide a legal excuse for his nonper-
      formance. To excuse performance in
      these circumstances would seriously
      hamper the conduct of business trans-
      actions and impair the validity of many
      contracts.

ANSWER OUTLINE

**Problem 2   Offer and Acceptance; Revocation;
                Rejection**

a.   Orange County Bank will prevail in ensuing law
      suit
        Offer was to enter unilateral contract requir-
          ing performance as authorized and only
          means of acceptance
            Therefore, promise to perform by
              Fennimore could not create contract
        Offer can be revoked at any time before
          acceptance
            Fennimore's timely revocation termin-
              ated offer
        Restatement of Contracts Rule - Modification
          of common law rules stated above
            Offeree's action of engaging in substan-
              tial action concerning requested
              performance can qualify as accept-
              ance of offer to enter unilateral
              contract
                Substantial action not present in
                  this case
        No fraud or misrepresentation by Fennimore
        Bank's justification for revoking its offer
          because of Fennimore's sale was immaterial

b.   Hernandez will prevail
        Offer is effective when communicated to
          offeree
        Counter offer effective when communicated
          to original offeror

General rule (acceptance upon dispatch) is that
    acceptance which arrives before counter offer
    creates a binding contract
        Exception applies if offeree first rejects
            offer (usually effective upon receipt)
            and then accepts offer (usually effective
            upon dispatch)
                First acceptance to arrive is effective

UNOFFICIAL ANSWER

Problem 2   Offer and Acceptance; Revocation;
               Rejection

Part a.

Orange County Bank will prevail. The fact situation
poses a classic illustration of a withdrawl of an offer
to enter into a unilateral contract. The bank's offer to
Fennimore called for the performance of an act (the
actual paying of the mortgage), not a promise to pay it,
as the means of acceptance. The language in the offer
is clear and unambiguous, providing a 5 percent discount on a mortgage if the mortgagor would pay the
entire mortgage in cash or by certified check by July
31, 1980, at the Second Street branch of the bank.
Thus, the bank's letter was an offer to enter into a
unilateral contract that required the performance of
the act as the authorized and exclusive means of acceptance. Fennimore's promise to perform the act was
ineffectual in creating a contract. Contract law generally provides that offers may be revoked at any time
prior to acceptance; even if the bank revoked its offer
the instant before the purported acceptance, it was a
timely revocation and the acceptance was too late.
The tender of performance would also be of no avail
since notice of revocation had been received on the
30th.

    In this situation, strict common law rules would
deny the creation of a contract. Some states, in recognition of the hardship of such results, have adopted
what is known as the *restatement of contracts* rule.
This modification of the common law rule in respect to
the unilateral contract rule holds that the unilateral
promise in an offer calling for an act becomes binding
as soon as part of the requested performance actually
has been rendered or a proper tender of performance
has been made. The courts have required substantial
action on the part of the offeree, which does not
appear to be present here.

    The fact that Fennimore was selling his property
and did not disclose the fact that he would have to pay
the mortgage off in any event is immaterial. There was
no material misrepresentation of fact made by him,
hence his action was not fradulent nor did he misrep-

resent. He was silent. Additionally, the fact that the
bank was using the sale as a reason for terminating the
offer was immaterial.

Part b.

Hernandez will prevail. An offer is not effective until
communicated to the offeree. The same rule applies to
counteroffers including a change in the price, as occurred here. Therefore, a counteroffer is not effective
until received by Austin, the original offeror. Hernandez's counteroffer does not destroy the offer until it
is received. Thus, Hernandez's telegram, which accepted Austin's offer and arrived ahead of Hernandez's
letter containing the counteroffer, is effective in creating a binding contract.

    This rule applies even if Hernandez had mailed a
letter that unequivocally accepted Austin's offer and
that would have been effective upon dispatch. The general rule that an acceptance is effective when dispatched is subject to an exception that is designed to prevent
entrapment of an offeror who is misled to his disadvantage by an offeree who attempts to take two inconsistent positions. Thus, when an offeree first rejects an
offer, then subsequently accepts it, the subsequent
acceptance will be considered effective upon dispatch
by an authorized means only if it arrives prior to the
offeror's receipt of the rejection. If the rejection arrives
first, the original offeror may treat the attempted
acceptance as a counteroffer which he is free to accept
or not. Were this not the rule, an offeror who, upon
receipt of a rejection, in good faith changed his position (that is, sold the goods to another customer),
could find himself having sold the same goods twice.

ANSWER OUTLINE

Problem 3   Substantial Performance; Effectiveness
               of Acceptance

a.   Result if dispute goes to court
      Common-law requires literal performance; any-
          thing less is a breach releasing either party from
          duty to perform
      Courts have developed doctrine of substantial
          performance as an exception concerning con-
          struction contracts
      If breach is immaterial; party who breached
          may recover, less damages. Party who
          breached must prove
      1. Defect was not structural in nature
      2. Breach was minor relative to total job (95% is
         a guide courts use)
      3. Breach was not intentional

Elements 1 and 2 appear to be met in this case

Satisfaction of element 3 is not determinable from facts given

Would be met if substitutions were due to mistake or mere negligence, and Silverwater would prevail

If substitution was willful, no recovery by Silverwater

b.   No contract for sale of real property

Offer is governed by common law of contracts

Offer stipulations stated that acceptance must be received before effective

Negated possibility of acceptance being effective even though sent by same means

Purported acceptance was counteroffer

Had to be accepted to create contract

Silence does not constitute acceptance unless

1. Parties intended silence as acceptance

2. Prior dealing indicates silence is acceptable

3. Custom of industry recognizes silence as acceptance

Above exceptions do not apply, and there is no contract

UNOFFICIAL ANSWER

Problem 3   Substantial Performance; Effectiveness of Acceptance

Parts a1. and a2.

The general common-law rules require literal performance by a party to a contract. Failure to literally perform constitutes a breach. Since promises are construed to be dependent upon each other, the failure by one party to perform releases the other. However, a strict and literal application of this type of implied condition often results in unfairness and hardship, particularly in cases such as this. Therefore, the courts developed some important exceptions to the literal performance doctrine. The applicable rule is known as the substantial performance doctrine, which applies to construction contracts and is a more specific statement of the material performance rule that applies to contracts other than construction contracts. The general rule holds that if the breach is immaterial, the party who breached may nevertheless recover under the contract, less damages caused by the breach. The substantial performance doctrine requires the builder (party breaching) to prove the following facts.

a.   The defect was not a structural defect.

b.   The breach was relatively minor in relation to the overall performance of the contract. The courts and texts sometimes talk in terms of a 95 percent or better performance.

c.   The breach must be unintentional or, to state it another way, the party breaching must have been acting in good faith.

It would appear that requirements a and b are clearly satisfied on the basis of the facts. Requirement c cannot be determined on the facts given. If Silverwater deliberately (with knowledge) substituted the improper and cheaper tile or sewerage pipes, then it may not be entitled to the benefit of the substantial performance exception. On the other hand, if these breaches were the result of an innocent oversight or mere negligence on its part, recovery should be granted. The recovery must be decreased by the amount of the damages caused by the breach. The substitute of sewer pipe of like quality and value would be considered substantial performance.

Part b.

No. The offer for the sale of real property is governed by the common law of contracts.

Anderson's letter constituted an offer that stated it would expire at a given time. In addition to stating the time, the letter indicated that acceptance "must be received in her (Anderson's) office" by said time. This language is clear and unambiguous and effectively negated the rule whereby acceptance may take place upon dispatch. Thus, despite use of the same means of communication, acceptance was not effective until receipt by Anderson on March 2, 1980. This was too late. Thus, the purported acceptance was a mere counteroffer by Heinz and had to be accepted in order to create a contract. Silence does not usually constitute acceptance. In fact, the common-law exceptions to this rule are limited in nature and narrowly construed. The law clearly will not permit a party to unilaterally impose silence upon the other as acceptance. The narrow exceptions are the following:

1.   The parties intended silence as acceptance.

2.   Prior dealing indicates that silence is an acceptable method of acceptance.

3.   The custom of the trade or industry recognizes silence as acceptance.

It is clear that our case is not within any of the exceptions; hence, silence does not constitute acceptance, and there is no contract.

MULTIPLE CHOICE QUESTIONS (1—32)

1.   Gibbeon Manufacturing shipped 300 designer navy blue blazers to Custom Clothing Emporeum. The blazers arrived on Friday, earlier than Custom had anticipated and on an exceptionally busy day for its receiving department. They were perfunctorily examined and sent to a nearby warehouse for storage until needed. On Monday of the following week, upon closer examination, it was discovered that the quality of the linings of the blazers was inferior to that specified in the sales contract. Which of the following is correct insofar as Custom's rights are concerned?

   a.   Custom can reject the blazers upon subsequent discovery of the defects.

   b.   Custom must retain the blazers since it accepted them and had an opportunity to inspect them upon delivery.

   c.   Custom's only course of action is rescission.

   d.   Custom had no rights if the linings were of merchantable quality.

2.   Which of the following requirements must be met for modification of a sales contract under the Uniform Commercial Code?

   a.   There must be consideration present if the contract is between merchants.

   b.   There must be a writing if the original sales contract is in writing.

   c.   The modification must satisfy the Statute of Frauds if the contract as modified is within its provisions.

   d.   The parol evidence rule applies and thus a writing is required.

3.   Barstow Hardware Company received an order for $850 of assorted hardware from Flanagan & Company. The shipping terms were F.O.B. Mannix Freight Line, seller's place of business, 2/10, net /30. Barstow packed and crated the hardware for shipment and it was loaded upon Mannix Freight's truck. While the goods were in transit to Flanagan, Barstow learned that Flanagan was insolvent in the equity sense (unable to pay its debts in the ordinary course of business). Barstow promptly wired Mannix Freight's office in Pueblo, Colorado, and instructed them to stop shipment of the goods to Flanagan and to store them until further instructions. Mannix complied with these instructions. Regarding the rights, duties, and liabilities of the parties, which of the following is correct?

   a.   Barstow's stoppage in transit was improper if Flanagan's assets exceeded its liabilities.

   b.   Flanagan is entitled to the hardware if it pays cash.

   c.   Once Barstow correctly learned of Flanagan's insolvency, it had no further duty or obligation to Flanagan.

   d.   The fact that Flanagan became insolvent in no way affects the rights, duties, and obligations of the parties.

4.   Ford bought a used typewriter for $625 from Jem Typewriters. The contract provided that the typewriter was sold "with all faults, as is, and at the buyer's risk." The typewriter broke down within a month. Ford took it back to Jem, and after prolonged arguing and negotiating, Jem orally agreed to reduce the price by $50 and refund that amount. Jem has reconsidered his rights and duties and decided not to refund the money. Under the circumstances, which of the following is correct?

   a.   The disclaimer of the implied warranties of merchantability and fitness is invalid.

   b.   The agreement to reduce the price is valid and binding.

   c.   Jem's promise is unenforceable since Ford gave no new consideration.

   d.   Since the contract as modified is subject to the statute of frauds, the modification must be in writing.

5.   Target Company, Inc. ordered a generator from Maximum Voltage Corporation. A dispute has arisen over the effect of a provision in the specifications that the generator have a 5,000 kilowatt capacity. The specifications were attached to the contract and were incorporated by reference in the main body of the contract. The generator did not have this capacity but instead had a maximum capacity of 4,800 kilowatts. The contract had a disclaimer clause which effectively negated both of the implied warranties of quality. Target is seeking to avoid the contract based upon breach of warranty and Maximum is relying on its disclaimer. Which of the following is a correct statement?

   a.   The 5,000 kilowatt term contained in the specifications does not constitute a warranty.

   b.   The disclaimer effectively negated any and all warranty protection claimed by Target.

   c.   The description language (5,000 kilowatt) contained in the specifications is an express warranty and has not been effectively disclaimed.

   d.   The parol evidence rule will prevent Target from asserting the 5,000 kilowatt term as a warranty.

6.   Buyer ordered goods from Seller. The contract required Seller to deliver them f.o.b. Buyer's place of business. Buyer inspected the goods, discovered they failed

to conform to the contract, and rightfully rejected them. In the event of loss of the goods, which of the following is a correct statement?

   a. Seller initially had the risk of loss and it remains with him after delivery.

   b. Risk of loss passes to Buyer upon tender of the goods f.o.b. Buyer's place of business.

   c. Buyer initially had the risk of loss, but it is shifted to Seller upon rightful rejection.

   d. If Seller used a public carrier to transport the goods to Buyer, risk of loss is on Buyer during transit.

7.   Milgore, the vice president of Deluxe Restaurants, telephoned Specialty Restaurant Suppliers and ordered a made-to-order dishwashing unit for one of its restaurants. Due to the specifications, the machine was not adaptable for use by other restauranteurs. The agreed price was $2,500. The machine was constructed as agreed but Deluxe has refused to pay for it. Which of the following is correct?

   a. Milgore obviously lacked the authority to make such a contract.

   b. The statute of frauds applies and will bar recovery by Specialty.

   c. Specialty can successfully maintain an action for the price.

   d. Specialty must resell the machine and recover damages based upon the resale price.

8.   Pure Food Company packed and sold quality food products to wholesalers and fancy food retailers. One of its most popular items was "southern style" baked beans. Charleston purchased a large can of the beans from the Superior Quality Grocery. Charleston's mother bit into a heaping spoonful of the beans at a family outing and fractured her jaw. The evidence revealed that the beans contained a brown stone, the size of a marble. In a subsequent lawsuit by Mrs. Charleston, which of the following is correct?

   a. Mrs. Charleston can collect against Superior Quality for negligence.

   b. Privity will not be a bar in a lawsuit against either Pure Food or Superior Quality.

   c. The various sellers involved could have effectively excluded or limited the rights of third parties to sue them.

   d. Privity is a bar to recovery by Mrs. Charleston, although her son may sue Superior Quality.

9.   Martha Supermarkets ordered 1,000 cases of giant pitted olives from Grove Packers and Wholesalers. The olives were to be packed, labelled and shipped in 30 days. The payment terms were 2/10, net/30 upon delivery. After the order was nearly ready for shipment, Grove learned that Martha was not paying its debts as they became due. Martha insisted on delivery according to the terms of the contract. Which of the following is correct?

   a. Upon discovery of Martha's financial condition, Grove was relieved from any duty under the contract.

   b. Martha has the right of performance since it was not insolvent in the bankruptcy sense.

   c. Grove must perform but it is entitled to demand cash.

   d. The terms of the contract provided credit to Martha and Grove is bound by it.

10.   Dupree buys and sells merchandise at wholesale. She is concerned with her insurance coverage on her purchases. Her desire is to insure the property at the earliest possible time legally permitted. Which of the following times or circumstances correctly indicates the earliest time permissible?

   a. At the time the goods are identified to the contract.

   b. When title to the goods has passed to her.

   c. When she has received possession of the goods.

   d. At the time the contract is made whether or not the goods are identified.

11.   Cox Manufacturing repudiated its contract to sell 300 televisions to Ruddy Stores, Inc. What recourse does Ruddy Stores have?

   a. It can obtain specific performance by the seller.

   b. It can recover punitive damages.

   c. It must await the seller's performance for a commercially reasonable time after repudiation if it wishes to recover anything.

   d. It can "cover," that is, procure the goods elsewhere and recover any damages.

12.   On March 11, Vizar Sales Corporation telegraphed Watson Company:

"Will sell 1,000 cases of coffee for $28 a case for delivery at our place of business on April 15. You may pick them up at our loading platform."

Watson telegraphed its acceptance on March 12. On March 20, coffee prices rose to $30 a case. Vizar telegraphed Watson on March 21 that it repudiated the sale and would not make delivery. The telegram was received by Watson on March 22 when the price was $32; Watson could have covered at that price but chose not to do so. On April 15 the coffee was selling at $35 a case. Watson tendered $28,000 to Vizar and indicated it was ready to take delivery. Vizar refused to deliver. What relief, if any, is Watson entitled to?

   a.   Specific performance, because it made a valid tender of performance.
   b.   Nothing, because it failed to cover.
   c.   Damages of $4,000 (the difference between the contract price and the fair market value at the time Watson learned of the breach).
   d.   Damages of $7,000 (the difference between the contract price and the fair market value at the time delivery should have been made).

13.   Kent, a wholesale distributor of cameras, entered into a contract with Williams. Williams agreed to purchase 100 cameras with certain optional attachments. The contract was made on October 1, 1976, for delivery by October 15, 1976; terms: 2/10, net 30. Kent shipped the cameras on October 6, and they were delivered on October 10. The shipment did not conform to the contract, in that one of the attachments was not included. Williams immediately notified Kent that he was rejecting the goods. For maximum legal advantage Kent's most appropriate action is to

   a.   Bring an action for the price less an allowance for the missing attachment.
   b.   Notify Williams promptly of his intention to cure the defect and make a conforming delivery by October 15.
   c.   Terminate his contract with Williams and recover for breach of contract.
   d.   Sue Williams for specific performance.

14.   Under a contract for sale on approval, unless otherwise agreed, what happens to "risk of loss" and "title" upon delivery to the buyer?

   a.   Risk of loss but not title passes to buyer.
   b.   Title but not risk of loss passes to buyer.
   c.   Risk of loss and title pass to buyer.
   d.   Neither risk of loss nor title pass to buyer.

15.   Franklin purchased 100 sets of bed frames from Tully Manufacturing, Inc. Franklin made substantial prepayments on the purchase price. Tully is insolvent and the goods have not been delivered as promised. Franklin wants the bed frames. Under the circumstances, which of the following will prevent Franklin from obtaining the bed frames?

   a.   The fact that he can obtain a judgment for damages.
   b.   The fact that he was not aware of Tully's insolvency at the time he purchased the bed frames.
   c.   The fact that the goods have not been identified to his contract.
   d.   The fact that he did not pay the full price at the time of the purchase even though he has made a tender of the balance and holds it available to Tully upon delivery.

16.   Gordon purchased 100 automatic sprinklers from Thompson, a jobber. Conrad was the rightful owner of the sprinklers which had been stolen from his warehouse. He had the sheriff repossess them and has asserted his ownership of them. Gordon's bill of sale specifically indicated that it made no implied warranties. The bill of sale did not contain any warranties of title. Which of the following is correct based on the above facts?

   a.   The title warranties have been effectively negated.
   b.   It is not possible to disclaim the title warranties.
   c.   Gordon's best course of action is to assert his superior title to the sprinklers since he is a good faith purchaser for value.
   d.   Thompson is liable in that he warranted that the title conveyed was good and his transfer rightful.

17.   Parks furnished specifications and ordered 1,000 specially-constructed folding tables from Metal Manufacturing Company, Inc. The tables were unique in design and had not appeared in the local market. Metal completed the job and delivered the order to Parks. Parks sold about 600 of the tables when Unusual Tables, Inc., sued both Parks and Metal for patent infringement. If Unusual wins, what is the status of Parks and Metal?

   a.   Metal is liable to Parks for breach of the warranty against infringement.
   b.   Parks is liable to Metal for breach of the warranty against infringement.
   c.   The warranty against infringement is not available to either Parks or Metal.
   d.   Parks and Metal are jointly and severally liable and, as such, must pay the judgment in equal amounts.

18. Donaldson sold Randal six bundles of mink skins. The contract contained no specific provision regarding title warranties. It did, however, contain a provision which indicated that the skins were sold "with all faults and defects." Two of the bundles of skins sold to Randal had been stolen and were reclaimed by the rightful owner. Which of the following is a correct statement?

    a. Since there was no express title warranty, Randal assumed the risk.

    b. The disclaimer "with all faults and defects" effectively negates any and all warranties.

    c. The contract automatically contained a warranty that the title conveyed is good and can only be excluded by specific language.

    d. The implied warranty of title is eliminated by the parol evidence rule.

19. Duval Liquor Wholesales, Inc., stored its inventory of goods in the Reliable Warehouse Company. Duval's shipments would arrive by truck and be deposited with Reliable who would in turn issue negotiable warehouse receipts to Duval. Duval would resell the liquor by transferring the negotiable warehouse receipts to the buyer who was responsible for transporting it to his place of business. In one of the sales of liquor to a retailer, the liquor was badly damaged and a question has arisen as to who has the risk of loss, Duval or the retailer. If the contract is silent on this point, when did the risk of loss pass to the retailer?

    a. When the goods have been placed on the warehouseman's delivery dock awaiting pick up by the retailer.

    b. When the goods have been identified to the contract.

    c. On his receipt of the negotiable warehouse receipts covering the goods.

    d. When the goods have been properly loaded upon the retailer's carrier.

20. Wexford Furniture, Inc., is in the retail furniture business and has stores located in principal cities in the United States. Its designers created a unique cocktail table. After obtaining prices and schedules, Wexford ordered 2,000 tables to be made to its design and specifications for sale as a part of its annual spring sales promotion campaign. Which of the following represents the earliest time Wexford will have an insurable interest in the tables?

    a. At the time the goods are in Wexford's possession.

    b. Upon shipment of conforming goods by the seller.

    c. When the goods are marked or otherwise designated by the seller as the goods to which the contract refers.

    d. At the time the contract is made.

21. Badger Corporation sold goods to Watson. Watson has arbitrarily refused to pay the purchase price. Under what circumstances will Badger not be able to recover the price if it seeks this remedy instead of other possible remedies?

    a. If Watson refused to accept delivery and the goods were resold in the ordinary course of business.

    b. If Watson accepted the goods but seeks to return them.

    c. If the goods sold were destroyed shortly after the risk of loss passed to the buyer.

    d. If the goods were identified to the contract and Badger made a reasonable effort to resell them at a reasonable price but was unable to do so.

22. Viscount Appliances sold Conway a refrigerator. Viscount wishes to disclaim the implied warranty of fitness for a particular purpose. Which of the following will effectively disclaim this warranty?

    a. The fact that the refrigerator is widely advertised and was sold under its brand name.

    b. A conspicuous written statement which states that "any and all warranty protection is hereby disclaimed."

    c. A conspicuous written statement indicating that "there are no warranties which extend beyond the description contained in the contract of sale."

    d. An inconspicuous written statement which specifically negates the warranty.

23. Devold Manufacturing, Inc., entered into a contract for the sale to Hillary Company of 2,000 solid-state CB radios at $27.50 each, terms 2/10, N/30, F.O.B. Hillary's loading platform. After delivery of the first 500 radios, a minor defect was discovered. Although the defect was minor, Hillary incurred costs to correct the defect. Hillary sent Devold a signed memorandum indicating that it would relinquish its right to recover the costs to correct the defect, provided that the balance of the radios were in conformity with the terms of the contract and the delivery dates were strictly adhered to. Devold met these conditions. Shortly before the last shipment of radios arrived, a dispute between the parties arose over an

unrelated matter. Hillary notified Devold that it was not bound by the prior generous agreement and would sue Devold for damages unless Devold promptly reimbursed Hillary. In the event of litigation, what would be the result and the basis upon which the litigation would be decided?

- a. Devold will lose in that Hillary's relinquishment of its rights was not supported by a consideration.
- b. Devold will win in that the defect was minor and the substantial performance doctrine applies.
- c. Hillary will lose in that the communication constituted a waiver of Hillary's rights.
- d. Hillary will win in that there was a failure to perform the contract, and Hillary suffered damages as a result.

24. Almovar Electronics was closing out several lines of electronic parts which were becoming outdated. It sent a letter on March 8 to Conduit Sales & Service Company, one of its largest retail customers, offering the entire lot at a substantial reduction in price. The offer indicated that it was for "immediate acceptance." The terms were "cash, pick up by your carrier at our loading dock and not later than March 15." It also indicated that the terms of the offer were not subject to variance. The letter did not arrive until March 10 and Conduit's letter accepting the offer was not mailed until March 12. The letter of acceptance indicated that Conduit would take the entire lot, would pay in accordance with the usual terms (2/10, net/30), and would pick up the goods on March 16. Which of the following best describe the legal relationship of the parties?

- a. The acceptance was not timely, hence no contract.
- b. The different terms of the acceptance are to be construed as proposals for changes in the contract.
- c. The different terms of the acceptance constituted a rejection of the offer.
- d. Since both parties were merchants and the changes in the acceptance were not material, there is a valid contract.

25. Wilson Corporation entered into a contract to sell goods to Marvin who has a place of business in the same town as Wilson. The contract was clear with respect to price and quantity, but failed to designate the place of delivery. Which of the following statements is correct?

- a. The contract is unenforceable because of indefiniteness.

- b. The place for delivery must be designated by the parties within five days or the contract is voidable.
- c. The seller's place of business is the proper place for delivery.
- d. The buyer's place of business is the proper place for delivery.

MAY 1981 QUESTIONS

26. The Uniform Commercial Code provides for a warranty against infringement. Its primary purpose is to protect the buyer of goods from infringement of the rights of third parties. This warranty

- a. Only applies if the sale is between merchants.
- b. Must be expressly stated in the contract or the Statute of Frauds will prevent its enforceability.
- c. Protects the seller if the buyer furnishes specifications which result in an infringement.
- d. Can **not** be disclaimed.

27. Brown ordered 100 cases of Delicious Brand peas at list price from Smith Wholesaler. Immediately upon receipt of Brown's order, Smith sent Brown an acceptance which was received by Brown. The acceptance indicated that shipment would be made within ten days. On the tenth day Smith discovered that all of its supply of Delicious Brand peas had been sold. Instead it shipped 100 cases of Lovely Brand peas, stating clearly on the invoice that the shipment was sent only as an accommodation. Which of the following is correct?

- a. Smith's shipment of Lovely Brand peas is a counteroffer, thus **no** contract exists between Brown and Smith.
- b. Smith's note of accommodation cancels the contract between Smith and Brown.
- c. Brown's order is a unilateral offer, and can only be accepted by Smith's shipment of the goods ordered.
- d. Smith's shipment of Lovely Brand peas constitutes a breach of contract.

28. Ace Auto Sales, Inc., sold Williams a secondhand car for $9,000. One day Williams parked the car in a shopping center parking lot. When Williams returned to the car, Montrose and several policemen were waiting. It turned out that the car had been stolen from Montrose who was rightfully claiming ownership. Subsequently, the car was returned by Williams to Montrose. Williams seeks recourse against Ace Auto Sales who

had sold him the car with the usual disclaimer of warranty. Which of the following is correct?

    a.   Since Ace Auto Sales' contract of sale disclaimed "any and all warranties" arising in connection with its sale to Williams, Williams must bear the loss.

    b.   Since Ace Auto and Williams were both innocent of any wrongdoing in connection with the theft of the auto, the loss will rest upon the party ultimately in possession.

    c.   Had Williams litigated the question of Montrose's ownership to the auto, he would have won since possession is nine-tenths of the law.

    d.   Ace Auto will bear the loss since a warranty of title in Williams' favor arose upon the sale of the auto.

29.   A dispute has arisen between two merchants over the question of who has the risk of loss in a given sales transaction. The contract does not specifically cover the point. The goods were shipped to the buyer who rightfully rejected them. Which of the following factors will be the most important factor in resolving their dispute?

    a.   Who has title to the goods.

    b.   The shipping terms.

    c.   The credit terms.

    d.   The fact that a breach has occurred.

30.   Doral Inc., wished to obtain an adequate supply of lumber for its factory extension which was to be constructed in the spring. It contacted Ace Lumber Company and obtained a 75-day written option (firm offer) to buy its estimated needs for the building. Doral supplied a form contract which included the option. Ace Lumber signed at the physical end of the contract but did not sign elsewhere. The price of lumber has risen drastically and Ace wishes to avoid its obligation. Which of the following is Ace's best defense against Doral's assertion that Ace is legally bound by the option?

    a.   Such an option is invalid if its duration is for more than two months.

    b.   The option is **not** supported by any consideration on Doral's part.

    c.   Doral is **not** a merchant.

    d.   The promise of irrevocability was contained in a form supplied by Doral and was **not** separately signed by Ace.

31.   Ambrose telephoned Miller Adding Machine Company and ordered 1,000 pocket calculators at $4.05 each. Ambrose agreed to pay 10% immediately and the balance within ten days after receipt of the entire shipment. Ambrose forwarded a check for $405.00 and Miller shipped 500 calculators the next day, intending to ship the balance by the end of the week. Ambrose decided that the contract was a bad bargain and repudiated it, asserting the Statute of Frauds. Miller sued Ambrose. Which of the following will allow Miller to prevail despite the Statute of Frauds?

    a.   The contract is **not** within the requirements of the statute.

    b.   Ambrose paid 10% down.

    c.   Miller shipped 500 of the calculators.

    d.   Ambrose admitted in court that it made the contract in question.

32.   Darrow purchased 100 sets of bookends from Benson Manufacturing, Inc. Darrow made substantial prepayments of the purchase price. Benson is insolvent and the goods have not been delivered as promised. Darrow wants the bookends. Under the circumstances, which of the following will prevent Darrow from obtaining the bookends?

    a.   The fact that he did **not** pay the full price at the time of the purchase even though he has made a tender of the balance and holds it available to Benson upon delivery.

    b.   The fact that he can obtain a judgment for damages.

    c.   The fact that he was **not** aware of Benson's insolvency at the time he purchased the bookends.

    d.   The fact that the goods have **not** been identified to his contract.

Problem 1   Breach of Warranty; Warranty of Title (1177,L7a & b)

(15 to 20 minutes)

Part a.   Max Motors, Inc., sold a 1973 used station wagon to Sarah Constance for $3,350. Constance has corresponded with Max Motors on several occasions and has alleged that Fogarty, an experienced salesman for Max Motors, made several express oral warranties in connection with her purchase of the car. Constance alleges that there has been a breach of warranty and as a result she has suffered damages to the extent of $1,025 for expenses incurred to repair the car. Constance also indicated that in the event she does not receive a refund of $1,025, she will take appropriate legal action to obtain satisfaction.

In various letters, Constance stated that she went to Max Motors and contacted Fogarty. Before she finally made a deal for the car, she asked many questions about the car. Fogarty assured her that the car was in good condition and that he had driven the car several times. In addition, Fogarty stated that "This is a car I can recommend and it is in A-1 shape."

Constance informed Fogarty that her husband had been transferred to another state, that her child was only two years old, and that she needed the car so she could join her husband. She stated that Fogarty assured her that he knew the car and knew the person who traded it in and it was "mechanically perfect." He also told her that, "it would get her any place she wanted to go and not to worry." Constance indicated she knew nothing about cars but would like to drive it. Fogarty replied this was not possible because he was the only man on duty at the lot that day and he could not leave to accompany her as required by company policy.

Constance stated she purchased the car in reliance on the statements made by Fogarty. Unfortunately, these statements proved to be incorrect. The car began knocking and finally broke down after being driven about 300 miles. The car was repaired by Master Mechanics and a copy of a receipted bill for $1,025 accompanied one of her letters to Max Motors.

Fogarty indicated that he believed what he stated was true, as far as he knew the car wasn't in bad condition, and he knew of no important defects in the car. He also indicated he told Constance that he could not warrant the car because it was over two years old and had in excess of 50,000 miles.

Required: Answer the following, setting forth reasons for any conclusions stated.

1.   Is it likely that Constance will prevail in a legal action against Max Motors? Discuss all relevant issues.

2.   Identify, but do not discuss, other warranties that Constance might rely upon in addition to the oral express warranties.

Part b.   A claim has been asserted against Ajax Motors for $7,000 arising out of the sale of a used 1975 automobile. Knox purchased the automobile in February 1977 and subsequently learned that it was a stolen car. The serial numbers had been changed, but it has been conclusively determined that the car belongs to Watts who has duly repossessed it. The contract contained a disclaimer which read as follows: "Ajax Motors hereby disclaims any and all warranties, express or implied, which are not contained in the contract." Knox has brought a legal action against Ajax Motors alleging breach of warranty.

Required: Answer the following, setting forth reasons for any conclusions stated.

What is the probable outcome of such a legal action? Discuss fully the legal basis upon which Knox is relying and any defense that Ajax Motors may assert.

Problem 2   Option Contract, Risk of Loss, Pre-Existing Duty, Contract Interference (1178,L5)

(20 to 25 minutes)

Part a.   Clauson Enterprises, Inc., was considering adding a new product line to its existing lines. The decision was contingent upon its being assured of a supply of an electronic component for the product at a certain price and a positive market study which clearly justified the investment in the venture.

Clauson's president approached Migrane Electronics and explained the situation to Migrane's president. After much negotiation, Migrane agreed to grant Clauson an option to purchase 12,000 of the necessary electronic components at $1.75 each or at the prevailing market price, whichever was lower. Clauson prepared the option below incorporating their understanding.

Option Agreement
Clauson Enterprises/Migrane Electronics

Migrane Electronics hereby offers to sell Clauson Enterprises 12,000 miniature solid state electronic breakers at $1.75 each or at the existing market price at the time of delivery, whichever is lower, delivery to be made in 12 equal monthly installments beginning one month after the exercise of this option. This option is irrevocable for six months from January 1, 1978.

Clauson Enterprises agrees to deliver to Migrane its market survey for the product line in which the component would be used if it elects not to exercise the option.

Both parties signed the option agreement and Migrane's president signed Migrane's corporate name alongside the last sentence of the first paragraph. On May 1, 1978, Migrane notified Clauson that it was revoking its offer. The market price for the component had increased to $1.85. On May 15, 1978, Clauson notified Migrane that it accepted the offer and that if Migrane did not perform, it would be sued and held liable for damages. Migrane replied that the offer was not binding and was revoked before Clauson accepted. Furthermore, even if it were binding, it was good for only three months as a matter of law.

Upon receipt of Migrane's reply, Clauson instituted suit for damages.

Required: Answer the following, setting forth reasons for any conclusions stated.

Who will prevail? Discuss all the issues and arguments raised by the fact situation.

Part b. On May 30, 1978, Hargrove ordered 1,000 spools of nylon yarn from Flowers, Inc., of Norfolk, Virginia. The shipping terms were "F.O.B., Norfolk & Western RR at Norfolk." The transaction was to be a cash sale with payment to be simultaneously exchanged for the negotiable bill of lading covering the goods. Title to the goods was expressly reserved in Flowers. The yarn ordered by Hargrove was delivered to the railroad and loaded in a boxcar on June 1, 1978. Flowers obtained a negotiable bill of lading made out to its own order. The boxcar was destroyed the next day while the goods were in transit. Hargrove refused to pay for the yarn and Flowers sued Hargrove for the purchase price.

Required: Answer the following, setting forth reasons for any conclusions stated.
Who will prevail?

Part c. Novack, an industrial designer, accepted an offer from Superior Design Corporation to become one of its designers. The contract was for three years and expressly provided that it was irrevocable by either party except for cause during that period of time. The contract was in writing and signed by both parties. After a year, Novack became dissatisfied with the agreed compensation which he was receiving. He had done a brilliant job and several larger corporations were attempting to lure him away.

Novack, therefore, demanded a substantial raise, and Superior agreed in writing to pay him an additional amount as a bonus at the end of the third year. Novack remained with Superior and performed the same duties he had agreed to perform at the time he initially accepted the position. At the end of the three years, Novack sought to collect the additional amount of money promised. Superior denied liability beyond the amount agreed to in the original contract.

Required: Answer the following, setting forth reasons for any conclusions stated.
Can Novack recover the additional compensation from Superior?

Part d. The basic facts are the same as stated in Part c except that one of Superior's competitors, Dixon Corporation, successfully lured Novack away from Superior by offering a substantially higher salary. Dixon did this with full knowledge of the terms of the original three-year contract between Novack and Superior.

Required: Answer the following, setting forth reasons for any conclusions stated.
1. Does Superior have any legal redress against Dixon?
2. Would Superior be successful if it seeks the equitable relief of specific performance (an order by the court compelling Novack to perform his contractual undertaking) for the remaining two years of the contract?

Problem 3   Consignments (580,L4a)

(7 to 10 minutes)

Part a.   After much study and deliberation, the marketing division of Majestic Enterprise, Inc., has recommended to the board of directors that the corporation market its products almost exclusively via consignment arrangements instead of other alternate merchandising-security arrangements. The board moved favorably upon this proposal.

Required:
Answer the following, setting forth reasons for any conclusions stated.
What are the key legal characteristics of a consignment?

MULTIPLE CHOICE ANSWERS

1.	a	8.	b	15.	c	22.	c	29.	d
2.	c	9.	c	16.	d	23.	c	30.	d
3.	b	10.	a	17.	b	24.	c	31.	d
4.	d	11.	d	18.	c	25.	c	32.	d
5.	c	12.	c	19.	c	26.	c		
6.	a	13.	b	20.	c	27.	d		
7.	c	14.	d	21.	a	28.	d		

EXPLANATION OF MULTIPLE CHOICE ANSWERS

1. (1180,L1,12) (a)   Answer (a) is correct since the buyer has a reasonable time in which to reject defective goods. Discovering the defect on Monday would be considered within a reasonable time, considering the goods had been delivered on Friday. Answer (d) is incorrect since the specification concerning the linings in the sales contract would be an express warranty which was breached when the linings were found to be inferior to what had been stated. Thus, the merchantable quality of the linings would be irrelevant.

2. (1180,L1,16) (c)   Under the U.C.C. the Statute of Frauds is applicable if the contract as modified is within the Statute. An example of this would be an oral contract for the sale of a car for $450 which is subsequently modified by the parties to a purchase price of $500. Such a modification must be in writing to be enforceable since it is within the statute of Frauds. Answer (a) is incorrect since under the U.C.C. modification of a pre-existing contract for the sale of goods needs no new consideration to be binding. The modification may be oral or written, depending on whether it involves an amount of $500 or more, so answer (b) is incorrect. Answer (d) is incorrect because the parol evidence rule does not apply to subsequent modifications of a written agreement, e.g. oral changes made after the original written agreement.

3. (1180,L1,17) (b)   When a seller discovers that the buyer is insolvent (this includes insolvency in the equity sense), the seller may stop the goods in transit and refuse delivery except for cash. If Flanagan pays cash he is entitled to the hardware. Thus, answer (b) is correct.

4. (580,L1,27) (d)   Even as modified, the contract would involve the sale of goods for $500 or more, thus the Statute of Frauds would require that such agreement be in writing. Answer (a) is incorrect because "with all faults, as is" does disclaim all implied warranties. Answer (c) is incorrect because a modification of a pre-existing contract for the sale of goods needs no new consideration.

5. (580,L1,32) (c)   The "5000 kilowatt" term is a statement of fact made as part of the basis of the bargain; thus it qualifies as an express warranty. Only the implied warranties were disclaimed, thus answer (c) is correct and answers (a) and (b) are incorrect. Answer (d) is incorrect because the parol evidence rule excludes oral statements from evidence when the agreement is in writing. The "5000 kilowatt" term was part of the written agreement, therefore the parol evidence rule would not exclude this term from the agreement.

6. (580,L1,33) (a)   In an f.o.b. point of destination contract the risk of loss transfers from seller to buyer upon tender of conforming goods. However, the seller did not deliver conforming goods and the risk of loss remains upon seller even after delivery. Thus answers (b), (c) and (d) are incorrect.

7. (580,L1,34) (c)   Since there are no prospective buyers of this unit due to its uniqueness of design, the seller can sue for the full contract price. Answer (a) is incorrect because the vice president would normally have authority to make such contracts. Answer (b) is incorrect because the Statute of Frauds allows enforcement of an oral contract for the sale of specially manufactured goods if substantial performance occurs before repudiation. Answer (d) is incorrect because Specialty may recover the full contract price for specially manufactured goods since there is no prospective market for this unit.

8. (580,L1,37) (b)   Both Pure Food and Superior Quality would be liable under the strict liability theory of product liability. If the product leaves the hands of the seller with a defect present that causes injury, the seller is liable for injury. Under strict liability there is no requirement of privity of contract between the seller and injured party. Even though Superior was not negligent they are still liable under strict liability. This liability cannot be excluded. If Mrs. Charleston were suing on the basis of breach of warranty she would have to show privity of contract. Answer (a) is incorrect because there is no negligence on the part of the seller, Superior Quality, but only on the manufacturer, Pure Food Company.

9. (580,L1,38) (c)   When the seller discovers that the buyer is insolvent, the seller may refuse delivery except for cash. Answer (c) is correct because Martha was insolvent in the "equity" sense. Answer (a) is incorrect because a buyer's insolvency does not discharge the seller's duty to perform. Answers (b) and (d) are incorrect because insolvency of the buyer in the "equity sense" is sufficient to permit the seller to demand cash before delivering the goods.

10. (580,L1,46) (a) Identification occurs when the seller designates what goods he is going to use to perform the contract. Once identification occurs the buyer has an insurable interest in the goods and can insure against any losses he might suffer if goods are damaged or destroyed.

11. (1179,L1,1) (d) The nonbreaching party under a contract for sale can attempt to mitigate damages by "cover," that is, by procuring the goods elsewhere and recovering as damages the difference between the contract price and the price of cover. Answer (a) is incorrect because specific performance is available only upon the damaged party showing that money damages are inadequate or other unique conditions exist which require actual performance. There is nothing here to indicate that the televisions are unavailable in the market or other unique conditions exist. Answer (b) is incorrect because punitive damages are never recoverable for breach of contract. Answer (c) is incorrect since a nonbreaching party need not wait after a breach occurs to begin proceedings to recover.

12. (1179,L1,13) (c) Watson should collect damages of $4,000 representing the difference between the contract price and the fair market value at the time he learned of the breach. The nonbreaching party in an anticipatory breach has a responsibility to mitigate damages upon learning of the breach. Answer (a) is incorrect because specific performance is available only when other legal remedies are inadequate. There is nothing to indicate that the coffee is unavailable or otherwise unique, and thus specific performance is not available. Answer (b) is incorrect because Watson is entitled to recover the damages resulting from the failure of Vizar to deliver the 1,000 cases of coffee at $28 a case. Furthermore, Watson presumably did cover after it became apparent on April 15 that Vizar would not deliver. Whether Watson actually purchases the coffee elsewhere (cover) is unimportant since one of the options of the nonbreaching party is to simply recover the difference between the contract price and the fair market value at the time of the breach. Answer (d) is incorrect because Watson is limited to the difference between the contract price and the fair market value at the time Watson learned of the breach.

13. (1176,L1,9) (b) Under the UCC, a seller has the right to cure non-conforming goods within the original time of the contract if he notifies the buyer. This would put Kent in the position of having fulfilled the contract and having complied with the UCC. Then Williams would be the one in breach of the contract if he does not pay on time.

If on the other hand, Kent does not cure the defect and brings an action for the price less an allowance, Williams would have the defense that the goods were non-conforming and he had the right to reject them. Then Kent could not recover for breach of contract, because it was he who breached it by tendering non-conforming goods. In the case of duplicatable cameras, specific performance would not be available to either party.

14. (577,L3,42) (d) Under the UCC both title and risk of loss remain with the seller until the buyer accepts the goods if it is a contract for "sale on approval." These contracts are used between sellers and consumers. Goods bought for resale may be bought under a contract for "sale or return." Under "sale and return," the seller retains title but the buyer has risk of loss.

15 (1178,L1,31) (c) Bed frames constitute goods and thus are regulated by the rules of the UCC. The UCC is liberal in allowing the buyer to select among a number of remedies upon the seller's breach. However, in order to obtain the particular goods, the buyer must prove that the particular goods are the ones that he contracted to buy. Lack of identification of the goods by the contract will prevent the buyer from proving which are the goods he contracted to buy. Answer (a) is incorrect because it essentially states the common law rule that specific performance is not available if a judgment for damages is available. However, under the UCC, if the seller becomes insolvent, the buyer may recover the goods if identified to the contract. Answer (b) is incorrect because being unaware of the seller's insolvency at the time of purchase would in no way impede the rights of the buyer described above. Answer (d) is incorrect because payment of a portion of the price, tender of the balance, and holding it available are circumstances which would greatly favor the distressed buyer's obtaining the particular goods.

16. (1178,L1,35) (d) A seller is liable for breach of warranty of title unless he specifically disclaimed such warranty at the time of sale. Since no mention was made of title, Thompson is held to have warranted good title to the 100 sprinklers purchased by Gordon. Thus, answer (a) is incorrect because there is no specific disclaimer of warranty of title. Answer (b) is incorrect because warranty of title may be specifically disclaimed. Answer (c) is incorrect because Gordon's best course of action is to pursue his warranty of title remedy rather than to attempt to establish superior title on the basis of being a good-faith pur-

chaser for value. Such action by Gordon would fail, since the facts indicate Conrad was the rightful owner from whom the goods had been stolen, and thus good title did not pass.

17. (1178,L1,36) (b) Parks, the purchaser, is liable to Metal, the seller, for breach of the warranty against infringement. Normally, it would be the seller who would be liable to the buyer for breach of the warranty against infringement, but when the buyer furnished the specifications for manufacture, the buyer must hold the seller harmless. Thus, answer (a) is incorrect. Also answer (c) is incorrect because the warranty against infringement is available. Answer (d) is incorrect because Parks furnished the specifications and Metal is an innocent party.

18. (579,L1,36) (c) A contract for the sale of goods automatically contains a warranty that the title to the goods is good, and the warranty can only be excluded by specific agreement in the contract. Thus answer (a) is incorrect, since no express title warranty need be given. Answer (b) is incorrect because the disclaimer "with all faults and defects" does not effectively negate the title warranty. Such a disclaimer will only disclaim implied warranties of quality and use. The parol evidence rule, as in answer (d), disallows oral evidence of agreements made prior to or contemporaneous with a written contract. It has nothing to do with a warranty of title.

19. (579,L1,39) (c) When goods are held by a warehouseman or other bailee and the seller is not to move the goods, the risk of loss passes to the buyer when he receives a negotiable document of title such as a warehouse receipt. Answers (a) and (d) are incorrect because the UCC specifies that risk of loss is to pass when the negotiable document of title passes. The parties may agree to pass the risk of loss at either of the times in answers (a) or (d), but it must be expressly stated to do so. Answer (b) is incorrect because identification of the goods to the contract helps determine when title passes, not when risk of loss passes. Risk of loss does not necessarily pass when title passes.

20. (578,L1,14) (c) Under the UCC, the buyer obtains an insurable interest in goods when they are identified to the contract. In the case of future goods, identification occurs when the goods are shipped, marked, or otherwise designated by the seller as the goods to which the contract refers. Answer (d) is incorrect because the insurable interest is not obtained at the time the contract is made. Answer (a) is incorrect because an insurable

interest can arise before the goods are in the buyer's possession. Answer (b) is incorrect because an insurable interest will be obtained before shipment when the goods are identified for shipment.

21. (578,L1,39) (a) A seller may not recover the contract price if buyer rejects delivery and the seller resells the goods in the ordinary course of business. The seller's damages is the difference between the contract price and the price at which the goods were sold (if less than the original contract price). Each example set out in answers (b), (c), and (d) presents an appropriate circumstance where a nonbreaching seller could rightfully recover the contract price.

22. (578,L1,40) (c) A disclaimer of implied warranty must be clear, conspicuous, and commonly understood as such. A conspicuous written statement stating "there are no warranties which extend beyond the description contained in the contract of sale" clearly states that there are no implied warranties. A statement of "any and all warranty protection is hereby disclaimed" (answer b) also adequately disclaims all implied warranties; but it also disclaims express warranties and all new appliances are sold with some type of warranty protection. Thus the disclaimer would be inconsistent and confusing. Answer (a) is incorrect because wide advertisement and brand name do not disclaim warranties. Answer (d) is incorrect because without exception, the UCC does not permit inconspicuous disclaimer of warranties.

23. (578,L1,41) (c) The communication constituted a waiver of Hillary's rights which is not retractable if it would be unjust because Devold relied on it. Waivers of claims arising out of an alleged breach of contract require no consideration to be valid under the UCC. Thus answer (a) is incorrect under the Code, although it would be correct under common law. Answer (b) is incorrect because the doctrine of substantial performance provides that performance is satisfied if deviations have been minor. However, damages would still be available except that Hillary waived his right to them. Answer (d) is incorrect because Hillary would win had he not, under the rules of the Code, waived his claim to damages.

24. (579,L1,35) (c) Under the UCC, additional terms in an acceptance are considered proposals for changes in the contract unless the offer precludes a variance of its terms. If the parties are merchants the additional terms become part of the contract unless the original offer precludes a change in terms, the new terms materially alter the original offer,

or the original offeror objects within a reasonable time. Almovar Electronics stated that the terms of the offer were not subject to variance. Therefore the different terms of the acceptance constituted a rejection of the offer. Answers (b) and (d) are incorrect because the original offer precluded acceptance with a variance of terms. Answer (a) is incorrect because an acceptance within a few days of receipt of the offer stating "for immediate acceptance" would satisfy the objective test of a "reasonable time."

25. (578,L1,43) (c) Open terms will not cause a contract for the sale of goods to fail for indefiniteness if there was an intent to contract and a reasonable basis for establishing a remedy is available. If the place of delivery is left open, the UCC provides that the seller's place of business shall be the proper place of delivery. Answer (a) is incorrect because the Code supplies the omitted delivery terms. Answer (b) is incorrect because no rule requires the parties to designate place of delivery within 5 days. Nor is the buyer's place of business (answer (d)) the proper place of delivery unless so stated in the contract.

MAY 1981 ANSWERS

26. (581,L1,14) (c) In a sale by a merchant, the merchant warrants that the goods are free from a rightful claim of infringement of patent or trademark by third parties. (A seller will be protected against liability under a warranty against infringement if the buyer furnishes the specifications used to manufacture the product that infringes upon another party's patent or trademark rights.) Answer (a) is incorrect because only the seller need be a merchant. Answer (b) is incorrect because a warranty against infringment is granted along with the warranty of title and thus, does not need to be expressly stated in the contract to be enforceable. Like the warranty of title, a warranty against infringement can be disclaimed by specific language or circumstances that indicate that this warranty is not extended. Therefore, answer (d) is incorrect.

27. (581,L1,15) (d) Shipment of a different brand of peas, even as an accommodation, constitutes a breach of contract because the terms of the contract have not been complied with. Answer (a) is incorrect because the shipment cannot be considered a counter-offer since there was already a contract in existence between Brown and Smith. Answer (b) is untrue because only the promised performance will discharge Smith, unless Brown accepts the accommodation. Answer (c) is incorrect since Brown's offer to Smith

constitutes a bilateral offer which was accepted by Smith's communication to Brown. This bilateral offer could have been accepted by delivery of the specified goods as well.

28. (581,L1,16) (d) In any contract for the sale of goods, unless specifically disclaimed, the seller extends a warranty of title to the buyer. Such a warranty is neither express nor implied but warrants that the seller has good title to the goods, that the transfer of said title is rightful, and that the buyer will have knowledge of all liens against the property at the time of transfer. Williams, the buyer, was not informed of all liens against the property, thus, Ace Auto must bear the loss since it violated the provisions of the title warranty. Answer (a) is incorrect because even if Ace disclaimed "any and all warranties", this would not discharge a warranty of title since specific reference to this warranty must be made in any disclaimer thereof. Answer (b) is incorrect because the seller will bear the loss in the event of defective title unless he properly disclaims that warranty. Answer (c) is also incorrect because possession of an item does not automatically result in the presumption of good title or ownership.

29. (581,L1,17) (d) Generally, risk of loss is determined by the following sequence of tests. First, if the parties have included provision for the allocation of loss as part of the contract, then that provision controls. If the contract is silent on this point, risk of loss is then assumed to be borne by any party who has breached the terms of the contract. Answer (a) is untrue since risk of loss under the UCC does not depend on which party has title at the time of loss. Answer (b) is incorrect since shipping terms (FOB shipping point/ destination) are used only if there is no contract provision or breaching party. Answer (c) is untrue since credit terms have no relevance to risk of loss.

30. (581,L1,18) (d) In order for a firm offer to be effective, it must be contained in writing signed by a merchant offeror. If the offeree supplies the form which contains a firm offer clause, the merchant offeror must separately sign that clause, otherwise it will be ineffective against the offeror. Answer (a) is incorrect since a firm offer is irrevocable for the stated period of time or, if none is stated, a reasonable period of time. However, this period of irrevocability can never exceed 3 months (90 days). Answer (b) is untrue since a firm offer made by a merchant (Ace) needs no consideration as long as the agreement is in a writing signed by merchant offeror. Answer (c) is incorrect since it is not necessary that the buyer be a merchant.

31. (581,L1,19) (d) One of the provisions of the Statute of Frauds is that a contract for the sale of

goods for $500 or more must be in writing. Since this contract was oral, one of the several exceptions under the Statute must exist if this contract is to be enforceable. If the party who seeks to avoid performance makes an admission of the contract's existence in a court of law or court document, the oral contract is enforceable to the extent of the admission. Answer (a) is incorrect since the sale in question involves the sale of goods for $4,050 so the Statue applies. Answer (b) is incorrect since partial payment ($405 for 500 calculators) will only allow enforcement of the contract to the extent of the part performance. Partial performance would also require a shipment and acceptance of the goods. Answer (c) is untrue because it only involves shipment and therefore, will not even result in enforceability of half the contract unless the goods are accepted.

32. (581,L1,20) (d) Upon identification of the goods that relate to a contract, several specific rights are granted to the buyer of these goods. Among these is the right to take delivery of goods upon insolvency of the seller if full or partial payment was made at the time of the purchase and any balance due is tendered to the seller. Since the question asks which condition will prevent recovery of the goods, lack of identification is correct because identification must occur before any rights of repossession accrue to the buyer. It is not necessary that the full price be paid at the time of purchase (a) as long as tender of the balance due is made to the seller. Answers (b) and (c) are incorrect since the fact that a buyer may obtain a judgment for damages to the goods by third parties or that a buyer is not aware of a seller's insolvency will not prevent the buyer from gaining possession of the goods.

ANSWER OUTLINE

Problem 1   Breach of Warranty; Warranty of Title

a1.   Yes. Constance will probably prevail against Max
Motors
The issue is whether Fogarty's statements constituted
a warranty
"Mechanically perfect" constitutes an affirmation
of fact, not sales talk
Affirmation of fact by seller becomes an express
warranty
Specific intention to make a warranty is not
necessary
Relative expertise of purchaser and seller is relevant
Seller's honest belief in truth of statements is irrelevant
Purchaser suffers detriment as a result of reliance on the
warranty
Warranty was not disclaimed by Fogarty
Warranties are not permitted to be disclaimed with-
out due notice

a2.   Constance might rely upon implied warranties of
Merchantability
Fitness for particular purpose

b.   Knox should prevail
Basis for recovery is title warranty per UCC
I.e., title is good and transferable
UCC does not indicate whether warranty is express
or implied
It may only be excluded by specific language
Ajax's defense is its disclaimer

UNOFFICIAL ANSWER

Problem 1   Breach of Warranty; Warranty of Title

a. 1.   Yes. The main issue is whether Fogarty's statements constitute an affirmation
of fact as contrasted with mere opinion.
This issue has been resolved in
many cases in favor of purchasers, such
as Constance. It often is difficult to draw
the line between an affirmation of fact,
which when relied upon constitutes a
warranty, and mere sales talk, which is
a statement of the seller's opinion. However, the combination of the various statements made by Fogarty and perhaps the
language "mechanically perfect" constituted
a warranty under the circumstances.
Furthermore, the relative expertise
of the parties is validly taken into account under such circumstances. Fogarty
was a used car salesman with long ex-

perience and was familiar with the
mechanical aspects of automobiles. It
would be only natural for Constance to
take his statements as being something
more than idle chatter. Her total lack
of knowledge of automobiles and their
engines would lead her to rely on Fogarty's representations.
In addition, all the other elements
necessary to establish an oral express
warranty are present. Fogarty's good
faith or honest belief in the truth of
his statements is irrelevant. Knowledge
of falsity has nothing to do with warranty. The Uniform Commercial Code
reads as follows: "Any affirmation of
fact or promise made by the seller to
the buyer which relates to the goods
and becomes part of the basis of the
bargain creates an express warranty that
the goods shall conform to the affirmation or promise." Additionally, the
code states, "It is not necessary to the
creation of an express warranty that the
seller use familiar words, such as warrants or guarantees or that. . .a specific
intention to make a warranty be present."
The facts clearly indicate that the
affirmation or promise was a basis of the
bargain; that is, that the language was
intended to be relied upon by the buyer
and it was. Finally, the buyer relied upon it to her detriment and suffered
damages as a result. Although the Uniform Commercial Code includes cautionary
language that an affirmation merely of the
value of the goods or a statement purporting
to be merely the seller's opinion or commen-
dation of the goods does not create a warranty, it appears that the facts clearly establish
an oral express warranty.
Another issue is the legal effect of
Fogarty's statement that he could not give
a warranty on the auto sold. Does this validly disclaim the oral express warranty protection? There is a general hostility manifested
by the Uniform Commercial Code and the
courts to allowing broad uninformative disclaimers to legally negate warranty protection. Warranties are not to be disclaimed
without due notice and fairness shown to
the purchaser under the circumstances. Where
there are words tending to negate an oral
express warranty, the purported disclaimer
shall be constructed wherever reasonable as

consistent with the warranty. Hence, a purported negation or limitation is inoperative to the extent that such a construction is unreasonable. Thus, it appears that the warranty has not been disclaimed.

2.   Constance might rely upon the implied warranties of merchantability and fitness for a particular purpose.

b.   The case should be decided in favor of Knox. The basis for recovery would be the title warranties provided under the Uniform Commercial Code which states that the title conveyed should be good and its transfer rightful, but here Watts was the rightful owner and entitled to repossess the car. The code does not indicate whether such a warranty is to be construed as an express or implied warranty. However, it can only be excluded by specific language or circumstances that give the buyer reason to know that the person selling does not claim title in himself. From this it would appear that a seller would have to clearly indicate that he does not purport to own the item in question and that the buyer is assuming the risk that the title is defective. Such was not the case. However, Ajax Motors will undoubtedly claim that the disclaimer is legally operative.

ANSWER OUTLINE

Problem 2   Option Contract, Risk of Loss, Pre-Existing Duty, Contract Interference

a.   Clauson will prevail. If no consideration, firm offer rule of UCC Article 3 applies
   Offer by merchant
   Signed writing
   Assurance that offer is not revocable
   Limited in all cases to three months
Three-month limit not applicable due to consideration
   I.e., a binding contract exists
   Clauson's acceptance was lawful and timely
   Clauson is entitled to recover damages

b.   Flowers will prevail
   Risk of loss on Hargrove per shipping terms
   Terms specified F.O.B. N&W RR at Norfolk
      I.e., specified shipper and F.O.B. shipping point
   Risk of loss passed to Hargrove when delivered to N&W
   Reservation of title has no effect on risk of loss

c.   Novack will not recover the additional compensation
   Pre-existing legal duty rule applies
      Contract modification for services requires consideration
      Novack's duties under revised contract unchanged
      UCC rule providing no consideration required to modify contract is applicable only to sale of goods

d1. Superior may recover damages from Dixon
   For intentional interference with contract right
   Dixon knew of prior contract
   Such intentional interference is a tort

d2. Superior cannot obtain specific performance
   Contract with Novack personal service contract
      Equitable remedies not available
      Would constitute involuntary servitude

UNOFFICIAL ANSWER

Problem 2   Option Contract, Risk of Loss, Pre-Existing Duty, Contract Interference

Part a.

Clauson Enterprises will prevail. The option in question is supported by consideration and consequently is a binding contract. The offer is definite and certain despite the fact that the pricing terms are not presently determinable. The Uniform Commercial Code is extremely liberal regarding satisfaction of the pricing terms.

Except for the presence of consideration in the form of the promise by Clauson to deliver the market survey to Migrane, the option would not have been binding beyond three months and Migrane would have prevailed. Section 2-205 of the Uniform Commercial Code provides as follows:

An offer by a merchant to buy or sell goods in a signed writing which by its terms gives assurance that it will be held open is not revocable, for lack of consideration, during the time stated or if no time is stated for a reasonable time, but in no event may such period of irrevocability exceed three months; but any such term of assurance on a form supplied by the offeree must be separately signed by the offeror.

It is apparent from the wording of this section that the option was valid without consideration, but only for three months. It was an offer by a merchant contained in a signed writing and clearly stated its irrevocability. Furthermore, the separately signed requirement where the form is supplied by the offeree was satisfied. But the section is inapplicable to the facts of this case since bargained-for consideration was present. The Uniform Commercial Code's three-month limitation does not apply to options where consideration is present. Hence, Clauson's acceptance was valid, and if Migrane refuses to perform, Clauson will be entitled to damages.

Part b.

Flowers will prevail because Hargrove has the risk of loss. The shipping terms determine who had the risk of loss. Section 2-509(1) of the Uniform Commercial Code provides that "Where the contract requires or authorizes the seller to ship the goods by carrier, (a) if it does not require him to deliver at a particular destination, the risk of loss passes to the buyer when the goods are duly delivered to the carrier, even though the shipment is under reservation. . . ."

The facts that title was reserved by Flowers and that Flowers retained the negotiable bill of lading do not affect the determination of who is to bear the risk of loss. The code makes it clear that title is irrelevant in determining the risk of loss.

Part c.

No. The pre-existing legal duty rule applies. Novack has not given any consideration for Superior's promise of additional compensation. The common law rules apply to contracts for services, and modifications of such contracts must be supported by consideration. In essence, Novack was already bound by a valid contract to perform exactly what he did perform under the modified contract. Hence, he did nothing more than he was legally obligated to do. As a result, there is no consideration to support Superior's promise to pay the bonus.

Section 2-209 of the Uniform Commercial Code, which provides that an agreement modifying a contract needs no consideration to be binding, is not applicable to an employment contract because section 2-209 covers only the sale of goods.

Part d.

1. Yes. A cause of action based upon Dixon's intentional interference with a contractual relationship would be available. All the requirements necessary to state such a cause of action are present, particularly the knowledge of the existing contractual relationship between Novack and Superior. The law treats Dixon's conduct as tortious and allows a recovery for damages against Dixon.

2. No. A court exercising its equity powers will not force a person to fulfill a contract for personal services. To do so smacks of involuntary servitude.

ANSWER OUTLINE

Problem 3   Consignments

a.   Key legal characteristics of consignments
            Consignor - owner of goods
            Consignee - agent who is to sell goods
      Characteristics
      1. Title stays with consignor
      2. Consignee has no obligation to purchase or pay for goods
      3. Consignee is paid a commission for goods sold
      4. Proceeds are consignor's

UNOFFICIAL ANSWER

Problem 3   Consignments

Part a.

A consignment is a selling arrangement between the owner, called the *consignor*, and the party who is to sell the goods, called the *consignee*. The consignee is appointed the agent to sell the owner's merchandise. The following are the key characteristics.

1.   Title to the goods remains at all times with the consignor.
2.   The consignee is at no time obligated to buy or pay for the goods.
3.   The consignee receives a commission for the goods sold.
4.   The proceeds belong to the consignor.

MULTIPLE CHOICE QUESTIONS (1—29)

1. Who among the following can personally qualify as a holder in due course?
   a. A payee.
   b. A reacquirer who was not initially a holder in due course.
   c. A holder to whom the instrument was negotiated as a gift.
   d. A holder who had notice of a defect but who took from a prior holder in due course.

2. The Mechanics Bank refused to pay a check drawn upon it by Clyde, one of its depositors. Which of the reasons listed below is **not** a proper defense for the bank to assert when it refused to pay?
   a. The bank believed the check to be an overdraft as a result of its misdirecting a deposit made by Clyde.
   b. The required indorsement of an intermediary transferee was missing.
   c. Clyde had orally stopped payment on the check.
   d. The party attempting to cash the check did not have proper identification.

3. Your client, Globe, Inc., has in its possession an undated instrument which is payable 30 days after date. It is believed that the instrument was issued on or about August 10, 1980, by Dixie Manufacturing, Inc., to Harding Enterprises in payment of goods purchased. On August 13, 1980, it was negotiated to Desert Products, Inc., and thereafter to Globe on the 15th. Globe took for value, in good faith and without notice of any defense. It has been learned that the goods shipped by Harding to Dixie are defective. Which of the following is correct?
   a. Since the time of payment is indefinite, the instrument is non-negotiable and Globe can **not** qualify as a holder in due course.
   b. By issuing an undated instrument payable 30 days after date, Dixie was reserving the right to avoid liability on it until it filled in or authorized the filling in of the date.
   c. Since the defense involves a rightful rejection of the goods delivered, it is valid against Globe.
   d. Globe can validly fill in the date and will qualify as a holder in due course.

4. A CPA's client has an instrument which contains certain ambiguities or deficiencies. In construing the instrument, which of the following is **incorrect**?
   a. Where there is doubt whether the instrument is a draft or a note, the holder may treat it as either.
   b. Handwritten terms control typewritten and printed terms, and typewritten terms control printed terms.
   c. An instrument which is payable only upon the happening of an event that is uncertain as to the time of its occurrence is payable at a definite time if the event has occurred.
   d. The fact that the instrument is antedated will not affect the instrument's negotiability.

5. Smith buys a TV set from the ABC Appliance Store and pays for the set with a check. Later in the day Smith finds a better model for the same price at another store. Smith immediately calls ABC trying to cancel the sale. ABC tells Smith that they are holding him to the sale and have negotiated the check to their wholesaler, Glenn Company, as a partial payment on inventory purchases. Smith telephones his bank, the Union Trust Bank, and orders the bank to stop payment on the check. Which of the following statements is correct?
   a. If Glenn can prove it is a holder in due course, the drawee bank, Union Trust, must honor Smith's check.
   b. Union Trust is **not** bound or liable for Smith's stop payment order unless the order is placed in writing.
   c. If Union Trust mistakenly pays Smith's check two days after receiving the stop order, the bank will **not** be liable.
   d. Glenn can **not** hold Smith liable on the check.

6. Marshall Franks purchased $1,050 worth of inventory for his business from Micro Enterprises. Micro insisted on the signature of Franks' former partner, Hobart, before credit would be extended. Hobart reluctantly signed. Franks delivered the following instrument to Micro:

January 15, 1980

We, the undersigned, do hereby promise to pay to the order of Micro Enterprises, Inc., One Thousand and Fifty Dollars ($1,050.00) on the 15th of April, 1980.

Marshall Franks
Marshall Franks

Norman Hobart
Norman Hobart

Memo:
N. Hobart signed as an
accommodation for Franks

Franks defaulted on the due date. Which of the following is correct?

    a.   The instrument is non-negotiable.

    b.   Hobart is liable on the instrument but only for $525.

    c.   Since it was known to Micro that Hobart signed as an accommodation party, Micro must first proceed against Franks.

    d.   Hobart is liable on the instrument for the full amount and is obligated to satisfy it immediately upon default.

7.   Rapid Delivery, Inc., has in its possession the following instrument which it purchased for value.

March 1, 1980

Thirty days from date, I, Harold Kales, do hereby promise to pay Ronald Green four hundred dollars and no cents ($400.00). This note is given for value received.

Harold Kales

Harold Kales

Which of the following is correct?

    a.   The instrument is negotiable.

    b.   The instrument is non-negotiable, and therefore Rapid has obtained no rights on the instrument.

    c.   Rapid is an assignee of the instrument and has the same rights as the assignor had on it.

    d.   The instrument is non-transferable on its face.

8.   Harrison obtained from Bristow his $11,500 check drawn on the Union National Bank in payment for bogus uranium stock. He immediately negotiated it by a blank indorsement to Dunlop in return for $1,000 in cash and her check for $10,400. Dunlop qualified as a holder in due course. She deposited the check in her checking account in the Oceanside Bank. Upon discovering that the stock was bogus, Bristow notified Union National to stop payment on his check, which it did. The check was returned to Oceanside Bank, which in turn debited Dunlop's account and returned the check to her. Which of the following statements is correct?

    a.   Dunlop can collect from Union National Bank since Bristow's stop payment order was invalid in that the defense was only a personal defense.

    b.   Oceanside's debiting of Dunlop's account was improper since she qualified as a holder in due course.

    c.   Dunlop can recover $11,500 from Bristow despite the stop order, since she qualified as a holder in due course.

    d.   Dunlop will be entitled to collect only $1,000.

9.   An otherwise valid negotiable bearer note is signed with the forged signature of Darby. Archer, who believed he knew Darby's signature, bought the note in good faith from Harding, the forger. Archer transferred the note without indorsement to Barker, in partial payment of a debt. Barker then sold the note to Chase for 80% of its face amount and delivered it without indorsement. When Chase presented the note for payment at maturity, Darby refused to honor it, pleading forgery. Chase gave proper notice of dishonor to Barker and to Archer. Which of the following statements best describes the situation from Chase's standpoint?

    a.   Chase can **not** qualify as a holder in due course for the reason that he did **not** pay face value for the note.

    b.   Chase can hold Barker liable on the ground that Barker warranted to Chase that neither Darby nor Archer had any defense valid against Barker.

    c.   Chase can hold Archer liable on the ground that Archer warranted to Chase that Darby's signature was genuine.

    d.   Chase can **not** hold Harding, the forger, liable on the note because his signature does **not** appear on it and thus, he made no warranties to Chase.

10.   Anderson agreed to purchase Parker's real property. Anderson's purchase was dependent upon his being able to sell certain real property that he owned. Anderson gave Parker an instrument for the purchase price. Assuming the instrument is otherwise negotiable, which one of the statements below, written on the face of the instrument, will render it non-negotiable?

    a.   A statement that Parker's cashing or indorsing the instrument acknowledges full satisfaction of Anderson's obligation.

    b.   A statement that payment of the instrument is contingent upon Anderson's sale of his real property.

    c.   A statement that the instrument is secured by a first mortgage on Parker's property and that upon default in payment the entire amount of the instrument is due.

    d.   A statement that the instrument is subject to the usual implied and constructive conditions applicable to such transactions.

11.   Mask stole one of Bloom's checks. The check was already signed by Bloom and made payable to Duval. The check was drawn on United Trust Company. Mask forged Duval's signature on the back of the check and cashed the check at the Corner Check Cashing Company which in turn deposited it with its bank, Town National Bank of Toka. Town National proceeded to collect on the check from United. None of the parties mentioned was negligent. Who will bear the loss assuming the amount cannot be recovered from Mask?

   a.   Bloom.
   b.   Duval.
   c.   United Trust Company.
   d.   Corner Check Cashing Company.

12.   Gomer developed a fraudulent system whereby he could obtain checks payable to the order of certain repairmen who serviced various large corporations. Gomer observed the delivery trucks of repairmen who did business with the corporations, and then he submitted bills on the bogus letterhead of the repairmen to the selected large corporations. The return envelope for payment indicated a local post office box. When the checks arrived, Gomer would forge the payees' signatures and cash the checks. The parties cashing the checks are holders in due course. Who will bear the loss assuming the amount cannot be recovered from Gomer?

   a.   The defrauded corporations.
   b.   The drawee banks.
   c.   Intermediate parties who indorsed the instruments for collection.
   d.   The ultimate recipients of the proceeds of the checks even though they are holders in due course.

13.   Barber has in his possession a negotiable instrument which he purchased in good faith and for value. The drawer of the instrument stopped payment on it and has asserted that Barber does not qualify as a holder in due course since the instrument is overdue. In determining whether the instrument is overdue which of the following is incorrect?

   a.   A reasonable time for a check drawn and payable in the United States is presumed to be 30 days after issue.
   b.   A reasonable time for a check drawn and payable in the United States is presumed to be 20 days after the last negotiation.
   c.   All demand instruments, other than checks, are not overdue until a reasonable time after their issue has elapsed.
   d.   The instrument will be deemed to be overdue if a demand for payment had been made and Barber knew this.

14.   Dodson drew a check to the order of Swanson for services which were partially rendered. The check was left blank because the exact amount was not known at the time of issue. The understanding between Dodson and Swanson was that Swanson would complete the job, fill in the check for the exact amount due which was estimated as $650, but which would in no event exceed $700. Swanson failed to complete the work as agreed, but filled in the amount of the check for $1,000. He then negotiated it to Irwin in satisfaction of a $500 debt, with the balance paid to Swanson in cash. Swanson has disappeared, Dodson stopped payment and Irwin is seeking to collect the $1,000 from Dodson. What will Irwin be able to collect?

   a.   Nothing.
   b. $500.
   c. $700.
   d. $1,000.

15.   Robb stole one of Markum's blank checks, made it payable to himself, and forged Markum's signature to it. The check was drawn on the Unity Trust Company. Robb cashed the check at the Friendly Check Cashing Company which in turn deposited it with its bank, the Farmer's National. Farmer's National proceeded to collect on the check from Unity Trust. The theft and forgery were quickly discovered by Markum who promptly notified Unity. None of the parties mentioned was negligent. Who will bear the loss, assuming the amount cannot be recovered from Robb?

   a.   Markum.
   b.   Unity Trust Company.
   c.   Friendly Check Cashing Company.
   d.   Farmer's National.

16.   Wilson drew a sight draft on Foxx, a customer who owed Wilson money on an open account, payable to the order of Burton, one of Wilson's creditors. Burton presented it to Foxx. After examining the draft as to its authenticity and after checking the amount against outstanding debts to Wilson, Foxx wrote on its face "Accepted -- payable in 10 days" and signed it. When Burton returned at the end of the ten days, Foxx told him he could not pay and was hard pressed for cash. Burton did not notify Wilson of these facts. Two days later when Burton again presented the instrument for payment, Burton was told that Foxx's creditors had filed a petition in bankruptcy that morning. Which of the following statements is correct?

   a.   The instrument in question is a type of demand promissory note.
   b.   Wilson had primary liability on the draft at its inception.
   c.   Foxx was secondarily liable on the instrument prior to acceptance.
   d.   Foxx assumed primary liability at the time of acceptance.

17.   Ajax, Inc., sold a refrigerator to Broadway Bill's Restaurant and accepted Broadway's negotiable promissory note for $600 as payment. The note was payable to Ajax's order one year after the date of issue. Thirty days after receiving the note, Ajax indorsed the note with a blank indorsement and sold it to National Bank for $550. National credited Ajax's checking account with $550, which brought Ajax's balance to $725. Ajax drew checks for a total of $675 which National honored. National then learned that the refrigerator had not been delivered by Ajax. The note is now due and unpaid. When National brings suit, Broadway pleads lack of consideration on the note. Which of the following is a valid statement with respect to the above facts?

    a.   The discount on the note is so great as to impugn National's taking in good faith.

    b.   In ascertaining the extent to which value had been given by National, the FIFO rule will apply to checks or notes deposited and the proceeds withdrawn.

    c.   Broadway has no liability on the note since it never received the refrigerator.

    d.   Broadway has only secondary liability on the note in question.

18.

```
                                    No. 111

DIANA DAVIDSON
21 West 21st Street
Toronto, Canada

                            April 1, 1977

Pay to the
order of      Stanley Stark      $1,000.00

One thousand & no/100's Canadian Dollars

                  Diana Davidson
                  Diana Davidson
```

FIRST NATIONAL TRUST
Buffalo, New York

For Finder's Fee

After examing the above instrument, which of the following conclusions is correct?

    a.   It is non-negotiable because it is payable in Canadian money.

    b.   It is a demand instrument but does not qualify as a negotiable instrument, because it is drawn in Canada and payable by a bank in the United States.

    c.   The instrument is a negotiable foreign check (draft), and in the event of dishonor a formal protest must be made by the party seeking recovery.

    d.   Diana Davidson is the maker of the instrument and as such is primarily liable thereon.

19.   Which of the following is a characteristic of the "without recourse" indorsement?

    a.   It can only be used where the instrument is a draft.

    b.   It puts the person acquiring it on notice of some defect or defense which could be asserted against the transferee of the instrument.

    c.   It modifies but does not completely eliminate the indorser's warranty liability to subsequent holders.

    d.   It will not limit the indorser's liability to an immediate transferee.

20.   Marlin ordered merchandise from Plant to be delivered the following day and gave Plant a check payable to its order drawn on Marlin's account in First Bank. It was agreed that the check would not be transferred unless delivery was received and accepted. The goods were not delivered and Marlin notified Plant that he exercised his right to rescind. Plant, nevertheless, negotiated the check for full value to Rose who took it in good faith and without notice of any defense. Rose then negotiated it for full value to Quirk who knew of Plant's breach of the agreement. Marlin promptly stopped payment on the check and refuses to pay it. Under these circumstances, which of the following statements is correct?

    a.   Marlin would have a valid defense in a suit by Rose for the amount of the check.

    b.   Marlin would have a valid defense in a suit by Quirk for the amount of the check.

    c.   Despite the fact that Quirk can not personally qualify as a holder in due course, he can assert Rose's standing as such.

    d.   A stop payment order will not prevent a holder in due course from collecting from the bank.

21.   Maxwell is a holder in due course of a check which was originally payable to the order of Clark and has the following indorsements on its back:

Clark

Pay to the order of White

Smithers

Without Recourse

White

Dobbins

Which of the following statements about this check is correct?

a. If the bank refuses to pay Maxwell's only recourse is to sue Dobbins.
b. The instrument was bearer paper in Dobbins' hands.
c. Clark's signature was not necessary to negotiate the instrument.
d. White has no warranty liability to Maxwell on the instrument.

22. An instrument reads as follows:

| $5,000.00 | Boise, Idaho | October 1, 1978 |

Thirty days after date I promise to pay to the order of

Cash _____ at 120 BROADWAY, New York City

Value received with interest at the rate of eight percent per annum.

This instrument arises out of a separate agreement.

No. 20   Due October 31, 1978   *A. G. Loeb*

Which of the following statements about this instrument is correct?

a. The instrument is negotiable.
b. The instrument is order paper.
c. The instrument is a time draft.
d. Failure to make a timely presentment will excuse Loeb from liability.

23. Filbert Corporation has in its possession an instrument which Groves, the maker, assured Filbert was negotiable. The instrument contains several clauses which are not typically contained in such an instrument and Filbert is not familiar with their legal effect. Which of the following will adversely affect the negotiability of the instrument?

a. A promise to maintain collateral and to provide additional collateral if the value of existing collateral decreases.
b. A term authorizing the confession of judgment on the instrument if not paid when due.
c. A statement to the effect that the instrument arises out of the November 1, 1978, sale of goods by Filbert to Groves.
d. A statement that it is payable only out of the proceeds from the resale of the goods sold by Filbert to Groves on November 1, 1978.

24. Mitchell sold his ranch to Campbell. Campbell tendered his uncertified check for $35,000 at the closing. Mitchell objected and asserted that the check had to be certified. An examination of the contract revealed that the usual certification requirement had been omitted. Mitchell begrudgingly accepted the check after a phone call to the bank confirmed that "the check is good." He promptly proceeded to Campbell's bank and requested that it be certified in that he needed a certified check for a closing the following day in connection with the purchase of another property. Regarding Mitchell's request for certification, which of the following is correct?

a. The bank is legally obligated to certify the check.
b. If the bank did certify the check, it constituted an acceptance and released Campbell.
c. The bank's oral statement that "the check is good" constituted an implied certification.
d. Once a check has been properly certified, further negotiation is prohibited.

25. Johnson lost a check that he had received for professional services rendered. The instrument on its face was payable to Johnson's order. He had indorsed it on the back by signing his name and printing "for deposit only" above his name. Assuming the check is found by Alcatraz, a dishonest person who attempts to cash it, which of the following is correct?

a. Any transferee of the instrument must pay or apply any value given by him for the instrument consistent with the indorsement.

b.   The indorsement is a blank indorsement and a holder in due course who cashed it for Alcatraz would prevail.

c.   The indorsement prevents further transfer or negotiation by anyone.

d.   If Alcatraz simply signs his name beneath Johnson's indorsement, he can convert it into bearer paper and a holder in due course would take free of the restriction.

26.   Archer has in his possession a bearer negotiable instrument. He took it by negotiation from Perth who had stolen it from Cox's office along with cash and other property. The robbery of Cox's office had received appropriate coverage in . the local papers in the area in which both Archer and Cox reside. Archer did not know that Perth had stolen the instrument when he purchased it at a 20% discount. Cox refuses to pay and Archer has commenced legal action asserting that he is a holder in due course. Which of the following statements is correct?

a.   Even if all other requisites are satisfied, Archer's title is defective in that there was no delivery by Cox of the instrument.

b.   Archer is a holder in due course and will prevail.

c.   Archer is prevented from qualifying as a holder in due course because there had been general notice published in the community about the robbery.

d.   The discount in and of itself prevents Archer from qualifying as a holder in due course or at least prevents him from so qualifying as to the 20%.

27.   Troy fraudulently induced Casper to make a negotiable instrument payable to the order of Troy in exchange for goods he never intended to deliver. Troy negotiated it to Gorden, who took with notice of the fraud. Gorden in turn negotiated it to Wagner, a holder in due course. Wagner presented it for payment to Casper, who refused to honor it. Wagner contacted Gorden who agreed to reacquire the instrument by negotiation from Wagner. Which of the following statements is correct?

a.   Casper would have been liable if Wagner had pursued his rights on the negotiable instrument.

b.   Gorden was initially a holder in due course as a result of the negotiation to him from Troy.

c.   Casper is liable to all parties except Troy in that it was his fault that the instrument was issued to Troy.

d.   Gorden can assert the rights of his prior holder in due course, Wagner, as a result of the repurchase.

28.   Franco & Sons, Inc., was engaged in the furniture manufacturing business. One of its bi-weekly paychecks was payable to Stein, who negotiated it to White in payment of a gambling debt. White proceeded to raise the amount of the check from $300 to $800 and negotiated it to Carson, a holder in due course, for cash. Upon presentment by Carson at the drawee bank, the teller detected the raising of the amount and contacted Franco who stopped payment on the check. Franco refuses to pay Carson. Carson is seeking to recover the $800. Under the circumstances, which of the following is a correct statement?

a.   Franco is liable, but only for $300.

b.   Franco is liable for the $800.

c.   Stein is liable for the $800.

d.   Franco has no liability to Carson.

29.   Grad arranged to borrow $500 on a time note from Paterson. Prior to delivery of the executed note to Paterson, Keller indorsed the note in blank as an accommodation for payee Paterson. Paterson negotiated the note to Meade by special indorsement. Meade negotiated it to Knight, a holder in due course. The note was not paid when due. Which of the following is correct?

a.   Keller has special defenses against a holder in due course because he is an accommodation indorser.

b.   Keller is primarily liable as a result of his accommodation indorsement.

c.   Knight need not give notice of dishonor to either Meade or Paterson.

d.   The fact that Keller indorsed the note prior to its being negotiated to Meade does not have any legal importance with respect to Knight's rights against Keller.

PROBLEMS

<u>Problem 1</u> Bank as Holder in Due Course; Material
Alteration; Non-negotiable Instrument
(1179,L3)

(20 to 25 minutes)

Part a. Glasco Machinery and Manufacturing,
Inc., sells industrial machinery to various customers
on credit terms of 20% down and three-month promissory notes for the balance.

Glasco was experiencing severe financial difficulty and desperately needed a loan for working capital and to stave off persistent creditors. Its bank insisted upon security for any loan it might make.
Glasco agreed to pledge $25,000 of its customer's
promissory notes as collateral for a $20,000 demand
loan. The notes pledged included some which Glasco
knew had been received on sales of defective machinery and several notes which Glasco's president
forged in anticipation of future shipments to customers.

After a short time Glasco's president saw that
detection was inevitable, withdrew all funds in the
bank, and absconded with the cash. The bank is
seeking to enforce payment of the notes against the
various parties.

Required: Answer the following, setting forth reasons
for any conclusions stated.

Discuss the bank's rights, if any, to collection
on the various promissory notes.

Part b. Grover had an $80 check payable to the
order of Parker that Parker had indorsed in blank. The
check was drawn by Madison on State Bank. Grover
deftly raised the amount to $800 and cashed it at
Friendly Check Cashing Company. Friendly promptly
presented it at State Bank where it was dishonored as
an overdraft. Grover has been apprehended by the police and is awaiting trial. He has no known assets.
Friendly is seeking collection on the instrument against
any or all of the other parties involved.

Required: Answer the following, setting forth reasons
for any conclusions stated.

Will Friendly recover against Madison, State
Bank, or Parker?

Part c. Horn Audio purchased some audio components from Samuels Sounds. The high quality audio
components were to be used by Horn in its expensive
customized sound systems to be sold to its customers.
Samuels fraudulently substituted a large number of
reconditioned audio components for the new ones that
Horn was shown and believed he had purchased. In
payment of the purchase, Horn executed and delivered
the following instrument to Samuels:

January 8, 1979

For value received, Horn Audio promises
to pay Three Thousand Dollars ($3,000.00)
to the order of Samuels Sounds, two weeks
after their receipt and out of the proceeds
from the resale of the audio components
this day purchased from Samuels Sounds
and used as major components in the customized sound system sold to our customers.

John Horn

Horn Audio

Samuels transferred the instrument to Wilmont
for value by signing it on the back and delivering it to
him. Wilmont had no knowledge of the fraudulent substitution of the audio components by Samuels. Several
months later, Wilmont presented the instrument to the
maker for payment. Horn refused to pay the instrument alleging fraud and breach of warranty. Furthermore, Horn stated that all the audio components were
returned to Samuels immediately upon discovery of
the facts. Wilmont has commenced legal action against
Horn on the instrument.

Required: Answer the following, setting forth reasons
for any conclusions stated.

Will Wilmont prevail in his legal action against
Horn on the instrument?

<u>Problem 2</u>   Negotiability of Instrument; Types of Indorsements (578,L2)

(25 to 30 minutes)

Part a.   Your CPA firm was engaged to audit the Meglo Corporation. During the audit you examined the following instrument:

April 2, 1977

Charles Noreen
21 West 21st Street
St. Louis, Missouri

I, Charles Noreen, do hereby promise to pay to Roger Smith, Two Thousand Dollars ($2,000) one year from date, with 8% interest upon due presentment.

FOR: Payment for used IBM typewriters.

Charles Noreen

Meglo purchased the instrument from Smith on April 10, 1977, for $1,700. Meglo received the instrument with Smith's signature and the words "Pay to the order of Meglo Corporation" on the back. Upon maturity, Meglo presented the instrument to Noreen, who refused to pay. Noreen alleged that the typewriters were defective and did not satisfy certain warranties given in connection with the purchase of the used IBM typewriters which were guaranteed for one year. Noreen had promptly notified Smith of this fact and had told him he would not pay the full amount due.

Required: Answer the following, setting forth reasons for any conclusions stated.

1. Is the instrument in question negotiable commercial paper?

2. Assuming that the instrument is negotiable, does Meglo qualify as a holder in due course entitled to collect the full $2,000?

3. Assuming that the instrument is negotiable, is Noreen's defense valid against a holder in due course?

4. Assuming that the instrument is nonnegotiable, what is the legal effect of the transfer by Smith to Meglo?

Part b.   Marvin Farber cashed a check for Harold Kern which was made to the order of Charles Walker by Marglow Investments & Securities. The check had the following indorsements on the back:

1. *Charles Walker*

2. without recourse
   Doris Williamson

3. Pay to the order of Harold Kern
   Jack Dixon

4. Pay to the order of Marvin Farber

Kern neglected to sign his indorsement when he gave the check to Farber, and Farber did not notice this until the following day. Before Farber could locate Kern and obtain his signature, Farber learned that Walker had fraudulently obtained the check from Marglow (the drawer). Farber finally located Kern and obtained his signature. Farber promptly indorsed the check in blank and cashed it at National Bank. National Bank presented the check for payment through normal banking channels, but it was dishonored by Marglow's bank pursuant to a valid stop order. National Bank contacted Farber and informed him of the situation. Farber repaid the amount and the check was returned to him with National Bank's blank indorsement on the back.

Required: Answer the following, setting forth reasons for any conclusions stated.

1. Identify the type of indorsement and indicate the liability for each indorsement numbered 1, 2, and 3 above.

2. Will Farber prevail in a legal action seeking payment of the check by Marglow?

MULTIPLE CHOICE QUESTIONS

1.	a	7.	c	13.	b	19.	c	25.	a
2.	a	8.	c	14.	d	20.	c	26.	b
3.	d	9.	b	15.	b	21.	b	27.	a
4.	c	10.	b	16.	d	22.	a	28.	a
5.	c	11.	d	17.	b	23.	d	29.	d
6.	d	12.	a	18.	c	24.	b		

EXPLANATION OF MULTIPLE CHOICE ANSWERS

1. (1180,L1,1)   (a)   The correct answer is (a) since the payee is the only holder who can meet the requirements of a holder in due course. A holder in due course must be a holder who gives executed value for the instrument (cannot be a gift). The holder in due course may have no knowledge of the fact that the instrument (principal only) is overdue nor knowledge of any defense on the instrument when he or she receives it. A holder in due course must also take the instrument in good faith. Answer (b) is incorrect since a holder who does not qualify as a holder in due course cannot better his rights by transferring the instrument through a HIDC. Answer (c) is incorrect because the holder failed to give value. The holder in answer (d) cannot qualify as HIDC since he has knowledge of a defense, but the holder does receive the rights of a HIDC since he acquired the instrument through a HIDC.

2. (1180,L1,2)   (a)   Answer (a) is not a proper defense for the bank to assert when it refused to pay. The bank is at fault by misdirecting the funds and has a duty to pay the check. Answers (b), (c) and (d) are all proper defenses for the bank. The oral stop payment order in answer (c) would effectively keep the bank from paying the check for a 14 day period.

3. (1180,L1,3)   (d)   An undated note is considered dated as of the day of issue. Thus Globe, the holder, has the authority to fill in the date with the day of issuance. After dating the instrument, Globe meets all the requirements of a HIDC. The fact that Globe received an undated instrument will not destroy its HIDC status. The time of payment is considered definite as soon as the appropriate date is entered. Answer (c) describes a personal defense (failure of consideration) which would not be good against a HIDC.

4. (1180,L1,4)   (c)   Answer (c) is the statement that is incorrect. In order to qualify as a draft, an instrument must be payable on demand or at a definite time. In the event the instrument rests on an uncertainty with respect to time (i.e., payable on the death of a certain person) it is nonnegotiable. To qualify as a negotiable instrument, one must be able to determine a definite time for payment from the face of the instrument. Answers (a), (b) and (d) all state proper rules of construction.

5. (1180,L1,5)   (c)   The correct answer is (c) since the bank is only liable to the drawer if failure to obey stop payment order caused the drawer a loss. Since Smith has no grounds for rescinding the sale, the Union Trust bank has no liability. Answer (a) is incorrect since a payee has no right to compel payment of a check by drawee bank. There is no privity of contract between the payee and drawee bank. Answer (b) is incorrect because the stop payment order can be oral or written. An oral order is effective for 14 days and a written order is effective for 6 months. A stop payment order does not destroy the drawer's liability on the instrument unless he has a valid defense, therefore, answer (d) is false.

6. (1180,L1,6)   (d)   An accommodating party (Hobart) is someone who lends his name to the instrument as security. Such a party is liable in the position he signs the instrument. In this case, Hobart signed as a co-maker and is therefore, primarily liable for the face value of the instrument. Micro can go against either Franks or Hobart on the due date. Hobart will be able to seek redress against Franks, the accommodated party. Therefore, answer (d) is correct. The instrument meets all the requirements of negotiability thus, answer (a) is incorrect.

7. (1180,L1,7)   (c)   Before an instrument qualifies as a negotiable instrument, it must be payable to order or to bearer. This instrument does not contain these words of negotiability; thus the law of assignments applies to the transfer of this nonnegotiable instrument. The assignee has the same rights as the assignor concerning this instrument. Thus, answer (c) is correct.

8. (1180,L1,8)   (c)   The only defenses good against a holder in due course are real defenses. In this case, the only defense Bristow can assert is fraud in the inducement, which is a personal defense, not good against a holder in due course. As a result, answer (c) is correct and Dunlop can recover the full $11,500 from Bristow. Bristow's only recourse will be against Harrison. Answer (a) is incorrect since the stop payment order requires the bank to refuse payment of the instrument. Oceanside's actions were proper under the circumstances making answer (b) incorrect. Answer (d) is also incorrect since Dunlop would be HIDC to the face value of the instrument since his check constitutes giving executed value for a negotiable instrument.

9. (1180,L1,9) (b) Barker, having received value for the instrument, has warranty liability to Chase, the immediate holder. Barker grants five warranties, one of which is that no defense is good on the instrument. Answer (b) is correct since this warranty was breached. If a holder performs the full agreed upon consideration or value promised for the instrument, he is a holder in due course to the face value of the instrument. This makes answer (a) incorrect. Answer (c) is incorrect because Archer's failure to endorse the instrument only extends his warranty liability (including the warranty that states all signatures are genuine) to the immediate holder, Barker. Answer (d) is incorrect since Harding is liable for the forgery he placed on the instrument.

10. (1180,L1,46) (b) Answer (b) will render the instrument nonnegotiable since such a statement would cause the instrument to be conditional by making payment dependent on an uncertain event. Answer (d) would not be placing any conditions on the instrument that would not already be present by operation of law. If the instrument states that it is "subject to" another agreement then this would condition the promise or order, and the instrument would be nonnegotiable. Normally a negotiable instrument can contain no other promise except the promise to pay money. However, the negotiable character of the instrument will not be destroyed by a second promise that concerns security for the instrument such as answer (c).

11. (580,L1,15) (d) Corner Check Cashing Company must bear the loss because as a holder obtaining payment, it warrants that it has good title to the instrument. However, it does not have good title because the forgery prevented good title from passing. Therefore answers (a) and (c) are incorrect because of Corner Check Cashing Company's warranty of good title. Answer (b) is incorrect because Duval has a real defense in that his indorsement was forged. Corner Check Cashing Company's only recourse is to recover from Mask.

12. (580,L1,19) (a) Normally forgeries of the payee's signature would be sufficient to relieve the defrauded corporations of any liability on these instruments. However, a drawer who voluntarily transfers payment to an imposter (Gomer) must bear the loss if a holder in due course subsequently tries to collect. Therefore, answer (a) is correct. Forgery is usually a real defense that would be good against all subsequent holders in due course but the imposter exception would allow the banks, intermediate parties and the recipients to avoid the loss. The rationale for such a result is the fact that the defrauded corporations were in the best position to keep the defense (forgery) from occurring.

13. (580,L1,22) (b) Under the law of commercial paper to qualify as a holder in due course, the holder must have no knowledge that the instrument is overdue. A check is considered overdue if outstanding more than 30 days after issue. All other demand instruments are overdue after a reasonable time has elapsed, or if the holder is aware demand has been made for payment. Therefore, answer (b) is incorrect because an instrument payable on its face to a specified person or bearer creates bearer paper (instead of order paper), because a special indorsement is payable to a named person and signed by the indorser.

14. (580,L1,24) (d) Irwin qualifies as a holder in due course and therefore can defeat any personal defense. The unauthorized completion of an incomplete instrument is a personal defense. Dodson's negligence precludes his claiming a real defense. Irwin can collect the full $1,000 from Dodson. Dodson's only recourse would be to sue Swanson.

15. (580,L1,30) (b) If the drawee bank (Unity Trust Company) pays a check on which the drawer's signature (Markum) was forged, the bank is bound by the acceptance and the drawee can only recover the money paid from the forger (Robb). Normally a person who presents an instrument for payment makes three warranties. These warranties are: warranty of title; warranty of no knowledge that the signature of the drawer is unauthorized; warranty of no material alterations. However, a holder in due course or someone with the rights of a holder in due course does not warrant to the drawee bank that the drawer's signature is genuine because the drawer bank is in a better position to determine the genuineness of the drawer's signature. Therefore, the drawee bank should bear the loss.

16. (1177,L3,34) (d) Foxx is the drawee of a draft and he had no liability until he signed it (no party is ever liable until he signs in some manner). When he signed (accepted) it, he assumed primary liability. Thus answer (d), but not answer (c), is correct. Answer (a) is incorrect because the instrument is a draft, i.e., an order directing another to pay. In contrast a note is a promise to pay. Answer (b) is incorrect because Wilson as drawer was only secondarily liable.

17. (1177,L3,37) (b) In ascertaining value given by a bank, FIFO is used. In this case the bank has given value of $500. While the bank credited Ajax's account for $550, Ajax only spent $500. Answer (a) is incorrect because a $50 discount is not so great

to affect good faith on a one-year note. Answer (c) is incorrect because Broadway has liability to the extent the bank is a holder in due course because non-delivery is a personal defense. Answer (d) is incorrect because as maker of a note, Broadway has primary liability.

18. (577,L2,20) (c) Drafts which are drawn or are payable outside the U.S. require a formal notice of dishonor (protest) to hold other parties (e.g., indorsers, drawer) liable when the instrument has been dishonored. Negotiability is not affected by payment in foreign currency, nor by being drawn in a foreign country and payable in the U.S. Diana Davidson is the drawer and is secondarily liable. She is not the maker because she did not promise to pay directly; instead she directed the bank to pay.

19. (577,L2,26) (c) A "without recourse" indorsement is a qualified indorsement which disclaims contractual liability if the instrument is dishonored. However, the qualified indorser still warrants good title, authorized signatures, no material alteration, etc. The "without recourse" indorsement modifies the indorser's liability to both immediate and subsequent transferees by changing the warranty from "no defense" to "no knowledge of any defense." It does not put any person on notice of a defect or defense against the transferee. A qualified incorsement can be used on any negotiable instrument including drafts, checks, and notes.

20. (1178,L1,42) (c) A person who takes a negotiable instrument from a holder in due course acquires the rights of the holder in due course. Quirk, who knew of the prior breach, is barred as qualifying personally as a holder in due course. However, he took from a holder in due course, and thus has the rights of the holder in due course. Answer (a) is incorrect because Rose qualifies as a holder in due course and Marlin's defense is not good against Rose. Answer (b) is incorrect because as explained above, Quirk has the rights of a holder in due course. Answer (d) is incorrect because a proper stop order payment will prevent a holder in due course from collecting from the bank. The bank is not obligated to the holder in due course, who must proceed against the drawee of the check.

21. (1178,L1,46) (b) The instrument is bearer paper in Dobbins' hands because under the UCC an indorsement that does not make the instrument payable to the order of someone converts the instrument to a bearer instrument. Answer (a) is incorrect because if the bank refuses to pay Maxwell, he, as a

holder in due course, has recourse to sue Dobbins, the prior indorsers, and the drawer. Answer (c) is incorrect because under the facts, this instrument was payable to the order of Clark, and therefore Clark's signature was necessary to further negotiate the instrument. Answer (d) is incorrect because White's qualified indorsement disclaimed his contract liability but he still has warranty liability to subsequent parties. Contract liability relates to the contract for which the negotiable instrument was given in consideration. Warranty liability relates to warranties made by an indorser of a negotiable instrument, e.g., good title, no material alterations, all signatures good, etc.

22. (1178,L1,50) (a) The instrument as drafted contains all of the requirements of negotiability. It is written and signed; it contains an unconditional promise to pay a sum certain; it is payable at a definite time; and it is payable to "order." Stating that the "instrument arises out of a separate agreement" is merely a reference and does not condition the promise to pay. Answer (b) is incorrect because payable to the order of cash is considered bearer paper. Answer (c) is incorrect because the instrument is a note and not a draft. Notes are a promise to pay and drafts are an order directing someone else to pay, e.g., a bank. Answer (d) is incorrect because failure to make a timely presentment will not generally excuse a maker from liability unless the instrument is payable at a bank (which it is not here) and the bank becomes insolvent. It is indorsers who are excused from liability when presentment for payment is late.

23. (579,L1,26) (d) A clause in an instrument stating that it is payable only out of the proceeds from the resale of certain goods would adversely affect the negotiability of the instrument, i.e., the instrument is not unconditional if payment is limited to a particular source. An instrument must be unconditional to be negotiable.

24. (579,L1,27) (b) When a holder obtains a bank's certification of a check, the drawer and all prior indorsers are released because the bank has assumed the obligation to pay the check. Answer (a) is incorrect because a bank is not legally obligated to certify a check, although this is a normal courtesy extended by banks. Answer (c) is incorrect because an oral statement by phone from a bank stating that a check from their customer is good does not constitute an implied certification. Certi-

fications must be in writing. Answer (d) is incorrect since certification of a check does not prevent the further negotiation of it.

25. (579,L1,28) (a) If an order instrument is indorsed with a restrictive indorsement, such as "for deposit only," and signed by the payee, then any transferee of the instrument must pay or apply any value given by them for the instrument consistent with the restrictive indorsement. Answer (b) is incorrect because the indorsement here is not a blank indorsement but a restrictive indorsement. Answer (c) is incorrect because restrictive indorsements that attempt to prevent further transfer or negotiation are of no effect. Answer (d) is incorrect because when a restrictive indorsement is placed on an instrument, all subsequent transferees must comply with the restriction in paying value for the instrument. Alcatraz would have notice that the indorsement was not complied with if the check was not held by a bank.

26. (579,L1,29) (b) Under the circumstances Archer is a holder who took the instrument for value, in good faith, and without notice that any person had an adverse claim against it. Thus Archer is a holder in due course and will prevail. Answer (a) is incorrect because a thief can pass good title of a negotiable bearer instrument to a holder in due course. Answer (c) is incorrect because general notice published in the community about the theft of the negotiable instrument is not sufficient notice to prohibit Archer from qualifying as a holder in due course. He must have actual notice. Answer (d) is incorrect because a 20% discount by itself is not unusual or sufficiently excessive to prevent the purchaser from qualifying as a holder in due course.

27. (579,L1,31) (a) Wagner, a holder in due course, could have held Casper fully responsible if Wagner had pursued his rights on the negotiable instrument. Casper's defense, fraud as to the underlying consideration, is a personal defense and is not effective against a holder in due course. Answer (b) is incorrect because Gorden initially took the instrument with notice of the fraud, and therefore cannot be a holder in due course. Answer (c) is incorrect because Casper has a personal defense and is only liable to holders in due course. Answer (d) is incorrect because Gorden previously held the instrument subject to the defense, and he cannot raise himself to the status of a holder in due course by

reacquiring the instrument. A person taking an instrument from a holder in due course only acquires the rights of a holder in due course if he never held the instrument subject to a defense.

28. (579,L1,32) (a) A holder in due course may enforce a materially altered check according to its original tenor. Thus, Franco is liable to Carson for the original tenor of the check, $300. Franco is not liable for the $800, as in answer (b), because the material alteration of the instrument is a real defense. Stein is not liable for the $800, as in answer (c), because he also has the real defense of material alteration. Answer (d) is incorrect because Franco is liable to Carson for $300.

29. (1177,L3,40) (d) Knight's rights against Keller are not affected by the time when Keller indorsed the note. If he had indorsed the note after Meade, Knight would know he was an accommodation indorser, but this would not affect Knight's rights. Answer (a) is incorrect because accommodation parties have no special defenses. They are liable in the capacity in which they sign. Answer (b) is incorrect because Keller is secondarily liable as indorser. Answer (c) is incorrect because Knight must give notice of dishonor to Meade and/or Paterson to hold them liable (as any indorser must be given notice).

ANSWER OUTLINE

Problem 1   Bank as Holder in Due Course; Material Alteration; Non-negotiable Instrument

a.   Bank's right to collect on the notes assumes negotiability

      Bank took notes for value in good faith

   Bank is a holder in due course to the extent of the loans

   Forgery and breach of contract are possible defenses

      Forgery is a real defense and bank cannot collect

      Breach is a personal defense and bank will collect

         Amount of collection will be based on whether bank took for value collectively

            And can proceed against each note in full

            Or each note is considered individually and bank can only collect 80% (20,000 loan/ 25,000 collateral)

b.   Friendly is holder in due course and can recover original amount

   Friendly can recover $80 from Madison, the maker or $800 if Madison was negligent in drafting check

   Friendly cannot recover from State Bank

      Because Friendly has no relationship to the bank

   Friendly can only recover $80 from Parker if maker dishonors

      Parkers alteration warranty was at time of transfer

         I.E., does not apply to subsequent alterations

c.   Wilmont will not prevail against Horn

      The note was not negotiable

         Not payable at a definite date

         Payable only from specified sales proceeds

            I.E., particular fund doctrine

   Wilmont is a transferee, not holder in due course

      And Horn negated his liability by returning goods

UNOFFICIAL ANSWER

Problem 1   Bank as Holder in Due Course; Material Alteration; Non-negotiable Instrument

    Part a.   The first issue to be decided is whether the bank is a holder in due course, which would require that the notes in question be negotiable and that the bank be a holder. When a bank is involved, these requirements usually would be met. The next question is whether the bank took for value and, if so, to what extent. Section 3-303 of the Uniform Commercial Code provides that a holder takes for value to the extent that he acquires a security interest in or a lien on the instrument. A lender taking one or several negotiable instruments as security for a loan becomes a holder in due course to the extent of the amount loaned (and not the face amount as would a holder in due course who purchased notes at a discount). Thus, the bank will not be entitled to recover more than the amounts it advanced. However, this creates a problem based upon the facts in this situation— Does the bank qualify as a holder in due course collectively against all the notes or is it limited to a collection of the amount loaned attributable to each note individually?

    There are two assertable defenses—forgery and breach of contract and/or warranty. Additionally, there are a number of notes against which no defense is applicable. Forgery is a real defense and is valid even against a holder in due course. As to the forged notes, the bank will not be able to collect anything from the purported makers. Breach of contract, or breach of warranty is only a personal defense and not assertable against a holder in due course. Thus, the bank will recover against the makers of those notes, but the question is to what extent? If each note is considered individually, then the bank can only collect 80 percent on each. If, however, the notes are considered to secure the loan collectively, then the bank will obtain a recovery of the overall amount loaned. This could increase the percentage payable due to the uncollectibility of the forged notes.

    Part b.   Grover materially altered the instrument within the meaning of Uniform Commercial Code Section 3-407, which provides that a holder in due course, such as Friendly, in all cases may enforce the instrument according to its original tenor. Thus, Friendly would be entitled to recover $80, the original tenor of the instrument, from Madison.

    Friendly is entitled to nothing from State Bank. The bank rightfully dishonored the instrument, but even had it done so wrongfully, Friendly has no relationship to the bank and hence no right to recover from it.

    Parker, as a transferor of the instrument by indorsement, gave certain implied warranties, including that the instrument had not been materially altered. This warranty is at the time of transfer and is not a warranty that the instrument will not be subsequently altered, as it was in this case. Although there would appear to be no recourse against Parker under the alteration warranty, in the event of dishonor by the maker, Parker is liable on the instrument according to its tenor ($80) at the time of indorsement.

There is one possibility for full recovery against Madison; Friendly must assert and prove that Madison was negligent in the way he drafted the instrument and thereby contributed to the alteration.

Part c. No. The instrument is not negotiable. First, it is not payable at a definite time, and second, it is payable only out of the proceeds from the resale of the audio components. This is referred as to the "particular fund doctrine." Once there has been an initial determination that the instrument is non-negotiable, it does not matter that the remaining steps for qualification as a holder in due course have been met. The defense is clearly a personal defense, but because Wilmont is a mere transferee (assignee), he has no better rights than Samuels. In light of the facts, Wilmont has no right to recovery because the goods were properly returned by Horn, and thus Wilmont will not prevail against Horn.

ANSWER OUTLINE

Problem 2   Negotiability of Instrument; Types of Indorsements

a1.   No, the instrument is not negotiable
        Because not payable to "order" or "bearer"
        Defect not cured by Smith's indorsement
        Reference to used typewriters not significant

a2.   Yes, Meglo would be a holder in due course
        Meglo took for value, without knowledge of defect, and not overdue
            $300 discount not sufficient to imply lack of good faith
        Meglo would collect $2,000

a3.   Noreen's defense would not be valid against holder in due course
        It is a personal defense

a4.   Meglo is not a holder in due course
        But is a transferee with transferor's rights
        Meglo will collect $2,000 less breach of warranty damages

b1.   Walker is a blank indorser
        Consists of only a signature
        Specifies no special indorsee
    Williamson is a "without recourse" or qualified indorser
    Dixon is a special indorser
        Specifies a special indorsee
        May be negotiated further by the special indorsee
    Indorsers give warranties upon transfer
        Liable to subsequent indorser or holder in order of indorsement
        Qualified indorsers avoid this liability

b2.   Farber will prevail against Marglow
        Even though Farber is not a holder in due course (HIDC)
            I.e., had notice of Marglow's defense prior to negotiation
        As transferee, Farber can assert the transferor's (Kern) status of HIDC
        But Farber cannot take the note back from a subsequent HIDC to obtain HIDC status

UNOFFICIAL ANSWER

Problem 2   Negotiability of Instrument; Types of Indorsements

Part a.

1.   No. Although it meets all of the other requisites of negotiability pursuant to the Uniform Commercial Code, it lacks the specific terminology of negotiability. That is, it is neither payable to Smith's "order" nor payable to "bearer." Consequently, it is a nonnegotiable promissory note. This defect is not cured by Smith's indorsement despite the fact he used the words "pay to the order of." The indication of the nature of the transaction is legally insignificant.

2.   Yes. The note is not overdue, and Meglo took it for value and without notice or knowledge of any defect in it. The only possible assertion that could be made by Noreen to defeat Meglo's status as a holder in due course is that the size of the discount was so large as to indicate a lack of good faith. In the absence of any further information, a $300 discount on a one-year note such as this is not of such amount as to suggest a lack of good faith. Under these circumstances Meglo would collect the full $2,000.

3.   No. It is a mere personal defense and as such would not prevail against a subsequent holder in due course.

4. Since the instrument is not negotiable it cannot be "negotiated" to another person so as to enable him to qualify as a holder in due course. However, the transferor does assign all his rights to collect on the promise. Therefore, even if the typewriters were defective, Meglo would be entitled to sue on the promise and collect the amount due, decreased by damages for breach of warranty.

Part b.

1. Walker (indorsement 1) is a blank indorser. A blank indorsement specifies no particular indorsee and may consist of a mere signature. Williamson (indorsement 2) is a "without recourse" or qualified indorser. As such, she does not guarantee payment. Furthermore, the warranty that no defense of any party is good against the indorser, which is given by other indorsers, is limited by a without-recourse indorsement to a warranty that the indorser has no knowledge of such defense.

Dixon (indorsement 3) is a special indorser. A special indorsement specifies the person to whom or to whose order it makes the instrument payable. Any instrument specially indorsed becomes payable to the order of the special indorsee and may be further negotiated only by that indorsement.

Indorsers in general have contract liability and also give certain warranties upon transfer. The Uniform Commercial Code provides that, unless otherwise agreed, indorsers are liable to one another in the order in which they indorse. This is presumed to be the order in which their signatures appear on the instrument. Both blank and special indorsers state that upon dishonor and notice, they will pay the instrument according to its tenor at the time of their indorsement to the holder or any subsequent indorser. The obligation is, in effect, a contractual undertaking to act as a guarantor. Walker and Dixon are subject to this liability; Williamson is not.

2. Yes. Although Farber cannot personally qualify as a holder in due course because he had notice of the defense (fraud) asserted by Marglow prior to the completion of the negotiation, he can assert the standing of his transferor (Kern). Thus Farber will prevail.

Farber could not assert a subsequent indorser-transferor's standing as a holder in due course (his bank's) in that the Uniform Commercial Code provides that a prior holder who had notice of a defense or claim against him cannot improve his position by taking it from a later holder in due course.

MULTIPLE CHOICE QUESTIONS (1–25)

1.   In the course of an examination of the financial statements of Control Finance Company for the year ended September 30, 1980, the auditors learned that the company has just taken possession of certain heavy industrial equipment from Arrow Manufacturing Company, a debtor in default. Arrow had previously borrowed $60,000 from Control secured by a security interest in the heavy industrial equipment. The amount of the loan outstanding is $30,000. Which of the following is correct regarding the rights of Control and Arrow?

   a.   Control is **not** permitted to sell the repossessed equipment at private sale.

   b.   Arrow has **no** right to redeem the collateral at any time once possession has been taken.

   c.   Control is **not** entitled to retain the collateral it has repossessed in satisfaction of the debt even though it has given written notice to the debtor and he consents.

   d.   Arrow is **not** entitled to a compulsory disposition of the collateral.

2.   The Jolly Finance Company provides the financing for Triple J Appliance Company's inventory. As a part of its sales promotion and public relations campaign, Jolly Finance placed posters in Triple J's stores indicating that Triple J is another satisfied customer of Jolly and that the goods purchased at Triple J are available through the financing by Jolly. Jolly also files a financing statement which covers the financed inventory. Victor Restaurants purchased four hi-fi sets for use in its restaurants and had read one of the Jolly posters. Triple J has defaulted on its loan and Jolly Finance is seeking to repossess the hi-fi sets. Which of the following is correct?

   a.   Jolly has a perfected security interest in the hi-fi sets which is good against Victor.

   b.   Victor's knowledge of the financing arrangement between Jolly and Triple J does **not** affect its right to the hi-fi sets.

   c.   Jolly's filing was unnecessary to perfect its security interest in Triple J's inventory since it was perfected upon attachment.

   d.   The hi-fi sets are consumer goods in Victor's hands.

3.   The Gordon Manufacturing Company manufactures various types of lathes. It sold on credit 25 general-use lathes to Hardware City, a large retail outlet. Hardware City sold one of the lathes to Johnson for use in his home repair business, reserving a security interest for the unpaid balance. However, Hardware City did **not** file a financing statement. Johnson's creditors are asserting rights against the lathe. Which of the following statements is correct?

   a.   The lathe is a consumer good in Johnson's hands.

   b.   No filing was necessary to perfect a security interest in the lathe against Johnson's creditors.

   c.   Gordon Manufacturing could assert rights against the lathe sold to Johnson in the event Hardware City defaults in its payments.

   d.   The lathe was inventory in both Gordon and Hardware's hands and is equipment in Johnson's, and both Gordon and Hardware City must file to perfect their interests.

4.   The Town Bank makes collateralized loans to its customers at 1% above prime on securities owned by the customer, subject to existing margin requirements. In doing so, which of the following is correct?

   a.   Notification of the issuer is necessary in order to perfect a security interest.

   b.   Filing is a permissible method of perfecting a security interest in the securities if the circumstances dictate.

   c.   Any dividend or interest distributions during the term of the loan belong to the bank.

   d.   A perfected security interest in the securities can only be obtained by possession.

5.   Bass, an automobile dealer, had an inventory of 40 cars and 10 trucks. He financed the purchase of this inventory with County Bank under an agreement dated July 7 that gave the bank a security interest in all vehicles on Bass' premises, all future aquired vehicles, and the proceeds thereof. On July 11, County Bank properly filed a financing statement that identified the collateral in the same way that it was identified in the agreement. On October 1, Bass sold a passenger car to Dodd for family use and a truck to Diamond Company for its hardware business. Which of the following is correct?

   a.   The security agreement may **not** provide for a security interest in future aquired vehicles even if the parties agree.

   b.   The passenger car sold by Bass to Dodd continues to be subject to the security interest of the County Bank.

   c.   The bank's security interest is perfected as of July 7 despite the fact it was **not** filed until July 11.

d.   The security interest of the County Bank does **not** include the proceeds from the sale of the truck to Diamond Company.

6.   Retailer Corp. was in need of financing. To secure a loan, it made an oral assignment of its accounts receivable to J. Roe, a local investor, under which Roe loaned Retailer on a continuing basis, 90% of the face value of the assigned accounts receivable. Retailer collected from the account debtors and remitted to Roe at intervals. Before the debt was paid, Retailer filed a petition in bankruptcy. Which of the following is correct?

a.   As between the account debtors and Roe, the assignment is **not** an enforceable security interest.

b.   Roe is a secured creditor to the extent of the unpaid debt.

c.   Other unpaid creditors of Retailer Corp. who knew of the assignment are bound by its terms.

d.   An assignment of accounts to be valid, requires the debtors owing the accounts to be notified.

7.   Which of the following is included within the scope of the Secured Transactions Article of the Code?

a.   The outright sale of accounts receivable.

b.   A landlord's lien.

c.   The assignment of a claim for wages.

d.   The sale of chattel paper as a part of the sale of a business out of which it arose.

8.   Williamson purchased from Dilworth Hardware a new lathe for his home workshop for cash. Two weeks later, Williamson was called by the Easy Loan Company. Easy explained to Williamson that it had been financing Dilworth's purchases from the manufacturers and that to protect its interest it had obtained a perfected security interest in Dilworth's entire inventory of hardware and power tools, including the lathe which Williamson bought. Easy further explained that Dilworth had defaulted on a payment due to Easy, and Easy intended to assert its security interest in the lathe and repossess it unless Williamson was willing to make payment of $200 for a release of Easy's security interest. If Williamson refuses to make the payment, which of the following statements is correct?

a.   Williamson will not take free of Easy's security interest if he was aware of said interest at the time he purchased the lathe.

b.   Even if Williamson had both actual notice and constructive notice via recordation of

Easy's interest, he will prevail if Easy seeks to repossess the lathe.

c.   Easy's security interest in the lathe in question is invalid against all parties unless its filing specifically described and designated the the particular lathe Williamson purchased.

d.   Williamson must pay the $200 or the lathe can be validly repossessed and sold to satisfy the amount Dilworth owes Easy and any excess paid to Williamson.

9.   Two Uniform Commerical Code concepts relating to secured transactions are "attachment" and "perfection." Which of the following is correct in connection with the similarities and differences between these two concepts?

a.   They are mutually exclusive and wholly independent of each other.

b.   Satisfaction of one automatically satisfies the other.

c.   Attachment relates primarily to the rights against the debtor and perfection relates primarily to the rights against third parties.

d.   It is not possible to have a simultaneous attachment and perfection.

10.   Which of the following requirements is not necessary in order to have a security interest attach?

a.   There must be a proper filing.

b.   The debtor must have rights in the collateral.

c.   Value must be given by the creditor.

d.   Either the creditor must take possession or the debtor must sign a security agreement which describes the collateral.

11.   In respect to obtaining a purchase money security interest, which of the following requirements must be met?

a.   The property sold may only be consumer goods.

b.   Only a seller may obtain a purchase money security interest.

c.   Such a security interest must be filed in all cases to be perfected.

d.   Credit advanced to the buyer must be used to obtain the property which serves as the collateral.

12.   Vista Motor Sales, a corporation engaged in selling motor vehicles at retail, borrowed money from Sunshine Finance Company and gave Sunshine a properly executed security agreement in its present and future inventory and in the proceeds therefrom

to secure the loan. Sunshine's security interest was duly perfected under the laws of the state where Vista does business and maintains its entire inventory. Thereafter, Vista sold a new pickup truck from its inventory to Archer and received Archer's certified check in payment of the full price. Under the circumstances, which of the following is correct?

- a. Sunshine must file an amendment to the financing statement every time Vista receives a substantial number of additional vehicles from the manufacturer if Sunshine is to obtain a valid security interest in subsequently delivered inventory.
- b. Sunshine's security interest in the certified check Vista received is perfected against Vista's other creditors.
- c. Unless Sunshine specifically included proceeds in the financing statement it filed, it has no rights to them.
- d. The term "proceeds" does not include used cars received by Vista since they will be resold.

13. Andrew asked Judy about the possibility of borrowing $10,000. Judy replied that she would be happy to make the loan if Andrew would provide collateral to secure payment. Andrew gave Judy his promissory note for $10,000, bearing interest at 7%, and delivered to Judy convertible bearer bonds with coupons attached. The bonds had a current market value of $12,000. During the period in which the loan was outstanding the bonds increased in market value to $18,000. In addition, one of the interest coupons became due. There is no express agreement between the parties as to their respective rights in the interest or profits. Under the circumstances, which of the following is correct?

- a. Judy owns the coupon representing matured interest due.
- b. Judy may elect to sell the bonds and retain the proceeds in excess of $12,000.
- c. If Judy sold the bonds to an innocent third party, the third party would obtain valid title.
- d. Such a financing arrangement must be filed in the appropriate recordation office in order to be valid.

14. Field warehousing is a well-established means of securing a loan. As such, it resembles a pledge in many legal respects. Which of the following is correct?

- a. The field warehouseman must maintain physical control of and dominion over the property.

- b. A filing is required in order to perfect such a financing arrangement.
- c. Temporary relinquishment of control for any purpose will suspend the validity of the arrangement insofar as other creditors are concerned.
- d. The property in question must be physically moved to a new location although it may be a part of the borrower's facilities.

15. Weatherall seeks to create a valid perfected security interest in goods under the provisions of the Uniform Commercial Code. Which of the following acts or actions will establish this?

- a. Weatherall obtains a written agreement under which Weatherall takes possession of the security.
- b. Weatherall obtains an unsigned written security agreement.
- c. Weatherall obtains a security agreement signed only by the debtor.
- d. Weatherall files a financing statement which is not in itself a security agreement.

16. Donaldson, Inc., loaned Watson Enterprises $50,000 secured by a real estate mortgage which included the land, buildings, and "all other property which is added to the real property or which is considered as real property as a matter of law." Star Company also loaned Watson $25,000 and obtained a security interest in all of Watson's "inventory, accounts receivable, fixtures, and other tangible personal property." There is insufficient property to satisfy the two creditors. Consequently, Donaldson is attempting to include all property possible under the terms and scope of its real property mortgage. If Donaldson is successful in this regard, then Star will receive a lesser amount in satisfaction of its claim. What is the probable outcome of Donaldson's action?

- a. Donaldson will not prevail if the property in question is detachable trade fixtures.
- b. Donaldson will prevail if Star failed to file a financing statement.
- c. Donaldson will prevail if it was the first lender and duly filed its real property mortgage.
- d. The problem will be decided by taking all of Watson's property (real and personal) subject to the two secured creditors' claims and dividing it in proportion to the respective debts.

17.   Galdstone Warehousing, Inc., is an independent bonded warehouse company. It issued a warehouse receipt for 10,000 bales of cotton belonging to Travis. The word "NEGOTIABLE" was conspicuously printed on the warehouse receipt it issued to Travis. The warehouse receipt also contained a statement in large, clear print that the cotton would only be surrendered upon return of the receipt and payment of all storage fees. Travis was a prominent plantation owner engaged in the cotton growing business. Travis pledged the warehouse receipt with Southern National Bank in exchange for a $50,000 personal loan. A financing statement was not filed. Under the circumstances, which of the following is correct?

  a.   Travis' business creditors cannot obtain the warehouse receipt from Southern National unless they repay Travis' outstanding loan.

  b.   The bank does not have a perfected security interest in the cotton since it did not file a financing statement.

  c.   Travis' personal creditors have first claim, superior to all other parties, to the cotton in question because the loan was a personal loan and constituted a fraud upon the personal creditors.

  d.   The fact that the word "NEGOTIABLE" and the statement regarding the return of the receipt were conspicuously printed upon the receipt is not binding upon anyone except Travis.

18.   Vega Manufacturing, Inc., manufactures and sells hi-fi systems and components to the trade and at retail. Repossession is frequently made from customers who are in default. Which of the following statements is correct concerning the rights of the defaulting debtors who have had property repossessed by Vega?

  a.   Vega has the right to retain all the goods repossessed as long as it gives notice and cancels the debt.

  b.   It is unimportant whether the goods repossessed are defined as consumer goods, inventory, or something else in respect to the debtor's rights upon repossession.

  c.   If the defaulting debtor voluntarily signs a statement renouncing his rights in the collateral, the creditor must nevertheless resell them for the debtor's benefit.

  d.   If a debtor has paid sixty percent or more of the purchase price of consumer goods in satisfaction of a purchase money security interest, the debtor has the right to have the creditor dispose of the goods.

19.   Draper Corporation, a retail merchant, was indebted to Cramer Corporation in the amount of $25,000 arising out of the sale of goods delivered to Draper on credit. Cramer and Draper signed a security agreement creating a security interest in certain collateral of Draper. The collateral was described in the security agreement as "the inventory of Draper Corporation, presently existing and thereafter acquired." This description of Draper's collateral

  a.   Is insufficient because it is too broad.

  b.   Is sufficient.

  c.   Must be more specific for the security interest to be perfected.

  d.   Is sufficient, but the security interest is valid only insofar as it is limited to Draper's presently existing inventory.

20.   Marcus purchased a Zomar 21-inch color television set from Hart Appliance, Inc. Marcus made a down payment of $100 and signed a negotiable promissory note and a security agreement. Hart Appliance did not file a financing statement covering the sale to Marcus.

  a.   Hart's failure to file the financing statement will allow subsequent creditors of Marcus to defeat Hart's security interest in the television set.

  b.   The sale of the television set by Marcus to a neighbor without disclosure of Hart's security interest in the set will result in the security interest being valid against the neighbor.

  c.   In order to perfect its security interest against any parties who subsequently assert rights against the television set, Hart must file the financing statement.

  d.   The transaction would be treated as a sale of consumer goods, subject to a purchase-money security interest in Hart.

21.   Your client, Ace Auto Sales, sold a 1974 Skylark Magnificent to Marcus on the installment basis. Marcus signed an installment agreement for the balance due ($2,000) on the purchase price. Ace's policy was not to file a financing statement in the appropriate recordation office. Marcus subsequently sold the car to Franks without disclosing the debt owed to Ace. Franks purchased the car in good faith, knowing nothing about the debt owed by Marcus to Ace. Marcus is bankrupt. Wallace, a general creditor of Marcus has asserted rights to the car in question. Under the circumstances

a. Marcus takes title free and clear of any claims because Ace did not file.

b. Ace can defeat the claim of Franks in that Franks is a mere third party beneficiary.

c. Ace's rights against Marcus under the contract of sale are unimpaired despite the lack of filing.

d. In the final analysis Wallace will prevail.

22. Wilcox Laboratories, Ltd., manufactures medical equipment for sale to medical institutions and retailers. Wilcox also sells directly to consumers in its wholly-owned retail outlets. Wilcox has created a subsidiary, Wilcox Finance Corporation, for the purpose of financing the purchase of its products by the various customers. In which of the following situations does Wilcox Finance not have to file a financing statement to perfect its security interest against competing creditors in the equipment sold by Wilcox?

a. Sales made to medical institutions.

b. Sales made to consumers who purchase for their own personal use.

c. Sales made to retailers who in turn sell to buyers in the ordinary course of business.

d. Sales made to any buyer when the equipment becomes a fixture.

23. Kelmore Appliances, Inc., sells various brand name appliances at discount prices. Kelmore maintains a large inventory which it obtains from various manufacturers on credit. These manufacturer-creditors have all filed and taken secured interests in the appliances and proceeds therefrom which they have sold to Kelmore on credit. Kelmore in turn sells to hundreds of ultimate consumers; some pay cash but most buy on credit. Kelmore takes a security interest but does not file a financing statement for credit sales. Which of the following is correct?

a. The appliances in Kelmore's hands are consumer goods.

b. Since Kelmore takes a purchase money security interest in the consumer goods sold, its security interest is perfected upon attachment.

c. The appliance manufacturers can enforce their secured interests against the appliances in the hands of the purchasers who paid cash for them.

d. A subsequent sale by one of Kelmore's customers to a bona fide purchaser will be subject to Kelmore's secured interest.

24. Robert Cunningham owns a shop in which he repairs electrical appliances. Three months ago Electrical Supply Company sold Cunningham, on credit, a machine for testing electrical appliances and obtained a perfected security interest at the time as security for payment of the unpaid balance. Cunningham's creditors have now filed an involuntary petition in bankruptcy against him. What is the status of Electrical in the bankruptcy proceeding?

a. Electrical is a secured creditor and has the right against the trustee if not paid to assert a claim to the electrical testing machine it sold to Cunningham.

b. Electrical must surrender its perfected security interest to the trustee in bankruptcy and share as a general creditor of the bankrupt's estate.

c. Electrical's perfected security interest constitutes a preference and is voidable.

d. Electrical must elect to resort exclusively to its secured interest or to relinquish it and obtain the same share as a general creditor.

25. Carter Corporation loaned $500,000 to Devon Corporation pursuant to an oral agreement granting a security interest in certain shares of stock held by Devon. Carter sought to have Devon sign a security agreement granting a security interest in the shares. Devon refused to sign any agreement, but instead delivered the stock certificates in question to Carter.

a. The security interest of Carter is not perfected until Devon signs the security agreement or Carter files a financing statement, whichever first occurs.

b. Carter must file a financing statement, or a copy of a security agreement, signed by the debtor to perfect its security interest.

c. Carter has a perfected security interest in the collateral.

d. Carter must sign the agreement, and a financing statement, and file either one of them to perfect its security interest in the shares of stock.

PROBLEMS

<u>Problem 1</u>   Perfection and Priorities (573,L5)
(15 to 20 minutes)

Baldwin Machine Shop, Inc., purchased a power lathe and took immediate delivery on June 10 from Yankee Machine Tools Corp. Baldwin agreed to pay the full price in cash within sixty days. Baldwin purchased a second lathe from Yankee on the same terms on July 7. Baldwin, although solvent, was experiencing cash difficulties and failed to pay Yankee for the lathes at the times agreed upon. The price of the two lathes still had not been paid in December when Baldwin ordered two more lathes from Yankee, agreeing to pay cash on delivery and also agreeing to pay for the first two lathes on delivery of the last two. In order to raise the cash necessary for this purpose, Baldwin negotiated a loan with First City Bank. The loan was closed on December 6. At the closing Baldwin executed a security agreement giving the bank a security interest in the four lathes and also executed and delivered a financing statement to the Bank in connection with the transaction. Baldwin then paid the loan proceeds to Yankee on December 6 and took delivery of the two new lathes. The Bank filed the financing statement on December 10.

Although the Bank did not know it at the time of the loan, Baldwin had given a security interest on June 1 in all of its machinery and equipment, including any machinery and equipment thereafter acquired, to Cairo Steel Corporation, a major steel supplier. Baldwin's objective was to secure credit purchases of steel from Cairo. Cairo filed the financing statement furnished by Baldwin concerning this transaction on December 8.

Six months have not elapsed, and Baldwin's financial condition has not improved. First City Bank is concerned about its security, having now learned of Cairo's security interest. You have acquired this information during the course of your examination of the Bank's financial statements.

Required:

What are the rights of First City Bank and Cairo Steel Corporation in Baldwin's lathes? Explain.

<u>Problem 2</u>   Perfection and Priorities (1178,L2a)

(10 to 15 minutes)

Part a.   National Finance Company engages in a wide variety of secured transactions which may be broken down into three categories.

I.   Consumer loans in connection with the purchase of automobiles, appliances, and furniture, National makes these loans in two ways. First, it makes direct loans to the consumer-borrower who then makes the purchase with the proceeds. Second, it is contacted by the seller and provides the financing for the purchase by the customer. In either case National takes a security interest in the property purchased.

II.   Collateralized loans to borrowers who deliver possession of property, such as diamonds, to National to secure repayment of their loans.

III.   Loans to merchants to finance their inventory purchases. National takes a security interest in the inventory and proceeds.

Except for category III, National does not file a financing statement.

Required: Answer the following, setting forth reasons for any conclusions stated.
1.   When does National's security interest in the various types of property attach?
2.   As a secured creditor, against what parties must National protect itself?
3.   Does National have a perfected security interest in any of the above property? If so, against whom?
4.   If the facts indicate that National does not have a perfected security interest against all parties, what should it do?
5.   Can National fully protect itself against all subsequent parties who might claim superior rights to the property involved?

<u>Problem 3</u>   Field Warehousing; Security Interest in
Negotiable Document of Title (580,L4b)

(7 to 10 minutes)

Part b.   Norwood Furniture, Inc., found that its credit rating was such that it was unable to obtain a line of unsecured credit. National Bank indicated that it would be willing to supply funds based upon a "pledge" of Norwood's furniture inventory which was located in two warehouses. The bank would receive notes and bearer negotiable warehouse receipts covering the merchandise securing the loans. An independent warehouseman was to have complete control over the areas in the warehouse set aside as field warehousing facilities. The Hastings Field Warehousing Corporation was selected to serve as the independent warehouseman. It was to retain keys to the posted area in which the inventory was contained. Negotiable bearer warehouse receipts were issued to Norwood when it delivered the merchandise to Hastings. The receipts were then delivered by Norwood to National to secure the loans which were made at 80% of the market value of the furniture indicated on the receipts. Upon occasion, Norwood would take temporary possession of the furniture for the purpose of packaging it, surrendering the warehouse receipt for this limited purpose. As orders were filled out of the field warehouse inventory, the requisite receipt would be relinquished by National, the merchandise obtained by Norwood, and other items substituted with a new receipt issued.

Required:

Answer the following, setting forth reasons for any conclusions stated.

1.   Based upon the facts given, is the field warehousing arrangement valid?

2.   When does a security interest in the negotiable warehouse receipts attach?

3.   What, if anything, is necessary to perfect a security interest in goods covered by negotiable warehouse receipts?

4.   What are the dangers, if any, that National faces by relinquishing the warehouse receipts to Norwood?

MULTIPLE CHOICE ANSWERS

1.	d	6.	a	11.	d	16.	a	21.	c
2.	b	7.	a	12.	b	17.	a	22.	b
3.	d	8.	b	13.	c	18.	d	23.	b
4.	d	9.	c	14.	a	19.	b	24.	a
5.	c	10.	a	15.	a	20.	d	25.	c

EXPLANATION OF MULTIPLE CHOICE ANSWERS

1. (1180,L1,31)   (d)   Upon default, the secured party normally has the right to retain (or sell) the collateral to satisfy the obligation. However, the secured party cannot retain the collateral if it is consumer goods and the debtor has paid 60% or more of the obligation. In such a case the debtor is entitled to a compulsory disposition of the goods. Controls security interest is in equipment not consumer goods, and Arrow has been paid only 50% of the obligation. Thus Arrow is not entitled to a compulsory disposition. Answer (d) is correct. Control can sell the possessed equipment at either a public or private sale. Either type of sale must be handled in a commercially reasonable manner. Thus answer (a) is incorrect. Arrow can redeem the collateral at any time up to when it is sold by paying the full obligation plus the expenses of the secured party. Control could retain the collateral if written notice of such was sent to the debtor and this debtor did not object within 21 days. This makes answers (b) and (c) incorrect.

2. (1180,L1,32)   (b)   A purchaser takes free of a perfected security interest in inventory if the purchaser buys from a dealer of goods in the ordinary course of business, even though the purchaser has knowledge of the security interest. In this question, the hi-fi sets are inventory, and Victor would qualify as a purchaser in the ordinary course of business. Thus answer (b) is correct and answer (a) is incorrect. Automatic perfection by attachment only occurs when a purchase-money security interest is taken in consumer goods. Jolly is taking a security interest in inventory, thus there would be no automatic perfection by attachment. This makes answers (c) and (d) incorrect.

3. (1180,L1,33)   (d)   The correct answer is (d) because the lathe is inventory, goods held for sale, in the hands of Gordon and Hardware. In Johnson's possession the lathe would be equipment, items used primarily in a business. Consumer goods are those items bought for use primarily for personal, family, or household purposes, making answer (a) incorrect. Filing the financing statement was necessary for perfection because the lathe was inventory and automatic perfection by attachment only applies to a security interest

in consumer goods. This makes answer (b) incorrect. Answer (c) is incorrect because a purchaser in the ordinary course of business (Johnson) will defeat a prior perfected security interest in inventory.

4. (1180,L1,34)   (d)   A perfected security interest in securities can only be obtained by possession. An exception to this rule is when the creditor temporarily returns the security to the debtor (for sale, exchange, etc.). In such situations, the creditor's security interest remains perfected for 21 days. However, a bona fide purchaser of the security will defeat the creditor's security interest. Thus, answer (d) is correct. To perfect a security interest in securities there is no need to notify the issuer. Dividends and interest earned during the secured transaction are the property of the debtor.

5. (1180,L1,35)   (c)   Answer (c) is correct because the security interest is perfected as of July 7, not July 11. Answer (a) is incorrect because after acquired property clause is very typical of a security agreement that creates a security interest in inventory. This provision creates a floating lien. Answer (b) is incorrect because a purchase in the ordinary course of business (Dodd) defeats a prior perfected security interest in inventory. Proceeds include what is received upon sale of the collateral. Country Bank does have a perfected security interest in the proceeds from the sale of a truck because the security agreement states proceeds are covered. The general rule states that security interest in proceeds is automatically perfected for a 10-day period if the security interest in the original collateral was perfected. However, if the security agreement states that the security interest is to cover proceeds, the perfected security interest will continue beyond the 10-day period without any additional filing. Thus answer (d) is incorrect.

6. (1180,L1,36)   (a)   A nonpossessary security interest in accounts can only be created by a written security agreement. Retailer Corp. and Roe engaged in an oral assignment of the accounts which would be unenforceable. Answer (a) is correct. A nonpossessary security interest in accounts can only be perfected by filing a financing statement.

7. (1180,L1,38)   (a)   The only item listed that is within the scope of article 9 (secured transactions) is the outright sale of accounts receivable.

8. (1179,L1,22) (b) Williamson is a buyer in the ordinary course of business and will defeat the rights of a secured creditor such as Easy Loan Company even if Williamson had both actual notice and/or constructive

notice of Easy's security interest. Answer (a) is incorrect because Williamson will take free of Easy's security interest as stated above even if he was aware of the interest at the time he purchased the lathe. Answer (c) is incorrect because Easy's security interest would be valid against appropriate parties if the security agreement contains a description which identifies the collateral. Answer (d) is incorrect as explained above, because Williamson purchased in good faith, paid value and dealt with a person who regularly deals in goods involved.

9. (1179,L1,23) (c)   The similarity and difference between the concepts of attachment and perfection are that attachments relate primarily to the rights of the secured party against the debtor and the collateral, whereas perfection relates primarily to the secured party's rights in the collateral against third parties. Attachment and perfection are not mutually exclusive and wholly independent of each other as in answer (a) since both are required to establish an effective secured transaction. Answer (b) is incorrect because satisfaction of one of these concepts does not automatically satisfy the other. To that extent, they are independent and the requirements of each must be satisfied. Answer (d) is incorrect because it is possible in limited circumstances to have a simultaneous attachment and perfection. This occurs in purchased money security interests in consumer goods.

10. (1179,L1,24) (a)   In order to have a security interest attached, it is not necessary that there be a proper filing. However, answers (b), (c), and (d) set out the 3 requirements which must be satisfied before a security agreement can attach in the collateral: the debtor must have rights in the collateral; value must be given by the creditor; and the creditor must take either possession of the collateral or the debtor must sign a security agreement which describes the collateral.

11. (1179,L1,25) (d)   In order to obtain a purchase money security interest, credit must be advanced to the buyer; in fact, this credit is used to obtain the property which security interest is not limited to consumer goods. Answer (b) as stated above is not correct because either a seller or other lender may obtain a purchase money security interest under appropriate circumstances. Answer (c) is incorrect because a purchase money security interest need not be filed in consumer goods transactions in order to be perfected.

12. (1179,L1,26) (b)   Under the facts given, Sunshine's security interest in the certified check that Vista received is perfected against Vista's other creditors. Answer (c) is incorrect because the security interest attaches to proceeds automatically without special mention in the financing statement. Answer (d) is incorrect because the term "proceeds" is broad enough to include anything received in exchange for the collateral including used motor vehicles, i.e., "trade ins." Answer (a) is incorrect because Sunshine covered itself in the executed security agreement by stating that the security agreement covered both present and future inventory. Therefore, an amendment is unnecessary every time Vista receives a substantial number of vehicles from the manufacturer.

13. (1177,L2,20) (c)   The bearer bonds are investment securities and a bona fide purchaser, i.e., one who takes innocently of any wrongdoing and in good faith, can take valid title. It is a similar situation to a holder in due course taking a negotiable instrument. Answer (a) is incorrect because Judy does not own the interest coupon but may keep the interest and reduce the obligation. Answer (b) is incorrect because Judy may not sell the bonds unless Andrew defaults. In any event Judy must turn over all proceeds in excess of $10,000. Answer (d) is incorrect because no financing arrangement need be filed because Judy has possession.

14. (1177,L2,24) (a)   A pledge is possession of the debtor's property by the creditor to secure a debt. This is the same as possessing collateral to perfect a security interest, i.e., the creditor must possess the collateral. This is done by the field warehouseman or his agent, by maintaining physical control and dominion over the property. Answer (b) is incorrect because filing is not required where there is possession. Answer (c) is incorrect because temporary relinquishment of control is acceptable to allow for an exchange of collateral, to allow the debtor to temporarily use or work on the goods. However, a holder in due course or bona fide purchaser who suffers legal detriment, i.e., purchases, lends money on, etc., during such interval will prevail. Answer (d) is incorrect because the collateral need not be moved to a new location; rather, it must be segregated and controlled.

15. (1177,L2,28) (a)   If Weatherall obtains a written security agreement (properly signed, etc.) and takes possession of the security, he will have a valid perfected security interest. Answer (b) is incorrect because the security agreement must be signed by the debtor to be valid. Answer (c) is incorrect because a security agreement alone without possession or filing is not perfected. Answer (d) is incorrect because a filed financing statement without having a security agreement does not create a security interest.

16. (578,L1,29) (a) Detachable trade fixtures are considered personal property, not real property. Therefore, a real estate mortgagee will not obtain a security interest in property classified as a detachable trade fixture. Answer (b) is incorrect because Donaldson's mortgage does not cover any personal property which is the issue here. Answer (c) is incorrect because the mortgage attaches only to real property. Thus property which is classified as personal will not be included whether the mortgage is recorded or not. Answer (d) is incorrect because the court's job is to distinguish between real and personal property and it lacks authority to divide disputed property in proportion to respective claims.

17. (578,L1,49) (a) Southern National Bank, by taking possession of the negotiable warehouse receipt, has perfected a security interest. The bank will not give up the negotiable document until the loan is repaid or it will lose perfection of its security interest. Answer (b) is incorrect because a financing statement need not be filed because possession of a negotiable document perfects a security interest in the goods represented by the document. Answer (c) is incorrect because taking a personal loan is not a fraud upon existing personal creditors and would not give the personal creditors any rights in the security. Answer (d) is incorrect because the word "negotiable" conspicuously printed on the warehouse receipt along with the statement is binding on all parties involved in the transaction.

18. (578,L1,50) (d) A secured creditor must sell consumer goods, i.e., cannot repossess and keep, if the debtor has paid 60 percent or more for them, unless the debtor waives this right in a signed writing. Answer (a) is incorrect because the creditor may propose to retain repossessed goods, but the creditor must sell them if the debtor objects. Answer (b) is incorrect because the distinction between consumer goods and other goods is important. Other goods may be retained unless the debtor objects, while consumer goods 60% paid for must be sold unless the debtor waives his right to a sale. Answer (c) is also incorrect because a defaulting debtor may voluntarily renounce his rights in the collateral and the creditor need not resell them for the debtor's benefit.

19. (575,L3,46) (b) The description of the collateral need be only so specific as to identify the collateral. The description is sufficient for the presently existing inventory and is also sufficient for the after-acquired inventory.

20. (1173,L1,6) (d) Assuming that Marcus purchased the television for his personal use, it would be a consumer good. Since Marcus used the television as collateral for the payments, it is a purchase-money security interest. A purchase-money security interest can be perfected by attachment alone if it is a consumer good. Hart, therefore, does not need to file a financing statement. The purchaser of a consumer good who purchases in good faith for personal use, takes free of the security interest.

21. (1175,L3,39) (c) A secured party need not file to retain a security interest or other rights under the contract with the debtor — filing is to protect the secured party from claims to the collateral by third parties. Franks is not a third party beneficiary, because he was not intended to acquire rights in the Ace—Marcus contract at the time of its formation. Neither is he an assignee of the installment contract since he was aware of it. A general creditor has no claim to specific property of a debtor but must reduce his claim to judgment prior to seeking attachment. However, an unrecorded or unfiled purchase money security interest should prevail over the judgment creditor.

22. (579,L1,14) (b) A purchase money security interest is automatically perfected without the necessity of filing a financing statement if the purchaser is a consumer who purchases for his own personal use. Answers (a), (c), and (d) are incorrect because in each of these cases a secured creditor must file a financing statement to perfect its security interest against competing creditors.

23. (579,L1,15) (b) When a creditor takes a purchase money security interest in consumer goods, the security interest is perfected upon attachment. Hence no filing is required by Kelmore. Answer (a) is incorrect because the appliances in Kelmore's possession before the sale would be classified as inventory and not as consumer goods. Answer (c) is incorrect because consumers who buy from dealers in the ordinary course of business take free and clear of pre-existing security interests even if they have knowledge of the security interests. Answer (d) is incorrect because a subsequent sale by one of Kelmore's customers to another bona fide consumer would not be subject to Kelmore's security interest. However, a subsequent purchaser would be subject to Kelmore's security interest if Kelmore had filed a financing statement at the time of the original consumer sale, rather than relying on perfection by attachment only.

24.   (579,L1,22)   (a)   Electrical, as a secured creditor, may assert a reclamation claim against the trustee in bankruptcy for the testing machine. Answer (b) is incorrect because the secured party may enforce its perfected security interest and then proceed as a general creditor against the bankrupt's estate to the extent the collateral does not satisfy the debt. Electrical's perfected security interest does not constitute a voidable preference as stated in answer (c) since the simultaneous sale and creation of the security interest is considered a fair exchange. Answer (d) is incorrect because a secured party is not forced to make an exclusive choice of remedy but may proceed against the security until it is exhausted and may then proceed in the bankruptcy action as a general creditor for any deficiency.

25.   (575,L3,42)   (c)   Carter has a perfected security interest in the collateral, because he has possession of the stock certificates and they are non-negotiable.   The agreement does not need to be in writing if the secured party has possession of the collateral.   Since the agreement need not be in writing, it need not be signed by either.

ANSWER OUTLINE

Problem 1   Perfection and Priorities

Cairo's security interest included after-acquired property
    Attaches automatically when property is acquired
      Cairo's security interest perfected on December 8
First City has a purchase-money security interest
Has ten days to perfect after debtor receives collateral
    Thus considered perfected on December 6
Thus, superior to Cairo's security interest
    Only on last two lathes
Cairo's security interest is superior on first two

UNOFFICIAL ANSWER

Problem 1   Perfection and Priorities

Since Cairo's security interest included after-acquired property, it would attach when Baldwin acquired the lathes. Cairo's interest however, was not perfected until the financing statement was filed on December 8. First City's security interest in the lathes attached on December 6 and was perfected on December 10. Ordinarily, priority among persons having perfected security interests in the same property is determined by the order in which they file to effect perfection. An exception to the general rule exists which favors a purchase-money security interest which is perfected at the time the debtor receives the collateral or within ten days thereafter A purchase-money security interest is one taken by a person who loans money to a second person to enable the second person to acquire the collateral to secure the loan.

As to the two lathes acquired by Baldwin on December 6, First City's security interest clearly was a purchase-money security interest, and since it was perfected within the specified ten-day period, it would be superior to Cairo's interest in the lathes acquired on December 6. With respect to the two lathes delivered to Baldwin in June and July, First City's security interest would seem not to be a purchase-money security interest since, at the time the loan was made, Baldwin had already acquired those lathes. Moreover, even if the Bank had a purchase-money security interest in the first two lathes, since the Bank did not perfect it within ten days after Baldwin had acquired the lathes, the interest would not be protected by the exception to the "first to file" rule discussed above. Accordingly, as to the first two lathes,

Cairo's security interest would take priority over that of First City.

ANSWER OUTLINE

Problem 2   Perfection and Priorities

a1. UCC provides security interests attach when
    Collateral is in possession of secured party
      Or debtor signs a security agreement
    Value is given by the creditor
    Debtor has rights in the collateral
  National transactions fulfill above criteria
    Transaction types I and III require security agreements
    Possession by creditor is sufficient for type II

a2. Secured creditors must protect themselves against
    Debtor
    Debtor's creditor
    Trustee in bankruptcy
    Subsequent purchasers for value

a3. National has security interest against debtor
    Security agreement is sufficient
  For others, creditor must have possession or file
   a financing statement
    Except financing statement is required to protect against subsequent purchasers of consumer goods
    Except subsequent purchasers of debtor's inventory take free of perfected security interest

a4. To perfect against all subsequent purchasers of consumer goods (type I), National should file a financing statement

a5. No, National may not protect itself against subsequent purchasers of goods in debtor's inventory
    I.e., protection is not possible without possession

UNOFFICIAL ANSWER

Problem 2   Perfection and Priorities

Part a.

1.   The Uniform Commercial Code provides that a security interest attaches in property when three events occur. First, collateral is in possession of the secured party pursuant to agreement, or the debtor has signed a security agreement that contains a description of the collateral. Second, value has been given by the creditor. Third, the debtor has rights in the collateral.

Insofar as National is concerned, a security interest in all three categories of secured transactions has attached. In categories I and III, there must be a security agreement signed by the debtor. Regarding the collateralized property in category II, possession pursuant to agreement without a signed writing is sufficient. In all instances, value has been given and the debtor has rights in the collateral.

2.   There are four potential parties against whom National must protect itself. These are the debtor, the debtor's creditors, the trustee in bankruptcy, and subsequent purchasers for value from the debtor.

3.   National's rights against the debtor are contained in the security agreement and the Uniform Commercial Code provisions relating to the agreement and the relationship between the parties. It is not necessary to file a financing statement in order to obtain these rights against the debtor; the agreement itself is sufficient.

To perfect a security interest against other parties, the creditor must either take possession (as in category II) or file a financing statement except where the creditor has taken "a purchase money security interest in consumer goods." In the latter case, perfection occurs at the time the security interest attaches, but it is only valid against the debtor's creditors and a trustee in bankruptcy and not against a bona fide purchaser unless a financing statement has been filed. Whether National uses either method described in category I to finance the purchase of the consumer goods, it will have a purchase money security interest if it gave value to enable the debtor to acquire rights in or the use of collateral if such value is in fact so used.

Where a creditor provides financing for a debtor to enable him to obtain and resell inventory items, the security interest is perfected by filing. However, since resale is clearly contemplated, purchasers for value take free of the perfected security interest.

4.   The only practical suggestion would be to file a financing statement in respect to the loans described in category I, which would then provide protection against subsequent purchasers from the debtor. National already is protected against the other parties in category I upon attachment of the security interest.

5.   No. As indicated above, where the goods are inventory in the hands of the debtor, a purchaser

for value in the ordinary course of business takes free of the creditor's perfected security interest. In such cases, it is not possible for the lender to completely protect itself against all parties without obtaining possession.

ANSWER OUTLINE

Problem 3   Field Warehousing; Security Interest in Negotiable Document of Title

b1.   Field warehousing arrangement is valid
Goods were under control of warehouse
Compliance with this requirement validates the arrangement

b2.   UCC provides that security interest in negotiable warehouse receipts attaches by
1. Creation of non-possessary interest thru written agreement
2. Creation of possessary interest by oral/written agreement

b3.   Nothing, possession of negotiable documents or title all that is needed to perfect security interest in goods covered by document

b4.   Dangers in relinquishing warehouse receipts to Norwood
May "duly negotiate" it to a holder who takes priority over earlier perfected security interest
Notice of security interest cannot be achieved by filing due negotiation of bearer document requires
1. Delivery
2. Good faith on part of holder
3. Value given
4. No notice of defense on document
5. Negotiated in ordinary course of business

UNOFFICIAL ANSWER

Problem 3   Field Warehousing; Security Interest in Negotiable Document of Title

Part b.

1.   Yes. Independent dominion and control by the field warehouseman is the essential test that must be met in order to create a valid security interest in the field warehoused goods. If the debtor (Norwood) were allowed to retain dominion and control of the goods placed in the field warehouse on its premises, the valid-

ity of the field warehousing arrangement would be questionable. But where the warehouseman is an independent warehousing company and where the formalities are adhered to (that is, posting, and the keys are in the warehouseman's exclusive control , the arrangement will withstand an attack upon its validity.

2.   The Uniform Commercial Code provides that a security interest attaches when

    a.   The collateral is in possession of the secured party pursuant to agreement or the debtor has signed a security agreement that contains a description of the collateral.
    b.   Value has been given.
    c.   The debtor has rights to the collateral.

    Typically the security interests in such situations arise upon delivery of the warehouse receipts to the creditor.

3.   Nothing. A security interest in goods covered by negotiable documents may be perfected by taking possession of the documents. When possession is obtained, no filing is necessary.

4.   The danger inherent in relinquishing the negotiable document of title to Norwood is that he may "duly negotiate" it to a holder. The code provides that "such holders take priority over an earlier security interest even though perfected. Filing . . . does not constitute notice of the security interest to such holders . . ."

    Negotiation of a negotiable bearer document of title is by delivery alone. The instrument is "duly negotiated" when negotiated "to a holder who purchases it in good faith without notice of any defense against or claim to it on the part of any person and for value, unless it is established that the negotiation is not in the regular course of business or financing or involved receiving the document in settlement or payment of a money obligation."

MULTIPLE CHOICE QUESTIONS (1—23)

1.   The federal bankruptcy act contains several important terms. One such term is "insider." The term is used in connection with preferences and preferential transfers. Which among the following is not an "insider?"

   a.   A secured creditor having a security interest in at least 25% or more of the debtor's property.

   b.   A partnership in which the debtor is a general partner.

   c.   A corporation of which the debtor is a director.

   d.   A close blood relative of the debtor.

2.   Bunker Industries, Inc., ceased doing business and is in bankruptcy. Among the claimants are employees seeking unpaid wages. The following statements describe the possible status of such claims in a bankruptcy proceeding or legal limitations placed upon them. Which one is an incorrect statement?

   a.   They are entitled to a priority.

   b.   If a priority is afforded such claims, it cannot exceed $2,000 per wage earner.

   c.   Such claims cannot include vacation, severance, or sick-leave pay.

   d.   The amounts of excess wages not entitled to a priority are mere unsecured claims.

3.   Merchant is in serious financial difficulty and is unable to meet current unsecured obligations of $25,000 to some 15 creditors who are demanding immediate payment. Merchant owes Flintheart $5,000 and Flintheart has decided to file an involuntary petition against Merchant. Which of the following is necessary in order for Flintheart to validly file?

   a.   Flintheart must be joined by at least two other creditors.

   b.   Merchant must have committed an act of bankruptcy within 120 days of the filing.

   c.   Flintheart must allege and subsequently establish that Merchant's liabilities exceed Merchant's assets upon fair valuation.

   d.   Flintheart must be a secured creditor.

4.   Hapless is a bankrupt. In connection with a debt owed to the Suburban Finance Company, he used a false financial statement to induce it to loan him $500. Hapless is seeking a discharge in bankruptcy. Which of the following is a correct statement?

   a.   Hapless will be denied a discharge of any of his debts.

   b.   Even if it can be proved that Suburban did not rely upon the financial statement, Hapless will be denied a discharge either in whole or part.

   c.   Hapless will be denied a discharge of the Suburban debt.

   d.   Hapless will be totally discharged despite the false financial statement.

5.   Moncrief is a surety on a $100,000 obligation owed by Vicars to Sampson. The debt is also secured by a $50,000 mortgage to Sampson on Vicars' factory. Vicars is in bankruptcy. Moncrief has satisfied the debt. Which of the following is a correct statement?

   a.   Moncrief is a secured creditor to the extent of the $50,000 mortgage and a general creditor for the balance.

   b.   Moncrief would not be entitled to a priority in bankruptcy, even though Sampson could validly claim it.

   c.   Moncrief is only entitled to the standing of a general creditor in bankruptcy.

   d.   Moncrief is entitled to nothing in bankruptcy since this was a risk he assumed.

6.   Which of the following provable debts is not discharged by bankruptcy?

   a.   Hospital bills.

   b.   Wages earned more than three months prior to commencement of bankruptcy proceedings.

   c.   Liability for breach of a fiduciary duty resulting from a fraud committed by the debtor-fiduciary.

   d.   Rent payments due which have accrued within three months of the filing of the petition in bankruptcy.

7.   Marco owns all the shares of stock of Digits Corporation. Digits is currently short of cash and has had to default on some of its current liabilities. Marco loaned Digits $2,000 to tide it over its crisis and obtained a note from Digits for the amount of the loan. If Digits is petitioned into bankruptcy, what is the status of Marco's loan?

   a.   It is a provable and allowable claim against the bankrupt's estate which is superior to the claims of other general creditors.

   b.   It is a provable and allowable claim against the bankrupt's estate together with the claims of all other general creditors.

   c.   It is invalid because the loan by Marco constituted an act of bankruptcy.

   d.   It is worthless because Marco is personally liable for the debts of Digits since he owns all of its stock.

8. Dunlop loaned Barkum $20,000 which was secured by a security agreement covering Barkum's machinery and equipment. A financing statement was properly filed covering the machinery and equipment. In addition, Delson was a surety on the Barkum loan. Barkum is now insolvent and a petition in bankruptcy has been filed against him. Delson paid the amount owed ($17,000) to Dunlop. The property was sold for $12,000. Which of the following is correct?

   a. Delson has the right of a secured creditor to the $12,000 via subrogation to Dunlop's rights and the standing of general creditor for the balance.

   b. To the extent Delson is not fully satisfied for the $17,000 he paid Dunlop, his claim against Barkum will not be discharged in bankruptcy.

   c. Delson's best strategy would have been to proceed against Barkum in his own right for reimbursement.

   d. Delson should have asserted his right of exoneration.

9. Barkam is starting a new business, Barkam Enterprises, which will be a sole proprietorship selling retail novelties. Barkam recently received a discharge in bankruptcy, but certain proved claims were unpaid because of lack of funds. Which of the following would be a claim against Barkam?

   a. The unpaid amounts owed to secured creditors who received less than the full amount after resorting to their security interest and receiving their bankruptcy dividend.

   b. The unpaid amounts owed to trade suppliers for goods purchased and sold by Barkam in the ordinary course of his prior business.

   c. A personal loan by his father made in an attempt to stave off bankruptcy.

   d. The unpaid amount of taxes due to the United States which became due and owing within three years preceding bankruptcy.

10. Markson is a general creditor of Black. Black filed a voluntary petition in bankruptcy. Markson is irate and wishes to have the bankruptcy court either deny Black a general discharge or at least not have his debt discharged. The discharge will be granted and it will include Markson's debt even if

   a. It is unscheduled.

   b. Markson extended the credit based upon a fraudulent financial statement.

   c. Markson was a secured creditor who was not fully satisfied from the proceeds

obtained upon disposition of the collateral.

   d. Black had received a previous discharge in bankruptcy within six years.

11. Which of the following statements best describes a composition agreement unanimously agreed to by all creditors?

   a. It provides for the appointment of a receiver to take over and operate the debtor's business.

   b. It is subject to approval by a federal district court judge.

   c. It provides for a discharge of the debts included in the composition agreement upon performance by the debtor.

   d. It binds only those creditors who do not subsequently withdraw from the agreement prior to its consummation.

12. Ted Dolson has filed a voluntary petition in bankruptcy. His assets are listed as $4,200 and his liabilities $18,750. His creditors include (1) three employees who have not been paid wages for six weeks at $100 per week per employee, (2) the United States government for $6,900 in back income and social security taxes, (3) his former wife for back alimony payments of $3,000, and (4) suppliers for goods purchased on open account for $7,050. In this situation

   a. All the debts in question are dischargeable in bankruptcy.

   b. Claims must be filed within three months of the filing of the petition in bankruptcy.

   c. The wage earners have the first priority after administration costs.

   d. The United States government claim will take precedence over the security interests of secured creditors.

13. Devlin made innocent misrepresentations concerning the sale of goods to Van Ness. Shortly thereafter Devlin became a bankrupt. Van Ness was permitted to file a claim for $5,000 for the loss sustained, but actually received only a 20% dividend from the bankrupt's estate. Within six months after the petition was filed but after his discharge, Devlin inherited some property. Van Ness desires to collect the remaining $4,000. Which of the following is correct?

   a. The misrepresentations relating to the sale of the merchandise preclude discharge of Van Ness's $4,000 unpaid claim.

b. Van Ness is entitled to a priority as a result of the misrepresentations.

c. Van Ness is entitled to recover a proportionate share of the inheritance up to the $4,000 deficiency.

d. Van Ness has irrevocably lost his right to the $4,000 unpaid claim as a result of Devlin's discharge in bankruptcy.

14. With respect to a bankruptcy offense, which of the following statements is correct?

a. The offense can only occur during the bankruptcy proceedings.

b. The offense includes the action by an officer of a corporation, in contemplation of a corporate bankruptcy proceeding, of concealing any property of the corporation.

c. The offense can only be committed by the bankrupt.

d. The offense cannot result in fines or imprisonment.

15. Austin owed $10,000 to Hubbel, $5,000 to †
Mavin, $8,000 to Drew, and $50,000 to other creditors. On March 16, 1977, a petition for Austin's involuntary bankruptcy was filed. On April 3, Austin was adjudged insolvent and a bankrupt under the Bankruptcy Reform Act, and a trustee in bankruptcy was appointed. Under the circumstances, which of the following is correct?

a. Assuming Austin was insolvent, payment of $10,000 to Hubbel on March 10 in satisfaction of Hubbel's unsecured claim would constitute a voidable preference.

b. All unsecured creditors would have to have joined in the filing of the bankruptcy petition.

c. An assignee for value of the claim for $5,000 owed by Austin to Mavin will only be able to submit a claim for the amount he paid for the assignment.

d. The trustee in bankruptcy will use the "first in time, first in right" rule with respect to the ultimate disposition of the bankrupt's estate.

16. Robert Cunningham owns a shop in which he repairs electrical appliances. Three months ago Electrical Supply Company sold Cunningham, on credit, a machine for testing electrical appliances and obtained a perfected security interest at that time to secure payment of the balance due. Cunningham's creditors have now filed an involuntary petition in

bankruptcy against him. What is the status of Electrical Supply?

a. Electrical Supply is a secured creditor that has the right, if not paid, to assert its rights against the machine sold to Cunningham to enforce its claim.

b. Electrical Supply must surrender its perfected security interest to the trustee in bankruptcy and share as a general creditor of the bankrupt's estate.

c. Electrical Supply's perfected security interest constitutes a preference and is voidable.

d. Electrical Supply must elect to resort exclusively to its secured interest or to relinquish it and obtain the same share as a general creditor.

17. A client has joined other creditors of the Ajax Demolition Company in a composition agreement seeking to avoid the necessity of a bankruptcy proceeding against Ajax. Which statement describes the composition agreement?

a. It provides for the appointment of a receiver to take over and operate the debtor's business.

b. It must be approved by all creditors.

c. It does not discharge any of the debts included until performance by the debtor has taken place.

d. It provides a temporary delay, not to exceed six months, insofar as the debtor's obligation to repay the debts included in the composition.

18. On January 10, 1978, Edwards gave Cantrell a mortgage on his office building to secure a past-due $40,000 obligation which he owed Cantrell. Cantrell promptly recorded the mortgage. On March 15, 1978, a petition in bankruptcy was filed against Edwards. Simpson, the trustee in bankruptcy, desires to prevent Cantrell from qualifying as a secured creditor. In seeking to set aside the mortgage, which of the following statements is correct?

a. The mortgage cannot be set aside since it is a real property mortgage and recorded.

b. Even if the mortgage is set aside, Cantrell has a priority in respect to the office building.

c. The mortgage can only be set aside if the mortgage conveyance was fraudulent.

d. The mortgage can be set aside if it was taken with knowledge of the fact that Edwards was insolvent in the bankruptcy sense.

19. You are setting up the accounts for Barkum Enterprises, which operates a retail novelties business. Barkum wants all true liabilities shown. He recently received a discharge in bankruptcy, but the following proved claims were unpaid because of lack of funds. Which would you consider to be a claim against him and his new venture?

    a. The unpaid amount owed to a secured creditor who received less than the full amount after resorting to his security interest.

    b. The unpaid amounts owed to his trade suppliers for goods sold by him in the ordinary course of his prior business.

    c. A personal loan by his father made in an attempt to stave off bankruptcy.

    d. The unpaid amount on the claim of a creditor who extended credit on the strength of a fraudulent financial statement.

MAY 1981 QUESTIONS

20. In a bankruptcy proceeding, the trustee

    a. Must be an attorney admitted to practice in the federal district in which the bankrupt is located.

    b. Will receive a fee based upon the time and fair value of the services rendered, regardless of the size of the estate.

    c. May **not** have had any dealings with the bankrupt within the past year.

    d. Is the representative of the bankrupt's estate and as such has the capacity to sue and be sued on its behalf.

21. Haplow engaged Turnbow as his attorney when threatened by several creditors with a bankruptcy proceeding. Haplow's assets consisted of $85,000 and his debts were $125,000. A petition was subsequently filed and was uncontested. Several of the creditors are concerned that the suspected large legal fees charged by Turnbow will diminish the size of the distributable estate. What are the rules or limitations which apply to such fees?

    a. None, since it is within the attorney-client privileged relationship.

    b. The fee is presumptively valid as long as arrived at in an arm's-length negotiation.

    c. Turnbow must file with the court a statement of compensation paid or agreed to for review as to its reasonableness.

    d. The trustee must approve the fee.

22. If a secured party's claim exceeds the value of the collateral of a bankrupt, he will be paid the total amount realized from the sale of the security and will

    a. Not have any claim for the balance.

    b. Become a general creditor for the balance.

    c. Retain a secured creditor status for the balance.

    d. Be paid the balance only after all general creditors are paid.

23. In order to establish a preference under the federal bankruptcy act, which of the following is the trustee required to show where the preferred party is **not** an insider?

    a. That the preferred party had reasonable cause to believe that the debtor was insolvent.

    b. That the debtor committed an act of bankruptcy.

    c. That the transfer was for an antecedent debt.

    d. That the transfer was made within 60 days of the filing of the petition.

REPEAT QUESTION

(581,L1,40)   Identical to item 17 above

PROBLEMS

Problem 1   Priority of Claimants (577,L7a)

(15 to 20 minutes)

Part a. The MIB Corporation has been petitioned into bankruptcy. The petition was filed February 1, 1977. Among its creditors are the following:

A.   Viscount Machine Manufacturing, Inc.
Viscount sold MIB two tractor trailers in August 1976, and filed and recorded its financing statement on December 15, 1976, after it learned that MIB was in severe financial difficulty. The outstanding balance due Viscount is $9,000 which is the current fair market value of the two tractor trailers. Viscount is attempting to repossess the tractor trailers in order to recover its outstanding balance.

B.   Second National County Bank
Second National holds a first mortgage on the real estate where MIB has its principal plant, office, and warehouse. The mortgage is for $280,750 representing the unpaid balance due on the original $350,000 mortgage. The property was sold for $290,000, its fair market value as established by bids received by the trustee. The mortgage was taken out two years ago and duly filed and recorded at that time.

C.   Marvel Supply Company
Marvel, a major supplier of parts, delivered $10,000 worth of parts to MIB on January 17, 1977. Upon delivery Marvel received 50% cash and insisted on the balance by the end of the month. When the balance was not paid, Marvel obtained from MIB a duly executed financing statement which Marvel filed on February 2, 1977.

D.   Sixty-five wage earners
This class of employee is mainly composed of the machine operators and others employed in MIB's plant and warehouse. They were not paid for the final month. All were paid at the minimum wage level and each has a claim for $400 which equals $26,000 in total.

E.   Federal, state, and local taxing authorities
MIB owes $6,800 in back taxes.

F.   Administration costs
These total $12,000.

G.   Various general creditors
Excluding items A through F stated above, general creditors have provable claims of $1,614,900. The bankrupt's total estate consists of $850,000 of assets in addition to the real estate described in B.

Required: Answer the following, setting forth reasons for any conclusions stated.

1.   Discuss the legal implications and the resulting rights of each of the persons or entities described above in A through G as a result of the facts given and the application of bankruptcy law to them.
2.   What is the bankruptcy dividend (percentage on the dollar) that each general creditor will receive? Show calculations in good form.

Problem 2   Security Interest as a Voidable
            Preference (1180,L3,b)

(7 to 10 minutes)

Part b. In connection with the audit of One-Up, Inc., a question has arisen regarding the validity of a $10,000 purchase money security interest in certain machinery sold to EssexCompany on March 2nd. Essex was petitioned into bankruptcy on May 1st by its creditors. The trustee is seeking to avoid One-Up's security interest on the grounds that it is a preferential transfer, hence voidable. The machinery in question was sold to Essex on the following terms: $1,000 down and the balance plus interest at nine percent (9%) to be paid over a three-year period. One-Up obtained a signed security agreement which created a security interest in the property on March 2nd, the date of the sale. A financing statement was filed on March 10th.

Required:
Answer the following, setting forth reasons for any conclusions stated.
1.   Would One-Up's security interest in the machinery be a voidable preference?
2.   In general, what are the requirements necessary to permit the trustee to successfully assert a preferential transfer and thereby set aside a creditor's security interest?

MULTIPLE CHOICE ANSWERS

1.	a	6.	c	11.	c	16.	a	21.	c
2.	c	7.	b	12.	c	17.	c	22.	b
3.	a	8.	a	13.	c	18.	d	23.	c
4.	c	9.	d	14.	b	19.	d		
5.	a	10.	c	15.	a	20.	d		

EXPLANATION OF MULTIPLE CHOICE ANSWERS

1. (580,L1,3) (a) Answer (a) is correct because a secured creditor is not an "insider" for the purposes of a preferential transfer. However, a partner is an insider with regard to the partnership, a director is an insider concerning the corporation, and a close relative is an insider to the debtor.

2. (580,L1,10) (c) Under the Bankruptcy Reform Act of 1978, a priority is given to claims of wage earners up to an amount of $2,000 per claimant, provided wages were earned within 90 days of the filing of the petition. This priority does include claims from vacation, severance and sick leave pay; therefore, answer (c) is the correct answer. If the individual wage earner's claim exceeds $2,000 it falls to the last priority under unsecured claims (general creditors).

3. (580,L1,31) (a) If the debtor has 12 or more creditors, 3 or more creditors who are owed at least $5,000 (together) above any security interest can file. Answer (b) is incorrect because the 1978 Bankruptcy Reform Act no longer includes "acts of bankruptcy." Answer (c) describes insolvency in the "bankruptcy" sense which is not required for involuntary bankruptcy. There is no need for Flintheart to be a secured creditor in order to sign an involuntary petition.

4. (580,L1,35) (c) If the debtor supplies false information to obtain credit, the debt incurred will not be discharged in a bankruptcy proceedings. Answer (a) is incorrect because only the debt involving the false information will not be discharged. All other dischargeable debts will be terminated at the end of the bankruptcy proceedings. Answer (b) is incorrect because the creditor must rely on the false information before the resulting debt becomes nondischargeable. Answer (d) is incorrect because Hapless will be denied a discharge of the Suburban debt.

5. (580,L1,42) (a) Once Moncrief, the surety, satisfies the debt, he is subrogated to the rights of Sampson, the creditor. Thus he becomes a secured creditor to the extent of the mortgage ($50,000) and a general creditor for the balance. Moncrief would have the same rights in the bankruptcy proceeding as Sampson could have exercised.

6. (1176,L2,18) (c) Debts created by fraud while acting in a fiduciary capacity are not discharged in bankruptcy. Hospital bills are not in any special class of debt in bankruptcy and are dischargeable. Wages earned and accrued are dischargeable.

7. (1176,L2,19) (b) A loan by a shareholder to the corporation is a provable and allowable claim whether or not it is evidenced by a note. With respect to the loan, Marco has the same status as the other general creditors. Answer (c) is no longer relevant under the new bankruptcy law contained in the Bankruptcy Reform Act of 1978. The debt is not worthless if it was a bona fide loan. Nor is Marco personally liable for the debts of Digits, as a stockholder he is only in a position to lose his capital contribution.

8. (579,L1,5) (a) When a surety properly pays a debtor's obligation, the surety is subrogated to the creditor's interest in property held as security for performance of the obligation. Accordingly the surety may enforce any lien, pledge, or mortgage which secured the debt. To the extent that the sale of the property fails to pay off the surety, the surety would become a general creditor in the bankruptcy action for the balance. Answer (b) is incorrect because an unpaid surety's claim will be discharged in bankruptcy just as a normal creditor's claim. Answer (c) is incorrect because once the debtor is adjudicated a bankrupt, the only option open to the surety would be to file as a creditor in the bankruptcy action. Answer (d) is incorrect because once the debtor has been adjudicated bankrupt the trustee controls the debtor's property and the remedy of exoneration will not be permitted. Exoneration is the right of a surety to require the debtor to pay the creditor if the debtor has the assets to do so.

9. (579,L1,16) (d) Any unpaid amount of taxes due to the United States or to any state or subdivision thereof from within three years preceding bankruptcy is not discharged by the bankruptcy proceeding. The unpaid balances owed to secured creditors, as in answer (a), or unpaid amounts owed to trade suppliers for goods purchased, as in answer (b), or a personal loan from the bankrupt's father made in an attempt to stave off bankruptcy, as in answer (c), are all items which would be discharged in bankruptcy. Once these claims are discharged, the bankrupt would no longer have to pay them.

10   (579,L1,24)   (c)   The requirement is the situation in which Markson's debt will be discharged. When a debtor files a voluntary petition in bankruptcy, a discharge will be granted and will include any amounts owed to secured creditors who were not fully paid from the proceeds of the collateral. A previous discharge within six years, as in answer (d), will bar a current discharge in bankruptcy. Also a debt will not be discharged in bankruptcy if the debt was created upon a fraudulent financial statement, as in answer (b), or has not been scheduled, as in answer (a). An unscheduled debt is one that has not been listed by the debtor and the creditor did not have notice of the bankruptcy proceeding.

11.   (1175,L1,9)   (c)   A composition agreement is an agreement between debtor and creditors that the creditors will take immediate payment of less than is due in satisfaction of the entire debt.   Answer (a) is likely to be a receivership or a step in bankruptcy.   Answer (b) is necessary for receiverships and arrangements with creditors but not compositions.   Answer (d) is incorrect because the creditors are bound when they agree, if there are two or more.

12.   (1175,L1,11)   (c)   After administration costs, wages earned within three months of date of filing have priority. However, wage priority is limited to $600 per workman. The taxes, wages earned within 3 months, and alimony payments are not dischargeable; they must be paid. If assets are insufficient to pay them, they will still be due after bankruptcy. Claims must be filed within six months of the first creditors' meeting. Secured interests have the highest priority, even over administration costs, because assets of the bankrupt validly encumbered by security interests do not vest in the trustee until after satisfaction of the secured party. The government claim for taxes comes after the wages earned within 3 months, with a maximum limit of $600. Wages greater than $600 or accruing longer than 3 months are processed as general claims.

13.   (1177,L2,23)   (c)   Title to any property inherited by a bankrupt within 6 months after petition for bankruptcy passes to the trustee. Therefore Van Ness can recover his share of this inheritance up to the amount of his claim. Answer (a) is incorrect because innocent misrepresentations do not preclude discharge of a debt in bankruptcy. Answer (b) is incorrect because there is no priority for misrepresentations. Answer (d) is incorrect because Van Ness can recover.

14.   (1177,L2,29)   (b)   Concealing property of a bankrupt is a bankruptcy offense. Answer (a) is incorrect because a bankruptcy offense, e.g., concealing assets, can be committed prior to the bankruptcy proceedings. Answer (c) is incorrect because this (as well as other bankruptcy offenses) can be committed by an officer of a bankrupt corporation as well as others who might conspire with a bankrupt. Answer (d) is incorrect because a bankruptcy offense can be punished by both fines and/or imprisonment.

15.   (1177,L2,32)   (a)   A voidable preference is a preferential transfer of property while insolvent and within four months prior to filing the petition. Payment of $10,000 to Hubbel is a preferential transfer, because it gives Hubbel a greater recovery on his debt than other unsecured creditors. Answer (b) is incorrect because at most, only three creditors need to join in filing the petition. If there are less than 12 creditors, only one need file. Answer (c) is incorrect because the assignee is owed the full $5,000 and can submit a claim for the full amount. Answer (d) is incorrect because the trustee must follow the priorities established under the Act in disposition of the estate.

16.   (578,L1,23)   (a)   Electrical Supply is a secured creditor because it has a security interest to protect its claim. A secured creditor has the right to assert its rights against the collateral to enforce its claim. Answer (b) is incorrect because a holder of a perfected security interest will prevail over a trustee in bankruptcy as long as the security interest is not a voidable preference. Answer (c) is incorrect because the transaction did not constitute a voidable preference since Cunningham received property equal to the debt established, i.e., it was a fair exchange. Electrical Supply is not required to resort exclusively to its secured interest. It may also share as a general creditor to the extent the secured interest is not adequate to cover the debt (answer (d)).

17.   (578,L1,24)   (c)   A composition with creditors is an agreement made between a debtor and creditors whereby the creditors agree with one another and the debtor to accept less than the full amount due. The composition does not discharge any of the debts until performance by the debtor has taken place. However, the agreement is valid from the time made. Answer (a) is incorrect because a composition does not provide for an appointment of receiver which is called a receivership. Answer (b) is incorrect because it need not be approved by all creditors, only those who wish to participate. Answer (d) is incorrect because a valid

composition discharges the unpaid portion of the debts and does not merely provide a temporary delay.

18. (578,L1,25) (d) The mortgage is a preference because it was made within 4 months of bankruptcy and gives Cantrell a greater recovery on his debt than other creditors of the general class he was in prior to the mortgage. A preference can be set aside by the trustee in bankruptcy. Answer (a) is incorrect because recording a mortgage does not prevent the trustee from setting it aside if it is a voidable preference. Answer (b) is incorrect because without the mortgage, the mortgagee is a general creditor with no priority to any asset. Answer (c) is incorrect because a fraudulent transfer is not necessary to have a voidable preference.

19. (578,L1,32) (d) Certain debts are not dischargeable in bankruptcy. A debt obtained by false pretenses is one which is not dischargeable in bankruptcy. Secured debts and trade debts are dischargeable. Loans from family are dischargeable whether made to stave off bankruptcy or not. Thus answers (a), (b), and (c) are generally discharged in bankruptcy.

MAY 1981 ANSWERS

20. (581,L1,41) (d) A trustee is the representative of the estate and has the capacity to sue and be sued. Answer (a) is false since a trustee is either elected by creditors or appointed by a judge to liquidate the estate. There is no requirement that the trustee be an attorney. Answer (b) is also incorrect since a trustee is compensated using a specified percentage of the estate, not by reference to value or amount of services rendered. Answer (c) is incorrect since it is permissible for the trustee to have dealings with the debtor within the prior year.

21. (581,L1,42) (c) According to the Rules of Bankruptcy Procedure, it is necessary to file a proof of claims against the debtor's estate. The filing must be timely (within a six-month period) or the claim will be barred. A claim that is filed on time is given prima facie validity and is approved unless there is an objection by one of the creditors. Answer (a) is incorrect since all claims are subject to filing and review. Answer (b) is also false because a fee may result from an arms-length negotiation and still be disallowed by Bankruptcy Procedure. Claims for services by an attorney of the debtor, to the extent a fee exceeds a reasonable value for services rendered, are disallowed. The court must

approve the reasonableness of the claim even if the transaction is an arms-length negotiation. Answer (d) is false because it is the courts, not the trustee, which approve the fees.

22. (581,L1,43) (b) A secured creditor has a security interest in the personal property of the debtor which is acting as collateral for the debt. In a bankruptcy proceeding, there is an order of priorities concerning distribution of the debtor's estate. Secured creditors are given first priority in the sense that property subject to a valid security interest is not part of the estate for distribution purposes but belongs to the secured creditor to the extent of his security interest. The secured party can either take the property or its cash equivalent. If the value of the property is insufficient to satisfy the claim, the secured creditor becomes a general creditor for the balance. After all secured creditors and priority claims are fully satisfied, all general creditors then share in the remaining assets of the debtor's estate. Answers (a), (b), and (d) are incorrect because the secured party does have a claim for the balance, but only as an unsecured general creditor.

23. (581,L1,44) (c) In order to establish a preference under the Bankruptcy Reform Act, the trustee is required to show that the transfer was made in payment of an antecedent debt (a debt incurred prior to the transfer as contrasted with a present transfer for value). As a result of such a transfer the preferred party receives more than he would in the bankruptcy proceedings. Answer (a) is untrue since, under the new Bankruptcy Reform Act of 1978 in order for the trustee to establish a preference, it is no longer a requirement to prove that the preferred party have reasonable cause to believe that the debtor is insolvent. Answer (b) is incorrect since, under the Act of 1978, acts of bankruptcy no longer exist. Answer (d) is incorrect since the transfer must be made within 90 days, not 60 days, of the filing of the bankruptcy petition.

ANSWER OUTLINE

Problem 1   Priority of Claimants

a1a. Viscount has a preference
> Which may be voided by the bankruptcy law
>> It was effected less than three months prior to filing

> Thus Viscount is a general creditor for $9,000

a1b. Second National is a secured creditor and will be paid in full from sale of real estate
> Balance of proceeds ($9,250) will go to general creditors

a1c. Marvel Supply is a general creditor for $5,000
> Financing statement after date of bankruptcy is invalid
> The $5,000 January 17 payment was valid
>> Exchange of one type of debtor asset for another

a1d. Wage earners are entitled to priority ($400 each)
> Payable after administration costs
>> But before taxes
> Priority limited to $2,000/employee
>> Within three months preceding filing

a1e. Unpaid taxes are a priority item
> Payable after administration costs and priority wages
> Taxes are not discharged in bankruptcy

a1f. Administration costs are a priority item
> First in position

a1g. General creditors receive pro rata distribution
> After all secured creditors and priority items

a2. See computation of bankruptcy dividend in Unofficial Answer below

UNOFFICIAL ANSWER

Problem 1   Priority of Claimants

a. 1.   A. Viscount Machine Manufacturing, Inc.
Viscount has a preference which is voidable under the bankruptcy laws. The trustee can attack the security interest asserted by Viscount because it was not perfected until December 15, 1976, which is less than three months prior to the filing of the petition in bankruptcy against MIB. Therefore, his secured position with respect to the tractor trailers will be denied, and he is placed in the general creditor category with respect to his $9,000 claim.

B. Second National County Bank
Second National is a bona fide secured creditor and as such will be paid in full ($280,750) from the proceeds of the sale of the real estate. The balance of the proceeds ($9,250) will be added to the funds which potentially are available to the general creditors.

C. Marvel Supply Company
Marvel Supply is a general creditor in the amount of $5,000. Filings made after the date of bankruptcy are invalid. The $5,000 cash payment does not present a problem in that it merely represents a contemporaneous exchange of one type of the debtor's assets for another at fair market value.

D. Sixty-five wage earners
The wage earners are entitled to a priority of $400 each, payable after administration costs but before taxes. Each employee is entitled to a priority not to exceed $2000 for wages earned within the three months preceding the filing of the bankruptcy petition.

E. Federal, state, and local taxing authorities
The unpaid taxes in question are also a priority item. They rank after the administration costs and the wage earners' claims. It should be noted that taxes which became due within three years preceding bankruptcy are not discharged in a bankruptcy proceeding.

F. Administration costs
As indicated above, administration costs (court, attorneys', trustees', and accountants' fees, etc.) are entitled to the first priority available against the unsecured assets of the debtor.

G. Various general creditors
The general creditors are entitled to a pro rata distribution of MIB's assets after all secured creditors and priority items are paid.

Note: Schedule for a.2. appears on the following page.

a. 2.   Computation of Bankruptcy Dividend

Assets Available to General Creditors

Before adjustments (G)		$ 850,000
Increased by excess proceeds from sale of real estate (B)		9,250
Subtotal		$ 859,250
Less priorities:		
Administrative costs (F)	$12,000	
Sixty-five wage earners (D)	26,000	
Federal, state, and local taxing authorities (E)	6,800	44,800
Total assets available to general creditors		$ 814,450

Liabilities of General Creditors

As stated (G)		$1,614,900
Increased by:		
Viscount's claim (A)	$ 9,000	
Marvel's claim (C)	5,000	14,000
Total		$1,628,900

Assets available ($814,450) ÷ liabilities applicable ($1,628,900) = 50% on the dollar; that is, 50 cents per dollar will be paid to general creditors.

ANSWER OUTLINE

Problem 2 Security Interest as a Voidable Preference

b1. No, security interest is not voidable preference
     Purchase money security interest perfected within 10 days after attachment is exempted from preference states

b2. Trustee may avoid any transfer of property as preferential which is;
1. To or for benefit of a creditor
2. For antecedent debt owed by debtor before such transfer
3. Made while debtor insolvent in bankrupt sense
   a. Transfer was to "insider"
   b. Transferee had reasonable cause to believe debtor insolvent at time of transfer
4. Transfer that enables creditor to receive more than in straight liquidation proceeding

UNOFFICIAL ANSWER

Problem 2 Security Interest as a Voidable Preference

Part b.

1.   No. The Bankruptcy Reform Act of 1978 has

not only modified the requirements for establishing a voidable preference, it has also specified transactions that do not constitute preferences. One such transaction is the creditor's taking a security interest in property acquired by the debtor as a contemporaneous exchange for new value given to the debtor to enable him to acquire such property (a purchase money security interest). The security interest must be perfected (filed) within 10 days after attachment. The act is in harmony with the secured transactions provisions of the Uniform Commercial Code. Thus, One-Up has a valid security interest in the machinery it sold to Essex.

2.   The Bankruptcy Reform Act of 1978 does not require that the creditor have knowledge or reasonable cause to believe the debtor is insolvent in the bankruptcy sense. Instead, under the act, where such insolvency exists on or within ninety days before the filing of the petition, knowledge of insolvency by the transferee need not be established. The act also assumes that the debtor's insolvency is presumed if the transfer alleged to be preferential is made within 90 days. Finally, the time period in which transfers may be set aside is 90 days unless the transferee is an "insider." If the transfer is to an insider, the trustee may avoid transfers made within one year prior to the filing of the petition. Thus, the trustee may avoid as preferential any transfer of property of the debtor that is

- To or for the benefit of a creditor.
- For or on account of an antecedent debt owed by the debtor before such transfer was made.
- Made while the debtor was insolvent in the bankruptcy sense (however, if the transfer is made within 90 days, the debtor's insolvency is presumed).
- Made on or within 90 days of the filing of the petition (or if made after the 90 days but within one year prior to the date of the filing of the petition and the transfer was to an "insider," it may be set aside if the transferee had reasonable cause to believe the debtor was insolvent at the time of the transfer).
- Such that it enables the creditor to receive more than he would if it were a straight liquidation proceeding.

The bankruptcy act contains a lengthy definition of the term "insider" that includes common relationships that the transferee has to the debtor, which, in case of an individual debtor, could be certain relatives, a partnership in which he is a general partner, his fellow general partners, or a corporation controlled by him.

MULTIPLE CHOICE QUESTIONS (1—30)

1. Dilworth provided collateral to Maxim to secure Dilworth's performance of an obligation owed to Maxim. Maxim also obtained the Protection Surety Company as a surety for Dilworth's performance. Dilworth has defaulted and Protection has discharged the obligation in full. Which of the following is the correct legal basis for Protection's assertion of rights to the collateral?

    a. Promissory estoppel.
    b. Exoneration.
    c. Indemnification.
    d. Subrogation.

2. Nolan Surety Company has agreed to serve as a guarantor of collection (a form of conditional guaranty) of the accounts receivable of the Dunbar Sales Corporation. The duration of the guarantee is one year and the maximum liability assumed is $3,000. Nolan charged the appropriate fee for acting in this capacity. Which of the following statements best describes the difference between a guarantor of collection and the typical surety relationship?

    a. A guaranty need not be in writing provided the duration is less than a year.
    b. The guarantor is not immediately liable upon default; the creditor must first proceed against the debtor.
    c. A guaranty is only available from a surety who is a compensated surety.
    d. A guaranty is only used in connection with the sale of goods which have been guaranteed by the seller.

3. Simpson and Thomas made separate contracts of suretyship with Allan to guarantee repayment of a $12,000 loan Allan made to Parker. Simpson's guarantee was for $12,000 and Thomas' for $8,000. In the event Simpson pays the full amount ($12,000), what may he recover from Thomas?

    a. Nothing since their contracts were separate.
    b. $4,800.
    c. $6,000.
    d. $8,000.

4. Cornwith agreed to serve as a surety on a loan by Super Credit Corporation to Fairfax, one of Cornwith's major customers. The relationship between Fairfax and Super deteriorated to a point of hatred as a result of several late payments on the loan. On the due date of the final payment, Fairfax appeared 15 minutes before closing and tendered payment of the entire amount owing to Super. The office manager of Super told Fairfax that he was too late and would have to pay the next day with additional interest and penalties. Fairfax again tendered the payment, which was again refused. It is now several months later and Super is seeking to collect from either Cornwith or Fairfax or both. What are Super's rights under the circumstances?

    a. It cannot collect anything from either party.
    b. The tender of performance released Cornwith from his obligation.
    c. The tender of performance was too late and rightfully refused.
    d. Cornwith is released only to the extent that the refusal to accept the tender harmed him.

5. A surety can avoid liability on his surety undertaking if he can show

    a. Death of the creditor.
    b. Bankruptcy of the creditor.
    c. A material alteration by the debtor and creditor of the contract which the surety guaranteed.
    d. Lack of capacity of the debtor.

6. Anthony is a surety on a debt owed by Victor to Day.

    a. Day must satisfy the Uniform Commercial Code's filing requirements in order to perfect his security interest.
    b. The surety undertaking need not be in writing if the surety is obtained by Victor at Day's request.
    c. The extension of credit by Day to Victor, contingent upon Anthony's agreeing to act as surety, provides the consideration for Anthony's promise.
    d. Upon default, Anthony would be allowed to deduct a personal claim that he has against Victor from his required payment to Day.

7. Barnes has agreed to become the conditional guarantor of collection on credit extended by Ace Supply Company on a contract for the sale of goods by Ace to Wilcox not exceeding $5,000.

    a. If Wilcox defaults, Barnes is immediately liable for the amount of the debt outstanding.
    b. A discharge in bankruptcy obtained by Wilcox will discharge Barnes.
    c. Upon default, Barnes must proceed against Wilcox on Ace's behalf if Ace so requests.
    d. Ace must first proceed against Wilcox before it is entitled to recover from Barnes.

8.   Under what conditions will both the debtor and the surety be able to avoid liability on a debt owed by the debtor to the creditor?

   a.   The debt exceeds $500 and the debtor's obligation is not contained in a signed writing.
   b.   The debtor lacks the capacity to enter into the contract wih the creditor.
   c.   There is a tender of payment by the surety.
   d.   The debtor is released by the creditor.

9.   In order to establish a co-surety relationship the two or more sureties must

   a.   Be aware of each other's existence at the time of their contract.
   b.   Sign the same contract creating the debt and the co-surety relationship.
   c.   Be bound to answer for the same debt or duty of the debtor.
   d.   Be bound for the same amount and share equally in the obligation to satisfy the creditor.

10.   A surety will not be liable on an undertaking if

   a.   The principal is a minor.
   b.   The underlying obligation was illegal.
   c.   The principal was insolvent at the time of the surety's agreement to act as surety.
   d.   The surety was mistaken as the legal implications of the surety agreement.

11.   What rights or defenses does a co-surety have?

   a.   The same legal rights against fellow sureties as a surety would have against a sub-surety.
   b.   The same rights as a single surety would have, but in addition, has the right of contribution from co-sureties.
   c.   A defense against liability for more than a proportionate share of the undertaking.
   d.   A defense against liability unless all co-sureties are sued jointly.

12.   Maxwell was the head cashier of the Amalgamated Merchants Bank. The Excelsior Surety Company bonded Maxwell for $200,000. An internal audit revealed a $1,000 embezzlement by Maxwell. Maxwell persuaded the bank not to report him, and he promised to pay the money back within ten days. The bank acquiesced and neither the police nor Excelsior was informed of the theft. Maxwell shortly thereafter embezzled $75,000 and fled. Excelsior refuses to pay. Is Excelsior liable? Why?

   a.   Excelsior is liable since the combined total of the embezzlements is less than the face amount of the surety bond.
   b.   Excelsior is liable for $75,000, but not the $1,000 since a separate arrangement was agreed to by Amalgamated with Maxwell.
   c.   Excelsior is liable since it is a compensated surety and as such assumed the risk.
   d.   Excelsior is not liable since the failure to give notice of the first embezzlement is a valid defense.

13.   Crawford and Blackwell separately agreed to act as sureties on a loan of $25,000 by Lux to Factor. Each promised to pay the full $25,000 upon default of Factor. Lux subsequently released Blackwell from his surety undertaking. Which of the following is a correct statement?

   a.   The release has no effect upon Crawford's right to contribution if he is obligated to pay.
   b.   The release of Blackwell had no effect upon Crawford's liability.
   c.   The release of Blackwell also totally released Crawford.
   d.   The release of Blackwell also released Crawford to the extent of $12,500.

14.   Alfred Matz negotiated with Basic Construction Company, Inc., to construct an apartment house. Desiring additional assurance of completion or payment of damages in the event of default, Matz insisted that a performance bond be posted. Basic obtained First Fidelity Surety Bonding Company as the surety on the undertaking. In addition to the normal terms of such contracts, First Fidelity insisted upon the right to complete the building in the event of default by Basic. The contract was drafted and signed by all the parties involved. Under the circumstances

   a.   Basic Construction is the third-party beneficiary of the contract.
   b.   If Basic Construction refuses to perform, Matz can obtain a court order obligating First Fidelity to complete construction.
   c.   First Fidelity has assumed the primary obligation to perform.
   d.   First Fidelity would be entitled to any and all rights that Matz would have against Basic in the event Basic defaults and First Fidelity pays.

15. George Parker wanted to purchase certain goods on credit from Charles Stabel with terms of payment of 2/10, net 30. Stabel required a surety on the obligation before he would agree to Parker's credit terms. As a personal favor, Sam Hayes, a well-known financier and friend, assumed the role as surety on the contract with Stabel. The goods were shipped to Parker on open account with the terms 2/10, net 30. Not having received payment after 20 days, Stabel went to Parker and persuaded him to execute a promissory note for the amount owed with the stipulation that payment would not be due until two months from the date of execution. Parker subsequently defaulted on the note, and Stabel sued Hayes on his surety promise. Under these circumstances

    a. Hayes' undertaking need not be in writing because it was gratuitous.

    b. Sale of the Parker note by Stabel would automatically release Hayes from all liability.

    c. Stabel's binding extension of time via the note relieved Hayes from liability.

    d. Hayes may withdraw from the surety agreement by giving prompt notice to Stabel prior to the extension of credit.

16. Sims became an agent for Paul with the power to sell goods furnished by Paul but with the requirement that Sims would guarantee payment to Paul for all credit sales made by Sims. Under the circumstances

    a. Sims is an agent coupled with an interest.

    b. The Statute of Frauds applies to the above arrangement regardless of the amount of sales Sims makes.

    c. Sims is a surety vis-a-vis any credit sales he makes on Paul's behalf.

    d. The relationship between Sims and Paul is subject to the Federal Fair Labor Standards Act.

17. The Martin Corporation was a small family-owned corporation whose owners were also the directors and officers. The corporation's bankers insisted that if any further credit were to be extended to the corporation the owners must guarantee payment by the corporation. This guaranty was agreed to by the owners in writing, and an additional $50,000 loan was granted to Martin Corporation. Which of the following best describes the legal significance of these events?

    a. The guaranty by the owners need not have been in writing since it was primarily for their own benefit.

    b. Once the owners agreed to the undertaking they automatically assumed responsibility for all of the corporation's prior debts.

    c. In the absence of specific provisions to the contrary, the owners are immediately liable on the debt in the event of the corporation's default.

    d. Since the owners each participated equally in the guaranty, each can be held liable by the bank, but only to the extent of his proportionate share in relation to the others.

18. Parker owed Charles $100,000 secured by a first mortgage on Parker's plant and land. Simons was the surety on the obligation but his liability was limited to $50,000. Parker defaulted on the debt and Charles demanded and received payment of $50,000 from Simons. Charles subsequently foreclosed the mortgage and upon sale of the mortgaged property netted $75,000. Simons claims a right of subrogation for his loss. Under the right of subrogation Simons should receive

    a. Nothing.

    b. $25,000.

    c. $37,500.

    d. $50,000.

19. Park owed Collins $1,000 and $2,000, respectively, on two separate unsecured obligations. Smythe had become a surety on the $2,000 debt at the request of Park when Park became indebted to Collins. Both debts matured on June 1. Park was able to pay only $600 at that time, and he forwarded that amount to Collins without instructions. Under these circumstances

    a. Collins must apply the funds pro rata in proportion to the two debts.

    b. Collins must apply the $600 to the $2,000 debt if there is no surety on the $1,000 debt.

    c. Smythe will be discharged to the extent of $400 if Collins on request of Smythe fails to apply $400 to the $2,000 debt.

    d. Collins is free to apply the $600 to the debts as he sees fit.

20. Which of the following transactions does not create a surety relationship?

    a. The assumption of a mortgage by the purchaser of a parcel of real estate.

    b. The blank indorsement of a check.

c.   Signing a nonnegotiable promissory note as an accommodation maker.

d.   Obtaining professional malpractice insurance by a CPA.

21.   Which of the following best describes what is required of a noncompensated surety?

a.   The noncompensated surety must have the legal capacity to make contracts generally.

b.   The noncompensated surety cannot be a corporation.

c.   The noncompensated surety benefits by a rule which requires a creditor to first proceed against the principal debtor before the surety can be held liable.

d.   The noncompensated surety must not directly or indirectly benefit from the undertaking.

22.   Franks is a surety on a $5,000 debt owed by Smith to Jones. Jones also holds as collateral property worth $4,000 belonging to Smith. Under these circumstances, which of the following statements is true?

a.   Franks has the right to the property immediately upon default.

b.   Jones need not first proceed against the collateral in order to hold Franks liable.

c.   Jones may return the collateral to Smith at any time prior to default without impairing his rights against Franks.

d.   Jones must file a financing statement in order to perfect his rights in the collateral he holds.

23.   Safety Surety Company, Inc., issued a surety bond for value received which guaranteed: (1) completion of a construction contract Poe had made with Cairns and (2) payment by Poe of his workmen. Poe defaulted and did not complete the contract. The workers were not paid for their last week's work. Poe had in fact become insolvent, and a petition in bankruptcy was filed two months after the issuance of the bond. What is the effect upon Safety as a result of the above events?

a.   If Safety pays the workers in full, it is entitled to the same priority in the bankruptcy proceedings that the workers would have had.

b.   If Safety pays damages to Cairns as a result of default on the contract, Safety is entitled to recover in the bankruptcy proceedings the entire amount it paid prior to the payment of the general creditors of Poe.

c.   If Safety has another separate claim against Cairns, Safety may not set it off against any rights Cairns may have under this contract.

d.   As a compensated surety, Safety would be discharged by Poe's bankruptcy.

24.   Martinson borrowed $50,000 from Wisdom Finance Company. The loan was evidenced by a non-negotiable promissory note secured by a first mortgage on Martinson's ranch. One of the terms of the note required acceleration of repayment in the event that Wisdom "deemed itself insecure." When the value of the property declined, Wisdom notified Martinson that pursuant to the terms of the note, it "deemed itself insecure" and demanded that either additional collateral or an acceptable surety be provided. Martinson arranged for Clark, a personal friend, to act as surety on the loan. Clark signed the note as an indorser and Wisdom agreed in writing not to accelerate repayment of the loan during the life of the debt. Martinson has defaulted. Which of the following is a correct statement?

a.   Clark's promise is not supported by consideration, hence is unenforceable.

b.   Clark is a guarantor of collection and his obligation is conditioned upon Wisdom's first proceeding against Martinson.

c.   Release of the mortgage by Wisdom would release Clark to the extent of the value of the property.

d.   Wisdom must first foreclose the mortgage before it can proceed against Clark.

25.   Quinn was the sole owner of Sunnydale Farms, Inc. The business was in dire need of additional working capital in order to survive. Click Company was willing to loan Sunnydale $12,000, but only if Click obtained a security interest in Sunnydale's machinery and equipment and a promise from Quinn to guarantee repayment of the loan. Click obtained both. Sunnydale was subsequently adjudged bankrupt. Click filed a reclamation claim for the machinery and equipment which was denied by the trustee in bankruptcy. The property was sold at public auction for $10,500. Click negotiated a settlement with the trustee whereby it received the $10,500 proceeds on the sale in full settlement of its claim against the bankrupt. Which of the following is a correct statement?

a.   Where a surety is the sole owner of the stock of the corporation whose debt he guarantees, he is a compensated surety.

b.   Click first had to exhaust his remedies against the property before he could sue Quinn.

c.   Quinn must pay Click the $1,500 difference, plus interest.

d.   The settlement released Quinn from his surety obligation.

MAY 1981 QUESTIONS

26.   Doral is the surety on a loan made by Nelson to Gordon. Which statement describes Doral's legal relationship or status among the respective parties?

a.   As between Gordon and Doral, Doral has the ultimate liability.

b.   Upon default by Gordon and payment by Doral, Doral is entitled to subrogation to the rights of Nelson or to obtain reimbursement from Gordon.

c.   Doral is a fiduciary insofar as Nelson is concerned.

d.   Doral is **not** liable immediately upon default by Gordon, unless the agreement so provides.

27.   Don loaned $10,000 to Jon, and Robert agreed to act as surety. Robert's agreement to act as surety was induced by (1) fraudulent misrepresentations made by Don concerning Jon's financial status and (2) a bogus unaudited financial statement of which Don had no knowledge, and which was independently submitted by Jon to Robert. Which of the following is correct?

a.   Don's fraudulent misrepresentations will **not** provide Robert with a valid defense unless they were contained in a signed writing.

b.   Robert will be liable on his surety undertaking despite the facts since the defenses are personal defenses.

c.   Robert's reliance upon Jon's financial statements makes Robert's surety undertaking voidable.

d.   Don's fraudulent misrepresentations provide Robert with a defense which will prevent Don from enforcing the surety undertaking.

28.   Welch is a surety on Stanton's contract to build an office building for Brent. Stanton intentionally abandoned the project after it was 85% completed because of personal animosity which developed toward Brent. Which of the following is a correct statement concerning the rights or responsibilities of the various parties?

a.   Any modification of the contract, however slight and even if beneficial to Welch, will release Welch.

b.   Welch would be ordered to specifically perform the completion of the building if Brent sought this remedy.

c.   Neither Stanton's failure to give Welch prior notice of its intention to abandon the project **nor** its actual abandonment of the project will release Welch.

d.   Welch can **not** engage a contractor to finish the job and obtain from Brent the balance due on the contract.

29.   Reginald, who is insolvent, defaulted on a loan upon which Jayne was the surety. Edward, the creditor, demanded payment from Jayne of the amount owed by Reginald. The loan was also secured by a mortgage which Edward has the right to foreclose. Which of the following is Jayne's best legal course of action?

a.   Seek specific performance by Reginald.

b.   Refuse to pay until Reginald has been petitioned into bankruptcy and the matter has been decided by the trustee in bankruptcy.

c.   Pay Edward and resort to the subrogation rights to the collateral.

d.   Refuse to pay because Edward must first resort to the collateral.

30.   Overall, Inc., owns 100% of the stock of Controlled Corporation, each being a separate entity. Overall telephoned the Factory Supply Company and ordered $400 of miscellaneous merchandise. Overall told Factory to ship the supplies to Controlled and Overall would pay for them. Factory did so and now seeks recovery of the price or damages. Which of the following is correct?

a.   Overall is a surety.

b.   The Statute of Frauds will **not** bar Factory from recovering from Overall.

c.   Controlled is the principal debtor.

d.   Overall and Controlled are jointly and severally liable on the contract.

PROBLEMS

Problem **1**   Modification of Surety's Contract;
            Surety's Right of Reimbursement
            (1179,L4)

(20 to 25 minutes)

Part a. The King Surety Company, Inc., wrote a performance bond for Allie Stores, Inc., covering the construction of a department store. Rapid Construction Company, the department store contractor, is a general contractor and is simultaneously working on several buildings. Until the entire building is completed, the bond contained a provision that obligated Allie to withhold 20% of the progress payments to be made to Rapid at various stages of completion. After approximately two-thirds of the project had been satisfactorily completed, Rapid pleaded with Allie to release the 20% withheld to date. Rapid indicated that he was having a cash flow problem and unless funds were released to satisfy the demands of suppliers, workmen, and other creditors, there would be a significant delay in the completion date of the department store. Rapid claimed that if the 20% withheld were released, the project could be completed on schedule. Allie released the amounts withheld. Two weeks later Rapid abandoned the project, citing as its reason rising cost which made the contract unprofitable. Allie has notified King of the facts and demands that either King complete the project or respond in damages. King denies liability on the surety bond.

Required: Answer the following, setting forth reasons for any conclusions stated.

Who will prevail?

Part b. Barclay Surety, Inc., is the surety on a construction contract that the Gilmore Construction Company made with Shadow Realty, Inc. By the terms of the surety obligation, Barclay is not only bound to Shadow, but also is bound to satisfy materialmen and laborers in connection with the contract. Gilmore defaulted, and Barclay elected to complete the project and pay all claims and obligations in connection with the contract, including all unpaid materialmen and laborers' claims against Gilmore. The total cost to complete exceeded the construction contract payments Barclay received from Shadow. Some of the materialmen who were satisfied had either liens or security interests against Gilmore. Gilmore has filed a voluntary bankruptcy petition.

Required: Answer the following, setting forth reasons for any conclusions stated.

What rights does Barclay have as a result of the above facts?

Problem **2** Effect of Contract Changes (1173,L7b&c)
            (10 to 15 minutes)

Part b.   Albert Gideon, Jr., doing business as Albert's Boutique, ordered $480 of mini-skirts from Abaco Fashions. Abaco refused to make delivery, having had previous collection problems with Gideon. Albert's father, Slade Gideon, a prominent manufacturer, called Abaco and said, "Ship the goods my son needs, and I will pay for them." Abaco delivered the mini-skirts, and they were received by Albert's Boutique. Albert's Boutique is in bankruptcy, and Slade Gideon refuses to pay. You are the accountant for Abaco Fashions.

Required:
    What are Abaco's rights against Slade Gideon? Explain.

Part c. Superior Construction Company, Inc., submitted the successful bid for the construction of your client's new factory. As part of the contract, Superior was required to obtain a performance bond from an acceptable surety company. Ace Surety, Inc., wrote the surety bond for the proposed building.

After the project was about one-third completed, Superior suggested several major changes in the contract. These included the expansion of the floor space by 10% and construction of an additional loading platform.

Required:
    1.   What problem does your client face if it agrees to the proposed changes? Explain.
    2.   What advice would you suggest in order to avoid this problem?

Problem **3** Surety's Consideration; Surety's Liability
            Upon Default (1180,L3a)

(7 to 10 minutes)

Part a. Hardaway Lending, Inc., had a 4-year $800,000 callable loan to Superior Metals, Inc., outstanding. The loan was callable at the end of each year upon Hardaway's giving 60 days written notice. Two and one-half years remained of the four years. Hardaway reviewed the loan and decided that Superior Metals was no longer a prime lending risk and it therefore decided to call the loan. The required written notice was sent to and received by Superior 60 days prior to the expiration of the second year. Merriweather,

Superior's chief executive officer and principal share-holder, requested Hardaway to continue the loan at least for another year. Hardaway agreed, provided that an acceptable commercial surety would guarantee $400,000 of the loan and Merriweather would person-ally guarantee repayment in full. These conditions were satisfied and the loan was permitted to continue.

The following year the loan was called and Sup-erior defaulted. Hardaway released the commercial surety but retained its rights against Merriweather and demanded that Merriweather pay the full amount of the loan. Merriweather refused, asserting the following:

- There was no consideration for his promise. The loan was already outstanding and he personally received nothing.
- Hardaway must first proceed against Superior be-fore it can collect from Merriweather.
- Hardaway had released the commercial surety, thereby releasing Merriweather.

Required:

Answer the following, setting forth reasons for any conclusions stated.

Discuss the validity of each of Merriweather's assertions.

MULTIPLE CHOICE ANSWERS

1.	d	7.	d	13.	d	19.	d	25.	d
2.	b	8.	d	14.	d	20.	d	26.	b
3.	b	9.	c	15.	c	21.	a	27.	d
4.	b	10.	b	16.	c	22.	b	28.	c
5.	c	11.	b	17.	c	23.	a	29.	c
6.	c	12.	d	18.	b	24.	c	30.	b

EXPLANATION OF MULTIPLE CHOICE ANSWERS

1. (580,L1,36) (d) Once a surety satisfies the obligation the surety is subrogated to the rights of the creditor. The surety is said to stand in the shoes of the creditor once the surety pays the debt. Promissory estoppel relates to consideration requirements of a contract. Exoneration is the surety's right to force the principal debtor to pay the debt on the due date if the surety is able to prove the debtor has sufficient funds. Indemnification is a right of an insured against an insurer.

2. (580,L1,39) (b) Guaranty of collection is a special form of suretyship agreement. The guarantor of collection is only liable if the creditor has attempted to collect from the principal debtor and was unable to do so. The normal surety is liable when the loan or obligation is due irrespective of whether the creditor has attempted to collect from the debtor. A guaranty is a promise to pay the debt of another, thus the statute of frauds would normally require that it be in writing. A guaranty can arise from a non-compensated, as well as a compensated, surety. A guaranty can be used in connection with all types of contracts.

3. (580,L1,41) (b) Simpson and Thomas would be co-sureties since they are guaranteeing the same obligation. If one co-surety satisfies the full obligation he then has the right of contribution, meaning that the other surety must contribute his proportionate share. Since Simpson guaranteed the full $12,000 and Thomas only guaranteed $8,000, their proportionate shares would be in a 3-to-2 ratio. Thus Thomas must pay Simpson $4,800.

4. (580,L1,44) (b) The tender of performance by the principal debtor completely releases the surety from his obligation. However, such tender does not release the principal debtor if the contractual duty consists of the obligation to pay money. If the contractual duty consisted of anything but the obligation to pay money, then the tender of such performance would have also released Fairfax.

5. (1176,L2,24) (c) Material alteration of the contract by the debtor and creditor is a defense for the surety, because it changes the risk of the undertaking which was guaranteed. If the surety consents to the alteration, the surety has no defense. Incapacity of the debtor does not affect the surety's liability. Nor does death or bankruptcy of the creditor release the surety, because the debtor's obligation still exists.

6. (1176,L2,26) (c) The consideration (credit) given by Day (creditor) to Victor (debtor) is extended to Anthony (surety) as long as Anthony's obligation to act as surety arises at the time of the debt transaction. Anthony is obligated to act at the time of the debt transaction by making the extension of credit contingent on Anthony's acting as surety. There are no filing requirements for a suretyship arrangement. A suretyship is not a security interest. The surety undertaking must be in writing, no matter who requests it, because it is an agreement to answer for the default of another. Anthony is entitled to the right of off-set for a claim against the creditor, Day, but not for a claim against the debtor, Victor.

7. (1176,L2,27) (d) Barnes is a conditional guarantor of collection, not a surety. Ace, as creditor, must first proceed against the debtor, Wilcox. Failing collection, Ace must give Barnes notice of his inability to collect, and then Barnes becomes liable as guarantor. Barnes need not proceed against Wilcox, Barnes is merely liable to pay Wilcox's debt to Ace. Barnes is subrogated to Ace's rights against Wilcox and may so proceed if he desires. A discharge in bankruptcy of the debtor does not discharge a surety.

8. (1176,L2,30) (d) If a creditor releases the debtor, the surety is also released unless the creditor reserved his rights against the surety. The surety agreement must be in writing but the debt need not unless the statute of frauds applies. It does not apply here because there are many ways in which a debt may exceed $500 without there having been a single sale of goods for $500. The debtor's lack of capacity will relieve the debtor of liability, but it is not a defense for the surety. Tender of payment by the surety will relieve the surety from liability, but not the debtor.

9. (1176,L2,31) (c) Co-sureties are two or more sureties bound to answer for the same debt or duty of the debtor. They need not be aware of each other's existence either at the time of

their contract or later. They need not sign the same contract. The only necessary connection is that they are both bound to answer for the same debt irrespective of the time they became bound. Co-sureties also need not be bound for the same amount, e.g., one could be bound for 60% and the other for 40%.

10. (577,L2,31) (b) A surety may exercise any defense on the contract which would have been available to the debtor except for the debtor's personal defenses. Illegality of the underlying obligation is a defense available to both the debtor and the surety. The surety cannot use the insolvency or minority of the principal debtor as a defense as this is a common reason for having a surety. Nor can the surety use his own mistake(s) as a defense.

11. (577,L2,32) (b) Co-sureties can be held jointly and severally liable for the full amount. Thus a creditor may proceed against only one surety. However, that surety can proceed against the other co-sureties for contribution. If the other co-sureties are insolvent, the solvent surety will have to pay the full amount (limited to the amount for which he agreed to be a surety). A sub-surety is a surety for the surety. Thus a sub-surety has the same rights against a surety—full reimbursement—that a surety has against the debtor.

12. (1178,L1,20) (d) The general rule is that a surety is released from liability for acts of the creditor which materially increase the surety's risk. In this case the failure of the creditor to give notice of the prior embezzlement materially increased the surety's risk. Answers (a) and (b) are incorrect because when the surety is released from liability it is immaterial that the embezzlements did not exceed the face value of the bond. Answer (c) is incorrect because Excelsior has not assumed the risk that the creditor would negligently and knowingly withhold material information from the surety.

13. (579,L1,7) (d) Unless there is a reservation of rights by the creditor against the co-sureties, release of one co-surety reduces the other co-surety's obligation by the same amount. Hence the release of Blackwell also released the co-surety, Crawford, to the extent of one-half the debt, or $12,500. Answers (a), (b), and (c) are incorrect because the actions of Lux did not totally release Crawford, but they did have an effect upon Crawford's liability and right to contribution.

14. (1174,L2,26) (d) Under the doctrine of subrogation, the surety steps into the creditor's shoes upon payment. So First Fidelity would be entitled to all rights that Matz would have against

Basic. Basic Construction is a party to the contract, not a third party beneficiary. First Fidelity has the right to complete the building, not the duty. First Fidelity is still a surety in its secondary obligation.

15. (1174,L2,29) (c) An extention of time to the debtor releases the surety because it is a material increase of the surety's risk. The surety agreement must be in writing whether compensative or gratuitous. Sale of the note would not affect the surety's risk. The surety may not withdraw from the surety agreement because the creditor detrimentally relied on him.

16. (1175,L1,12) (c) Sims is a del credere agent. Although technically del credere agents are not sureties, in essence Sims is a surety under the broad definition since he guarantees payment to Paul. Sims is an agent but not coupled with an interest; he has no ownership rights. The Statute of Frauds is not applicable to del credere agent's guarantees because such promises are considered to be primary. The Fair Labor Standards Act is not applicable to outside salesmen such as Sims. The "best" answer is (c).

17. (576,L1,11) (c) As sureties, the owners are immediately liable on the debts if the corporation defaults. No notice need be given them. If the guarantee was primarily for the owners' benefit, the guarantee would not need to be in writing. But since the benefit only accrues to the owners indirectly (through the corporation), it is not considered to be primarily for their benefit. They only guaranteed one loan and did not assume responsibility for other debts. The bank can hold any one of them fully liable for the entire debt and the others may be required to contribute their proportionate share to the one held liable.

18. (576,L1,12) (b) Upon payment to the creditor, the surety is subrogated to the creditor's rights against the debtor. The creditor is entitled to satisfy any part of his debt from collateral held by him, but any remaining collateral must be turned over to the surety. Charles was satisfied by $50,000 from Simons and $50,000 from the collateral. Simons is subrogated to the remaining $25,000 and can still proceed against Parker for the remaining $25,000.

19. (574,L1,13) (d) When a debtor has more than one debt outstanding with the same creditor and makes a part payment, the debtor may give instructions as to which debt the part payment is to apply. If the debtor makes no instructions the creditor is free to apply the part payment to whichever debt he chooses. The fact that one debt is guaranteed by a surety makes no difference in the absence of instructions by the debtor. So Collins can apply the $600 to the debts as he sees fit.

20. (1177,L2,17) (d) A suretyship relationship exists when one person agrees to be answerable for the debt or default of another. Unlike a suretyship relation, insurance is the distribution of the cost of risk over a large number of individuals. Malpractice insurance is spreading the cost of possible professional liability over a large number of professionals. Answer (a) is incorrect because a person who assumes a mortgage is a surety for the original mortgagor who remains primarily liable. Answer (b) is incorrect because a person who endorses a check in blank is a surety in that he promises to pay if the check is dishonored (endorsement "without recourse" disclaims this liability). Answer (c) is incorrect because an accommodation maker of a nonnegotiable note is a surety in that he promises to pay if the maker does not.

21. (1177,L2,18) (a) Suretyship contracts are required to meet the general requirements of contract law and therefore the surety (whether compensated or not) must have the legal capacity to contract. Suretyship law allows the contract element of consideration to be satisfied by the extension of the debtor's consideration to the surety and this is then called a non-compensated (accommodation) surety. Answer (b) is incorrect because like a compensated surety, an uncompensated surety can be a corporation. Answer (c) is incorrect because the creditor need not proceed against the debtor first under either surety arrangement. Answer (d) is incorrect, because an uncompensated surety may benefit in any way a compensated surety could.

22. (1177,L2,19) (b) A creditor who holds collateral need not proceed against the collateral to hold the surety liable. Answer (a) is incorrect because the surety, Franks, has a right to the collateral if he pays the creditor for the debt. Answer (c) is incorrect because Jones may not return the collateral to the debtor or Franks is released as surety to the extent of the collateral. As surety he relied on the creditor, Jones, holding it. Answer (d) is incorrect because Jones need not file a financing statement as his possession perfects his rights in the collateral.

23. (578,L1,46) (a) A surety who pays is subrogated to the rights of the party to whom payment is made. Hence Safety would occupy the same priority of the workers. Answer (b) is incorrect because Cairns is a general creditor and Safety would only have the rights of a general creditor if it pays Cairns. Answer (c) is incorrect because a surety may set off any claim the surety has against the party to whom payment is owed. Answer (d) is incorrect because a surety, whether compensated or not, is not discharged by the bankruptcy of the debtor. Debtor bankruptcy is a major reason for having a surety arrangement.

24. (579,L1,1) (c) Clark became a surety by indorsing the existing promissory note. Since Clark is a surety, release of the collateral by the creditor (Wisdom) would release the surety (Clark) to the extent of the value of the collateral released. Answer (a) is incorrect because Clark's promise to act as surety by indorsing the promissory note was supported by consideration: the creditor agreed not to accelerate repayment of the loan during the life of the debt. Answer (b) is incorrect because Clark is a surety, and his obligation is not conditioned upon Wisdom's first proceeding against Martinson. Clark is liable if Martinson does not pay the note when it is presented to him at maturity. Answer (d) is incorrect because Wisdom need not foreclose the mortgage before it can proceed against Clark. Clark is responsible immediately upon default, presentment, or notice of dishonor.

25. (579,L1,6) (d) Release of a debtor by the creditor releases the surety also. Thus the settlement negotiated between the trustee in bankruptcy and creditor released Quinn, the surety, from any further obligation. Thus answer (c) is incorrect because Quinn need not pay Click the creditor the $1,500 deficiency. Answer (b) is incorrect because Quinn agreed to be an ordinary surety, for which there is no requirement that the creditor exhaust his remedies against the property. Answer (a) is incorrect because a surety is not compensated merely because he is the sole stockholder of a corporation whose debt he guarantees.

MAY 1981 ANSWERS

26. (581,L1,35) (b) A surety, who satisifies the obligation of the debtor, will be subrogated to the rights of the creditor. The right of subrogation means that upon satisfaction of the creditor, the surety has the same rights as the creditor had against the debtor. This includes the rights in any collateral the creditor

might be holding to insure performance by the principal debtor. The surety also has the right of reimbursement which means once the surety satisfies the obligation, the principal debtor must repay the surety.
Answer (a) is incorrect because the principal debtor,
not the surety, always has ultimate liability. Answer
(c) is incorrect since there is no fiduciary relationship
between surety and creditor. Answer (d) is incorrect
because normally a surety is immediately liable upon
default by the debtor. Only in a guaranty of collection
does the creditor have to exhaust his remedies against
debtor before being able to proceed against the surety.

27. (581,L1,36)   (d)   If the creditor obtains the
surety's promise by fraud, the surety has a valid
defense against the creditor. The fact that the creditor's fraud was not contained in a signed writing
(answer a) will not invalidate the surety's defense.
Answer (b) is incorrect because the fact that fraud in
the inducement is a personal defense has relevance
only under the law of negotiable instruments, not the
law of suretyship. Fraud by the principal debtor on
the surety will not permit the surety to avoid liability
to the creditor (answer c).

28. (581,L1,37)   (c)   Unless the contract is a
conditional guaranty, it is unnecessary for creditors to
give notice of the debtor's default to the surety. With
or without notice, upon default the surety is liable for
the performance guaranteed under the agreement.
Answer (a) is incorrect because any modifications of
the contract that have the possibility of increasing the
surety's risk would release the surety. Brent could sue
the surety for compensatory damages, not specific
performance; therefore, answer (b) is incorrect. Answer
(d) is incorrect since if Welch, the surety, did satisfy
the obligation by engaging a contractor to finish the
job, Welch could collect the balance due on the agreement.

29. (581,L1,38)   (c)   Upon payment by the
surety, the surety will be subrogated (stand in the
shoes of the creditor) to the rights of the creditor.
Edward, the creditor, had a right to foreclose the mortgage; therefore, when Jayne pays the obligation, she
also has the right to foreclose on the mortgage. Answer
(a) is incorrect because money damages would be a
sufficient remedy, consequently specific performance
would not be available. Answer (b) is incorrect since
bankruptcy of the principal debtor is not a defense
that the surety can use against the creditor. Answer
(d) is incorrect since the creditor has no obligation to
resort to the collateral before proceeding against the
surety for satisfaction. However, if the creditor does
not use the collateral, he must hold the collateral for
the benefit of the surety.

30. (581,L1,39)   (b)   Overall's promise is not a
promise to pay the debt of another. Consequently,
it need not be in writing to be enforceable because it
does not fall within the suretyship section of the
Statute of Frauds. Answers (a), (c) and (d) are incorrect because the agreement is a third party beneficiary contract, not a suretyship agreement. Controlled
never incurred an obligation concerning the goods
delivered to them. Overall is the debtor who entered
a contract with Factory for the benefit of Controlled.

ANSWER OUTLINE

**Problem 1   Modification of Surety's Contract;
Surety's Right of Reimbursement**

a.   King (Surety) will prevail
    The creditor modified the surety contract
        Without the surety's consent
    Noncompensated surety is discharged on any modification
    Compensated surety is discharged if change materially increases risk
        If not material, surety's liability is decreased
    Here the change materially increased the risk
        The released monies were not committed to the project
        The withheld monies induced builder to complete
        The withheld monies reduced surety's exposure

b.   Barclay is entitled to reimbursement from Gilmore
    But since Gilmore is bankrupt
        Normally Barclay would have same position as other creditors
        Except Barclay is subrogated to materialmen and laborers' rights
            Liens and security interests of materialmen
            Limited priorities of wage earners

UNOFFICIAL ANSWER

**Problem 1   Modification of Surety's Contract
Surety's Right of Reimbursement**

Part a.   King Surety Company will prevail. The creditor (Allie), without King's consent, has modified the surety contract. Under these circumstances, a noncompensated surety would be discharged without question; however, a compensated surety is not discharged completely unless the modification materially increases the risk. If the risk is not materially increased, the obligation is decreased to the extent of the loss. In this case, there was a material increase in the risk. First, there is nothing to indicate that the monies released by Allie were committed by Rapid to the particular project (Allie's department store) because Rapid had several simultaneous projects. Moreover, it is clear that the monies withheld provided a strong inducement for a builder such as Rapid to complete the undertaking since the expected final payment would have been large in relation to the final outlays

to complete construction. Finally, the withheld payments reduced the exposure of the surety to the extent of 20 percent.

Part b.   Barclay is, of course, entitled to reimbursement from Gilmore. However, since Gilmore is bankrupt, Barclay will receive the same percentage on the dollar as will all other general creditors of Gilmore's estate. However, Barclay is subrogated to the rights of the materialmen and laborers it has satisfied. Specifically, it would have the right to assert the liens and security interests of the materialmen. Furthermore, wage earners are entitled to a limited priority in a bankruptcy proceeding, which Barclay could assert.

ANSWER OUTLINE

Problem 2 Effect of Contract Changes

b.   Abaco can collect from Slade Gideon
    Slade is liable on contract immediately
        I.e., third party beneficiary contract
    Statute of Frauds Writing not required for less than $500 of goods
        Also, delivery and acceptance satisfies

c1.   Suggested changes materially alter original contract
    Material alterations discharge surety
    Client will lose surety protection if changes are made

c2.   Client should obtain surety's consent
    Otherwise reject suggested changes

UNOFFICIAL ANSWER

Problem 2   Effect of Contract Changes

Part b.   Abaco can proceed successfully against Slade Gideon to collect the debt. Slade Gideon created a direct obligation to Abaco (a third-party beneficiary contract) by his statement, "Ship the goods my son needs, and I will pay for them." The Statute of Frauds is not at issue because the debt is for less than $500. Were the Statute of Frauds at issue, it would have been satisfied by the shipment of the merchandise by Abaco and its receipt by Albert's Boutique.

Part c.

1.   The suggested changes represent material alterations of the original construction contract. If the client agrees to the proposed changes, it faces the loss of the surety company's protection.

Material alteration of the contract affords the surety a defense against recovery on its undertaking.

2.   The client should either obtain a consent to the changes from the surety company in writing or reject the proposed changes.

ANSWER OUTLINE

Problem 3   Surety's Consideration; Surety's Liability
            Upon Default

a.   Hardaway's foregoing legal right to call the loan
          acts as adequate consideration
     Fact that loan is already outstanding is irrelevant
     There is no requirement that creditor first
          proceed against debtor
     Creditor may proceed against either debtor or
          surety
     Release of commercial surety partially released
          Merriweather
     Right of contribution has been impaired to the
          extent contribution could have been demand-
          ed from surety

UNOFFICIAL ANSWER

Problem 3   Surety's Consideration; Surety's Liability
            Upon Default

Part a.

The first two defenses asserted by Merriweather are invalid. The third defense is partially valid.

     Consideration on Hardaway's part consisted of foregoing the right to call the Superior Metals loan. The fact that the loan was already outstanding is irrelevant. By permitting the loan to remain outstanding for an additional year instead of calling it, Hardaway relinquished a legal right, which is adequate consideration for Merriweather's surety promise. Consideration need not pass to the surety; in fact, it usually primarily benefits the principal debtor.

     There is no requirement that the creditor first proceed against the debtor before it can proceed against the surety, unless the surety undertaking expressly provides such a condition. Basic to the usual surety undertaking is the right of the creditor to proceed immediately against the surety. Essentially, that is the reason for the surety.

     Hardaway's release of the commercial surety from its $400,000 surety undertaking partially released Merriweather. The release had the legal effect of impairing Merriweather's right of contribution against its cosurety (the commerical surety). Thus, Merriweather

is released to the extent of 1/3 ($400,000 (commerical surety's guarantee)/$1,200,000 (the aggregate of the cosureties's guarantees)) of the principal amount ($800,000), or $266,667.

MULTIPLE CHOICE QUESTIONS (1—33)

1. Wallers and Company has decided to expand the scope of its business. In this connection, it contemplates engaging several agents. Which of the following agency relationships is within the Statute of Frauds and thus should be contained in a signed writing?

    a. An irrevocable agency.

    b. A sales agency where the agent normally will sell goods which have a value in excess of $500.

    c. An agency for the forthcoming calendar year which is entered into in mid-December of the prior year.

    d. An agency which is of indefinite duration but which is terminable upon one month's notice.

2. A power of attorney is a useful method of creation of an agency relationship. The power of attorney

    a. Must be signed by both the principal and the agent.

    b. Exclusively determines the purpose and powers of the agent.

    c. Is the written authorization of the agent to act on the principal's behalf.

    d. Is used primarily in the creation of the attorney-client relationship.

3. Agents sometimes have liability to third parties for their actions taken for and on behalf of the principal. An agent will **not** be personally liable in which of the following circumstances?

    a. If he makes a contract which he had no authority to make but which the principal ratifies.

    b. If he commits a tort while engaged in the principal's business.

    c. If he acts for a principal which he knows is nonexistent and the third party is unaware of this.

    d. If he acts for an undisclosed principal as long as the principal is subsequently disclosed.

4. Mayberry engaged Williams as her agent. It was mutually agreed that Williams would **not** disclose that he was acting as Mayberry's agent. Instead he was to deal with prospective customers as if he were a principal acting on his own behalf. This he did and made several contracts for Mayberry. Assuming Mayberry, Williams or the customer seeks to avoid liability on one of the contracts involved, which of the following statements is correct?

    a. Williams has **no** liability once he discloses that Mayberry was the real principal.

    b. Mayberry must ratify the Williams contracts in order to be held liable.

    c. The third party may choose to hold either Williams or Mayberry liable.

    d. The third party can avoid liability because he believed he was dealing with Williams as a principal.

5. Park Manufacturing hired Stone as a traveling salesman to sell goods manufactured by Park. Stone also sold a line of products manufactured by a friend. He did **not** disclose this to Park. The relationship was unsatisfactory and Park finally fired Stone after learning of Stone's sales of the other manufacturer's goods. Stone, enraged at Park for firing him, continued to make contracts on Park's behalf with both new and old customers that were almost uniformly disadvantageous to Park. Park, upon learning of this, gave written notice of Stone's discharge to all parties with whom Stone had dealt. Which of the following statements is **incorrect**?

    a. Park can bring an action against Stone to have him account for any secret profits.

    b. Prior to notification, Stone retained some continued authority to bind Park despite termination of the agency relationship.

    c. New customers who contracted with Stone for the first time could enforce the contracts against Park if they knew that Stone had been Park's salesman but were unaware that Stone was fired.

    d. If Park had promptly published a notification of termination of Stone's employment in the local newspapers and in the trade publications, he would **not** be liable for any of Stone's contracts.

6. Michaels appointed Fairfax as his agent. The appointment was in writing and clearly indicated the scope of Fairfax's authority and also that Fairfax was **not** to disclose that he was acting as an agent for Michaels. Under the circumstances

    a. Fairfax is an agent coupled with an interest.

    b. Michaels must ratify any contracts made by Fairfax on behalf of Michaels.

    c. Fairfax's appointment had to be in writing to be enforceable.

    d. Fairfax has the implied and apparent authority of an agent.

7.   Magnus Real Estate Developers, Inc., wanted to acquire certain tracts of land in Marshall Township in order to build a shopping center complex. To accomplish this goal, Magnus engaged Dexter, a sophisticated real estate dealer, to represent them in the purchase of the necessary land without revealing the existence of the agency. Dexter began to slowly but steadily acquire the requisite land. However, Dexter made the mistake of purchasing one tract outside the description of the land needed. Which of the following is correct under these circumstances?

a.   The use of an agent by Magnus, an undisclosed principal, is manifestly illegal.

b.   Either Magnus or Dexter may be held liable on the contracts for the land, including the land that was not within the scope of the proposed shopping center.

c.   An undisclosed principal such as Magnus can have no liability under the contract since the third party believed he was dealing with Dexter as a principal.

d.   An agent for an undisclosed principal assumes no liability as long as he registers his relationship to the principal with the clerk of the proper county having jurisdiction.

8.   Wanamaker, Inc., engaged Anderson as its agent to purchase original oil paintings for resale by Wanamaker. Anderson's express authority was specifically limited to a maximum purchase price of $25,000 for any collection provided it contained a minimum of five oil paintings. Anderson purchased a seven-picture collection on Wanamaker's behalf for $30,000. Based upon these facts, which of the following is a correct legal conclusion?

a.   The express limitation on Anderson's authority negates any apparent authority.

b.   Wanamaker cannot ratify the contract since Anderson's actions were clearly in violation of his contract.

c.   If Wanamaker rightfully disaffirms the unauthorized contract, Anderson is personally liable to the seller.

d.   Neither Wanamaker nor Anderson is liable on the contract since the seller was obligated to ascertain Anderson's authority.

9.   Ozgood is a principal and Flood is his agent. Ozgood is totally dissatisfied with the agency relationship and wishes to terminate it. In which of the following situations does Ozgood not have the power to terminate the relationship?

a.   Ozgood and Flood have agreed that their agency is irrevocable.

b.   Flood has been appointed as Ozgood's agent pursuant to a power of attorney.

c.   Flood is an agent coupled with an interest.

d.   The agency agreement is in writing and provides for a specific duration which has not elapsed.

10.   Wilcox works as a welder for Miracle Muffler, Inc. He was specially trained by Miracle in the procedures and safety precautions applicable to installing replacement mufflers on automobiles. One rule of which he was aware involved a prohibition against installing a muffler on any auto which had heavily congealed oil or grease or which had any leaks. Wilcox disregarded this rule, and as a result an auto caught fire causing extensive property damage and injury to Wilcox. Which of the following statements is correct?

a.   Miracle is not liable because its rule prohibited Wilcox from installing the muffler in question.

b.   Miracle is not liable to Wilcox under the workmen's compensation laws.

c.   Miracle is liable irrespective of its efforts to prevent such an occurrence and the fact that it exercised reasonable care.

d.   Wilcox does not have any personal liability for the loss because he was acting for and on behalf of his employer.

11.   Halliday engaged Fox as her agent. It was mutually agreed that Fox would not disclose that he was acting as Halliday's agent. Instead he was to deal with prospective customers as if he were a principal acting on his own behalf. This he did and made several contracts for Halliday. Assuming Halliday, Fox, or the customer seeks to avoid liability on one of the contracts involved, which of the following statements is correct?

a.   The third party may choose to hold either Fox or Halliday liable.

b.   The third party can avoid liability because he believed he was dealing with Fox as a principal.

c.   Halliday must ratify the Fox contracts in order to be held liable.

d.   Fox has no liability once he discloses that Halliday was the real principal.

12.   Smith has been engaged as a general sales agent for the Victory Medical Supply Company. Victory, as Smith's principal, owes Smith several duties which are implied as a matter of law. Which of the following duties is owed by Victory to Smith?

a.   Not to compete.
b.   To reimburse Smith for all expenditures as long as they are remotely related to Smith's employment and not specifically prohibited.
c.   Not to dismiss Smith without cause for one year from the making of the contract if the duration of the contract is indefinite.
d.   To indemnify Smith for liability for acts done in good faith upon Victory's orders.

13.   Winter is a sales agent for Magnum Enterprises. Winter has assumed an obligation to indemnify Magnum if any of Winter's customers fail to pay. Under these circumstances, which of the following is correct?
a.   Winter's engagement must be in writing regardless of its duration.
b.   Upon default, Magnum must first proceed against the delinquent purchaser-debtor.
c.   The above facts describe a del credere agency relationship and Winter will be liable in the event his customers fail to pay Magnum.
d.   There is no fiduciary relationship on either Winter's or Magnum's part.

14.   Gladstone has been engaged as sales agent for the Doremus Corporation. Under which of the following circumstances may Gladstone delegate his duties to another?
a.   Where an emergency arises and the delegation is necessary to meet the emergency.
b.   Where it is convenient for Gladstone to do so.
c.   Only with the express consent of Doremus.
d.   If Doremus sells its business to another.

15.   Futterman operated a cotton factory and employed Marra as a general purchasing agent to travel through the southern states to purchase cotton. Futterman telegraphed Marra instructions from day to day as to the price to be paid for cotton. Marra entered a cotton district in which she had not previously done business and represented that she was purchasing cotton for Futterman. Although directed by Futterman to pay no more than 25 cents a pound, Marra bought cotton from Anderson at 30 cents a pound, which was the prevailing offering price at that time. Futterman refused to take the cotton. Under these circumstances, which of the following is correct?
a.   The negation of actual authority to make the purchase effectively eliminates any liability for Futterman.
b.   Futterman is not liable on the contract.
c.   Marra has no potential liability.
d.   Futterman is liable on the contract.

16.   Harper was employed as a carpenter by the Ace Construction Company. He negligently constructed a scaffold at one of Ace's construction sites. The scaffold collapsed and injured Dirks (a fellow employee), Franklin (a supplier), and Harper.
a.   Ace Construction Company is not liable to Franklin if Harper disobeyed specific instructions regarding construction of the scaffold.
b.   Ace Construction Company is liable to Franklin even though Harper was grossly negligent.
c.   Harper is not personally liable to Dirks or Franklin.
d.   Harper cannot obtain workmen's compensation.

17.   Under which of the following circumstances will an agent acting on behalf of a disclosed principal not be liable to a third party for his actions?
a.   He signs a negotiable instrument in his own name and does not indicate his agency capacity.
b.   He commits a tort in the course of discharging his duties.
c.   He is acting for a non-existent principal which subsequently comes into existence after the time of the agent's actions on the principal's behalf.
d.   He lacks specific express authority but is acting within the scope of his implied authority.

18.   What fiduciary duty, if any exists in an agency relationship?
a.   The principal owes a fiduciary duty to his agent.
b.   The agent owes a fiduciary duty to third parties he deals with for and on behalf of his principal.
c.   The agent owes a fiduciary duty to his principal.
d.   There is no fiduciary duty in an agency relationship.

19.   Brian purchased an electric typewriter from Robert under a written contract. The contract provided that Robert retained title until the purchase price was fully paid and granted him the right to repossess the typewriter if Brian failed to make any of the required ten payments. Arthur, an employee of Robert, was instructed to repossess the machine on the basis that Brian had defaulted in making the third payment. Arthur took possession of the typewriter and delivered it to Robert. It was then discovered that Brian was not in default. Which of

the following conclusions is supported by the above facts?

    a.   Arthur is not liable to Brian.

    b.   Brian can sue either or both Arthur and Robert for damages, but can collect only once.

    c.   Neither party is liable since it was apparently an honest mistake.

    d.   If Arthur is sued and must pay the judgment obtained against him, he has no rights against Robert.

20. Wilkinson is a car salesman employed by Fantastic Motors, Inc. Fantastic instructed Wilkinson not to sell a specially equipped and modified car owned by the company. Fantastic had decided to use this car as a "super" demonstrator to impress potential purchasers. The car had just arrived from Detroit, had been serviced, and was parked alongside other similar models. Barkus "fell in love" with the car and, after some negotiation with Wilkinson, signed a contract to purchase the car. Barkus gave Wilkinson a check for 20% of the purchase price and executed a note and a purchase money security agreement. Wilkinson forged Fantastic's name on the check and disappeared. Fantastic seeks to repossess the car from Barkus. What is the probable outcome of the above facts?

    a.   Fantastic will be permitted to repossess the car but must compensate Barkus for any inconvenience.

    b.   Barkus will be permitted to keep the car if Barkus assumes the loss on the check given to Wilkinson.

    c.   Fantastic will be permitted to repossess the car because there was an express prohibition against the sale of this car.

    d.   Barkus will be permitted to keep the car because Wilkinson had the apparent authority to bind Fantastic to the contract of sale.

21. Farley Farms, Inc., shipped 100 bales of hops to Burton Brewing Corporation. The agreement specified that the hops were to be of a certain grade. Upon examining the hops, Burton claimed that they were not of that grade. Farley's general sales agent who made the sale to Burton agreed to relieve Burton of liability and to have the hops shipped elsewhere. This was done, and the hops were sold at a price less than Burton was to have paid. Farley refused to accede to the agent's acts and sued Burton for the amount of its loss. Under these circumstances

    a.   Farley will prevail only if the action by its agent was expressly authorized.

    b.   Even if Farley's agent had authority to make such an adjustment, it would not be enforceable against Farley unless ratified in writing by Farley.

    c.   Because the hops were sold at a loss in respect to the price Burton had agreed to pay, Burton would be liable for the loss involved.

    d.   Farley is bound because its agent expressly, impliedly, or apparently had the authority to make such an adjustment.

22. In order to hold the principal liable under the ratification doctrine for the unauthorized act of a party purporting to act as his agent

    a.   The principal need not have been in existence at the time the contract was made.

    b.   The purported agent must have been acting for an undisclosed principal.

    c.   The principal must have full knowledge of the facts regarding the action taken on his behalf.

    d.   The ratification must be in writing and made within a reasonable time after the unauthorized action was taken on his behalf.

23. Joe Walters was employed by the Metropolitan Department Store as a driver of one of its delivery trucks. Under the terms of his employment he made deliveries daily along a designated route and brought the truck back to the store's garage for overnight storage. One day instead of returning to the garage as required, he drove the truck twenty miles north of the area he covered expecting to attend a social function unrelated to his employment or to his employer's affairs. Through his negligence in operating the truck while enroute, Walters seriously injured Richard Bunt. Walters caused the accident and was solely at fault. Bunt entered suit in tort against the store for damages for personal injuries, alleging that the store, as principal, was responsible for the tortious acts of its agent. Under these circumstances

    a.   Metropolitan is not liable because Walters was an independent contractor.

    b.   Metropolitan is not liable because Walters had abandoned his employment and was engaged in an independent activity of his own.

c.   Metropolitan is liable based upon the doctrine of respondant superior.

d.   Bunt can recover damages from both Walters and Metropolitan.

24.   Badger Corporation engaged Donald Keller as one of its sales representatives to sell automotive parts. Keller signed an employment contract which required him to obtain home-office approval on any contract in excess of $500 entered into by Keller on Badger's behalf. The industry custom and most of Badger's agents had authority to make such contracts if they did not exceed $1,000. Keller signed a contract on Badger's behalf with Zolar Garages, Inc. for $850. Badger rejected the contract and promptly notified Zolar of its decision. Under these circumstances

a.   Keller is a del credere agent.

b.   Keller did not have express authority to make the Zolar contract.

c.   Keller had the implied authority to make the contract.

d.   Badger's prompt disaffirmance of Keller's action retroactively terminated any liability it might have had.

25.   An agent's power to bind his principal to a contract is generally terminated

a.   Automatically upon the commission of a tort by the agent.

b.   Instantly upon the death of the principal.

c.   Upon the bankruptcy of the agent.

d.   Without further action by the principal upon the resignation of the agent.

26.   Normally a principal will not be liable to a third party

a.   On a contract signed on his behalf by an agent who was expressly forbidden by the principal to make it and where the third party was unaware of the agent's limitation.

b.   On a contract made by his agent and the principal is not disclosed, unless the principal ratifies it.

c.   For torts committed by an independent contractor if they are within the scope of the contract.

d.   On a negotiable instrument signed by the agent in his own name without revealing he signed in his agency capacity.

27.   Dolby was employed as an agent for the Ace Used Car Company to purchase newer model used cars. His authority was limited by a $3,000 maximum price for any car. A wholesaler showed him a 1938 classic car which was selling for $5,000. The wholesaler knew that Ace only dealt in newer model used cars and that Dolby had never paid more than $3,000 for any car. Dolby bought the car for Ace, convinced that it was worth at least $7,000. When he reported this to Williams, Ace's owner, Williams was furious but he nevertheless authorized processing of the automobile for resale. Williams also began pricing the car with antique car dealers who indicated that the current value of the car was $4,800. Williams called the wholesaler, told him that Dolby had exceeded his authority, that he was returning the car, and that he was demanding repayment of the purchase price. What is the wholesaler's best defense in the event of a lawsuit?

a.   Dolby had apparent authority to purchase the car.

b.   Dolby's purchase was effectively ratified by Ace.

c.   Dolby had express authority to purchase the car.

d.   Dolby had implied authority to purchase the car.

MAY 1981 QUESTIONS

28.   Barton, a wealthy art collector, orally engaged Deiter to obtain a rare and beautiful painting from Cumbers, a third party. Cumbers did not know that Barton had engaged Deiter to obtain the painting for Barton because as Barton told Deiter "that would cause the price to skyrocket." Regarding the liability of the parties if a contract is made or purported to be made, which of the following is correct?

a.   Since the appointment of Deiter was oral, no agency exists, and any contract made by Deiter on Barton's behalf is invalid.

b.   Because Barton specifically told Deiter not to reveal for whom he (Deiter) was buying the painting, Deiter can not be personally liable on the contract made on Barton's behalf.

c.   If Deiter makes a contract with Cumbers which Deiter breaches, Cumbers may, after learning of the agreement between Barton and Deiter, elect to recover from either Barton or Deiter.

d.   If Deiter makes a contract to purchase the painting, without revealing he is Barton's agent, Cumbers has entered into a contract which is voidable at his election.

29.   Moderne Fabrics, Inc., hired Franklin as an assistant vice president of sales at $2,000 a month. The

employment had no fixed duration. In light of their relationship to each other, which of the following is correct?

a. Franklin has a legal duty to reveal any interest adverse to that of Moderne in matters concerning his employment.

b. If Franklin voluntarily terminates his employment with Moderne after working for it for several years, he can **not** work for a competitor for a reasonable period after termination.

c. Moderne can dismiss Franklin only for cause.

d. The employment contract between the parties must be in writing.

30 Sly was a general agent of the Cute Cosmetics Company with authority to sell, make collections, and adjust disputes. Sly was caught padding his monthly expense account by substantial amounts and was dismissed. Cute hired another general agent, Ready, to replace Sly. Ready was slowly but steadily calling upon Sly's accounts to make sales and was informing them that Sly's services had been terminated. Cute also published a notice in the appropriate trade journals and the local newspaper announcing the replacement of Sly with Ready. Sly, after he was let go, called on all the customers who had outstanding accounts payable and quickly made whatever collections he could in cash and absconded. Which of the following statements is correct regarding Cute's legal right against the customers?

a. Cute can regain possession of the goods since title did **not** pass because Sly's actions constituted a fraud.

b. Cute can obtain payment from the customers despite Sly's wrongful acts since it had published a notice of Sly's dismissal.

c. Cute will have to absorb the loss since Sly had continuing implied authority to make collections.

d. Cute will have to absorb the loss unless Cute can prove the customers had actual notice of Sly's dismissal.

31. Marcross is an agent for Fashion Frocks, Ltd. As such, Marcross made a contract for and on behalf of Fashion Frocks with Sowinski Fabrics which was not authorized and upon which Fashion has disclaimed liability. Sowinski has sued Fashion on the contract asserting that Marcross had the apparent authority to make it. In considering the factors which will determine the scope of Marcross' apparent authority, which of the following would **not** be important?

a. The custom and usages of the business.

b. Previous acquiescence by the principal in similar contracts made by Marcross.

c. The express limitations placed upon Marcross' authority which were **not** known by Sowinski.

d. The status of Marcross' position in Fashion Frocks.

32. Duval Manufacturing Industries, Inc., orally engaged Harris as one of its district sales managers for an 18-month period commencing April 1, 1980. Harris commenced work on that date and performed his duties in a highly competent manner for several months. On October 1, 1980, the company gave Harris a notice of termination as of November 1, 1980, citing a downturn in the market for its products. Harris sues seeking either specific performance or damages for breach of contract. Duval pleads the Statute of Frauds and/or a justified dismissal due to the economic situation. What is the probable outcome of the lawsuit?

a. Harris will prevail because he has partially performed under the terms of the contract.

b. Harris will lose because his termination was caused by economic factors beyond Duval's control.

c. Harris will lose because such a contract must be in writing and signed by a proper agent of Duval.

d. Harris will prevail because the Statute of Frauds does **not** apply to contracts such as his.

33. Jason Manufacturing Company wished to acquire a site for a warehouse. Knowing that if it negotiated directly for the purchase of the property the price would be substantially increased, it employed Kent, an agent, to secure lots without disclosing that he was acting for Jason. Kent's authority was evidenced by a writing signed by the proper officers of Jason. Kent entered into a contract in his own name to purchase Peter's lot, giving Peter a negotiable note for $1,000 signed by Kent as first payment. Jason wrote Kent acknowledging the purchase. Jason also disclosed its identity as Kent's principal to Peter. In respect to the rights and liabilities of the parties, which of the following is a correct statement?

a. Peter is **not** bound on the contract since Kent's failure to disclose he was Jason's agent was fraudulent.

b. Jason, Kent and Peter are potentially liable on the contract.

c. Unless Peter formally ratifies the substitution of Jason for Kent, he is **not** liable.

d. Kent has **no** liability since he was acting for and on behalf of an existing principal.

PROBLEMS

Problem 1   Ratification; Agency Coupled With an Interest (580,L5a &b)

(10 to 15 minutes)

Part a.   Vogel, an assistant buyer for the Granite City Department Store, purchased metal art objects from Duval Reproductions. Vogel was totally without express or apparent authority to do so, but believed that his purchase was a brilliant move likely to get him a promotion. The head buyer of Granite was livid when he learned of Vogel's activities. However, after examining the merchandise and listening to Vogel's pitch, he reluctantly placed the merchandise in the storeroom and put a couple of pieces on display for a few days to see whether it was a "hot item" and a "sure thing" as Vogel claimed. The item was neither "hot" nor "sure" and when it didn't move at all, the head buyer ordered the display merchandise repacked and the entire order returned to Duval with a letter that stated the merchandise had been ordered by an assistant buyer who had absolutely no authority to make the purchase. Duval countered with a lawsuit for breach of contract.

Required:
Answer the following, setting forth reasons for any conclusions stated.
Will Duval prevail?

Part b.   Foremost Realty, Inc., is a real estate broker that also buys and sells real property for its own account. Hobson purchased a ranch from Foremost. The terms were 10% down with the balance payable over a 25 year period. After several years of profitable operation of the ranch, Hobson had two successive bad years. As a result, he defaulted on the mortgage. Foremost did not want to foreclose, but instead offered to allow Hobson to remain on the ranch and suspend the payment schedule until Foremost could sell the property at a reasonable price. However, Foremost insisted that it be appointed as the irrevocable and exclusive agent for the sale of the property. Although Hobson agreed, he subsequently became dissatisfied with Foremost's efforts to sell the ranch and gave Foremost notice in writing terminating the agency. Foremost has indicated to Hobson that he does not have the legal power to do so.

Required:
Answer the following, setting forth reasons for any conclusions stated.
Can Hobson terminate the agency?

Problem 2   Vicarious Liability (1178,L3a&b)

(10 to 15 minutes)

Part a.   Rapid Delivery Service, Inc., hired Dolson as one of its truck drivers. Dolson was carefully selected and trained by Rapid. He was specifically instructed to obey all traffic and parking rules and regulations. One day while making a local delivery, Dolson double parked and went into a nearby customer's store. In doing so, he prevented a car legally parked at the curb from leaving. The owner of the parked car, Charles, proceeded to blow the horn of the truck repeatedly. Charles was doing this when Dolson returned from his delivery. As a result of a combination of several factors, particularly Charles' telling him to "move it" and that he was "acting very selfishly and in an unreasonable manner," Dolson punched Charles in the nose, severely fracturing it. When Charles sought to restrain him, Dolson punched Charles again, this time fracturing his jaw. Charles has commenced legal action against Rapid.

Required: Answer the following, setting forth reasons for any conclusions stated.
1.   Will Charles prevail?
2.   What liability, if any, would Dolson have?

Part b.   Harold Watts was employed by Superior Sporting Goods as a route salesman. His territory, route, and customers were determined by Superior. He was expected to work from 9:00 AM to 5:00 PM, Monday through Friday. He received a weekly salary plus time and one-half for anything over 40 hours. He also received a small commission on sales which exceeded a stated volume. The customers consisted of sporting goods stores, department stores, athletic clubs, and large companies which had athletic programs or sponsored athletic teams. Watts used his personal car in making calls or, upon occasion, making a delivery where the customer was in a rush and the order was not large. Watts was reimbursed for the use of the car for company purposes. His instructions were to assume the customer is always right and to accommodate the customer where to do so would cost little and would build goodwill for the company and himself.
One afternoon while making a sales call and dropping off a case of softballs at the Valid Clock Company, the personnel director told Watts he was planning to watch the company's team play a game at a softball field located on the other side of town, but that his car would not start. Watts said, "Don't

worry, it will be my pleasure to give you a lift and I would like to take in a few innings myself." Time was short and while on the way to the ballpark, Watts ran a light and collided with another car. The other car required $800 of repairs and the owner suffered serious bodily injury.

Required: Answer the following, setting forth reasons for any conclusions stated.

    1. What is Superior's potential liability, if any, to the owner of the other car?

    2. What is Valid's potential liability, if any, to the owner of the other car?

MULTIPLE CHOICE ANSWERS

1.	c	8.	c	15.	d	22.	c	29.	a
2.	c	9.	c	16.	b	23.	b	30.	d
3.	a	10.	c	17.	d	24.	b	31.	c
4.	c	11.	a	18.	c	25.	b	32.	c
5.	d	12.	d	19.	b	26.	d	33.	b
6.	d	13.	c	20.	d	27.	b		
7.	b	14.	a	21.	d	28.	c		

EXPLANATION OF MULTIPLE CHOICE ANSWERS

1.   (1180,L1,25)   (c)   Answer (c) is correct in that it describes the only agency relationship that falls within the Statute of Frauds, one not capable of being performed within one year. The agency relationship described is for one year, but to be an enforceable relationship as an oral agreement, it must be capable of being performed within one year of the date of formation of the relationship. Since the date of formation and the date of the beginning of performance differ, the contract is not capable of being performed in one year and must be in writing to be enforceable. Since the relationship described in answer (d) could be performed in one month it is enforceable as an oral agreement. The relationships described in answers (a) and (b) do not fall within the Statute of Frauds and are enforceable as oral agreements.

2.   (1180,L1,26)   (c)   A power of attorney is a written document authorizing another to act as one's agent. The written authorization must only be signed by the principal. Besides the express authority granted in the power of attorney, the agent can also have implied and apparent powers by which to bind the principal. Thus, answer (c) is correct.

3.   (1180,L1,27)   (a)   The correct answer is (a) since an agent, after the principal ratifies an unauthorized act, is acting within his authority and is free of any liability on the contract. An agent is personally liable for all torts he commits; therefore, answer (b) is incorrect. An agent is liable if he acts for a principal which he knows is non-existent and knows the third party is unaware of this. Thus, answer (c) is incorrect. If an agent contracts for an undisclosed principal, the agent remains liable to the third party even though he is acting within the scope of his authority. The agent, however, has recourse against the principal. The third party can sue either the principal or agent. As a result, answer (d) is incorrect.

4.   (1180,L1,28)   (c)   In an undisclosed principal relationship, the third party has the option of holding the principal or agent liable, making answer (c) correct.

Answer (a) is incorrect since in an undisclosed principal relationship the agent is always liable even though acting within the scope of his authority. Answer (b) is incorrect because Williams had been expressly authorized to make these contracts. Consequently, there would be no need for Mayberry to ratify these agreements. They are binding due to Williams' express authority. Answer (d) is incorrect because an undisclosed principal relationship is legal. The only time an undisclosed principal could not enforce an agreement against the third party would be when the contract specifically excluded an undisclosed principal as a party to the agreement.

5.   (1180,L1,29)   (d)   When termination of an agency relationship occurs by means other than operation of law (such as unilateral action upon the part of the principal), the principal is obligated to give two types of notice. First, constructive notice by publication to all third parties who have had no prior dealings with the agent. This is effective to terminate the agent's authority to bind the principal even if the third party does not read the publication. Secondly, the principal must give actual notice to all parties that had prior dealings with the agent. If the principal does not give proper notice upon termination the agent has apparent authority to bind the principal. This makes answer (d) correct since it contains the incorrect statement. An agency is a fiduciary relationship in which the agent owes good faith and loyalty to the principal. The agent is precluded from dealing for his own interests (secret profits). Violation of the agent's fiduciary duty allows the principal to sue for the secret profits. This makes answer (a) incorrect because it contains a true statement.

6.   (1180,L1,30)   (d)   The correct answer is (d). This is a legal contract establishing Fairfax as an agent with express, implied, and apparent authority. Answer (a) is incorrect because an agent coupled with an interest is a relationship where the agent has a property or security interest in the relationship (beyond sharing in the commissions); and as a result, the principal needs to terminate the relationship. The principal needs to ratify only those contracts outside the agent's scope of authority (express or implied). This explains why answer (b) is false. Answer (c) is incorrect since the creation of a principal agency relationship through contract needs to be in writing only if it is not capable of being performed in one year.

7.   (1179,L1,31) (b)   Either Magnus (the undisclosed principal) or Dexter (the agent) may be held liable on the contract for all land entered into by Dexter on Magnus's behalf including the parcel not wanted by Mag-

nus. Dexter executed the contract within the scope of the agency relationship and thus Dexter's actions are binding on Magnus. Also, Dexter is liable on each of the contracts because he failed to disclose that he was acting as agent for Magnus Corporation. Answer (a) is incorrect because the practice of using an agent to represent an undisclosed principal has been accepted by the courts as being legal and ethical. Answer (c) is incorrect because an undisclosed principal has full liability under a contract made by his agent even though the third party is not aware of the existence of the principal at the time of the contract. Answer (d) is incorrect because there is no provision for an agent of an undisclosed principal registering his relationship with any public official. In order to avoid liability, the agent must fully disclose his principal before the contract is made.

8.   (1179,L1,33) (c)   If the principal, Wanamaker, rightfully disaffirms the unauthorized contract by Anderson, the agent, Anderson is personally liable to the seller on the theory of the implied warranty of authority. Anderson warranted to the seller that he had authority to bind Wanamaker to the sale contract. Answer (a) is incorrect because an express limitation on an agent's authority does not negate any apparent authority. Apparent authority is based on prior action and on what is customary in the general business community. Answer (b) is incorrect because Wanamaker, the principal, could ratify the contract made by Anderson since Anderson was purporting to act for Wanamaker. Answer (d) is incorrect because the agent is always liable on a contract that he makes on behalf of his principal on the theory that he warrants to the third party that he has authority. The seller should have ascertained Anderson's authority in order to assure that he had an enforceable contract against Wanamaker.

9.   (1179,L1,50) (c)   Normally, a principal has the power to terminate an agency relationship even though it would constitute a breach to do so. However, where the agency is an agency coupled with an interest, i.e., where the agent owns part of the subject matter, the principal does not have the power to terminate the relationship. Answer (a) is incorrect because a principal can elect to terminate and be liable for breach of contract even though he has agreed that the agency is irrecoverable. Answer (b) is incorrect because an appointment of an agent pursuant to a power of attorney does not deprive the principal of the power to terminate the relationship. Answer (d) is incorrect because an agency agreement, even if in writing, and even if it provides for a specific duration, can be terminated by the principal in violation of the agreement. However, this action does subject the principal to a suit for damages.

10.   (578,L1,1)   (c)   The principal or employer is liable for injurious acts caused by its agents or employees who are acting within the course and scope of their employment. The fact that the principal had a rule designed to prevent such an injurious act is not a legal defense. Thus answer (a) is incorrect. Answer (b) is incorrect because the employer is liable to the employee under the workmen's compensation laws for a job-related injury even if the employee disobeyed instructions or was negligent. Answer (d) is incorrect because even though the employer is liable, the negligent employee is not excused from personal liability for negligent acts. If Miracle is held liable, e.g., for property damage by the lessor, Miracle will be subrogated to the third party's rights against Wilcox.

11.   (578,L1,2)   (a)   Halliday is an undisclosed principal. A third party who contracts with the agent of the undisclosed principal may choose to hold either the agent or principal liable. Answer (b) is incorrect because third-party unawareness of the principal does not release the principal from any contract. Answer (c) is incorrect because an undisclosed principal is liable for contracts made by the agent and ratification by the principal is not necessary. Answer (d) is incorrect because an agent who acts for an undisclosed principal remains liable even after the principal is disclosed.

12.   (578,L1,3)   (d)   A principal (employer) owes a duty to its agent (employee) to indemnify the agent for acts carried out in good faith upon the principal's (employer's) behalf. Answer (a) is incorrect because a principal owes no duty not to compete with its agent. It is the agent who has a duty not to compete with its principal. Answer (b) is incorrect because a principal has the duty to reimburse an agent only for expenditures directly related to employment. Answer (c) is incorrect because agency agreements of an indefinite duration are generally implied to continue from pay period to pay period and may be terminated by notice of either party.

13.   (578,L1,4)   (c)   An agent who sells on credit and guarantees the accounts to his principal is known as a del credere agent. Answer (a) is incorrect because a del credere agent's guarantee is not a suretyship agreement and is not required to be in writing. Answer (b) is incorrect because Winter promised to indemnify Magnum if the customers failed to pay; the agreement did not require Magnum to try to collect from the customers. Answer (d) is incorrect because as an agent, Winter is a fiduciary and owes the duty of loyalty, good faith, obedience, duty to account, not to commingle, etc.

14. (578,L1,5) (a) Generally an agency relationship involves trust and confidence and therefore cannot be delegated without consent. However, an agent would have implied authority to delegate duties in an emergency where the delegation is necessary to meet the emergency. Answer (b) is incorrect because convenience is not an adequate excuse to delegate an agent's duties. Answer (c) is incorrect because express consent is not always necessary to make a delegation, as the authority to delegate can arise from implications such as the type of business, usage, prior conduct, and the emergency doctrine as explained above. Answer (d) is incorrect because if a principal sells his business, the agency is likely to terminate rather than authorize a sales agent to delegate his duties to another.

15. (578,L1,10) (d) The principal, Futterman, is liable for the acts of his general agent, even though the agent violated rules which were unknown to the third party. Answer (a) is incorrect because even though Marra did not have actual authority to buy at 30 cents a pound, she had apparent authority to do so (because she was a general purchasing agent). Answer (b) is incorrect because Futterman is liable on this contract. Answer (c) is incorrect because Marra has potential liability both to third parties for violating her warranty of authority and to her principal for disregarding proper instructions.

16. (1176,L2,21) (b) Ace, as employer, is liable for the acts of its employees committed during the course and scope of employment. Harper may also be liable for gross negligence, but that does not relieve the employer of liability. Nor is the employer relieved of liability if the employee disobeyed specific instructions, if the act was in the course of employment. Harper is not relieved of liability, because Ace can also be held liable. Harper can obtain workmen's compensation even though the accident was his fault. The purpose of the workmen's compensation laws is to aid injured employees, not to find fault.

17. (1176,L2,29) (d) An agent for a disclosed principal having authority, whether express or implied, is not personally liable. An agent who signs a negotiable instrument in his own name without indicating his capacity as an agent is personally liable. Although the principal may be liable for an agent's tort, the agent is also personally liable. An agent is liable to third parties if he contracts on behalf of a non-existent principal whether or not the principal later comes into existence.

18. (577,L2,22) (c) An agent is a fiduciary to his principal and must act in the best interests of the principal and with complete loyalty. An agent owes no duty to third parties other than to act in a legal or non-negligent manner. The principal does not owe a fiduciary duty to the agent; he merely has a duty to compensate the agent, indemnify him for expenses and liability, and not to discredit him or interfere with his work.

19. (577,L2,24) (b) The buyer under a retained title contract is fully entitled to possession until retaken by due process. Taking possession of property of another without legal justification constitutes the tort of conversion. Mistake or lack of criminal intent is not a defense. Both the agent and principal are liable for damages. The principal is liable because he directed the tort and it was committed within the course and scope of the agency relationship. Agents are liable to third persons for their torts even if committed in performance of the agency. However an agent that follows instructions and performs in a non-negligent manner is entitled to reimbursement from the principal.

20. (577,L2,27) (d) Whether a contract made by an agent is binding on the principal depends on authority. While the agent, Wilkinson, lacked express or implied authority (and in fact had specific instructions not to sell this car), he nevertheless had apparent authority insofar as third persons without knowledge were concerned. A contract based on apparent authority is enforceable if it is the type usually or customarily made by similar agents in the performance of their employment relationships. In general, established business customs permit a new car salesman to bind his principal to a contract for the sale of an automobile from inventory, accept a down payment by check, and make the usual warranties and financing arrangements. The buyer can keep the car and the principal, Fantastic Motors, is deemed to have received the check when it was delivered to an agent with apparent authority.

21. (1175,L1,15) (d) A general sales agent such as Farley's would have implied or apparent authority, if not express authority, to make such an adjustment and this would bind the principal, Farley. Farley will prevail only if his agent did not have any authority. Ratification is only used where the agent did not have authority in the first place, i.e., for an authorized act, and it need not be in writing. Burton would be liable for the loss only if he had breached. Since Farley arguably breached by shipping the wrong

grade, and also because the parties have negotiated a modification, accord, or rescission, Burton is not liable.

22. (576,L3,47) (c) The principal must have full knowledge of the facts for a ratification to be effective. Another requirement is that the principal must have been in existence and have legal capacity at the time the contract was made. The agent must have purported to act on behalf of the one who later ratifies. Ratification need not be in writing unless the act performed would have required written authorization, and an election to reject or ratify must be made by the principal within a reasonable time after discovery.

23. (1174,L1,14) (b) The mere fact that Metropolitan has employed Walters to drive its truck, is not sufficient to impose liability on Metropolitan for injuries negligently caused by Walters if the use was outside the scope of employment. The test is generally whether the agent was involved in the advancement of the principal's business. Walters was clearly beyond the scope of his employment as he was travelling outside his route for a personal reason, and therefore his principal is not liable for his negligent acts.

24. (1174,L1,9) (b) Express authority is that authority which the principal specifically gives to the agent. Keller was specifically instructed to make contracts up to $500 without Badger's further approval. He did not have express authority to make the $850 contract with Zolar.

25. (1174,L1,11) (b) Death, as well as insanity, immediately terminates any authority previously granted. The termination is automatic and does not depend on notification of any third party or the agent.

26. (575,L2,31) (d) An undisclosed principal is not liable to a third party on a negotiable instrument signed by only the agent. A principal is liable to a third party on a contract signed by the agent, if the third party has reason to believe the agent is acting under authorization. An undisclosed principal is liable on a contract made by his agent unless the third party holds the agent responsible; the agent fully performs the contract; or the contract is a negotiable instrument. Although an independent contractor is not an agent, a principal is liable for the torts committed by any type of an employee acting within the scope of employment.

27. (579,L1,40) (b) After discovering that the agent had disobeyed instructions and exceeded his authority, Ace nevertheless proceeded to process the car for resale. This constitutes an effective ratification since it is approval after the fact. Answer (a) is incorrect because the wholesaler knew from previous dealings that Ace Used Car Company only dealt in newer model used cars and Dolby had never paid more than $3,000 for any car; thus apparent authority is missing. Answer (c) is incorrect because Dolby had express instructions not to pay more than $3,000 and to purchase only newer model vehicles. Answer (d) is incorrect because implied authority is that authority which is deemed necessary to carry out an agent's express authority. Since he did not have express authority, he did not have implied authority either.

MAY 1981 ANSWERS

28. (581,L1,29) (c) Upon learning the identity of the undisclosed principal, the third party may sue the agent and the principal but may only elect to recover from one of them. Answer (a) is incorrect because an agency relationship could result from an express (oral or written) or implied agreement as well as by estoppel. Answer (b) is incorrect because an agent for an undisclosed or partially disclosed principal is fully liable for performance on contracts the agent makes. This is true even though the contracts are within the agent's scope of authority. Answer (d) is incorrect since the fact that an agency relationship is undisclosed will not allow the third party to avoid liability under a contract made by an agent acting within the scope of his authority.

29. (581,L1,30) (a) An agency relationship is a fiduciary relationship which means that the agent owes great trust and loyalty to the principal while acting as an agent. An agent with interests adverse to his principal must disclose these facts to the principal. Answer (b) is incorrect since the employment contract did not contain a restrictive covenant prohibiting competition. The agent may work for a competitor but has a duty not to disclose confidential information if detrimental to his old principal. Answer (c) is incorrect because a principal can normally dismiss the agent without cause even though the principal may be liable for breach. Answer (d) is incorrect since the contract is capable of being performed in one year; the oral contract is enforceable.

30.   (581,L1,31)   (d)   Termination of an agency relationship can occur by operation of law (e.g., death or insanity of either party, bankruptcy of the principal) or by acts of the parties (e.g., terms of the agreement, mutual recission, unilateral acts of either party). When termination occurs by acts of the parties, the principal must give actual notice to all parties who had previously dealt with the agent. All parties that knew of the relationship but had never dealt with Sly need only receive constructive notice through publication in an appropriate trade journal or newspaper. Answer (b) is incorrect since Cute did not give actual notice to the prior customers. Consequently, Sly retained apparent authority, not implied, to make collections and sell goods. Therefore, answers (a) and (b) are incorrect.

31.   (581,L1,32)   (c)   A third person's reasonable interpretation of a principal's representations measures apparent authority. Express limitations on Marcross' authority, which were not known by Sowinski, are called secret limitations. These limitations do not alter an agent's apparent authority since the third party can assume there are no limits on the agent's normal authority unless informed to the contrary. Answer (a) is incorrect since an agent's normal authority is measured in relation to the custom and usages of the business. Answer (b) is incorrect since previous acquisitions will influence a third party's interpretation of an agent's authority. Answer (d) is incorrect because apparent authority may be inferred from the position or status of the agent.

32.   (581,L1,33)   (c)   The Statute of Frauds provides that contracts not performable within one year must be in writing to be enforceable. Since the Duval-Harris contract cannot be performed within one year (18 month duration), it is required to be in writing to be enforceable. Answer (a) is incorrect since Harris' past performance would allow him to recover any amount owed him from services rendered before termination. However, it will not enable him to enforce the executory portion (unperformed part) of the oral contract. Answer (b) is incorrect since the economic factors cited by Duval would not be proper grounds for avoidance of the contract. Economic factors do not qualify as an objective impossibility which would excuse Duval's duty to perform. Answer (d) is incorrect since the Statute of Frauds does apply.

33.   (581,L1,34)   (b)   All three parties are potentially liable on the contract. A principal, whether disclosed, undisclosed or partially disclosed, will be liable for the contracts of his agent if these agreements are within the scope of the agent's express, implied or apparent authority. Answers (a) and (c) are incorrect because an undisclosed agency relationship is not fraudulent or illegal and will effectively bind the third party to the agreement without that party's subsequent ratification. Answer (d) is incorrect because an agent, acting on behalf of an undisclosed or partially disclosed principle, is personally liable for performance of the contract even though the agreement was within the agent's scope of authority.

ANSWER OUTLINE

Problem 1   Ratification; Agency Coupled With an Interest

a.   Yes, Duval will prevail in breach of contract action

    Initially Vogel (agent) had no express or apparent authority; however, principal ratified unauthorized contract by

        Retaining and displaying goods

        Lack of timely notification of refusal of goods

    Granite would not be liable if immediate notification had occurred

b.   May Hobson terminate agency unilaterally

    No, most agency-principal relationships terminable by either party

    However, agency coupled with an interest is irrevocable

        As mortgagee of defaulting mortgagor, creditor has interest in property

UNOFFICIAL ANSWER

Problem 1   Ratification; Agency Coupled With an Interest

a.   Yes. Despite the stated lack of express or apparent initial authority of Vogel, Granite City Department Store's agent, there would appear to be a ratification by the principal.

    It is clear from the facts stated that Granite would not have been liable on the Vogel contract if the head buyer had immediately notified Duval and returned the goods. Instead the head buyer retained the goods and placed some on display in an attempt to sell them. Had they proved to be a "hot" item, undoubtedly the art objects would have been gratefully kept by Granite. Granite wants to reject the goods if they don't sell. Such conduct is inconsistent with a repudiation based upon the agent's lack of express or apparent authority. The retention of the goods for the time indicated, the attempted sale of the goods, and a failure to notify Duval in a timely way, when taken together, constitute a ratification of the unauthorized contract.

b.   No. The facts reveal an agency coupled with an interest and therefore an irrevocable agency. Most agency-principal relationships are terminable by either party. However, one clearly recognized exception to this generally prevailing rule is that the agency may not be terminated when the agent has an interest in property that is the subject of the agency. This agency, coupled with an interest rule, applies here since the creditor (Foremost Realty, Inc.) has the requisite interest in the property because it is the mortgagee-creditor of the defaulting mortgagor-debtor. Thus, the appointment by Hobson of Foremost as the irrevocable agent for the sale of the mortgaged property cannot be terminated unilaterally by Hobson.

ANSWER OUTLINE

Problem 2   Vicarious Liability

a1.   Yes, Rapid is probably liable for Dolson's action

    Master is liable for servants' tortious conduct

    Employee's conduct must be within scope of employment

    Employer's lack of fault does not relieve liability

a2.   Dolson is liable to Charles

    For tortious injury inflicted

    Rapid's liability does not relieve Dolson from liability

b1.   Superior is liable to the owner of the other car

    Watt's automobile trip was within scope of employment with Superior

b2.   Valid has no liability to the owner of the other car

    Valid's personnel director was not negligent re accident

    Valid had no control or responsibility over Watts

UNOFFICIAL ANSWER

Problem 2   Vicarious Liability

Part a.

1.   Probably yes. A master is liable for his servant's unauthorized tortious conduct within the scope of employment. This is true despite the fact that the master is in no way personally at fault or has forbidden the type of conduct engaged in by the servant. A servant is normally an employee who renders personal service to his employer and whose activities are subject to the control of the employer. A truck driver such as Dolson would clearly fall within such a description. Once this has been established, the question is whether the assaults committed upon Charles by Dolson were within

the scope of his employment. When the intentional use of force is involved, the courts have taken an expansive view insofar as imposition of liability upon the employer. If the servant's actions are predictable, there is likelihood that liability will be imposed upon the master. Where the servant deals with third persons in carrying out his job, the courts ask whether the wrongful act which occurred was likely to arise out of the performance of his job. Additionally, consideration is given to whether any part of his motive was the performance of his job, or if not, whether it was a normal reaction to a situation created by the job. Truck drivers using force in situations involving parking space or after a collision resulting in a dispute are not uncommon. The courts have usually imposed liability in cases such as this unless the assault was unrelated to the job, was solely personal, or was outrageous.

2. Dolson is liable to Charles for the tortious injury inflicted. The fact that Dolson may have been acting as a servant of Rapid and may impose liability upon his employer does not relieve him from liability.

Part b.

1. Superior Sporting Goods is liable for the negligence of its servant-agent Watts. The requisite control of his activities is apparent from the facts. Furthermore, based upon the instructions Watts received, it would appear that he was acting within the scope of his employment. In fact, one could conclude from the facts that Watts had express authority to make a trip such as the one he made when the accident occurred. He specifically was told to generally accommodate the customer where to do so would cost little and would build goodwill for the company and himself. This appears to be exactly what he did. Superior will undoubtedly attempt to assert the "independent frolic" doctrine and claim that Watts had abandoned his employment in order to pursue his own interests or pleasures. However, the deviation was not great, it took place during normal working hours, and, most importantly, was at the request of a customer and was a type of conduct Superior specifically encouraged.

2. Valid Clock Company has no liability. Its agent was not at fault, nor can it be reasonably argued that an agency relationship was created between itself and Watts because its personnel director accepted the ride offered by Watts. The requisite control of Watts' physical activities by Valid is not present.

MULTIPLE CHOICE QUESTIONS (1—30)

1. Perone was a member of Cass, Hack & Perone, a general trading partnership. He died on August 2, 1980. The partnership is insolvent, but Perone's estate is substantial. The creditors of the partnership are seeking to collect on their claims from Perone's estate. Which of the following statements is correct insofar as their claims are concerned?

    a. The death of Perone caused a dissolution of the firm, thereby freeing his estate from personal liability.

    b. If the existing obligations to Perone's personal creditors are all satisfied, then the remaining estate assets are available to satisfy partnership debts.

    c. The creditors must first proceed against the remaining partners before Perone's estate can be held liable for the partnership's debts.

    d. The liability of Perone's estate can **not** exceed his capital contribution plus that percentage of the deficit attributable to his capital contribution.

2. The partnership agreement of one of your clients provides that upon death or withdrawal, a partner shall be entitled to the book value of his or her partnership interest as of the close of the year preceding such death or withdrawal and nothing more. It also provides that the partnership shall continue. Regarding this partnership provision, which of the following is a correct statement?

    a. It is unconscionable on its face.

    b. It has the legal effect of preventing a dissolution upon the death or withdrawal of a partner.

    c. It effectively eliminates the legal necessity of a winding up of the partnership upon the death or withdrawal of a partner.

    d. It is **not** binding upon the spouse of a deceased partner if the book value figure is less than the fair market value at the date of death.

3. Watson decided to withdraw from the Sterling Enterprises Partnership. Watson found Holmes as a prospective purchaser and his successor as a partner in the partnership. The other partners agreed to admit Holmes as a general partner in Watson's place. As a part of the agreement between Watson and Holmes, Holmes promised to satisfy any prior partnership debts for which Watson might be liable. What potential liability does Holmes or Watson have to firm creditors?

    a. Holmes has no liability for the obligations arising before he entered the partnership.

    b. Holmes is liable for the obligations arising before he entered the partnership, but only to the extent of partnership property.

    c. Holmes is fully liable to firm creditors for liabilities occurring before and after his entry into the partnership.

    d. Watson's liability to firm creditors has been extinguished.

4. One of your audit clients, Major Supply, Inc., is seeking a judgment against Danforth on the basis of a representation made by one Coleman, in Danforth's presence, that they were in partnership together doing business as the D & C Trading Partnership. Major Supply received an order from Coleman on behalf of D & C and shipped $800 worth of goods to Coleman. Coleman has defaulted on payment of the bill and is insolvent. Danforth denies he is Coleman's partner and that he has any liability for the goods. Insofar as Danforth's liability is concerned, which of the following is correct?

    a. Danforth is **not** liable if he is **not** in fact Coleman's partner.

    b. Since Danforth did **not** make the statement about being Coleman's partner, he is **not** liable.

    c. If Major Supply gave credit in reliance upon the misrepresentation made by Coleman, Danforth is a partner by estoppel.

    d. Since the "partnership" is operating under a fictitious name (the D & C Partnership) a filing is required and Major Supply's failure to ascertain whether there was in fact such a partnership precludes it from recovering.

5. In the course of your audit of James Fine, doing business as Fine's Apparels, a sole proprietorship, you discovered that in the past year Fine had regularly joined with Charles Walters in the marketing of bathing suits and beach accessories. You are concerned whether Fine and Walters have created a partnership relationship. Which of the following factors is the **most** important in ascertaining this status?

    a. The fact that a partnership agreement is **not** in existence.

    b. The fact that each has a separate business of his own which he operates independently.

    c. The fact that Fine and Walters divide the net profits equally on a quarterly basis.

    d. The fact that Fine and Walters did **not** intend to be partners.

6. Ms. Walls is a limited partner of the Amalgamated Limited Partnership. She is insolvent and her debts exceed her assets by $28,000. Goldsmith, one of Walls' largest creditors, is resorting to legal process to obtain the payment of Walls' debt to him. Goldsmith has obtained a charging order against Walls' limited partnership interest for the unsatisfied amount of the debt. As a result of Goldsmith's action, which of the following will happen?

    a.   The partnership will be dissolved.

    b.   Walls' partnership interest must be redeemed with partnership property.

    c.   Goldsmith automatically becomes a substituted limited partner.

    d.   Goldsmith becomes in effect an assignee of Walls' partnership interest.

7. Jon and Frank Clarke are equal partners in the partnership of Clarke & Clarke. Both Jon Clarke and the partnership are bankrupt. Jon Clarke personally has $150,000 of liabilities and $100,000 of assets. The partnership's liabilities are $450,000 and its assets total $250,000. Frank Clarke, the other partner, is solvent with $800,000 of assets and $150,000 of liabilities. What are the rights of the various creditors of Jon Clarke, Frank Clarke and the partnership?

    a.   Jon Clarke must divide his assets equally among his personal creditors and firm creditors.

    b.   Frank Clarke will be liable in full for the $200,000 partnership deficit.

    c.   Jon Clarke's personal creditors can recover the $50,000 deficit owed to them from Frank Clarke.

    d.   Frank Clarke is liable only for $100,000, his equal share of the partnership deficit.

8. King, Kline and Fox were partners in a wholesale business. Kline died and left to his wife his share of the business. Kline's wife is entitled to

    a.   The value of Kline's interest in the partnership.

    b.   Kline's share of specific property of the partnership.

    c.   Continue the partnership as a partner with King and Fox.

    d.   Kline's share of the partnership profits until her death.

9. Which of the following will not result in a dissolution of a partnership?

    a.   The bankruptcy of a partner as long as the partnership itself remains solvent.

    b.   The death of a partner as long as his will provides that his executor shall become a partner in his place.

    c.   The wrongful withdrawal of a partner in contravention of the agreement between the partners.

    d.   The assignment by a partner of his entire partnership interest.

10. Teal and Olvera were partners of the T & O Real Estate Investment Company. They decided to seek more capital in order to expand their participation in the booming real estate business in the area. They obtained five individuals to invest $100,000 each in their venture as limited partners.

Assuming the limited partnership agreement is silent on the point, which of the following acts may Teal and Olvera engage in without the written consent of all limited partners?

    a.   Admit an additional person as a general partner.

    b.   Continue the partnership business upon the death or retirement of a general partner.

    c.   Invest the entire amount ($500,000) of contributions by the limited partners in a single venture.

    d.   Admit additional limited partners from time to time in order to obtain additional working capital.

11. Which of the following is a correct statement concerning the similarities of a limited partnership and a corporation?

    a.   Shareholders and limited partners may both participate in the management of the business and retain limited liability.

    b.   Both are recognized for federal income tax purposes as taxable entities.

    c.   Both can only be created pursuant to a statute and each must file a copy of their respective certificates with the proper state authorities.

    d.   Both provide insulation from personal liability for all of the owners of the business.

12. Marshall formed a limited partnership for the purpose of engaging in the export-import business. Marshall obtained additional working capital from Franklin and Lee by selling them each a limited partnership interest. Under these circumstances the limited partnership

    a.   Will generally be treated as a taxable entity for federal income tax purposes.

    b.   Will lose its status as a limited partnership if there is ever more than one general partner.

    c.   Can limit the liability of all partners.

    d.   Can only be availed of if the state in which it is created has adopted the Uniform Limited Partnership Act or a similar statute.

13. A general partner will not be personally liable for which of the following acts or transactions committed or engaged in by one of the other partners or by one of the partnership's employees?

    a.   The gross negligence of one of the partnership's employees while carrying out the partnership business.

    b.   A contract entered into by the majority of the other partners but to which the general partner objects.

    c.   A personal mortgage loan obtained by one of the other partners on his residence to which that partner, without authority, signed the partnership name on the note.

    d.   A contract entered into by the partnership in which the other partners agree among themselves to hold the general partner harmless.

14. Grand, a general partner, retired, and the partnership held a testimonial dinner for him and invited ten of the partnership's largest customers to attend. A week later a notice was placed in various trade journals indicating that Grand had retired and was no longer associated with the partnership in any capacity. After the appropriate public notice of Grand's retirement, which of the following best describes his legal status?

    a.   The release of Grand by the remaining partners and the assumption of all past and future debts of the partnership by them via a "hold harmless" clause constitutes a novation.

    b.   Grand has the apparent authority to bind the partnership in contracts he makes with persons who have previously dealt with the partnership and are unaware of his retirement.

    c.   Grand has no liability to past creditors upon his retirement from the partnership if they have all been informed of his withdrawal and his release from liability, and if they do not object within 60 days.

    d.   Grand has the legal status of a limited partner for the three years it takes to pay him the balance of the purchase price of his partnership interest.

15. A limited partner

    a.   May not withdraw his capital contribution unless there is sufficient limited-partnership property to pay all general creditors.

    b.   Must not own limited-partnership interests in other competing limited partnerships.

    c.   Is automatically an agent for the partnership with apparent authority to bind the limited partnership in contract.

    d.   Has no liability to creditors even if he takes part in the control of the business as long as he is held out as being a limited partner.

16. Absent any contrary provisions in the agreement, under which of the following circumstances will a limited partnership be dissolved?

    a.   A limited partner dies and his estate is insolvent.

    b.   A personal creditor of a general partner obtains a judgment against the general partner's interest in the limited partnership.

    c.   A general partner retires and all the remaining general partners do not consent to continue.

    d.   A limited partner assigns his partnership interest to an outsider and the purchaser becomes a substituted limited partner.

17. A limited partner's capital contribution to the limited partnership

    a. Creates an intangible personal property right of the limited partner in the limited partnership.

    b. Can be withdrawn at the limited partner's option at any time prior to the filing of a petition in bankruptcy against the limited partnership.

    c. Can only consist of cash or marketable securities.

    d. Need not be indicated in the limited partnership's certificate.

18. The Statute of Frauds requires a written partnership agreement when the partnership

    a. By its terms has a duration of more than one year.

    b. Has assets in excess of $5,000.

    c. Is engaged in the real-estate business.

    d. Contains members who reside in different states.

19. Webster, Davis, and Polk were general partners in the antique business. Webster contributed his illustrious name, Davis managed the partnership, and Polk contributed the capital. Absent an agreement to the contrary, which of the following provisions would automatically prevail?

    a. Polk has the majority vote in respect to new business.

    b. Polk has assumed the responsibility of paying Webster's personal debts upon insolvency of the partnership.

    c. Webster, Davis, and Polk share profits and losses equally.

    d. Davis is entitled to a reasonable salary for his services.

20. In 1970, Allen, Burton, and Carter became equal partners for the purpose of buying and selling real estate for profit. For convenience, title to all property purchased was taken in the name of Allen. Allen died with partnership real estate and partnership personal property standing in his name valued at $25,000 and $5,000, respectively. The partnership had no debts. Allen's wife claims a dower right in the real property. Allen had bequeathed all his personal property to his children who claim an absolute one-third interest in the $5,000 of personal property. In this situation

    a. Allen's wife has a valid dower right to all the real property held in her deceased husband's name.

    b. Partnership property is subject to a right of survivorship in the surviving partners; hence, Allen's wife is entitled only to his share of undistributed partnership profits.

    c. Allen's children are entitled to one-third of all partnership personal property.

    d. Allen's estate is entitled to settlement for the value of his partnership interest.

21. General Cosmetics, a limited partnership created pursuant to the Uniform Limited Partnership Act, is in liquidation. Some of the limited partners are also creditors of the partnership. Under the circumstances, how should the liquidation be accomplished?

    a. First satisfy all creditors, including any creditors who are also limited partners, in order of priority as provided by law.

    b. Distribute any excess remaining after the satisfaction of creditors to limited partners with the exception of undistributed profits to which the general partners may be entitled.

    c. Satisfy all outside creditors, excluding any limited partners who are also creditors, and then satisfy limited partners for all their claims.

    d. Satisfy all partners whether general or limited for their original capital contribution after all creditors have been satisfied.

22. Fox, Harrison, and Dodge are the general partners of Great Expectations, a limited partnership. There are 20 limited partners. The general partners wish to add two more general partners and sell additional limited partnership interests to the public. The limited partnership certificate is silent on these matters. The general partners

    a. Can admit the two additional partners as general partners without the consent of the limited partners if the general partners vote unanimously to do so.

    b. Cannot admit additional limited partners unless there is unanimous written consent or ratification of their action by the limited partners.

    c. Can admit additional limited partners if a majority of the general and limited partners consent to do so.

    d. Cannot admit any general or limited partners without amending the written partnership agreement.

23. Martin Cosgrove induced Harold Watts, Charles Randall, and James Howard to join him in a partnership venture. Cosgrove is a sophisticated investor. He proposed that Watts, Randall, and Howard each contribute $100,000 cash to a limited partnership which would consist of himself as general partner and the others as limited partners. Cosgrove was to contribute $50,000, but he was to share equally in all profits and assume all losses in excess of $50,000 upon dissolution. Under these circumstances

   a. The purported creation of a limited partnership is invalid because there must be at least two general partners.
   b. Creditors of the limited partnership would have to sue Cosgrove for any deficiency of assets in liquidation in excess of $50,000 before being able to resort to limited-partnership property above this amount.
   c. If one of the limited partners agreed in the certificate to contribute $100,000 cash but instead contributed $90,000 in cash and $10,000 in services, he may be held liable to the partnership creditors for $10,000.
   d. The limited partnership can properly be called the Cosgrove, Watts, Randall & Howard Investing Company, Limited Partnership.

24. Kimball, Thompson, and Darby formed a partnership. Kimball contributed $25,000 in capital and loaned the partnership $20,000; he performed no services. Thompson contributed $15,000 in capital and part-time services, and Darby contributed only his full-time services. The partnership agreement provided that all profits and losses would be shared equally. Three years after the formation of the partnership, the three partners agreed to dissolve and liquidate the partnership. Firm creditors, other than Kimball, have bona fide claims of $65,000. After all profits and losses have been recorded there are $176,000 of assets to be distributed to creditors and partners. When the assets are distributed

   a. Darby receives nothing since he did not contribute any property.
   b. Thompson receives $45,333 in total.
   c. Kimball receives $62,000 in total.
   d. Each partner receives one-third of the remaining assets after all the firm creditors, including Kimball, have been paid.

25. Bonanza Real Estate Ventures is a limited partnership created pursuant to the law of a state which has adopted the Uniform Limited Partnership Act. It has three general partners and 1,100 limited partners living in various states. The limited partnership interests were offered to the general public at $5,000 per partnership interest. Johnson purchased a limited-partnership interest in the Bonanza Real Estate Ventures. As such, he

   a. Cannot assign his limited-partnership interest to another person without the consent of the general partners.
   b. Is entitled to interest on his capital contribution.
   c. Is a fiduciary vis-a-vis the limited partnership and its partners.
   d. Must include his share of the limited-partnership taxable profits in his taxable income even if he does not withdraw anything.

26. The partnership of Baker, Green, and Madison is insolvent. The partnership's liabilities exceed its assets by $123,000. The liabilities include a $25,000 loan from Madison. Green is personally insolvent, his personal liabilities exceed his personal assets by $13,500. Green has filed a voluntary petition in bankruptcy. Under these circumstances, partnership creditors

   a. Must proceed jointly against the partnership and all the general partners so that losses may be shared equitably among the partners.
   b. Rank first in payment and all (including Madison) will share proportionately in the partnership assets to be distributed.
   c. Will have the first claim to partnership property to the exclusion of the personal creditors of Green.
   d. Have the right to share pro rata with Green's personal creditors Green's personal assets.

27. Jack Gordon, a general partner of Visions Unlimited, is retiring. He sold his partnership interest to Don Morrison for $80,000. Gordon assigned to Morrison all his rights, title, and interests in the partnership and named Morrison as his successor partner in Visions. In this situation

   a. The assignment to Morrison dissolves the partnership.
   b. Absent any limitation regarding the assignment of a partner's interest, Gordon is free to assign it at his will.

c. Morrison is entitled to an equal voice
and vote in the management of the
partnership, and he is entitled to exercise all the rights and privileges that
Gordon had.

d. Morrison does not have the status of
a partner, but he can, upon demand,
inspect the partnership accounting records.

28. For which of the following purposes is a general partnership recognized as an entity by the Uniform Partnership Act?
a. Insulation of the partners from personal
liability.
b. Taking of title and ownership of property.
c. Continuity of existence.
d. Recognition of the partnership as the
employer of its members.

29. In determining the liability of a partnership
for the acts of a partner purporting to act for the
partnership without the authorization of his fellow
partners, which of the following actions will bind
the partnership?
a. A written admission of liability in a lawsuit brought against the partnership.
b. Signing the partnership name as a surety
on a note for the purchase of that partner's summer home.
c. An assignment of the partnership assets
in trust for the benefit of creditors.
d. The renewal of an existing supply contract which the other partners had decided
to terminate and which they had specifically voted against.

30. Which of the following is a correct statement
with respect to the rights of a limited partner?
a. The limited partner will only have taxable income if the limited partnership
makes a distribution in the tax year.
b. The partnership is required to purchase
the limited partnership interest at the
current book value if the limited partner demands this.
c. The limited partner may assign his partnership interest to whomsoever he wishes
at any time.
d. The limited partner must first offer his
interest to the partnership before he may
sell to another party.

PROBLEMS

Problem 1   Assumed Name Statute; Fiduciary
Responsibility; Dissolution; Assignment of Partnership Interest (579,L4)

(20 to 25 minutes)

Part a. Strom, Lane, and Grundig formed a partnership on July 1, 1974, and selected "Big M Associates" as their partnership name. The partnership agreement specified a fixed duration of ten years for the
partnership. Business went well for the partnership for
several years and it established an excellent reputation
in the business community. In 1978, Strom, much to
his amazement, learned that Grundig was padding his
expense accounts by substantial amounts each month
and taking secret kick-backs from certain customers
for price concessions and favored service. Strom informed Lane of these facts and they decided to seek
an accounting of Grundig, a dissolution of the firm
by ousting Grundig, and the subsequent continuation
of the firm by themselves under the name, "Big M
Associates."

Required: Answer the following, setting forth reasons
for any conclusions stated.

1.   Were there any filing requirements to be
satisfied upon the initial creation of the partnership?

2.   What will be the basis for the accounting
and dissolution and should such actions be successful?

3.   Can Strom and Lane obtain the right to
continue to use the firm name if they prevail?

Part b. Palmer is a member of a partnership. His
personal finances are in a state of disarray, although he
is not bankrupt. He recently defaulted on a personal
loan from the Aggressive Finance Company. Aggressive
indicated that if he did not pay within one month, it
would obtain a judgment against him and levy against
all his property including his share of partnership property and any interest he had in the partnership. Both
Palmer and the partnership are concerned about the
effects of this unfortunate situation upon Palmer and
the partnership.

Required: Answer the following, setting forth reasons
for any conclusions stated.

1.   Has a dissolution of the partnership occurred?

2.   What rights will Aggressive have against the
partnership or Palmer concerning Palmer's share of
partnership property or his interest in the partnership?

3.   Could Palmer legally assign his interest in
the partnership as security for a loan with which to pay
off Aggressive?

Problem 2   Wrongful Dissolution; Limited Partnership (580,L5c & d)

(10 minutes)

Part c.   Whipple, Ryan, and Lopez decided to
pool their assets and talents in a partnership. The partnership was to provide management consulting services.
The partnership agreement provided the following:

- All policy questions regarding the scope,
nature, billings, size, and future expansion
of the business are to be decided by a
majority vote of the partners. Each partner
shall be bound by the decision reached.

- Since each party to this agreement has discontinued a profitable individual business
at great financial sacrifice, it is mutually
agreed that this partnership shall be irrevocable for a period of five (5) years from
the date of execution.

For the first year things went smoothly for the
partnership. The relationship of the partners was amic-
able as they integrated the three separate businesses
into one. However, in the middle of the second year,
policy disputes began to arise. In virtually every instance, Ryan and Lopez opposed Whipple on matters
of expansion and billing rates. At the end of the second
year, Whipple announced "he had had enough." He indicated that the ultra-conservative thinking of his
partners was deplorable and he could not remain in the
partnership under the circumstances. He immediately
resigned as a partner, re-established his own business,
and actively competed with the partnership. Many of
his former clients followed him.

Required:
Answer the following, setting forth reasons for
any conclusions stated.
What recourse, if any, do Ryan and Lopez, or the
partnership, have against Whipple?

Part d.   Marvello and Stein decided to promote
the Beacon Limited Partnership and to act as the general
partners thereof. The partnership was to engage in the

machinery leasing business. The general partners had no previous experience in this business nor did they have what one would call exemplary personal characters. However, by grandiose claims, pressure tactics, and extolling the supposed tax benefits of the investment they managed to sell 250 limited partnership interests at $2,000 each. All this was done via a "private placement" as the promoters called it. The venture got off the ground. However, largely through the incompetence of the general partners, the partnership lost a substantial amount of money in the first year of operations. The limited partners are shocked by the performance of the general partners and the heavy losses incurred. They also have been informed by their tax advisors that there are definite limits on the tax benefits they were promised.

Required:

Answer the following, setting forth reasons for any conclusions stated.

1.   What are the rights of the limited partners under common law?

2.   Has there been any violation of the federal securities laws, and do the limited partners have any rights thereunder?

3.   What is the maximum federal income tax loss that an individual limited partner may take on his or her investment?

Problem 3   Criteria for Partnership; Liability of Partners (578,L5)

(15 to 20 minutes)

Part a. Millard rented office space in a building owned by Burbank. Millard was in the import-export business and was desperately in need of additional cash. Therefore, he decided to use Burbank's name in conjunction with his own as if they were partners in order to obtain credit from several lenders. He placed a nameplate on his door with the legend "Millard & Burbank" and had the same name listed on the directory in the lobby. In addition, he had business cards and stationery printed with the same title. Finally, he placed an announcement in the local paper that Burbank had joined him in the newly-created partnership of Millard & Burbank. Burbank's rental agent saw the partnership name on the door, saw the listing in the lobby directory, and informed Burbank of the situation. Burbank read the notice in the local paper. In response to this misrepresentation, Burbank told his rental agent to remove the listing in the lobby and to tell Millard to stop the nonsense. These instructions were not followed. In the interim, Millard was negotiating

a $10,000 loan with Easy Credit Corporation, one of the other tenants in the office building. Dunlop, one of Easy's officers, had seen the "partnership" nameplate on Millard's door, the listing in the lobby, and the notice in the paper. Therefore, based exclusively upon the credit standing of Burbank, the loan was made. Millard defaulted on the loan and is hopelessly insolvent. Easy demanded payment from Burbank who refused to pay and denied any liability as Millard's partner.

Required: Answer the following, setting forth reasons for any conclusions stated.

1.   Are Millard and Burbank partners in fact?

2.   Under what legal theory could Easy prevail?

Part b. Idaho Mining & Minerals was formed 10 years ago by five individuals as a general partnership. After several years of losses the partnership finally began to show a modest profit from its operations which has increased steadily. The current picture is one of justified optimism. The most recent year showed a profit in excess of $250,000, and realistic projections indicate profits in excess of $1 million within five years. The partners are considering incorporating the business and going public sometime in the future. The partners are concerned about the implications of incorporating from the standpoint of (1) their liability after incorporation, with particular emphasis on possible liability for claims against the corporation and pre-existing claims against the partnership, and (2) the tax implications to them of a transfer of the business to a newly-created corporation.

Their concern is predicated upon the following facts. There is a significant lawsuit against the partnership which is believed to be baseless but which could nevertheless result in serious liability. Furthermore, the tax basis of their respective partnership interests is low in relation to the current fair market value of the partnership's assets.

Required: Answer the following, setting forth reasons for any conclusions stated.

1.   Explain the legal liability and implications of the proposed incorporation to the partners and the corporation.

2.   What are the federal income tax implications to the partners as to recognition of gain or loss as a result of a transfer of the partnership assets to a newly-created corporation?

MULTIPLE CHOICE ANSWERS

1.	b	7.	b	13.	c	19.	c	25.	d
2.	c	8.	a	14.	b	20.	d	26.	c
3.	c	9.	d	15.	a	21.	a	27.	b
4.	c	10.	c	16.	c	22.	b	28.	b
5.	c	11.	c	17.	a	23.	c	29.	d
6.	d	12.	d	18.	a	24.	c	30.	c

EXPLANATION OF MULTIPLE CHOICE ANSWERS

1. (1180,L1,19)   (b)   In a partnership, a general partner has unlimited liability for the partnership debts. Upon the death of a partner, this liability continues and is assumed by the deceased partner's estate. Under the doctrine of marshalling of assets, personal creditors have first priority to Perone's personal assets, with any excess going to the partnership creditors. This makes answer (b) correct and answers (a) and (d) incorrect. Answer (c) is incorrect since each partner, including a deceased partner's estate, is individually liable for the entire amount of partnership debts. However, if a partner pays more than his share of the partnership debts, he can sue his co-partners to recover the excess.

2. (1180,L1,20)   (c)   Such a partnership agreement does not prevent the dissolution of the partnership upon the death or withdrawal of a partner; it merely eliminates the necessity of the second step in the termination of the partnership which is the winding up process. Such an agreement is enforceable. Answer (c) is the correct answer.

3. (1180,L1,21)   (c)   Normally, an incoming partner is liable for existing partnership obligations only to the extent of his/her capital contributions. However, a new partner can become personally liable for these debts through an assumption or a novation. The agreement that Watson and Holmes entered into would constitute an assumption of the prior partnership debts by Holmes. This makes answer (c) correct.

4. (1180,L1,22)   (c)   A partnership can be created by estoppel. This occurs when a third party changes his position in reliance upon a misrepresentation of the fact that a partnership exists. Danforth is a partner by estoppel. Danforth does not need to make a statement to become a partner by estoppel; his silence would be sufficient considering he is present at the time Coleman represents that they are partners. Answer (c) is correct.

5. (1180,L1,23)   (c)   Two or more persons sharing profits of a business is prima facie evidence (raises a presumption) that a partnership exists. This presumption is overcome if it can be shown that the sharing of profits are for: services rendered, interest on loans, payment of debts, rent, any other reasonable explanation. The lack of intent or lack of a partnership agreement will not necessarily determine whether a partnership exists. Answer (c) is the correct answer.

6. (1180,L1,24)   (d)   Goldsmith's charging order would in effect make him assignee of Wall's partnership interest. A limited partner may assign his partnership interest to whomever he wishes at any time. However, the assignee will not become a partner without consent of the existing partners. Goldsmith's charging order would operate as an involuntary assignment of Wall's limited partnership interest. Goldsmith would have a right to Wall's share of the profits plus Wall's capital contributions if the partnership is dissolved. Answer (a) is incorrect because an assignment of any type of partnership interest (general or limited) does not dissolve a partnership.

7. (1179,L1,15)   (b)   Frank Clarke, as a partner, is fully liable for all of the partnership debts. Answer (a) is incorrect because Jon Clarke's personal creditors under the marshalling of assets rule have first priority over his personal assets to the exclusion of the firm creditors. Answer (c) is incorrect because a partner is not responsible for the personal obligations of his partners in the absence of highly unusual circumstances. Answer (d) is incorrect because as stated in (b) above, Frank Clarke is fully liable for all partnership debts and not merely his equal or pro rata share of the partnership deficit.

8. (1179,L1,16)   (a)   When a partner dies, his heirs or those named in his will are entitled to the value of the deceased partner's interest in the partnership. The heirs do not become and are not entitled to become partners as in answer (c) and the survivors acquire no interest in specific property of the partnership as in (b). The heirs are only entitled to the deceased partner's interest in the partnership. Answer (d) is incorrect because the surviving wife of a deceased partner is only entitled to her husband's rights at the time of his death.

9. (1179,L1,17)   (d)   The assignment by a partner of his entire partnership interest does not dissolve a partnership. Answer (a) is incorrect because the bankruptcy of a partner or of the partnership itself results in dissolution. Answer (b) is incorrect because the death of a partner generally results in a court ordered dissolution even if there is a purported agreement which attempts to substitute an executor as a partner in place of the

decedent. Answer (c) is incorrect because the wrongful withdrawal of a partner even though in contravention of the partnership agreement will result in a dissolution of the partnership.

10.   (1179,L1,18) (c) The investment decisions of the T & O Investment Limited Partnership are properly made by the general partners without consent of limited partners. The Uniform Limited Partnership Act specifically prohibits a limited partner from taking an active part in management decisions. Answers (a), (b), and (d) are each acts which are beyond the general partner's authorities: admitting another person as a general partner, r, continuing the partnership on the death, retirement, or insanity of a general partner, or admitting additional limited partners.

11.   (1179,L1,30) (c) The clear similarity of a limited partnership and a corporation is that both can only be created pursuant to a statute and each must file a copy of their respective certificates with the proper state authorities. Answer (a) is incorrect because limited partners in a limited partnership may not participate in management of a business and retain their limited liability. Answer (b) is incorrect because the limited partnership is not generally recognized for federal income tax purposes as a taxable entity. Income and losses flow through the partnership to the partners. Answer (d) is incorrect because general partners which are required in each limited partnership are not insulated from personal liability.

12. (1177,L1,7) (d) Limited partnerships are special creations of the state and are only valid in states where they are authorized, e.g., by the Uniform Limited Partnership Act. Answer (a) is incorrect because limited partnerships, like general partnerships, are not treated as taxable entities. Profits and losses flow through to the partners. Answer (b) is incorrect because a limited partnership may have any number of general partners or limited partners. Answer (c) is incorrect because there must be at least one general partner and his liability cannot be limited.

13.   (1177,L1,12) (c) A partner who signs the partnership name to his personal mortgage has attempted to make the partnership a guarantor or surety. Unanimous consent is needed or the other partners will not be personally liable since apparent authority is lacking. General partners are personally liable for the partnership's debts and liabilities. Answer (a) is incorrect because gross negligence of an employee may create such a liability. Answer (b) is incorrect because partnership business is carried out by majority

rule and each partner will be personally liable whether he objected or not. Answer (d) is incorrect because the other partners can agree not to hold a partner liable among themselves but they cannot prevent his being held personally liable by third parties.

14.   (1176,L1,10) (b) Until actual notice is received by persons who have previously dealt with the partnership. Grand has apparent authority to contractually bind the partnership. Grand will also be liable for subsequent liabilities until actual notice is given creditors who previously dealt with the partnership. The release of Grand and assumption of debts by the partnership is not a novation, because the creditors have not agreed to release Grand. Grand will remain liable to past creditors until the debts are satisfied or there is a novation. Grand will be a creditor, not a limited partner, while the partnership is paying him off.

15.   (1176,L1,11) (a) Limited partners may not withdraw their capital contributions so as to impair a creditor's status. Unless there is sufficient partnership property to pay all general creditors, withdrawal of limited partner capital impairs a creditor's status. Limited partners are not restricted in owning competing interests (but general partners are), because limited partners do not participate in management, i.e., they are merely investors. Limited partners are not agents and do not have apparent authority. General partners are agents, because they participate in management. If limited partners take part in the management of a business, they become liable as general partners.

16.   (1176,L1,13) (c) If a general partner retires and the others do not consent to continue, the partnership is dissolved. Such dissolution can be avoided by a provision in the partnership agreement. If a limited partner dies (whether or not his estate is insolvent) or if he assigns his partnership interest, there is no dissolution. Remember a limited partner is similar to a stockholder of a corporation. A partnership is not dissolved if a creditor obtains a judgment against a partner's partnership interest. The creditor only has the right to income from the partnership interest; the creditor is not a substituted partner and does not have the right to manage or inspect the books.

17. (1176,L1,15) (a) A limited partner's (as does a general partner's) capital contribution creates an intangible property right in the partnership. Limited partners have no right to any specific partnership property, but rather a share of the total. The capital contribution cannot be withdrawn if it will impair a creditor's status, i.e., there must be enough partnership property to satisfy all creditors. A limited partner may contribute property just as a general partner may. A limited partner cannot contribute services if they will involve managing or operating the business. Each limited partner's capital contribution is one of the required inclusions in the limited partnership certificate (generally required to be filed).

18. (1174,L1,2) (a) Contracts which by their terms are not to be performed within one year from the making thereof are covered by the Statute of Frauds. Therefore, the partnership agreement described in answer (a) would have to be in writing. Answers (b), (c), and (d) do not present situations covered by the provision.

19. (1174,L1,4) (c) Absent an agreement to the contrary, partnership profits and losses are shared equally. All partners have equal rights in the management and none of the partners are entitled to compensation for acting in partnership affairs. While each partner is personally liable for partnership debts, partners are not liable for personal debts of another partner.

20. (1174,L1,6) (d) The property held by Allen was partnership property. This property is subject to a right of survivorship in the surviving partners. The deceased's estate has a right to settlement for the value of his partnership interest. Allen's wife would have dower's rights in this settlement or would be entitled to a forced share with the remainder going to his children.

21. (1174,L1,7) (a) The order of distribution of assets in a limited partnership differs from that of a general partnership. First priority belongs to creditors of the partnership, including limited partners who are also creditors. Next are limited partners in respect to their share of undistributed profits and other compensation by way of income on their contribution. The capital contributions of limited partners are then distributed, followed by claims of general partners other than for capital

and profits. If there are assets still remaining, the general partners receive any undistributed profits. Last in order of distribution are the general partners' capital contributions.

22. (575,L1,5) (b) Admission of additional limited partners or additional general partners to a limited partnership requires unanimous written consent or ratification of the act by the present limited partners. Therefore, (b) is the best answer.

23. (575,L2,18) (c) Only one general partner is required in limited partnership. The firm name cannot contain the name of a limited partner. The assets of the firm contain the limited partnership assets and creditors of the firm can reach these assets without suing Cosgrove. Thus, (c) is the best answer. A limited partner's contribution must be in either cash or property and cannot consist of services. A limited partner is liable to the partnership, and to its creditors, for any difference between his contribution as actually made and that stated in the certificate as having been made. The $10,000 in services would not count in computing the limited partner's contribution, so he is liable for this amount.

24. (575,L2,19) (c) The firm has $176,000 in assets. After payment to creditors of $65,000, the firm would have $111,000. The firm would have to repay Kimball's loan of $20,000, leaving $91,000. Capital contributions would then be repaid, $25,000 to Kimball and $15,000 to Thompson. The remaining $51,000 in profit would be divided equally among Kimball, Thompson, and Darby, or $17,000 each. Kimball, therefore, would receive $20,000 as repayment of his loan, $25,000 as repayment of his capital contribution, and $17,000 in profits for a total of $62,000.

25. (575,L2,20) (d) Limited partners are merely investors in the partnership enterprise. They are not entitled to interest on their capital investment. They do not have any say in the management and owe no fiduciary duty to the partnership. The limited partnership interest is personal property and assignable without the consent of the other members. Any share of the profits of the limited partnership accruing to the special partner is personal income and taxable as such, regardless of whether the profits have been withdrawn.

26. (575,L2,23) (c) Creditors of the partnership must first proceed against the partnership to satisfy their respective claims. Should the partnership assets be insufficient, they may proceed against any and all of the partners as they may choose. Liabilities to partners other than for capital and profits do not have equal priority with claims of outside creditors. Claims of outside creditors have priority. Partnership creditors have priority in distribution of partnership assets, and personal creditors have priority over partnership creditors in the distribution of the personal assets of a partner.

27. (575,L2,24) (b) A partner's right to share in profits and receive a share upon dissolution of the partnership is assignable. The right to participate in management, however, is not assignable without consent of all the partners. A partner may not assign his right to access to the firm's books or records. The assignment of these rights would, in effect, make the assignee a partner. No person may be admitted as a partner without the consent of all existing partners. A partner cannot, by selling his interest in the partnership to a third person, make the latter a partner in the firm against the will and consent of the other parties.

28. (1178,L1,16) (b) While a partnership is not a legal entity, it is recognized as an entity for the purpose of taking title and ownership of property under the Uniform Partnership Act. Answer (a) is incorrect because partners are liable for most acts of other partners and debts of the partnership. Answer (c) is incorrect because there is no continuity of existence of partnerships as in the case of corporations. Partnerships are automatically dissolved by the death or withdrawal of a partner. Answer (d) is incorrect because a partnership is not recognized as an entity so as to give recognition to the partnership as the employer of its partners. The partners are considered self-employed.

29. (1178,L1,23) (d) A partner has apparent authority to renew an existing supply contract which is apparently for the purpose of carrying on the partnership business in a usual way. In the absence of knowledge by a third party that such action was unauthorized by other partners, the contract renewal is binding on the partnership. The matters described in answers (a), (b), and (c) are actions requiring unanimous consent of the partners:

1. Written admission of liability of partnership in a lawsuit.
2. Committing partnership as surety on a partner's personal debt.
3. Assignment of partnership assets to creditors.

Therefore a partner does not have apparent authority to bind the partnership in these matters because third parties are supposed to be aware of the requirement of unanimity.

30. (1178,L1,26) (c) In general, a limited partner may assign his partnership interest to whomever he wishes at any time. However, the assignee will not become a partner without agreement by the other partners. Answer (a) is incorrect because a limited partner's taxable income is based on the earnings of the limited partnership whether or not a distribution of such earnings is made. Answer (b) is incorrect as a general statement of limited partnership law, because the partnership is not required to purchase a limited partner's interest unless the partnership agreement specifically so provides. Answer (d) is incorrect because the right of first refusal by the partnership does not exist unless specifically stated in the limited partnership agreement.

ANSWER OUTLINE

Problem 1   Assumed Name Statute; Fiduciary Responsibility; Dissolution; Assignment of Partnership Interest

a1.   Yes, fictitious name statute must be complied with since partnership name is not actual name of partners

Requires recording in public records

Purpose is to advise public who real parties are

But no filing of the partnership agreement is required

a2.   Each partner is a fiduciary for all partnership related affairs per uniform partnership act (UPA)

UPA holds breach of fiduciary duty to be grounds for accounting

Courts grant partnership dissolution when

Partner breaches fiduciary duty to partnership

Persistent breach of partnership agreement by partner makes it impractical to carry on partnership business

Dissolution and accounting should be granted

Grundig breached fiduciary duty by

Dishonesty with partners

Stealing from partners

Involved partnership in illegal price discrimination

a3.   Yes, continuing partners should obtain right to use firm name

UPA provides for continuation of business in same firm name when partnership has

Fixed duration (10 years here) and

Dissolution is a violation of the partnership agreement

Here, because Grundig's conduct is wrongful

b1.   No, partner default on personal debt does not cause dissolution

Only bankruptcy of partner causes dissolution

Facts state Palmer was not bankrupt

Threats or action against partner's interest in partnership does not cause dissolution

b2.   Partner creditors have no rights against partnership property

Only partners have rights to use partnership property for partnership purposes

Aggressive has right to obtain first a judgment against Palmer and then a charging order

Charging order entitles creditor to obtain debtor's future distributions from the partnership

b3.   Yes, partner may assign his partnership interest

Unless prohibited by partnership agreement

Does not cause dissolution

Does not make assignee a partner

Assignee only entitled to assignor's profits and capital distributions

UNOFFICIAL ANSWER

Problem 1   Assumed Name Statute; Fiduciary Responsibility; Dissolution; Assignment of Partnership Interest

Part a.

1.   Yes. Although no filing of the partnership agreement is required, virtually all states have statutes that require registration of fictitious or assumed names used in trade or business. The purpose of such statutes is to disclose the real parties in interest to creditors and those doing business with the company. This is typically accomplished by filing in the proper office of public records the names and addresses of the parties doing business under an assumed name. The statutes vary greatly in detail (e.g., some states require newspaper publication).

2.   The facts indicate a clear breach of fiduciary duty by Grundig. Section 21 of the Uniform Partnership Act holds every partner accountable as a fiduciary. It provides that "every partner must account to the partnership for any benefit, and hold as trustee for it any profits derived by him without the consent of other partners from any transactions connected with the . . . conduct . . . of the partnership or from any use by him of its property." Grundig's conduct is squarely within the act's language. Section 22 of the act gives any partner a right to a formal accounting of partnership affairs if there is a breach of fiduciary duty by a fellow partner.

Section 32 (c) and (d) of the act provides for a dissolution by court decree upon application of a partner whenever—

- A partner has been guilty of conduct that tends to prejudicially affect the business.

- A partner willfully or persistently commits a breach of the partnership agreement or otherwise so conducts himself in matters relating to the partnership business that it is not reasonably practicable to carry on the business in partnership with him.

Certainly Grundig's conduct would appear to fall within one or both of the above categories. He breached his fiduciary duty, was dishonest with his fellow partners, was in fact stealing from his partners, and may have involved the partnership in illegal price discrimination. Thus, the grant of application for dissolution would be appropriate.

3.   Probably yes. Section 38(2)(b) of the Uniform Partnership Act relating to the right to continue the business in the same firm name, under the circumstances described, is narrowly drawn. This provision was designed to cover situations where partnerships have fixed durations and one of the partners has caused a dissolution wrongfully "in contravention of the partnership agreement." The facts indicate that Big M Associates did have a fixed duration (10 years); consequently, this requirement is met. While the acts by Grundig are not in contravention of any specific express language of the partnership agreement, as would be the case where a partner wrongfully withdraws, the courts treat other types of wrongful conduct to be in contravention of the partnership agreement and thus, to be the basis for dissolution. Strom and Lane could obtain the right to continue to use the firm name for the duration of the partnership agreement if Grundig's conduct was deemed both wrongful and in contravention of the agreement.

Part b.
1.   No. Since the facts clearly indicate that Palmer is not bankrupt, his financial problems will not precipitate a dissolution of the partnership. However, if Palmer were bankrupt, the Uniform Partnership Act (Sec. 31(5) specifically provides that the bankruptcy of one of the partners causes a dissolution. The fact that creditors take action against a delinquent partner's interest in the partnership, although annoying and inconvenient, does not result in a dissolution.

2.   Aggressive will have no rights to the partnership property either directly or indirectly by asserting Palmer's rights. In fact, Palmer only has the right to the use of partnership property for partnership purposes. Since partnership property is insulated from attack by

Aggressive, Aggressive will assert its rights against Palmer's partnership interest. The method used to reach this interest is to reduce its claim against Palmer to a judgment and then obtain from the court a "charging order" to enable Aggressive to collect on the judgment. In effect, Aggressive has obtained a right comparable to a lienholder against Palmer's interest in the partnership. The "charging order" would provide Aggressive with the right to payments (earnings or capital distributions) that would ordinarily go to Palmer, the partner-debtor.

3.   Yes. There is nothing in the Uniform Partnership Act that prevents a partner from assigning all or part of his interest in a partnership. The assignment may be outright or for the more common purpose of securing a loan. If there is to be any such restriction on a partner's right to assign his partnership interest, the partnership agreement must so provide. Section 27 of the Uniform Partnership Act specifically provides that a partner's assignment of his partnership interest does not cause a dissolution. The act limits such an assignment to the partner's right to share in profits and capital distributions but does not make the assignee a partner.

ANSWER OUTLINE

Problem 2   Wrongful Dissolution; Limited Partnership

c.   Recourse of Ryan and Lopez against Whipple
Whipple's withdrawl caused dissolution
Dissolution in contravention of partnership agreement
Consequences of wrongful withdrawal
Other partners have right to damages for breach
Other partners may continue business in same name
May possess partnership property
Must secure bond or pay Whipple value of partnership interest less damages
Under common law partnership may not sue; not legal entity
Other partners may seek to recover damages caused by Whipple's competition
May seek to enjoin Whipple from competing with partnership for term of the agreement

d1.   Limited partners may:
Request an accounting
Sue general partners for negligence or breach of
fiduciary responsibility

d2.   Yes, federal securities laws were violated
Sale of limited partnership interest qualifies as
security offering under 1933 act
Failure to register violates act and gives
purchaser absolute right of recission
Promoter's misstatements violate act and give
purchasers right to damages or restitution

d3. $2,000, at-risk limitation (amount of contribu-
tion plus liability for which partner is personally
obligated) applies

UNOFFICIAL ANSWER

Problem 2   Wrongful Dissolution; Limited Partnership

c.   Whipple's withdrawal from the partnership
caused a dissolution. The Uniform Partnership Act
provides that the dissolution of a partnership is the
change in the relation of the partners caused by any
partner's ceasing to be associated in carrying on the
business. Furthermore, the dissolution was in contravention of the partnership agreement, which provided
an irrevocable term of five years. Whipple resigned after
two years.

There are several consequences of such wrongful
conduct. First, with respect to Whipple, who caused
the dissolution wrongfully, the other partners have the
right to damages for breach of the agreement. These
may be charged against him in an accounting or by an
action at law. In addition, if the partners who have not
caused the dissolution desire to continue the business
in the same name, they may do so during the agreed
term of the partnership. In doing so, they may possess
the partnership property, provided they secure a bond
approved by the court or pay to the partner who
caused the dissolution wrongfully, the value of his
interest in the partnership, less damages and indemnify
him for all present and future liabilities.

The partnership cannot sue in the partnership
name according to the common law rule, since it is not
a legal entity. A growing number of states (some thir-
teen) have changed this rule, but the Uniform Partnership Act is silent on the point.

The final action that could be taken by the partners is to seek to recover for damages caused as a result
of Whipple's establishing his own business in competition with the partnership and to seek some form of

injunctive relief in equity that wholly or partly precludes him from competing for the remainder of the
five years.

Part d.

1.   The limited partners would have a common-law
right to sue the general partners for damages based
upon their negligence or breach of fiduciary duty.
They can seek an accounting and raise these claims in
that proceeding.

2.   Yes. The Securities Act of 1933 applies to the
offering and sale of the limited partnership interests,
which are treated as "securities" within the meaning of
the act. The failure to register at all violates the act and
gives an absolute right of rescission to the investors.
Additionally, the promoter's representations may have
contained material misstatements of fact, in violation
of the Securities Act of 1933 and Securities Exchange
Act of 1934. For these violations, either damages or
restitution may be available.

3.   The 1976 Tax Reform Act significantly limited
the availability of loss deductions generated by limited
partnerships beyond the amount of the limited partner's
contribution and any additional liability upon which
he was personally obligated. The Internal Revenue
Code accomplished this by enacting an "at-risk" limitation on the limited partner's deductions. Normally, this
will equal his contribution, which becomes his basis
and does not include the liabilities incurred by the
partnership. In the absence of special circumstances,
the maximum loss available for income tax purposes in
this fact situation would be $2,000 per limited partner-
ship interest purchased.

ANSWER OUTLINE

Problem 3   Criteria for Partnership; Liability of
Partners

a1.   No partnership in fact exists between Millard
and Burbank
Based on criteria for determining whether a
partnership exists
Sharing profits and losses
Joint property ownership, etc.
Exercise of management functions

a2.   Easy may recover if Burbank is "partner by
estoppel"
If Burbank allowed Millard to use his name
as partner
May be in fact or inferred from evidence

Based on Burbank's conduct, i.e., inaction
Thus Burbank may be a partner by estoppel

b1. Partners remain jointly and severally liable for
partnership debts after incorporation
Unless creditors grant a novation
Transfer of assets to corporation does not
diminish liabilities
No personal liability for debts subsequent to
incorporation
Corporation may assume partnership liabilities
If not expressly assumed, liability may be
imposed

b2. No tax gain or loss is recognized on incorporation
of partnership
Tax-free exchange per sections 351 and 368c of
the Code
The gain is postponed
Basis in partnership becomes basis in stock

UNOFFICIAL ANSWER

Problem 3   Criteria for Partnership; Liability of
Partners

Part a.

1.   No. The Uniform Partnership Act provides the
criteria for determining whether a partnership exists
between two or more parties. Although there are
several other factors, such as sharing in losses, joint
ownership of property, and exercise of management
functions, the most important single factor is whether
the parties share in profits. Under the facts of the
case presented, there is a total lack of any of the
factors necessary to establish the existence of an
actual partnership between Millard and Burbank.

2.   Since Millard and Burbank are not in fact
partners, the only legal theory upon which Easy
might recover is that Burbank is a "partner by
estoppel." This theory is contained in section
16 (1) of the Uniform Partnership Act:

When a person, by words spoken or written
or by conduct, represents himself, or consents to another representing him to anyone,
as a partner in an existing partnership or
with one or more persons not actual partners, he is liable to any such person to
whom such representation has been made,
who has, on the faith of such representation, given credit to the actual or apparent
partnership, and if he has made such repre-

sentation or consented to its being made in
a public manner he is liable to such person,
whether the representation has or has not
been made or communicated to such person
so giving credit by or with the knowledge of
the apparent partner making the representation or consenting to its being made.

The central issue is apparent from a reading
of the facts and the statute. Did Burbank "consent"?
There is a split of authority on the question of
whether Burbank's inaction constituted consent. It
has been held that persons are liable if they have
been held out as partners and know that they
are being so held out, unless they prevent it,
even if to do so they have to take affirmative
action. On the other hand, the partnership act
takes the position that to be held as a partner,
one must consent to the holding out and that
consent is a matter of fact to be proven as any
other fact. Since "consent" is to be proven as
any other fact, it can be inferred from circum-
stantial evidence, that is, the conduct of one held
out taken in light of all the surrounding circumstances. Based upon Burbank's failure to do virtually anything under the circumstances, it would not
be surprising if Burbank were held to have consented.

Part b.

1.   The partners will remain jointly and severally
liable for the debts of the partnership. The fact
that the partnership transfers all of its assets to
a corporation in no way diminishes their liability
to the partnership creditors who could have held
the partners personally liable. Obviously, parties
dealing with the corporation after the transfer
will not be able to assert rights against the former
partners who are now shareholders.
The corporation's liability for the debts of
the former partnership, particularly the contingent
liability, would normally be provided for by an
express assumption of liability by the successor.
If this were a purchase by an unrelated third-
party corporation, the partners would, of course,
insist upon the inclusion of an express assumption. This is also common in circumstances described in the fact situation where a new corporation is created by the partners who in turn own
its shares and the corporation acquires the property
and carries on the business of the partnership. Where
there is an express assumption, the Uniform Partnership Act expressly provides that the creditors
of the dissolved partnership are also creditors of
the "person" (here a corporation) continuing the

business. The same result is obtained by resort to the third-party creditor beneficiary doctrine. But unless the creditors agree, the partners remain liable for the partnership debts.

Even where there is no express assumption by the successor, liability may be imposed upon the "person" (corporation) continuing the business, based upon one of the following theories. First, the courts may find a contractual obligation or promise implied in fact based upon the presumed intention of the parties. Second, the corporation may be disregarded and treated as the mere alter ego of the parties or as a sham.

2.   As a general rule, there is no recognition of gain or loss upon the change in form from the partnership to the corporate status. This is a tax-free exchange within the provisions of sections 351 and 368(c) of the Internal Revenue Code. The gain is, in effect, postponed, and each partner's respective basis and holding period for his partnership interest becomes the basis and holding period for the stock in the corporation.

MULTIPLE CHOICE QUESTIONS (1—40)

1. Hargrove lost some stock certificates of the Apex Corporation which were registered in his name, but which he had indorsed in blank. Flagg found the securities and sold them through a brokerage house to Waldorf. Apex, unaware of Hargrove's problem, transferred them to Waldorf. Hargrove is seeking to recover the securities or damages for their value. Which of the following is correct?

    a. The stock in question is transferable but Waldorf takes subject to Hargrove's claim of title.

    b. Waldorf is a holder in due course of a negotiable instrument and therefore will prevail.

    c. Apex is liable for wrongfully transferring Hargrove's stock to Waldorf.

    d. Waldorf qualifies as a bona fide purchaser and acquires the stock free of Hargrove's adverse claim.

2. Barton Corporation and Clagg Corporation have decided to combine their separate companies pursuant to the provisions of their state corporation laws. After much discussion and negotiation, they decided that a consolidation was the appropriate procedure to be followed. Which of the following is an incorrect statement with respect to the contemplated statutory consolidation?

    a. A statutory consolidation pursuant to state law is recognized by the Internal Revenue Code as a type of tax-free reorganization.

    b. The larger of the two corporations will emerge as the surviving corporation.

    c. Creditors of Barton and Clagg will have their claims protected despite the consolidation.

    d. The shareholders of both Barton and Clagg must approve the plan of consolidation.

3. Mark Corporation is a moderate-sized closely held corporation which is 80% owned by Joseph Mark. The remaining 20% of stock is owned by Mark's wife, sons, daughter, and parents. One son, David Mark, who recently graduated from business school, has been hired by the corporation as financial vice president at a salary of $60,000 per year. Other members of the family are either officers or directors of the corporation and are all generously compensated. Joseph Mark is paid $300,000 as Chairman of the Board and Chief Executive Officer. The corporation is profitable, solvent, and meeting all claims as they become due. Who of the following would have standing to attack the reasonableness of the salary payments?

    a. The creditors of the corporation.

    b. The attorney general of the state in which Mark is incorporated.

    c. The Internal Revenue Service.

    d. The Securities and Exchange Commission.

4. The Board of Directors of Wilcox Manufacturing Corporation, a publicly held corporation, has noted a significant drop in the stock market price of its 7% preferred stock and proposes to purchase some of the stock. The proposed purchase price is substantially below the redemption price of the stock. The Board has decided to acquire 100,000 shares of said preferred stock and either place it in the treasury or retire it. Under these circumstances, which of the following is a correct statement?

    a. The corporation will realize a taxable gain as a result of the transaction.

    b. The preferred stock so acquired must be retired and may not be held as treasury stock.

    c. The corporation may not acquire its own shares unless the articles of incorporation so provide.

    d. Such shares may be purchased by the corporation to the extent of unreserved and unrestricted earned surplus available therefor.

5. A major characteristic of the corporation is its recognition as a separate legal entity. As such it is capable of withstanding attacks upon its valid existence by various parties who would wish to disregard its existence or "pierce the corporate veil" for their own purposes. The corporation will normally be able to successfully resist such attempts except when

    a. The corporation was created with tax savings in mind.

    b. The corporation was created in order to insulate the assets of its owners from personal liability.

    c. The corporation being attacked is a wholly owned subsidiary of its parent corporation.

    d. The creation of and transfer of property to the corporation amounts to a fraud upon creditors.

6. Golden Enterprises, Inc., entered into a contract with Hidalgo Corporation for the sale of its mineral holdings. The transaction proved to be *ultra vires*. Which of the following parties, for the reason stated, may properly assert the *ultra vires* doctrine?

a. Golden Enterprises to avoid performance.
b. A shareholder of Golden Enterprises to enjoin the sale.
c. Hidalgo Corporation to avoid performance.
d. Golden Enterprises to rescind the consummated sale.

7. Grandiose secured an option to purchase a tract of land for $100,000. He then organized the Dunbar Corporation and subscribed to 51% of the shares of stock of the corporation for $100,000, which was issued to him in exchange for his three-month promissory note for $100,000. Controlling the board of directors through his share ownership, he had the corporation authorize the purchase of the land from him for $200,000. He made no disclosure to the board or to other shareholders that he was making a $100,000 profit. He promptly paid the corporation for his shares and redeemed his promissory note. A disgruntled shareholder subsequently learned the full details of the transaction and brought suit against Grandiose on the corporation's behalf. Which of the following is a correct statement?

a. Grandiose breached his fiduciary duty to the corporation and must account for the profit he made.
b. The judgment of the board of directors was conclusive under the circumstances.
c. Grandiose is entitled to retain the profit since he controlled the corporation as a result of his share ownership.
d. The giving of the promissory note in exchange for the stock constituted payment for the shares.

8. Destiny Manufacturing, Inc., is incorporated under the laws of Nevada. Its principal place of business is in California and it has permanent sales offices in several other states. Under the circumstances, which of the following is correct?

a. California may validly demand that Destiny incorporate under the laws of the state of California.
b. Destiny must obtain a certificate of authority to transact business in California and the other states in which it does business.
c. Destiny is a foreign corporation in California, but not in the other states.
d. California may prevent Destiny from operating as a corporation if the laws of California differ regarding organization and conduct of the corporation's internal affairs.

9. Plimpton subscribed to 1,000 shares of $1 par value common stock of the Billiard Ball Corporation at $10 a share. Plimpton paid $1,000 upon the incorporation of Billiard and paid an additional $4,000 at a later time. The corporation subsequently became insolvent and is now in bankruptcy. The creditors of the corporation are seeking to hold Plimpton personally liable. Which of the following is a correct statement?

a. Plimpton has no liability directly or indirectly to the creditors of the corporation since he paid the corporation the full par value of the shares.
b. As a result of his failure to pay the full subscription price, Plimpton has unlimited joint and several liability for corporate debts.
c. Plimpton is liable for the remainder of the unpaid subscription price.
d. Had Plimpton transferred his shares to an innocent third party, neither he nor the third party would be liable.

10. Randolph Corporation would like to pay cash dividends on its common shares outstanding. Under corporate law, Randolph may not pay these dividends if it is insolvent or would be rendered so by the payment. For this purpose, an insolvent corporation is one which

a. Is unable to pay its debts as they become due in the usual course of its business.
b. Has an excess of liabilities over assets.
c. Has an excess of current liabilities over current assets.
d. Has a deficit in earned surplus.

11. Unless otherwise provided by a corporation's articles of incorporation or by-laws, a board of directors may act without a meeting if written consent setting forth the action so taken is signed by

a. A plurality of them.
b. A majority of them.
c. Two-thirds of them.
d. All of them.

12. Surplus of a corporation means
a. Net assets in excess of stated capital.
b. Liquid assets in excess of current needs.
c. Total assets in excess of total liabilities.
d. Contributed capital.

13. For legal purposes, net assets of a corporation means the amount
   a. By which current assets exceed its current liabilities.
   b. By which liquid assets exceed its current liabilities.
   c. By which total assets exceed its total liabilities.
   d. Of its current assets.

14. Mr. Parker has been issued 100 shares of common stock of Capital, Inc., having a par value of $30 per share. What aggregate consideration must Mr. Parker pay for the shares of stock if he is to escape any contingent liability in connection with these shares in the future?
   a. At least $30.
   b. At least $3,000.
   c. Less than $3,000.
   d. Between $30 and $3,000.

15. Caskill Corporation issued 100 shares of its $10 par value common stock to Mr. Jason, its vice-president, for a price of $1,000. In consideration he paid $200 cash, gave a note for $400, cancelled $300 salary owed him for services rendered to the corporation, and promised to render $100 worth of future services. His shares are
   a. Paid in full.
   b. 50% paid for.
   c. 90% paid for.
   d. 20% paid for.

16. Miller Corporation declared a common stock dividend of 1 common share for every 10 common shares outstanding. The owners' equity accounts of the corporation immediately prior to the declaration of the common stock dividend were as follows:

Stated capital (10,000 shares of common stock issued and outstanding,
$1 par value per share) $10,000
Earned surplus (retained earnings)   4,000

No other transactions are relevant. Immediately after the issuance of the common stock dividend, stated capital will amount to
   a. $11,000.
   b. $10,000.
   c. $9,000.
   d. $1,000.

17. Dexter, Inc., was incorporated in its home state. It expanded substantially and now does 20% of its business in a neighboring state in which it maintains a permanent facility. It has not filed any papers in the neighboring state.

   Which of the following statements is incorrect?
   a. Dexter has automatically appointed the secretary of state of the neighboring state as its agent for the purpose of service of legal process if it failed to appoint or maintain a registered agent in that state.
   b. Dexter will be able to maintain an action or suit in the neighboring state if it subsequently obtains a certificate of authority.
   c. Dexter can not defend against a suit brought against it in the neighboring state's courts.
   d. The attorney general of the neighboring state can recover all back fees and franchise taxes which would have been imposed plus all penalties for failure to pay same.

18. Which of the following can not properly be received as the consideration for the issuance of shares?
   a. Promissory notes.
   b. Services actually performed for the corporation.
   c. Shares of stock of another corporation.
   d. Intangible property rights.

19. Watson entered into an agreement to purchase 1,000 shares of the Marvel Corporation, a corporation to be organized in the near future. Watson has since had second thoughts about investing in Marvel. Under the circumstances, which of the following is correct?
   a. A written notice of withdrawal of his agreement to purchase the shares will be valid as long as it is received prior to incorporation.
   b. A simple transfer of the agreement to another party will entirely eliminate his liability to purchase the shares of stock.
   c. Watson may not revoke the agreement for a period of six months in the absence of special circumstances.
   d. Watson may avoid liability on his agreement if he can obtain the consent of the majority of other individuals committed to purchase shares to release him.

20. Derek Corporation decided to acquire certain assets belonging to the Mongol Corporation. As consideration for the assets acquired, Derek issued 20,000 shares of its no-par common stock with a stated value of $10 per share. The value of the assets

acquired subsequently turned out to be much less than the $200,000 in stock issued. Under the circumstances, which of the following is correct?

a. It is improper for the board of directors to acquire assets other than cash with no-par stock.

b. Only the shareholders can have the right to fix the value of the shares of no-par stock exchanged for assets.

c. In the absence of fraud in the transaction, the judgment of the board of directors as to the value of the consideration received for the shares shall be conclusive.

d. Unless the board obtained an independent appraisal of the acquired assets' value, it is liable to the extent of the overvaluation.

21. The Zebra Corporation is neither de jure nor de facto. As such it

a. Can nevertheless recover on a loan which it made to one of its suppliers.

b. Cannot be held liable for torts commited by its agents.

c. Cannot be treated as a corporation for tax purposes.

d. Can nevertheless validly continue to do business as a corporation without fear of legal action by the state as long as it is solvent and pays taxes.

Items 22, 23, and 24 are based on the following information:

Korn was one of several promoters interested in organizing Alpha Corporation. Korn entered into an employment contract for the services of Wentz. It was mutually understood that Wentz would perform certain duties and that these might be performed in behalf of a corporation yet to be formed. Korn also entered into an agreement with Bates Company for services to be rendered by the corporation at a future date.

The corporation was formed and began operations, but a defective filing prevented compliance with the requirements for legal incorporation.

22. Failure to comply strictly with all of the filing requirements probably resulted in

a. A de jure corporation.

b. A de facto corporation for some purposes, at least.

c. The formation of a partnership.

d. The unenforceability of all agreements mentioned.

23. Assume that Alpha Corporation was properly formed and Wentz performed services for the corporation in accordance with his agreement with Korn. If Wentz seeks to recover the compensation agreed upon in his agreement with Korn

a. The corporation is probably liable to Wentz for the salary under the agreement if it adopted the agreement.

b. The corporation is probably automatically bound by the preincorporation agreement of Korn as its agent.

c. Absent express adoption of the agreement by Alpha's board of directors, Wentz may recover for his services to the corporation only from Korn.

d. Any obligation Korn undertook under the agreement is terminated if Wentz assumes a position with the corporation at the salary specified in the agreement.

24. After proper incorporation of Alpha, it was decided to purchase a plant site. Gold, a newly elected director, has owned a desirable site for many years. He purchased the property for $60,000, and its present fair value is $100,000. What would be the result if Gold offered the property to Alpha for $100,000 in an arm's-length transaction with full disclosure at a meeting of the seven directors of the corporation?

a. The sale would be proper only upon requisite approval by the appropriate number of directors and at no more than Gold's cost, thus precluding his profiting from the sale to the corporation.

b. The sale would be void under the self-dealing rule.

c. The sale would be proper and Gold would not have to account to the corporation for his profit if the sale was approved by a disinterested majority of the directors.

d. The sale would not be proper, if sold for the present fair value of the property, without the approval of all of the directors in these circumstances.

Items 25, 26, and 27 are based on the following information.

Coe Corporation is authorized to issue 15,000 shares of $100 par value common stock of which 10,000 shares are issued and, of these, 500 shares are held as treasury stock. The treasury stock was appropriately acquired under applicable state law.

25. A shareholder owning 5% of the outstanding stock of Coe has asked the corporation to repurchase his shares of stock. Should Coe want to repurchase the stock, which of the following statements best describes the effect to the corporation?

    a. The repurchase of the shares by the corporation would normally require stockholder approval.

    b. Absent stockholder approval, shares may be repurchased by the corporation only by affording all stockholders a right of pro rata redemption.

    c. Repurchased shares must normally be retired if they were never authorized.

    d. Repurchase of the shares may not be made if such repurchase would render the corporation insolvent.

26. At a meeting of seven members of Coe's board of directors which constituted a quorum, the directors voted four to three to acquire the assets of Zeta Company in exchange for 300 shares of Coe's common stock. In this circumstance

    a. The board could not properly act on such a matter without attendance by all board members.

    b. If the board's action provided for the exchange of 300 shares for Zeta's assets, the board's action would be proper regardless of the preemptive rights of shareholders.

    c. The board's action was not proper because the action required the affirmative vote of at least five directors.

    d. Shareholder approval would be required for the action of the board to be effective, whether treasury stock or previously authorized but unissued stock is to be exchanged for Zeta's assets.

27. The treasury stock held by Coe

    a. Is treated as issued and outstanding stock.

    b. May be resold without regard to preemptive rights.

    c. May be voted by management.

    d. Normally entitles a purchaser at a later date to an amount equal to all dividends per share paid while the shares were held by the corporation as treasury stock.

28. Delray Corporation has a provision in its corporate charter as follows: "Holders of the noncumulative preferred stock shall be entitled to a fixed annual dividend of 8% before any dividend shall be paid on common stock." There are no further provisions relating to preferences or statements regarding voting rights. The preferred stock apparently

    a. Is noncumulative, but only to the extent that the 8% dividend is not earned in a given year.

    b. Is nonvoting unless dividends are in arrears.

    c. Has a preference on the distribution of the assets of the corporation upon dissolution.

    d. Is not entitled to participate with common stock in dividend distribution beyond 8%.

29. Under which of the following circumstances would a corporation's existence terminate?

    a. The death of its sole owner-shareholder.

    b. Its becoming insolvent.

    c. Its legal consolidation with another corporation.

    d. Its reorganization under the federal bankruptcy laws.

30. Donald Walker is a dissident stockholder of the Meaker Corporation which is listed on a national stock exchange. Walker is seeking to oust the existing board of directors and has notified the directors that he intends to sue them for negligence. Under the circumstances, Walker

    a. Can be validly denied access to the corporate financial records.

    b. Can be legally prohibited from obtaining a copy of the stockholder list because his purpose is not bona fide.

    c. Must show personal gain on the part of the directors if he is to win his lawsuit.

    d. Can insist that the corporation mail out his proxy materials as long as he pays the cost.

31. Walter Thomas as the promoter of Basic Corporation made a contract for and on behalf of Basic with Fair Realty Corporation for the purchase of an office building. Thomas did not disclose that the corporation had not been created. Thomas will not have any liability on the contract

    a. Because he made it in the name of the corporation.

    b. If the corporation subsequently adopts the contract.

    c. If the corporation and Fair Realty enter into a novation regarding the contract.

    d. If the corporation comes into existence and rejects the contract.

32. Hobson, Jones, Carter, and Wolff are all medical doctors who have worked together for several years. They decided to form a corporation and their attorney created a typical professional corporation for them. Which of the following is correct?

    a. Such a corporation will not be recognized for federal tax purposes if one of its goals is to save taxes.

    b. The state in which they incorporated must have enacted professional corporation statutes permitting them to do so.

    c. Upon incorporation, the doctor-shareholder is insulated from personal liability beyond his capital contribution.

    d. The majority of states prohibit the creation of professional corporations by doctors.

MAY 1981 QUESTIONS

33. Universal Joint Corporation has approached Minor Enterprises, Inc., about a tax-free statutory merger of Minor into Universal. The stock of both corporations is listed on the NYSE. Which of the following requirements or procedures need **not** be complied with in order to qualify as a statutory merger pursuant to state and federal law?

    a. The boards of directors of both corporations must approve the plan of merger.

    b. Universal, the surviving corporation, must apply for and obtain a favorable revenue ruling from the Treasury Department.

    c. The boards of both corporations must submit the plan of merger to their respective shareholders for approval.

    d. The securities issued and exchanged by Universal for the shares of Minor must be registered since they are considered to be "offered" and "sold" for purposes of the Securities Act of 1933.

34. The consideration for the issuance of shares by a corporation may **not** be paid in

    a. Tangible property.

    b. Intangible property.

    c. Services to be performed for the corporation.

    d. Services actually performed for the corporation.

35. Bixler obtained an option on a building he believed was suitable for use by a corporation he and two other men were organizing. After the corporation was sucessfully promoted, Bixler met with the Board of Directors who agreed to acquire the property for $200,000. Bixler deeded the building to the corporation and the corporation began business in it. Bixler's option contract called for the payment of only $155,000 for the building and he purchased it for that price. When the directors later learned that Bixler paid only $155,000, they demanded the return of Bixler's $45,000 profit. Bixler refused, claiming the building was worth far more than $200,000 both when he secured the option and when he deeded it to the corporation. Which of the following statements correctly applies to Bixler's conduct?

    a. It was improper for Bixler to contract for the option without first having secured the assent of the Board of Directors.

    b. If, as Bixler claimed, the building was fairly worth more than $200,000, Bixler is entitled to retain the entire price.

    c. Even if, as Bixler claimed, the building was fairly worth more than $200,000, Bixler nevertheless must return the $45,000 to the corporation.

    d. In order for Bixler to be obligated to return any amount to the corporation, the Board of Directors must establish that the building was worth less than $200,000.

36. Delta Corporation has decided to purchase $2,000,000 of its own outstanding shares. In connection with this acquisition, which of the following is a correct statement?

    a. The shares may **not** be acquired out of capital surplus.

    b. The share in question must be classified as treasury shares if **not** cancelled.

    c. A subsequent offering of the acquired shares to the public in interstate commerce would be exempt from SEC registration.

    d. If the shares are acquired at a price less than the original offering price, the corporation has realized a taxable capital gain.

37. The stock of Crandall Corporation is regularly traded over the counter. However, 75% is owned by the founding family and a few of the key executive officers. It has had a cash dividend record of paying out annually less than 5% of its earnings and profits over the past 10 years. It has, however, declared a 10% stock dividend during each of these years. Its accumulated earnings and profits are beyond the reasonable current and anticipated needs of the business. Which of the following is correct?

    a. The shareholders can compel the declaration of a dividend only if the directors' dividend policy is fraudulent.

b.   The Internal Revenue Service can **not** attack the accumulation of earnings and profits since the Code exempts publicly held corporations from the accumulations provisions.

c.   The fact that the corporation was paying a 10% stock dividend, apparently in lieu of a cash distribution, is irrelevant insofar as the ability of the Internal Revenue Service to successfully attack the accumulation.

d.   Either the Internal Revenue Service or the shareholders could successfully obtain a court order to compel the distribution of earnings and profits unreasonably accumulated.

38.   Global Trucking Corporation has in its corporate treasury a substantial block of its own common stock, which it acquired several years previously. The stock had been publicly offered at $25 a share and had been reacquired at $15. The board is considering using it in the current year for various purposes. For which of the following purposes may it validly use the treasury stock?

a.   To pay a stock dividend to its shareholders.

b.   To sell it to the public without the necessity of a registration under the Securities Act of 1933, since it had been previously registered.

c.   To vote it at the annual meeting of shareholders.

d.   To acquire the shares of another publicly held company without the necessity of a registration under the Securities Act of 1933.

39.   The Larkin Corporation is contemplating a two-for-one stock split of its common stock. Its $4 par value common stock will be reduced at $2 after the split. It has 2 million shares issued and outstanding out of a total of 3 million authorized. In considering the legal or tax consequences of such action, which of the following is a correct statement?

a.   The transaction will require both authorization by the Board of Directors and approval by the shareholders.

b.   The distribution of the additional shares to the shareholders will be taxed as a dividend to the recipients.

c.   Surplus equal to the par value of the existing number of shares issued and outstanding must be transferred to the stated capital account.

d.   The trustees of trust recipients of the additional shares must allocate them ratably between income and corpus.

40.   At their annual meeting, shareholders of the Laurelton Corporation approved several proposals made by the Board of Directors. Among them was the ratification of the salaries of the executives of the corporation. In this connection, which of the following is correct?

a.   The shareholders can **not** legally ratify the compensation paid to director-officers.

b.   The salaries ratified are automatically valid for federal income tax purposes.

c.   Such ratification by the shareholders is required as a matter of law.

d.   The action by the shareholders serves the purpose of confirming the board's action.

PROBLEMS

Problem 1   Dividends; Contracts with Director; Director Fiduciary Responsibility (579,L3)

(25 to 30 minutes)

Part a.   The Decimile Corporation is a well-established, conservatively-managed, major company. It has consistently maintained a $3 or more per share dividend since 1940 on its only class of stock, which has a $1 par value. Decimile's board of directors is determined to maintain a $3 per share annual dividend distribution to maintain the corporation's image in the financial community, to reassure its shareholders, and to prevent a decline in the price of the corporation's shares which would occur if there were a reduction in the dividend rate. Decimile's current financial position is not encouraging although the corporation is legally solvent. Its cash flow position is not good and the current year's earnings are only $0.87 per share. Retained earnings amount to $17 per share. Decimile owns a substantial block of Integrated Electronic Services stock which it purchased at $1 per share in 1950 and which has a current value of $6.50 per share. Decimile has paid dividends of $1 per share so far this year and contemplates distributing a sufficient number of shares of Integrated to provide an additional $2 per share.

Required: Answer the following, setting forth reasons for any conclusions stated.

1.   May Decimile legally pay the $2 per share dividend in the stock of Integrated?

2.   As an alternative, could Decimile pay the $2 dividend in its own authorized but unissued shares of stock? What would be the **legal** effect of this action upon the corporation?

3.   What are the federal income tax consequences to the noncorporate shareholders—

(a)   If Decimile distributes the shares of Integrated?

(b)   If Decimile distributes its own authorized but unissued stock?

Part b.   Clayborn is the president and a director of Marigold Corporation. He currently owns 1,000 shares of Marigold which he purchased several years ago upon joining the company and assuming the presidency. At that time, he received a stock option for 10,000 shares of Marigold at $10 per share. The option is about to expire but Clayborn does not have the money to exercise his option. Credit is very tight at present and most of his assets have already been used to obtain loans. Clayborn spoke to the chairman of Marigold's board about his plight and told the chairman that he is going to borrow $100,000 from Marigold in order to exercise his option. The chairman was responsible for Clayborn's being hired as president of Marigold and is a close personal friend of Clayborn. Fearing that Clayborn will leave unless he is able to obtain a greater financial interest in Marigold, the chairman told Clayborn: "It is okay with me and you have a green light." Clayborn authorized the issuance of a $100,000 check payable to his order. He then negotiated the check to Marigold in payment for the shares of stock.

Required: Answer the following, setting forth reasons for any conclusions stated.

What are the legal implications, problems, and issues raised by the above circumstances?

Part c.   Towne is a prominent financier, the owner of 1% of the shares of Toy, Inc., and one of its directors. He is also the chairman of the board of Unlimited Holdings, Inc., an investment company in which he owns 80% of the stock. Toy needs land upon which to build additional warehouse facilities. Toy's president, Arthur, surveyed the land sites feasible for such a purpose. The best location in Arthur's opinion from all standpoints, including location, availability, access to transportation, and price, is an eight-acre tract of land owned by Unlimited. Neither Arthur nor Towne wish to create any legal problems in connection with the possible purchase of the land.

Required: Answer the following, setting forth reasons for any conclusions stated.

1.   What are the legal parameters within which this transaction may be safely consummated?

2.   What are the legal ramifications if there were to be a $50,000 payment "on the side" to Towne in order that he use his efforts to "smooth the way" for the proposed acquisition?

Problem 2   Pre-Incorporation Contracts; Director Fiduciary Responsibility (578,L4)

(25 to 30 minutes)

Part a.   Grace Dawson was actively engaged in the promotion of a new corporation to be known as Multifashion Frocks, Inc. On January 3, 1978, she obtained written commitments for the purchase of shares totaling $600,000 from a group of 15 potential investors. She was also assured orally that she would be engaged as the president of the corporation upon the commencement of business. Helen Banks was the principal investor, having subscribed to $300,000 of the shares of Multifashion. Dawson immediately began work on the incorporation of Multifashion, made several contracts for and on its behalf, and made cash expenditures of $1,000 in accomplishing these goals. On February 15, 1978, Banks died and her estate has declined to honor the commitment to purchase the Multifashion shares. At the first shareholders' meeting on April 5, 1978, the day the corporation came into existence, the shareholders elected a board of directors. With shareholder approval, the board took the following actions:

1. Adopted some but not all of the contracts made by Dawson.
2. Authorized legal action, if necessary, against the Estate of Banks to enforce Banks' $300,000 commitment.
3. Declined to engage Dawson in any capacity (Banks had been her main supporter).
4. Agreed to pay Dawson $750 for those cash outlays which were deemed to be directly beneficial to the corporation and rejected the balance.

Required: Answer the following, setting forth reasons for any conclusions stated.

Discuss the legal implications of each of the above actions taken by the board of directors of Multifashion.

Part b. Duval is the chairman of the board and president of Monolith Industries, Inc. He is also the largest individual shareholder, owning 40 percent of the shares outstanding. The corporation is publicly held, and there is a dissenting minority. In addition to his position with Monolith, Duval owns 85 percent of Variance Enterprises, a corporation created under the laws of the Bahamas. During 1977 Carlton, the president of Apex Industries, Inc., approached Duval and suggested that a tax-free merger of Monolith and Apex made good sense to him and that he was prepared to recommend such a course of action to the Apex board and to the shareholders. Duval studied the proposal and decided that Apex was a most desirable candidate for acquisition. Duval informed the president of Variance about the overture, told him it was a real bargain, and suggested

that Variance pick it up for cash and notes. Not hearing from Duval or Monolith, Carlton accepted an offer from Variance and the business was sold to Variance. Several dissenting shareholders of Monolith learned the facts surrounding the Variance acquisition and have engaged counsel to represent them. The Variance acquisition of Apex proved to be highly profitable.

Required: Answer the following, setting forth reasons for any conclusions stated.

Discuss the rights of the dissenting Monolith shareholders and the probable outcome of a legal action by them.

Problem 3   Declaration of Dividends (1180,L2a)

(7 to 10 minutes)

Part a. The Dexter Corporation has not paid a dividend since 1970 on its 7% non-cumulative preferred stock. In the years 1970-1973 the company had net losses which threatened to impair its financial position. Since 1974 the company has had earnings sufficient to pay the preferred stock dividend. In fact, earnings have gradually increased since 1974, and by 1976 Dexter had recouped all losses which occurred in the years 1970-1973. During the years 1974-1979 the profits were credited to retained earnings.

The funds were neither committed to physical plant or equipment nor did the board indicate that it had long range plans calling for such a commitment. Preferred shareholders had complained at board meetings regarding the repeated passing over of preferred dividends. The board's actions were explained on the grounds of pessimism about the company's and the economy's outlook and therefore, the need to build up adequate additional reserves to provide for the possibility of future losses. The board's outlook during the time in question could properly be categorized as one of pessimism and conservatism.

On January 15, 1980, the board decided to pay the 7% divdend on the preferred stock and a large dividend on the common stock. The preferred shareholders were irate. A group of preferred shareholders have commenced a suite seeking an injunction against Dexter and its board of directors prohibiting the payment of dividends on the common stock unless it first pays dividends on the non-cumulative preferred for previous years to the extent that the corporation had net earnings available for payment.

Required:
Answer the following, setting forth reasons for any conclusions stated.
Will the preferred shareholders prevail?

MULTIPLE CHOICE ANSWERS

1.	d	9.	c	17.	c	25.	d	33.	b
2.	b	10.	a	18.	a	26.	b	34.	c
3.	c	11.	d	19.	c	27.	b	35.	c
4.	d	12.	a	20.	c	28.	d	36.	b
5.	d	13.	c	21.	a	29.	c	37.	c
6.	b	14.	b	22.	b	30.	d	38.	a
7.	a	15.	b	23.	a	31.	c	39.	a
8.	b	16.	a	24.	c	32.	b	40.	d

EXPLANATION OF MULTIPLE CHOICE ANSWERS

1. (1180,L1,10)   (d) If stock certificates endorsed in blank are lost and then later sold by the finder to a bona fide purchaser, the BFP will take the certificates free of any claims by the prior owner. Waldorf purchased for value, in good faith and without notice of any adverse claim, thus he qualifies as a BFP. Neither Apex nor Waldorf would have any liability to Hargrove. This makes answer (d) correct.

2. (580,L1,6)   (b)   A consolidation is the unifying of two or more corporations into one new corporation, extinguishing both existing corporations. Therefore, answer (b) is the correct answer since neither corporation will survive the consolidation. Answer (a) is incorrect because under the Internal Revenue Code reorganizations, including statutory mergers or consolidations, receive non-recognition treatment for tax purposes. Answer (c) is incorrect because the rights of the creditors of the consolidating corporations are in no way impaired by the consolidation. Before a corporation can engage in a consolidation or merger, shareholder approval must be obtained. Approval by a majority is normally sufficient but some states demand approval by two-thirds of the shareholders.

3. (580,L1,7)   (c)   The correct answer is (c) because the Internal Revenue Service has the right to attack the reasonableness of salary payments and not permit the deduction on the tax return. The attorney general and Securities and Exchange Commission have no authority to question the reasonableness of salary payments.

4. (580,L1,8)   (d)   Answer (d) is the correct choice because a corporation is limited to the amount of unappropriated retained earnings for purchases of treasury stock. Answer (a) is incorrect because no treasury stock transactions, either purchases or sales, result in taxable gains or losses. Answer (b) is incorrect because it is legal to hold preferred or common shares as treasury stock. Answer (c) is also incorrect because it is *not* required to be stated in the articles

of incorporation that a corporation be allowed to reacquire outstanding shares of its own stock.

5. (580,L1,9)   (d)   A corporation is recognized as a separate legal entity except when the creation of or transfer of property to the corporation is used to perpetrate a fraud upon creditors. In these situations, the courts may disregard the entity and "pierce the corporate veil," leaving the shareholders with unlimited liability for corporate obligations. Therefore, the correct answer is (d). One advantage of a corporation is the limited liability of its owners, thus this is a proper motive for creating a corporation. Creating a corporation for tax savings is also a valid reason for forming a corporation. Answer (c) is incorrect because a wholly owned subsidiary is recognized as a separate legal entity unless it is merely an "agent" or instrumentality of its parent corporation.

6. (580,L1,12)   (b)   An *ultra vires* doctrine applies when a corporation enters a contract outside the scope of its express or implied authority granted by its articles of incorporation. Answer (b) is correct because since the state or shareholder has the right to object to an *ultra vires* act, a competitor could not object. A shareholder can institute a derivative action against directors and officers to recover damages for such acts. Answers (a) and (c) are incorrect because when an *ultra vires* contract has been executed on one side, most state courts hold the nonperforming party may not raise the defense of *ultra vires.* Answer (d) is incorrect because when both parties have performed, neither party may sue to rescind an *ultra vires* contract.

7. (580,L1,13)   (a)   Grandiose has a fiduciary duty to the corporation through his ability to control the board of directors. He is in effect a director since he has 51% control. A director may deal with the corporation only if he does so openly and in good faith, i.e., permitting the board to decide free from Grandiose's influence. If a profit is derived at the corporations's expense, the director must account for the profit made. Answer (b) is incorrect because the board is not independent of the interested party. Answer (c) is incorrect because Grandiose must account for the profit to the corporation. Answer (d) is incorrect because a promissory note is not valid to support the sale of stock. The purchase of shares requires the exchange of cash, property, or past services.

8. (580,L1,14)   (b)   A corporation "doing business" in a state other than that of incorporation must comply with that state's license requirements. This usually requires filing a certificate of authority. The concept of doing business involves something more than

isolated transactions. Answer (a) is incorrect because a corporation is not required to incorporate in a state in which it does business. Answer (c) is incorrect because Destiny is a foreign corporation in any state in which it does business other than that state in which it is incorporated. Answer (d) is incorrect because Destiny needs to comply only with the incorporation laws in its state of incorporation, in this case, Nevada.

9.   (580,L1,16)   (c)   Plimpton has breached his subscription contract with the Billiard Ball Corporation, and is therefore liable for the remainder of the unpaid subscription price. Shares may be purchased for money, services already rendered, and property. Promissory notes are not proper consideration for the purchase of shares. Plimpton is liable to creditors for the balance due on the subscription price. This is true even if Plimpton transfers the shares to an innocent third party. The issuing corporation has a lien on those shares that have not been paid for fully. However, this lien would not be effective against an innocent third party purchaser unless the lien was conspicuously noted on the stock certificate. Plimpton's failure to pay the full purchase price of the shares would not change his limited liability concerning corporate debts.

10.   (577,L1,15)   (a)   A corporation may not pay dividends if it is insolvent or would become insolvent as a result of paying the dividends. For this purpose, insolvency in the equity sense is used, i.e., unable to pay debts as they become due in the usual course of business. In contrast, the bankruptcy definition of insolvency is liabilities in excess of assets. Thus current liabilities, current assets and earned surplus do not determine solvency in the equity sense.

11.   (576,L2,21)   (d)   Normally a board of directors may only act at a meeting, and the common-law rule is that a quorum is a majority. But recently the law has developed to allow a board of directors to act more informally, i.e., without a meeting, if there is unanimous consent and if not so precluded by the articles of incorporation or the by-laws. Thus all the directors must consent.

12.   (1175,L2,22)   (a)   Surplus of a corporation means net assets in excess of stated capital. Liquid assets in excess of current needs are net quick assets. Total assets in excess of total liabilities is net assets. Contributed capital is capital paid into the corporation not in the conduct of business, i.e., not earned surplus (retained earnings).

13.   (1175,L2,26)   (c)   Net assets of a corporation means the amount by which total assets exceed total liabilities. Current assets less current liabilities is known as working capital. Liquid assets less current liabilities is known as a net quick asset.

14.   (1175,L2,28)   (b)   Mr. Parker must pay par value or greater ($30 times 100 shares) to escape any contingent liability. The answer is $3,000 because the question asked how much must he pay for the "shares" of stock, not how much per share (or the answer would be $30). If he pays less than par value, he may be liable to creditors for the difference between the amount paid and par value. Stock issued for less than par or stated value is known as watered stock (a form of fraud on the corporation's creditors).

15.   (1175,L2,29)   (b)   Mr. Jason's shares are 50% paid for. He has paid $200 cash and cancelled $300 salary owed him. Obligations for future services (promise to render $100 worth of) and for future payment (note for $400) are not valid payment for capital stock. If and when he performs the services and pays the note, his shares will be fully paid.

16.   (1175,L2,30)   (a)   Since there were 10,000 shares outstanding, a dividend of one share for every 10 shares outstanding had an effect of increasing outstanding shares by 1,000. Stated value is $1, so stated capital must be increased by $1,000. The $1,000 is transferred from earned surplus (retained earnings) to stated capital which results in $11,000 in stated capital.

17.   (1178,L1,10)   (c)   Note the requirement is the statement which is incorrect; although Dexter may not bring an action in a state where it has not properly registered to do business, any corporation may defend itself if it is sued. Answers (a), (b), and (d) are not the correct choice because their statements are generally true. Answer (a) is incorrect because it is common for state laws to provide the secretary of state as an agent for purposes of legal service on corporations that have failed to appoint a registered agent in that state. Answer (b) is incorrect because it is generally true that a corporation can cure the failure to register properly and after so doing is permitted to maintain an action in that state's courts. Answer (d) is incorrect because the attorney general of each state can recover all back fees and franchise taxes plus penalties against corporations who failed to register.

18. (1178,L1,14) (a)   Promissory notes (executory promises) are not sufficient consideration for the issuance of shares of corporate stock. Services actually performed, shares of stock in another corporation, and intangible property rights do constitute good consideration for the issuance of corporate stock. Consideration for the issuance of stock must actually be received. Promises to perform in the future are not adequate.

19. (1178,L1,15) (c)   The subscriber, Watson, may not revoke the agreement to purchase stock in the Marvel Corporation for a period of six months in the absence of special circumstances. Under the Model Business Corporation Act, preincorporation stock subscriptions are deemed to be continuing offers which are irrevocable for purposes of administrative convenience for a period of six months. Answer (a) is incorrect because a notice indicating withdrawal, even if written, will not be valid until the expiration of six months. Answer (b) is incorrect because a simple transfer of an agreement does not constitute a novation and thus the assigning party remains liable. Answer (d) is incorrect also because a subscriber can only avoid liability during the six-month period by obtaining the unanimous consent of the other subscribers.

20. (1178,L1,19) (c)   The board of directors has the power and duty to determine the value of property received for stock. In the absence of fraud, such judgment shall be conclusive. Answer (a) is incorrect because cash, property, and services performed are all good consideration for both par and no-par stock. Answer (b) is incorrect because, as stated above, it is within the power and duty of the board of directors to fix the value of property received for stock. Shareholders have no right to determine the value of no-par stock. Answer (d) is not as correct because directors are merely required to exercise ordinary care and prudence in the exercise of their duties. They are not liable for honest mistakes in judgment.

21. (1174,L3,39) (a)   Even though an association may not attain the status of a de jure or de facto corporation, it might be deemed a corporation by estoppel as to a specific transaction. Corporation by estoppel is an equitable doctrine to which courts resort to prevent injustice. Thus, an association might be held liable for torts of its agents or treated as a corporation for tax purposes on this doctrine. The association could also recover on a loan which it made in order that the borrower would not be unjustly enriched. The corporation by estoppel doctrine applies only to specific transactions, however, and the association faces the danger of legal action by the state.

22. (574,L3,39) (b)   Alpha would not obtain the status of a de jure corporation because of the failure to comply with all the filing requirements. Therefore, answer (a) is false. Since there was a valid law under which the corporation could have been formed; a bona fide attempt was made to comply with the filing requirements; and corporate powers were exercised; a de facto corporation would be held to exist. The shareholders would not be treated as partners, but would have limited liability and agreements entered would be enforceable against the corporation if they would have been enforceable against a de jure corporation. The status of the corporation could only be attacked by the state in a quo warranto proceeding.

23. (574,L3,40) (a)   If pre-incorporation agreements are to be enforced against the resulting corporation, the corporation (after coming into existence) must adopt the agreements. The corporation is not automatically bound by any pre-incorporation agreement. Therefore, answer (b) is false. Answer (c) is false, because express adoption of a pre-incorporation agreement is not necessary. Adoption may be implied from the corporation's acts, such as receiving the benefits of Wentz's services. Even if the agreement is adopted, either expressly or by implication, Korn is still liable under the contract. Answer (a) is the best answer, since in that situation, the corporation adopted the contract and bound itself to the terms of the contract.

24. (574,L3,41) (c)   Directors may deal with the corporation if there is full disclosure and a disinterested majority approves the transaction. This is the situation in answer (c). Gold is not required to sell the property at the price which he acquired the property, nor would the sale be void under the self-dealing rule. The self-dealing rule allows a director to deal with the corporation as long as the transaction is conducted openly and approved by a disinterested majority. Nor is there any reason to require Gold to sell the property to the corporation at Gold's purchase price. Gold has owned the land for numerous years and should be expected to receive a profit from his investment.

25. (574,L3,47) (d)   A corporation may repurchase its own stock only out of existing, earned, and/or capital surplus and may not do so if this would

cause the corporation to become insolvent. Stockholder approval is not required for the repurchase of the corporation stock by the corporation, nor must the corporation afford other shareholders a right of pro rata redemption. Repurchased shares may either be retired or retained as treasury stock.

26. (574,L3,48) (b) In this situation, Loe is issuing 300 shares of previously authorized stock in exchange for the assets of Zeta. As long as this action does not "water" previously issued stock, it may be accomplished by a majority vote of the board of directors present at the directors' meeting, provided a quorum is present. Shareholder approval is not required and present shareholders have no preemptive rights since such rights apply only to newly authorized capital stock. "Watered stock" is stock issued for overvalued assets.

27. (574,L3,49) (b) Treasury stock is stock which is authorized, issued, but not outstanding, having been either returned to or acquired by the corporation. Treasury stock cannot be voted or participate in dividends or distributions. It can, however, be resold without regard to par value or pre-emptive rights at the decision of the board of directors.

28. (1174,L3,33) (d) For non-cumulative preferred stock, if a dividend is not paid, the obligation to pay the dividend ceases even though it is earned, should there be a valid business reason for retention of the earnings. Usually preferred stock has no voting rights, but absent the usual provision in the certificate of incorporation which provides that preferred has no voting rights, preferred stock has the same voting rights as common stock. The preferences given preferred stock must be stated. Therefore, in this situation, the 8% non-cumulative preferred has no preference in the distribution of assets nor may it participate in earnings over and above the 8% annual dividend.

29. (1174,L3,35) (c) One of the attributes of a corporation is its perpetual existence irrespective of the lives of its owners. The death of a corporation's sole shareholder would not result in the termination. Ownership would change to the deceased's heirs. The insolvency or appointment of a receiver does not terminate the existence of a corporation. Reorganization under the federal bankruptcy laws may result in the termination of the corporation, and the creation of a new corporation to conduct the business of the old corporation (this is not always the case). The best answer to this question is (c). In a consolidation with another corporation, both of the consolidating corporations are terminated and a new corporation

is formed. By definition, a consolidation cannot occur without the termination of a corporation's existence.

30. (1174,L3,36) (d) A stockholder has a common law right to inspect the books of the corporation including the list of stockholders. This right may not be denied unless the stockholder's purpose is hostile to the corporation or the stockholder is attempting to use the corporation's books and records for unwarranted purposes. Stockholders may readily inspect the books in attempt to uncover corporate mismanagement. A dissident stockholder must also be given a list of corporation's shareholders if he is attempting to oust the management and proposes a proxy fight. Federal securities regulation requires that the corporation supply such a list and also mail the dissident's proxy material. The dissident shareholder, however, must pay the cost of the mailing. Regarding Walker's planned negligence suit, it is unnecessary that he prove personal gain on the part of the directors. Directors are liable for damages resulting from lack of reasonable care regardless of personal gain.

31. (1174,L3,38) (c) Thomas, because he was acting for a non-existent principal and had knowledge that Fair Realty was unaware, is personally liable to Fair Realty on the contract. The corporation cannot subsequently adopt the contract, because this would be a ratification of an agent's unauthorized act. For a ratification to be effective, the principal must have been in existence at the time the act occurred. However, a novation regarding the contract would relieve Thomas of liability. A novation would determine the old contract and would substitute Basic for Thomas, discharging all of Thomas' contractual obligations.

32. (1178,L1,22) (b) Professional corporations are only allowed in states which have enacted statutes permitting their incorporation. They are not normally allowed under the general corporation statutes. Answer (a) is incorrect because such a corporation will be recognized for federal tax purposes even if its goal is to save taxes. Answer (c) is incorrect because the typical statute provides that the professional being incorporated remains personally liable for his professional acts. His liability will only be limited for ordinary business debts of the corporation. Answer (d) is incorrect because most states now permit the creation of professional corporations by doctors and similar professional persons.

MAY 1981 ANSWERS

33. (581,L1,21)   (b)   There is no provision requiring the surviving corporation of a tax-free statutory merger to apply for and obtain a favorable revenue ruling from the Treasury Department. Answers (a) and (c) are incorrect because the board of directors and shareholders of both corporations must approve the merger. Answer (d) is incorrect since only securities issued in conjunction with a court supervised reorganization are exempt from the registration requirements of the Securities Act of 1933. For purposes of the act, the shares exchanged between Union and Universal would be "offered" and "sold".

34. (581,L1,22)   (c)   Consideration for the issuance of shares by a corporation may be paid in cash, property or prior services. The following items do not constitute consideration for common stock: promise to perform future services, promise to pay (e.g., a promissory note). Answer (c), services to be performed for the corporation, is the only one that would not act as consideration for the issuance of shares. Answers (a), (b) and (d) all qualify as proper consideration for shares.

35. (581,L1,23)   (c)   Promoters are persons who originate and organize the formation of a corporation. They have a fiduciary duty to act for the corporation and its shareholders. For Bixler to retain the profits made from the sale of property to the corporation, he must make full disclosure to and receive approval from either the board of directors or existing shareholders. Since Bixler did not comply with these procedures, the $45,000 would be considered secret profits and must be returned to the corporation even though the building might have a market value of $200,000. Thus, answers (b) and (d) are incorrect. Answer (a) is incorrect since the promoter may enter into preincorporation contracts (e.g., employment contracts, options on property) on behalf of the corporation. The corporation is not liable on these contracts until it adopts such agreements or enters a novation (a second agreement whereby corporation replaces the promoter under the same terms as the preincorporation contract). The corporation cannot ratify the agreement since the corporate entity was not in existence when the promoter entered the contract.

36. (581,L1,24)   (b)   When a corporation purchases its own stock these shares are classified as treasury shares if not cancelled. Treasury shares are issued but not outstanding; these shares cannot be voted on and do not receive dividends. Answer (a) is incorrect because a corporation is required to purchase treasury stock with capital surplus. Capital surplus consists of earned surplus (retained earnings) and paid-in-surplus (the amount paid for stock over par or stated value). It is illegal for a corporation to buy treasury stock with legal capital (par value of issued stock). Answer (c) is untrue because the corporation would have to comply with SEC requirements when the treasury stock was resold. Answer (d) is incorrect since a corporation never recognizes gains or losses on transactions with its own stock.

37. (581,L1,25)   (c)   The fact that the corporation was paying a 10% stock dividend instead of a cash distribution would not hinder the IRS from attacking the accumulation of earnings. Answer (a) is incorrect because stockholders can compel the declaration of a dividend when withholding dividends would be a clear abuse of the board of directors' discretion, even when such a dividend policy is not fraudulent. The Code does not exempt publicly held corporations from the accumulation provisions, therefore, answer (b) is incorrect. Answer (d) is incorrect because the IRS cannot compel the corporation to distribute earnings and profits that have unreasonably accumulated. However, the corporation is subject to an additional tax on earnings retained in excess of $150,000 if such retention is unreasonable.

38. (581,L1,26)   (a)   Treasury stock may be disposed of at the discretion of the board of directors through a sale or through the declaration of dividends to shareholders. Answer (b) is incorrect since the original public offering was sufficiently long ago to require the filing of a new registration statement before selling these treasury shares. Answer (c) is incorrect because treasury shares cannot be voted. Answer (d) is incorrect because treasury shares exchanged for the stock of another publicly held corporation are considered to be "offered" and "sold" for the purposes of the Securities Act of 1933. Therefore, a registration statement would have to be filed and approved before the transaction could be completed.

39. (581,L1,27)   (a)   Both the board of directors and the shareholders of a corporation must approve a fundamental change in the corporate structure. Examples of fundamental corporate changes would be: dissolution of corporation, amendment of corporate charter, increase of capital stock, etc. Larkin would need to amend its corporate charter to increase the number of authorized shares before engaging in the stock split. Answer (b) is incorrect because stock splits are normally exempt from income tax because the shareholder-recipient maintains the same proportionate interest of ownership. Answer (c) is incorrect because a stock split decreases the par value in proportion to the increase in the number of shares.

Therefore, total par value is unchanged. Answer (d) is incorrect because trustees are to include shares received through a stock split or stock dividend in the principal (corpus) of the trust. Cash dividends are considered income when allocating trust items between principal (corpus) and income beneficiaries.

40. (581,L1,28)   (d)   The compensation of corporate officers is fixed by a resolution of the board of directors. If none is fixed, the law implies that the officer is paid a reasonable sum for his services. Any action by the shareholders serves merely to confirm the board's action concerning the officers' salaries. It is not needed as a matter of law, therefore, answer (c) is incorrect. Answer (a) is incorrect because the directors can confirm the officers' salaries even though not legally needed. Answer (b) is incorrect because the IRS has the power to attack any officer's salary as unreasonable. If the compensation is deemed unreasonable, the IRS treats the excessive amount as a constructive dividend.

ANSWER OUTLINE

Problem 1   Dividends; Contracts with Director;
             Director Fiduciary Responsibility

a1.   Yes, property dividends may be paid by corporations
          With investments in stock of other companies
          Issuing company must be solvent
          Limited to unrestricted retained earnings (earned surplus)
             Decimile has retained earnings of $17/share

a2.   Yes, stock dividends may be paid by corporations
          The dividends must be charged to unrestricted retained earnings
             At not less than par value
          With the amount to be credited to stated capital

a3(a) Issuance of stock of another company is a property dividend
          Recipients must report FMV as dividend income
          Dividend income is ordinary income
             Subject to $100 dividend exclusion
          Recipient's basis in property dividend is FMV when received

a3(b) If Decimile Corporation issues its own stock as dividend
          It is a non-taxable transaction
          Recipients must reallocate original cost to total shares owned after distribution

b.   Loans by corporations must be for benefit of corporation
          If for corporate benefit, board of directors may approve
          Otherwise, stockholder approval is required
          Here, loan is for corporate benefit
             But chairman lacked authority and may be personally liable
             Board of directors should ratify, or recall loan

c1.   To avoid contracts with interested directors being void or voidable
          The relationship of interested directors is disclosed to those approving the contracts or
          Approval by board of directors without counting votes of interested directors, or
             Interested directors may be counted to establish quorum
          Shareholders, knowing of director interest, approve the contract, or
          The transaction must be fair and reasonable to corporation

c2.   Side payments to corporate directors violate fiduciary duty
          And probably constitutes a criminal act
          Towne must return money to Toy
          Toy Corporation could treat transaction as voidable

UNOFFICIAL ANSWER

Problem 1   Dividends; Contract with Director;
             Director Fiduciary Responsibility

Part a.

1.   Yes. The Model Business Corporation Act authorizes the declaration and payment of dividends in cash, property, or the shares of the corporation as long as the corporation is not insolvent and would not be rendered insolvent by the dividend payment. The act limits the payment of dividends in cash or property to the unreserved and unrestricted earned surplus of the corporation. Decimile meets this requirement since it has retained earnings of $17 per share. Thus, payment of the dividend in the shares of Integrated is permitted.

2.   Yes. The Model Business Corporation Act permits dividends to be declared and paid in the shares of the corporation. However, where the dividend is paid in its authorized but unissued shares, the payment must be out of unreserved and unrestricted surplus. Furthermore, when the shares paid as a dividend have a par value, they must be issued at not less than par value. Concurrent with the dividend payment, an amount of surplus equal to the aggregate par value of the shares issued as a dividend must be transferred to stated capital.

3.   (a) If the shares of Integrated stock are paid as a dividend to the noncorporate shareholders, the shareholders must include the fair market value of the Integrated shares as dividend income received. Such income is ordinary income subject to a $100 dividend exclu-

sion. The recipient taxpayer will have as a tax basis for the Integrated shares an amount equal to the fair market value of the stock received.

(b) If the shares of Decimile stock are paid as a dividend, the recipient taxpayer is not subject to tax upon receipt of the shares. Internal Revenue Code Section 305 provides that such stock dividends are not taxable. However, the recipient must allocate his basis (typically his cost) for the shares he originally owned to the total number he owned after the distribution.

Part b.

The Model Business Corporation Act specifically deals with loans to employees and directors. If the loan is not for the benefit of the corporation, then such a loan must be authorized by the shareholders. However, the board of directors may authorize loans to employees when and if the board decides that such loan or assistance may benefit the corporation. It would appear that the loan was made for the benefit of the corporation so the latter rule applies. However, the chairman's individual authorization clearly does not meet these statutory requirements and could subject him to personal liability. Therefore, a meeting of the board should be called to consider the ratification or recall of the loan.

Part c.

1.   The Model Business Corporation Act allows such transactions between a corporation and one or more of its directors or another corporation in which the director has a financial interest. The transaction is neither void nor voidable even though the director is present at the board meeting which authorized the transaction or because his vote is counted for such purpose if—

- The fact of such relationship or interest is disclosed or known to the board of directors or committee that authorizes, approves, or ratifies the contract or transaction by a vote or consent sufficient for the purpose without counting the votes or consents of such interested directors; or

- The fact of such relationship or interest is disclosed or known to the shareholders entitled to vote and they authorize, approve, or ratify such contract or transaction by vote or written consent; or

- The contract or transaction is fair and reasonable to the corporation. Common or interested directors may be counted in determining the presence of a quorum at a meeting of the board of

directors or a committee thereof that authorizes, approves, or ratifies such contract or transaction.

2.   A $50,000 payment to Towne would be a violation of his fiduciary duty to the corporation. In addition, it might be illegal depending upon the criminal law of the jurisdiction. In any case he would be obligated to return the amount to the corporation. Furthermore, the payment would constitute grounds for permitting Toy to treat the transaction as voidable.

ANSWER OUTLINE

Problem 2   Pre-Incorporation Contracts; Director Fiduciary Responsibility

a1.   Pre-incorporation contracts are not binding on new corporations
    Unless subsequently adopted by the new corporation
    Because corporation was not in existence at time of contract
    A new corporation enjoying benefits implies adoption
  Promoter has liability for the contract prior to incorporation
    Even after adoption by the corporation (as surety)
      Unless a novation releases promoter

a2.   Pre-incorporation subscribers are liable for stock subscriptions
    For a period of six months
    Unless revocation is allowed by the subscription agreement
    Or unless consented to by all other subscribers
  Subscriber's responsibility transfers to subscriber's estate

a3.   New corporation may adopt or reject pre-incorporation contracts
    Including employment contracts
    Permits corporations to make their own contracts
    Provides protection against self-serving promoter contracts

a4.   Dawson may be entitled to $1,000 if corporation received benefits
    I.e., per the doctrine of implied adoption (receiving benefits)
    Or under the doctrine of unjust enrichment

b. Corporate directors and officers are fiduciaries
    May not personally benefit through corporate deals
    Dissenting shareholders may recover from self-serving directors
    By suing derivatively on behalf of the corporation
    Thus it appears dissenting stockholders may have the Variance-Apex transaction voided
    Or have Apex transferred to Monolith including profits
    Alternatively, damages may be recovered directly from Duval

UNOFFICIAL ANSWER

Problem 2   Pre-Incorporation Contracts; Director Fiduciary Responsibility

Part a.

In general, pre-incorporation contracts are not binding upon a newly created corporation prior to their adoption by its board of directors. Overall, one would conclude that the board acted properly and legally with respect to the actions taken. Each item is discussed separately below.

1. The board's action was proper and within its discretion. Care, however, should be taken to avoid an implied adoption by having the corporation avail itself of some or all of the benefits of a contract while purporting to reject the contract. The corporation is not legally bound prior to adoption, because it was not in existence at the time the contract was made. Dawson, on the other hand, has liability on the contracts she made prior to incorporation. Moreover, with respect to the contracts adopted by the corporation, she assumes the status of a surety unless a novation was entered into, releasing Dawson of all liability. The nonexistent principal rule would apply to Dawson unless the contract she made was contingent upon the corporation's adopting it after coming into existence.

2. An exception is made to the general rule of pre-incorporation actions insofar as stock subscriptions are concerned. Due to necessity and practical considerations, the parties who agree to provide the capital vital to the corporation's creation are not permitted to withdraw their commitments for six months. The Model Business Corporation Act provides that "a subscription for shares of a corporation to be organized shall be irrevocable for a period of six months, unless provided by the terms of the subscription agreement or unless all of the subscribers consent to the revocation of such subscriptions." Hence, the subscription by Banks is valid and is a bona fide claim against the Estate of Banks.

3. The board of a newly created corporation is, at its inception, free to either adopt or reject pre-incorporation contracts made on behalf of the corporation. This general rule also applies to the employment contract of a promoter such as Dawson. The rationale for this rule is founded upon the belief that the corporation should not be shackled by commitments that it did not have an opportunity to adequately consider. In addition, promoters as a class have often abused their power and made what have proved to be self-serving contracts. Thus, the board acted properly, and it need not engage Dawson.

4. The only problem that arises is that Dawson was not paid in full. She might be entitled to the full $1,000 under two possible theories. The first is a contract implied in fact (an implied adoption) by the board accepting all the benefits of the $1,000 expenditure. The other theory would be a contract implied in law based upon unjust enrichment. Under this theory, if Dawson can prove that the corporation did receive benefits which were worth $1,000, she can recover the additional $250.

Part b.

Directors and officers of a corporation are fiduciaries in their relationship to the corporation they serve. As such, they can neither directly nor indirectly benefit in their dealings with or for the corporation. They cannot engage in transactions that are in violation of their fiduciary duty to protect and further the best interests of their principal. Making a secret profit or acquiring a personal advantage out of their office is an act which the corporation may seek to have set aside as voidable.

Based upon this general statement of directors' and officers' fiduciary duty, it appears that the dissenting shareholders could sue derivatively on behalf of Monolith. That is, they could institute legal action on behalf of and in the name of Monolith to set aside the Variance-Apex transaction and have the business transferred to Monolith along with the profits earned during the interim. As an alternative, they could seek to recover directly from Duval damages that would be payable to Monolith.

The result seems clear in light of the facts. First, the opportunity came to Duval in his capacity as the chairman of the board and president of Monolith. Next, he did not pursue the matter but instead informed Variance's president of the opportunity to purchase Apex. Duval's conduct appears to be a case of self-dealing, duplicity, secrecy, and perhaps deceit. Taking the law and all the circumstances surrounding the purchase of Apex assets by Variance, Monolith's dissenting shareholders would probably be successful in a derivative shareholder action.

ANSWER OUTLINE

Problem 3   Declaration of Dividends

a.   No, preferred stockholders will not prevail
        Stockholder - Corporation relationship essentially contractual
        Noncumulative preferred stock
            Dividends declared at discretion of board of directors
            Passed over dividends are lost
        Judgement of board of directors concerning dividends not overruled unless there is dishonesty or clear abuse of discretion

UNOFFICIAL ANSWER

Problem 3   Declaration of Dividends

Part a.

No. The stock in question was noncumulative preferred. The relationship of the preferred shareholders to the corporation is essentially contractual and the stock certificate is, in fact, the contract. The contract agreed to by the owners of this preferred stock was essentially that if the board of directors passed over the declaration of the preferred dividend in a given year or years, it would not accumulate but would be lost. Whether or not to declare a dividend is within the discretion of the board. Its judgment is not over-ridden by the courts unless there is dishonesty or a clear abuse of discretion. The fact that there were earnings sufficient to pay preferred dividends after 1973, that the funds were not actually expended for purchase of physical plant or property, or that the earnings were not being accumulated for the purpose of expansion are not sufficient to persuade a court to grant the injunction. Although the board was pessimistic and conservative, that would not

be an abuse of their discretion. The Model Business Corporation Act states that "the board of directors of a corporation may, from time to time, declare . . . dividends," thus retaining discretion in the board regarding dividend declaration. In conclusion, the law respects the business judgment of directors in determining whether to declare dividends. The board is afforded wide discretion in such matters, and unless there is an abuse of such discretion, a court will not interfere with its judgment.

MULTIPLE CHOICE QUESTIONS (1-25)

1. Divco Corporation manufactured and sold a high quality line of distinctive calculators. In order to fully realize the potential of the products, it decided to engage in a franchising arrangement with selected outlets throughout the country. Its basic arrangement was to grant to each dealer the exclusive right to sell in a designated area and each dealer agreed not to sell outside its allotted geographic area. Which of the following **best** describes the status of the law?

    a. Such arrangements are *per se* illegal.

    b. Divco **must** sell on consignment, thereby retaining title, in order to avoid illegality.

    c. Such franchising arrangements will be tested under the rule of reason and as long as they are found to be reasonable they are legal.

    d. Such arrangements are specifically declared to be illegal under existing antitrust statutes.

2. Jay Manufacturing Company sells high quality, high-priced lawn mowers to retailers throughout the United States. Jay unilaterally announced suggested retail prices in its advertisements. Jay also informed retailers that its products would not be sold to them if the retailers used them as "loss leaders" or "come-ons." There was no requirement that any retailer agree to sell at the suggested prices or refrain from selling at whatever price they wished. Monroe Sales, Inc., a large home supply discounter, persistently engaged in loss-leader selling of the Jay mower. Jay has terminated sales to Monroe and declined to do any further business with it. Monroe claims that Jay has violated the antitrust laws. Under the circumstances, which is a correct statement?

    a. The arrangement in question is an illegal joint boycott.

    b. The arrangement in question amounts to price-fixing and is illegal per se.

    c. The mere unilateral refusal to deal with Monroe is not illegal under antitrust laws.

    d. Even if it were found that in fact the over-whelming preponderance of retailers had willingly agreed to follow the suggested prices, Jay would not have violated antitrust laws.

3. Congress recently amended the antitrust laws to provide stiffer penalties and increased sanctions for violation of the various acts' provisions. Which of the following represents an incorrect statement of the changed provisions?

    a. The maximum fine for corporations was increased to one million dollars.

    b. Violations of the Sherman Act are now classified as felonies with a maximum prison term of 3 years.

    c. Punitive damages obtainable in private anti-trust actions have been increased from 3 times to 5 times actual damages.

    d. The maximum fine for individuals has been increased to $100,000.

4. Marble Manufacturing, Inc., produces a high quality, trademarked line of distinctive clocks which it sells to selected wholesalers and retailers. The clocks are sold in free and open competition with the clocks of many other manufacturers. The selection of the wholesalers and retailers is dependent upon their agreeing to the pricing policies of Marble. Several other manufacturers also have similar marketing arrangements. The above-described marketing arrangement is

    a. Legal, in that Marble is merely "meeting the competition" of other clock manufacturers.

    b. Legal, since it is a permissible resale price maintenance agreement.

    c. Fully subject to the general antitrust prohibitions against price fixing.

    d. To be tested under the rule of reason, since the agreement is not among competitors but rather between a supplier and its customers.

5. The Duplex Corporation has been charged by the United States Justice Department with an "attempt to monopolize" the duplex industry. In defending itself against such a charge, Duplex will prevail if it can establish

    a. It had no intent to monopolize the duplex industry.

    b. Its percentage share of the relevant market was less than 50%.

    c. Its activities do not constitute an unreasonable restraint of trade.

    d. It does not have monopoly power.

6. The Flick Corporation sold various interrelated products that it manufactured. One of the items was manufactured almost exclusively by Flick and sold throughout the United States. Flick realized the importance of this product to its purchasers and decided to capitalize on the situation by requiring all purchasers to take at least two other products in order to obtain the item over which it has almost complete market control. At Flick's spring sales meeting, its president informed the entire sales force that they were to henceforth sell only to those customers who agreed to take the additional products. As a result of this plan, gross

sales of the additional items increased by more than $1 million. Which of the following best describes the legality of the above situation?

    a.   It is illegal only if the products are patented products.

    b.   It is an illegal tying arrangement.

    c.   It is legal as long as the price charged to retailers for the other products is competitive.

    d.   It is legal if the retailers do not complain about purchasing the other products.

7.   Wanton Corporation, its president, and several other officers of the corporation are found guilty of conspiring with its major competitor to fix prices. Which of the following sanctions would not be applicable under federal antitrust laws?

    a.   Suspension of corporate right to engage in interstate commerce for not more than one year.

    b.   Treble damages.

    c.   Seizure of Wanton's property illegally shipped in interstate commerce.

    d.   Fines against Wanton and fines and imprisonment of its president and officers.

8.   Which of the following activities engaged in by a corporation will not be deemed illegal under the antitrust law?

    a.   A price-fixing agreement with competitors aimed at lowering prices to a reasonable level.

    b.   The charging of a price aimed at maximizing its profits based upon economic analysis of supply and demand for its products.

    c.   Participating in a plan suggested by the trade association aimed at territorial allocations of markets to cut costs.

    d.   The payment of brokerage commissions to the purchasers of goods.

9.   The Donner Corporation has obtained a patent on a revolutionary coin-operated washing machine. It is far superior to the existing machines currently in use. Which of the following actions taken by Donner will not result in a violation of federal antitrust law?

    a.   Maintaining the resale price for machines it sells to distributors.

    b.   Obtaining a near total monopolization of the market as a result of the patent.

    c.   Requiring the purchasers of the machines to buy from Donner all their other commonplace supplies connected with the use of the machine.

    d.   Joining in a boycott with other appliance manufacturers to eliminate a troublesome discount distributor.

10.   Expansion Corporation is an aggressive, large-sized conglomerate. It is seeking to obtain control of several additional corporations including Resistance Corporation. Expansion does not currently buy from, sell to, or compete with Resistance. Which of the following statements applies to this proposed take-over?

    a.   Since **Expansion** does not buy from, sell to, or compete with Resistance, antitrust laws do not apply.

    b.   If Expansion can consummate the acquisition before there is an objection to it, the acquisition cannot subsequently be set aside.

    c.   The acquisition is likely to be declared illegal if there will be reciprocal buying and there is a likelihood that other entrants into the market would be precluded.

    d.   The acquisition is legal on its face if there will be cost efficiency resulting from combined marketing and advertising.

11.   The Justice Department is contemplating commencing an action against Lion Corporation for monopolizing the off-shore oil drilling business in violation of Section 2 of the Sherman Act. Which of the following would be **Lion's** best defense against such an action?

    a.   Since the drilling is off-shore, interstate commerce is not involved.

    b.   The monopoly was originally the result of a long since expired patent.

    c.   Lion had no specific wrongful intent to monopolize.

    d.   Lion's market share is such that it does not have the power to fix prices or to exclude competitors.

12.   Marvel Toys, Inc., manufactures and sells toys to Gem Stores, a large department store chain, and to Fantastic Discounts, a major toy retailer, at prices below its sales price of similar toys to other retailers in the market area. Its pricing policy vis-a-vis Gem is based solely upon the fact that Gem is a new customer and the low prices were quoted in order to obtain its business and thereby eliminate Marvel's unused production capacity. For Fantastic, the lower prices are charged in order to meet the identical prices legally charged by a competitor. In assessing the potential violation of antitrust laws against price discrimination, it would appear that Marvel Toys

a. Has not violated the antitrust laws as long as none of its competitors can show damages.

b. Has a valid defense with respect to its sales to Gem.

c. Has not violated the antitrust laws with respect to its sales to Fantastic.

d. Will not have committed any violation if it was operating at a loss at the time of the sales.

13. Paperbox Company is one of four equal-sized paper-carton container companies whose sales constitute 90% of paper container sales in the relevant market. Competition has been intense. In order to control costs within reasonable limits the chief executive officers of the four companies have agreed that they will set a maximum price, agreed upon by them, to be paid for the pulp they purchase. From an antitrust standpoint

a. No antitrust violation occurs if the price set is reasonable.

b. The agreement is a per se violation of the antitrust laws.

c. No antitrust violation occurs if the suppliers of raw pulp agree that the price is reasonable and works in the best interest of all parties.

d. The agreement will not violate the antitrust laws if it can be shown that it is necessary to prevent insolvency of one of the parties to the agreement who controls 30% of the market.

14. In attacking a corporation having 15% of the relevant market in a highly concentrated (oligopolistic) industry, the Justice Department will most likely prevail under the Sherman Act's monopoly provisions if it shows that

a. A significant amount of sales in interstate commerce is involved.

b. The five leading corporations in the industry controlled 60% of the relevant market.

c. The corporation through product innovation has improved its percentage shares from 12.5% to 15% over the past three years.

d. The corporation has manifested a specific intent to monopolize.

15. Pickwick is a troublesome chain store appliance dealer. He constantly engaged in price cutting on widely advertised name products in order to lure customers to his store so that he could sell them other products. The "big three" manufacturers agreed that Pickwick could no longer sell their products unless he ceased and desisted from such practices. Pickwick refused and the three manufacturers promptly cut off his supply of their branded products. Which of the following is a correct statement?

a. Since the conduct described was unilateral, and Pickwick did not agree to stop his price cutting, the manufacturers' conduct is legal.

b. The conduct described is a joint boycott, and as such is illegal per se.

c. If the harm to the public was minor, and the products were readily available from other appliance dealers in a market marked by free and open competition, there would be no violation of the law.

d. Since a businessman has the freedom to choose with whom he will deal, the conduct in question is not illegal under antitrust law.

16. George Corporation entered into contracts to supply all of the requirements of 1,000 dealers in New England. In these contracts the dealers agreed not to sell products competitive with those of George. These dealers constituted 20% of the total number of dealers in the area. George Corporation may

a. Be enjoined from enforcing the contracts if they might substantially lessen competition.

b. Be enjoined only to the extent that its own outlets operated by its agents are involved.

c. Not be enjoined because only 20% of the New England dealers are involved.

d. Be enjoined for violating the Robinson-Patman Act.

17. You were the auditor examining the financial statements of Mason Corporation and noted an extraordinary increase in the sales of certain items. Further inquiry revealed that Mason sold various interrelated products which it manufactured. One of the items was manufactured almost exclusively by them. This unique product was in great demand and was sold throughout the United States. Mason realized the importance of the product to its purchasers and decided to capitalize on the situation

by requiring all purchasers to take at least two of its other products if they wished to obtain the item over which it had almost complete market control. At the spring sales meeting the president of Mason informed the entire sales force that they were to henceforth sell only to those customers who agreed to take the additional products. He indicated that this was a great opportunity to substantially increase sales of other items. Under the circumstances, which of the following best describes the situation?

    a.   The plan is both ingenious and legal and should have been resorted to long ago.

    b.   The arrangement is an illegal tying agreement; hence per se illegal.

    c.   Since Mason did not have complete market control over the unique product in question, the arrangement is legal.

    d.   As long as the other products which must be taken are sold at a fair price to the buyers, the arrangement is legal.

18. Over a six-year period, Yeats Corporation acquired 46% of the outstanding stock of Glick, Inc. More than 40% of the shares so acquired were purchased from Glick's past and present directors. Both Glick and Yeats have capital, surplus, and undivided profits aggregating more than $1,000,000. Yeat's current directors owned stock in both corporations and were on the board of directors of each. Yeats utilized his ownership control to elect the remaining members of the board of directors and its own slate of officers for Glick. Glick and Yeats are manufacturers of goods which are in competition with each other throughout the United States. Since Yeats acquired control of Glick, Yeats' percentage share of the nationwide market has remained relatively stable. However, Yeats and Glick each by agreement have ceased marketing in certain geographical territories where it is more advantageous for the other to sell. Which of the following statements applies to the above situation?

    a.   There is nothing in the facts as revealed above which would constitute a violation of the federal antitrust laws.

    b.   The interlocking directorate is not illegal because less than 50% of the Glick stock is owned by Yeats.

    c.   The interlocking directorate is a clear violation of the federal antitrust laws.

    d.   There is no current violation of the federal antitrust law because there has been no marked improvement in the competitive position of Yeats or Glick.

19. The four largest manufacturers in their industry

have had a combined share of the market in excess of 80% each year for several years. As members of a trade association, certain officers of these corporations meet periodically to discuss various topics of mutual interest. Matters discussed include engineering design, production methods, product costs, market shares, merchandising policy, and inventory levels. Open discussion of pricing is scrupulously avoided. However, the representatives usually see each other after the association meetings and pricing is frequently discussed. These representatives have maintained prices in accordance with an informal oral agreement terminable at will by any company wishing to withdraw. They have never reduced their agreement to a written document or memorandum. The four corporations compete with each other in interstate commerce. Which of the following applies?

    a.   The members of the trade association may validly appoint the trade association as their representative to set minimum prices.

    b.   If the trade association suggested it, the distributors of the four corporations may legally enter an agreement among themselves to follow the industry leader's pricing policy.

    c.   The trade association could legally allocate marketing areas among its members.

    d.   The four corporations have illegally entered into a price maintenance agreement among themselves.

20. Super Sports, Inc., sells branded sporting goods and equipment throughout the United States. It sells to wholesalers, jobbers, and retailers who in turn resell the goods to their respective customers. The wholesalers and jobbers, who do not sell at retail, are charged lower prices than retailers, but are required to purchase in larger quantities than retailers with the cost savings inherent in such purchases accounting for the lower prices. The retailers are all charged the same prices but receive discounts for quantity purchases based exclusively upon the cost savings resulting from such quantity purchases. Girard, one of Super's retail customers, has demanded discounts comparable to those available to the wholesalers and jobbers in its vicinity. Super has refused to acquiesce in this demand. Therefore, Girard sues Super alleging an illegal price discrimination in violation of the Robinson-Patman Act. Which defense by Super listed below will be most likely to prevail?

    a.   Girard does not have the right to sue under the Robinson-Patman Act.

    b.   The discounts are functional, that is, Super's wholesalers and jobbers do not compete with retailers such as Girard.

c.   Super does not have the requisite intent to discriminate among its purchasers.

d.   The prices Super charges are reasonable, and its profit margins are low.

21.   The following facts arose during the examination of the financial statements of Western Manufacturing, Inc. Western, a large manufacturer of industrial products, is attempting to acquire a controlling block of shares of Davis, Inc., a competing manufacturer. Davis' market share is about 40% in the section of the United States in which Western and Davis compete. Western's share of this market is about 35%. Four other firms compete for the remaining 25%. Western's share of the national market is 20% and Davis' share is 8%. In the event that the Justice Department seeks to prevent the above acquisition, which of the following is the most likely result?

a.   The court would grant an injunction prohibiting the acquisition in question.

b.   The court would dismiss the Justice Department's action in that the relative shares of the two corporations are less than 30% if the entire United States is taken as the geographic market.

c.   The court would permit the acquisition and agree to review the case after a year's experience under the merger to determine its actual effect upon competition.

d.   The court would dismiss the Justice Department's action if Western could show that the acquisition would result in significant business efficiencies.

22.   Wonder Electronix, Inc., entered into "reasonable" minimum price-resale-maintenance agreements with the distributors of its trademarked products. The distributors willingly accepted the minimum price and it was in fact a "reasonable" price for the products. What is the legal status of this arrangement?

a.   It is subject to the rule of reason as contrasted with the per se illegality rule applicable to such price fixing among competitors.

b.   It is subject to the per se illegality rule.

c.   It will not be illegal if the product bears the label, trademark, or brand name of Wonder and it competes with like products of Wonder's competitors.

d.   It is exempt from antitrust law if the product is patented.

MAY 1981 QUESTIONS

23.   The Aden Corporation entered into its standard dealership contract with the Downtown Corporation. The contract provided Downtown with an exclusive right to sell Aden's products in Columbia County. Which of the following provisions, if included as a part of the contract, will **not** create a potential antitrust problem?

a.   Aden retains all rights, title, and interest to the goods shipped to Downtown.

b.   Downtown agrees to certain resale price ranges stipulated by Aden.

c.   Downtown may **not** sell any product which Aden Corporation designates as being competitive with its products.

d.   Downtown agrees **not** to sell to certain retailers designated by Aden as price cutters.

24.   The Radiant Furnace Company entered into agreements with retail merchants whereby they agreed not to sell beneath Radiant's minimum "suggested" retail price of $850 in exchange for Radiant's agreeing not to sell its furnaces at retail in their respective territories. The agreement does not preclude the retail merchants from selling competing furnaces. What is the legal status of the agreement?

a.   It is illegal even though the price fixed is reasonable.

b.   It is legal if the product is a trade name or trademarked item.

c.   It is legal if the power to fix maximum prices is **not** relinquished.

d.   It is illegal unless it can be shown that the parties to the agreement were preventing cut-throat competition.

25.   Global Reproductions, Inc., makes and sells high quality, expensive lithographs of the works of famous artists. It sells to art wholesalers throughout the United States. It requires that its wholesalers not purchase lithographs of competing companies during the three-year duration of the contract. They may sell all other types of pictures, including oil, watercolor and charcoal. The Federal Trade Commission has attacked the legality of this exclusive dealing arrangement. This exclusive dealing arrangement

a.   Is legal *per se* since its duration is less than five years.

b.   Could be found to be illegal under the Sherman, Clayton, and Federal Trade Commission Acts.

c.   Will be tested under the rule of reason, and only if found to be unreasonable, will be declared illegal.

d.   Is legal since the wholesalers are permitted to sell all other types of pictures.

PROBLEM

Problem 1   Price Fixing and Discrimination (577,L6)

(15 to 20 minutes)

Part b. The CPA firm of Christopher and Diana was engaged to audit the books of Starr Antenna Company. An examination of Starr's files revealed the threat of a lawsuit by Charles Grimm, the owner of Grimm's TV Sales and Service Company. An analysis of the pertinent facts revealed the following.

Grimm's complaint arose because Grimm could not obtain the quantity of television antennas ordered from Starr. The three other antenna manufacturers, who supplied the tri-state area in which Starr did business, would not sell antennas to Grimm. Grimm knows that several other retailers are encountering similar problems with Starr and the three major competitors. Diana, the partner in charge of the audit, found this to be a strange situation and talked with Baxter, Starr's Vice President of Marketing. Baxter explained that about a year ago there had been a period of "cutthroat" competition among the four major antenna manufacturers involved. In order to avoid a repetition of this disastrous situation, they had entered into an unwritten gentlemen's agreement to "limit output per manufacturer to the amount produced in the year immediately preceding that in which the cutthroat competition had occurred." They also agreed that each manufacturer would not sell to the acknowledged customers of the others. Baxter said there was still plenty of competition for new customers in the tri-state area and that they were contemplating raising the production limitation by 25%. He said that "this arrangement had made life a lot easier and profitable for all concerned." He also indicated that the prices charged were "reasonable" to the purchasers.

Required: Answer the following, setting forth reasons for any conclusions stated.

What are the legal problems and implications of the above facts?

Part c. The General Pen Company is one of the largest manufacturers of fountain pens and does business in every state in the United States. General developed a new line of prestige pens called the "Diamond Line" which it sold at a very high price. In order to uphold its prestige and quality appeal, General decided to maintain a high resale price. Consequently, it obtained agreements from department stores, jewelers, and other outlets not to sell the pen below the $15 suggested retail price. The Double Discount Department Store refused to sign the agreement and used the pen as a sales gimmick to attract customers. Double advertised and sold Diamond Line pens for $12, to which General objected. Double threatened General with a treble damage action for price-fixing if it did not withdraw its objections.

Required: Answer the following, setting forth reasons for any conclusions stated.

What are the legal problems and implications of the above facts?

Problem 2   Price Discrimination (1180,L2b)
(10 to 12 minutes)

Part b. In 1979 Banner was one of 38 retail Marco gasoline stations in greater Fort Wayne, Massachusetts, and one of 8 such stations in its particular sales territory. The nearest competing Marco station was 11 blocks away. Banner's supplier, Marvel Company, was a major integrated refiner and distributor of petroleum products. Like other Marco stations in Fort Wayne, Banner purchases gasoline from Marvel at 94.1 cents per gallon and resold it at 98.9 cents per gallon.

In September of 1979 Best by Test Oil Company, operator of a chain of 65 retail gasoline stations, opened its only Best by Test station in Fort Wayne diagonally across the street from Banner and began selling its gasoline at 96.9 cents per gallon. Best by Test was exclusively a retailer and did not compete with Marvel. This differential of 2 cents per gallon between Banner's and Best by Test's retail prices was the normal differential between "major" and "non-major" brands of gasoline. Subsequently however, beginning in December, Best by Test from time to time reduced its price, sometimes to 91.9 cents or 90.9 cents per gallon, and on each occasion Banner's sales suffered. Banner sought assistance from Marvel to meet Best by Test's competition. After four months of watchful waiting, Marvel gave Banner a discount of 1.7 cents per gallon in April 1980 to permit the latter to reduce its retail price to 95.9 cents per gallon to counter a Best by Test retail price of 94.9 cents per gallon, later lowered to 93.9 cents per gallon. At this point, other Marco dealers, located within a three and one-half mile radius of Banner, suffered substantial declines in sales; they had not received any discount from Marvel and had not reduced their retail prices. They observed some of their former customers buying gasoline from Banner. Those Marco retail stations which suffered losses as a result of Marvel's pricing policies have claimed a violation of federal antitrust law by Marvel and have brought legal action against it to recover damages.

Required:

Answer the following, setting forth reasons for any conclusions stated.

1.   Will the Marco retail stations which suffered losses prevail?

2.   What probable defense will Marvel assert in order to avoid liability?

MULTIPLE CHOICE ANSWERS

1.	c	6.	b	11.	d	16.	a	21.	a
2	c	7.	a	12.	c	17.	b	22.	b
3.	c	8.	b	13.	b	18.	c	23.	a
4.	c	9.	b	14.	d	19.	d	24.	a
5.	a	10.	c	15.	b	20.	b	25.	b

EXPLANATION OF MULTIPLE CHOICE ANSWERS

1. (1180,L1,18)   (c)   Under a recent change in anti-trust law, an agreement between a manufacturer (franchiser) and a dealer (franchisee) which gives the dealer an exclusive right to sell in a designated area and each dealer agrees not to sell outside this area is tested under the rule of reason. In the past, such franchising agreements creating vertical territorial limitations were illegal per se unless the franchiser retained title to the goods involved. However, that has been changed by a recent supreme court ruling, making answer (c) correct.

2. (580,L1,1)   (c)   A joint boycott requires that two or more parties agree not to deal with a third party. The mere unilateral refusal to deal with Monroe would not be a joint boycott under the provisions of the Sherman Antitrust Act. Since there is no agreement to fix prices between Monroe and Jay this activity is not a per se violoation. However, if an overwhelming preponderance of the retailers had agreed to follow the price, then there would be an agreement that constituted price fixing, which is illegal per se.

3. (580,L1,2)   (c)   Answer (c) is the correct answer because treble damages is still an appropriate sanction under the antitrust laws. Answers (a), (b), and (d) are incorrect because these state sanctions are presently existing under the antitrust laws.

4. (580,L1,4)   (c)   Marble's refusal to sell to retailers who do not follow Marble's pricing policy is sufficient activity to constitute price fixing, an illegal per se violation of the Sherman Antitrust Act. Answer (a) is incorrect because price fixing is an illegal per se violation meaning that there is no justification (meeting the competition) for engaging in such activity. Answers (b) and (d) are incorrect because vertical price fixing (resale price maintenance agreement) is also illegal per se since the repeal of the Miller-Tydings Act no longer allows fair trade laws. Thus the rule of reason does not apply to this type of violation.

5. (580,L1,5)   (a)   The charge is "an attempt to monopolize," not to create a monopoly. Therefore, the government will need to show such intent on the part of Duplex. The fact that Duplex has a small per-centage of the relevant market (answer (b)) or that the corporation cannot control prices or exclude competition (monopolistic powers) (answer (d)) would not be valid defenses. The charge pertains to Section 2, not Section 1, of the Sherman Antitrust Act; therefore the fact that Duplex's activities do not constitute an unreasonable restraint of trade would not be a proper defense.

6. (1179,L1,6)   (b)   The requirement by the Flick Corporation that its customers buy at least 2 products in order to obtain the item they want is an illegal tying arrangement. Answer (a) is incorrect because illegal tying arrangements are determined on the basis of economic policy and are not affected by whether the products are patented or not. Answer (c) is incorrect because under the antitrust laws, it is immaterial that prices are competitive under an otherwise illegal tying arrangement. Generally, the courts treat tying arrangements as illegal per se so long as the dollar volume is not insignificant, i.e., where the seller has sufficient economic power to impose an appreciable restraint on free competition in the tied product. Answer (d) is incorrect because the illegality is based on the above explanation and not on whether the retailers complain about the tying arrangement.

7. (1179,L1,21)   (a)   The suspension of a corporation's right to engage in interstate commerce as a result of violations of the antitrust act is not one of the authorized sanctions under federal antitrust laws. Treble damages as in answer (b) are available to injured parties. Answer (c), seizure of property being illegally shipped in interstate commerce in violation of the antitrust laws, is also an authorized sanction. Likewise, fine and imprisonment of the corporation's officers, as in answer (d), are also authorized sanctions.

8. (1179,L1,34)   (b)   It is permissible under the antitrust laws for a corporation to charge a price aimed at maximizing profits based upon economic analysis of supply and demand. Answer (a) is illegal: price fixing is a per se violation of the antitrust laws, even if it results in lower prices. Answer (c) also is a violation of the antitrust laws: participation in a plan of allocating sales market. The fact that it was actually offered by a trade association is immaterial. Answer (d), the payment of broker commissions to purchasers of goods, is generally deemed to be a violation of the Robinson-Patman Act. The effect of such rebates constitutes price discrimination between purchasers.

9. (1179,L1,35) (b)   The obtaining of a near total monopoly of a market for a particular product as a result of a patent does not generally result in violation of the federal antitrust laws. The issuance of the patent,

which is an exception to the antitrust laws, results in the monopoly being "thrust upon" the patent holder. Answer (a) is incorrect because an attempt by a seller to maintain the resale price for his product is a violation of the antitrust laws. Answer (c) is incorrect because it is an illegal tying arrangement to require the purchasers to buy all their common place supplies as a condition for obtaining the desired machines. Answer (d) is incorrect because joint boycotts aimed at excluding certain troublesome buyers from the market restrain trade and are per se illegal activities.

10.   (1179,L1,36) (c)   Even though Expansion Corporation does not currently buy from, sell to, or compete with Resistance Corporation, the acquisition is likely to be declared illegal if there will be reciprocal buying and other entrants into the market may be precluded. The antimerger section of the Clayton Act prohibits mergers which will substantially lessen competition or tend to create a monopoly. Answer (a) is incorrect because the fact that Expansion and Reliance do not do business with each other does not mean that the antitrust laws do not apply. Section 7 of the Clayton Act is intended to cope with monopolistic trends in their incipiency stage before Sherman Act violations occur. Answer (b) is incorrect because the government may proceed against a merger at any time if the merger threatens to restrain commerce. A government proceeding after the merger is accomplished seeks divesture. Answer (d) is incorrect because mergers or acquisitions are not legal just because there may appear to be cost efficiencies resulting from combined marketing, advertising, and other activities. Acquisitions are considered to be legal if it is apparent that competition has not or will not be lessened.

11.   (1179,L1,37) (d)   The best defense against an allegation of monopolizing under Section 2 of the Sherman Act is to demonstrate that the defendant's market share is not large enough to permit price fixing or exclusion of competitors. In making such a determination, the court looks primarily to the percentage share of the relevant market. Answer (a) is incorrect because the antitrust laws apply to all US companies wherever they operate. Furthermore, the acts prescribe activity which has an effect on interstate commerce, i.e., the activity does not have to be in interstate commerce. Answer (b) is not the best defense since the monopoly was a result of an expired, rather than a current, patent. Answer (c) is incorrect because no specific wrongful intent to monopolize need be proven by the Justice Department.

12.   (1175,L3,46)   (c)   Marvel Toys has not violated antitrust laws with respect to Fantastic, because meeting lawful competition is a defense

to price discrimination.   Price discrimination cannot be used to obtain new customers such as Gem.   Antitrust laws are violated whether or not competitors can show damages and whether or not the violator was operating at a loss.

13.   (1175,L3,47)   (b)   Fixing prices is a per se violation whether or not the price is reasonable. It does not matter if the suppliers agree the price is reasonable; fixing prices is not justifiable. The purpose of the antitrust laws is to promote competition by prohibiting friendly or hostile actions that undermine competition.   Maximum as well as minimum prices are included.   The fact that a company is failing can be a defense to a merger, but not to price fixing.

14.   (576,L1,13)   (d)   The Justice Department will most likely prevail if the corporation has manifested an intent to monopolize, because the Sherman Act forbids the formation of, or the attempt to form, monopolies.   A significant amount of sales in interstate commerce is not necessary, because any sales in interstate commerce will suffice.   If the top five corporations have 60% of the market, 15% is not likely to be a monopoly.   Similarly, an increase from 12.5% to 15% over three years is not a monopoly or substantial evidence of an attempt to monopolize, especially in light of the product innovation.

15.   (1178,L1,1)   (b)   An agreement between competitors to jointly boycott a troublesome buyer is a per se violation of the antitrust laws. Each of the "big three" manufacturers individually could have made the decision to cease doing business with Pickwick but they may not do so in concert. Answer (a) is incorrect because the manufacturers acted in concert and this is illegal whether or not their action is unilateral in regard to Pickwick. Answer (c) is incorrect because the agreement between the three manufacturers constituted a per se violation of the antitrust laws, and thus it is not necessary to show the specific effect or harm caused by the activity. The term "per se violation" means without legal justification. Answer (d) is incorrect because while it is true that a business person acting independently has the freedom to choose with whom he will deal, the conduct described in this question involves acting in concert with competitors.

16.   (1174,L3,43)   (a)   Sale of commodities on the condition that the purchaser would not deal in the commodities of a competitor of the seller

where the effect of the transaction is to substantially lessen competition are prohibited by Section 3 of the Clayton Act. If the contracts do substantially lessen competition, then George Corp. can be enjoined from enforcing the contracts.

17.   (1177,L3,46)   (b)   An arrangement requiring the buyer to take one or more other products as a condition to buying the desired product is called tying. It is illegal per se as a practical matter (because the seller will have to be in a monopolistic position to be able to force other products on a seller). Answer (c) is incorrect because even though Mason did not have total control, it did have monopolistic control. Answer (d) is incorrect because the practice is per se illegal. The price of the tied products is not considered.

18.   (578,L1,7)   (c)   The Clayton Act prohibits interlocking directorates where either corporation has shareholder's equity (capital, surplus, and undivided profits) of more than $1 million, and competition is substantially lessened. Answer (b) is incorrect because the interlocking directorate prohibition is not dependent on ownership of 50% or more of another corporation. Answers (a) and (d) are incorrect because serious violations of the antitrust laws have occurred. Yeat's and Glick's share of the market has not changed, but competition has been substantially lessened by their division of markets which is in itself a per se violation of the federal antitrust laws.

19.   (578,L1,8)   (d)   An express formal agreement is not required to constitute an illegal price maintenance agreement. The four manufacturers have, by their informal oral agreement, agreed and conspired to fix prices which is a per se violation of the federal antitrust laws. Answer (a) is incorrect because prices may not be set by a trade association any more legally than if done by the members themselves. Answer (b) is likewise incorrect because any pricing agreement is illegal even if it is to follow the industry leader's pricing, no matter who suggests it. Answer (c) is also incorrect because a trade association can no more legally allocate markets than can the members.

20.   (578,L1,9)   (b)   Price discrimination is illegal if the effect would substantially lessen competition. In this case, the price discrimination is based on cost savings and the competition is not between competitors. The wholesalers are charging the same price and the retailers are charging the same price (except for a functional discount based on quantity cost savings). Answer (a) is incorrect because Girard has the right to sue. There has been price discrimination and it is up to the court to determine whether or not it is legal. Answer (c) is incorrect because intent to discriminate is not a factor in the legality of price discrimination. Answer (d) is incorrect because reasonable prices or low profit margins are not a justification for price discrimination. It is the competition between the buyers which is being protected and not the profits of the seller.

21.   (1178,L1,5)   (a)   Answer (a) is the most likely result, i.e., the court would grant an injunction prohibiting Western from acquiring control of Davis. In looking at Western's percentage share of the relevant market after the acquisition, it is apparent that they would have more than 30% of the market where they compete. This creates a presumption that the merger is unlawful. Answer (b) is not so likely because share of the market analysis should be applied to the section of the country where they compete and not to the United States as a whole. Answer (c) is unlikely because the facts in this case indicate such a clear violation of the anti-merger provisions of the law. Nonetheless, it is possible for the government to review a merger after it has occurred. Answer (d) is unlikely because significant business efficiency resulting from a merger does not insulate it from attack by the Justice Department under the antitrust laws. The major exception is if the acquired company was a failing company and there was no other purchaser whose acquisition would be less anticompetitive.

22.   (1178,L1,6)   (b)   Whether resale price maintenance agreements are reasonable or not, they are not permitted by antitrust laws and are per se violations. Answer (a) is incorrect because impositions on how a buyer can resell goods are per se illegal just as are price fixing agreements. Answers (c) and (d) are incorrect because neither patents, labels, trademarks, nor brand names give a seller the right to make impositions on how a buyer can resell goods.

MAY 1981 ANSWERS

23.   (581,L1,55)   (a)   This agreement is an example of vertical territorial allocation which is judged under the rule of reason. The fact Aden retains title to the goods would not create a potential antitrust problem but serve to substantiate the fact that the rule of reason (i.e., the agreement can be legally justified) should be applied. Answer (b) is incorrect because the provision would qualify as vertical price

fixing which is illegal per se (i.e., no legal justification). Answer (c) is incorrect because the provision
would create an exclusive dealing contract which could
result in an antitrust violation. Answer (d) is incorrect
because the provision would result in the creation of
a joint boycott which is illegal per se.

24.   (581,L1,56)   (a)   The agreement is an example of vertical price fixing which is illegal per se
under the Sherman Act. This means there is no legal
justification for entering into this type of agreement.
Proof of engaging in this type of activity is sufficient
to constitute a violation, even though the price charged
is reasonable. Such activity had been allowed under the
Fair Trade laws but these laws were recently repealed.
Answers (b), (c) and (d) are all incorrect because they
do not state legal justification for entering a vertical
price fixing agreement.

25.   (581,L1,57)   (b)   The contract provision described in the question is an exclusive dealing arrangement. While the Clayton Act is usually referred to in
determining the legality of such arrangements, both
the Sherman and Federal Trade Commission Acts
contain provisions governing exclusive dealings contracts. Basically, the criterion used to judge the legality
of this type of contract is one of quantitative sub-
stantiality, i.e., the contract provision will be judged
according to objective standards such as the percentage
of market control gained through such restrictions
or the dollar amount of transactions involved (e.g.,
contracts involving $500,000 are normally considered
to be illegal automatically). Since these standards are
objective in nature, use of the rule of reason answer
(c) is normally not accepted as justification once the
dollar or percentage limits are exceeded. Answer (a)
is incorrect as exclusive dealings contracts are not
illegal per se under the various Acts, and the duration
of a contract provision will not determine whether or
not an agreement is illegal per se. Answer (d) is incorrect because whether the wholesalers are allowed to
sell other pictures would be irrelevant in deciding
whether this exclusive dealing contract restricts competition in lithographs.

ANSWER OUTLINE

Problem 1   Price Fixing and Discrimination

b. There is a possible violation of the Sherman Act
   The manufacturers conspired to restrain interstate
   commerce
      I.e., they agreed to limit output and allocate cus-
      tomers
   This is similar to price-fixing and is per se illegal
      The specific circumstances do not affect the illegality
      Oral understanding
      To eliminate destructive price cutting
      To charge reasonable prices

c. General Pen's price-fixing arrangement is illegal
      I.e., Double Discount has a valid cause of action
   Price-fixing used to be legal if per state price main-
      tenance law
   General Pen comes within these "fair trade laws"
   In 1975 Congress removed this exception which was
      previously permitted
   Thus Pen's arrangement is not legal.

UNOFFICIAL ANSWER

Problem 1   Price Fixing and Discrimination

b.   The fact situation described poses obvious violations of the Sherman Act. First, the four competing antenna manufacturers entered into an
illegal "contract, combination, or conspiracy"
in restraint of interstate commerce when they
agreed to limit their output. This is akin to
price fixing and is, per se, illegal. The fact
that the understanding was oral does not matter, nor does it matter that their goal was to
eliminate destructive price cutting or charge
reasonable prices. Additionally, the agreement
among the four antenna manufacturers to allocate customers among themselves is another
clearly anticompetitive device which has been
placed in the, per se, illegal category. The
anticompetitive effects are so obvious that
this kind of conduct has been held to be
without legal justification.

c.   The problem raised by the facts is whether the
price-fixing arrangement engaged in by General
Pen Company is illegal. Normally, price fixing
is, per se, illegal. However, Congress originally
permitted an exception to this blanket prohibition. In effect the price-fixing agreement was
legal if there was (1) a state law permitting
resale price maintenance (a manufacturer fixing

the minimum price at which purchasers could
sell); (2) free and open competition among
other makers of the product; and (3) one or
more retail sellers agreeing to retail price maintenance. The facts of the case indicate that
General Pen comes within the scope of the pri-
or "fair trade" laws. However, in 1975, Congress amended the law concerning resale price
maintenance and removed the exception previously permitted under the Sherman Act. Consequently, resale price maintenance (vertical
price fixing) is now illegal. Thus, Double Discount has a valid cause of action against General
Pen based upon the amended statute.

ANSWER OUTLINE
Problem 2   Price Discrimination

b1.   Yes, Marco stations that suffered losses will
     prevail
     Violation of Robinson - Patman Act
       Price discrimination among Marvel's custo-
       mers
         Allows Banner to undersell its com-
         petitors
         Competitors suffer decreased sales and loss
         of customers
b2.   Reduced prices to meet prices of competitors
      Must be competitor of firm cutting its prices
      Best by test is not a competitor of Marvel

UNOFFICIAL ANSWER
Problem 2   Price Discrimination

Part b.

1.   Yes, Marvel's price discrimination is a violation
of the Robinson-Patman Act, and the defense of
"meeting competition" is not available. The price
discrimination involved is at the buyer level, a secondary-line price discrimination. That is, it was a price
discrimination among various customers (the retail gas
stations) of the manufacturer or producer (Marvel)
that enables the customer receiving the lower price to
undersell its competitors. Marvel's selling to Banner at
1.7¢ less than it sold to its other service stations is
squarely within the proscribed conduct. Where there
is such a secondary-line price discrimination, the
requirement of "injury to competition" is met if there
is a reasonable possibility that competition will be

adversely affected. Here, the decreased sales and loss of customers by the other stations would satisfy such a requirement, and thus, there is a prima facie Robinson-Patman violation.

2.   Marvel's chief defense would be that it had reduced its prices to meet the lower prices of a competitor. However, the facts indicate that Marvel and Best by Test did not compete since Best was not a supplier. The price reduction being met must be that of a competitor of the firm cutting its price, not a competitor of a purchaser of that firm. Thus, the good faith "meeting competition" defense is not available.

MULTIPLE CHOICE QUESTIONS (1—22)

1. The Securities Exchange Act of 1934 requires that certain persons register and that the securities of certain issuers be registered. In respect to such registration under the 1934 Act, which of the following statements is **incorrect**?

    a.   All securities offered under the Securities Act of 1933 also must be registered under the 1934 Act.

    b.   National securities exchanges must register.

    c.   The equity securities of issuers, which are traded on a national securities exchange, must be registered.

    d.   The equity securities of issuers having in excess of $1 million in assets and 500 or more stockholders which are traded in interstate commerce must be registered.

2. Theobold Construction Company, Inc., is considering a public stock offering for the first time. It wishes to raise $1.2 million by a common stock offering and do this in the least expensive manner. In this connection, it is considering making an offering pursuant to Regulation A. Which of the following statements is correct regarding such an offering?

    a.   Such an offering can **not** be made to more than 250 people.

    b.   The maximum amount of securities permitted to be offered under Regulation A is $1 million.

    c.   Only those corporations which have had an initial registration under the Securities Act of 1933 are eligible.

    d.   Even if Regulation A applies, Theobold is required to distribute an offering circular.

3. Shariff is a citizen of a foreign country. He has just purchased six percent (6%) of the outstanding common shares of Stratosphere Metals, Inc., a company listed on a national stock exchange. He has instructed the brokerage firm that quietly and efficiently handled the execution of the purchase order that he wants the securities to be held in street name. What are the legal implications of the above transactions? Shariff must

    a.   Immediately have the securities registered in his own name and take delivery of them.

    b.   Sell the securities because he has violated the anti-fraud provisions of the Securities Exchange Act of 1934.

    c.   Notify Stratosphere Metals, Inc., of his acquisition and file certain information as to his identity and background with the SEC.

    d.   Notify the SEC and Stratosphere Metals, Inc., only if he acquires ten percent (10%) or more of Stratosphere's common shares.

4. Which of the following statements concerning the scope of Section 10(b) of the Securities Exchange Act of 1934 is correct?

    a.   In order to come within its scope, a transaction must have taken place on a national stock exchange.

    b.   It applies exclusively to securities of corporations registered under the Securities Exchange Act of 1934.

    c.   There is an exemption from its application for securities registered under the Securities Act of 1933.

    d.   It applies to purchases as well as sales of securities in interstate commerce.

5. Which of the following statements is correct regarding qualification for the private placement exemption from registration under the Securities Act of 1933?

    a.   The instrumentalities of interstate commerce must **not** be used.

    b.   The securities must be offered to **not** more than 35 persons.

    c.   The minimum amount of securities purchased by each offeree must **not** be less than $100,000.

    d.   The offerees **must** have access to or be furnished with the kind of information that would be available in a registration statement.

6. The Foreign Corrupt Practices Act of 1977 prohibits bribery of foreign officials. Which of the following statements correctly describes the Act's application to corporations engaging in such practices?

    a.   It only applies to multinational corporations.

    b.   It applies to all domestic corporations engaged in interstate commerce.

    c.   It only applies to corporations whose securities are registered under the Securities Exchange Act of 1934.

    d.   It applies only to corporations engaged in foreign commerce.

7. Taylor is the executive Vice President for Marketing of Reflex Corporation and a member of the Board of Directors. Based on information obtained during the course of his duties, Taylor concluded that Reflex's profits would fall by 50% for the quarter and 30% for the year. He quietly contacted

his broker and disposed of 10,000 shares of his Reflex stock at a profit, some of which he had acquired within 6 months of the sale. In fact, Reflex's profits did not fall, but its stock price declined for unrelated reasons. Taylor had also advised a friend to sell her shares and repurchase the stock later. She followed Taylor's advice, sold for $21, and subsequently repurchased an equal number of shares at $11. A shareholder has commenced a shareholder derivative action against Taylor and the friend for violation of the Securities Exchange Act of 1934. Under these circumstances, which of the following is correct?

    a.   Taylor is not an insider in relation to Reflex.

    b.   Taylor must account to the corporation for his short-swing profit.

    c.   Taylor and the friend must both account to the corporation for their short-swing profits.

    d.   Neither Taylor nor the friend has incurred any liability under the 1934 act.

8.   Which of the following is exempt from registration under the Securities Act of 1933?

    a.   First mortgage bonds.

    b.   The usual annuity contract issued by an insurer.

    c.   Convertible preferred stock.

    d.   Limited partnership interests.

9.   Under the Securities Act of 1933, an accountant may be held liable for any materially false or misleading financial statements, including an omission of a material fact therefrom, provided the purchaser

    a.   Proves reliance on the registration statement or prospectus.

    b.   Proves negligence or fraud on the part of the accountant.

    c.   Brings suit within four years after the security is offered to the public.

    d.   Proves a false statement or omission existed and the specific securities were the ones offered through the registration statement.

10.   Whitworth has been charged by Bonanza Corporation with violating the Securities Exchange Act of 1934. Whitworth was formerly the president of Bonanza, but he was ousted as a result of a proxy battle. Bonanza seeks to recover from Whitworth any and all of his short-swing profits. Which of the following would be a valid defense to the charges?

    a.   Whitworth is a New York resident, Bonanza was incorporated in New York, and the transactions were all made through

the New York Stock Exchange; therefore, an interstate commerce was not involved.

    b.   Whitworth did not actually make use of any insider information in connection with the various stock transactions in question.

    c.   All the transactions alleged to be in violation of the 1934 act were purchases made during February 1979 with the corresponding sales made in September 1979.

    d.   Whitworth's motivation in selling the stock was solely a result of the likelihood that he would be ousted as president of Bonanza.

11.   The Securities and Exchange Commission is not empowered to

    a.   Obtain an injunction which will suspend trading in a given security.

    b.   Sue for treble damages.

    c.   Institute criminal proceedings against accountants.

    d.   Suspend a broker-dealer.

12.   Under the Securities Act of 1933, subject to some exceptions and limitations, it is unlawful to use the mails or instruments of interstate commerce to sell or offer to sell a security to the public unless

    a.   A surety bond sufficient to cover potential liability to investors is obtained and filed with the Securities and Exchange Commission.

    b.   The offer is made through underwriters qualified to offer the securities on a nationwide basis.

    c.   A registration statement has been properly filed with the Securities and Exchange Commission, has been found to be acceptable, and is in effect.

    d.   The Securities and Exchange Commission approves of the financial merit of the offering

13.   Under which of the following circumstances is a public offering of securities exempt from the registration requirements of the Securities Act of 1933?

    a.   There was a prior registration within one year.

    b.   The corporation is a public utility subject to regulation by the Federal Power Commission.

    c.   The corporation was closely held prior to the offering.

d.   The issuing corporation and all prospective security owners are located within one state, and the entire offering, sale, and distribution is made within that state.

14.   The Securities Act of 1933, in general, exempts † certain small stock offerings from full registration. What is the maximum dollar amount which would qualify for this exemption?
a. $300,000.
b. $1,500,000
c. $750,000.
d. $1,000,000.

15.   The Securities Act of 1933 specifically exempts from registration, securities offered by any person
a.   Other than an issuer, underwriter, or dealer.
b.   Who is an issuer of a public offering.
c.   If the securities in question have previously been registered.
d.   In a small company.

16.   The Securities Act of 1933 applies to the
a.   Sale in interstate commerce of insurance and regular annuity contracts.
b.   Sale by a dealer of securities issued by a bank.
c.   Sale through a broker of a controlling person's investment in a public corporation.
d.   Sale in interstate commerce of bonds issued by a charitable foundation.

17.   Issuer, Inc., a New York corporation engaged † in retail sales within New York City, was interested in raising $1,600,000 in capital.   In this connection it approached through personal letters eighty-eight people in New York, New Jersey, and Connecticut, and then followed up with face-to-face negotiations where it seemed promising to do so.   After extensive efforts in which Issuer disclosed all the information that these people requested, nineteen people from these areas purchased Issuer's securities.   Issuer did not limit its offers to insiders, their relatives, or wealthy or sophisticated investors.   In regard to this securities issuance
a.   The offering is probably exempt from registration under federal securities law as a private placement.

b.   The offering is probably exempt from registration under federal securities law as a small offering.
c.   The offering is probably exempt from registration under federal securities law as an intrastate offering.
d.   The offering probably is not exempt from registration under federal securities law.

18.   Mr. Jackson owns approximately 40% of the shares of common stock of Triad Corporation. The rest of the shares are widely distributed among 2,000 shareholders. Jackson needs funds for other business ventures and would like to raise about $2,000,000 through the sale of some of his Triad shares. He accordingly approached Underwood & Sons, an investment banking house in which he knew one of the principals, to purchase his Triad shares and distribute the shares to the public at a reasonable price through its offices in the United States. Any profit on the sales could be retained by Underwood pursuant to an agreement reached between Jackson and Underwood. In this situation
a.   The securities to be sold probably do not need to be registered with the Securities and Exchange Commission.
b.   Underwood & Sons probably is not an underwriter as defined in the federal securities law.
c.   Jackson probably is considered an issuer under federal securities law.
d.   Under federal securities law, no prospectus is required to be filed in connection with this contemplated transaction.

19.   Young owns 200 shares of stock of Victory Manufacturing Company. Victory is listed on a national stock exchange and has in excess of one million shares outstanding. Young claims that Truegood, a Victory director, has purchased and sold shares in violation of the insider trading provisions of the Securities Exchange Act of 1934. Young has threatened legal action. Which of the following statements is correct?
a.   Truegood will have a valid defense if he can show he did not have any insider information which influenced his purchases or sales.
b.   Young can sue Truegood personally, but his recovery will be limited to his proportionate share of Truegood's profits plus legal expenses.

c.   In order to prevail, Young must sue for and on behalf of the corporation and establish that the transactions in question occurred within less than six months of each other and at a profit to Truegood.

d.   Since Young's stock ownership is less than 1%, his only recourse is to file a complaint with the SEC or obtain a sufficient number of other shareholders to join him so that the 1% requirement is met.

20.   Tweed Manufacturing, Inc., plans to issue $5 million of common stock to the public in interstate commerce after its registration statement with the SEC becomes effective.   What, if anything, must Tweed do in respect to those states in which the securities are to be sold?

a.   Nothing, since approval by the SEC automatically constitutes satisfaction of any state requirements.

b.   Make a filing in those states which have laws governing such offerings and obtain their approval.

c.   Simultaneously apply to the SEC for permission to market the securities in the various states without further clearance.

d.   File in the appropriate state office of the state in which it maintains its principal office of business, obtain clearance, and forward a certified copy of that state's clearance to all other states.

21.   Harvey Wilson is a senior vice president, 15% shareholder and a member of the Board of Directors of Winslow, Inc.   Wilson has decided to sell 10% of his stock in the company.   Which of the following methods of disposition would subject him to SEC registration requirements?

a.   A redemption of the stock by the corporation.

b.   The sale by several brokerage houses of the stock in the ordinary course of business.

c.   The sale of the stock to an insurance company which will hold the stock for long-term investment purposes.

d.   The sale to a corporate officer who currently owns 5% of the stock of Winslow and who will hold the purchased stock for long-term investment.

22.   The Securities Exchange Act of 1934 holds certain insiders liable for short-swing profits under section 16(b) of the act.   Which of the following classes of people would not be insiders in relation to the corporation in which they own securities?

a.   An executive vice president.

b.   A major debenture holder.

c.   An 11% owner, 8% of which he owns in his or her own name and 3% in an irrevocable trust for his or her benefit for life.

d.   A director who owns less than 10% of the shares of stock of the corporation.

PROBLEMS

<u>Problem 1</u>   Registration; Deceptive Devices; Insider
Information (1176,L7)

(20 to 25 minutes)

Darius Corporation has 1,000,000 shares of
common stock outstanding of which 450,000 shares
are publicly traded over-the-counter and 550,000 are
owned by Lynn, its president. The market price of
the stock has ranged from $3 to $4 per share over
the past year. Lynn obtained his Darius shares on
August 10, 1976, when Darius acquired a company
wholly owned by Lynn pursuant to an exchange
of 550,000 Darius shares for all of the shares of
Lynn's company. The Darius shares received by
Lynn were unregistered and contained a legend
which restricted transfer except on the opinion
of counsel that the shares were transferable. The
number of Darius shares held by the public was
450,000 both before and after the August 10 exchange.

On September 22, 1976, Archer & Co.,
Lynn's broker, purchased from Lynn, for its
own account and in ten separate transactions,
a total of 10,000 shares of Darius at $4.50
per share. The next day Archer purchased from
Lynn in eight separate transactions an additional
8,000 shares in total at $5.50 per share, again
for its own account. These were the only transactions on September 22 and 23, and trading
in Darius shares over-the-counter had otherwise
been light in recent months. On September 24,
1976, Archer circulated a story that there was
an active demand for Darius shares. Within a
few days, Darius stock was quoted over-the-
counter at $9 per share.

On September 30, 1976, Archer sold, as
agent for Lynn, 50,000 of Lynn's Darius shares
for $9 a share to buyers in several states which
Archer had solicited in the open market. Archer
also sold for $9 per share the 18,000 Darius
shares purchased the prior week for its own account. Soon thereafter, trading activity in Darius
stock subsided to its normally light volume which
was reflected in the market price retreat to $3
per share.

Required: Answer the following, setting forth
reasons for any conclusions stated.

a.   What is the general statutory rule requiring registration under the Securities Act of
1933, and would the Darius shares sold by

Archer be exempt as a so-called "transactions
by any person other than an issuer, underwriter
or dealer" or as a so-called "brokers' transaction?

b.   Did Archer violate the Securities Exchange Act of 1934 when buying and selling
the 18,000 shares of Darius?

c.   Is Lynn liable to Darius under the
Securities Exchange Act of 1934 because he
sold 68,000 shares of Darius?

<u>Problem 2</u>   Reg. A and Rule 10b-5 (1178,L4)

(20 to 25 minutes)

Part a. Glover Corporation is a small rapidly-
expanding manufacturing company. In 1977 Glover
made a public offering of its shares for $400,000
in accordance with Regulation A, issued by the
Securities and Exchange Commission pursuant to
the Securities Act of 1933. The shares are not
listed on any exchange, but are sometimes bought
and sold in interstate commerce. At the end of
1977 Glover had total assets of $900,000, 429
shareholders, and sales of $650,000 for the year.

Required: Answer the following, setting forth
reasons for any conclusions stated.

1.   What is a Regulation A offering and what
are the general requirements which must be met
in order to qualify for making such an offering?

2.   What difference is there in the potential
liability of the parties making an offering under
Regulation A as contrasted with a full registration?

3.   What are the time limitations in which an
aggrieved party may commence an action for
failure to comply with the Securities Act of 1933?

4.   What are the major provisions of the
Securities Exchange Act of 1934 which do not
apply to Glover and its officers, directors, and
principal shareholders after the public offering
and which major provisions do apply?

Part b. Gordon & Groton, CPAs, were the
auditors of Bank & Company, a brokerage firm and
member of a national stock exchange. Gordon &
Groton examined and reported on the financial
statements of Bank which were filed with the
Securities and Exchange Commission.

Several of Bank's customers were swindled
by a fraudulent scheme perpetrated by Bank's
president who owned 90% of the voting stock of
the company. The facts establish that Gordon &
Groton were negligent but not reckless or grossly

negligent in the conduct of the audit and neither participated in the fraudulent scheme nor knew of its existence.

The customers are suing Gordon & Groton under the antifraud provisions of Section 10(b) and Rule 10b-5 of the Securities Exchange Act of 1934 for aiding and abetting the fraudulent scheme of the president. The customers' suit for fraud is predicated exclusively on the nonfeasance of the auditors in failing to conduct a proper audit, thereby failing to discover the fraudulent scheme.

Required: Answer the following, setting forth reasons for any conclusions stated.

   1.   What is the probable outcome of the lawsuit?

   2.   What other theory of liability might the customers have asserted?

MULTIPLE CHOICE ANSWERS

1.	a	6.	b	11.	b	16.	c	21.	b
2.	d	7.	b	12.	c	17.	d	22.	b
3.	c	8.	b	13.	d	18.	c		
4.	d	9.	d	14.	b	19.	c		
5.	d	10.	c	15.	a	20.	b		

EXPLANATION OF MULTIPLE CHOICE ANSWERS

1. (1180,L1,39)   (a)   The correct answer is (a). The Securities Act of 1933 applies to the initial issuance of securities and has the purpose of providing investors with full and fair disclosure concerning these securities. The Securities Exchange Act of 1934 generally applies to the subsequent trading of securities but not necessarily all securities required to register under the 1933 Act. Each of the following are required to register under the 1934 Act: (1) national securities exchange; (2) brokers and dealers, (3) dealers in municipal securities, (4) securities that are traded on any national exchange, (5) equity securities traded in interstate commerce having in excess of $1 million in assets and 500 or more shareholders.

2. (1180,L1,40)   (d)   The correct answer is (d). Small issues (up to $1,500,000) may be exempt from the full registration requirements of the SEC Act of 1933 if there is a notification filing with the SEC and an offering circular under Regulation A. A Regulation A offering can be made to any number of people as long as issuance does not exceed $1,500,000. A corporate issuer need not show an initial registration under the Securities Act of 1933 before being eligible to make a Regulation A offering.

3. (1180,L1,41)   (c)   According to the tender offer provisions of the Securities Exchange Act of 1934, anyone who acquired more than 5% of a company's equity securities must notify the issuer and disclose his/her identity and other relevant facts to SEC. If a tender offer is involved (in this question it was not present), the purchaser must give this information to the SEC and shareholders before making the offer. Thus, answer (c) is correct.

4. (1180,L1,42)   (d)   Answer (d) is correct because under Rule 10b-5 (Securities Exchange Act of 1934) it is unlawful to use any manipulative or deceptive devices in the purchase or sale of securities if the mail, interstate commerce, or a national stock exchange is used. Answer (a) is incorrect because it is unlawful to use the mail or any instrumentality of interstate commerce in addition to a national stock exchange. The rule is not limited to securities subject to the 1934 Act but applies to any sale of a security if interstate commerce is used. Therefore, answers (b) and (c) are incorrect.

5. (1180,L1,43)   (d)   The correct statement is (d). Answer (b) is wrong since it is SEC practice, not law, to limit the number of offerees to 35. Answer (c) is false because there is no minimum dollar amount requirement to comply with concerning the private placement exemption. Answer (a) is not one of the qualifications for the private placement exemption.

6. (1180,L1,44)   (b)   Answer (b) is correct. The Foreign Corrupt Practices Act of 1977 applies to any U.S. business enterprise engaged in interstate commerce including companies required to register with the SEC under the 1934 Act and domestic business organizations. Answers (a), (c), and (d), therefore, are incorrect.

7. (1179,L1,27) (b)   Taylor, as executive vice president and a member of the Board of Directors, is classified by the 1934 Securities Act as an insider and therefore must account to the corporation for short-swing profit on stock which he acquired within 6 months of sale, or profits that he acquired from unfairly using inside information about the company for his personal gain. Answer (a) is incorrect because an officer and director is an insider. Answer (c) is incorrect because there is no provision requiring the friend who acquired information from an insider to account to the corporation for his/her short-swing profits. Answer (d) is incorrect because as stated above, Taylor is liable under the 1934 Securities Act for the short-swing profits.

8. (1179,L1,18) (b)   Usual insurance and annuity contracts (including variable annuities) issued by an insurance company are exempt from the Securities Act of 1933. Answers (a), (c), and (d) are incorrect because each is regulated first mortgage bonds, convertible preferred stock, and limited partnership interests.

9. (1179,L1,29) (d)   Under the Securities Act of 1933, an accountant is liable to a purchaser of securities if the purchaser proves a false financial statement (including statements with a material omission), and the specific securities were ones offered through a registration statement. Answer (a) is incorrect because the purchaser need not prove reliance on the registration statement or prospectus. Instead, the burden is shifted from the plaintiff to the defendant accountant to show that he is not responsible for the investment loss by the purchaser, i.e., accountant must prove due diligence. Answer (b) is incorrect because the purchaser need not prove negligence or fraud on the part of the accountant

Again, all that need be proven is the misstatement or omission. Answer (c) is incorrect because the maximum time limitation for bringing such an action is 3 years after the security is offered to the public.

10.   (1179,L1,32) (c)   Transactions in excess of 6 months are not short-swing profits since the statute defines short-swing as 6 months or less. Purchase of the stock in February and sale in September is more than 6 months. Answer (a) is incorrect because the securities were traded on the New York Stock Exchange. Thus, Bonanza stock was offered, if not sold, to persons in very many states. Answer (b) is not a good defense because the 1934 statute provides that all short-swing profits by an insider belong to the corporation, i.e., proving that insider information was used is not necessary. Answer (d) is not a good defense because the motivation in selling the stock is not relevant. The issue is whether or not the stock was sold in less than a 6 month period. The insider's motive and intent are irrelevant.

11.   (577,L1,1)   (b)   The SEC is not empowered to sue for treble damages. Treble damages are a civil remedy for those injured by an antitrust violation. The SEC may take administrative action to suspend a broker-dealer when there has been a violation of the federal securities laws. The SEC also may institute criminal proceedings against accountants or others for willful violations of the Securities Acts. Also, the SEC may seek and obtain preliminary and final injunctions to prevent trading which is in violation of the Act.

12.   (577,L1,3)   (c)   Unless a registration statement has been filed with the SEC and accepted, it is generally unlawful under the 1933 Act to offer or sell securities to the public using instruments of interstate commerce. There is no exception to registration by obtaining a surety bond. Nor does it matter who makes the offer; qualified underwriters are subject to the same rules. The SEC never evaluates the financial merit of an offering. Instead, the SEC requires full and fair disclosure so that investors can make their own determination. Registration statements are the vehicles of full and fair disclosures.

13.   (577,L1,4)   (d)   There is an exemption from the registration requirements for transactions which take place wholly within one state. It is called an intrastate offering. No purchaser or offeree can reside in another state, nor can any offer, sale, or distribution be made in another state. Each new offering of the issuer corporation's securities must be registered. Public utilities are not exempt, nor does it matter whether the issuing corporation was closely held or publicly held prior to the offering.

14.   (576,L2,29)   (b)   An issuance of up to $1,500,000 may be exempt if notification, filing, offering circular, and other specified conditions of SEC Regulation A are met. These requirements are not as onerous or costly as full registration but meet the objective of amply protecting the investing public by requiring disclosure and notification of material facts. In essence, the filing or registration, offering circular, and other requirements of this regulation are designed to be less formal than issues exceeding $1,500,000 It should be noted that the antifraud provisions apply to Regulation A offerings as well as any sale of a security using interstate commerce.

15.   (576,L2,30)   (a)   There is a broad specific exemption for securities offered by any person other than an issuer, underwriter, or dealer. Thus under the Acts public offerings of securities are regulated, but private offerings are exempted. This exemption permits most investors to sell their own securities without registration, prospectus, or other regulations except the antifraud provisions. To avoid circumvention of the Act, the SEC has promulgated a number of complicated provisions dealing with this exemption when the security sold is "restricted" or the seller is a "controlling person."

16.   (1173,L2,23)   (c)   Securities issued by banks or charitable institutions and insurance and regular annuity contracts are exempted from securities regulation. Answer (c) is correct because sale of a controlling person's stock through a broker has been ruled to be a distribution of securities. Thus, the distribution must comply with the registration requirements of the Securities Act of 1933.

17.   (575,L1,15)   (d)   The offering is of sufficient size and made to a sufficiently sizable number of persons not limited to insiders or sophisticated investors, that it would not be exempt as either a private offering or as a small offering. Because the offerees and the subsequent purchasers were not all residents of the state in which Issuer, Inc., does all its business, the intrastate offering would not be available either. Therefore, the offering would probably not be exempt from registration requirements of federal securities regulation.

18.   (578,L1,6)   (c)   Jackson is considered to be an issuer under the Securities Act of 1933. The definition of issuer includes a controlling person.

Jackson is a controlling person because as substantial holder (40%), he has the power to influence the management and policies of the corporation. This transaction does not come within any exception and therefore is required to be registered with the SEC. Thus answer (a) is incorrect since a registration is required. Answer (b) is incorrect because Underwood & Sons is an underwriter. It has purchased securities from an issuer for public distribution. Answer (d) is incorrect since this is a public sale of securities under the provisions of the Securities Act of 1933, i.e., all registration requirements including the filing of a prospectus are necessary.

19. (1178,L1,33) (c) A stockholder of a corporation whose stock is traded on an exchange may sue for and on behalf of the corporation for profits on insider purchases and sales of company stock occurring within less than six months of each other. Insiders are corporate directors and officers; also stockholders owning more than 10% of any class of stock are insiders. Answer (a) is incorrect because insiders are liable for any profit from the purchase and sale of securities held for less than six months whether or not they have insider information. Answer (b) is incorrect because Young cannot sue Truegood personally, but instead must do so for and on behalf of the corporation. Answer (d) is incorrect because no rule requires a stockholder to own 1% or more of the stock of the corporation if the stockholder is seeking enforcement of the insider trading provisions of the Securities Act of 1934.

20. (579,L1,43) (b) Anyone planning to issue common stock must make a filing in those states that have laws governing such offerings and obtain their approval in addition to meeting the registration requirements of the SEC. Answer (a) is incorrect since approval by the SEC does not automatically constitute satisfaction of state "blue-sky" laws. Answer (c) is incorrect because the issuer must apply to each state for permission to market the securities in addition to the SEC. Answer (d) is incorrect because each state makes its own approval of the stock issue; it cannot be done by one state for the other states.

21. (579,L1,48) (b) Wilson, the officer and stockholder of Winslow, Inc., will be required to comply with SEC registration requirements if he chooses to dispose of his 15% stock in the corporation by having it sold by several brokerage houses in the ordinary course of business. Wilson is deemed to be a controlling person, i.e., one who has the power to influence

management and policies of the issuer, and thus his stock would be considered to be restricted stock. Sale by a controlling person through a broker is not exempted from SEC registration if more than 1% of the outstanding stock is sold. Answer (a) is incorrect because a redemption of stock is not an offering to the public and therefore not covered by the 1933 Act. Answers (c) and (d) are not subject to the SEC registration requirements because they are private placements of securities to sophisticated investors.

22. (579,L1,49) (b) A major debenture holder is not considered an insider. Insiders are defined as officers, directors, and owners of greater than 10% of any class of the issuer's securities. Therefore answers (a) and (d) are incorrect. Answer (c) is incorrect because beneficial ownership will satisfy the over 10% ownership requirement. Stock held by an irrevocable trust is beneficially owned by the beneficiary.

ANSWER OUTLINE

Problem 1   Registration; Deceptive Devices;
             Insider Information

a. SEC registration statement required for interstate sales
   18,000 shares purchased and sold by Archer were not
     exempt
   Nor the 50,000 shares sold by Archer for Lynn
   Archer was an underwriter
       For an issuer (Lynn)
   Broker transaction exemption not available
       Seller and broker cannot solicit orders
       Broker can act only as agent not principal
       Broker can only receive customary commission

b. Archer violated 1934 Act
   Act prohibits fraudulent schemes
       Archer's multiple transaction purchases to raise
         price of Darius stock
       Active demand story

c. Lynn is liable to Darius
   1934 Act prohibits use of inside information
   Insider profit recoverable by corporation
       If purchase and sale occur in less than 6 months

UNOFFICIAL ANSWER

Problem 1   Registration; Deceptive Devices;
             Insider Information

a.   The Securities Act of 1933 provides that it
     is unlawful for any person, directly or in-
     directly, to sell a security in interstate com-
     merce unless a registration statement for such
     security is in effect. Here, there was no reg-
     istration statement in effect with respect to
     the Darius shares sold by Archer; thus, these
     shares appear to have been sold in contra-
     vention of the registration requirement of
     the 1933 act.

         It might be argued, however, that
     these unregistered shares were sold pursuant
     to an exemption from the registration re-
     quirements of the 1933 act. One exemption
     is that accorded "transactions by any per-
     son other than an issuer, underwriter or
     dealer." The term "underwriter" generally
     means any person who has purchased from
     an issuer with a view toward, or offers or
     sells for an issuer in connection with, the
     distribution of any security. For purposes
     of determining whether a person is an
     underwriter, an "issuer" includes, in addi-
     tion to the corporation issuer-in-fact, any

person directly or indirectly controlling
the corporate issuer. Here, Lynn owns 55%
of the shares of Darius Corporation and is,
thus, a person in control of the issuer.
Archer, having purchased for its own account 18,000 shares from Lynn and having resold the shares within a week, most
likely would be an underwriter under the
1933 act. The reason is that Archer appears to have purchased Darius Securities
from an issuer with a view to distributing
them to the public. Lynn is deemed to be
an issuer of Darius securities because he is
a controlling shareholder. Similarly the sale
of 50,000 shares by Archer as agent for
Lynn would appear not to come within
this exemption because Archer has made
a sale for an issuer in connection with the
distribution of the Darius shares to the
public.

    Another exemption from registration
under the 1933 act is the one granted for
"brokers' transactions." Generally, this exemption applies to ordinary brokers' transactions,
that is, where neither the seller nor his broker
solicits orders to buy the security involved,
where the broker does no more than execute
the order to sell as agent, and where the
broker receives no more than the customary
broker's commission. Here, in connection with
the sale of Lynn's 50,000 shares, Archer solicited buyers for Darius shares. And regarding
the 18,000 shares, Archer purchased them as
principal for its own account rather than as
agent on behalf of Lynn. For these reasons,
the brokers' transactions exemption would not
appear to be available in the given circumstances.

b.   Yes. Under the Securities Exchange Act of
     1934, it is unlawful for any person, direct-
     ly or indirectly, by the use of any means of
     interstate commerce or the mails, in connec-
     tion with the purchase or sale of any security,
     to employ any manipulative or deceptive de-
     vice or fraudulent scheme or practice, or to
     misstate, or omit to state, any material fact.
     The purchases by Archer from Lynn in mul-
     tiple transactions and the subsequent circula-
     tion of a story that there was active demand
     for Darius shares would be considered a man-
     ipulative or deceptive device to raise the price
     of the stock for personal gain at the public's
     expense.

c.   Yes. To prevent the unfair use of inside information that may have been obtained by a
beneficial owner of more than 10% of any
class of equity security of the issuer, the
1934 act provides that any profit realized
by the beneficial owner from any purchase
and sale of that security within any period
of less than six months shall be recoverable
by the issuer. Here, Lynn has purchased and
sold 68,000 Darius common shares within a
six-month period, while owning up to 55%
of Darius common stock. Thus, Lynn would
be liable under this provision to pay Darius
the profits he realized on these transactions.

ANSWER OUTLINE

Problem 2   Reg. A and Rule 10b-5

a1.   Regulation A exempts small offerings from full
registration
    Not to exceed $1,500,000
    Permits less documentation than full regis-
    tration
    Sale only by offering circular
    Financial statements may be unaudited

a2.   Liability is the same for Regulation A offerings
as for all other SEC offerings

a3.   The Securities Act of 1933 Statute of Limitations
is
    One year after discovery of untrue statement
    or omission
        Or after such discovery should have been
        made
    Or three years after security was bought
    Whichever is shorter

a4.   The 1934 Act does not apply to Glover
    It has less than $1 million in assets and 500
    shareholders
    Not listed on a national stock exchange
    Thus, it is not subject to reporting requirements,
    proxy rules, insider trading provisions, or tender
    rules
    But the anti-fraud provisions of the act do apply

b1.   The case should be dismissed
    Section 10(b) and Rule 10b-5 suits must establish
    fraud
    Here the CPA neither knew nor participated in
    the fraud
    Mere negligence is insufficient to establish fraud
    Knowledge of fraud is necessary in action for
    fraud under 10(b)

b2.   Alternate theories of liability might be
    Common law action for negligence
        Appears to lack privity requirement
        The foreseeable beneficiaries would not
        likely extend to Bank's customers
    Section 17 of the Securities and Exchange Act of
    1934
        Requires brokers to submit audited statements
        to SEC
        Thus, failure of accountant to perform proper
        audit creates liability

UNOFFICIAL ANSWER

Problem 2   Reg. A and Rule 10b-5

Part a.

1.   The Securities Act of 1933 gives the Securities and Exchange Commission authority to exempt
certain small public offerings from full registration.
The dollar amount of the offering may not exceed
$1.5 million (until recently increased, this amount
was $500,000). In order to obtain an exemption,
the issuer must meet the filing requirements contained in Regulation A. These requirements are
not as onerous as a full registration, although considerable documentation is required. The financial
statements generally need not be audited, and supplemental disclosures are not as extensive. Sales
must be made only by an offering circular, which
is similar to a prospectus, and it must be supplied
to each purchaser.

2.   None. The same liabilty for a false statement
or a material omission that applies to a full registration applies to a Regulation A offering.

3.   The act contains a two-part statute of limitations. First, any action must be brought within one
year after discovery of the untrue statement or omission or after such discovery should have been made
by the exercise of reasonable diligence. Second, in
no event can an action be brought more than three
years after the security was bought in good faith.

4.   Because of its size (less than $1 million assets
and less than 500 shareholders) and the fact that
it is not listed on a national stock exchange, Glover
is not required to register under the Securities Exchange Act of 1934. Consequently, it is not subject to the act's corporate reporting requirements,
proxy rules, insider trading provisions, or tender
rules. However, the antifraud provisions of the act
apply.

Part b.

1.   The case should be dismissed. A suit under Section 10(b) and Rule 10b-5 of the Securities Exchange Act of 1934 must establish fraud. Fraud is an intentional tort and as such requires more than a showing of negligence. Although the audit was admittedly improper and performed in a negligent manner, the CPAs neither participated in the fraudulent scheme nor did they know of its existence. The element of scienter or guilty knowledge must be present in order to state a cause of action for fraud under Section 10(b) of the Securities Exchange Act of 1934.

2.   The plaintiffs might have stated a common law action for negligence. However, they may not be able to prevail due to the privity requirement. There was no contractual relationship between the defrauded parties and the CPA firm. Although the exact status of the privity rule is unclear, it is doubtful that the simple negligence in this case would extend Gordon & Groton's liability to the customers who transacted business with Bank. However, the facts of the case as presented in court would determine this.

Another possible theory which has been attempted recently in the courts is liability under Section 17 of the Securities Exchange Act of 1934, which requires registered brokers to submit audited financial statements to the SEC. The plaintiff claimed that the accountant failed to perform a proper audit and thereby created liability to the customers of the brokerage firm who suffered losses as a result of the financial collapse of the brokerage firm. The Second Circuit Court of Appeals decided 2 to 1 that the plaintiff had stated a cause of action. The case is now on appeal to the Supreme Court.

MULTIPLE CHOICE QUESTIONS (1–25)

1. Jackson Enterprises dismissed its auditors for cause. The CPA firm failed to complete its audit within the time stipulated due to its own inefficiency. Under the circumstances
   a. The client has the right to all of the CPA's working papers relating to the engagement which are retained by the CPA.
   b. The CPA firm is entitled to recover the full fee agreed upon less a per diem diminution of 5% for each day delayed.
   c. Recovery by the CPA firm in quasi-contract will not be available if as a result of the delay the audit is worthless to Jackson.
   d. If Jackson sues the CPA firm for damages for breach of contract, recovery will be denied because it is commonly recognized that unless the contract so stipulates, time is not of the essence.

2. The traditional common-law rules regarding accountants' liability to third parties for negligence
   a. Remain substantially unchanged since their inception.
   b. Were more stringent than the rules currently applicable.
   c. Are of relatively minor importance to the accountant.
   d. Have been substantially changed at both the federal and state levels.

3. A third-party purchaser of securities has brought suit based upon the Securities Act of 1933 against a CPA firm. The CPA firm will prevail in the suit brought by the third party even though the CPA firm issued an unqualified opinion on materially incorrect financial statements if
   a. The CPA firm was unaware of the defects.
   b. The third-party plaintiff had no direct dealings with the CPA firm.
   c. The CPA firm can show that the third party plaintiff did not rely upon the audited financial statements.
   d. The CPA firm can establish that it was not guilty of actual fraud.

4. Henry Lamb worked for several years for a major CPA firm which has offices in 37 states.

He resigned his position with the CPA firm, then returned to his home state where he opened his own CPA practice. Under the circumstances
   a. Lamb will be liable for damages to his former employer if he engages in the practice of accounting in any state in which the firm has offices.
   b. Lamb will be liable for damages to his former employer if he accepts as his client any party, solicited or unsolicited, who had been a client of his former employer immediately prior to his being retained by said client.
   c. He must obtain permission of the state board of accountancy in the state in which he was previously employed in order to relocate.
   d. He must be licensed to practice as a CPA in his home state.

5. Martinson is a duly licensed CPA. One of his clients is suing him for negligence alleging that he failed to meet generally accepted auditing standards in the current year's audit thereby failing to discover large thefts of inventory. Under the circumstances
   a. Martinson is not bound by generally accepted auditing standards unless he is a member of the AICPA.
   b. Martinson's failure to meet generally accepted auditing standards would result in liability.
   c. Generally accepted auditing standards do not currently cover the procedures which must be used in verifying inventory for balance-sheet purposes.
   d. If Martinson failed to meet generally accepted auditing standards, he would undoubtedly be found to have committed the tort of fraud.

6. Walters & Whitlow, CPAs, failed to discover a fraudulent scheme used by Davis Corporation's head cashier to embezzle corporate funds during the past five years. Walters & Whitlow would have discovered the embezzlements promptly if they had not been negligent in their annual audits. Under the circumstances, Walters & Whitlow will normally not be liable for
   a. Punitive damages.
   b. The fees charged for the years in question.
   c. Losses occurring after the time the fraudulent scheme should have been detected.

d.   Losses occurring prior to the time the fraudulent scheme should have been detected and which could have been recovered had it been so detected.

7.   Martin Corporation orally engaged Humm & Dawson to audit its year-end financial statements. The engagement was to be completed within two months after the close of Martin's fiscal year for a fixed fee of $2,500. Under these circumstances what obligation is assumed by Humm & Dawson?

a.   None, because the contract is unenforceable since it is not in writing.

b.   An implied promise to exercise reasonable standards of competence and care.

c.   An implied obligation to take extraordinary steps to discover all defalcations.

d.   The obligation of an insurer of its work which is liable without fault.

8.   Which of the following can a CPA firm legally do?

a.   Accept a competing company in the same industry as another of its clients.

b.   Establish an association of CPAs for the purpose of determining minimum fee schedules.

c.   Effectively disclaim liability to third parties for any and all torts.

d.   Effectively establish an absolute dollar limitation on its liability for a given engagement.

9.   Winslow Manufacturing, Inc., sought a $200,000 loan from National Lending Corporation. National Lending insisted that audited financial statements be submitted before it would extend credit. Winslow agreed to this and also agreed to pay the audit fee. An audit was performed by an independent CPA who submitted his report to Winslow to be used solely for the purpose of negotiating a loan from National. National, upon reviewing the audited financial statements, decided in good faith not to extend the credit desired. Certain ratios, which as a matter of policy were used by National in reaching its decision, were deemed too low. Winslow used copies of the audited financial statements to obtain credit elsewhere. It was subsequently learned that the CPA, despite the exercise of reasonable care, had failed to discover a sophisticated embezzlement scheme by Winslow's chief accountant. Under these circumstances, what liability does the CPA have?

a.   The CPA is liable to third parties who extended credit to Winslow based upon the audited financial statements.

b.   The CPA is liable to Winslow to repay the audit fee because credit was not extended by National.

c.   The CPA is liable to Winslow for any losses Winslow suffered as a result of failure to discover the embezzlement.

d.   The CPA is not liable to any of the parties.

10.   A CPA is subject to criminal liability if the CPA

a.   Refuses to turn over the working papers to the client.

b.   Performs an audit in a negligent manner.

c.   Willfully omits a material fact required to be stated in a registration statement.

d.   Willfully breaches the contract with the client.

11.   A CPA was engaged by Jackson & Wilcox, a small retail partnership, to examine its financial statements. The CPA discovered that due to other commitments, the engagement could not be completed on time. The CPA, therefore, unilaterally delegated the duty to Vincent, an equally competent CPA. Under these circumstances, which of the following is true?

a.   The duty to perform the audit engagement is delegable in that it is determined by an objective standard.

b.   If Jackson & Wilcox refuses to accept Vincent because of a personal dislike of Vincent by one of the partners, Jackson & Wilcox will be liable for breach of contract.

c.   Jackson & Wilcox must accept the delegation in that Vincent is equally competent.

d.   The duty to perform the audit engagement is nondelegable and Jackson & Wilcox need not accept Vincent as a substitute if they do not wish to do so.

12.   Gaspard & Devlin, a medium-sized CPA firm, employed Marshall as a staff accountant. Marshall was negligent in auditing several of the firm's clients. Under these circumstances which of the following statements is true?

a.   Gaspard & Devlin is not liable for Marshall's negligence because CPAs are generally considered to be independent contractors.

b.   Gaspard & Devlin would not be liable for Marshall's negligence if Marshall disobeyed specific instructions in the performance of the audits.

c.   Gaspard & Devlin can recover against its insurer on its malpractice policy even if one of the partners was also negligent in reviewing Marshall's work.

d.   Marshall would have no personal liability for negligence.

13. Sharp, CPA, was engaged by Peters & Sons, a partnership, to give an opinion on the financial statements which were to be submitted to several prospective partners as part of a planned expansion of the firm. Sharp's fee was fixed on a per diem basis. After a period of intensive work, Sharp completed about half of the necessary field work. Then due to unanticipated demands upon his time by other clients, Sharp was forced to abandon the work. The planned expansion of the firm failed to materialize because the prospective partners lost interest when the audit report was not promptly available. Sharp offers to complete the task at a later date. This offer was refused. Peters & Sons suffered damages of $4,000 as a result. Under the circumstances, what is the probable outcome of a lawsuit between Sharp and Peters & Sons?

a.   Sharp will be compensated for the reasonable value of the services actually performed.

b.   Peters & Sons will recover damages for breach of contract.

c.   Peters & Sons will recover both punitive damages and damages for breach of contract.

d.   Neither Sharp nor Peters & Sons will recover against the other.

14. Josephs & Paul is a growing medium-sized partnership of CPAs. One of the firm's major clients is considering offering its stock to the public. This will be the firm's first client to go public. Which of the following is true with respect to this engagement?

a.   If the client is a service corporation, the Securities Act of 1933 will not apply.

b.   If the client is not going to be listed on an organized exchange, the Securities Exchange Act of 1934 will not apply.

c.   The Securities Act of 1933 imposes important additional potential liability on Josephs & Paul.

d.   As long as Josephs & Paul engages exclusively in intrastate business, the federal securities laws will not apply.

15. Magnus Enterprises engaged a CPA firm to perform the annual examination of its financial statements. Which of the following is a correct statement with respect to the CPA firm's liability to Magnus for negligence?

a.   Such liability can not be varied by agreement of the parties.

b.   The CPA firm will be liable for any fraudulent scheme it does not detect.

c.   The CPA firm will not be liable if it can show that it exercised the ordinary care and skill of a reasonable man in the conduct of his own affairs.

d.   The CPA firm must not only exercise reasonable care in what it does, but also must possess at least that degree of accounting knowledge and skill expected of a CPA.

16. The Apex Surety Company wrote a general fidelity bond covering defalcations by the employees of Watson, Inc. Thereafter, Grand, an employee of Watson, embezzled $18,900 of company funds. When his activities were discovered, Apex paid Watson the full amount in accordance with the terms of the fidelity bond, and then sought recovery against Watson's auditors, Kane & Dobbs, CPAs. Which of the following would be Kane & Dobbs' best defense?

a.   Apex is not in privity of contract.

b.   The shortages were the result of clever forgeries and collusive fraud which would not be detected by an examination made in accordance with generally accepted auditing standards.

c.   Kane & Dobbs were not guilty either of gross negligence or fraud.

d.   Kane & Dobbs were not aware of the Apex-Watson surety relationship.

17. The CPA firm of Knox and Knox has been subpoenaed to testify and produce its correspondence and working papers in connection with a lawsuit brought against Johnson, one of its clients. Regarding the attempted resort to the privileged communication rule in seeking to avoid admission of such evidence in the lawsuit, which of the following is correct?

a.   Federal law recognizes such a privilege if the accountant is a Certified Public Accountant.

b.   The privilege is available regarding the working papers since the accountant is deemed to own them.

c.   The privilege is as widely available as the attorney-client privilege.

d.   In the absence of a specific statutory provision, the law does not recognize the existence of the privileged communication rule between an accountant and his client.

18.   A CPA firm is being sued by a third party purchaser of securities sold in interstate commerce to the public. The third party is relying upon the Securities Act of 1933. The CPA firm had issued an unqualified opinion on incorrect financial statements. Which of the following represents the best defense available to the CPA firm?

a.   The securities sold had not been registered with the SEC.

b.   The CPA firm had returned the entire fee it charged for the engagement to the corporation.

c.   The third party was not in privity of contract with the CPA firm.

d.   The action had not been commenced within one year after the discovery of the material misrepresentation.

19.   On July 25, 1978, Archer, the president of Post Corporation, with the approval of the board of directors, engaged Biggs, a CPA, to examine Post's July 31, 1978, financial statements and to issue a report in time for the annual stockholders' meeting to be held on September 5, 1978. Notwithstanding Biggs' reasonable efforts, the report was not ready until September 7 because of delays by Post's staff. Archer, acting on behalf of Post, refused to accept or to pay for the report since it no longer served its intended purpose. In the event Biggs brings a legal action against Post, what is the probable outcome?

a.   The case would be dismissed because it is unethical for a CPA to sue for his fee.

b.   Biggs will be entitled to recover only in quasi contract for the value of the services to the client.

c.   Biggs will not recover since the completion by September 5th was a condition precedent to his recovery.

d.   Biggs will recover because the delay by Post's staff prevented Biggs from performing on time and thereby eliminated the timely performance condition.

MAY 1981 QUESTIONS

20.   DMO Enterprises, Inc., engaged the accounting firm of Martin, Seals & Anderson to perform its annual audit. The firm performed the audit in a competent, nonnegligent manner and billed DMO for $16,000, the agreed fee. Shortly after delivery of the audited financial statements, Hightower, the assistant controller, disappeared, taking with him $28,000 of DMO's funds. It was then discovered that Hightower had been engaged in a highly sophisticated, novel defalcation scheme during the past year. He had previously embezzled $35,000 of DMO funds. DMO has refused to pay the accounting firm's fee and is seeking to recover the $63,000 that was stolen by Hightower. Which of the following is correct?

a.   The accountants can **not** recover their fee and are liable for $63,000.

b.   The accountants are entitled to collect their fee and are **not** liable for $63,000.

c.   DMO is entitled to rescind the audit contract and thus is **not** liable for the $16,000 fee, but it can **not** recover damages.

d.   DMO is entitled to recover the $28,000 defalcation, and is **not** liable for the $16,000 fee.

21.   The CPA firm of Knox & Knox has been subpoenaed to testify and produce its correspondence and workpapers in connection with a lawsuit brought by a third party against one of their clients. Knox considers the subpoenaed documents to be privileged communication and therefore seeks to avoid admission of such evidence in the lawsuit. Which of the following is correct?

a.   Federal law recognizes such a privilege if the accountant is a Certified Public Accountant.

b.   The privilege is available regarding the working papers since the CPA is deemed to own them.

c.   The privileged communication rule as it applies to the CPA-client relationship is the same as that of attorney-client.

d.   In the absence of a specific statutory provision, the law does **not** recognize the existence of the privileged communication rule between a CPA and his client.

22.   Major, Major & Sharpe, CPAs, are the auditors of MacLain Industries. In connection with the public offering of $10 million of MacLain securities, Major expressed an unqualified opinion as to the financial statements. Subsequent to the offering, certain misstatements and omissions were revealed. Major has been sued by the purchasers of the stock offered pursuant to the registration statement which included the financial statements audited by Major. In the ensuing lawsuit by the MacLain investors, Major will be able to avoid liability if

a.   The errors and omissions were caused primarily by MacLain.

b.   It can be shown that at least some of the investors did **not** actually read the audited financial statements.

c.   It can prove due diligence in the audit of the financial statements of MacLain.

d.   MacLain had expressly assumed any liability in connection with the public offering.

23.   Donalds & Company, CPAs, audited the financial statements included in the annual report submitted by Markum Securities, Inc., to the Securities and Exchange Commission. The audit was improper in several resepcts. Markum is now insolvent and unable to satisfy the claims of its customers. The customers have instituted legal action against Donalds based upon section 10b and rule 10b-5 of the Securities Exchange Act of 1934. Which of the following is likely to be Donalds' best defense?

a.   They did **not** intentionally certify false financial statements.

b.   Section 10b does **not** apply to them.

c.   They were **not** in privity of contract with the creditors.

d.   Their engagement letter specifically disclaimed any liability to any party which resulted from Markum's fradulent conduct.

24.   The 1976 Tax Reform Act substantially changed the regulation of tax return preparers by

a.   Granting the Internal Revenue Service the power to seek injunctive relief against a wrongdoing preparer.

b.   Providing criminal sanctions.

c.   Imposing civil liability regardless of whether the preparer does the preparation for compensation.

d.   Expanding the legal remedies of the client for whom the return was prepared.

25.   If a CPA firm is being sued for common law fraud by a third party based upon materially false financial statements, which of the following is the best defense which the accountants could assert?

a.   Lack of privity.

b.   Lack of reliance.

c.   A disclaimer contained in the engagement letter.

d.   Contributory negligence on the part of the client.

PROBLEMS

Problem 1   Effect of Disclaimer on Liability; Partnership Liability; Third Party Liability (577,L4)   (20 to 25 minutes)

The CPA firm of Martinson, Brinks & Sutherland, a partnership, was the auditor for Masco Corporation, a medium-sized wholesaler. Masco leased warehouse facilities and sought financing for leasehold improvements to these facilities. Masco assured its bank that the leasehold improvements would result in a more efficient and profitable operation. Based on these assurances, the bank granted Masco a line of credit.

The loan agreement required annual audited financial statements. Masco submitted its 1975 audited financial statements to the bank which showed an operating profit of $75,000, leasehold improvements of $250,000, and net worth of $350,000. In reliance thereon, the bank loaned Masco $200,000. The audit report which accompanied the financial statements disclaimed an opinion because the cost of the leasehold improvements could not be determined from the company's records. The part of the audit report dealing with leasehold improvements reads as follows:

Additions to fixed assets in 1975 were found to include principally warehouse improvements. Practically all of this work was done by company employees and the cost of materials and overhead were paid by Masco. Unfortunately, fully complete detailed cost records were not kept of these leasehold improvements and no exact determination could be made as to the actual cost of said improvements. The total amount capitalized is set forth in note 4.

In late 1976 Masco went out of business, at which time it was learned that the claimed leasehold improvements were totally fictitious. The labor expenses charged as leasehold improvements proved to be operating expenses. No item of building material cost had been recorded. No independent investigation of the existence of the leasehold improvements was made by the auditors.

If the $250,000 had not been capitalized, the income statement would have reflected a substantial loss from operations and the net worth would have been correspondingly decreased.

The bank has sustained a loss on its loan to Masco of $200,000 and now seeks to recover damages from the CPA firm, alleging that the accountants negligently audited the financial statements.

Required: Answer the following, setting forth reasons for any conclusions stated.

a.   Will the disclaimer of opinion absolve the CPA firm from liability?

b.   Are the individual partners of Martinson, Brinks & Sutherland, who did not take part in the audit, liable?

c.   Briefly discuss the development of the common law regarding the liability of CPAs to third parties.

Problem 2   Antifraud Section of Security Act of 1934; Liability and Defenses Under Sec. 11(A) of 1933 Act (1180,L4)

(15 to 20 minutes)

Part a. Whitlow & Company is a brokerage firm registered under the Securities Exchange Act of 1934. The Act requires such a brokerage firm to file audited financial statements with the SEC annually. Mitchell & Moss, Whitlow's CPAs, performed the annual audit for the year ended December 31, 1979, and rendered an unqualified opinion, which was filed with the SEC along with Whitlow's financial statements. During 1979 Charles, the president of Whitlow & Company, engaged in a huge embezzlement scheme that eventually bankrupted the firm. As a result substantial losses were suffered by customers and shareholders of Whitlow & Company, including Thaxton who had recently purchased several shares of stock of Whitlow & Company after reviewing the company's 1979 audit report. Mitchell & Moss' audit was deficient; if they had complied with generally accepted auditing standards, the embezzlement would have been discovered. However, Mitchell & Moss had no knowledge of the embezzlement nor could their conduct be categorized as reckless.

Required:

Answer the following, setting forth reasons for any conclusions stated.

1.   What liability to Thaxton, if any, does Mitchell & Moss have under the Securities Exchange Act of 1934?

2.   What theory or theories of liability, if any, are available to Whitlow & Company's customers and shareholders under the common law?

Part b. Jackson is a sophisticated investor. As such, she was initially a member of a small group who was going to participate in a private placement of $1 million of common stock of Clarion Corporation. Numerous meetings were held among management and the investor group. Detailed financial and other information was supplied to the participants. Upon the eve of completion of the placement, it was aborted when one major investor withdrew. Clarion then decided to offer $2.5 million of Clarion common stock to the public pursuant to the registration requirements of the Securities Act of 1933. Jackson subscribed to $300,000 of the Clarion public stock offering. Nine months later, Clarion's earnings dropped significantly and as a result the stock dropped 20% beneath the offering price. In addition, the Dow Jones Industrial Average was down 10% from the time of the offering.

Jackson has sold her shares at a loss of $60,000 and seeks to hold all parties liable who participated in the public offering including Allen, Dunn, and Rose, Clarion's CPA firm. Although the audit was performed in conformity with generally accepted auditing standards, there were some relatively minor irregularities. The financial statements of Clarion Corporation, which were part of the registration statement, contained minor misleading facts. It is believed by Clarion and Allen, Dunn and Rose, that Jackson's asserted claim is without merit.

Required:

Answer the following, setting forth reasons for any conclusions stated.

1.   Assuming Jackson sues under the Securities Act of 1933, what will be the basis of her claim?

2.   What are the probable defenses which might be asserted by Allen, Dunn, and Rose in light of these facts?

Problem 3   Liability Under Tax Reform Act of 1976 and Securities Act of 1933 (580,L2)

(20 to 25 minutes)

Part a.   For the first time in the history of federal income tax law, Congress enacted legislation in 1976 that imposed civil liabilities and penalties upon individuals who are guilty of certain misconduct in connection with their preparing income tax returns for a fee. Prior provisions of the Internal Revenue Code which dealt with criminal fraud remained unchanged.

Required:

Answer the following, setting forth reasons for any conclusions stated.

What potential civil liabilities and penalties to the United States government should the practitioner be aware of in connection with the improper preparation of a federal income tax return, and what types of conduct would give rise to these liabilities and penalties?

Part b.   The directors of Clarion Corporation, their accountants, and their attorneys met to discuss the desirability of this highly successful corporation going public. In this connection, the discussion turned to the potential liability of the corporation and the parties involved in the preparation and signing of the registration statement under the Securities Act of 1933. Craft, Watkins, and Glenn are the largest shareholders. Craft is the Chairman of the Board; Watkins is the Vice Chairman; and Glenn is the Chief Executive Officer. It has been decided that they will sign the registration statement. There are two other directors who are also executives and shareholders of the corporation. All of the board members are going to have a percentage of their shares included in the offering. The firm of Witherspoon & Friendly, CPAs, will issue an opinion as to the financial statements of the corporation which will accompany the filing of the registration statement, and Blackstone & Abernathy, Attorneys-at-Law, will render legal services and provide any necessary opinion letters.

Required:

Answer the following, setting forth reasons for any conclusions stated.

Discuss the types of potential liability and defenses pursuant to the Securities Act of 1933 that each of the above parties or classes of parties may be subject to as a result of going public.

MULTIPLE CHOICE ANSWERS

1.	c	6.	a	11.	d	16.	b	21.	d
2.	d	7.	b	12.	c	17.	d	22.	c
3.	c	8.	a	13.	b	18.	d	23.	a
4.	d	9.	d	14.	c	19.	d	24.	a
5.	b	10.	c	15.	d	20.	b	25.	b

EXPLANATION OF MULTIPLE CHOICE ANSWERS

1. (1175,L2,17) (c) If the audit is worthless to Jackson, then time was of the essence. In such a case the injured party has a right to reject performance entirely. Also, if the audit is worthless, Jackson has received no unjust enrichment (the basis for quasi-contract recovery) for the CPA firm to recover. Working papers belong to the auditor and clients have no right to them. There is no doctrine for an auditor's fee to be reduced for each day the audit is not completed. Even if time is not made expressly of the essence, it may be inferred from the nature of the agreement. And in any event, the failure to meet the deadline of a contract entitles the non-breaching party to recover damages.

2. (1175,L2,18) (d) Federal and state statutes have substantially changed the accountants' liability to third parties for negligence. The Securities Act of 1933 is an example of much more stringent rules than the traditional common-law. At the state level, the liability for gross negligence or constructive fraud has arisen. The common-law rules are still important to the CPA, because they determine liability in areas outside the scope of these statutes.

3. (1175,L2,19) (c) Under the Securities Act of 1933 the third party need not prove reliance on the statements, but the CPA may avoid liability if he can prove that the third party's loss was due to another cause (in effect show that the third party did not rely on the statement). Unawareness or no actual fraud does not relieve the CPA of liability, because negligence is enough to create liability. The third party need only purchase the covered securities; direct dealings are not necessary.

4. (1175,L2,20) (d) A CPA must be licensed in the state in which he is going to practice on his own. State boards have no control over an accountant leaving the state. Lamb, as a former employee, cannot be precluded from competing with his former employer. Nor can he be precluded from accepting a client of his former employer as his own client, but to solicit one would violate the Code of Professional Ethics. A more difficult question is whether the courts would enforce an express agreement for an accountant not to compete with his former employer.

5. (1175,L2,21) (b) Any auditor is required to perform his work with reasonable care which is partly determined by compliance with GAAS. Failure to meet GAAS would indicate negligence, resulting in liability to the client. All auditors may be bound by GAAS which do cover procedures to verify inventory. Fraud is intentional deceit and would not exist merely from failure to follow GAAS.

6. (1175,L2,23) (a) CPAs normally would not be liable for punitive damages for simple negligence. Punitive damages are usually reserved for malicious or outrageous acts,e.g., fraud. They may be liable for their fees, because they did not do a competent job. Both losses occurring after the fraud should have been discovered, and those occurring before the fraud that could have been recovered, are chargeable to the CPAs, because it is their fault that the corporation sustained the losses.

7 (1176,L1,1) (b) When accepting an auditing engagement, an accountant makes an implied promise to exercise reasonable standards of competence and care. What is considered reasonable depends on the contract with the client, GAAP, GAAS, court decisions, statutes, and custom. There is no obligation to discover all defalcations if it would take extraordinary steps unless contracted to do so. Accountants only insure losses arising from their work that use of reasonable care would have avoided. The contract does not need to be in writing to be enforceable, because it is a contract for services (not land, goods, or intangibles) which can be performed within one year.

8. (1176,L1,2) (a) There is no reason why a CPA firm cannot accept a company competing with an existing client. Such a restriction would limit CPA firms to few clients. Minimum fee schedules (price fixing) are a per se violation of the Sherman Act (whether or not carried out by an association of CPAs). No one except the government can effectively disclaim tort liability to third parties. A CPA firm could limit tort liability with its client if fairly bargained for, i.e., if the limitation was not unconscionable. The same principle applies to putting a dollar limitation on its liability.

9.   (1176,L1,3)   (d)   The CPA is not liable to any of the parties. The CPA would be liable to Winslow or to third parties if he was negligent or fraudulent. A CPA is not responsible for undetected defalcations if reasonable care was used in performing the audit. The CPA did not condition the audit fee upon National's extension of credit. The offer of services on a basis contingent with findings would be a violation of Rule 302 of the Code of Professional Ethics.

10.   (1177,L1,1)   (c)   Criminal liability is only incurred by violating a statute. A CPA who willfully omits a material fact required to be stated in a registration statement is in violation of the Securities Acts and is subject to criminal liability. Civil liability is incurred by violating a legal duty owed to another. Answers (b) and (d) are incorrect because performing an audit in a negligent manner and willfully breaching a contract are violations of a legal duty owed to another and give rise to civil liability. Answer (a) is incorrect because a CPA owns his workpapers and has no duty to turn them over to a client.

11.   (1177,L1,3)   (d)   The duty to perform the audit is not delegable, because the audit is a contract for personal services based on personal trust or character. Only in certain cases, i.e., where services are mechanical and only the end result is desired, can personal services be delegated, e.g., moving goods, but never an audit. Jackson and Wilcox need not accept Vincent as a substitute, but they may if they wish. Thus answers (a) and (c) are incorrect. Answer (b) is incorrect because since Jackson and Wilcox have no duty to accept Vincent, they may refuse him for any reason, even personal dislike.

12.   (1177,L1,4)   (c)   Gaspard & Devlin can recover on its malpractice insurance no matter who in the firm was negligent, i.e., a malpractice policy insures negligence. Although CPA firms and individual practitioners are independent contractors, the firm independently contracted with the client. Answer (a) is incorrect because the firm as employer is liable for the negligence of its employees acting within the course and scope of their employment. Answer (b) is incorrect because Marshall's disobeyance of instructions would not matter because the firm is responsible for the actions of its employees. Answer (d) is incorrect because Marshall may be held personally liable either by the client, or by the firm if it is held liable by the client.

13.   (1177,L1,5)   (b)   The probable outcome is that Peters & Sons will recover their damages, because Sharp knew the purpose of the audit and it was Sharp's fault that the audit was not finished. Answer (a) is incorrect because Sharp will not be compensated, since he breached the contract and Peters & Sons realized no value from his work. Answer (c) is incorrect because punitive damages are not usually allowed for breach of contract. Punitive damages are allowed for fraud, gross negligence, and intentionally inflicted wrongs.

14.   (1177,L1,9)   (c)   Before the client goes public, Josephs & Paul is only liable to the client and known intended third-party beneficiaries (i.e., users) of the financial statements, absent fraud or constructive fraud. After the client "goes public" and becomes subject to the 1933 Act, Josephs & Paul may be held liable by any purchaser of the securities for any misleading statement in addition to incurring criminal liability. Answer (a) is incorrect because the Securities Act of 1933 covers the initial sales of securities regardless of the seller's form of organization. Answer (b) is incorrect because the Securities Exchange Act of 1934 applies to over-the-counter stocks in addition to securities listed on organized exchanges. Answer (d) is incorrect because the securities acts apply to securities sold in interstate commerce or through the mails even if the seller or its CPAs conducts business wholly intrastate.

15.   (1178,L1,2)   (d)   A CPA firm must exercise reasonable care and also must possess that degree of accounting knowledge and skill expected of an average CPA. Answer (a) is incorrect because a CPA's liability can be varied by agreement between the CPA and the client. Answer (b) is incorrect because a CPA firm is not liable for failing to detect fraudulent schemes provided their negligence did not prevent discovery. Answer (c) is incorrect because a CPA firm must exercise the care and skill of an average CPA rather than that of a reasonable person who is not trained as a CPA.

16.   (1178,L1,3)   (b)   A CPA is not normally liable to third parties unless he is negligent. He is not negligent if he performs his work with reasonable care as an average CPA in accordance with GAAS. Therefore the best defense for the CPAs would be that the forgeries and fraud were not the type ordinarily detected by an examination made in accordance with GAAS. Answer (a) is not the best defense because privity of contract is not needed to hold a CPA liable if he is grossly negligent or fraudulent. Answer (c) is not the

best defense because only ordinary negligence is necessary to hold a CPA liable by third parties if the accountant knows they are the intended beneficiaries of his work. Answer (d) is not the best defense because a CPA is liable to any third party who relies on his work if the CPA has committed fraud or constructive fraud (gross negligence).

17. (1178,L1,4) (d) At common law there is no rule granting privileged communication between an accountant and client. Thus, unless a statute specifically provides the privilege, none exists. Answer (a) is incorrect because no such federal rule exists. Answer (b) is incorrect because while it is true the accountant is deemed to own the audit work papers, that does not constitute a privilege to resist a properly served subpoena. Answer (c) is incorrect because, unlike the attorney-client privilege which is widely available, no such privilege generally exists for accountants.

18. (1178,L1,11) (d) The best defense for the CPA firm is that the third-party purchaser failed to commence his action within one year after discovery of the untrue statement or omission, or after such discovery should have been made by the exercise of reasonable diligence. This is the statute of limitations under the Securities Act of 1933. Answer (a) is not the best defense, because these securities should have been registered with the SEC and therefore the CPA firm can be held liable under the 1933 Act whether or not the securities were registered. Answer (b) is not the best defense because an accountant can be held liable whether or not he was paid. Answer (c) is not the best defense because the Securities Act of 1933 eliminates the necessity for privity of contract.

19. (1178,L1,32) (d) Accountants are responsible for performing contracts with their clients in accordance with the contractual terms. Additionally the rules of contracts also apply, and since Biggs was prevented from performing timely due to the client's delays, Biggs will recover his fees. Answer (a) is incorrect because a suit by an accountant to collect his fee would be handled as would any other contract for personal services. Similarly, answer (b) is incorrect because Biggs may recover in full under the contract. Answer (c) is incorrect because the the client prevented Biggs from meeting the deadline.

MAY 1981 ANSWERS

20. (581,L1,1) (b) In this case, a client is seeking to sue its auditor because defalcations perpetrated by management were not discovered during an annual audit. A client may sue its auditor under common law for breach of fiduciary duty, negligence, gross negligence or fraud. The auditor is obligated to plan the audit, to search for such irregularities, and to investigate matters coming to the auditor's attention that might indicate the existence of irregularities, but the auditor does not guarantee that these activities will be discovered. If the auditor is not negligent in the performance of his duties (e.g., he does not violate GAAS), he will not be liable for irregularities not discovered during the audit. In addition, the absence of negligence also precludes the client from withholding the auditor's fee. Thus, answer (b) is correct since the question specifically indicates that the auditor performed the audit in a "competent, non-negligent manner". Answers (a), (c), and (d) are incorrect since they all indicate some degree of liability on the part of the auditor.

21. (581,L1,2) (d) Under common law, no provision exists which grants privileged communication status to CPA-client relationships. Under the Code of Ethics, a CPA is generally prohibited from revealing client information without the client's permission except in situations involving a CPA firm's peer review evaluation, AICPA trial board inquiries, and information subpoenaed by a court of law. In the preceding situation, the CPA has no right to withhold client information from the requesting authorities. However, some state statutes do grant privileged communication status to confidential communications between a client and his accountant. But, unless such a state statute exists, no law will permit a CPA to avoid testifying in a lawsuit brought against his client. Answer (a) is incorrect because no federal law recognizes a privileged status of CPA-client relations. Answer (b) is incorrect because the fact that a CPA owns the workpapers has no effect on a CPA's duty to disclose information contained therein in the situations described above. Answer (c) is incorrect because the law does recognize the privileged nature of an attorney-client relationship; thus, this type of relationship is not the same as a CPA-client relationship.

22. (581,L1,3) (c) The SEC Act of 1933 concerns the regulation of initial public offerings of stock. The Act requires the filing of a registration statement including a certified financial statement. Any person acquiring a security covered by the registration can sue the accountant, if the certified financial

statements contained false statements or omitted material facts. The presence of such misstatements and omissions is prima facie evidence that the accountant is liable. This means that plaintiff-purchaser does not have the burden of proving the accountant's negligence; the accountant must prove he was not negligent and that he acted with due diligence (skill and care of the average accountant). Answer (a) is incorrect since the auditor's certification of the financial statements covers management's representations. The fact that the errors were caused by MacLain's actions will not relieve the auditor of liability. Answer (b) is also incorrect since the plaintiff does not have to prove reliance on the financial statements or that the loss was suffered from the misstatement. Answer (d) is incorrect since MacLain's express assumption of liability will not relieve the auditor.

23.   (581,L1,4)   (a)   The SEC Act of 1934 has antifraud provisions. These provisions apply to all transactions involving interstate commerce, mail, or transactions on the national exchange involving the purchase or sale of securities. Rule 10B5 makes it unlawful for any person to defraud, make untrue statements of material facts or omit material facts on the financial statements or engage in a business which operates as a fraud on persons involved in the purchase or sale of the securities. The correct answer is (a) since this would be the best defense. Scienter by the auditor must be established to hold them liable. This means that the defendant had knowledge of false statements or that the statement was made with a reckless disregard of the truth. Answer (b) is incorrect because Rule 10B5 applies to the accountants. Answer (c) is incorrect because privity (a contract between the creditors and the accountants) is not required to hold accountants liable. Answer (d) is incorrect since the auditor cannot disclaim liability in this manner.

24.   (581,L1,5)   (a)   This question deals with the substantial changes enacted by the Tax Reform Act of 1976. The principal effect of this act was to allow the IRS to seek an injunction against tax preparers who engage in the following activities: conduct subject to civil or criminal penalties under the Internal Revenue Code, misrepresentation of a preparer's qualifications to practice, guarantees that clients will receive refunds or tax credits on returns, or any other fraudulent or deceptive conduct. The only answer which reflects the above changes is answer (a). Answers (b) and (d) are incorrect because the 1976 Act did not substantially change either the criminal sanctions already available under previous acts (b) or the legal remedies available for clients (d). Answer (c) is incorrect because a preparer is always liable whether or not he prepares a return for compensation; in either case he must

sign the tax return without modifying the liability clause contained therein.

25.   (581,L1,6)   (b)   Under common law, a plaintiff must typically prove that: 1) there was negligence or fraud on the part of the preparer, 2) that misleading statements were prepared or distributed, 3) that the plaintiff relied on those misleading statements, and 4) that a loss resulted from this reliance. If a plaintiff is unable to prove, or if the auditor is able to disprove, any of these four requirements, the auditor will not be held liable. Thus, answer (b), in which the auditor attacks the validity of one of the above four conditions (reliance on the misleading statements) is correct in that this is the best defense of those listed in the possible answers. Answer (a) is incorrect because in cases of actual or constructive fraud, privity of third parties is not necessary in order to bring suit. Answer (c) is incorrect because a disclaimer contained in an engagement letter is not effective in relieving an accountant's liability for certified statements. Answer (d) is incorrect in that a client's negligence will not absolve the auditor of his responsibilities to third parties in any situation.

ANSWER OUTLINE

Problem 1   Effect of Disclaimer on Liability; Partnership Liability; Third Party Liability

a.   The disclaimer will not absolve CPA's liability
        The CPA was negligent
            No measures to determine leasehold improvement existence
            No notice of non-verification of existence
        Bank relied on CPA's report
        Generally CPA is not liable after proper disclaimer
            But here disclaimer implied improvements existed

b.   Yes. All partners are liable
        Even those who did not take part in the audit
        Partners are jointly and severally liable
        All partners are personally responsible for the firm's liability

c.   CPA liability to third parties for negligence is based on the doctrine of privy of contract
        But CPA is liable to client for ordinary negligence
        CPA may also be liable to third parties for fraud or gross negligence constituting fraud
        CPA may also be liable to third-party beneficiaries for ordinary negligence
        In the 1950s and 60s, liability began to expand
        Now a CPA may be found liable for ordinary negligence
            To a reasonably definable class of persons whom the CPA might reasonably foresee to rely on his report

UNOFFICIAL ANSWER

Problem 1   Effect of Disclaimer on Liability; Partnership Liability; Third Party Liability

a.   No. The disclaimer of opinion will not absolve the CPA firm from liability. The auditor was negligent by failing either to take adequate measures to determine whether the leasehold improvements existed or to give notice that their existence had not been verified. As a result of such negligence and the bank's reliance upon the report, the CPA firm would be liable to the bank.

An auditor generally will not be held responsible for limitations on the audit if the auditor's report gives adequate notice of them. A disclaimer of opinion is the means used by the auditor to give adequate notice of limitations. Although the CPA firm attempted to disclaim an opinion on the financial statements, the wording in the auditor's report was suffi-

ciently unclear that it is doubtful a court would find the report accomplished its intended purpose. The disclaimer said only that the "actual cost" of the improvements could not be determined, and the explanation strongly implied that the improvements actually existed and had substantial value (by use of such phrases as "were found" and "work was done") when in fact they did not exist. Consequently, the report was misleading.

b.   Yes. The individual partners of the CPA firm are liable even though they did not take part in the audit. A partnership is an entity that is an association of two or more persons as co-owners to carry on a business for profit. All partners are jointly and severally liable and therefore personally responsible for the firm's liability to the bank. The individual partners may have to satisfy the bank's claim from their personal assets, even though they did not personally take part in the audit.

c.   Determination of the liability of a CPA to third parties requires balancing two conflicting recognized interests of the law:

(1)   The CPA's reasonable right to self-protection from claims of unknown persons whom the CPA has no reason to suspect would rely on his report, and

(2)   The important public policy of protecting third parties who rely upon financial statements from the adverse effects of incompetent performance by professionals.

The *Ultramares* case in 1931 firmly established the doctrine of privity of contract leaving a CPA liable for simple or ordinary negligence only to a client. However, the opinion in that case indicated that a CPA could be liable to third parties if the conduct of the examination or preparation of the auditor's report involved fraud or negligence so gross as to permit an inference of fraud.

An additional basis upon which a third party could recover is as a third-party beneficiary. This relationship would be found in cases where it was clearly indicated that the engagement was undertaken for and was intended to benefit the third party, typically a lender.

The position of courts in upholding the doctrine of privity of contract began to change in the 1950s and 1960s. Court decisions began to reflect the view that CPAs owe a duty of care not only to their own clients but also to those whom they should know will rely on their reports in the transactions for which these reports are prepared. The courts began to rule that the CPA is liable for negligence for careless financial misrepresentations relied upon by foreseen and limited classes of persons. This extended the CPA's liability to third parties for simple or ordinary negligence to reasonably limited and reasonably definable classes of persons whom the CPA might reasonably expect would rely upon his report.

ANSWER OUTLINE

Problem 2   Antifraud Section of Security Act of 1934; Liability and Defenses Under Sec. 11(A) of 1933 Act

a1.   Under antifraud provision in section 10(b) of SEC Act of 1934, Thaxton is required to show
    Misstatement or omission of material fact in financials utilized in purchasing Whitlow & Co. stock
    Loss resulted from purchase of stock
    Loss resulted from reliance on misleading financials
    Auditors acted with knowledge (scienter)
    Facts indicate that proof of first three requirements by Thaxton is probable; however, facts show that auditors did not have knowledge
a2.   Negligence as evidenced by failure to comply with GAAS; if auditors were negligent, customers and shareholders must show
    They had third party beneficiary status relative to auditor's contract to audit Whitlow & Co., or
    A legal duty to act without negligence was due to them

b1.   Basis of claim is that loss was sustained from using misleading statements; section 11(a) of 1933 SEC Act applies
    Potential liability arises if minor irregularities result in certification of materially false or misleading financials
    Jackson's case asserts that financials contain false statement and that damages were sustained
    Jackson does not have to prove reliance of negligence (company or auditor)
    To avoid liability defendant must supply acceptable defenses

b2.   Probable defenses which Allen, Dunn and Rose might assert are
    Jackson knew of false statement or omission in audited financials included in registration statement
        Jackson (plaintiff) may not recover if proof exists that she had knowledge of "untruth or omission"
        Facts indicate Jackson may have had adequate knowledge
    False statement or omission was not material; test is whether investor would have been influenced not to purchase stock if right information had been disclosed
    Loss did not result from false statement or omission
        Portion of loss probably resulted from stock market decline
        Lack of evidence linking earnings decline to false statement or omission would give auditors defense
    Departure from GAAS did not represent noncompliance with due diligence standard

UNOFFICIAL ANSWER

Problem 2   Antifraud Section of Security Act of 1934; Liability and Defenses Under Sec. 11(A) of 1933 Act

Part a.

1.   In order for Thaxton to hold Mitchell & Moss liable for his losses under the Securities Exchange Act of 1934, he must rely upon the antifraud provisions of section 10(b) of the act. In order to prevail Thaxton must establish that
·   There was an omission or misstatement of a material fact in the financial statements used in connection with his purchase of the Whitlow & Company shares of stock.
·   He sustained a loss as a result of his purchase of the shares of stock.
·   His loss was caused by reliance on the misleading financial statements.
·   Mitchell & Moss acted with scienter.
    Based on the stated facts, Thaxton can probably prove the first three requirements cited above. To prove the fourth requirement, Thaxton must show that Mitchell & Moss had knowledge (scienter) of the fraud or recklessly disregarded the truth. The facts clearly indicate that Mitchell & Moss did not have knowledge of the fraud and did not recklessly disregard the truth.

2.   The customers and shareholders of Whitlow & Company would attempt to recover on a negligence theory based on Mitchell & Moss' failure to comply with GAAS. Even if Mitchell & Moss were negligent, Whitlow & Company's customers and shareholders must also establish either that—

·   They were third party beneficiaries of Mitchell & Moss' contract to audit Whitlow & Company, *or*

·   Mitchell & Moss owed the customers and shareholders a legal duty to act without negligence.

Although recent cases have expanded a CPA's legal responsibilities to a third party for negligence, the facts of this case may fall within the traditional rationale limiting a CPA's liability for negligence; that is, the unfairness of imputing an indeterminate amount of liability to unknown or unforeseen parties as a result of mere negligence on the auditor's part. Accordingly, Whitlow & Company's customers and shareholders will prevail only if (1) the courts rule that they are either third-party beneficiaries or are owed a legal duty and (2) they establish that Mitchell & Moss was negligent in failing to comply with generally accepted auditing standards.

Part b.

1.   The basis of Jackson's claim will be that she sustained a loss based upon misleading financial statements. Specifically, she will rely upon section 11(a) of the Securities Act of 1933, which provides the following:

> In case any part of the registration statement, when such part became effective, contained an untrue statement of a material fact or omitted to state a material fact required to be stated therein or necessary to make the statements therein not misleading, any person acquiring such security (unless it is proved that at the time of such acquisition he knew of such untruth or omission) may, either at law or in equity, in any court of competent jurisdiction, sue . . . every accountant . . . who has with his consent been named as having prepared or certified any part of the registration statement . . .

To the extent that the relatively minor irregularities resulted in the certification of materially false or misleading financial statements, there is potential liability. Jackson's case is based on the assertion of such an untrue statement or omission coupled with an allegation of damages. Jackson does not have to prove reliance on the statements nor the company's or auditor's negligence in order to recover the damages. The burden is placed on the defendant to provide defenses that will enable it to avoid liability.

2.   The first defense that could be asserted is that Jackson knew of the untruth or omission in audited financial statements included in the registration statement. The act provides that the plaintiff may not recover if it can be proved that at the time of such acquisition she knew of such "untruth or omission."

Since Jackson was a member of the private placement group and presumably privy to the type of information that would be contained in a registration statement, plus any other information requested by the group, she may have had sufficient knowledge of the facts claimed to be untrue or omitted. If this be the case, then she would not be relying on the certified financial statements but upon her own knowledge.

The next defense assertable would be that the untrue statement or omission was not material. The SEC has defined the term as meaning matters about which an average prudent investor ought to be reasonably informed before purchasing the registered security. For section 11 purposes, this has been construed as meaning a fact that, had it been correctly stated or disclosed, would have deterred or tended to deter the average prudent investor from purchasing the security in question.

Allen, Dunn, and Rose would also assert that the loss in question was not due to the false statement or omission; this is, that the false statement was not the cause of the price drop. It would appear that the general decline in the stock market would account for at least a part of the loss. Additionally, if the decline in earnings was not factually connected with the false statement or omission, the defendants have another basis for refuting the causal connection between their wrongdoing and the resultant drop in the stock's price.

Finally, the accountants will claim that their departure from generally accepted auditing standards was too minor to be considered a violation of the standard of due diligence required by the act.

ANSWER OUTLINE

Problem 3   Liability Under Tax Reform Act of 1976 and Securities Act of 1933

a.   Potential liabilities and penalties for tax practitioner

    1976 tax reform act imposed civil liabilities and penalties

        Basis for liability is understatement of taxpayer's liability

        Understatement due to negligence, penalty = $100/return

        Willful understatement, penalty = $500/return

        Burden of proof lies with preparer

1976 Tax Reform Act established new procedures for preparers and associated penalties

1. $25 for failure to give copy of return to taxpayer
2. $50 for failure to retain a copy of returns prepared or a list of taxpayers
3. $25 for absence of identification number on return
4. $25 for failure to sign return
5. $500 for each taxpayer's income tax check negotiated by preparer

1976 tax reform act gave IRS power to seek injunctive relief for:

1. Conduct subject to disclosure requirement penalties or understatement-of-liability penalties
2. Conduct subject to criminal penalties
3. Misrepresentation of preparers' eligibility to practice or his experience
4. Guarantee of tax refund or of allowance of credit
5. Other fraudulent or deceptive conduct

b.   Potential liability and defenses pursuant to the Securities Act of 1933

Act permits suit of various parties connected with registration statement

For untrue statement of or omission of material fact

Issuers, signers, directors, underwriters, and experts have potential liability

Any acquirer may sue unless knowledge of untruth or omission is proved

All directors and signers are issuers

May be sued in that capacity

Liable without fault for entire registration statement

Accountants and lawyers are experts

Not liable for portions on which they did not render expert opinion

Benefit of "due diligence" defense

Act provides certain defenses based on amount of damages and relationship to misstatements or omissions

UNOFFICIAL ANSWER

Problem 3   Liability Under Tax Reform Act of 1976 and Securities Act of 1933

Part a.

The 1976 Tax Reform Act substantially changed the liability imposed upon individuals who prepare income tax returns for compensation. In addition to disclosure requirements and ethical standards, the act imposed civil liability and penalties and empowered the government to obtain injunctive relief.

The basis for liability under the 1976 Tax Reform Act is an understatement of the taxpayer's federal income tax liability. A final determination of the taxpayer's tax liability by the Internal Revenue Service or the courts is not a necessary condition for establishing an understatement of that liability. Where the understatement is due to the negligent or intentional disregard of the income tax rules or regulations, the penalty is $100. The penalty does not extend to the employer of a tax return preparer solely by reason of the relationship. In the event of a trial of the question of the proper assessment of the penalty, the preparer has the burden of proving he was not at fault.

Where it is found that the preparer willfully understated the taxpayer's liability, the penalty is $500 per return. Where the willful understatement of liability also constitutes a negligent or intentional disregard for the rules and regulations, as it usually will, the combined penalty is a maximum of $500.

The 1976 Tax Reform Act also established new procedures for return preparers. Noncompliance with these procedures subjects the preparer to the following penalties.

1. $25 for failure to furnish a copy of the completed return to the taxpayer.
2. $50 for failure to retain either a copy of all returns prepared or a list of all taxpayers and their identification numbers.
3. $25 for failure to reflect the preparer's identification number on the tax return.
4. $25 for failure to sign the return.
5. $500 for each taxpayer's income tax check endorsed or otherwise negotiated by the preparer.

Finally, the Internal Revenue Service has the power to seek injunctive relief by enjoining a preparer from engaging in prohibited practices; or, if his conduct has repeatedly violated the proscribed practices, he may be enjoined from practicing as an income tax return preparer.

The specific practices of an income tax return preparer that can initiate an action to enjoin on the part of the service are the following:

1. Conduct subject to disclosure requirement penalties and understatement-of-taxpayer-liability penalties.
2. Conduct subject to criminal penalties under the Internal Revenue Code.
3. Misrepresentation of (a) the return preparer's eligibility to practice before the IRS or (b) his experience or education as an income tax return preparer.

4. Guarantee of payment of a tax refund or of allowance of a tax credit.
5. Other fraudulent or deceptive conduct that substantially interferes with proper administration of the internal revenue laws.

Part b.

The Securities Act of 1933 permits an aggrieved party to sue various parties connected with the registration statement for an untrue statement of a material fact in the registration statement or the omission of a material fact required to be stated therein or necessary to make the statements therein not misleading. Those having potential liability include issuers of the security, those who signed the registration statement, every director, underwriter, and expert.

Any acquirer of the security may sue unless it is proved that at the time of such acquisition he knew of such untruth or omission.

Since all the directors and signers are also issuers along with the corporation, they may be sued in that capacity, since with the one exception mentioned above, issuers may not avoid liability for untrue statements or omissions. They are insurers of the truth contained in the registration statement; that is, they are liable without fault.

Contrast their liability with that of the accountants and lawyers who are both experts. As such, they are not liable for parts of the registration statement on which they did not render an expert opinion. Moreover, as experts, they have the benefit of the "due diligence" defense. That is, liability can be avoided if it can be shown by the expert that he had, after reasonable investigation, reasonable ground to believe and did believe at the time such part of the registration statement became effective that the parts for which he gave expert opinion were true and that there was no omission to state a material fact required to be stated.

The act also provides certain defenses based on the amount of damages and their relationship to the misstatements or omissions.

MULTIPLE CHOICE QUESTIONS (1—26)

1. Ichi Ban Mopeds, Inc., is a Japanese manufacturer which has a manufacturing facility in the United States. United States business comprises ten percent (10%) of the sales of Ichi Ban of which four percent (4%) is manufactured at its United States facility. Under these circumstances
   a. Ichi Ban is exempt from state workmen's compensation laws.
   b. Ichi Ban is exempt from the Fair Labor Standards Act provided it is governed by comparable Japanese law.
   c. Ichi Ban is subject to generally prevailing federal and state laws applicable to American employees with respect to its employees at the United States facility.
   d. Ichi Ban could legally institute a policy which limited promotions to Japanese-Americans.

2. Harris was engaged as a crane operator by the Wilcox Manufacturing Corporation, a company complying with state worker's compensation laws. Harris suffered injuries during regular working hours as a result of carelessly climbing out on the arm of the crane to make an adjustment. While doing so, he lost his balance, fell off the arm of the crane and fractured his leg. Wilcox's safety manual for the operation of the crane strictly forbids such conduct by an operator. Wilcox denies any liability, based upon Harris' gross negligence, his disobedience and a waiver of all liability signed by Harris shortly after the accident. Wilcox further asserts that Harris is **not** entitled to worker's compensation because he is a skilled worker and is on a guaranteed biweekly salary. Which of the following is a correct statement insofar as Harris' rights are concerned?
   a. If he elects to sue under common law for negligence, his own negligence will result in a denial of recovery.
   b. Harris is **not** entitled to worker's compensation because he is **not** an "employee."
   c. Harris is **not** entitled to recovery because his conduct was a clear violation of the safety manual.
   d. Harris waived his rights by signing a waiver of liability.

3. Which of the following is a correct statement regarding the federal income tax treatment of social security tax payments and retirement benefits?
   a. The employer's social security tax payments are **not** deductible from its gross income.

   b. Social security retirement benefits are fully includable in the gross income of the retiree if he earns an amount in excess of certain established ceilings.
   c. Social security retirement benefits are excludable from the retiree's gross income even if the retiree has recouped all he has contributed.
   d. The employee's social security tax payments are deductible from the employee's gross income.

4. Which of the following provisions is a part of the Social Security law?
   a. Social Security benefits must be fully funded and payments, current and future, must constitutionally come only from Social Security taxes.
   b. Upon the death of an employee prior to his retirement, his estate is entitled to recieve the amount attributable to his contributions as a death benefit.
   c. A self-employed person must contribute an annual amount which is less than the combined contributions of an employee and his or her employer.
   d. Social Security benefits are taxable as income when they exceed the individual's total contributions.

5. At age 66, Jonstone retired as a general partner of Gordon & Co. He no longer participates in the affairs of the partnership but does receive a distributive share of the partnership profits as a result of becoming a limited partner upon retirement. Jonstone has accepted a part-time consulting position with a corporation near his retirement home. Which of the following is correct regarding Jonstone's Social Security situation?
   a. Jonstone's limited partner distributive share will be considered self-employment income for Social Security purposes up to a maximum of $10,000.
   b. There is no limitation on the amount Jonstone may earn in the first year of retirement.
   c. Jonstone will lose $1 of Social Security benefits for each $1 earnings in excess of a statutorily permitted amount.
   d. Jonstone will be subject to an annual earnings limitation until he attains a stated age which, if exceeded, will reduce the amount of Social Security benefits.

6. Yeats Manufacturing is engaged in the manufacture and sale of convertible furniture in interstate commerce. Yeats' manufacturing facilities are located in a jurisdiction which has a compulsory workmen's compensation act. Hardwood, Yeats' president, decided that the company should, in light of its safety record, choose to ignore the requirement of providing workmen's compensation insurance. Instead, Hardwood indicated that a special account should be created to provide for such contingencies. Basset was severely injured as a result of his negligent operation of a lathe which accelerated and cut off his right arm. In assessing the potential liability of Yeats, which of the following is a correct answer?

    a. Federal law applies since Yeats is engaged in interstate commerce.

    b. Yeats has no liability, since Basset negligently operated the lathe.

    c. Since Yeats did not provide workmen's compensation insurance, it can be sued by Basset and cannot resort to the usual common law defenses.

    d. Yeats is a self-insurer, hence it has no liability beyond the amount of the money in the insurance fund.

7. The federal Social Security Act applies in general to both employers and employees. Hexter Manufacturing is a small business as defined by the Small Business Administration. Regarding Hexter's relationship to the requirements of the Social Security Act, which of the following is correct?

    a. Since Hexter is a small business, it is exempt from the Social Security Act.

    b. Social Security payments made by Hexter's employees are tax deductible for federal income tax purposes.

    c. Hexter has the option to be covered or excluded from the provisions of the Social Security Act.

    d. The Social Security Act applies to both Hexter and its employees.

8. The Fair Labor Standards Act

    a. Applies to all employees whether or not engaged in interstate commerce.

    b. Requires that double time be paid to any employee working in excess of eight hours in a given day.

    c. Prohibits discrimination based upon the sex of the employee.

    d. Requires all employees doing the same job to receive an equal rate of pay.

9. Martin Wilson was hired by Gismore Enterprises, Inc., as an operator of a drill press. Gismore is fully covered by workmen's compensation insurance. Wilson did not believe in the safety regulations posted by management, hence, he removed the protective shields designed to prevent any possible injury to his hands. In this way he could meet production standards with a minimal effort and collect production bonuses. In the process of his work, Wilson unfortunately caught his hand in the drill press and the operating physician decided that amputation was the only alternative if Wilson's life were to be saved. Wilson seeks to recover. In this situation

    a. Wilson can recover in negligence against Gismore.

    b. Wilson will be denied all recovery because of his assumption of the risk.

    c. If Wilson was working overtime, workmen's compensation rules would not apply.

    d. Even if Wilson is guilty of contributory negligence, workmen's compensation rules provide for recovery.

10. The federal Fair Labor Standards Act

    a. Prohibits any employment of a person under 16 years of age.

    b. Requires payment of time-and-one-half for overtime to actors engaged in making television productions.

    c. Contains an exemption from the minimum-wage provision for manufacturing plants located in areas of high unemployment.

    d. Prohibits the delivery by a wholesaler to a dealer in another state of any goods where the wholesaler knew that oppressive child labor was used in the manufacture of the goods.

11. If an employer carried workmen's compensation coverage on his employees, an injured employee would

    a. Probably be covered even if the injury was caused by a co-worker.

    b. Not be covered if the injury was caused by grossly negligent maintenance by the employer.

    c. Probably not be covered if the injury was due to a violation of plant rules in operating the machine.

    d. Be covered if the employee was driving to work from his home.

12. Busby & Nelson, a general partnership, is a small furniture manufacturing company located in a southwestern state. It sells most of its products to fine furniture stores in Chicago, Los Angeles, and New York. It employs 50 skilled workmen and 10 other employees. Busby & Nelson has elected not to be covered under the state law which provides for elective workmen's compensation coverage because its safety standards are excellent, and there has not been a serious employee injury for several years. Busby & Nelson

  a. Would not be held liable for workmen's compensation to an injured employee if the injury was due to the employee's negligence.

  b. Is obligated to pay workmen's compensation benefits to its employees even though such coverage was optional.

  c. Is subject to lawsuits for damages by injured employees and may not assert the common-law defenses such as contributory negligence.

  d. Cannot create any type of pension plan for the partners and its employees which will permit payments thereto to be deducted in whole or part for federal-income-tax purposes.

13. Workmen's compensation laws

  a. Are uniform throughout the United States with the exception of Louisiana.

  b. Have not been adopted by all states except where required by federal law.

  c. Do not preclude an action against a third party who has caused an injury.

  d. Do not cover employees injured outside the jurisdiction.

14. The Federal Social Security Act

  a. Applies to self-employed businessmen.

  b. Excludes professionals such as accountants, lawyers, and doctors.

  c. Provides for a deduction by the employee against his federal income tax.

  d. Applies to professionals at their option.

15. Which of the following classes of employees is exempt from both the minimum wage and maximum hours provisions of the Federal Fair Labor Standards Act?

  a. Members of a labor union.

  b. Administrative personnel.

  c. Hospital workers.

  d. No class of employees is exempt.

16. The Jax Corporation owned and operated a modern, highly efficient sawmill. Forrester was one of its saw operators. Jax Corporation was subject to periodic inspections of its operations by both governmental and insurance company inspectors regarding its safety standards. It was agreed by virtually everyone involved in examining Jax's safety standards and equipment that they were outstanding and far above the minimum level which most other mills in the state met. Forrester was an employee of long standing and a man of firm convictions. He believed that many of the rules and required safety equipment were nothing more than a "bloody nuisance." Forrester repeatedly disregarded them when he could do so without being caught. Unfortunately, one day Forrester was seriously injured while using a power saw. He lost his left hand. Had he followed proper procedures and used the required safety equipment the injury would not have occurred. What circumstance described above would preclude Forrester from recovering under workmen's compensation?

  a. Forrester's gross negligence.

  b. Agreement by all inspectors that safety standards were outstanding and far above minimum levels.

  c. Forrester's disregard of safety standards only when he could do it without being caught.

  d. None of the circumstances described above would preclude Forrester's recovery under workmen's compensation.

17. During the 1976 examination of the financial statements of Viscount Manufacturing Corporation, the CPAs noted that although Viscount had 860 full-time and part-time employees, it had completely overlooked its reponsibilities under the Federal Insurance Contributions Act (FICA). Under these circumstances, which of the following is true?

  a. No liability under the act will attach if the employees voluntarily relinquish their rights under the act in exchange for a cash equivalent paid directly to them.

  b. If the union which represents the employees has a vested pension plan covering the employees which is equal to or exceeds the benefits available under the act, Viscount has no liability.

  c. Since employers and employees owe FICA taxes at the same rate and since the employer must withhold the employees' tax from their wages as paid, Viscount must remit to the government a tax double the amount assessed directly against the employer.

  d. The act does not apply to the part-time employees.

18. Fashion Industries, Inc., manufactures dresses which it sells throughout the United States and South America. Among its 5,000 employees in 1976 were 165 youngsters aged 14 and 15 who worked in a wide range of jobs and were paid at a rate less than the minimum wage. Which statement is correct in accordance with the general rules of the Fair Labor Standards Act?

    a. Fashion was exempt from regulation because less than 5% of its employees were children.

    b. Fashion did not violate the law since both male and female youngsters were paid at the same rate and only worked on Saturdays.

    c. Fashion violated the law by employing children under 16 years of age.

    d. Fashion was exempt from regulation if more than 10% of its sales were in direct competition with foreign goods.

19. The theatrical agency of Power & Tyrone employs two people full time. Which of the following is true with regard to federal unemployment insurance?

    a. In terms of industry and number of employees, Power & Tyrone is within the class of employers covered by the federal unemployment tax.

    b. Service agencies are exempt.

    c. Since the number of employees is small, an exemption can be obtained from coverage if a request is filed with the appropriate federal agency.

    d. If the employees all reside in one state and do not travel interstate on company business, Power & Tyrone is exempt from compliance with the act.

20. Barnaby is an employee of the Excelsior Manufacturing Company, a multi-state manufacturer of toys. The plant in which he works is unionized and Barnaby is a dues paying member. Which statement is correct insofar as the Federal Fair Labor Standards Act is concerned?

    a. Excelsior is permitted to pay less than the minimum wage to employees since they are represented by a bona fide union.

    b. The act allows a piece-rate method to be employed in lieu of the hourly rate method where appropriate.

    c. The act excludes from its coverage the employees of a labor union.

    d. The act sets the maximum number of hours that an employee can work in a given day or week.

21. Jones has filed a claim with the appropriate Workmen's Compensation Board against the Atlas Metal & Magnet Company. Atlas denies liability under the State Workmen's Compensation Act. In which of the following situations will Jones recover from Atlas or its insurer?

    a. Jones intentionally caused an injury to himself.

    b. Jones is an independent contractor.

    c. Jones is basing the claim upon a disease unrelated to the employment.

    d. Jones and another employee of Atlas were grossly negligent in connection with their employment, resulting in injury to Jones.

22. Wilton was grossly negligent in the operation of a drill press. As a result he suffered permanent disability. His claim for workmen's compensation will be

    a. Reduced by the percentage share attributable to his own fault.

    b. Limited to medical benefits.

    c. Denied.

    d. Paid in full.

23. Jane Sabine was doing business as Sabine Fashions, a sole proprietorship. Sabine suffered financial reverses and began to use social security and income taxes withheld from her employees to finance the business. Sabine finally filed a voluntary petition in bankruptcy. Which of the following would not apply to her as a result of her actions?

    a. She would remain liable for the taxes due.

    b. She is personally liable for fines and imprisonment.

    c. She could justify her actions by showing that the use of the tax money was vital to continuation of the business.

    d. She may be assessed penalties up to the amount of taxes due.

MAY 1981 QUESTIONS

24. Stephens is an employee of the Jensen Manufacturing Company, a multi-state manufacturer of roller-skates. The plant in which he works is unionized and Stephens is a dues paying union member. Which statement is correct insofar as the Federal Fair Labor Standards Act is concerned?

    a. The Act allows a piece-rate method to be employed in lieu of the hourly-rate method where appropriate.

    b. Jensen is permitted to pay less than the minimum wage to employees since they are represented by a bona fide union.

c.   The Act sets the maximum number of hours that an employee can work in a given day or week.

d.   The Act excludes from its coverage the employees of a labor union.

25.   The Social Security Act provides for the imposition of taxes and the disbursement of benefits. Which of the following is a correct statement regarding these taxes and disbursements?

a.   Only those who have contributed to Social Security are eligible for benefits.

b.   As between an employer and its employee, the tax rates are the same.

c.   A deduction for federal income tax purposes is allowed the employee for Social Security taxes paid.

d.   Social Security payments are includable in gross income for federal income tax purposes unless they are paid for disability.

26.   Musgrove Manufacturing Enterprises is subject to compulsory worker's compensation laws in the state in which it does business. It has complied with the state's worker's compensation provisions. State law provides that were there has been compliance, worker's compensation is normally an exclusive remedy. However, the remedy will **not** be exclusive if

a.   The employee has been intentionally injured by the employer personally.

b.   The employee dies as a result of his injuries.

c.   The accident was entirely the fault of a fellow-servant of the employee.

d.   The employer was only slightly negligent and the employee's conduct was grossly negligent.

Problem 1   Workmen's Compensation (1178,L3c)

(5 to 10 minutes)

Part c. Eureka Enterprises, Inc., started doing business in July 1977. It manufactures electronic components and currently employs 35 individuals. In anticipation of future financing needs, Eureka has engaged a CPA firm to audit its financial statements. During the course of the examination, the CPA firm discovers that Eureka has no workmen's compensation insurance, which is in violation of state law, and so informs the president of Eureka.

Required: Answer the following, setting forth reasons for any conclusions stated.

1. What is the purpose of a state workmen's compensation law?

2. What are the legal implications of not having workmen's compensation insurance?

MULTIPLE CHOICE ANSWERS

1.	c	7.	d	13.	c	19.	a	25.	b
2.	a	8.	c	14.	a	20.	b	26.	a
3.	c	9.	d	15.	b	21.	d		
4.	c	10.	d	16.	d	22.	d		
5.	d	11.	a	17.	c	23.	c		
6.	c	12.	c	18.	c	24.	a		

EXPLANATION OF MULTIPLE CHOICE ANSWERS

1. (1180,L1,58) (c) Since Ichi Ban Mopeds, Inc., is doing business in the United States, it is subject to applicable federal and state laws concerning the employees at the United States facility. This includes state workmen's compensation laws, the Fair Labor Standards Act, and many other regulatory statutes. Answer (d) is incorrect because Title VII of Civil Rights Act of 1964 states that employers cannot discriminate on the basis of religion, sex or national origin unless the above categories are bona fide occupational qualifications reasonably necessary to normal business operation. National origin would not be a bona fide occupational qualification for promotion.

2. (1180,L1,59) (a) The correct answer is (a) since if Harris elects to sue under common law for negligence, the employer can use the defense of contributory negligence which will prevent Harris from recovering. Since the purpose of the workmen's compensation laws is to give employees certainty of benefits for job-related injuries and diseases, most state statutes prohibit waiver of these benefits by employees. Thus answer (d) is wrong. Workmen's compensation laws destroy the employer's common law defenses of: assumption of risk; negligence of a fellow employee; contributory negligence. Even though the employee's conduct that caused the injury was a violation of prescribed safety rules, the employee will recover under workmen's compensation laws if the injury occurred on the job. Thus answer (d) is incorrect. Answer (b) is incorrect because a skilled worker on a guaranteed biweekly salary is not exempted from the provisions of workmen's compensation laws. However, workmen's compensation laws do not cover all employees; some exemptions are: agricultural workers; domestic workers; causal employees; employers who employ below a fixed number of employees.

3. (1180,L1,60) (c) Out of social concern for the well-being of the elderly, social security income may be excluded from gross income, when filing a federal tax return. Therefore answer (b) is incorrect. Answer (a) is false since the employer may deduct all ordinary and necessary business expense including social security tax. Answer (d) is incorrect because federal tax laws provide that since social security benefits are not included in gross income, social security payments cannot be deducted from gross income during the taxpayer's working years.

4. (580,L1,17) (c) Answer (c) is correct because annual contributions made by a self-employed individual amount to 8.1% of the first $25,900 (for 1980) of self-employment income, whereas the contributions of an employee and his or her employer amount to 12.26% of the first $25,900 (for 1980) of wages. Answer (a) is incorrect because it is legal to fund Social Security benefits from sources other than Social Security taxes. Answer (b) is incorrect because upon death of an individual, the amount of death benefits have no relation to the amount of contributions paid by the individual. Answer (d) is incorrect because benefits received in excess of the individual's total contributions are not taxable as income.

5. (580,L1,18) (d) Answer (d) is correct because there is no limit on earnings after age 72 under the Social Security laws. Answer (a) is incorrect because under Social Security law an individual's wages normally shall be computed without regard to any maximum limitations and a partner's distributive share will be excluded entirely if certain requirements are met. Answer (b) is incorrect because the limitation on Jonstone's earnings may occur in the first year if he had excess earnings above the statutorily permitted amount. Answer (c) is incorrect because Social Security law does reduce benefits on the basis of a complicated statutory formula that would not result in a loss of $1 of Social Security benefits for each $1 of earnings in excess of a statutorily permitted amount.

6. (1179,L1,48) (c) The usual result when the employer fails to provide workmens compensation insurance is that the injured employee may sue in a common law action, and the employer cannot resort to the usual common law defenses (such as contributory negligence, assumption of risk, or fellow servant rule). Answer (a) is incorrect because there is no federal law applying to workmens compensation. Workmens compensation is regulated by state statutes, which are only affected by federal guidelines. Answer (b) is incorrect because the employer does have liability for job-related injuries even if the injured employee was negligent. Answer (d) is incorrect in that Yeats is not a self-insuror because the problem indicates that he is doing business in a state that has a compulsory workmens compensation act, i.e., does not recognize self-insurance plans.

7. (1179,L1,49) (d) The Social Security Act applies to both Hexter and its employees. The fact that Hexter Manufacturing is defined as a small business by the Small Business Administration Act is of no legal consequence. Answer (a) is incorrect because its size cannot exempt a business from social security. Answer (b) is incorrect because social security payments made by an employee are not deductible for federal income tax purposes. The social security tax and the income tax are separate taxes. Answer (c) is incorrect since Hexter has no option but must be covered by the provisions of the Social Security Act. Participation is mandatory.

8. (1174,L2,30) (c) Employers must be engaged in interstate commerce to be subject to the act. If applicable, the Act requires 1½ times to be paid for overtime. It is not necessary for all employees doing the same job to be paid the same.

9. (1174,L2,32) (d) Workmen's compensation is an alternative to a tort cause of action. Consequently, tort defenses such as assumption of risk and contributory negligence will not deny recovery. Workmen's compensation applies whenever employees are on the job.

10. (574,L3,42) (d) Some child labor, such as newspaper carrying, is not covered by FLSA. Professionals, such as actors, are exempt from the provisions. Finally, being in an area of high or low unemployment does not excuse compliance with the Act.

11. (574,L3,43) (a) Workmen's compensation is a form of strict liability on the employer in exchange for the employee's forbearance of the right to sue in tort. Negligence by the employee or the employer is not a factor in workmen's compensation. However, to be compensable, the injury must have happened on the job. Injuries sustained driving to work would not be covered.

12. (575,L3,44) (c) If an employer elects not to be covered by workmen's compensation and an employee is injured, the employee may sue in tort and the employer is not entitled to use the common law defenses such as contributory negligence. This is a method to influence employers to adopt workmen's compensation. If the election not to have workmen's compensation is valid, the employer is not liable for workmen's compensation payments, but can be sued in tort.

13. (575,L3,35) (c) All states have workmen's compensation laws, but they are not uniform, and each state has its own rules and regulations. It is entirely possible for WC to cover employees outside their state if they are working for their home state employer. WC compensates an injured employee, but does not preclude an action against the third party who caused the accident. Where the employer pays WC premiums, this right of action against third parties normally belongs to the employer.

14. (1176,L3,47) (a) The Federal Social Security Act specifically applies to those who are self-employed and provides a separate contribution rate for them. It includes all employees and self-employed persons whether or not professionals. Professionals do not have an option of whether or not to participate. Employees do not get a tax deduction unless their FICA withholdings exceed the amount required by law to be withheld.

15. (577,L1,13) (b) Administrative personnel are exempt from the minimum wage and maximum hours provisions of the FLSA as are executive and professional employees. Labor union members and hospital workers are covered by the FLSA.

16. (577,L1,14) (d) Claims for recovery under workmen's compensation must arise out of and in the course of employment, i.e., from injury on the job. An employee can recover even if the injury is his own fault and he was grossly negligent. Neither his disregard of the safety standards nor the quality of the safety standards will affect his recovery.

17. (1177,L1,13) (c) It is the employer's duty to withhold FICA taxes from the employee and remit both these and the employer share to the government. If the employer neglects to withhold, the employer is liable for both the employer and employee taxes, i.e., to pay double. Answer (a) is incorrect because FICA is mandatory and employees may not relinquish their rights. Answer (b) is incorrect because pension plans and other benefits are no substitute for FICA. Answer (d) is incorrect because FICA applies to all employees whether part-time or full-time.

18. (1177,L1,14) (c) It is a violation of the FLSA to employ children under the age of 16 except in very limited circumstances. Answer (a) is incorrect because there are no exemptions based on the number of children employed. Answer (b) is incorrect because equal pay and weekend work do not excuse employing children under 16. Answer (d) is incorrect because competition with foreign or any other goods is also not an excuse. Child labor exceptions are agriculture,

child actors, employment by a parent, and newspaper delivery.

19. (1177,L1,15) (a) Federal unemployment tax must be paid if there are one or more employees being paid wages. Answer (b) is incorrect because service agencies are included as is any other business. Answer (c) is incorrect because there is no exemption for few employees. Answer (d) is incorrect even if the employees do not leave the state; as long as some part of the business concerns interstate commerce or the mails are used, the business is included.

20. (578,L1,47) (b) The Fair Labor Standards Act (FLSA) prescribes the minimum wages which may be paid to employees. The FLSA allows methods of payment other than an hourly rate, including the piece-rate method, if it at least equals the hourly minimum. Answers (a) and (c) are incorrect because union employees are covered by the FLSA as are non-union employees and they may not be paid less than the minimum wage. Answer (d) is incorrect because the FLSA does not set the maximum number of hours that employees can work, but instead provides for minimum wages and payment for overtime.

21. (578,L1,48) (d) Workmen's compensation provides benefits to employees who are injured on the job even though the employee may have been negligent, or even grossly negligent. Answer (a) is incorrect, because workmen's compensation does not provide benefits for injuries which the worker intentionally inflicts. Answer (b) is incorrect also because an independent contractor is not an employee and therefore is not entitled to workman's compensation coverage. Answer (c) is incorrect because an injury must be job-related to obtain workmen's compensation benefits.

22. (579,L1,47) (d) A worker injured in a job-related activity will be paid the full amount specified by the applicable workmen's compensation act despite the fact that the worker may have been grossly negligent. Hence, answer (a) is incorrect because the workmen's compensation laws do not reduce benefits by the percentage share attributable to the worker's own fault. Answer (b) is incorrect because workmen's compensation benefits are not limited to medical benefits. Answer (c) is incorrect because in no event should benefits for job-related injuries or diseases be denied an injured worker except if willfully inflicted or if they result from intoxication or mutual altercations.

23. (579,L1,50) (c) The requirement is the statement that would not apply to Jane Sabine's actions. An employer who withholds social security and income taxes from employees may not justify using such funds to finance her business even if such action were vital to continuation of the business. Such action is a criminal act and would subject the perpetrator to absolute liability. Even should she be adjudicated a bankrupt, she would, as in answer (a), remain personally liable for taxes due. As in answer (b), she would be personally liable for fines and imprisonment. Also in answer (d), she may be assessed penalties up to the amount of the taxes due (100%).

MAY 1981 ANSWERS

24. (581,L1,58) (a) Under the Fair Labor Standards Act an employer can substitute a piece-rate method of payment for the hourly rate. Answers (b) and (d) are incorrect since the fact that the employees are represented by a union would be irrelevant when applying this act. Union members are covered by the act and must be paid at least the statutory minimum wage. Answer (c) is incorrect since the act does not specify the maximum number of hours an employee can work in a given day. The act does stipulate that an employee is to be paid time and a half for hours worked in excess of 40 hours per week.

25. (581,L1,59) (b) An employer is required to match contributions of employees to the Social Security System on a dollar-for-dollar basis. Answer (a) is incorrect since benefits may be paid to the surviving spouse or other dependents of a deceased individual who was covered under the Social Security System. Answer (c) is incorrect since the amount of Social Security taxes paid is not an allowable deduction on an individual's tax return. Payments to the system are taxed in full when made, and are recovered on a tax-free basis when received by the individual in the form of benefits. Answer (d) is incorrect because Social Security payments are not included in the gross income of a taxpayer.

26. (581,L1,60) (a) If the employer intentionally injures the employee, the employee would not only have a right to proceed under worker's compensation, but could sue the employer in a civil court of law on the basis of an intentional tort. Answers (b), (c) and (d) are incorrect because they do not state grounds that would allow the injured employee to sue in a civil court of law if covered by a proper worker's compensation plan. Even though the injury was caused by contributory negligence of the employee or the act of a fellow servant, the injured employee could still recover, but recovery under worker's compensation would be the exclusive remedy.

ANSWER OUTLINE

Problem 1   Workmen's Compensation

c1.   Workmen's comp compensates employees injured
       at work
            Benefits available to injured, survivors, or de-
            pendents

c2.   Workmen's comp is generally mandatory by
       statute
            Employers with no workmen's comp have
            liability
            Also precludes common-law defenses of
               Fellow-servant
               Assumption of risk
               Contributory negligence
            Employer may also be liable for workmen's
               comp benefits, also fines and possibly
               imprisonment

UNOFFICIAL ANSWER

Problem 1   Workmen's Compensation

Part c.

1.   Workmen's compensation laws provide a system of compensation for employees who are injured,
disabled, or killed as a result of accidents or occupational diseases in the course of their employment.
Benefits also extend to survivors or dependents of
these employees.

2.   In all but a distinct minority of jurisdictions,
workmen's compensation coverage is mandatory. In
those few jurisdictions that have elective workmen's
compensation, employers who reject workmen's
compensation coverage are subject to common law
actions by injured employees and are precluded from
asserting the defenses of fellow-servant, assumption
of risk, and contributory negligence. The number of
such jurisdictions having elective compensation coverage has been constantly diminishing. The penalty in
these jurisdictions is the loss of the foregoing defenses.
      The more common problem occurs in connec-
tion with the failure of an employer to secure compensation coverage even though he is obligated to
do so in the majority of jurisdictions. The one
uniform effect of such unwise conduct on the part
of the employer is to deny him the use of the
common law defenses mentioned above.
      In addition to the foregoing, an increasing
number of states have provided for the payment
of workmen's compensation by the state to the
injured employee of the uninsured employer. The
state in turn proceeds against the employer to
recover the compensation cost and to impose
penalties that include fines and imprisonment.
Other jurisdictions provide for a penalty in the
form of additional compensation payments over
and above the basic amounts, or they require an
immediate lump-sum payment.

MULTIPLE CHOICE QUESTIONS (1–31)

1. Gilgo has entered into a contract for the purchase of land from the Wicklow Land Company. A title search reveals certain defects in the title to the land to be conveyed by Wicklow. Wicklow has demanded that Gilgo accept the deed and pay the balance of the purchase price. Furthermore, Wicklow has informed Gilgo that unless Gilgo proceeds with the closing, Wicklow will hold Gilgo liable for breach of contract. Wicklow has pointed out to Gilgo that the contract says nothing about defects and that he must take the property "as is." Which of the following is correct?

  a. Gilgo can rely on the implied warranty of merchantability.

  b. Wicklow is right in that if there is **no** express warranty against title defects, none exists.

  c. Gilgo will prevail because he is entitled to a perfect title from Wicklow.

  d. Gilgo will win if the title is **not** marketable.

2. Marks is a commercial tenant of Tudor Buildings, Inc. The term of the lease is five years and two years have elapsed. The lease prohibits subletting, but does **not** contain any provision relating to assignment. Marks approached Tudor and asked whether Tudor could release him from the balance of the term of the lease for $500. Tudor refused unless Marks would agree to pay $2,000. Marks located Flint who was interested in renting in Tudor's building and transferred the entire balance of the lease to Flint in consideration of his promise to pay Tudor the monthly rental and otherwise perform Marks' obligations under the lease. Tudor objects. Which of the following statements is correct?

  a. A prohibition of the right to sublet contained in the lease completely prohibits an assignment.

  b. The assignment need **not** be in writing.

  c. The assignment does **not** extinguish Marks' obligation to pay the rent if Flint defaults.

  d. The assignment is invalid without Tudor's consent.

3. Carr owns 100 acres of undeveloped land on the outskirts of New Town. He bought the land several years ago to build an industrial park in the event New Town grew and prospered. The land was formerly used for grazing and truck gardening. A subsequent inspection revealed that several adjacent landowners recently had been using a shortcut across his land in order to reach a newly constructed highway. Which of the following is a correct statement?

  a. There is a danger that the adjacent land-owners will obtain title by adverse possession.

  b. Since Carr has properly recorded his deed, the facts do not pose a problem for him.

  c. There is a danger that an easement may be created.

  d. Since the adjacent landowners are trespassers, Carr has nothing to fear.

4. Dombres is considering purchasing Blackacre. The title search revealed that the property was willed by Adams jointly to his children, Donald and Martha. The language contained in the will is unclear as to whether a joint tenancy or a tenancy in common was intended. Donald is dead and Martha has agreed to convey her entire interest by quit-claim deed to Dombres. The purchase price is equal to the full fair market price of the property. Dombres is not interested in anything less than the entire title to the tract. Under the circumstances, which of the following is correct?

  a. There is a statutory preference which favors the finding of a joint tenancy.

  b. Whether the will created a joint tenancy or a tenancy in common is irrelevant since Martha is the only survivor.

  c. Dombres will not obtain title to the entire tract of land by Martha's conveyance.

  d. There is no way or means whereby Dombres may obtain a clear title under the circumstances.

5. Marcross and two business associates own real property as tenants in common that they have invested in as a speculation. The speculation proved to be highly successful, and the land is now worth substantially more than their investment. Which of the following is a correct legal incident of ownership of the property?

  a. Upon the death of any of the other tenants, the deceased's interest passes to the survivor(s) unless there is a will.

  b. Each of the co-tenants owns an **undivided** interest in the whole.

  c. A co-tenant cannot sell his interest in the property without the consent of the other tenants.

  d. Upon the death of a co-tenant, his estate is entitled to the amount of the original investment, but not the appreciation.

6. Carter wished to obtain additional working capital for his construction company. His bankers indicated that they would be willing to lend the company $50,000 if the bank could obtain a first mortgage on

the real property belonging to the business. Carter reluctantly acquiesced and mortgaged all his real property to secure repayment of the loan. Unknown to the bank one portion of the real property was already mortgaged to Johnson for $30,000, but Johnson had neglected to record the mortgage. The bank promptly recorded its mortgage. Which of the following is correct regarding the rights of the parties?

    a. Johnson's failure to record makes the mortgage invalid against Carter.

    b. The bank's mortgage will have a priority over Johnson's mortgage.

    c. Both mortgagees would share the proceeds from any foreclosure on a pro rata basis.

    d. The bank will be deemed to have notice of Johnson's mortgage and will take subject to the mortgage.

7. Dunbar Dairy Farms, Inc., pursuant to an expansion of its operations in Tuberville, purchased from Moncrief a 140-acre farm strategically located in the general area in which Dunbar wishes to expand. Unknown to Dunbar, Cranston, an adjoining landowner, had fenced off approximately five acres of the land in question. Cranston installed a well, constructed a storage shed and garage on the fenced-off land, and continuously farmed and occupied the five acres for approximately 22 years prior to Dunbar's purchase. Cranston did this under the mistaken belief that the five acres of land belonged to him. Which of the following is a correct answer in regard to the five acres occupied by Cranston?

    a. Under the circumstances Cranston has title to the five acres.

    b. As long as Moncrief had properly recorded a deed which includes the five acres in dispute, Moncrief had good title to the five acres.

    c. At best, the only right that Cranston could obtain is an easement.

    d. If Dunbar is unaware of Cranston's presence and Cranston has failed to record, Dunbar can oust him as a trespasser.

8. Gail Monet has decided to make certain gifts to her family. Her goal is to reduce her estate and income taxes. Which of the following need not be present in order for Monet to make valid gifts?

    a. Monet must be competent to make the gifts in question.

    b. Monet must have some purpose or motive other than, or in addition to, the mere saving of taxes.

    c. There must be delivery of the gifts to the donees.

    d. The gifts must be made voluntarily and with the requisite donative intent.

9. Farber sold his house to Ronald. Ronald agreed among other things to pay the existing mortgage on the house. The Safety Bank, which held the mortgage, released Farber from liability on the debt. The above described transaction (relating to the mortgage debt) is

    a. Invalid in that the bank did not receive any additional consideration from Farber.

    b. Not a release of Farber if Ronald defaults, and the proceeds from the sale of the mortgaged house are insufficient to satisfy the debt.

    c. A novation.

    d. A delegation.

10. Vance obtained a 25-year leasehold interest in an office building from the owner, Stanfield.

    a. Vance's interest is non-assignable.

    b. The conveyance of the ownership of the building by Stanfield to Wax will terminate Vance's leasehold interest.

    c. Stanfield's death will not terminate Vance's leasehold interest.

    d. Vance's death will terminate the leasehold interest.

11. An easement cannot be

    a. Created by reservation.

    b. The mere right to the use of another's land but must be obtained for the benefit of the land owned by the party obtaining the easement.

    c. Obtained by prescription if the claimant's use of the land has been interrupted by the prompt action of the landowner.

    d. Conveyed by the easement owner to another party who purchases the land owned by the easement owner.

12. A real estate mortgage

    a. Need not be in writing.

    b. Creates an intangible personal property right for the mortgagee.

    c. If properly recorded, gives constructive notice to subsequent purchasers and mortgagees of the recording mortgagee's interest.

    d. Is not assignable by the mortgagee.

13. Jane Luft, doing business as Luft Enterprises, owned a tract of land upon which she had intended to build an additional retail outlet. There is an existing first mortgage of $70,000 on the property which is held by the First County National Bank. Luft decided not to expand, and a buyer, Johnson, offered $150,000 for the property. Luft accepted and received a certified check for $80,000 plus a signed statement by Johnson promising to pay the existing mortgage. What are the legal rights of the indicated parties?

    a. Luft remains liable to First County despite Johnson's promise to pay.

    b. First County must first proceed against Johnson on the mortgage before it has any rights against Luft.

    c. The delegation of the debt is invalid if Johnson does not have a credit rating roughly comparable to Luft's.

    d. The bank is the incidental beneficiary of Johnson's promise to pay the mortgage.

14. Which of the following is true with respect to an easement created by an express grant?

    a. The easement will be extinguished upon the death of the grantee.

    b. The easement cannot be sold or transferred by the owner of the easement.

    c. The easement gives the owner of the easement the right to the physical possession of the property subject to the easement.

    d. The easement must be in writing to be valid.

15. Donaldson, Inc., loaned Watson Enterprises $50,000 secured by a real estate mortgage which included the land, buildings, and "all other property which is added to the real property or which is considered as real property as a matter of law." Wilkins also loaned Watson $25,000 and obtained a security interest in all of Watson's "inventory, accounts receivable, fixtures, and other tangible personal property." Watson defaulted and there is insufficient property to fully satisfy the two creditors. There is some doubt as to the nature of certain property and Donaldson is attempting to include all the property under the terms and scope of its real property mortgage. What is the probable outcome for Donaldson?

    a. Donaldson will prevail in that real property is preferred over personal property.

    b. Assuming Donaldson was the first lender and duly filed its real property mortgage, Donaldson will prevail in respect to all property necessary to satisfy its $50,000 loan.

    c. If the fixtures in question are detachable trade fixtures, Donaldson will not prevail in its attempt to include them.

    d. The problem will be decided by taking all of Watson's property (real and personal) subject to the two secured creditors' claims and dividing it in proportion to the respective debts.

16. Abrams owned a fee simple absolute interest in certain real property. Abrams conveyed it to Fox for Fox's lifetime with the remainder interest upon Fox's death to Charles. What are the rights of Fox and Charles in the real property?

    a. Charles may not sell his interest in the property until the death of Fox.

    b. Fox has a possessory interest in the land and Charles has a future interest.

    c. Charles must outlive Fox in order to obtain any interest in the real property.

    d. Any conveyance by either Fox or Charles must be joined in by the other party in order to be valid.

17. Fitz decided to purchase a two-acre tract in an industrial park from Expansion, Inc., the developer. The usual contract of sale was drafted and signed by the parties. However, it was silent in respect to marketable title and the type of deed to be delivered at the closing. What effect does the omission of these items from the contract have?

    a. The contract is subject to an implied covenant that Fitz will receive marketable title at the closing.

    b. Expansion must deliver a warranty deed with full covenants.

    c. In the event Expansion decides to withdraw the property from the market because of rising land prices, Fitz could obtain damages but not specific performance.

    d. Fitz should have a title search within 30 days after the closing in order to make sure the title is clear.

18. Maxwell purchased real property from Plumb and received a warranty deed at the closing. Maxwell neglected to record the deed. In this situation

    a. A subsequent purchaser from Plumb will obtain a better title to the real property than Maxwell even if the subsequent purchaser is aware of Maxwell's prior purchase.

b. Maxwell must record his deed in order to perfect his rights against Plumb.

c. Recordation would provide constructive notice of Maxwell's rights to subsequent purchasers of the real property even though they do not have actual notice.

d. Maxwell lacks an insurable interest in the property and any fire insurance he obtains is void.

19. Your client, Albert Fall, purchased a prominent industrial park from Josh Barton. At the closing, Barton offered a quitclaim deed. The contract of sale called for a warranty deed with full covenants.

a. Fall should accept the quitclaim deed since there is no important difference between a quitclaim deed and a warranty deed.

b. An undisclosed mortgage which was subsequently discovered would violate one of the covenants of a warranty deed.

c. Fall cannot validly refuse to accept Barton's quitclaim deed.

d. The only difference between a warranty deed with full covenants and a quitclaim deed is that the grantor of a quitclaim does not warrant against defects post his assumption of title.

20. Franklin's will left his ranch "to his wife, Joan, for her life, and upon her death to his sons, George and Harry, as joint tenants." Because of the provisions in Franklin's will

a. Joan cannot convey her interest in the ranch except to George and Harry.

b. The ranch must be included in Joan's estate for federal estate tax purposes upon her death.

c. If George predeceases Harry, Harry will obtain all right, title, and interest in the ranch.

d. Joan holds the ranch in trust for the benefit of George and Harry.

21. Unlimited Fashions, Inc., leased a store in the Suburban Styles Shopping Center for five years at $1,500 a month. The lease contained a provision which prohibited assignment of the lease. After occupying the premises for two years, Unlimited sublet the premises to Fantastic Frocks for the balance of its term, less one day, at $2,000 per month. Unlimited moved out on a Sunday and removed all its personal property and trade fixtures such as portable clothing racks, cash registers, detachable counters,

etc. Which of the following best describes the legal status of the parties involved?

a. Unlimited has not breached its contract with Suburban.

b. Suburban is entitled to the additional $500 rental paid each month by Fantastic to Unlimited.

c. Removal of the trade fixtures in question by Unlimited was improper and it can be held liable to Suburban for their fair value.

d. Fantastic is a tenant of Suburban.

22. Norton owned and operated a trucking business. He was financially hard pressed and obtained a loan from the First State Bank "secured by his equipment and including all other chattels and personal property used in his business." The loan security agreement was properly filed in the county records office. In addition, Norton obtained a loan from the Title Mortgage Company; the loan was secured by a first mortgage on all the real property used in the trucking business. Norton is now insolvent and a petition in bankruptcy has been filed. Which of the following is a correct statement concerning the security interest in the properties;

a. If Title Mortgage failed to record its mortgage, the trustee in bankruptcy will be able to defeat Title's security interest.

b. Norton's central air conditioning and heating system is included in First State's security interest.

c. If Title Mortgage did not record its mortgage, First State is entitled to all fixtures, including those permanently annexed to the land.

d. A sale of all the personal and real business property by Norton to a bona fide purchaser will defeat First State's security interest unless First State recorded its security interest in both the appropriate real and personal property recordation offices.

23. Harrison purchased Bigacre from Whitmore. The deed described the real property conveyed and the granting clause read: "Seller hereby releases, surrenders, and relinquishes to buyer any right, title, or interest that he may have in Bigacre." The deed contained no covenants. What is Harrison's legal status concerning title to Bigacre?

a. Harrison has obtained a quitclaim deed.

b. If an adverse claimant ousts Harrison from Bigacre, Harrison will have recourse against Whitmore.

c. The only warranty contained in the deed is an implied warranty of marketability of title.

d. Harrison's deed is neither insurable nor recordable.

24. Miltown borrowed $60,000 from Strauss upon the security of a first mortgage on a business building owned by Miltown. The mortgage has been amortized down to $50,000. Sanchez is buying the building from Miltown for $80,000. Sanchez is paying only the $30,000 excess over and above the mortgage. Sanchez may buy it either "subject to" the mortgage, or he may "assume" the mortgage. Which is a correct statement under these circumstances?

a. The financing agreement ultimately decided upon must be recorded in order to be binding upon the parties.

b. The financing arrangement is covered by the Uniform Commercial Code if Sanchez takes "subject to" the existing first mortgage.

c. Sanchez will acquire no interest in the property if he takes "subject to" instead of "assuming" the mortgage.

d. Sanchez would be better advised to take "subject to" the mortgage rather than to "assume" the mortgage.

25. Lutz sold his moving and warehouse business, including all the personal and real property used therein, to Arlen Van Lines, Inc. The real property was encumbered by a duly-recorded $300,000 first mortgage upon which Lutz was personally liable. Arlen acquired the property subject to the mortgage but did not assume the mortgage. Two years later, when the outstanding mortgage was $260,000, Arlen decided to abandon the business location because it had become unprofitable and the value of the real property was less than the outstanding mortgage. Arlen moved to another location and refused to pay the installments due on the mortgage. What is the legal status of the parties in regard to the mortgage?

a. Lutz must satisfy the mortgage debt in the event that foreclosure yields an amount less than the unpaid balance.

b. If Lutz pays off the mortgage, he will be able to successfully sue Arlen because Lutz is subrogated to the mortgagee's rights against Arlen.

c. Arlen took the real property free of the mortgage.

d. Arlen breached its contract with Lutz when it abandoned the location and defaulted on the mortgage.

26. In connection with the audit of Fiske & Company, you found it necessary to examine a deed to certain property owned by the client. In this connection, which of the following statements is correct?

a. A deed purporting to convey real property, but which omits the day of the month, is invalid.

b. A deed which lacks the signature of the grantor is valid.

c. A quitclaim deed which purports to transfer to the grantee "whatever title the grantor has" is invalid.

d. A deed which purports to convey real property and recites a consideration of $1 and other valuable consideration is valid.

27. Paxton owned Blackacre, and he obtained a $10,000 loan from a bank secured by a real property mortgage on Blackacre. The mortgage was properly recorded. Paxton subsequently sold Blackacre to Rogers, expressly warranting that there were no mortgages on the property. Rogers was unaware of the bank's interest in the property. Paxton has disappeared, and the bank has demanded payment from Rogers. Rogers has refused, and the bank is seeking to foreclose its mortgage. Which of the following statements is correct?

a. Rogers is personally liable on the mortgage loan.

b. As a bona fide purchaser for value, Rogers will prevail and retain the property free of the mortgage.

c. The bank will prevail in its foreclosure action.

d. The bank must obtain a judgment against Paxton before it can foreclose the mortgage.

28. Charles is a commercial tenant of Luxor Buildings, Inc. The term of the lease is five years and two years have elapsed. The lease prohibits subletting, but does not contain any provision relating to assignment. Charles approached Luxor and asked whether Luxor could release him from the balance of the term of the lease for $500. Luxor refused unless Charles would agree to pay $2,000. Charles located Whitney who was interested in renting in Luxor's building and transferred the entire balance of the lease to Whitney in consideration of his promise to pay Luxor the monthly rental and otherwise perform Charles' obligations under the lease. Luxor ob-

jects. Which of the following statements is correct?

    a.   The assignment is invalid without Luxor's consent.

    b.   The assignment does not extinguish Charles' obligation to pay the rent if Whitney defaults.

    c.   The assignment need not be in writing.

    d.   A prohibition of the right to sublet contained in the lease completely prohibits an assignment.

MAY 1981 QUESTIONS

29.   Glover Manufacturing, Inc., purchased a four-acre tract of commercially zoned land. A survey of the tract was made prior to the closing, and it revealed an unpaved road which passed across the northeast corner of the land. The title search revealed a mortgage held by Peoples National Bank, which was satisfied at the closing by the seller out of the funds received from Glover. The title search did not indicate the existence of any other adverse interest which would constitute a defect in title. There was no recordation made in connection with the unpaved road. Which of the following statements is correct regarding Glover's title and rights to the land against the claims of adverse parties?

    a.   The unpaved road poses **no** potential problem if Glover promptly fences off the property and puts up "no trespassing" signs.

    b.   Glover does **not** have to be concerned with the unpaved road since whatever rights the users might claim were negated by failing to record.

    c.   The mere use of the unpaved road as contrasted with the occupancy of the land can **not** create any interest adverse to Glover.

    d.   The unpaved road revealed by the survey may prove to be a valid easement created by prescription.

30.   Golden sold his moving and warehouse business, including all the personal and real property used therein, to Clark Van Lines, Inc. The real property was encumbered by a duly-recorded $300,000 first mortgage upon which Golden was personally liable. Clark acquired the property subject to the mortgage but did not assume the mortgage. Two years later, when the outstanding mortgage was $260,000, Clark decided to abandon the business location because it had become unprofitable and the value of the real property was less than the outstanding mortgage. Clark moved to another location and refused to pay the installments due on the mortgage. What is the legal status of the parties in regard to the mortgage?

    a.   Clark took the real property free of the mortgage.

    b.   Clark breached its contract with Golden when it abandoned the location and defaulted on the mortgage.

    c.   Golden must satisfy the mortgage debt in the event that foreclosure yields an amount less than the unpaid balance.

    d.   If Golden pays off the mortgage, he will be able to successfully sue Clark because Golden is subrogated to the mortgagee's rights against Clark.

31.   Tremont Enterprises, Inc., needed some additional working capital to develop a new product line. It decided to obtain intermediate term financing by giving a second mortgage on its plant and warehouse. Which of the following is true with respect to the mortgages?

    a.   If Tremont defaults on both mortgages and a bankruptcy proceeding is initiated, the second mortgagee has the status of general creditor.

    b.   If the second mortgagee proceeds to foreclose on its mortgage, the first mortgagee must be satisfied completely before the second mortgagee is entitled to repayment.

    c.   Default on payment to the second mortgagee will constitute default on the first mortgage.

    d.   Tremont can **not** prepay the second mortgage prior to its maturity without the consent of the first mortgagee.

PROBLEMS

Problem 1   Assignment of Lease; Fixture; Real vs. Personal Property (579,L5)

(15 to 20 minutes)

Part a. Hammar Hardware Company, Inc., purchased all the assets and assumed all the liabilities of JoMar Hardware for $60,000. Among the assets and liabilities included in the sale was a lease of the building in which the business was located. The lessor-owner was Marathon Realty, Inc., and the remaining unexpired term of the lease was nine years. The lease did not contain a provision dealing with the assignment of the leasehold. Incidental to the purchase, Hammar expressly promised JoMar that it would pay the rental due Marathon over the life of the lease and would hold JoMar harmless from any future liability thereon.

When Marathon learned of the proposed transaction, it strenuously objected to the assignment of the lease and to the occupancy by Hammar. Later, after this dispute was resolved and prior to expiration of the lease, Hammar abandoned the building and ceased doing business in that area. Marathon has demanded payment by JoMar of the rent as it matures over the balance of the term of the lease.

Required: Answer the following, setting forth reasons for any conclusions stated.

1.   Was the consent of Marathon necessary in order to assign the lease?

2.   Is JoMar liable on the lease?

3.   If Marathon were to proceed against Hammar, would Hammar be liable under the lease?

Part b. The Merchants and Mechanics County Bank expanded its services and facilities as a result of the economic growth of the community it serves. In this connection, it provided safe deposit facilities for the first time. A large vault was constructed as a part of the renovation and expansion of the bank building. Merchants purchased a bank vault door from Foolproof Vault Doors, Inc., for $65,000 and installed it at the vault entrance. The state in which Merchants was located had a real property tax but did not have a personal property tax. When the tax assessor appraised the bank building after completion of the renovation and expansion, he included the bank vault door as a part of the real property. Merchants has filed an objection claiming the vault door was initially personal property and remains so after installation in the bank.

There are no specific statutes or regulations determinative of the issue. Therefore, the question will be decided according to common law principles of property law.

Required: Answer the following, setting forth reasons for any conclusions stated.

1.   What is the likely outcome as to the classification of the bank vault door?

2.   The above situation involves a dispute between a tax authority and the owner of property. In what other circumstances might a dispute arise with respect to the classification of property as either real or personal property?

Problem 2   Landlord-Tenant Problems (574,L4b)

(10 to 15 minutes)

Part b.   Reynolds leased a manufacturing building from Philip under a written lease for a period of five years at a specified rental and with a provision that the lessor would keep the structure in repair.

Reynolds subleased a portion of the lower floor to Signor giving him access through a hallway from the main entrance. Philip subsequently mortgaged the building, and Central Savings, the mortgagee, ultimately foreclosed and acquired good title to the property. Reynolds was unable to get Central Savings to make certain minor repairs and had withheld rent in an amount equal to the repairs he was forced to make. Central Savings meanwhile notified both Reynolds and Signor that the lease was terminated and that both were to pay rent directly to it for one month and then vacate.

Required:
1.   Discuss Reynolds' right to withhold rent in the amount of repairs.
2.   Absent a breach by the tenants, discuss Central Savings' right to:
       a.   Evict the tenants.
       b.   Require Signor to pay the rent directly to it.

<u>Problem 3</u> Purchase Subject to Mortgage **(580,L4c)**

(7 to 10 minutes)

Part c. Newfeld purchased a parcel of land in New City from Stoneham Realty. His plan was to construct a professional building and parking lot on the property. In order to do this, Newfeld needed financing and approached the New City National Bank for a first mortgage loan. The proposal looked good to New City National and they loaned Newfeld **$200,000** to help finance the venture. Newfeld engaged builders who accomplished the construction of the building and the parking lot. After two years of ownership and operation of the building and lot, Newfeld decided to sell. Robbins agreed to purchase Newfeld's interest but indicated she was not willing to assume the existing mortgage. It was finally agreed that the entire property would be transferred to Robbins subject to the New City National's first mortgage. Robbins subsequently defaulted.

Required: Answer the following, setting forth reasons for any conclusions stated.

     1.   Who is expected to make the payments during the remaining life of the mortgage?

     2.   What rights does New City Bank have against Robbins and Newfeld upon default?

     3.   Assume that the bank has to resort to foreclosure and that after the debt, interest, and all expenses have been paid, there is $2,000 remaining. Who is entitled to this amount?

MULTIPLE CHOICE ANSWERS

1.	d	8.	b	15.	c	22.	a	29.	d
2.	c	9.	c	16.	b	23.	a	30.	c
3.	c	10.	c	17.	a	24.	d	31.	b
4.	c	11.	c	18.	c	25.	a		
5.	b	12.	c	19.	b	26.	d		
6.	b	13.	a	20.	c	27.	c		
7.	a	14.	d	21.	a	28.	b		

EXPLANATION OF MULTIPLE CHOICE ANSWERS

1. (1180,L1,47) (d) In a contract for the sale of real property, unless expressly disclaimed, there is an implied promise that the seller will provide a marketable title. A marketable title is one reasonably free from doubt. It does not contain: encumbrances; encroachments; restrictions, except for zoning laws. However, to be marketable, a title does not have to be perfect. Third parties may have rights to temporary use and possession of the property. Thus, answer (d) is correct, and answers (b) and (c) are incorrect. Answer (a) is incorrect because the implied warranty of merchantability is granted in a sale of goods by a merchant not in the sale of real property.

2. (1180,L1,48) (c) A tenant may engage in an assignment or a sublease unless expressly prohibited by the lease. An assignment of the lease is the transfer by the lessee of his entire interest without reserving any right of re-entry. The assignor remains liable on the lease despite the assignment. Answer (c) is correct. Answer (a) is incorrect because a clause in the lease prohibiting a sublease does not prohibit an assignment. Since there were 3 years left on the lease when assigned, it was not capable of being performed within one year and consequently the agreement to transfer such an interest must be in writing [answer (b)]. There is no need for the landlord to consent to the assignment unless the lease expressly prohibited assignment.

3. (580,L1,11) (c) One method of creating an easement is by prescription. This occurs when a person uses someone else's land in a wrongful, continuous, open and notorious manner for the prescribed statutory period of time. The adjacent landowner appears to be engaging in this type of use. The landowners are merely using the property, not possessing it, thus adverse possession is not present. Prescription can occur even though the owner has recorded the deed. Anyone obtaining an easement would initially be a trespasser since the use must be wrongful.

4. (580,L1,26) (c) When the deed is unclear as to whether a joint tenancy or tenancy in common was intended, there is a statutory presumption in favor of tenancy in common. Thus, Donald and Martha were tenants in common and when Donald died his interest passed to his heirs. Thus, if Dombres wanted to obtain the entire title, he would have to purchase the interest of Donald's heirs, as well as Martha's interest.

5. (1179,L1,10) (b) The correct legal incident of ownership of property as tenants in common is that each of the co-tenants owns an undivided interest in the whole. Answer (a) is incorrect because upon the death of any of the other tenants in common, the deceased tenant's interest will pass to his heirs and not to the surviving co-tenants. Answer (c) is incorrect because a co-tenant in common can sell his interest in the property without the consent of the other co-tenants. Answer (d) is incorrect because upon the death of a co-tenant, his estate owns the same interest as the decedent.

6. (1179,L1,40) (b) The bank's mortgage will have a priority over Johnson's mortgage because the bank appears to have been without knowledge of the unrecorded mortgage of Johnson and thus takes priority over it. Answer (a) is incorrect because the failure to record a mortgage does not make it invalid against the debtor. An unrecorded mortgage subjects the mortgage holder to losing his priority to a third party. Answer (c) is incorrect because where there are conflicting mortgages, the mortgages do not share the collateral on a pro rata basis. Rather, a priority is established. Here the bank has the highest priority and would be paid in full first and Johnson's mortgage would be paid second. Answer (d) is incorrect because the bank did not have actual notice of Johnson's mortgage. Also, the mortgage was not recorded, the bank had no constructive notice.

7. (1179,L1,41) (a) Cranston has acquired title to the 5 acres by adverse possession. Even though by mistake, Cranston did occupy the property under the claim of right doctrine, hostile to the actual owner in an open, notorious, and exclusive manner for a continuous period which would be sufficient under common law and most jurisdictions. Answer (b) is incorrect because an actual owner of rural property can lose title by adverse possession as described above. Answer (c) is incorrect because at best, Cranston could, and apparently did, obtain full ownership of the property by adverse possession. Note that "at worst," Cranston could only obtain an easement but answer (c) said "at best." Answer (d) is incorrect because a purchaser of real

property is deemed to have constructive notice of the presence of all persons located on the property that he is buying. Thus, in law, Dunbar is on notice of Cranston's presence.

8.   (1179,L1,43)   (b)   A purpose or motive other than to save taxes is not required in order to make a valid gift. Answers (a), (c), and (d) set out the requisite elements necessary to make a valid gift, i.e., there must be the requisite donative intent by a competent party, delivery, and acceptance.

9.   (1176,L3,40)   (c)   A novation (a substituted contract) in a mortgage transaction occurs when the purchaser agrees to assume the mortgage and the mortgagee agrees to release the original mortgagor with the purchaser as replacement. It is not invalid. In consideration for releasing Farber, the bank got Ronald to be personally liable on the debt. After the novation Farber has no liability even if Ronald defaults and the proceeds from the sale of the house are insufficient to satisfy the debt. A delegation is when a party to a contract turns over his duties to another party. Duties are delegated and rights are assigned. A delegant is still liable if the delagatee defaults, but Farber (as delegant) had no liability because of the novation.

10.   (1176,L3,41)   (c)   A lease is not terminated by the death of either the lessor or the lessee. Thus neither Stanfield's death nor Vance's death will terminate the lease. Transfer of ownership of leased property also does not terminate a lease. Therefore if Stanfield conveys to Wax, Wax will take subject to the lease. As a general rule a lessee may assign or sublet a leasehold interest in accordance with reasonable restrictions in the lease; thus Vance's interest is assignable.

11.   (1176,L3,42)   (c)   To obtain an easement by prescription (by use which is adverse or hostile to the owner), the claimant's use of the land must not be interrupted by the landowner for the statutory period. Answer (a) is incorrect because an easement can be created by reservation, e.g., sell the land but reserve the right to cross it. Answer (b) is incorrect because an easement appurtenant is an easement on one parcel of land for the benefit of another parcel of land. There is also an easement in gross which is a personal right to use another's land without any benefit to another parcel of land. Answer (d) is incorrect because an easement owner can convey his

easement to a new owner of the land in question but he cannot convey it to a third party who has no interest in the land.

12.   (1176,L3,44)   (c)   A real estate mortgage can be recorded similarly to a deed of sale (mortgages are interests in land). If recorded it gives constructive notice to subsequent purchasers and mortgagees. They are deemed to know of the mortgage as a matter of law. A mortgage must be in writing because it is a grant of an interest in land. However, equity will enforce an oral mortgage between the parties unless the rights of third parties intervene. It is not an intangible personal property right but rather a security interest in real property. A mortgagee may assign a mortgage; assignment does not affect the mortgagor.

13.   (577,L2,29)   (a)   Luft is the mortgagor and remains liable on the mortgage until it is paid or the mortgagee releases her. Although Johnson became liable on the mortgage by assuming it, the mortgagee may choose to proceed against either Luft or Johnson first. Commonly, the mortgagee will foreclose on the land first. However, the grantor, Luft, is in the nature of a surety and can be sued immediately upon default. Luft may delegate the debt without reference to Johnson's credit rating. Tne bank is a creditor beneficiary, not an incidental beneficiary.

14.   (577,L3,36)   (d)   An easement is the right to make use of another's land. This right if established by an express grant is an "interest in land" which under the statute of frauds requires a writing to be valid. The owner of an easement does not have the right to possess the land, he can only use it. In most cases an easement will not terminate upon the death of the grantee unless specifically stated in the grant or the easement is personal, such as an easement in gross. As a general rule only certain types of easements are not assignable and even these can be made assignable by proper wording and intent in the grant.

15.   (577,L3,37)   (c)   Real property includes land and things attached to land. Personal property includes everything that is not real property. Fixtures are usually considered real property but business or trade fixtures which are easily detachable are considered personal property. Therefore if the fixtures in question are detachable trade fixtures, Watson will prevail as to them because they are not covered by Donaldson's mortgage. It does not matter that Donaldson was first if they are not covered by the mortgage. The property will not be

divided because each of them has a security interest or lien in different kinds of property. There is no preference of real property over personal property.

16.   (577,L3,40)   (b)   Abrams has created a life estate in Fox which will terminate on his death and a remainder interest for Charles or his heirs which will begin on Fox's death. Charles' right to possession is a future interest while Fox has a present possessory interest. Charles owns this future interest right now and Fox's death is necessary for Charles or his heirs to take possession. Either party may sell or convey their interest in the property at any time without the permission of the other.

17.   (577,L3,44)   (a)   If a contract for the sale of land is silent as to warranties of title, there is an implied promise that seller will provide a marketable title (one reasonably free from doubt). There is no implied promise to deliver a warranty deed. Such a promise must be stated in the contract. Fitz must have a title search done before he closes the sale or it will be too late. Fitz could maintain an action for specific performance if Expansion tries to withdraw because land is a unique item and specific performance is a remedy for breach of a contract on sale of land.

18.   (576,L2,23)   (c)   Recording deeds to real property provides constructive notice to subsequent purchasers which means that a subsequent purchaser cannot take in good faith, i.e., he has notice as a matter of law that the property has already been sold. If a subsequent purchaser is aware of Maxwell's prior purchase, he is not a good faith purchaser and cannot obtain a better title even if Maxwell has not recorded. Maxwell must record his deed to protect himself from third parties, because if he does not record and a third party buys the property without actual knowledge of his purchase, the third party will get a superior title. Actual notice would result from occupation of the property by Maxwell or otherwise showing that a third party was aware of Maxwell's unrecorded interest.

19.   (1173,L3,40)   (b)   There is an important difference between a quitclaim deed and a warranty deed in that the quitclaim deed does not contain any of the warranties of a warranty deed. An undisclosed mortgage violates a covenant that the deed is free from encumbrances. If the deed does not comply with the contract of sale, Fall does not have to accept it.

20.   (575,L1,8)   (c)   Joan has a life estate and may convey it to anyone. Upon Joan's death the ranch becomes the estate of George and Harry and will not be included in Joan's estate. George and Harry have joint tenancy so if George dies first, Harry obtains all rights, title, and interest in the ranch. The holder of a life estate does not hold it in trust for the future interests.

21.   (575,L1,11)   (a)   Unlimited has not breached its contract with Surburban, because a prohibition against an assignment is not a prohibition against a sublet. Fantastic is a tenant of Unlimited, not of Surburban. Therefore, Surburban is not entitled to the increased rentals collected by Unlimited. Unlimited remained a tenant because it subletted rather than assigned and therefore can properly remove the trade fixtures.

22.   (575,L1,12)   (a)   If the mortgage is not recorded, the trustee will be able to reduce the title mortgage's status as a priority creditor. The air conditioning and heating system are permanent fixtures which are not included in First State's security interest and First State cannot be entitled to them. The sale of all the business assets is a bulk transfer and the first purchaser cannot be a bona fide purchaser.

23.   (575,L2,17)   (a)   Harrison obtained a quitclaim deed which contains no covenants of warranty. It is only a transfer of whatever interests the seller had. A quitclaim deed can be both insurable and recordable.

24.   (1177,L2,21)   (d)   Miltown remains primarily liable on the mortgage unless Strauss gives Miltown a novation. A novation is a "release." If Sanchez takes "subject to" the mortgage he will not be personally liable as he would be if he "assumes" the mortgage. If Sanchez cannot keep up the payments, Strauss will have to recover from Miltown or foreclose on the land. Answer (a) is incorrect because the agreement need not be recorded to be binding upon the parties; recording is to protect from third parties. Answer (b) is incorrect because the UCC is not involved as the transaction involves real property. Answer (c) is incorrect because Sanchez will have the same ownership interest in the property with either a "subject to" or by "assuming" the mortgage.

25.   (578,L1,28)   (a)   The original mortgagor remains liable unless there has been a novation (a release) despite the fact that there may have

been subsequent sales of the property. Answer (b) is incorrect because Lutz will have no rights against Arlen because Arlen took the property subject to the mortgage and therefore never assumed personal liability on the mortgage. Answer (c) is incorrect because Arlen did not take the property free of the mortgage. The property was at all times subject to the mortgage. Answer (d) is incorrect because Arlen did not breach the contract by defaulting on the mortgage (unless he expressly promised Lutz he would pay the mortgage). Arlen did not assume the mortgage but only took the property subject to the mortgage.

26. (578,L1,31) (d) A deed conveying real property is valid whether or not consideration is given. Delivery of the deed conveys title. Answer (a) is incorrect because a deed is not invalid due to the omission of the day of the month of a transaction. A replacement deed should be filed which corrects the date omission. Answer (b) is incorrect because a deed which lacks a signature or other authenticating mark is invalid. Answer (c) is incorrect because a quitclaim deed is a conveyance without warranties of what title the grantor holds. It is a valid deed, but does not warrant what rights are being deeded.

27. (1178,L1,43) (c) The bank will prevail in its foreclosure action. The bank properly recorded the mortgage and thereby gave valid notice to all other parties. Answer (a) is incorrect because Rogers did not assume the mortgage and does not become personally liable on the mortgage loan. Answer (b) is incorrect because despite being a bona fide purchaser, Rogers had constructive notice prior to his purchase, because the mortgage was properly recorded. Answer (d) is incorrect because the mortgagee bank need not obtain a judgment against Paxton, the debtor, before it can foreclose its mortgage. The purpose of a mortgage is to gain a security interest in the property to avoid having to resort to personal judgments.

28. (1178,L1,48) (b) An assignment of a lease by the original tenant does not extinguish the tenant's obligation to pay the rent if the subsequent tenant defaults. Answer (a) is incorrect because leases are generally considered to be assignable unless prohibited by the lease. Answer (d) is incorrect because a prohibition against the right to sublet does not prohibit an assignment. Answer (c) is incorrect because leases that exceed one year are generally considered to be an interest in real property and under the Statute of Frauds transfer of an interest in real property requires a writing.

MAY 1981 ANSWERS

29. (581,L1,52) (d) An easement can be created by prescription when a person uses someone else's land in a wrongful, open and notorious manner continuously for the period of time prescribed by statute (normally 20 years). Answer (a) is incorrect because, if the property was not fenced until after the statutory period had expired, the easement would have already been created by prescription. Answer (b) is incorrect because an easement gained by prescription is valid without recording such interest. Answer (c) is incorrect because adverse use creates an easement, while adverse occupancy (adverse possession) results in ownership of the property.

30. (581,L1,53) (c) Golden, the original debtor, must satisfy the mortgage debt in the event that the foreclosure yields an amount less than the unpaid balance. Golden was originally liable on the mortgage, and no novation or release was granted by the mortgagor when Golden sold the warehouse to Clark. Answer (a) is incorrect because Clark did not take the property free of the mortgage. The property was subject to the mortgage at all times, but Clark was not personally liable as he did not assume the mortgage. Answer (b) is incorrect because Clark bought the property only subject to the mortgage and therefore, did not breach his agreement with Golden when he abandoned the location and stopped making the mortgage payments. Answer (d) is incorrect because Golden will not be able to sue Clark because Clark did not contract to be liable on the mortgage debt. Thus, there is no one for Golden to be subrogated to.

31. (581,L1,54) (b) Upon foreclosure, the first mortgagee has priority and must be paid in full before any payment is made to a subsequent mortgagee (second or third mortgagees). Answer (a) is incorrect because a second mortgagee remains a secured creditor in the bankruptcy proceedings although his interest is inferior to a first mortgagee. The doctrine of marshalling of assets may help a second mortgagee since it allows him to compel a first mortgagee to foreclose on other property available to the first mortgagee as security before foreclosing on property which a second mortgagee has a claim on. Answer (c) is incorrect because default of the second mortgage does not constitute a default of the first mortgage. Answer (d) is incorrect since second mortgages are sometimes obtained for a short period of time and can be paid off before maturity without consent of first mortgagee.

ANSWER OUTLINE

Problem 1   Assignment of Lease; Fixture; Real vs. Personal Property

a1.   No, lessor's consent is not necessary to assign a lease unless lease prohibits assignment
     Rare for court to prohibit assignment
        Exception might be lease involving personal trust

a2.   Yes, assignor of a contract remains liable unless
        Novation granted i.e., creditor released assignor
     JoMar has only delegated the duty to pay to Marathon
     JoMar becomes a surety as part of the transaction

a3.   Yes, Hammar is liable to Marathon
        Marathon is a third party creditor beneficiary
            Hammar promised JoMar he would pay Marathon
            Privity and consideration requirements do not apply

b1.   The vault door will probably be classified as real property
     Criteria for determining whether personal property has become real property are:
        Annexation: The method and permanence of physical attachment
        Adaptation: Extent to which the door is necessary to the purpose of real property
        Intent: Intent of party affixing as to whether property to remain as personal or become real property
     Above criteria indicate bank vault door has become real property

b2.   Other situations requiring classification of property as real or personal:
        Real property mortgagees vs. creditors of mortgagor with security interest in personal property
            Which assets secure what debtors?
        Landlord vs. tenant upon expiration of lease
            What property may tenant remove?
        Beneficiaries of a will vs. the executor
            Distribution based on classification of property as real or personal?
        Seller vs. buyer of real property
            What does contract to sell include?
        Real property mortgagees vs. mortgagors
            What property is included in mortgage?

UNOFFICIAL ANSWER

Problem 1   Assignment of Lease; Fixture; Real vs. Personal Property

Part a.

1.   No. In the absence of a restriction on the right to assign specifically stated in the lease, a lessee may assign his leasehold interest to another. Only in unusual circumstances, where the lease involves special elements of personal trust and confidence as contrasted with mere payment for occupancy, will the courts limit the right to assign.

2.   Yes. Although JoMar may effectively assign the lease, which in effect is an assignment of the right to occupy the leasehold premises and a delegation of its duty to pay Marathon, it cannot shed its liability to Marathon for the rental payments. In the absence of a release, JoMar remains liable. The transaction described in the fact situation is in the nature of a surety relationship.

3.   Yes. Marathon is a third-party creditor beneficiary of Hammar's promise to JoMar. As such, Marathon can assert rights on the promise even though it was not a party to the contract. Marathon is not barred by lack of privity or the fact that it gave no consideration to Hammar for the promise.

Part b.

1.   Based upon the facts of the problem and the legal criteria discussed below, the vault door will probably be classified as real property. The criteria applicable are these:

•   Annexation—the mode and degree to which the chattel is physically attached to the real property.

- Adaptation—the extent to which the chattel is used in promoting the purpose for which the real property is used.

- Intention—whether the chattel was intended as a permanent improvement of the real property.

Applying these criteria to the facts demonstrates that the degree of annexation of a vault door is by necessity very high. Furthermore, the adaption of the personal property (the vault door) to the use of the real property by the bank also argues for a finding in favor of real property classification. Finally, the last criterion, the intent of the bank to make a permanent improvement of the real property, appears to have been satisfied. Taking these criteria together, it would appear that the bank door has become real property.

2.   In addition to tax collectors, disputes involving the categorization of property as real or personal have arisen in respect of—

- Real property mortgagees versus creditors of the same debtor who have a security interest in personal property (chattel mortgagees).

- Landlord versus tenant upon expiration of the lease and the question of what property may be removed.

- Takers under a will versus the executor in cases where different takers will receive the property, based upon its classification.

- The seller versus the purchaser of real property, where a dispute arises concerning the removal of certain property by the seller.

- The mortgagor versus mortgagee, when the question arises regarding what property is included under the scope of the mortgage.

ANSWER OUTLINE

Problem 2   Landlord-Tenant Problems

b1.   Reynolds has no right to withhold rent in amount of repairs
    Covenant by lessor and lessee deemed independent
      Unless different intent shown
    No constructive eviction here because defects were minor

b2a.   Unless Reynolds breaches, Reynolds cannot be evicted
    Lease term not affected by subsequent change of ownership

b2b.   Reynolds can sublet unless prohibited by lease
    Signor is sublessee and tenant of Reynolds
    Central Savings has no right to collect from Signor

UNOFFICIAL ANSWER

Problem 2   Landlord-Tenant Problems

Part b.

1.   Reynolds has no right to withhold rent in the amount of repairs. Covenants by lessor and lessee are deemed independent unless it is clear that the parties intended the contrary. However, if the breach were sufficiently serious, it might furnish the basis for a claim of constructive eviction. This does not seem to be the case on the facts.

2.   (a)   Central Savings has no right to evict the tenants. When the lease preceded the mortgage, the tenant's term is not affected by the later mortgage absent an agreement by the tenant to the contrary.

    (b)   Signor is a sublessee and, as such, a tenant of Reynolds. Absent a provision in the lease prohibiting the sublease, Reynolds committed no breach by the subletting, and the sublessee, as a tenant of the sublessor, has no direct obligations to the lessor.

ANSWER OUTLINE

Problem 3   Purchase Subject to Mortgage

c1.   Robbins is expected to make payments on mortgage on transferred property
    Robbins purchased property subject to mortgage
      No personal liability to mortgagee
      If she defaults
        Bank-mortgagee has right to foreclose on property and use proceeds from sale to pay obligation

c2.   Rights of bank against Robbins and Newfeld
upon default
    No rights against Robbins; she did not assume
       mortgage, but Robbins is subject to foreclosure
       action
    Newfeld remains liable

c3.   Right to excess amount upon foreclosure belongs
to Robbins
    Mortgagee not entitled to profit
    Newfeld not entitled to excess
       Not the owner
       Did not satisfy debt
       Had been fully paid for equity interest

UNOFFICIAL ANSWER

Problem 3 Purchase Subject to Mortgage

Part c.

1.   Despite the absence of a legal obligation to do so,
Robbins is expected to make the remaining mortgage
payments. She is the legal owner, subject to the mortgage, and has parted with money sufficient to purchase
Newfeld's equity interest. If Robbins defaults, she will
lose the money already invested in the purchase. Normally one would default only if the value of the property is less than the mortgage outstanding.

2.   New City has no rights against Robbins upon default. Not having assumed the mortgage, Robbins has
no personal liability to pay the mortgage. Newfeld
remains liable on his original promise; the sale to
Robbins does not alter his liability.

3.   The $2,000 belongs to Robbins. The mortgagee
is not entitled to reap a profit as a result of the foreclosure but is only entitled to complete satisfaction,
principal, interest, and expenses. Newfeld is not entitled to anything since he is not the owner, did not
satisfy the debt, and has been fully paid for his equity
interest by Robbins.

MULTIPLE CHOICE QUESTIONS (1—27)

1.   Bernard Manufacturing, Inc., owns a three-story building which it recently purchased. The purchase price was $200,000 of which $160,000 was financed by the proceeds of a mortgage loan from the Cattleman Savings and Loan Association. Bernard immediately procured a standard fire insurance policy on the premises for $200,000 from the Magnificent Insurance Company. Cattleman also took out fire insurance of $160,000 on the property from the Reliable Insurance Company of America. The property was subsequently totally destroyed as a result of a fire which started in an adjacent loft and spread to Bernard's building. Insofar as the rights and duties of Bernard, Cattleman, and the insurers are concerned, which of the following is a correct statement?

   a.   Cattleman Savings and Loan lacks the requisite insurable interest to collect on its policy.

   b.   Bernard Manufacturing can only collect $40,000.

   c.   Reliable Insurance Company is subrogated to Cattleman's rights against Bernard upon payment of Cattleman's insurance claim.

   d.   The maximum amount that Bernard Manufacturing can collect from Magnificent is $40,000, the value of its insurable interest.

2.   Real Life Insurance Company has refused to pay on a $50,000 term life insurance policy taken out by Dodson. The circumstances surrounding Dodson's procuring the policy are as follows: Maxwell, an acquaintance of Dodson's, contacted him one day and asked him if he would like to make $100. Dodson said, "Sure, as long as it is easy money." Maxwell assured Dodson that the only thing Dodson had to do was sign an application for insurance, submit to a physical, name Maxwell as the beneficiary, and subsequently assign the policy to Maxwell. Maxwell paid Dodson the $100 and reimbursed him for the premium. Two years after taking out the policy, Dodson died. Maxwell presented the policy to Real Life for payment and it refused to pay. Which of the following is correct?

   a.   Real Life must pay the $50,000 to Maxwell since he is the beneficiary.

   b.   Dodson's estate is entitled to the $50,000 proceeds of the life insurance policy.

   c.   Maxwell will recover the $50,000 since the policy was assigned to him.

   d.   Maxwell will recover nothing in that he lacked an insurable interest in Dodson's life.

3.   Morse is seeking to collect on a property insurance policy covering certain described property which was destroyed. The insurer has denied recovery based upon Morse's alleged lack of an insurable interest in the property. In which of the situations described below will the insurance company prevail?

   a.   The property has been willed to Morse's father for life and, upon his father's death, to Morse as the remainderman.

   b.   The insured property does **not** belong to Morse, but instead to a corporation which he controls.

   c.   Morse is **not** the owner of the insured property but a mere long-term lessee.

   d.   The insured property belongs to a general trade debtor of Morse and the debt is unsecured.

4.   The Fargo Corporation provides its employees with free group life insurance of $1,000 for each $1,000 of annual salary. Maxwell is an Executive Vice President of Fargo and receives a salary of $100,000 a year. Consistent with state laws, Maxwell has assigned the group policy to his wife Joan. Regarding the group policy and its assignment, which of the following is correct?

   a.   The assignee of a group policy **must** have an insurable interest in the life of the insured.

   b.   The assignment of the policy to Joan transferred all the legal incidents of ownership to her.

   c.   Maxwell does **not** have any income for income tax purposes as a result of Fargo's payment of the insurance premiums.

   d.   The proceeds from the group policy will be an asset of Maxwell's estate upon his death.

5.   Which of the following defenses by a life insurance company would be unsuccessful by reason of the incontestable clause?

   a.   A limitation upon the scope of the causes of death which the policy covers.

   b.   Cancellation of the policy due to nonpayment of premiums.

   c.   A material misstatement of fact by the insured relating to his health.

   d.   Lack of an insurable interest on the part of the party who insured the deceased.

6. Newton is an employee of the Black Motor Company. She is covered to the extent of $50,000 by a group term life insurance policy which covers all the full-time employees of Black. She pays no premiums on the policy. Regarding the legal and tax aspects of this policy, which of the following is a correct statement?

    a. Black is not entitled to a deduction for the premiums paid on the policy.

    b. Newton must include the annual premium to purchase the $50,000 policy in her gross income.

    c. Newton is obligated to name the Black Motor Company as the contingent beneficiary.

    d. The policy is cancelled upon her terminating her employment unless she elects to pay the premiums herself at the non-group rate.

7. Rollo Trading Corporation insured its 15 automobiles for both liability and collision. Poindexter, one of its salesmen, was in an automobile accident while driving a company car on a sales trip. The facts clearly reveal that the accident was solely the fault of Connors, the driver of the other car. Poindexter was seriously injured, and the automobile was declared a total loss. The value of the auto was $2,850. Which of the following is an incorrect statement regarding the rights and liabilities of Rollo, its insurer, Poindexter, and Connors?

    a. Rollo's insurer has no liability whatsoever since the accident was the result of Connors' negligence.

    b. Rollo's insurer is liable for $2,850, less any deductible, on the collision policy, but will be subrogated to Rollo's rights.

    c. Rollo's insurer must defend Rollo against any claims by Poindexter or Connors.

    d. Poindexter has an independent action against Connors for the injuries caused by Connors' negligence.

8. Hazard & Company was the owner of a building valued at $100,000. Since Hazard did not believe that a fire would result in a total loss, it procured two standard fire insurance policies on the property. One was for $24,000 with the Asbestos Fire Insurance Company and the other was for $16,000 with the Safety Fire Insurance Company. Both policies contained standard pro rata and 80% coinsurance clauses. Six months later, at which time the building was still valued at $100,000, a fire occurred which resulted in a loss of $40,000. What is the total amount Hazard can recover on both policies and the respective amount to be paid by Asbestos?

    a. $0 and $0.

    b. $20,000 and $10,000.

    c. $20,000 and $12,000.

    d. $40,000 and $20,000.

9. Charleston, Inc., had its warehouse destroyed by fire. Charleston's property was insured against fire loss by the Conglomerate Insurance Company. An investigation by Conglomerate revealed that the fire had been caused by a disgruntled employee whom Charleston had suspended for one month due to insubordination. Charleston seeks to hold its insurer liable for the $200,000 loss of its warehouse. Which of the following is correct insofar as the dispute between Charleston and the Conglomerate Insurance Company?

    a. Since the loss was due to the deliberate destruction by one of Charleston's employees, recovery will be denied.

    b. Conglomerate must pay Charleston, but it will be subrogated to Conglomerate's rights against the wrongdoing employee.

    c. The fact that the employee has been suspended for one month precludes recovery against Conglomerate.

    d. Arson is excluded from the coverage of most fire insurance policies, and therefore Conglomerate is not liable.

10. Alphonse, a sole CPA practitioner, obtained a malpractice insurance policy from the Friendly Casualty Company. In regard to this coverage

    a. Issuance of an unqualified opinion by Alphonse when he knows the statements are false does not give Friendly a defense.

    b. The policy would automatically cover the work of a new partnership formed by Alphonse and Borne.

    c. Friendly will not be subrogated to rights against Alphonse for his negligent conduct of an audit.

    d. Coverage includes injury to a client resulting from a slip on a rug negligently left loose in Alphonse's office.

11. Digital Sales, Inc., leased office space from Franklin Rentals for a five-year period. The lease did not contain any provisions regarding insurance by the lessee. During the term of the lease the office building was gutted by a fire that started in an adjacent building and spread to Franklin's building. In this situation

    a. Digital has an implied obligation to insure the portion of the building it leased, to protect its interest in the property and that of the lessor.

b. Digital has an insurable interest in the building, but only to the extent of the value of its leasehold.

c. If the building is fully occupied and leased on long-term leaseholds, Franklin has no insurable interest.

d. If Franklin sold the building, it could nevertheless continue the insurance coverage and collect on the policy because its insurable interest in the building runs from its prior ownership.

12. The partnership of Cox & Hayes, CPAs, is a medium-sized accounting firm. The senior staff member, Walton, is the office manager. The office building is owned by the partnership and title is duly recorded in the partnership name. With regard to life and property insurance, which of the following is true?

a. Only the partnership, not the partners, has an insurable interest in the lives of the partners.

b. The partnership does not have an insurable interest in the life of Walton because he is not a partner.

c. Each individual partner has an insurable interest in the partnership property even though title to the property is in the partnership name.

d. Only the partnership can insure the firm's office building against property damage.

13. On November 1, 1977, Brady applied for a life insurance policy on her own life for $50,000, naming her son as beneficiary. The application which Brady signed contained the following clause:

The insurance hereby applied for shall not take effect until (1) a written or printed policy shall have been actually delivered to and accepted by the insured (Brady), while in good health, and (2) the first premium thereon is paid.

What is the legal effect of the above clause?

a. One or both of the above provisions is invalid as a matter of public policy.

b. If Brady paid the premium at the time she took out the policy and was at that time "in good health," the policy is legally binding irrespective of her having suffered a serious accident prior

to the insurance policy being written and delivered.

c. If the insurance company wrote the policy and delivered it to a general agent who held it for safekeeping until Brady picked it up, the policy would be in effect if Brady was in good health when the policy was delivered to the agent even though Brady died before picking it up.

d. Under no circumstances will Brady prevail unless she physically picks up the policy while "in good health."

14. When Wayne died in 1976 his will created a testamentary trust out of the residue of his estate for the benefit of his wife during her lifetime and the remainder to his son, Eric, upon Mrs. Wayne's death. The residue of the estate included rental property subject to a $45,000 first mortgage. Probate of the estate has been completed, and the property deeded to the trustee to hold pursuant to the terms of the will. Carlton, Wayne's attorney and advisor, was named as executor and the Jefferson Trust Company was named as the sole trustee. Which of the following parties does not have an interest in the trust property sufficient to obtain fire insurance on said property?

a. The son, Eric.
b. Wayne's wife.
c. The first mortgagee.
d. Eric's wife.

15. Adams Company purchased a factory and warehouse from Martinson for $150,000. Adams obtained a $100,000 real estate mortgage loan from a local bank and was required by the lender to pay for the cost of title insurance covering the bank's interest in the property. In addition, Adams was required to obtain fire insurance sufficient to protect the bank against loss due to fire. The co-insurance factor has been satisfied. Under these circumstances, which of the following is correct?

a. Adams can purchase only $50,000 of title insurance since it already obtained a $100,000 title policy for the bank equal to the bank loan.

b. The bank could not have independently obtained a fire insurance policy on the property because Adams has legal title.

c. If Adams obtained a $150,000 fire insurance policy which covered its interest and the bank's interest in the property and there is an estimated $50,000 of fire loss, the insurer will typically be obligated to pay the owner and the bank the amounts equal to their respective interests as they may appear.

d. If Adams obtained a $100,000 fire insurance policy covering the bank's interest and $150,000 covering his own interest, each would obtain these amounts upon total destruction of the property.

16. Peters leased a restaurant from Brady with all furnishings and fixtures for a period of five years with an option to renew for two additional years. Peters made several structural improvements and modifications to the interior of the building. He obtained a fire insurance policy for his own benefit insuring his interest in the property for $25,000. The restaurant was totally destroyed by an accidental fire. Peters seeks recovery from his insurer. Subject to policy limits, which of the following is correct?

a. Peters is entitled to recover damages to the extent of the value of his leasehold interest.

b. Peters is entitled to recover for lost profits due to the fire even though the policy is silent on the point.

c. Peters must first seek redress from the owner before he is entitled to recover.

d. Peters will not recover because he lacks the requisite insurable interest in the property.

17. When an insured owns a life insurance policy on his life and has borrowed against it without repaying the loan at the time of his death

a. No proceeds are payable if the loan was equal to full cash surrender value prior to the death of the insured.

b. The face amount must be paid to a beneficiary irrevocably named prior to the loan where no notice of the loan was given to the beneficiary.

c. The policy becomes incontestable to the extent of the amount of the loan.

d. The insurer may withhold the amount of the loan and interest from proceeds otherwise payable on the insured's death even though after the loan the policy was assigned for consideration to a third party who had no notice of the loan.

18. Margo, Inc., insured its property against fire with two separate insurance companies, Excelsior and Wilberforce. Each carrier insured the property for its full value, and neither insurer was aware that the other had also insured the property. The policies were the standard fire insurance

policies used throughout the United States. If the property is totally destroyed by fire, how much will Margo recover?

a. Nothing because Margo has engaged in an illegal gambling venture.

b. The full amount from both insurers.

c. A ratable or pro rata share from each insurer, not to exceed the value of the property insured.

d. Only 80% of the value of the property from each insurer because of the standard co-insurance clause.

19. A typical term life insurance policy

a. Builds up a cash value during its duration against which the policyholder can borrow.

b. Is assignable.

c. Creates a vested interest in the named beneficiary.

d. Does not require an insurable interest in the person taking out the policy as do other types of life insurance policies.

20. The Devon Insurance Company issued a $50,000 whole life insurance policy to Finn. Finn's age was incorrectly stated in the application, and, as a result, she paid a smaller premium than that applicable to her age. Devon denies liability asserting as its defense a material misrepresentation by Finn. Under the circumstances, how much will Finn's beneficiary collect?

a. The entire amount of the policy if the incontestable clause applies.

b. Nothing, unless the beneficiary can establish that Finn was unaware of her correct age.

c. The amount of insurance that the premium would have purchased if the correct age had been stated.

d. The amount of premium Finn paid during her lifetime with interest at the legal rate.

21. Nabor, Inc., purchased a three-year fire insurance policy from the Fidelity Insurance Company covering its factory and warehouse. Which of the following statements is correct as a general rule of insurance law?

a. The policy will not cover the intentional destruction of the property by a third party.

b. The policy will not cover the destruction of the property if it is caused by the gross negligence of an employee of Nabor.

c. If Nabor sells the insured property to a third party and assigns the insurance policy to the buyer, it continues in effect.

d. If Nabor sells the insured property, but retains the fire insurance policy, it will not be able to collect on the policy in the event of its destruction by fire.

22. Wilson obtained a fire insurance policy on his dairy farm from the Columbus Insurance Company. The policy was for $80,000 which was the value of the property. The policy was the standard fire insurance policy sold throughout the United States. A fire occurred late one night and caused a $10,000 loss. Which of the following will prevent Wilson from recovering the full amount of his loss from Columbus Insurance?

a. The coinsurance clause.

b. Wilson had a similar policy with another insurance company for $40,000.

c. The fact that 50% of the loss was caused by smoke and water damage.

d. The fact that his negligence was the primary cause of the fire.

23. Dobbins insured his life for $100,000 naming his wife as beneficiary. After the policy had been in effect for ten years and had a cash surrender value in excess of $15,000, Dobbins assigned the policy to Suburban National Bank to secure a $20,000 loan. A copy of the assignment was filed with Suburban at its home office. Dobbins has died and his widow and Suburban are seeking to recover on the $100,000 life insurance policy. Which of the following is correct?

a. Suburban's recovery is limited to the amount of the loan outstanding plus interest.

b. The assignment to Suburban was void without the beneficiary's consent.

c. Suburban will be denied recovery due to a lack of an insurable interest.

d. The widow had a vested interest in the insurance policy in question.

MAY 1981 QUESTIONS

24. On October 15, 1980, Golden made a loan of $100,000 to Phillips and obtained a mortgage for $50,000 on Phillips' home as security for the loan. The home was worth $50,000. The following day Golden, to protect himself further, took out a fire insurance policy on Phillips' home in the sum of $50,000 with himself as beneficiary, and also a policy on Phillips' life in the same sum, with himself as beneficiary. Golden paid the premiums on both policies for one year. On March 1, 1981, Phillips paid his debt to Golden in full and the mortgage was satisfied and cancelled. On April 15, 1981, Phillips' home was completely destroyed by fire, and Phillips, trapped in the house, died in the flames. At this time, the two policies were still in effect and there had been no change in the beneficiary. On which, if any, policy is Golden entitled to collect?

a. Life insurance policy only.

b. Fire insurance policy only.

c. Both insurance policies.

d. Neither insurance policy.

25. Lincoln loaned Osgood $20,000 and obtained an unsecured negotiable promissory note for that amount. Lincoln wishes to obtain a life insurance policy on Osgood's life as added protection on the loan. With respect to Lincoln's obtaining an insurance policy on Osgood's life, which of the following is true?

a. Lincoln has an insurable interest in Osgood's life and may legally assign the insurance policy to a transferee of the note.

b. If Osgood consented to Lincoln's insuring him for an amount substantially in excess of the loan, Lincoln would be able to recover the face amount of the policy.

c. Lincoln does **not** have an insurable interest since the note is negotiable.

d. The only policy that Lincoln may legally obtain is a term policy.

26. Larkin insured his own life for $40,000 and named his wife as beneficiary. He took out the policy on July 15, 1978. He has paid all premiums as they became due. The policy included the following two provisions:

. The Insured represents that the statements he has made in the application for insurance and in the questionnaire submitted in connection with his physical health are true and are a part of the policy issued to him.

. This Policy shall be incontestable after it has been in force for a period of two years from the date of issue, except for failure to pay premiums.

Larkin died on January 10, 1981, and the insurance company cancelled the policy on February 1, 1981, upon learning that Larkin had lied about his health. Larkin's widow seeks recovery of the $40,000 from the insurer. What will be the probable outcome of the dispute between the widow and the insurers?

    a.   The widow will receive a refund of all the premiums paid.

    b.   The widow will receive nothing because of the false health statements made by Larkin at the inception of the policy.

    c.   The widow will receive the full $40,000.

    d.   The widow will receive a refund of all the premiums paid plus accrued interest.

27.   Burt owns an office building which is leased to Hansen Corporation under the terms of a long-term lease. Both Burt and Hansen have procured fire insurance covering the building. Which of the following is correct?

    a.   Both Burt and Hansen have separate insurable interests.

    b.   Burt's insurable interest is limited to the book value of the property.

    c.   Hansen has an insurable interest in the building, but only to the extent of the value of any additions or modifications it has made.

    d.   Since Burt has legal title to the building, he is the only party who can insure the building.

PROBLEMS

Problem 1   Insurable Interests (1176,L6b&c)

(15 to 20 minutes)

Part b.   Balsam was a partner in the firm Wilkenson, Potter & Parker. The firm had a buy-out arrangement whereby the partnership funded the buy-out agreement with insurance on the lives of the partners payable to the partnership. When the insurance policies were obtained by the part-nership, Balsam understated his age by three years. Eight years later, Balsam decided to sell his part-nership interest to Gideon. The sale was consum-mated and the other partners admitted Gideon as a partner in Balsam's place. The partnership never-theless retained ownership in the policy on the life of Balsam and continued to pay the premiums there-on. Balsam died one year later. The insurance com-pany refuses to pay the face value of the policy claiming that the partnership is only entitled to the amount of the premiums paid. As a basis for this position, the insurance company asserts lack of an insurable interest and material misrepresentation.

Required: Answer the following, setting forth reasons for any conclusions stated.

Will Wilkenson, Potter & Parker prevail in an action against the insurance company? Give specific attention to the assertions of the in-surance company.

Part c.   Anderson loaned the Drum Cor-poration $60,000. The loan was secured by a first mortgage on Drum's land and the plant thereon. Anderson independently procured a fire insurance policy for $60,000 on the mort-gaged property from the Victory Insurance Company. Six years later when the mortgage had been amortized down to $52,000, the plant was totally destroyed by a fire caused by faulty electrical wiring in the rear storage area.

Required: Answer the following, setting forth reasons for any conclusions stated.

1.   Anderson seeks recovery of $60,000 from the Victory Insurance Company. How much will it collect?
2.   Upon payment by Victory Insurance Company, what rights does **Victory** have?

Problem 2   Insurable Interest (1174,L7c)

(5 to 10 minutes)

Part c.   Marvel Enterprises, Inc., contracted to buy Jonstone's factory and warehouse. The con-tract provided that if title did not pass to Marvel prior to October 1, 1974, Marvel would have the right to possession on that date pending conveyance of title upon delivery of the deed. The contract also provided that the purchase price was to be adjusted depending upon the actual acreage con-veyed as determined by an independent survey. This provision was subject to a further stipulation: the maximum purchase price would not exceed $450,000 nor be less than $425,000 as long as the survey did not reveal major variances nor render title unmarketable.

All the requisite paperwork was not in order by October 1, 1974, and Marvel exercised its option to take possession on that date. Concurrently, Mar-vel obtained a fire insurance policy on the factory and warehouse effective October 1, 1974. The closing was finally scheduled for October 17, 1974. The survey confirmed the acreage described in the con-tract of sale, and Marvel tendered the balance of the purchase price on October 17, 1974. During the interim period, however, the factory and ware-house were totally destroyed by fire and Marvel seeks to recover on its fire insurance policy. The insurance company denies liability.

Required:
Discuss Marvel's rights to recover from the insurance company.

MULTIPLE CHOICE ANSWERS

1.	c	7.	a	13.	c	19.	b	25.	a
2.	d	8.	c	14.	d	20.	c	26.	c
3.	d	9.	b	15.	c	21.	d	27.	a
4.	b	10.	c	16.	a	22.	b		
5.	c	11.	b	17.	d	23.	a		
6.	d	12.	c	18.	c	24.	a		

EXPLANATION OF MULTIPLE CHOICE ANSWERS

1. (1180,L1,53) (c) Answer (c) is correct because under a fire insurance policy, an insurer who pays a claim is subrogated (succeeds to the rights of the insured) to any rights that the insured had against a third party. Answer (a) is incorrect since Cattleman, as mortgagee, has an insurable interest to the extent of the outstanding debt ($160,000). If the policy is a valued policy, then Bernard will collect $200,000. If it is an open policy, then Bernard will collect the market value of the building at the time of destruction up to a maximum of $200,000. Thus, answer (b) and (d) are incorrect.

2. (1180,L1,54) (d) The party purchasing a life insurance policy must have an insurable interest in the life covered by the policy at the time the policy is issued. To have an insurable interest in someone's life the insured must be related by blood or have a substantial economic interest in having the life continue. Even though Dodson signed the insurance application, Maxwell would be considered the insured. Thus to collect on the policy Maxwell would have to prove that he had an insurable interest in Dodson's life at the time the policy was issued. Since Maxwell does not have an insurable interest, Real Life could successfully contest payment of this policy. This is true even if the policy contained an incontestability clause. Lack of insurable interest at time policy was issued is always proper grounds for insurer to refuse payment of a life insurance policy.

3. (1180,L1,55) (d) Concerning a property insurance policy, the insured must have an insurable interest in the property when the loss occurs. To have an insurable interest in property, a person must have both a legal interest and a possibility of monetary loss. An unsecured creditor does not have an insurable interest in the property of the debtor. However, a vested remainder-man would have an insurable interest, as would a shareholder in the property of the corporation, and as would a lessee in the property that is the subject of the leasehold.

4. (1180,L1,56) (b) Due to the assignment of the policy, Joan received the incidents of ownership of this policy. Answer (a) is incorrect because an insurable interest in a life insurance policy need only be present at the time the policy is purchased, not at insured's death. Answer (c) is incorrect since the premiums paid by the employer are taxable as income to the employee. Answer (d) is incorrect because the proceeds from the group policy will not be included in Maxwell's estate due to the fact that he transferred the incidents of ownership of the policy before his death. Proceeds would be included if Maxwell had retained the incidents of ownership at the time of death.

5. (1180,L1,57) (c) When a life insurance policy contains an incontestability clause, the policy may not be contested because of concealments or misstatements after a stated time (generally 2 years) except for: nonpayment of premiums; no insurable interest; no proof of death; risk not covered by policy.

6. (580,L1,43) (d) Answer (d) is the correct statement in that an employee upon termination has the option, if so provided by the insuring party, to continue coverage if the insured party continues making the premium payments. Answer (a) is incorrect because a corporation may deduct group term life insurance premiums paid by the employer. Answer (b) is incorrect because it is excluded as taxable income for coverage up to $50,000. Answer (c) is incorrect because the insured party has the right to name any party as beneficiary and is not required to name the corporation as beneficiary.

7. (580,L1,47) (a) Rollo Trading Corporation's insurer does have liability even though the accident was the result of Connor's negligence. Rollo had collision coverage under the insurance policy, therefore the insurer is liable for any damages to Rollo's car caused by collision, irrespective of whose negligence caused the damage. Most policies contain $50- or $100-deductible clauses concerning collision coverage. One of the insurer's obligations under an auto insurance policy is to defend the insured against any lawsuits arising from operation of the vehicle covered by the policy. Poindexter has a right to sue Connors for injuries caused by Connor's negligence.

8. (580,L1,48) (c) When there is a partial loss for property covered under a policy with a co-insurance clause, the following formula is applied to determine the recovery:

$$\frac{\text{Face value of policy}}{\text{Fair value of property} \times \text{co-insurance \%}} \times \text{Loss}$$

$$\frac{\$16,000}{\$100,000 \times 80\%} \times \$40,000 = \frac{\text{Recovery}}{\$8,000}$$

$$\frac{\$24,000}{\$100,000 \times 80\%} \times \$40,000 = \frac{\$12,000}{\$20,000}$$

Thus answer (c) is the correct answer.

9. (1179,L1,12) (b) Under the facts, Conglomerate must pay Charleston, the insured, but Conglomerate upon payment will be subrogated to the Charleston rights against the employee who committed arson. Answer (a) is incorrect since the typical fire policy does not exclude recovery by the insured if a fire is caused by deliberate or negligent destruction by the insured's employees. Answer (c) is incorrect because the fact that the employee has been suspended for 1 month is of no legal consequence. Answer (d) is incorrect because arson by anyone other than the insured is generally an included risk under standard fire insurance policies.

10. (574,L3,53) (c) The insurance company would not be subrogated to the rights against its insured who holds a malpractice policy for negligence. The reason for a malpractice insurance policy is to protect the insured against this type of action. Malpractice insurance would not cover intentional wrongs such as fraud. A malpractice policy would not automatically cover the new partnership, because the character of the new partner is crucial to the risk that the insurance company takes. Injuries such as a slip on a rug are not covered under malpractice insurance, but under personal liability.

11. (575,L2,32) (b) One has an insurable interest where there is a legal interest and a possibility of pecuniary loss. A lessee, Digital in this case, has an insurable interest to the extent of the value of the leasehold. The lessee has no obligation to insure the building it leases unless so provided in the lease, because the lessor has an insurable interest in the building, even if it is fully occupied. Upon the sale of a building, the prior owner loses his insurable interest because he no longer has an ownership interest.

12. (1177,L1,2) (c) Each partner has an insurable interest in partnership property, because each partner has an ownership interest in partnership property even though title is in the partnership. Therefore each partner could insure the office

building (although the total insurance recoverable is the value of the building which would be apportioned among the partners). Partners have insurable interests in the lives of other partners to pay off estates and prevent liquidation of the partnership. A partnership, as employer, has an insurable interest in key employees because their death would be a substantial loss to the business.

13. (1177,L1,10) (c) A general agent is one who has broad authority as contrasted to the limited authority of a special agent. When an insurance company unconditionally issues a life insurance policy and (1) mails it to the insured, or (2) delivers it to its own agent for delivery to the insured, without further duties to be performed, the courts usually hold that a constructive delivery to the insured has occurred prior to physical delivery. This is based on the assumption that the agent is agent for both the company and for the insured. Therefore, if Brady was in good health when the agent accepted the policy for her, the terms of the clause are met. Answer (a) is incorrect because neither provision is invalid; they are merely conditions precedent to liability of the insurer. Answer (b) is incorrect because Brady must believe she is in good health when she takes delivery of the policy or she has breached her warranty and the policy is voidable by the insurer. Answer (d) is incorrect because if Brady believes she is in good health but actually is not, then the policy is good and she has not breached a warranty.

14. (1177,L3,47) (d) In order to have an insurable interest in property, one must have both a legal interest and a possibility of pecuniary loss. Eric's wife has no legal interest, because she will have no ownership interest when it passes to Eric. Eric has a future legal interest in the property and may insure it to insure his interest. Wayne's wife has a present life estate which is an ownership (legal) interest. The first mortgagee has a secured interest which satisfies the legal interest requirement.

15. (578,L1,17) (c) Where both the owner and a mortgagee are insured under a policy, typically a loss payable clause will allow the mortgagee to collect to the extent of his loss. Answer (d) is incorrect because the policy is probably open or unvalued rather than a stated value policy. Unless it is a stated value policy, the insurance company will only be liable for the smaller of the policy face value or the FMV of the loss at the time of the loss. Answer (b) is incorrect because a mortgagee has an insurable interest and can independently obtain a fire

insurance policy on mortgaged property. Answer (a) is incorrect because an owner of property can purchase any amount of title insurance that the insurance company agrees to sell.

16. (578,L1,20) (a) A lessee has an insurable interest to the extent of the value of his leasehold interest. Therefore Peters is entitled to recover damages to the extent of the value of his leasehold interest, not to exceed the $25,000 policy limit. Answer (b) is incorrect because lost profits are not recoverable unless specifically included in the policy. Answer (c) is incorrect because an insured party may recover upon loss and need not seek redress from any other party first. Peter's insurance carrier would obtain by right of subrogation, however, any potential claim he has against the owner. Answer (d) is incorrect because a lessee has an insurable interest in leased property.

17. (574,L3,45) (d) When an insured borrows on a life insurance policy, the insured's estate does not have to repay the loan. The assignment of a policy to a third party with no notice of the loan has no effect on the insurance company. The cash surrender value is not necessarily equal to the face of the policy. An irrevocably named beneficiary only has rights to the remaining proceeds of the policy. The loan does not affect the incontestability of the policy.

18. (1175,L3,38) (c) A person who insures with multiple policies can only collect the proportionate amount of the loss from each insurer. The limit of recovery is the value of the loss. There is nothing illegal about insuring with more than one policy or to insure for more than the value of the property. A co-insurance clause must be stated in the policy and does not affect recovery if insurance is carried for full value.

19. (576,L2,31) (b) A typical term life policy is assignable just as any other life policy unless it is specifically made non-assignable, which is not common. Only if the policy is not assignable does it create a vested interest in the beneficiary. A term policy does not build up a cash value as does ordinary life policies, and therefore is much cheaper. All life insurance policies, including term, require an insurable interest in the person taking out the policy.

20. (577,L1,5) (c) If an insured's age is misstated, either the premium must be adjusted, or after death the beneficiary will be paid the amount of in-

surance the premiums would have purchased using the correct age of the insured. The incontestable clause does prevent most other misrepresentations from being used as a defense by the insurance company. However, it does not bar an adjustment to reflect the correct age. The beneficiary does not need to establish Finn's good faith. Since the beneficiary can recover the insurance, the insurance company has earned the premiums paid.

21. (1178,L1,13) (d) For fire insurance, the owner of the policy must have an insurable interest when the loss occurs. If Nabor sells the property it will no longer have an insurable interest and may not collect on the policy. Answer (a) is incorrect because the purpose of fire insurance is to cover all fires execpt for intentional destruction of the insured property by the owner. Likewise answer (b) is incorrect because the general rules of insurance law provide for recovery under the policy even if destruction of the property is caused by gross negligence of an employee of the insured. Answer (c) is incorrect because a fire insurance policy cannot be validly assigned without approval by the insurance company.

22. (579,L1,2) (b) When a property owner has insured his property with more than one insurance company, each insurance company is required to pay a pro rata share of the loss. If Wilson had both an $80,000 policy and a $40,000 policy on the same property, the $80,000 policy must pay two-thirds and the $40,000 policy one-third of any loss (limited to $80,000 and $40,000 respectively). Answer (a) is incorrect because a coinsurance clause applies only when the property owner has underinsured his property; Wilson insured his property for its value. Answer (c) is incorrect since damage from smoke and water in addition to fire damage is recoverable under the standard fire policy sold in the United States. Answer (d) is incorrect since negligence is not a bar to recovery under a standard fire insurance policy.

23. (579,L1,3) (a) The life insurance policy was assigned to Suburban Bank only as collateral for the loan. Hence, the assignee's recovery is limited to the amount of the loan outstanding, plus interest. Answer (c) is incorrect because the insured purchased the policy and he has an insurable interest on his own life. The assignee of a life insurance policy is not required to have an insurable interest. Answer (d) is incorrect since the beneficiary is not recognized as having a vested interest unless the beneficiary designation is made irrevocable. Hence, the insured has the power to change the name of the beneficiary without the consent of the beneficiary, which means answer (b) is incorrect, also.

MAY 1981 ANSWERS

24. (581,L1,45)   (a)   In order for a valid insurance policy to exist, the insured party must have an insurable interest in the property or life that is being insured. With respect to property, an insurable interest exists when a person has a legal or equitable interest in the property and will either suffer a loss upon the property's destruction or benefit from the property's continued existence. An insurable interest in property must be present at the time the property is destroyed in order for the insured party to collect on the policy. An insurable interest in a person's life can arise from a relationship of great love and affection (family members have insurable interests in each other), or from an economic relationship (debtor/creditor, partnership/partner, corporation/employee). Unlike an interest in property, an insurable interest in a life need only be present at the time the policy is taken out. Golden (the creditor) has an insurable interest in the life of the debtor (Phillips) to the extent of the unsecured debt owed. Since this is a life insurance policy, the creditor need not have an insurable interest in the life of the debtor at the time of the debtor's death. Thus, Golden could collect on the policy even if the loan had been repaid in full at the time of Phillips' death. Answers (c) and (d) are incorrect because Golden will not collect on the fire insurance policy, since Golden had no interest in the property at the time of its destruction (the mortgage had been canceled). Answer (d) is incorrect since Golden will collect on the life insurance policy.

25. (581,L1,46)   (a)   An insurable interest in the life of another is present when the insured party has a relationship of great love and affection (e.g., a family member) or of economic dependancy (e.g., debtor/creditor) in the life of the insured. Such an interest need only be present at the time the insurance policy is taken out. In this problem, Lincoln (the creditor) has an insurable interest in Osgood (the debtor) to the extent of any unsecured debt ($20,000). Answer (c) is incorrect because life insurance contracts may usually be assigned (an assignment changes the beneficiary named in the policy). Normally, a life insurance policy contains a provision that allows the owner to change the beneficiary. However, if the policy does not contain such a provision, the beneficiary's rights are vested and the owner of the policy can only assign it with the consent of the beneficiary. Answer (b) is incorrect because a creditor may not insure against the death of a debtor for more than the amount of the unsecured debt, even with the debtor's permission to do so. Answer (d) is incorrect because Lincoln is not limited to obtaining a term policy. A term policy provides for coverage during a fixed period of time

(e.g., 10 years), and the insurer is liable only if the insured dies within the term of the policy. A term policy, unlike a straight life insurance policy, has no cash surrender value.

26. (581,L1,47)   (c)   The provision in the policy concerning Larkin's health is a warranty. A warranty is a statement of fact contained in an insurance policy which either diminishes the risk of the insurer's loss or guards against an undisclosed fact which would increase the insurer's risk. The legal consequence of a false warranty is that the policy is voidable by the insurer (common law). However, by statute warranties in life insurance policies are treated as representations—the result that the misrepresentation must be material before the insurer can void the policy. Larkin's policy also contained an incontestability clause, which states the insurer cannot contest payment of the policy after being in effect for 2 years except for nonpayment of premiums. Since Larkin's policy has been in force for more than 2 years, the insurance company could not use Larkin's misrepresentation to void the policy. Answers (a), (b), and (d) are incorrect since the widow will collect the full $40,000.

27. (581,L1,48)   (a)   A person has an insurable interest in property if he will benefit by its continued existence or suffer from its destruction and has a legal or equitable interest in the property (e.g., a mortgagee, mortgagor, tenant in rented property, or partner in partnership property). Both Burt (owner of legal title) and Hansen (tenant in leased property) have an insurable interest, therefore, answer (a) is true. Answer (b) is incorrect because Burt has an insurable interest to the extent of any economic loss he might suffer. Such a loss would normally be measured by market value of the property, not book value. Answer (c) is also false because the tenant has an insurable interest for the amount of economic loss he will suffer in the event the property is destroyed. This amount may be greater or less than the value of the additions or modifications. The tenants would measure their economic loss in reference to items such as the expense of finding a new office building or new business space.

ANSWER OUTLINE

Problem 1   Insurable Interests

b.   The insurance company must pay
      An insurable interest in Balsom existed
          I.e., there was an economic interest
      Insurable interest only required at policy inception
      Age misrepresentation does not void policy
          But does reduce amount recoverable
          To the insurance purchasable with premiums
          paid

c1.   Anderson's recovery (insurable interest) is principal
      plus
          Interest at time of the fire
          Limited to policy face value

c2.   Victory is subrogated to Anderson's rights
          I.e., to receive mortgage payments

UNOFFICIAL ANSWER

Problem 1   Insurable Interests

b.   Yes. An insurable interest in the life of an-
      other is present here since the firm had a
      substantial economic interest in the life of
      Balsam at the time the policy was procured.
      It is well recognized that an entity has the
      requisite standing to procure insurance on its
      key participants. Certainly a general partner
      qualifies as a key participant. In addition,
      the funding of buy-out agreements is essen-
      tial in many instances, and insurance law
      recognizes this economic necessity. The in-
      surable interest required for a life insurance
      policy need only exist at the inception of
      the policy. Balsam's subsequent retirement
      does not invalidate it.
          The fact that Balsam misrepresented
      his age will not cause the loss of the entire
      insurance proceeds. The general rule provides
      that such a misrepresentation merely reduces
      the amount recoverable to that which the
      premiums would purchase if the correct age
      had been stated.

c.   1.   Anderson's insurable interest equals the
            extent of the mortgage debt outstand-
            ing. Thus, his recovery is limited to
            the $52,000 debt outstanding plus ac-
            crued interest on the debt, but the
            total recovery cannot exceed $60,000,
            the maximum coverage under the poli-
            cy.

2.   Upon payment, Victory is subrogated to
      the rights of Anderson and will succeed
      to Anderson's rights to receive payments
      under the terms of the mortgage and
      mortgage bond. If Drum Corporation
      fails to continue the payments, Victory
      may foreclose on the mortgage.

ANSWER OUTLINE

Problem 2   Insurable Interest

c.   Marvel (the insured) will recover from insurance
      company
      Insurable interest requirement satisfied
          Purchaser of real property in possession prior
          to closing has risk of loss
          Contract to purchase alone may also be suffi-
          cient

UNOFFICIAL ANSWER

Problem 2   Insurable Interest

Part c. Marvel will recover against the insurance
company for the value of the insured property
destroyed, i.e., the factory and warehouse.
      The insurance company is undoubtedly as-
serting a lack of insurable interest on Marvel's part
in that legal title had not been transferred to it at
the time of the fire. However where a purchaser,
pursuant to a contract of sale of real property,
takes possession of the premises prior to the
closing, the risk of loss is his. Thus, the insurable interest requirement has been satisfied and
Marvel may recover. It may also be argued that a
valid insurable interest is created by the contract
alone.

MULTIPLE CHOICE QUESTIONS (1—26)

1. The Marquis Trust has been properly created and it qualifies as a real estate investment trust (REIT) for federal income tax purposes. As such, it will
   a. Be taxed as any other trust for income tax purposes.
   b. Have been created under the Federal Trust Indenture Act.
   c. Provide limited liability for the parties investing in the trust.
   d. Be exempt from the Securities Act of 1933.

2. James Gordon decided to create an inter vivos trust for the benefit of his grandchildren. Gordon wished to bypass his own children and to provide an independent income for his grandchildren. He did not, however, wish to completely part with the assets he would transfer to the trust. Therefore, he transferred the assets to the York Trust Company in trust for the benefit of his grandchildren irrevocably for a period of 21 years. In relation to the Gordon trust and the rights and duties of the parties in respect to it
   a. Such a trust is quite useful in skipping generations and tying up the ownership of property, since its duration can be potentially infinite.
   b. The trust is **not** recognized as a legal entity for tax purposes, thus Gordon must include the trust income with his own.
   c. York has legal title to the trust property, the grandchildren have equitable title, and Gordon has a reversionary interest.
   d. If the trust deed is silent on the point, York must **not** sell or otherwise dispose of the trust assets without Gordon's advice and consent.

3. Paul Good's will left all of his commercial real property to his wife Dorothy for life and the remainder to his two daughters, Joan and Doris, as tenants in common. All beneficiaries are alive and over 21 years of age. Regarding the rights of the parties, which of the following is a correct statement?
   a. Dorothy may **not** elect to take against the will and receive a statutory share instead.
   b. The daughters **must** survive Dorothy in order to receive any interest in the property.
   c. Either of the daughters may sell her interest in the property without the consent of their mother or the other daughter.
   d. If only one daughter is alive upon the death of Dorothy, she is entitled to the entire property.

4. Larson is considering the creation of either a lifetime (inter vivos) or testamentary (by his will) trust. In deciding what to do, which of the following statements is correct?
   a. If the trust is an inter vivos trust, the trustee must file papers in the appropriate state office roughly similar to those required to be filed by a corporation to qualify.
   b. An inter vivos trust must meet the same legal requirements as one created by a will.
   c. Property transferred to a testamentary trust upon the grantor's (creator's) death is **not** included in the decedent's gross estate for federal tax purposes.
   d. Larson can retain the power to revoke an inter vivos trust.

5. An executor named in the decedent's will
   a. Must consent to serve, have read the will, and be present at the execution of the will.
   b. Need **not** serve if he does **not** wish to do so.
   c. Must serve without compensation unless the will provides otherwise.
   d. Can **not** be the principal beneficiary of the will.

6. The Astor Bank and Trust Company is the trustee of the Wayne Trust. A significant portion of the trust principal has been invested in AAA rated public utility bonds. Some of the bonds have been purchased at face value, some at a discount, and others at a premium. Which of the following is a proper allocation of the various items to income?
   a. The income beneficiary is entitled to the entire interest without dilution for the premium paid but is not entitled to the proceeds attributable to the discount upon collection.
   b. The income beneficiary is entitled to the entire interest without dilution and to the proceeds attributable to the discount.
   c. The income beneficiary is only entitled to the interest less the amount of the premium amortized over the life of the bond.
   d. The income beneficiary is entitled to the full interest and to an allocable share of the gain resulting from the discount.

7.   Waldorf's last will and testament named Franklin as the executor of the will. In respect to Franklin's serving as executor, which of the following is correct?

   a.   He serves without compensation unless the will provides otherwise.

   b.   He is at liberty to purchase the estate's property the same as any other person dealing at arm's length.

   c.   Waldorf must have obtained Franklin's consent in writing to serve as executor.

   d.   Upon appointment by the court, he serves as the legal representative of the estate.

8.   At his death, Filmore owned a $100,000 life insurance policy on his life in which he designated his wife as the beneficiary. The insurer paid the proceeds of the policy directly to Mrs. Filmore after his death. Which of the following is a correct statement?

   a.   If Filmore's will designates a person other than his wife to receive the proceeds of the insurance policy, such a designation will not be valid.

   b.   Upon receipt of the proceeds, Mrs. Filmore will have received $100,000 of taxable income, but income averaging is permitted.

   c.   The insurance proceeds are not includible in Filmore's estate for federal estate tax purposes.

   d.   Filmore, having designated his wife as the beneficiary of the policy, could not change the beneficiary unless she died or they were divorced.

9.   Mullins created a trust pursuant to her last will and testament which named her husband as the life income beneficiary and her children as the remaindermen. She is dead. Which of the following does not apply to the above-described trust?

   a.   It is a testamentary trust.

   b.   The husband has the right to appoint the ultimate beneficiaries.

   c.   The children have a vested interest in the trust.

   d.   The trustee owes a fiduciary duty to both the husband and the children.

10.   Woodrow died and left a will that named as co-executors the Fundamental Trust Company and Harlow, who is one of the residuary legatees. The will was silent on various points indicated below. Which of the following is correct?

   a.   If Woodrow's will was not properly executed, it will not be admitted to probate and his property will be distributed according to the intestate succession laws even though this is contrary to Woodrow's wishes as stated in the will.

   b.   Since Harlow is one of the residuary legatees, Harlow cannot serve as executor since this would represent a conflict of interest and also would violate Harlow's fiduciary duty.

   c.   All taxes paid will be allocated to the residuary estate and not apportioned.

   d.   The executors have complete discretion insofar as investing the estate's assets during the term of their administration.

11.   James Gordon decided to create an inter vivos trust for the benefit of his grandchildren. He wished to bypass his own children, and to provide an independent income for his grandchildren. He did not, however, wish to completely part with the assets he would transfer to the trust. Therefore, he transferred the assets to the York Trust Company, in trust for the benefit of his grandchildren irrevocably for a period of 12 years. Which of the following is correct regarding the trust?

   a.   The trust will fail for want of a proper purpose.

   b.   The trust income will not be taxable to Gordon during its existence.

   c.   Gordon retains beneficial title to the property transferred to the trust.

   d.   If Gordon demands the return of the trust assets prior to the 12 years, York must return them to him since he created the trust and the assets will eventually be his again.

Items **12** and **13** are based on the following information:

   Martin is the trustee of the Baker Trust which has assets in excess of $1 million. Martin has engaged the CPA firm of Hardy & Fox to prepare the annual accounting statement for the allocation of receipts and expenditures between income and principal. The trust indenture provides that "receipts and expenses are to be allocated to income or principal according to law."

12.   Which of the following receipts should be allocated to income?

   a.   Rights to subscribe to shares of the distributing corporation.

   b.   Sale of rights to subscribe to shares of the distributing corporation.

   c.   A 2% stock dividend.

   d.   Rights to subscribe to shares of another corporation.

13. Which of the following receipts from real property should be allocated to principal?

    a.   An unexpected payment of nine months' arrears in rental payments.

    b.   A six-month prepayment of rent.

    c.   Insurance proceeds for the destruction of a garage on one of the properties.

    d.   Interest on a purchase money mortgage arising from the sale of a parcel of the trust's real property.

14. Allgood is a trustee of a trust in which Lance is the life beneficiary and Ronald is the remainderman who is entitled to the corpus (principal) upon the death of Lance. Five thousand shares of stock in Parkard Company make up a portion of the trust. In September 1977, Parkard declared a 10% stock dividend out of the earnings accumulated after the trust was created. Parkard also issued rights to subscribe to new stock, and the trustee sold these stock rights for $5,000. Regarding Allgood's duties as the trustee, which of the following is correct, assuming there is no express provision covering the point in the trust indenture?

    a.   The proceeds from the subsequent sale of the 10% stock dividend must be divided proportionately between the beneficiaries.

    b.   The proceeds from the sale of the stock rights must be added to the corpus (principal) of the trust.

    c.   Allgood has discretion insofar as determining the proper share the beneficiaries are to receive in connection with the $5,000.

    d.   Allgood was obligated to obtain the consent of the beneficiaries prior to selling the stock rights.

15. Harris is the trustee named in Filmore's trust. The trust named Filmore as the life beneficiary, remainder to his children at age 21. The trust consists of stocks, bonds, and three pieces of rental income property. Which of the following statements best describes the trustee's legal relationships or duties?

    a.   The trustee has legal and equitable title to the rental property.

    b.   The trustee must automatically reinvest the proceeds from the sale of one of the rental properties in like property.

    c.   The trustee is a fiduciary with respect to the trust and the beneficiaries.

    d.   The trustee must divide among all the beneficiaries any insurance proceeds received in the event the real property is destroyed.

16. Kilgore created an irrevocable fifteen-year trust for the benefit of his minor children. At the end of the fifteen years, the principal (corpus) reverts to Kilgore. Kilgore named the Reliable Trust Company as trustee and provided that Reliable would serve without the necessity of posting a bond. In understanding the trust and rules applicable to it, which of the following is correct?

    a.   The trust is not a separate legal entity for federal tax purposes.

    b.   The facts indicate that the trust is a separate legal entity for both tax and non-tax purposes.

    c.   Kilgore may revoke the trust after eleven years, since he created it, and the principal reverts to him at the expiration of the fifteen years.

    d.   If Kilgore dies ten years after creation of the trust, it is automatically revoked and the property is distributed to the beneficiaries of his trust upon their attaining age 21.

17. Fifteen years ago Madison executed a valid will. He names his son, Walker, as the executor of his will and left two-thirds of his estate to his wife and the balance equally to his children. Madison is now dead and the approximate size of his estate is one million dollars. Which of the following statements is correct?

    a.   The will is invalid because it was executed at a time which is beyond the general statute of limitations.

    b.   The estate is not recognized as a taxable entity for tax purposes.

    c.   All the property bequeathed to his wife will be excluded from the decedent's estate for federal estate tax purposes.

    d.   Walker must, in addition to being named in the will, be appointed or approved by the appropriate state court to serve as the executor.

18. The normal types of questions relating to estates and trusts which might be referred from a law firm to a CPA firm would include problems which involve

    a.   The order of distribution under the intestate succession laws.

    b.   Whether an ancillary proceeding is required.

    c.   The amount of property or money to be received by the income beneficiaries as contrasted with the amount to be accumulated for the remainderman.

    d.   Whether a will has been effectively revoked.

19. Madison died 15 years after executing a valid will. He named his son, Walker, as the executor of his will. He left two-thirds of his estate to his wife and the balance equally to his children. Which of the following is a right or duty of Walker as executor?

    a. Walker must post a surety bond even if a provision in the will attempts to exempt him from this responsibility.

    b. Walker has an affirmative duty to discover, collect, and distribute all the decedent's assets.

    c. If the will is silent on the point, Walker has complete discretion insofar as investing the estate's assets during the term of his administration.

    d. Walker can sell real property without a court order, even though he has not been expressly authorized to do so.

20. The intestate succession distribution rules

    a. Do not apply to property held in joint tenancy.

    b. Do not apply to real property.

    c. Effectively prevent a decedent from totally disinheriting his wife and children.

    d. Apply to situations where the decedent failed to name an executor.

21. Which of the following receipts should be allocated by a trustee exclusively to income?

    a. A stock dividend.

    b. An extraordinary year-end cash dividend.

    c. A liquidating dividend whether in complete or partial liquidation.

    d. A stock split.

22. The Unity Trust Company is the trustee of a trust which has large real estate investments. Which of the following receipts or charges should be allocated by the trustee to income?

    a. Paving assessment for a new street.

    b. Prepaid rent received from tenants.

    c. A loss on the sale of one of the rental properties.

    d. The proceeds from an eminent domain proceeding.

23. Which of the following receipts or disbursements by a trustee should be credited to or charged against income?

    a. Amortization payment on real property subject to a mortgage.

    b. Capital gain distributions received from a mutual fund.

    c. Stock rights received from the distributing corporation.

    d. The discount portion received on redemption of treasury bills.

MAY 1981 QUESTIONS

24. With respect to trusts, which of the following states an **invalid** legal conclusion?

    a. The trustee must obtain the consent of the majority of the beneficiaries if a major change in the investment portfolio of the trust is to be made.

    b. For federal income tax purposes, a trust is entitled to an exemption similar to that of an individual although **not** equal in amount.

    c. Both the life beneficiaries of a trust and the ultimate takers have rights against the trustee, and the trustee is accountable to them.

    d. A trust is a separate taxable entity for federal income tax purposes.

25. The last will and testament of Jean Bond left various specific property and sums of money to relatives and friends. She left the residue of her estate equally to her favorite niece and nephew. Which of the various properties described below will become a part of Bond's estate and be distributed in accordance with her last will and testament?

    a. A joint savings account which listed her sister, who is still living, as the joint tenant.

    b. The entire family homestead which she had owned in joint tenancy with her older brother who predeceased her and which was still recorded as jointly owned.

    c. Several substantial gifts that she made in contemplation of death to various charities.

    d. A life insurance policy which designated a former partner as the beneficiary.

26. Shepard created an inter vivos trust for the benefit of his children with the remainder to his grandchildren upon the death of his last surviving child. The trust consists of both real and personal property. One of the assets is an apartment building. In administering the trust and allocating the receipts and disbursements, which of the following would be **improper**?

    a. The allocation of forfeited rental security deposits to income.

    b. The allocation to principal of the annual service fee of the rental collection agency.

    c. The allocation to income of the interest on the mortgage on the apartment building.

    d. The allocation to income of the payment of the insurance premiums on the apartment building.

PROBLEM

Problem 1   Trust Principal and Income (576,L7b)

(7 to 10 minutes)

Part b.   You have been assigned by a CPA firm to work with the trustees of a large trust in the preparation of the first annual accounting to the court. The income beneficiaries and the remaindermen are in dispute as to the proper allocation of the following items on which the trust indenture is silent:

(1)   Costs incurred in expanding the garage facilities of an apartment house owned by the trust and held for rental income.

(2)   Real estate taxes on the apartment house.

(3)   Cost of casualty insurance premiums on the apartment house.

(4)   A two-for-one stock split of common stock held by the trust for investment.

(5)   Insurance proceeds received as the result of a partial destruction of an office building which the trust owned and held for rental income.

(6)   Costs incurred by the trust in the sale of a tract of land.

(7)   Costs incurred to defend title to real property held by the trust.

Required:

1.   Explain briefly the nature of a trust, the underlying concepts in the allocation between principal and income, and the importance of such allocations.

2.   Indicate the allocations between principal and income to be made for each of the above items.

MULTIPLE CHOICE ANSWERS

1.	c	7.	d	13.	c	19.	b	25.	b
2.	c	8.	a	14.	b	20.	a	26.	b
3.	c	9.	b	15.	c	21.	b		
4.	d	10.	a	16.	b	22.	b		
5.	b	11.	b	17.	d	23.	d		
6.	a	12.	d	18.	c	24.	a		

EXPLANATION OF MULTIPLE CHOICE ANSWERS

1.   (1180,L1,45)   (c)   The certificateholders (owners) of a real estate investment trust have limited liability. Their liability is limited to their investment in the trust similar to the limited liability of a shareholder in a corporation and a limited partner. Thus answer (c) is correct. Answer (d) is incorrect because the sale of an interest in a real estate investment trust is the sale of a security under the Securities Act of 1933. Consequently, the seller of these interests would have to comply with the registration requirements of this act. A real estate investment trust does not fall within the provisions of the Federal Trust Indenture Act. This makes answer (b) incorrect. The normal trust, as distinguished from a real estate investment trust, is a taxable entity for income tax purposes, while a real estate investment trust is not a taxable entity. Ordinary income passes through to the investors and each investor pays income tax on his/her share.

2.   (1180,L1,49)   (c)   A trust is a fiduciary relationship in which one person, the trustee, has legal title to the property and another person, the beneficiary, has equitable title. Upon termination of the trust, the property is disposed of according to the stated desires of the settlor (creator of the trust). Thus, answer (c) is correct. Answer (a) is incorrect because a trust is considered a taxable entity for income tax purposes. If a trust deed is silent, the trustee has the authority to sell trust property if necessary to carry out the trust purpose. This makes answer (d) incorrect. Answer (a) is incorrect because the rule against perpetuities states that the duration of a trust cannot be infinite and can never exceed "a life in being plus 21 years." The rationale behind this rule is to prevent the tying up of title to property for an unreasonable length of time.

3.   (1180,L1,50)   (c)   The will created a life estate in Dorothy, the wife, and a vested remainder in fee simple that the daughters owned as tenants in common. This means that the daughters' ownership rights to the property came into existence when Paul, the decedent, died, even though their right of possession does not occur until Dorothy dies, and her life estate terminates. One daughter could sell her interest without the consent of either of the other two parties. Answer (c) is

correct. Answer (a) is incorrect because a spouse under the concept of statutory share has the right to denounce the will and elect to take stated share (normally 1/3) of the dead spouse's estate. Answer (d) is incorrect because the daughters received the remainder as tenants in common, not as joint tenants. Tenancy in common does not have the right of survivorship thus, if one of the daughters predeceased Dorothy, the interest of the dead daughter would pass by the deceased daughter's estate.

4.   (1180,L1,51)   (d)   A settlor may revoke a trust if the trust instrument reserves this right. Thus, answer (d) is correct. Creation of an inter vivos (living) trust only need be in writing when the trust involves real property, or where performance is not capable of being completed in one year from the date of creation. Inter vivos trusts involving personal property can be oral. Testamentary trusts must meet the same legal requirements for a valid will (i.e., in writing, signed, witnessed, etc.). Thus, answers (a) and (b) are incorrect. Answer (c) is incorrect because property in a testamentary trust is considered to have been transferred at the decedent's death and is therefore part of the decedent's gross estate for federal estate tax purposes.

5.   (1180,L1,52)   (b)   An executor is the personal representative of the decedent that is named in a will. If the decedent died intestate, then, the court would appoint an administrator as the personal representative. The person named as executor can decline to serve; in which case, the court will then appoint an executor. If the will does not provide compensation for the services of an executor, the court will order that the person serving in this capacity receive a reasonable fee for services rendered. The executor can be the principal beneficiary of the will, but need not have read the will nor be present at the signing of the will.

6.   (580,L1,28)   (a)   Normally the income beneficiary is entitled to all interest earned by the items making up the corpus of the trust and the principal beneficiary is charged with any loss or gain relevant to the value of the corpus of the trust. Thus, answer (a) is correct.

7.   (580,L1,40)   (d)   An executor is the legal representative of an estate when the decedent died testate (with a valid will). The executor has the right to be compensated unless the will denies such right. He is in a fiduciary relationship with the estate and thus is not like any other person dealing at arm's length. There is no need to obtain the consent in writing of the individual designated as executor. Naturally, the designated person can decline serving in such a capacity.

8. (580,L1,45) (a) Answer (a) is correct because the naming of a beneficiary in the insurance contract takes precedence over the declaration in a will of who will receive the proceeds of the policy. Answer (b) is incorrect because life insurance proceeds are excluded from taxable income if paid in a lump sum by reason of death. But for estate tax purposes, the proceeds are to be included in Filmore's estate, therefore answer (c) is incorrect. Answer (d) is incorrect because if so provided in the insurance contract, an insured party may change the beneficiary at his/her option. The standard life insurance policy has such a provision.

9. (580,L1,50) (b) Mullins has created a present life interest for her husband with a future interest in her children. Since the husband only has a life interest he has no right to appoint the ultimate beneficiaries; therefore, answer (b) is an incorrect statement and does not apply to the trust. Mullins has created the trust in her will and it is to take effect on her death, therefore it is a testamentary trust. Upon the creation of a future interest, if the only requirement for enjoyment of this interest is the death of the holder of the prior interest, then the future interest is said to be vested as compared to contingent. The trustee of a trust owes a fiduciary duty to all beneficiaries of the trust.

10. (1179,L1,20) (a) If the will is not properly executed, it cannot be admitted to probate and therefore Woodrow's property would be distributed according to intestate succession laws even though this is contrary to Woodrow's wishes as stated in the ineffective will. Answer (b) is incorrect because it is permissable to have a legatee also serve as an executor. Legatee/executors are not deemed to represent a conflict of interest or a violation of the fiduciary duty. Answer (c) is incorrect because unless the will indicates otherwise, taxes will be apportioned to all bequests and not allocated to the residuary estate. Answer (d) is incorrect because the executors do not have complete discretion in investing an estate's assets during the term of administration. The executors must comply with restraints set out by the probate court and the various state statutes.

11. (1179,L1,44) (b) In a properly drafted inter vivos trust, irrevocable for a period of 12 years, the trust income will not be taxable to the donor (settlor) during its existence but will be taxable to the beneficiaries. Answer (a) is incorrect because the trust as described will not fail for lack of a proper purpose. The property that has been transferred to the trust must be managed; thus the trust is an active one with a proper purpose since the trustee must actually perform these duties. Answer (c) is incorrect because the settlor, Gordon, does not retain the beneficial title to the trust since the duration of the trust is sufficiently long. The beneficiary holds the beneficial title to the property. Answer (d) is incorrect because under the facts as stated, Gordon has created an irrevocable trust. Thus, he may not demand return of the trust assets prior to the expiration of the 12 years. The only possibility of this occuring is if the settlor and all beneficiaries agree to a termination prior to the expiration of the 12 years.

12. (1179,L1,46) (d) Rights to subscribe to shares of another corporation should be allocated to income. Answer (a), subscription rights to the distributing corporation, (b) sale of subscription rights to the distributing corporation, and (c), a stock dividend, are examples of items that should be allocated to principal.

13. (1179,L1,47) (c) Insurance proceeds for the destruction of a garage located on the trust property should be allocated to principal since the insurance proceeds represent a change in the form of principal. The rental payments in answer (a), the prepayment of rent in answer (b) and the interest on a purchased money mortgage in answer (d) are all items that should be allocated to income.

14. (1177,L3,44) (b) Answer (a) is incorrect because the $5,000 proceeds must be added to the corpus (principal) of the trust. The stock rights are considered trust property rather than income. Answer (c) is incorrect because Allgood does not have discretion to allocate the $5,000 proceeds. The treatment as capital is determined under the Uniform Principal and Income Act. Answer (d) is incorrect because the trustee did not need consent to sell the stock rights. He was only under a duty to act in the best interests of the trust and beneficiaries.

15. (578,L1,30) (c) A trustee of a trust is a fiduciary with respect to the trust and the beneficiaries. Answer (a) is incorrect because a trustee has legal title but the beneficiaries have equitable title to trust property. Answer (b) is incorrect because a trustee need not automatically reinvest proceeds from a sale but instead may use appropriate discretion in accordance with established standards. Answer (d) is incorrect because the insurance proceeds are not divided among beneficiaries. Insurance proceeds are allocated to the corpus of the trust for the benefit of the remainderman.

16.   (578,L1,33)   (b)   A trust may be a legal
entity for both tax and non-tax purposes even if
the settlor is also the remainderman. The settlor is
the person who contributes property to a trust.
A remainderman is the person who receives the
trust corpus at the termination of the trust. Answer
(a) is incorrect because the trust is a separate legal
entity for federal tax purposes. Answer (c) is incorrect because the settlor of a trust may not revoke the trust unless he reserved the right of
revocation or unless all the beneficiaries agree.
Answer (d) is incorrect because if Kilgore dies after
10 years the trust will continue for the remaining
5 years for the benefit of the children and will then
pass to his heirs or devisees.

17.   (578,L1,34)   (d)   An executor, in addition to
being named in the will, must be appointed or approved by the appropriate state court. Answer (a) is
incorrect because a will is valid at the time of death
of the testator and is not regulated by the ordinary
statute of limitations. Answer (b) is incorrect because an estate of a deceased person is recognized
as a taxable entity. Answer (c) is incorrect because
a marital deduction bequeathed to a spouse is deducted from an estate for federal estate tax purpose but it may not exceed 50% of the estate.

18.   (1176,L3,46)   (c)   A law firm might refer
the determination of trust income and trust principal to a CPA firm. This is an accounting problem and not a legal problem although the rules
of law must be applied in the process. Intestate
succession, revocation of a will, and ancillary proceedings are legal problems not within a CPA's expertise.

19.   (577,L3,41)   (b)   As executor of his father's
will, Walker has the affirmative duty to carry out the
wishes of his father. He must collect all debts, pay all
expenses, and carry out the distribution of the assets
to those specified. The will may provide that a surety
bond is not necessary for the executor but the probate
court in its discretion may not comply with this provision. An executor may not sell real property without
the court's approval unless the will specifically grants
this power. Unless the will grants unlimited discretion,
Walker must conform to various prudent investment
guidelines in the management of the estate's assets
during administration.

20.   (1178,L1,34)   (a)   Property held in joint tenancy
passes to the survivor whether or not there is a will.
The intestate succession rules apply to persons who die
intestate, i.e., without a will. Answer (b) is incorrect

because intestate succession applies to all property of
a decedent dying without a will. Answer (c) is
incorrect because the intestate succession rules do not
effectively prevent a decedent from totally disinheriting
his wife and children because such effect might be
accomplished by other estate planning devises such as
a will. Answer (d) is incorrect because the failure to
name an executor would not have the effect of converting a decedent from the status of testate to intestate. An administrator would be appointed by the
court in place of an executor.

21.   (1178,L1,37)   (b)   Under the Uniform Principal
and Income Act a year-end cash dividend, whether
regular or extraordinary, should be allocated by a
trustee exclusively to income. Stock dividends,
liquidating dividends, and stock splits are all examples of receipts which should be allocated to principal.

22.   (1178,L1,38)   (b)   Rental income, whether prepaid,
current, or in arrears, is properly allocated by a trustee
to income. Permanent improvements to the trust property
such as a paving assessment are properly allocated to
principal. A loss on a sale of rental properties and proceeds from an eminent domain proceeding are also
examples of charges and receipts which should be
made to principal.

23.   (1178,L1,40)   (d)   In allocating between income
and principal of a trust, the trustee should credit the
discount portion received on redemption of treasury
bills to income. This is essentially interest, which is
an income item. The mortgage payments in answer
(a), the capital gains distribution in answer (b), and
the stock rights received from a distributing corporation in answer (c) are all examples of receipts or disbursements which a trustee should allocate to principal.

MAY 1981 ANSWERS

24.   (581,L1,49)   (a)   A trust is a fiduciary relationship wherein one person (trustee) holds legal title
to property for the benefit of another (beneficiary).
A trustee has the power to do what is necessary to
fulfill the terms of the trust. A trustee cannot spec-
ulate, must diversify and can make major changes in
an investment portfolio without the consent of beneficiaries. Answer (b) is not incorrect because a simple
trust is entitled to a $300 per year exemption for
federal tax purposes which is similar to an individual's
exemption. Answer (c) is not incorrect because a
trustee is a fiduciary to the beneficiaries and can take
no personal advantage from his position. All bene-

ficiaries can sue for mismanagement, conversion or waste by the trustee. A trustee must also keep trust assets separate from his personal assets and be accountable for both trust assets and his actions. Answer (d) is not an incorrect statement since a trust is a separate taxable entity for federal income tax purposes although it may not be subject to any tax.

25. (581,L1,50)   (b)   A joint tenancy is a form of concurrent property ownership in which the joint tenants have a right of survivorship in the property concurrently held. Thus, if a joint tenant dies, that tenant's interest in the property is divided equally among the surviving joint tenants. The deceased tenant's interest in the property will not pass to his heirs. Since Jean had full ownership of the property upon her brother's death and on her death, such property is properly included in her estate. Answer (a) is incorrect because, upon Jean's death, her sister will receive full ownership of the savings account regardless of any provision to the contrary in a will. Answer (c) is incorrect since gifts made in contemplation of death are irrevocable once made. Answer (d) is incorrect since a life insurance policy will pass to the named beneficiary without regard to the will of the deceased.

26. (581,L1,51)   (b)   An inter vivos trust comes into existence while the settlor (grantor) is living. The allocation of trust items to principal and income is governed by the Uniform Principal and Income Act (adopted by most states). Allocations made to trust principal include: original trust property, proceeds and gains from sale of trust property, insurance received on destruction of property, new property purchased with principal or proceeds from the principal, stock dividends and splits and a reserve for depreciation. Disbursements from trust principal are for reduction of indebtedness, litigation over trust property, permanent improvements and costs related to purchase/sale of trust property. Income includes profits from trust principal, e.g., rent, interest, cash dividends and royalties. Expenses from income include interest, insurance premiums, taxes, repairs, and depreciation. The annual service fee should be allocated to income because it is an expense associated with administration and management of trust property. It should not be allocated to principal. Answers (a), (c), and (d) are all proper allocations to income.

ANSWER OUTLINE

Problem 1   Trust Principal and Income

b1.   Trust involves transfer of income-producing property
　　　To a trustee
　　　Trustee takes legal title
　　　Trustee is a fiduciary for beneficiaries
　　Principal and income are allocated by
　　　Trust agreement, otherwise
　　　Law of jurisdiction where trust is located, or
　　　Uniform Principal and Income Act
　　Principal is the trust property
　　　Which may change in composition
　　　Less expenses incurred in protecting title
　　Income is that produced by trust property
　　　Less ordinary operating expenses.
　　Allocation of principal and income is important
　　　For distribution of benefits of trust
　　　Income to beneficiary
　　　Principal to remainderman at end of trust

b2 | | | |
|---|---|---|
| (1) | Expanding garage | Principal |
| (2) | Real estate taxes | Income |
| (3) | Casualty insurance premiums | Income |
| (4) | Common stock split | Principal |
| (5) | Insurance proceeds | Principal |
| (6) | Land sale | Principal |
| (7) | Defense of property title | Principal |

UNOFFICIAL ANSWER

Problem 1   Trust Principal and Income

b.   1.   A trust generally involves a transfer of income-producing property (principal) by will, deed, or indenture to a trustee who takes legal title to the property subject to a fiduciary obligation to manage and conserve the property for the benefit of others who are described as beneficiaries. A trust generally provides that the trustee shall invest the trust principal and pay the income therefrom to the income beneficiary and at the termination of the trust transfer the trust principal to the remainderman. The property that composes the principal of the trust may change from time to time as the trustee sells and reinvests the proceeds.

　　　The will or trust agreement can provide the rules for allocation of items between principal and income. In the absence of specific trust provisions, the law of the jurisdiction in which the trust is located will govern. For this purpose, most jurisdictions have adopted the Uniform Principal and Income Act or some variation thereof. Income produced by the investment and management of the trust principal is kept separate for distribution to the income beneficiary. However, ordinary operating expenses incurred by the trust in generating earnings are charged against income. Similarly, expenses incurred in acquiring or protecting the trustee's title to principal are charged against principal. Thus, the allocation between principal and income of a trust is of great importance because it affects the respective benefits derived from the trust by the income beneficiary and the remainderman.

2. | | | |
|---|---|---|
| (1) | Principal |
| (2) | Income |
| (3) | Income |
| (4) | Principal |
| (5) | Principal |
| (6) | Principal |
| (7) | Principal |

CHAPTER FOUR

FINANCIAL ACCOUNTING PROBLEMS AND SOLUTIONS

Financial accounting is the most tested and broadest topic on both the practice and theory sections of the examination. Theory, tested from 1:30 to 5:00, Friday afternoon, generally includes 60 individual multiple choice questions and 4 essay questions. Practice, tested from 1:30 to 6:00, Wednesday and Thursday afternoons, generally contains 3 overall multiple choice problems and 2 practice problems each afternoon. Each overall practice multiple choice problem contains 20 individual questions, for a total of 60 multiple choice questions.

The questions were categorized into eleven groups to help you modularize your study program. The eleven groups consist of common topics in intermediate and advanced accounting. The first topic, "miscellaneous financial," is a catchall category containing revenue recognition, installment sales, accounting changes, interim reporting, etc. "Present value applications" consists of bond, lease, and pension topics. Inflation accounting includes price level, replacement and current costs, and foreign exchange. The frequency of appearance of each of these eleven topics on both the practice and theory examinations since 1977 is presented on pages 443 and 444.

Each of the essay questions and practice problems are coded as to month-year, section, and problem number, e.g., (579,P4) indicates May 1979, problem 4 of Practice I. Note P = Practice I, Q = Practice II, and T = Theory. Explanations to multiple choice answers are similarly coded except an additional number indicates the question number, e.g., (579,Q1,7) where 7 is the individual multiple choice question number.

Theory questions are generally 20-30 minutes and practice problems are 40-60 minutes in length.

FINANCIAL PROBLEM INDEX

	Exam Reference	Number of Minutes	Problem Page No.	Answer Page No.
Miscellaneous Financial (MISC)				
Multiple Choice				
29 - Basic Concepts			445	466
5 - Error Correction			447	470
18 - Accounting Changes			448	471
18 - Financial Statements			451	474

*Also see the solutions approach problem in Chapter 9 of Volume I on page 706.

	Exam Reference	Number of Minutes	Problem Page No.	Answer Page No.
Present Value Applications (PV)				
Multiple Choice				
22 - Fundamental Concepts			649	668
17 - Bonds			652	671
- Debt Restructure (none to date)				
19 - Leases			655	673
14 - Pensions			659	676
Problems				
Fundamental Concepts				
1. Valuation of Notes	1172,T3	25-30	662	678
2. Noninterest Bearing Note	579,P4c	15-20	662	679
Bonds				
3. Effective Interest and Early Extinguishment of Debt	1178,T5	15-20	662	681
4. Accounting for Bonds	1180,T4	15-25	663	682
5. Issuance and Extinguishment	1179,P5	40-50	663	683
6. Discount Calculation	1178,P3a	15-20	663	685
Debt Restructure				
7. Entries for Modification of Terms	Kieso & Weygandt, 3rd Ed., p. 639-adapted	40-50	664	686
Leases				
8. Description of Lease Accounting	580,T3	15-25	664	689
9. Capital Leases	1178,T4	20-25	665	690
10. Lessee's Capital Lease	572,Q4-adapted	40-50	665	691
Pensions				
11. Definitions	578,T4	20-25	666	693
12. Plan Calculations	1173,T5	25-30	666	696
Inflation Accounting (INFL)				
41 Multiple Choice				
1. Current Valuation of Assets	578,T6	25-30	705	715

	Exam Reference	Number of Minutes	Problem Page No.	Answer Page No.
Sample Practice I Examination		220-270	1013	1068
Sample Practice II Examination		220-270	1025	1071
Sample Theory Examination		150-210	1059	1086

Some problems were altered to make them applicable due to changes in GAAP and/or to improve the pedagogy. The altered problems are designated by the symbol †.

FREQUENCY OF PRACTICE TOPICS APPEARING ON THE EXAM

EXAM	MISC	WC	INV	FA	TAX	STK	PV	INFO	RATO	PART	ICON	COST*	QUAN	GOV	ITAX	TPRO	PTAX	CTAX
5/77	6MC 1	2MC 2	3MC	3MC	2MC	4MC 1/3	3MC	3MC	2MC		4MC 1/3	12MC 1	6MC	2MC	12MC	4MC		1
11/77	4MC	5MC	4MC	7MC	2MC	6MC	3MC 2/3	1/3	3MC	1/3	1MC 2	14MC 1	6MC	1	1	1MC	3MC	13MC
5/78	4MC	4MC 1	2MC	4MC 1	2MC	4MC 1	4MC	3MC	2MC	3MC	3MC	15MC 1	2MC	1	13MC	4MC		1
11/78	7MC 1	3MC	2MC 1	5MC	1MC	7MC	7MC 1	3MC	1MC		3MC	14MC 1	4MC	1	1	2MC	2MC	13MC
5/79	4MC	7MC 1/2	1	6MC 1	1MC	5MC	6MC 1/2	4MC	2MC	2MC	3MC	17MC 1	3MC	1	19MC	1MC		1
11/79	4MC	1MC	1MC 1	5MC 1	2MC	4MC	4MC 1	2MC	3MC	3MC	8MC	18MC	2MC 1	1	19MC	1MC		1
5/80	3MC	8MC 1/3	3MC	3MC	1MC	5MC 1	6MC 2/3	2MC	2MC	3MC	4MC 1	17MC 1	3MC	1	19MC	4MC	3MC	14MC
11/80	5MC	4MC 1	2MC 1	5MC	1MC 11MC	6MC		2MC	2MC		2MC 1	17MC 1	3MC	1	17MC	10MC	3MC	10MC
5/81	8MC 14MC	14MC	3MC	6MC	3MC	9MC 1	6MC 1 1/2	2MC	7MC		1MC 1/2	20MC 1		1	19MC	3MC	3MC	15MC

Cost accounting topics are subdivided further in Chapter 5.

NOTE:

See page 14 for a complete explanation of the above coding. Explanation of topic abbreviations appears below.

MISC	(Mod. 23)	Miscellaneous Financial	PV	(Mod. 29)	Present Value Applications
WC	(Mod. 24)	Working Capital	INFL	(Mod. 30)	Inflation Accounting
INV	(Mod. 25)	Inventory	RATO	(Mod. 31)	Ratio Analysis
FA	(Mod. 26)	Fixed Assets	PART	(Mod. 32)	Partnerships
TAX	(Mod. 27)	Tax Deferrals	ICON	(Mod. 33)	Investments and Consolidations
STK	(Mod. 28)	Stockholders' Equity	COST	(Mod. 34)	Cost Accounting

QUAN	(Mod. 38)	Quantitative Methods
GOV	(Mod. 39)	Governmental Accounting
ITAX	(Mod. 40)	Individual Taxation
TPRO	(Mod. 41)	Transactions in Property
PTAX	(Mod. 42)	Partnership Taxation
CTAX	(Mod. 43)	Corporate Taxation

FREQUENCY OF THEORY TOPICS APPEARING ON THE EXAM

EXAM	MISC	WC	INV	FA	TAX	STK	PV	INFL	RATO	PART	ICON	COST*	QUAN	GOV
May 1977	6MC 1	3MC	3MC	3MC 1/2	3MC	7MC	2MC	2MC 1/2			4MC 1	7MC 1	4MC	1
Nov 1977	8MC 1	2	2MC	1MC	2MC	2MC	6MC	1MC 1				16MC 1		6MC
May 1978	11MC 1	6MC		1MC 1	1MC	1MC	3MC 1	1MC 2			1MC	18MC 1	1MC	6MC
Nov 1978	9MC 1	4MC	2MC	2MC	1MC	3MC 1	1MC 3	3MC			2MC	12MC 1	2MC	9MC
May 1979	3MC 2	3MC	1MC	2MC 1	2MC	1MC 1	3MC	1MC			3MC 1	17MC 1	4MC	10MC
Nov 1979	10MC 2	3MC	2MC	1MC	1MC 1/2	4MC 1/2	6MC 1	2MC			2MC 1	5MC 1	4MC	10MC
May 1980	7MC 1/2	9MC	4MC	3MC	2MC	1MC 1	6MC 1	4MC	2MC		4MC 1	7MC 1 1/2	1MC	10MC
Nov 1980	11MC	4MC 1/2	3MC 1/2	3MC 1	1MC	1MC 1	3MC 1	2MC			2MC	16MC 1	4MC	10MC
May 1981	11MC 1/5	5MC	1MC 4/5	4MC		7MC 1	6MC 1	1MC 1	3MC		2MC 1	10MC 1	2MC	10MC

*Cost accounting topics are subdivided further in Chapter 5.

NOTE:

See page 14 for a complete explanation of the above coding. Explanation of topic abbreviations appears below.

MISC	(Mod. 23) Miscellaneous Financial	PV	(Mod. 29) Present Value Applications	QUAN	(Mod. 38) Quantitative Methods
WC	(Mod. 24) Working Capital	INFL	(Mod. 30) Inflation Accounting	GOV	(Mod. 39) Governmental Accounting
INV	(Mod. 25) Inventory	RATO	(Mod. 31) Ratio Analysis	ITAX	(Mod. 40) Individual Taxation
FA	(Mod. 26) Fixed Assets	PART	(Mod. 32) Partnerships	TPRO	(Mod. 41) Transactions in Property
TAX	(Mod. 27) Tax Deferrals	ICON	(Mod. 33) Investments and Consolidations	PTAX	(Mod. 42) Partnership Taxation
STK	(Mod. 28) Stockholders' Equity	COST	(Mod. 34) Cost Accounting	CTAX	(Mod. 43) Corporate Taxation

MULTIPLE CHOICE QUESTIONS

BASIC CONCEPTS (1—29)

1. When a specific customer's account receivable is written off as uncollectible, what will be the effect on net income under each of the following methods of recognizing bad debt expense?

	Allowance	*Direct Write Off*
a.	None	Decreased
b.	Decreased	None
c.	Decreased	Decreased
d.	None	None

2. Which of the following is an accrued liability?
   a. Cash dividends payable.
   b. Wages payable.
   c. Rent revenue collected one month in advance.
   d. Portion of long-term debt payable in current year.

3. Objectivity is assumed to be achieved when an accounting transaction
   a. Is recorded in a fixed amount of dollars.
   b. Involves the payment or receipt of cash.
   c. Involves an arm's-length transaction between two independent parties.
   d. Allocates revenues or expenses in a rational and systematic manner.

4. The concept of consistency is sacrificed in the accounting for which of the following income statement items?
   a. Discontinued operations.
   b. Loss on disposal of a segment of a business.
   c. Extraordinary items.
   d. Cumulative effect of change in accounting principle.

5. The computation of the current value of an asset using the present value of future cash flows method does *not* include the
   a. Cost of alternate uses of funds given up.
   b. Productive life of the asset.
   c. Applicable interest rate.
   d. Future amounts of cash receipts or cash savings.

6. When bad debt expense is estimated on the basis of the percentage of past actual losses from bad debts to past net credit sales, and this percentage is adjusted for anticipated conditions, the accounting concept of

   a. Matching is being followed.
   b. Matching is **not** being followed.
   c. Substance over form is being followed.
   d. Going concern is **not** being followed.

7. Which of the following is a deferred cost that should be amortized over the periods estimated to be benefited?
   a. Prepayment of three-year insurance premiums on machinery.
   b. Security deposit representing two-months' rent on leased office space.
   c. Advance from customer to be returned when sale completed.
   d. Property tax for this year payable next year.

8. The principle of objectivity includes the concept of
   a. Summarization.
   b. Classification.
   c. Conservatism.
   d. Verifiability.

9. Historical cost is a measurement base currently used in financial accounting. Which of the following measurement bases is (are) also currently used in financial accounting?

	Current selling price	Discounted cash flow	Replace- ment cost
a.	Yes	No	Yes
b.	Yes	Yes	Yes
c.	Yes	No	No
d.	No	Yes	Yes

10. What is the underlying concept that supports the immediate recognition of a loss?
    a. Conservatism.
    b. Consistency.
    c. Judgment.
    d. Matching.

11. Under what condition is it proper to recognize revenues prior to the sale of merchandise?
    a. When the ultimate sale of the goods is at an assured sales price.
    b. When the revenue is to be reported as an installment sale.
    c. When the concept of internal consistency (of amounts of revenue) must be complied with.
    d. When management has a long-established policy to do so.

12. Rent revenue collected one month in advance should be accounted for as
   a. Revenue in the month collected.
   b. A current liability.
   c. A separate item in stockholders' equity.
   d. An accrued liability.

13. One of the basic features of financial accounting is the
   a. Direct measurement of economic resources and obligations and changes in them in terms of money and sociological and psychological impact.
   b. Direct measurement of economic resources and obligations and changes in them in terms of money.
   c. Direct measurement of economic resources and obligations and changes in them in terms of money and sociological impact.
   d. Direct measurement of economic resources and obligations and changes in them in terms of money and psychological impact.

14. Which of the following is an example of the concept of conservatism?
   a. Stating inventories at the lower of cost or market.
   b. Stating inventories using the FIFO method in periods of rising prices.
   c. Using the percentage-of-completion method in the first year of a long-term construction contract.
   d. Using the interest method instead of the straight-line method to record interest in the first year of a long-term receivable.

15. Continuation of an accounting entity in the absence of evidence to the contrary is an example of the basic concept of
   a. Accounting entity.
   b. Consistency.
   c. Going concern.
   d. Substance over form.

16. Depreciation measurement should be based on
   a. Past input exchange price.
   b. Current input exchange price.
   c. Future input exchange price.
   d. Current output exchange price.

17. What theory of ownership equity is enumerated by the following equation: assets minus liabilities minus preferred stock equity equals common stock equity?
   a. Fund.
   b. Enterprise.
   c. Entity.
   d. Residual equity.

18. There has been considerable discussion regarding the nature of accounting principles (standards). One source delineates three levels: pervasive, broad operating, and detailed. Which of these three levels should be viewed as composing "generally accepted accounting principles"?
   a. Pervasive only.
   b. Pervasive and broad operating only.
   c. Broad operating and detailed only.
   d. Pervasive, broad operating, and detailed.

19. During the lifetime of an entity accountants produce financial statements at arbitrary points in time in accordance with which basic accounting concept?
   a. Objectivity.
   b. Periodicity.
   c. Conservatism.
   d. Matching.

20. Which of the following asset valuation methods is not a violation of the accounting concept of historical cost?
   a. Net present value of future cash flows.
   b. Replacement cost.
   c. Market value.
   d. General price-level restatement.

21. Generally, revenues should be recognized at a point when
   a. Management decides it is appropriate to do so.
   b. The product is available for sale to the ultimate consumer.
   c. An exchange has taken place and the earnings process is virtually complete.
   d. An order for a definite amount of merchandise has been received for shipment FOB destination.

22. Why are certain costs of doing business capitalized when incurred and then depreciated or amortized over subsequent accounting cycles?
   a. To reduce the federal income tax liability.
   b. To aid management in the decision-making process.
   c. To match the costs of production with revenues as earned.
   d. To adhere to the accounting concept of conservatism.

23.   What accounting concept justifies the usage of accruals and deferrals?

    a.   Going concern.
    b.   Materiality.
    c.   Consistency.
    d.   Stable monetary unit.

24.   Which of the following principles best describes the conceptual rationale for the methods of matching depreciation expense with revenues?

    a.   Associating cause and effect.
    b.   Systematic and rational allocation.
    c.   Immediate recognition.
    d.   Partial recognition.

25.   Which of the following is not a basis for the immediate recognition of a cost during a period?

    a.   The cost provides no discernible future benefit.
    b.   The cost recorded in a prior period no longer produces discernible benefits.
    c.   The federal income tax savings using the immediate write-off method exceed the savings obtained by allocating the cost to several periods.
    d.   Allocation of the cost on the basis of association with revenue or among several accounting periods is considered to serve no useful purpose.

MAY 1981 QUESTIONS

26.   The valuation of a promise to receive cash in the future as present value on the financial statements of a business entity is valid because of the accounting concept of

    a.   Entity.
    b.   Materiality.
    c.   Going concern.
    d.   Neutrality.

27.   Which of the following is an example of the expense recognition principle of associating cause and effect?

    a.   Allocation of insurance cost.
    b.   Sales commissions.
    c.   Depreciation of fixed assets.
    d.   Officers' salaries.

28.   Accruing net losses on firm purchase commitments for inventory is an example of the accounting concept of

    a.   Conservatism.
    b.   Realization.
    c.   Consistency.
    d.   Materiality.

29.   Which of the following accounting concepts states that an accounting transaction should be supported by sufficient evidence to allow two or more qualified individuals to arrive at essentially similar measures and conclusions?

    a.   Matching.
    b.   Objectivity.
    c.   Periodicity.
    d.   Stable monetary unit.

MULTIPLE CHOICE QUESTIONS

ERROR CORRECTION (30—34)

Items 30 and 31 are based on the following information:

The Shannon Corporation began operations on January 1, 1978. Financial statements for the years ended December 31, 1978, and 1979, contained the following errors:

	December 31,	
	1978	*1979*
Ending inventory	$16,000 understated	$15,000 overstated
Depreciation expense	$ 6,000 understated	—
Insurance expense	$10,000 overstated	$10,000 understated
Prepaid insurance	$10,000 understated	—

In addition, on December 31, 1979, fully depreciated machinery was sold for $10,800 cash, but the sale was not recorded until 1980. There were no other errors during 1978 or 1979 and no corrections have been made for any of the errors.

30.   Ignoring income taxes, what is the total effect of the errors on 1979 net income?

    a.   Net income overstated by $30,200.
    b.   Net income overstated by $11,000.
    c.   Net income overstated by $5,800.
    d.   Net income understated by $1,800.

31.   Ignoring income taxes, what is the total effect of the errors on the amount of working capital at December 31, 1979?

    a.   Working capital overstated by $4,200.
    b.   Working capital understated by $5,800.
    c.   Working capital understated by $6,000.
    d.   Working capital understated by $9,800.

Items 32, 33, and 34 are based on the following information:

Declaration, Inc., is a calendar-year corporation. Its financial statements for the years 1974 and 1973 contained errors as follows:

	1974	1973
Ending inventory	$1,000 understated	$3,000 overstated
Depreciation expense	$ 800 understated	$2,500 overstated

32. Assume that the proper correcting entries were made at December 31, 1973. By how much will 1974 income before income taxes be overstated or understated?

    a. $200 understated.
    b. $500 overstated.
    c. $2,700 understated.
    d. $3,200 understated.

33. Assume that no correcting entries were made at December 31, 1973. Ignoring income taxes, by how much will retained earnings at December 31, 1974, be overstated or understated?

    a. $200 understated.
    b. $500 overstated.
    c. $2,700 understated.
    d. $3,200 understated.

34. Assume that no correcting entries were made at December 31, 1973, or December 31, 1974, and that no additional errors occurred in 1975. Ignoring income taxes, by how much will working capital at December 31, 1975, be overstated or understated?

    a. $0.
    b. $1,000 overstated.
    c. $1,000 understated.
    d. $1,700 understated.

MULTIPLE CHOICE QUESTIONS

ACCOUNTING CHANGES (35–52)

35. Which of the following should be disclosed in the Summary of Significant Accounting Policies?
    a.   Composition of inventory (raw materials, work-in-process, and finished goods).
    b.   Basis of consolidation.
    c.   Depreciation expense amount.
    d.   Adequacy of pension plan assets in relationship to vested benefits.

36. From inception of operations, Essex Corporation recognized income in its financial statements and for income tax reporting under the completed-contract method of reporting income from long-term construction contracts. On January 1, 1979, Essex changed to the percentage-of-completion method of income recognition for financial statement reporting but not for income tax reporting. Essex can justify the change.

As of December 31, 1978, Essex compiled data showing that income under the completed-contract method aggregated $350,000. If the percentage-of-completion method had been used, the accumulated income for these contracts through December 31, 1978, would have been $440,000. Assume that the income tax rate for all years is 50%. The cumulative effect of changing from the completed-contract method to the percentage-of-completion method must be reported by Essex in the 1979

    a.   Retained earnings statement as a $45,000 credit adjustment to the beginning balance.
    b.   Income statement as a $45,000 credit.
    c.   Retained earnings statement as a $90,000 credit adjustment to the beginning balance.
    d.   Income statement as a $90,000 credit.

37. APB Opinion No. 22, "Disclosure of Accounting Policies,"
    a.   Requires description of every accounting policy followed by a reporting entity.
    b.   Provides a specific listing of all types of accounting policies which must be disclosed.
    c.   Requires disclosure of the format for the statement of changes in financial position.
    d.   Requires description of all significant accounting policies to be included as an integral part of the financial statements.

Items 38 and 39 are based on the following information:

Bond Company purchased a machine on January 1, 1975, for $3,000,000. At the date of acquisition, the machine had an estimated useful life of six years with no salvage. The machine is being depreciated on a straight-line basis. On January 1, 1978, Bond determined, as a result of additional information, that the machine had an estimated useful life of eight years from the date of acquisition with no salvage. An accounting change was made in 1978 to reflect this additional information.

38. Assuming that the direct effects of this change are limited to the effect on depreciation and the related tax provision, and that the income tax rate was 50% in 1975, 1976, 1977 and 1978, what should be reported in Bond's income statement for the year ended December 31, 1978, as the cumulative effect on prior years of changing the estimated useful life of the machine?
    a. $0
    b. $187,500
    c. $250,000
    d. $375,000

39. What is the amount of depreciation expense on this machine that should be charged in Bond's income statement for the year ended December 31, 1978?
    a. $100,000
    b. $300,000
    c. $375,000
    d. $500,000

40. Presenting consolidated financial statements this year when statements of individual companies were presented last year is
    a.   A correction of an error.
    b.   An accounting change that should be reported prospectively.
    c.   An accounting change that should be reported by restating the financial statements of all prior periods presented.
    d.   Not an accounting change.

41. Which type of accounting change should always be accounted for in current and future periods?
    a.   Change in accounting principle.
    b.   Change in reporting entity.
    c.   Change in accounting estimate.
    d.   Correction of an error.

42. The Raider Company changed its method of pricing inventories from first-in, first-out to last-in, first-out. What type of accounting change does this represent?
    a.   A change in accounting estimate for which the financial statements for the prior periods included for comparative purposes should be presented as previously reported.
    b.   A change in accounting principle for which the financial statements for prior periods included for comparative purposes should be presented as previously reported.
    c.   A change in accounting estimate for which the financial statements for prior periods included for comparative purposes should be restated.
    d.   A change in accounting principle for which the financial statements for prior periods included for comparative purposes should be restated.

43. Accounting changes are often made and the monetary impact is reflected in the financial statements of a company even though, in theory, this may be a violation of the accounting concept of
    a.   Materiality.
    b.   Consistency.
    c.   Conservatism.
    d.   Objectivity.

44. When a company makes a change in accounting principle, prior year financial statements are not generally restated to reflect the change. The Accounting Principles Board decided that this procedure would prevent a dilution of public confidence in financial statements but recognized that this procedure conflicts with the accounting concept of
    a.   Materiality.
    b.   Conservatism.
    c.   Objectivity.
    d.   Comparability.

45. Which of the following is (are) the proper time period(s) to record a change in accounting estimate?
    a.   Current period and prospectively.
    b.   Current period and retroactively.
    c.   Retroactively only.
    d.   Current period only.

46. The Greeley Company was formed on January 1, 1975, and used an accelerated method of depreciation on its machinery until January 1, 1977. At that time, Greeley adopted the straight-line method of depreciation

for the machinery previously acquired as well as for any new machinery acquired in 1977.

Information concerning depreciation amounts under each method is as follows:

Year	Depreciation if accelerated method used	Depreciation if straight-line method used
1975	$300,000	$200,000
1976	400,000	250,000
1977	450,000	280,000

Assume that the direct effects of this change are limited to the effect on depreciation and the related tax provisions, and that the income tax rate was 50% in each of these years. What should be reported in Greeley's income statement for the year ended December 31, 1977, as the cumulative effect on prior years of changing to a different depreciation method?

a. $0.
b. $125,000.
c. $210,000.
d. $250,000

47. Which of the following describes a change in reporting entity?

a. A company acquires a subsidiary that is to be accounted for as a purchase.
b. A manufacturing company expands its market from regional to nationwide.
c. A company acquires additional shares of an investee and changes from the equity method of accounting to consolidation of the subsidiary.
d. A business combination is made using the pooling of interests method.

MAY 1981 QUESTIONS

48. On January 1, 1980, Belmont Company changed its inventory cost flow method to the FIFO cost method from the LIFO cost method. Belmont can justify the change, which was made for both financial statement and income tax reporting purposes. Belmont's inventories aggregated $4,000,000 on the LIFO basis at December 31, 1979. Supplementary records maintained by Belmont showed that the inventories would have totaled $4,800,000 at December 31, 1979, on the FIFO basis. Ignoring income taxes, the adjustment for the effect of changing to the FIFO method from the LIFO method should be reported by Belmont in the 1980

a. Income statement as an $800,000 debit.

b. Retained earnings statement as an $800,000 debit adjustment to the beginning balance.
c. Income statement as an $800,000 credit.
d. Retained earnings statement as an $800,000 credit adjustment to the beginning balance.

49. Flex Company owns a machine that was bought on January 2, 1977, for $94,000. The machine was estimated to have a useful life of five years and a salvage value of $6,000. Flex uses the sum-of-the-years digits method of depreciation. At the beginning of 1980, Flex determined that the useful life of the machine should have been four years and the salvage value $8,800. For the year 1980, Flex should record depreciation expense on this machine of

a. $11,100.
b. $14,800.
c. $17,600.
d. $21,300.

50. An example of a special change in accounting principle that should be reported by restating the financial statements of prior periods is the change from the

a. Straight-line method of depreciating plant equipment to the sum-of-the-years-digits method.
b. Sum-of-the-years-digits method of depreciating plant equipment to the straight-line method.
c. LIFO method of inventory pricing to the FIFO method.
d. FIFO method of inventory pricing to the LIFO method.

51. Which of the following should be disclosed in the Summary of Significant Accounting Policies?

a. Rent expense amount.
b. Maturity dates of long-term debt.
c. Methods of amortizing intangibles.
d. Composition of plant assets.

52. How should a change in accounting estimate that is recognized by a change in accounting principle be reported?

	Change in accounting estimate	Change in accounting principle
a.	No	No
b.	Yes	Yes
c.	No	Yes
d.	Yes	No

REPEAT QUESTION

(581,P1,8)   Identical to item 46 above

MULTIPLE CHOICE QUESTIONS

FINANCIAL STATEMENTS (53–70)

53. An extraordinary item is one which
   a. Occurs infrequently and is uncontrollable in nature.
   b. Occurs infrequently and is unusual in nature.
   c. Is material and is unusual in nature.
   d. Is material and is uncontrollable in nature.

Items 54 and 55 are based on the following information:

The following condensed statement of income of Helen Corporation, a diversified company, is presented for the two years ended December 31, 1979 and 1978:

	1979	1978
Net sales	$10,000,000	$9,600,000
Cost of sales	6,200,000	6,000,000
Gross profit	3,800,000	3,600,000
Operating expenses	2,200,000	2,400,000
Operating income	1,600,000	1,200,000
Gain on sale of division	900,000	—
	2,500,000	1,200,000
Provision for income taxes	1,250,000	600,000
Net income	$ 1,250,000	$ 600,000

On January 1, 1979, Helen entered into an agreement to sell for $3,200,000 the assets and product line of one of its separate operating divisions. The sale was consummated on December 31, 1979, and resulted in a gain on disposition of $900,000. This division's contribution to Helen's reported income before income taxes for each year was as follows:

    1979 $(640,000) loss
    1978 $(500,000) loss

Assume an income tax rate of 50%.

54. In the preparation of a revised comparative statement of income, Helen should report income from continuing operations after income taxes for 1979 and 1978, respectively, amounting to
   a. $1,120,000 and $600,000.
   b. $1,120,000 and $850,000.
   c. $1,250,000 and $600,000.
   d. $1,250,000 and $850,000.

55. In the preparation of a revised comparative statement of income, Helen should report under the caption "Discontinued Operations" for 1979 and 1978, respectively
   a. Income of $130,000 and a loss of $250,000.
   b. Income of $130,000 and $0.
   c. Income of $260,000 and a loss of $500,000.
   d. A loss of $640,000 and a loss of $500,000.

56. When a segment of a business has been discontinued during the year, the gain or loss on disposal should
   a. Be an extraordinary item.
   b. Exclude operating losses during the phase-out period.
   c. Include operating losses of the current period up to the measurement date.
   d. Be net of applicable income taxes.

57. The Chance Company, a holding company, has two operating subsidiaries; one manufacturing wheelbarrows and the other manufacturing toothbrushes. The wheelbarrow subsidiary has been unprofitable, and in late December 1975, Chance contracted to sell that subsidiary to another company for $60,000. The sale will be effective on April 1, 1976. Chance will continue to operate the wheelbarrow subsidiary during the first three months of 1976, even though those operations are expected to result in a $10,000 loss (before income taxes) during that period.

At December 31, 1975, the carrying amount of Chance's investment in the wheelbarrow subsidiary is $100,000. Both the $40,000 loss on the sale of the investment and the $10,000 operating loss will be deductible on Chance's 1976 income tax return, resulting in an anticipated tax savings of $25,000 at an assumed 50% tax rate.

Chance's statement of income for its year ended December 31, 1975, should include a "loss on disposal of wheelbarrow subsidiary, net of applicable income tax benefit" in the amount of
   a. $0.
   b. $20,000.
   c. $25,000.
   d. $30,000.

58. Which of the following events would be accounted for as a prior period adjustment?
   a. Change in the depreciable lives of fixed assets.
   b. Change in amount of opening retained earnings balance due to an error in a prior period.

c. Change in the method of computing depreciation of fixed assets.
d. Change in inventory cost flow assumption from first-in, first-out to weighted average.

59. How should an unusual event not meeting the current criteria for an extraordinary item be disclosed in the financial statements?
a. Shown as a separate item in operating revenues or expenses and supplemented by a footnote if deemed appropriate.
b. Shown in operating revenues or expenses but not shown as a separate item.
c. Shown after ordinary net earnings but before extraordinary items.
d. Shown after extraordinary items net of income tax but before net earnings.

60. Each of the following areas must always have a footnote included in the financial statements commenting on normal transactions within that area except
a. Assets acquired by lease.
b. Trade accounts receivable.
c. Pension plans.
d. Employee stock options.

61. On October 1, 1978, The Ajax Company consigned one hundred television sets to M & R Retailers, Inc. Each television set had a cost of $150. Freight on the shipment was paid by Ajax in the amount of $200.

On December 1, 1978, M & R submitted an account sales stating that it had sold sixty sets and it remitted the $12,840 balance due. The remittance was net of the following deductions from the sales price of the televisions sold:

Commission (20% of sales price)

Advertising $500
Delivery and installation charges   100

What was the total sales price of the television sets sold by M & R?
a. $13,440.
b. $15,000.
c. $16,800.
d. $17,000.

62. A review of the December 31, 1978, financial statements of Rhur Corporation revealed that under the caption "extraordinary losses," Rhur reported a total of $260,000. Further analysis revealed that the $260,000 in losses was comprised of the following items:

1. Rhur recorded a loss of $50,000 incurred in the abandonment of equipment formerly used in the business.
2. In an unusual and infrequent occurrence, a loss of $75,000 was sustained as a result of hurricane damage to a warehouse.
3. During 1978, several factories were shut down during a major strike by employees. Shutdown expenses totaled $120,000.
4. Uncollectible accounts receivable of $15,000 were written off as uncollectible.

Ignoring income taxes, what amount of loss should Rhur report as extraordinary on its 1978 Statement of Income?
a. $50,000.
b. $75,000.
c. $135,000.
d. $260,000.

63. When a company discontinues an operation and disposes of the discontinued operation (segment), the transaction should be included in the earnings statement as a gain or loss on disposal reported as
a. A prior period adjustment.
b. An extraordinary item.
c. An amount after continuing operations and before extraordinary items.
d. A bulk sale of fixed assets included in earnings from continuing operations.

64. Which of the following items, if material in amount, would normally be considered an extraordinary item for reporting results of operations?
a. Utilization of a net operating loss carryforward.
b. Gains or losses on disposal of a segment of a business.
c. Adjustments of accruals on long-term contracts.
d. Gains or losses from a fire.

65. A transaction that is material in amount, unusual in nature, and infrequent in occurrence, should be presented in the income statement separately as a component of income
a. Net of applicable income taxes.
b. As a prior period adjustment.
c. From continuing operations.
d. From discontinued operations.

MAY 1981 QUESTIONS

Items 66 and 67 are based on the following data: Marvel Construction Co., Inc., had a net income of

$600,000 for the year ended December 31, 1980, after inclusion of the following special events that occurred during the year:

- The decision was made on January 2 to discontinue the cinder block manufacturing segment.
- The cinder block manufacturing segment was actually sold on July 1.
- Operating income from January 1 to June 30 for the cinder block manufacturing segment amounted to $90,000 before taxes.
- Cinder block manufacturing equipment with a book value of $250,000 was sold for $100,000.

Marvel was subject to income tax at the rate of 40%.

66. Marvel's after-tax income from continuing operations for the year ended December 31, 1980, was
   a. $360,000.
   b. $564,000.
   c. $600,000.
   d. $636,000.

67. Marvel's aggregate income tax expense for the year ended December 31, 1980, should be
   a. $216,000.
   b. $240,000.
   c. $264,000.
   d. $400,000.

68. An example of an item which should be reported as a prior period adjustment is the
   a. Collection of previously written-off accounts receivable.
   b. Payment of taxes resulting from examination of prior year income tax returns.
   c. Correction of error in financial statements of a prior year.
   d. Receipt of insurance proceeds for damage to building sustained in a prior year.

69. A transaction that is material in amount, unusual in nature, but **not** infrequent in occurrence, should be presented separately as a (an)
   a. Component of income from continuing operations, but **not** net of applicable income taxes.
   b. Component of income from continuing operations, net of applicable income taxes.
   c. Extraordinary item, net of applicable income taxes.
   d. Prior period adjustment, but **not** net of applicable income taxes.

70. An extraordinary item should be reported separately as a component of income
   a. Before cumulative effect of accounting changes and after discontinued operations of a segment of a business.
   b. Before cumulative effect of accounting changes and before discontinued operations of a segment of a business.
   c. After cumulative effect of accounting changes and after discontinued operations of a segment of a business.
   d. After cumulative effect of accounting changes and before discontinued operations of a segment of a business.

MULTIPLE CHOICE QUESTIONS

INTERIM FINANCIAL REPORTING (71—82)

71. The computation of a company's third quarter provision for income taxes should be based upon earnings

    a.   For the quarter at an expected annual effective income tax rate.

    b.   For the quarter at the statutory rate.

    c.   To date at an expected annual effective income tax rate less prior quarters' provisions.

    d.   To date at the statutory rate less prior quarters' provisions.

72. Bailey Company, a calendar year corporation, has the following income before income tax provision and estimated effective annual income tax rates for the first three quarters of 1979:

Quarter	Income before income tax provision	Estimated effective annual tax rate at end of quarter
First	$60,000	40%
Second	70,000	40%
Third	40,000	45%

Bailey's income tax provision in its interim income statement for the third quarter should be

    a. $18,000

    b. $24,500

    c. $25,500

    d. $76,500

73. On January 1, 1979, Builder Associates entered into a $1,000,000 long-term, fixed-price contract to construct a factory building for Manufacturing Company. Builder accounts for this contract under the percentage-of-completion and estimated costs at completion at the end of each quarter for 1979 were as follows:

Quarter	Estimated Percentage of Completion	Estimated Costs at Completion
1	10%	$750,000
2*	10%	$750,000
3	25%	$960,000
4*	25%	$960,000

*No work performed in the 2nd and 4th quarters.

What amounts should be reported by Builder as "Income on Construction Contract" in its quarterly income statements based on the above information?

	Gain (Loss) for the Three Months Ended			
	March 31, 1979	June 30, 1979	September 30, 1979	December 31, 1979
a.	$0	$0	$0	$10,000
b.	$25,000	$0	$(15,000)	$0
c.	$25,000	$0	$0	$0
d.	$25,000	$0	$ 6,000	$0

74. In August 1978 Ella Company spent $150,000 on an advertising campaign for subscriptions to the magazine it sells on getting ready for the skiing season. There are only two issues; one in October and one in November. The magazine is only sold on a subscription basis and the subscriptions started in October 1978. Assuming Ella's fiscal year ends on March 31, 1979, what amount of expense should be included in Ella's quarterly income statement for the three months ended December 31, 1978, as a result of this expenditure?

    a. $37,500

    b. $50,000

    c. $75,000

    d. $150,000

75. In considering interim financial reporting, how did the Accounting Principles Board conclude that such reporting should be viewed?

    a.   As a "special" type of reporting that need not follow generally accepted accounting principles.

    b.   As useful only if activity is evenly spread throughout the year so that estimates are unnecessary.

    c.   As reporting for a basic accounting period.

    d.   As reporting for an integral part of an annual period.

76. On January 1, 1976, Perry Inc., paid property taxes on its plant for the calendar year 1976 amounting to $40,000. In March 1976, Perry made its annual major repairs to its machinery amounting to $120,000. These repairs will benefit the entire calendar year's operations. How should these expenses be reflected in Perry's quarterly income statements?

| | Three Months Ended | | | |
	March 31, 1976	June 30, 1976	September 30, 1976	December 31, 1976
a.	$ 22,000	$46,000	$46,000	$46,000
b.	$ 40,000	$40,000	$40,000	$40,000
c.	$ 70,000	$30,000	$30,000	$30,000
d.	$160,000	$0	$0	$0

77. The Harris Corporation has an incentive commission plan for its salesmen, entitling them to an additional sales commission when actual quarterly sales exceed budgeted estimates. An analysis of the account "incentive commission expense" for the year ended December 31, 1977, follows:

Amount	For Quarter Ended	Date Paid
$40,000	December 31, 1976	January 23, 1977
28,000	March 31, 1977	April 24, 1977
15,000	June 30, 1977	July 19, 1977
23,000	September 30, 1977	October 22, 1977

The incentive commission for the quarter ended December 31, 1977, was $27,000. This amount was recorded and paid in January 1978. What amount should Harris record as incentive commission expense for 1977?

    a. $133,000.
    b. $106,000.
    c. $93,000.
    d. $66,000.

78. An inventory loss from market decline of $600,000 occurred in May 1978. The Kup Company recorded this loss in May 1978 after its March 31, 1978, quarterly report was issued. None of this loss was recovered by the end of the year. How should this loss be reflected in Kup's quarterly income statements?

| | Three Months Ended | | | |
	March 31, 1978	June 30, 1978	September 30, 1978	December 31, 1978
a.	$ 0	$ 0	$ 0	$600,000
b.	$ 0	$200,000	$200,000	$200,000
c.	$ 0	$600,000	$ 0	$ 0
d.	$150,000	$150,000	$150,000	$150,000

79. Which of the following methods of inventory valuation is allowable at interim dates but not at year-end?

    a. Weighted average.
    b. Estimated gross profit rates.
    c. Retail method.
    d. Specific identification.

80. Which of the following is an inherent difficulty in the determination of the results of operations on an interim basis?

    a. Cost of sales reflects only the amount of product expense allocable to revenue recognized as of the interim date.
    b. Depreciation on an interim basis is a partial estimate of the actual annual amount.
    c. Costs expensed in one interim period may benefit other periods.
    d. Revenues from long-term construction contracts accounted for by the percentage-of-completion method are based on annual completion and interim estimates may be incorrect.

MAY 1981 QUESTIONS

81. In January 1980 Horner Company paid $80,000 in property taxes on its plant for the calendar year 1980. Also in January 1980 Horner estimated that its year-end bonus to executives for 1980 would be $320,000. What is the amount of the expenses related to these two items that should be reflected in Horner's quarterly income statement for the three months ended June 30, 1980 (second quarter)?

    a. $0.
    b. $ 20,000.
    c. $ 80,000.
    d. $100,000.

82. For interim financial reporting, an inventory loss from a temporary market decline in the first quarter which can reasonably be expected to be restored in the fourth quarter

    a. Should be recognized as a loss proportionately in each of the first, second, third, and fourth quarters.
    b. Should be recognized as a loss proportionately in each of the first, second, and third quarters.
    c. Need **not** be recognized as a loss in the first quarter.
    d. Should be recognized as a loss in the first quarter.

MULTIPLE CHOICE QUESTIONS

SEGMENT REPORTING (83—88)

83. Selected data for a segment of a business enterprise are to be separately reported in accordance with FASB Statement No. 14 when the revenues of the segment exceed 10 percent of the
   a. Combined net income of all segments reporting profits.
   b. Total revenues obtained in transactions with outsiders.
   c. Total revenues of all the enterprise's industry segments.
   d. Total combined revenues of all segments reporting profits.

84. The Jonas Company is a diversified company that discloses supplemental financial information as to industry segments of its business. The following information is available for 1979:

	Sales	Traceable Costs	Allocable Costs
Product A	$400,000	$225,000	
Product B	300,000	240,000	
Product C	200,000	135,000	
	$900,000	$600,000	$150,000

Allocable costs are allocated based on the ratio of a segment's income before allocable costs to total income before allocable costs. This should be considered an appropriate method of allocation. What is the operating profit for Product B for 1979?
   a. $0
   b. $10,000
   c. $30,000
   d. $50,000

85. In financial reporting for segments of a business enterprise, the operating profit or loss of a segment should include
   a. Federal income taxes.
   b. Interest expense even though segment's operations are not principally of a financial nature.
   c. Revenue earned at the corporate level.
   d. Common costs allocated on a reasonable basis.

86. The profitability information that should be reported for each reportable segment of a business enterprise consists of
   a. An operating profit or loss figure consisting of segment revenues less traceable costs and allocated common costs.
   b. An operating profit or loss figure consisting of segment revenues less traceable costs but not allocated common costs.
   c. An operating profit or loss figure consisting of segment revenues less allocated common costs but not traceable costs.
   d. Segment revenues only.

MAY 1981 QUESTIONS

87. Plains, Inc., engages in three lines of business, each of which is considered to be a significant industry segment. Company sales aggregated $1,800,000 in 1980, of which Segment No. 3 contributed 60%. Traceable costs were $600,000 for Segment No. 3 out of a total of $1,200,000 for the company as a whole. In addition $350,000 of common costs are allocated based on the ratio of a segment's income before common costs to the total income before common costs. What should Plains report as operating profit for Segment No. 3 in 1980?
   a. $200,000.
   b. $270,000.
   c. $280,000.
   d. $480,000.

88. In financial reporting for segments of a business enterprise, the operating profit or loss of a segment should include among other items
   a. Traceable costs.
   b. Foreign income taxes.
   c. Extraordinary items.
   d. Loss on discontinued operations.

PROBLEMS: BASIC CONCEPTS

Problem 1   Revenue Recognition   (1174,T4)

(25 to 30 minutes)

Part a.   The earning of revenue by a business enterprise is recognized for accounting purposes when the transaction is recorded. In some situations, revenue is recognized approximately as it is earned in the economic sense. In other situations, however, accountants have developed guidelines for recognizing revenue by other criteria; such as, at the point of sale.

Required (ignore income taxes):

1. Explain and justify why revenue is often recognized as earned at time of sale.

2. Explain in what situations it would be appropriate to recognize revenue as the productive activity takes place.

3. At what times, other than those included in 1. and 2. above, may it be appropriate to recognize revenue? Explain.

Part b.   Income measurement can be divided into different income concepts classified by income recipients. The following income concepts are tailored to the listed categories of income recipients.

Income Concepts	Income Recipients
1. Net income to residual equity holders.	Common stockholders.
2. Net income to investors.	Stockholders and long-term debt holders.
3. Value-added income.	All employees, stockholders, governments, and some creditors

Required:

For each of the concepts listed above, explain in separately numbered paragraphs what major categories of revenue, expense, and other items would be included in the determination of income.

Problem 2   Accounting Entity   (572,T5)

(25 to 30 minutes)

The concept of the accounting entity often is considered to be the most fundamental of accounting concepts, one that pervades all of accounting.

Required:

a.   1.   What is an accounting entity? Explain.

2.   Explain why the accounting entity concept is so fundamental that it pervades all of accounting.

b.   For each of the following indicate whether the accounting concept of entity is applicable; discuss and give illustrations.

1.   A unit created by or under law.

2.   The product-line segment of an enterprise.

3.   A combination of legal units and/or product-line segments.

4.   All of the activities of an owner or a group of owners.

5.   An industry.

6.   The economy of the United States.

Problem 3   Fictitious Statements About GAAP (577,T5)

(20 to 30 minutes)

Three independent, unrelated statements follow regarding financial accounting. Each statement contains some unsound reasoning.

Statement I

One function of financial accounting is to measure a company's net earnings for a given period of time. An earnings statement will measure a company's true net earnings if it is prepared in accordance with generally accepted accounting principles. Other financial statements are basically unrelated to the earnings statement. Net earnings would be measured as the difference between revenues and expenses. Revenues are an inflow of cash to the enterprise and should be realized when recognized. This may be accomplished by using the sales basis or the production basis. Expenses should be matched with revenues to measure net earnings. Usually, variable expenses are assigned to the product, and fixed expenses are assigned to the period.

Statement II

One function of financial accounting is to accurately present a company's financial position at a given point in time. This is done with a statement of financial position, which is prepared using historical-cost valuations for all assets and liabilities except inventories. Inventories are stated at first-in, first-out (FIFO), last-in, first-out (LIFO), or average valuations. The statement of financial position must be prepared on a consistent basis with prior years' statements.

In addition to reflecting assets, liabilities, and stockholders' equity, a statement of financial position should, in a separate section, reflect a company's reserves. The section should include three different types of reserves: depreciation reserves, product warranty reserves, and retained earnings reserves. All three of these types of reserves are established by a credit to the reserve account.

Statement III

Financial statement analysis involves using ratios to test past performance of a given company. Past performance is compared to a predetermined standard, and the company is evaluated accordingly. One such ratio is the current ratio, which is computed as current assets divided by current liabilities, or as monetary assets divided by monetary liabilities. A current ratio of 2 to 1 is considered good for companies; but the higher the ratio, the better the company's financial position is assumed to be. The current ratio is dynamic because it helps to measure fund flows.

Required:

Identify the areas that are not in accordance with generally accepted accounting principles or are untrue with respect to the financial statement analysis discussed in each of the statements and explain why the reasoning is incorrect. Complete your identification and explanation of each statement before proceeding to the next statement.

Problem 4   Accrual vs. Cash Basis (1179,T3)

(15 to 20 minutes)

Generally accepted accounting principles require the use of accruals and deferrals in the determination of income.

Required:

a.   How does accrual accounting affect the determination of income? Include in your discussion what constitutes an accrual and a deferral, and give appropriate examples of each.

b.   Contrast accrual accounting with cash accounting.

Problem 5   Bad Debts (1179,T2a)

(10 to 15 minutes)

When a company has a policy of making sales for which credit is extended, it is reasonable to expect a portion of those sales to be uncollectible. As a result of this, a company must recognize bad debt expense. There are basically two methods of recognizing bad debt expense: (1) direct write-off method, and (2) allowance method.

Required:

1.   Describe fully both the direct write-off method and the allowance method of recognizing bad debt expense.

2.   Discuss the reasons why one of the above methods is preferable to the other and the reason why the other method is not usually in accordance with generally accepted accounting principles.

PROBLEMS: ERROR CORRECTION

Problem 6   Schedule of Error Effects (577,Q3)

(40 to 50 minutes)

You have been engaged to examine the financial statements of Zurich Corporation for the year ended December 31, 1976. In the course of your examination you have ascertained the following information:

1. A check for $1,500 representing the repayment of an employee advance was received on December 29, 1976, but was not recorded until January 2, 1977.

2. Zurich uses the allowance method of accounting for uncollectible trade accounts receivable. The allowance is based upon 3% of past due accounts (over 120 days) and 1% of current accounts as of the close of each month. Due to a changing economic climate, the amount of past due accounts has increased significantly, and management has decided to increase the percentage based on past due accounts to 5%. The following balances are available:

	As of Nov. 30, 1976 Dr. (Cr.)	As of Dec. 31, 1976 Dr. (Cr.)
Accounts Receivable	$390,000	$430,000
Past due accounts (included in accounts receivable)	12,000	30,000
Allowance for uncollectible accounts	(28,000)	9,000

3. The merchandise inventory on December 31, 1975, did not include merchandise having a cost of $7,000 which was stored in a public warehouse. Merchandise having a cost of $3,000 was erroneously counted twice and included twice in the merchandise inventory on December 31, 1976. Zurich uses a periodic inventory system.

4. On January 2, 1976, Zurich had a new machine delivered and installed in its main factory. The cost of this machine was $97,000, and the machine is being depreciated on the straight-line method over an estimated useful life of 10 years. When the new machine was installed, Zurich paid for the following items which were not included in the cost of the machine, but were charged to repairs and maintenance:

Delivery expense	$ 2,500
Installation costs	8,000
Rearrangement of related equipment	4,000
	$14,500

5. On January 1, 1975, Zurich leased a building for 10 years at a monthly rental of $12,000. On that date, Zurich paid the landlord the following amounts:

Rent deposit	$ 6,000
First month's rent	12,000
Last month's rent	12,000
Installation of new walls and offices	80,000
	$110,000

The entire amount was charged to rent expense in 1975.

6. In January 1975, Zurich issued $200,000 of 8%, 10-year bonds at 97. The discount was charged to interest expense in 1975. Interest on the bonds is payable on December 31st of each year. Zurich has recorded interest expense of $22,000 for 1975 and $16,000 for 1976.

7. On May 3, 1976, Zurich exchanged 500 shares of treasury stock (its $50 par value common stock) for a parcel of land to be used as a site for a new factory. The treasury stock had cost $70 per share when it was acquired and on May 3, 1976, it had a fair market value of $80 per share. Zurich received $2,000 when an existing building on the land was sold for scrap. The land was capitalized at $40,000, and Zurich recorded a gain of $5,000 on the sale of its treasury stock.

8. The account "advertising and promotion" included an amount of $75,000 which represented the cost of printing sales catalogues for a special promotional campaign in January 1977.

9. Zurich adopted a pension plan on January 2, 1976, for eligible employees to be administered by a trustee. Based upon actuarial computations, the annual normal pension cost was $70,000 and the present value of past service cost on that date was $900,000. The company has decided to use the maximum provision for pension expense and to fund past service cost. On December 31, 1976, Zurich remitted to the trustee $970,000 and charged this amount to the account "pension expense."

10. Zurich was named as a defendant in a law suit by a former customer. Zurich's counsel has advised management that Zurich has a good defense and that counsel does not anticipate that there will be any impairment of Zurich's assets or that any significant liabilities will be incurred as a result of this litigation. Management, however, wishes to be conservative and, therefore, has established a loss contingency of $100,000.

Required:

Prepare a schedule showing the effect of errors upon the financial statements for 1976. The items in the schedule should be presented in the same order as the facts are given with corresponding numbers 1 through 10. Use the following columnar headings for your schedule:

No.	Explanation	Income Statement Dr. (Cr.)	Balance Sheet December 31, 1976 Dr. (Cr.)	Account

Problem 7   Journal Entries and Schedule   (1178,Q3)

(50 to 60 minutes)

The Noble Corporation is in the process of negotiating a loan for expansion purposes. The books and records have never been audited and the bank has requested that an audit be performed. Noble has prepared the following comparative financial statements for the years ended December 31, 1977, and 1976:

BALANCE SHEET
As of December 31, 1977 and 1976

	1977	1976
Assets		
Current Assets		
Cash	$ 163,000	$ 82,000
Accounts receivable	392,000	296,000
Allowance for un-collectible accounts	(37,000)	(18,000)
Marketable securities, at cost	78,000	78,000
Merchandise inventory	207,000	202,000
Total current assets	$ 803,000	$640,000
Fixed Assets		
Property, plant and equipment	167,000	169,500
Accumulated depreciation	(121,600)	(106,400)
Total fixed assets	45,400	63,100
Total assets	$ 848,400	$703,100
Liabilities and Stockholders' Equity		
Liabilities		
Accounts payable	$ 121,400	$196,100
Stockholders' equity		
Common stock, par value $10, authorized 50,000 shares, issued and outstanding 20,000 shares	260,000	260,000
Retained earnings	467,000	247,000
Total stockholders' equity	727,000	507,000
Total liabilities and stockholders' equity	$ 848,400	$703,100

STATEMENT OF INCOME
For the Years Ended December 31, 1977 and 1976

	1977	1976
Sales	$1,000,000	$900,000
Cost of sales	430,000	395,000
Gross profit	570,000	505,000
Operating expenses	210,000	205,000
Administrative expenses	140,000	105,000
	350,000	310,000
Net income	$ 220,000	$195,000

During the course of the audit, the following additional facts were determined:

1. An analysis of collections and losses on accounts receivable during the past two years indicates a drop in anticipated losses due to bad debts. After consultation with management it was agreed that the loss experience rate on sales should be reduced from the recorded 2% to 1%, beginning with the year ended December 31, 1977.

2. An analysis of marketable securities revealed that this investment portfolio consisted entirely of short-term investments in marketable equity securities that were acquired in 1976. The total market valuation for these investments as of the end of each year was as follows:

December 31, 1976	$81,000
December 31, 1977	$62,000

3. The merchandise inventory at December 31, 1976, was overstated by $4,000 and the merchandise inventory at December 31, 1977, was overstated by $6,100.

4. On January 2, 1976, equipment costing $12,000 (estimated useful life of ten years and residual value of $1,000) was incorrectly charged to operating expenses. Noble records depreciation on the straight-line method. In 1977 fully depreciated equipment (with no residual value) that originally cost $17,500 was sold as scrap for $2,500. Noble credited the proceeds of $2,500 to property and equipment.

5. An analysis of 1976 operating expenses revealed that Noble charged to expense a three-year insurance premium of $2,700 on January 15, 1976.

Required:

    a.   Prepare the journal entries to correct the books at December 31, 1977. The books for 1977 have not been closed. Ignore income taxes.

    b.   Prepare a schedule showing the computation of corrected net income for the years ended December 31, 1977 and 1976, assuming that any adjustments are to be reported on comparative statements for the two years. The first items on your schedule should be the net income for each year. Ignore income taxes. (Do not prepare financial statements.)

PROBLEMS: ACCOUNTING CHANGES

Problem 8   Description of Types (580,T4a)

        (10 to 15 minutes)

    The various types of accounting changes may significantly affect the presentation of both financial position and results of operations for an accounting period and the trends shown in comparative financial statements and historical summaries.

Required:

    1.   Describe a change in accounting principle and how it should be reported in the income statement of the period of the change.

    2.   Describe a change in accounting estimate and how it should be reported in the income statement of the period of the change.

    3.   Describe a change in reporting entity and how it should be reported. Give an appropriate example of a change in reporting entity.

PROBLEMS: FINANCIAL STATEMENTS

Problem 9   Statement Deficiencies (579,T2)

        (20 - 25 minutes)

    Shown below are the financial statements issued by Allen Corporation for its fiscal year ended October 31, 1978:

Allen Corporation
STATEMENT OF FINANCIAL POSITION
October 31, 1978

Assets

Cash	$ 15,000
Accounts receivable, net	150,000
Inventory	120,000
Total current assets	285,000
Trademark (Note 3)	250,000
Land	125,000
Total assets	$660,000

Liabilities

Accounts payable	$ 80,000
Accrued expenses	20,000
Total current liabilities	100,000
Deferred income tax payable (Note 4)	80,000
Total liabilities	180,000

Stockholders' Equity

Common stock, par $1 (Note 5)	$100,000	
Additional paid-in capital	180,000	
Retained earnings	200,000	480,000
Total liabilities and stockholders' equity		$660,000

Allen Corporation
EARNINGS STATEMENT
For the fiscal year ended October 31, 1978

Sales		$1,000,000
Cost of goods sold		750,000
Gross margin		250,000
Expenses:		
Bad debt expense	$ 7,000	
Insurance	13,000	
Lease expenses (Note 1)	40,000	
Repairs and maintenance	30,000	
Pensions (Note 2)	12,000	
Salaries	60,000	162,000
Earnings before provision for income tax		88,000
Provision for income tax		28,740
Net earnings		$ 59,260
Earnings per common share outstanding		$ 0.5926

Allen Corporation
STATEMENT OF RETAINED EARNINGS
For the fiscal year ended October 31, 1978

Retained earnings, November 1, 1977		$150,000
Extraordinary gain, net of income tax		25,000
Net earnings for the fiscal year ended October 31, 1978		59,260
		234,260
Dividends ($0.3426 per share)		34,260
Retained earnings, October 31, 1978		$200,000

FOOTNOTES

Note 1 — Long-Term Lease

Under the terms of a 5-year noncancelable lease for buildings and equipment, the Company is obligated to make annual rental payments of $40,000 in each of the next four fiscal years. At the conclusion of the lease period, the Company has the option of purchasing the leased assets for $20,000 (a bargain purchase option) or entering into another 5-year lease of the same property at an annual rental of $5,000.

Note 2— Pension Plan

Substantially all employees are covered by the Company's pension plan. Pension expense is equal to the total of pension benefits paid to retired employees during the year.

Note 3 — Trademark

The Company's trademark was purchased from Apex Corporation on January 1, 1976, for $250,000.

Note 4 — Deferred Income Tax Payable

The entire balance in the deferred income tax payable account arose from tax-exempt municipal bonds that were held during the previous fiscal year giving rise to a difference between taxable income and reported net earnings for the fiscal year ended October 31, 1977. The deferred liability amount was calculated on the basis of expected tax rates in future years.

Note 5 — Warrants

On January 1, 1977, one common stock warrant was issued to stockholders of record for each common share owned. An additional share of common stock is to be issued upon exercise of ten stock warrants and receipt of an amount equal to par value. For the six months ended October 31, 1978, the average market value for the Company's common stock was $5 per share and no warrants had yet been exercised.

Note 6 — Contingent Liability

On October 31, 1978, the Company was contingently liable for product warranties in an amount estimated to aggregate $75,000.

Required:

Review the preceding financial statements and related footnotes. Identify any inclusions or exclusions from them that would be in violation of generally accepted accounting principles, and indicate corrective action to be taken. Do **not** comment as to format or style. Respond in the following order:

- Statement of Financial Position.
- Footnotes.
- Earnings Statement.
- Statement of Retained Earnings.
- General.

Problem 10   Discontinued Operations (1176,Q5)

(40 to 50 minutes)

The Century Company, a diversified manufacturing company, had four separate operating divisions engaged in the manufacture of products in each of the following areas: food products, health aids, textiles, and office equipment.

Financial data for the two years ended December 31, 1975, and 1974 are presented below:

	Net Sales	
	1975	1974
Food products	$3,500,000	$3,000,000
Health aids	2,000,000	1,270,000
Textiles	1,580,000	1,400,000
Office equipment	920,000	1,330,000
	$8,000,000	$7,000,000

	Cost of Sales	
	1975	1974
Food products	$2,400,000	$1,800,000
Health aids	1,100,000	700,000
Textiles	500,000	900,000
Office equipment	800,000	1,000,000
	$4,800,000	$4,400,000

	Operating Expenses	
	1975	1974
Food products	$ 550,000	$ 275,000
Health aids	300,000	125,000
Textiles	200,000	150,000
Office equipment	650,000	750,000
	$1,700,000	$1,300,000

On January 1, 1975, Century adopted a plan to sell the assets and product line of the office equipment division and expected to realize a gain on this disposal. On September 1, 1975, the division's assets and product line were sold for $2,100,000 cash resulting in a gain of $640,000 (exclusive of operations during the phase-out period).

The company's textiles division had six manufacturing plants which produced a variety of textile products. In April 1975, the company sold one of these plants and realized a gain of $130,000. After the sale, the operations at the plant that was sold were transferred to the remaining five textile plants which the company continued to operate.

In August 1975, the main warehouse of the food products division, located on the banks of the Bayer River, was flooded when the river overflowed. The resulting damage of $420,000 is not included in the financial data given above. Historical records indicate that the Bayer River normally overflows every four to five years causing flood damage to adjacent property.

For the two years ended December 31, 1975, and 1974, the company had interest revenue earned on investments of $70,000 and $40,000 respectively.

For the two years ended December 31, 1975, and 1974, the company's net income was $960,000 and $670,000 respectively.

The provision for income tax expense for each of the two years should be computed at a rate of 50%.

Required:

Prepare in proper form a comparative statement of income of the Century Company for the two years ended December 31, 1975, and December 31, 1974. Footnotes are not required.

Problem 11   Statement Interrelationships

(575,P4)   (50 to 60 minutes)

This question concerns the various interrelationships among financial statements, accounts (or groups of accounts) among those statements, and accounts (or groups of accounts) within each statement. The following information is presented for Woods Company for the year ended December 31, 1974:

- The Statement of Changes in Financial Position.
- Selected information from the Income Statement.

Statement of Changes in Financial Position

Working capital, January 1, 1974		$16,500
Add resources provided:		
Operations:		
Net loss for 1974	$(2,885)	
Adjustments not involving working capital:		
Bond premium amortization	(500)	
Deferred income taxes	(200)	
Depreciation expense	3,000	
Goodwill amortization for 1974	2,000	
Total from operations		1,415
Portion of proceeds of equipment sold representing undepreciated cost		10,000
Proceeds from reissue of treasury stock		11,400
Par value of common stock issued to reacquire preferred stock		7,500
Total resources provided		30,315
Subtract resources applied:		
Purchase of land		14,715
Current maturity of long-term bond debt		7,200
Par value of preferred stock reacquired by issuing common stock		7,500
Total resources applied		29,415
Increase in working capital		900
Working capital, December 31, 1974		$17,400

Information from the Income Statement

Bad debt expense		$750
Bond interest expense (net of amortization of bond premium)		$3,500
Loss before tax adjustment		$(3,900)
Less:		
Income tax adjustment (refund due)	$815	
Deferred income taxes	200	1,015
Net loss after tax adjustment		$(2,885)

Information Regarding January 1 and December 31 Balance Sheets

The book value of the equipment sold was two-thirds of the cost of that equipment.

Selected Ratios

	January 1, 1974 (prior to restatement)	December 31, 1974
Current ratio	?	3 to 1
Total stockholders' equity divided by total liabilities	4 to 3	?

Information Regarding the Correction of an Error

Woods Company had neglected to amortize $2,000 of goodwill in 1973. The correction of this material error has been appropriately made in 1974.

Balance Sheet

	January 1, 1974 (prior to restatement)	December 31, 1974
Current assets	$22,000	$ (5)
Building and equipment	92,000	(6)
Accumulated depreciation	(25,000)	(7)
Land	(1)	(8)
Goodwill	12,000	(9)
Total assets	$ (?)	$ (?)
Current liabilities	$ (2)	(10)
Bonds payable (8%)	(3)	(11)
Bond premium	(?)	(12)
Deferred income taxes	(4)	1,700
Common stock	66,000	(13)
Paid-in capital	13,000	(14)
Preferred stock	16,000	(15)
Retained earnings (deficit)	(6,000)	(16)
Treasury stock (at cost)	(9,000)	0
Total liabilities and stockholders' equity	$ (?)	$ (?)

- Selected information regarding the January 1 and December 31 Balance Sheets.
- Information regarding the correction of an error.
- Partially completed Balance Sheets at January 1 (prior to restatement) and December 31. The omitted account and groups-of-account balances are numbered from (1) through (16) and can be calculated from the other information given.

Required:

Number your answer sheet from (1) through (16). Place the correct balance for each balance-sheet account or group of accounts next to the corresponding number on your answer sheet. Show supporting computations in good form. (One account balance and the totals are shown as a question mark(?). Calculation of these amounts may be necessary to calculate the numbered balances, but is not required to be shown separately in your numbered answers.) Do not recopy the balance sheets. Calculations of answers need not follow the numerical order of these blanks 1 through 16. Do not restate the January 1 balance sheet for the error.

PROBLEMS: INTERIM REPORTING

Problem 12   Treatment of Selected Items (1178,T6)

(15 to 20 minutes)

Interim financial reporting has become an important topic in accounting. There has been considerable discussion as to the proper method of reflecting results of operations at interim dates. Accordingly, the Accounting Principles Board issued an opinion clarifying some aspects of interim financial reporting.

Required:
   a.   Discuss generally how revenue should be recognized at interim dates and specifically how revenue should be recognized for industries subject to large seasonal fluctuations in revenue and for long-term contracts using the percentage-of-completion method at annual reporting dates.
   b.   Discuss generally how product and period costs should be recognized at interim dates. Also discuss how inventory and cost of goods sold may be afforded special accounting treatment at interim dates.
   c.   Discuss how the provision for income taxes is computed and reflected in interim financial statements.

PROBLEMS: SEGMENT REPORTING

Problem 13   Definitions and Tests (579,T5)

(15 to 20 minutes)

Part a.   In order to properly understand current generally accepted accounting principles with respect to accounting for and reporting upon segments of a business enterprise, as stated by the Financial Accounting Standards Board in its Statement 14, it is necessary to be familiar with certain unique terminology.

Required:

With respect to segments of a business enterprise, explain the following terms:

   1.   Industry segment.
   2.   Revenue.
   3.   Operating profit and loss.
   4.   Identifiable assets.

Part b.   A central issue in reporting on industry segments of a business enterprise is the determination of which segments are reportable.

Required:

   1.   What are the tests to determine whether or not an industry segment is reportable?

   2.   What is the test to determine if enough industry segments have been separately reported upon and what is the guideline on the maximum number of industry segments to be shown?

MULTIPLE CHOICE ANSWERS

BASIC CONCEPTS

1.	a	7.	a	13.	b	19.	b	25.	c
2.	b	8.	d	14.	a	20.	d	26.	c
3.	c	9.	b	15.	c	21.	c	27.	b
4.	d	10.	a	16.	a	22.	c	28.	a
5.	a	11.	a	17.	d	23.	a	29.	b
6.	a	12.	b	18.	d	24.	b		

EXPLANATION OF MULTIPLE CHOICE ANSWERS

1. **(1180,T1,1)** **(a)** The requirement is the effect, on net income, of writing off a specific customer's account receivable under both the allowance and direct write-off methods. The solutions approach is to prepare journal entries for both methods. Allowance:

Allowance for Doubtful Accounts   XXX
   Accounts Receivable   XXX

Direct Write-Off:

Bad Debt Expense   XXX
   Accounts Receivable   XXX

In the Allowance method, the journal entry does not include any income statement accounts, so there is no effect on net income. In the Direct Write-Off method, the journal entry includes a debit to an expense account, indicating decreased net income.

2. **(1180,T1,3)** **(b)** An accrued liability results from recording an expense which has been incurred but not paid. Wages payable is an example of an expense incurred but not paid. The other choices are liabilities, but not accrued liabilities. Cash dividends payable and the current portion of long-term debt do not result from expenses. Rent revenue collected in advance is an example of an unearned revenue.

3. **(1180,T1,5)** **(c)** Objectivity is assumed to be achieved when an exchange involves an arm's length transaction between two independent parties. When two independent parties negotiate a deal which is fair to both, we can assume the result is objective. Choices (a) and (b) are incorrect because they do not automatically indicate objectivity. For example, a corporation may pay a fixed cash salary to a major stockholder; this is not necessarily objective because the parties involved are not independent. Choice (d) is incorrect because revenue and expense allocation is by nature a somewhat subjective process; such allocation, therefore, cannot be assumed to be objective.

4. **(1180,T1,6)** **(d)** The concept of consistency is sacrificed in accounting for the cumulative effect of a change in accounting principle. The principle of consistency requires that similar events be accounted for in a similar fashion from year to year. Discontinued operations (a), losses on disposal (b), and extraordinary items (c), while they may not occur every year, are accounted for consistently when they do occur. However, by definition, a change in accounting principle indicates that a different principle or method has been used for the same type of transactions.

5. **(1180,T1,7)** **(a)** When computing the current value of an asset using the present value method, the future amounts of cash receipts or cash savings (d) over the productive life of the asset (b) are discounted at the applicable interest rate (c). The cost of alternate uses of funds given up (a) is not considered in the computation.

6. **(1180,T1,12)** **(a)** When bad debt expense is estimated based on a percentage of credit sales, the matching principle is being followed. The entity is attempting to estimate what part of this year's sales will not be collected, thereby matching this year's expense with this year's sales. It is important to note that either choice (a) or (b) must be correct. One states that matching is_ followed, the other that matching _is not_ followed. Obviously either matching is or is not followed; there is no other alternative.

7. **(580,T1,8)** **(a)** A deferred cost is a cost which has been paid in advance of its use in the business and is, therefore, an asset which will provide future benefits such as the prepayment of insurance premiums. Answer (b) is incorrect because a deposit to cover potential damages will not necessarily provide benefits in the future; it would be more properly labelled a receivable. Answers (c) and (d) are incorrect because both are liabilities rather than assets.

8. **(580,T1,26)** **(d)** Objectivity and verifiability both refer to the adequacy of evidence concerning the validity of accounting data. Summarization refers to the compilation of numerical data, classification to the categorization of financial data, and conservatism to the avoidance of overstating assets and income.

9. **(580,T1,28)** **(b)** Current selling price is used as a measurement base, for example, in the case of precious metals having a fixed selling price with no substantial cost of marketing (ARB 43, Chapter 4, para 16). Discounted cash flow is used as a measurement base for assets capitalized under long-term leases

(SFAS 13, para 10). Replacement cost is used as a measurement base for inventories when the replacement cost has fallen below historical cost (ARB, 43, Chapter 4, para 9).

10. (580,T1,29) (a) Conservatism refers to a tendency on the part of accountants and management of preferring understatement of income to overstatement of income. Thus, immediate recognition of a loss would be preferable to deferring the loss. The lower of cost or market rule applied to short-term investments and inventory is a prime example of accounting conservatism. See para 171 of APB Statement 4. Consistency refers to achieving comparability over time by using the same accounting procedures, methods, etc. Judgment refers to the need for subjective decision-making in financial accounting, because the financial accounting process cannot be reduced to a set of inflexible rules. For example, there are numerous estimates in accounting that are based upon so many variables that detailed rules cannot be prescribed. Matching refers to the attempt of comparing revenues and expenses in specific periods of time. The objective is to determine the amount of income or loss.

11. (1179,T1,5) (a) The requirement is the condition permitting revenue recognition prior to the sale of merchandise. Per para 1 of Chapter 1A of ARB 43, profit is to be considered realized when a sale in the ordinary course of business is effected. Statement 9 (para 16) of Chapter 4 of ARB 43 indicates that inventory valuation above cost can only be justified by the following: an inability to determine approximate costs, immediate marketability at a quoted price, and the characteristic of unit interchangeability. Thus, a condition permitting recognition of revenue prior to sale would be an assured sales price. Answer (b) is incorrect because, with the installment sales method, revenue recognition is deferred until cash is collected (as a result of the questionability of collection of the sales price). Answer (c) is incorrect because the concept of internal consistency of amounts of revenue is a nonsense term. Answer (d) is incorrect because a long established management policy of noncompliance with GAAP does not justify the noncompliance.

12. (1179,T1,14) (b) Revenue collected one month in advance should be accounted for as a current liability. Current liabilities are obligations whose liquidation is reasonably expected to require the use of existing resources properly classifiable as current assets or the creation of other current liabilities. This includes collections received in advance of delivery of goods or services per para 7 of Chapter 3A of ARB 43. Answer (a) is incorrect because recognition of revenue in the

month collected would be the cash rather than the accrual basis of accounting. Answer (c) is incorrect because deferred revenue is not included in stockholder's equity. Answer (d) is incorrect because an accrued liability relates to an expense rather than to deferred revenue.

13. (1179,T1,18) (b) A basic feature of financial accounting is direct measurement of economic resources and obligations and changes in them in terms of money, per para 118 of APB 4. There are 13 basic features listed, including accounting entity, going concern, time periods, measurement in terms of money, accrual, exchange price, approximation, judgment, general purpose financial information, fundamentally related statements, substance over form, and materiality. Answers (a), (c), and (d) are incorrect because financial accounting does not measure economic resources in terms of sociological and/or psychological impact.

14. (1179,T1,19) (a) Application of lower of cost or market rules to inventory is an application of the concept of conservatism. Conservatism is considered a modifying convention in para 171 of APB Statement 4. Answer (b) is incorrect because the FIFO method in periods of rising prices results in a higher inventory than the LIFO or average cost methods. Answer (c) is incorrect because the percentage-of-completion method in the first year of a long-term contract results in the recognition of profit and the deferral of an increased cost (by the amount of the profit recognition). Answer (d) is incorrect because more interest is recognized under the interest method in the first year of a long-term non-interest bearing receivable than under the straight-line method. Under the interest method, a constant rate of interest is applied to the net book value (present value) of the receivable each year. In the first year, the present value of the receivable will be low and accordingly, a smaller amount of interest income will be recognized per the interest method than the straight-line method. As the non-interest bearing receivable is increased each period by the amount of income recognized, the receivable at the end of the period will also be less.

15. (1179,T1,27) (c) The continuation of an accounting entity in the absence of evidence to the contrary is the going concern assumption. See para 117 of APB Statement 4. Answer (a) is incorrect because an accounting entity refers to a specific business enterprise for which financial statements are prepared per para 116 of APB Statement 4. Answer (b) is incorrect because consistency is an important factor in comparability within a single enterprise because it permits meaningful comparisons between financial statements of an enterprise

at different times, per para 96-98 of APB 4. Answer (d) is incorrect because substance over form emphasizes the economic substance of events when the legal form may differ from the economic substance, per para 127 of APB 4.

16. (1176,T1,1)   (a)   Chapter 9A of ARB 43 prescribes depreciation to be calculated on the original historical cost (para 7). This position is further supported in para 17 of APB 6. The past input exchange price is the historical cost. The current input exchange price is the current replacement cost. The future input exchange price is the future replacement cost. The current output exchange price is the current market value. Thus, answer (a) historical cost is correct.

17. (1176,T1,8)   (d)   Residual interest is the interest in the economic resources of an enterprise remaining after economic obligations, i.e., A − L = SE (para 59 APB Statement 4). The fund theory is based on the equation, assets equals liabilities or sources of assets. The emphasis is on the assets, the credit side of the balance sheet just indicates the sources of the assets. The enterprise theory of ownership, like the entity theory, is concerned with the ownership of the assets or the credit side of the balance sheet in contrast to the fund theory. The enterprise theory considers the corporation to be a social enterprise for the benefit of many parties including creditors, employees, customers, etc. The entity theory emphasizes the business as a separate legal entity apart from the personal affairs and interests of the owners.

18. (577,T1,8)   (d)   The source for the three levels of accounting principles (pervasive, broad operating, and detailed) is APB Statement 4. Per the statement, GAAP incorporate the consensus at any time as to the economic resources and obligations which should be recorded as assets and liabilities and the recording, measurement, and disclosure of changes therein. See para 27-31 of APB Statement 4.

19. (1178,T1,6)   (b)   A basic assumption underlying accounting methodology is that the economic life of a business enterprise can be broken down into short periods (usually one year) for financial reporting purposes. The financial reporting periods are of equal length to facilitate comparison. See the discussion of timeliness and time periods as a basic feature of financial accounting in paras 92 and 119 of APB Statement 4. Answer (a) is incorrect because objectivity is often called verifiability,

which is a qualitative objective of accounting per para 90 of APB Statement 4. Answer (c) is incorrect because conservatism, a modifying convention, permits understating net income and net assets rather than overstatement (para 171, APB Statement 4). Answer (d) is incorrect because matching is the entire process of income determination, i.e., matching of revenues and expenses (footnote 43 to para 147 of APB Statement 4).

20. (579,T1,19)   (d)   General price-level adjusted statements do not result in deviation from the concept of historical cost per para 28 of APB Statement 3. Rather, the units of measure (dollars) are restated to reflect changes in the general purchasing power. Answer (a), net present value, answer (b), replacement costs, and answer (c), market value, are all estimates of future economic utility (market value) and thus are deviations from the concept of historical cost.

21. (578,T1,3)   (c)   Revenue is recognized when an exchange has taken place (providing an objective measure of value) and the earnings process is virtually complete. See para 150 of APB Statement 4. Also see para 1 of Chapter 1a of ARB 43, which indicates profit is realized at the point of sale in the ordinary course of business, unless collection is not reasonably assured.
   Answer (b) is incorrect because an exchange has not taken place proving either the salability of the product or establishing its value. Answer (a) is incorrect because management does not determine accounting rules. Instead accounting rules are applied to the economic events incurred by an enterprise. Answer (d) is incorrect because title transfer has not taken place until the merchandise is received at the destination. FOB means free on board destination, and the risk of loss and title to the goods remains with the seller until the goods reach their destination.

22. (578,T1,5)   (c)   Costs associated with future revenue production are deferred as assets to those periods in which they contribute to the production of revenue. See para 155 of APB Statement 4. The objective is to associate, or match, the cause (cost and expenses) with the effect (revenues). Alternatively, costs which cannot be associated directly with revenue but are known to benefit future periods are amortized in a systematic and rational manner. See para 157-159 of APB Statement 4. Answer (d) is incorrect because conservatism would dictate expensing rather than deferring costs. Answer (b) is incorrect because improper matching of revenues and expenses would confuse management rather than aiding in its decision-making

process. Answer (a) is incorrect because deferral of costs increases, rather than decreases, federal tax liability.

23. (578,T1,7)   (a)   The going concern concept or postulate means that an enterprise is going to continue in the future in the absence of information to the contrary. Thus accruals and deferrals may be used to allocate the effects of multi-period transactions to the period in which they belong. For example, revenues and expenses may be deferred to future periods if revenue or expense is to be recognized in the future. Conversely, revenue or expense can be recognized in the current period even though the cash flow will occur in future periods (para 117 of Statement 4). The principle of materiality simply means that only material items need be of concern in financial reporting decisions. Answer (b) is incorrect because consistency is an objective of financial accounting which enhances comparability across time by requiring the use of the same accounting procedures, methods, etc., period after period. Answer (d), stable monetary unit, refers to the implicit assumption in financial statements that the purchasing power of the monetary unit (dollar) is stable enough not to warrant the use of price-level adjusted statements.

24. (578,T1,18)   (b)   Depreciation is usually matched with revenue on the basis of allocating the cost of an asset to future periods based upon the expiration of time. See para 159 of APB Statement 4. Answer (a), associating cause and effects, refers to product-type expenses such as cost of goods sold. Note: while depreciation of production facilities can become a product expense, the depreciation is usually allocated to time periods on a systematic and rational basis. Answer (d), immediate recognition, refers to expensing costs immediately because the benefits of the cost cannot be associated with any particular period.

25. (578,T1,25)   (c)   Income tax savings should not be a justification for adoption of accounting procedures. The objective of financial statements is to fairly present in accordance with GAAP. When items are expensed for tax purposes and deferred for accounting purposes, a timing difference occurs and an adjustment of deferred taxes is appropriate. When expense for tax purposes exceeds expense per books, the deferred taxes account should be credited as the tax expense per books will exceed the taxes payable. Answers (a), (b), and (d) are stated as reasons for immediate recognition of expense in para 160 of APB Statement 4.

26. (581,T1,2)   (c)   The requirement is the concept that establishes the validity of presenting a promise to receive cash in the future at its present value on the financial statements. The going concern principle implies that a firm will remain in existence long enough to collect the receivable, justifying its recording. Answer (a) is incorrect because the entity concept means that the activity of a business enterprise can be kept separate and distinct from its owners. Answer (b), materiality, applies to information which is significant enough to affect evaluations of investment decisions. Neutrality, (answer d), is defined as freedom from bias.

27. (581,T1,3)   (b)   The requirement is for an example of the "associating cause and effect expense recognition principle". Cause and effect presumes that some costs are recognized as expenses on the basis of a presumed direct association with specific revenue (APB Statement 9, para 21); sales commissions (answer b) fits this category. Answers (a) and (c) are incorrect because these costs are expensed using the "systematic" and "rational" allocation expense principle. Answer (d) is an example of the "immediate recognition" expense principle.

28. (581,T1,4)   (a)   The requirement is the accounting concept which supports the accrual of net losses on a firm's purchase commitments. Conservatism refers to a preference on the part of accountants for understating rather than overstating when doubt exists (e.g., the salability of inventory). Accruing these losses is preferable to waiting until the firm purchase commitments are consummated. Realization (answer b) specifies when revenue should be recognized. Consistency (answer c) refers to achieving comparability overtime by using the same accounting methods, etc. Materiality (answer d) refers to information which is significant enough to affect investor evaluations of investment alteratives.

29. (581,T1,5)   (b)   The requirement is the accounting concept which states that an accounting transaction should be supported by sufficient evidence to allow two or more qualified individuals to arrive at essentially similar measures and conclusions. Objectivity refers to the availability and adequacy of evidence which establishes the validity of the data being considered (APB Statement 4, para 90). Matching (answer a) refers to relating expenses with revenues or periods of time. Periodicity (answer c) is a basic assumption that the economic life of a business enterprise can be broken down into short periods for financial reporting purposes (APB Statement 4, paras 92 and 119).

MULTIPLE CHOICE ANSWERS

ERROR CORRECTION

30. a   31. a   32. a   33. c   34. a

EXPLANATION OF MULTIPLE CHOICE ANSWERS

30. (1180,Q1,7)   (a)   The requirement is the total effect of several errors on 1979 net income. The requirement for the second problem in this set is the total effect of the same errors on the amount of working capital at 12/31/79. The overstatement or understatement of a year-end current asset or liability affects the amount of working capital. The solutions approach is to identify the effect of each error separately:

Error	Effect on 1979 income	Effect on 12/31/79 WC
Beginning inventory understated	$16,000 over	—
Ending inventory overstated	15,000 over	$15,000 over
1978 depreciation understated	—	—
1978 insurance expense overstated	—	—
1979 insurance expense understated	10,000 over	—
Prepaid insurance understated at 12/31/78	—	—
Sale of machinery	10,800 under	10,800 under
Total effect	$30,200 over	$ 4,200 over

The understatement of 1979 beginning inventory means cost of goods sold is also understated; therefore, net income is overstated. The overstatement of ending inventory means less cost assigned to cost of goods sold which also results in an overstatement of income. Only the overstatement of inventory and understatement of cash affected working capital.

31. (1180,Q1,8)   (a)   See explanation for (1180,Q1,7).

32.   (576,P1,3)   (a)   If the accounts are correct at the beginning of 1974, the only errors are an understatement of ending inventory of $1,000 which results in an overstatement of cost of goods

sold, and an understatement of depreciation expense. The $1,000 overstatement of cost of goods sold is offset by the $800 understatement of depreciation expense, resulting in an understatement of income of $200.

33.   (576,P1,4)   (c)   The requirement is the effect of the 1973 and 1974 errors on 1974 ending retained earnings. It is useful to note that the inventory errors are counterbalancing, in that the $3,000 overstatement of inventory at the end of 1973 overstates retained earnings at the end of 1973 but understates income in 1974. Thus the $3,000 inventory error is nullified in 1974 ending retained earnings. The depreciation errors, however, are not counterbalancing until the assets have been sold. In this case the $2,500 overstatement in 1973 is offset by the $800 understatement in 1974. to give a net overstatement of depreciation expense of $1,700. This $1,700 coupled with the overstatement of cost of sales during 1974 of $1,000 results in a $2,700 understatement of retained earnings at the end of 1974.

34.   (576,P1,5)   (a)   The requirement is to compute the error in working capital at the end of 1975 assuming no errors occurring in 1975. Since ending inventory at the end of 1975 will be presumably correct, and the depreciation expense, accumulated depreciation, etc. do not affect working capital, there should be no overstatement or understatement of working capital. It is important for you to recognize the need for a time diagram and care in reading dates, as many of you have missed this problem because you did not realize that the requirement was with respect to 1975 rather than 1974.

MULTIPLE CHOICE ANSWERS

ACCOUNTING CHANGES

35.	b	39.	b	43.	b	47.	d	51.	c
36.	a	40.	c	44.	d	48.	d	52.	d
37.	d	41.	c	45.	a	49.	b		
38.	a	42.	b	46.	b	50.	c		

EXPLANATION OF MULTIPLE CHOICE ANSWERS

35.   (1180,T1,9)   (b)   The requirement is which of the four choices should be disclosed in the Summary of Significant Accounting Policies. APB 22 recommends that the Summary identify the accounting policies followed by the reporting entity. The basis of consolidation is a significant accounting policy which should be disclosed. The items given in the other choices should also be disclosed in the statements or footnotes, but do not constitute accounting policies.

36.   (580,P1,1)   (a)   The requirement is to compute the cumulative effect of a change in accounting principle from the completed-contract method to the percentage-of-completion method as well as to indicate the appropriate location of the cumulative effect in Essex's 1979 financial statements. Per para 27 of APB 20, a change in method of accounting for long-term contracts is one of three changes requiring retroactive restatement of all prior periods presented. The cumulative effect at the beginning of each period to be added or subtracted from the opening balance of retained earnings is the difference between the $440,000 of income which would have resulted from using the percentage-of-completion method had Essex used this method since its inception and the $350,000 of income since inception under the completed-contract method. The cumulative effect of $90,000 must be reduced by the income tax effect at the 50% tax rate resulting in a net cumulative effect of $45,000. Answers (b) and (d) are incorrect because this type of accounting change is one of the special changes requiring restatement of all prior periods presented. Answer (c) is incorrect because it does not reflect the related tax effect.

37.   (580,T1,23)   (d)   Para 8 of APB 22 requires a description of all significant accounting policies to be included as an integral part of the financial statements. It does not require a description of every policy nor does it list which types of policies need to be disclosed.

38.   (1179,P1,1)   (a)   The requirement is the cumulative effect of a change in the estimated life of a machine from 6 years to 8 years at the beginning of the fourth year. Para 31 of APB 20 requires that changes in accounting estimates, e.g., useful life of an asset, should be reflected in the period of change and in future periods. Also, there should be no restatement of amounts recorded in prior statements (para 19). Thus, the cumulative effect on previous periods resulting from a change in the estimated useful life of the asset is zero.

39.   (1179,P1,2)   (b)   The requirement is the amount of depreciation expense for the year in which the remaining useful life is revised from three to five years. Per para 31 of APB 20, changes in accounting estimates are reflected prospectively, i.e., no retroactive adjustment. Accordingly, the solutions approach is to determine the amount of depreciation to date, subtract it from the depreciation base (here, cost because there is no salvage value), and divide by the remaining 5-year useful life. As computed below, the depreciation base beginning in 1978 is $1,500,000. The depreciation taken in 1975-1977 was $1,500,000 ($3,000,000 ÷ 6 years x 3 years). The remaining depreciation base of $1,500,000 ($3,000,000 − $1,500,000) is divided by 5 years, resulting in $300,000 per year depreciation.

$3,000,000	Cost (no salvage)
1,500,000	1975, 1976, 1977 depreciation
$1,500,000	to be depreciated in 1978-1982

$1,500,000 ÷ 5 years = $300,000

40.   (1179,T1,28)   (c)   Per para 34 of APB 20, accounting changes that result from a change in the business entity should be reflected in financial statements that are restated. Here, the statements of individual companies are being combined into consolidated statements as a result of a business combination. Answer (a) is incorrect because there would not be a correction of an error unless the financial statements ought to have been consolidated in previous years when the statements of individual companies were presented. Answer (b) is incorrect because only changes in accounting estimates should be accounted for prospectively per para 31 of APB 20. Answer (d) is incorrect because presenting consolidated statements when statements of individual companies have been presented previously is a change in accounting entity, which is considered an accounting change.

41.   (1176,T1,4)   (c)   APB 20 prescribes accounting for accounting changes. Only changes in accounting estimates should be accounted for in current and future periods (para 31). Changes in accounting principles are either accounted for by retroactive restatement or adjustment in the period of change for the cumulative effect of

the change depending on the nature of change (para 19 and 27). Changes in reporting entities require retroactive restatement (para 34). Correction of an error in previously issued statements is a prior period adjustment (para 36).

42. (1176,T1,5) **(b)** A change from FIFO to LIFO is a change in accounting principle, not a change in accounting estimate. It is not a special change requiring retroactive restatement of prior periods (para 27, APB 20). Rather the change from FIFO to LIFO requires the cumulative effect of the change, less tax effects, to be shown in the income statement (below income from ordinary operations) in the year of the change. Using this cumulative effect approach, there is no adjustment of prior periods' statements. See para 19 and 20 of APB 20. Note, however, that disclosure of the effect of retroactive application to prior periods is required on a pro forma basis, i.e., not in the financial statements themselves (para 21).

43. (1178,T1,4) **(b)** Accounting changes violate the consistency concept (para 98 of APB Statement 4). Consistency permits comparability through time for a single enterprise. Consistency is an important aspect of the qualitative objective of comparability. Answer (a) is incorrect because materiality, a basic feature of accounting, concerns information only significant enough to affect evaluations of investment decisions (para 128, APB Statement 4). Answer (c) is incorrect because conservatism, a modifying convention, permits understating net income and net assets rather than overstating them (para 171, APB Statement 4). Answer (d) is incorrect because objectivity, often called verifiability, is a qualitative objective of accounting (para 90 of APB Statement 4). Verifiable information is that which "would be substantially duplicated by independent measurers using the same measurement methods."

44. (1178,T1,5) **(d)** When changes in accounting principle are made, statements of prior years are restated only in four special cases (changing from LIFO, changing method of accounting for long-term contracts, changing to or from full cost method in extractive industries, and changes made by a company for its first issuance of statements). All other changes are given "cumulative effect" treatment. The rationale for generally not restating prior financial statements is to prevent a weakening of investor confidence in previously determined accounting numbers. Therefore, "cumulative effect" treatment is used even though

prior year statements will not be comparable with current year statements, which use the new principle. Materiality (answer a) is a constraint which states that information need not be disclosed if it is not significant enough to influence users (see SFAC 2). Conservatism (answer b) is a modifying convention which calls for understatement rather than overstatement of income and assets when uncertainty is present (APB Statement 4). Objectivity (answer c), referred to as reliability in SFAC 2, is a qualitative characteristic of accounting information. Objectivity consists of verifiability, representational faithfulness, and neutrality.

45. (1178,T1,20) **(a)** The requirement is the proper time period(s) to record a change in accounting estimate. Per para 31 of APB 20, a change in accounting estimate should be accounted for in the period of change and in future periods if the change affects both. If the change only affects the current period, only the current period will be affected. Answers (b) and (c) are incorrect because there should be no retroactive restatement or reporting of retroactive pro forma amounts. Thus answer (a) is superior to answer (d) because it reflects the possibility that changes in accounting estimates will affect more than the present period.

46. (578,P1,17) **(b)** The requirement is the cumulative effect on prior years of changing from accelerated depreciation to straight-line depreciation in 1977. The cumulative effect of an accounting change is computed on beginning retained earnings of the year in which the change was made per para 20 of APB 20. Since $700,000 of accelerated depreciation had been taken up to the beginning of 1976, and $450,000 of straight-line depreciation would have been taken (per the computations below), the cumulative effect before income taxes is $250,000. Since the effective tax rate is 50%, the cumulative effect net of taxes is $125,000.

	Accelerated	Straight-Line
1975	$300,000	$200,000
1976	400,000	250,000
	$700,000	$450,000

47. (578,T1,6) **(d)** Para 34 of APB 20 indicates that accounting changes which produce a different reporting entity, i.e., a new reporting entity, are changes in an accounting entity which should be presented by restating the financial statements of all prior periods presented. Examples are poolings, presenting consolidated statements in the place of previously issued individual statements of related companies, changing specific subsidiaries comprising a consolidated group, and changing companies which have previously been reported as a combined group. Answers (a) and (c) do not indicate a different reporting entity; they indicate changed conditions due to economic events, i.e., purchase of a subsidiary. Answer (b) is incorrect because the change in reporting is based upon a change in markets.

MAY 1981 ANSWERS

48.   (581,P1,13)   (d)   The requirement is to determine whether the cumulative effect of changing from LIFO to FIFO is a debit or credit as well as to indicate the appropriate location of the cumulative effect in Belmont's 1980 financial statements. The solutions approach is to prepare the journal entry to restate the inventory from $4,000,000 up to $4,800,000. Since the inventory account must be debited, the cumulative effect is a credit.

Inventory	$800,000	
?		$800,000

Generally, the cumulative effect of any accounting change should be shown in the income statement between extraordinary items and net income. However, one of the exceptions to this general rule per APB 20 is a change from LIFO to any other inventory valuation method. These exceptions require an adjustment to beginning retained earnings and retroactive restatement of prior years' financial statements.

49.   (581,Q2,24)   (b)   The requirement is the amount of depreciation expense to be recorded by Flex in 1980, when the estimates of useful life and salvage value are revised. Per para 31 of APB 20, changes in accounting estimates are reflected prospectively (no cumulative effect treatment or retroactive restatement). The first step is to calculate depreciation recorded in 1977 through 1979 before the estimates were revised. Depreciation for those first three years would be 12/15 (5/15 + 4/15 + 3/15) of cost minus salvage ($94,000 − $6,000), or $70,400. Therefore, the net book value at the beginning of 1980 is $23,600 ($94,000 − $70,400). Using the new estimated life of 4 years, 1980 becomes the last year of the machine's useful life. Therefore, the machine must be depreciated down from the net book value ($23,600) to the new estimated salvage of $8,800. Depreciation for 1980 is $14,800 ($23,600 − $8,800).

50.   (581,T1,23)   (c)   The requirement is an example of a special change in accounting principle that should be reported by restating the financial statements of prior periods. Accounting changes are generally handled by a cumulative-effect type adjustment in the income statement in the year of the change. In special circumstances, a change in accounting principle may be handled retroactively (APB 20, para 27). One of the changes that should be accorded this treatment is a change from the LIFO method of inventory pricing to any other method. Answers (a), (b) and (d) are incorrect because they are all cumulative effect type changes.

51.   (581,T1,28)   (c)   The requirement is an example of an item that should be disclosed in the Summary of Significant Accounting Policies. APB 22 recommends that when financial statements are issued, a statement identifying the accounting policies adopted and followed by the reporting entity should be presented as an integral part of the financial statements. The accounting policies are the specific accounting principles and the methods of applying the principles that have been adopted for preparing the financial statements. Answers (a), (b) and (d) are incorrect because these items are not accounting principles and methods for applying the adopted principles; these items would, however, be disclosed in footnotes in other parts of the financial statements.

52.   (581,T1,29)   (d)   The requirement is how a change in accounting estimate that is recognized by a change in accounting principle is reported. Per para 31 of APB 20, the effect of a change in accounting estimate should be handled prospectively; that is, no attempt should be made to go back and restate prior years financial statements. Changes in accounting principles are handled by a cumulative effect type adjustment in the income statement. APB 20, para 32 states that a change in accounting estimate that is recognized in whole or in part by a change in accounting principle should be reported as a change in an estimate because the cumulative effect attributable to the change in accounting principle usually cannot be separated from the current or future effects of the change in estimate.

MULTIPLE CHOICE ANSWERS

FINANCIAL STATEMENTS

53. b	57. c	61. c	65. a	69. a
54. b	58. b	62. b	66. d	70. a
55. a	59. a	63. c	67. d	
56. d	60. b	64. a	68. c	

EXPLANATION OF MULTIPLE CHOICE ANSWERS

53. (1180,T1,13)   (b)   Para 20 of APB 30 lists two main criteria for extraordinary items: unusual nature and infrequency of occurrence. Materiality is also a factor in determining if an item is given extraordinary treatment in the financial statements, but it is not a distinguishing feature of extraordinary items. Uncontrollability is not one of the criteria specified in APB 30 for determining whether an item is extraordinary.

54. (1180,Q1,2)   (b)   The requirement is the amount of income from continuing operations after income taxes for 1979 and 1978 to be reported on a revised comparative income statement. Helen discontinued a segment in 1979. APB Opinion 30 requires that "financial statements of <u>current</u> and <u>prior</u> periods . . . should disclose the results of operations of the disposed segment, less applicable taxes, as a separate component of income . . ." Therefore, the discontinued operations should be reported separately, net of taxes, for both 1979 and 1978. Income from continuing operations must be adjusted so the effect of the discontinued segment is taken out:

	1979	1978
Operating income, as reported	$1,600,000	$1,200,000
Add back loss from discontinued operations	640,000	500,000
Income from continuing operations, before taxes	2,240,000	1,700,000
Less 50% income taxes	(1,120,000)	(850,000)
Income from continuing operations	$1,120,000	$ 850.000

Under the caption "Discontinued Operations", Helen should report:

	1979	1978
Loss from operations	$(640,000)	$(500,000)
Gain on sale	900,000	—
	260,000	(500,000)
50% tax effect	(130,000)	250,000
Discontinued operations	$ 130,000	$(250,000)

55. (1180,Q1,3)   (a)   See explanation for (1180, Q1,2).

56. (580,T1,11)   (d)   Para 8 of APB 30 requires the gain or loss due to discontinued operations to be shown net of applicable taxes. The same opinion distinguishes discontinued operations from extraordinary items (answer (a)). Answers (b) and (c) are also incorrect; the gain or loss due to discontinued operations includes operating losses during the phase-out period (from the measurement date to the disposal date) but excludes operating losses prior to the measurement date.

57. (577,Q1,1)   (c)   Once a decision has been made to dispose of the segment (measurement date), the results of the discontinued operations and any gain or loss from disposal of the segment should be reported separately from continuing operations. These amounts should be disclosed after income from continuing operations but before extraordinary items and the cumulative effect of accounting changes. See para 8 of APB 30. If a loss is expected from the proposed sale or abandonment of the segment, the estimated loss should be recognized as of the measurement date. If a gain is expected on the discontinuance, it should not be recognized until the disposal date. The computation of gain or loss from the disposal of a segment should include the expected income (loss) from operations between the measurement date and the disposal date. However, if net income is expected from operations, it should only be recognized to the extent of other losses from the disposal. Any excess net income should be recognized when realized (para 15, APB 30.)

58. (1178,T1,8)   (b)   The requirement is which of the answers illustrates a prior period adjustment. Per SFAS 16, prior period adjustments consist of only 1) corrections of errors in the financial statements of prior periods, and 2) realization of income tax benefits of preacquisition operating loss carryforwards of purchased subsidiaries. Answer (a) is incorrect because changes in depreciable lives of fixed assets are changes in estimates and accounted for per APB 20, para 31. Answers (c) and (d) are incorrect because a change in the method of computing depreciation on fixed assets is a change in accounting principle accounted for per para 19 of APB 20.

59. (1178,T1,17)   (a)   The requirement is how to disclose an unusual event not meeting the criteria for an extraordinary item, i.e., one that is not infrequent even though unusual. Items unusual <u>or</u> infrequent are to be disclosed separately in the operating section of the income statement and also may be supplemented by a footnote (para 26 of APB 30).

Note that such items should not be shown net of income taxes. Answer (b) is incorrect because unusual events, even though not infrequent, should be shown as a separate item. Answers (c) and (d) are incorrect because unusual events should be shown in the operating section of the income statement.

60. (1178,T1,44) (b) The requirement is a type of transaction that does not require special footnote disclosures. As trade accounts receivable arise in the normal course of business, no special disclosures are necessary. In contrast, assets acquired by lease (SFAS 13, para 16), pension plans (APB 8, para 46), and employee stock option plans are more unusual (ARB 43, Chapter 13B, para 15). These specific type transactions require extended disclosure in financial statements.

61. (579,Q1,6) (c) The requirement is the total sales price of television sets sold by a consignee. The problem indicates $12,840 was remitted by the consignee after 20% commission and after the deduction of $600 in advertising and delivery expenses. Thus the total sales price is equal to the $12,840 remitted plus a 20% commission on the sales price plus $500 in advertising plus $100 in delivery. Accordingly, an equation can be set up and solved to determine sales as illustrated below.

$$\text{Sales} = \$12,840 + \$600 + .20 \text{ sales}$$
$$.8 \text{ Sales} = \$13,440$$
$$\text{Sales} = \$16,800$$

62. (579,Q1,13) (b) The requirement is the amount of extraordinary losses which should be reported by Rhur Corporation. Extraordinary losses are those that are both unusual and infrequent per para 20 of APB 30. Only the $75,000 hurricane damage is unusual and infrequent. The $50,000 equipment abandonment loss, the $120,000 strike loss and the $15,000 writeoff of accounts receivable are all prohibited by para 23 of APB 30.

63. (1177,T1,18) (c) APB 30 prescribes reporting for discontinued operations (and extraordinary items). Both the gain or loss from discontinued operations and the gain or loss on sale of the segment should be shown after income from continuing operations, but before any extraordinary items or cumulative effects of accounting changes (para 8, APB 30). Prior period adjustments are reported at the beginning of the retained earnings statement. Extraordinary items are reported after discontinued operations and before the cumulative effects of accounting changes (all of which follow income from continuing operations).

64. (578,T1,24) (a) Accounting for extraordinary items is specified in APB 30. Extraordinary items are those which are both unusual and infrequent. Unusual means possessing a high degree of abnormality and being clearly unrelated to the ordinary activities of an entity. Infrequency indicates no reasonable expectation of reoccurrence in the foreseeable future. Thus, very few items are extraordinary. Answer (c) is incorrect because adjustments of accrual for long-term contracts are usual rather than unusual. Answer (d) is incorrect because gains or losses from a fire are not infrequent because they can be reasonably expected to recur. Answer (b) is incorrect because gains or losses on disposal of a segment are to be accounted for separately in the income statement and specifically not as an extraordinary item per para 8 of APB 30. Answer (a), utilization of an operating loss carryforward, is specifically deemed to be an extraordinary item per para 45 of APB 11.

65. (580,T1,15) (a) Para 20 of APB 30 defines extraordinary items as events and transactions that are distinguished by their unusual nature and by their infrequency of occurrence. Answers (b) and (d) are incorrect because they refer to other components of income. Answer (c) is incorrect because extraordinary items are presented in a separate section of the income statement below income from continuing operations. Answer (a) is correct because extraordinary items must be shown net of applicable income taxes.

MAY 1981 ANSWERS

66. (581,Q2,39) (d) The requirement is Marvel's after-tax income from continuing operations for 1980. Per para 8 of APB 30, results of continuing operations should be reported separately from discontinued operations. Both the income earned by the discontinued segment during 1980 and the loss on disposal qualify as discontinued operations. The solutions approach is to visualize the lower segment of the income statement:

Income from cont. operations, before taxes
− Income tax expense - cont. oper.

Income from cont. oper.
+/− Discontinued oper., net of tax

Net Income

The next step is to fill in these income statement items. Net income ($600,000) is given. Discontinued operations include the $90,000 operating income and a $150,000 loss on disposal ($100,000 selling price less $250,000 book value). This nets out to a $60,000 loss on discontinued operations, which must be expressed net of the 40% tax effect; the after-tax loss is $36,000.

Finally, by working up from the bottom of the income statement, after-tax income from continuing operations can be computed as $636,000.

Net income + loss from discont. oper. = after-tax inc. from contin. oper.
$600,000 + $36,000 = $636,000

67. (581,Q2,40) (d) This question is an example of a problem which a CPA candidate can solve very simply, or waste time with a more complicated solution. The complicated solution would be to compute income tax expense on continuing operations and discontinued operations separately, then add these two amounts together. A much simplier solutions approach is

Total Pretax Income — Aggregate Income Tax Expense = Net Income
100%   —   40%
     = 60%

Therefore, if net income is $600,000, total pretax income must be $1,000,000, and aggregate income tax expense is $400,000.

68. (581,T1,13) (c) The requirement is an example of an item which should be reported as a prior period adjustment. The correction of an accounting error in prior years financial statements is one of the items that should be reported as a prior period adjustment. Answer (a) is an example of an accounting estimate, which means that at the time of the write-off, the best available information was used for the determination of the uncollectibility. Answer (b) is incorrect only in the context that the examination was performed by the Internal Revenue Service and not by the company. If the latter, payment of additional taxes would have been an error to be accounted for as a prior period adjustment. Answer (d) is incorrect because it assumes that the collection of insurance proceeds was not anticipated in the previous year.

69. (581,T1,21) (a) The requirement is the presentation on the income statement of a transaction that is material in amount, unusual in nature, but not infrequent in occurrence. To be classified as an extraordinary item net of applicable taxes on the income statement, a material item must be both unusual in nature and infrequent in occurrence (APB 30, para 20). If an item does not meet the criteria above, it is shown with the normal, recurring revenues, costs, and expenses from continuing operations before taxes. Answer (b) is incorrect because these items are not shown net of tax. Answer (c) is incorrect because the "infrequent occurrence" criterion is not met. Answer (d) is incorrect because the transaction does not represent the correction of an error on a prior years' financial statements.

70. (581,T1,22) (a) The requirement is the location in the income statement where extraordinary items are reported. Per para 11 of APB 30, items that are considered either a discontinuance of a segment of a business, (APB 30, para 13) an extraordinary item (APB 30, para 20), or a cumulative effect of an accounting change (APB 20, para 7) should be shown as separate items, net of tax, on the income statement, in the order listed.

MULTIPLE CHOICE ANSWERS

INTERIM FINANCIAL REPORTING

71. c	74. d	77. c	80. c	82. c
72. b	75. d	78. c	81. d	
73. b	76. b	79. b		

EXPLANATION OF MULTIPLE CHOICE ANSWERS

71. (1180,T1,16) (c) FASB Interpretation 18 requires computation of quarterly income tax provisions by applying the estimated annual effective tax rate to year-to-date ordinary income to obtain the year-to-date tax. From this amount is subtracted prior quarters' provisions applicable to ordinary income to obtain the current quarter's tax. In other words, the "change in estimate" approach is used. The income tax effects of capital gains are assigned to the quarter in which the related item occurred.

72. (1180,P1,9) (b) The requirement is Bailey's income tax provision (expense) in its interim income statement for the third quarter. FASB Interpretation 18 states that the tax provision for an interim period is the tax for the year to date (estimated annual rate times year-to-date income) less the total tax provisions reported for previous interim periods.

Year to date tax (45%)($170,000)	$76,500
Previously reported tax (40% x $130,000)	52,000
Third quarter tax provision	$24,500

73. (580,P1,8) (b) The requirement is to compute the income to be recognized in quarterly (interim) financial statements on a construction contract using the percentage-of-completion method. The solutions approach is to compute the income on the contract at the end of each quarter by (1) applying the estimated percentage of completion to the total estimated income to be recognized on the contract, and (2) subtracting the income recognized in preceding quarters to arrive at the income for the latest quarter. In the second and fourth quarters there was no work done on the contract and no change in the total estimated cost of completion. In quarter three the estimated costs of completion are revised upward. Since the cumulative income to date is less than income recognized in the first quarter, it is necessary to recognize a loss in the second quarter. The loss is handled as a change in accounting estimate rather than restating the first quarter.

Quarter 1:

   10% ($1,000,000 − $750,000) = $25,000 income
recognized

Quarter 2:

   -0-

Quarter 3:

   25% ($1,000,000 − $960,000) = $10,000 income
earned to date

   $10,000 income to date − $25,000 income recognized in previous periods = $(15,000) loss for
quarter

Quarter 4:

   -0-

74. (1179,P1,11) (d) The requirement is the amount of advertising expense to be included in a quarterly statement when the advertising relates only to revenue productivity of that particular quarter. Since the advertising relates only to the quarter ended 12/31/78, all the advertising should be expensed in that quarter. Per para 15a of APB 28, expenses other than product costs should be allocated among interim periods based on an estimate of the benefit received or activity associated with the period. Since the advertising will only benefit the quarter in which the magazines are sold, all of the expense should be allocated to the interim period ending 12/31/78.

75. (1176,T1,18) (d) The basic premise of APB 28 is that each interim period is an integral part of an annual period (para 9). Thus, interim reporting is not a special type reporting and must follow GAAP. The major issues concerning interim reporting are situations where activity is not evenly spread, i.e., is seasonal. The costs of seasonal activities require estimates, e.g., annual rate of federal income tax. As an integral part of an annual period, an interim period is not a basic accounting period.

76. (577,P1,13) (b) Costs should be charged to income in interim periods as they are incurred or allocated among periods based upon estimated benefits therefrom. See para 15a, APB 28. Since the property taxes and the machinery repairs benefit the entire calendar year, the $160,000 should be allocated evenly among the four quarters. Also see para 16a and 16c of APB 28.

77. (1178,Q1,2) (c) The requirement is the incentive commission expense for 1977. The 1977 commission expense does not include the expense for the last quarter of 1976 paid in 1977, but does include the fourth quarter 1977 expenses of $27,000 paid in 1978. Accordingly, the commission expense is $93,000.

First quarter	$28,000
Second quarter	15,000
Third quarter	23,000
Fourth quarter	27,000
1977 Commission exp.	$93,000

78. (579,P1,7) (c) The requirement is how to reflect a $600,000 inventory market decline occurring in the second quarter when none of the losses are recovered by the end of the year. Per para 14(c) of APB 28, inventory losses from market declines should not be deferred beyond the interim period when the decline in market value occurs. If market recoveries occur in subsequent interim periods, they should be reported as gains in the subsequent periods. If the market decline can reasonably be expected to be restored in the fiscal year, the temporary decline should not be recognized. Since in this question the decline was permanent, the entire $600,000 should all be recognized in the second quarter.

79.. (579,T1,3) (b) The requirement is the inventory valuation method acceptable for interim statements but not acceptable for annual statements. Per para 14a of APB 28, estimated gross profit rates may be used to estimate interim inventory. If this procedure is followed, the method should be disclosed as well as any significant subsequent adjustments. Answer (a), weighted average, answer (c), retail method, and answer (d), specific identification, are all generally accepted inventory valuation methods.

80. (1177,T1,13) (c) The requirement is specification of a major problem in measuring income in interim periods. The most serious problem specified is dealing with costs that are expensed in one interim period but may provide benefits to other interim periods. See para 4, 15, and 16 of APB 28. Answer (a) is incorrect because cost of sales consists of product expenses which are relatively easy to define. Once the sale has been recorded, the cost of sales is determinable. Answer (b) is incorrect because depreciation in an interim period can be based upon a proportionate amount of the annual rate, i.e., the estimates have been made on an annual basis and only have to be broken down as to the interim periods. Answer (d) is incorrect because revenue from percentage of completion estimates of long-term construction contracts is as accurate for interim periods as it is for annual periods.

MAY 1981 ANSWERS

81. (581,P1,6) (d) The requirement is the amount of expense to reflect in Horner's quarterly income statement for the second quarter. According to para 15a of APB 28, costs should be charged to income in interim periods as they are incurred or allocated among the periods based upon estimated benefits received. Since both the property taxes and executive bonus benefit the entire calendar year, the $400,000 total expense should be allocated evenly among the four quarters.

82. (581,T1,32) (c) The requirement is the proper treatment in interim financial reporting of an inventory loss from a temporary market decline in the first quarter which can reasonably be expected to be restored in the fourth quarter. Per APB 28, para 14, companies that prepare interim financial statements should generally use the same inventory pricing methods (FIFO, LIFO, average, etc.) and make provisions for write-downs to market at interim dates on the same basis as used at annual inventory dates. Inventory losses from market declines should not be deferred beyond the interim period in which the decline occurs. Subsequent recoveries from increases in market prices in the same fiscal year on the same inventory should be recognized as gains in the interim period of the market increase. However, APB 28, para 14(c) allows for not recognizing a loss in interim periods from a decline in market prices of inventory if these declines are temporary and can reasonably be expected to be restored in the fiscal year.

MULTIPLE CHOICE ANSWERS

SEGMENT REPORTING

83. c   85. d   86. a   87. a   88. a
84. c

EXPLANATION OF MULTIPLE CHOICE ANSWERS

83. (1180,T1,28)   (c)   SFAS 14 requires that selected data for a segment be reported separately if one of three criteria are met. One of these criteria is met when the revenues of the segment exceed 10% of the combined revenues of all industry segments.

84. (580,Q1,15)   (c)   The requirement is the operating profit for Product B, which would be equal to its sales less traceable and allocable costs. The allocable costs are to be allocated on the ratio of a segment's income before allocable costs to total income before allocable costs as shown below:

	Product A	Product B	Product C
Traceable costs	$225,000	$240,000	$135,000
Income	$175,000	$ 60,000	$ 65,000
Total income	÷300,000	÷300,000	÷300,000
Allocation percentage	=58%	=20%	=22%
Total allocable costs	x150,000	x150,000	x150,000
Assignment of allocable costs to products	$ 87,000	$ 30,000	$ 33,000

Thus, operating profit for Product B would be $300,000, less $240,000 and $30,000, or $30,000.

85. (580,T1,38)   (d)   SFAS 14, para 10d, describes which elements are to be included in and excluded from the operating profit and loss of a segment. Answers (a), (b), and (c) are specifically excluded. Costs incurred by the enterprise that are not directly traceable to an industry segment (common costs) are to be allocated on a reasonable basis to those segments for whose benefit the expenses were incurred.

86. (1179,T1,25) (a)   For each reportable segment of a business enterprise, required profitability disclosure is the operating profit or loss. Operating profit or loss is the segment's revenue less traceable costs and allocated common costs. Operating expenses which are not directly traceable to an industry segment will be allocated on a reasonable basis among all industry segments, per para 10d of SFAS 14. Answer (b) is incorrect because allocated common costs are a de-

duction in determining segment operating profit or loss. Answer (c) is incorrect because traceable costs are deducted in determining segment operating profit or loss. Answer (d) is incorrect because operating expenses and allocated common costs must be deducted from segment revenue to compute segment operating profit or loss.

MAY 1981 ANSWERS

87.   (581,P1,4)   (a)   The requirement is the amount reported as operating profit for Segment No. 3 in 1980. The solutions approach is to first visualize Segment 3's income statement. Then write in the headings and information given. The common costs and operating profit are filled in after they are determined.

Sales	$1,080,000	(60%)($1,800,000)
Traceable Costs	(600,000)	(given)
Common Costs	(280,000)	(80%)($ 350,000)
Operating Profit	$ 200,000	

Common costs are allocated based on the ratio of a segment's income before common costs to the company's total income before common costs. Segment 3 has income before common costs of $480,000 ($1,080,000 − $600,000). The company's total income before common costs is $600,000 ($1,800,000 − $1,200,000). Therefore, Segment No. 3's share of the common costs is 80% ($480,000 ÷ $600,000).

88. (581,T1,39)   (a)   The requirement is to identify an item that should be included in the calculation of the operating profit or loss of a segment. Per para 10(d) of SFAS 14, the operating profit or loss of an industry segment is its revenue minus all operating expenses. As used therein, operating expenses include those expenses that relate to both sales to unaffiliated customers and revenue from intersegment sales. Costs that are not traceable to segments shall be allocated on a reasonable basis among those industry segments for whose benefit the expenses were incurred. The items listed in answers (b) and (c) are explicitly excluded from the calculation of segmental operating profit and loss and answer (d) is implicitly excluded because a loss from discontinued operations relates to a particular segment.

ANSWER OUTLINE: BASIC CONCEPTS

Problem 1   Revenue Recognition

1. Part a requires justification for revenue recognition at the point of sale, situations where revenue is recognized as it is produced, and other revenue recognition points. Part b requires delineation of revenue, expense, and other income determination items for three concepts of income: net income to common stockholders, net income to investors, and net income to all participants in the business enterprise.

2. You should organize your solution in the outline format of the requirements. Each of the three requirements under both a and b should contain two short paragraphs of discussion.

3. Revenue is recognized at the point of sale out of convention and also is the "best" of the alternative recognition points. If output is sold as it is produced, e.g., service industries, newspapers, etc., revenue is recognized as production takes place. Alternatives to point of sale are cash collection, e.g., the installment method of accounting for receivables, and production, e.g, mining of valuable minerals or meat packing.

4. Net income to common stockholders is the residual after payment of all other production costs, e.g., labor, interest, raw materials, etc. Net income to investors would be the residual income plus interest paid on long-term debt. The value added concept of income is the value of the output less the value of all inputs.

UNOFFICIAL ANSWER: BASIC CONCEPTS

Problem 1   Revenue Recognition

a. 1. Most merchandising concerns deal in finished products and would recognize revenue at the point of sale. This is often identified as the moment when title legally passes from seller to purchaser. At the point of sale there is an arm's-length transaction to objectively measure the amount of revenue to be recognized. With accounting theory based heavily on objective measurement, it is logical that point-of-sale transaction revenue recognition would be used by many firms, especially merchandising concerns.

Other advantages of point-of-sale timing for revenue recognition include the following:

It is a discernible event (as contrasted to the accretion concept).

The seller has completed his part of the bargain — that is, the revenue has been earned with the passage of title when the goods are delivered.

Realization has occurred in the sense that cash or near-cash assets have been received ——there is some merit in holding that it is not earned revenue until cash or near-cash assets have been received.

The seller's costs have been incurred with the result that net income can be measured.

2. For service-type firms, accounting recognition of revenue approximates the earning process. The recognition of revenue for accounting purposes takes place (is recorded) during the period the services are rendered. Although it is theoretically possible to continuously accrue revenue as the services are rendered, for practical reasons revenue is usually accrued periodically with emphasis on the appropriate period of recognition. Theoretically, the revenue is properly recognized in the accounting period in which the revenue-generating activity takes place.

In some non-service firms, revenue can be recognized as the productive activity takes place instead of at a later period (as at point of sale). The most common situation where revenue is recognized as production takes place has been through the application of percentage-of-completion accounting to long-term construction contracts. Under this procedure revenue is approximated, based on degree of contract performance to date, and recorded as earned in the period in which the productive activity takes place.

A similar situation is present where, applying the accretion concept, the recognition of revenue takes place when increased values arise from natural growth or an aging process. In an economic sense, increases in the value of inventory give rise to revenue.

Revenue recognition by the accretion concept is not the result of recorded transactions, but is accomplished by the process of making comparative inventory valuations. Examples of applying the accretion concept would include the aging of certain liquors and wines, growing timber, and raising livestock.

3. Revenue is sometimes recognized at completion of the production activity, or after the point of sale. The recognition of revenue at completion of production is justified only if certain conditions are present. The necessary conditions are that there must be a relatively stable market for the product, marketing costs must be nominal, and the units must be homogeneous. The three necessary conditions are not often present except in the case of certain precious metals and agricultural products. In these situations it has been considered appropriate to recognize revenue at the completion of production.

In rare situations it may be necessary to postpone the recognition of revenue until after the point of sale. The circumstances would have to be unusual to postpone revenue recognition beyond the point of sale because of the theoretical desirability to recognize revenue as early in the earning process as possible. A situation where it would be justified to postpone revenue recognition until a time after the point of sale would be where there is substantial doubt as to the ultimate collectibility of the receivable.

b. 1. Net income to the residual equity holders would be determined by including all revenues, expenses, gains, and losses in the computation of net income. The net income would include all extraordinary gains and losses, and gains and

losses from discontinued operations of a segment of a business, but would exclude any prior period adjustments. The net income determined in accordance with these limitations (as discussed in Accounting Principles Board Opinion, Numbers 9 and 30) must be reduced by any current period claim the preferred equity holders have on net income.

The resulting amount is the amount of net income available to the residual equity holders. Accordingly, the amount of income accruing to the residual equity holders would be the reported net income of the corporation reduced by the amount of prior claim of any preferential class(es) of stock.

2. The net income to investors would be the amount of net income normally reported on the income statement plus the interest (net of income tax effect) on long-term debt. Thus, net income to investors includes all revenues, expenses, gains, losses, extraordinary items, and gains and losses from discontinued operations of a segment of a business, but excludes financing charges for long-term debt.

3. The value-added concept of income is the broadest of the operational-approach concepts to income determination. The value-added concept is a special net-income concept closely akin to the gross-national-product (GNP) determination.

The value added is the value of the output of the firm less the value of supplies, goods, fuels, electrical energy, and similar items (often called transfers in GNP determination) acquired from other firms and individuals. Thus, all employees, governments, and owners, and many creditors are recipients of the income when following this concept.

The value-added concept requires the recognition of income during production because all values are expressed in terms of the product selling price.

ANSWER OUTLINE: BASIC CONCEPTS

Problem 2   Accounting Entity

a1. Accounting entity is a specific firm or enterprise
       Apart from owners
       And other separate legal enterprises
     Can also be a unit controlling resources
       Individual
       Profit-seeking company
       Not-for-profit enterprise
     Alternatively in terms of an economic interest group
       E.g., owners
       Approach used for financial reports

a2. Accounting entity defines boundaries of accounting
       information system
       Determines data to be included in system
       E.g., transaction between entity and third parties
     All other accounting concepts are in reference to the
       entity
       It is the most basic premise of the accounting model

b1. Legal units are the most common accounting entities
       Corporations, partnerships, and proprietorships

b2. Product lines are also entities

b3. A group of legal entities may be an accounting entity
       E.g., consolidated statements
       Combination of product-line segments

b4. Accounting entities can be in terms of owners
       E.g., personal financial statements
       Estate reporting

b5. Accounting entity could embrace an industry
       E.g., industry financial data

b6. USA economy is entity for GNP data

UNOFFICIAL ANSWER: BASIC CONCEPTS

Problem 2   Accounting Entity

a.   1.   The conventional or traditional approach
           has been to define the accounting entity
           in terms of a specific firm or enterprise
           unit that is separate and apart from the
           owner or owners and from other enter-
           prises having separate legal and account-
           ing frames of reference. For example,
           partnerships and sole proprietorships
           were accounted for separately from the
           owners although such a distinction might
           not exist legally. Thus it was recognized
           that the transactions of the enterprise
           should be accounted for and reported
           upon separately from those of the owners.

           An extension of this approach is to
           define the accounting entity in terms of
           an economic unit that controls resources,
makes and carries out commitments and
conducts economic activity. In the
broadest sense an accounting entity could
embrace any object, event or attribute of
an object or event for which there is an
input-output relationship. Such an accounting entity may be an individual, a
profit-seeking or not-for-profit enterprise
or any subdivision or attribute thereof
for which a system of accounts is maintained. Thus this approach is oriented
toward the unit for which financial reports are prepared.

An alternative approach is to define
the accounting entity in terms of an
area of economic interest to a particular individual, group or institution. The
boundaries of such an economic entity
would be identified by determining (1)
the interested individual, group or
institution and (2) the nature of that
individual's, group's or institution's
interest. Thus this approach is oriented
to the users of financial reports.

2.   The accounting entity concept defines
      the area of interest and thus narrows
      the range and establishes the boundaries
      of the possible objects, activities or
      attributes of objects or activities that
      may be selected for inclusion in account-
      ing records and reports. Further, postu-
      lates as to the nature of the entity
      also may aid in determining (1) what
      information to include in reports of
      the entity and (2) how to best present
      information of the entity so that rela-
      vant features are disclosed and irrelevant
      features do not cloud the presentation.

      The applicability of all the other
      generally accepted concepts (or princi-
      ples or postulates) of accounting (e.g.,
      continuity, money measurement and
      time periods) depends upon the estab-
      lished boundaries and nature of the
      accounting entity. The other account-
      ing concepts lack significance without
      reference to an entity. The entity
      must be defined before the balance of
      the accounting model can be applied
      and the accounting can begin. Thus
      the accounting entity concept is so
      fundamental that it pervades all of
      accounting.

b.   1.   Yes, units created by or under law

would include corporations, partnerships, and occasionally sole proprietorships. Thus legal units probably are the most common types of accounting entities.

2. Yes, a product line or other segment of an enterprise, such as a division, department, profit center, branch or cost center, could be an accounting entity. The stimuli for financial reporting by segment include investors, the Securities and Exchange Commission, financial executives and the accounting profession.

3. Yes, most large corporations issue consolidated financial reports for two or more legal entities that constitute a controlled economic entity. Accounting for investments in subsidiary companies by the equity method also is an example of an accounting unit that extends beyond the legal entity. The financial reports for a business enterprise that includes two or more product-line segments would also be a form of a consolidated report that most commonly would be considered to be the report of a single legal entity.

4. Yes, although the accounting entity often is defined in terms of a business enterprise that is separate and distinct from other activities of the owner or owners, it also is possible for an accounting entity to embrace all of the activities of an owner or a group of owners. Examples include financial statements for an individual (personal financial statements) and the financial report of a person's estate.

5. Yes, the accounting entity could embrace an industry. Examples include financial data compiled for an industry by a trade association (industry averages) or by the federal government. Probably the best examples of an industry being the accounting entity are in the accounting systems prescribed by the Federal Power Commission and the Federal Communications Commission which defines the original cost of an asset in terms of the cost to the person first devoting it to public service.

6. Yes, the accounting entity concept can embrace the economy of the United States. An example is the national in-

come accounts compiled by the U. S. Department of Commerce. Another area where the entity concept is applicable is in the yet to be developed area of socio-economic accounting.

ANSWER OUTLINE: BASIC CONCEPTS

Problem 3   Fictitious Statements About GAAP

Statement I

   "True" earnings not determinable due to estimates
   GAAP is to fairly present
   All statements related to income statement
   Revenues are more than cash inflow
   Revenues recognized when realized
   Sales revenues recognized when realized
      Production revenues recognized when earned
   Production basis justifiable if reasonably estimable
      and realization is reasonably assured
   Some expenses cannot be matched with revenues
   Period vs. product (manufacturing) expenses

Statement II

   "Fairly" rather than "accurately"
   Various valuation methods are in balance sheet
   Inventories are at lower of cost or market
   Consistency is important
   A separate "reserve" section is unacceptable
   Reserve not proper terminology, instead
      Accumulated depreciation
      Warranty liability
      Retained earnings appropriations

Statement III

   Statement analysis involves future estimates
   Involves application of analytic tools for decision making
   Current ratio is not monetary assets ÷ monetary liabilities
   Current ratio must be in context of type of company
   High ratio does not automatically mean better
      E.g., high ratio may indicate idle assets
   Current ratio is not dynamic, i.e., measured at a point in time

UNOFFICIAL ANSWER: BASIC CONCEPTS

Problem 3   Fictitious Statements About GAAP

Statement I

The function of financial accounting is to provide quantitative financial information intended to help make economic decisions about a business enterprise. Measurement of net earnings is certainly one aspect of the above generalization. Nonetheless, it is not possible to measure true net earnings because of the flexibility permitted by generally accepted accounting principles and because of the estimates and judgment factors inherent in the financial accounting process. The intent behind generally accepted accounting principles is to fairly present net earnings. Other financial statements, the statement of financial position and the statement of changes in financial position, are definitely related to the earnings statement of a company. Although each financial statement discloses a different aspect of the company, all of these financial statements are based on the same underlying data. These financial statements, therefore, inherently articulate with each other.

Revenues are gross increases in assets or gross decreases in liabilities resulting from an enterprise's earnings-directed activities that can change owners' equity. In other words, revenues are more than just an inflow of cash; not all cash inflows are revenues, for example, borrowing money or issuing capital stock. It is incorrect to state that revenues are realized when they are recognized. These concepts should be distinguished. Revenues are theoretically earned throughout the entire production and distribution process, although the recognition or recording is generally based on more practical considerations. Revenues are realized when evidenced by other new liquid assets. Revenue recognition refers to recording revenues in the accounts.

The general procedure followed in the sales basis of revenue recognition clearly recognizes revenues when they are realized. The production basis of revenue recognition is a variation from the sales basis because the former tends to recognize revenues when they are earned, as opposed to realized. The production basis, for example, percentage-of-completion contracts, is justifiable if total profit can be reasonably estimated and ultimate realization is reasonably assured.

To the extent possible, expenses should be matched with revenues; nevertheless, such cause and effect association is not always possible. Some expenses are recognized by systematic and rational allocation to periods. Other expenses are recognized because their incurrence provides no discernible future benefits.

Product expenses (manufacturing expenses), whether variable or fixed, should be assigned to the product. Period expenses, whether variable or fixed, are generally those that are far removed from production, for example, marketing, general, and administrative expenses, and are, therefore, assigned to the period.

Statement II

Measurement of financial position is one aspect of the function of financial accounting; nonetheless, financial accounting strives for fair presentation rather than "accurate" presentation. The term "accurate" is invalid because of the flexibility permitted by generally accepted accounting principles and because of the estimates and judgment factors inherent in the accounting process.

A statement of financial position is actually a mixture of various valuations for assets and liabilities. For example, monetary assets, such as cash and accounts receivable, are generally reflected at net realizable value; fixed assets are generally reflected at historical cost; long-term liabilities are generally reflected at present value at inception; and leases are also generally reflected at present value. Deferred taxes are reflected at a nondiscounted amount.

Inventories should be reflected at lower-of-cost-or-market valuation. FIFO, LIFO, and average cost are not methods of inventory valuation. They are assumptions regarding the flow of units or costs and are all based on historical costs. Consistency is a vital part of the financial accounting process; but consistency does not preclude an accounting change if such a change is warranted. Therefore there will be circumstances in which the need for consistency will be superseded by other needs such as preferred methods of accounting or economic reality.

A statement of financial position should not have a separate section for reserves. The three types of reserves cited (depreciation, product warranty, and retained earnings) should be classified among the assets, liabilities, and stockholders' equity sections as explained below. The use of the term "reserve" in these cases is not proper. The generally accepted meaning of reserve indicates that an amount of retained earnings has been appropriated for a specific purpose.

A depreciation reserve should be called "allowance for depreciation" or "accumulated depreciation." It is established by charging an expense and should be classified as a contra-asset account.

A reserve for product warranty is established by charging an expense and should be classified as a liability. It should be considered current or noncurrent depending on the amounts estimated to be liquidated each future period.

A retained earnings reserve is established by charging retained earnings. It does not affect net earnings. It is merely an appropriation of retained earnings and should be so reflected on a statement of financial position as part of stockholders' equity.

Statement III

Financial statement analysis is the judgmental process which aims to evaluate the current and past financial positions and results of operations of a company with the primary objective of determining the best possible estimates and predictions about future conditions and performance. The process of financial statement analysis consists of applying analytical tools and techniques to financial statements in order to derive from them measurements and relationships that are significant and useful for decision making. This definition stresses two aspects. First, financial statement analysis is intended to aid decision making which is usually future oriented. The past is used as a guide to the future. Second, while ratios are an important tool for the analyst, they are not the only such tool. Other tools and techniques of financial statement analysis include comparative financial statements showing year-to-year amount changes, index number trend series showing year-to-year percentage changes, and common-size financial statements showing percentage relationships within a given statement. Other tools also include cash forecasts, analysis of changes in financial position, analysis of variation in gross margin, and analysis of cost-volume-earnings (profit) relationships.

The use of financial ratios involves more than merely comparing the results to a predetermined standard. Other sources of comparison are industry averages and trends within the company.

The current ratio cannot be computed as monetary assets divided by monetary liabilities because "monetary" is not synonymous with "current." A monetary asset or liability is an account that will be received or paid in a predetermined fixed amount of dollars regardless of the effect of inflation or deflation. Examples of monetary assets and liabilities include cash, accounts receivable (current and noncurrent) in stated amounts of cash, and accounts payable and other debt (current and noncurrent) in stated amounts of cash. A nonmonetary asset or liability is an account that is not stated in a fixed amount of dollars, and can be adjusted subsequent to its creation to reflect the effects of inflation or deflation. An example of a nonmonetary asset is inventory. In the event that prices increase, the sales price of that inventory can be adjusted accordingly. The elements of the current ratio, therefore, contain both monetary and nonmonetary components and cannot be defined as monetary assets divided by monetary liabilities. A current ratio of 2:1 is considered good for many companies, but such an evaluation is a function of the type of company and industry. Therefore, a blanket standard is misleading. It is better to view standard performance in terms of ranges rather than single amounts. In other words, a predetermined standard range may be from 1.8:1 and 2.2:1. A company's ratio that falls outside this range, either below or above, should be carefully analyzed. In other words, a higher ratio is not necessarily advantageous. For example, too high a current ratio may indicate excessive idle funds which should be put to better use.

The current ratio is not dynamic and does not measure fund flows. It is a static concept which com-

pares certain elements at a point in time. It measures the ability of present current assets to cover existing liabilities. It is probably more a test of liquidation than of a going concern because current assets and current liabilities are, in reality, revolving, that is, being continuously replaced with new current assets and new current liabilities. This replacement is better evaluated by future activity, such as sales, earnings, or working-capital flow, than by a static measure.

ANSWER OUTLINE: BASIC CONCEPTS

Problem 4   Accrual vs. Cash Basis

a.   Accrual accounting recognizes asset and liability effects of transactions in periods to which they relate
            To match revenues and expenses
            I.E., revenue and expense are not only recognized when received or paid
            Revenues are recognized and recorded when earned
            Expenses are recognized and recorded as follows:
                Associating cause and effect
                    Direct association of expense with specific revenue
                Systematic and rational allocation
                    Allocation among periods benefited
                Immediate recognition
                    No future benefit from costs incurred this period
                    No future benefit from costs incurred in prior period
                    Allocation serves no useful purpose
        Accrual
            Transaction affecting income but is not reflected in cash
                Accrued revenue is revenue earned, but not collected
                    E.G., Interest revenue earned but not collected
                Accrued expense is expense incurred but not paid
                    E.G., salaries incurred but not paid by year-end
        Deferral
            Transaction reflected in cash, but not in income
                Deferred revenue is revenue collected, but not yet earned
                    E.G., rent collected in advance for future periods
                Deferred expense is expense paid, but not yet incurred
                    E.G., insurance premiums paid for future periods

b.   Cash basis accounting reflects effects on assets and liabilities only when cash is paid or collected
Accrual accounting reflects these effects in periods to which they relate
Thus, cash basis does not properly match revenue and expense and is not per GAAP

UNOFFICIAL ANSWER: BASIC CONCEPTS

Problem 4   Accrual vs. Cash Basis

a.   Accrual accounting recognizes and reports the effects of transactions and other events on the assets and liabilities of a business enterprise in the time periods to which they relate rather than only when cash is received or paid. Accrual accounting attempts to match revenues and the expenses associated with those revenues in order to determine net income for an accounting period. Revenues are recognized and recorded as earned. Expenses are recognized and recorded as follows:

- Associating Cause and Effect. Some expenses are recognized and recorded on a presumed direct association with specific revenue.

- Systematic and Rational Allocation. In the absence of a direct association with specific revenue, some expenses are recognized and recorded by attempting to allocate expenses in a systematic and rational manner among the periods in which benefits are provided.

- Immediate Recognition. Some costs are associated with the current accounting period as expenses because (1) costs incurred during the period provide no discernible future benefits, (2) costs recorded as assets in prior periods no longer provide discernible benefits, or (3) allocating costs either on the basis of association with revenues or among several accounting periods is considered to serve no useful purpose.

An accrual represents a transaction that affects the determination of income for the period but has not yet been reflected in the cash accounts of that period. Accrued revenue is revenue earned but not yet collected in cash. An example of accrued revenue is accrued interest revenue earned on bonds from the last interest payment date to the end of the accounting period. An accrued expense is an expense incurred but not yet paid

in cash. An example of an accrued expense is salaries incurred for the last week of the accounting period that are not payable until the subsequent accounting period.

A deferral represents a transaction that has been reflected in the cash accounts of the period but has not yet affected the determination of income for that period. Deferred (prepaid) revenue is revenue collected or collectible in cash but not yet earned. An example of deferred (prepaid) revenue is rent collected in advance by a lessor in the last month of the accounting period, which represents the rent for the first month of the subsequent accounting period. A deferred (prepaid) expense is an expense paid or payable in cash but not yet incurred. An example of a deferred (prepaid) expense is an insurance premium paid in advance in the current accounting period, which represents insurance coverage for the subsequent accounting period.

b.   In cash accounting, the effects of transactions and other events on the assets and liabilities of a business enterprise are recognized and reported only when cash is received or paid; while in accrual accounting, these effects are recognized and reported in the time periods to which they relate. Because cash accounting does not attempt to match revenues and the expenses associated with those revenues, cash accounting is not in conformity with generally accepted accounting principles.

ANSWER OUTLINE: BASIC CONCEPTS

Problem 5   Bad Debts

a1.   Direct write-off method requires identification of specific uncollectible balances before expense recognition, then

Bad debt expense	XXX	
Accounts receivable		XXX

Allowance method requires estimate of bad debt expense prior to identification of specific bad debts, then

Record estimated bad debts at year-end as expense

Bad debt expense	XXX	
Allowance for doubtful accounts		XXX

When specific bad debts are identified, then

Allowance for doubtful
  accounts   XXX
      Accounts receivable   XXX

No expense recognized when accounts are
  written off

Two methods of estimating bad debts expense
  As a percentage of accounts receivable at
    year-end
  As a percentage of sales of the period

a2. Allowance method is preferable

Credit sale costs are matched with revenue
Gives proper carrying value of accounts
  receivable

Direct write-off method is inferior and generally
  not per GAAP

May be written off in a period subsequent to
  sale
I.E., does not comply with matching concept
Proper carrying value for accounts receivable
  not achieved

UNOFFICIAL ANSWER: BASIC CONCEPTS

Problem 5   Bad Debts

1. There are basically two methods of recogniz-
    ing bad debt expense: (1) direct write-off and
    (2) allowance.

    The direct write-off method requires the iden-
    tification of specific balances that are deemed
    to be uncollectible before any bad debt expense
    is recognized. At the time that a specific account
    is deemed uncollectible, the account is removed
    from accounts receivable and a corresponding
    amount of bad debt expense is recognized.
    The allowance method requires an estimate of
    bad debt expense for a period of time by refer-
    ence to the composition of the accounts receiv-
    able balance at a specific point in time (aging)
    or to the overall experience with credit sales
    over a period of time. Thus, total bad debt
    expense expected to arise as a result of opera-
    tions for a specific period is estimated, the valua-
    tion account (allowance for doubtful accounts)

is appropriately adjusted, and a corresponding
amount of bad debt expense is recognized. As
specific accounts are identified as uncollectible,
the account is written off; that is, it is removed
from accounts receivable and a corresponding
amount is removed from the valuation account
(allowance for doubtful accounts). Net accounts
receivable do not change, and there is no charge
to bad debt expense when specific accounts are
identified as uncollectible and written off using
the allowance method.

2. The allowance method is preferable because it
    matches the cost of making a credit sale with the
    revenues generated by the sale in the same period
    and achieves a proper carrying value for accounts
    receivable at the end of a period. Since the direct
    write-off method does not recognize the bad
    debt expense until a specific amount is deemed
    uncollectible, which may be in a subsequent
    period, it does not comply with the matching
    concept and does not achieve a proper carrying
    value for accounts receivable at the end of a
    period.

SOLUTION GUIDE: ERROR CORRECTION

Problem 6   Schedule of Error Effects

1. The problem presents a series of factual situations
    and requires the correcting or adjusting entry for
    each situation.

2. Thus the solutions approach is to consider each
    of the ten factual situations as independent prob-
    lems.

2.1 A cash cutoff error has occurred inasmuch as
     cash was received before year-end, but not
     credited to receivables until the following period.
     The correcting entry is to debit cash and to
     credit accounts receivable for $1,500.

2.2 At the end of the year the allowance for bad
     debts should be $5,500 (1% of $400,000 plus
     5% of $30,000). Since the allowance account
     has a $9,000 <u>debit</u> balance, a credit to the
     allowance account and a debit in the income
     statement of $14,500 is required.

2.3 Beginning inventory was understated by $7,000. The correcting entry is to debit current cost of sales and credit beginning retained earnings for $7,000. The ending inventory was overstated by $3,000 which requires a debit to current cost of sales and a credit to inventory for $3,000.

2.4 The costs of the delivery expense, installation costs, and related rearrangement costs for new equipment is a capital expenditure. Thus the $14,500 should be debited to machinery and credited to repairs and maintenance in the income statement. In turn, the $14,500 should be amortized over the 10-year life, requiring a $1,450 debit to the income statement and a $1,450 credit to accumulated depreciation.

2.5 Of the $110,000 expensed in 1975, only the first month's rent ($12,000) and amortization of the leasehold improvements (10% of $80,000) should have been expensed. Thus the correcting entry is to capitalize the incorrectly expensed expenditures.

Rent deposit	$ 6,000	
Prepaid rent	12,000	
Leasehold improve-ments	80,000	
Retained earnings		$98,000

The entry to record leasehold amortization in 1975 is:

Retained earnings	$ 8,000	
Leasehold im-provement		$ 8,000

The entry to record the 1976 amortization is:

Amortization exp.	$ 8,000	
Leasehold im-provement		$ 8,000

2.6 As indicated, the $6,000 of bond discount was expensed in 1975 rather than being capitalized and amortized over the ten-year life of the bonds. Thus the correcting entry to capitalize the discount is:

Bond discount	$ 6,000	
Retained earnings		$ 6,000

The entry to record the amortization is:

Bond discount amort. (1976)	$ 600	
Retained earnings (1975)	600	
Bond discount		$ 1,200

2.7 The gain on disposal of treasury stock was incorrectly credited to income rather than to paid-in capital. Also the $2,000 proceeds from sale of existing buildings should have been considered as a reduction in the cost of land, as the property was purchased as a building site.

The solutions approach to a complicated error situation is to determine what entry was made and what entry should have been made. Then reverse the entry that was made and make the correct entry. The entries made were:

Land	$40,000	
Treasury stock		$35,000
Gain on sale of treasury stock		5,000

Cash	$ 2,000	
Misc. or scrap income		$ 2,000

The entries that should have been made were:

Land	$40,000	
Treasury stock		$35,000
Paid-in capital		5,000

Cash	$ 2,000	
Land		$ 2,000

Thus the net correcting entries are to debit the income statement and credit land for $2,000, as well as to debit the gain on sale of treasury stock and credit paid-in capital for $5,000.

2.8 The $75,000 incurred in 1976 for 1977 sales catalogues should be deferred and expensed in 1977. Thus the correcting entry is to credit the 1976 income statement and debit prepaid advertising for $75,000.

2.9 Per APB 8, the maximum amount of past service costs that can be expensed in any year is 10%. Normal costs are to be expensed each year. Thus past costs of $90,000 (10% of $900,000) and normal costs of $70,000 may be expensed in 1976. Based on the entry expensing $970,000, the correcting entry is:

Deferred pension costs	$810,000	
Income statement		$810,000

2.10 Since it is not probable that a reasonably estimable loss will occur (SFAS 5), no loss or related liability should be recorded. Thus the entry to record the loss contingency should be reversed.

UNOFFICIAL ANSWER: ERROR CORRECTION

Problem 6   Schedule of Error Effects

No.	Explanation	Income Statement Dr. (Cr.)	Balance Sheet December 31. 1976 Dr. (Cr.)	Account
1.	Cash and accounts receivable misstated		$ 1,500	Cash
			(1,500)	Accounts receivable
2.	Adjustment of allowance for uncollectibles:			
	Adjust balance at December 31, 1976	$ 14,500	(14,500)	Allowance for uncollectible accounts
3.	Merchandise inventory—misstated:			
	December 31, 1975	7,000	(7,000)	Retained earnings
	December 31, 1976	3,000	(3,000)	Merchandise inventory
4.	Machinery cost—incorrect:			
	Adjustment of cost	(14,500)	14,500	Machinery
	Adjustment of depreciation	1,450	(1,450)	Accumulated depreciation
5.	1975 rent expense—incorrect:			
	Adjustment for rent deposit		6,000	Rent deposit
			(6,000)	Retained earnings
	Prepaid rent (last month)		12,000	Prepaid rent
			(12,000)	Retained earnings
	Record leasehold improvement		80,000	Leasehold improvements
			(80,000)	Retained earnings
	Amortization expense	8,000	8,000	Retained earnings
			(16,000)	Leasehold improvements
6.	Bond discount—incorrect:			
	Record discount		(6,000)	Retained earnings
			6,000	Bond discount
	Amortization of discount	600	600	Retained earnings
			(1,200)	Bond discount
7.	Adjustment of cost of land:			
	Sale of building for scrap	2,000	(2,000)	Land
	Gain on issuance of treasury stock—incorrect	5,000	(5,000)	Capital in excess of par value
8.	Prepaid advertising	(75,000)	75,000	Prepaid advertising and promotion
9.	Pension expense—misstated—*Schedule A*	(810,000)	810,000	Deferred pension cost
10.	Reversal of contingency loss provision	(100,000)	100,000	Estimated contingency loss

Schedule A

ADJUSTMENT OF PENSION EXPENSE
(Not Required)

Pension expense recorded		$970,000
Less correct amount of pension expense:		
Normal cost	$ 70,000	
Past service cost ($900,000 × 10%)	90,000	$160,000
Adjustment—representing deferred pension cost		$810,000

SOLUTION GUIDE: ERROR CORRECTION

Problem 7   Journal Entries and Schedule

1. The requirement is to prepare journal entries to correct the books of Noble Corporation at 12/31/77 assuming the books have not been closed. Part b requires a schedule of corrections to net income for years 1977 and 1976.

2. The solutions approach is to begin by understanding the requirements and studying the financial statements. Each of the five paragraphs of supplementary information should then be analyzed to determine the required adjusting entries.

2.1 Since the bad debt expense should be reduced from 2% of sales to 1% of sales beginning in 1977, $10,000 should be credited to administrative expenses with a corresponding debit to the allowance for uncollectible accounts. In 1977, $20,000 ($1,000,000 x 2%) of expense was recorded and only $10,000 should have been recorded.

2.2 Since the market value of the short-term investment in marketable equity securities decreased below cost by $16,000 ($78,000 cost and $62,000 market) as of 12/31/77, an allowance account should be set up for $16,000 with the corresponding debit to a loss account. Per para 8-11 of SFAS 12, portfolios of short-term investments in marketable equity securities should be carried at the lower of cost or market. The excess of aggregate cost over market should be accounted for in a valuation allowance account. Changes in the valuation allowance account for the current portfolio of marketable equity securities should be reflected in income.

2.3 Inventory should be credited by $6,100, because the 1977 year-end inventory was overstated by $6,100. Since beginning inventory was overstated by $4,000, the net effect on 1977 income was only $2,100 (overstatement of beginning inventory understates income and overstatement of ending inventory overstates income). The overstatement of beginning inventory of $4,000 requires an adjustment to beginning retained earnings.

Retained earnings	$4,000	
Cost of sales		$4,000
Cost of sales	$6,100	
Inventory		$6,100

2.4 Equipment costing $12,000 at the beginning of 1976 was incorrectly expensed and $12,000 should be debited to equipment. Depreciation of the equipment is $1,100 per year ($12,000 cost minus $1,000 salvage value divided by 10-year life). Accordingly additional 1977 depreciation expense is $1,100, and $2,200 of additional accumulated depreciation should be reflected at the end of 1977. Correct 1976 income with a $10,900 credit to retained earnings ($12,000 equipment cost that was expensed minus $1,100 of depreciation not recorded).

When fully depreciated fixed assets are sold, the fixed asset and related accumulated depreciation should be removed from the books. Since the $2,500 received was already credited to equipment, an additional credit of $15,000 ($17,500 − $2,500) is needed. Debit accumulated depreciation for $17,500, and credit a gain for $2,500.

2.5 The $2,700 insurance premium for a three-year policy purchased in January 1976 should be expensed at the rate of $900 per year in 1976, 1977, and 1978. Accordingly at the end of 1977 $900 should be debited to prepaid insurance (for 1978) and $900 should be recorded as 1977 expense with a $1,800 credit to retained earnings to correct 1976 income.

2.6 Your earlier analysis of the balance sheet should have noted that 20,000 shares of $10-par common stock are outstanding, but the common stock account shows a balance of $260,000. Thus $60,000 of paid-in capital in excess of par value is included in the capital stock account. Accordingly, $60,000 should be transferred from the common stock account to the paid-in capital on common stock account.

3. Part b requires a schedule correcting reported 1976 and 1977 income (see Unofficial Answer following). Reflect the adjustments recorded in part a.

UNOFFICIAL ANSWER: ERROR CORRECTION

Problem 7   Journal Entries and Schedule

Part a.

Noble Corporation
ADJUSTING JOURNAL ENTRIES
December 31, 1977

	Debit	Credit
(1)		
Allowance for uncollectible accounts	$10,000	
Administrative expenses		$10,000
To reflect reduction in loss experience rate		
(2)		
Unrealized loss on marketable securities	16,000	
Allowance to reduce marketable securities to market		16,000
To reduce marketable securities to market valuation		

(3)

Retained earnings	4,000	
Cost of sales	2,100	
Merchandise inventory		6,100

To adjust for overstatements in opening and closing inventories

(4)

Equipment	12,000	
Operating expenses	1,100	
Retained earnings		10,900
Accumulated depreciation		2,200

To adjust for misposting of equipment purchase in 1976

	Debit	Credit
(5)		
Accumulated depreciation	$17,500	
Equipment		$15,000
Other income		2,500

To adjust for misposting of equipment sale

(6)

Prepaid expenses	900	
Operating expenses	900	
Retained earnings		1,800

To adjust for nonrecognition of prepaid expense in 1976

(7)

Common stock	60,000	
Capital in excess of par		60,000

To adjust for capital contributed in excess of par value

Part b.

Noble Corporation
COMPUTATION OF CORRECTED NET INCOME
For the years ended December 31, 1977 and 1976

	1977 Debit (Credit)	1976 Debit (Credit)
Reported income	$(220,000)	$(195,000)
Change in accounts receivable loss experience rate from 2% to 1%	(10,000)	—
Unrealized loss on marketable securities reduced to market	16,000	—
Ending merchandise inventories overstated:		
December 31, 1976	(4,000)	4,000
December 31, 1977	6,100	
Misposting of equipment purchase:		
Decrease in operating expenses—1976		(10,900)
Increase in operating expenses—1977	1,100	
Misposting of proceeds of equipment sold	(2,500)	
Recognition of prepaid insurance	900	(1,800)
Corrected net income	$(212,400)	$(203,700)

ANSWER OUTLINE: ACCOUNTING CHANGES

Problem 8   Description of Types

a1.   Change in accounting principle
    Use of different and preferable generally accepted principle from one used previously
    Recognize cumulative effect of change in net income of current period
        Net of tax difference in beginning retained earnings
            Retained earnings per books — retained earnings if new principle had been used
        Reporting cumulative effect type accounting changes
            Show between extraordinary items and net income
            Show per-share amount of cumulative effect
            Show pro-forma amounts (total and per-share) for all periods presented
                Pro-forma amounts represent results if new principle used in all affected periods presented

a2.   Change in accounting estimate
    Results from new events, more experience, or more information
    Account for in current and any future periods affected

a3.   Change in reporting entity
    Results in financial statements which represent a different reporting entity
    Restate financials of all prior periods presented
    e.g.,
        Change in composition of companies included in consolidated financial statements
        Business combination accounted for as pooling-of-interest

UNOFFICIAL ANSWER: ACCOUNTING CHANGES

Problem 8   Description of Types

1.   A change in accounting principle results from adoption of a generally accepted accounting principle differenct from the one used previously for reporting purposes. A change in accounting principle is characteristically a change from one generally accepted accounting principle to a preferable one.

A change in accounting principle should be recognized by including the cumulative effect of changing to a new accounting principle in net income of the period of the change. The amount of the cumulative effect is the difference between (a) the amount of retained earnings at the beginning of the period of change and (b) the amount of retained earnings that would have been reported at that date if the new accounting principle had been applied retroactively for all prior periods that would have been affected and by recognizing only the direct effects of the change and related income tax effect. The amount of the cumulative effect should be shown in the income statement between the captions "extraordinary items" and "net income." The per-share information shown on the face of the income statement should include the per-share amount of the cumulative effect of the accounting change. Pro-forma disclosure of the effect of retroactive restatement should be shown on the face of the income statement.

It should be noted, however, that Accounting Principles Board Opinion No. 20 describes a few specific changes in accounting principles that should be reported by restating the financial statements of prior periods.

2.   A change in accounting estimate occurs as new events occur, as more experience is acquired, or as additional information is obtained.

A change in accounting estimate should be accounted for in (a) the period of change if the change affects that period only or (b) the period of change and future periods if the change affects both.

3.   A change in reporting entity is a special type of change in accounting principle that results in financial statements, which, in effect, are those of a different reporting entity.

A change in reporting entity should be reported by restating the financial statements of all prior periods presented in order to show financial information for the new reporting entity for all periods.

Presenting consolidated statements in place of statements of individual companies and a business combination accounted for by the pooling-of-interests method are two examples of a change in reporting entity.

ANSWER OUTLINE: FINANCIAL STATEMENTS

Problem 9   Statement Deficiencies

2   Statement of financial position
    Deferred income tax liability should not be shown
        It is a permanent not a timing difference
    Amortize trademark over forty years
        Using straight-line method
    Accounts receivable should be at gross
        Less an allowance for doubtful accounts
    Number of common shares should be disclosed
        Authorized, issued, and outstanding

FOOTNOTES

Footnote 1 — Lease is a capital, not operating, lease due to the bargain purchase option
    Lease expense is misstated in income statement
    Present value of minimum lease payments is an asset on the balance sheet
    The capitalized amount should be amortized over the life of the asset

Footnote 2 — Pay-as-you-go is unacceptable pension method
    It is cash basis rather than accrual basis
    Acceptable pension accounting methods include
        Unit credit
        Entry age normal
        Individual level premium
        Attained age normal
        Aggregate method

Footnote 3 — Trademark - appears to be appropriate

Footnote 4 — Deferred income tax payable is incorrect
    Based on a permanent not a timing difference
    Also based on liability rather than deferral method
    (used anticipated rather than current tax rates)

Footnote 5 — Stock warrants - appears appropriate

Footnote 6 — Warranty liability should be accrued and expensed in the income statement
    Because the loss is probable and reasonably estimable

A footnote of significant accounting policies should disclose
    Inventory accounting methods
    Amortization of trademark
    Basis for valuation of land
    Pension plan accounting procedures
    Capitalized lease amortization

Income statement errors
    EPS is incorrect
        Outstanding warrants require dual presentation
            Primary EPS
            Fully diluted EPS
        Dilutive effect of warrants is omitted
        Extraordinary item is not reflected in EPS
        EPS should be presented for
            Earnings before extraordinary items
            Extraordinary items
            Net Income
        The extraordinary item belongs in the income statement not in statement of retained earnings

    Statement of retained earnings
        The extraordinary item belongs in the income statement
        Correction of deferred taxes accounting would be a prior period adjustment

    Statement of changes in financial position is missing

UNOFFICIAL ANSWER: FINANCIAL STATEMENTS

Problem 9   Statement Deficiencies

Statement of Financial Position

The deferred income tax liability should not be shown on the statement because it arose from a permanent difference, not a timing difference. The trademark should be amortized over a maximum period of forty years, using the straight-line method of amortization. Accounts receivable should be shown at the gross amount and an amount net of the allowance for doubtful accounts. Also, the number of common shares authorized, issued, and outstanding should be disclosed in the stockholders' equity section.

Footnotes

The lease discussed in footnote 1 is a capital lease because of the bargain purchase option. Therefore, lease expense shown in the earnings statement is incorrect. The present value of the future minimum lease payments (net of executory costs and any profit thereon) should be determined and recorded on the statement of financial position as an asset. The cost of the leased assets is then matched with earnings as amortization expense over the life of the assets and the cost of the deferral of payment as interest expense over the life of the lease.

The pay-as-you-go or terminal funding methods are not generally accepted methods of accounting for pension cost. An acceptable method, such as unit credit, entry age normal, individual level premium, aggregate, or attained age normal should be adopted in order to reflect the cost of providing pension benefits.

Even though there is no income tax deferral to be recorded on the statement of financial position because the difference between taxable income and accounting income is a permanent difference, not a timing difference that would turn around at a later date, footnote 4 describes an incorrect method of determining the deferral. Had the deferred income tax recognition been required to be used, the deferral method is the generally accepted method, not the liability method.

The warranty contingency meets the two tests for the accrual of a contingent loss (probable, and amount reasonably estimable) and should be accrued as a liability and an expense shown in the earnings statement.

Preceding the footnotes to the financial statements, or as the initial footnote, there should be a description of all significant accounting policies used by the company. Based on the statements as presented, this footnote should address itself to the following areas: (1) inventory, (2) amortization of trademark, (3) basis for valuation of land, (4) pension plan accounting procedures, and (5) capitalized lease amortization.

Earnings Statement

An analysis of the earnings statement discloses the following violations of generally accepted accounting principles.

Earnings per share as shown is incorrect for several reasons. First, the title "earnings per common share" is incorrect because there are warrants outstanding calling for a dual presentation using the titles "primary earnings per share" and "fully diluted earnings per share." The amount shown as earnings per share is incorrect for three reasons:

1. The dilutive effect of the warrants outstanding is not considered (that is, not properly accounted for using the treasury stock method).

2. The extraordinary item should be considered in the computation of primary and fully diluted earnings per share.

3. Primary earnings per share and fully diluted earnings per share should be stated for earnings before extraordinary items, for extraordinary items, and for net earnings.

Net earnings are incorrect because the extraordinary gain is omitted. To correct this, the extraordinary gain should be taken out of the statement of retained earnings and shown in the earnings statement.

Statement of Retained Earnings

The extraordinary item does not belong in this statement; properly, it should be reflected in the earnings statement. Also, the correction of the deferred tax amount should be reflected in this statement as a correction of an error made in a prior period.

General

The statement of changes in financial position is missing; one should be prepared and included with the other statements and disclosures in order to make this a complete set of financial statements.

SOLUTION GUIDE: FINANCIAL STATEMENTS

Problem 10   Discontinued Operations

1. The requirement is comparative income statements for 1975 and 1974. This problem is an application of APB 30—"Reporting the Results of Operations."

2. The solutions approach is to visualize the net sales, cost of sales, operating expense, income, taxes, etc., format of the income statement based on the combined sales, cost of sales, operating expenses, etc., data given at the beginning of the problem. The next step is to work through each paragraph of additional information making adjustments to the basic data.

2.1 Since the office equipment division was discontinued during 1975, the operating results of the office equipment division should be excluded from 1975 and 1974 continuing operations (para 8, APB 30). Thus the net sales, cost of sales, and operating expenses of the office equipment division should be excluded from continuing operations and included in a separate section before extraordinary items and the cumulative effect of accounting changes. The $640,000 gain on sale of the office equipment division is offset against the $530,000 loss from operations in the unofficial solution. These discontinued items should be shown net of taxes.

2.2 The sale of one of the textile manufacturing plants resulted in a gain of $130,000 which should be disclosed as a separate component of income from continuing operations (para 26, APB 30). It is not an extraordinary item, because it is not both unusual and infrequent as required by APB 30, para 20. It is, however, unusual, i.e., it is unrelated to the ordinary typical activities of the company.

2.3 The flood damage to the food products warehouse is also unusual but not infrequent. Para 20 of APB 30 defines infrequency as an event which would not reasonably be expected to recur in the future. Since it is unusual but not infrequent, the $420,000 loss should be disclosed as a separate component of income from continuing operations. Both the $420,000 flood loss and the $130,000 gain on sale of plant should not be shown net of taxes (para 26, APB 30).

2.4   The interest revenue on investments should be shown separately as other revenue in the income statements.

2.5   The net income figures of $960,000 and $670,000 provide numbers to reconcile to at the bottom of the income statement.

2.6   The income tax rate of 50% should be applied first to income from continuing operations and then from each component of discontinued operations.

UNOFFICIAL ANSWER: FINANCIAL STATEMENTS

Problem 10   Discontinued Operations

The Century Company
COMPARATIVE STATEMENT OF INCOME
For the Two Years Ended December 31, 1975 and December 31, 1974

	1975	1974
Net sales	$7,080,000	$5,670,000
Cost of sales	4,000,000	3,400,000
Gross profit on sales	3,080,000	2,270,000
Operating expenses	1,050,000	550,000
Operating income	2,030,000	1,720,000
Other revenue and (expenses):		
Interest revenue	70,000	40,000
Gain on sale of plant	130,000	—
Loss due to flood damage	(420,000)	—
	(220,000)	40,000
Income from continuing operations before income taxes	1,810,000	1,760,000
Less provision for income taxes	905,000	880,000
Income from continuing operations	905,000	880,000
Discontinued operations:		
(Loss) from operations of discontinued office equipment division	—	(420,000)
Less applicable income taxes	—	210,000
	—	(210,000)
Gain on disposal of office equipment division	110,000	—
Less applicable income taxes	55,000	—
	55,000	
Net income	$ 960,000	$ 670,000

SOLUTION GUIDE: FINANCIAL STATEMENTS

Problem 11   Statement Interrelationships

1.   An efficient solutions approach is essential to this problem. The unofficial answer provides an explanation of each item but not how to work the problem.

2.   Glance over the text of the problem and study the requirements. Note that the first paragraph provides a table of contents to the problem.

3.   Study the balance sheets to determine which items are required. For example, land is the only required asset at the beginning of the year and all assets are required at the end of the year. Similarly, all liabilities and stockholder equity items except deferred taxes and treasury stock are required at the end of the year. At the beginning of the year, all of the liabilities are required.

4.   After becoming acquainted with the accounts and the balance sheet, begin working through the data in the problem. Make notes relating items in the statement data to both balance sheets. For example: the net loss of $2,885 will affect retained earnings. Also, the entry to correct the failure to amortize $2,000 of goodwill last year will reduce retained earnings. As there are no other items in the statements that affect retained earnings, retained earnings is reduced from a $6,000 deficit to a $10,885 deficit. The important point is to get started through the use of these intermediary solutions.

4.1   Another intermediary solution is to note that the stockholders' equity/total liabilities is a 4 to 3 ratio. The effect is to be able to compute that all of the liabilities total $60,000. If the total liabilities are $60,000, total liabilities and stockholders' equity is $140,000. Thus, if total assets are $140,000, land is $39,000.

5.   The important point is to get started as illustrated in the above paragraphs. There is no best solution. Any series of intermediary solutions will bring you closer to a completed worksheet. In reading the unofficial answer which follows, remember that you cannot work the problem in chronological order.

UNOFFICIAL ANSWER: FINANCIAL STATEMENTS

Problem 11   Statement Interrelationships

(1) $39,000.   This balance is calculated by knowing that total assets prior to restatement (see note) are $140,000 because the total of liabilities and stockholders' equity prior to restatement is $140,000. Total stockholders' equity equals $80,000 ($66,000 + $13,000 + $16,000 − $6,000 − $9,000). Total stockholders' equity divided by total liabilities is 4 to 3; hence, total liabilities equal $60,000 ($80,000 ÷ 1⅓). Thus the total of liabilities and stockholders' equity is $140,000 ($60,000 + $80,000). The balance for land is thus calculated as follows: ($140,000 − $12,000 + $25,000 − $92,000 − $22,000 = $39,000).

(2) $5,500.   Current assets minus beginning working capital ($22,000 − $16,500).

(3) $50,000.   Bond interest expense plus bond premium amortization ($3,500 + $500) equals the stated interest ($4,000). The stated interest divided by the interest rate ($4,000 ÷ 8%) equals the face value of the bonds ($50,000).

(4) $1,900.   Balance per ending balance sheet plus debit to this account during the year ($1,700 + $200).

(5) $26,100.   Let X equal current liabilities. Current assets minus current liabilities equals working capital. Current assets are three times current liabilities (3X − X = $17,400). X (current liabilities) equals $8,700 and 3X (current assets) equals $26,100.

(6) $77,000.   Balance per opening balance sheet less cost of equipment sold during the year ($92,000 − $15,000). The undepreciated cost of the equipment sold was two-thirds of the cost. Therefore, cost was $15,000 ($10,000 ÷ 2/3) and accumulated depreciation was $5,000.

(7) $(23,000).   See (6). Balance per opening balance sheet plus depreciation expense for the year less accumulated depreciation on equipment sold ($25,000 + $3,000 − $5,000).

(8) $53,715.   Balance per opening balance sheet plus acquisition (purchase of land) ($39,000 + $14,715).

(9) $8,000.   Balance per opening balance sheet prior to restatement less goodwill amortization for 1974 and 1973 (see note) ($12,000 − $2,000 − $2,000).

(10) $8,700.   See (5).

(11) $42,800.   Balance per opening balance sheet less current maturity of long-term bond debt ($50,000 − $7,200).

(12) $2,100.   Balance per opening balance sheet less bond premium amortization ($2,600 − $500).

(13) $73,500.   Balance per opening balance sheet plus par value of common stock issued to reacquire preferred stock ($66,000 + $7,500).

(14) $15,400.   Balance per opening balance sheet plus excess of proceeds from reissue of treasury stock over cost of treasury stock ($13,000 + $2,400). (Excess equals proceeds from reissue of treasury stock less treasury stock (at cost) per the opening balance sheet) ($11,400 − $9,000).

(15) $8,500.   Balance per opening balance sheet less par value of preferred stock reacquired by issuing common stock ($16,000 − $7,500).

(16) $(10,885).   Balance per opening balance sheet prior to restatement plus 1974 net loss after tax adjustment plus prior period adjustment (correction of error) (see note) ($6,000 debit + $2,885 + $2,000).

Note:

A material error requires that the prior financial statement be restated. The goodwill and retained earnings at January 1 would be restated by reducing each by $2,000. Total assets and equities would then be $138,000. Actual restatement, however, is not required as part of this answer.

ANSWER OUTLINE: INTERIM REPORTING

Problem 12   Treatment of Selected Items

a. Recognition of revenue in interim statements
   Recognize revenue as is recognized for annual
   statements
   I.e., normally point of sale or performance
   of service
   Seasonal variations should be disclosed by footnote
   Long-term contract recognized same as for annual
   statements

b. Recognition of costs in interim statement
   Also the same as in annual statements
   Product cost should be matched with associated
   revenues
   Period costs should be expensed as incurred
   Or allocated to interim periods based on time
   expired, etc.
   Recognize gains or losses in full when incurred
   Unless type to be deferred at year-end
   Cost allocation among interim periods must be
   reasonable
   Interim inventory valuation exceptions
   Gross profit method may be used to estimate
   inventory and cost of goods sold
   Temporary liquidation of LIFO inventory tiers
   may be ignored
   Difference in carrying value and replacement
   cost is a current liability
   Inventory market value declines are recognized as
   they occur
   Standard cost variances are treated as for annual
   statements

c. Recognition of income taxes in interim statements
   Expense is based upon the expected annual rate
   Rate based on income for book purposes rather
   than tax purposes
   Compute expected annual rate based on expected
   Annual earnings
   Investment tax credits
   Foreign tax rates
   Percentage depletion, capital gains rates
   And other tax-planning alternatives
   Calculation excludes
   Extraordinary items
   Discontinued operations
   Cumulative effect of changes
   These items are reported net of tax effect
   Compute provision for interim taxes on a cumula-
   tive basis

E.g., compute tax to date and adjust for taxes
recognized in previous interim periods

No retroactive adjustments for changes in expected rate

UNOFFICIAL ANSWER: INTERIM REPORTING

Problem 12   Treatment of Selected Items

a.   Sales and other revenues should be recognized for interim financial statement purposes in
the same manner as revenues are recognized for
annual reporting purposes. This means normally
at the point of sale or, in the case of services,
at completion of the earnings process.

In the case of industries whose sales vary
greatly due to the seasonal nature of business, revenues should still be recognized as earned, but a
disclosure should be made of the seasonal nature
of the business in the notes.

In the case of long-term contracts recognizing
earnings on the percentage-of-completion basis, the
current state of completion of the contract should
be estimated and revenue recognized at interim
dates in the same manner as at the normal year end.

b.   For interim reporting purposes, product costs
(costs directly attributable to the production of
goods or services) should be matched with the product and associated revenues in the same manner
as for annual reporting purposes.

Period costs (costs not directly associated
with the production of a particular good or service) should be charged to earnings as incurred or
allocated among interim periods based on an estimate of time expired, benefit received, or other
activity associated with the particular interim period(s).
Also, if a gain or loss occurs during an interim period
and is a type that would not be deferred at year
end, the gain or loss should be recognized in full
in the interim period in which it occurs. Finally,
in allocating period costs among interim periods,
the basis for allocation must be supportable and
may not be based on merely an arbitrary assignment of costs between interim periods.

The AICPA Accounting Principles Board allowed for some variances from the normal method
of determining cost of goods sold and valuation
of inventories at interim dates in Opinion no. 28,
but these methods are allowable only at interim
dates and must be fully disclosed in a footnote
to the financial statements. Some companies use
the gross profit method of estimating cost of goods
sold and ending inventory at interim dates instead

of taking a complete physical inventory. This is an allowable procedure at interim dates, but the company must disclose the method used and any significant variances that subsequently result from reconciliation of the results obtained using the gross profit method and the results obtained after taking the annual physical inventory.

At interim dates, companies using the LIFO cost-flow assumption may temporarily have a reduction in inventory level that results in a liquidation of base period tiers of inventory. If this liquidation is considered temporary and is expected to be replaced prior to year end, the company should charge cost of goods sold at current prices. The difference between the carrying value of the inventory and the current replacement cost of the inventory is a current liability for replacement of LIFO base inventory temporarily depleted. When the temporary liquidation is replaced, inventory is debited for the original LIFO value and the liability is removed.

Inventory losses from a decline in market value at interim dates should not be deferred but should be recognized in the period in which they occur. However, if in a subsequent interim period the market price of the written-down inventory increases, a gain should be recognized for the recovery up to the amount of the loss previously recognized. If a temporary decline in market value below cost can reasonably be expected to be recovered prior to year end, no loss should be recognized.

Finally, if a company uses a standard costing system to compute cost of goods sold and to value inventories, variances from the standard should be deferred instead of being immediately recognized.

c.   The AICPA Accounting Principles Board stated that the provision for income taxes shown in interim financial statements must be based upon the effective tax rate expected for the entire annual period for ordinary earnings. The effective tax rate is, in accordance with previous APB opinions, based on earnings for financial statement purposes as opposed to taxable income which may consider timing differences. This effective tax rate is the combined federal and state(s) income tax rate applied to expected annual earnings, taking into consideration all anticipated investment tax credits, foreign tax rates, percentage depletion capital gains rates, and other available tax planning alternatives. Ordinary earnings do not include unusual or extraordinary items, discontinued operations, or cumulative effects of changes in accounting principles, all of which will be separately reported or reported net of their related tax effect in reports for the interim period or for the fiscal year. The amount shown as the provision for income

taxes at interim dates should be computed on a year-to-date basis. For example, the provision for income taxes for the second quarter of a company's fiscal year is the result of applying the expected rate to year-to-date earnings and subtracting the provision recorded for the first quarter. There are several variables in this computation (expected earnings may change, tax rates may change), and the year-to-date method of computation provides the only continuous method of approximating the provision for income taxes at interim dates. However, if the effective rate or expected annual earnings change between interim periods, the change is not reflected retroactively but the effect of the change is absorbed in the current interim period.

ANSWER OUTLINE: SEGMENT REPORTING

Problem 13 Definitions and Tests

a1.   Industry segment — Enterprise component providing products or services to unaffiliated customers

   Specification of unaffiliated customers precludes reporting vertically integrated operations as segments

a2.   Segment revenue — Sales revenues from all unaffiliated and intersegment sales (or transfers)

   Intersegment sales accounted for at internal transfer prices

   Interest is included if receivables are segment identifiable assets

   Except interest on loans to other segments

a3.   Segment operating profit — Revenue minus all operating expenses

   Operating expenses include those for unaffiliated and intersegment sales

   Nondirect operating expenses should be allocated to segments on a reasonable basis

   Intersegment purchases accounted at internal transfer price

   Items not included in determining operating profit

   Revenue earned at the corporate level and not derived from the operations of any industry segment.

   General corporate expenses
   Interest expense
   Domestic and foreign income taxes
   Income or loss of unconsolidated subsidiaries

           Discontinued operations gains or
             losses
           Extraordinary items
           Minority interest
           Cumulative affect of an accounting
             principle change

a4.   Identifiable assets — Assets used by industry
      segment
           Including allocated portion of jointly
             used assets
           And adjusted for appropriate valuation
             allowances e.g., goodwill allocable to
             a particular segment
           But not general corporate assets
           And not intersegment loans (unless a
             financing segment)

b1.   Segments are reportable
           If segment revenue is 10% or more of
             total revenue
           If operating profit (or loss) is 10% or more
             of operating profits for all segments re-
             porting profits or operating losses for
             all segments reporting losses
           If assets are 10% or more of all segment
             assets
           Other segments may be required for
             interperiod comparability

b2.   Separately reported segments must account
      for 75% of revenues to unaffiliated custom-
      ers
           If not, additional segments must be report-
             ed to meet the criteria
      Separately reported segments should not
      exceed 10

UNOFFICIAL ANSWER: SEGMENT REPORTING

Problem 13   Definitions and Tests

Part a.

1.   An industry segment is a component of an enterprise engaged in providing a product or service or
group of related products or services primarily
to unaffiliated customers for a profit. By defining an industry segment in terms of products
and services sold primarily to unaffiliated customers, it can be seen that vertically integrated
operations of an enterprise are not segments.

2.   The revenue of an industry segment includes
revenue both from sales to unaffiliated customers and from intersegment sales or transfers, if any, of products and services similar
to those sold to unaffiliated customers. Interest earned from sources outside the enterprise
and from intersegment trade receivables is included in revenue if the asset on which the interest is earned is included among the industry
segment's identifiable assets, but interest earned on advances or loans to other industry segments is not included unless the primary function of the segment is financial in nature. Also,
revenue from intersegment sales or transfers is
accounted for on the basis used by the enterprise to price the intersegment sales or transfers.

3.   The operating profit or loss of an industry segment is its revenue minus all operating expenses.
Operating expenses include expenses that relate
to both revenue from sales to unaffiliated customers and revenue from intersegment sales or
transfers. An enterprise's operating expenses
that are not directly traceable to an industry
segment should be allocated on a reasonable
basis among those segments for whose benefit
the expenses were incurred. Intersegment purchases should be accounted for on the same
basis as intersegment sales or transfers. Statement of Financial Accounting Standards no. 14
does, however, specify certain items of revenue
and expense that should not be considered in
determining operating profit or loss for an industry segment:

   a.   Revenue earned at the corporate level and
not derived from the operations of any industry segment.
   b.   General corporate expenses.
   c.   Interest expense (unless the segment's
principal purpose is of a financial nature).
   d.   Domestic and foreign income taxes.
   e.   Equity in the earnings or losses of unconsolidated subsidiaries.
   f.   Gains or losses on discontinued operations.
   g.   Extraordinary items.
   h.   Minority interest.
   i.   Cumulative effect of a change in accounting principles.

4.   The identifiable assets of an industry segment are
those tangible and intangible enterprise assets
that are used by the industry segment, including
assets used exclusively by that segment and an

allocated portion of assets used jointly by two or more segments. Goodwill allocable to a particular industry segment is a part of that segment's identifiable assets. However, assets maintained for general corporate purposes (i.e., those not used in the operations of any industry segment) should not be allocated to industry segments. Identifiable assets of industry segments should not include loans or transfers to other segments unless the primary business of the segment is financial in nature. The identifiable assets of an industry segment also include the appropriate valuation allowances, such as allowance for doubtful accounts, accumulated depreciation, and marketable securities valuation allowance.

The Financial Accounting Standards Board has stated that if an enterprise has many reportable segments, benefit to the reader may be lost if more than 10 segments are reported. In such a situation, the board suggests combining related reportable segments until the total is ten or fewer.

Part b.

1. There are three basic tests to be applied to segments of an industry to see if they are significant enough to be separately reportable. If a segment meets any one of the tests it is deemed significant and reportable.

    The first test is based upon revenue. If a segment's revenue from sales to unaffiliated customers and intersegment sales and transfers is equal to 10 percent or more of the enterprise's combined revenues, the segment is reportable.

    The second test is based upon operating profits or losses. There are two subtests in this category based upon absolute amounts of operating profits or losses. A segment is deemed reportable if the operating profit or loss shown by the segment is equal to or greater than 10 percent of the higher of the following two absolute amounts:

    > Sum of all operating profits for all segments reporting operating profits.
    > Sum of all operating losses for all segments reporting operating losses.

    Third, a segment is significant and reportable if the identifiable assets of the segment equal or exceed 10 percent of the combined identifi-

able assets of all of the industry segments within the enterprise.

Finally, all segments, whether deemed reportable or not, must be reviewed from the standpoint of interperiod comparability, because the primary purpose of presenting segment information is to aid the financial statement reader.

2. Statement of Financial Accounting Standards no. 14 states that enough industry segments must be separately reported so that the total of revenues from sales to unaffiliated customers for the reportable segments equals or exceeds 75 percent of the combined revenues from sales to unaffiliated customers for the entire enterprise. If applying the prescribed tests does not yield the required percentage of revenues described above, additional segments must be reported on until the 75 percent test is met.

MULTIPLE CHOICE QUESTIONS (1—63)

1.   A characteristic of all assets and liabilities comprising working capital is that they are
   a.   Cash equivalents.
   b.   Current.
   c.   Monetary.
   d.   Marketable.

2.   For a marketable equity securities portfolio included in noncurrent assets, which of the following should be included in net income of the period?
   a.   Realized gains during the period.
   b.   Unrealized losses during the period.
   c.   Accumulated changes in the valuation allowance.
   d.   Increases in the valuation allowance during the period.

3.   Which of the following need *not* be disclosed in a statement of changes in financial position as a source and use of funds?
   a.   Acquisition of fixed assets in exchange for capital stock.
   b.   Dividend paid in capital stock of the company (stock dividend).
   c.   Retirement of a bond issue through the issuance of another bond issue.
   d.   Conversion of convertible debt to capital stock.

4.   How should the amortization of bond discount for a bond issuer be shown on the statement of changes in financial position (defining funds as working capital)?
   a.   Need **not** be shown.
   b.   Use of funds.
   c.   Expense **not** requiring the use of funds.
   d.   Contra-expense item **not** providing funds.

5.   Taylor Company was involved in a tax dispute with the Internal Revenue Service at the close of its year ended December 31, 1979. The company's tax counsel believes that an unfavorable outcome is probable. A reasonable estimate of additional tax payments is in the range between $300,000 and $800,000, but $500,000 is a better estimate than any other amount in that range. The situation was unchanged when the financial statements were issued on March 5, 1980. What amount of additional taxes should be accrued and charged to income in 1979?
   a. $0
   b. $300,000
   c. $500,000
   d. $800,000

6.   On January 10, 1979, Wayne, Inc., purchased 5,000 shares of Jason Corporation's common stock at $60 per share. The purchase is a long-term investment and is less than 20% of Jason's outstanding shares. This investment is appropriately reflected in Wayne's balance sheet as a noncurrent marketable equity security at December 31, 1979. The market value of Wayne's investment in Jason's common stock was as follows:

| | Market Value | |
Date	Per share	Total
December 15, 1979	$47	$235,000
December 31, 1979	46	230,000

On December 15, 1979, Wayne determined that there had been an other than temporary decline in the market value. What amount should Wayne record as a loss in its income statement for the year ended December 31, 1979?
   a. $0
   b. $ 5,000
   c. $65,000
   d. $70,000

7.   An analysis of Pickwick Corporation's short-term marketable equity securities portfolio acquired in 1979 reveals the following totals at the end of its 1979 calendar year:

Aggregrate cost	$90,000
Aggregate market value	80,000
Aggregate lower of cost or market value applied to each security in the portfolio	76,000

What is the amount of the valuation allowance that Pickwick should record at December 31, 1979?
   a. $0
   b. $ 4,000
   c. $10,000
   d. $14,000

8. The December 31, 1979, trial balance of the Mark Company before adjustments included the following accounts:

	Debit	Credit
Allowance for doubtful accounts	$ 2,000	
Sales		$830,000
Sales returns and allowances	10,000	

Mark estimates its bad debts based upon 2% of net sales. What amount should Mark record as bad debt expense for 1979?

    a. $14,400
    b. $14,600
    c. $16,400
    d. $16,600

9. A truck owned and operated by Green Company was involved in an accident with an auto driven by White on November 15, 1979. Green received notice on January 10, 1980, of a lawsuit for $750,000 damages for a personal injury suffered by White. The company counsel believes it is probable that the plaintiff will be successful against the company for an estimated amount of $250,000. Counsel also believes there is a chance the plaintiff will be awarded as much as $350,000. Green's accounting year ends on December 31, and the 1979 financial statements were issued on March 15, 1980. What amount of loss, if any, must be accrued by a charge to income in 1979?

    a. $0
    b. $250,000
    c. $350,000
    d. $750,000

10. The net income for the year ended December 31, 1979, for Diamond Company was $2,500,000. Additional information is as follows:

Depreciation of fixed assets	$2,900,000
Dividends paid on preferred stock	200,000
Long-term debt:	
Bond discount amortization	50,000
Interest expense	800,000
Provision for doubtful accounts	
on long-term receivables	250,000
Amortization of goodwill	90,000

What should be the working capital provided from operations in the statement of changes in financial position for the year ended December 31, 1979?

    a. $5,490,000
    b. $5,540,000
    c. $5,790,000
    d. $5,990,000

11. The following information was taken from the accounting records of Oregon Corporation for 1979:

Proceeds from issuance of preferred	
stock	$4,000,000
Dividends paid on preferred stock	400,000
Bonds payable converted to	
common stock	2,000,000
Purchases of treasury stock, common	500,000
Sale of plant building	1,200,000
2% stock dividend on common stock	300,000

Oregon's statement of changes in financial position for the year ended December 31, 1979, should show the following sources and uses of funds, based on the information above:

	Sources	Uses
a.	$5,200,000	$1,200,000
b.	$5,500,000	$1,200,000
c.	$7,200,000	$2,900,000
d.	$7,500,000	$3,200,000

12. The following bank reconciliation is presented for the Kingston Company for the month of November 1979:

Balance per bank statement,		
11/30/79		$18,040
Add: Deposit in transit		4,150
		22,190
Less: Outstanding checks	$ 6,300	
Bank credit recorded in error	20	6,320
Balance per books, 11/30/79		$15,870

Data for the month of December 1979 follows:

Per bank

December deposits	$26,100
December disbursements	22,420
Balance, 12/31/79	21,720

All items that were outstanding as of November 30, cleared through the bank in December, including the bank credit. In addition, $2,500 in checks were outstanding as of December 31, 1979. What is the balance of cash per books at December 31, 1979?

    a. $19,220
    b. $19,240
    c. $21,720
    d. $24,220

13. The following information is available for the Leer Company:

Credit sales during 1979	$200,000
Allowance for doubtful accounts at December 31, 1978	2,400
Accounts receivable deemed worthless and written off during 1979	3,200

During 1979 Leer estimated that its bad debt expense should be 1% of all credit sales.

As a result of a review and aging of accounts receivable in early January 1980, it has been determined that an allowance for doubtful accounts of $2,200 is needed at December 31, 1979. What amount should Leer record as bad debt expense for the year ended December 31, 1979?

    a. $2,000
    b. $3,000
    c. $3,200
    d. $4,200

14. A new product introduced by Maude Corporation carries a two-year warranty against defects. The estimated warranty costs related to dollar sales are as follows:

Year of sale	3%
Year after sale	5%

Sales and actual warranty expenditures for the years ended December 31, 1978, and 1979 are as follows:

	Sales	Actual Warranty Expenditures
1978	$400,000	$10,000
1979	500,000	35,000

What amount should Maude report as its estimated warranty liability as of December 31, 1979?

    a. $ 2,000
    b. $12,000
    c. $27,000
    d. $37,000

15. An analysis and aging of the accounts receivable of the Franklin Company at December 31, 1979, revealed the following data:

Accounts receivable	$450,000
Allowance for uncollectible accounts per books	25,000
Accounts deemed uncollectible	32,000

Based upon the above data, the net realizable value of the accounts receivable at December 31, 1979, was

    a. $393,000
    b. $418,000
    c $425,000
    d. $443,000

16. The Vandiver Corporation provides an incentive compensation plan under which its president receives a bonus equal to 10% of the corporation's income in excess of $100,000 before income tax but after the bonus. If income before income tax and bonus is $320,000 and the effective tax rate is 40%, the amount of the bonus would be

    a. $20,000.
    b. $22,000.
    c. $29,090.
    d. $32,000.

17. The carrying amount of a current marketable equity securities portfolio in the balance sheet of a company shall be the aggregate

    a.   Cost of the portfolio, whether it is higher than or lower than the aggregate market value of the portfolio.
    b.   Cost of the portfolio, when it is higher than the aggregate market value of the portfolio.
    c.   Market value of the portfolio, when it is higher than or lower than the aggregate cost of the portfolio.
    d.   Market value of the portfolio, when it is lower than the aggregate cost of the portfolio.

18. If a company issues both a balance sheet and an income statement with comparative figures from last year, a statement of changes in financial position

    a.   Is no longer necessary; but may be issued at the company's option.
    b.   Should not be issued.
    c.   Should be issued for each period for which an income statement is presented.
    d.   Should be issued for the current year only.

19. Which of the following items is included on a statement of changes in financial position only because of the all-financial-resources concept?

    a.   Depreciation.
    b.   Issuance (sale) of common stock.
    c.   Purchase of treasury stock.
    d.   Retirement of long-term debt by issuance of preferred stock.

20.   The working capital format is an acceptable format for presenting a statement of changes in financial position. Which of the following formats is (are) also acceptable?

	Cash	Quick assets
a.	Acceptable	Not acceptable
b.	Not acceptable	Not acceptable
c.	Not acceptable	Acceptable
d.	Acceptable	Acceptable

21.   Which of the following must be disclosed in a statement of changes in financial position or in a related tabulation for at least the current period?
   a.   Net change in each balance sheet account.
   b.   Net change in each element of working capital.
   c.   Gross changes in depreciable assets.
   d.   Earnings per share.

22.   When the accounts receivable of a company are sold outright to a company which normally buys accounts receivable of other companies without recourse, the accounts receivable have been
   a.   Pledged.
   b.   Assigned.
   c.   Factored.
   d.   Collateralized.

23.   Reserves for contingencies for general or unspecified business risks should
   a.   Be accrued in the financial statements and disclosed in the notes thereto.
   b.   Not be accrued in the financial statements but should be disclosed in the notes thereto.
   c.   Not be accrued in the financial statements and need not be disclosed in the notes thereto.
   d.   Be accrued in the financial statements but need not be disclosed in the notes thereto.

24.   The following information on selected cash transactions for 1978 has been provided by the Smith Company:

Proceeds from short-term borrowings	$1,200,000
Proceeds from long-term borrowings	4,000,000
Purchases of fixed assets	3,200,000
Purchases of inventories	8,000,000
Proceeds from sale of Smith's common stock	2,000,000

What is the increase in working capital for the year ended December 31, 1978, as a result of the above information?
   a. $ 800,000
   b. $2,000,000
   c. $2,800,000
   d. $4,000,000

25.   The Supple Food Company distributes to consumers coupons which may be presented (on or before a stated expiration date) to grocers for discounts on certain products of Supple. The grocers are reimbursed when they send the coupons to Supple. In Supple's experience, 40% of such coupons are redeemed, and generally one month elapses between the date a grocer receives a coupon from a consumer and the date Supple receives it. During 1978 Supple issued two separate series of coupons as follows:

Issued On	Total Value	Consumer Expiration Date	Amount Disbursed as of 12/31/78
1/1/78	$100,000	6/30/78	$34,000
7/1/78	120,000	12/31/78	40,000

The December 31, 1978 balance sheet should include a liability for unredeemed coupons of
   a. $0
   b. $ 8,000
   c. $14,000
   d. $32,000

26.   On the December 31, 1978 balance sheet of the Stat Company, the current assets were comprised of the following items:

Cash	$ 70,000
Accounts receivable	120,000
Inventories	60,000
	$250,000

An examination of the accounts revealed that the accounts receivable were composed of the following items:

Accounts receivable

Trade accounts	$ 93,000
Allowance for uncollectible accounts	(2,000)
Claim against shipper for goods lost in transit (November 1978)	3,000
Selling price of unsold goods sent by Stat on consignment at 130% of cost (and not included in Stat's ending inventory)	26,000
	$120,000

What is the correct amount of current assets as of December 31, 1978?

- a. $221,000
- b. $224,000
- c. $244,000
- d. $250,000

27. Information concerning the debt of the Gallery Company is as follows:

Short-term borrowings:

Balance at December 31, 1974	$ 1,200,000
Proceeds from borrowings in 1975	1,500,000
Payments made in 1975	(1,400,000)
Balance at December 31, 1975	$ 1,300,000

Current portion of long-term debt:

Balance at December 31, 1974	$ 5,500,000
Transfers from caption "Long-Term Debt"	6,000,000
Payments made in 1975	(5,500,000)
Balance at December 31, 1975	$ 6,000,000

Long-term debt:

Balance at December 31, 1974	$42,500,000
Proceeds from borrowings in 1975	18,000,000
Transfers to caption "Current Portion of Long-Term Debt"	(6,000,000)
Payments made in 1975	(10,000,000)
Balance at December 31, 1975	$44,500,000

Assuming funds are defined as working capital, how should the above information be shown on Gallery's statement of changes in financial position for the year ended December 31, 1975?

	Source	Use
a.	$16,000,000	$18,000,000.
b.	$17,400,000	$19,500,000.
c.	$18,000,000	$16,000,000.
d.	$25,500,000	$22,900,000.

Items 28 and 29 are based on the following information:

Patsy Corp., has estimated its activity for December 1976. Selected data from these estimated amounts are as follows:

- Sales $350,000
  Gross profit (based on sales) 30%
  Increase in trade accounts receivable during month $10,000
  Change in accounts payable during month $0
  Increase in inventory during month $5,000

- Variable selling, general and administrative expenses (S,G&A) includes a charge for uncollectible accounts of 1% of sales.
  - Total S,G&A is $35,500 per month plus 15% of sales.
  - Depreciation expense of $20,000 per month is included in fixed S,G&A.

28. On the basis of the above data, what are the estimated cash receipts from operations for December?

- a. $336,500.
- b. $340,000.
- c. $346,500.
- d. $350,000.

29. On the basis of the above data, what are the estimated cash disbursements from operations for December?

- a. $309,500.
- b. $313,000.
- c. $314,500.
- d. $318,000.

30. For the month of December 1975, the records of Ranger Corporation show the following information:

Cash received on accounts receivable	$35,000
Cash sales	30,000
Accounts receivable, December 1, 1975	80,000
Accounts receivable, December 31, 1975	74,000
Accounts receivable written off as uncollectible	1,000

The corporation uses the direct write-off method in accounting for uncollectible accounts receivable. What are the gross sales for the month of December 1975?

- a. $59,000.
- b. $60,000.
- c. $65,000.
- d. $72,000.

31. At the close of its first year of operations, December 31, 1975, the Walker Company had accounts receivable of $250,000, which were net of the related allowance for doubtful accounts. During 1975, the company had charges to bad debt expense of $40,000 and wrote off, as uncollectible, accounts receivable of $10,000. What should the company report on its balance sheet at December 31, 1975, as accounts receivable before the allowance for doubtful accounts?

    a. $250,000.
    b. $260,000.
    c. $280,000.
    d. $300,000.

32. The Hutch Company sells household furniture. Customers who purchase furniture on the installment basis make payments in equal monthly installments over a two-year period, with no down payment required. Hutch's gross profit on installment sales equals 60% of the selling price of the furniture.

For financial accounting purposes, sales revenue is recognized at the time the sale is made. For income tax purposes, however, the installment method is used. There are no other book and income tax accounting differences, and Hutch's income tax rate is 50%.

If Hutch's December 31, 1976, balance sheet includes a deferred tax credit of $30,000 arising from the difference between book and tax treatment of the installment sales, it should also include installment accounts receivable of

    a. $30,000.
    b. $50,000.
    c. $60,000.
    d. $100,000.

33. The statement of changes in financial position discloses changes in financial position during the year and also

    a.   Summarizes the financing and investing activities of an entity.
    b.   Reports the changes in net working capital as opposed to cash.
    c.   Relates changes in net monetary assets to net working capital.
    d.   Reflects transactions that affect current financial position.

34. On a statement of changes in financial position, depreciation is treated as an adjustment to reported net earnings because depreciation

    a.   Is a direct source of funds.
    b.   Reduces reported net earnings but does not involve an outflow of funds.
    c.   Reduces reported net earnings and involves an inflow of funds.
    d.   Is an inflow of funds to a reserve account for replacement of assets.

35. Selected information from the 1976 accounting records of the Soccer Company is as follows:

Working capital provided from operations	$ 2,000,000
Collection of short-term receivables	40,000,000
Payments of accounts payable	30,000,000
Capital expenditures	2,800,000
Proceeds from long-term borrowings	1,500,000
Payments on long-term borrowings	500,000
Dividends on common stock	900,000
Purchases of treasury stock	200,000
Sales of stock to officers and employees	100,000
Working capital at December 31, 1975	18,000,000

Assuming funds are defined as working capital, what should be the working capital at December 31, 1976, shown on Soccer's statement of changes in financial position for the year ended December 31, 1976?

    a. $17,200,000.
    b. $17,300,000.
    c. $18,200,000.
    d. $27,200,000.

36. When preparing a statement of changes in financial position using the cash basis for defining funds, an increase in ending inventory over beginning inventory will result in an adjustment to reported net earnings because

    a.   Funds were increased since inventory is a current asset.
    b.   The net increase in inventory reduced cost of goods sold but represents an assumed use of cash.
    c.   Inventory is an expense deducted in computing net earnings, but is not a use of funds.
    d.   All changes in non-cash accounts must be disclosed under the all financial resources concept.

37. A net unrealized gain on a company's long-term portfolio of marketable equity securities should be reflected in the current financial statements as

    a.   An extraordinary item shown as a direct increase to retained earnings.

b.   A current gain resulting from holding marketable equity securities.
c.   A footnote or parenthetical disclosure only.
d.   A valuation allowance and included in the equity section of the statement of financial position.

38.   The working capital provided from operations in Seat's statement of changes in financial position for 1978 was $8,000,000. For 1978, depreciation on fixed assets was $3,800,000, amortization of goodwill was $100,000, and dividends on common stock were $2,000,000. Based on the information given above, Seat's net income for 1978 was
    a. $2,100,000.
    b. $4,100,000.
    c. $8,000,000.
    d. $11,900,000.

39.   In an effort to increase sales, Nick Razor Blade Company inaugurated a sales promotional campaign on June 30, 1978, whereby Nick placed a coupon in each package of razor blades sold, the coupons being redeemable for a premium. Each premium costs Nick $.50 and 5 coupons must be presented by a customer to receive a premium. Nick estimated that only 60% of the coupons issued will be redeemed. For the six months ended December 31, 1978, the following information is available:

Packages of Razor Blades Sold	Premiums Purchased	Coupons Redeemed
800,000	60,000	200,000

What is the estimated liability for premium claims outstanding at December 31, 1978?
    a. $20,000.
    b. $28,000.
    c. $36,000.
    d. $48,000.

40.   Dobbin Corporation, a manufacturer of household paints, is preparing annual financial statements at December 31, 1978. Because of a recently proven health hazard in one of its paints, the government has clearly indicated its intention of having Dobbin recall all cans of this paint sold in the last six months. The management of Dobbin estimates that this recall would cost $1,000,000. What accounting recognition, if any, should be accorded this situation?
    a.   No recognition.
    b.   Footnote disclosure.
    c.   Operating expense of $1,000,000.
    d.   Extraordinary loss of $1,000,000.

41.   During 1978 Boyd Corporation, which uses the allowance method of accounting for uncollectible accounts, recorded charges to bad debt expense of $50,000 and in addition it wrote off, as uncollectible, accounts receivable of $42,000. As a result of these transactions, working capital was decreased by
    a. $50,000.
    b. $42,000.
    c. $8,000.
    d. $0.

42.   A marketable equity security must have a ready market in order to be classified as current, and
    a.   Be available to management for use in short run operations.
    b.   Be traded on a recognized national exchange.
    c.   Have a current market value in excess of original cost.
    d.   Have been owned less than one year.

43.   Kirt, Incorporated, had net income for 1977 of $3,000,000. Additional information is as follows:

Amortization of goodwill	$ 80,000
Depreciation on fixed assets	3,200,000
Long-term debt:	
Bond discount amortization	130,000
Interest expense	2,600,000
Provision for doubtful accounts:	
Current receivables	700,000
Long-term receivables	210,000

Assuming funds are defined as working capital, what should be the working capital provided from operations in the statement of changes in financial position for the year ended December 31, 1977?
    a. $6,200,000.
    b. $6,410,000.
    c. $6,620,000.
    d. $9,220,000.

44.   If a marketable equity security which was classified as noncurrent in a prior period were to be reclassified as current in the current period, what would be the effect upon the valuation allowance attendant to that security assuming no change in its market value?
    a.   The valuation allowance should be reclassified to current also.
    b.   The valuation allowance should be recognized as a loss in the current period.
    c.   The valuation allowance should be adjusted to zero and the security reclassified at cost.
    d.   The valuation allowance should be recognized as a gain in the subsequent period.

45. On its December 31, 1977, balance sheet, the Noble Corporation reported the following as investments in long-term marketable equity securities:

Investment in long-term marketable
equity securities at cost $300,000
Less allowance to reduce long-term
equity securities to market   28,000
                                          $272,000

At December 31, 1978, the market valuation of the portfolio was $298,000. What should Noble report on its 1978 Statement of Income as a result of the increase in the market value of the investments in 1978?

a. $0.
b. Unrealized loss of $2,000.
c. Realized gain of $26,000.
d. Unrealized gain of $26,000

46. Which of the following is the proper accounting treatment of a gain contingency?

a. An accrued amount.
b. Deferred earnings.
c. An account receivable with an additional disclosure explaining the nature of the transaction.
d. A disclosure only.

MAY 1981 QUESTIONS

47. During 1978 Lawton Company introduced a new line of machines that carry a three-year warranty against manufacturer's defects. Based on industry experience, warranty costs are estimated at 2% of sales in the year of sale, 4% in the year after sale, and 6% in the second year after sale. Sales and actual warranty expenditures for the first three-year period were as follows:

	Sales	Actual warranty expenditures
1978	$ 200,000	$ 3,000
1979	500,000	15,000
1980	700,000	45,000
	$1,400,000	$63,000

What amount should Lawton report as a liability at December 31, 1980?

a. $0.
b. $ 5,000.
c. $ 68,000.
d. $105,000.

48. The working capital of Rogers Company at December 31, 1979, was $10,000,000. Selected information for the year 1980 for Rogers is as follows:

Working capital provided from
operations $1,700,000
Capital expenditures   3,000,000
Proceeds from short-term borrowings   1,000,000
Proceeds from long-term borrowings   2,000,000
Payments on short-term borrowings   500,000
Payments on long-term borrowings   600,000
Proceeds from issuance of common stock   1,400,000
Dividends paid on common stock   800,000

What is Rogers' working capital at December 31, 1980?

a. $10,700,000.
b. $11,200,000.
c. $11,500,000.
d. $12,000,000.

49. Fulton Cereal Company inaugurated a new sales promotional program. For every 10 cereal box tops returned to the company, customers receive an attractive prize. Fulton estimates that only 30% of the cereal box tops reaching the consumer market will be redeemed.

Additional information is as follows:

	Units	Amounts
Sales of cereal boxes	2,000,000	$1,400,000
Purchase of prizes	36,000	18,000
Prizes distributed to customers	28,000	

At the end of its year, Fulton recognized a liability equal to the estimated cost of potential prizes outstanding. What is the amount of this estimated liability?

a. $ 4,000.
b. $16,000.
c. $18,000.
d. $42,000.

50. Bold Company estimates its annual warranty expense at 2% of annual net sales. The following data are available:

Net sales for 1980 $ 4,000,000

Warranty liability account:
  December 31, 1979 $60,000 credit
  Warranty payments
    during 1980   50,000 debit

After recording the 1980 estimated warranty expense, the warranty liability account would show a December 31, 1980, balance of

a. $10,000.
b. $70,000.

c. $80,000.
d. $90,000.

51.   Steven Corporation began operations in 1980. For the year ended December 31, 1980, Steven made available the following information:

Total merchandise purchases for the year	$350,000
Merchandise inventory at December 31, 1980	70,000
Collections from customers	200,000

All merchandise was marked to sell at 40% above cost. Assuming that all sales are on a credit basis and all receivables are collectible, what should be the balance in accounts receivable at December 31, 1980?

a. $ 50,000.
b. $192,000.
c. $250,000.
d. $290,000.

Items 52. through 55. related to data to be reported in the Statement of Changes in Financial Position of Debbie Dress Shops, Inc., based on the following information:

Debbie Dress Shops, Inc.
BALANCE SHEETS

	December 31,	
	1980	1979
Assets		
Current assets:		
Cash	$ 300,000	$ 200,000
Accounts receivable – net	840,000	580,000
Merchandise inventory	660,000	420,000
Prepaid expenses	100,000	50,000
Total current assets	1,900,000	1,250,000
Long-term investments	80,000	–
Land, buildings and fixtures	1,130,000	600,000
Less accumulated depreciation	110,000	50,000
	1,020,000	550,000
Total assets	$3,000,000	$1,800,000

	December 31,	
	1980	1979
Equities		
Current liabilities:		
Accounts payable	$ 530,000	$ 440,000
Accrued expenses	140,000	130,000
Dividends payable	70,000	–
Total current liabilities	740,000	570,000
Note payable – due 1983	500,000	–
Stockholders' equity:		
Common stock	1,200,000	900,000
Retained earnings	560,000	330,000
	1,760,000	1,230,000
Total liabilities and stockholders' equity	$3,000,000	$1,800,000

Debbie Dress Shops, Inc.
INCOME STATEMENTS

	Year ended December 31,	
	1980	1979
Net credit sales	$6,400,000	$4,000,000
Cost of goods sold	5,000,000	3,200,000
Gross profit	1,400,000	800,000
Expenses (including income taxes)	1,000,000	520,000
Net income	$ 400,000	$ 280,000

Additional information available included the following:

- Although the Corporation will report all changes in financial position, management has adopted a format emphasizing the flow of cash.
- All accounts receivable and accounts payable relate to trade merchandise. Accounts payable are recorded net and always are paid to take all of the discount allowed. The Allowance for Doubtful Accounts at the end of 1980 was the same as at the end of 1979; no receivables were charged against the Allowance during 1980.
- The proceeds from the note payable were used to finance a new store building. Capital stock was sold to provide additional working capital.

52. Cash collected during 1980 from accounts receivable amounted to
   a. $5,560,000.
   b. $5,840,000.
   c. $6,140,000.
   d. $6,400,000.

53. Cash payments during 1980 on accounts payable to suppliers amounted to
   a. $4,670,000.
   b. $4,910,000.
   c. $5,000,000.
   d. $5,150,000.

54. Cash receipts during 1980 which were not provided by operations totaled
   a. $140,000.
   b. $300,000.
   c. $500,000.
   d. $800,000.

55. Cash payments for non-current assets purchased during 1980 were
   a. $ 80,000
   b. $530,000.
   c. $610,000.
   d. $660,000.

Items 56. and 57. are based on the following information:

Magnolia, Inc.
BALANCE SHEETS

| | December 31, | |
	1980	1979
Current assets	$ 474,000	$ 320,000
Equipment	1,230,000	1,200,000
Accumulated depreciation	(436,000)	(420,000)
Goodwill	480,000	500,000
Total assets	$1,748,000	$1,600,000
Current liabilities	$ 360,000	$ 160,000
Bonds payable	400,000	600,000
Discount on bonds	(12,000)	(20,000)
Common stock	1,112,000	1,112,000
Retained earnings (deficit)	(112,000)	(252,000)
Total liabilities and stockholders' equity	$1,748,000	$1,600,000

You have discovered the following facts:
- During 1980, Magnolia sold at no gain or loss equipment with a book value of $76,000 and purchased new equipment costing $150,000.
- During 1980, bonds with a face and book value of $200,000 were extinguished, with no gain or loss. They were not current liabilities prior to their extinguishment.
- Retained earnings was affected only by the 1980 net income or loss.

56. How much working capital was provided by operations during 1980?
   a. $208,000.
   b. $212,000.
   c. $220,000.
   d. $228,000.

57. Assume that $200,000 face value of bonds became current at December 31, 1980, to be repaid in early 1981. What should be the change in working capital under this assumption after considering all changes in financial position?
   a. $ 46,000 increase.
   b. $ 46,000 decrease.
   c. $246,000 increase.
   d. $246,000 decrease.

Items 58. and 59. pertain to classification of short-term obligations expected to be refinanced, and are based on the following data:

Royal Corporation's liabilities at December 31, 1980, were as follows:

Trade accounts payable	$100,000
16% notes payable issued November 1, 1980, maturing July 1, 1981	30,000
14% debentures payable issued February 1, 1980; final installment due February 1, 1985; balance at December 31, 1980, including annual installment of $50,000 due February 1, 1981	300,000
	$430,000

Royal's December 31, 1980, financial statements were issued on March 31, 1981. On January 5, 1981, the entire $300,000 balance of the 14% debentures was refinanced by issuance of a long-term obligation. In addition, on March 1, 1981, Royal consummated a noncancelable agreement with the lender to refinance the 16% note payable on a long-term basis, on readily determinable terms that have not yet been implemented. Both parties are financially capable of honoring the agreement, and there have been no violations of any of the agreement's provisions.

58. The total amount of Royal's short-term obligations that may properly be excluded from current liabilities at December 31, 1980, is
- a. $0.
- b. $30,000.
- c. $50,000.
- d. $80,000.

59. Assume the same facts for Royal Corporation's liabilities, except that the agreement with the lender to refinance the 16% note payable on a long-term basis is cancelable at any time upon ten days' notice by the lender. The total amount of Royal's short-term obligations that may properly be excluded from current liabilities at December 31, 1980, is
- a. $0.
- b. $30,000.
- c. $50,000.
- d. $80,000.

60. Volner Company's fire insurance premiums were increased from $60,000 to $200,000 in 1980. To avoid paying such a substantial additional expense, Volner increased the deductible on its policy from $100,000 to $1,000,000. Volner's income tax rate is 40%. At December 31, 1980, how much of a contingent liability should Volner accrue to cover possible future fire losses?
- a. $0.
- b. $ 540,000.
- c. $ 600,000.
- d. $1,000,000.

61. How should a loss contingency that is reasonably possible and for which the amount can be reasonably estimated be reported?

	Accrued	*Disclosed*
a.	Yes	No
b.	No	Yes
c.	Yes	Yes
d.	No	No

62. In a statement of changes in financial position (defining funds as working capital) bad debt expense should be added back to net income when it relates to

	Current receivables	*Long-term receivables*
a.	Yes	Yes
b.	Yes	No
c.	No	No
d.	No	Yes

63. Gain contingencies are usually recognized in the income statement when
- a. Realized.
- b. Occurrence is reasonably possible and the amount can be reasonably estimated.
- c. Occurrence is probable and the amount can be reasonably estimated.
- d. The amount can be reasonably estimated.

REPEAT QUESTIONS

(581,Q1,5)   Identical to item 31 above
(581,T1,26)   Identical to item 36 above

PROBLEMS

Problem 1   Marketable Equity Securities (SFAS 12)

(1177,T4)   (20 to 25 minutes)

Part a. The Financial Accounting Standards Board issued its Statement Number 12 to clarify accounting methods and procedures with respect to certain marketable securities. An important part of the statement concerns the distinction between non-current and current classification of marketable securities.

Required:

1.   Why does a company maintain an investment portfolio of current and noncurrent securities?
2.   What factors should be considered in determining whether investments in marketable equity securities should be classified as current or noncurrent, and how do these factors affect the accounting treatment for unrealized losses?

Part b. Presented below are four unrelated situations involving marketable equity securities:

Situation I

A noncurrent portfolio with an aggregate market value in excess of cost includes one particular security whose market value has declined to less than one-half of the original cost. The decline in value is considered to be other than temporary.

Situation II

The statement of financial position of a company does not classify assets and liabilities as current and noncurrent. The portfolio of marketable equity securities includes securities normally considered current that have a net cost in excess of market value of $2,000. The remainder of the portfolio has a net market value in excess of cost of $5,000.

Situation III

A marketable equity security, whose market value is currently less than cost, is classified as noncurrent but is to be reclassified as current.

Situation IV

A company's noncurrent portfolio of marketable equity securities consists of the common stock of one company. At the end of the prior year the market value of the security was fifty percent of original cost, and this effect was properly reflected in a valuation allowance account. However, at the end of the current year the market value of the security had appreciated to twice the original cost. The security is still considered noncurrent at year end.

Required:

What is the effect upon classification, carrying value, and earnings for each of the above situations. Complete your response to each situation before proceeding to the next situation.

Problem 2   Statement of Changes (1177,T5)

(20 to 25 minutes)

The statement of changes in financial position is normally a required basic financial statement for each period for which an earnings statement is presented. The reporting entity has flexibility in form, content, and terminology of this statement to meet the objectives of differing circumstances. For example, the concept of "funds" may be interpreted to mean, among other things, cash or working capital. However, the statement should be prepared based on the "all financial resources" concept.

Required:

a.   What is the "all financial resources" concept?
b.   What are two types of financial transactions which would be disclosed under the "all financial resources" concept that would not be disclosed without this concept?
c.   What effect, if any, would each of the following seven items have upon the preparation of a statement of changes in financial position prepared in accordance with generally accepted accounting principles using the cash concept of funds?
1.   Accounts receivable — trade.
2.   Inventory.
3.   Depreciation.
4.   Deferred income tax credit from interperiod allocation.
5.   Issuance of long-term debt in payment for a building.
6.   Payoff of current portion of debt.
7.   Sale of a fixed asset resulting in a loss.

Problem 3 Statement of Changes (1180,Q4)

(45 to 55 minutes)

Presented below are comparative statements of financial position of Kenwood Corporation as of December 31, 1979, and December 31, 1978, respectively.

Kenwood Corporation
Statement of Financial Position

	December 31, 1979	December 31, 1978	Increase (Decrease)
Assets			
Current assets:			
Cash	$ 100,000	$ 90,000	$ 10,000
Accounts receivable (net of allowance for uncollectible accounts of $10,000 and $8,000, respectively)	210,000	140,000	70,000
Inventories	260,000	220,000	40,000
Total current assets	570,000	450,000	120,000
Land	325,000	200,000	125,000
Plant and equipment	580,000	633,000	(53,000)
Less: accumulated depreciation	(90,000)	(100,000)	10,000
Patents	30,000	33,000	(3,000)
Total assets	$1,415,000	$1,216,000	$199,000
Liabilities and Shareholders' Equity			
Liabilities:			
Current liabilities:			
Accounts payable	$ 260,000	$ 200,000	$ 60,000
Accrued expenses	200,000	210,000	(10,000)
Total current liabilities	460,000	410,000	50,000
Deferred income taxes	140,000	100,000	40,000
Long-term bonds (due December 15, 1990)	130,000	180,000	(50,000)
Total liabilities	730,000	690,000	40,000
Shareholders' equity:			
Common stock, par value $5, authorized 100,000 shares, issued and outstanding 50,000 and 42,000 shares, respectively	250,000	210,000	40,000
Additional paid-in capital	233,000	170,000	63,000
Retained earnings	202,000	146,000	56,000
Total shareholders' equity	685,000	526,000	159,000
Total liabilities and shareholders' equity	$1,415,000	$1,216,000	$199,000

Presented below is the income statement of Kenwood Corporation for the year ended December 31, 1979.

Kenwood Corporation
INCOME STATEMENT
For the Year Ended December 31, 1979

Sales	$1,000,000
Expenses:	
Cost of sales	560,000
Salary and wages	190,000
Depreciation	20,000
Amortization	3,000
Loss on sale of equipment	4,000
Interest	16,000
Miscellaneous	8,000
Total expenses	801,000
Income before income taxes and extraordinary item	199,000
Income taxes	
Current	50,000
Deferred	40,000
Provision for income taxes	90,000
Income before extraordinary item	109,000
Extraordinary item — gain on repurchase of long-term bonds (net of $10,000 income tax)	12,000
Net income	$ 121,000

Earnings per share:	
Income before extraordinary item	$2.21
Extraordinary item	.24
Net income	$2.45

Additional Information:

· On February 2, 1979, Kenwood issued a 10% stock dividend to shareholders of record on January 15, 1979. The market price per share of the common stock on February 2, 1979, was $15.

· On March 1, 1979, Kenwood issued 3,800 shares of common stock for land. The common stock and land had current market values of approximately $40,000 on March 1, 1979.

· On April 15, 1979, Kenwood repurchased long-term bonds with a face value of $50,000. The gain of $22,000 was reported as an extraordinary item on the income statement.

· On June 30, 1979, Kenwood sold equipment costing $53,000, with a book value of $23,000, for $19,000 cash.

· On September 30, 1979, Kenwood declared and paid a $0.04 per share cash dividend to shareholders of record August 1, 1979.

· On October 10, 1979, Kenwood purchased land for $85,000 cash.

· Deferred income taxes represent timing differences relating to the use of accelerated depreciation methods for income tax reporting and straight-line depreciation methods for financial statement reporting.

Required:

Using the working-capital concept of funds, prepare a statement of changes in financial position of Kenwood Corporation for the year ended December 31, 1979. (Do not prepare a schedule of changes in working capital.)

Problem 4 ___ Loss Contingencies (SFAS 5) (1177,T6)

(25 to 30 minutes)

Part a. The two basic requirements for the accrual of a loss contingency are supported by several basic concepts of accounting. Three of these concepts are: periodicity (time periods), measurement, and objectivity.

Required:

Discuss how the two basic requirements for the accrual of a loss contingency relate to the three concepts listed above.

Part b. The following three independent sets of facts relate to (1) the possible accrual or (2) the possible disclosure by other means of a loss contingency.

Situation I

A company offers a one-year warranty for the product that it manufactures. A history of warranty claims has been compiled and the probable amount of claims related to sales for a given period can be determined.

Situation II

Subsequent to the date of a set of financial statements, but prior to the issuance of the financial statements, a company enters into a contract which will probably result in a significant loss to the company. The amount of the loss can be reasonably estimated.

Situation III

A company has adopted a policy of recording self-insurance for any possible losses resulting from injury to others by the company's vehicles. The premium for an insurance policy for the same risk from an independent insurance company would have an annual cost of $2,000. During the period covered by the financial statements, there were no accidents involving the company's vehicles which resulted in injury to others.

Required:

Discuss the accrual and/or type of disclosure necessary (if any) and the reason(s) why such disclosure is appropriate for each of the three independent sets of facts above. Complete your response before proceeding to the next situation.

Problem **5**   Statement of Changes (578,Q3)

(50 to 60 minutes)

The management of Hatfield Corporation, concerned over a decrease in working capital, has provided you with the following comparative analysis of changes in account balances between December 31, 1976, and December 31, 1977:

	December 31,		Increase
Debit Balances	1977	1976	(Decrease)
Cash	$ 145,000	$ 186,000	$ (41,000)
Accounts receivable	253,000	273,000	(20,000)
Inventories	483,000	538,000	(55,000)
Securities held for plant expansion purposes	150,000	—	150,000
Machinery and equipment	927,000	647,000	280,000
Leasehold improvements	87,000	87,000	—
Patents	27,800	30,000	(2,200)
	$2,072,800	$1,761,000	$311,800

Credit Balances

	1977	1976	Increase (Decrease)
Allowance for uncollectible accounts receivable	$ 14,000	$ 17,000	$ (3,000)
Accumulated depreciation of machinery and equipment	416,000	372,000	44,000
Allowance for amortization of leasehold improvements	58,000	49,000	9,000
Accounts payable	232,800	105,000	127,800
Cash dividends payable	40,000	—	40,000
Current portion of 6% serial bonds payable	50,000	50,000	—
6% serial bonds payable	250,000	300,000	(50,000)
Preferred stock	90,000	100,000	(10,000)
Common stock	500,000	500,000	—
Retained earnings	422,000	268,000	154,000
Totals	$2,072,800	$1,761,000	$311,800

Additional Information

During 1977 the following transactions occurred:

· New machinery was purchased for $386,000. In addition, certain obsolete machinery, having a book value of $61,000, was sold for $48,000. No other entries were recorded in Machinery and Equipment or related accounts other than provisions for depreciation.

· Hatfield paid $2,000 legal costs in a successful defense of a new patent. Amortization of patents amounting to $4,200 was recorded.

· Preferred stock, par value $100, was purchased at 110 and subsequently cancelled. The premium paid was charged to retained earnings.

· On December 10, 1977, the board of directors declared a cash dividend of $0.20 per share payable to holders of common stock on January 10, 1978.

· A comparative analysis of retained earnings as of December 31, 1977 and 1976, is presented below:

| | December 31, | |
	1977	1976
Balance, January 1	$268,000	$131,000
Net income	195,000	172,000
	463,000	303,000
Dividends declared	(40,000)	(35,000)
Premium on preferred stock repurchased	(1,000)	—
	$422,000	$268,000

Required:

    a.   Prepare a statement of changes in financial position of Hatfield Corporation for the year ended December 31, 1977, based upon the information presented above. The statement should be prepared using a working-capital format.

    b.   Prepare a schedule of changes in working capital of Hatfield Corporation for the year ended December 31, 1977.

PROBLEMS

Problem 6   Contingencies: Conditions and Disclosures (1180,T3a)

(10 to 15 minutes)

    Part a. Loss contingencies may exist for companies.

Required:

    1.   What conditions should be met for an estimated loss from a contingency to be accrued by a charge to income?

    2.   When is disclosure required, and what disclosure should be made for an estimated loss from a loss contingency that need not be accrued by a charge to income?

MULTIPLE CHOICE ANSWERS

1.	b	14.	c	27.	c	40.	c	53.	d
2.	a	15.	b	28.	a	41.	a	54.	d
3.	b	16.	a	29.	c	42.	a	55.	c
4.	c	17.	d	30.	b	43.	c	56.	d
5.	c	18.	c	31.	c	44.	b	57.	d
6.	d	19.	d	32.	d	45.	a	58.	d
7.	c	20.	d	33.	a	46.	d	59.	c
8.	c	21.	b	34.	b	47.	d	60.	a
9.	b	22.	c	35.	a	48.	a	61.	b
10.	c	23.	c	36.	b	49.	b	62.	d
11.	c	24.	c	37.	c	50.	d	63.	a
12.	a	25.	b	38.	b	51.	b		
13.	b	26.	c	39.	b	52.	c		

EXPLANATION OF MULTIPLE CHOICE ANSWERS

1. (1180,T1,4)   (b)   Working capital is current assets less current liabilities. Therefore, all assets and liabilities comprising working capital are current. The other choices describe some, but not all, working capital items. For example, prepaid items are not cash equivalents (b); inventory (c) is not a monetary item; and marketable (d) is a term not normally used to describe liabilities.

2. (1180,T1,23)   (a)   Realized gains and losses are always included in net income of the period. For noncurrent marketable equity securities, cumulative unrealized losses net of recoveries are shown as a deduction from owner's equity instead of being recognized in net income.

3. (1180,T1,29)   (b)   The requirement is which of the four choices need not be disclosed as a source and use of funds in a statement of changes in financial position. APB 19 requires that the "all financial resources" concept be followed in preparing these statements; all transactions which significantly affect the enterprise's financing and investing activities must be included in the statement. However, some transactions are excepted from this treatment because they do not provide or use resources. Stock dividends are an example of this type of transaction discussed in APB 19. All the other transactions listed must be shown in the statement of changes in financial position.

4. (1180,T1,30)   (c)   The requirement is how the amortization of bond discount should be shown on the statement of changes for a bond issuer. The amortization of bond discount results in an expense which reduces net income, but does not cause an increase or decrease in working capital. The amortization, therefore, must be added back to net income to arrive at working capital provided from operations. It must be shown on the statement [as opposed to answer (a)], does not use funds, [opposite of answer (b)], and is not a contra-expense [answer (c)].

5. (1180, P1,2)   (c)   The requirement is what amount of additional taxes should be accrued and charged to income in 1979. Para 8 of SFAS 5 requires that estimated losses from loss contingencies be accrued if the contingency is probable (as is stated in this question) and reasonably estimable. FASB Interpretation 14 states that the loss should be recorded at the best estimate within the range of possible loss, $500,000 in this case, or at the minimum if no best estimate exists.

6. (1180,P1,13)   (d)   The requirement is the amount which should be recorded as a loss in Wayne, Inc.'s income statement from an other than temporary decline in the market value of a noncurrent marketable equity security. Per para 21 of SFAS 12, the loss realized in this situation is measured as the difference between their cost and market value on the balance sheet date.

1/10/79	Cost	
	5,000 shares x $60 =	$300,000
12/31/79	Market value	
	5,000 shares x $46 =	230,000
Realized loss to be recognized		$ 70,000

7. (1180,P1,20)   (c)   The requirement is the amount of the valuation allowance that Pickwick should record for its short-term marketable equity securities portfolio. Para 8 of SFAS 12 requires that the carrying amount of such portfolios be reported at the lower of aggregate cost or aggregate market value (not LCM applied on a security by security basis). The aggregate market value of $80,000 is less than aggregate cost of $90,000.

8. (1180,Q1,14)   (c)   The requirement is the amount Mark should record as bad debt expense for 1979. Since Mark estimates bad debt by applying an experience percentage (2%) to net sales, the balance on the allowance account can be ignored. Bad debt expense is 2% times net sales ($830,000–$10,000), or $16,400.

9.   (580, P1,4)   (b)   The requirement is to determine the amount of the loss that must be accrued by Green Company for their December 31, 1979, financial statements. Per SFAS 5, para 8, a loss contingency should be accrued and charged to income if information available prior to the issuance of financial statements (March 15, 1980) indicates that at the balance sheet date the loss is (1) probable, and (2) can be reasonably estimated. Answer (b) is correct because it meets both of these criteria. Answer (a) is incorrect because the given information indicates that a loss should be recognized. Answers (c) and (d) are incorrect because they do not represent the amount of probable loss.

10.   (580,P1,18)   (c)   The requirement is to compute the amount of working capital provided by operations for the year ended December 31, 1979. The solutions approach is to begin with net income and add back those items that did not require the use of working capital. Items not requiring the use of working capital include depreciation expense, amortization of bond discount, provision for long-term doubtful accounts and amortization of goodwill. Note that these items are not considered sources of working capital but are necessary adjustments because they were deducted from revenue to obtain net income. Note that the provision for doubtful accounts on short-term receivables would not be added back, because the effect of recording these is to decrease accounts receivable (net), an element of working capital). Dividends are a distribution of income and working capital. Therefore, they are neither added to nor subtracted from net income in computing the amount of working capital from operations.

Net income		$2,500,000
Add:		
Depreciation	$2,900,000	
Bond disc. amort.	50,000	
Provision for doubt-ful accounts on L-T receivables	250,000	
GW amort.	90,000	3,290,000
		$5,790,000

11.   (580,P1,19)   (c)   The requirement is sources and uses of funds for 1979. The solutions approach is to analyze each item to determine its effect on working capital. Bonds payable converted to common stock is a source and a use of equal amounts. Consequently working capital is not affected. However, these transactions must be

shown in the statement of changes in financial position. The 2% stock dividend is one of the items that is not reported in the statement of changes in financial position (per APB 19, para 14f) as it is merely an adjustment within the stockholders' equity accounts that does not affect the resources of the firm.

Sources		Uses	
$4,000,000	Iss. of pref. stk.	$ 400,000	Pref. stk. div.
2,000,000	Conv. bonds to CS	2,000,000	Bonds pay.
1,200,000	Sale of plant	500,000	Treas. stock
$7,200,000		$2,900,000	

12.   (580,Q1,1)   (a)   The requirement is the balance of cash per books as 12/31/79. The deposits and disbursements per the bank for December must be adjusted to reflect deposits in transit and outstanding checks in the November bank statement as shown in the schedule below:

Balance per books, 11/30/79	$15,870
Add: Deposits ($26,100 [Dec.] − $4,150 [Nov. dep. in transit])	21,950
Book error	20
	$37,840
Deduct: Checks ($22,420 [Dec.] − $6,300 [Nov. O/S] + $2,500 [Dec. O/S])	(18,620)
Balance per books 12/31/79	$19,220

13.   (580,Q1,3)   (b)   The requirement is the amount of bad debt expenses for 1979. The information implies that Leer is changing from a percentage-of-sales to an aging approach for determining bad debts expense. The solutions approach is to prepare a T-account for the allowance for doubtful accounts. The beginning balance was $2,400, bad debts of $3,200 were written off during the year, and the ending balance is determined to be $2,200. Therefore, the 1979 expense must be $3,000, the adjustment needed to create the required balance.

Allowance for Doubtful Accounts

		$2,400	Beg. balance
Written off	$3,200		
		3,000	1979 expenses
		$2,200	Ending balance

14.   (580,Q1,12)   (c)   The requirement is the balance in the estimated warranty liability account at the end of 1979. The solutions approach is to prepare

a T-account for the liability. The estimated warranty costs are 8% of sales. Thus, the liability account is credited for $32,000 in 1978 and $40,000 in 1979. Since only $45,000 of actual expenditures were made to date, there is a $27,000 balance.

	Warranty Liability	
	$32,000	1978 sales
	$40,000	1979 sales
Expenditures (both years) $45,000		
Balance		$27,000

15.   (580,Q1,17)   (b)   The requirement is for the net realizable value of the accounts receivable at December 31, 1979. The gross amount of $450,000 less uncollectible accounts per the aging schedule of $32,000 results in a net realizable amount of $418,000. Implied in the information given is that the balance of allowance for uncollectible accounts per books is before adjustment for the $32,000 balance needed.

16.   (580,Q1,20)   (a)   The requirement is the amount of the bonus, given that the bonus is to equal 10% of income in excess of $100,000 before deducting taxes, but after deducting the bonus. Therefore the tax rate can be ignored in this problem and bonus would be 10% of $220,000 minus 10% of the bonus on $20,000, as computed below.

$$B = 10\% (\$320,000 - \$100,000 - B)$$
$$B = \$22,000 - .1\ B$$
$$1.1B = \$22,000$$
$$B = \$20,000$$

17.   (580,T1,2)   (d)   Para 8 of SFAS 12 requires that the carrying amount of a marketable equity securities portfolio be reported at the lower of its aggregate cost or market value determined at the balance sheet date. Both answers (a) and (c) are incorrect because they limit the valuation of the portfolio to reflect cost (answer (a)) and market value (answer (c)) only. Answer (b) is incorrect since it states the valuation to be the higher of cost or market.

18.   (580,T1,16)   (c)   Para 7, APB 19, requires that when a balance sheet, income statement and statement of retained earnings are issued, a statement of changes in financial position must be presented for each period for which an income statement is presented. Answers (a), (b), and (d) all contradict the requirement of APB 19.

19.   (580,T1,17)   (d)   Under the all-financial-resources concept, all significant financing and investing activities should be included on the statement of changes in financial position even though cash or working capital are not affected. Specific examples which are found in para 8 of APB 19 include the conversion of long-term debt to capital stock. Answers (b) and (c) both directly affect working capital, while depreciation is included in the statement of changes in financial position as an adjustment of net income.

20.   (580,T1,18)   (d)   The requirement is whether or not cash and/or quick assets are/is an acceptable format for the statement of changes in financial position. Para 11 of APB 19 permits both of these formats.

21.   (580,T1,20)   (b)   Para 12 of APB 19 requires the disclosure of net changes in each element of working capital for at least the current period either in the statement of changes in financial position or in a related tabulation.

22.   (580,T1,22)   (c)   Factoring (answer (c)) is the term used for the sale of accounts receivable. Neither pledging (answer (a)) nor assigning (answer (b)) of accounts receivable results in a sale of the accounts; they are merely different methods of providing security in order to obtain financing. Collateralizing (answer (d)) is a term not normally used for methods of financing receivables.

23.   (580,T1,25)   (c)   Para 14 of FASB 5 states that no accrual, loss, or disclosure should be made for general or unspecified business risks and that they need not be disclosed.

24.   (1179,P1,18)   (c)   The requirement is the increase in working capital as a result of a series of transactions. The solutions approach is to identify the transactions affecting working capital. Proceeds from short-term borrowings do not affect working capital because both current assets and current liabilities are increased. Proceeds from long-term borrowings increase working capital because current assets are increased. Noncurrent liabilities are also increased but do not affect working capital. Purchases of fixed assets decrease working capital as current liabilities are increased or current assets are decreased. Purchases of inventories do not affect working capital because inventory is increased by decreasing current assets and/or increasing current liabilities. Proceeds from sale of

common stock increase current assets (stockholders' equity is also increased). Thus, the long-term borrowing, fixed asset purchases, and stock sale transactions affect working capital as detailed below.

1978 Working Capital Changes

Long-term borrowings	$4,000,000
FA purchases	(3,200,000)
Stock sale	2,000,000
	$2,800,000 increase

25. (1179,Q1,2) (b) The requirement is the liability for unredeemed promotional coupons at 12/31/78. Two separate series of promotional coupons were issued during 1978. The first series expired on 6/30/78 and the problem indicated that one month elapses between the date the grocers receive the coupons from consumers and the date that Supple receives them. Accordingly, no additional liability should be accrued for the first series. The second series, which expired on 12/31/78, required disbursements of $40,000 on total coupon value issued of $120,000. Since Supple's experience is 40% of the coupons are redeemed, the overall disbursement is expected to be $48,000 (40% of $120,000). Thus, an accrued liability of $8,000 ($48,000 - $40,000) is required.

26. (1179,Q1,13) (c) The requirement is the correct amount of current assets as of 12/31/78. The balance sheet presentation included cash, accounts receivable, and inventories of $250,000. The additional detail of accounts receivable indicates that goods out on consignment are included in accounts receivable at their selling price, rather than being included in inventory at their cost. Since the selling price of the consigned goods is 130% of cost, the cost of the $26,000 of goods at retail is $20,000 ($26,000 ÷ 130%). Thus, current assets are overstated by $6,000 and should be reduced from $250,000 to $244,000.

27. (1176,P1,15) (c) The requirement is to determine the disclosures required on the statement of changes regarding debt. Since short-term borrowings and the current portion of long-term debt are working capital items, no detail of their changes need be disclosed in the statement of changes. Thus, one must focus on long-term debt. There was a source or borrowing of $18,000,000 and payments and transfers of $16,000,000. Thus long-term debt provided $18,000,000 of working capital, and used $16,000,000 of working capital. See para 12 and 13 of APB 19.

28. (1176,P2,35) (a) Estimated cash receipts for December are the sales figure of $350,000 less bad debts of $3,500 less the $10,000 increase in accounts receivable.

CR	
$350,000	Sales
− 3,500	Bad debts
− 10,000	Increase in AR
$336,500	

29. (1176,P2,36) (c) The estimated cash disbursements for December are 70% (1.00 − GP%) of the $350,000 of sales, plus $5,000 of inventory increase, plus SG&A of $64,500. The $64,500 of SG&A consists of $35,500 plus 15% of sales, totalling $88,000 adjusted for noncash items of $20,000 depreciation and $3,500 of bad debts.

CD		SG&A	
$350,000		$35,500	Fixed
70%		52,500	Variable
$245,000		−20,000	Depreciation
+ 5,000	Inventory incr.	− 3,500	Bad debts
+64,500	SG&A	$64,500	
$314,500			

30. (1176,Q1,8) (b) The requirement is gross sales. Add cash sales of $30,000, credit sales of $35,000, the accounts written off of $1,000 and subtract the decrease in receivable of $6,000. The decrease in receivables must be considered a reduction in sales, because $6,000 of the $35,000 were not sales of this period but rather collections of sales of a previous period. The $1,000 written off was sold and is part of gross sales even though not collectible.

Cash sales	$30,000
Charge sales	+35,000
AR decrease	− 6,000
AR writeoff	+ 1,000
Gross sales	$60,000

31. (1176,Q1,13) (c) The requirement is the amount of accounts receivable before the allowance for doubtful accounts at 12-31-75. If we know the balance in accounts receivable is $250,000 after deducting the allowance for doubtful accounts, we only have to compute the amount in the allowance for doubtful accounts and add it to $250,000. The allowance account was credited for $40,000 (bad debts expense) and debited for $10,000 (receivable write-offs). Adding the $30,000 balance in the allowance for doubtful accounts to the $250,000 of net receivables provides $280,000 of gross receivables at 12-31-75.

32. (577,Q1,12) (d) The requirement is the amount of installment accounts receivable at the end of 1976. The deferred tax credit of the $30,000 exists because installment profit has been reported per books, but not on the tax return. Thus for every dollar of gross profit receivable, there should be $.50 in the deferred tax credit account. Thus the $30,000 credit indicates that there is $60,000 of gross profit in the receivable. Given a 60% gross profit rate, the receivable must equal $100,000.

33. (577,T2,23) (a) The statement of changes in financial position summarizes the financing and investing activities of the enterprise, regardless of whether working capital items are directly affected, e.g., acquisition of property by issuance of stock. See para 7 and 8 of APB 19. Answer (b) is incorrect because the cash approach as well as the net working capital approach may be used (para 9). Answer (c) is incorrect because no computation of changes in net monetary assets is made in the statement of changes in financial position. Answer (d) is incorrect because financing and investing activities affecting only non-current items are also reflected, e.g., issuance of stock for fixed assets.

34. (577,T2,24) (b) Depreciation does not affect working capital. Depreciation however must be added back to net income when using net income as a proxy for working capital generated by operations. In the calculation of net income, depreciation is a negative item but does not cause an outflow or reduction of working capital. See para 10 of APB 19.

35. (1177,P1,17) (a) The requirement is to compute the amount of working capital at the end of 1976. The solutions approach is to add all of the increases and subtract all of the decreases in working capital to the balance at the end of 1975. The solution is presented below. All items are included except collection of short-term receivables and payments of accounts payable which are implicitly included in the computation determining working capital provided by operations.

Beginning balance	18,000
Operations	+ 2,000
Capital expenditures	− 2,800
Long-term borrowings	+ 1,500
Long-term debt repayment	− 500
Dividends	− 900
Treasury stock purchase	− 200
Sale of stock	+ 100
	17,200

36. (1178,T1,21) (b) The requirement is the effect of an increase in ending inventory on a cash basis statement of changes in financial position. Reported net income must be adjusted in computing cash provided by operations because the increase in inventory reduced cost of sales and thus increased income but did not increase cash. Answer (a) is incorrect because an increase in inventory decreases cash. Answer (c) is incorrect because inventory is not an expense in computing net income even though a change in inventory is an adjustment to cost of goods sold. Answer (d) is incorrect because all changes in non-cash accounts must be disclosed under the cash basis approach to the statement of changes in financial position, not the all financial resources concept. The all financial resources concept includes investing and financing transactions that do not affect cash, such as a direct exchange of long-term debt for assets.

37. (578,T1,11) (c) Unrealized gain on marketable equity securities is only disclosed in the financial statements per para 12 of SFAS 12. Gains are only reflected in the financial statements when they are realized, i.e., upon sale. If in the previous period, a valuation account had been set up to reduce the aggregate non-current marketable equity security cost to market, this entry would be reversed. There would, however, be no effect on the income statement. The end of the year financial statements would present noncurrent marketable equity securities at cost. Parenthetical or footnote disclosure would indicate their market value (para 12).

38. (579,P1,16) (b) The requirement is the net income given working capital provided by operations of $8,000,000, depreciation of $3,800,000, goodwill amortization of $100,000, and dividends on common stock of $2,000,000. To compute the working capital provided by operations, net income is adjusted for non-working capital income and expense items. Thus depreciation of $3,800,000 and $100,000 of goodwill amortization would be added to net income. Thus the net income is computed as $4,100,000 by

working the schedule below from bottom to top. Note that dividends on common stock do not affect the adjustment of net income to working capital provided by operations.

Net income	$4,100
Depreciation	3,800
Goodwill amortization	100
Working capital from operations	$8,000

39. (579,Q1,2) (b) The requirement is the liability for premium claims at 12/31/78. During the six months the premium plan has been in effect, 800,000 packages of blades containing coupons have been sold, of which 60% are estimated to be redeemed. The total expected redemptions of 480,000 (800,000 x 60%) coupons must be reduced by the 200,000 of coupons already redeemed. The resulting 280,000 coupons to be redeemed will result in the issuance of 56,000 premiums (280,000 ÷ 5), which cost $.50 each, resulting in a liability of $28,000.

40. (579,Q1,5) (c) The requirement is the amount, if any, to be accrued for a loss contingency. Since there are both a clear intention by the government to have the Dobbin Corporation recall its paint, and also the management can estimate the cost of the recall at $1,000,000, this contingent loss should be recorded in the financial statements per SFAS 5, para 8. The estimated loss would be classified as an ordinary item per para 20 of APB 30, because it is probably not both unusual and infrequent. To be unusual, the event must possess a high degree of abnormality and be unrelated to the ordinary operations of the entity. Infrequency means that it should not reasonably be expected to occur in the foreseeable future taking into account the environment in which the entity operates. Given the environment of paint, chemical, etc. manufacturers, government recalls of products are not "infrequent" and possibly not "unusual." Product recalls are not highly abnormal, and they might occur in the future.

41. (579,Q1,20) (a) The requirement is the effect on working capital of charging $50,000 to bad debts expense and writing off uncollectible accounts of $42,000. Charging bad debts expense reduces working capital because a contra-current asset account (allowance for doubtful accounts) is increased. The writeoff of uncollectible accounts, however, has no effect on working capital as both the current

asset account and the contra-current asset account are reduced by the same amount. Accordingly, working capital would be decreased by only the $50,000 charged to bad debts expense (and credited to the allowance for doubtful accounts).

42. (579,T1,15) (a) The requirement is an attribute (in addition to having a ready market) for classifying marketable equity securities as current. In order to be classified as current, they must also be available for management's use within the current operating cycle. The definition of current assets is "cash and other assets or resources commonly identified as those which are reasonably expected to be realized in cash or sold or consumed during a normal operating cycle of a business" (para 4, Chapter 3, ARB 43). Answer (b) is incorrect because it is concerned with the marketability rather than whether the security is current or noncurrent. Answer (c) is incorrect because it is concerned with the market value relative to the original cost, which has nothing to do with the balance-sheet classification of the security. Answer (d) is incorrect because availability for use in the near future, not length of past holding, is relevant to the current-noncurrent classification.

43. (1178,P1,18) (c) The requirement is the amount of working capital provided from operations per the working capital concept. The approach is to adjust net income of $3,000,000 for items affecting net income but not affecting working capital. The $80,000 amortization of goodwill, $3,200,000 depreciation of fixed assets, $130,000 of bond discount amortization, and $210,000 of doubtful accounts on long-term receivables all are charged against net income but do not affect working capital. Accordingly they must be added back to working capital which results in working capital provided by operations of $6,620,000.

Note that the amortization of bond discounts has the effect on increasing interest expense without affecting the amount paid in cash as interest expense. Also note that the provision for doubtful accounts on current receivables reduces working capital and also reduces income, i.e., no adjustment is required. Conversely provisions for doubtful accounts on long-term receivables do not affect working capital, but reduce income, i.e., an adjustment is required.

Net income	$3,000,000
Goodwill amortization	80,000
Depreciation expense	3,200,000
Discount amortization	130,000
Bad debts on noncurrent receivables	210,000
Working capital from operations	$6,620,000

44. (1178,T1,11) (b)   The requirement is the effect on the valuation allowance of a marketable equity security that was reclassified from noncurrent to current. When there is a change in classification of a security between current and noncurrent, any excess of cost over market is charged to income as a realized loss, and the market value becomes the new cost basis. Thus the valuation allowance account is recognized as a loss in the period of reclassification. See para 10 of SFAS 12. The entry to reclassify the marketable equity security would be:

Loss on reclassification	(plug)	
Marketable equity securities -		
current	(market)	
Marketable equity securities -		
noncurrent		(cost)
Net unrealized loss on non-		(cost-
current securities		market)

45. (579,Q1,3) (a)   The requirement is the effect on income of an increase in market value of noncurrent marketable equity securities. Para 11 of SFAS 12 requires that the debit resulting from the establishment of an allowance account to reduce noncurrent marketable equity securities to market be carried as a deferred debit in the shareholder equity section, i.e., it is not recognized in income. Thus when the market value increases, the decrease in the valuation account will also result in a corresponding decrease in the deferred debit carried in the equity section of the balance sheet. Thus no income results from an increase in market value of noncurrent marketable equity securities.

46. (578,T1,22) (d)   While SFAS 5, Accounting for Contingencies, superseded ARB 50, the FASB did not change the accounting for gain contingencies. Contingencies usually are not reflected in the accounts but adequate disclosure should be made without misleading users concerning the likelihood of realization of the gain. See para 17 of SFAS 5.

MAY 1981 ANSWERS

47. (581,P1,3) (d)   The requirement is the amount to be reported as a warranty liability at 12/31/80. The solutions approach is to prepare a T-account for the liability. The liability is credited for total estimated warranty expense, which is 12% of 1978-80 sales. The liability is debited when actual warranty expenditures are made. Since the expenditures made are less than the total estimated expense to date, a credit balance of $105,000 results.

Warranty Liability

$ 63,000	$168,000
Expenditures	(12%)($1,400,000)
End. bal. 105,000	Estimated expense
	$105,000 End. bal.

48. (581,P1,10) (a)   The requirement is Roger's working capital at 12/31/80. The solutions approach is to visualize a working capital "T"-account.

Working Capital

Beginning balance	
+ Sources	— Uses
Ending balance	

Note that the proceeds from and payments on short-term borrowings do not affect the amount of working capital because in both transactions, only current accounts (cash and short-term debt) are involved. The remaining items must be identified as sources or uses and placed in the "T"-account described above.

Working Capital

Beginning balance	$10,000,000		
Sources:		Uses:	
From operations	1,700,000		Cap. expenditures
		$ 3,000,000	
From LT borrowing	2,000,000	600,000	LT debt payments
From iss. C.S.	1,400,000	10,700,000	Ending balance
Ending balance $10,700,000			

49. (581,Q1,7) (b)   The requirement is the amount of estimated premium liability to be recognized at year-end. Only 30% of the 2,000,000 box tops, or 600,000 box tops, are expected to be redeemed. Since 10 box tops are required per prize, 60,000 prizes will be distributed. Of this total, 28,000 prizes have already been distributed, leaving a liability of 32,000 prizes at $ .50 each ($18,000 ÷ 36,000 prizes purchased). Therefore, the liability is $16,000.

50. (581,Q1,9) (d)   The requirement is the amount of warranty liability to be reported by Bold Company at 12/31/80. The solutions approach is to prepare a T-account for the liability. The estimated warranty expense is 2% of annual net sales. Therefore,

the liability account is credited for $80,000 (2% of $4,000,000) in 1980. Since $50,000 of warranty expenditures were made during 1980, the ending balance in the liability account is $90,000.

Warranty Liability

		$60,000	12/31/79 bal.
1980 expend.	$50,000	$80,000	1980 exp.
		$90,000	12/31/80 bal.

51. (581,Q1,19)   (b)   The requirement is the balance in accounts receivable at 12/31/80. The solutions approach is to first compute 1980 sales, then prepare a T-account for accounts receivable. 1980 cost of goods sold is $280,000 ($350,000 purchases less $70,000 ending inventory). Note that beginning inventory is zero because the company began operations in 1980. Since all merchandise was marked to sell at 40% above cost, 1980 credit sales are $392,000 ($280,000 cost of goods sold x 140%). The T-account analysis below indicates that accounts receivable at 12/31/80 is $192,000.

Accounts Receivable

1/1/80 bal.	$0		
Credit Sales	$392,000	$200,000	Collections
12/31/80 Bal.	$192,000		

52. (581,Q2,25)   (c)   The requirement is cash collected during 1980 from accounts receivable. The solutions approach is to prepare a T-account for accounts receivable. The allowance account has no effect on this analysis, because the problem states that the balance in this account has not changed and no accounts receivable were written off. Net credit sales are the only debit to accounts receivable because all accounts receivable relate to trade merchandise. In the T-account below, you must solve for the missing credit to determine that $6,140,000 was collected on account during 1980.

AR - Net

12/31/79 balance	$ 580,000		
1980 Net Credit Sales	6,400,000	?	1980 Collections
12/31/80 balance	$ 840,000		

Author's Note: Based on the information given in this problem, no bad debt expense was recorded during 1980. However, unrealistic as this assumption might be, it is important to simply work with the information as given.

53. (581,Q2,26)   (d)   The requirement is cash payments during 1980 on accounts payable. The solutions approach is to visualize the accounts payable T-account.

Accounts Payable

		$440,000	12/31/79
Payments	?	?	Purchases
		$530,000	12/31/80

It is apparent that in order to determine payments to suppliers, purchases of trade merchandise must first be computed. The cost of goods sold statement can be used to compute purchases.

Beginning Inventory	$	420,000
+ Purchases	+	?
− Ending Inventory	−	660,000
Cost of Goods Sold	$	5,000,000

Purchases = $5,000,000 − ($420,000 − $660,000)
   = $5,240,000

Finally, the purchases are entered into the accounts payable T-account, and payments to suppliers of $5,150,000 can be plugged in.

Accounts Payable

		$ 440,000	12/31/79
Payments	5,150,000	5,240,000	Purchases
		$ 530,000	12/31/80

54. (581,Q2,27)   (d)   The requirement is cash receipts during 1980 which were not provided by operations. In solving the 2 remaining items, the solutions approach is to work through the comparative balance sheets noting increases and decreases; the additional information given must be considered in connection with these changes. These cash receipts include proceeds from long-term borrowing, and issuance of capital stock.

Proceeds from long-term note	$500,000
Proceeds from issuance of common stock	$300,000
	$800,000

55. (581,Q2,28)   (c)   The requirement is cash payments for noncurrent assets purchased during 1980. The two noncurrent assets shown on the balance sheet (long-term investments and land, building, and fixtures) have increased from 12/31/79 to 12/31/80, indicating cash purchases since the additional information does not suggest any other means of acquisition. Therefore, cash payments include $80,000 for long-term investments and $530,000 ($1,130,000 − $600,000) for land, building and fixtures.

56. (581,Q2,29)   (d)   The requirement is the amount of working capital provided by operations in 1980. Working capital provided by operations is net income adjusted for any revenues or expenses which do not provide or use working capital. Since the deficit was affected only by net income, the $140,000

decrease in the retained earnings deficit is the 1980 net income. The next step is to examine the comparative balance sheets and additional information to locate any net income adjustments. There are three such items: depreciation expense (computed below), goodwill amortization ($500,000 − $480,000 = $20,000) and bond discount amortization ($20,000 − $12,000 = $8,000). Note that no part of the $8,000 reduction in the bond discount account relates to the bonds extinguished, since the face and book value of these bonds were the same.

In order to determine the amount of depreciation expense, both the equipment and accumulated depreciation accounts have to be analyzed. The equipment T-account analysis reveals that the cost of equipment sold was $120,000.

Equipment			
12/31/79	$1,200,000		
Purchase	$ 150,000	?	Sale
12/31/80	$1,230,000		

The equipment sold had a book value of $76,000; if it originally cost $120,000, the accumulated depreciation at the time of sale was $44,000. The accumulated depreciation T-account below indicates that 1980 depreciation expense is $60,000.

Accumulated Deprec.			
		$420,000	12/31/79
Sale $44,000		?	Deprec. exp.
		$436,000	12/31/80

The working capital provided by operations is computed below. Because all three adjustments are expenses which do not involve an outflow of working capital, they are added back to net income.

Net income	$140,000
Add back:	
Deprec. Exp.	60,000
Goodwill Amort.	20,000
Bond Discount Amort.	8,000
Working Capital Provided by Operations	$228,000

57. (581,Q2,30)   (d)   The requirement is the change in working capital, assuming that $200,000 face value of bonds became current at 12/31/80. The solutions approach is to prepare a schedule of changes in working capital based on the balance sheets given, and subtract the decrease in working capital caused by reclassification of the bonds payable as a current liability.

	12/31/80	12/31/79	Change in Working Capital
Current Assets	$ 474,000	$ 320,000	$ 154,000
Current Liab.	$(360,000)	$(160,000)	$(200,000)
	$ 114,000	$ 160,000	

Change in WC before bond reclassification	$(46,000)
Bond reclassification	$(200,000)
Decrease in working capital	$(246,000)

Note that it must be assumed that none of the unamortized bond discount relates to the bonds reclassified, or the answer would not match any of the four choices given.

58. (581,Q2,31)   (d)   The requirement is the total amount of Royal's short-term obligations that may properly be excluded from current liabilities at 12/31/80. Per SFAS 6, an enterprise may exclude a short-term obligation from current liabilities only if (1) it intends to refinance the obligation on a long-term basis and (2) it demonstrates an ability to consummate the refinancing. The $50,000 current installment of the 14% debentures qualify for exclusion because those debentures were actually refinanced on a long-term basis. When a financing agreement is used to provide evidence of ability to consummate, the agreement must: be noncancellable; be long-term; and, possess readily determinable terms. In addition, the company must not be in violation of the agreement, and both the lender and investor must be financially capable of honoring the agreement. Since all these requirements are met by the described financing agreement, the $30,000 note payable may also be excluded from current liabilities.

59. (581,Q2,32)   (c)   Refer to the discussion of the previous question. Since the financing agreement is no longer noncancellable, the $30,000 note payable may not be excluded from current liabilities. However, the $50,000 current installment of the 14% debentures may be excluded as discussed in the previous question.

60. (581,Q2,37)   (a)   The requirement is the amount of contingent liability Volner should accrue to cover possible future fire losses. Per para 28 of SFAS 5, a contingent liability should not be accrued for uninsured risks. Contingent liabilities are accrued only when the event creating the contingency (in this case, the fire) has already occurred. Also, a company cannot have an obligation to itself to replace damaged property so no real liability exists either before or after the event occurs.

61. (581,T1,10) (b) The requirement is how a loss contingency that is reasonably possible and for which the amount can be reasonably estimated should be reported. FASB 5 requires recognition of a loss if it is probable at the balance sheet date that a liability has been incurred and the amount of the loss can be reasonably estimated. If no accrual is made for a loss contingency because one or both of the following conditions above are not met, SFAS 5, para 10, requires disclosure of the contingency be made when there is at least a reasonable possibility that a loss may have been incurred.

62. (581,T1,27) (d) The requirement is whether debt expense that relates to current and/or long-term receivables should be added back to net income in a statement of changes in financial position in which working capital flows are emphasized. In these statements, a separate schedule of current assets and current liabilities is used to compute the change in working capital. The solutions approach to this question is to make the journal entry to record bad debt expense.

Bad debts expense	XXX	
Allow. for bad		
debts: Current		XXX
Allow. for bad		
debts: Long-term		XXX

Note that the bad debts expense is a deduction in determining net income. The credit to the account "allowance for bad debts: current" does reduce working capital and working capital from operations. However, the long-term allowance account does not affect working capital. Note that all of the expense in the above entry has been deducted in arriving at net income. Since the portion credited to the long-term receivable did not affect working capital, this amount should be added to net income; it is like depreciation.

63. (581,T1,36) (a) The requirement is to identify the point at which gain contingencies are usually recognized in the income statement. "Contingency" designates a claim or right whose existence is uncertain but which may become valid property rights eventually. Accountants have adopted a conservative policy in the area of gain contingencies. Accordingly, the following provision of para 3 of ARB 50 shall be applicable. It states that gain contingencies are not reflected in the accounts since to do so might be to recognize revenue prior to its realization.

ANSWER OUTLINE

Problem 1   Marketable Equity Securities (SFAS 12)

a1.   Current marketable securities
        Provide a return on liquid investments
        Are an investment of idle excess funds
        Noncurrent marketable investments
            Provide dividend or interest earnings
            Can provide appreciation of market value
            Can create desirable relationships with suppliers,
              etc.

a2.   Current assets are resources to be converted into
       cash or sold or consumed
            During the operating cycle, or one year, which-
              ever is less
            Current securities are readily marketable
                And intended to be liquidated
        Noncurrent securities must also be marketable
            Intended to be held for more than one year
        Feasibility of disposal must also be considered
        Writedowns to market are
            Recognized in earnings for current marketable
              securities
            Deferred as part of shareholders' equity for non-
              current securities
                Unless permanent decline, then recognize loss

b1.   Permanent decline in market value of noncurrent
       security
        Write security down
        Recognize loss in current period
        No writeup for subsequent market value recovery

b2.   Nonclassified balance sheet
        All equity securities are considered noncurrent
        Use cost, because aggregate market exceeds cost
          by $3,000
        Thus, no effect on earnings

b3.   Reclassification of noncurrent marketable equity
       security with market below cost
            Transfer from noncurrent to current
                Market is new basis if less than cost
                Difference is loss in current period

b4.   Noncurrent marketable equity securities below
       cost and then above cost
            For noncurrent, market below cost results in
              debit valuation account in shareholders' equity
            When market increases over cost
                Valuation account reduced to zero
                Carrying value cannot exceed cost
                Thus no effect on earnings

UNOFFICIAL ANSWER

Problem 1   Marketable Equity Securities (SFAS 12)

a. 1.   A company invests in marketable equity securi-

ties that are classified as current assets primarily to earn interest or dividends on cash used as emergency funds and excess cash being held by the company. Easy and quick access to these funds is a primary requirement for this type of investment, and as a result, these investments must be considered nearly as liquid as cash.

Investments in marketable equity securities that are classified as noncurrent assets are made by a company with the intent to hold them for a period in excess of one operating cycle (or one year if the normal operating cycle is less than one year). While the ultimate reason for a company's investing in noncurrent securities of another company is to improve earnings, this may be accomplished by investing for several specific reasons. The first reason might be for dividends (or interest) paid on the investment. Second, a company may feel that the security will appreciate in market value. Third, the company may desire to assure itself of a satisfactory operating relationship with another company in terms of supply or distribution. None of these reasons requires the immediate liquidity of the investment.

2.   The general classification of any asset as being current in nature is that the asset will be converted to cash, sold, or consumed during the normal operating cycle of the business or within one year, if the operating cycle is less than one year. In the case of marketable equity securities classified as current, the above general rule is complied with by meeting the following two requirements: (1) the security must be readily marketable; (2) it must be the intention of management to dispose of the investment within the next succeeding operating cycle or fiscal year if the normal operating cycle is less than one year. Because of this assumed liquidity, it follows that any reduction in market value below original cost should be immediately reflected in earnings, since the original intent was to use the funds as cash within the current operating cycle (or year if the normal operating cycle is less than one year).

Noncurrent assets represent amounts that are not expected to be converted to cash, sold, or consumed within the normal operating cycle of the business (or within one year if the operating cycle is less than one year). While noncurrent marketable equity securities have a ready market, the central point to be considered in classification is the intent of management. Management must have determined that the security is to be held for greater than one cycle (or year, as the case may be) in order for the security to be classified as noncurrent. Because of the intent of management to retain the investment regardless of the current market situation, any reduction in market value below cost, other than a permanent decline, should properly be deferred until such time as management's intent is to liquidate the investment in the current operating cycle (or year, if the normal operating cycle is less than one year).

It can be seen from the foregoing discussion that any given security, if it initially meets the requirements of being readily marketable, can be classified either as current or noncurrent depending on the intent of management. However, the intent of management (presumably related to the company's investment objectives) must be mitigated by the additional factor of feasibility. Management must consider such factors as cash flow or asset stewardship in determining whether or not its intent is feasible under prevailing business conditions.

b.   Situation I

If the market value of an equity security declines in value below cost and the decline in value is considered to be other than temporary, a realized loss should be recognized and reflected in the determination of net earnings for the current period. A transaction of this nature reduces the cost basis of the security, and the new cost basis should not be adjusted for subsequent recoveries in market value.

Situation II

In the case of a statement of financial position that does not classify assets and liabilities between current and noncurrent, the entire portfolio of marketable equity securities should be treated as if it were noncurrent in nature. The carrying value of marketable equity securities should be the lower of cost or market value at the date of the statement of financial position. From the facts given, it can be determined that the aggregate market valuation exceeds cost; thus, the carrying value of the portfolio would be at cost. Therefore, there would be no effect on earnings.

Situation III

If there is a change in the classification of a marketable equity security between current and noncurrent, the security shall be transferred between the corresponding portfolios at the lower of its cost or market value at the date of transfer. If the market value is less than cost, the market value shall become the new cost basis, and the difference shall be accounted for as if it were a realized loss and included in the determination of net earnings.

Situation IV

A valuation allowance is created to reflect a net unrealized loss in the aggregate for a given portfolio of securities. In the facts given, the portfolio in question consists of one security that had decreased in value in a prior year and had appreciated to a value in excess of cost in the current period. Since the carrying value of the security is the lower of cost or market, the valuation allowance established in the prior year must be adjusted to zero, resulting in carrying the security at original cost at the end of the current period. Since this is a noncurrent security, the adjustment of the valuation allowance will affect the equity section of the statement of financial position and have no effect on current earnings.

ANSWER OUTLINE

Problem 2   Statement of Changes

a.   All financial resources concept
    Discloses all material financing transactions
    Even those not affecting funds

b.   Item disclosed per all financial resources concept
    Acquisition of noncurrent assets with
        Noncurrent debt
        Other noncurrent assets
        Equity securities
    Reduction of long-term debt by
        Other long-term debt
        Issuance of noncurrent assets
        Issuance of equity

c.   Treatment per cash concept of funds
    1. Change in accounts receivable is source or use of cash
    2. Change in inventory represents source or use of cash
    3. Depreciation is non-cash expense
        Add back to operating earnings
    4. Change in deferred tax credits is source or use of cash
    5. Long-term debt issued for building does not affect cash
        A financing and investing transaction per all financial resources concept

6. Reduction of current debt is use of cash
7. Loss on fixed asset sale is added back to income
   Proceeds are a source of cash

UNOFFICIAL ANSWER

Problem 2   Statement of Changes

a. The "all financial resources" concept requires that all material financial transactions be disclosed in the statement of changes in financial position. Transactions that technically do not increase or decrease funds (regardless of the concept of funds employed) but that represent significant financing and investing activities entered into by an entity must also be disclosed within this statement. Disclosure of a significant transaction that does not increase or decrease "funds" is made by showing one side of the transaction as a source of funds and the other side of the transaction as a corresponding use of funds.

b. Opinion 19 of the Accounting Principles Board states that all important changes in financial position should be disclosed. Inasmuch as all changes in financial position with respect to "funds" (i.e., cash, working capital, quick assets, etc.) are disclosed in the normal preparation of the statement, the "all financial resources" concept refers to those transactions that affect financial position but do not increase or decrease "funds." These transactions would include the following:

1.   Purchase of noncurrent assets by the issuance of capital stock or long-term debt, or a reduction in another noncurrent asset.

2.   Reduction of a long-term liability by the issuance of capital stock or the incurrence of another long-term liability, or a reduction in a noncurrent asset.

c. The effects and procedural considerations required by Opinion 19 of the Accounting Principles Board of the seven account balances (transactions) upon the preparation of a statement of changes in financial position using the cash concept of funds are as follows.

(1)   Accounts receivable—trade are generated as a result of credit sales. A balance in accounts receivable—trade represents sales (a part of operating earnings) not represented by cash. An increase in the accounts receivable—trade balance indicates that the actual cash generated is equal to sales as reported on the earnings statement less the increase in accounts receivable—trade balance. Conversely, a net decrease in the accounts receivable—trade balance would have to be added to sales as reported on the earnings statement to arrive at cash generated from sales. In the preparation of a statement of changes in financial position the increase (decrease) in this account balance between two periods represents a use (source) of funds.

(2)   Inventory is a component part of cost-of-goods-sold. The net change in inventory balances affects the cash used for cost-of-goods-sold. An increase in ending inventory over beginning inventory reduces the cost-of-goods-sold. However, cash was presumed to be used to increase the inventory balance. An increase in the inventory balance represents a "use" of cash. When there is an increase in inventory balances, the cash used for cost-of-goods-sold is the cost-of-goods-sold as shown in the current earnings statement plus the increase in inventory balance.

   A similar analysis leads to the conclusion that a decrease in ending inventory balance with respect to beginning inventory balance gives rise to a net increase in cost-of-goods-sold as shown in the current earnings statement but a reduction in the cash so used.

(3)   Depreciation represents a systematic allocation of the cost of a fixed asset to the accounting periods benefited by the asset. The process of recognizing depreciation does not affect cash. Operating earnings is determined using depreciation as an expense, so in determining cash generated from operations, depreciation must be added back to operating earnings.

(4)   Deferred income taxes are the difference between income taxes matched against earnings and the actual amount paid or payable for the period. If the balance of deferred income tax credits, for example, increases between two periods, the amount of income taxes paid was less than the indicated income tax expense. Therefore, an increase in deferred income tax credits represents an expense not requiring cash and thus must be added back to net earnings in a manner similar to depreciation.

   Conversely, if deferred income tax credits decrease, the amount "paid" was greater than the current income tax expense and represents a "use" of funds.

(5) The purchase of a building by issuing long-term debt obviously does not require the use of funds using the cash concept. However, APB Opinion 19 requires that all important changes in financial position be disclosed. The purchase of the building must be shown as a "use" of funds and the issuance of long-term debt must be shown as a "source" of funds.

(6) The payment of the current portion of debt using the cash concept of funds represents a use of funds.

(7) In the sale of a fixed asset there are two component parts to be considered in the transaction: (1) recovery of book value and (2) resultant gain or loss on the transaction. Only the resultant gain or loss is reflected in net earnings, and the gain or loss is not the result of ordinary operations for statement of changes in financial position purposes (although it is part of ordinary operations for earnings statement purposes). The gain (loss) should be deducted from (added to) net earnings, and the total proceeds from the sale of the fixed asset should be shown as a source of cash. In general practice, the earnings effect is left in the net earnings (loss) figure and only the book value is added back as a source of funds.

SOLUTION GUIDE

Problem 3   Statement of Changes

1. The requirement is to prepare a statement of changes in financial position using the working capital concept of funds; a schedule of changes in working capital is not required.

2. This solution guide uses the "direct" approach to preparing the statement of changes in financial position. Under this approach the increases or decreases in the non-current accounts are analyzed by relating them to the additional text information; supporting schedules, including journal entries and "T" accounts are used, as necessary, in arriving at the sources and uses. Some of the sources and uses are identified directly in the additional information, e.g., a statement that $XXXX of cash dividends were declared. These can be entered directly in the sources or uses section of the statement (uses in the case of dividends); no further analysis is necessary. Once the increases, decreases and addi-

tional information have been analyzed, there may still be some unexplained increases and/or decreases; e.g., if an increase in equipment is unexplained, assume working capital was used to acquire equipment.

> *Author's note: The AICPA solution to this problem includes a work sheet (not required). We (the authors) believe that such an approach is too time consuming because of the necessity to copy the accounts and numbers (increases and decreases) from the exam booklet onto a worksheet, identify (write) the source and use items on the worksheet, and finally transfer the information to the required statement. We believe use of the direct approach enables candidates to analyze carefully the more complex transactions but avoids wasting valuable time transferring information on and off of a worksheet.*

3. The solutions approach is to set up a skeleton statement entering the company title, etc. and the main headings.
   FINANCIAL RESOURCES PROVIDED
   Working Capital from Operations
   Working Capital from Other Sources
   Financial Resources not Affecting Working Capital
   FINANCIAL RESOURCES USED
   Working Capital Uses
   Financial Resources not Affecting Working Capital

3.1 Begin by entering the income before extraordinary item in the operations section; as explained below, per APB 19, the extraordinary item must be separately reported in a statement of changes in financial position.

3.2 The next step is to analyze the additional information given in the problem which is marked with a bullet. As the total amount of each change (increase or decrease) in the "noncurrent accounts" is explained, make a mark next to the dollar amount of the increase or decrease. If only part of a change is explained, note the amount explained next to the total amount of the increase or decrease. As noted above, it may be necessary to use journal entries and or "T" accounts for analyzing some of the changes.

3.3 The first item of additional information is not used in the required statement of changes in financial position because stock dividends are not shown in this statement per APB 19; however, it is necessary to analyze this change in the accounts affected to ensure that all changes are explained. Enter (4,200 shares x $ 5 par value) or $21,000 next to the $40,000 increase in the common stock account. Also note the ($63,000 market value of stock — $21,000 par value) $42,000 next to the $63,000 increase in additional paid-in capital.

3.4 The issuance of common stock for land is shown under both the sources and uses section as "financial resources not affecting working capital" at $40,000. Note the $40,000 next to the $125,000 increase in land, (3,800 shares x $5) or $19,000 next to the common stock account, and ($40,000 fair value — $19,000 par value) or $21,000 next to additional paid-in capital. The changes in common stock and additional paid-in capital have now been explained. Note that the constructor of this problem intentionally made the total change in the common stock account ($40,000) the same as the fair value of that transaction and the total change in the additional paid-in capital account ($63,000) the same as the total amount of retained earnings to be capitalized. A more systematic approach for the first two transactions is to enter these transactions into "T" accounts. Use abbreviations liberally in these "T" accounts.

CS	
210,000	Beg. Bal.
21,000	Stock dividend
19,000	Issued for land
250,000	End Bal.

APIC	
170,000	Beg. Bal.
42,000	Stock dividend
21,000	Issued for land
233,000	End Bal.

R.E.			
Stock dividend	63,000	146,000	Beg. Bal.
Cash dividend	2,000	121,000	Net income
(see 3.7 below)		202,000	End Bal.

3.5 Per APB 19, working capital effect of the extraordinary item of $12,000 ($22,000 gain net of $10,000 of income taxes) must be reported separately from working capital from operations in the statement of changes. The journal entry to record the bond reacquisition was

Bonds payable	50,000	
Gain		22,000
Cash		28,000

The income tax effect can also be reflected in an entry:

Income tax expense— extraordinary item	$10,000	
Income tax payable		$10,000

The working capital effect of the above entries is a decrease of ($28,000 decrease in cash + $10,000 increase in income taxes payable). This amount ($38,000) can also be obtained by deducting the net gain of $12,000 from the $50,000 par value of the bonds reacquired. Although APB 19 is not specific on the treatment of the book value portion of these transactions, there is a preference in practice for combining the two components (see AICPA solution). Place a mark beside the $50,000 increase in bonds payable and enter the $38,000 extraordinary item under the uses section of the statement.

3.6   The $4,000 loss on sale of equipment did not require the use of working capital; therefore, $4,000 is added to income before extraordinary item. The $19,000 realized on the sale of equipment is shown under working capital from "other source." The $53,000 decrease in equipment has been explained. The accumulated depreciation is analyzed as follows:

		Accum. Deprec.	
Deprec.	30,000	100,000	Beg. Bal.
		20,000	Equip. sold
		90,000	End Bal.

The $20,000 of depreciation must be added back since it was deducted in arriving at net income, the starting point in computing funds from operations, but did not require working capital.

3.7   The cash dividends of $2,000 (50,000 shares x $.04) are a use of working capital.

3.8   The purchase of land for $85,000 is a use of working capital. The total change of $125,000 in the land account has now been explained.

3.9   The $40,000 increase in deferred income taxes must be added to the income from operations section, because although the $40,000 was deducted (income tax expense) in determining income before extraordinary items, it did not require the use of working capital because a current liability was not credited for the $40,000.

3.10 The only change in a noncurrent account which has not been dealt with is the $3,000 decrease in patents. The $3,000 is an addition to net income for the same reason cited above for depreciation.

3.11 In solving these problems, valuable time should not be spent trying to reconcile the change in working capital derived from the change in the current assets and current liabilities with the change reflected in the required statement of changes in financial position. The target amount is:

Increase in current assets	$120,000
Less: increase in current liabilities	50,000
Net increase in working capital	$ 70,000

UNOFFICIAL ANSWER

Problem 3   Statement of Changes

Kenwood Corporation
STATEMENT OF CHANGES IN FINANCIAL POSITION
For the Year Ended December 31, 1979

Financial Resources Provided

Working capital provided from operations:

Income before extraordinary item		$109,000
Add items not affecting working capital in the current period		
Depreciation	$20,000	
Amortization	3,000	
Loss on sale of equipment	4,000	
Deferred income taxes	40,000	67,000
Working capital provided from operations		176,000
Working capital from other sources		
Proceeds from sale of equipment		19,000
Financial resources not affecting working capital		
Issuance of common stock to purchase land		40,000
Total financial resources provided		$235,000

Financial Resources Used

Working capital used		
Extraordinary item— repurchase of long-term bonds (including income tax of $10,000 on the gain) (50,000 - 12,000)		$ 38,000
Cash dividends (50,000 shs. x $0.04)		2,000
Purchase of land		85,000
Financial resources not affecting working capital		
Purchase of land by issuance of common stock		40,000
Total financial resources used		165,000
Increase in working capital		$ 70,000

ANSWER OUTLINE

Problem 4   Loss Contingencies (SFAS 5)

a.   Accrual of loss contingency — SFAS 5
         Recognize loss if asset impairment, viability,
            etc., is probable
            And subject to estimate
         Periodicity
            Write down asset or reflect liability in period
               event occurs
            Failure to accrue loss will overstate income
         Measurement
            Since timing and magnitude are not exactly
               known
            Make reasonable estimate of loss contingency
         Objectivity
            Loss estimate by independent parties should
               be similar
            Loss must be probable before accrual
            Future should confirm existence of the loss

b1.   Warranty
            Liability is probable
            Amount is estimable
               Based upon past experience
            Thus the liability and expense should be accrued
               Further disclosure may be necessary

b2.   Subsequent event
            No liability incurred during period
            Thus the event should not be accrued
            Use footnote disclosure
            Should include nature and estimate of loss

b3.   Self-insurance
            No loss contingency occurred during current
               period
            Thus no loss should be recorded
            Cannot record amount not paid to insurance
               company
            Footnote should disclose self-insurance policies

UNOFFICIAL ANSWER

Problem 4   Loss Contingencies (SFAS 5)

a. The two basic requisites for the accrual of a loss
contingency (probability of loss and reasonable estimation) are the results of the interaction of several concepts of accounting theory. Three of these
concepts are (1) periodicity (time periods), (2)
measurement, and (3) objectivity. The first of
these concepts relates to the first characteristic
of an event necessary before accruing a loss
contingency, and the second and third concepts
listed relate to the second necessary requirement
for the accrual of a loss contingency.

   The first requirement that must be satisfied for the accrual of a loss contingency is that
at a time prior to the issuance of the financial
statements there is an indication that it is probable
that an asset has been impaired or a liability
has been incurred at the date of the financial
statements. A basic objective in the recognition
of losses is to record them in the particular
period in which they are incurred. With respect
to the accrual of a loss contingency, a probable
loss should be recognized in the same period in
which it resulted in the probable impairment of
an asset or the probable incurrence of a liability.
The failure to accrue the loss contingency in the
period of occurrence will generally overstate earnings initially and understate earnings in future
periods.

   The second requirement for the accrual of
a loss contingency states that the amount of the
loss must be reasonably estimable. The concept of
measurement requires that the event must be quantifiable in terms of a standard unit of measure (dollars). In the case of a loss contingency related
to the period covered in the current financial
statements, the exact timing and magnitude of the
loss may not be known in advance, but based on
past experience or other methods of analysis, a
reasonable estimate of the loss contingency can
be made. In making the estimate, the probability
that a reasonable amount will be determined statistically is enhanced by a large population of accounts
from which the probable loss will occur (law of
large numbers).

   Also related to the reasonable estimation of
the probable future loss, the concept of objectivity
requires that the estimate be supported by quantitative data. The basis for the estimate must yield
essentially the same estimate when computed by
different individuals using the available supporting
data. The concept of objectivity is supportive of
the contention that future events will confirm the
occurrence of a loss at the date of the financial
statements. Of course the loss must be probable
as well as estimable and justified in light of future
events.

b. Situation I

   When a company sells a product subject to a
warranty, it is probable that there will be expenses incurred in future accounting periods relating
to revenues recognized in the current period. As

such, a liability has been incurred to honor the warranty at the same date as the recognition of the revenue. Based on prior experience or technical analysis, the occurrence of warranty claims can be reasonably estimated and a probable dollar estimate of the liability can be made. The contingent liability for warranties meets both of the requirements for the accrual of a loss contingency, and the estimated amount of the loss should be reflected in the financial statements. In addition to recording the accrual, it may be advisable to disclose the factors used in arriving at the estimate by means of a footnote especially when there is a possibility of a greater loss than was accrued.

Situation II

Even though (1) there is a probable loss on the contract, (2) the amount of the loss can be reasonably estimated and (3) the likelihood of the loss was discovered prior to the issuance of the financial statements, the fact that the contract was entered into subsequent to the date of the financial statements precludes accrual of the loss contingency in financial statements for periods prior to the incurrence of the loss. However, the fact that a material loss has been incurred subsequent to the date of the financial statements but prior to their issuance should be disclosed by means of a footnote in the financial statements. The disclosure should contain the nature of the contingency and an estimate of the amount of the probable loss or a range into which the loss will probably fall.

Situation III

The fact that a company chooses to self-insure the contingency of injury to others caused by its vehicles is not basis enough to accrue a loss contingency that has not occurred at the date of the financial statements. An accrual or "reserve" cannot be made for the amount of insurance premium that would have been paid had a policy been obtained to insure the company against this particular risk. A loss contingency may only be accrued if prior to the date of the financial statements a specific event has occurred that will impair an asset or create a liability and

an amount related to that specific occurrence can be reasonably estimated. The fact that the company is self-insuring this risk should be disclosed by means of a footnote to alert the financial statement reader to the exposure created by the lack of insurance.

SOLUTION GUIDE

Problem 5   Statement of Changes

1. The requirement is a statement of changes in financial position for 1977 using the working-capital format. A schedule of changes in working capital is also required.

2. The solutions approach is to begin by preparing a schedule of changes in working capital to determine the net change in working capital for 1977. List the change in each current asset and current liability account to compute the change in working capital. In this problem there is a net decrease in working capital of $280,800. Thus in the statement of changes in financial position, uses of working capital will exceed sources of working capital by $280,800.

3. The solutions approach to prepare the statement of changes in financial position is to analyze each noncurrent account in the balance sheet and the paragraphs of related information to determine if working capital has been provided or used.

3.1 Begin by reviewing the comparative balance sheets. The $150,000 increase in securities held for plant expansion is a noncurrent item and is a use of working capital. The $280,000 increase in machinery indicates a use of working capital, although there may have been a sale of machinery and equipment to provide working capital. There do not appear to be any changes in leasehold improvements. The decrease in the patent accounts indicates patent amortization which was charged against income, but did not require the use of working capital. The increase in accumulated depreciation on machinery indicates a depreciation charge in the income statement which did not require the use of working capital. The same is true for the amortization of leasehold improvements. The $50,000 decrease in bonds indicates the use of working capital. The decrease in preferred stock indicates a use of working capital. The increase in retained earnings indicates a source of working capital from income, possibly net of a use of working capital for the payment of dividends. Now analyze each paragraph of additional information and impact their effect on the previous analysis.

Net income		$195,000
Loss on sale of machinery	$13,000	
Depreciation expense	89,000	
Amortization of leasehold improvements	9,000	
Amortization of patents	4,200	
		115,200
		$310,200

The Unofficial Answer appears on the next page.

3.2 The $386,000 purchase of machinery is a use of working capital. The sale of obsolete machinery for $48,000 is a source of working capital. Use the T-account analysis of the machinery account below to determine that the original cost of the machinery sold was $106,000. Given that the old equipment had a book value of $61,000, there had to be $45,000 of accumulated depreciation on the machinery sold. The T-account analysis of accumulated depreciation below indicates that 1977 depreciation had to be $89,000 in order to obtain a net increase in accumulated depreciation of $44,000. The $89,000 is added back to income, because it was deducted from income and did not require the use of working capital.

Machinery		
Purchase	$386,000	
Sale	_____	$106,000
Net increase	$280,000	

Accumulated Depreciation		
Old machinery	$ 45,000	
1977 deprec.		$ 89,000
Net increase		$ 44,000

3.3 The $2,000 of legal costs required the use of working capital and were capitalized as patents. The $4,200 patent amortization was charged to income, but did not require a use of working capital. Accordingly, the $4,200 should be added back to income.

3.4 The repurchase of the preferred stock was an $11,000 use of working capital which also resulted in a $1,000 debit to retained earnings.

3.5 The cash dividend declared of $40,000 was a use of working capital.

3.6 Conveniently, an analysis of retained earnings explains the $154,000 increase in retained earnings during 1977. All has been accounted for except for the $195,000 which is net income. Net income must be adjusted by the items as shown below (discussed above) indicating working capital provided from operations of $310,200.

UNOFFICIAL ANSWER

Problem 5   Statement of Changes

a.

Hatfield Corporation
STATEMENT OF CHANGES
IN FINANCIAL POSITION
For the year ended December 31, 1977

Sources of working capital

Working capital provided from operations			
Net income		$195,000	
Add items not requiring an outlay of working capital			
Loss on sale of machinery	$13,000		
Depreciation expense	89,000		
Amortization of leasehold improvements	9,000		
Amortization of patents	4,200	115,200	
Working capital provided from operations		310,200	
Working capital provided from other sources			
Sale of machinery		48,000	
Total sources of working capital			$ 358,200

Uses of working capital

Declaration of cash dividends	$ 40,000	
Repurchase and retirement of preferred stock	11,000	
Payment of legal fees in defense of patent	2,000	
Purchase of securities for plant expansion	150,000	
Purchase of new machinery	386,000	
Provision for current portion of 6% serial bonds payable	50,000	
Total uses of working capital		639,000
Decrease in working capital		$ (280,800)

b.

Hatfield Corporation
SCHEDULE OF CHANGES IN WORKING CAPITAL
For the year ended December 31, 1977

	December 31, 1977	December 31, 1976	Increase (Decrease) in working capital
Composition of working capital			
Current assets			
Cash	$145,000	$186,000	$ (41,000)
Accounts receivable, net	239,000	256,000	(17,000)
Inventories	483,000	538,000	(55,000)
Total current assets	867,000	980,000	(113,000)
Current liabilities			
Accounts payable	232,800	105,000	(127,800)
Cash dividends payable	40,000		(40,000)
Current portion of 6% serial bonds payable	50,000	50,000	—
Total current liabilities	322,800	155,000	(167,800)
Working capital	$544,200	$825,000	
Decrease in working capital			$ (280,800)

ANSWER OUTLINE

Problem 6   Contingencies: Conditions and Dis-
                                closures

a1.   Conditions necessary to accrue an estimated loss
         contingency are
         It is probable that an asset has been impaired or
         a liability incurred at financial statement date,
         and amount of loss can be reasonably estimated

a2.   Disclose unaccrued loss contingencies if
         reasonable possibility exists that loss may have
         been incurred
         Disclose loss contingency involving unasserted
         claim when it is probable that the claim will be
         asserted, and reasonably possible that the out-
         come will be unfavorable
         Disclosure should indicate:
         Nature of contingency, and
         Estimate of possible loss, range of loss, or that
         an estimate cannot be made

UNOFFICIAL ANSWER

Problem 6   Contingencies: Conditions and Dis-
                              closures

Part a.
1.   An estimated loss from a loss contingency shall
be accrued by a charge to income if both of the following conditions are met:
   • Information available prior to issuance of the
      financial statements indicates that it is probable
      that an asset had been impaired or a liability had
      been incurred at the date of the financial state-
      ments. It is implicit in this condition that it
      must be probable that one or more future events
      will occur confirming the fact of the loss.
   • The amount of loss can be reasonably estimated.

2.   Disclosure should be made for an estimated loss
from a contingency that need not be accrued by a
charge to income when there is at least a reasonable
possibility that a loss may have been incurred. The
disclosure should indicate the nature of the contingency and should estimate the possible loss or range
of loss or state that such an estimate cannot be made.
       Disclosure of a loss contingency involving an un-
asserted claim is required when it is probable that the
claim will be asserted and there is a reasonable possibility that the outcome will be unfavorable.

MULTIPLE CHOICE QUESTIONS (1–46)

1. When should an indicated loss on a long-term contract be recognized under the completed-contract method and the percentage-of-completion method, respectively?

	Completed-Contract	Percentage-of-Completion
a.	Immediately	Immediately
b.	Immediately	Over the life of the project
c.	Completion of contract	Over the life of the project
d.	Completion of contract	Immediately

2. Goods on consignment should be included in the inventory of
a. The consignor but **not** the consignee.
b. Both the consignor and the consignee.
c. The consignee but **not** the consignor.
d. Neither the consignor nor the consignee.

3. Which of the following inventory cost flow methods could use dollar-value pools?
a. Conventional (lower of cost or market) retail.
b. Weighted average.
c. FIFO.
d. LIFO.

4. On January 1, 1979, Jay Company changed to the weighted-average cost method from the first-in, first-out (FIFO) cost method for inventory cost flow purposes. Jay can justify the change, which was made for both financial statement and income tax reporting purposes. The change will result in a $120,000 decrease in the beginning inventory at January 1, 1979. Ignoring income taxes, the cumulative effect of changing to the weighted-average method from the FIFO method must be reported by Jay in the 1979
a. Income statement as a $120,000 debit.
b. Retained earnings statement as a $120,000 debit adjustment to the beginning balance.
c. Income statement as a $120,000 credit.
d. Retained earnings statement as a $120,000 credit adjustment to the beginning balance.

5. The following information is available for the Silver Company for the three months ended March 31, 1979:

Merchandise inventory, Janaury 1, 1979	$ 900,000
Purchases	3,400,000
Freight-in	200,000
Sales	4,800,000

The gross margin recorded was 25% of sales. What should be the merchandise inventory at March 31, 1979?
a. $ 700,000
b. $ 900,000
c. $1,125,000
d. $1,200,000

6. The Kirby Construction Company has consistently used the percentage-of-completion method of recognizing income. In 1978 it began a construction project to erect a building for $3,000,000. The project was completed during 1979. Under this method, the accounting records disclosed the following:

	1978	1979
Progress billings during year	$1,100,000	$1,900,000
Cost incurred during year	900,000	1,800,000
Collections on billings during year	700,000	2,300,000
Estimated cost to complete	1,800,000	—

What amount of income should Kirby have recognized in 1978?
a. $100,000
b. $110,000
c. $150,000
d. $200,000

7. Estimates of price-level changes for specific inventories are required for which of the following inventory methods?
a. Dollar-value LIFO.
b. Weighted average cost.
c. FIFO.
d. Conventional retail.

8. If the conventional (lower of cost or market) retail inventory method is used, which of the following calculations would include (exclude) net markdowns?

	Cost ratio (percentage)	Ending inventory at retail
a.	Include	Include
b.	Include	Exclude
c.	Exclude	Include
d.	Exclude	Exclude

9. The calculation of the income recognized in the second year of a four-year construction contract which is accounted for using the percentage-of-completion method is based on the
    a. Cumulative actual costs incurred only.
    b. Incremental cost for the second year only.
    c. Estimated costs at the inception of the contract.
    d. Latest available estimated costs.

10. An example of an inventory accounting policy that should be disclosed is the
    a. Effect of inventory profits caused by inflation.
    b. Composition of inventory into raw materials, work-in-process, and finished goods.
    c. Identification of major suppliers.
    d. Method used for inventory pricing.

11. The Good Trader Company values its inventory by using the retail method (FIFO basis, lower of cost or market). The following information is available for the year 1978.

	Cost	Retail
Beginning inventory	$ 80,000	$140,000
Purchases	297,000	420,000
Freight-in	4,000	
Shortages	——	8,000
Markups (net)	——	10,000
Markdowns (net)	——	2,000
Sales	——	400,000

At what amount would The Good Trader Company report its ending inventory?
    a. $112,000
    b. $113,400
    c. $117,600
    d. $119,000

12. The percentage-of-completion method of accounting for long-term construction-type contracts is preferable when
    a. Estimates of cost to complete and extent of progress toward completion are reasonably dependable.
    b. The collectibility of progress billings from the customer is reasonably assured.
    c. A contractor is involved in numerous projects.
    d. The contracts are of a relatively short duration.

13. On May 2, 1975, a fire destroyed the entire merchandise inventory on hand of Sanchez Wholesale Corporation. The following information is available:

Sales, January 1 through May 2, 1975	$360,000
Inventory, January 1, 1975	80,000
Merchandise purchases, January 1 through May 2, 1975 (including $40,000 of goods in transit on May 2, 1975, shipped F.O.B. shipping point)	330,000
Markup percentage on cost	20%

What is the estimated inventory on May 2, 1975, immediately prior to the fire?
    a. $70,000.
    b. $82,000.
    c. $110,000.
    d. $122,000.

14. The following information is available for The Gant Company for 1976:

Freight-in	$ 20,000
Purchase returns	80,000
Selling expenses	200,000
Ending inventory	90,000

The cost of goods sold is equal to 700% of selling expenses.

What is the cost of goods available for sale?
    a. $1,390,000.
    b. $1,490,000.
    c. $1,500,000.
    d. $1,590,000.

15. Moore Corporation has two products in its ending inventory, each accounted for at the lower of cost or market. A profit margin of 30% on selling price is considered normal for each product. Specific data with respect to each product follows:

	Product # 1	Product # 2
Historical cost	$17.00	$ 45.00
Replacement cost	15.00	46.00
Estimated cost to dispose	5.00	26.00
Estimated selling price	30.00	100.00

In pricing its ending inventory using the lower of cost or market, what unit values should Moore use for products #1 and #2 respectively?

- a. $15.00 and $44.00.
- b. $16.00 and $44.00.
- c. $16.00 and $45.00.
- d. $17.00 and $46.00.

16. Jamison Corporation's inventory cost on its statement of financial position was lower using first-in, first-out than last-in, first out. Assuming no beginning inventory, what direction did the cost of purchases move during the period?

- a. Up.
- b. Down.
- c. Steady.
- d. Cannot be determined.

17. When valuing raw materials inventory at lower of cost or market, what is the meaning of the term "market"?

- a. Net realizable value.
- b. Net realizable value less a normal profit margin.
- c. Current replacement cost.
- d. Discounted present value.

18. A company using a periodic inventory system neglected to record a purchase of merchandise on account at year end. This merchandise was omitted from the year-end physical count. How will these errors affect assets, liabilities, and stockholders' equity at year end and net earnings for the year?

	Assets	Liabilities	Stock-holders' Equity	Net Earnings
a.	No effect	understate	overstate	overstate.
b.	No effect	overstate	understate	understate.
c.	Understate	understate	no effect	no effect.
d.	Understate	no effect	understate	understate.

19. How should earned but unbilled revenues at the balance-sheet date on a long-term construction contract be disclosed if the percentage-of-completion method of revenue recognition is used?

- a. As construction in progress in the current-asset section of the balance sheet.
- b. As construction in progress in the noncurrent-asset section of the balance sheet.
- c. As a receivable in the noncurrent-asset section of the balance sheet.
- d. In a footnote to the financial statements until the customer is formally billed for the portion of work completed.

20. Which of the following statements is not valid as it applies to inventory costing methods?

- a. If inventory quantities are to be maintained, part of the earnings must be invested (plowed back) in inventories when FIFO is used during a period of rising prices.
- b. LIFO tends to smooth out the net income pattern since it matches current cost of goods sold with current revenue, when inventories remain at constant quantities.
- c. When a firm using the LIFO method fails to maintain its usual inventory position (reduces stock on hand below customary levels) there may be a matching of old costs with current revenue.
- d. The use of FIFO permits some control by management over the amount of net income for a period through controlled purchases, which is not true with LIFO.

21. During 1972 R Corp., a manufacturer of chocolate candies, contracted to purchase 100,000 pounds of cocoa beans at $1.00 per pound, delivery to be made in the spring of 1973. Because a record harvest is predicted for 1973, the price per pound for cocoa beans had fallen to $.80 by December 31, 1972.

Of the following journal entries, the one which would properly reflect in 1972 the effect of the commitment of R Corp. to purchase the 100,000 pounds of cocoa is

		Debit	Credit
a.	Cocoa inventory	100,000	
	Accounts payable		100,000
b.	Cocoa inventory	80,000	
	Loss on purchase commitments (an expense account)	20,000	
	Accounts payable		100,000
c.	Loss on purchase commitments (an expense account)	20,000	
	Accrued loss on purchase commitments (a liability account)		20,000
d.	No entry would be necessary in 1972.		

22. During the course of your examination of the financial statements of H Co., a new client, for the year ended December 31, 1972, you discover the following:

Inventory at January 1, 1972, had been overstated by $3,000.

Inventory at December 31, 1972, was understated by $5,000.

An insurance policy covering three years had been purchased on January 2, 1971, for $1,500 . The entire amount was charged as an expense in 1971.

During 1972 the company received a $1,000 cash advance from a customer for merchandise to be manufactured and shipped during 1973. The $1,000 had been credited to sales revenue. The company's gross profit on sales is 50%.

Net income reported on the 1972 income statement (before reflecting any adjustments for the above items) is $20,000.

The proper net income for 1972 is
a. $26,500.
b. $23,500.
c. $16,500.
d. $20,500.

23.   Goldstein Co., a specialty clothing store, uses the retail-inventory method. The following information relates to 1973 operations:

Inventory January 1, 1973, at cost	$14,200
Inventory January 1, 1973, at sales price	20,100
Purchases in 1973 at cost	32,600
Purchases in 1973 at sales price	50,000
Additional markups on normal sales price	1,900
Sales (including $4,200 of items which were marked down from $6,400)	60,000

The cost of the December 31, 1973, inventory determined by the retail-inventory method is
a. $9,800.
b. $6,370.
c. $6,743.
d. $6,543.

24.   Q Co. prepares monthly income statements. A physical inventory is taken only at year end; hence, month-end inventories must be estimated. All sales are made on account. The rate of mark-up on cost is 50%. The following information relates to the month of June 1973.

Accounts receivable, June 1, 1973	$10,000
Accounts receivable, June 30, 1973	15,000
Collection of accounts receivable during June 1973	25,000
Inventory, June 1, 1973	18,000
Purchases of inventory during June, 1973	16,000

The estimated cost of the June 30, 1973, inventory would be
a. $12,000.
b. $14,000.
c. $19,000.
d. $22,000.

25.   Buildit Construction Corporation contracted to construct a building for $400,000. Construction began in 1976 and was completed in 1978. Data relating to the contract are summarized below:

	Year ended December 31,	
	1976	1977
Costs incurred	$200,000	$110,000
Estimated costs to complete	100,000	—

Buildit uses the percentage-of-completion method as the basis for income recognition. For the years ended December 31, 1976, and 1977, respectively, Buildit should report income of
a. $0 and $90,000.
b. $45,000 and $45,000.
c. $66,667 and $23,333.
d. $90,000 and $0.

26.   When inventory declines in value below original (historical) cost, and this decline is considered other than temporary, what is the maximum amount that the inventory can be valued at?
a.   Sales price net of conversion costs.
b.   Net realizable value.
c.   Historic cost.
d.   Net realizable value reduced by a normal profit margin.

27.   How should the balances of progress billings and construction in progress be shown at reporting dates prior to the completion of a long-term contract?
a.   Progress billings as deferred income, construction in progress as a deferred expense.
b.   Progress billings as income, construction in progress as inventory.
c.   Net, as a current asset if debit balance and current liability if credit balance.
d.   Net, as income from construction if credit balance, and loss from construction if debit balance.

28. Assuming no beginning inventory, what can be said about the trend of inventory prices if cost of goods sold computed when inventory is valued using the FIFO method exceeds cost of goods sold when inventory is valued using the LIFO method?

    a.   Prices decreased.
    b.   Prices remained unchanged.
    c.   Prices increased.
    d.   Price trend cannot be determined from information given.

29. For annual reporting purposes, Storrar Co. appropriately accounts for revenues from long-term construction-type contracts under the percentage-of-completion method. In December 1975, for budgeting purposes, Storrar estimated that these revenues would be $1,600,000 for 1976. Favorable business conditions occurred in October 1976 and, as a result, Storrar recognized revenues of $2,000,000 for the year ended December 31, 1976. If the percentage-of-completion method had been used for the quarterly income statements on the same basis followed for the year end income statement, revenues would have been as follows:

Three months ended March 31, 1976	$ 300,000
Three months ended June 30, 1976	400,000
Three months ended September 30, 1976	200,000
Three months ended December 31, 1976	1,100,000
Total	$2,000,000

What amount of revenues from long-term construction-type contracts should be reflected in Storrar's quarterly income statement for the three months ended December 31, 1976?

    a. $500,000.
    b. $800,000.
    c. $1,100,000.
    d. $2,000,000.

Items 30 and 31 are based on the following information:

The following information was available from the inventory records of the Alexander Company for January 1977:

	Units	Unit Cost	Total Cost
Balance at January 1, 1977	2,000	$ 9.775	$19,550

Purchases:

January 6, 1977	1,500	10.300	15,450
January 26, 1977	3,400	10.750	36,550

Sales:

January 7, 1977	1,800
January 31, 1977	3,200
Balance at January 31, 1977	1,900

30. Assuming that Alexander maintains perpetual inventory records, what should be the inventory at January 31, 1977, using the weighted moving average inventory method, rounded to the nearest dollar?

    a. $19,523.
    b. $19,703.
    c. $19,950.
    d. $19,998.

31. Assuming that Alexander does not maintain perpetual inventory records, what should be the inventory at January 31, 1977, using the weighted average inventory method, rounded to the nearest dollar?

    a. $19,523.
    b. $19,703.
    c. $19,950.
    d. $19,998.

32. If a unit of inventory has declined in value below original cost, but the market value exceeds net realizable value, the amount to be used for purposes of inventory valuation is

    a.   Net realizable value.
    b.   Original cost.
    c.   Market value.
    d.   Net realizable value less a normal profit margin.

33. Which method of inventory pricing best approximates specific identification of the actual flow of costs and units in most manufacturing situations?

    a.   Average cost.
    b.   First-in, first-out.
    c.   Last-in, first-out.
    d.   Base stock.

Items 34 and 35 are based on the following information:

In 1974, Long Corporation began construction work under a three-year contract. The contract price is $800,000. Long uses the percentage-of-cost-completion method for financial-accounting purposes.

The income to be recognized each year is based on the proportion of cost incurred to total estimated costs for completing the contract. The financial-statement presentations relating to this contract at December 31, 1974, follow:

Balance Sheet

Accounts receivable—construction contract billings		$15,000
Construction in progress	$50,000	
Less contract billings	47,000	
Cost-of-uncompleted contract in excess of billings		3,000

Income Statement

Income (before tax) on the contract recognized in 1974	$10,000

34. How much cash was collected in 1974 on this contract?
  a. $15,000.
  b. $32,000.
  c. $35,000.
  d. $47,000.

35. What was the initial estimated total income before tax on this contract?
  a. $10,000.
  b. $30,000.
  c. $160,000.
  d. $200,000.

Items **36** and **37** are based on the following information:

The Quick Sales Company uses the retail-inventory method to value its merchandise inventory. The following information is available:

	Cost	Retail
Beginning inventory	$40,000	$70,000
Purchases	290,000	400,000
Freight-in	2,000	—
Markups (net)	—	3,000
Markdowns (net)	—	5,000
Employee discounts	—	1,000
Sales		390,000

36. What is the ending inventory at retail?
  a. $71,000.
  b. $72,000.
  c. $77,000.
  d. $78,000.

37. If the ending inventory is to be valued at the lower of cost or market, what is the cost to retail ratio?
  a. $332,000 ÷ $468,000.
  b. $332,000 ÷ $472,000.
  c. $332,000 ÷ $473,000.
  d. $332,000 ÷ $474,000.

38. When using the periodic-inventory method, which of the following generally would not be separately accounted for in the computation of cost of goods sold?
  a. Trade discounts applicable to purchases during the period.
  b. Cash (purchase) discounts taken during the period.
  c. Purchase returns and allowances of merchandise during the period.
  d. Cost of transportation-in for merchandise purchased during the period.

39. The September 30, 1975, physical inventory of Clinton Company appropriately included $3,800 of merchandise which was not recorded as purchases until October, 1975. What effect will this error have on September 30, 1975, assets, liabilities, retained earnings, and earnings for the year then ended, respectively?
  a. No effect ; overstate ; understate ; understate.
  b. No effect; understate; understate; overstate.
  c. Understate; no effect; overstate; overstate.
  d. No effect; understate; overstate; overstate.

40. For the year 1975, the gross profit of Dumas Company was $96,000; the cost of goods manufactured was $340,000; the beginning inventories of goods in process and finished goods were $28,000 and $45,000, respectively; and the ending inventories of goods in process and finished goods were $38,000 and $52,000, respectively. The sales of Dumas Company for 1975 must have been
  a. $419,000.
  b. $429,000.
  c. $434,000.
  d. $436,000.

41. The Hastings Company began operations on January 1, 1976, and uses the FIFO method in costing its raw material inventory. Management is contemplating a change to the LIFO method and is interested in determining what effect such a change will have on net income. Accordingly, the following information has been developed:

Final Inventory	1976	1977
FIFO	$240,000	$270,000
LIFO	200,000	210,000

Net Income		
(computed under the FIFO method)	120,000	170,000

Based upon the above information, a change to the LIFO method in 1977 would result in net income for 1977 of

- a. $110,000.
- b. $150,000.
- c. $170,000.
- d. $230,000.

42.   The inventory account of Benson Company at December 31, 1976, included the following items:

	Inventory Amount
Merchandise out on consignment at sales price (including markup of 40% on selling price)	$7,000
Goods purchased, in transit (shipped f.o.b. shipping point)	6,000
Goods held on consignment by Benson	4,000
Goods out on approval (sales price $2,500, cost $2,000)	2,500

Based on the above information, the inventory account at December 31, 1976, should be reduced by

- a. $7,300.
- b. $12,500.
- c. $13,500.
- d. $19,500.

MAY 1981 QUESTIONS

43.   The following data were available from the records of the Bricker Department Store for the year ended December 31, 1980:

	At cost	At retail
Merchandise inventory, January 1, 1980	$180,000	$260,000
Purchases	660,000	920,000
Markups		20,000
Markdowns		80,000
Sales		960,000

Using the retail method, an estimate of the merchandise inventory at December 31, 1980, valued at the lower of average cost or market, would be

- a. $220,000.
- b. $160,000.
- c. $120,000.
- d. $112,000.

44.   Mercer Construction Company recognizes income under the percentage-of-completion method of reporting income from long-term construction contracts. During 1978 Mercer entered into a fixed-price contract to construct a bridge for $15,000,000. Contract costs incurred and estimated costs to complete the bridge were as follows:

	Cumulative contract costs incurred	Estimated costs to complete
At December 31, 1978	$ 1,000,000	$8,000,000
At December 31, 1979	5,500,000	5,500,000
At December 31, 1980	10,000,000	2,000,000

How much income should Mercer recognize on the above contract for the year ended December 31, 1980?

- a. $ 500,000.
- b. $ 833,333.
- c. $1,350,000.
- d. $2,500,000.

45.   Hestor Company's records indicate the following information:

Merchandise inventory, January 1, 1980	$ 550,000
Purchases, January 1 through December 31, 1980	2,250,000
Sales, January 1 through December 31, 1980	3,000,000

On December 31, 1980, a physical inventory determined that ending inventory of $600,000 was in the warehouse. Hestor's gross profit on sales has remained constant at 30%. Hestor suspects some of the inventory may have been taken by some new employees. At December 31, 1980, what is the estimated cost of missing inventory?

- a. $100,000.
- b. $200,000.
- c. $300,000.
- d. $700,000.

46. When progress billings are sent on a long-term contract, what type of account should be credited under the completed-contract method and percentage-of-completion method?

	Completed-contract	Percentage-of-completion
a.	Revenue	Revenue
b.	Revenue	Contra asset
c.	Contra asset	Revenue
d.	Contra asset	Contra asset

Problem 1   Change to LIFO (1176,T5)

(20 to 25 minutes)

Part a.   Inventory may be computed under one of various cost-flow assumptions. Among these assumptions are first-in, first-out (FIFO) and last-in, first-out(LIFO). In the past, some companies have changed from FIFO to LIFO for computing portions or all of their inventory.

Required:

1.   Ignoring income tax, what effect does a change from FIFO to LIFO have on net earnings and working capital? Explain.

2.   Explain the difference between the FIFO assumption of earnings and operating cycle and the LIFO assumption of earnings and operating cycle.

Part b.   Companies using LIFO inventory sometimes establish a "Reserve for the Replacement of LIFO Inventory" account.

Required:

Explain why and how this "Reserve" account is established and where it should be shown on the statement of financial position.

Problem 2   Various Methods (1179, P4)

(40 to 45 minutes)

Problem 2 consists of three unrelated parts.

Part a.   The Frate Company was formed on December 31, 1978. The following information is available from Frate's inventory records for Product Ply:

	Units	Unit Cost
January 1, 1979		
(beginning inventory)	800	$ 9.00
Purchases:		
January 5, 1979	1,500	$10.00
January 25, 1979	1,200	$10.50
February 16, 1979	600	$11.00
March 26, 1979	900	$11.50

A physical inventory on March 31, 1979 shows 1,600 units on hand.

Required:
Prepare schedules to compute the ending inventory at March 31, 1979, under each of the following inventory methods:

1.   FIFO
2.   LIFO
3.   Weighted average

Show supporting computations in good form.

Part b.   The Red Department Store uses the retail inventory method. Information relating to the computation of the inventory at December 31, 1978, is as follows:

	Cost	Retail
Inventory at January 1, 1978	$ 32,000	$ 80,000
Sales		600,000
Purchases	270,000	590,000
Freight in	7,600	
Markups		60,000
Markup cancellations		10,000
Markdowns		25,000
Markdown cancellations		5,000
Estimated normal shrinkage is 2% of sales.		

Required:
Prepare a schedule to calculate the estimated ending inventory at the lower of average cost or market at December 31, 1978, using the retail inventory method. Show supporting computations in good form.

Part c.   On November 21, 1978, a fire at Hodge Company's warehouse caused severe damage to its entire inventory of Product Tex. Hodge estimates that all usable damaged goods can be sold for $10,000. The following information was available from Hodge's accounting records for Product Tex:

Inventory at November 1, 1978	$100,000
Purchases from November 1, 1978, to date of fire	140,000
Net sales from November 1, 1978, to date of fire	220,000

Based on recent history, Hodge had a gross margin (profit) on Product Tex of 30% of net sales.

Required:

Prepare a schedule to calculate the estimated loss on the inventory in the fire, using the gross margin (profit) method. Show supporting computations in good form.

Problem 3   LIFO Problem (576,P4)

(40 to 50 minutes)

Number 3 consists of three unrelated parts.

Part a.   The Topanga Manufacturing Company manufactures two products: Mult and Tran. At December 31, 1974, Topanga used the first-in, first-out (FIFO) inventory method. Effective January 1, 1975, Topanga changed to the last-in, first-out (LIFO) inventory method. The cumulative effect of this change is not determinable and, as a result, the ending inventory of 1974 for which the FIFO method was used, is also the beginning inventory for 1975 for the LIFO method. Any layers added during 1975 should be costed by reference to the first acquisitions of 1975 and any layers liquidated during 1975 should be considered a permanent liquidation.

The following information was available from Topanga's inventory records for the two most recent years:

	Mult		Tran	
	Units	Unit Cost	Units	Unit Cost
1974 purchases:				
January 7	5,000	$4.00	22,000	$2.00
April 16	12,000	4.50		
November 8	17,000	5.00	18,500	2.50
December 13	10,000	6.00		
1975 purchases:				
February 11	3,000	7.00	23,000	3.00
May 20	8,000	7.50		
October 15	20,000	8.00		
December 23			15,500	3.50
Units on hand:				
December 31, 1974	15,000		14,500	
December 31, 1975	16,000		13,000	

Required:

Compute the effect on income before income taxes for the year ended December 31, 1975, resulting from the change from the FIFO to the LIFO method.

Part b.   The Barometer Company manufactures one product. On December 31, 1972, Barometer adopted the dollar-value LIFO inventory method. The inventory on that date using the dollar-value LIFO inventory method was $200,000. Inventory data are as follows:

Year	Inventory at respective year-end prices	Price index (base year 1972)
1973	$231,000	1.05
1974	299,000	1.15
1975	300,000	1.20

Required:

Compute the inventory at December 31, 1973, 1974, and 1975, using the dollar-value LIFO method for each year.

Part c.   The Jericho Variety Store uses the LIFO retail inventory method. Information relating to the computation of the inventory at December 31, 1975, follows:

	Cost	Retail
Inventory, January 1, 1975	$ 29,000	$ 45,000
Purchases	120,000	172,000
Freight-in	20,000	
Sales		190,000
Net markups		40,000
Net markdowns		12,000

Required:

Assuming that there was no change in the price index during the year, compute the inventory at December 31, 1975 using the LIFO retail inventory method.

Problem 4   Inventory Errors (1178,P4)

(20 to 30 minutes)

Part a.   The Allen Company is a wholesale distributor of automotive replacement parts. Initial amounts taken from Allen's accounting records are as follows:

Inventory at December 31, 1977 (based
on physical count of goods in Allen's
warehouse on December 31, 1977) $1,250,000

Accounts payable at December 31, 1977:

Vendor	Terms	Amount
Baker Company	2% 10 days, net 30	$ 265,000
Charlie Company	Net 30	210,000
Dolly Company	Net 30	300,000
Eager Company	Net 30	225,000
Full Company	Net 30	—
Greg Company	Net 30	—
		$1,000,000
Sales in 1977		$9,000,000

Additional information is as follows:

1. Parts held on consignment from Charlie to Allen, the consignee, amounting to $155,000, were included in the physical count of goods in Allen's warehouse on December 31, 1977, and in accounts payable at December 31, 1977.

2. $22,000 of parts which were purchased from Full and paid for in December 1977 were sold in the last week of 1977 and appropriately recorded as sales of $28,000. The parts were included in the physical count of goods in Allen's warehouse on December 31, 1977, because the parts were on the loading dock waiting to be picked up by customers.

3. Parts in transit on December 31, 1977 to customers, shipped F.O.B. shipping point, on December 28, 1977, amounted to $34,000. The customers received the parts on January 6, 1978. Sales of $40,000 to the customers for the parts were recorded by Allen on January 2, 1978.

4. Retailers were holding $210,000 at cost ($250,000 at retail), of goods on consignment from Allen, the consignor, at their stores on December 31, 1977.

5. Goods were in transit from Greg to Allen on December 31, 1977. The cost of the goods was $25,000, and they were shipped F.O.B. shipping point on December 29, 1977.

6. A quarterly freight bill in the amount of $2,000 specifically relating to merchandise purchases in December 1977, all of which was still in the inventory at December 31, 1977, was received on January 3, 1978. The freight bill was not included in either the inventory or in accounts payable at December 31, 1977.

7. All of the purchases from Baker occurred during the last seven days of the year. These items have been recorded in accounts payable and accounted for in the physical inventory at cost before discount. Allen's policy is to pay invoices in time to take advantage of all cash discounts, adjust inventory accordingly, and record accounts payable, net of cash discounts.

Required:
Prepare a schedule of adjustments to the initial amounts using the format shown below. Show the effect, if any, of each of the transactions separately and if the transactions would have no effect on the amount shown, state NONE.

	Inventory	Accounts Payable	Sales
Initial amounts	$1,250,000	$1,000,000	$9,000,000
Adjustments—increase (decrease)			
1			
2			
3			
4			
5			
6			
7			
Total adjustments			
Adjusted amounts	$	$	$

Problem 5   Long-Term Contracts (579,T4)

(15 to 20 minutes)

In accounting for long-term contracts (those taking longer than one year to complete), the two methods commonly followed are the percentage-of-completion method and the completed-contract method.

Required:

a.   Discuss how earnings on long-term contracts are recognized and computed under these two methods.

b.   Under what circumstances is it preferable to use one method over the other?

c.   Why is earnings recognition as measured by interim billings not generally accepted for long-term contracts?

d.   How are job costs and interim billings reflected on the balance sheet under the percentage-of-completion method and the completed-contract method?

Problem 6   L.T. Contracts: Theoretical Justifications (1180,T3b)

(10 to 15 minutes)

Part b. Income determination for long-term construction contracts presents special problems because the construction work often extends over two or more accounting periods. The two methods commonly followed are the percentage-of-completion method and the completed-contract method.

Required:

Evaluate the use of the percentage-of-completion method for income determination purposes for long-term construction contracts. Discuss only theoretical arguments.

Problem 7   Long-Term Contracts (1180,P4)

(45 to 55 minutes)

Problem 7 consists of two unrelated parts.

Part a.   Curtiss Construction Company, Inc., entered into a firm fixed-price contract with Axelrod Associates on July 1, 1977, to construct a four-story office building. At that time, Curtiss estimated that it would take between two and three years to complete the project. The total contract price for construction of the building is $4,000,000. Curtiss appropriately accounts for this contract under the completed-contract method in its financial statements and for income tax reporting. The building was deemed substantially completed on December 31, 1979. Estimated percentage-of completion, accumulated contract costs incurred, estimated costs to complete the contract, and accumulated billings to Axelrod under the contract were as follows:

	At December 31, 1977	At December 31, 1978	At December 31, 1979
Percentage-of-completion	10%	60%	100%
Contract costs incurred	$ 350,000	$2,500,000	$4,250,000
Estimated costs to complete the contract	$3,150,000	$1,700,000	
Billings to Axelrod	$ 720,000	$2,160,000	$3,600,000

Required:
1.   Prepare schedules to compute the amount to be shown as "cost of uncompleted contract in excess of related billings" or "billings on uncompleted contract in excess of related costs" at December 31, 1977, 1978, and 1979. Ignore income taxes. Show supporting computations in good form.
2.   Prepare schedules to compute the profit or loss to be recognized as a result of this contract for the years ended December 31, 1977, 1978, and 1979. Ignore income taxes. Show supporting computations in good form.

Part b.   On April 1, 1979, Butler, Inc., entered into a cost-plus-fixed-fee contract to construct an electric generator for Dalton Corporation. At the contract date, Butler estimated that it would take two years to complete the project at a cost of $2,000,000. The fixed fee stipulated in the contract is $300,000. Butler appropriately accounts for this contract under the percentage-of-completion method. During 1979 Butler incurred costs of $700,000 related to the project, and the estimated cost at December 31, 1979, to complete the contract is $1,400,000. Dalton was billed $500,000 under the contract.

Required:
Prepare a schedule to compute the amount of gross profit to be recognized by Butler under the contract for the year ended December 31, 1979. Show supporting computations in good form.

MULTIPLE CHOICE ANSWERS

1.	a	11.	a	21.	c	31.	b	41.	a
2.	a	12.	a	22.	a	32.	a	42.	a
3.	d	13.	c	23.	b	33.	b	43.	d
4.	a	14.	b	24.	b	34.	b	44.	a
5.	b	15.	c	25.	c	35.	c	45.	a
6.	a	16.	b	26.	b	36.	c	46.	d
7.	a	17.	c	27.	c	37.	c		
8.	c	18.	c	28.	a	38.	a		
9.	d	19.	a	29.	c	39.	d		
10.	d	20.	d	30.	c	40.	b		

EXPLANATION OF MULTIPLE CHOICE ANSWERS

1.   (1180,T1,2)   (a)   The requirement is when to recognize an indicated loss on a long-term contract under both the completed-contract and percentage-of-completion methods. ARB 45 requires that expected losses should be recognized immediately under both methods.

2. (1180,T1,17)   (a)   Goods on consignment remain the property of the consignor until sold (i.e., legal title to the goods does not pass to the consignee). The consignee bears no responsibility except for adequate care of the consigned merchandise. Therefore, consigned goods are included only in the inventory of the consignor.

3. (1180,T1,18)   (d)   A variation of LIFO, dollar-value LIFO, uses dollar-value pools; to qualify for inclusion in a dollar-value LIFO pool the items must be "similar" rather than "identical" as is the case under unit LIFO. No other inventory methods utilize dollar-value pools.

4.   (1180,P1,3)   (a)   The requirement is to compute the cumulative effect of a change in accounting principle from the weighted-average method to the FIFO method for inventory cost flow purposes, as well as to indicate its appropriate placement in the 1979 financial statements. Except for specific exceptions, APB No. 20 requires that changes in accounting principle be reported in the income statement rather than as an adjustment in the retained earnings statement. To determine whether the cumulative effect is a debit or credit, it is helpful to visualize the journal entry to record this change. The decrease in the inventory would be recorded as a credit; therefore, the income statement effect would be a debit.

Cumulative effect of accounting change	120,000	
Inventory		120,000

5.   (1180,Q1,11)   (b)   The requirement is the amount of merchandise inventory at 3/31/79. The information given indicates that the gross margin method for estimating inventory is to be used. The solutions approach is to set up the problem in the form of the cost of goods sold section of the income statement.

Beginning inventory		$ 900,000
Add: Purchases	$3,400,000	
Freight-In	200,000	3,600,000
Cost of goods available		4,500,000
Deduct:		
Cost of goods sold (estimated)		($3,600,000)
Ending inventory		$ 900,000

Cost of goods sold is estimated by taking 75% of sales ($4,800,000). Since gross margin is 25% of sales, the ratio of CGS to sales is 75%.

6.   (580,Q1,5)   (a)   The requirement is the amount of income under the percentage-of-completion method for 1978. The solutions approach is to first determine the expected total income on the contract which is the contract price of $3,000,000 less the costs incurred to date of $900,000 and expected remaining costs of $1,800,000, leaving income of $300,000. The percentage of the job completed ($900,000 cost to date ÷ $2,700,000 expected costs) is multipled by the expected profits of $300,000 to yield the profit to be recognized in 1978 of $100,000. The formula for recognizing profit on long-term contracts is shown below. Note that total expected losses would be recognized immediately, i.e., not prorated.

$$\frac{\text{costs to date}}{\text{total expected costs}} \times \text{expected profit} = \text{profit recognized to date}$$

7.   (580,T1,3)   (a)   Dollar-value LIFO utilizes specific price indexes to price the increase or decrease in inventory pools of similar items. The IRS allows retailers to use published government index numbers while manufacturers must develop their own. Remember that income tax accounting dictates the accounting for inventories when LIFO is used. Estimates of price level changes are not required for the other methods mentioned.

8.   (580,T1,4)   (c)   The conventional retail method uses a more conservative or lower inventory figure obtained by including net markups but excluding net markdowns in determining the denominator of the cost-to-retail ratio. This lower inventory figure approximates the lower of cost or market. The ending inventory at retail selling price should include net markdowns.

9.   (580,T1,6)   (d)   The calculation of income recognized in this problem would be based on the ratio of cumulative actual costs incurred divided by the latest available estimated total costs. Answer (b) is incorrect because using the incremental costs for the second year as the base would give a percentage-of-completion equal to or greater than 100%. The estimated costs at the inception of the contract (answer (c)) may no longer be accurate or relevant. Answer (a) is incorrect for the same reason as for answer (b)).

10.   (580,T1,24)   (d)   Para 6 of APB Opinion No. 22 defines the accounting policies of a reporting entity as the specific accounting principles and the methods of applying those principles that have been adapted for preparing the financial statements. Using this definition, the only accounting policy listed among the answers is the method used for inventory pricing.

11.   (1179,Q1,9)   (a)   The requirement is the ending inventory for Good Trader Company based on the retail method (FIFO basis, lower of cost or market). The solutions approach is to set up a cost to retail schedule as illustrated below. The first step is to determine the ending inventory at retail which is $160,000. Note that the inventory flow is FIFO. Thus, ending inventory will be made up of this period's purchases. The cost/retail ratio to be applied to the ending inventory is 301/430, which is 70%. Note that the freight-in applies to this year's purchases, and an assumption is usually made that markups apply only to purchases. Thus, 70% of $160,000 is $112,000, which is ending inventory.

	Cost	Retail
BI	$ 80,000	$140,000
Purchases	+297,000	+420,000
Freight-in	+4,000	
Markups (net)		+10,000
Goods available	$381,000	$570,000
Shortages		−8,000
Markdowns (net)		−2,000
Sales		−400,000
EI		$160,000

301 ÷ 430 = 70%
$160,000 x 70% = $112,000

12.   (1179,T1,15)   (a)   The percentage-of-completion method for long-term contracts is preferable over the completed contract method when estimates of cost to complete and extent of progress made toward completion are reasonably dependable per para 15 of ARB 45. Answer (b) is incorrect because under either method of accounting for long-term contracts, a reserve for doubt-

ful accounts should be established for noncollectible billings. Answer (c) is incorrect because if the contractor is involved in numerous projects, the completed contracts method may approximate the results of percentage-of-completion, as there would be a number of projects being completed each period. Answer (d) is incorrect because the completed contract method is not appropriate for short-term contracts.

13.   (1176,Q1,15)   (c)   Note the requirement is the inventory immediately prior to the fire, not the fire loss as is frequently asked. Thus, the $40,000 of goods in transit shipped F.O.B. shipping point are included. The solutions approach is to add beginning inventory and purchases and subtract out cost of sales as computed below. Note that the markup percentage is on cost, not retail, i.e., $360,000 ÷ 120% equals $300,000 of cost of sales.

BI	$ 80,000
Purchases	330,000
	410,000
Sales (cost)	300,000
	$110,000

14.   (577,Q1,13)   (b)   The requirement is goods available for sale. Goods available for sale are equal to ending inventory plus cost of sales or beginning inventory plus purchases. Cost of goods sold is 7 times the selling expense of $200,000, or $1,400,000. Add the $90,000 of ending inventory to the $1,400,000 to obtain goods available for sale of $1,490,000.

15.   (577,Q1,14)   (c)   The requirement is to price products 1 and 2 at the lower of cost or market. See Chapter 4 of ARB 43, para 9. The lower of cost or market rule is applied by selecting the lower of cost or market. Cost is historical cost. Market is replacement cost subject to a ceiling and a floor, i.e., maximum and minimum. The maximum (ceiling) is net realizable value which is selling price less disposal costs, and the minimum (floor) is the net realizable value less normal profit, i.e., the ceiling less normal profit. To recap, first compute market and then compare it with cost. As computed below, the net realizable value (ceiling) is the selling price less the cost of disposal, or $25 and $74 respectively. The net realizable value minus profit (floor) is $16 and $44 respectively. Since the replacement cost for product 1 of $15 is below the floor, market is the floor, or $16. The replacement cost of $46 for product 2 is within the floor-ceiling range, and thus market for product 2 is $46. The lower of cost or

market is $16 (market) for product 1, and $45 (cost) for product 2.

	1	2
NRV	$30 - $5	$100 - $26
NRV - profit	25 - 9	74 - 30
Replacement	15	46
Market	16	46
Cost	17	45
Lower	16	45

16.   (577,T1,10) (b) If FIFO results in a lower ending inventory than LIFO, prices have to have been decreasing during the period. In FIFO, the beginning inventory is sold first and the ending inventory is made up of the latest purchases. The opposite is true of LIFO where latest purchases are sold first, and the beginning inventory is reflected in the ending inventory. Thus when prices decrease, FIFO would tend to indicate a lower ending inventory than LIFO.

17.   (577,T1,11) (c) The lower of cost or market inventory method is prescribed in Chapter 4 of ARB 43, para 9. Market is defined as current replacement cost subject to a maximum of net realizable value, i.e., estimated selling price less disposal cost, and a minimum of net realizable value less normal profit.

18.   (577,T2,25) (c) When inventory is excluded from both purchases and ending inventory, there is no effect on net income or shareholders' equity, because ending inventory is subtracted from the sum of purchases plus beginning inventory to determine cost of sales. Failure to record inventory, however, does understate the inventory and the liability accounts. Thus answer (c) is correct.

19. (1174,T1,18) (a) Earned but unbilled revenues at the balance sheet date on long term construction contracts should be classified as a current asset. The accounting is specified in paragraph 5 of ARB 45. As construction costs are incurred they are debited to a construction in progress account. Since these costs have not been billed to the customer at the balance sheet date, they should not be classified as receivables.

20.   (1174,T2,22) (d) Under FIFO, current purchases usually become part of ending inventory rather than cost of goods sold and thus do not affect current income. Under LIFO, however, current purchases are normally included in cost of goods sold and thus net income could be affected by controlled purchases.

21.   (1173,P1,11) (c) Losses on purchase commitments, if material, should be recognized in the accounts. See statement number 10 (Paragraph 17) of Chapter 4 of ARB 43. In this question there is a purchase commitment loss of $.20 per pound on 100,000 lbs. of cocoa beans. The loss should be accrued by debiting a loss account and crediting a liability or deferred revenue account. Next period when the cocoa beans are purchased at $.80, purchases will be debited at $.80, and accrued loss on purchase commitments will be debited for $.20 per pound.

22.   (1173,P1,12) (a) The effect of beginning inventory overstatement is understatement of the current years income, because cost of goods sold is overstated. The effect of understatement of ending inventory will be understatement of current income, because cost of goods sold will be overstated. The three year insurance policy was expensed in 1971, and $500 should have been expensed in 1972. All of the $1,000 should be adjusted out of 1972 income (no costs of sales was expensed this period). The adjustments are summarized below.

Reported income	20,000
B. I. overstatement	+ 3,000
E. I. understatement	+5,000
1972 insurance	− 500
Deferred revenue	−1,000
	$26,500

23.   (574,Q1,14) (b) The cost of ending inventory by the retail method is determined by multiplying the ending inventory at retail by the cost to retail ratio. The cost to retail ratio is determined by the ratio of cost of goods available for sale to goods available for sale at retail. The computations are scheduled below. Note that markups and not markdowns are included to determine the goods available for sale ratio and markdowns as well as sales are subtracted from goods available at retail to determine ending inventory at retail.

	Cost	Retail
Beginning inventory	14,200	20,100
Purchases	32,600	50,000
Markups		1,900
Ratio is 65%	46,800	72,000
Markdowns		2,200
Sales		60,000
Ending inventory		9,800

65% of $9,800 = $6,370

24. (1173,P1,10) (b) The ending inventory is determined by T-account analysis of accounts receivable and cost of goods sold. Sales at retail are $30,000 as evidenced by the T-account analysis of AR below. Markup of 50% of cost is a markup of 1/3 on retail and thus sales at cost are $20,000. The T-account analysis of C of S indicates ending inventory of $14,000.

		AR		
Beg.	10,000	Collections	25,000
Sales	30,000	End	15,000

		C of S		
Beg.	18,000	C of S	20,000
Pur.	16,000	End.	14,000

25. (1178,Q1,13) (c) The requirement is the profits on a long-term construction contract for 1976 and 1977 using the percentage-of-completion method. The percentage-of-completion method recognizes income over the life of contract in contrast to the completed-contract method which recognizes income only when the contract is complete. Each year the estimated percentage-of-completion is multipled times the expected profit. Thus in 1976 the estimated percentage-of-completion is two-thirds ($200,000 of cost incurred over the $200,000 of costs incurred plus $100,000 of estimated remaining costs). The total expected profit is the $400,000 contract price less the total expected costs of $300,000. As computed below, 1976 percentage-of-completion profit is $66,667. In the last year of a construction contract, the total profit is known. The actual total profit on the contract less all previously recognized profit is the amount of profit to be recognized in the last year. In 1977 the total profit is known to be $90,000 ($400,000 − $310,000) and since $66,667 was recognized in 1976, the 1977 profit is $23,333 as computed below.

$$1976 \quad \frac{\$200,000}{\$200,000 + \$100,000} (\$400,000 - \$300,000)$$
$$= \$66,667$$

1977 $400,000 − $310,000 − $66,667 = $23,333

26. (1178,T1,12) (b) The requirement is the maximum amount at which inventory can be valued provided that market is less than historical cost. Per para 9 of Chapter 4 of ARB 43, market cannot exceed net realizable value (nor can it be less than net realizable value reduced by normal profit margins).

Net realizable value is selling price less estimated completion and disposal costs. Note that whether the decline is considered temporary or other than temporary has no effect on inventory valuation.

27. (1178,T1,40) (c) The requirement is how to report progress billings and construction in progress prior to completion of a long-term contract. Per para 4 and 5 of ARB 45, construction in progress, which is a deferred cost, should be shown net of progress billings which are deferred revenues. If a debit balance, construction in progress net of progress billings is a current asset; and it is a current liability if a credit balance. Answer (a) is incorrect because it does not indicate construction in progress and progress billings are to be offset. Answer (b) is incorrect because progress billings are a deferred revenue rather than income. Answer (d) is incorrect because the billings may not be on a proportionate basis, i.e., 75% of the costs may already have been incurred and only 50% of the contract billed per the construction contract.

28. (579,T1,11) (a) The requirement is the trend in prices if cost of goods sold per FIFO exceeds cost of goods sold per LIFO. The price level has decreased if cost of goods sold per FIFO exceeds cost of goods sold per LIFO (with no beginning inventory). FIFO indicates that goods purchased at the beginning of the year are included in cost of goods sold, first-in, first-out. In contrast, LIFO means the latest purchases are included in cost of goods sold, last-in, first-out. Thus when FIFO cost of goods sold exceeds LIFO cost of goods sold, the prices are decreasing during the period.

29. (1177,P1,10) (c) The requirement is the amount of revenue to be recognized on the interim income statement for the last three months of the year. Since $1,100,000 would have been recognized in the last three months based upon the method to determine annual income, it is the amount of revenue to be recognized in the interim period. In other words, the same accounting principles are used in the preparation of interim statements as for annual statements. See para 10 of APB 28. Para 11 specifically states that revenues should be recognized during an interim period on the same basis as followed for the annual period.

30. (1177,P1,12) (c) The requirement is the ending inventory using the moving average inventory method. The moving average inventory method requires that a new unit cost be computed each time new goods are purchased. A computation is not

needed when goods are sold, because the inventory account is credited at the average price. The computations below result in an ending inventory quantity of 1,900 units, to be priced at $10.50 each, resulting in an ending inventory quantity of $19,950. Note that no calculation is needed after computing the unit price for the last purchase

$$
\begin{array}{rl}
2,000 & \$19,550 \\
+1,500 & 15,450 \\
\hline
3,500 & \$35,000 = \$10.00 \\
-1,800 & 18,000 \\
\hline
1,700 & \$17,000 = \$10.00 \\
+3,400 & 36,550 \\
\hline
5,100 & \$53,550 = \$10.50 \\
-3,200 & \\
\hline
1,900 &
\end{array}
$$

1,900 x $10.50 = $19,950

31. (1177,P1,13) (b) The requirement is the ending inventory based upon the weighted average (not moving average) method. The weighted average method is simply a weighted average unit cost of inventory throughout the period. Thus the total number of units available for sale is divided into their total cost (here $71,550 ÷ 6,900 units). The ending inventory of 1,900 units times the average unit cost of $10.37 is **$19,703.**

$$
\begin{array}{rl}
2,000 & \$19,550 \\
1,500 & 15,450 \\
3,400 & 36,550 \\
\hline
6,900 & 71,550 = \$10.37
\end{array}
$$

1,900 x $10.37 = **$19,703.**

32. (1177,T1,17) (a) When inventory is to be valued at less than cost (written down to market), market is defined as the replacement cost not to exceed net realizable value (sales price less disposal costs and costs to complete) or to be less than net realizable value less a normal profit margin. In this problem the market value is below cost but exceeds net realizable value. Thus inventory will be written down to net realizable value if net realizable value is less than original cost. See para 9 of Chapter 4 of ARB 43.

33. (1177,T1,19) (b) Most manufacturing operations process and sell inventory in the order it is received, i.e., the first items in are the first to be sold, which is FIFO. LIFO and base stock would mean that inventory that is originally purchased would be kept on hand and never sold. An example of a base stock

situation might be a sand and gravel storage area. Average cost would imply that inventories were continually mixed and there was always some of the original inventory on hand.

34. (575,P1,13) (b) In long-term construction accounting, the account "construction in progress" is a deferred debit: it consists of all of the costs to date (and profits recognized to date under the percentage-of-completion method). "Contract billings" is a deferred credit: as the customer is billed, receivables is debited and contract billings is credited. In this problem contract billings totaled $47,000. Thus $47,000 has been billed and $15,000 is still outstanding, which means $32,000 has been collected.

35. (575,P1,14) (c) To date $10,000 has been recognized on a total of cost plus profits in the "construction in progress account" of $50,000. Thus the ratio of profit to cost plus profit is 20%. The contract price is $800,000 and the estimated total income is $160,000.

36. (1175,Q1,16) (c) The goods available at retail before markups and markdowns, etc., is $470,000. The $470,000 was marked up $3,000, marked down $5,000, and then $391,000 of retail merchandise was sold. Thus the ending retail inventory is $77,000. While only $390,000 was recorded in sales, $391,000 of retail merchandise was sold less $1,000 of employee discounts.

37. (1175,Q1,17) (c) As discussed in problem above, the cost/retail ratio is the cost of goods available over the retail value of goods available. For valuation at the lower of cost or market (or at the conservative retail method), markups but not markdowns are included in goods available. Thus the goods available at retail are the beginning inventory plus purchases plus markups ($70,000 + $400,000 + $3,000).

38. (1175,T1,1) (a) Traditionally, purchases are recorded net of trade discounts. Thus if something were selling with a 30% trade discount, one would record it at the net amount rather than the gross amount. Purchase discounts are usually recorded separately, i.e., purchases are recorded at gross and purchase discounts are recorded when taken. Purchase returns and allowances are generally accounted for separately as is transportation-in.

39. (1175,T1,11) (d) The physical inventory was correct but the purchase and payable were not recorded until the next period. Thus assets are properly stated; liabilities are understated; retained earnings and earnings are overstated because purchases (and thus cost of sales) are understated. Notice that we worked the problem without becoming concerned with the alternative answers until we determined the solution.

40. (576,Q1,15) (b) The solutions approach is to set up the T account for the finished goods inventory so that you can determine the cost of sales. Cost of sales plus gross profit of $96,000 will equal sales. Notice that the problem gives you beginning and ending inventory for the work-in-process account which are not relevant to the problem. The beginning finished goods inventory of $45,000 plus the cost of goods manufactured of $340,000 provides $385,000 available for sale. The $52,000 of ending inventory is subtracted to obtain $333,000 for cost of sales. Add the $333,000 of cost of sales to gross profit of $96,000 to obtain $429,000 for sales.

FG Inventory

BI	$ 45,000	C of S	$333,000
CGM	340,000	EI	52,000
	$385,000		$385,000

41. (578,Q1,7) (a) The requirement is 1977 income if a change is made to LIFO in 1977. Changing to LIFO is a cumulative effect type change. The new accounting principle is used in the year of change and the cumulative effect of the change in beginning retained earnings is included as a separate item in the income statement after income from continuing operations and before net income. The effect on beginning retained earnings of changing from FIFO to LIFO is to reduce beginning retained earnings by $40,000 since inventory per FIFO was $40,000 greater than per LIFO. Think of a balance sheet: if you decrease inventory by $40,000 what else decreases? retained earnings. During 1977 the difference between FIFO inventory and LIFO inventory increases by $20,000 [(($240,000 − $200,000) at beginning of year compared to ($270,000 − $210,000) at year-end]. Thus the direct effect is $60,000. The change in operating income for 1977 is −$20,000, and the cumulative effect on beginning retained earnings is −$40,000 (both are reported in the income statement).

1977 income per FIFO	$170,000
FIFO to LIFO as of 1/1/77	−40,000
FIFO to LIFO in 1977	−20,000
1977 income per LIFO	$110,000

Note that changing to LIFO is a change for which the cumulative effect may not be determinable (see para 26, APB 20). If it is not determinable, use LIFO as ending inventory and pick up the entire effect in income in the year of change. For example, in this problem the whole $60,000 would be reflected in operating income.

42. (578,Q1,17) (a) The requirement is the amount inventory should be reduced as the result of overstated items. The merchandise on consignment should be priced at cost, not retail, i.e., reduced by 40% of $7,000, or $2,800. The title of goods purchased FOB shipping point has transferred to Benson when in transit. Thus, no adjustments are necessary. The goods held on consignment by Benson are not owned by Benson, and accordingly should not be included in the inventory. The goods out on approval, i.e., no sale has taken place, should be priced at cost, not retail, i.e., reduced by $500 ($2,500 − $2,000).

Consignment inventory profit	$−2,800
Goods held on consignment	−4,000
Profit on goods not sold	− 500
	$−7,300

MAY 1981 ANSWERS

43. (581,P1,2) (d) The requirement is the lower of average cost or market amount of the 12/31/80 inventory, using the retail method. The solutions approach is to set up a schedule to compute ending inventory at retail and the cost-to-retail ratio. To approximate lower of cost or market, markups are included in the denominator of the ratio but markdowns are not. The effect is to make the denominator larger which results in a lower, more conservative, inventory valuation.

	Cost	Retail
1/1/80 inventory	$180,000	$ 260,000
Purchases	660,000	920,000
Markups		20,000
Cost/Retail	$840,000	$1,200,000
Markdowns		(80,000)
Sales		(960,000)
Ending inventory at retail		$ 160,000

Cost/Retail Ratio $840/$1,200 = 70%

The last step is to multiply the cost-to-retail ratio by the ending inventory at retail to find ending inventory at cost.

($160,000)(70%) = $112,000

44.   (581,P1,5)   (a)   The requirement is the amount of income Mercer should recognize in 1980 on a long term contract, using the percentage-of-completion method. The income to be recognized in 1980 will be the difference between total income earned in 1978-1980 less the amount of income recognized in 1978-79. At 12/31/79, the contract was 50% complete ($5,500,000 ÷ $11,000,000) based on estimates available then. At that time, the total expected income was $4,000,000 ($15,000,000 contract price − $11,000,000 estimated total costs). Therefore, the income recognized as of 12/31/79 was 50% of $4,000,000, or $2,000,000. At 12/31/80, the contract is 5/6 complete ($10,000,000 ÷ $12,000,000), and the total expected income is $3,000,000 ($15,000,000 contract price − $12,000,000 estimated total costs). Therefore, the income earned as of 12/31/80 is 5/6 of $3,000,000, or $2,500,000. Income to be recognized in 1980 is $500,000 as illustrated below:

$$\begin{pmatrix} \text{Income} \\ \text{earned as of} \\ \text{12/31/80} \end{pmatrix} - \begin{pmatrix} \text{Income} \\ \text{previously} \\ \text{recognized} \end{pmatrix} = \begin{pmatrix} \text{Income to be} \\ \text{recognized} \\ \text{in 1980} \end{pmatrix}$$

$$\$2,500,000 - \$2,000,000 = \$500,000$$

45.   (581,Q1,14)   (a)   The requirement of this problem is to find the cost of missing inventory at the end of the year. The solution approach to this problem is to calculate the estimated amount of inventory and compare this amount to the actual inventory on hand to determine the loss.

Set up a schedule using the format of the income statement.

Cost of G.S.
Beg. Inv.	$ 550,000	
+ Purchases	2,250,000	
Goods avail.	$2,800,000	
− End Inv.	?	
(70% x $3,000,000)		$2,100,000
		$ 900,000

* The cost of goods sold as a percentage of sales is 100% minus the 30% gross profit rate. The estimated ending inventory is $2,800,000 goods available less $2,100,000 cost of G.S. or $700,000. The estimated cost of the missing inventory is $700,000 − $600,000 = $100,000.

46.   (581,T1,35)   (d)   The requirement is the type of account that should be credited under the completed-contract method and the percentage-of-completion method to record progress billings. Under the percentage-of-completion method, income is recognized periodically on the basis of the percentage of the job that is complete. The completed-contract method recognizes income from the job only when the contract is completed. This is the only difference in accounting for the two methods. For both methods, when progress billings are sent, an account called "Billings on Construction in Process" is credited for the amount billed. This is shown on the balance as a contra-account to the "Construction in Process" account.

ANSWER OUTLINE

Problem 1   Change to LIFO

a1.   LIFO matches most recent costs with revenues
LIFO inventory is priced at earliest costs
In rising prices, LIFO reports less income
   (Assuming stable or increasing inventory)
In falling prices, LIFO reports more income
   (Assuming stable or increasing inventory)
Decreasing inventories tend to have the oppo-
   site effect

a2.   FIFO combines operating and holding gains
   Operating cycle is cash-inventory-cash
Earnings are net of actual goods sold
LIFO profits provide for inventory replacement
In contrast, LIFO excludes holding gains
   Operating cycle is inventory-cash-inventory

b.   Reserve account is used when LIFO inventory
   decreases
Otherwise early inventory costs are matched with
   current revenues
Cost temporary inventory decrease at current prices
Reserve account set up for excess of replacement cost
   over LIFO carrying cost
Reserve account is a current liability

UNOFFICIAL ANSWER

Problem 1   Change to LIFO

a.   1.   When using LIFO, the most recently incurred costs are included in cost of
goods sold on the earnings statement,
and the earlier costs are included in
the inventory reported on the statement of financial position. When using
FIFO, the earlier costs are included in
cost of goods sold on the earnings
statement, and the later, more current
costs are included in the inventory on
the statement of financial position.

   If all prices remain constant
and inventory quantities remain constant, there will be no effect upon
net earnings or working capital resulting from the use of LIFO rather
than FIFO.

   If prices are rising and inventory
quantities remain constant or increase,
LIFO will produce a larger cost of
goods sold and a smaller net earnings.
The change from FIFO to LIFO would,
thus, reduce net earnings. Likewise, rising prices yield a lower LIFO inventory
cost on the statement of financial position than the corresponding FIFO inven-

tory cost. Therefore, the change to LIFO
would reduce working capital.

   If prices are falling and inventory
quantities remain constant or increase,
LIFO would produce a smaller cost of
goods sold and, therefore, a larger net
earnings than FIFO. The change to
LIFO would, thus, increase net earnings. Likewise, falling prices yield a
higher LIFO inventory cost on the
statement of financial position than the
corresponding FIFO inventory cost.
Therefore, the change to LIFO would
increase working capital.

   If inventory quantities decrease,
the relative effects of using LIFO rather
than FIFO cannot be determined without giving consideration to the direction of price changes and the magnitude
of the inventory change.

2.   The use of FIFO as an inventory method
results in recognizing all elements of earnings at the time of sale. Holding gains
(or losses) are combined with the operating (trading) earnings and are not
separately identified. Holding gains arise
from holding inventory during periods
of rising prices. Operating earnings result from selling a product at a price
above current cost.

   Under FIFO, the operating cycle
is viewed as cash to merchandise and
back to cash again; therefore, reported
earnings should be net of goods (actually) sold. An assumed FIFO cost flow
generally is a good approximation of
specific identification for most goods in
most industries. According to FIFO proponents, FIFO generally matches the
actual cost of the (actual) goods sold
with the revenue produced.

   Because FIFO ignores the cost of
the replacement of the inventory at possible higher prices (in a period of rising
prices), it includes a "paper" profit that
is not really available for distribution to
owners because it is needed to replace
inventory.

   The use of LIFO as an inventory
method matches the most recently incurred costs with the revenue produced.
It, therefore, largely excludes holding gains
from the reported earnings if inventory
quantity remains constant or increases.
Reported earnings from the period are
more likely to include a deduction for

goods sold in an amount that approximates more closely the higher cost required to replace inventory (during periods of rising prices) and, thereby, represent the distributable earnings accruing to the owners under the going-concern concept. The operating cycle is viewed as merchandise to cash and back to merchandise. In other words, LIFO proponents claim that the actual flow of goods should not be a determinant of net earnings.

b. The account "Reserve for Replacement of LIFO Inventory" may also be called "Excess of Replacement Cost over LIFO Cost of Basic Inventory Temporarily Liquidated." The use of this account arises when there are less units in ending inventory than in beginning inventory for a company using LIFO. This sale of part of the inventory results in matching some older, lower costs (assuming rising prices) with current revenues. Furthermore, if the inventory is replaced, the new inventory cost would exceed the prior, basic inventory cost, because replacement would be at higher prices. In other words, this decline in inventory would lead to the reporting of an amount of net earnings that is distorted simply because replacement did not occur prior to the end of the accounting period.

Assuming that the inventory decline is temporary, LIFO proponents would suggest avoiding this potential distortion by charging cost of goods sold with current costs even though some of the goods sold may have been carried at older, lower costs. The reserve account is then credited for the excess of the current replacement cost over the LIFO carrying cost for the inventory temporarily liquidated, as the alternative account title implies. When this inventory is replenished, the temporary reserve (credit) is removed, and the goods acquired are placed in inventory at their old LIFO costs. While it exists, the reserve account should be shown among the current liabilities on the statement of financial position to currently reflect the expected reduction of reported working capital of this amount when the goods are replaced.

Under the dollar-value LIFO method, changes in actual units are ignored, and the concern shifts to dollars invested in inventories. This often permits rather drastic shifts in inventory mix without causing a

recovery of any of the older LIFO costs. This may be affected by the number of inventory pools a firm establishes; the fewer the inventory pools, the less likelihood of any invasion of LIFO base costs.

SOLUTION GUIDE

Problem 2   Various Methods

1. The problem consists of 3 unrelated parts requiring inventory calculations.

2. Part a requires March ending inventory per FIFO, LIFO, and weighted average. Note that the inventory calculations are based on a physical system rather than on a perpetual inventory system. In order to make perpetual computations, sales data would also have to be presented.

   2.1 FIFO, first-in-first-out, indicates that the beginning inventory was sold first and ending inventory consists of the latest purchases. Accordingly, the 1,600 units of ending inventory consist of 900 units @ $11.50, 600 units @ $11.00, and 100 units @ $10.50.

   2.2 LIFO, last-in-first-out, indicates that the latest purchases were sold first and ending inventory consists of the beginning inventory and first purchases. Accordingly, the 1,600 units of ending inventory consist of 800 units @ $9.00 (beginning inventory) and 800 units at $10.00.

   2.3 Per weighted average, the ending inventory of 1,600 is priced at the weighted average of units available for sale during the period which is $10.35. The total number of units available for sale was 5,000 and their cost $51,750 ($51,750 ÷ 5,000 = $10.35). Thus the ending inventory is valued at $16,560 (1,600 units @ $10.35).

3. Part b requires ending inventory at the lower of average cost or market using the retail inventory method. The retail inventory method determines the cost of inventory by multiplying the cost-retail ratio times ending inventory at retail. Average cost or market refers to the cost-retail ratio, which is determined by dividing goods available for sale at cost by goods available for sale at retail. For example, if the computation were on a FIFO basis, the cost-retail ratio would be made up of purchases at cost divided by purchases at retail.

3.1   The first step is to compute ending inventory at retail. This is done by determining goods available at retail (beginning inventory, purchases, freight-in, net markups) and subtracting sales, markdowns, and shrinkage. Goods available at retail ($720,000) consists of $80,000 BI, $590,000 purchases, and $50,000 net markups. Ending inventory at retail ($88,000) requires subtraction of $600,000 sales, $20,000 net markdowns, and $12,000 shrinkage.

3.2   The cost-retail ratio is computed as the cost of goods available for sale of $309,600 ($32,000 BI, $270,000 purchases and $7,600 freight-in) over the $720,000 goods available at retail or 43% ($309,600/$720,000).

3.3   The cost of the ending inventory at the lower of average cost or market using the retail inventory method is $37,840 ($88,000 ending inventory at retail times the cost-retail ratio of 43%).

4.   Part c requires calculation of an estimated fire loss using the gross profit method. Generally the gross profit method requires computation of an ending inventory based upon beginning inventory, purchases, and sales which must be reduced by cost of sales given a gross profit rate.

4.1   The beginning inventory of $100,000 plus the purchases of $140,000 equals goods available of $240,000. Since sales of $220,000 (30% gross profit) were made in November prior to the fire, the $240,000 goods available must be reduced by the $154,000 ($220,000 @ 70%) cost of sales resulting in ending inventory of $86,000 ($240,000 − $154,000).

4.2   The $86,000 estimated inventory at the time of fire must be reduced by the $10,000 salvage value of the inventory to determine the fire loss of $76,000.

UNOFFICIAL ANSWER

Problem 2   Various Methods

Part a.

1.   *Frate Company*
COMPUTATION OF INVENTORY FOR
PRODUCT PLY UNDER FIFO
INVENTORY METHOD
March 31, 1979

	Units	Unit Cost	Total Cost
March 26, 1979	900	$11.50	$10,350
February 16, 1979	600	11.00	6,600
January 25, 1979 (portion)	100	10.50	1,050
March 31, 1979, inventory	1,600		$18,000

2.   *Frate Company*
COMPUTATION OF INVENTORY FOR
PRODUCT PLY UNDER LIFO
INVENTORY METHOD
March 31, 1979

	Units	Unit Cost	Total Cost
Beginning inventory	800	$ 9.00	$ 7,200
January 5, 1979	800	10.00	8,000
March 31, 1979, inventory	1,600		$15,200

3.

Frate Company
COMPUTATION OF INVENTORY FOR
PRODUCT PLY UNDER WEIGHTED
AVERAGE INVENTORY METHOD
March 31, 1979

	Units	Unit Cost	Total Cost
Beginning inventory	800	$ 9.00	$ 7,200
January 5, 1979	1,500	10.00	15,000
January 25, 1979	1,200	10.50	12,600
February 16, 1979	600	11.00	6,600
March 26, 1979	900	11.50	10,350
	5,000		$51,750
Weighted average cost ($51,750 ÷ 5,000)		$10.35	
March 31, 1979, inventory	1,600	$10.35	$16,560

Part b.

Red Department Store
COMPUTATION OF ESTIMATED INVENTORY
USING RETAIL INVENTORY METHOD
December 31, 1978

	Cost	Retail
Inventory at January 1, 1978	$ 32,000	$ 80,000
Purchases	270,000	590,000
Freight in	7,600	
Net markups (60,000 − 10,000)		50,000
Goods available for sale	$309,600	720,000
Cost ratio ($309,600 ÷ $720,000)	43%	
Sales		600,000
Net markdowns (25,000 − 5,000)		20,000
Estimated normal shrinkage (2% X 600,000)		12,000
		632,000
Estimated inventory at retail at December 31, 1978		$ 88,000
Estimated inventory at December 31, 1978, lower of cost or market ($88,000 X 43%)	$ 37,840	

Part c.

Hodge Company
CALCULATION OF ESTIMATED LOSS ON
INVENTORY IN THE FIRE USING GROSS
MARGIN (PROFIT) METHOD
November 21, 1978

Inventory at November 1, 1978		$100,000
Purchases from November 1, 1978, to date of fire		140,000
Cost of goods available for sale		240,000
Estimated cost of goods sold		
Net sales from November 1, 1978, to date of fire	$220,000	
Less estimated gross margin (profit) ($220,000 X 30%)	66,000	154,000
Estimated cost of inventory at date of fire		86,000
Less salvage goods		10,000
Estimated loss on inventory in the fire		$ 76,000

SOLUTION GUIDE

Problem 3   LIFO Problem

1.   The requirement in part a is to determine the effect on 1975 income of changing from FIFO to LIFO at the beginning of 1975.

1.1   Use a Time Diagram to determine that the difference in income is due to the difference in ending 1975 inventory.

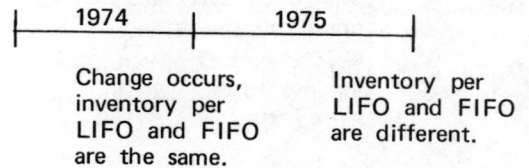

1974	1975
Change occurs, inventory per LIFO and FIFO are the same.	Inventory per LIFO and FIFO are different.

1.2   Calculate FIFO for 1975 ending inventories, i.e., ending inventory priced at latest costs.

Mult	16,000 @ $8.00 =	$128,000
Tran	13,000 @ 3.50 =	45,500
	Ending 1975 FIFO	$173,500

1.3   Calculate LIFO inventories, i.e., ending inventory is beginning inventory adjusted for change during 1975. Beginning inventory is ending 1974 inventory at LIFO.

Mult
  Beginning

        10,000 @ $6.00 = $60,000
         5,000 @ 5.00 = 25,000

                                    $85,000
        Increase of 1,000 @ $7.00   7,000
                                    $92,000

  Tran
    Beginning

          14,500 @ $2.50 = $36,250
    Decrease of 1,500 @ $2.50 = 3,750

                                $ 32,500

            Ending 1975 LIFO $124,500

1.4 Since LIFO of $124,500 is used instead of FIFO of $173,500, income is $49,000 less than if FIFO had been used. Note this same approach could be used on cost of sales.

2. The requirement is to calculate the dollar LIFO inventory value at the end of 1973, 1974, 1975.

2.1 Reduce the year-end inventory values to base year dollars.

2.2 Multiply the base year and subsequent layers times their respective price levels.

3. The requirement is ending inventory per LIFO retail.

3.1 Compute the cost to retail ratio for 1975 purchases.

3.2 Determine ending inventory at retail.

3.3 Multiply the cost to retail ratio times the increase in retail inventory during the year.

3.4 Add the cost of the increase in inventory to the cost of beginning inventory.

UNOFFICIAL ANSWER

Problem 3   LIFO Problem

a.

The Topanga Manufacturing Company
**EFFECT ON INCOME BEFORE INCOME TAXES—
CHANGE FROM FIFO TO LIFO INVENTORY
METHOD**
For the Year Ended December 31, 1975

Inventory at December 31, 1975
if on FIFO Inventory Method:
Mult—16,000 units x $8.00
  (October 15, 1975 unit cost) $128,000
Tran—13,000 units x $3.50
  (December 23, 1975 unit cost)   45,500 $173,500

Inventory at December 31, 1975
on LIFO Inventory Method:
Mult
  Beginning inventory:
    5,000 units x $5.00
    (November 8, 1974 unit cost)   25,000
    10,000 units x $6.00
    (December 13, 1974 unit cost)   60,000
                                     85,000
  Layer added in 1975:
    1,000 units x $7.00
    (February 11, 1975 unit cost)   7,000
                                               92,000
Tran
  Beginning inventory:
    14,500 units x $2.50
    (November 8, 1974 unit cost)   36,250
  Layer liquidated in 1975:
    1,500 units x $2.50
    (November 8, 1974 unit cost)   (3,750)
                                               32,500
                                              124,500

Decrease in income before
  income taxes—change from FIFO
  to LIFO inventory method $ 49,000

b.

The Barometer Company
DOLLAR-VALUE LIFO COMPUTATIONS

Year	Inventory at Respective Year-end Prices	Price Index (Base Year 1972)	Inventory at Base Year (1972) Prices
1973	$231,000	1.05	$220,000
1974	299,000	1.15	260,000
1975	300,000	1.20	250,000

December 31, 1973:

Base	$200,000
1973 layer at 1973 cost	
($220,000 − $200,000 = $20,000) x 1.05	21,000
	$221,000

December 31, 1974:

Base	$200,000
1973 layer at 1973 cost	21,000
1974 layer at 1974 cost	
($260,000 − $220,000 = $40,000) x 1.15	46,000
	$267,000

December 31, 1975:

Base	$200,000
1973 layer at 1973 cost	21,000
1974 layer at 1974 cost	
($250,000 − $260,000 = ($10,000) +	
$40,000 = $30,000) x 1.15	34,500
	$255,500

c.

The Jericho Variety Store
LIFO RETAIL COMPUTATION
December 31, 1975

	Cost	Retail
Purchases	$120,000	$172,000
Freight-in	20,000	
Net markups		40,000
Net markdowns		(12,000)
	$140,000	200,000
Cost ratio ($140,000 ÷ $200,000)	70%	
Sales		190,000
1975 layer:		
At retail		10,000
At cost ($10,000 x 70%)	$ 7,000	
Inventory, January 1, 1975 (base)	$ 29,000	$ 45,000
Inventory, December 31, 1975	$ 36,000	$ 55,000

SOLUTION GUIDE

Problem 4   Inventory Errors

1. Part a requires the effect of seven situations on inventory, accounts payable, and sales. The solution's format is presented in the problem. Thus the solutions approach is to analyze each of the seven situations on Allen Company's inventory, accounts payable, and sales. Note that the requirement and preliminary data should be studied first.

1.1 The $155,000 of inventory consigned to Allen Company by Charlie Company is not inventory of Allen (title has not passed from Charlie to Allen as the merchandise is consigned) and should not be included in either inventory or accounts payable. Thus $155,000 should be deducted from both inventory and accounts payable. There is no effect on sales.

1.2 The $22,000 of parts that were sold in 1977 and property recorded as sales in 1977 should not be in Allen's inventory. Rather the $22,000 should be in cost of sales. Thus $22,000 should be deducted from inventory. There is no effect on accounts payable and the sales have already been recorded appropriately per the problem.

1.3 Since the sale of parts was made F.O.B. shipping point on December 28, title passes on December 28. Thus the $34,000 of parts should be in cost of sales, and the $40,000 selling price should be in 1977 sales. There is no effect on accounts payable. Note that the sales entry in 1978 should be reversed but is not part of the requirement of this problem.

1.4 The goods out on consignment are Allen's property and should be included in inventory. Since the inventory at December 31 is based on goods in Allen's warehouse, the $210,000 of consignment inventory is not included in ending inventory. Thus the inventory should be increased by $210,000. There is no effect on accounts payable or sales.

1.5 Since the goods were shipped to Allen F.O.B. shipping point on December 29, they are properly includable in Allen's inventory and accounts payable as of the end of the year. As the goods were in transit on December 31, they were not included in inventory. Accordingly both inventory and accounts payable should be increased by $25,000. There is no effect on sales.

1.6 Since the freight-in pertains to merchandise properly included in inventory as of December 31, $2,000 should be added to both inventory and accounts payable (the liability has not been recorded). There is no effect on sales.

1.7 Since Allen's policy is to pay invoices to obtain cash discounts and adjust inventory accordingly, the $265,000 of purchases from Baker Company should be adjusted to reflect the 2% discount. Thus $5,300 ($265,000 x 2%) should be subtracted from inventory and accounts payable. There is no effect on sales.

UNOFFICIAL ANSWER

Problem 4   Inventory Errors

Part a.

	Inventory	Accounts Payable	Sales
Initial amounts	$1,250,000	$1,000,000	$9,000,000
Adjustments: Increase (decrease)			
1.	(155,000)	(155,000)	NONE
2.	(22,000)	NONE	NONE
3.	NONE	NONE	40,000
4.	210,000	NONE	NONE
5.	25,000	25,000	NONE
6.	2,000	2,000	NONE
7. ($265,000 x 2%)	(5,300)	(5,300)	NONE
Total adjustments	54,700	(133,300)	40,000
Adjusted amounts	$1,304,700	$ 866,700	$9,040,000

ANSWER OUTLINE

Problem 5   Long-Term Contracts

a. Percentage-of-completion revenue is the total revenue times the percent complete. The percentage may be based on

> Engineering reports
> Direct labor costs or hours

Usually the percentages are derived several ways and compared

> Revenue is reduced by direct contract costs of the period
> Previously recognized profits must be subtracted in subsequent periods

Completed contract earnings are recognized at completion, in the period of completion

> The contract price is revenue
> All the costs incurred are expensed

If a loss is expected per either completed-contract or percentage-of-completion, a provision for the entire loss is recognized immediately

b. Percentage-of-completion method is preferable

> When estimates of completion are reasonably dependable

Completed-contract is preferable

> When completion percentages are not dependable

c. Interim billings often are not meaningfully related to the work performed on the contract

> Billings may be accelerated at the beginning to provide working capital to the contractor

> Income recognized on a billing basis would permit manipulation of income

d. Percentage-of-completion on the balance sheet

> A schedule of contract costs incurred during the period

> Gross profit based on degree of completion by contract

> Total billings rendered on each contract

> Excess of costs and profits over billings is a current asset

> Excess of billings over costs and profits are a current liability

Completed-contract method on the balance sheet

Same as percentage-of-completion except there are no estimated profits

Excess of costs over billings is a current asset

Excess of billings over costs is a current liability

UNOFFICIAL ANSWER

Problem 5   Long-Term Contracts

a. The revenue recognized on a long-term contract under the percentage-of-completion method is determined by applying a percentage representing the degree of completion to the total contract price at the end of the accounting period. The percentage is derived by dividing the costs incurred to date by the total estimated costs of the entire contract based on the most recent information. The percentage may also be derived by other measures of progress, such as engineering or architectural estimates, the ratio of direct labor costs incurred to date to total estimated labor costs, or the ratio of direct labor hours incurred to estimated total direct labor hours. Percentages derived under these various methods should yield essentially comparable data. The revenue so derived is then reduced by the direct contract costs to determine the gross profit recognized in the initial period.

b. The percentage-of-completion method is preferable when estimates of the bases upon which progress is measured are reasonably dependable. The completed-contract method is preferable when inherent hazards or lack of dependable estimates cause the forecasts to be of doubtful value.

c. Interim billings on long-term contracts are not generally accepted as a method of recognizing earnings because such billings often do not bear a meaningful relationship to the work performed on the contract. Typically, billings may be accelerated in the early stages of the contract to provide the contractor with the working capital needed to begin performance. If earnings were recognized on a billings basis, it would be possible for a contractor to materially distort the contractor's earnings merely by rendering billings without regard to any degree of progress on the contract.

d. Under the percentage-of-completion method, a schedule is made of the contracts in process, showing the total costs incurred as of the end of a given period, the estimated gross profit recognized based on the degree of completion, and the total billings rendered on each individual contract. If costs incurred plus recognized profits exceed the related billings on a contract, this net figure is shown as a current asset. This treatment shows that the contractor has not fully billed the customer for work performed to date and has a claim against the customer for that portion of work completed but not yet billed. If billings on a contract exceed costs incurred plus estimated profits, this net figure is shown as a current liability, which means that the contractor has overbilled the customer for work done to date and must complete the work represented by the excess billings. Under the completed-contract method, the treatment of excess costs and billings is the same as under the percentage-of-completion method except that estimated profits are not computed because profit recognition is deferred until a contract is completed. The excess of costs over related billings on a contract is a current asset while the excess of billings over related costs on a contract is a current liability.

In subsequent periods, since the percentage-of-completion method described produces cumulative results, gross profit recognized in prior periods must be subtracted to obtain current earnings to be recognized.

Under the completed-contract method, no earnings are recognized until the contract is substantially completed. For the period in which completion occurs, gross revenues include the total contract price. Total job costs incurred are deducted from gross revenues, resulting in recognition of the entire amount of gross profit in the completion period. If it is expected that a loss will occur on the contract, a provision for loss should be recognized immediately.

ANSWER OUTLINE

Problem 6   L.T. Contracts: Theoretical Justifications

b. Arguments for the percentage-of-completion method

Matches revenue with effort by recognizing income as work is performed

Allows comparability between accounting periods

Arguments against the percentage-of-completion method based on cost estimates for unfinished work

Lacks objectivity and verifiability

Is a departure from the realization concept which requires completion of earnings process before recognizing revenue

Less conservative than completed-contract

However, anticipated losses are recognized

UNOFFICIAL ANSWER

Problem 6   L.T. Contracts: Theoretical Justifications

Part b.

Arguments for the percentage-of-completion method are that it recognizes income periodically as work is performed on a contract, thus matching revenue with effort and allowing for comparability between accounting periods.

Arguments against the percentage-of-completion method are that it recognizes income based on estimates for unperformed work that may involve unforeseen costs and possible losses, thus resulting in a lack of objectivity and verifiability. Furthermore, the realization concept is not strictly adhered to when revenue is recognized before a sale is completed, and it is less conservative than the completed-contract method because income is recognized before the total income for the completed job is certain. It should be noted, however, that when the current estimate of total contract costs indicates a loss, in most circumstances provision should be made for the loss on the entire contract

ANSWER OUTLINE

Problem 7   Long-Term Contracts

1.   Problem 7 consists of two unrelated parts consisting of preparing schedules for a "firm fixed-price contract" accounted for under the completed-contract method and a cost-plus-fixed-fee contract accounted for by the percentage-of-completion method.

2.   Part A has two requirements. The first requirement is to prepare a schedule to show the "cost of uncompleted contract in excess of related billings" or "billings on uncompleted contract in excess of related costs" at 12-31-77, 78 and 79.

2.1   The first requirement can be mapped onto a schedule as follows:

Curtiss Construction Company
"Costs in Excess of Related Billings" or
"Billings in Excess of Related Costs"
at December 31,

	1977	1978	1979
Contract costs incurred to date			
Billings to Axelrod to date			

Note that we have started to prepare a single schedule whereas the AICPA solution (shown in the problem outline following this solution guide) has a separate schedule for each year.

2.2   The next step is to use the data given to complete the above schedule. The first line in the table of information (percentage-of-completion) is not needed since the fourth sentence indicated that "Curtiss appropriately uses the completed-contract method . . ." The second and third lines, contract costs incurred and billings to Axelrod are cumulative numbers so they can be entered directly into the skeleton schedule above.

Curtiss Construction Company
"Costs in Excess of Billings" of
"Billings in Excess of Related Costs"
at December 31,

	1977	1978	1979
Contract costs incurred to date	$350,000	$2,500,000	$4,250,000
Billings to Axelrod to date	720,000	2,160,000	3,600,000
Costs in excess of billing:		$ 340,000	$ 650,000
Billings in Excess of Costs	$370,000		

Our solution agrees with the AICPA's up to this point; however, an alternative exists in this problem with respect to the losses which are computed in 1978 and 1979 in 3 below. The AICPA solution to this problem deducts the amount of the credit which results when the loss for 1978 and 1979 is recorded from the costs in excess of related billings for each year. If we did the same thing in our schedule above we would get the identical amounts ($140,000 in 1978 and $400,000 in 1979) as the AICPA did. The alternative to the netting of the credit which arises when recording the 1978 and 1979 losses is to show the credit amount for each year as a liability. See journal entries under 3.3 below.

Current liabilities	1978	1979
Estimated liability on long-term contract	$200,000	$250,000

Author's note: Candidates who were aware of this alternative would, presumably, not have to show the liability presentation above since the requirement doesn't mention it.

3. The second requirement of Part A is to prepare a schedule of profit or loss for the years 1977, 1978 and 1979.

(3.2 Con't)

3.1 Remember that Curtiss uses the completed-contract method for this project; therefore, (para 11, ARB 45) no income should be recognized until the project is completed. However, if a loss is expected from the contract, the entire estimated amount of the loss from the contract is going to result. The contract is substantially complete at December 31, 1979; therefore, if the contract shows a net profit at the end of 1979, such profit should be recognized in 1979.

3.2 As in the first requirement, a more efficient approach than the use of single year schedules shown in the AICPA solution is to prepare one schedule for the three years.

Curtiss Construction Co.
Profit or Loss Recognized on Contract
For the Year Ended December 31

	1977	1978	1979
Contract Price:	$4,000,000	$4,000,000	$4,000,000
Estimated Total Costs :			
Costs incurred to date	$ 350,000	$2,500,000	$4,250,000
Estimated costs to complete	3,150,000	1,700,000	–0–
Estimated total costs for the three year period, actual for 1979	$3,500,000	$4,200,000	$4,250,000
Estimated total income loss for three year period, actual for 1979	500,000	(200,000)	(250,000)
Loss previously recognized			(200,000)
Estimated amount of income (loss) recognized in the current period, actual for 1979	–0–	(200,000)	(50,000)

3.3 Journal entries (not required) to record the loss are

1978 Loss on L-T
  Construction
  Constract   200,000
    Estimated Liability
    for Loss on
    L-T contract   200,000
  To record estimated loss
  on L-T contract

1979 Loss on L-T
  Construction
  Contract   50,000
    Estimated Liability
    for Loss on
    L-T contract   50,000
  To record additional
  loss on L-T Contract

4. Part B requires the computation of the amount of gross profit to be recognized by Butler Corp. for the year ended December 31, 1979 on a cost-plus-fixed-fee contract. Butler appropriately uses the percentage-of-completion method for this contract.

4.1 Butler will earn $300,000 in total income from this project, regardless of the actual costs incurred, since it is a cost-plus-fixed-fee contract. The amount to be recognized in 1979 is computed as follows:

$$\frac{\text{Costs incurred to date}}{\text{*Total estimated costs}} \times \frac{\text{Fixed}}{\text{Fee}} = \frac{\text{Income}}{\text{recognized for 1979}}$$

$$\frac{\$700,000}{\text{*}\$700,000 + \$1,400,000} \times \$300,000 =$$

$\underline{\$100,000}$ Income recognized for 1979

* Costs incurred to date plus estimated costs to complete the project.

Note that the $500,000 billed under the contract is not relevant in determining the amount of gross profit to be recognized.

UNOFFICIAL ANSWER

Problem 7　Long-Term Contracts

Part a.

1.　　　*Curtiss Construction Company, Inc.*
COMPUTATION OF BILLINGS ON UNCOMPLETED CONTRACT IN EXCESS OF RELATED COSTS
December 31, 1977

Partial billings on contract during 1977	$720,000
Deduct construction costs incurred during 1977	350,000
Balance, December 31, 1977	$370,000

Curtiss Construction Company, Inc.
COMPUTATION OF COSTS OF UNCOMPLETED CONTRACT IN EXCESS OF RELATED BILLINGS
December 31, 1978

Balance, December 31, 1977—excess of billings over costs	$ (370,000)
Add construction costs incurred during 1978 ($2,500,000 − $350,000)	2,150,000
	1,780,000
Deduct provision for loss on contract recognized during 1978 ($2,500,000 + $1,700,000 − $4,000,000)	200,000
	1,580,000
Deduct partial billings during 1978 ($2,160,000 − $720,000)	1,440,000
Balance, December 31, 1978	$ 140,000

Curtiss Construction Company, Inc.
COMPUTATION OF COSTS RELATING TO SUBSTANTIALLY COMPLETED CONTRACT IN EXCESS OF BILLINGS
December 31, 1979

Balance, December 31, 1978—excess of costs over billings	$ 140,000
Add construction costs incurred during 1979 ($4,250,000 − $2,500,000)	1,750,000
	1,890,000
Deduct loss on contract recognized during 1979 ($4,250,000 − $4,000,000 − $200,000)	50,000
	1,840,000
Deduct partial billings during 1979 ($3,600,000 − $2,160,000)	1,440,000
Balance, December 31, 1979	$ 400,000

2.　　　*Curtiss Construction Company, Inc.*
COMPUTATION OF PROFIT OR LOSS TO BE RECOGNIZED ON UNCOMPLETED CONTRACT
Year Ended December 31, 1977

Contract price		$4,000,000
Deduct contract costs		
Incurred to December 31, 1977	$ 350,000	
Estimated costs to complete	3,150,000	
Total estimated contract cost		$3,500,000
Estimated gross profit on contract at completion		$ 500,000
Profit to be recognized		$ 0

(The completed-contract method recognizes income only when the contract is completed, or substantially so.)

Curtiss Construction Company, Inc.
COMPUTATION OF LOSS TO BE RECOGNIZED ON UNCOMPLETED CONTRACT
Year ended December 31, 1978

Contract price	$4,000,000
Deduct contract costs	
Incurred to December 31, 1978	2,500,000
Estimated costs to complete	1,700,000
Total estimated contract cost	4,200,000
Loss to be recognized	$ (200,000)

(The completed-contract method requires that provision should be made for an expected loss.)

Curtiss Construction Company, Inc.
COMPUTATION OF LOSS TO BE RECOGNIZED
ON SUBSTANTIALLY COMPLETED CONTRACT
Year Ended December 31, 1979

Contract price	$4,000,000
Deduct contract costs incurred	4,250,000
Loss on contract	(250,000)
Deduct provision for loss booked at	
December 31, 1978	200,000
Loss to be recognized	$ (50,000)

Part b.

Butler, Inc.
COMPUTATION OF GROSS PROFIT TO BE
RECOGNIZED ON UNCOMPLETED CONTRACT
Year Ended December 31, 1979

Total contract price	
Estimated contract cost at	
completion ($700,000 + $1,400,000)	$2,100,000
Fixed fee	300,000
Total	2,400,000
Total estimated cost	2,100,000
Gross profit	$ 300,000
Percentage-of-completion	
($700,000 ÷ $2,100,000)	33-1/3%
Gross profit to be recognized	
($300,000 x 33-1/3%)	$ 100,000

MULTIPLE CHOICE QUESTIONS (1—40)

1. A consideration in determining the useful life of an intangible asset is **not** the
    a. Legal, regulatory, or contractual provisions.
    b. Provisions for renewal or extension.
    c. Expected actions of competitors.
    d. Initial cost.

2. When the fair value is determinable, a nonreciprocal transfer of a nonmonetary asset to another entity should be recorded at the
    a. Fair value of the asset received, but no gain or loss should be recognized on the disposition of the asset.
    b. Fair value of the asset transferred, and a gain or loss should be recognized on the disposition of the asset.
    c. Recorded amount of the asset transferred.
    d. Recorded amount of the asset received.

3. An activity that would be expensed currently as research and development costs is the
    a. Adaptation of an existing capability to a particular requirement or customer's need as a part of continuing commercial activity.
    b. Legal work in connection with patent applications or litigation, and the sale or licensing of patents.
    c. Engineering follow-through in an early phase of commercial production.
    d. Testing in search for or evaluation of product or process alternatives.

4. Shaw Company purchased a machine on January 1, 1978, for $350,000. The machine has an estimated useful life of five years and a salvage value of $50,000. The machine is being depreciated using the double-declining balance method. The asset balance net of accumulated depreciation at December 31, 1979, should be
    a. $126,000
    b. $158,000
    c. $170,000
    d. $224,000

5. In January 1980, Kemper Construction Company exchanged an old truck, which cost $54,000 and was one-third depreciated, and paid $35,000 cash for a used crane having a current fair value of $65,000. At what amount should the crane be recorded on the books of Kemper?
    a. $54,000
    b. $65,000
    c. $71,000
    d. $89,000

6. During 1979, the Commander Corporation acquired 3 pieces of machinery at an auction for a lump sum price of $240,000. In addition, Commander paid $12,000 to have the machines installed. An appraisal disclosed the following values:

Machine A	$ 50,000
Machine B	$150,000
Machine C	$100,000

What costs should be assigned to Machines A, B, and C, respectively?
    a. $40,000, $120,000, and $ 80,000.
    b. $42,000, $126,000, and $ 84,000.
    c. $50,000, $150,000, and $100,000.
    d. $84,000, $ 84,000, and $ 84,000.

7. On January 2, 1975, Hermes Corporation acquired a patent for $192,000. The patent had a remaining legal life of twelve years and an estimated useful life of eight years. In January 1979, Hermes paid $12,000 in legal fees in a successful defense of the patent. What should Hermes record as patent amortization for 1979?
    a. $16,000
    b. $24,000
    c. $25,500
    d. $27,000

8. The Plaza Company was organized late in 1978 and began operations on January 1, 1979. Plaza is engaged in conducting market research studies on behalf of manufacturers. Prior to the start of operations, the following costs were incurred:

Attorney's fees in connection with organization of Plaza	$ 4,000
Improvements to leased offices prior to occupancy	7,000
Meetings of incorporators, state filing fees and other organization expenses	5,000
	$16,000

Plaza has elected to record amortization of organization costs over the maximum period allowable under generally accepted accounting principles. What is the amount of organization costs amortized for 1979?

    a. $ 225
    b. $ 400
    c. $1,800
    d. $3,200

9.   In January 1978 Solataire Company purchased equipment for $60,000, to be used in its manufacturing operations. The equipment was estimated to have a useful life of 8 years, with salvage value estimated at $6,000. Solataire considered various methods of depreciation and selected the sum-of-the-years-digits method of depreciation. On December 31, 1979, the related allowance for accumulated depreciation will have a balance

    a. $7,500 less than under the straight-line method.
    b. $7,500 less than under the double-declining balance method.
    c. $9,000 greater than under the straight-line method.
    d. $9,000 greater than under the double-declining balance method.

10.   During 1979 The Simon Company sustained a loss of $72,000 when a fire destroyed its merchandise inventory. The merchandise had a fair value of $100,000 immediately before the loss. The loss was covered by an insurance policy with a face value of $70,000 and an 80% coinsurance clause. What is the amount of the indemnity collectible as a result of this loss?

    a. $57,600
    b. $63,000
    c. $70,000
    d. $72,000

11.   Company A and Company B exchanged non-monetary assets with no monetary consideration involved and no impairment of value. The exchange did not culminate an earning process for either Company A or Company B. The accounting for the exchange should be based on the

    a.   Recorded amount of the asset received.
    b.   Recorded amount of the asset relinquished.
    c.   Fair value of the asset received.
    d.   Fair value of the asset relinquished.

12.   A method which excludes salvage value from the base for the depreciation calculation is

    a.   Straight-line.
    b.   Sum-of-the-years-digits.
    c.   Double-declining-balance.
    d.   Productive-output.

13.   On January 1, 1970, Burry Corporation purchased for $76,000, equipment having a useful life of ten years and an estimated salvage value of $4,000. Burry has recorded monthly depreciation of the equipment on the straight-line method. On December 31, 1978, the equipment was sold for $15,000. As a result of this sale, Burry should recognize a gain of

    a. $0
    b. $ 3,800
    c. $ 7,400
    d. $11,400

14.   On December 1, 1978, Dartmouth Corporation exchanged 1,000 shares of its $25 par value common stock held in treasury for a parcel of land to be held for a future plant site. The treasury shares were acquired by Dartmouth at a cost of $40, and on the exchange date the common shares of Dartmouth had a fair market value of $55 per share. Dartmouth received $5,000 for selling scrap when an existing building was removed from the site. Based upon these facts, the land should be capitalized at

    a. $35,000
    b. $40,000
    c. $50,000
    d. $55,000

15.   In January 1978, the Under Mine Corporation purchased a mineral mine for $3,400,000 with removable ore estimated by geological surveys at 4,000,000 tons. The property has an estimated value of $200,000 after the ore has been extracted. The company incurred $800,000 of development costs preparing the mine for production. During 1978, 400,000 tons were removed and 375,000 tons were sold. What is the amount of depletion that Under Mine should record for 1978?

    a. $375,000
    b. $393,750
    c. $400,000
    d. $420,000

16.   Which of the following principles best describes the current method of accounting for research and development costs?

    a.   Associating cause and effect.
    b.   Systematic and rational allocation.
    c.   Income tax minimization.
    d.   Immediate recognition as an expense.

17.   The Ackley Company exchanged 100 shares of Burke Company common stock, which Ackley was holding as an investment, for a piece of equipment from the Flynn Company. The Burke

Company common stock, which had been purchased by Ackley for $30 per share, had a quoted market value of $34 per share at the date of exchange. The piece of equipment had a recorded amount on Flynn's books of $3,100. What journal entry should Ackley have made to record this exchange?

		Debit	Credit
a.	Equipment	$3,000	
	Investment in Burke		
	Co. com. stk.		$3,000
b.	Equipment	3,100	
	Investment in Burke		
	Co. com. stk.		3,000
	Other income		100
c.	Equipment	3,100	
	Other expense	300	
	Investment in Burke		
	Co. com. stk.		3,400
d.	Equipment	3,400	
	Investment in Burke		
	Co. com. stk.		3,000
	Other income		400

18. Minor Baseball Company had a player contract with Doe that was recorded in its accounting records at $145,000. Better Baseball Company had a player contract with Smith that was recorded in its accounting records at $140,000. Minor traded Doe to Better for Smith by exchanging each player's contract. The fair value of each contract was $150,000. What amount should be shown in the accounting records after the exchange of player contracts?

	Minor	Better
a.	$140,000	$140,000
b.	$140,000	$145,000
c.	$145,000	$140,000
d.	$150,000	$150,000

19. On February 1, 1977, Reflection Corporation purchased a parcel of land as a factory site for $50,000. An old building on the property was demolished, and construction began on a new building which was completed on November 1, 1977. Costs incurred during this period are listed below:

Demolition of old building	$ 4,000
Architect's fees	10,000
Legal fees for title investigation and purchase contract	2,000
Construction costs	500,000

(Salvaged materials resulting from demolition were sold for $1,000.)

Reflection should record the cost of the land and new building respectively as
- a. $52,000 and $513,000.
- b. $53,000 and $512,000.
- c. $53,000 and $510,000.
- d. $55,000 and $510,000.

20. On January 1, 1976, Kent Corporation purchased a machine for $50,000. Kent paid shipping expenses of $500 as well as installation costs of $1,200. The machine was estimated to have a useful life of ten years and an estimated salvage value of $3,000. In January 1977 additions costing $3,600 were made to the machine in order to comply with pollution control ordinances. These additions neither prolonged the life of the machine nor did they have any salvage value. If Kent records depreciation under the straight-line method, depreciation expense for 1977 is
- a. $4,870.
- b. $5,170.
- c. $5,270.
- d. $5,570.

21. On July 1, 1976, Carol Corporation purchased factory equipment for $25,000. Salvage value was estimated to be $1,000. The equipment will be depreciated over ten years using the double-declining-balance method. Counting the year of acquisition as one-half year, Carol should record depreciation expense for 1977 on this equipment of
- a. $3,840.
- b. $4,500.
- c. $4,800.
- d. $5,000.

22. Which of the following research and development related costs should be capitalized and amortized over current and future periods?
- a. Research and development general laboratory building.
- b. Inventory used for a specific research project.
- c. Administrative salaries allocated to research and development.
- d. Research findings purchased from another company to aid a particular research project currently in process.

23. In January 1975 Tracy Corporation purchased a patent for a new consumer product for $180,000. At the time of purchase, the patent was valid for

fifteen years. Due to the competitive nature of the product however, the patent was estimated to have a useful life of only ten years. During 1978 the

product was permanently removed from the market under governmental order because of a potential health hazard present in the product. What amount should Tracy charge to expense during 1978, assuming amortization is recorded at the end of each year?

a. $12,000.
b. $18,000.
c. $126,000.
d. $144,000.

24.   On December 1, 1976, Hobart Company acquired a new delivery truck in exchange for an old delivery truck that it had acquired in 1973. The old truck was purchased for $7,000 and had a book value of $2,800. On the date of the exchange the old truck had a market value of $3,000. In addition, Hobart paid $3,500 cash for the new truck, which had a list price of $8,000. At what amount should Hobart record the new truck for financial accounting purposes?

a. $6,300.
b. $6,500.
c. $7,000.
d. $8,000.

25.   Eastside Corporation purchased a machine on July 1, 1973, for $75,000. The machine was estimated to have a useful life of 10 years with an estimated salvage value of $5,000. During 1976 it became apparent that the machine would become uneconomical after December 31, 1980, and that the machine would have no scrap value. Accumulated depreciation on this machine as of December 31, 1975, was $17,500. What should be the charge for depreciation in 1976 under generally accepted accounting principles?

a. $10,000.
b. $11,500.
c. $12,750.
d. $17,500.

26.   The general ledger of the Flint Corporation as of December 31, 1976, includes the following accounts:

Organization costs	$ 5,000
Deposits with advertising agency (will be used to promote good-will)	8,000
Discount on bonds payable	15,000
Excess of cost over book value of net assets of acquired subsidiary	70,000
Trademarks	12,000

In the preparation of Flint's balance sheet as of December 31, 1976, what should be reported as total intangible assets?

a. $87,000.
b. $92,000.
c. $95,000.
d. $110,000.

27.   A schedule of machinery owned by Lester Manufacturing Company is presented below:

	Total Cost	Estimated Salvage Value	Estimated Life in Years
Machine A	$550,000	$50,000	20
Machine B	200,000	20,000	15
Machine C	40,000	—	5

Lester computes depreciation on the straight-line method. Based upon the information presented, the composite life of these assets (in years) should be

a.   13.3.
b.   16.0.
c.   18.0.
d.   19.8.

28.   Howard Co. incurred research and development costs in 1977 as follows:

Materials used in research and development projects	$ 400,000
Equipment acquired that will have alternate future uses in future research and development projects	2,000,000
Depreciation for 1977 on above equipment	500,000
Personnel costs of persons involved in research and development projects	1,000,000
Consulting fees paid to outsiders for research and development projects	100,000
Indirect costs reasonably allocable to research and development projects	200,000
	$4,200,000

The amount of research and development costs charged to Howard's 1977 income statement should be
   a. $1,500,000.
   b. $1,700,000.
   c. $2,200,000.
   d. $3,500,000.

29.   Brower Corporation owns a manufacturing plant in the country of Oust. On December 31, 1977, the plant had a book value of $5,000,000 and an estimated fair market value of $8,000,000. The government of Oust has clearly indicated that it will expropriate the plant during the coming year and will reimburse Brower for 40% of the plant's estimated fair market value. What journal entry should Brower make on December 31, 1977, to record the intended expropriation?

		Debit	Credit
a.	Estimated loss on expropriation of foreign plant	$1,800,000	
	Allowance for estimated loss on foreign plant		$1,800,000
b.	Estimated loss on expropriation of foreign plant	3,000,000	
	Allowance for estimated loss on foreign plant		3,000,000
c.	Receivable due from foreign government	3,200,000	
	Investment in foreign plant		3,200,000
d.	Loss on expropriation of foreign plant	1,800,000	
	Receivable due from foreign government	3,200,000	
	Investment in foreign plant		5,000,000

30.   On January 2, 1975, Mogul Company acquired equipment to be used in its manufacturing operations. The equipment has an estimated useful life of 10 years and an estimated salvage value of $5,000. The depreciation applicable to this equipment was $24,000 for 1977, computed under the sum-of-the-years-digits

method. What was the acquisition cost of the equipment?
   a. $165,000.
   b. $170,000.
   c. $240,000.
   d. $245,000.

31.   In January 1977 Action Corporation entered into a contract to acquire a new machine for its factory. The machine, which had a cash price of $150,000, was paid for as follows:

Down payment	$ 15,000
Notes payable in 10 equal monthly installments	120,000
500 shares of Action common stock with an agreed value of $50 per share	25,000
Total	$160,000

Prior to the machine's use, installation costs of $4,000 were incurred. The machine has an estimated useful life of 10 years and an estimated salvage value of $5,000. What should Action record as depreciation expense for 1977 under the straight-line method?
   a. $15,900.
   b. $15,500.
   c. $15,000.
   d. $14,900.

32.   In 1978 Murray Corporation developed a new product that will be marketed in 1979. In connection with the development of this product, the following costs were incurred in 1978:

Research and development departmental costs	$200,000
Materials and supplies consumed	50,000
Compensation paid to research consultants	60,000
	$310,000

It is anticipated that these costs will be recovered in 1981. What is the amount of research and development costs that Murray should record in 1978 as a charge to income?
   a. $0.
   b. $60,000.
   c. $250,000.
   d. $310,000.

33.   What is the proper time or time period over which to match the cost of an intangible asset with revenues if it is likely that the benefit of the asset

will last for an indeterminate but very long period of time?

a. Forty years.
b. Fifty years.
c. Immediately.
d. At such time as diminution in value can be quantitatively determined.

MAY 1981 QUESTIONS

34. On January 1, 1979, Current Company purchased a new machine for $5,000,000. The new machine has an estimated useful life of five years and the salvage value was estimated to be $500,000. Current uses the sum-of-the-years'-digits method of depreciation. The amount of depreciation expense for 1980 (the second year) would be

a. $ 800,000.
b. $1,200,000.
c. $1,333,333.
d. $1,500,000.

35. On January 1, 1980, Richmond, Inc., signed a fixed-price contract to have Builder Associates construct a major plant facility at a cost of $4,000,000. It was estimated that it would take three years to complete the project. Also on January 1, 1980, to finance the construction cost, Richmond borrowed $4,000,000 payable in 10 annual installments of $400,000 plus interest at the rate of 11%. During 1980 Richmond made deposit and progress payments totaling $1,500,000 under the contract; the average amount of accumulated expenditures was $650,000 for the year. The excess borrowed funds were invested in short-term securities, from which Richmond realized investment income of $250,000. What amount should Richmond report as capitalized interest at December 31, 1980?

a. $ 71,500.
b. $165,000.
c. $190,000.
d. $440,000.

36. During 1980 Trencher, Inc., incurred research and development costs as follows:

Experimental and development cost of a new process patented in December 1980	$250,000
Testing for evaluation of new products	300,000
Modification of the formulation of a chemical product	150,000
Research and development costs reimbursable under a contract with Quality Chemicals Corporation	500,000

What amount should Trencher report as research and development expense in its income statement for the year ended December 31, 1980?

a. $0.
b. $450,000.
c. $700,000.
d. $950,000.

37. Town Corporation purchased factory equipment that was installed and put into service January 2, 1979, at a total cost of $64,000. Salvage value was estimated at $4,000. The equipment is being depreciated over eight years using the double-declining balance method. For the year 1980, Park should record depreciation expense on this equipment of

a. $11,250.
b. $12,000.
c. $15,000.
d. $16,000.

38. Which of the following should be expensed as incurred by the franchisee for a franchise with an estimated useful life of ten years?

a. Amount paid to the franchisor for the franchise.
b. Periodic payments to a company, other than the franchisor, for that company's franchise.
c. Legal fees paid to the franchisee's lawyers to obtain the franchise.
d. Periodic payments to the franchisor based on the franchisee's revenues.

39. When a fixed asset with a five-year estimated useful life is sold during the second year, how would the use of the sum-of-the-years-digits method of depreciation instead of the straight-line method of depreciation affect the gain or loss on the sale of the fixed asset?

	Gain	*Loss*
a.	Decrease	Increase
b.	Increase	Decrease
c.	No effect	No effect
d.	No effect	Decrease

40. Which of the following depreciation methods is computed in the same way as depletion is computed?

a. Straight-line.
b. Sum-of-the-years-digits.
c. Double-declining-balance.
d. Productive-output.

REPEAT QUESTIONS

(581,Q1,3)   Identical to item 14 above
(581,Q1,8)   Identical to item 24 above
(581,T1,20)   Identical to item 12 above

Problem 1   Accounting for R&D (578,T5)

(20 to 25 minutes)

The Thomas Company is in the process of developing a revolutionary new product. A new division of the company was formed to develop, manufacture, and market this new product. As of year end (December 31, 1977) the new product has not been manufactured for resale; however, a prototype unit was built and is in operation.

Throughout 1977 the new division incurred certain costs. These costs include design and engineering studies, prototype manufacturing costs, administrative expenses (including salaries of administrative personnel), and market research costs. In addition, approximately $500,000 in equipment (estimated useful life—10 years) was purchased for use in developing and manufacturing the new product. Approximately $200,000 of this equipment was built specifically for the design development of the new product; the remaining $300,000 of equipment was used to manufacture the pre-production prototype and will be used to manufacture the new product once it is in commercial production.

Required:
    a.   What is the definition of "research" and of "development" as defined in Statement of Financial Accounting Standards No. 2?
    b.   Briefly indicate the practical and conceptual reasons for the conclusion reached by the Financial Accounting Standards Board on accounting and reporting practices for research and development costs.
    c.   In accordance with Statement of Financial Accounting Standards No. 2, how should the various costs of Thomas described above be recorded on the financial statements for the year ended December 31, 1977?

Problem 2   Property, Plant, and Equipment (1180,T2)

(15 to 25 minutes)

Among the principal topics related to the accounting for the property, plant, and equipment of a company are acquisition and retirement.

Required:
    a.   What expenditures should be capitalized when equipment is acquired for cash?
    b.   Assume that the market value of equipment acquired is not determinable by reference to a similar purchase for cash. Describe how the acquiring company should determine the capitalizable cost of equipment purchased by exchanging it for each of the following:
        1.   Bonds having an established market price.
        2.   Common stock not having an established market price.
        3.   Similar equipment having a determinable market value.
    c.   Describe the factors that determine whether expenditures relating to property, plant, and equipment already in use should be capitalized.
    d.   Describe how to account for the gain or loss on the sale of property, plant, and equipment for cash.

Problem 3 Property, Plant and Equipment (576,T3)

(20 to 25 minutes)

Part a.   Property, plant, and equipment (plant assets) generally represent a material portion of the total assets of most companies. Accounting for the acquisition and usage of such assets is, therefore, an important part of the financial reporting process.

Required:

    1.   Distinguish between revenue and capital expenditures and explain why this distinction is important.

    2.   Briefly define depreciation as used in accounting.

    3.   Identify the factors that are relevant in determining the annual depreciation and explain whether these factors are determined objectively or whether they are based on judgment.

    4.   Explain why depreciation is usually shown in the sources of funds section of the statement of changes in financial position.

Part b.   A company may acquire plant assets (among other ways) for cash, on a deferred-payment plan, by exchanging other assets, or by a combination of these ways.

Required:

1. Identify six costs that should be capitalized as the cost of land. For your answer, assume that land with an existing building is acquired for cash and that the existing building is to be removed in the immediate future in order that a new building can be constructed on that site.

2. At what amount should a company record a plant asset acquired on a deferred-payment plan?

3. In general, at what amount should plant assets received in exchange for other nonmonetary assets be recorded? Specifically, at what amount should a company record a new machine acquired by exchanging an older, similar machine and paying cash?

Problem 4   Fixed Assets and Depreciation (578,P5)

(50 to 60 minutes)

This problem consists of two unrelated parts.

Part a. At December 31, 1976, certain accounts included in the property, plant and equipment section of the Townsand Company's balance sheet had the following balances:

Land	$100,000
Buildings	800,000
Leasehold improvements	500,000
Machinery and equipment	700,000

During 1977 the following transactions occurred:
· Land site number 621 was acquired for $1,000,000. Additionally, to acquire the land Townsand paid a $60,000 commission to a real estate agent. Costs of $15,000 were incurred to clear the land. During the course of clearing the land, timber and gravel were recovered and sold for $5,000.
· A second tract of land (site number 622) with a building was acquired for $300,000. The closing statement indicated that the land value was $200,000 and the building value was $100,000. Shortly after acquisition, the building was demolished at a cost of $30,000. A new building was constructed for $150,000 plus the following costs:

Excavation fees	$11,000
Architectural design fees	8,000
Building permit fee	1,000
Imputed interest on funds used during construction	6,000

The building was completed and occupied on September 30, 1977.

· A third tract of land (site number 623) was acquired for $600,000 and was put on the market for resale.
· Extensive work was done to a building occupied by Townsand under a lease agreement that expires on December 31, 1986. The total cost of the work was $125,000, which consisted of the following:

Painting of ceilings	$ 10,000	estimated useful life is one year
Electrical work	35,000	estimated useful life is ten years
Construction of extension to current working area	80,000	estimated useful life is thirty years
	$125,000	

The lessor paid one-half of the costs incurred in connection with the extension to the current working area.

· During December 1977 costs of $65,000 were incurred to improve leased office space. The related lease will terminate on December 31, 1979, and is not expected to be renewed.
· A group of new machines was purchased under a royalty agreement which provides for payment of royalties based on units of production for the machines. The invoice price of the machines was $75,000, freight costs were $2,000, unloading charges were $1,500, and royalty payments for 1977 were $13,000.

Required:
1. Prepare a detailed analysis of the changes in each of the following balance sheet accounts for 1977:

Land
Buildings
Leasehold improvements
Machinery and equipment

Disregard the related accumulated depreciation accounts.

2. List the items in the fact situation which were not used to determine the answer to 1. above, and indicate where, or if, these items should be included in Townsand's financial statements.

Part b. On January 1, 1975, Barth Company, a small machine-tool manufacturer, acquired for $1,000,000 a piece of new industrial equipment. The new equipment was eligible for the investment tax credit and Barth took full advantage of the credit and accounted for the amount using the flow-through method. The new equipment had a useful life of five years and the salvage value was estimated to be $100,000. Barth estimates that the new equipment can produce 10,000 machine tools in its first year. Production is then estimated to decline by 1,000 units per year over the remaining useful life of the equipment.

The following depreciation methods may be used:

- Double-declining-balance
- Straight-line
- Sum-of-the-years-digits
- Units-of-output

Required:

1. Which depreciation method would result in the maximization of profits for financial statement reporting for the three-year period ending December 31, 1977? Prepare a schedule showing the amount of accumulated depreciation at December 31, 1977, under the method selected. Show supporting computations in good form. Ignore present value, income tax, and deferred income tax considerations in your answer.

2. Which depreciation method would result in the minimization of profits for income tax reporting for the three-year period ending December 31, 1977? Prepare a schedule showing the amount of accumulated depreciation at December 31, 1977, under the method selected. Show supporting computations in good form. Ignore present value considerations in your answer.

Problem 5   Fixed Assets (1174,Q5b)

(20 to 25 minutes)

Part b. Number your answer sheet from 1 to 14. For each numbered item on the following schedule supply the correct amount next to the corresponding number on your answer sheet. Round each answer to the nearest dollar. Do not recopy the schedule. Show supporting computations in good form.

Thompson Corporation, a manufacturer of steel products, began operations on October 1, 1972. The accounting department of Thompson has started the fixed-asset and depreciation schedule presented on the following page. You have been asked to assist in completing this schedule. In addition to ascertaining that the data already on the schedule are correct, you have obtained the following information from the company's records and personnel:

Depreciation is computed from the first of the month of acquisition to the first of the month of disposition.

Land A and Building A were acquired from a predecessor corporation. Thompson paid $812,500 for the land and building together. At the time of acquisition, the land had an appraised value of $72,000 and the building had an appraised value of $828,000.

Land B was acquired on October 2, 1972, in exchange for 3,000 newly issued shares of Thompson's common stock. At the date of acquisition, the stock had a par value of $5 per share and a fair value of $25 per share. During October 1972 Thompson paid $10,400 to demolish an existing building on this land so it could construct a new building.

Construction of Building B on the newly acquired land began on October 1, 1973. By September 30, 1974, Thompson had paid $210,000 of the estimated total construction costs of $300,000. Estimated completion and occupancy are July 1975.

Certain equipment was donated to the corporation by a local university. An independent appraisal of the equipment when donated placed the fair value at $16,000 and the salvage value at $2,000.

Machinery A's total cost of $110,000 includes installation expense of $550 and normal repairs and maintenance of $11,000. Salvage value is estimated at $5,500. Machinery A was sold on February 1, 1974.

On October 1, 1973, Machinery B was acquired with a down payment of $4,000 and the remaining payments to be made in ten annual installments of $4,000 each beginning October 1, 1974. The prevail-

Thompson Corporation
FIXED ASSET AND DEPRECIATION SCHEDULE
For Fiscal Years Ended September 30, 1973, and September 30, 1974

Assets	Acquisition Date	Cost	Salvage	Depreciation Method	Estimated Life in Years	Depreciation Expense Year Ended September 30, 1973	Depreciation Expense Year Ended September 30, 1974
Land A	October 1, 1972	$ (1)	N/A	N/A	N/A	N/A	N/A
Building A	October 1, 1972	(2)	$47,500	Straight Line	(3)	$14,000	$ (4)
Land B	October 2, 1972	(5)	N/A	N/A	N/A	N/A	N/A
Building B	Under Construction	210,000 to date	–	Straight Line	Thirty	–	(6)
Donated Equipment	October 2, 1972	(7)	2,000	150% Declining Balance	Ten	(8)	(9)
Machinery A	October 2, 1972	(10)	5,500	Sum of Years' Digits	Ten	(11)	(12)
Machinery B	October 1, 1973	(13)	–	Straight Line	Fifteen	–	(14)

N/A — Not applicable

ing interest rate was 8%. The following data were abstracted from present-value tables:

Present value of $1.00 at 8%

10 years	.463
11 years	.429
15 years	.315

Present value of annuity of $1.00
in arrears at 8%

10 years	6.710
11 years	7.139
15 years	8.559

MULTIPLE CHOICE ANSWERS

1.	d	9.	c	17.	d	25.	b	33.	a
2.	b	10.	b	18.	c	26.	a	34.	b
3.	d	11.	b	19.	d	27.	b	35.	a
4.	a	12.	c	20.	c	28.	c	36.	c
5.	b	13.	b	21.	b	29.	a	37.	b
6.	b	14.	c	22.	a	30.	b	38.	d
7.	d	15.	c	23.	c	31.	d	39.	b
8.	a	16.	d	24.	a	32.	d	40.	d

EXPLANATION OF MULTIPLE CHOICE ANSWERS

1.   (1180,T1,15)   (d)   In determining the useful life of an intangible asset, any factor which can contribute to lengthening or shortening that life must be considered. APB 17 lists several factors to be considered, including legal, regulatory, or contractual provisions; provisions for renewal or extension; and expected actions of competitors. Initial cost, while used to determine amortization amount, has no bearing on useful life.

2.   (1180,T1,24)   (b)   APB 29 requires recording nonreciprocal transfers at fair value when it is determinable. Answer (a) is incorrect because no asset is received in this case. Answers (c) and (d) are incorrect because fair value is determinable.

3.   (1180,T1,27)   (d)   SFAS 2 requires that all research and development costs be charged to expense as incurred. Para 9-10 of that statement provide guidelines by listing specific examples of activities which are and are not considered R & D. Testing in search for or evaluation of product or process alternatives is an example given of R & D, while the other choices are not considered R & D.

4.   (1180, P1,1)   (a)   The requirement is the net book value of a machine at the end of 1979, which is 2 years after it was purchased for $350,000. The machine has an estimated useful life of five years and a salvage value of $50,000. The salvage value is not relevant since the double-declining balance method is being used. The depreciation rate is the straight-line percentage (100% ÷ 5) or 20% X 2 or 40%. Depreciation expense for the first two years is:

   1978: ($350,000)(40%) = $140,000

   1979: ($350,000 − $140,000)(40%) = $84,000

The net book value is the cost ($350,000) less the accumulated depreciation ($140,000 + $84,000) = $126,000.

5.   (1180,P1,6)   (b)   The requirement is the proper amount at which to record a used crane acquired in exchange for a used truck. This exchange involves similar productive assets as defined in para 21 of APB 29. In recording such exchanges, it is necessary to determine if the fair market value of the asset given up, or fair market value received if more clearly determinable, is greater or less than the book value of the asset given up. If greater, a gain results; however, the gain is not recognized and the acquired asset is recorded at the sum of the book values given up. If less, there is a loss which should be recognized immediately. Since it is necessary to test for a gain or loss, a helpful approach is to prepare the journal entry to record the exchange.

Crane	65,000	
Loss on Sale	6,000	
* Accum. Depr.	18,000	
Truck		54,000
Cash		35,000

   * 1/3(54,000)

Because the fair value of the truck is not given, the fair values of the crane acquired ($65,000) is compared to the book value given up, ($36,000 + $35,000) giving a loss of $6,000.

6.   (1180,Q1,9)   (b)   The requirement is the costs to be assigned to Machines A, B and C in a lump sum purchase. Note that the 4 choices show 4 different values for both machine A and machine B; therefore, to answer this problem, only the cost assigned to A or B need be computed. The total cost to be allocated among the three machines is the cost to acquire ($240,000) and prepare for use ($12,000), a total of $252,000. $300,000 is the total appraised value of the three machines. This total cost is allocated on the basis of relative appraised value:

Machine A
($ 50,000/$300,000) ($252,000) = $ 42,000

Machine B
($150,000/$300,000) ($252,000) = $126,000

Machine C
($100,000/$300,000) ($252,000) = $ 84,000

7.   (1180,Q1,15)   (d)   The requirement is the amount Hermes should record as patent amortization for 1979. The patent was acquired at a cost of $192,000 at the beginning of 1975 and is being amortized over a useful life of eight years (useful life is used because it is shorter than the legal life). Yearly amortization for 1975 thru 1978 was:

   $192,000 ÷ 8 yrs. = $24,000/year

By the beginning of 1979, the net amount left in the

patent account was $192,000 − (4) ($24,000), or $96,000. In early 1979, Hermes paid $12,000 in legal fees to successfully defend the patent, which should be capitalized as a cost of the patent. The new amount in the patent account is then $108,000 ($96,000 + $12,000), to be amortized over the remaining 4 years of the useful life. Amortization for 1979 is $108,000 ÷ 4 yrs. = $27,000/year.

8. (580,Q1,2) (a) Organizational costs that are amortizable include the attorney's fees and meetings of incorporators, state filing fees, and other organizational expenses. Leasehold improvements are assets to amortize but not as organization costs. For financial accounting, intangible assets are generally amortized over a 40-year period.

Attorney's fees	$4,000
Meetings, etc.	5,000
	$9,000 ÷ 40 yrs. = $225/year

9. (580,Q1,11) (c) The solutions approach is to compute the balance of accumulated depreciation under the three methods offered as alternatives. If the SYD method is used for book purposes, accumulated depreciation account balance is $9,000 greater than under the straight-line method.

SYD:

($54,000)(8/36) = $12,000	(1978)
($54,000)(7/36) = 10,500	(1979)
$22,500	

S/L:

($54,000)(1/8) = $ 6,750	(1978)
($54,000)(1/8) = 6,750	(1979)
$13,500	

DDB:

($60,000)(25%)= $15,000	(1978)
($45,000)(25%)= 11,250	(1979)
$26,250	

10. (580,Q1,14) (b) The requirement is for the amount of loss that will be collected from the insurance company. Since there is an 80% coinsurance clause, Simon Co. and the insurance company are co-insurers. The formula for coinsurance when there is one policy is:

$$\frac{\text{Face of policy}}{\text{Insurance required}} \times \text{amount of loss} = \text{amount collectible}$$

$$\frac{\$70,000}{80\% (\$100,000)} \times \$72,000 = \$63,000$$

11. (580,T1,30) (b) When nonmonetary assets are exchanged with no monetary consideration involved, no gain is recognized if the earnings process is not culminated. Therefore the accounting for such an exchange must be based on the recorded amount of the asset relinquished. See APB 29, para 21.

12. (580,T1,35) (c) All acceptable financial accounting depreciation methods make an adjustment to the depreciation base for salvage value except the declining-balance methods which use net book value as the base.

13. (1179,Q1,4) (b) The requirement is the gain on sale of equipment at 12/31/78. The equipment was purchased on 1/1/70 for $76,000, with a useful life of 10 years and a salvage value of $4,000 (straight-line depreciation was used). The equipment was sold for $15,000 at 12/31/78. The calculations required to compute the gain are presented below. First, depreciation of $7,200 per year is calculated. Next, 9 years' depreciation of $64,800 (and book value of $11,200) are calculated. Finally, the gain is $3,800.

$$\frac{\$76,000 - \$4,000}{10 \text{ years}} = \$7,200/\text{year depreciation}$$

9 years x $7,200 = $64,800 depreciation to 12/31/78
$76,000 cost - $64,800 depreciation = $11,200
book value
$15,000 sales price - $11,200 book value = $3,800 gain

14. (1179,Q1,10) (c) The requirement is at what value a future plant site should be capitalized. The land was acquired in exchange for treasury stock that had a fair market value of $55,000 (1,000 shares at $55). Para 18 of APB 29 indicates that nonmonetary transactions should be based on fair values. Also, $5,000 was received for scrap from an existing building that was removed from the plant site. This $5,000 is a reduction of the cost of the plant site, resulting in a capitalized value of $50,000 ($55,000 - $5,000).

15. (1179,Q1,16) (c) The requirement is the 1978 depletion for Under Mine. The solutions approach is to determine the depletion expense per ton as illustrated below. The $4,000,000 estimated net cost of the mine divided by the 4,000,000 estimated removable tons results in a depletion rate of $1 per ton. Since 400,000 tons were removed, the depletion expense would be $400,000. Since 375,000 tons were sold, there would be an inventory of $25,000 at $1 per ton.

Mine cost	$3,400,000
Development cost	+800,000
Salvage value	−200,000
Cost to be depreciated	$4,000,000

÷ est. recover.   4,000,000 tons
                           = $1/ton

16. (1179,T1,9) (d) Research and development costs are expensed when incurred per para 12 of SFAS 2. Answer (a) is incorrect because if R&D were accounted for by associating cause and effect, R&D would be capitalized and amortized to the periods in which the R&D produced revenue. Answer (b) is incorrect because systematic and rational allocation implies capitalization and amortization. Answer (c) is incorrect because the method of accounting for R&D for financial reporting purposes does not determine the method to be used for income tax purposes. Thus, R&D may be expensed for tax purposes regardless of what is done for financial reporting purposes.

17. (1176,P1,18) (d) This is a non-monetary exchange which is covered by APB 29. APB 29 (para 18) requires that non-monetary transactions generally be based on fair values. The $34 market value per share of Burke stock (100 shares) establishes the fair value of the machine at $3,400. Thus, the Ackley Company records the equipment at $3,400; credits the investment in Burke stock for the $30/share carrying value ($3,000); and records other income of $400.

18. (1178,P1,17) (c) The requirement is the asset carrying values on the books of two baseball companies after exchanging player contracts. Generally, non-monetary exchanges are recorded at fair market value per APB 29. The exception (for which the non-monetary exchange is recorded on a cost basis) is when the exchange is not the culmination of an earnings process per para 21. More specifically, an exchange of a productive asset not held for sale in the ordinary course of business for a similar productive asset is not the culmination of an earning process. Accordingly the exchange of player contracts should be accounted for at cost. Thus, Minor exchanged a player contract that had a cost of $145,000 for another contract which will now be valued at $145,000. Better Company exchanged a contract that had a cost of $140,000 for another contract. Thus the other contract will be valued by Better at $140,000.

19. (1178,Q1,10) (d) The requirement is land cost and new building cost. The cost of the land includes the original cost of $50,000 plus the old building demolition cost of $4,000, plus the title investigation and purchase contract costs of $2,000, less the demolition salvage value of $1,000, which totals $55,000. The building cost is the architect's fees of $10,000 and the construction cost of $500,000.

20. (1178,Q1,11) (c) The requirement is depreciation expense for 1977 based on the straight-line method for a machine purchased in the beginning of 1976. The machine cost is $51,700 ($50,000 cost plus shipping cost of $500 and installation cost of $1,200). The depreciation base is $48,700 (cost of $51,700 less salvage value of $3,000) resulting in an annual depreciation cost of $4,870 ($48,700 ÷ 10 yr.). The pollution control additions of $3,600 made at the beginning of 1977 are to be amortized over the remaining nine years with no salvage value, resulting in a $400 per year cost. Thus the depreciation for 1977 is $5,270 ($4,870 + $400).

21. (1178,Q1,8) (b) The requirement is depreciation expense in 1977 based upon the double-declining-balance method. Note that the double-declining-balance method takes twice the straight-line rate times the net book value each year. Salvage value is ignored except that the book value of the asset is not depreciated below salvage value. Note that the machine was purchased midway in 1976. Thus depreciation must be computed for 1976 as one-half year's depreciation; the first year's depreciation would be one-half of 20% of the original cost of $25,000. In 1977 the beginning book value is $22,500 (cost of $25,000 less 1976 depreciation of $2,500). Depreciation for 1977 is 20% times the book value of $22,500.

1976	$2,500 = .5(25,000 x 20%)
1977	$4,500 = (25,000 − 2,500) x 20%

22. (1178,T1,19) (a) The requirement is the research and development cost which should be capitalized and amortized over current and future periods. Per SFAS 2, all R&D costs are expensed except equipment and facilities that are acquired for R&D and have alternative future uses which are capitalized and amortized. Presumably a general laboratory building would have alternative future uses, e.g., can be sold, and should be capitalized and amortized. Answer (b) is incorrect because inventory used for a specific research project should be expensed when incurred (para 11a). Answer (c) is incorrect because administrative salaries allocated to R&D should be expensed per para 11e. Answer (d) is incorrect because research purchased from another company to aid a particular research project currently in process does not have an alternative future use (if it did have an alternative future use, i.e., possible sale, it could be capitalized and amortized).

23. (579,Q1,14) (c) The requirement is the amount of expense that should be recorded as a result of owning a patent that was purchased for $180,000 4 years ago that is now worthless. In 1975, 1976, and 1977, the patent was amortized $18,000 per year or a total of $54,000. Since the patent was deemed to be worthless in 1978, the remaining book value of $126,000 should be expensed in 1978. Note that the capitalization and amortization of a patent (R&D) purchased from others is not a violation of para 11 of SFAS 2. Intangibles purchased from others having alternative future uses, e.g., potential sale, are to be capitalized and amortized.

24. (1177,Q1,1) (a) The requirement is the amount at which to record the new truck. The solutions approach is to prepare the journal entry to record the trade-in of the old truck for the new truck.

New truck	$6,300	
Acc. Dep.	4,200	
Cash		$3,500
Old truck		7,000

Note that there is no gain recorded on the trade-in of the old truck, because the exchange is one productive asset for a similar productive asset. Thus there is no culmination of the earnings process. See para 21b of APB 29. Note that the gain of $200 ($3,000 FMV less book value of $2,800) is deferred to future periods as a result of recording the new truck at $6,300 rather than at $6,500.

25. (1177,Q1,2) (b) The requirement is the depreciation to be charged in 1976. During 1976 the machine's expected useful life was decreased. Retirement was expected to be at the end of 1980 instead of the end of 1983, and the scrap value of $5,000 was decreased to zero. This is a change in accounting estimate and accounted for prospectively, i.e., no retroactive adjustments nor restatement of prior periods (para 31, APB 20). Thus the unamortized cost as of the beginning of 1976 of $57,500 ($75,000 cost less $17,500 accumulated depreciation) must be amortized over the remaining five years (1976 through 1980). The resulting depreciation for 1976 is $11,500 ($57,500 ÷ 5).

26. (1177,Q1,4) (a) APB 17 requires the cost of intangible assets acquired from others (including goodwill acquired in a business combination) to be recorded as assets (para 24). These assets should be amortized to income over the period to be benefited (not to exceed 40 years). See para 29 of APB 17. Here total intangible assets are $87,000 ($5,000 of organization costs, $70,000 of goodwill, and $12,000 in trademarks). The deposits with the advertising agency are a prepaid expense. When the advertising agency performs the services contracted, the $8,000 will be expensed. The $15,000 of discount on bonds payable is a deferred charge which is considered a contra long-term liability.

27. (1177,Q1,5) (b) The requirement is the composite life of the asset. The solutions approach is to determine the annual straight-line depreciation and divide the annual depreciation into the total amount to be depreciated. Per the schedule below, the annual depreciation is $45,000, which when divided into the total depreciation base of $720,000, indicates a composite life of 16 years.

Machine A	$500 dep. base ÷ 20 yrs =	$25 dep.
Machine B	180 dep. base ÷ 15 yrs =	12 dep.
Machine C	40 dep. base ÷ 5 yrs =	8 dep.
	$720 total dep. base	$45 total dep.

$$720 ÷ \$45 = 16 \text{ years}$$

Composite depreciation permits assets to be grouped for depreciation purposes precluding individual records for each asset. When applied to similar assets, the method is sometimes called group depreciation. Generally major repair and replacement expenditures are charged to the accumulated depreciation account. Relatedly, gains and losses on disposal of individual assets are usually not recognized, i.e., they are charged to the accumulated depreciation account.

28. (578,P1,1) (c) Generally SFAS 2 requires that R&D expenses be expensed as incurred. Para 11 provides detailed guidance as to costs includable as R&D. Generally materials, personnel, related contract services by others, and reasonable indirect costs are includable in R&D. In addition, the costs of equipment, facilities, and intangibles purchased from others that have alternative future uses are capitalized and expensed over their useful lives. Thus, in this problem, all of the items are probably expensed except the equipment purchased (of which the depreciation for 1977 is included). Thus the 1977 R&D cost charged to income is the $4,200,000 total costs incurred in the problem less the $2,000,000 equipment purchase.

29. (578,Q1,6) (a) The requirement is the entry to record the contingent expropriation. Since Brower Corporation will receive $3,200,000 (40% of the FMV of $8,000,000), and the book value is now $5,000,000, an estimated loss of $1,800,000 is probable. Accordingly a loss should be recorded, and a contra asset, or estimated liability, should also be recorded. Answers (b) and (c) are incorrect because they are for the wrong amount. Answer (d) is incorrect because it records the expropriation of the foreign plant which has not yet occurred.

30. (578,Q1,15) (b) The requirement is the acquisition cost of the equipment given SYD, 10-year life, salvage value of $5,000, and 1977 depreciation of $24,000. The denominator of the SYD fraction is 55, as computed below. In 1977 the SYD fraction becomes 8/55. Set up an equation as below indicating 8/55 of the cost minus salvage value is equal to 1977 depreciation of $24,000. Solve for cost by multiplying both sides by 55/8, as illustrated below.

$$\frac{n(n+1)}{2} = 55, \quad \begin{array}{l} 1975 = 10/55 \\ 1976 = 9/55 \\ 1977 = 8/55 \end{array}$$

$$8/55 \,(\text{cost} - \$5,000) = \$24,000$$
$$\text{cost} - \$5,000 = \$24,000 \times 55/8$$
$$\text{cost} - \$5,000 = \$165,000$$
$$\text{cost} = \$170,000$$

31. (578,Q1,16) (d) The 1977 straight-line depreciation is required. The machine would be recorded initially at the purchase price of $150,000. The installation cost of $4,000 increased the cost to $154,000 which is reduced by the $5,000 salvage to $149,000. As the depreciation is 10% per year, 1977 depreciation will be $14,900.

32. (579,Q1,17) (d) The requirement is the amount of R&D that should be expensed in 1978 for a new product to be marketed in 1979. Para 12 of SFAS 2 requires all R&D to be expensed in the year incurred. The only exceptions are intangible assets and fixed assets, purchased from others, which have alternative future uses (which should be capitalized and amortized over their useful lives). Thus all of the $310,000 should be expensed in 1978.

33. (579,T1,12) (a) Per para 29 of APB 17, intangibles are not to be amortized over a period greater than 40 years using the straight-line method.

MAY 1981 ANSWERS

34. (581,P1,9) (b) The requirement is the amount of depreciation expense for the second year using sum-of-the-years'-digits depreciation. The machine has a useful life of five years. The SYD denominator is $15[(5 \times 6) \div 2]$. The numerator would be 5 the first year, and 4 the second year. The depreciation base is cost ($5,000,000) less salvage value ($500,000), or $4,500,000. Depreciation for the second year is computed below:

$$(4/15)(\$4,500,000) = \$1,200,000$$

35. (581,P1,11) (a) The requirement is the amount Richmond should report as capitalized interest at 12/31/80. The amount of interest eligible for capitalization is

$$\left(\begin{array}{c} \text{Average} \\ \text{Accumulated} \\ \text{Expenditures} \end{array}\right) \left(\begin{array}{c} \text{Interest} \\ \text{Rate} \end{array}\right) \left(\begin{array}{c} \text{Construction} \\ \text{Period} \end{array}\right)$$

Note that this follows the basic interest formula, Principle x Interest x Time. Since Richmond has outstanding debt incurred specifically for the construction project, in an amount greater than the average accumulated expenditures of $650,000, the interest rate of 11% is used for capitalization purposes (SFAS 34, para 12). Therefore, the amount of interest to be capitalized is $71,500.

$$(\$650,000)(11\%)(1 \text{ year}) = \$71,500$$

36. (581,P1,14) (c) The requirement is the amount Trencher should report as R & D expense in its 1980 income statement. Generally, SFAS 2 requires that R & D costs be expensed as incurred. However, R & D costs incurred for other entities under a contractual agreement may be capitalized. Therefore, the $500,000 charge is capitalized while the remaining $700,000 is expensed as R & D.

37. (581,Q1,2) (b) The requirement is the DDB depreciation expense for 1980 on equipment put into service on 1/2/79. When using the DDB method, salvage value is ignored (except that the asset is not depreciable below salvage). The straight-line rate is doubled and applied each year to the beginning net book value. The solutions approach is to calculate 1979 depreciation first so the 1/1/80 net book value can be determined. Since the asset has an 8-year life, the DDB rate is $1 \div 8 \times 2 = 2 \div 8$ or 25%. Thus, 1979 and 1980 depreciation are $16,000 and $12,000, respectively.

Original cost	$64,000
1979 depreciation (25% x $64,000)	−16,000
1/1/80 net book value	$48,000
1980 depreciation (25% x $48,000)	$12,000

38. (581,T1,7) (d) The requirement is the item which should be expensed as incurred by a franchisee. Answers (a), (b) and (c) all represent payments by the franchise as part of the purchase of the franchise. These payments relate to the future right to use the asset and are, therefore, capitalized and amortized over the estimated useful life of the franchise or 40 years, whichever is shorter, as an operating expense. In this case, the payments in items (a), (b), and (c) would be amortized over the ten-year estimated useful life. Item (d) represents annual payments made under the franchise agreement and should be entered as operating expenses in the period in which they were incurred. They do not represent an asset to the franchise since they do not relate to future rights to use the franchise.

39. (581,T1,14) (b) The requirement is the effect on the gain or loss on the sale of a fixed asset before the end of its useful life if the sum-of-the-years-digits method of depreciation is used instead of the straight-line method. The sum-of-the-years-digits method is an accelerated method of depreciation which means that a larger portion of the asset's cost is charged against income in the early years of the asset's life than in the later years. Therefore, if the asset is sold in year two, the sum-of-the-years-digits method would have provided larger depreciation deductions than the straight-line method; this would result in a correspondingly lower adjusted basis for the sum-of-years-digits. If the proceeds from the subsequent sale are greater than both adjusted bases, the one with the lower basis (SYD method) would show a higher gain. If the proceeds are less than both adjusted bases, the lower basis would result in a lower loss.

40. (581,T1,17) (d) The requirement is the depreciation method that is computed in the same way as depletion is computed. Of the four answers given, answer (d), productive-output, is the only method which computes depreciation based on consumption, which is the basic concept behind a depletion calculation.

ANSWER OUTLINE

Problem 1   Accounting for R&D

a. Research — planned search or critical investigation
>   Aimed at discovery of new knowledge to produce
>>   New products and significant benefit to existing products

>   Development — translation of research findings
>>   Into new product or product betterment designs

b. SFAS 2 reduced the alternatives of accounting for R&D
>   Practice alternatives were
>>   Expense as incurred
>>   Capitalize when incurred with subsequent amortization
>>   Selective capitalization
>>   Capitalize until future benefits determined

>   Alternative rationale were
>>   Associating cause and effect
>>   Systematic and rational allocation
>>   Immediate recognition

>   FASB determined the "immediate recognition" principle applied
>>   Uncertainties of future R&D benefits and lack of objective criteria undermined the capitalization method

c. Expense as R&D
>   Design and engineering studies
>   Prototype manufacturing costs
>   R&D administrative costs
>   Cost of R&D equipment to be used only for one product

>   Capitalize and depreciate remaining $300,000 of equipment
>>   Such depreciation is R&D cost

>   Market research and related costs are not R&D
>>   Are period costs appearing separately from R&D

UNOFFICIAL ANSWER

Problem 1   Accounting for R&D

a.   Research, as defined in Statement of Financial Accounting Standards no. 2, is "planned search or critical investigation aimed at discovery of new knowledge with the hope that such knowledge will be useful in developing a new product or service . . . or a new process or technique . . . or in bringing about a significant improvement to an existing product or process."

Development, as defined in Statement of Financial Accounting Standards no. 2, is "the translation of research findings or other knowledge into a plan or design for a new product or process or for a significant improvement to an existing product or process whether intended for sale or use."

b.   The current accounting and reporting practices for research and development costs were promulgated by the Financial Accounting Standards Board (FASB) in order to reduce the number of alternatives that previously existed and to provide useful financial information about research and development costs. The FASB considered four alternative methods of accounting: (1) charge all costs to expense when incurred; (2) capitalize all costs when incurred; (3) selective capitalization; and (4) accumulate all costs in a special category until the existence of future benefits can be determined. The FASB concluded that all research and development costs should be charged to expense as incurred. (Statement of Financial Accounting Standards no. 2 does not apply to activities that are unique to enterprises in the extractive industries, and accounting for the costs of research and development activities conducted for others under a contractual arrangement is a part of accounting for contracts in general and is beyond the scope of that statement.)

In reaching this decision, the FASB considered the three pervasive principles of expense recognition: (1) associating cause and effect; (2) systematic and rational allocation, and (3) immediate recognition. The FASB found little or no evidence of a direct causal relationship between current research and development expenditures and subsequent future benefits. The high degree of uncertainty surrounding future benefits, if any, of individual research and development projects makes it doubtful that there is any useful purpose to be served by capitalizing the costs and allocating them over future periods. In view of the above, the FASB concluded that the first two principles of expense recognition do not apply, but rather that the "immediate recognition" principle of expense recognition should apply.

The high degree of uncertainty about whether research and development expenditures will provide any future benefits, the lack of objectivity in setting criteria, and the lack of usefulness of the resulting information led the FASB to reject the alternatives of capitalization, selective capitalization, and accumulation of costs in a special category.

c.   In accordance with Statement no. 2 of the Financial Accounting Standards Board, the following costs attributable only to research and development should be expensed as incurred:

- Design and engineering studies.

- Prototype manufacturing costs.

- Administrative costs related solely to research and development.

- The cost of equipment produced solely for development of the product ($200,000).

The remaining $300,000 of equipment should be capitalized and shown on the statement of financial position at cost. The depreciation expense resulting from the current year is a part of research and development expense for the year. The market research direct costs and related administrative expenses are not research and development costs. These costs are treated as period costs and are shown as expense items in the current earnings statement.

ANSWER OUTLINE

Problem 2   Property, Plant, and Equipment

a.   Expenditures to be capitalized in cash acquisition of equipment include
   Invoice price (net of discounts, even if not taken), plus
   All costs incurred in acquiring equipment and preparing it for use
      e.g., freight, installation, breaking-in costs, etc.

b.   Capitalizable cost of equipment having no "cash equivalent price" is determined as follows:
b1.   If equipment is acquired by giving bonds with an established market price, capitalize equipment at market value of consideration given up, which is market value of bonds
b2.   If equipment is acquired by giving common stock, capitalize equipment at market value given or received whichever is more evident (independent appraisal may be used)
b3.   If equipment is acquired by giving similar equipment, capitalize acquired equipment at lower of recorded amount of equipment relinquished or market value of equipment received

c.   Factors which determine whether expenditures relating to property, plant, and equipment in use should be capitalized
   Amount is relatively large
   Non-recurring in nature
   Extend useful life of the property, plant, and equipment
   Increase the usefulness of the property, plant, and equipment

d.   Accounting for gain or loss on sale of property, plant, and equipment
   Remove net book value (cost less accumulated depreciation) from accounts
   Gain = excess of cash received over net book value
   Loss = excess of net book value over cash received

UNOFFICIAL ANSWER

Problem 2   Property, Plant, and Equipment

a.   The expenditures that should be capitalized when equipment is acquired for cash should include the invoice price of the equipment (net of discounts) plus all incidental outlays relating to its purchase or preparation for use, such as insurance during transit, freight, duties, ownership search, ownership registration, installation, and breaking-in costs. Any available discounts, whether taken or not, should be deducted from the capitalizable cost of the equipment.

b.
1.   When the market value of the equipment is not determinable by reference to a similar cash purchase, the capitalizable cost of equipment purchased with bonds having an established market price should be the market value of the bonds.

2.   When the market value of the equipment is not determinable by reference to a similar cash purchase, and the common stock used in the exchange does not have an established market price, the capitalizable cost of equipment should be the equipment's estimated fair value if that is more clearly evident than the fair value of the common stock. Independent appraisals may be used to determine the fair values of the assets involved.

3.   When the market value of equipment acquired is not determinable by reference to a similar cash purchase, the capitalizable cost of equipment

purchased by exchanging similar equipment having a determinable market value should be the lower of the recorded amount of the equipment relinquished or the market value of the equipment exchanged.

c. The factors that determine whether expenditures relating to property, plant, and equipment already in use should be capitalized are as follows:
· Expenditures are relatively large in amount.
· They are nonrecurring in nature.
· They extend the useful life of the property, plant, and equipment.
· They increase the usefulness of the property, plant, and equipment.

d. The net book value at the date of the sale (cost of the property, plant, and equipment less the accumulated depreciation) should be removed from the accounts. The excess of cash from the sale over the net book value removed is accounted for as a gain on the sale, while the excess of net book value removed over cash from the sale is accounted for as a loss on the sale.

ANSWER OUTLINE

Problem 3   Property, Plant and Equipment

a1. Revenue expenditures benefit only current period
        Are expensed in the period incurred
    Capital expenditures benefit several periods
        Are expensed in periods benefited
    Distinction determines timing of expense recognition
        Affects periodic earnings
        And reported assets
    When revenue expenditures are capitalized
        Current earnings are overstated
        Assets are overstated
        Future earnings are understated

The reverse is true if a capital item is expensed.

a2. Depreciation allocates historical cost to periods benefited
        Process of cost allocation, not valuation
        Not intended to provide replacement funds
        Application of matching concept

a3. Factors in determining annual depreciation
        Original cost
        Estimated salvage value
        Estimated useful life
        Depreciation method

a4. Depreciation reduces net earnings
        Does not require an outflow of funds
        Add back to earnings to calculate funds provided by operations
    Depreciation is not a direct source of funds
        Thus, indirect source through tax savings

b1. Costs of land are listed in the Unofficial Answer below, items (a) through (k)

b2. Record deferred-payment plan cost at equivalent cash price
        Impute interest rate if necessary
        To determine present value
            Interest portion of contract is interest expense

b3. Generally value asset acquisitions at fair value
        Of asset given or received
        Whichever is more clearly evident
    No gain recognized on exchange of productive assets
        New cost is undepreciated cost of old assets plus cash paid

UNOFFICIAL ANSWER

Problem 3   Property, Plant and Equipment

a.   1.   Relative to plant assets, a cost incurred or an expenditure made, that is assumed to benefit only the current accounting period is called a revenue expenditure and is charged to expense in the period believed to benefit. A capital expenditure is similarly a cost incurred or an expenditure made but is expected to yield benefits either in all future accounting periods (acquisition of land) or in a limited number of accounting periods. Capital expenditures (if material in amount) are capitalized, that is, recorded as assets, and, if related to assets of limited life, amortized over the periods believed to benefit.

The distinction between capital and revenue expenditures is of significance because it involves the timing of the recognition of expense, and consequently, the determination of periodic earnings. It also affects the amounts reported as assets whose costs generally have to be recouped from future periods' revenues.

If a revenue expenditure is improperly capitalized, current earnings are overstated, assets are overstated, and future earnings are understated for all the periods to which the improperly capitalized cost is amortized. If the cost is not amortized, future earnings will not be affected but assets and retained earnings will continue to be overstated for as long as the cost remains on the books. If a nonamortizable capital expenditure is improperly expensed, current earnings are understated and assets and retained earnings are understated for all foreseeable periods in the future. If an amortizable capital expenditure is improperly expensed, current earnings are understated, assets and retained earnings are understated, and future earnings are overstated for all periods to which the cost should have been amortized.

2. Depreciation is the accounting process of allocating an asset's historical cost (recorded amount) to the accounting periods benefitted by the use of the asset. It is a process of cost allocation, not valuation. Depreciation is not intended to provide funds for an asset's replacement; it is merely an application of the matching concept.

3. The factors relevant in determining the annual depreciation for a depreciable asset are the initial recorded amount (cost), estimated salvage value, estimated useful life, and depreciation method.

   Assets are typically recorded at their acquisition cost, which is in most cases objectively determinable. But cost assignments in other cases—"basket purchases" and the selection of an implicit interest rate in asset acquisition under deferred-payment plans—may be quite subjective involving considerable judgment.

   The salvage value is an estimate of an amount potentially realizable when the asset is retired from service. It is initially a judgment factor and is affected by the length of its useful life to the enterprise.

   The useful life is also a judgment factor. It involves selecting the "unit" of measure of service life and estimating the number of such units embodied in the asset. Such units may be measured in terms of time periods or in terms of activity (for example, years or machine hours). When selecting the life, one

should select the lower (shorter) of the physical life or the economic life to this user. Physical life involves wear and tear and casualties; economic life involves such things as technological obsolescence and inadequacy.

   Selecting the depreciation method is generally a judgment decision; but, a method may be inherent in the definition adopted for the units of service life, as discussed earlier. For example, if such units are machine hours, the method is a function of the number of machine hours used during each period. A method should be selected that will best measure the portion of services expiring each period. Once a method is selected, it may be objectively applied by using a predetermined, objectively derived formula.

4. Because revenue usually represents an inflow of funds, and expense usually represents an outflow of funds, net earnings represent a net inflow of funds. Depreciation reduces reported net earnings but does not involve an outflow of funds. Therefore, it is added back to reported net earnings to calculate funds provided by operations. On a statement of changes in financial position, depreciation should be clearly shown as an adjustment to net earnings not requiring a use of funds rather than be shown as a source of funds. Depreciation is not a direct source of funds. It can be considered an indirect source only through income tax savings.

b. 1. The following costs, if applicable, should be capitalized as a cost of land:

   (a) Negotiated purchase price
   (b) Brokers' commission
   (c) Legal fees
   (d) Title fee
   (e) Recording fee
   (f) Escrow fees
   (g) Surveying fees
   (h) Existing unpaid taxes, interest, or liens assumed by the buyer
   (i) Clearing, grading, landscaping, and subdividing
   (j) Cost of removing old building (less salvage)
   (k) Special assessments such as lighting or sewers if they are permanent in nature.

2. A plant asset acquired on a deferred-payment plan should be recorded at an equivalent cash price excluding interest. If interest is not stated in the sales contract, an imputed interest should be determined. The asset should then be recorded at its present value, which is computed by discounting the payments at the stated or imputed interest rate. The interest portion (stated or imputed) of the contract price should be charged to interest expense over the life of the contract.

3. In general, plant assets should be recorded at the fair value of the consideration given or the fair value of the asset received, whichever is more clearly evident. This general theoretical preference is somewhat constrained by the requirements of APB Opinion No. 29.

Specifically when exchanging an old machine and paying cash for a new machine, the new machine should be recorded at the amount of monetary consideration (cash) paid plus the undepreciated cost of the nonmonetary asset (old machine) surrendered if there is no indicated loss. An indicated loss should be recognized; this would reduce the recorded amount of the new machine. No indicated gain, however, should be recognized by the party paying monetary consideration.

SOLUTION GUIDE

Problem 4   Fixed Assets and Depreciation

1. Part a requires an analysis of the changes in the land, buildings, leasehold improvements, and machinery accounts based upon 1977 transactions. A related requirement is to list the items presented in the problem which do not affect the analysis of the four asset accounts.

2. The solutions approach is to analyze each of the six paragraphs of the additional information to determine the effect on the four asset accounts and to identify data having no effect.

2.1 The $1,070,000 spent to acquire land site number 621 is an increase in the land account. The $60,000 real estate fee and the clearing cost of $15,000 less the $5,000 received for timber and gravel are capitalized as part of land. The rationale is that $1,070,000 had to be spent to acquire a "land site."

2.2 Similarly, land site number 622 cost $330,000 ($300,000 for land and $30,000 for building demolition). The property was bought as a land site as evidenced by the demolition of the building shortly after acquisition.

A new building was constructed for $150,000 plus excavation fees ($11,000), architectural design fees ($8,000), and a building permit fee ($1,000). Thus, the total cost of the new building was $170,000, which is an increase in the buildings account. Imputed interest on funds used during construction is not considered a cost of the building. Imputed interest is not reflected anywhere in traditional financial statements, i.e., imputed interest is not included in the traditional accounting model. This position was reaffirmed in SFAS No. 34.

2.3 Land site number 623, acquired at a cost of $600,000, was purchased for resale, and therefore would not be presented as land on the balance sheet. Rather, it would be presented as land held for resale (possibly an inventory-type item).

2.4 Of the $125,000 spent on the building leased by Townsand, only $75,000 would be capitalized as leasehold improvements. The $10,000 of painting is maintenance, and would be expensed (not capitalized) in 1977. The electrical work of $35,000 would be capitalized as a leasehold improvement and amortized over the useful life of 10 years, which is the remaining life of the lease. Of the $80,000 cost to extend the working area, $40,000 is to be paid by the lessor. The remaining $40,000 will be capitalized as a leasehold improvement and amortized over the remaining life of the lease, which is ten years (even though the useful life of the asset is 30 years).

2.5 The $65,000 improvements to leased office space is capitalized as a leasehold improvement and amortized during 1978 and 1979, the remainder of the office lease.

2.6 The cost of the new machines purchased was $78,500, which includes freight ($2,000) and unloading charges ($1,500). All the costs associated with putting an asset in initial operating condition and location are capitalized. The $13,000 royalty payments for 1977 are expenses.

3. Beginning with the beginning balance of each of the four asset accounts, reflect the adjustments required by the foregoing analysis.

3.1 Also prepare a list of the items not affecting the four asset accounts: imputed interest, land held for resale, painting, and royalty payments.

4. Part b requires (1) the depreciation method to maximize profits for a three-year period; and (2) the depreciation method to minimize profits for a three-year period.

5. The solutions approach is to prepare a depreciation schedule for each of the four methods suggested in the problem.

	DDB	SL	SYD	Output
1975	400,000	180,000	300,000	225,000
1976	240,000	180,000	240,000	202,500
1977	144,000	180,000	180,000	180,000
3-year dep.	784,000	540,000	720,000	607,500

5.1 The double-declining-balance method ignores the salvage value of $100,000. Accordingly, twice the straight-line rate of 20%, or 40%, is taken times the cost of $1,000,000. In 1977, 40% is taken times the net book value of $360,000 ($600,000 − $240,000).

5.2 The straight-line method is simply 20% of $900,000 ($1,000,000 cost − $100,000 salvage value) in each of the years.

5.3 The sum-of-the-years'-digits method depreciates cost less salvage value of $900,000 based upon 5/15, 4/15, 3/15, 2/15, 1/15 over a five-year period. The denominator is computed by the formula n ([n + 1] / 2) which is 5 (6/2), or 15.

5.4 The units-of-output method allocates cost less salvage value or $900,000, based upon 40,000 units of output (10,000 the first year, 9,000 the second year, etc.). Thus each 1,000 units of output results in a depreciation charge of $22,500. Thus the 10,000 units of output in the first year results in $225,000 deprecition, the 9,000 units in year 2 results in $202,500 depreciation, etc.

6. Maximization of profits requires the depreciation method resulting in the least depreciation over the three-year period, which is the straight-line method. The minimization of profits requires the depreciation method resulting in the most depreciation, which is the double-declining-balance method. Prepare formal solutions with supporting computations per the requirement.

UNOFFICIAL ANSWER

Problem 4   Fixed Assets and Depreciation

Part a.

1.   Townsand Company
ANALYSIS OF LAND ACCOUNT
for 1977

Balance at January 1, 1977			$ 100,000
Land site number 621			
Acquisition cost		$1,000,000	
Commission to real estate agent		60,000	
Clearing costs	$15,000		
Less amounts recovered	5,000	10,000	
Total land site number 621			1,070,000
Land site number 622			
Land value		200,000	
Building value		100,000	
Demolition cost		30,000	
Total land site number 622			330,000
Balance at December 31, 1977			$1,500,000

Townsand Company
ANALYSIS OF BUILDINGS ACCOUNT
for 1977

Balance at January 1, 1977		$800,000
Cost of new building constructed on land site number 622		
Construction costs	$150,000	
Excavation fees	11,000	
Architectural design fees	8,000	
Building permit fee	1,000	170,000
Balance at December 31, 1977		$970,000

Townsand Company
ANALYSIS OF LEASEHOLD IMPROVEMENTS ACCOUNT
for 1977

Balance at January 1, 1977	$500,000
Electrical work	35,000
Construction of extension to current work area ($80,000 x ½)	40,000
Office space	65,000
Balance at December 31, 1977	$640,000

Townsand Company
ANALYSIS OF MACHINERY AND EQUIPMENT ACCOUNT
for 1977

Balance at January 1, 1977		$700,000
Cost of new machines acquired		
Invoice price	$75,000	
Freight costs	2,000	
Unloading charges	1,500	78,500
Balance at December 31, 1977		$778,500

2.   Items in the fact situation which were not used to determine the answer to 1, above, and where, or if, these items should be included in Townsand's financial statements are as follows:

· Imputed interest of $6,000 on funds used during construction should not be included anywhere in Townsand's financial statements.
· Land site number 623, which was acquired for $600,000, should be included in Townsand's balance sheet as land held for resale.
· Painting of ceilings for $10,000 should be included as a normal operating expense in Townsand's income statement.
· Royalty payments of $13,000 should be included as a normal operating expense in Townsand's income statement.

Part b.

1.   The straight-line method of depreciation would result in the maximization of profits for financial statement reporting for the three-year period ending December 31, 1977.

Barth Company
ACCUMULATED DEPRECIATION USING STRAIGHT-LINE METHOD
December 31, 1977

$$\frac{\text{Cost} - \text{salvage value}}{\text{Useful life}}$$

$$\frac{\$1,000,000 - \$100,000}{5 \text{ years}} = \$180,000$$

Year	Depreciation expense	Accumulated depreciation
1975	$180,000	$180,000
1976	180,000	$360,000
1977	180,000	$540,000
	$540,000	

2.   The double-declining-balance method* of depreciation would result in the minimization of profits for income tax reporting for the three-year period ending December 31, 1977.

Barth Company
ACCUMULATED DEPRECIATION USING DOUBLE-DECLINING-BALANCE METHOD
December 31, 1977

Straight-line rate is 5 years or 20%.
Double-declining-balance rate is 40% (20% x 2).
Ignore salvage value.

Year	Book value at beginning of year	Depreciation expense	Accumulated depreciation
1975	$1,000,000	$400,000	$400,000
1976	600,000	240,000	$640,000
1977	360,000	144,000	$784,000
		$784,000	

---

*Under generally accepted accounting principles, the sum-of-the-years-digits method of depreciation would result in higher profits for the three-year period because the cost of the equipment should be reduced by salvage value. However, the Internal Revenue Code permits a taxpayer to reduce salvage value by up to 10% of basis for income tax reporting; and if this option were taken, the sum-of-the-years-digits method would result in lower profits for income tax reporting for the three-year period.

SOLUTION GUIDE

Problem 5   Fixed Assets

1. Review the fixed asset and depreciation schedule
    prior to reading the text of part b. After gain-
    ing familiarity with the schedule, work through
    the text of the problem computing items miss-
    ing in the schedule. The unofficial answer con-
    tains explanations of the computations.

UNOFFICIAL ANSWER

Problem 5   Fixed Assets

b.   *Computations for Fixed Asset and*
                                 Depreciation Schedule

(1)	$ 65,000.	Allocated in proportion to ap-praised values (72/900 x $812,500).
(2)	$747,500.	Allocated in proportion to ap-praised values (828/900 x $812,500).
(3)	Fifty years.	Cost less salvage ($747,500 − $47,500) divided by annual de-preciation ($14,000).
(4)	$ 14,000.	Same as prior year since it is straight-line depreciation.
(5)	$ 85,400.	[Number of shares (3,000) times fair value ($25)] plus demo-lition cost of existing building ($10,400).
(6)	None.	No depreciation before use.
(7)	$ 16,000.	Fair market value.
(8)	$ 2,400.	Cost ($16,000) times percentage (15%).
(9)	$ 2,040.	Cost ($16,000) less prior year's de-preciation ($2,400) equals $13,600. Multiply $13,600 times 15%.

(10)	$ 99,000.	Total cost ($110,000) less repairs and maintenance ($11,000).
(11)	$ 17,000.	Cost less salvage ($99,000 − $5,500) times 10/55.
(12)	$ 5,100.	Cost less salvage ($99,000 − $5,500) times 9/55 times one-third of a year.
(13)	$ 30,840.	[Annual payment ($4,000) times present value of annuity at 8% for 10 years (6.71)] plus down payment ($4,000). This can be computed from an annuity due table since the payments are at the beginning of each year. To convert from an annuity in arrears to an annuity due factor, proceed as follows: For eleven payments use the present value in arrears for 10 years (6.710) plus 1.00. Multiply this factor (7.710) times $4,000 annual payment.
(14)	$ 2,056.	Cost ($30,840) divided by esti-mated life (15 years).

MULTIPLE CHOICE QUESTIONS (1—26)

1. In accounting for income taxes, interest received on municipal obligations is an example of
   a. Intraperiod tax allocation.
   b. Interperiod tax allocation.
   c. A permanent difference.
   d. A timing difference.

2. Arnold Company depreciates its machinery using an accelerated method of depreciation for income tax reporting and the straight-line method for financial statement reporting. For the 1979 calendar year, depreciation on machinery amounted to $900,000 under the accelerated method and $550,000 under the straight-line method. Also in 1979, Arnold received interest on municipal obligations of $150,000. Assuming an income tax rate of 40%, by what amount should the Deferred Income Tax account change?
   a. $0
   b. $ 80,000
   c. $140,000
   d. $200,000

3. The books of The Hazel Company for the year ended December 31, 1979, showed income of $180,000 before provision for income tax. In computing the taxable income for federal income tax purposes, the following timing differences were taken into account:

Depreciation deducted for tax purposes in excess of depreciation recorded on the books	$8,000
Income from installment sale reportable for tax purposes in excess of income recognized on the books	$6,000

What should Hazel record as its current federal income tax liability at December 31, 1979, assuming a corporate income tax rate of 50%?
   a. $86,000
   b. $89,000
   c. $90,000
   d. $91,000

4. Which of the following interperiod tax allocation methods uses the tax rates in effect at the origination of the timing differences and does not adjust for subsequent changes in tax rates?
   a. Deferred method.
   b. Liability method.
   c. Net of tax method.
   d. Net present value method.

5. An example of intraperiod income tax allocation is
   a. Interest income on municipal obligations.
   b. Estimated expenses for major repairs accrued for financial statement purposes in one year, but deducted for income tax purposes when paid in a subsequent year.
   c. Rental income included in income for income tax purposes when collected, but deferred for financial statement purposes until earned in a subsequent year.
   d. Reporting the cumulative effect on prior years of changing to a different depreciation method in the income statement, net of direct tax effects.

6. In 1978, West Company accrued, for financial statement reporting, estimated losses on disposal of unused plant facilities of $800,000. The facilities were sold in March 1979. Also, in 1978 West paid $100,000 of premiums on officers' life insurance. Assuming that the effective income tax rate was 40%, the amount reported in the provision for deferred income taxes in West's income statement for the year ended December 31, 1978, should be a
   a. $320,00 credit.
   b. $320,000 debit.
   c. $360,000 credit.
   d. $360,000 debit.

7. Which of the following requires intraperiod tax allocation?
   a. Extraordinary gains or losses as defined by the Accounting Principles Board.
   b. That portion of dividends reduced by the dividends received deduction by corporations under existing federal income tax law.
   c. The excess of accelerated depreciation used for tax purposes over straight-line depreciation used for financial reporting purposes.
   d. All differences between taxable income and financial statement earnings.

8. The amount of income tax applicable to transactions that must be reported using intraperiod income tax allocation is computed
   a. By multiplying the item by the effective income tax rate.
   b. As the difference between the tax computed based on taxable income without including the item and the tax computed based on taxable income including the item.

c.   As the difference between the tax com-
     puted on the item based on the amount
     used for financial reporting and the amount
     used in computing taxable income.

d.   By multiplying the item by the difference
     between the effective income tax rate
     and the statutory income tax rate.

9.   Interperiod income tax allocation is justified
by the basic theory that income taxes should be
treated as which of the following?

a.   An expense.

b.   A distribution of earnings.

c.   A distribution of earnings for the cur-
     rent portion and an expense for the de-
     ferred portion.

d.   An expense for the current portion and
     a distribution of earnings for the de-
     ferred portion.

10.   In 1975, the Chrol Company formed a
foreign subsidiary. Income before United States
and foreign income taxes for this wholly-owned
subsidiary was $500,000 in 1975. The income
tax rate in the country of the foreign subsidiary
was 40%. None of the earnings of the foreign
subsidiary have been remitted to Chrol; however,
there is nothing to indicate that these earnings
will not be remitted to Chrol in the future.

The country of the foreign subsidiary does
not impose a tax on remittances to the United
States. A tax credit is allowed in the United
States for taxes payable in the country of the
foreign subsidiary.

Assuming the income tax rate in the United
States is 48%, what is the total amount of income taxes relating to the foreign subsidiary that
should be shown in the income statement of
Chrol in 1975?

a. $0.

b. $40,000.

c. $200,000.

d. $240,000

11.   Burns Co., an installment seller of furniture,
records sales on the accrual basis for financial-
reporting purposes but on the installment method
for tax purposes. As a result, $50,000 of deferred
income taxes have been accrued at December 31,
1974. In accordance with trade practice, installment accounts receivable from customers are shown
as current assets, although the average collection
period is approximately three years.

At December 31, 1974, Burns Co. has recorded a $20,000 deferred income tax debit aris-
ing from a book accrual of noncurrent deferred
compensation expense which is not presently tax
deductible.

Also, at December 31, 1974, Burns has
accrued $15,000 of deferred income taxes result-
ing from the use of accelerated depreciation for
tax purposes and straight-line depreciation for
financial-reporting purposes.

How should the deferred income taxes be
shown on Burns' December 31, 1974 balance sheet?

a.   Current deferred income tax debit of
     $50,000; noncurrent deferred income
     tax debit of $20,000; and noncurrent
     deferred income tax credit of $15,000.

b.   Current deferred income tax credit of
     $50,000; current deferred income tax
     debit of $20,000; and noncurrent
     deferred income tax credit of $15,000.

c.   Noncurrent deferred income tax debit
     of $20,000; and noncurrent deferred
     income tax credit of $65,000.

d.   Current deferred income tax credit of
     $50,000; and noncurrent deferred in-
     come tax debit of $5,000.

12.   Interperiod income tax allocation in corporate financial statements can best be justified by
which of the following accounting concepts or
principles?

a.   Conservatism.

b.   Matching.

c.   Realization.

d.   Objectivity.

13.   Tramway Corporation is a stable, going concern which each year invests about $25,000 in
new plant and equipment as an equal amount
of older equipment is retired. It has been reporting income for both tax and financial-statement
purposes by using straight-line depreciation, but it
has now changed to accelerated depreciation for
tax purposes. This difference in depreciation
methods will cause a deferred tax credit which
over the years will build up

a.   And then remain relatively constant.

b.   Rapidly and then slowly increase.

c.   Indefinitely.

d.   Rapidly and then slowly decline.

14. Baker, Inc., owns 35% of the outstanding stock of Cable, Inc. During the calendar year 1974, Baker's "Investment in Cable" account appeared as follows:

Balance, January 1, 1974	$650,000
Equity in 1974 earnings of Cable	100,000
Dividends received from Cable—1974	(20,000)
Balance, December 31, 1974	$730,000

Baker feels that its equity in Cable's undistributed earnings will be realized in the form of future dividends. Assuming a 40% income tax rate, by how much should deferred income taxes be affected because of these facts?
  a. $4,800.
  b. $6,000.
  c. $7,200.
  d. $9,000.

15. The Carine Company, which was formed on January 1, 1975, adopted a policy of deferring investment tax credits for accounting purposes. Investment tax credits of $100,000 were available in 1975 on equipment that was purchased on January 1, 1975. The equipment has an estimated ten-year life. What is the amount of investment tax credit that should be credited to income in 1975?
  a. $10,000.
  b. $14,286.
  c. $90,000.
  d. $100,000.

16. A company has four "deferred income tax" accounts arising from timing differences involving: (1) current assets, (2) noncurrent assets, (3) current liabilities, and (4) noncurrent liabilities. The presentation of these four "deferred income tax" accounts in the statement of financial position should be shown as
  a. A single net amount.
  b. A net current and a net noncurrent amount.
  c. Four accounts with no netting permitted.
  d. Valuation adjustments of the related assets and liabilities that gave rise to the deferred tax.

17. Which of the following situations would require use of interperiod tax allocation procedures?
  a. Research and development costs are deducted for income tax purposes in the year incurred.
  b. A material gain on a sale-leaseback transaction is taxed in the year of sale.

  c. Unamortized discount and call premium on an early extinguishment of debt are deducted for income tax purposes in the year of extinguishment.
  d. The amount of a material loss on the sale of an asset differs for tax and accounting purposes because of different bases for this asset. The different bases are due to a quasi-reorganization recognized for accounting but not for income tax purposes.

18. The Skipper Company, a calendar-year company, began operations in 1975 and, for that year, reported an operating loss of $140,000. For 1976, the company reported operating income (before income taxes) of $300,000.

Assuming an income tax rate of 50%, what should Skipper record in 1976 as a tax benefit arising from the operating loss carryforward?
  a. $0.
  b. $70,000.
  c. $80,000.
  d. $150,000.

19. Gomer Corporation reported the following results for its first three years of operations:

1974 - Operating income (before income taxes)	$ 10,000
1975 - Operating loss (before income taxes)	(200,000)
1976 - Operating income (before income taxes)	350,000

There were no permanent or timing differences during these years. For the year ended December 31, 1976, what should Gomer record as its current income tax liability, assuming a corporate income tax rate of 45% for all years?
  a. $67,500.
  b. $72,000.
  c. $90,000.
  d. $157,500.

20. For financial statement reporting, the Lexington Corporation recognizes royalty income in the period earned. For income tax reporting, royalties are taxed when collected. At December 31, 1976, unearned royalties of $400,000 were included in Lexington's balance sheet. All of these royalties had been collected in 1976. During 1977, royalties of $600,000 were collected. Unearned royalties in Lexington's December 31, 1977, balance sheet amounted to $350,000. Assuming that the income tax rate was 50%, the amount reported in the pro-

vision for deferred income taxes in Lexington's income statement for the year ended December 31, 1977, should be a
- a. $25,000 debit.
- b. $175,000 credit.
- c. $200,000 debit.
- d. $300,000 credit.

21. In 1977, Sarli, Inc., accrued, for financial statement reporting, estimated expenses for major repairs of $400,000. The repairs were paid for in 1978. For income tax reporting, these expenses are deducted when paid. Also in 1977, Sarli received $100,000 of interest income on municipal obligations. Assuming that the income tax rate was 50%, the amount reported in the provision for deferred income taxes in Sarli's income statement for the year ended December 31, 1977, should be a
- a. $150,000 debit.
- b. $150,000 credit.
- c. $200,000 credit.
- d. $250,000 credit.

Items 22 and 23 are based on the following information:

Pacter Co., an installment seller, earns a $300 pretax gross profit on each installment sale. For financial reporting purposes the entire $300 is recognized at the time of sale, but for income tax purposes the installment method of accounting is used.

Assume Pacter makes one sale in 1978, another sale in 1979, and a third sale in 1980. In each case, one-third of the gross sales price is collected in the year of sale, one-third in the next year, and the final installment in the next year.

22. Assuming an income tax rate of 50%, the amount[†] which should be shown on Pacter's December 31, 1980, balance sheet as "deferred income taxes" relative to the three sales is
- a. $100.
- b. $150.
- c. $200.
- d. $300.

23. Assume that on January 1, 1980, the tax rate increased to 60% from 50%. The appropriate amount to report as "deferred income taxes" under the "gross change method" on Pacter's December 31, 1980, balance sheet is
- a. $120.
- b. $170.
- c. $270.
- d. $300.

MAY 1981 QUESTIONS

24. In 1980 Waldo Company paid the annual premiums of $80,000 on officers' life insurance (on which the company is the beneficiary) and received interest income of $120,000 on municipal obligations. Also in 1980 Waldo collected $200,000 in royalties. For income tax reporting, the royalties are taxed when collected. For financial statement reporting, the royalties are recognized as income in the period earned. The unearned portion of the royalties collected in 1980 amounted to $150,000 at December 31, 1980. Assuming that the income tax rate is 40%, what amount of deferred taxes would be recorded as a result of these transactions?
- a. $ 60,000.
- b. $ 76,000.
- c. $ 96,000.
- d. $108,000.

25. On January 2, 1978, Gow Corporation bought a press for $22,000, with an estimated useful life of four years and a salvage value of $6,000. Straight-line depreciation is used for financial statement purposes and the sum-of-the-years digits method is used for income tax purposes. Assuming an income tax rate of 50%, and no other timing differences, what amount should be reported in the balance sheet as deferred income taxes at December 31, 1980?
- a. $ 400 debit.
- b. $1,200 credit.
- c. $1,600 credit.
- d. $2,400 credit.

26. Boa Constructors, Inc., had an operating loss carryforward of $100,000 at December 31, 1979, for which the tax benefit was fully realized at the end of 1980, when the income tax rate was 40%. For the year ended December 31, 1980, the tax benefit should be reported in the income statement as
- a. A $40,000 reduction in income tax expense.
- b. An extraordinary item of $40,000.
- c. An operating gain of $40,000.
- d. An extraordinary item of $100,000.

Problem 1 Tax Allocation and Investment Credit

   (576,T6) (20 to 25 minutes)

   Part a.   Income tax allocation is an integral part of generally accepted accounting principles. The applications of intraperiod tax allocation (within a period) and interperiod tax allocation (among periods) are both required.

Required:

   1.   Explain the need for intraperiod tax allocation.

   2.   Accountants who favor interperiod tax allocation argue that income taxes are an expense rather than a distribution of earnings. Explain the significance of this argument. Do not explain the definitions of expense or distribution of earnings.

   3.   Indicate and explain whether each of the following independent situations should be treated as a timing difference or a permanent difference.

   a.   Estimated warranty costs (covering a three-year warranty) are expensed for accounting purposes at the time of sale but deducted for income tax purposes when incurred.

   b.   Depreciation for accounting and income tax purposes differs because of different bases of carrying the related property. The different bases are a result of a business combination treated as a purchase for accounting purposes and as a tax-free exchange for income tax purposes.

   c.   A company properly uses the equity method to account for its 30% investment in another company. The investee pays dividends that are about 10% of its annual earnings.

   4.   Discuss the nature of the deferred income tax accounts and possible classifications in a company's statement of financial position.

   Part b.   The investment tax credit can be accounted for by one of two "generally accepted" methods for accounting purposes.

Required:

   Identify and explain these two accounting methods for the investment tax credit. Do not discuss income tax computations of the investment tax credit.

Problem 2 Calculation of Deferred Taxes (1176,P5a)
                (25 to 30 minutes)

   Part a.   The Mikis Company has supplied you with information regarding its 1975 income tax expense for financial statement reporting as follows:

   •   The provision for current income taxes (exclusive of investment tax credits) was $600,000 for the year ended December 31, 1975. Mikis made estimated tax payments of $550,000 during 1975.

   •   Investment tax credits of $100,000 arising from fixed assets put into service in 1975 were taken for income tax reporting in 1975. Mikis defers investment tax credits and amortizes them to income over the productive life of the related assets for financial statement reporting. Unamortized deferred investment tax credits amounted to $400,000 at December 31, 1975, and $375,000 at December 31, 1974.

   •   Mikis generally depreciates fixed assets using the straight-line method for financial statement reporting and various accelerated methods for income tax reporting. During 1975, depreciation on fixed assets amounted to $900,000 for financial statement reporting and $950,000 for income tax reporting. Commitments for the purchase of fixed assets amounted to $450,000 at December 31, 1975. Such fixed assets will be subject to an investment tax credit of 10%.

   •   For financial statement reporting, Mikis has accrued estimated losses from product warranty contracts prior to their occurrence. For income tax reporting, no deduction is taken until payments are made. At December 31, 1974, accrued estimated losses of $200,000 were included in the liability section of Mikis' balance sheet. Based on the latest available information, Mikis estimates that this figure should be 30% higher at December 31, 1975. Payments of $250,000 were made in 1975.

• In 1970, Mikis acquired another company for cash. Goodwill resulting from this transaction was $800,000 and is being amortized over a forty-year period for financial statement reporting. The amortization is not deductible for income tax reporting.

• Mikis has a wholly-owned foreign subsidiary. In 1975, this subsidiary had income before United States and foreign income taxes of $175,000 and a provision for taxes in its own country of $70,000. No earnings were remitted to Mikis in 1975. For United States income tax reporting, Mikis will receive a tax credit for $70,000 when these earnings are remitted. Mikis provides taxes on the unremitted earnings of this subsidiary for financial statement reporting.

• Premiums paid on officers' life insurance amounted to $80,000 in 1975. These premiums are not deductible for income tax reporting.

• Assume that the United States income tax rate was 48%.

Required:

1. What amounts should be shown for (1) provision for current income taxes; (2) provision for deferred income taxes; and (3) investment tax credits recognized in Mikis' income statement for the year ended December 31, 1975? Show supporting computations in good form.

2. Identify any information in the fact situation which was not used to determine the answer to (1) above and explain why this information was not used.

Problem 3   Gross vs. Net Change Method

(1179, T4a) (5 to 10 minutes)

Part a. Deferred income taxes are required under generally accepted accounting principles. Accounting Principles Board Opinion No. 11 requires the use of the deferred method of comprehensive interperiod tax allocation. Two ways to account for timing differences under the deferred method are: (1) gross change method, and (2) net change method.

Required:

1. Describe the gross change method.
2. Describe the net change method.

MULTIPLE CHOICE ANSWERS

1.	c	7.	a	13.	a	19.	b	25.	b
2.	c	8.	b	14.	a	20.	a	26.	b
3.	b	9.	a	15.	a	21.	c		
4.	a	10.	d	16.	b	22.	b		
5.	d	11.	d	17.	b	23.	b		
6.	a	12.	b	18.	b	24.	a		

EXPLANATION OF MULTIPLE CHOICE ANSWERS

1.   (1180,T1,8)   (c)   In accounting for income taxes, interest received on municipal obligations is an example of a permanent difference. Municipal interest is included in financial income as earned, but is never included in taxable income. Therefore it is not a timing difference (d), and no interperiod tax allocation (b) is necessary. Intraperiod tax allocation (a) is incorrect because there is no income tax expense associated with municipal interest income.

2.   (1180,P1,19)   (c)   The requirement is the change in Arnold's Deferred Income Tax account. The interest on municipal obligations can be ignored since it is a permanent difference; only timing differences affect Deferred Taxes. The choice of different depreciation methods for tax and financial reporting purposes results in a timing difference of $350,000 ($900,000 − $550,000). The change (increase) in the Deferred Tax account would be the tax effect of the timing difference, (40%)($350,000) or $140,000.

3.   (580,Q1,7)   (b)   The requirement is the federal income tax liability at 12/31/79. To determine this liability the income per books of $180,000 must be adjusted to taxable income, as shown below:

Income per books	$180,000
Add tax income in excess	
of book income	6,000
	$186,000
Deduct tax depreciation in	
excess of book depreciation	(8,000)
Taxable income	$178,000

The tax liability, then, based on the given tax rate of 50% would be $89,000.

4.   (580,T1,12)   (a)   Under the deferred method, adjustments are not made for subsequent changes in the tax rate. The liability method does require adjustment and the net of tax method allows for either rates when the timing difference originated or expected rates when reversal is scheduled to occur. The net present value method is a capital budgeting technique, not an interperiod tax allocation method. See APB 11, para 19-21.

5.   (580,T1,13)   (d)   Intraperiod income tax allocation refers to the allocation of taxes within a period; interperiod tax allocation refers to allocation among periods. Intraperiod tax allocation must be applied to income from continuing operations, discontinued operations, extraordinary items, changes in accounting principles (answer (d)), and prior period adjustments. Answer (a) concerns a permanent difference, for which no income tax allocation is necessary, and both answers (b) and (c) refer to timing differences, for which interperiod allocation would be applied.

6.   (1179,P1,12)   (a)   The requirement is the amount of provision for deferred income taxes in the income statement resulting from an accrual of an estimated $800,000 loss on disposal of unused plant facilities, given a tax rate of 40%. The accrual of $800,000 of estimated losses is a timing difference because it will not be deductible for tax purposes until the loss is incurred. Accordingly, no credit will arise for income tax purposes until the loss is incurred. Thus, interperiod tax allocation (APB 11) requires that the anticipated $320,000 credit (40% of the $800,000 loss) be reflected in the income statement in 1978. The requirement is for the provision for deferred income taxes in the income statement, which would eliminate confusion over the meaning of "provision for deferred income taxes," as it must be a nominal account to be in the income statement. Also note that the $100,000 premium on officers' life insurance is not a timing difference. It is either an expense for both tax and book purposes or it is a permanent difference.

7.   (1179,T1,17)   (a)   Intraperiod tax allocation requires allocation of a period's income taxes among income from continuing operations, extraordinary items, prior period adjustments, and direct entries to other stockholder equity accounts, per para 51 of APB 11. Intraperiod tax allocation is in contrast to interperiod tax allocation, which results in allocation of taxes among periods. Answer (b) is incorrect because the effect of the dividends received deduction is a permanent difference and thus requires neither intraperiod or interperiod tax allocation. Answer (c) is incorrect because the excess of accelerated depreciation used for tax purposes over straight-line depreciation used for book purposes is an interperiod timing difference, which requires interperiod tax allocation. Answer (d) is incorrect because all differences between taxable income and financial statement earnings are either timing differences or permanent differences, neither of which requires intraperiod tax allocations.

8. (579,T1,9) (b) Intraperiod income tax allocation of annual tax expense must be made to income from ordinary operations, discontinued operations, extraordinary items, cumulative effect of an accounting change, and prior period adjustments. The tax effect to be associated with any of the special items (other than income from ordinary operations) is computed by determining the income tax on overall taxable income and comparing it with the income tax on ordinary operations. If more than one special item exists, the difference between tax on ordinary operations and tax on overall taxable income must be allocated among the special items. See para 52 of APB 11 and Interpretation No. 19 of APB 11.

9. (579,T1,14) (a) Interperiod income tax allocation is based on the fact that income taxes are an expense of the business enterprise (para 14(b), APB 11). Interperiod tax allocation is an accrual approach of accounting for income tax expense. In the absence of interperiod allocation, income taxes would be expensed when payable, i.e., cash basis accounting. Answers (b), (c), and (d) are incorrect because income taxes are not considered a distribution of earnings but rather are an expense of doing business.

10. (576,P1,11) (d) APB 23 (para 10) requires that parent companies consider undistributed earnings of a subsidiary as a timing difference unless there is definite evidence that the subsidiary's earnings will be remitted in a tax free liquidation or will not be remitted in the future. Thus the taxes on the $500,000 of income will be 48%. Foreign taxes will be 40% and domestic taxes will be 8% (48% less the 40% credit for foreign taxes per the problem).

11. (575,Q1,4) (d) APB 11, para 57, requires that deferred taxes be classified into two categories, current and noncurrent. The classification should parallel the classification of the accounts that gave rise to the deferred taxes. In the current problem, the $50,000 of deferred taxes resulting from the accrual method of financial reporting and installment method for tax reporting results in a $50,000 deferred credit. It is current because the installment receivables are classified as current. It is a credit balance because the installment method defers the recognition of revenue and payment of taxes. The $20,000 deferred debit is noncurrent because the deferred compensation expense is noncurrent. The $15,000 of deferred taxes resulting from the use of accelerated depreciation for tax purposes and straight-line for financial

reporting has a credit balance, because the accelerated depreciation for tax purposes defers payment of taxes. It is noncurrent because the assets are not current assets. Thus on the balance sheet the current deferred taxes will have a $50,000 credit balance. The noncurrent deferred taxes will have a $5,000 debit balance ($20,000 debit less $15,000 credit).

12. (575,T1,9) (b) Interperiod income tax allocation is based upon the matching principle. In tax allocation, federal tax expense is reported in the year in which income is reported for financial reporting purposes. It is the application of accrual accounting to federal income tax expense. See para 36 of APB 11.

13. (575,T1,17) (a) The deferred credit will build up in the first few years and then remain relatively constant because a constant amount of equipment will be purchased and retired each year. Thus in every year approximately the same amount of equipment will be depreciated at accelerated rates and approximately the same amount of equipment will be depreciated at decelerated rates, e.g., every year $25,000 will be depreciated at the first year's depreciation rate and $25,000 will be depreciated at the last year's depreciation rate.

14. (1175,P1,8) (a) APB 24 requires that investors accounting for investments under the equity method consider the undistributed earnings as a timing difference. The tax rate applicable should be based upon the expectation of dividends or sale of the investment. See para 7 and 8 of APB 24. In this problem the assumption is that the $80,000 of undistributed earnings will be remitted as dividends. Thus the 40% tax rate is applied to the $80,000 of undistributed dividends less the 85% dividends received exclusion permitted by the IRS. Thus the 40% would apply to $12,000 of taxable income, which is $4,800.

15. (576,P1,6) (a) There are two methods of accounting for the investment credit, the deferred method and the flow-through method. The flow-through method recognizes investment credits as a reduction in tax expense in the year that they become available. The deferred method considers investment tax credits as a reduction in the cost of assets, and the credits are amortized over the useful life of the assets. Thus with a 10 year life, the $100,000 should be amortized 10% per year or $10,000.

16. (1176,T1,6)   (b) Deferred taxes rising from timing differences should be classified in two categories on the balance sheet. The first category is the net current amount and the second is the net noncurrent amount. See para 57 of APB 11. Answer (d), "valuation adjustments of the related assets and liabilities" is a net of tax method which in addition to being a nonacceptable disclosure procedure, is unacceptable as a method of interperiod tax allocation (para 21).

17. (1176,T1,7)   (b) If a material gain on a sale-leaseback transaction is taxed in the year of sale, interperiod tax allocation is required because the gain must be deferred and amortized in proportion to the amortization of the leased asset (para 33 of SFAS 13). Answer (a) is incorrect because R&D costs must be expensed in the year incurred (para 12 SFAS 2). Answer (c) is incorrect because losses on early extinguishment of debt are to be recognized in the year of extinguishment for financial accounting purposes (para 20 of APB 26). Answer (d) is incorrect because it describes a permanent difference between taxable income and accounting income which does not affect other periods and thus does not require interperiod tax allocation (para 33 and 34 of APB 11).

18. (577,Q1,10)   (b) The requirement is the amount of the tax benefit recognizable in 1976 from the operating loss carryforward. Operating loss carryforwards are generally recognized in the year that they are actually realized (here, 1976). See para 45 of APB 11. Since the tax rate is 50%, a tax benefit of $70,000 will be recognized in 1976 as an extraordinary item (note this treatment per para 45 of APB 11 was not superseded by APB 30).

19. (1177,Q1,13) (b) The requirement is the income tax liability in the third year of operations. Since the respective operating results were a $10,000 profit, $200,000 loss, and $350,000 profit, the operating loss in the second year of $200,000 will be carried back $10,000 to the first year and $190,000 will offset income in the third year. Thus the income tax liability in the third year will be $350,000 less $190,000, or $160,000 times 45%, which is $72,000. Note that the requirement is the current tax liability.

The effect of the operating loss carryforward is $190,000 times 45%, or $85,500, which would be reported as an extraordinary item on the income statement (para 61, APB 11). The expense associated with

operating income would be 45% of the $350,000 of operating income (i.e., $157,500) which is required by para 52 of APB 11 (intraperiod tax allocation). To recap:

1976 tax expense	
(45% of $350,000)	$157,500
Operating loss carryforward	
Extraordinary item	
(45% of $190,000)	85,500
1976 taxes payable	$ 72,000

20. (578,P1,2)   (a) The requirement is the change in the deferred tax account in 1977. The solutions approach is a T-account analysis of the unearned royalty account and the journal entry to record the current year's taxes, as illustrated below. The unearned royalty account indicates a beginning balance of $400,000 and 1977 collections of $600,000, and 1977 earnings of $650,000, leaving an ending balance of $350,000. The tax expense for the year would be 50% of the 1977 earnings of $650,000 and the tax liability would be 50% of the 1977 collections of $600,000. The increase of $25,000 in the deferred taxes account requires a $25,000 debit in the income statement.

	Unearned Royalties	
Beginning balance		$ 400,000
1977 collections		600,000
1977 earnings	$ 650,000	
Ending balance	350,000	
	$1,000,000	$1,000,000
Tax expense	$ 325,000	
Deferred taxes		$ 25,000
Tax liability		300,000

21. (578,P1,15)   (c) The requirement is the provision for deferred income taxes on the income statement which is the effect on tax expense due to the change in the deferred taxes account. The deferred taxes account is only affected by timing differences, and the municipal obligation interest income is a permanent difference and has no effect on deferred taxes. The $400,000 of expenses reported in 1977 reduce 1977 tax expense per books, but do not reduce the tax liability. At the 50% tax rate, the tax payable will be $200,000 (50% of $400,000) greater than the tax expense. Thus tax expense (provision for deferred taxes) will be credited for $200,000. Note that the Institute refers to "provision for deferred taxes" as the tax expense effect of the adjustment to the deferred tax account.

22.   (574,Q1,7)   (b)   As of the end of 1980, there is $200 of gross margin deferred from the sale in 1980 and $100 of gross margin deferred from the sale in 1979. Fifty percent of the $300 deferred gross margin should appear as deferred income taxes on the balance sheet.

23.   (574,Q1,8)   (b)   Under the "gross change method" the amount of deferred income taxes is found by multiplying an originating timing difference by the tax rate in effect in the year in which the timing difference originates. When the timing difference reverses the deferred income tax account is reduced by the amount originally recorded for the specific timing difference. Consequently, the balance in deferred income taxes at December 31, 1980 consists of

1979 sale: $100 deferred gross margin x 50% = $ 50

1980 sale: $200 deferred gross margin x 60% = 120
                                                 $170

Note that if the "net change method" were used the balance would be $150 because the $200 originating timing difference from the 1980 sale would be netted against the two $100 reversals relating to the 1978 and 1979 sales respectively.

Deferred Income Taxes

	100 ($200 x 50%)	:1978
	50 ($200 − $100)50%	:1979
	-0- [$100 − ($100 + $100)] 60%	:1980
Balance 150		
	150 Balance	

MAY 1981 ANSWERS

24.   (581,P1,19)   (a)   The requirement is the amount of deferred taxes which would be recorded by Waldo in 1980. The annual premiums on officer's life insurance and the interest income on municipal obligation are permanent differences. Both of these items affect accounting income, but never enter into the computation of taxable income. The royalties collected represent a timing difference. The full $200,000 is taxable income and will increase accounting income eventually. However, only the $50,000 earned in 1980 will be recognized as accounting income currently. The solutions approach is to prepare the journal entry to record income taxes.

Income Tax Expense $20,000
Deferred Taxes $60,000
  Income Tax Currently Payable $80,000

$20,000 = (40%)($ 50,000)

$80,000 = (40%)($200,000)

25.   (581,Q2,33)   (b)   The requirement is to calculate the amount reported as deferred income taxes at the end of 1980. Deferred income taxes are caused by timing differences, which arise due to a difference between financial accounting methods and tax methods. To calculate the balance in deferred taxes, the total timing differences must be determined and multiplied by the tax rate. The depreciation expense in this problem is the only timing difference. The solution approach is to compute the amount of expense reported on the income statement and tax return each year. The depreciable base is $16,000 ($22,000 cost less $6,000 salvage value).

	Tax.	Books
1980	$ 6,400 (4/10 x 16,000)	$ 4,000 16,000 x ¼%
1981	$ 4,800 (3/10 x 16,000)	$ 4,000 16,000 x ¼%
1982	$ 3,200 (2/10 x 16,000)	$ 4,000 16,000 x ¼%
	$14,400	$12,000

Therefore, the total timing difference is $2,400 ($14,400 − $12,000) and this amount multiplied by a tax rate of 50% results in deferred taxes of $1,200. Since the expense on the tax return is greater than the expense on the income statement, taxable income will be less than accounting income. Therefore, the $1,200 deferred taxes will be recorded as a credit.

Tax Expense   XXXX
  Deferred Taxes   1,200
  Tax Payable   XXXX

26.   (581,Q2,36)   (b)   The requirement of this problem is to calculate the tax benefit arising from a net operating loss carryforward and indicate how this benefit is reported on the income statement. According to APB 11, the tax benefit should be reported as an extraordinary item. The amount reported is the amount of the loss ($100,000) multiplied by the tax rate (40%), or $40,000. Note that if in 1979, realization of the carryforward was assured beyond any reasonable doubt, the tax benefit of the loss carryforward would be recognized as an operating item in 1979.

ANSWER OUTLINE

Problem 1 Tax Allocation and Investment Credit

a1. Intraperiod allocation relates tax expense to each element of earnings, e.g., operating NI, extraordinary items, etc.

a2. Interperiod allocation matches tax expense with earnings

a3. Warranty costs — timing difference
   Depreciation — permanent difference
   Equity method — timing difference

a4. Deferred tax is difference between tax expense and tax liability
   Separate current and noncurrent deferred amounts
   Net current and net noncurrent acceptable
    Not net of taxes method

b. Accounting for investment tax credit
   Deferral method
    Spread credit over life of asset
    Treats credit as reduction in asset cost
   Flow-through method
    Reduce tax expense by credit in year of purchase
    Credit earned when purchased

UNOFFICIAL ANSWER

Problem 1 Tax Allocation and Investment Credit

a. 1. Intraperiod tax allocation is necessary to obtain an appropriate relationship between income tax expense and each element of earnings (continuing operations, discontinued operations, extraordinary items, and cumulative effects of accounting changes) or between income tax expense and prior-period adjustments. Income tax expense attributable to earnings before extraordinary items is computed based solely on the earnings before extraordinary items to prevent distortion of the results of continuing operations. The extraordinary items are shown net of the corresponding income tax consequences as an adjustment to beginning retained earnings.

  2. Some accountants cite the argument that income taxes are an expense rather than a distribution of earnings. They apply the matching concept of accrual accounting, thus relating the income taxes presented on the earnings statement to the earnings that gave rise to those taxes. Their argument is that income tax expense for financial reporting should be related to the respective pretax accounting earnings. Implicit in this argument is the notion that a distribution of earnings is not allocated to periods.

3. a. Timing difference. The full estimated three years of warranty expenses reduce the current year's pretax accounting earnings, but will reduce taxable income in varying amounts each respective year, as incurred. Assuming the estimate as to each warranty is valid, the total amounts deducted for accounting and for tax purposes will be equal over the three-year period for a given warranty. This is an example of an expense that, in the first period, reduces pretax accounting earnings more than taxable income and, in later years, reverses and reduces taxable income without affecting pretax accounting earnings.

  b. Permanent difference. This difference in depreciation for pretax accounting earnings and taxable income will never reverse because the depreciation is based on different recorded amounts of the assets in question. The income tax expense per books would be reflected based on the amount actually paid (or due) in this situation.

  c. Timing difference. The investor's share of earnings of an investee (other than subsidiaries and corporate joint ventures) accounted for by the equity method is included in pretax accounting earnings, while only dividends received are included in taxable income. This difference between pretax accounting earnings and taxable income is assumed to be related either to probable future dividend distributions or to anticipated realization on disposal of the investment and is a factor in determining income tax expense. Future dividends imply ordinary income, and future disposal of an investment implies capital-gains income. Because dividend income is subject to an 85% dividends-received deduction, the effective rate would, in this case, be lower for the ordinary dividend income than for capital gains.

4. The deferred income tax account mathematically represents the balancing figure accounting for the difference between the income tax expense that has been matched with pretax accounting earnings and the income tax payable (amount based on taxable income that will actually be paid to the government plus any allowance for possible deficiency upon an Internal Revenue Service audit).

    A debit balance in a deferred income tax account should be classified as a deferred charge. A credit balance in a deferred income tax account should be classified as a deferred credit. In accordance with Accounting Principles Board Statement No. 4, the deferred charge is considered an asset even though it may not possess the usual characteristics of assets, and the deferred credit is considered a liability even though the income tax may never have to be paid.

    Another possible classification of the debit or credit balance in deferred income taxes is a net of tax presentation. Under this approach each tax allocation account (or portions thereof) is reported as an offset to, or a valuation factor for, the asset or liability that gave rise to the tax effect. Net of tax presentation is an extension of a valuation concept and treats the tax effects as valuation concept and treats the tax effects as valuation adjustments of the related assets and liabilities. The Accounting Principles Board specifically stated that the net of tax presentation should not be used for financial reporting, because deferred taxes are not considered elements of valuation of assets and liabilities.

    Four possible deferred income tax accounts may arise. These are a current deferred charge, a noncurrent deferred charge, a current deferred credit, and a noncurrent deferred credit. These could be classified on a statement of financial position as follows:

(a) Separate current and noncurrent amounts. In this form of presentation all statements-of-financial-position accounts resulting from income tax allocation are classified into four separate categories—current assets, noncurrent assets, current liabilities, and noncurrent liabilities.

(b) Net current and net noncurrent amounts. In this form of presentation all statement-of-financial-position accounts resulting from income tax allocation are classified into two categories—net current amount and net noncurrent amount.

(c) Single amount. In this form of presentation all statement-of-financial-position accounts resulting from income tax allocation are combined in a single amount.

The Accounting Principles Board has selected the net current and net noncurrent classification. Deferred charges and deferred credits relating to timing differences represent the cumulative recognition given to their tax effects and, as such, do not represent receivables or payables in the usual sense. They should be classified in two categories—one for net current amount and the other for the net noncurrent amount. The current portions of such deferred charges and credits should be those amounts that relate to assets and liabilities classified as current. Thus, if installment receivables are a current asset, the deferred credits representing the tax effects of uncollected installment sales should be a current item; if an estimated provision for warranties is a current liability, the deferred charge representing the tax effect of such provision should be a current item. Likewise, the noncurrent portions of deferred income taxes should be those amounts that relate to assets and liabilities classified as noncurrent. The Accounting Principles Board has specified that deferred taxes should not be part of the stockholders' equity section of the statement of financial position.

b. The investment tax credit may be accounted for either by the deferral or the flow-through method. The deferral method involves spreading the investment tax credit over the life of the related asset rather than reducing the income tax expense in the year in which the asset is placed in service and is the preferred choice in the opinion of the Accounting Principles Board. This method records the investment tax credit as a deferred credit and amortizes it over the productive life of the related asset by a credit to income tax expense each year. The theory behind this method is that the company benefits by using an asset, not by acquiring it.

The flow-through (tax-reduction) method of accounting for the investment tax credit involves reducing the income tax expense for the full amount of the tax credit in the year the credit is taken on the income tax return. Reported earnings after tax would then be higher than earnings after tax where the deferral method is used. The tax credit is generally earned for tax purposes when an asset meeting the legal conditions is placed in service. The theory behind this method is that the benefit (tax savings) should be recognized in the year it actually occurs, which is the year in which the asset is placed in service. Furthermore, the tax credit is entirely subject to the income tax laws and should, therefore, be considered as another element in the tax computation and reflected only when actually used. It is neither a permanent nor a timing difference because it does not affect either pretax accounting earnings or taxable income.

SOLUTION GUIDE

Problem 2   Calculation of Deferred Taxes

1. The most difficult aspect is determining the requirements. The provision for current income taxes is meant to be the tax liability currently payable. The provision for deferred income taxes is the adjustment to the deferred income tax account. Total tax expense is the sum of current and deferred. Also required is the adjustment to the deferred investment tax credit.

2. The solutions approach is to prepare the journal entry to record the tax expense, tax deferrals, and tax liability. After attempting to get a handle on the requirements, one should read through the data, paragraph by paragraph, making the computations necessary to prepare the journal entry for taxes. Also, note that information not used should be checked for listing per the second requirement.

2.1 The investment tax credits of $100,000 will reduce the provision for current income taxes (tax liability) from $600,000 to $500,000. Note that this is the amount due to the federal government before consideration of prepayments,

etc. The $550,000 estimated tax payments are not relevant to the requirements.

2.2 If the beginning balance of deferred investment tax credits was $375,000, $100,000 of credits was recognized for tax purposes, and the ending balance was $400,000; $75,000 in credits was reflected in tax expense for book purposes. The required entry is to increase the deferred tax credit account by $25,000, i.e., $100,000 was recognized on the tax return, but only $75,000 on the books.

2.3 The depreciation per the tax return exceeded depreciation per books by $50,000. Given the 48% tax rate, this will require an increase in deferred taxes of $24,000. The commitments to purchase additional fixed assets are not relevant to the requirements as the investment credit is not applicable until the assets are purchased and put in service.

2.4 The warranty expense per books exceeded the warranty expense per tax return by the increase in the liability account (from $200,000 to $260,000). The warranty expense is not deductible on the tax return until paid. At 48% this $60,000 of expense per books, not allowed on the tax return, is a debit to deferred taxes of $28,800 (expense per books exceeded expense per tax return).

2.5 The goodwill resulting from acquisition of another company under the purchase method will never be deductible for tax purposes and thus is a permanent difference. It does not affect the deferred tax account, and is not considered in this problem.

2.6 Because the earnings of the foreign subsidiary have not been remitted, they are not taxable in the current period, but the tax expense should be accrued as the income is accrued for book purposes. Upon remittance, 48% of the $175,000 would be taxable (48% of $175,000 is $84,000) less the foreign tax credit of $70,000. Thus, while not payable in the current period, $14,000 of tax expense should be accrued for book purposes and thus increases deferred taxes by that amount.

2.7 The premiums on officers' life insurance are not deductible and thus a permanent difference. As a permanent difference they are not considered in determining the tax journal entry.

2.8 The solutions approach to record the tax liability, tax expense, and changes in the deferred tax accounts results in the following entries:

1) Income Tax Expense   600,000
      Income Tax Payable   600,000
2) Income Tax Payable   550,000
      Cash   550,000
3) Income Tax Payable   100,000
      Investment Tax Credit   100,000
4) Investment Tax Credit 75,000
      Income Tax Expense   75,000
5) Income Tax Expense   9,200*
      Deferred Income Taxes   9,200

*net effect of adjustment in 2.3, 2.4, and 2.6 previously.

3. To recap, the information not relevant to the solution was:
   - Commitments to purchase assets of $450,000.
   - Goodwill amortization of $20,000.
   - Officer life insurance premiums of $80,000.
   - Estimated taxes of $550,000.

The Unofficial Answer appears on the next page. An alternative schedule for requirement 1 is presented below.

MIKIS CO.
INCOME TAX SECTION
of INCOME STATEMENT
For the Year Ended
12-31-75
Alternative to AICPA's Solution

Income Tax Expense:

		(1)
*Current Portion		$600,000
Deferred Portion		
Depreciation 48% ($50,000)	$24,000	
Warranty (Sched. 2)	(28,800)	(2)
Foreign Income (Sched. 3)	14,000	+ 9,200
Income Tax Expense Before Invest. Tax Credit		$609,200
Less: Investment Tax Credit Recognized (Sched. 4)	(3)	− 75,000
Income Tax Expense		$534,200

* Income Tax Payable without consideration of $100,000 allowable Investment Tax Credit.

Note: Requirements 1. (1), (2), (3) are identified in the right hand column.

Problem 2   Calculation of Deferred Taxes
a.

Mikis Company
INCOME TAX SECTION OF INCOME STATEMENT
For the Year Ended December 31, 1975

Provision for current income taxes (*Schedule 1*)		$500,000
Provision for deferred income taxes:		
Excess of depreciation for income tax reporting over depreciation for financial statement reporting ($50,000 × 48%)	$24,000	
Excess of product warranty expense for financial statement reporting over product warranty expense for income tax reporting (*Schedule 2*)	(28,800)	
Unremitted earnings of wholly owned foreign subsidiary (*Schedule 3*)	14,000	
		9,200
Investment tax credits recognized (*Schedule 4*)		25,000
		$534,200

Schedule 1

Computation of Provision for Current Income Taxes

Provision for current income taxes (exclusive of investment tax credits)	$600,000
Investment tax credits taken for income tax reporting in 1975	(100,000)
Provision for current income taxes	$500,000

Schedule 2

Computation of Excess of Product Warranty Expense for Financial Statement Reporting Over Product Warranty Expense for Income Tax Reporting, Net of Income Tax Effect

Accrued estimated losses from product warranty contracts at December 31, 1974	$200,000
Payments made in 1975 (expense for income tax reporting)	250,000
	50,000
Accrued estimated losses from product warranty contracts at December 31, 1975 ($200,000 × 130%)	260,000
Amount charged to expense in 1975 for financial statement reporting	$310,000
Amount charged to expense in 1975 for financial statement reporting	$310,000
Payments made in 1975 (expense for income tax reporting)	250,000
	60,000
Income tax effect	48%
Excess of product warranty expense for financial statement reporting over product warranty expense for income tax reporting, net of income tax effect	$ 28,800

Schedule 3

Computation of Unremitted Earnings of Wholly Owned
Foreign Subsidiary, Net of Income Tax Effect

Income from wholly owned foreign subsidiary before United States and foreign income taxes	$175,000
Income tax effect	48%
Total income taxes to be provided	84,000
Income taxes included in provision for current income taxes	70,000
Unremitted earnings of wholly owned foreign subsidiary, net of income tax effect	$ 14,000

Schedule 4

Computation of Investment Tax Credits Recognized

Unamortized deferred investment tax credits at December 31, 1974	$375,000
Investment tax credits deferred for financial statement reporting in 1975	100,000
	475,000
Unamortized deferred investment tax credits at December 31, 1975	400,000
Investment tax credits amortized during 1975	75,000
Investment tax credits taken for income tax reporting in 1975	100,000
Investment tax credits recognized	$ 25,000

2. Information in the fact situation that was not used to determine the answer to 1 above was as follows:

- Estimated tax payments of $550,000. Because this was a payment against a liability, there was no effect on Mikis's income statement for the year ended December 31, 1975.

- Commitments for the purchase of fixed assets of $450,000. Because this was merely a commitment and not a liability of Mikis, there was no effect on Mikis's income statement for the year ended December 31, 1975.

- Goodwill amortization of $20,000. Because the amortization was not deductible for income tax reporting, it was a permanent difference.

- Premiums paid on officers' life insurance of $80,000. Because this expense was not deductible for income tax reporting, it was a permanent difference.

SOLUTION GUIDE

Problem 3   Gross vs. Net Change Method

a1.   Gross change method
   Timing differences originating in current period are reflected at current tax rates
   Timing differences reversing in current period are reflected at tax rates existing in the deferred taxes account

a2.   Net change method applies the current rate to the net change in originating and reversing timing differences

UNOFFICIAL ANSWER

Problem 3   Gross vs. Net Change Method

a.   1.   Under the gross change method, the tax effects of timing differences originating in the current period are determined at the current income tax rates. The tax effects of timing differences originating in prior periods and reversing in the current period are determined at the applicable income tax rates reflected in the accounts as of the beginning of the current period.

      2.   Under the net change method, the tax effects of the net change in the originating and reversing timing differences are determined at the current income tax rates.

MULTIPLE CHOICE QUESTIONS (1–61)

1. In applying the treasury stock method of computing the dilutive effect of outstanding options or warrants, for quarterly fully diluted earnings per share, when is it appropriate to use the ending market price of common stock as the assumed repurchase price?
   a. Always.
   b. Never.
   c. When the ending market price is higher than the average market price and the exercise price.
   d. When the ending market price is lower than the average market price and higher than the exercise price.

2. Information relating to the capital structure of Vauxhall Corporation is as follows:

	December 31	
	1978	1979
Outstanding shares of:		
Common stock	200,000	200,000
Preferred 6% stock, $100 par, convertible into 3 shares of common stock for each share of preferred	10,000	10,000

The preferred stock was issued at par on July 1, 1978, when the bank prime interest rate was 9.5%. During 1979, Vauxhall paid dividends of $6 per share on its preferred stock. The net income for the year ended December 31, 1979, is $860,000. The primary earnings per common share, rounded to the nearest penny, for the year ended December 31, 1979, should be
   a. $3.74
   b. $4.00
   c. $4.10
   d. $4.30

3. Weaver Company had 100,000 shares of common stock issued and outstanding at December 31, 1978. On July 1, 1979, Weaver issued a 10% stock dividend. Unexercised stock options to purchase 20,000 shares of common stock (adjusted for the 1979 stock dividend) at $20 per share were outstanding at the beginning and end of 1979. The average market price of Weaver's common stock (which was not affected by the stock dividend) was $25 per share during 1979. Net income for the year ended December 31, 1979, was $550,000. What should be Weaver's 1979 primary earnings per common share, rounded to the nearest penny?
   a. $4.82
   b. $5.00
   c. $5.05
   d. $5.24

4. Elaine Corporation was organized on January 1, 1979, with an authorization of 1,000,000 shares of common stock with a par value of $5 per share.

During 1979, the corporation had the following capital transactions:

January 4 — issued 200,000 shares @ $5 per share.
April 8 — issued 100,000 shares @ $7 per share.
June 9 — issued 30,000 shares @ $10 per share.
July 29 — purchased 50,000 shares @ $4 per share.
December 31 — sold 50,000 shares held in treasury @ $8 per share.

Elaine used the cost method to record the purchase and reissuance of the treasury shares. What should be the balance in the account "capital in excess of par value" as of December 31, 1979?
   a. $400,000
   b. $450,000
   c. $500,000
   d. $550,000

5. Newton Corporation was organized on January 1, 1977. On that date it issued 200,000 shares of its $10 par value common stock at $15 per share (400,000 shares were authorized). During the period January 1, 1977, through December 31, 1979, Newton reported net income of $750,000 and paid cash dividends of $380,000. On January 5, 1979, Newton purchased 12,000 shares of its common stock at $12 per share. On December 31, 1979, 8,000 treasury shares were sold at $8 per share. Newton used the cost method of accounting for treasury shares. What is the total stockholders' equity of Newton as of December 31, 1979?
   a. $3,290,000
   b. $3,306,000
   c. $3,338,000
   d. $3,370,000

6. Sprint Company has 1,000,000 shares of common stock authorized with a par value of $3 per share, of which 600,000 shares are outstanding. When the market value was $8 per share, Sprint issued a stock dividend whereby for each six shares held one share was issued as a stock dividend. The par value of the stock was not changed. What entry should Sprint make to record this transaction?

a.	Retained earnings	$300,000	
	Common stock		$300,000
b.	Additional paid-in capital	300,000	
	Common stock		300,000

c.   Retained earnings   800,000
        Common stock   300,000
        Additional paid-in
          capital   500,000
d.   Additional paid-in
        capital   800,000
        Common stock   300,000
        Retained earnings   500,000

7.   The following information was abstracted from the accounts of the Oar Corporation at December 31, 1979:

Total income since incorporation	$840,000
Total cash dividends paid	260,000
Proceeds from sale of donated stock	90,000
Total value of stock dividends distributed	60,000
Excess of proceeds over cost of treasury stock sold	140,000

What should be the current balance of retained earnings?
   a. $520,000
   b. $580,000
   c. $610,000
   d. $670,000

8.   The following changes in account balances of the Marvel Corporation during 1979 are presented below:

	Increase
Assets	$356,000
Liabilities	108,000
Capital stock	240,000
Additional paid-in capital	24,000

Assuming there were no charges to retained earnings other than for a dividend payment of $52,000, the net income for 1979 should be
   a. $16,000
   b. $36,000
   c. $52,000
   d. $68,000

9.   On June 30, 1979, the stockholders' equity section of Comet Corporation was as follows:

Common stock, par value $25; authorized 500,000 shares; issued and outstanding 300,000 shares	$ 7,500,000
Additional paid-in capital	1,400,000
Retained earnings	1,890,000
	$10,790,000

On July 1, 1979, the board of directors of Comet declared a 5% stock dividend on common stock, to be distributed on August 10, 1979, to shareholders of record on July 31, 1979. The market price of Comet's common stock on each of these dates was as follows:

July 1	$30
July 31	31
August 10	32

What is the amount of the charge to retained earnings as a result of the declaration and distribution of this stock dividend?
   a. $375,000
   b. $450,000
   c. $465,000
   d. $480,000

Items 10 and 11 are based on the following information:

The Gaston Company has sustained heavy losses over a period of time and conditions warrant that Gaston undergo a quasi-reorganization at December 31, 1979.

Selected balance sheet items prior to the quasi-reorganization are as follows:

•   Inventory was recorded in the accounting records at December 31, 1979, at its market value of $6,000,000. Cost was $6,500,000.
•   Property, plant and equipment was recorded in the accounting records at December 31, 1979, at $12,000,000, net of accumulated depreciation. The appraised value was $8,000,000.
•   Stockholders' equity on December 31, 1979, was as follows:

Common stock, par value $10 per share; authorized, issued and outstanding, 700,000 shares	$7,000,000
Capital in excess of par	1,600,000
Retained earnings (deficit)	(900,000)
	$7,700,000

•   Under the terms of the quasi-reorganization, the par value of the common stock is to be reduced from $10 per share to $5 per share.

10.   Immediately after the quasi-reorganization has been accomplished, the total of stockholders' equity should be
   a. $3,300,000
   b. $3,500,000
   c. $3,700,000
   d. $4,200,000

11. Immediately after the quasi-reorganization has been accomplished, retained earnings (deficit) should be

    a. $0
    b. $ (200,000)
    c. $(4,400,000)
    d. $(4,900,000)

Items 12. and 13. are based on the following information:

Information relating to the capital structure of the Galaxy Company is as follows:

	December 31	
	1978	1979
Outstanding shares of:		
Common stock	90,000	90,000
Convertible preferred stock	10,000	10,000
9% convertible bonds	$1,000,000	$1,000,000

During 1979 Galaxy paid dividends of $2.50 per share on its preferred stock. The preferred stock is convertible into 20,000 shares of common stock and is considered a common stock equivalent. The 9% convertible bonds are convertible into 30,000 shares of common stock, but are not considered common stock equivalents. The net income for the year ended December 31, 1979, is $485,000. Assume that the income tax rate is 50%.

12. What should be the primary earnings per share, rounded to the nearest penny, for the year ended December 31, 1979?

    a. $3.79
    b. $4.21
    c. $4.41
    d. $4.73

13. What should be the fully diluted earnings per share, rounded to the nearest penny, for the year ended December 31, 1979?

    a. $3.79
    b. $3.96
    c. $4.11
    d. $4.51

14. The Culture Corporation had the following classes of stock outstanding as of December 31, 1979:

Common stock, $20 par value, 20,000 shares outstanding.
Preferred stock, 6%, $100 par value, cumulative and fully participating, 1,000 shares outstanding.

Dividends on preferred stock have been in arrears for 1977 and 1978. On December 31, 1979, a total cash dividend of $90,000 was declared. What are the amounts of dividends payable on both the common and preferred stock, respectively?

    a. $57,600 and $32,400.
    b. $62,400 and $27,600.
    c. $67,200 and $22,800.
    d. $72,000 and $18,000.

15. Theodore Corporation's stockholders' equity section of its December 31, 1978, balance sheet was as follows:

Common stock, authorized 1,000,000 shares; issued 900,000 shares; outstanding 800,000 shares; $10 par value	$ 9,000,000
Capital in excess of par	2,200,000
Retained earnings	5,600,000
Less shares held in treasury, 100,000 shares at cost	(800,000)
Total stockholders' equity	$16,000,000

During 1979 Theodore reissued 50,000 shares of the treasury stock at $12 per share. No other treasury stock transactions occurred during 1979. What amount and type of income should be reported on this transaction on the financial statements for the year ended December 31, 1979?

    a. $0.
    b. $100,000 ordinary income.
    c. $200,000 ordinary income.
    d. $200,000 extraordinary income.

16. Jordon Corporation has 80,000 shares of $50 par value common stock authorized, issued and outstanding. All 80,000 shares were issued at $55 per share. Retained earnings of the company amounts to $160,000. If 1,000 shares of Jordon common stock are reacquired at $62 and the par value method of accounting for treasury stock is used, stockholders' equity would decrease by

    a. $0.
    b. $50,000.
    c. $55,000.
    d. $62,000.

17. The issuer should directly charge retained earnings for the market value of the shares issued in a (an)

    a.   Pooling of interests.
    b.   2 for 1 stock split.
    c.   Employee stock bonus.
    d.   10 percent stock dividend.

18.   Faucet Company has 2,500,000 shares of common stock outstanding on December 31, 1977. An additional 500,000 shares of common stock were issued on April I, 1978, and 250,000 more on July 1, 1978. On October 1, 1978, Faucet issued 5,000, $1,000 face value, 7% convertible bonds. Each bond is convertible into 40 shares of common stock. The bonds were not considered common stock equivalents at the time of their issuance, and no bonds were converted into common stock in 1978. What is the number of shares to be used in computing primary earnings per share and fully diluted earnings per share, respectively, for the year ended December 31, 1978?

    a.   2,875,000 and 2,975,000.
    b.   2,875,000 and 3,075,000.
    c.   3,000,000 and 3,050,000.
    d.   3,000,000 and 3,200,000.

19.   At December 31, 1977, the Merlin Company had 50,000 shares of common stock issued and outstanding. On April 1, 1978, an additional 10,000 shares of common stock were issued. Merlin's net income for the year ended December 31, 1978, was $172,500. During 1978 Merlin declared and paid $100,000 cash dividends on its nonconvertible preferred stock. The earnings per common share, rounded to the nearest penny, for the year ended December 31, 1978, should be

    a. $1.26
    b. $1.32
    c. $3.00
    d. $3.14

20.   On August 1, 1979, Winston Company reacquired 4,000 shares of its $15 par value common stock for $18 per share. Winston uses the cost method to account for treasury stock. What journal entry should Winston make to record the acquisition of treasury stock?

		Debit	Credit
a.	Treasury stock	$60,000	
	Additional paid-in capital	12,000	
	Cash		$72,000
b.	Treasury stock	60,000	
	Retained earnings	12,000	
	Cash		72,000
c.	Retained earnings	72,000	
	Cash		72,000
d.	Treasury stock	72,000	
	Cash		72,000

21.   When treasury stock is purchased for more than the par value of the stock and the cost method is used to account for treasury stock, what account(s) should be debited?

    a.   Treasury stock for the par value and additional paid-in capital for the excess of the purchase price over the par value.
    b.   Additional paid-in capital for the purchase price.
    c.   Treasury stock for the purchase price.
    d.   Treasury stock for the par value and retained earnings for the excess of the purchase price over the par value.

22.   At the date of the financial statements, common stock shares issued would exceed common stock shares outstanding as a result of the

    a.   Declaration of a stock split.
    b.   Declaration of a stock dividend.
    c.   Purchase of treasury stock.
    d.   Payment in full of subscribed stock.

23.   Conditions warranted that a company have a quasi-reorganization. Immediately after the quasi-reorganization, the retained earnings account

    a.   Has a zero balance.
    b.   Remains the same as it was before the quasi-reorganization.
    c.   Is frozen and dated, and subsequent transactions will be shown separately.
    d.   Has a debit balance equal to the write-down of the assets which were overstated.

24.   When computing primary earnings per share, common stock equivalents are

    a.   Ignored.
    b.   Recognized whether they are dilutive or anti-dilutive.
    c.   Recognized only if they are anti-dilutive.
    d.   Recognized only if they are dilutive.

25.   Raulo Corporation owned 1,000,000 shares of marketable equity securities of Sub Corporation. On December 31, 1976, when Raulo's account "investment in common stock of Sub Corporation" had a carrying value of $8 per share, Raulo distributed these shares to its stockholders as a dividend. Raulo originally paid $10 for each share. Sub has 2,000,000 shares issued and outstanding, which are traded on a national stock exchange. The quoted market price for a Sub share was $4 on the declaration date and $3 on the distribution date.

What would be the reduction in Raulo's stockholders' equity as a result of the above transaction? (Do not consider income tax effects,)

    a. $3,000,000.
    b. $4,000,000
    c. $8,000,000.
    d. $10,000,000.

26.   A company reacquires shares of its own stock and reports the transaction in the theoretically correct manner. What effect will this transaction have on stockholders' equity and earnings per share respectively?

    a.   Decrease and decrease.
    b.   Increase and no effect.
    c.   Decrease and increase.
    d.   Increase and decrease.

27.   The nature of primary earnings per share involving adjustment for stock options can be described as

    a.   Historical because earnings are historical.
    b.   Historical because it indicates the firm's valuation.
    c.   Pro forma because it indicates potential changes in number of shares.
    d.   Pro forma because it indicates potential changes in earnings.

Items 28. and 29. are based on the following information:

A company wishes to raise funds by issuing either bonds or cumulative preferred stock.

28.   How will the annual interest or dividend affect total liabilities each year?

    a.   Interest is a current liability each year (until paid).
    b.   Cumulative preferred dividends are a current liability each year (until paid).
    c.   Both interest and cumulative preferred dividends are current liabilities each year (until paid).
    d.   Interest and cumulative preferred dividends in arrears are current liabilities each year (until paid).

29.   How will the annual interest or dividend affect annual net earnings available to common stockholders each year?

    a.   Annual net earnings available to common stockholders are reduced by annual interest but not by preferred dividends.
    b.   Annual net earnings available to common stockholders are reduced by preferred dividends but not by annual interest.
    c.   Annual net earnings available to common stockholders are reduced by annual interest and preferred dividends.
    d.   Annual net earnings available to common stockholders are not reduced by annual interest or preferred dividends.

30.   How should cumulative preferred dividends in arrears be shown in a corporation's statement of financial position?

    a.   Footnote.
    b.   Increase in stockholders' equity.
    c.   Increase in current liabilities.
    d.   Increase in current liabilities for the amount expected to be declared within the year or operating cycle, and increase in long-term liabilities for the balance.

31.   On January 1, 1977, Wilson, Inc., declared a 5% stock dividend on its common stock when the market value of the common stock was $15 per share. Stockholders' equity before the stock dividend was declared consisted of:

Common stock, $10 par value. Authorized 200,000 shares; issued and outstanding 100,000 shares	$1,000,000
Additional paid-in capital on common stock	150,000
Retained earnings	700,000
Total stockholders' equity	$1,850,000

What was the effect on Wilson's retained earnings as a result of the above transaction?

    a.   No effect.
    b. $50,000 decrease.
    c. $75,000 decrease.
    d. $150,000 decrease.

32.   On July 1, 1976, Austin Company granted Harry Ross, an employee, an option to buy 500 shares of Austin common stock at $30 per share. The option was exercisable for five years from the date of the grant. Ross exercised his option on October 1, 1976, and sold his shares on December 2, 1976. The quoted market prices of Austin common stock during 1976 were as follows:

July 1	$30 per share
October 1	35 per share
December 2	37 per share

As a result of the option granted to Ross, Austin should recognize additional compensation expense for 1976 on its books of

- a. $0.
- b. $1,000.
- c. $2,500.
- d. $3,500.

33. The term "reserve" in financial statements should be used to identify

- a. The decline in value of fixed assets that must be replaced in the future.
- b. An amount of funds being accumulated to satisfy or lessen the effect of an unresolved contingency.
- c. An amount of retained earnings identified for a specific purpose.
- d. The probable amount of uncollectible accounts receivable.

34. A company issued a new class of convertible preferred stock during the year. At the date of issuance the cash yield on the stock was sixty percent of the bank prime interest rate, however, by the end of the year the cash yield was equal to ninety percent of the bank prime interest rate. At the end of the year what type of classification should this security receive for computation of earnings per share?

- a. Long-term debt equivalent.
- b. Other potentially dilutive security.
- c. Convertible preferred stock.
- d. Common stock equivalent security.

35. An analysis of stockholders' equity of Medina Corporation as of January 1, 1977, is as follows:

Common stock, par value $20; authorized 100,000 shares; issued and outstanding 60,000 shares	$1,200,000
Capital in excess of par value	140,000
Retained earnings	760,000
Total	$2,100,000

Medina uses the cost method of accounting for treasury stock and during 1977 entered into the following transactions:

- Acquired 1,000 shares of its stock for $35,000.
- Sold 600 treasury shares at $38 per share.
- Retired the remaining treasury shares.

Assuming no other equity transactions occurred during 1977, what should Medina report at December 31, 1977, as capital in excess of par value?

- a. $156,800.
- b. $150,800.
- c. $140,000.
- d. $135,800.

36. With respect to the computation of earnings per share, which of the following would be most indicative of a simple capital structure?

- a. Common stock, preferred stock, and convertible securities outstanding in lots of even thousands.
- b. Earnings derived from one primary line of business.
- c. Ownership interest consisting solely of common stock.
- d. Equity represented materially by liquid assets.

37. On July 1, 1977, Round Company issued for $525,000 a total of 5,000 shares of $100 par value, 7% noncumulative preferred stock along with one detachable warrant for each share issued. Each warrant contains a right to purchase one share of Round's $10 par value common stock for $15 a share. The market price of the rights on July 1, 1977, was $2.25 per right. On October 31, 1977, when the market price of the common stock was $19 per share and the market value of the rights was $3.00 per right, 4,000 rights were exercised. As a result of the exercise of the 4,000 rights and the issuance of the related common stock, what journal entry would Round make?

		Debit	Credit
a.	Cash	$60,000	
	Common stock		$40,000
	Additional paid-in capital		20,000
b.	Cash	$60,000	
	Common stock rights outstanding	9,000	
	Common stock		$40,000
	Additional paid-in capital		29,000
c.	Cash	60,000	
	Common stock rights outstanding	12,000	
	Common stock		40,000
	Additional paid-in capital		32,000

d.	Cash	60,000	
	Common stock rights		
	outstanding	16,000	
	Common stock		40,000
	Additional paid-in		
	capital		36,000

38. In 1976, Orlando, Inc., issued for $105 per share, 8,000 shares of $100 par value convertible preferred stock. One share of preferred stock can be converted into three shares of Orlando's $25 par value common stock at the option of the preferred shareholder. In August 1977, all of the preferred stock was converted into common stock. The market value of the common stock at the date of the conversion was $30 per share. What total amount should be credited to additional paid-in capital as a result of the issuance of the preferred stock and its subsequent conversion into common stock?

   a. $80,000.
   b. $120,000.
   c. $200,000.
   d. $240,000.

39. The Amlin Corporation was incorporated on January 1, 1977, with the following authorized capitalization:

   20,000 shares of common stock, no par value, stated value $40 per share.
   5,000 shares of 5% cumulative preferred stock, par value $10 per share.

During 1977 Amlin issued 12,000 shares of common stock for a total of $600,000 and 3,000 shares of preferred stock at $16 per share. In addition, on December 20, 1977, subscriptions for 1,000 shares of preferred stock were taken at a purchase price of $17. These subscribed shares were paid for on January 2, 1978. What should Amlin report as total contributed capital on its December 31, 1977, balance sheet?

   a. $520,000.
   b. $648,000.
   c. $665,000.
   d. $850,000.

40. The computation of earnings per share in accordance with generally accepted accounting principles may involve the consideration of securities deemed common stock equivalents. Common stock equivalents are an example of

   a. Form over substance.
   b. Substance over form.
   c. Form over accounting principle.
   d. Substance over accounting principle.

41. The par-value method of accounting for treasury stock differs from the cost method in that

   a. No gains or losses are recognized on the sale of treasury stock using the par-value method.
   b. Any gain is recognized upon repurchase of stock but a loss is treated as an adjustment to retained earnings.
   c. It reverses the original entry to issue the common stock with any difference between carrying value and proceeds adjusted through paid-in capital and treats a subsequent resale like a new issuance of common stock.
   d. It reverses the original entry to issue the common stock with any difference being shown as an ordinary gain or loss and does not recognize any gain or loss on a subsequent resale of the stock.

42. At December 31, 1978, the Suppa Company had 500,000 shares of common stock issued and outstanding, 400,000 of which had been issued and outstanding throughout the year and 100,000 of which were issued on October 1, 1978. Net income for the year ended December 31, 1978, was $2,144,000. What should be Suppa's 1978 earnings per common share, rounded to the nearest penny?

   a. $4.29.
   b. $4.76.
   c. $5.04.
   d. $5.36.

43. Cash dividends on the $10 par value common stock of Ray Company were as follows:

1st quarter of 1978	$ 800,000
2nd quarter of 1978	900,000
3rd quarter of 1978	1,000,000
4th quarter of 1978	1,100,000

The 4th quarter cash dividend was declared on December 20, 1978, to stockholders of record on December 31, 1978. Payment of the 4th quarter cash dividend was made on January 9, 1979.

In addition, Ray declared a 5% stock dividend on its $10 par value common stock on December 1, 1978, when there were 300,000 shares issued and outstanding and the market value of the common stock was $20 per share. The shares were issued on December 21, 1978.

What was the effect on Ray's stockholders' equity accounts as a result of the above transactions?

	Common Stock	Additional Paid-In Capital	Retained Earnings
a.	$ 0	$ 0	$3,800,000 debit
b.	$150,000 credit	$ 0	$3,950,000 debit
c.	$150,000 credit	$150,000 credit	$4,100,000 debit
d.	$300,000 credit	$300,000 debit	$3,800,000 debit

44. Presented below is the stockholders' equity section of Caper Corporation at December 31, 1977:

Common stock, par value $20; authorized 50,000 shares; issued and outstanding 30,000 shares	$600,000
Capital in excess of par value	150,000
Retained earnings	230,000
	$980,000

During 1978 the following transactions occurred relating to stockholders' equity:

1,000 shares were reacquired at $28 per share.
900 shares were reacquired at $30 per share.
1,500 shares of treasury stock were sold at $32 per share.

For the year ended December 31, 1978, Caper reported net income of $110,000. The state in which Caper is incorporated places a restriction on the distribution of retained earnings equal to the cost of treasury stock. Assuming Caper accounts for treasury stock under the cost method, what should it report as total stockholders' equity on its December 31, 1978, balance sheet?

   a. $1,071,000.
   b. $1,078,000.
   c. $1,083,000.
   d. $1,090,000.

45. Spare Corporation had two issues of securities outstanding: common stock and a 5% convertible bond issue in the face amount of $10,000,000. Interest payment dates of the bond issue are June 30th and December 31st. The conversion clause in the bond indenture entitles the bondholders to receive forty shares of $20 par value common stock in exchange for each $1,000 bond. On June 30, 1978, the holders of $900,000 face value bonds exercised the conversion privilege. The market price of the bonds on that date was $1,100 per bond and the market price of the common stock was $35. The total unamortized bond discount at the date of conversion was $500,000. In applying the book value method, what amount should Spare credit to the account "capital in excess of par," as a result of this conversion?

   a. $135,000.
   b. $180,000.
   c. $460,000.
   d. $540,000.

46. Dilutive common stock equivalents must be used in the computation of

   a. Fully diluted earnings per share only.
   b. Primary earnings per share only.
   c. Fully diluted and primary earnings per share.
   d. Other potentially dilutive securities only.

MAY 1981 QUESTIONS

47. Redford Corporation's capital structure at December 31, 1979, was as follows:

	Shares issued and outstanding
Common stock	100,000
Nonconvertible preferred stock	20,000

On July 1, 1980, Redford issued a 10% stock dividend on its common stock, and paid a cash dividend of $2.00 per share on its preferred stock. Net income for the year ended December 31, 1980, was $780,000. What should be Redford's 1980 earnings per common share?

   a. $6.73.
   b. $7.05.
   c. $7.09.
   d. $7.80.

48. At December 31, 1979, Sonic Company had 20,000 shares of common stock issued and outstanding and 5,000 shares of nonconvertible preferred stock issued and outstanding. Sonic's net income for the year ended December 31, 1980, was $120,000. During 1980 Sonic declared and paid $50,000 cash dividends on common stock and $8,000 cash dividends on the nonconvertible preferred stock. There were no common stock or preferred stock transactions during the year. The earnings per common share for the year ended December 31, 1980, should be

   a. $3.50.
   b. $4.80.
   c. $5.60.
   d. $6.00.

49. Livingston Corporation has incurred losses from operations for several years. At the recommendation of the newly hired president, the board of directors voted to implement a quasi-reorganization, subject to stockholder approval. Immediately prior to the restatement, on June 30, 1980, Livingston's balance sheet was as follows:

Current assets	$ 550,000
Property, plant, and equipment (net)	1,350,000
Other assets	200,000
	$2,100,000
Total liabilities	$ 600,000
Common stock	1,600,000
Additional paid-in capital	300,000
Retained earnings (deficit)	(400,000)
	$2,100,000

The stockholders approved the quasi-reorganization effective July 1, 1980, to be accomplished by a reduction in other assets of $150,000, a reduction in property, plant, and equipment (net) of $350,000, and appropriate adjustment to the capital structure. To implement the quasi-reorganization, Livingston should reduce the common stock account in the amount of

    a. $0.
    b. $100,000.
    c. $400,000.
    d. $600,000.

Items 50. and 51. are based on the following information:

On January 1, 1980, Karva Company granted James Dean, the president, an option to purchase 1,000 shares of Karva's $30 par value common stock at $40 per share. The option becomes exercisable on January 1, 1982, after Dean has completed two years of service.

50. Assume that the quoted market prices of Karva's $30 par value common stock were as follows:

January 1, 1980	$40
December 31, 1980	55

As a result of the option granted to Dean, Karva should recognize compensation expense in 1980 of

    a. $0.
    b. $ 5,000.
    c. $ 7,500.
    d. $15,000.

51. Assume that the quoted market prices of Karva's $30 par value common stock were as follows:

January 1, 1980	$45
December 31, 1980	55

As a result of the option granted to Dean, Karva should recognize compensation expense in 1980 of

    a. $0.
    b. $2,500.
    c. $5,000.
    d. $7,500.

52. On July 1, 1980, Metaro Corporation purchased for $108,000, 2,000 shares of Jean Corporation's newly issued 6% cumulative $20 par value preferred stock. Each share also had one stock warrant attached, which entitled the holder to acquire, at $19, one share of Jean $10 par value common stock for each two warrants held. On July 2, 1980, the market price of the preferred stock (without warrants) was $50 per share and the market price of the stock warrants was $10 per warrant. On September 1, 1980, Metaro sold all the stock warrants for $19,800.

What should be the gain on the sale of the stock warrants?

    a. $0.
    b. $ 800.
    c. $1,800.
    d. $9,800.

53. On December 31, 1979, the stockholders' equity section of Mercedes Corporation was as follows:

Common stock, par value $5; authorized 30,000 shares; issued and outstanding, 9,000 shares	$ 45,000
Additional paid-in capital	58,000
Retained earnings	73,000
Total stockholders' equity	$176,000

On April 1, 1980, the board of directors declared a 10% stock dividend, and accordingly 900 additional shares were issued, when the fair market value of the stock was $8 per share. For the three months ended March 31, 1980, Mercedes sustained a net loss of $16,000.

What amount should Mercedes report as retained earnings as of April 1, 1980?

    a. $49,800.
    b. $52,500.
    c. $54,300.
    d. $57,000.

54. The following capital stock information pertains to Palisades Corporation:

	Number of shares issued	Amount
Common stock, $10 par value; 300,000 shares authorized:		
January 1, 1980	45,000	$450,000
Sold on May 1, 1980	3,000	30,000
Total, December 31, 1980	48,000	$480,000
Preferred stock, 9%, cumulative nonconvertible, $100 par value; 10,000 shares authorized	1,000	$100,000

The number of shares on which the 1980 earnings per share computation should be based is
a. 46,500.
b. 47,000.
c. 48,000.
d. 49,000.

55. What is most likely effect of a stock split on the par value per share and the number of shares outstanding?

	Par value per share	Number of shares outstanding
a.	Decrease	Increase
b.	Decrease	No effect
c.	Increase	Increase
d.	No effect	No effect

56. How should the excess of the subscription price ove. the par value of common stock subscribed be recorded?
a. As additional paid-in capital when the subscription is received.
b. As additional paid-in capital when the subscription is collected.
c. As retained earnings when the subscription is received.
d. As additional paid-in capital when the capital stock is issued.

57. Assume the cost method of accounting for treasury stock transactions is used. Any excess of the amount received upon resale over the price paid for the treasury stock should be shown as an
a. Increase in additional paid-in capital.
b. Increase in retained earnings.
c. Element of operating income.
d. Extraordinary gain.

58. For a compensatory stock option plan for which the date of grant and the measurement date are the same, compensation cost should be recognized in the income statement
a. At the date of retirement.
b. Of each period in which services are rendered.
c. At the exercise date.
d. At the adoption date of the plan.

59. When computing fully diluted earnings per share, convertible securities that are **not** common stock equivalents are
a. Ignored.
b. Recognized whether they are dilutive or anti-dilutive.
c. Recognized only if they are dilutive.
d. Recognized only if they are anti-dilutive.

60. For purposes of computing the weighted-average number of shares outstanding during the year, a midyear event that must be treated as occurring at the beginning of the year is the
a. Declaration and payment of stock dividend.
b. Purchase of treasury stock.
c. Sale of additional common stock.
d. Issuance of stock warrants.

61. For a compensatory stock option plan for which the date of the grant and the measurement date are the same, what account is credited at the date of the grant?
a. Retained earnings.
b. Stock options outstanding.
c. Deferred compensation cost.
d. Compensation expense.

REPEAT QUESTION

(581,Q1,6)　　Identical to item 34 above

PROBLEMS

Problem 1   Earnings Per Share (574,T6)

(25 to 30 minutes)

"Earnings per share" (EPS) is the most featured single financial statistic about modern corporations. Daily published quotations of stock prices have recently been expanded to include a "times earnings" figure for many securities which is based on EPS. Often the focus of analysts' discussions will be on the EPS of the corporations receiving their attention.

Required:

a. Explain how dividends or dividend requirements on any class of preferred stock that may be outstanding affect the computation of EPS.

b. One of the technical procedures applicable in EPS computations is the "treasury-stock method."

1. Briefly describe the circumstances under which it might be appropriate to apply the treasury-stock method.

2. There is a limit to the extent to which the treasury-stock method is applicable. Indicate what this limit is and give a succinct indication of the procedures that should be followed beyond the treasury-stock limits.

c. Under some circumstances convertible debentures would be considered "common stock equivalents" while under other circumstances they would not.

1. When is it proper to treat convertible debentures as common stock equivalents? What is the effect on computation of EPS in such cases?

2. In case convertible debentures are not considered as common stock equivalents, explain how they are handled for purposes of EPS computations.

Problem 2   Common Stock Equivalents (1178,T2)

(15 to 20 minutes)

The earnings per share data required of a company depend on the nature of its capital struc-

ture. A corporation may have a simple capital structure and only compute "earnings per common **share**" or may have a complex capital structure and **have to** compute "primary earnings per share" and "fully diluted earnings per share."

Required:

a. Define the term "common stock equivalent" and describe what securities would be considered common stock equivalents in the computation of earnings per share.

b. Define the term "complex capital structure" and discuss the disclosures (both financial and explanatory) necessary for earnings per share when a corporation has a complex capital structure.

Problem 3   Primary vs Fully Diluted EPS (580,T2b)

(10 to 15 minutes)

Part b.   Public enterprises are required to present earnings per share data on the face of the income statement.

Required:

Compare and contrast primary earnings per share with fully diluted earnings per share for each of the following:

1. The effect of common stock equivalents on the number of shares used in the computation of earnings per share data.

2. The effect of convertible securities that are **not** common stock equivalents on the number of shares used in the computation of earnings per share data.

3. The effect of antidilutive securities.

Problem 4   EPS (Darren Company) (575,Q4)

(40 to 50 minutes)

The following schedule sets forth the short-term debt, long-term debt, and stockholders' equity of Darren Company as of December 31, 1974. The president of Darren has requested that you assist the controller in preparing figures for earnings per share computations.

Short-term debt:	
Notes payable - banks	$ 4,000,000
Current portion of long-term debt	10,000,000
Total short-term debt	$ 14,000,000
Long-term debt:	
4% convertible debentures due April 15, 1986	$ 30,000,000
Other long-term debt less current portions	20,000,000
Total long-term debt	50,000,000
Stockholders' equity:	
$4.00 cumulative, convertible preferred stock; par value $20 per share; authorized 2,000,000 shares; issued and outstanding 1,200,000 shares; liquidation preference $30 per share aggregating $36,000,000	24,000,000
Common stock; par value $1 per share; authorized 20,000,000 shares; issued 7,500,000 shares including 600,000 shares held in treasury	7,500,000
Additional paid-in capital	4,200,000
Retained earnings	76,500,000
Total	112,200,000
Less cost of 600,000 shares of common stock held in treasury (acquired prior to 1974)	900,000
Total stockholders' equity	111,300,000
Total long-term debt and stockholders' equity	$161,300,000

The "Other long-term debt" and the related amounts due within one year are amounts due on unsecured promissory notes which require payments each year to maturity. The interest rates on these borrowings range from 6% to 7%. At the time that these monies were borrowed, the bank prime interest rate was 7%.

The 4% convertible debentures were issued at their face value of $30,000,000 in 1956 when the bank prime interest rate was 5%. The debentures are due in 1986 and until then are convertible into the common stock of Darren at the rate of 25 shares for each $1,000 debenture.

The $4.00 cumulative, convertible preferred stock was issued in 1973. The stock had a market value of $75 at the time of issuance when the bank prime interest rate was 9%. On July 1, 1974, and on October 1, 1974,

holders of the preferred stock converted 80,000 and 20,000 preferred shares, respectively, into common stock. Each share of preferred stock is convertible into 1.2 shares of common stock.

On April 1,1974, Darren acquired the assets and business of Brett Industries by the issuance of 800,000 shares of Darren common stock in a transaction appropriately accounted for as a purchase.

On October 1, 1973, the company granted options to its officers and selected employees to purchase 100,000 shares of Darren's common stock at a price of $33 per share. The options are not exercisable until 1976.

The average and ending market prices during 1974 of Darren common stock were as follows:

	Average Market Price	Ending Market Price
First Quarter	$31	$29
Second Quarter	33	32
Third Quarter	35	33
Fourth Quarter	37	34
Average for the year	34	—
December 31, 1974	—	34

Dividends on the preferred stock have been paid through December 31,1974. Dividends paid on the common stock were $0.50 per share for each quarter.

The net income of Darren Company for the year ended December 31, 1974, was $8,600,000. There were no extraordinary items. The provision for income taxes was computed at a rate of 48%.

Required:

a. Prepare a schedule which shows the adjusted number of shares for 1974 to compute:
    1. Primary earnings per share.
    2. Fully diluted earnings per share.

b. Prepare a schedule which shows the adjusted net income for 1974 to compute:
    1. Primary earnings per share.
    2. Fully diluted earnings per share.
Do not compute earnings per share.

Problem 5   Categories of Stockholders' Equity

(576,T7) (20 to 25 minutes)

Part a.   A corporation's capital (stockholders' equity) is a very important part of its statement of financial position.

Required:

Identify and discuss the general categories of capital (stockholders' equity) for a corporation. Be sure to enumerate specific sources included in each general category.

Part b.   Stock splits and stock dividends may be used by a corporation to change the number of shares of its stock outstanding.

Required:

1.   What is meant by a stock split effected in the form of a dividend?

2.   From an accounting viewpoint, explain how the stock split effected in the form of a dividend differs from an ordinary stock dividend.

3.   How should a stock dividend which has been declared but not yet issued be classified in a statement of financial position? Why?

Part c.   Jones Company has adopted a traditional stock option plan for its officers and other employees. This plan is properly considered a compensatory plan.

Required:

Discuss how accounting for this plan will affect net earnings and earnings per share. Ignore income tax considerations and accounting for income tax benefits.

Problem 6   Stock Option Plans (580,T4b)

(10 to 15 minutes)

Part b.   A corporation has a noncompensatory stock purchase plan for all of its employees and a compensatory stock option plan for some of its corporate officers.

Required:

1.   Compare and contrast the accounting at the date the stock is issued for the noncompensatory stock purchase plan and the compensatory stock option plan.

2.   What entry should be made for the compensatory stock option plan at the date of the grant?

Problem 7   Stock Appreciation Rights (Adapted from Kieso and Weygandt, Intermediate Accounting, 3rd edition, p. 762)

(15 to 25 minutes)

Futuristic Products Company establishes a stock appreciation rights program which entitles its new president, Jill Castleberry, to receive cash for the difference between the market price of the stock and a preestablished price of $30 (also market price) on December 31, 1980 on 20,000 SARs. The date of grant is December 31, 1980 and the required employment (service) period is three years. President Castleberry exercises all of the SARs in 1986. The market value of the stock fluctuates as follows: 12/31/81—$36; 12/31/82—$39; 12/31/83—$45; 12/31/84—$36; 12/31/85—$48.

Required:

1.   Prepare a five-year (1981-1985) schedule of compensation expense pertaining to the 20,000 SARs granted President Castleberry.

2.   Prepare the journal entry for compensation expense in 1981, 1984, and 1985 relative to the 20,000 SARs.

Problem 8   Treasury Stock (1179,T2b)

(10 to 15 minutes)

For numerous reasons a corporation may reacquire shares of its own capital stock. When a company purchases treasury stock, it has two options as to how to account for the shares: (1) cost method, and (2) par value method.

Required:

Compare and contrast the cost method with the par value method for each of the following:

1.   Purchase of shares at a price less than par value.

2. Purchase of shares at a price greater than par value.
3. Subsequent resale of treasury shares at a price less than purchase price, but more than par value.
4. Subsequent resale of treasury shares at a price greater than both purchase price and par value.
5. Effect on net income.

<u>Problem 9</u>   Stockholders' Equity Transactions
              (578,P3)
              (50 to 60 minutes)

This problem consists of two unrelated parts.

Part a.   Howard Corporation is a publicly-owned company whose shares are traded on a national stock exchange. At December 31, 1976, Howard had 25,000,000 shares of $10 par value common stock authorized, of which 15,000,000 shares were issued and 14,000,000 shares were outstanding.

The stockholders' equity accounts at December 31, 1976, had the following balances:

Common stock	$150,000,000
Additional paid-in capital	80,000,000
Retained earnings	50,000,000
Treasury stock	18,000,000

During 1977, Howard had the following transactions:

· On February 1, 1977, a secondary distribution of 2,000,000 shares of $10 par value common stock was completed. The stock was sold to the public at $18 per share, net of offering costs.

· On February 15, 1977, Howard issued at $110 per share, 100,000 shares of $100 par value, 8% cumulative preferred stock with 100,000 detachable warrants. Each warrant contained one right which with $20 could be exchanged for one share of $10 par value common stock. On February 15, 1977, the market price for one stock right was $1.

· On March 1, 1977, Howard reacquired 20,000 shares of its common stock for $18.50 per share. Howard uses the cost method to account for treasury stock.

· On March 15, 1977, when the common stock was trading for $21 per share, a major stockholder donated 10,000 shares which are appropriately recorded as treasury stock.

· On March 31, 1977, Howard declared a semiannual cash dividend on common stock of

$0.10 per share, payable on April 30, 1977, to stockholders of record on April 10, 1977. The appropriate state law prohibits cash dividends on treasury stock.

· On April 15, 1977, when the market price of the stock rights was $2 each and the market price of the common stock was $22 per share, 30,000 stock rights were exercised. Howard issued new shares to settle the transaction.

· On April 30, 1977, employees exercised 100,000 options that were granted in 1975 under a noncompensatory stock option plan. When the options were granted, each option had a preemptive right and entitled the employee to purchase one share of common stock for $20 per share. On April 30, 1977, the market price of the common stock was $23 per share. Howard issued new shares to settle the transaction.

· On May 31, 1977, when the market price of the common stock was $20 per share, Howard declared a 5% stock dividend distributable on July 1, 1977, to stockholders of record on June 1, 1977. The appropriate state law prohibits stock dividends on treasury stock.

· On June 30, 1977, Howard sold the 20,000 treasury shares reacquired on March 1, 1977, and an additional 280,000 treasury shares costing $5,600,000 that were on hand at the beginning of the year. The selling price was $25 per share.

· On September 30, 1977, Howard declared a semiannual cash dividend on common stock of $0.10 per share and the yearly dividend on preferred stock, both payable on October 30, 1977, to stockholders of record on October 10, 1977. The appropriate state law prohibits cash dividends on treasury stock.

· On December 31, 1977, the remaining outstanding rights expired.

· Net income for 1977 was $25,000,000.

Required:

Prepare a work sheet to be used to summarize, for each transaction, the changes in Howard's stockholders' equity accounts for 1977. The columns on this work sheet should have the following headings:

Date of transaction (or beginning date)
Common stock—number of shares
Common stock—amount
Preferred stock—number of shares
Preferred stock—amount
Common stock warrants—number of rights
Common stock warrants—amount
Additional paid-in capital
Retained earnings
Treasury stock—number of shares
Treasury stock—amount

Show supporting computations in good form.

Part b. Tomasco, Inc., began operations in January 1973 and had the following reported net income or loss for each of its five years of operations:

1973	$ 150,000	loss
1974	130,000	loss
1975	120,000	loss
1976	250,000	income
1977	1,000,000	income

At December 31, 1977, the Tomasco capital accounts were as follows:

Common stock, par value $10 per share; authorized 100,000 shares; issued and outstanding 50,000 shares $ 500,000

4% nonparticipating noncumulative preferred stock, par value $100 per share; authorized, issued and outstanding 1,000 shares   100,000

8% fully participating cumulative preferred stock, par value $100 per share; authorized, issued and outstanding 10,000 shares   1,000,000

Tomasco has never paid a cash or stock dividend. There has been no change in the capital accounts since Tomasco began operations. The appropriate state law permits dividends only from retained earnings.

Required:

Prepare a work sheet showing the maximum amount available for cash dividends on December 31, 1977, and how it would be distributable to the holders of the common shares and each of the preferred shares. Show supporting computations in good form.

MULTIPLE CHOICE ANSWERS

1.	c	14.	b	27.	c	40.	b	53.	a
2.	a	15.	a	28.	a	41.	c	54.	b
3.	a	16.	d	29.	c	42.	c	55.	a
4.	d	17.	d	30.	a	43.	c	56.	a
5.	a	18.	c	31.	c	44.	c	57.	a
6.	c	19.	a	32.	a	45.	a	58.	b
7.	a	20.	d	33.	c	46.	c	59.	c
8.	b	21.	c	34.	d	47.	a	60.	a
9.	b	22.	c	35.	d	48.	c	61.	b
10.	c	23.	a	36.	c	49.	d		
11.	a	24.	d	37.	b	50.	a		
12.	c	25.	c	38.	d	51.	b		
13.	a	26.	c	39.	c	52.	c		

EXPLANATION OF MULTIPLE CHOICE ANSWERS

1. (1180,T1,11)   (c)   The treasury stock method is used to measure the extent of dilution in terms of the number of incremental shares issued for which no proceeds from any assumed conversion are added to the firm's assets. It is used only when the exercise price is below the market price for all of three consecutive months with the most recent month being the last month of the period. APB 15 states that when applying the treasury stock method to compute fully diluted EPS, the ending market price of common stock should be used as the assumed purchase price when it is higher than average market price. AICPA Interpretation 60 of APB 15 reasserts that this rule should also be followed for quarterly computations.

2. (1180,P1,4)   (a)   The requirement is to compute primary earnings per share (PEPS). The solutions approach is to first determine EPS based only on common stock outstanding to use as a "benchmark" against which to measure potential dilution:

$$\frac{\$860,000 \quad \$60,000}{\text{net income} - \text{preferred dividend}} = \$4.00$$
$$200,000 \text{ shares}$$

The next step is to find EPS assuming conversion

$$\frac{\$860,000 \text{ net income}}{200,000 \text{ shares} + 30,000 \text{ shares}} = \$3.74$$

Since $3.74 is less than $4.00, the preferred stock is dilutive. Finally, it is necessary to determine if the preferred stock is a common stock equivalent (CSE). The 6% dividend rate is less than 2/3 of 9.5% prime rate; therefore, this security is a CSE, and PEPS is $3.74. Fully diluted earnings per share (FDEPS) is also $3.74. (Note that if the preferred stock had not been a CSE, PEPS and FDEPS would have been $4.00 and $3.74 respectively).

3. (1180,P1,10)   (a)   The requirement is Weaver's 1979 primary earnings per share (PEPS). Common shares outstanding at the beginning of the year were 100,000, and 10,000 shares were issued as a stock dividend. The stock dividend is a retroactive adjustment for EPS calculations, all 110,000 shares are treated as being outstanding for the entire year. Stock options are always common stock equivalents, and the treasury stock method is used to determine the number of incremental shares in computing PEPS.

Proceeds from exercise (20,000 shares x $20)	$400,000
Shares issued upon exercise	20,000
Treasury shares purchasable ($400,000 ÷ $25)	16,000
Incremental shares	4,000

Primary earnings per share is the net income of $550,000 divided by 114,000 shares, or $4.82.

4. (1180,Q1,1)   (d)   The requirement is the balance of "capital in excess of par value" at year-end. The solutions approach is to identify the change in that account resulting from each transaction described.

	Effect
January 4 — shares issued at par	$ 0
April 8 — shares issued at $2 above par (100,000)(S2)	$200,000
June 9 — shares issued at $5 above par (30,000)($5)	$150,000
July 29 — purchased treasury shares	$ 0
December 31 — sold treasury shares at $4 above cost (50,000)($4)	$200,000
Change in "capital in excess of par"	$550,000

Since Elaine uses the cost method of accounting for treasury shares, there is no effect on "capital in excess of par" when the shares are purchased, but the account is increased when the treasury shares are reissued above cost.

5. (1180,Q1,4)   (a)   The requirement is the total stockholders' equity at 12/31/79. The cost method of accounting for treasury shares is used. The solutions approach is to identify the effect of each transaction on stockholders' equity.

		Effect
1/1/77	200,000 shares issued for $15	$3,000,000
77-79	Net income	750,000
77-79	Dividends	(380,000)
1/5/79	Purchased 12,000 treasury shares at $12	(144,000)
12/31/79	Sold 8,000 treasury shares at $8	64,000
12/31/79	Stockholders' equity	$3,290,000

When treasury shares were purchased on 1/5/79, the transaction is recorded at cost. When resold, the following entry would be made:

Cash	$64,000	
* Retained Earnings	$32,000	
Treasury stock		$96,000

*8,000($12 cost − $8 reissue price)

The debit to Retained Earnings decreases stockholders' equity, while the credit to Treasury Stock increases stockholders' equity. The net effect is an increase of $64,000.

6.   (1180,Q1,5)   (c)   The requirement is the entry to record a stock dividend of one share for every six held. Chapter 7 of ARB 43 requires that a stock dividend of less than 20-25% should be recorded by transferring from retained earnings to common stock and paid-in capital an amount equal to the fair value of the stock dividend. This dividend is a 1/6 or 16.7% dividend, so the fair value of $800,000 (100,000 shares $8) is debited to Retained Earnings and credited to common stock and additional paid-in capital.

7.   (1180,Q1,6)   (a)   The requirement is the current balance of retained earnings. Retained earnings is increased by income and decreased by dividends:

$$\frac{\text{Retained}}{\text{earnings}} = \text{income} - \frac{\text{cash}}{\text{dividends}} - \frac{\text{stock}}{\text{dividends}}$$

$$\$840,000 - \$260,000 - \$60,000 = \underline{\$520,000}$$

The proceeds from selling donated stock and the excess of proceeds over cost of treasury stock sold would be credited to paid-in capital.

8. (1180,Q1,12)   (b)   The requirement is the net income for 1979. First the change in owners equity can be determined:

$$\Delta \text{ A} - \Delta \text{ L} = \Delta \text{OE}$$
$$\$356,000 - \$108,000 = \Delta \text{OE}$$
$$\$248,000 = \Delta \text{OE}$$

Three items caused this change in owners' equity: a change in contributed capital (+$240,000 + $24,000), dividends (−52,000), and net income. The net income,

then can be isolated in the following equation:

$$\Delta \text{ OE} = \Delta \text{contributed capital} + \text{NI} - \text{Dividends}$$
$$\$248,000 = \$264,000 + \text{NI} - \$52,000$$
$$\text{NI} = \$36,000.$$

9. (1180,Q1,16)   (b)   The requirement is the amount of the charge to retained earnings as a result of the declaration and distribution of the stock dividend. Chapter 7 of ARB 43 requires that a stock dividend of less than 20-25% be recorded at fair market value of the shares to be issued. This FMV should be measured as of the date of declaration, July 1. The charge to retained earnings is 5% of the shares outstanding (5% x 300,000) times $30 FMV or $45,000.

10. (1180,Q1,17)   (c)   The requirement is the total of stockholders' equity immediately after the quasi-reorganization. The second problem of the pair requires the amount of retained earnings (deficit) immediately after the quasi-reorganization. In a quasi-reorganization, assets are revalued at current values, and the deficit is eliminated by being charged against paid-in capital. The new balance of stockholders' equity is equal to the old balance, less any writedown of assets. The only assets to be written down are property, plant and equipment from $12 million to $8 million. The new amount of stockholders' equity is the 12/31/79 balance of $7,700,000 less the writedown of P,P and E ($4,000,000) equals $3,700,000. One major purpose of a quasi-reorganization is to establish the balance of retained earnings at zero by writing an accumulated deficit off against paid in capital. Therefore, the retained earnings balance after the reorganization will be "0".

11. (1180,Q1,18)   (a)   See explanation for (1180,Q1,17).

12.   (580,P1,5)   (c)   The requirements are to compute the primary and fully diluted earnings per share (next question). The solutions approach is to first determine the earnings per share based on the weighted number of shares outstanding to use as a "benchmark" against which to measure potential dilution.

1. Compute EPS on weighted average number of shares outstanding:

a) $485,000 net income − $25,000 pref. div. = $460,000 income available for distribution to common stockholders

b) $460,000 available income ÷ 90,000 weighted average number of common shares outstanding during 1979 = $5.11 per share EPS on weighted average number of shares.

The next step is to determine which, if any, of the potentially dilutive securities are dilutive.

2. Dilution test for potentially dilutive securities:

   a) Preferred stock

      (1) ($2.50 div.x 10,000 shares of pref. stk.) ÷ 20,000 shares of com. stk. if conv. from pref. stk. = $1.25 per com. share

      (2) Since $1.25 per share (if the preferred stock was converted) is less than $5.11 per share (if the preferred stock was not converted), the preferred stock is dilutive.

   b) Bonds

      (1) (9% interest rate x $1,000,000 par value of bonds x [1—tax rate]) ÷ 30,000 shares of common stock if bonds were converted = $1.50 per common share

      (2) Since $1.50 per share (if the bonds were converted) is less than $5.11 per share, the bonds are dilutive.

The final step is to prepare a schedule to compute primary and fully diluted EPS. Note that when starting with net income no adjustment is needed for preferred dividends if conversion is assumed. See EPS in the Stockholders' Equity section of Chapter 9, Volume I, for further explanation of the above approach.

	PEPS	FDEPS
Dollars for numerator		
Net income*	$485,000	$485,000
Conv. bond int.		45,000
EPS dollars	$485,000	$530,000
Shares for denominator		
Outstanding shares	90,000	90,000
Conv. pref. stk.	20,000	20,000
Conv. bonds		30,000
No. of shares	110,000	140,000

$485,000 ÷ 110,000 = $4.41 PEPS

$530,000 ÷ 140,000 = $3.79 FDEPS

*Note: When starting with net income no adjustment is needed for preferred dividends if conversion is assumed.

13. (580,P1,6) (a)   See preceding answer for explanation.

14. (580,Q1,13) (b)   The requirement is to allocate the $90,000 cash dividends between preferred and common stockholders. Cumulative preferred stock requires the years in arrearage to be paid first. This amount [(6%)($100)(1,000 shares)(2 yrs)] is $12,000. The $12,000 in arrears plus the current year's $6,000 for preferred is to be deducted from the $90,000 total cash dividend. Common stock is then given 6%. This amounts to (6% x $20 x 20,000) = $24,000. The remaining $48,000 ($90,000 — $18,000 — $24,000) is allocated among the classes of stock in proportion to their relative shares of total stockholders' equity. Preferred shareholders have equity of $100,000 over the total equity of $500,000; this, multiplied by $48,000, is the participating portion for preferred stockholders. The common stockholders' share of the $48,000 is $400,000 ÷ $500,000, or 80%.

	Preferred	Common	Total
6% '77-'78 arrearage	$12,000	—	$12,000
1979 current	6,000	$24,000	30,000
	$18,000	$24,000	$42,000
Participating	9,600	38,400	48,000
	$27,600	$62,400	$90,000

15. (580,Q1,16) (a)   Selling treasury shares at a gain results in an increase in Capital in Excess of Par Treasury Stock. No gain or loss is reported on the income statement for treasury stock transactions. They are adjustments of owners' equity accounts.

16. (580,Q1,19) (d)   When using the par value method of recording acquisitions of treasury stock, the Treasury Stock account is debited for the par value of the stock. The additional paid-in capital account should be reduced for the amount originally credited for the number of shares involved. Any further reductions must reduce the Retained Earnings account. All of the debits reduce stockholders' equity.

Treasury Stock	$50,000	
Add'l. Pd.-in Cap.	5,000	
R.E.	7,000	
Cash		$62,000

17. (580,T1,39) (d)   Issuance of a stock dividend of less than 20-25% is accounted for by transferring from retained earnings to paid-in capital an amount equal to the fair value of the stock issued, as explained in ARB 43, Chapter, para 10-13. In a pooling of interests, the book value of assets received is used to record the transaction. Pure stock splits result in no accounting entries. An employee stock bonus would result in a charge to an expense account.

18.   (1179,P1,5) (c) The requirement is the number of shares to be used in computing primary earnings per share (PEPS) and fully diluted earnings per share (FDEPS) in 1978. The solutions approach is to start with the beginning number of shares outstanding and adjust that figure for each issuance of stock during the year and for the convertible bonds issued on 10/1/78. On 1/1/78, 2,500,000 shares were outstanding. The April 1 issuance of 500,000 shares results in a weighted average of 375,000 shares (500,000 x 75%), because the shares were outstanding for 3/4 of a year. The July 1 issuance of 250,000 shares is equivalent to 125,000 shares (250,000 x 50%), because the shares were outstanding for 1/2 of the year. The October 1 issuance of convertible bonds is not relevant to PEPS because the bonds were not considered common stock equivalents and were not converted into stock during the year. For FDEPS, however, the bonds would be considered converted. Since there were 5,000 bonds, each convertible into 40 shares of stock, this results in an additional 50,000 equivalent shares (5,000 bonds x 40 shares x ¼ yr.). Thus there would be 3,000,000 shares outstanding for PEPS and 3,050,000 shares outstanding for FDEPS.

1/1/78 O/S	2,500,000
4/1/78 issuance	375,000
7/1/78 issuance	125,000
PEPS	3,000,000 shares
Convertible bonds	50,000
FDEPS	3,050,000 shares

19.   (1179,P1,6) (a) The requirement is the 1978 EPS. EPS is a ratio of adjusted net income over adjusted shares outstanding. Net income must be adjusted for preferred dividends, i.e., preferred dividends are not considered an expense and are not available to common stockholders. Shares outstanding must be adjusted to determine the weighted average of those shares outstanding during the year. Thus, the $172,500 must be reduced by the $100,000 dividend to the preferred stockholders. The 50,000 shares outstanding at the beginning of the year must be adjusted to reflect the 10,000 shares that were outstanding for 9 months, resulting in a total weighted average of 57,500 shares outstanding. The final computation is the $72,500 of adjusted earnings divided by 57,500 shares, resulting in a $1.26 of EPS.

20.   (1179,P1,20) (d) The requirement is the journal entry to reflect the acquisition of treasury stock under the cost method. The cost method of accounting for

treasury stock requires that treasury stock be debited for the acquisition costs (in this case, $72,000). Upon resale, any difference between the carrying value and the selling price is accounted for per para 12 of APB 6. An excess of the sales price over cost is credited to paid-in capital from treasury stock. Any excess of cost over sales price is debited to paid-in capital and/or retained earnings. The cost method of accounting for treasury stock is in contrast to the par value method. Per the par value method, treasury stock is debited for par value upon reacquisition. The excess of cost over par value is charged to the paid-in capital account and/or retained earnings. When the treasury stock is reissued, the excess of selling price over par value is credited to paid-in capital from treasury stock transactions.

21.   (1179,T1,6) (c) The requirement is the debit when treasury stock is repurchased for more than par under the cost method. Under the cost method of accounting for treasury stock, treasury stock is debited for the amount paid for the treasury stock. At resale or retirement, the original cost is credited with any gain going to paid-in-capital and any loss to paid-in-capital or retained earnings (see para 12 of APB 6). Answers (a) and (d) are incorrect because they describe the par value method rather than the cost method of accounting for treasury stock. Answer (b) is incorrect because paid-in-capital is never debited for the purchase price of treasury stock.

22.   (1179,T1,7) (c) Common shares issued would exceed common shares outstanding if treasury stock existed. The number of shares outstanding would be less than those originally issued because treasury shares would have been repurchased from those originally issued. Answers (a), (b), and (d) are incorrect because issuance of stock by stock split, stock dividends, or stock subscriptions results in the same number of shares outstanding as were issued. Declaration of either a stock dividend or a stock split does not increase either shares issued or shares outstanding (it is the distribution of splits and dividends that increases both).

23.   (1179,T1,23) (a) Immediately after quasi-reorganization, retained earnings should have a zero balance, per para 10 of Chapter 7 of ARB 43. The purpose of a quasi-reorganization is to revalue assets and eliminate a deficit. This will allow reporting of an income in the future and presumably resumption of payment of dividends. Assets are written down and the deficit in retained earnings is eliminated by debits to other capital accounts. Answer (b) is incorrect because the new retained earnings account will have a zero balance. Answer (c) is incorrect because retained earnings is ad-

justed to zero by debits to other shareholder equity accounts. The new retained earnings account must be dated for 10 years per ARB 46. Answer (d) is incorrect because the debit balance in retained earnings is removed by an appropriate credit to other shareholder equity accounts.

24. (1179,T1,29) (d) Common stock equivalents are only considered in computing primary earnings per share if they are dilutive, i.e., if they reduce EPS. See para 30 of APB 15, and also note that the same is true for fully diluted earnings per share. Thus, only common stock equivalents, contingent issuances, etc., which reduce earnings per share figures, should be included in that computation. Answers (a), (b), and (c) are incorrect because common stock equivalents are included in EPS computations only if they are dilutive.

25. (577,Q1,5) (c) The requirement is the reduction in Raulo's stockholders' equity resulting from the issuance of the property dividend. The property dividend consists of 1,000,000 shares carried at $8 per share. Para 23 of APB 29 indicates that the distribution should be accounted for at its fair value (either $4 or $3 per share). The requirement, however, is the reduction in stockholders' equity which will be the entire $8,000,000, because any portion of the $8,000,000 not charged to retained earnings as a dividend will flow through to retained earnings as a loss on the transaction. In other words, an asset with a carrying value of $8,000,000 is being severed from assets. Also the $2,000,000 reduction ($10 to $8 per share) in carrying value was already a debit in shareholders' equity. See para 11 of SFAS 12.

26. (577,T1,1) (c) Reacquisition of treasury stock decreases stockholders' equity and increases earnings per share. The solutions approach is to study each requirement separately. The solutions approach for the effect on shareholders' equity can be determined by visualizing a T-account balance sheet whereby assets are reduced to reacquire treasury stock and there is a corresponding reduction in shareholders' equity. The solutions approach for earnings per share is to recognize that EPS is a ratio consisting of a numerator and denominator. While the numerator will not be affected, the denominator is decreased since there are fewer shares outstanding, thus increasing the ratio.

27. (577,T2,28) (c) When the treasury stock method is incorporated in a primary earnings per share calculation, the figure becomes pro forma because it involves hypothetical exercise of the options or warrants as of

the beginning of the period and then a subsequent hypothetical repurchase of stock at the average market price during the year with the hypothetical funds. See para 36-38 of APB 15.

28. (577,T2,32) (a) Only bond interest is a current liability. Cumulative preferred dividends may carry restrictions on financing or investing activities of the corporation, but are not liabilities until declared by the board of directors.

29. (577,T2,33) (c) Annual net earnings available to common stockholders, e.g., the numerator in EPS calculations, are reduced by both bond interest and preferred dividends. The interest reduces income in the income statement (and also reduces tax expense). The preferred dividends are subtracted from net income in computing net earnings available to common stockholders.

30. (1176,T1,12) (a) Cumulative preferred dividends in arrears should be disclosed in aggregate and on a per share basis. See footnote 16 to para 50 of APB 15. Cumulative preferred dividends are those which must be paid in subsequent years if not declared in any one year; they have a cumulative preference prior to the payment of common stock dividends. There is no entry to record a liability, because a liability to pay dividends does not exist until they have been declared. Cumulative dividends in arrears are not an increase in stockholders' equity. If anything, preferred dividends in arrears increase the equity of preferred stockholders and reduce the equity of common stockholders.

31. (1177,P1,18) (c) Stock dividends, as distinguished from stock splits, are accounted for by capitalizing the fair market value of the additional shares issued. See para 10 of Chapter 7b of ARB 43. In the case of stock splits there is no capitalization of retained earnings. Rather the par or stated value is assumed to be adjusted to allow the additional shares to be issued with the amount of legal capital remaining the same. In some cases the par or stated value may not be changed. Then the par or stated value of the additional shares issued must be capitalized (para 15 of Chapter 7b of ARB 43).

The solutions approach is to journalize the stock dividend declaration. Note that common stock dividend distributable is credited instead of common stock. Only the declaration of a stock dividend has been made. When the stock dividend is distributed, the common stock dividend distributable will be debited and common stock credited for the par or stated value issued. The common stock dividend distributable account is not a liability account; rather it is a shareholders' equity account.

Retained earnings	$75,000	
Com. stk. div. dist.		$50,000
Add'l. paid-in capital		25,000

32. (1177,Q1,14) (a) The requirement is the amount of compensation expense to be recognized as a result of granting a stock option. Since the market price of the stock at the time the option was granted ($30/share) is the same or less than the option price ($30/share), there is no compensation expense. See para 12 of Chapter 13b of ARB 43.

33. (1177,T1,11) (c) The requirement is the use of the term "reserve" in financial statements. Generally the term "reserve" has fallen into disfavor and is not used in the account titles of financial statements. It has been used to describe a contra-asset account, such as "Reserve for Depreciation." It has also been used to describe a liability account such as "Reserve for Taxes." Additionally, "reserve" has been used to describe an appropriation of retained earnings such as a "Reserve for Contingencies." It has also been used to describe accumulation of specific assets, such as a sinking fund "Reserve for Retirement of Bonds." Para 60 and 64 of Accounting Terminology Bulletin No. 1 recommends the third usage, i.e., an appropriation of retained earnings.

34. (1177,T1,22) (d) The convertible preferred stock is a common stock equivalent because <u>at issuance</u> the cash yield was less than 66 2/3% of the then current bank prime interest rate. Note that the determination of common stock equivalency status is made at the time the security is issued (para 31, APB 15).

35. (578,Q1,12) (d) The requirement is the ending balance of capital in excess of par value. The solutions approach is to journalize the entries for each of the three transactions as illustrated below. The second transaction results in paid-in capital in excess of par value of $1,800, as $1,800 more was received for the treasury stock than was originally paid (see the first entry). The third entry results in a charge of $6,000 to paid-in capital in excess of par value at retirement. This assumes that the paid-in capital in excess of par value included paid-in capital from other than original issuance, e.g., gains

on treasury stock transactions. See para 12 of APB 6.

Treasury shares	$35,000	
Cash		$35,000

Cash	$22,800	
Treasury shares		$21,000
Paid-in excess		1,800

Common stock	$ 8,000	
Paid-in excess	6,000	
Treasury shares		$14,000

36. (578,T1,14) (c) A simple capital structure is one which includes only common stock. It does not have any potentially dilutive convertible securities, options or warrants. See para 14 of APB 15. Answer (a) is incorrect because preferred stock and convertible securities raise the possibility of dilution which would require primary earnings per share and possibly fully diluted earnings per share figures. Answers (b) and (d) are incorrect because they do not relate to the capital structure of the business enterprise.

37. (1178,P1,19) (b) The requirement is the journal entry to reflect the exercise of 4,000 common stock rights that were previously issued with preferred stock. The solutions approach is to prepare the journal entry to reflect the original issuance of the preferred stock.

Cash	$525,000	
Preferred stock		$500,000
Com. stock rights		11,250
Paid in on pref.		13,750

When the 5,000 shares of preferred were issued, $525,000 was received which is a debit to cash. The credit is to $500,000 of preferred stock (5,000 shares at $100 par). The allocation to the stock rights is $11,250 (5,000 rights at $2.25 per right). Since only the market value of the rights at the date of issuance is given, the assumption is made that the value of each preferred stock is $102.75 (each unit of 1 preferred share and 1 common stock right has a value of $105).

When the rights are exercised, cash of $60,000 (4,000 rights at $15) and the stock rights of $9,000 (4,000 rights at $2.25) are debited. Common stock is credited for par

(4,000 shares at $10) and the difference of $29,000 ($60,000 + $9,000 − $40,000) is paid in excess of common par.

Cash	$60,000		
Com. stock rights	9,000		
Common stock		$40,000	
Paid in on com.		29,000	

38. (1178,P1,20) (d) Conversion of convertible securities into common stock can either be accounted for at the cost (carrying value) of the security being converted or the market value of the common stock issued for the convertible securities. The majority treatment, however, is the carrying value.

The solutions approach is to prepare the journal entry to reflect the exchange as illustrated below. No value is assigned to the conversion feature. The convertible preferred stock was originally issued for a total of $840,000 ($40,000 had been paid in excess of preferred par value). Thus the entry to record the exchange at the carrying value of the convertible preferred is to debit preferred stock for $800,000 and paid-in capital on preferred for $40,000. Since 24,000 shares of $25 par common are issued, there is a credit of $600,000 to common stock. The remaining credit is to paid-in capital on common for $240,000. Note the problem requires the total amount to be credited to paid-in capital. If the problem had specified the net amount, $200,000 ($240,000 credit less $40,000 debit) would be appropriate.

Preferred stock	$800,000	
Paid-in on preferred	40,000	
Common stock		$600,000
Paid-in on common		240,000

39. (1178,Q1,5) (c) The requirement is the total contributed capital as of 12/31/77. Total contributed capital is total legal capital plus other paid-in amounts. Thus the $600,000 received for common and the $48,000 received for preferred are part of contributed capital. Also, when the 1,000 shares of preferred were subscribed for $17 in December, the following entry was made:

Stock subscriptions receivable	$17,000	
Pref. stock subscribed		$10,000
Paid-in on preferred		7,000

Both the preferred stock subscribed and the paid-in

capital on preferred are considered contributed capital. Thus the contributed capital consists of:

Common	$600,000
Preferred	48,000
Preferred subscribed	17,000
	$665,000

40. (1178,T1,2) (b) The requirement is what is the nature of common stock equivalents. "A common stock equivalent is a security which is not, in form, a common stock but which usually contains provisions to enable its holders to become a common stockholder and which, because of its terms and the circumstances under which it was issued, is in substance equivalent to a common stock" (APB 15, para 25). Thus, securities which are not common stock in form, but are in substance, are treated as common stock in EPS calculations. This is known as putting substance over form. Substance over form is a basic accounting feature discussed in paragraphs 25 and 127 of APB Statement 4. Answer (a) is incorrect because if form were permitted over substance, accounting statements would not be realistic. Answers (c) and (d) are incorrect because the issue is not either form or substance vis-a-vis accounting principles.

41. (1178,T1,24) (c) The requirement is the difference between the par value method and the cost method of accounting for treasury stock. Upon purchase of treasury stock, the par value method records the treasury stock at par value with debits to paid-in capital for any amounts recorded when the stock was issued. Also the difference between the amount paid for the preferred stock and its carrying value is an adjustment to paid-in capital or retained earnings (para 12 of APB 6).

Treasury stock	(par value)
Paid in capital	(recorded at issuance of stock)
Paid in cap. or RE	(plug)
Cash	(amount paid for TS)

Subsequent sales are treated as a new issuance.

In contrast, the cost method records treasury stock acquisitions at their cost. Answers (a), (b), and (d) are all incorrect because differences between carrying values and proceeds or cash outlays on treasury stock transactions are never taken to the income statements as gains or losses. Rather they are reflected in the capital accounts with gains going to paid-in capital and losses being charged to either paid-in capital or retained earnings. See para 12 of APB 6.

42. (579,P1,4) (c) The requirement is 1978 EPS. Earnings per share is a ratio of adjusted earnings over adjusted shares outstanding. In this problem there was $2,144,000 of net income with no adjustments. The 500,000 shares outstanding at year end included 100,000 issued on 10/1/78. Para 47 of APB 15 requires EPS to be computed based on the weighted average of the shares outstanding during the year. Thus the 100,000 shares issued on 10/1/78 were equivalent to 25,000 shares outstanding for the year, and the ratio is $2,144,000/425,000 shares, which equals $5.04.

43. (579,P1,13) (c) The requirement is the effect of a series of transactions on the common stock, paid-in capital, and retained earnings of Ray Company. The solutions approach is to journalize the entries affecting the three accounts. First the cash dividends should be recorded as a $3,800,000 debit to retained earnings with a credit to cash and dividends payable as illustrated below. Next make the entry for the issuance of a 15,000 share (300,000 shares x 5%) stock dividend when the market price is $20/share and par value is $10/share. The entries result in debits to retained earnings of $4,100,000 and credits to common stock and paid in capital of $150,000 each.

Retained earnings	$3,800,000	
Cash		$2,700,000
Dividends payable		1,100,000
Retained earnings	$ 300,000	
Stock		$ 150,000
Paid-in capital		150,000

44. (579,Q1,1) (c) The requirement is the total shareholders' equity at the end of 1978. The solutions approach is to analyze each of the transactions that occurred during the year as illustrated in the journal entries below. Next analyze the effect of each entry on the beginning shareholders' equity of $980,000. Both treasury stock acquisitions reduce total shareholders' equity. The sale of treasury stock and the reported net income increase shareholders' equity. The fact that the state of incorporation places a restriction on distribution of retained earnings equal to the cost of the treasury stock only means that retained earnings will be divided into appropriated and unappropriated (this has no effect on total shareholders' equity).

Journal Entries			Effect on Share-holders' Equity
			980 Beg. bal.
TS	$28		
Cash		$28	−28
TS	27		
Cash		27	−27
Cash	48		
TS (FIFO)		43	
Pd.-in cap.		5	+48
NI	110		
RE		110	+110
			1,083 End. bal.

45. (579,Q1,4) (a) The requirement is the credit to "capital in excess of par" as a result of conversion of $900,000 of convertible bonds to common stock. The solutions approach is to prepare the journal entry to record the conversion at book value to determine the credit to paid-in capital. Since $900,000 of bonds was converted, bonds payable must be debited. Common stock of $800 (40 shares of $20 par) is issued for each $1,000 bond. Thus $720,000 (900 x $800) is credited to common stock. The credit to discount on bonds payable is 9% (900 bonds converted ÷ 10,000 bonds outstanding) of the total unamortized discount at the time of conversion. Thus the credit to discount on bonds payable is $45,000, which in turn requires a credit of $135,000 to paid-in capital to balance the journal entry.

Bonds payable	$900,000	
Common stock		$720,000
Discount on BP		45,000
Paid-in capital		135,000

46. (579,T1,18) (c) Dilutive common stock equivalents are used in the computation of both fully diluted and primary earnings per share. A common stock equivalent is a security that is not in the form of a common stock but contains a provision to enable its holder to become a common stockholder and thus is in substance equivalent to common stock. See paras 24 and 40 of APB 15.

MAY 1981 ANSWERS

47. (581,P1,12) (a) The requirement is to compute Redford's 1980 earnings per common share. The solutions approach is to recall the distinction between a simple and a complex capital structure. This problem deals with a simple capital structure, because no potentially dilutive securities exist. The earnings available to the common stockholders is computed as $780,000 net income — ($2 x 20,000) preferred dividends = $740,000. The number of common shares outstanding is computed as 100,000 shares outstanding for the entire year plus the 10,000 (100,000 x .10) shares issued on July 1, 1980. Remember that stock splits and stock dividends are retroactive adjustments of the number of outstanding common shares and are not weighted by the number of months the stock dividend has been outstanding (APB 15, para 48). Thus, the total common shares assumed to be outstanding during 1980 is 110,000. The EPS is computed as

$$\frac{\text{Earnings available to the C.S. Holder}}{\text{Weighted average number of shares of C.S. outstanding}} = \frac{\$740,000}{110,000} = \$6.73$$

48.   (581,P1,18)   (c)   The requirement is to compute the earnings per common share for Sonic Company. Since Sonic Company has no potentially dilutive securities, the specific requirement is to find EPS for a simple capital structure. The formula is

$$\text{EPS} = (\text{Net income} - \text{Pref. dividends}) \div \begin{array}{l}\text{weighted}\\\text{average}\\\text{number of}\\\text{shares}\end{array}$$

The numerator in this problem is $112,000 ($120,000 net income — $8,000 preferred dividends). Recall that preferred dividends are always deducted for <u>cumulative</u> preferred stock and for <u>noncumulative</u> only if declared. Although this problem does not indicate whether the preferred stock is cumulative, the fact that dividends were declared is a sufficient indication that they should be deducted. Since no common stock transactions occurred during the period, the denominator for the EPS computation is simply the 20,000 shares of common stock outstanding. The EPS is computed as $112,000 ÷ 20,000 = $5.60.

49.   (581,P1,20)   (d)   The requirement is to compute the amount of the reduction in common stock as a result of a quasi-reorganization. The solutions approach is to prepare the journal entries to give effect to the quasi-reorganization.

Step 1: Revalue all assets to their current values by adjusting the deficit in retained earnings.

RE	500,000	
P, P & E		350,000
OA		150,000

Step 2: Create enough paid-in-capital to eliminate the $900,000 deficit in retained earnings, which results after the above entry is posted. Since a $300,000 balance already exists in paid-in-capital, the additional amount needed is $600,000.

CS	600,000	
Paid-in Capital		600,000

Step 3: Eliminate the deficit in Retained Earnings.

Paid-in-Capital	900,000	
RE		900,000

The answer ($600,000) is derived in the second entry; the third entry is not necessary if you remembered that common stock would not be further affected.

50.   (581,Q1,10)   (a)   The requirement is to determine the appropriate compensation expense for 1980. The future compensation expense is calculated as the difference between the option price and the market price of the stock on the date the option was granted times the number of shares which can be purchased under the option. On the date of grant, the option price was $40 per share and the market price was $40 per share, therefore, the difference is zero and the compensation expense is zero.

51.   (581,Q1,11)   (b)   The requirement is the same as for the above item. If the market price is $45 per share on the grant date and the option price is $40 per share, the total compensation expense is $5 x 1,000 shares or $5,000. However, this total compensation should be allocated over the number of periods the employee is required to provide service in order to be able to exercise the option. In this problem, two years of service are required; therefore, the compensation expense is $5,000 ÷ 2, or $2,500 per year.

52.   (581,Q1,12)   (c)   The requirement is to determine the gain on the sale of stock warrants. The solution approach is to calculate the amount of purchase price allocated to the stock and the amount allocated to the warrants. This allocation is made on the basis of the ratios of the relative fair market values of the stock and warrants over the total fair market value of stock and warrants. The combined fair market value is $60 ($50 stock + $10 warrants). The allocation is:

Warrants: $10/$60 x $108,000 = $18,000
Stock: $50/$60 x $108,000 = $90,000

The final step is to compute the gain or loss on the sale of warrants by comparing the purchase price allocated to the warrants with the selling price of the warrants. The selling price was $19,800 and the allocation of purchase price to the warrants was $18,000; therefore, the gain on the sale of warrants was $1,800.

53.   (581,Q1,13)   (a)   The requirement is to determine the balance in retained earnings on 4/1/80. The solutions approach to this problem is to make the entries in a T-account. Solve for the debit to retained earnings due to the stock dividend. When the

stock dividend is less than 20-25%, the retained earnings account is debited for the number of shares issued multiplied by the market price per share. The stock dividend is stated as 10%; therefore, the market price is used and the debit to retained earnings is for 900 shares times $8 per share or $7,200. Retained earning is also debited for the $16,000 loss.

	R.E.		
Stk. Dividend	$ 7,200	$73,000	Beg. Balance
Loss	16,000		
		$49,800	End Balance

54. (581,Q2,23) (b) The requirement in this problem is to solve for the number of shares for calculating earnings per share. Palisades Corporation has a simple capital structure; therefore, a single earnings per share figure is calculated. It is based on the weighted average number of shares of common stock outstanding during the year. When stock is sold during the year, the shares issued must be weighted for the period of time they are outstanding. The weighted average is calculated by multiplying the number of shares issued by the fraction of a year during which the stock was outstanding [3,000 x (8 ÷ 12)], or 2,000 shares. The total number of shares is:

$$45,000 + 2,000 = 47,000 \text{ shares}$$

55. (581,T1,1) (a) The requirement is the most likely effect of a stock split on the par value per share and the number of shares outstanding. A stock split results in a decrease in the par value per share and a corresponding increase in the number of shares outstanding.

56. (581,T1,12) (a) The requirement is the treatment of the excess of the subscription price over the par value of common stock subscribed. The excess is recorded as additional paid-in capital when the subscription is received.

57. (581,T1,16) (a) The requirement is how an excess of the amount received upon resale over the price paid for treasury stock should be shown when the cost method of accounting for treasury stock transactions is used; the excess is credited to additional paid-in capital. Answer (b) is wrong because the reissuance of treasury stock is considered a transaction related to the capital of company; retained earnings is never credited. Answers (c) and (d) are wrong because per para 27 of APB 9, charges or credits resulting from transactions in a company's own capital stock should be excluded from the determination of net income or the results from operations under all circumstances.

58. (581,T1,19) (b) The requirement is when should the compensation cost for a compensatory stock option plan be recognized when the date of grant

and the measurement date are the same. Per para 12 of APB 25, compensation cost in stock option plans should be recognized as an expense of one or more periods in which an employee renders the services. The measurement date for determining the compensation cost is the first date on which are known both (1) the number of shares an individual employee is entitled to received, and (2) the option or purchase price, if any. That date for many or most plans is the date an option is granted. The compensation cost is measured as the difference between the quoted market price of the stock at the measurement date and the amount, if any, the employee is required to pay.

59. (581,T1,24) (c) The requirement is the treatment of convertible securities that are not common stock equivalents in computing fully diluted earnings per share. Convertible securities which are not common stock equivalents enter into the computation of fully diluted earnings per share only if they are dilutive. The if-converted method is used to determine the incremental effect of the conversion assumption.

60. (581,T1,25) (a) The requirement is the midyear event that must be treated as ocurring at the beginning of the year for the purposes of computing the weighted average number of shares outstanding during the year. The computation of earnings per share data should be based on the weighted average number of common shares and common share equivalents outstanding during each period presented. Per para 3A of APB 15, if the number of common shares outstanding increases as a result of a stock dividend or stock split, the computation should give retroactive recognition to the beginning of the period in which they were declared or issued.

61. (581,T1,38) (b) The requirement is the account which is credited at the date of grant for a compensatory stock option plan for which the date of the grant and the measurement date are the same. The measurement date per para 10 of APB 15 is that date on which are known both (1) the number of shares that an individual employee is entitled to receive and (2) the option or purchase price, if any. The date of grant is that date when the corporation foregoes the principal alternative use (sale) of the shares. When these dates coincide, the amount of compensation expense is the difference between the market price and the option price at the date of grant. Also, APB 25 specifies that the compensation expense should be recognized in the period(s) in which the employee performs services. Thus, deferred compensation cost (answer (c)) is debited and stock options outstanding is credited. The deferred compensation expense account is a contra stockholders' equity account and is shown as an offset to the stock options outstanding account in the Stockholders' Equity section of the balance sheet.

ANSWER OUTLINE

Problem 1   Earnings Per Share

a.   For EPS, subtract preferred dividends from net
income
    For noncumulative, only when declared
    Always if dividend is cumulative
    Except when assuming conversion
        Must be common stock equivalents for PEPS
        Determined at time of issuance
        (2/3 prime interest rate)
        Or if included in FDEPS

b1.   TS method used when option price less than market
price
    Usually for substantially all of the three months
        preceding year-end
If option price exceeded market price, options are
antidilutive
    Not included in EPS calculations

b2.   TS method limited to reacquisition of 20% of out-
standing
Any remaining funds are considered to reduce debt
    Any further remaining funds assumed invested in
        securities
All net of tax effects

c1.   Convertible bonds are CSE if they yield less than
2/3 prime rate
    Determined at issuance
    Are included in both PEPS and FDEPS if dilutive
    Interest saving less tax effect added to EPS numerator
    Shares from conversion added to EPS denominator

c2.   Convertible bonds, not CSE, are included in FDEPS
    If dilutive
    Interest saving less tax effect added to EPS numerator
    Shares from conversion added to EPS denominator

UNOFFICIAL ANSWER

Problem 1   Earnings Per share

a.   Dividends on outstanding preferred stock must
be subtracted from net income or added to
net loss for the period before computing EPS
on the common shares. This generalization
will be modified by the various features and
different requirements preferred stock may
have with respect to dividends. Thus, if
preferred stock is cumulative, it is necessary
to subtract its current dividend requirements
from net income (or to add them to net
loss) in order to arrive at the amount into
which to divide outstanding common shares
to compute EPS on the latter. This must

be done regardless of whether or not the
preferred dividends were **actually** declared.
Where the preferred shares are noncumulative,
only preferred dividends actually declared
during the current period need be subtracted
from net income (or added to net loss) to
arrive at the amount to be used in EPS
calculations.

In case the preferred shares are convertible
into common stock, when assuming conversion,
dividend requirements on the preferred shares
are not deducted from net income. This
applies when testing for potential dilution to
determine whether or not the diluted EPS
figures for the period are lower than primary
EPS figures. Diluted EPS figures are reported
if they are lower by 3% or more than the
primary EPS figure; if the degree of dilution
is less than 3%, diluted figures are not reported.

It is possible for preferred stock to be a
common stock equivalent. A common stock
equivalent is a security which is not, in form,
a common stock but which contains provision
to enable its holder to become a common
stockholder and which, because of the terms
and circumstances under which it was issued,
is in substance equivalent to a common stock.
The basic test for convertible preferred shares
is applied when the shares are first issued. If
at that time the cash yield (dividend rate) of
the convertible preferred shares is less than
two-thirds of the then-current bank prime
interest rate, they should be considered common stock equivalents. Common stock equivalents are added to common shares outstanding
to determine primary EPS. If preferred shares
are accorded this treatment, their dividends
are not subtracted from income for EPS
calculation purposes.

b.   1.   When options and warrants to buy common stock are outstanding and their
exercise price (i.e., proceeds the corporation would derive from issuance of common stock pursuant to the warrants and
options) is less than the average price at
which the company could acquire its
outstanding shares as treasury stock, the
treasury stock method is generally applicable. In these circumstances, existence
of the options and warrants would be
dilutive. However, if the exercise price
of options and warrants exceeded the

average price of common stock, the cash proceeds from their assumed exercise would provide for repurchasing more common shares than were issued when the warrants were exercised, thereby reducing the number of shares outstanding. In these circumstances assumed exercise of the warrants would be anti-dilutive, so exercise would not be presumed for purposes of computing primary EPS.

2. The application of the treasury-stock method is modified if the number of common shares issuable upon the exercise of warrants and options exceeds 20% of the number of common shares outstanding at the end of the period. The applicable procedure in such event is to assume that all warrants and options have been exercised and the aggregate proceeds therefrom are applied in two steps. First, funds are applied to repurchase outstanding common shares at the average market price during the period (treasury-stock method) but not to exceed 20% of the outstanding shares. Next, the balance of funds are applied to reduce any short-term or long-term borrowings and any remaining funds are assumed to be invested in United States government securities or commercial paper, with appropriate recognition of any income tax effects.

c. 1. Convertible debentures are common stock equivalents when at the time of their issuance their cash yield rate of interest (or lowest scheduled rate in the first five years thereafter) is less than two-thirds of the then-current bank prime interest rate. If their conversion would have a dilutive effect, then for purposes of calculating primary EPS, their interest (less tax effect) is added to net income as the numerator of the EPS calculation while the number of shares resulting from their assumed conversion is added to the denominator portion of the EPS calculation.

2. In case convertible debentures are not treated as common stock equivalents (therefore, are not treated as having

been converted for purposes of calculating primary EPS) they might still be accorded the treatment of conversion for purposes of calculating fully diluted EPS figures. For this to happen, other elements would also have to enter into the fully diluted EPS calculations in conjunction with convertible debentures and the convertible debentures would have had to be issued at an original interest rate of more than two-thirds the prime interest rate. In arriving at the calculation of fully diluted EPS figures where convertible debentures are assumed to be converted, their interest (less tax effect) is added back to net income as the numerator element of the EPS calculation while the number of shares of common stock into which they would be convertible is added to the shares outstanding to arrive at the denominator element of the calculation.

ANSWER OUTLINE

Problem 2   Common Stock Equivalents

a. Common stock equivalents (CSE) are equivalent to common stock
    But are not in the form of common stock
    E.g., CSE values are determined by common stock characteristics or conversion features
  CSEs are reflected in both primary and fully diluted EPS
    If their effect is dilutive
  Convertible securities are CSE if
    They yield less than 2/3 of the prime rate at issuance
    Or have same terms as other outstanding CSE
    Or another convertible CSE is issued with same terms
  Options, warrants, etc., are always CSE
    Including convertible securities requiring cash payments
  Participating securities with common stock features are CSE
  Contingent issuances, based only on passage of time, are CSE

b. Complex capital structure has potentially dilutive convertible securities, options, etc., which could dilute EPS
  A complex capital structure requires dual EPS presentation
    Primary earnings per share (PEPS)
      Based on outstanding stock and CSE
    Fully diluted earnings per share (FDEPS)

Based on all contingent issuances of common stock

Required disclosures for complex capital structure

Summary descriptions of outstanding securities

Schedule explaining computation of PEPS and FDEPS

Number of shares issued upon conversion, etc.

The effect on EPS of conversion as if they had taken place at the beginning of the period

Effect on EPS of intended use of stock sale proceeds to retire debt

UNOFFICIAL ANSWER

Problem 2   Common Stock Equivalents

a.   A common stock equivalent is a security which, because of the terms and the circumstances under which it was issued, is in substance equivalent to common stock. The securities are not common stock in form, but a characteristic of a common stock equivalent is that a large part of its value is derived from its common stock characteristics or conversion privileges. Common stock equivalents are included in both primary and fully diluted earnings-per-share computations only when their effect is dilutive.

Convertible securities that yield less than two-thirds of the bank prime interest rate at the time of issuance are considered common stock equivalents. Also, convertible securities issued with the same terms as those of an outstanding common stock equivalent, regardless of their yield, are considered common stock equivalents. Outstanding convertible securities that were not originally a common stock equivalent become a common stock equivalent if another convertible security with the same terms is issued and classified as a common stock equivalent.

Options and warrants, stock purchase contracts, and certain agreements to issue common stock in the future are considered to be common stock equivalents. Convertible securities that allow or require the payment of cash at the exercise date are considered to be equivalent to warrants.

Some participating securities and two-class common stock are considered to be common stock equivalents if their participation features enable the holders to share in the earnings potential on the same basis as that of common stockholders.

Finally, contingent shares are common stock equivalents if they are to be issued in the future upon the mere passage of time.

b.   A capital structure is regarded as complex when it includes potentially dilutive convertible securities, options, warrants, or other rights that upon conversion or exercise could, in the aggregate, dilute earnings per common share.

When a corporation has a complex capital structure, there should be a dual presentation with equal prominence on the face of the earnings statement. This presentation is to include a primary earnings per share that is based on outstanding common shares and securities equivalent to common shares that have a dilutive effect divided into net earnings adjusted for any interest or dividends paid on the common stock equivalents. Also included in this presentation is the calculation of the fully diluted earnings per share. This is a pro forma presentation which reflects dilution of earnings per share that would have occurred if all contingent issues of common stocks that would individually reduce earnings per share had taken place at the beginning of the year.

Additional disclosures when a complex structure exists include (1) a summary description explaining pertinent rights and privileges of the various outstanding securities, (2) a schedule or note explaining the basis upon which primary and fully diluted earnings per share are calculated, (3) a disclosure of the numbers of shares issued upon conversion, exercise, or satisfaction of required conditions during at least the most recent fiscal period and any other subsequent period presented. If conversion during the current period would have affected primary earnings per share if they had taken place at the beginning of the period, then supplementary information should be furnished for the latest period showing what primary earnings per share would have been if such conversion had taken place at the beginning of that period. If the proceeds from a sale of common stock or common stock equivalents are used to retire or there is the intent to retire preferred stock or debt, then disclosure should be made of what the earnings per share would have been if the retirement had taken place at the beginning of the period.

ANSWER OUTLINE

Problem 3   Primary vs Fully Diluted EPS

b.   Primary earnings per share computation versus fully diluted earnings per share computation

b1.   Common stock equivalents, if dilutive, increase number of shares for both

b2.   Convertible securities not common stock equivalents, if dilutive, increase number of shares for fully diluted

b3. Antidilutive securities are not included.in either earnings per share figures

UNOFFICIAL ANSWER

Problem 3   Primary vs Fully Diluted EPS

Part b.

1. Common stock equivalents are included in the computation of the number of shares for both primary earnings per share and fully diluted earnings per share as long as the common stock equivalents have a dilutive effect.

2. Convertible securities that are not common stock equivalents are excluded from the computation of the number of shares for primary earnings per share; however, they are included in the computation of the number of shares for fully diluted earnings per share as long as they have a dilutive effect.

3. Antidilutive securities are excluded from both primary earnings per share and fully diluted earnings per share.

SOLUTION GUIDE

Problem 4   EPS (Darren Company)

An alternative solution has been substituted for the AICPA unofficial answer.

1. The requirements are twofold: number of shares and adjusted net income for both PEPS and FDEPS. Before immersing yourself in the details of the problem, quickly review the basic rules in APB 15. This will preclude your confusing APB 15 rules as a result of reading all of the details of the problem.

2. Work through the problem beginning with the debt and stockholders' equity information. Since there were various issuances of stock during the year, you need to compute a weighted average. Thus, you need to subtract the shares issued throughout the year from the 6,900,000 shares outstanding at year end. You may wish to construct a time diagram to indicate the issuances throughout the year. You can also use a time diagram to simplify the weighted average computation of shares outstanding during the year. As indicated in schedule 1 below, the weighted average of shares outstanding throughout the year is 6,634,000 shares.

3. Next work through all of the extra information in the problem.

3.1 The other long-term debt provides you with an interest rate of 6-7% which could have been, but was not, necessary in the treasury stock method of accounting for stock options.

3.2 The first step is to compute "benchmark" EPS, the first two columns of the second table in the solution. This EPS of $ .54 will be used to determine dilution. Note that supporting schedules 2 and 3 are needed before the "benchmark" can be computed.

3.3 The 4% convertible debentures are anti-dilutive. The effect of converting a debenture would be to divide 25 shares into the interest savings of $40 ($1,000 bond @ 4%) less income taxes at 48%. The effect would be to divide about $20 by 25 shares, which results in an eighty cent plus EPS.

3.4 The convertible preferred is also anti-dilutive, because the $4 dividend would be divided by 1.2 shares, resulting in an EPS of over $3.

3.5 The options are common stock equivalents and are dilutive at the end of the year as the option price of $33 is less than the average market price. Thus you must apply the treasury stock method to the options. While there are several possible applications of the method, the unofficial answer assumes one-fourth of the options are exercised in the third period and one-fourth of the options are exercised in the fourth period. The proceeds received are used to repurchase the stock at year-end. The net effect is to increase the denominator of the EPS ratio by 4,132 shares. Note that no further adjustment is necessary for FDEPS as ending market price of the stock is the same as the average market price.

4. In computing fully diluted earnings the only adjustment required is to assume that all the preferred that were converted during the year were converted at the beginning of the year. Any conversion which takes place during a year is rolled back to the beginning of the year when computing fully diluted EPS, even though conversion is anti-dilutive. This is done only for shares actually converted. See note to unofficial solution.

ALTERNATIVE SOLUTION

Problem 4   EPS (Darren Company)

Tests for Common Stock
Equivalency and Dilution

Potentially Dilutive Securities	Incremental Effects Per Share	Benchmark EPS = $.54 Dilutive or Antidilutive	Equivalency Status
1. Convertible Debentures	$\frac{\$40(1-.48)}{25 \text{ shares}} = \$ .83$	Antidilutive	No; 4% > (2/3)(5%)
2. Convertible Preferred Stock	$\frac{\$4}{1.2 \text{ Shares}} = \$3.33$	Antidilutive	Yes; 5-1/3% < (2/3)(9%)
3. Options	Primary and Fully Diluted: $\frac{\text{No numerator effect}}{4,132 \text{ shares (schedule 1)}}$	Dilutive	Always

Computations of Primary and
Fully Diluted EPS

Items	Benchmark EPS Numerator	Denominator	Primary Numerator	Denominator	Fully Diluted Numerator	Denominator
Net Income	$ 8,600,000		$ 8,600,000		$ 8,600,000	
Pref. Dividend (schedule 2)	(5,020,000)		(5,020,000)		(4,800,000)	
Common Shares (schedule 3)		6,634,000		6,634,000		6,634,000
Conv. Pref. Stock (120,000 − 54,000)						66,000
Options				4,132		4,132
Totals	$ 3,580,000 ÷	6,634,000	$ 3,580,000 ÷	6,638,132	$ 3,800,000 ÷	6,704,132
Key to Problem Requirements			(b.1)	(a.1)	(b.2)	(a.2)
EPS	$ .54 [*]		$ .54		$ .57	

[*]EPS would be reported at $.54 as in the case of a simple capital structure. See complete explanatory note on the next page.

Note:

Earnings per share would be reported as $.54 (benchmark EPS). Because the 3% dilution test is not met, a dual presentation is not required. Because they are anti-dilutive, the convertible debentures are omitted from the calculation of fully diluted earnings per share. They are omitted from the calculation of primary earnings per share because they are not common stock equivalents. Because it is anti-dilutive, the convertible preferred stock _not_ actually converted is omitted from the calculation of primary and fully diluted earnings per share.

The convertible preferred stock actually converted during the year is included in the weighted average number of shares actually outstanding for calculating primary earnings per share. Its effect on the weighted average number of shares actually outstanding is from the date of conversion to the end of the year.

For fully diluted earnings per share, the actual conversion of shares is *assumed* at the beginning of the year. This conversion is *assumed* for fully diluted earnings per share only, *not* for primary earnings per share. The "if converted" method for fully diluted earnings per share must be applied to these securities from the beginning of the year even if the effect is anti-dilutive. The dividends actually paid on these shares converted must be added back to the adjusted net income for fully diluted earnings per share. This is a technicality which will not likely appear on the exam again. *(Professional Standards, Volume Three, Accounting, Commerce Clearing House, Inc., AC § U 2011.152.)*

Schedule 1

Schedule of Shares Assumed Reacquired with Proceeds

First Quarter — Not computed since the average quarterly market price ($31) did not exceed the exercise price ($33)	---
Second Quarter — Not computed since the average quarterly market price ($33) did not exceed the exercise price ($33)	---
Third Quarter — 100,000 shares x ¼ x $33 exercise price = $825,000; $825,000 ÷ $35 average quarterly market price	23,571
Fourth Quarter — 100,000 shares x ¼ x $33 exercise price = $825,000; $825,000 ÷ $37 average quarterly market price	22,297
Total shares assumed reacquired with proceeds	45,868

Shares represented by options outstanding (100,000 x ½ yr.)	50,000
Shares assumed acquired	45,868
Denominator shares	4,132

Schedule 2

Preferred Stock Dividend Schedule

Shares outstanding all year	1,200,000
Preferred stock dividend	x $ 4
Fully diluted effect	$4,800,000
Shares converted:	
80,000 x $2	160,000
20,000 x $3	60,000
Primary effect	$5,020,000

Schedule 3

Common Shares for "Benchmark" EPS

Shares outstanding from January 1, 1974:		
Total shares issued at December 31, 1974		7,500,000
Less: Treasury stock	600,000	
Shares issued in acquisition of Brett Industires	800,000	
Shares converted from preferred	120,000	(1,520,000)
Shares outstanding from January 1, 1974		5,980,000
Shares issued in acquisition of Brett Industries in a purchase transaction:		
Issued April 1, 1974 (800,000 x ¾)		600,000
Shares issued upon conversion of 100,000 shares of preferred stock:		
Issued July 1, 1974 (96,000 x ½)	48,000	
Issued October 1, 1974 (24,000 x ¼)	6,000	54,000
		6,634,000

ANSWER OUTLINE

Problem 5   Categories of Stockholders' Equity

a.   Contributed capital is amount paid in for all stock
      and amounts capitalized by board of directors,
      including
           Legal capital
           Premiums over par
           Donations of assets
           Assessments on stockholders
           Stock subscription forfeitures
           Gains on treasury stock
           Excess on common par issued for convertibles
           Acquisiton of TS below par
           Tax benefits on certain stock options
      Retained earnings are net earnings less
           Net losses from operations
           Dividends (cash or stock)
           Net effects of prior period adjustments
           Retained earnings may be appropriated or unap-
               propriated
      Appraisal capital is the recognized revaluation of assets
           Not a conventional accounting procedure

b1.   A stock split is a proportional distribution of stock
       to stockholders
            In excess of 20%-25% of the outstanding shares
            Causes material decrease in market value
            May be called a stock split "effected as a dividend"

b2.   Stock dividend: Dr retained earnings for dividend
       market value
       Stock split: no change in shareholders' equity accounts
            Just a change in par or stated value

b3.   Unissued stock dividends are disclosed in shareholders'
       equity
            Not a liability, as they may be rescinded
            Do not require the use of corporate assets
            Disclose number of shares to be issued

c.   Reduce net income if compensation expense is
       recognized
            By amount market price exceeds option price
                At measurement date
            Expense recognized in periods earned by employee
            EPS reduced by reduced income
                Number of shares outstanding increased

UNOFFICIAL ANSWER

Problem 5   Categories of Stockholders' Equity

a.   The general categories of a corporation's capi-
      tal are contributed (invested) capital, earned
      capital (retained earnings), and appraisal capi-
      tal.

Contributed capital represents the amounts paid in for all classes of shares of stock and the amounts capitalized by order of the corporation's board of directors. Included in contributed capital is legal capital, which is usually the aggregate par value or stated value of the shares issued. Legal capital is usually not subject to withdrawal; it is intended to protect corporate creditors. Contributed capital also includes other amounts in addition to the legal capital. These amounts are generally referred to as additional paid-in capital and include the following:

· Premiums over the par (stated) value of the stock issued (including stock dividends).
· Donations of assets to the corporation by stockholders or others.
· Assessments on stockholders.
· Forfeitures of stock subscriptions.
· Excess of proceeds from reissuing treasury stock over its cost.
· Conversion of convertible bonds or preferred stock.
· Reacquisition of outstanding shares at an amount below par (stated) value.
· Tax benefits from certain stock options.

Retained earnings are the accumulated net earnings of a corporation in excess of any net losses from operations and dividends (cash or stock). Total retained earnings should also include prior-period adjustments as direct increases or decreases and may include certain reserves. These reserves are appropriations of retained earnings as unavailable for dividends. These reserves and related restrictions may arise as a result of a restriction in a bond indenture or other formal agreement or they may be created at the discretion of the board of directors.

Appraisal capital represents the recognized upward revaluation of net assets. This capital is unrealized from a conventional accounting point of view and should, therefore, be segregated from contributed capital and retained earnings. Because such write-ups are a departure from generally accepted accounting principles, their use is usually restricted to situations where state law provides for the creation of appraisal surplus and the payment of dividends therefrom. Even if legally acceptable, the creation of appraisal surplus can present some significant reporting problems.

b. 1. A stock split effected in the form of a dividend is a distribution of corporate stock to present stockholders in proportion to each stockholder's current holdings and can be expected to cause a material decrease in the market value per share of the stock. Accounting Research Bulletin No. 43 specifies that a distribution in excess of 20% to 25% of the number of shares previously outstanding would cause a material decrease in the market value. This is a characteristic of a stock split as opposed to a stock dividend, but, for legal reasons, the term "dividend" must be used for this distribution. From an accounting viewpoint, it should be disclosed as a stock split effected in the form of a dividend because it meets the accounting definition of a stock split as explained above.

2. The stock split effected in the form of a dividend differs from an ordinary stock dividend in the amount of other paid-in capital or retained earnings to be capitalized. An ordinary stock dividend involves capitalizing (charging) retained earnings equal to the market value of the stock distributed. A stock split effected in the form of a dividend involves no charge to retained earnings or other paid-in capital if the par (stated) value of the stock is reduced in inverse proportion to the distribution. If the stock's par (stated) value is not reduced in inverse proportion to the distribution of stock, other paid-in capital or retained earnings would be charged for the par (stated) value of the additional shares issued.

Another distinction between a stock dividend and a stock split is that a stock dividend usually involves distributing additional shares of the same class of stock with the same par or stated value. A stock split usually involves distributing additional shares of the same class of stock but with a proportionate reduction in par or stated value. The aggregate par or stated value would then be the same before and after the stock split.

3. A declared but unissued stock dividend should be classified as part of corporate capital rather than as a liability in a statement of financial position. A stock dividend affects only capital accounts; that is, retained earnings are decreased and contributed capital is increased. Thus, there is no debt to be paid, and, consequently, there is no severance of corporate assets when a stock dividend is issued. Furthermore, stock dividends declared can be revoked by a corporation's board of directors any time prior to issuance. Finally, the corporation usually will formally announce its intent to issue a specific number of additional shares, and these shares must be reserved for this purpose.

c. Accounting for this stock option plan will reduce net earnings if compensation expense is to be recognized. If the option price equals or exceeds the stock's market price at the measurement date, which is the date of grant for a traditional stock option plan, no compensation is recognized, and, accordingly, there is no effect on net earnings.

If the option price is less than the stock's market price at the measurement date, the difference is considered compensation. This compensation should be recognized as an expense of one or more periods in which an employee performs services. The period or periods benefitted may be specified in the plan or may be inferred from the terms or from the past pattern of such plans. Compensation expense would, of course, reduce net earnings each period.

Earnings per share computations are based on adjusted net earnings divided by adjusted number of shares. The adjusted net earnings are affected as discussed above. The adjusted number of shares may include potential common stock represented by these options, thereby diluting the earnings per share because the options are common stock equivalents.

ANSWER OUTLINE

Problem 6   Stock Option Plans

b1.   Accounting for stock purchase (option) plans at stock issue date

	Noncompensatory Plan	
·Cash	XXX	
Capital Stock (par value)		XXX
Additional paid-in capital		XXX
	Compensatory Plan	
Cash	XXX	
Compensation Expense(1)	XXX	
Capital stock (par value)		XXX
Additional paid-in capital(2)		XXX

(1) Dr. stock options outstanding if expense recorded previously

(2) Credit = (debit to cash + debit to options outstanding or compensation expense) — credit to capital stock

b2. Accounting for compensatory stock option plan at date of grant

When Date of Grant and Measurement Date Coincide

Compensation expense or deferred compensation	XXX(1)	
Stock options outstanding		XXX

(1) Amount = Market price of stock — option price

When Date of Grant and Measurement Date Do Not Coincide

No entry is made

UNOFFICIAL ANSWER

Problem 6   Stock Option Plans

Part b.

1.   For the noncompensatory stock purchase plan, the entry at the date the stock is issued is as follows:

- Debit to cash (or appropriate liability account if amounts were previously withheld through payroll deductions) for the cash price.
- Credit to capital stock for the par value of the stock.
- Credit to additional paid-in capital for the excess of the cash price over the par value.

For the compensatory stock option plan, the entry at the date the stock is issued is as follows:

- Debit to cash for the cash price.
- Debit to stock options outstanding (when the compensation expense has already been recognized) or debit to compensation expense.
- Credit to capital stock for the par value of the stock.
- Credit to additional paid-in capital for the excess of (a) the debit to cash (cash price) and (b) the debit to stock options outstanding, over the par value.

2.   If the date of the grant and the measurement date are the same, the entry for the compensatory stock option plan at the date of the grant is to debit compensation or deferred compensation expense and credit stock options outstanding for the excess of the market price of the stock over the option price.

If the date of the grant and the measurement date are different, no entry is made for the compensatory stock option plan at the date of the grant.

SOLUTION GUIDE

Problem 7   Stock Appreciation Rights

1.   The requirements are to prepare a five year schedule of compensation expense related to SAR's and to prepare journal entries for three of those years. Before attempting the schedule, refresh your memory concerning what SAR's are and the way in which we account for them under FASB Interpretation No. 28.

2.   Recall that SAR's entitle the holder to receive share appreciation, i.e., the excess of the stock's market price at the date of exercise over a pre-established price. The appreciation may be paid in cash (as in this problem), shares of stock; or a combination of both. This means that unlike stock compensation plans, in which the expense of the plan to the company can generally be measured at the date of grant, the compensation expense for SAR's cannot be accurately measured until they are exercised.

3.   Until that date, however, the matching principle indicates that compensation expense must be recorded. This is accomplished by establishing an accrued liability during the service period on the basis of the difference between the market price for the period and the pre-established price, i.e., what could be called an "esti-measurable" expense at any given point. Using the data from the problem this means:

3.1   With a three year service period, year one must accrue a liability of 1/3 of the appreciation esti-measurable <u>at that point</u>. Year two must have accrued 2/3 of the appreciation esti-measurable, and at year three, 100% of apprecia-tion esti-measurable must be accrued. After that the accrued liability at the end of each period should equal what the <u>total</u> expense to the company <u>would be</u> if the holder exercised the SAR's at that point.

3.2   This means that compensation expense will be charged or credited each year until exercise with the amount needed to maintain the accrued liability balance at 33-1/3%, 66-2/3%, 100%, 100% . . . esti-measurable compensation. Note that compensation expense recorded <u>to date</u> must equal the balance of the esti-measurable liability accrued to date. It should be obvious that if at any time the market price of the stock is below the pre-established price, the company does not in fact have a liability and therefore the compensation expense recognized to date would be zero.

UNOFFICIAL ANSWER
Problem 7   Stock Appreciation Rights

(a)

Solution
Schedule of Compensation Expense
Stock Appreciation Rights (20,000)

Date	Market Price	Pre-Estab-lished Price	Esti-Measurable Compensa-tion	% To Be Accrued	Esti-Measurable Liability Accrued To Date	Period's Compensa-tion Expense	Comp. Exp. To Date
12/31/81	$36	$30	$120,000	33-1/3%	$ 40,000	$ 40,000	$ 40,000
12/31/82	39	30	180,000	66-2/3%	120,000	80,000	120,000
12/31/83	45	30	300,000	100%	300,000	180,000	300,000
12/31/84	36	30	120,000	100%	120,000	(180,000)	120,000
12/31/85	48	30	360,000	100%	360,000	240,000	360,000

(b)

1981	Compensation Expense - SAR's	40,000	
	Liability under Stock Appreciation Plan		40,000
1984	Liability under Stock Appreciation Plan	180,000	
	Compensation Expense - SAR's		180,000
1985	Compensation Expense - SAR's	240,000	
	Liability under Stock Appreciation Plan		240,000

ANSWER OUTLINE

Problem 8   Treasury Stock

b1.   Accounting for treasury stock when purchase price is less than par value

Cost method — Debit treasury stock for purchase price

Par method — Debit treasury stock for par value of shares
Credit paid-in capital for excess

b2.   Treasury stock when purchase price is greater than par value

  Cost method — Debit treasury stock for purchase price

  Par method — Debit treasury stock for par value of shares
        Debit excess to paid-in capital and/or retained earnings

b3.   Treasury stock when sold at less than purchase price, but more than par value

  Cost method — Credit treasury stock for cost
        Debit excess first to paid-in capital from prior treasury stock transactions and then to retained earnings

  Par method — Credit treasury stock for par
        Credit excess to paid-in capital

b4.   Treasury stock when sold at more than purchase price and par

  Cost method — Credit treasury stock for cost
        Credit excess to paid-in capital

  Par method — Credit treasury for par
        Credit excess to paid-in capital

b5.   Treasury stock transactions do not affect net income.

UNOFFICIAL ANSWER

Problem 8   Treasury Stock

1.   Under the cost method, treasury stock is debited for the purchase price of the shares even though the purchase price is less than the par value.

Under the par value method, treasury stock is debited for the par value of the shares, and a separate paid-in capital account is credited for the excess of the par value over the purchase price.

2.   Under the cost method, treasury stock is debited for the purchase price of the shares.

Under the par value method, treasury stock is debited for the par value of the shares, and the debit for the excess of the purchase price over the par value is assigned to additional paid-in capital arising from past transactions in the same class of stock and/or retained earnings.

3.   Under the cost method, treasury stock is credited for the original cost (purchase price) of the shares, and the excess of the original cost (purchase price) over the sales price first is debited to additional paid-in capital from earlier sales or retirements of treasury stock, and any remainder then is debited to retained earnings.

Under the par value method, treasury stock is credited for the par value of the shares, and the excess of the sales price over the par value is credited to additional paid-in capital from sale of treasury stock.

4.   Under the cost method, treasury stock is credited for the original cost (purchase price) of the shares, and the excess of the sales price over the original cost (purchase price) is credited to additional paid-in capital from sale of treasury stock.

Under the par value method, treasury stock is credited for the par value of the shares, and the excess of the sales price over the par value is credited to additional paid-in capital from sale of treasury stock.

5.   There is no effect on net income as a result of treasury stock transactions.

SOLUTION GUIDE

Problem 9   Stockholders' Equity Transactions

1.   Part a requires a worksheet to summarize stockholder equity transactions in 1977. The column headings are provided. Note that the beginning balances are indicated and should be put at the top of the worksheet including number of shares data.

2.   Since 12 transactions are indicated for 1977, the solutions approach is to analyze each transaction in terms of its journal entry.

2.1   February 1

Cash	$36,000,000	
Common stock		$20,000,000
Paid-in capital		16,000,000

(Sale of 2,000,000 shares common stock ($10 par) at $18/share)

2.2   February 15

Cash	$11,000,000	
Preferred stock		$10,000,000
Paid-in capital		900,000
Common stock warrants		100,000

(Sale of 100,000 shares of preferred stock ($100 par) and detachable common stock warrants at $110/share; allocate $1 to each warrant)

2.3   March 1

Treasury stock— common	$ 370,000	
Cash		$ 370,000

(Reacquisition of 20,000 shares treasury stock— common at $18.50/share)

2.4   March 15

Treasury stock— common	$ 210,000	
Donated capital		$ 210,000

(Donation of 10,000 shares of treasury stock— common when market was $21/share)

2.5   March 31

Retained earnings	$ 1,597,000	
Cash		$ 1,597,000

($.10/share cash dividend on common)

Beginning O/S	15,000,000 shares
Less beginning T/S	(1,000,000)
Sale	2,000,000
TS purchase	(20,000)
TS donation	(10,000)
	15,970,000 shares @ $.10
	= $1,597,000 dividend

2.6   April 15

Common stock warrants	$ 30,000	
Cash	600,000	
Common stock		$ 300,000
Paid-in capital		330,000

(Exercise of 30,000 of the outstanding common stock warrants; exercise price $20/share)

2.7   April 30

Cash	$ 2,000,000	
Common stock		$ 1,000,000
Paid-in capital		1,000,000

(Sale of 100,000 common shares to employees at $20/share per noncompensatory stock options—no value was attributed to the options when granted)

2.8   May 31

Retained earnings	$16,100,000	
Common stock		$ 8,050,000
Paid-in capital		8,050,000

(5% common stock dividend, $10 par and $20 market)

Beginning O/S	15,000,000 shares
Less beginning TS	(1,000,000)
Sale	2,000,000
TS purchase	(20,000)
TS donation	(10,000)
Exercise of warrants	30,000
Sale to employees	100,000
	16,100,000 x 5% =
	805,000 shares

2.9   June 30

Cash	$ 7,500,000	
Treasury stock- common		$ 5,970,000
Paid-in capital		1,530,000

(Sale of 300,000 treasury shares at $25; 20,000 shares acquired on March 1 cost $370,000, and the 280,000 other shares cost $5,600,000)

2.10 September 30

> | Retained earnings | $ 2,520,500 | |
> |---|---|---|
> | Common stock dividend payable | | $ 1,720,500 |
> | Preferred stock dividend payable | | 800,000 |
>
> (Preferred stock of $10,000,000 at 8% equals $800,000. Common stock shares outstanding are 17,205,000 — 16,100,000 in 2.8 above plus 805,000 stock dividend plus 300,000 TS sale — at $.10 is $1,720,500)

2.11 December 31

> | Common stock warrants | $ 70,000 | |
> |---|---|---|
> | Paid-in capital | | $ 70,000 |
>
> (Expiration of 70,000 warrants at $1—of the 100,000 issued, only 30,000 were exercised)

2.12 December 31

> | P&L account | $25,000,000 | |
> |---|---|---|
> | Retained earnings | | $25,000,000 |
>
> (net income for 1977)

3. Based on the analysis of each of the transactions, record the amounts in the summary worksheet previously prepared (note that the number of shares and rights is also required). This could have been done simultaneously with the analysis of each transaction.

4. Part b requires a worksheet showing the maximum amount available for cash dividends at 12/31/77 for Tomasco and how it would be distributed to common and preferred stockholders.

4.1 The solutions approach is to understand the capital structure which consists of a common stock, a 4% nonparticipating noncumulative preferred stock, and an 8% fully-participating cumulative preferred stock. Also the business had operated for five years and no dividends have been paid. Dividends are payable only from retained earnings.

4.2 Retained earnings at the end of 1977 are $850,000:

> | 1973 | $ (150,000) |
> |---|---|
> | 1974 | (130,000) |
> | 1975 | (120,000) |
> | 1976 | 250,000 |
> | 1977 | 1,000,000 |
> | | $ 850,000 |

4.3 The 4% nonparticipating noncumulative preferred will receive only $4,000 (4% of $100,000). Since this preferred stock is noncumulative there are no dividends in arrears.

4.4 The 8% fully-participating cumulative preferred will receive $400,000 as a result of the cumulative preferred status, i.e., 5 years at 8% of $1,000,000. The remaining retained earnings would be prorated between the 8% participating preferred and the common after $40,000 of dividends are allocated to common to compensate for the 8% allocated to the preferred in 1977.

> | Retained earnings available | $850,000 |
> |---|---|
> | 4% nonparticipating noncumulative preferred 1977 payment | (4,000) |
> | 8% participating cumulative preferred 1973—77 payment | (400,000) |
> | 8% of $500,000 of common to offset 1977 8% dividend for participating preferred | (40,000) |
> | To be prorated between participating, preferred, and common | $406,000 |

$$\text{Common} \quad \frac{\$500,000}{\$1,000,000 + \$500,000^*} \times \$406,000$$

$$= \$135,333$$

$$\text{Preferred} \quad \frac{\$1,000,000}{\$1,000,000 + \$500,000^*} \times \$406,000$$

$$= \$270,667$$

*$1,000,000 of preferred O/S and $500,000 of common O/S

4.5 Recap:

> | 4% nonparticipating noncumulative preferred | $ 4,000 |
> |---|---|
> | 8% participating cumulative preferred | 670,667 |
> | Common | 175,333 |
> | | $850,000 |

Schedules from Unofficial Answers were not used because they duplicate our Solution Guide

Howard Corporation

SUMMARY OF STOCKHOLDERS' EQUITY ACCOUNTS TRANSACTIONS

For 1977

Date of Transaction	Common Stock		Preferred Stock		Common Stock Warrants		Additional Paid-in Capital	Retained Earnings	Treasury Stock	
	Number of Shares	Amount	Number of Shares	Amount	Number of Rights	Amount			Number of Shares	Amount
Beginning 2/1/77	15,000,000	$150,000,000					$ 80,000,000	$50,000,000	1,000,000	$18,000,000
(See SG 2.1*) 2/15/77	2,000,000	20,000,000					16,000,000			
(See SG 2.2) 3/1/77			100,000	$10,000,000	100,000	$100,000	900,000			
(See SG 2.3) 3/15/77									20,000	370,000
(See SG 2.4) 3/31/77							210,000		10,000	210,000
(See SG 2.5) 4/15/77								(1,597,000)		
(See SG 2.6) 4/30/77	30,000	300,000			(30,000)	(30,000)	330,000			
(See SG 2.7) 5/31/77	100,000	1,000,000					1,000,000			
(See SG 2.8) 6/30/77	805,000	8,050,000					8,050,000			
(See SG 2.9) 9/30/77							1,530,000		(300,000)	(5,970,000)
(See SG 2.10) 12/31/77								(2,520,500)		
(See SG 2.11) 12/31/77					(70,000)	(70,000)	70,000			
(See SG 2.12)								25,000,000		
	17,935,000	$179,350,000	100,000	$10,000,000	-0-	$ -0-	$108,090,000	$54,782,500	730,000	$12,610,000

*SG = Solution Guide

UNOFFICIAL ANSWER

Problem 9   Stockholders' Equity Transactions

Tomasco, Inc.
MAXIMUM CASH DIVIDEND DISTRIBUTION
December 31, 1977

	Common stock	4% Preferred stock	8% Preferred stock	Total
8% preferred stock, dividends in arrears for 1973–1976 ($1,000,000 × 8% × 4 years)			$320,000	$320,000
4% preferred stock dividends for 1977 ($100,000 × 4%)		$4,000		4,000
8% preferred stock dividends for 1977 ($1,000,000 × 8%)			80,000	80,000
Distribution of remaining retained earnings *(Schedule 1)*	$175,333		270,667	446,000
	$175,333	$4,000	$670,667	$850,000

Schedule 1

Distribution of Remaining Retained Earnings

	Common stock	8% Preferred stock	Total
Dividends on common stock at preferred rate ($500,000 × 8%)	$ 40,000		$ 40,000
Distribution of remaining retained earnings of $406,000* based on the ratio of par values:			
Common stock $\left(\dfrac{\$\ 500,000}{\$1,500,000} \times \$406,000\right)$	135,333		⎫
8% preferred stock $\left(\dfrac{\$1,000,000}{\$1,500,000} \times \$406,000\right)$		$270,667	⎬ 406,000 ⎭
	$175,333	$270,667	$446,000

*$850,000 — $320,000 — $4,000 — $80,000 — $40,000

MULTIPLE CHOICE QUESTIONS

FUNDAMENTAL CONCEPTS (1—22)

1. On January 1, 1980, Liberty Company sold a machine to Bell Corporation in an "arms length" transaction. Bell signed a noninterest bearing note requiring payment of $20,000 annually for ten years. The first payment was made on January 1, 1980. The prevailing rate of interest for this type of note at date of issuance was 12%. Information on present value factors is as follows:

Period	Present value of $1 at 12%	Present value of ordinary annuity of $1 at 12%
9	0.361	5.328
10	0.322	5.650

Liberty should record the above sale in January 1980 at

- a. $ 64,400
- b. $ 84,980
- c. $113,000
- d. $126,560

2. On January 1, 1979, the Carpet Company lent $100,000 to its supplier, Loom Corporation, evidenced by a note, payable in 5 years. Interest at 5% is payable annually with the first payment due on December 31, 1979. The going rate of interest for this type of loan is 10%. The parties agreed that Carpet's inventory needs for the loan period will be met by Loom at favorable prices. Assume that the present value (at the going rate of interest) of the $100,000 note is $81,000 at January 1, 1979. What amount of interest income, if any, should be included in Carpet's 1979 income statement?

- a. $0
- b. $4,050
- c. $5,000
- d. $8,100

3. On May 1, 1980, a company purchased a new machine which it does not have to pay for until May 1, 1982. The total payment on May 1, 1982, will include both principal and interest. Assuming interest at a 10% rate, the cost of the machine would be the total payment multiplied by what time value of money concept?

- a. Future amount of annuity of 1.
- b. Future amount of 1.
- c. Present value of annuity of 1.
- d. Present value of 1.

4. The Bay Company sold some machinery to the Inlet Company on January 1, 1976. The cash selling price would have been $379,100. Inlet entered into an installment sales contract which required annual payments of $100,000, including interest at 10%, over five years. The first payment was due on December 31, 1976. What amount of interest income should be included in Bay's 1978 income statement (the third year of the contract)?

- a. $24,180
- b. $24,871
- c. $37,910
- d. $50,000

5. On January 1, 1975, the Fulmar Company sold personal property to the Austin Company. The personal property had cost Fulmar $40,000. Fulmar frequently sells similar items of property for $44,000. Austin gave Fulmar a noninterest bearing note payable in six equal annual installments of $10,000 with the first payment due December 31, 1975. Collection of the note is reasonably assured. A reasonable rate of interest for a note of this type is 10%. The present value of an annuity of $1 in arrears at 10% for six periods is 4.355. What amount of sales revenue from this transaction should be reported in Fulmar's income statement for the year ended December 31, 1975?

- a. $10,000.
- b. $40,000.
- c. $43,550.
- d. $44,000.

6. The Mitchell Company received a seven-year noninterest bearing note on February 22, 1974, in exchange for property it sold to the Grispin Company. There was no established exchange price for this property and the note has no ready market. The prevailing rate of interest for a note of this type was 10% on February 22, 1974, 10.2% on December 31, 1974, 10.3% on February 22, 1975, and 10.4% on December 31, 1975. What interest rate should be used to calculate the interest revenue from this transaction for the year ended December 31, 1975 and 1974, respectively?

- a. 0% and 0%.
- b. 10% and 10%.
- c. 10% and 10.3%.
- d. 10.2% and 10.4%.

7. At the beginning of 1973, Garmar Company received a three-year noninterest-bearing $1,000 trade note. The market rate for equivalent notes was 8% at that time. Garmar reported this note as $1,000 trade notes receivable on its 1973 year-end statement of financial position and $1,000 as sales revenue for 1973. What effect did this accounting for the note have on Garmar's net earnings for 1973, 1974, and 1975, and its retained earnings at the end of 1975, respectively?

   a.   Overstate, understate, understate, zero.

   b.   Overstate, understate, understate, understate.

   c.   Overstate, overstate, understate, zero.

   d.   No effect on any of these.

8. The figure .9423 is taken from the column marked 2% and the row marked three periods in a certain interest table. From what interest table is this figure taken?

   a.   Amount of $1.

   b.   Amount of annuity of $1.

   c.   Present value of $1.

   d.   Present value of annuity of $1.

9. A businessman wants to withdraw $3,000 (including principal) from an investment fund at the end of each year for five years. How should he compute his required initial investment at the beginning of the first year if the fund earns 6% compounded annually?

   a. $3,000 times the amount of an annuity of $1 at 6% at the end of each year for five years.

   b. $3,000 divided by the amount of an annuity of $1 at 6% at the end of each year for five years.

   c. $3,000 times the present value of an annuity of $1 at 6% at the end of each year for five years.

   d. $3,000 divided by the present value of an annuity of $1 at 6% at the end of each year for five years.

10. On December 31, 1976, Majestic Corporation sold for $15,000 an old machine having an original cost of $50,000 and a book value of $6,000. The terms of the sale were as follows:

   $5,000 down payment

   $5,000 payable on December 31 of the next two years

The agreement of sale made no mention of interest, however, 10% would be a fair rate for this type of transaction. What should be the amount of the notes receivable net of the unamortized discount on December 31, 1976, rounded to the nearest dollar?

   a. $8,678.

   b. $9,091.

   c. $10,000.

   d. $11,000.

11. On August 1, 1978, Bamco Corporation purchased a new machine on a deferred payment basis. A down payment of $1,000 was made and 4 monthly installments of $2,500 each are to be made beginning on September 1, 1978. The cash equivalent price of the machine was $9,500. Bamco incurred and paid installation costs amounting to $300. The amount to be capitalized as the cost of the machine is

   a. $9,500.

   b. $9,800.

   c. $11,000.

   d. $11,300.

12. Which of the following transactions would require the use of the present value of an annuity due concept in order to calculate the present value of the asset obtained or liability owed at the date of incurrence?

   a.   A capital lease is entered into with the initial lease payment due upon the signing of the lease agreement.

   b.   A capital lease is entered into with the initial lease payment due one month subsequent to the signing of the lease agreement.

   c.   A ten-year 8% bond is issued on January 2 with interest payable semi-annually on July 1 and January 1 yielding 7%.

   d.   A ten-year 8% bond is issued on January 2 with interest payable semi-annually on July 1 and January 1 yielding 9%.

13. An accountant wishes to find the present value of an annuity of $1 payable at the beginning of each period at 10% for eight periods. He has only one present-value table which shows the present value of an annuity of $1 payable at the end of each period. To compute the present-value factor he needs, the accountant would use the present-value factor in the 10% column for

   a.   Seven periods.

   b.   Seven periods and add $1.

   c.   Eight periods.

   d.   Nine periods and subtract $1.

Items **14** through **17** apply to the appropriate use of present-value tables. Given below are the present-value factors for $1.00 discounted at 8% for one to five periods. Each of the following items is based on 8% interest **compounded** annually from day of deposit to day of withdrawal.

Periods	Present value of $1 discounted at 8% per period
1	0.926
2	0.857
3	0.794
4	0.735
5	0.681

14. What amount should be deposited in a bank today to grow to $1,000 three years from today?

   a. $\dfrac{\$1,000}{0.794}$

   b. $1,000 x 0.926 x 3.

   c. ($1,000 x 0.926) + ($1,000 x 0.857) + ($1,000 x 0.794).

   d. $1,000 x 0.794.

15. What amount should an individual have in his bank account today before withdrawal if he needs $2,000 each year for four years with the first withdrawal to be made today and each subsequent withdrawal at one-year intervals? (He is to have exactly a zero balance in his bank account after the fourth withdrawal.)

   a. $2,000 + ($2,000 x 0.926) + ($2,000 x 0.857) + ($2,000 x 0.794).

   b. $\dfrac{\$2,000}{0.735}$ x 4.

   c. ($2,000 x 0.926) + ($2,000 x 0.857) + ($2,000 x 0.794) + ($2,000 x 0.735).

   d. $\dfrac{\$2,000}{0.926}$ x 4.

16. If an individual put $3,000 in a savings account today, what amount of cash would be available two years from today?

   a. $3,000 x 0.857.

   b. $3,000 x 0.857 x 2.

   c. $\dfrac{\$3,000}{0.857}$.

   d. $\dfrac{\$3,000}{0.926}$ x 2.

17. What is the present value today of $4,000 to be received six years from today?

   a. $4,000 x 0.926 x 6.

   b. $4,000 x 0.794 x 2.

   c. $4,000 x 0.681 x 0.926.

   d. Cannot be determined from the information given.

18. Calculation of the amount of the equal periodic payments which would be equivalent to a year 0 outlay of $1,000 is most readily effected by reference to a table which shows the

   a. Amount of 1.

   b. Present value of 1.

   c. Amount of an annuity of 1.

   d. Present value of an annuity of 1.

MAY 1981 QUESTIONS

19. Stark, Inc., has $1,000,000 of notes payable due June 15, 1981. At the financial statement date of December 31, 1980, Stark signed an agreement to borrow up to $1,000,000 to refinance the notes payable on a long-term basis. The financing agreement called for borrowings not to exceed 80% of the value of the collateral Stark was providing. At the date of issue of the December 31, 1980, financial statements the value of the collateral was $1,200,000 and was not expected to fall below this amount during 1981. On the December 31, 1980, balance sheet, Stark should classify

   a. $40,000 of notes payable as short-term and $960,000 as long-term obligations.

   b. $200,000 of notes payable as short-term and $800,000 as long-term obligations.

   c. $1,000,000 of notes payable as short-term obligations.

   d. $1,000,000 of notes payable as long-term obligations.

20. Electro Corporation bought a new machine and agreed to pay for it in equal annual installments of $5,000 at the end of each of the next five years. Assume a prevailing interest rate of 15%. The present value of an ordinary annuity of $1 at 15% for five periods is 3.35. The future amount of an ordinary annuity of $1 at 15% for five periods is 6.74. The present value of $1 at 15% for five periods is 0.5. How much should Electro record as the cost of the machine?

   a. $12,500.

   b. $16,750.

   c. $25,000.

   d. $33,700.

21. Glen, Inc., purchased certain plant assets under a deferred payment contract on December 31, 1980. The agreement was to pay $10,000 at the time of purchase and $10,000 at the end of each of the next five years. The plant assets should be valued at
   a. The present value of a $10,000 ordinary annuity for five years.
   b. $60,000.
   c. $60,000 plus imputed interest.
   d. $60,000 less imputed interest.

22. A two-year note was issued in an arm's-length transaction at face value solely for cash at the beginning of this year. There were no other rights or privileges exchanged. The interest rate is specified at 10 percent per year. Principal and interest are payable at maturity. The prevailing rate of interest for a loan of this type is 15 percent per year. What annual interest rate should be used to record interest expense for this year and next year?

	This year	Next year
a.	10 percent	15 percent
b.	10 percent	10 percent
c.	15 percent	10 percent
d.	15 percent	15 percent

MULTIPLE CHOICE QUESTIONS

BONDS (23–39)

23. On July 1, 1979, Glenn Company purchased Dell Corporation 10-year, 9% bonds with a face value of $200,000, for $216,000, which included $6,000 of accrued interest. The bonds, which mature on March 1, 1986, pay interest semiannually on March 1 and September 1. Glenn uses the straight-line method of amortization. The amount of income Glenn should report for the calendar year 1979 as a result of the above long-term investment would be
   a. $ 7,800
   b. $ 8,250
   c. $ 9,000
   d. $15,000

24. On January 1, 1974, Provident Corporation issued for $1,040,000, one thousand of its 9%, $1,000 callable bonds. The bonds are dated January 1, 1974, and mature on January 1, 1984. Interest is payable semi-annually on July 1 and January 1. The bonds can be called by the issuer at 101 at any time after December 31, 1978.

   On July 1, 1979, Provident called in all of the bonds and retired them. Assume that Provident uses the straight-line method of amortizing bond premium. Ignoring income taxes, what is the amount of gain or loss that Provident should record on this early extinguishment of debt in its income statement for the year ended December 31, 1979?
   a. $ 8,000 gain.
   b. $10,000 loss.
   c. $12,000 gain.
   d. $30,000 gain.

25. On March 1, 1979, Danna Corporation issued $500,000 of 8% nonconvertible bonds at 103 which are due on February 28, 1999. In addition, each $1,000 bond was issued with 30 detachable stock warrants, each of which entitled the bondholder to purchase, for $50, one share of Danna common stock, par value $25. On March 1, 1979, the fair market value of Danna's common stock was $40 per share and the fair market value of each warrant was $4. What amount of the proceeds from the bond issue should Danna record as an increase in stockholders' equity?
   a. $0
   b. $ 15,000
   c. $ 60,000
   d. $375,000

26. On January 1, 1975, Gilbert Corporation issued $1,200,000 of 6% ten-year bonds at 103. The bonds are callable at the option of Gilbert at 105. Gilbert has recorded amortization of the bond premium on the straight-line method (which was not materially different from the interest method).

On December 31, 1979, Gilbert repurchased $600,000 of the bonds in the open market at 98. Gilbert has recorded interest and amortization for 1979. Ignoring income taxes and assuming that all amounts involved are material, Gilbert should report the gain from this reacquisition as
   a.   Other income of $21,000.
   b.   An extraordinary gain of $21,000.
   c.   Other income of $42,000.
   d.   An extraordinary gain of $42,000.

27. On March 1, 1980, Williams Corporation issued at 103 plus accrued interest, one hundred of its 9%, $1,000 bonds. The bonds are dated January 1, 1980, and mature on January 1, 1990. Interest is payable semiannually on January 1 and July 1. Williams paid bond issue costs of $5,000. Based on the information above, Williams would realize net cash receipts from the bond issuance of
   a. $ 98,000.
   b. $ 99,500.
   c. $103,000.
   d. $104,500.

28. Gains or losses from the early extinguishment of debt, if material, should be
   a.   Amortized over the remaining original life of the extinguished issue.
   b.   Amortized over the life of the new issue.
   c.   Recognized as an extraordinary item in the period of extinguishment.
   d.   Recognized in income before taxes in the period of extinguishment.

29. On April 7, 1975, the Script Corporation sold a $1,000,000 twenty-year, 8 percent bond issue for $1,030,000. Each $1,000 bond has a detachable warrant that permits the purchase of one share of the corporation's common stock for $30. The stock has a par value of $25 per share. Immediately after the sale of the bonds, the corporation's securities had the following market values:

8% bond without warrants	$1,020
Warrants	10
Common stock	28

What accounts should the corporation credit to record the sale of the bonds?

a.	Bonds payable	$1,000,000
	Premium on bonds payable	2,000
	Common stock warrants outstanding	28,000
b.	Bonds payable	1,000,000
	Premium on bonds payable	5,000
	Common stock warrants outstanding	25,000
c.	Bonds payable	1,000,000
	Premium on bonds payable	20,000
	Common stock warrants outstanding	10,000
d.	Bonds payable	$1,000,000
	Premium on bonds payable	30,000

30. On September 1, 1975, the Consul Company acquired $10,000 face value 8% bonds of Envoy Corporation at 104. The bonds were dated May 1, 1975, and mature on April 30, 1980, with interest payable each October 31 and April 30.

What entry should Consul make to record the purchase of the bonds on September 1, 1975?

a.	Investment in bonds	$10,400	
	Interest receivable	266	
	Cash		$10,666
b.	Investment in bonds	10,666	
	Cash		10,666
c.	Investment in bonds	10,666	
	Accrued interest receivable		266
	Cash		10,400
d.	Investment in bonds	10,000	
	Premium on bonds	666	
	Cash		10,666

31. The December 31, 1978, general ledger of The North Company contained an account "6% Bonds Payable." This account had a balance of $95,000 as of that date. Further examination revealed that the bonds had a face value of $100,000, with a yield of 8% and were issued at a discount. The amortization of the bond discount was recorded under the effective interest method. Interest was paid on January 1 and July 1 of each year. On July 1, 1979, several years before their maturity, North retired the bonds at 102, excluding accrued interest. What is the extraordinary loss that North should record on the early retirement of the bonds on July 1, 1979?
   a. $4,200
   b. $6,200
   c. $7,000
   d. $7,800

32. When the interest payment dates of a bond are May 1 and November 1, and a bond issue is sold on June 1, the amount of cash received by the issuer will be

a. Decreased by accrued interest from June 1 to November 1.

b. Decreased by accrued interest from May 1 to June 1.

c. Increased by accrued interest from June 1 to November 1.

d. Increased by accrued interest from May 1 to June 1.

33. The generally accepted method of accounting for gains or losses from the early extinguishment of debt is based on the assumption that any gain or loss on the transaction reflects

a. An adjustment to the cost basis of the asset obtained by the debt issue.

b. An amount that should be considered a cash adjustment to the cost of any other debt obtained over the remaining life of the old debt instrument.

c. An amount received or paid to obtain a new debt instrument and, as such, should be amortized over the life of the new debt.

d. A change in the market rate of interest which should be recognized in the period of extinguishment.

34. On October 1, 1978, Mann Company purchased 500 of the $1,000 face value, 8% bonds of Womann, Incorporated, for $540,000, which includes accrued interest of $10,000. The bonds, which mature on January 1, 1985, pay interest semiannually on January 1 and July 1. Assuming that Mann uses the straight-line method of amortization and that the bonds are appropriately recorded as a long-term investment, the bonds should be shown on Mann's December 31, 1978, balance sheet at

a. $528,400.

b. $528,800.

c. $530,000.

d. $540,000.

MAY 1981 QUESTIONS

35. On January 1, 1980, Battle Corporation sold at 97 plus accrued interest, two hundred of its 8%, $1,000 bonds. The bonds are dated October 1, 1979, and mature on October 1, 1989. Interest is payable semi-annually on April 1 and October 1. Accrued interest for the period October 1, 1979, to January 1,

1980, amounted to $4,000. As a result, on January 1, 1980, Battle would record bonds payable, net of discount, at

a. $190,000.

b. $194,000.

c. $196,000.

d. $198,000.

36. On January 1, 1981, Welling Company purchased 100 of the $1,000 face value, 8%, ten-year bonds of Mann, Inc. The bonds mature on January 1, 1991, and pay interest annually on January 1. Welling purchased the bonds to yield 10% interest. Information on present value factors is as follows:

Present value of $1 at 8% for 10 periods	0.4632
Present value of $1 at 10% for 10 periods	0.3855
Present value of an annuity of $1 at 8% for 10 periods	6.7101
Present value of an annuity of $1 at 10% for 10 periods	6.1446

How much did Welling pay for the bonds?

a. $ 87,707.

b. $ 92,230.

c. $ 95,477.

d. $100,000.

37. Elba Corporation issued $200,000 face amount of 8% bonds with interest payable on April 1 and October 1. The bonds were callable at 105. Interest and amortization of bond discount have been accounted for up to October 1, 1980, at which date the bonds were called. Unamortized bond discount on that date amounted to $16,000. Ignoring the income tax effect, what was Elba's gain or loss on the bond retirement?

a. $ 6,000 gain.

b. $ 6,000 loss.

c. $10,000 loss.

d. $26,000 loss.

38. How should the value of warrants attached to a debt security be accounted for?

a. No value assigned.

b. A separate portion of paid-in capital.

c. An appropriation of retained earnings.

d. A liability.

39. How should the cash proceeds from convertible bonds sold at issue date at par be recorded?

a. As additional paid-in capital for the portion of the proceeds attributable to the conversion feature and as a liability for the portion of the proceeds attributable to the debt.

b. As retained earnings for the portion of the proceeds attributable to the conversion feature and as a liability for the portion of the proceeds attributable to the debt.
c. As a liability for the entire proceeds.
d. As additional paid-in capital for the portion of the proceeds attributable to the conversion feature and as retained earnings for the portion of the proceeds attributable to the debt.

MULTIPLE CHOICE QUESTIONS

LEASES (40—58)

40. Benedict Company leased equipment to Mark, Inc., on January 1, 1978. The lease is for an eight-year period expiring December 31, 1985. The first of 8 equal annual payments of $600,000 was made on January 1, 1978. Benedict had purchased the equipment on December 29, 1977, for $3,200,000. The lease is appropriately accounted for as a sales-type lease by Benedict. Assume that the present value at January 1, 1978, of all rent payments over the lease term discounted at a 10% interest rate was $3,520,000. What amount of interest income should Benedict record in 1979 (the second year of the lease period) as a result of the lease?

a. $261,200
b. $292,000
c. $320,000
d. $327,200

41. Arrow Company purchased a machine on January 1, 1979, for $1,440,000 for the purpose of leasing it. The machine is expected to have an eight-year life from date of purchase, no residual value, and be depreciated on the straight-line basis. On February 1, 1979, the machine was leased to Baxter Company for a three-year period ending January 31, 1982, at a monthly rental of $30,000. Additionally, Baxter paid $72,000 to Arrow on February 1, 1979, as a lease bonus. What is the amount of income before income taxes that Arrow should report on this leased asset for the year ended December 31, 1979?

a. $172,000
b. $187,000
c. $222,000
d. $237,000

42. Lease Y contains a bargain purchase option and the lease term is equal to 75 percent of the estimated economic life of the leased property. Lease Z contains a bargain purchase option and the lease term is equal to less than 75 percent of the estimated economic life of the leased property. How should the lessee classify these leases?

	Lease Y	Lease Z
a.	Operating lease	Operating lease
b.	Operating lease	Capital lease
c.	Capital lease	Capital lease
d.	Capital lease	Operating lease

43. In a lease that is recorded as a sales-type lease by the lessor, the difference between the gross investment in the lease and the sum of the present values of the two components of the gross investment should be recorded as

a. Unearned income.
b. Manufacturer's or dealer's profit.
c. Rental income.
d. Deferred charge.

Items 44 and 45 are based on the following information:

Fox Company, a dealer in machinery and equipment, leased equipment to Tiger, Inc., on July 1, 1979. The lease is appropriately accounted for as a sale by Fox and as a purchase by Tiger. The lease is for a 10-year period (the useful life of the asset) expiring June 30, 1989. The first of 10 equal annual payments of $500,000 was made on July 1, 1979. Fox had purchased the equipment for $2,675,000 on January 1, 1979, and established a list selling price of $3,375,000 on the equipment. Assume that the present value at July 1, 1979, of the rent payments over the lease term discounted at 12% (the appropriate interest rate) was $3,165,000.

44. What is the amount of profit on the sale and the amount of interest income that Fox should record for the year ended December 31, 1979?
a. $0 and $159,900.
b. $490,000 and $159,900.
c. $490,000 and $189,900.
d. $700,000 and $189,900.

45. Assuming that Tiger uses straight-line depreciation, what is the amount of depreciation and interest expense that Tiger should record for the year ended December 31, 1979?
a. $158,250 and $159,900.
b. $158,250 and $189,900.
c. $168,750 and $159,900.
d. $168,750 and $189,900.

46. Rent collected in advance by the lessor for an operating lease is a (an)
a. Accrued liability.
b. Deferred asset.
c. Accrued revenue.
d. Deferred revenue.

Items 47 and 48 are based on the following information:

The Morn Company leased equipment to the Lizard Company on May 1, 1978. At that time the collectibility of the minimum lease payments was not reasonably predictable. The lease expires on May 1, 1980. Lizard could have bought the equipment from Morn for $900,000 instead of leasing it. Morn's accounting records showed a book value for

the equipment on May 1, 1978, of $800,000. Morn's depreciation on the equipment in 1978 was $200,000. During 1978 Lizard paid $240,000 in rentals to Morn, incurred maintenance and other related costs under the terms of the lease of $18,000 in 1978. After the lease with Lizard expires, Morn will lease the equipment to the Cold Company for another two years.

47. The income before income taxes derived by Morn from this lease for the year ended December 31, 1978, should be
a. $ 22,000
b. $100,000
c. $122,000
d. $240,000

48. Ignoring income taxes, the amount of expense incurred by Lizard from this lease for the year ended December 31, 1978, should be
a. $ 22,000
b. $200,000
c. $218,000
d. $240,000

49. In a lease that is appropriately recorded as a direct financing lease by the lessor, unearned income
a. Should be amortized over the period of the lease using the interest method.
b. Should be amortized over the period of the lease using the straight-line method.
c. Does not arise.
d. Should be recognized at the lease's expiration.

50. On January 1, 1976, The Anson Company leased a machine to Scovil Company. The lease was for a 10-year period, which approximated the useful life of the machine. Anson purchased the machine for $80,000 and expects to earn a 10% return on its investment, based upon an annual rental of $11,836 payable in advance each January 1st.

Assuming that the lease was a financing lease, what should be the interest entry on Anson's books on December 31, 1976?

a.	Cash	$ 3,836	
	Interest revenue		$3,836
b.	Unearned interest		
	revenue	6,816	
	Interest revenue		6,816
c.	Cash	8,000	
	Interest revenue		8,000
d.	Cash	11,836	
	Interest revenue		8,000
	Equipment		3,836

51. What is the cost basis of an asset acquired by a lease which is in substance an installment purchase?

a. The net realizable value of the asset determined at the date of the lease agreement plus the sum of the future minimum lease payments under the lease.

b. The sum of the future minimum lease payments under the lease.

c. The present value of the amount of future minimum lease payments under the lease (exclusive of executory costs and any profit thereon) discounted at an appropriate rate.

d. The present value of the market price of the asset discounted at an appropriate rate as an amount to be received at the end of the lease.

52. Generally accepted accounting principles require that certain lease agreements be accounted for as purchases. The theoretic basis for this treatment is that a lease of this type

a. Effectively conveys all of the benefits and risks incident to the ownership of property.

b. Is an example of form over substance.

c. Provides the use of the leased asset to the lessee for a limited period of time.

d. Must be recorded in accordance with the concept of cause and effect.

53. On June 30, 1977, Gulch Corporation sold equipment to an unaffiliated company for $550,000. The equipment had a book value of $500,000 and a remaining useful life of 10 years. That same day, Gulch leased back the equipment at $1,500 per month for 5 years with no option to renew the lease or repurchase the equipment. Gulch's equipment rent expense for this equipment for the year ended December 31, 1977, should be

a. $4,000.

b. $5,000.

c. $9,000.

d. $11,000.

54. An office equipment representative has a machine for sale or lease. If you buy the machine, the cost is $7,596. If you lease the machine, you will have to sign a noncancellable lease and make 5 payments of $2,000 each. The first payment will be paid on the first day of the lease. At the time of the last payment you will receive title to the machine. The present value of an ordinary annuity of $1 is as follows:

Number of Periods	Present Value		
	10%	12%	16%
1	0.909	0.893	0.862
2	1.736	1.690	1.605
3	2.487	2.402	2.246
4	3.170	3.037	2.798
5	3.791	3.605	3.274

The interest rate implicit in this lease is approximately

a. 10%.

b. 12%.

c. Between 10% and 12%.

d. 16%.

55. The Standard Company leased a piece of equipment to the Piping Company on July 1, 1977, for a one-year period expiring June 30, 1978, for $90,000 a month. On July 1, 1978, Standard leased this piece of equipment to the Tacking Company for a three-year period expiring June 30, 1981, for $100,000 a month. The original cost of the piece of equipment was $6,000,000. The piece of equipment which has been continually on lease since July 1, 1973, is being depreciated on a straight-line basis over an eight-year period with no salvage value. Assuming that both the lease to Piping and the lease to Tacking are appropriately recorded as operating leases for accounting purposes, what is the amount of income (expense) before income taxes that each would record as a result of the above facts for the year ended December 31, 1978?

	Standard	Piping	Tacking
a.	$ 390,000	($540,000)	($600,000)
b.	$ 390,000	($540,000)	($975,000)
c.	$1,140,000	($165,000)	($225,000)
d.	$1,140,000	($915,000)	($600,000)

56. Based solely upon the following sets of circumstances indicated below, which set gives rise to a sales type or direct financing lease of a lessor?

	Transfers ownership by end of lease?	Contains bargain purchase provision?	Collectibility of lease payments assured?	Any important uncertainties?
a.	No	Yes	Yes	No
b.	Yes	No	No	No
c.	Yes	No	No	Yes
d.	No	Yes	Yes	Yes

MAY 1981 QUESTIONS

57.   Howard Company sublet a portion of its warehouse for five years at an annual rental of $18,000, beginning on May 1, 1980. The tenant paid one year's rent in advance, which Howard recorded as a credit to unearned rental income. Howard reports on a calendar-year basis. The adjustment on December 31, 1980, should be

		Dr.	Cr.
a.	No Entry		
b.	Unearned rental income	$ 6,000	
	Rental income		$ 6,000
c.	Rental income	$ 6,000	
	Unearned rental income		$ 6,000
d.	Unearned rental income	$12,000	
	Rental income		$12,000

58.   For a capital lease, an amount equal to the present value at the beginning of the lease term of minimum lease payments during the lease term, excluding that portion of the payments representing executory costs such as insurance, maintenance, and property taxes to be paid by the lessor, together with any profit thereon, should be recorded by the lessee as a (an)

a.   Expense.
b.   Liability but **not** an asset.
c.   Asset but **not** a liability.
d.   Asset and a liability.

MULTIPLE CHOICE QUESTIONS

PENSIONS (59—72)

59. The pension expense accrued by a company will be increased by interest equivalents when
   a. Amounts funded are less than pension cost accrued.
   b. Amounts funded are greater than pension cost accrued.
   c. The plan is fully vested.
   d. The plan is fully funded.

60. Which of the following disclosures concerning pension plans should be made in a company's financial statements or their notes?
   a. A statement of a company's accounting and funding policies.
   b. The amount of retirement benefits paid during the year.
   c. A description of the actuarial assumptions made.
   d. The amount of unfunded past service costs.

61. In accounting for the cost of pension plans, an acceptable actuarial cost method for financial purposes is
   a. Pay-as-you-go.
   b. Terminal funding.
   c. Entry age normal.
   d. Turnover.

62. The maximum annual provision for pension cost permitted is normal cost, plus
   a. 10 percent of past service cost (until fully amortized).
   b. A provision for vested benefits.
   c. 10 percent of past service cost (until fully amortized), plus 10 percent of any increases or decreases in prior service cost arising on amendments of the plan, plus interest equivalents on the difference between provisions and amounts funded.
   d. Interest equivalents on any unfunded prior service cost, plus a provision for the excess of the actuarially computed value of vested benefits over the total of the pension fund if such excess is not at least 5 percent less than the comparable excess at the beginning of the year.

63. The vested benefits of an employee in a pension plan represent

   a. Benefits to be paid to the retired employee in the current year.
   b. Benefits to be paid to the retired employee in the subsequent year.
   c. Benefits accumulated in the hands of an independent trustee.
   d. Benefits that are not contingent on the employee's continuing in the service of the employer.

64. The past service costs in a pension plan
   a. Should be charged to income in the year of the inception of the pension plan.
   b. Should be funded in the year of the inception of the pension plan.
   c. Represent pension cost assigned to years prior to the current balance sheet date.
   d. Represent pension cost assigned to years prior to the inception of the pension plan.

65. APB Opinion No. 8 sets minimum and maximum limits on the annual provision for pension cost. An amount that is always included in the calculation of both the minimum and maximum limit is
   a. Amortization of past service cost.
   b. Normal cost.
   c. Interest on unfunded past and prior service costs.
   d. Retirement benefits paid.

66. The Pasther Company has a contributory pension plan for all of its employees. In 1975, a total of $100,000 was withheld from employees' salaries and deposited into a pension fund administered by an outside trustee. In addition, Pasther deposited $200,000 of its own money into the fund in 1975. Based on the report of Pasther's outside actuaries which was received in December 1975, the 1975 actuarial cost of the pension plan was $320,000. As a result of this report, Pasther deposited $20,000 of its own money into the fund on January 12, 1976. How much should the provision for pension cost be in Pasther's 1975 income statement?
   a. $200,000.
   b. $220,000
   c. $300,000.
   d. $320,000.

67. In March 1975, Rocka Company adopted a pension plan for its eligible employees. Unfunded past service cost was determined to be $7,000,000 and this amount will be paid in 10 annual installments of $1,000,000 to an outside funding agency administering the plan.

Additional Information:

		1976	1977

Past service cost will be amortized
over 20 years.

Normal cost for 1975 (remitted to
funding agency in 1975). $560,000

Amortization of past service cost
for 1975.   650,000

	1976	1977
12-year accrual	$100,000	$100,000
Reduction for interest	–	835
Past service pension cost	100,000	99,165
10-year funding	113,909	113,909
Balance sheet—deferred charge:		
Balance	13,909	28,653
Increase	13,909	14,744

What is the deferred pension cost for 1975?
a. $350,000.
b. $440,000.
c. $500,000.
d. $560,000.

69. If normal cost for 1976 was $70,000, Johnson should record pension expense in 1976 of
    a. $70,000.
    b. $113,909.
    c. $170,000.
    d. $183,909.

68. What is the difference between the terms past service costs and prior service costs?
    a. Past service costs refer to costs applicable to periods prior to a particular date of actuarial valuation, and prior service costs refer to costs applicable to employee service prior to the inception of a pension plan.
    b. Past service costs refer to costs applicable to employee service prior to the inception of a pension plan, and prior service costs refer to costs applicable to periods prior to a particular date of actuarial valuation.
    c. Past service costs refer to costs applicable to a pension plan for an employee who enters the plan after the inception of the plan in order to bring the employee's benefits into line with the other participants in the plan, and prior service costs refer to changes in prior period pension costs that are caused by a change in actuarial valuation.
    d. There is no difference between the two terms, and they may be used interchangeably.

Items 69 and 70 are based on the following information:

The Johnson Corporation adopted a pension plan in 1976 on a funded, noncontributory basis. Johnson elected to amortize past service costs over twelve years and to fund past service costs over ten years. Normal costs are to be funded as incurred each year. The following schedule reflects both amortization of the past service cost and funding for the years 1976 and 1977.

70. If normal cost in 1977 was $75,000, the entry that Johnson should make in 1977 to record pension expense and funding is

		Debit	Credit
a.	Pension expense	$100,000	
	Deferred charge — funding in excess of costs	13,909	
	Cash		$113,909
b.	Pension expense (normal cost)	$ 75,000	
	Pension expense (past service)	99,165	
	Deferred charge — funding in excess of costs	14,744	
	Cash		$188,909
c.	Pension expense	$175,000	
	Deferred charge — funding in excess of costs	13,909	
	Cash		$188,909
d.	Pension expense (normal cost)	$ 75,000	
	Pension expense (past service)	100,000	
	Deferred charge — funding in excess of costs	14,744	
	Cash		$189,744

7.1. In which of the following pension instances would the accrual of past service costs have to be reduced for interest presumed earned?

    a. When past service costs have been fully accrued prior to funding.

    b. When pension expense exceeds the maximum allowable accrual.

    c. When past service costs have been fully funded prior to accrual.

    d. When interest presumed earned on previously accrued past service cost exceeds interest presumed earned on unaccrued past service cost.

MAY 1981 QUESTIONS

72. On January 1, 1980, Pierce, Inc., adopted a noncontributory pension plan for all of its eligible employees. The plan requires Pierce to make annual payments to the designated trustee three months after the end of each year. The first payment was due on March 31, 1981. Information relating to the plan is as follows:

Normal cost for 1980	$ 200,000
Past service cost at January 1, 1980 (unfunded)	1,000,000
Funds held by the trustee are expected to earn an 8% return.	

Assuming that Pierce elects to maximize its pension expense in accordance with GAAP, what would be the amount of accrued pension expense at December 31, 1980?

    a. $216,000.

    b. $280,000.

    c. $300,000.

    d. $380,000.

REPEAT QUESTION

(581,T1,37)   Identical to item 64 above

PROBLEMS: FUNDAMENTAL CONCEPTS

Problem 1　　Valuation of Notes　(1172,T3)

(25 to 30 minutes)

Business transactions often involve the exchange of property, goods, or services for notes or similar instruments that may stipulate no interest rate or an interest rate that varies from prevailing rates.

Required:

a. When a note is exchanged for property, goods, or services, what value should be placed upon the note:

1. If it bears interest at a reasonable rate and is issued in a bargained transaction entered into at arm's length; Explain.

2. If it bears no interest and/or is not issued in a bargained transaction entered into at arm's length? Explain.

b. If the recorded value of a note differs from the face value:

1. How should the difference be accounted for? Explain.

2. How should this difference be presented in the financial statements? Explain.

Problem 2　　Noninterest Bearing Note (579,P4c)

(15 to 20 minutes)

On January 1, 1977, the Lock Company sold property to the Key Company which originally cost Lock $600,000. Key gave Lock a $900,000 noninterest bearing note payable in six equal annual installments of $150,000, with the first payment due and paid on January 1, 1977. There was no established exchange price for the property and the note has no ready market. The prevailing rate of interest for a note of this type is 12%. The present value of an annuity of $1 in advance for six periods at 12% is 4.605.

Required:

1. Prepare a schedule computing the balance in Lock's net receivables from Key at December 31, 1978, based on the above facts. Show supporting computations in good form.

2. Prepare a schedule showing the income or loss before income taxes for the years ended December 31, 1977, and 1978, that Lock should record as a result of the above facts.

PROBLEMS: BONDS

Problem 3 Effective Interest and Early Extinguishment of Debt (1178,T5)

(15 to 20 minutes)

Part a. The appropriate method of amortizing a premium or discount on issuance of bonds is the effective interest method.

Required:

1. What is the effective interest method of amortization and how is it different from and similar to the straight-line method of amortization?

2. How is amortization computed using the effective interest method, and why and how do amounts obtained using the effective interest method differ from amounts computed under the straight-line method?

Part b. Gains or losses from the early extinguishment of debt that is refunded can theoretically be accounted for in three ways:

- Amortized over remaining life of debt.
- Amortized over the life of the new debt issue.
- Recognized in the period of extinguishment.

Required:

1. Discuss the supporting arguments for each of the three theoretic methods of accounting for gains and losses from the early extinguishment of debt.

2. Which of the above methods is generally accepted and how should the appropriate amount of gain or loss be shown in a company's financial statements?

Problem 4   Accounting for Bonds (1180,T4)

(15 to 25 minutes)

One way for a corporation to accomplish long-term financing is through the issuance of long-term debt instruments in the form of bonds.

Required:

a.   Describe how to account for the proceeds from bonds issued with detachable stock purchase warrants.

b.   Contract a serial bond with a term (straight) bond.

c.   For a five-year term bond issued at a premium, why would the amortization in the first year of the life of the bond differ using the interest method of amortization instead of the straight-line method? Include in your discussion whether the amount of amortization in the first year of the life of the bond would be higher or lower using the interest method instead of the straight-line method.

d.   When a bond issue is sold between interest dates at a discount, what journal entry is made and how is the subsequent amortization of bond discount affected? Include in your discussion an explanation of how the amounts of each debit and credit are determined.

e.   Describe how to account for and classify the gain or loss from the reacquisition of a long-term bond prior to its maturity.

Problem 5   Issuance and Extinguishment (1179,P5)

(40 to 50 minutes)

Problem 2 consists of three unrelated parts.

a.   On January 1, 1979, the Hopewell Company sold its 8% bonds that had a face value of $1,000,000. Interest is payable at December 31, each year. The bonds mature on January 1, 1989. The bonds were sold to yield a rate of 10%. The present value of an ordinary annuity of $1 for 10 periods at 10% is 6.1446. The present value of $1 for 10 periods at 10% is 0.3855.

Required:

Prepare a schedule to compute the total amount received from the sale of the bonds. Show supporting computations in good form.

b.   On September 1, 1978, the Junction Company sold at 104, (plus accrued interest) four thousand of

its 9%, ten-year, $1,000 face value, nonconvertible bonds with detachable stock warrants. Each bond carried two detachable warrants; each warrant was for one share of common stock, at a specified option price of $15 per share. Shortly after issuance, the warrants were quoted on the market for $3 each. No market value can be determined for the bonds above. Interest is payable on December 1, and June 1. Bond issue costs of $40,000 were incurred.

Required:

Prepare in general journal format the entry to record the issuance of the bonds. Show supporting computations in good form.

c.   On December 1, 1976, the Cone Company issued its 7%, $2,000,000 face value bonds for $2,200,000, plus accrued interest. Interest is payable on November 1 and May 1. On December 31, 1978, the book value of the bonds, inclusive of the unamortized premium, was $2,100,000. On July 1, 1979, Cone reacquired the bonds at 98, plus accrued interest. Cone appropriately uses the straight-line method for the amortization of bond premium because the results do not materially differ from using the interest method.

Required:

Prepare a schedule to compute the gain or loss on this early extinguishment of debt. Show supporting computations in good form.

Problem 6   Discount Calculation (1178,P3a)

(15 to 20 minutes)

On January 1, 1978, MyKoo Corporation issued $1,000,000 in five-year, 5% serial bonds to be repaid in the amount of $200,000 on January 1, of 1979, 1980, 1981, 1982, and 1983. Interest is payable at the end of each year. The bonds were sold to yield a rate of 6%. Information on present value and future amount factors is as follows:

Present value of an ordinary annuity of $1 for 5 years		Future amount of an ordinary annuity of $1 for 5 years	
5%	6%	5%	6%
4.3295	4.2124	5.5256	5.6371

Number	Present Value of $1		Future Amount of $1	
of years	5%	6%	5%	6%
1	.9524	.9434	1.0500	1.0600
2	.9070	.8900	1.1025	1.1236
3	.8638	.8396	1.1576	1.1910
4	.8227	.7921	1.2155	1.2625
5	.7835	.7473	1.2763	1.3382

Required:

1.   Prepare a schedule showing the computation of the total amount received from the issuance of the serial bonds. Show supporting computations in good form.

2.   Assume the bonds were originally sold at a discount of $26,247. Prepare a schedule of amortization of the bond discount for the first two years after issuance, using the interest (effective rate) method. Show supporting computations in good form.

PROBLEMS: DEBT RESTRUCTURE

Problem 7   Entries for Modification of Terms
              (Adapted from Kieso and Weygandt,
              Intermediate Accounting, 3rd edition, p. 639)

(40 to 50 minutes)

Irish, Inc. owes English Bank a 10-year, 19% note in the amount of $110,000 plus $11,000 of accrued interest. The note is due today 12/31/78. Because Irish, Inc. is in financial trouble, English agrees to accept 40,000 shares of Irish's $1.00 par value common stock which is selling for $1.25, forgive the accrued interest, reduce the face amount of the note to $60,000, extend the maturity date to 12/31/81, and reduce the interest rate to 5%. Interest will continue to be due on 12/31 each year.

Required:

a.   Prepare all the necessary journal entries on the books of Irish, Inc. from restructure through maturity.

b.   Prepare all the necessary journal entries on the books of English Bank from restructure through maturity.

c.   Assume that instead of Irish, Inc. giving English Bank the 40,000 shares of common stock, a piece of land with a book value of $50,000 and a fair value of $55,000 is given as part of the restructure arrangement. All other facts remain unchanged.

1.   Prepare the entries on the books of both entities on 12/31/78.

2.   Describe verbally how the interest revenue (English Bank) and interest expense (Irish, Inc.) for 1979, 1980, and 1981 would be determined.

PROBLEMS: LEASES

Problem 8   Description of Lease Accounting (580,T3)

(15 to 25 minutes)

Part a.   Capital leases and operating leases are the two classifications of leases described in FASB pronouncements, from the standpoint of the **lessee**.

Required:

1.   Describe how a capital lease would be accounted for by the lessee both at the inception of the lease and during the first year of the lease, assuming the lease transfers ownership of the property to the lessee by the end of the lease.

2.   Describe how an operating lease would be accounted for by the lessee both at the inception of the lease and during the first year of the lease, assuming equal monthly payments are made by the lessee at the beginning of each month of the lease. Describe the change in accounting, if any, when rental payments are not made on a straight-line basis.

Do **not** discuss the criteria for distinguishing between capital leases and operating leases.

Part b.   Sales-type leases and direct financing leases are two of the classifications of leases described in FASB pronouncements, from the standpoint of the **lessor**.

Required:

Compare and contrast a sales-type lease with a direct financing lease as follows:

1.   Gross investment in the lease.
2.   Amortization of unearned interest income.
3.   Manufacturer's or dealer's profit.

Do **not** discuss the criteria for distinguishing between the leases described above and operating leases.

Problem 9   Capital Leases (1178,T4)

(20 to 25 minutes)

Milton Corporation entered into a lease arrangement with James Leasing Corporation for a certain machine. James's primary business is leasing and it is not a manufacturer or dealer. Milton will lease the machine for a period of three years which is 50% of the machine's economic life. James will take possession of the machine at the end of the initial three-year lease and lease it to another smaller company that does not need the most current version of the machine. Milton does not guarantee any residual value for the machine and will not purchase the machine at the end of the lease term.

Milton's incremental borrowing rate is 10% and the implicit rate in the lease is 8½%. Milton has no way of knowing the implicit rate used by James. Using either rate, the present value of the minimum lease payments is between 90% and 100% of the fair value of the machine at the date of the lease agreement.

Milton has agreed to pay all executory costs directly and no allowance for these costs is included in the lease payments.

James is reasonably certain that Milton will pay all lease payments, and, because Milton has agreed to pay all executory costs, there are no important uncertainties regarding costs to be incurred by James.

Required:
a. With respect to Milton (the lessee) answer the following:
1.   What type of lease has been entered into? Explain the reason for your answer.
2.   How should Milton compute the appropriate amount to be recorded for the lease or asset required?
3.   What accounts will be created or affected by this transaction and how will the lease or asset and other costs related to the transaction be matched with earnings?
4.   What disclosures must Milton make regarding this lease or asset?

b. With respect to James (the lessor) answer the following:
1.   What type of leasing arrangement has been entered into? Explain the reason for your answer.

2.   How should this ease be recorded by James and how are the appropriate amounts determined?
3.   How should James determine the appropriate amount of earnings to be recognized from each lease payment?
4.   What disclosures must James make regarding this lease?

Problem 10 Lessee's Capital Lease †
(572,Q4)

(40 to 50 minutes)

In 1977, the Archibald Freight Company negotiated and closed a long-term lease contract for newly constructed truck terminals and freight storage facilities. The buildings were erected to the company's specifications on land owned by the company. On January 1, 1978, Archibald Freight Company took possession of the leased properties. On January 1, 1978 and 1979 the company made cash payments of $1,200,000 which were recorded as rental expenses.

Although the terminals have a composite useful life of forty years, the noncancellable lease runs for twenty years from January 1, 1978 with a favorable purchase option available upon expiration of the lease. You have determined that the leased properties and related obligations should be accounted for as a capital lease. Internal Revenue Service agents have indicated that purchase accounting will be required for tax purposes and that an assessment will be made for deficiencies in 1978 income taxes.

The twenty-year lease is effective for the period January 1, 1978 through December 31, 1997. Advance rental payments of $1,000,000 are payable to the lessor on January 1 of each of the first ten years of the lease term. Advance rental payments of $300,000 are due on January 1 for each of the last ten years of the lease. The company has an option to purchase all of these leased facilities for $1 on December 31, 1997. It also must make annual payments to the lessor of $75,000 for property taxes and $125,000 for insurance. The lease was negotiated to assure the lessor a 6 percent rate of return. Archibald, who is aware of the lessor's rate of return, has an incremental borrowing rate of 8%.

Selected present value factors are as follows:

| | For an ordinary annuity of $1 at | | For $1 at | |
Periods	6%	8%	6%	8%
1	.943396	.925926	.943396	.925926
2	1.833393	1.783265	.889996	.857339
8	6.209794	5.746639	.627412	.540269
9	6.801692	6.246888	.591898	.500249
10	7.360087	6.710081	.558395	.463193
19	11.158117	9.603599	.330513	.231712
20	11.469921	9.818147	.311805	.214548

Required: Round all of the computations to the nearest dollar.

a.   Prepare a schedule to compute for Archibald Freight Company the discounted present value of the terminal facilities and related obligation at January 1, 1978.

b.   Prepare a schedule to compute an estimate of Archibald Freight Company's deficiency in federal income taxes for 1978. Assume the following:

1. The discounted present value of the terminal facilities and related obligation at January 1, 1978 was $10,000,000.

2. The cost of the leased properties is to be amortized by the straight-line method with an estimate of zero salvage value.

3. The effective tax rate is 40 percent.

c.   Assuming again that the discounted present value of terminal facilities and related obligation at January 1, 1978 was $10,000,000, prepare journal entries for Archibald Freight Company to record the:

1. Cash payment to the lessor on January 1, 1980.

2. Depreciation expense for the year ended December 31, 1980.

3. Interest expense for the year ended December 31, 1980.

PROBLEMS: PENSIONS

Problem 11   Definitions (578,T4)

(20 to 25 minutes)

Part a.   Generally accepted accounting principles require that pension costs be accounted for on the accrual basis. The various components of pension expense include (but are not limited to): 1. normal cost, 2. past service cost, 3. prior service cost, and 4. interest.

Required:

Define each of the four terms designated above and discuss how each of the costs is accounted for under generally accepted accounting principles.

Part b.   The accounting for past service cost has been a controversial issue. Some members of the profession advocate the accrual of past service cost only to the extent funded, and others advocate the accrual of past service cost regardless of the amount funded.

Required:

1. What are the arguments in favor of accruing past service cost only to the extent funded?
2. What are the arguments in favor of accruing past service cost regardless of the amount funded?

Problem 12   Plan Calculations (1173,T5)

(25 to 30 minutes)

Casey and Lewis Printers, Inc., was organized in 1955 and established a formal pension plan on January 1, 1969, to provide retirement benefits for all employees. The plan is noncontributory and is funded through a trustee, the First National Bank, which invests all funds and pays all benefits as they become due. Vesting occurs when the employee retires at age sixty-five. Original past service cost of $110,000 is being amortized over 15 years and funded over 10 years on a present-value basis at 5%. The Company also funds an amount equal to current normal cost net of actuarial gains and losses. There have been no amendments to the plan since inception.

The independent actuary's report follows:

Casey & Lewis Printers, Inc.
BASIC NONCONTRIBUTORY PENSION
PLAN
Actuarial Report as of June 30, 1973

I. **Current Year's Funding and Pension Cost**

Normal cost (before adjustment for actuarial gains) computed under the entry-age-normal method		$34,150
Actuarial gains:		
Investment gains (losses):		
Excess of expected dividend income over actual dividend income		(350)
Gain on sale of investments		4,050
Gains in actuarial assumptions for:		
Mortality		3,400
Employee turnover		5,050
Reduction in pension cost from closing of plant		8,000
Net actuarial gains		$20,150
Normal cost (funded currently) $14,000		14,000
Past service costs:		
Funding	14,245	
Amortization		10,597
Total funded	28,245	
Total pension cost for financial statement purposes		$24,597

II. **Fund Assets**

Cash	$ 4,200
Dividends receivable	1,525
Investment in common stock, at cost (market value, $177,800)	162,750
	$168,475

III. **Actuarial Liabilities**

Number of employees	46
Number of employees retired	0
Yearly earnings of employees	$598,000
Actuarial liability	$145,000

IV. **Actuarial Assumptions**

Interest	5%
Mortality	1951 Group Annuity Tables
Retirement	Age 65

Required:

a. On the basis of requirements for accounting for the cost of pension plans, evaluate the (1) treatment of actuarial gains and losses and (2) computation of pension cost for financial-statement purposes. Ignore income tax considerations.

b. Independent of your answer to part a., assume that the total amount to be funded is $32,663, the total pension cost for financial-statement purposes is $29,015, and all amounts presented in Parts II, III, and IV of the actuary's report are correct. In accordance with Accounting Principles Board Opinion Number 8, write a footnote for the financial statements of Casey & Lewis Printers, Inc., for the year ended June 30, 1973.

MULTIPLE CHOICE ANSWERS

FUNDAMENTAL CONCEPTS

1.	d	6.	b	11.	b	16.	c	21.	d
2.	d	7.	a	12.	a	17.	c	22.	b
3.	b	8.	c	13.	b	18.	d		
4.	b	9.	c	14.	d	19.	a		
5.	d	10.	a	15.	a	20.	b		

EXPLANATION OF MULTIPLE CHOICE ANSWERS

1.   (1180,P1,8)   (d)   The sale of the machine in January 1980 should be recorded at the present value of the note receivable per APB 21. The first payment on the note is on the date of sale. Therefore, the payments constitute an annuity due of 10 payments and 9 discount periods, the factor for which is the PV factor for a nine year ordinary annuity plus 1.000, or 6.328. The sale should be recorded at (6.328)($20,000) or $126,560.

2.   (580,P1,14)   (d)   The requirement is the amount of interest income to be included in Carpet's 1979 income statement. The solutions approach is to recognize that (1) a note has been issued for cash and a future benefit, and (2) the provision for interest on the loan is not reasonable (per APB 21, para 7). The difference between the face value of the note ($100,000) and its present value ($81,000) represents interest on notes receivable of $19,000. Using an effective interest approach, interest income for Carpet is computed as follows:

   10% (imputed rate) x $81,000 (present value of the discounted note) = $8,100 interest income

3.   (580,T1,48)   (b)   The cost of the machine is the present value of the one lump-sum payment being made two years from the purchase date. The present value of an annuity of 1 is not used because a series of payments is not involved.

4.   (1179,P1,10)   (b)   The requirement is the amount of interest income to be recognized in 1978. On 1/1/76, the installment sale resulted in a $379,100 receivable. The receivable carries a 10% interest rate, and $100,000 has been paid at the end of each year. The solutions approach is to prepare an amortization schedule as illustrated below. Note that the payments are made at the end of the year. Accordingly, 10% of the principal balance at the beginning of the year will be interest revenue for each year. The $100,000 payment less the interest revenue will be the principal reduction at the end of each year as illustrated below. Thus, in 1978, $24,871 should be reflected as interest income.

AMORTIZATION SCHEDULE
$100,000 per year paid

	Beginning Principal	Interest Revenue	Principal Reduction
1976	379,100	37,910	62,090
1977	317,010	31,701	68,299
1978	248,711	24,871	75,129

5.   (1176,P1,10)   (d)   The preferable method of determining the note's present value is based either on the established exchange price of the goods or the market value of the note. (see para 9 of APB 21). Here only the established exchange price ($44,000) is given. Of the $60,000 received, $44,000 is the current selling price and $16,000 is deferred income (interest).

If neither the established exchange price of the goods or the market price of the note is evident, one must impute the interest rate (para 10). In this case the interest rate would be 10% and the present value $43,550. The term "annuity in arrears" means that the payments were to occur at the end of each of the 6 years (an annuity in advance is one in which the payments are at the beginning of each year).

6.   (1176,P1,11)   (b)   The determination of an interest rate to value a note should be made at the time the note is issued and not changed thereafter. See the last sentence in para 12 of APB 21. Thus, interest revenue would be calculated at 10% throughout the life of the note.

7.   (1176,T1,15)   (a)   The requirement is to determine the effect of errors on 1973, 1974, 1975 income and ending 1975 retained earnings. The solutions approach is to draw a time diagram as illustrated below. In 1973, sales will be overstated because the note and sales were recorded at the gross rather than the net present value (as required per para 12, APB 21). In 1974, interest income from the note will not be recorded, thus, understating income. The same will be true in 1975. The end of 1975 retained earnings will be the same. The effect of the error is to overstate 1973 income by the understatement of interest income in 1974 and 1975.

1973	1974	1975
over	under	under

8.   (1176,T2,35)   (c)   The amount of $1 or the amount of an annuity of $1 are concerned with the future value of an amount invested today or a series of future payments. The present value of $1 and the present value of annuity of $1 are concerned with the value today of a future payment or series of future payments. Since the time value of money factor (TVMF) .9423 is less than 1, the answer has to be the present value of $1 or the present value of an annuity of $1. If it were the present value of an annuity of $1 (the present value of three future payments), the TVMF would have to be over 1 and somewhat less than 3. Thus, .9423 is the   present value of $1 to be received three years in the future.

9.   (1176,T2,36)   (c)   The requirement is the computation to determine the present value (value today) of a $3,000 payment at the end of each year, for five years. Thus, one multiplies the amount to be received at the end of each year ($3,000), times the time value of money factor for the present value of a payment at the end of each year, for five years (i.e., an annuity) at 6%. Answer (a) describes the amount of money one would have on hand at the end of the fifth year if $3,000 were deposited at the end of each year, for five years. Answers (b) and (d) are not generally relevant, as TVMFs are usually multiplied times the payment to get a present or future value.

PV or FV = TVMF x Payment(s)

10.   (1177,Q1,11) (a)   The requirement is the present value of $5,000 one year from now and $5,000 two years from now if the interest rate is 10%. Remember that present value (future value) equals a time value of money factor times the payment. The present value TVMF at 10% is $(1/1.1)^n$ Thus the present value of $5,000 in one year is $5,000 ÷ 1.1. Similarly, the present value of $5,000 two years from now is $5,000 ÷ 1.21 $[1.1^2]$ due to compounding.

$$5,000 ÷ 1.1\ \ = 4,545$$
$$5,000 ÷ 1.21 = \underline{4,132}$$
$$8,677$$

11. (1178,Q1,6)   (b)   The requirement is the cost of the machine purchased on the installment basis. Since the cash equivalent price was $9,500, the $11,000 total payment (4 payments at $2,500 plus the $1,000 down payment) is considered $1,500

interest and $9,500 machine cost. The $300 installation cost is also capitalized, as all costs required to get goods in their operating condition and location should be capitalized. Thus the total cost of the machine is $9,800.

12.   (579,T1,10)   (a)   The requirement is the situation which illustrates an annuity due. An annuity due (annuity in advance) is when the first payment takes place at the beginning of the first period, in contrast to an ordinary annuity (annuity in arrears), in which the first payment takes place at the end of the first period. In answer (a), the inital lease payment is due at the beginning of the first period. Answers (b), (c) and (d) all illustrate situations in which the first lease or interest payment occurs at the end of the first period.

13.   (576,T2,29)   (b)   The solutions approach to time value of money problems is a time diagram as illustrated below. As the problem indicates, it is an annuity in advance of eight payments, i.e., payments are made at the beginning of the period in contrast with an ordinary annuity wherein payments are made at the end of each period. Given a table for an ordinary annuity (or an annuity in arrears), simply note that it is an annuity of 7 payments plus the present value of the first payment. The present value of the first payment is 1, i.e., there is no discount. Thus the present value of an annuity in advance of 8 payments is the present value of an ordinary annuity for 7 payments plus 1.

PERIODS	1	2	3	4	5	6	7	8
Annuity in Advance	1	2	3	4	5	6	7	8
Annuity in Arrears		1	2	3	4	5	6	7

14.   (1174,T2,23)   (d)   The question asks for the present value of $1,000 to be received 3 years from today. The table presented is the present value of an amount. Simply take the present value factor of .794 times $1,000. Answer (a) is incorrect because it is the future value of $1,000 deposited today, i.e., if you deposit $1,000 today earning interest at 8% per year, the future value will be $1,000 divided by .794. Answers (b) and (c) imply annuities which are incorrect for this question.

15. (1174,T2,24) (a) This question involves an annuity, because there are to be annual payments of the same amount. The question asks for the present value of a $2,000 payment today and every year thereafter for a total of 4 payments. Thus one must compute the present value of the four payments. The present value of $2,000 today is $2,000. The present value of $2,000 one year from now is .926 X $2,000. The present value of $2,000 two years from now is $2,000 X .857. Answer (c) would have been correct if the first of the four payments were to be received at the end of the first year instead of the beginning of the first year. When the first payment of an annuity is received at the end of the first year, it is called an ordinary annuity. When the first payment of an annuity is received at the beginning of the first year, it is called an annuity due. Present value of an annuity tables are usually presented assuming an ordinary annuity, i.e., the first payment comes at the end of the first period.

16. (1174,T2,25) (c) The question calls for the future value of an amount rather than a present value of an amount. Present value of an amount is the reciprocal of the future value of an amount. For example, the present value of $10 to be received one year from now is $10/1+i and the value of $10 in one year is simply 1+i X $10. In this case we wish to find the future value of $3,000 two years from now so we divide $3,000 by the present value factor for n = 2 and i = 8%.

17. (1174,T2,26) (c) The present value of $4,000 six years from today would be the present value of $4,000 one year from today discounted back an additional five years, i.e., to find the present value factors for 6 years multiply the present value factor for 1 year times the present value for 5 years.

18. (1170,T1,7) (d) When dealing with a series of equal periodic payments, one is concerned with an annuity. When one is concerned with the value today, i.e., year zero, present value is appropriate rather than future value (often referred to as the "amount of").

MAY 1981 ANSWERS

19. (581,P1,15) (a) The requirement is to compute the amount of the $1,000,000 obligation maturing on June 15, 1981 that can be classified as long-term and the amount that will be classified as short-term. In order for a currently maturing liability to be classified as long-term, a company must show intent and ability to refinance the obligation. (SFAS 6, para 11) Stark, Inc., intends to refinance the entire $1,000,000; however, Stark only has the ability to refinance (.8 x $1,200,000) $960,000 due to the financing agreement that limits borrowing to 80% of the value of collateral. Thus, $40,000 ($1,000,000 − $960,000) is considered short-term and $960,000 is considered long-term.

20. (581,Q2,34) (b) The requirement is to calculate the cost of a machine to be paid for in five, $5,000 installments. Because the payments are equal, this is an annuity problem, and since the payments take place at the end of the period, it is an ordinary annuity. The cost of the machine is equal to the present value of the $5,000 ordinary annuity. The present value of the annuity is calculated by multiplying the amount of each payment ($5,000) by the factor for the present value of an ordinary annuity of $1.00 at 15% for 5 periods (3.35). Therefore, the cost of the machine is $16,750.

21. (581,T1,6) (d) The requirement is the amount that plant assets should be valued at when such assets are purchased under a deferred payment contract. Assets purchased on a deferred payment contract should be accounted for at the present value of the consideration to be exchanged between the contracting parties at the date of the transaction; this is necessary in order to properly reflect cost. The asset should not, therefore, be valued at $60,000, but at the present value of the total $60,000 in payments. To estimate the present value of these payments under these circumstances, an appropriate interest rate must be imputed. Answer (a) is incorrect because it does not take into consideration the $10,000 down payment. Answer (b) is incorrect because it does not take into consideration imputed interest on the obligation. Answer (c) is incorrect because imputed interest is deducted from the face of the obligation.

22. (581,T1,18) (b) The requirement is the annual interest rate that should be used to record interest expense on a two-year note which was issued in an arms-length transaction at face value solely for cash. APB 21, para 6 and para 10 state that when a note is issued solely for cash and no other right or privilege is exchanged, it is presumed to have a present value at issuance measured by the cash proceeds exchanged, and the interest factor is thus assumed to be the stated or coupon rate. Since the note issued solely for cash has a present value equal to the cash proceeds, interest expense other than that provided by the coupon or stated rate should not be imputed. If the parties also exchanged unstated or stated rights or privileges, a premium or discount is recorded, and the effective interest rate would differ from the stated rate.

MULTIPLE CHOICE ANSWERS

BONDS

23.	b	27.	b	31.	b	35.	b	39. c
24.	a	28.	c	32.	d	36.	a	
25.	c	29.	c	33.	d	37.	d	
26.	b	30.	a	34.	b	38.	b	

EXPLANATION OF MULTIPLE CHOICE ANSWERS

23. (1180,P1,12) **(b)** The requirement is the income Glenn should report for 1979 from a long-term investment in bonds. The bonds were purchased on July 1, so Glenn should recognize a half-year's cash interest less 6 months premium amortization. The cash interest for a half-year is ($200,000) (9%) (6/12) = $9,000 . The bond premium is $216,000 − 6,000 − 200,000 = $10,000. Since the bonds will be outstanding 80 months from the date of purchase, the bond premium amortization for the six months of 1979 in which Glenn held the investment is ($10,000)(6/80) = 750. Therefore, the income to be recognized would be $9,000 less $750 or $8,250.

24. (1180,P1,15) **(a)** The requirement is the amount of gain or loss that Provident should record on its early extinguishment of debt; the gain or loss is the difference between the carrying amount of the bonds and the cash paid to retire the bonds. In this case, the carrying amount of the bonds is the face value of the bonds plus the unamortized premium:

Unamortized
premium $= \$40,000 - (\$40,000)(\frac{5.5}{10}) =$ $18,000

Carrying
amount   = $1,000,000 + $18,000   = $1,018,000
Cash paid   = $1,000,000 × 101%   = $1,010,000

Gain: $1,018,000 − $1,010,000 = $8,000

The solutions approach might also include preparing the journal entry to record the retirement:

Bonds payable	1,000,000	
Bond Premium	18,000	
Cash		1,010,000
Gain on Retirement		8,000

25. (1180,Q1,19) **(c)** The requirement is the amount of the proceeds from the bond issue (with detachable warrants) which should be recorded as an increase in stockholders' equity. APB 14 states that the proceeds from the sale of debt with detachable stock warrants should be allocated between the two securities (debt and equity). 500 bonds ($500,000/$1,000) are issued with 30 warrants each, for a total of 15,000 warrants. Stockholders' equity is credited with the FMV of the warrants issued, (15,000) ($4), or $60,000.

26. (1180,Q1,20) **(b)** The requirement is the amount and classification of the gain to be recognized from the reacquisition of $600,000 of bonds issued 5 years earlier. The bonds were originally issued at 103% of par value or $618,000, which resulted in recording a premium of $18,000. At the time of retirement, the premium has been amortized for five years of the ten years the bonds were scheduled to be outstanding. Therefore, (5/10) ($18,000) or $9,000 has been amortized, leaving $9,000 of premium on the books. The solutions approach is to prepare the journal entry to record the retirement:

Bonds Payable	$600,000	
Bond Premium	$ 9,000	
*Cash		$588,000
Gain on retirement		$ 21,000

*($600,000) (98%)

This gain of $21,000 is classified as an extraordinary item per para 8 of FASB 4.

27. (580,P1,20) **(b)** The requirement is the amount of cash realized on the issuance of bonds. The solutions approach is to adjust the issue price for the accrued interest and issuance costs. Note that a 6% annual rate is 1% for 60 days. To obtain 9% for 60 days, move the decimal point two places to the left for 1% of $100,000 ($1,000) and add ½ of $1,000 for the additional 3%.

$103,000	Bond issue price
(5,000)	Issue costs
1,500	Accrued interest
$ 99,500	

28. (580,T1,10) **(c)** SFAS 4, para 8, states that gains and losses from extinguishment of debt shall be included in the determination of net income and classified as an extraordinary item. Answers (a) and (b) defer recognition of the gain or loss, while answer (d) does not classify the gain or loss as extraordinary.

29. (1176,Q1,3) **(c)** The proceeds of bonds issued with detachable purchase warrants should be allocated based upon fair market values at the time of issuance and accounted for separately. See para 16 of APB 14. In this instance, the portion attributed to warrants is 10 over 1,030 and the portion attributable to bonds is 1,020 over 1,030. Since the $1,030 was received for each bond, $10 would be credited to warrants and $1,020 credited to bonds payable ($1,000 to the liability and $20 to the premium account). The solutions approach is to journalize the entry.

Cash	$1030	
Stk. warrants		$ 10
Bonds payable		$1,000
Bond prem.		$ 20

30. (1176,Q1,11) (a) The solutions approach to a journal entry is to debit and credit individual accounts as they become apparent. First recognize that there is to be a debit to investment in bonds for $10,400. Second, there is accrued interest that is purchased and paid for which requires a debit to interest receivable or interest income. Third, there is a credit to cash for the sum of $10,400 plus the accrued interest. The accrued interest is from April 30 to September 1 or four months. For a year the interest is $800 (8% of $10,000). So four months' interest would be one-third of $800 or $266. Thus the cash paid must equal $10,666 including the accrued interest.

Investment in bonds	$10,400	
Interest receivable	266	
Cash		$10,666

31. (1179,Q1,14) (b) The requirement is the amount of extraordinary loss on retirement of $100,000 of bonds at 7/1/79. Bonds payable had a balance of $95,000 at 1/1/79 with a 6% nominal contract rate that were sold to yield 8%. Amortization of discount was under the effective interest method. The solutions approach is to determine the book value of the bonds at 7/1/79 and compare that to the $102,000 paid to retire the bonds. As calculated below, the effective interest was $3,800 for the 6 months ended 7/1/79, and the interest paid was $3,000, which resulted in $800 of discount amortization. Thus, the book value increased from $95,000 to $95,800 at 7/1/79. Since $102,000 was paid to liquidate a $95,800 liability, a $6,200 loss was incurred.

```
    95,000
      .04  (semi-annual)
 $ 3,800  effective interest
   3,000  cash paid (3% semi-annual of $100,000)
 $   800  discount amortization
```

Bond book value
```
   95,000  1/1/79 balance
      800  7/1/79 amortization
 $95,800  7/1/79
```
$102,000 paid - $95,800 liability = $6,200 loss

32. (1179,T1,1) (d) The requirement is the effect of selling a bond issue on June 1 when interest payment dates are May 1 and November 1. When the bond issue is sold on June 1, the purchaser will pay for the accrued interest from May 1 to June 1. On the following November 1, the bondholder will receive six months' interest. In other words, six months' interest is paid to bondholders at the interest payment date regardless of how long the bondholder has owned the bonds. If a bondholder sells the bonds between interest payment dates, the seller will receive interest for the number of days the bonds have been held since the last interest payment date. Answers (a) and (c) are incorrect because there is no adjustment for the amount of interest remaining within the bond interest period. Answer (b) is incorrect because the amount of cash received is increased rather than decreased for interest from the last payment date to the date of the sale of bonds.

33. (1177,T1,14) (d) Gain or loss on early extinguishment of debt is recognized in the period of extinguishment per para 20 of APB 26. The difference between the carrying value on the books and the market value (this difference giving rise to the gain or loss) is caused by changes in the market rate of interest subsequent to the date of issuance. See para 8 of APB 26. If the interest method recommended by APB 21 is used to amortize premium or discount on long-term liabilities, the book value and market value should coincide if the overall market rate of interest has not changed from the time of issuance.

34. (579,P1,8) (b) The requirement is the amount of the long-term investment in bonds at 12/31/78. Note that the bonds were purchased on 10/1/78 for $530,000 ($540,000 less $10,000 in accrued interest). The bonds mature on 1/1/85, resulting in 75 months of amortization. The monthly amortization is $400 ($30,000 divided by 75). Three months of amortization (Oct.-Dec.) would be $1,200, resulting in a bond book value of $528,800 ($530,000 − $1,200).

MAY 1981 ANSWERS

35. (581,P1,16) (b) The requirement is to compute the amount at which the bonds payable will be recorded, net of discount. The solutions approach is to remember that the quoted price of 97 only refers to the issue price of the bond itself. Thus, the bonds payable would be recorded at $194,000 ($200,000 × .97). The information given on accrued interest is peripheral to the problem.

36. (581,P2,31) (a) The requirement is to compute how much Welling paid for the $100,000 bonds of Mann, Inc. The solutions approach is to recall that the market price of a bond is equal to the present value of the (1) maturity value and (2) future cash interest receipts. The present value of the maturity value and interest receipts is computed using the yield or market rate, not the nominal rate. Thus, the amount paid for the bonds is:

amount		factor		
100,000	x	.3855	=	$38,550
8,000	x	6.1446	=	49,157
				$87,707

37. (581,Q2,21) (d) The requirement is the amount of gain or loss Elba must recognize from the bond retirement. Gain or loss will be the difference between the carrying value of the bonds and the call price on the date of retirement. The carrying value is the $200,000 face value of the bonds less the $16,000 bond discount, or $184,000. The call price Elba must pay to retire the bonds is 105% of the face value of the bonds, or $210,000. Thus, the loss is equal to:

$210,000	Call Price
− 184,000	Carrying Value
$ 26,000	Loss

38. (581,T1,9) (b) The requirement is to identify the proper accounting for the value of warrants attached to a debt security. Per APB 14, para 16, convertible debt with <u>detachable</u> stock warrants should be accounted for by allocating the issue price between the warrants (paid-in capital) and the bonds (debt) by using the relative sales value of the two securities at time of issuance. If the stock warrants are <u>non-detachable</u>, however, no value is assigned to the warrants (paid-in capital). The wording of this question makes it difficult to say whether (a) or (b) is the best answer. If the word "value" is emphasized, the best answer is (b). On the other hand, if we focus on the word "attached", answer (a) would seem to be a better choice. Answer (c), an appropriation of retained earnings, makes no sense because the event that is to be accounted for relates to an investment by bondholders. Answer (d), a liability, likewise makes no sense because warrants represent equity.

39. (581,T1,15) (c) The requirement is how the cash proceeds from convertible bonds sold at issue date at par should be recorded. APB 14, para 10 recommends that no portion of the proceeds from the issuance of convertible debt should be accounted for as attributable to the conversion feature. The main reason given for this treatment is the inseparability of the debt and conversion option.

MULTIPLE CHOICE ANSWERS

LEASES

40.	a.	44.	b	48.	d	52.	a	56.	a
41.	a	45.	a	49.	a	53.	a	57.	d
42.	c	46.	d	50.	b	54.	d	58.	d
43.	a	47.	a	51.	c	55.	a		

EXPLANATION OF MULTIPLE CHOICE ANSWERS

40. (1180,P1,14) (a) The requirement is the amount of interest income Benedict should record in the second year of an eight-year lease period. The income recorded would be 10% of the present value of the lease receivable balance outstanding in year 2 (1979). The interest can be computed using an amortization table.

	(1)Cash received	(2)10% Interest	P.V. of lease payments received
1/1/78			3,520,000
1/1/78	600,000		2,920,000
12/31/78		292,000	3,212,000
1/1/79	600,000		2,612,000
12/31/79		261,200	

(1) decreases in P.V. of lease payments
(2) increases in P.V. of lease payments

41. (1180,P1,16) (a) The requirement is the amount of income Arrow should report on the leased asset for 1979. Income from the lease is the monthly rental plus a proportionate fraction of the lease bonus less any depreciation expense.

Rental income = 11 months x $30,000	= $330,000
Lease bonus income = $72,000 x 11/36	= $ 22,000
Depreciation expense = $\dfrac{\$1,440,000}{8 \text{ years}}$	= ($180,000)
Income from leased asset	$172,000

Note that the lease bonus is recognized as income proprotionately over the 36 month lease period. The leased asset is depreciated for a full year since it has an 8-year life from the *date of purchase* (January 1).

42. (1180,T1,21) (c) The requirement is the classification of two leases by the lessee. SFAS 13 states that a lease shall be classified as a capital lease by the lessee if one or more of the four criteria are met. The criteria include a bargain purchase option, which both Lease Y and Lease Z contain. Therefore both would be classified as capital leases.

43. (1180,T1,22)   (a)   The difference between the gross investment in the lease and the sum of the present value of the two components (lease payments receivable + unguaranteed residual value) is unearned income. Answer (b) is incorrect because dealer's profit is the difference between the present value of the two components of gross investment and the cost of the leased asset. Answer (c) pertains to operating leases and deferred charges , answer (d), does not arrise in connection with the difference described.

44. (580,P1,10)   (b)   The requirement is to compute the gross profit and interest income of Fox as well as the interest expense and depreciation expense for Tiger. The situation is a sales-type lease for Fox and a capital lease for Tiger. Fox's gross profit is the difference between the present value of the lease payments (sales) and the cost of goods sold ($3,165,000 − $2,675,000 = $490,000 gross profit). Interest income for Fox is found by subtracting the first lease payment ($500,000) from the present value of the lease payments ($3,165,000). The difference is the outstanding balance for the first year ($2,665,000). Interest under the effective method is 12% (effective rate) x ½ year x $2,665,000 outstanding balance = $159,900 interest income in 1979.

45. (580,P1,11)   (a)   Tiger's interest expense is equal to the interest income recorded by Fox because Tiger capitalizes on an amount equal to the sales price. Straight-line depreciation is $3,165,000 ÷ 10 x ½ year = $158,250.

46. (580,T1,7)   (d)   Collection of rent in advance for an operating lease would be recorded by a debit to cash and a credit to a liability account (because the lessor owes the lessee use of the rented facilities). Therefore answers (b) and (c) are incorrect because no asset other than cash is involved and no revenue has been earned. Answers (a) and (d) are both liabilities. Accrued liability, answer (a), relates to an expense which has been incurred but has not been recorded or paid. Deferred revenue, answer (d), is revenue received before it has been earned.

47. (1179,P1,14)   (a)   The requirement is the amount of 1978 income before taxes for a lessor. First, note that the lease shall be accounted for as an operating lease, because the payments are not reasonably predictable, per para 8 of SFAS 13. The lessor's income per the operating method is the $240,000 rental income less the 1978 depreciation of $200,000 and maintenance and related costs of $18,000, which results in a $22,000 income for 1978.

48. (1179,P1,15)   (d)   The requirement is the amount of lease expense for the lessee under an operating lease. The operating method is appropriate because the collectibility of the minimum lease payments was not reasonably predictable (see para 8 of SFAS 13). The lease expense to the lessee is the lease payment of $240,000.

49. (1179,T1,12)   (a)   Lessors account for unearned income on direct financing leases by amortizing the interest income over the period of the lease using the interest method. This is per para 18b of SFAS 13. The entry to record a direct financing lease by a lessor is

    Gross lease receivable
        Leased property
        Unearned lease income

The unearned lease income is recognized over the life of the lease to provide a constant rate of return on the net lease receivable, which is the gross receivable minus the unearned lease revenue.

50. (577,Q1,2)   (b)   The requirement is the journal entry to record interest for 1976. An effective rate of interest of 10% is given. Since $11,836 was paid in advance on January 1, 1976, the amount of principle outstanding for the year was $68,164 ($80,000 minus $11,836). The interest would be 10% of $68,164, or $6,816. Para 18 of SFAS 13 requires that financing leases be recorded at gross, i.e., the total of lease payments be debited to lease receivables as illustrated below.

1-1-76	Lease receivable	$118,360	
	Machine		$80,000
	Unearned interest		38,360
1-1-76	Cash	$11,836	
	Lease receivable		$11,836
12-31-76	Unearned interest	$ 6,816	
	Interest revenue		$ 6,816

51. (1177,T1,5)   (c)   Lessees record leased assets which are in substance an installment purchase by debiting the asset and crediting a liability for the present value of the future minimum lease payments (para 10 of SFAS 13). Also see para 5j for the definition of minimum lease payments. The other answers are incorrect because the asset and liability are simply recorded at the present value of all future payments that nave to be made for the asset.

52. (1177,T1,20)   (a)   Lease agreements are to be recorded as purchases when in fact they are pur-

chases, i.e., conveying benefits and risks incident to ownership of the property (para 61, SFAS 13). Answer (b) is incorrect because when a lease agreement is required to be capitalized, it is substance over form rather than form over substance. Answer (c) is incorrect because capital leases provide use of the leased asset for an extended period of time, usually the useful life of the asset. Answer (d) is incorrect because capitalized lease transactions are not recorded on the basis of cause and effect, but rather substance over form.

53. (578,Q1,14) (a) The requirement is 6 months' rent expense resulting from an equipment sale on 6/30/77 and leaseback. Para 33 of SFAS 13 requires that profit or loss on the sale of assets which are leased back be deferred and amortized in proportion to rental payments over the lease if it is an operating lease. Accordingly the $50,000 of gain on sale of the equipment must be amortized over the remaining lease life of five years. Thus, for the last six months of 1977, $5,000 of the gain will be recognized, reducing the lease expense from $9,000 to $4,000.

54. (1178,P2,39) (d) The requirement is the implicit rate of interest in the lease given that $7,596 is the cash price or present value. The lease payments are an annuity in advance (note the table is given for an ordinary annuity, or annuity in arrears) of $2,000 each. The solutions approach is to compute the present value at 10%, 12%, and 16% of the annuity. The time value of money factor for an ordinary annuity of 4 years is multipled times $2,000 to obtain the present value of the payments for the beginning of the years 2 through 5. The present value of the $2,000 paid at the beginning of the year one is $2,000 which must be added to the present value of the annuity. As the table below indicates, the present value of the annuity in advance at 16% is $7,596.

	10%	12%	16%
TVMF			
(n = 4)	3.170	3.037	2.798
x $2,000	$6,340	$6,074	$5,596
+ $2,000	$8,340	$8,074	$7,596

55. (579,P1,11) (a) The requirement is the income (expense) for a lessor and two lessees regarding a piece of equipment on lease during 1978. Since it is an operating lease, the lessor (Standard) will recognize a total of $1,140,000 rental income (6 months' rent at $90,000 and 6 months' rent at $100,000). The lessor's depreciation will be $750,000 ($6,000,000 asset costs ÷ 8 yr.). Note that the requirement is

for income (not total revenue), which is $390,000 ($1,140,000 − $750,000).

The first lessee (Piping) will incur lease expense of $540,000 ($90,000 for 6 months). The second lessee (Tacking) will incur lease expense of $600,000 ($100,000 for 6 months).

56. (579,T1,6) (a) Per paras 7 and 8 of SFAS 13, for a lease to be classified as a sales-type or direct-financing-type lease, it must meet at least one of the four capital lease criteria. In addition, the collectibility of the lease payments must be assured, and there must be no important uncertainties. These last two conditions result in only answer (a) being correct. "Transfers ownership by end of lease" and "contains bargain purchase provision" are two of the four capital lease criteria. Note only one of these capital lease criteria must be met, and the lease be collectible and without important uncertainties.

MAY 1981 ANSWERS

57. (581,Q2,38) (d) The requirement of this problem is to make the necessary adjusting entry on December 31 to record the appropriate rental income. The solutions approach is to determine how much of the annual rental payment is earned income and how much should be deferred to the next period. The amount earned this period is calculated by multiplying the annual payment by the number of months this year used up over the total 12 months which is $18,000 x 8/12 or $12,000. The adjusting entry is:

Unearned rental income	12,000	
Rental income		12,000

58. (581,T1,8) (d) The requirement is how a lessee should record the amount equal to the present value of the minimum lease payments at the beginning of the lease term of a capital lease. Per SFAS 13, para 10, the lessee shall record a capital lease as an asset and a liability at an amount equal to the present value at the beginning of the lease term of the minimum lease payments during the lease term excluding executory cost.

MULTIPLE CHOICE ANSWERS

PENSIONS

59.	a	62.	c	65.	b	68.	b	71.	c
60.	a	63.	d	66.	b	69.	c	72.	c
61.	c	64.	d	67.	a	70.	b		

EXPLANATION OF MULTIPLE CHOICE ANSWERS

59. (1180,T1,25)   (a)   The pension expense accrued by a company will be increased by interest equivalents when "amounts funded are less than pension cost accrued." When a pension plan is underfunded, the amount of earnings actuarially assumed will not exist. Therefore, expense is increased by the amount of missing earnings (interest equivalents). Answer (b), "funding greater than pension cost accrued," would result in a decrease in pension expense for interest equivalents. Vesting (answer c) is not directly related to interest equivalents. If the plan is fully funded (answer d) there would not be an increase for interest equivalents.

60.   (580,T1,21)   (a)   Para 46 of APB 8 lists five items which should be disclosed concerning pension plans. These items are a statement identifying employee groups covered, a statement of accounting and funding policies answer (a), the provision for pension cost for the period, the excess of vested benefits over the amount funded or accrued, and the nature and effect of significant matters affecting comparability for all periods presented.

61.   (580,T1,33)   (c)   The entry age normal actuarial cost method is described in Appendix A of APB 8 as being an acceptable method, while terminal funding is designated as being not acceptable. Pay-as-you-go is not an actuarial method, and simply recognizes pension cost when benefits are paid (cash basis) and is thus unacceptable. Turnover is not a method but a term which means termination of employment for a reason other than death or retirement.

62.   (580,T1,34)   (c)   APB 8, para 17, permits a maximum annual provision for pension cost including normal cost plus the three elements identified in answer (c). Remember that normal cost plus the two elements in answer (d) comprise the minimum annual provision allowed.

63.   (1179,T1,8) (d)   Vested benefits in a pension plan are benefits that are not contingent on an employee continued service. The benefits are earned regardless of continued employment. Answers (a) and (b) are incorrect because benefits to be paid in any particular year do not include all benefits earned by an employee. Answer (c) is incorrect because benefits in the hands of a trustee are funded benefits, not vested benefits.

64.   (1179,T1,20) (d)   Past service costs in a pension plan represent costs assigned to years prior to the inception of the plan, per Appendix B of APB 8. Past costs are differentiated from normal costs and prior service costs. Normal cost is the cost assigned to a period subsequent to the inception of the plan per an actuarial cost method. Prior service cost is the pension cost assigned to years prior to the date of a particular actuarial evaluation. Accordingly, prior service costs include any remaining unamortized past service costs. Answer (a) is incorrect because past service costs may not be charged to income over a period less than 10 years. Answer (b) is incorrect because APB 8 does not contain funding requirements. APB 8 is concerned only with the accounting requirements for pension plans. Answer (c) is incorrect because pension costs assigned to years prior to the current balance sheet date are prior service costs.

65.   (1179,T1,21) (b)   An item that is included in the calculation of both the minimum and maximum annual pension expense is normal cost. The minimum consists of 1) normal costs, 2) interest on unfunded prior service costs, and 3) provision for vested benefits. The maximum consists of 1) normal costs, 2) 10% of past service costs, 3) 10% of increases or decreases in prior service costs from plan amendments, and 4) interest equivalents on difference between amounts expensed and amounts funded.

66.   (1176,P1,5)   (b)   A contributory pension plan is one in which employees, as well as employer, contribute to the cost of the plan. In 1975 the total actuarial cost of the plan was $320,000 of which $100,000 was contributed by employees. Actuarial cost is normal cost per APB 8 (see para 17 and Appendix B). Thus, the cost to the Pasther Company was $220,000. Since the Pasther Company is on an accrual basis, the fact that only $200,000 was actually paid in 1975 has no effect.

67.   (577,Q1,11)   (a)   The requirement is deferred pension costs for 1975. The solutions approach is to prepare the journal entry for the pension plan. Cash of $1,000,000 for past service costs and $560,000 for normal costs is paid out. The pension expense for the year is $650,000 of past service cost

amortization plus the normal cost of $560,000. The excess of cash payment over the current year's pension expense ($350,000) is deferred to future periods.

Pension expense	$1,210,000	
Deferred pension expense	350,000	
Cash		$1,560,000

68. (1177,T1,15) (b) Past service costs are the costs attributable to years of service prior to the inception of a pension plan. Prior service costs are those costs attributable to prior service as of a certain valuation date. Prior costs also include any remaining past service costs. Other prior costs arise from amendments to the plan, i.e., retroactive increases in benefits. See Appendix B — Glossary of APB 8. Answer (a) is incorrect because the definitions of past service costs and prior costs are interchanged.

69. (1178,Q1,14) (c) The requirement is pension expense for 1976 which consists of past cost and normal cost. In 1976, the normal costs are given as $70,000. While only $100,000 of past costs are going to be expensed in 1976, $113,909 is going to be funded. The result is a debit to deferred charges. The solutions approach is to record the entry for past pension cost in 1976 as illustrated below. Thus the $100,000 of past costs plus $70,000 normal costs results in pension expense of $170,000.

Pension expense	$100,000	
Deferred pension costs	13,909	
Cash		$113,909

70. (1178,Q1,15) (b) The requirement is the entry to record 1977 pension expense. Since the $75,000 normal cost was funded, and $113,909 of past cost is funded, the credit to cash is $188,909. Normal cost is given as $75,000. The problem indicates deferred charges increased by $14,744. Thus the past cost is a plug figure of $99,165 which consists of past costs amortization of $100,000 less $835 of interest equivalents. The $835 of interest equivalent is the interest earned on the amount that had been funded in 1976 in excess of the 12-year accrual.

Pension expense (normal)	$75,000	
Pension expense (past)	99,165	
Deferred pension costs	14,744	
Cash		$188,909

71. (579,T1,8) (c) The requirement is the situation in which amortization of past service costs would have to be reduced for interest presumed earned. Pension actuarial methods assume interest is being earned on funds assumed to be deposited. A typical assumption is that deposits are made as expense is accrued. When past service costs have been funded prior to accrual, there would be interest earned that was not expected in the actuarial assumptions. Para 17, APB 8, requires that interest adjustments be made when amounts deposited vary from actuarial assumptions. Answer (a) is incorrect because if past service costs have been accrued, but not funded, an additional pension cost provision would have to be made for the interest that was not earned on the unfunded amounts. Answer (b) is incorrect because the interest equivalents are determined by the relationship of pension cost accruals to pension funding, rather than between the amount of expense recorded and the maximum amount that could be recorded per APB 8. Answer (d) is incorrect because no interest is presumed earned on unaccrued costs.

MAY 1981 ANSWERS

72. (581,P1,7) (c) The requirement is to compute the **maximum** amount that Pierce can record as pension expense. The solutions approach is to remember that the maximum pension expense recorded in any one year should not be more than the total of

1. Normal Cost
2. 10% of past service cost
3. 10% of prior costs arising from amendments
4. Interest equivalent on any difference between amounts funded and amounts expensed.

Thus, the maximum pension expense allowed under APB 8 is $200,000 normal cost + $100,000 ($1,000,000 × .10) PSC amortization = $300,000.

ANSWER OUTLINE: FUNDAMENTAL CONCEPTS

Problem 1   Valuation of Notes

a1.   Notes should be valued at present value
     Also should be FMV of property exchanged
     At face if at a reasonable interest rate
   Notes consist of two elements
     Principal for property received
     Interest to compensate for use of funds

a2.   Value noninterest-bearing notes at FMV of property
     Or FMV of note, whichever is clearer
   If FMV of note cannot be established, impute interest rate
     Establish when note is issued based on
        Credit standing of issuer
        Restrictive covenants
        Collateral
        Payment and other terms
        Tax consequences to buyer and seller
        No subsequent change for changed interest rate
   Should not be less than debtor would pay elsewhere
   Objective is to approximate reasonable rate

b1.   Difference between FMV and face value is discount
   or premium
     Amortize as interest
     To result in a constant rate of interest
     I.e., the interest method
   May use other methods if not materially different

b2.   Discount or premium is offset to note
     I.e., not separate asset or liability
     Nor deferred charge or deferred credit
   Disclose effective interest rate
     Amortization is interest in income statement

UNOFFICIAL ANSWER: FUNDAMENTAL CONCEPTS

Problem 1   Valuation of Notes

a.   1.   A note received in exchange for property, goods, or services should be recorded at its present value which is presumably the value of the property exchanged. In the case of a note bearing interest at a reasonable rate and issued in an arm's-length transaction, the face value of the note should be used, as explained below.

      A note received for property, goods, or services represents two elements, which may or may not be stipulated in the note: (1) the principal amount, equivalent to the bargained exchange price of the property, goods, or services as established between the seller and the buyer and (2) an interest factor to compensate the seller over the life of the note for the use of funds he would have received in a cash transaction at the time of the exchange. Notes so exchanged are accordingly valued and accounted for at the present value of the consideration exchanged between the contracting parties at the date of the transaction in a manner similar to that followed for a cash transaction.

When a note is exchanged for property, goods, or services in a bargained transaction entered into at arm's length, there is a presumption that the rate of interest stipulated by the parties to the transaction represents fair and adequate compensation to the seller for the use of the related funds. In these circumstances the note's present value is identical with its face value. Furthermore, where the rate of interest is reasonable and separately stated, the face value of the note is equal to the bargained exchange price for the property.

2.   When a note bears no interest (or has a stated interest rate that differs sharply from the prevailing rate) and/or is not issued in an arm's-length transaction, the present value must be determined through consideration of the economic substance of the transaction.

The note and the sales price of the property, goods, or services exchanged for the note should be recorded at the fair value of the property, goods, or services or at an amount that reasonably approximates the market value of the note, whichever is the more clearly determinable. That amount may or may not be the same as the face amount; any resulting discount or premium should be accounted for as an element of interest over the life of the note.

In the absence of established exchange prices for the related property, goods, or services or evidence of the market value of the note, the present value of a note that stipulates no interest (or a rate of interest that differs sharply from the prevailing rate) should be determined by discounting all future payments on the note, using an imputed rate of interest as described below. This determination should be made at the time the note is issued; any subsequent changes in prevailing interest rates should be ignored.

The variety of transactions encountered precludes any specific interest rate from being applicable in all circumstances. However, some general guides may be stated. The choice of a rate may be affected by the credit standing of the issuer, restrictive covenants, the collateral, payment, other terms pertaining to the debt, and the tax consequences to the buyer and seller. The prevailing rates for similar instruments of issuers with similar credit ratings will normally help determine the appropriate interest rate. In any event, the rate used for valuation purposes will normally be at least equal to the rate at which the debtor can obtain financing of a similar nature from other sources at the date of the transaction. The objective is to approximate the rate that would have resulted if an independent borrower and an independent lender had negotiated a similiar transaction under comparable terms and conditions with the option to pay the cash price upon purchase or to give a note for the amount of the purchase that bears the prevailing rate of interest to maturity.

b. 1.   If the recorded value of a note differs from its face value, the difference should be treated as discount or premium and amortized as interest over the life of the note in such a way as to result in a constant rate of interest when applied to the amount outstanding at the beginning of any given period. This is the "interest" method. Other methods of amortization may be used if the results obtained are not materially different from those which would result from the "interest" method.

2.   The discount or premium is not an asset or liability separable from the note that gives rise to it. Therefore, the discount

or premium should be reported in the balance sheet as a direct deduction from or addition to the face amount of the note. It should not be classified as a deferred charge or deferred credit. The description of the note should include the effective interest rate. A valid alternative would be to report the note at its net value, disclosing the face amount of the note and the effective rate of interest on the face of the financial statements or in the notes to the statements.

Amortization of discount or premium should be reported as interest in the income statement.

SOLUTION GUIDE: FUNDAMENTAL CONCEPTS

Problem 2   Noninterest Bearing Note

This problem requires (1) the net receivable from Key at 12/31/78 and (2) the related income or loss before taxes for 1977 and 1978. The receivable is noninterest bearing and was received by Lock Company upon sale of property.

1.   The solutions approach is to determine the present value of the note at the beginning of 1977, and then to compute the interest income on the note in 1977 and 1978.

2.   Since there was no established exchange for the property, the present value of the note should be determined using the prevailing market interest rate for the type of note being discounted per paras 12-14 of APB 21. Thus the note should have been discounted at the prevailing interest rate of 12%. The time value of money factor for the present value of an annuity in advance (i = 12%, n = 6 where the first payment is made at the beginning of the first period) is 4.605. The present value of the note at the beginning of 1979 was $690,750 ($150,000 x 4.605).

3.   The interest for 1977 is $64,890 which is computed as 12% of the net receivable during 1977. The net receivable during 1977 was the present value of the future payments at 1/1/77 of $690,750 minus the $150,000 initial payment. Thus 1977 interest income should have been $64,890 ($540,750 x 12%).

4. The interest income in the second year should be $54,677 which is 12% of the net receivable during 1978 of $455,640 ($690,750 original present value minus 1/1/77 payment of $150,000 plus 1977 interest of $64,890 minus 1/1/78 payment of $150,000).

5. Finally, note that profit on sale on the property in 1977 was $90,750 (the sales price of $690,750 minus $600,000 original cost).

UNOFFICIAL ANSWER: FUNDAMENTAL CONCEPTS

Problem 2   Noninterest Bearing Note

1.   *Lock Company*
COMPUTATION OF BALANCE IN NET RECEIVABLES FROM KEY
December 31, 1978

	Prin-cipal	Un-earned interest	Net receiv-able
Sales price ($150,000 X 4.605)	$900,000	$209,250	$690,750
Payment made on January 1, 1977	150,000	—	150,000
	750,000	209,250	540,750
Interest income for 1977 (Schedule 1)	—	64,890	64,890
Balance at December 31, 1977	750,000	144,360	605,640
Payment made on January 1, 1978	150,000	—	150,000
	600,000	144,360	455,640
Interest income for 1978 (Schedule 2)	—	54,677	54,677
Balance at December 31, 1978	$600,000	$ 89,683	$510,317

2.   *Lock Company*
INCOME BEFORE INCOME TAXES
For the years ended December 31, 1977 and 1978

	1977	1978
Profit on sale:		
Sales price ($150,000 X 4.605) $690,750		
Cost of property 600,000	$ 90,750	—
Interest income (Schedules 1 and 2)	64,890	$54,677
Income before income taxes	$155,640	$54,677

Schedule 1

Computation of Interest Income for 1977

Sales price	$690,750
Payment made on January 1, 1977	150,000
	540,750
Interest rate	12%
Interest income	$ 64,890

Schedule 2

Computation of Interest Income for 1978

Balance at December 31, 1977 ($540,750 + $64,890)	$605,640
Payment made on January 1, 1978	150,000
	455,640
Interest rate	12%
Interest income	$ 54,677

SOLUTION GUIDE: BONDS

Problem 3   Effective Interest and Early Extinguishment of Debt

a1.   Effective interest method applies constant interest rate to net book value of debt

Straight-line method applies a constant dollar amortization over life of debt

    Results in a changing effective interest rate on net book value of debt

Both methods compute premium or discount as difference between maturity value of debt and issuance proceeds

a2.   Interest method requires computation of effective interest rate

Effective rate discounts future principal and interest payments to equal proceeds of bond issue

Interest expense is the effective rate times the net book value of the debt (maturity value adjusted by discount or premium)

Amortization is difference between interest expense and interest paid

Amortization increases when debt premium exists

    Due to decreasing carrying value of the debt

    And corresponding decrease in interest expense

Amortization increases in the case of a discount

    Due to the increasing carrying value of the debt

    And corresponding increase in interest expense

Thus amortization varies due to the changing book value of the debt per the interest method

In contrast straight-line amortization yields a constant amortization over life of debt

b1.   Three methods of accounting for debt refunding

    Amortize gain or loss over remaining life of old debt

    Gain or loss is cost of interest savings on existing debt

        Refunding occurs due to interest savings

    Gain or loss to be amortized over the life of new debt

        Gain or loss affects the cost of obtaining a new debt

        Thus benefits life of new debt

        And should be amortized over life of that debt

    Gain or loss recognized in period of refunding

        Refunding gain or loss the same as other debt extinguishments

            Generally gain or loss is recognized in year of extinguishment

        Recognizes change in value of the debt

        Relates its interest fluctuations to prior periods

            If debt was carried at market, no extinguishment gain or loss would exist

Call premiums and unamortized discount are adjustments to interest cost of bond extinguished

    Gain or loss should be recognized immediately

b2.   The immediate recognition principle is only acceptable method

    If material, it is an extraordinary item

UNOFFICIAL ANSWER: BONDS

Problem 3   Effective Interest and Early Extinguishment of Debt

Part a.

1.   The effective interest method of amortization of bond discount or premium applies a constant interest rate to the carrying value of debt as opposed to the straight-line method that applies a constant dollar amount over the life of the debt resulting in a changing effective interest rate paid based on the carrying value of the debt. Either method, however, computes the premium or discount to be amortized as the difference between the par value of the debt and the proceeds from the issuance.

2.   Before the interest method of amortization can be used, the effective yield or interest rate of the bond must be computed. The effective yield rate is the interest rate that will discount the two components of the debt instrument to the amount received at issuance. The two components in the value of a bond are the present value of the principal amount due at the end of the bond term and the present value of the annuity represented by the periodic interest payments during

the life of the bond. Interest expense using the interest method is based upon the effective yield or interest rate multiplied by the carrying value of the bond (par value effected for unamortized premium or discount). The amount of amortization is the difference between recognized interest expense and the interest actually paid (par value multiplied by nominal rate). When a premium is being amortized, the dollar amount of the periodic amortization will increase over the life of the instrument due to the decreasing carrying value of the bond instrument multiplied by the constant effective interest rate, which is subtracted from the amount of cash interest paid. In the case of a discount, the dollar amount of the periodic amortization will increase over the life of the bond due to the increasing carrying value of the bond instrument multiplied by the constant effective interest rate from which is subtracted the amount of cash interest paid. The varying amounts of amortization occur because of the changing carrying value of the bond over the life of the instrument.

In contrast, the straight-line method of amortization yields a constant dollar amount of amortization based upon the life of the instrument regardless of effective yield rates demanded in the marketplace.

Part b.

1.   *Gain or loss to be amortized over the remaining life of old debt.* The basic argument supporting this method is that if refunding is done to obtain debt at a lower cash outlay (interest cost), then the gain or loss is truly a cost of obtaining the reduction in cash outlay. As such, the new rate of interest alone does not reflect the cost of the new debt, but a portion of the gain or loss on the extinguishment of the old instrument must be matched with the nominal interest to reflect the true cost of obtaining the new debt instrument. This argument states that this matching must continue for the unexpired life of the old debt in order to reflect the true nature of the transaction and cost of obtaining the new debt instrument.

Gain or loss to be amortized over the life of the new debt instrument. This argument states that the gain or loss from early extinguishment of debt actually affects the cost of obtaining a new debt instrument. However, this method asserts that the effect should be matched with the interest expense of the new debt for the entire life of the new debt instrument. This argument is based on the assumption that the debt was refunded to take advantage of new lower interest rates or to avoid projected high interest rates in the future and that any gain or loss on early extinguishment should be reflected as an element of this decision and total interest cost over the life of the new instrument should be stated to reflect this decision.

Gain or loss recognized in the period of extinguishment. Proponents of this method state that the early extinguishment of debt to be refunded actually does not differ from other types of extinguishment of debt where the consensus is that any gain or loss from the transaction should be recognized in full in current net earnings. The early extinguishment of the debt is prompted for the same reason that other debt instruments are extinguished, namely, that the value of the debt instrument has changed in light of current financial circumstances and early extinguishment of the debt would produce the most favorable results. Also, it is argued that any gain or loss on the extinguishment is directly related to market interest fluctuations related to prior periods. If the true market interest rate had been known at the time of issuance, there would be no gain or loss at the time of extinguishment. Also, even if market interest rates were not known but the carrying value of the bond was periodically adjusted to market, any gain or loss would be reflected at the interim dates and not in a future period. The call premium paid on extinguishment and any unamortized premium or discount are actually adjustments to the actual effective interest rate over the outstanding life of the bond. As such, any gain or loss on the early extinguishment of debt is related to prior-period valuation differences and should be recognized immediately.

2.   The immediate recognition principle is the only acceptable method of reflecting gains or losses on the early extinguishment of debt, and these amounts, if material, must be reflected as extraordinary items.

SOLUTION GUIDE: BONDS

Problem 4   Accounting for Bonds

a.   Accounting for proceeds from bonds issued with detachable stock purchase warrants
    Portion of proceeds allocable to warrants should be accounted for as paid-in capital
    Remainder of proceeds should be allocated to the debt security
        Discount (or, infrequently, a decreased premium) usually results

b.   Serial bond matures at a series of installment dates; term bond matures entirely on a single date

c.   Difference between interest method and straight-line method of bond premium amortization .

      Interest method uses constant interest rate applied to changing balance (carrying value)

      Use of straight-line method results in recognition of equal amount of premium amortization each period

      Amount of amortization in year 1 would be lower using interest method than if straight-line method were used

d.   Entry to record bonds issued between interest dates is

Cash (amount = bond price + accrued interest)	XXX	
Discount on bonds payable	XXX	
Bonds payable (par)		XXX
Accrued interest payable (or interest expense)		XXX

      Amortization is affected because discount should be amortized over the period from date of sale (not date of bond) to the maturity date

e.   Gain (loss) on reacquisition of long-term bond prior to maturity; classify by purpose of reacquisition

      To meet sinking fund requirements - ordinary income

      All other reacquisitions - if material, extraordinary item (net of tax)

UNOFFICIAL ANSWER: BONDS

Problem 4   Accounting for Bonds

a.   Because detachable stock purchase warrants are equity instruments that have a separate fair value at the issue date, the portion of the proceeds from bonds issued with detachable stock purchase warrants allocable to the warrants should be accounted for as paid-in capital. The remainder of the proceeds should be allocated to the debt security portion of the transaction. This usually results in issuing the debt security at a discount (or, occasionally, a reduced premium).

b.   A serial bond progressively matures at a series of stated installment dates, for example, one-fifth each year. A term (straight) bond completely matures on a single date.

c.   The amortization in the first year of the life of a five-year term bond issued at a premium would differ using the interest method instead of the straight-line method because the interest method employs a uniform interest rate based upon a changing balance,

whereas the straight-line method provides for the recognition of an equal amount of premium amortization each period. Because the interest method provides for an increasing premium amortization each period, the amount of amortization in the first year of the life of the bond would be lower.

d.   The journal entry to record a bond issue sold between interest dates is as follows:

·   Debit cash for the price of the bond plus the accrued interest from the last interest date.

·   Debit discount on bonds payable for the amount of discount to be amortized over the remaining life of the issue.

·   Credit bonds payable for the par value of the bonds.

·   Credit accrued interest payable (or interest expense) for the accrued interest from the last interest date.

      The subsequent amortization of bond discount is affected when a bond issue is sold between interest dates because the discount should be amortized over the period from the date of sale (not the date of the bond) to the maturity date.

e.   The gain or loss from the reacquisition of a long-term bond prior to its maturity should be included in the determination of net income for the period reacquired and, if material, classified as an extraordinary item, net of related income taxes.

SOLUTION GUIDE: BONDS

Problem 5   Issuance and Extinguishment

1.   This problem consists of 3 unrelated parts concerning bonds payable.

2.   Part a. requires a schedule computing the total amount received from the sale of $1,000,000 of 8% bonds. The bonds mature ten years after the date of sale, and interest is paid at the end of each year. The bonds were sold to yield a 10% return to the purchaser.

    2.1   The solutions approach is to compute the present value of the $1,000,000 maturity value, and the present value of the annuity of the ten $80,000 (8% of $1,000,000) interest payments.

    2.2   The present value of $1,000,000 ten years in the future is $1,000,000 times .3855 (the present value of $1 for 10 periods at 10%).

2.3 The present value of 10 annual payments of $80,000 is $80,000 times 6.1446 (the present value of an ordinary annuity of $1 for 10 periods).

3. Part b. requires the general journal entry to record the issuance of 4,000 bonds with detachable stock purchase warrants. Each bond carried two warrants and the warrants had a quoted market price of $3 shortly after issuance.

3.1 The $100,000 bonds were sold for 104 or $4,160,000 plus accrued interest less issue costs. The accrued interest is for 3 months (June-August) which is 25% of the annual interest cost of $360,000 ($4,000,000 @ 9%) or $90,000. The bond issue costs were $40,000. Thus cash is to be debited for $4,210,000 ($4,160,000 + $90,000 − $40,000).

3.2 The bond issue costs of $40,000 are debited as a deferred charge per para 16 of APB 21.

3.3 The credits are to bonds payable $4,000,000, interest expense or payable $90,000, stock warrants $24,000, and bond premium $136,000. The stock warrants are credited for $6 (2 warrants per bond @ $3) times 4,000 bonds. No allocation of the net proceeds is made between the bonds and the warrants, because no market value was established for the bonds. The $136,000 credit to bond premium is the $160,000 (4% of $4,000,000) less the $24,000 assigned to stock warrants.

4. Part c. requires a schedule to compute the gain or loss on the reacquisition of $2,000,000 of 7% bonds. The bonds were issued on 1/1/76 for $2,200,000. Interest is payable on November 1 and May 1. Note that the premium has been amortized on a straight-line basis.

4.1 The solutions approach is to determine the book value of the bonds at the date of sale (7/1/79) and compare it with the reacquisition price.

4.2 If the book value of the bonds was $2,200,000 on 12/1/76 and $2,100,000 on 12/31/78, 25 months have resulted in $100,000 of amortization, i.e., $4,000/month.

4.3 Thus the book value of the bonds will be $2,076,000 (2,100,000 less 6 months at $4,000) on 7/1/79. The bonds were repurchased for $1,960,000 (2,000 bonds @ $980). Thus the gain is $116,000 ($2,076,000 liability extinguished for $1,960,000). Note that the accrued interest on the bonds at issuance or reacquisition has no effect on the bond book value, reacquisition cost, or gain or loss.

UNOFFICIAL ANSWER: BONDS

Problem 5   Issuance and Extinguishment

Part a.

Hopewell Company
COMPUTATION OF TOTAL AMOUNT RECEIVED FROM SALE OF BONDS
January 1, 1979

Present value of the future principle ($1,000,000 X 0.3855)	$385,500
Present value of future annual interest payments ($80,000 ($1,000,000 X 8%) X 6.1446)	491,568
Amount received from sale of bonds	$877,068

Part b.

Junction Company
JOURNAL ENTRY
September 1, 1978

	Debit	Credit
Cash	$4,210,000	
Bond issue costs deferred	40,000	
Bonds payable (4,000 X $1,000)		$4,000,000
Premium on bonds payable (Schedule 1)		136,000
Detachable stock warrants (Schedule 1)		24,000
Bond interest expense (Schedule 2)		90,000

To record the issuance of the bonds.

Schedule 1

Premium on Bonds Payable and
Value of Stock Warrants

Sales price (4,000 X $1,040)	$4,160,000
Face value of bonds	4,000,000
	160,000
Deduct value assigned to stock warrants (4,000 X 2 = 8,000 warrants X $3)	24,000
Premium on bonds payable	$ 136,000

Schedule 2

Accrued Bond Interest to Date of Sale

Face value of bonds	$4,000,000
Interest rate	9%
Annual interest	$ 360,000
Accrued interest (3 months) — ($360,000 X 3/12)	$ 90,000

Part c.

Cone Company
**COMPUTATION OF GAIN ON EARLY
EXTINGUISHMENT OF DEBT**
July 1, 1979

Book value of bonds on December 1, 1976	$2,200,000
Book value of bonds on December 31, 1978	2,100,000
Amortization for 25 months	$ 100,000
Monthly amortization ($100,000 ÷ 25)	$ 4,000
Book value of bonds on December 31, 1978	$2,100,000
Amortization for 1979 to July 1, 1979 ($4,000 X 6 months)	24,000
Book value of bonds on July 1, 1979	2,076,000
Cost of reacquisition (2,000 X $980)	1,960,000
Gain on early extinguishment of debt	$ 116,000

SOLUTION GUIDE: BONDS

Problem 6   Discount Calculation

1. Part a requires 1) the total amount received from the issuance of $1,000,000 of serial bonds, and 2) an amortization schedule of bond discount assuming the bonds were sold at a $26,247 discount.

2. The amount to be received from the issuance of serial bonds is the present value of the principal and interest payments to be made on the bonds. Interest is to be paid annually at the end of each year. Thus the solutions approach is to determine the cash flow at the beginning of years 1979 through 1983 and then compute the present value of each cash flow at a discount rate of 6% as illustrated below. Note that the principal payment for each of the years 1979 through 1983 is $200,000.

Year	Interest Payment*	Total Payment	TVMF (6%)	Present Value
1/1/79	$50,000	$250,000	.9434	$235,850
1/1/80	40,000	240,000	.8900	213,600
1/1/81	30,000	230,000	.8396	193,108
1/1/82	20,000	220,000	.7921	174,262
1/1/83	10,000	210,000	.7473	156,933
		Net cash proceeds of bond issue		$973,753

*5% of $1,000,000 for 1978, 5% of $800,000 for 1979, etc.

2.1 An alternative solution would be to compute the present value of each interest payment separately and then compute the present value of the principal repayments as the present value of an annuity of $200,000 for five years.

3. The second requirement of part a is to prepare a bond discount amortization schedule for the first two years if the bonds were sold at a $26,247 discount.

4. Recall that under the interest method, interest income or interest expense is the effective rate times the outstanding book value of the receivable or payable. The cash payment is the contract rate times the maturity or face value. The difference between the interest income or expense and the cash receipt or cash payment is the amortization of discount or premium.

4.1 If the discount is $26,247, the net book value during 1978 is $973,753 ($1,000,000 − $26,247). The interest expense for MyKoo Corporation in 1978 would be $58,425 ($973,753 x 6%). Since the cash payment is $50,000 ($1,000,000 x 5%), the amortization is $8,425 ($58,425 − $50,000). The entry is

Bond interest expense $58,425
  Cash $50,000
  Bond discount   8,425

4.2 During 1979 the carrying value of the bonds is $782,178 ($1,000,000 maturity value minus $200,000 principal payment minus $17,822 bond discount). Recall that the original discount of $26,247 was amortized by $8,425 during 1978. Thus the interest expense in 1979, the second year of the issue, is $46,930 ($782,178 x 6%), and the interest payment is $40,000 ($800,000 x 5%). The resulting amortization is $6,930. The entry is:

Bond interest expense $46,930
  Cash $40,000
  Bond discount   6,930

UNOFFICIAL ANSWER: BONDS

Problem 6   Discount Calculation

Schedule for Problem 6 appears on following page

SOLUTION GUIDE: DEBT RESTRUCTURE

Problem 7   Entries for Modification of Terms

1. SFAS No. 15 prescribed the accounting treatment for "troubled" debt which is either satisfied by the exchange of an asset or equity interest, is extended with a modification of terms, or a combination of the two. This problem deals with a combination situation whereby the debt is partially satisfied by English Bank accepting shares of Irish, Inc.'s stock (requirements a and b) or land (requirement c) and then extending the debt and modifying its terms.

2. A quick review of the steps to take in debt restructuring problems should make this problem straight-forward.

2.1 If the debt is forgiven entirely by an asset or equity interest transferred, the difference between the book value of the debt including accrued interest and the FMV of the transfer is a "gain" to the debtor and a "loss" to the creditor.

2.2 If the debt is only partially satisfied by the transfer of an asset or equity interest (the situation in this problem), the debt is first reduced by the FMV of the transfer.

2.3 The difference between the pre-restructure debt amount and the FMV is treated as modification of terms. The steps to take are:
  Calculate the total future cash flows under the new terms.
  Compare the total future cash flows to the loan payable or loan receivable balance on each set of books.

2.4 If the total future cash flows are less than the debt, write the debt down to equal the future cash flows recognizing a gain (debtor) and loss (creditor). In this case the remaining debt is equal to the PV of future cash flows. Consequently, there is no future interest to be recognized, i.e., each cash payment is applied totally against the debt.

Problem 6

1.

MyKoo Corporation
SCHEDULE OF TOTAL AMOUNT RECEIVED FOR SERIAL BOND

Present value of amount to be paid on January 1 each year
for 5 years at an annual yield of 6% ($200,000 × 4.2124) $842,480

Present value of interest to be paid at the end of each year
for 5 years at an annual yield of 6% computed as follows:

Date	Bonds outstanding	Interest at 5%	Present value factor at 6%	Present value of interest payments
12/31/78	$1,000,000	$50,000	.9434	$47,170
12/31/79	800,000	40,000	.8900	35,600
12/31/80	600,000	30,000	.8396	25,188
12/31/81	400,000	20,000	.7921	15,842
12/31/82	200,000	10,000	.7473	7,473

Total present value of interest payments   131,273

$973,753

2.

MyKoo Corporation
AMORTIZATION OF BOND DISCOUNT
Interest (Effective Rate) Method

Year	(A) Carrying value of bonds ($1,000,000 − E − F)	(B) Effective interest expense (6% × A)	(C) Interest payments	(D) Amortization of bond discount (B − C)	(E) Bond discount balance (E − D)	(F) Cumulative principal payments
Issue	$973,753				$26,247	
1	782,178	$ 58,425	$ 50,000	$ 8,425	17,822	$ 200,000
2	589,108	46,930	40,000	6,930	10,892	400,000
3	394,454	35,346	30,000	5,346	5,546	600,000
4	198,121	23,667	20,000	3,667	1,879	800,000
5	0	11,879*	10,000	1,879	0	1,000,000
		$176,247	$150,000	$26,247		

*Rounding differences ignored.
Note: Computations for years 3, 4, and 5 are not part of requirement but are included in answer so that complete schedule can be presented.

2.5 If the future cash flows are greater than the debt, there is no gain or loss recognized. In this situation the debt on the books is the PV of the future cash flows, i.e., the cash flows discounted at some effective interest rate have a PV equal to the debt before restructure. The rate which will equate the future cash flow and debt must be determined and interest expense and revenue will be recognized for each cash payment using the effective interest method.

UNOFFICIAL ANSWER: DEBT RESTRUCTURE

Problem 7   Entries for Modification of Terms

Debt on books at restructure	$110,000 + $11,000 = $121,000	
FMV of stock transferred	40,000 x $1.25 =	50,000
Debt after transfer of stock		$ 71,000
Cash flow under new terms $60,000 + ($60,000 x .05 x 3)=		$ 69,000
Excess of debt over total cash flow		($ 2,000)

Since the total future cash flow is less than the debt on the books at restructure recognize gain or loss and apply each future cash payment totally against debt.

a. Entries by Irish, Inc.:

1978

Accrued interest payable	$11,000	
Notes payable ($110,000 − $69,000)	41,000	
Common stock		$40,000
Additional paid-in capital		10,000
Gain on restructure (extraordinary)		2,000

1979, 1980, and 1981

Notes payable	$ 3,000	
Cash		$ 3,000

Also in 1981

Notes payable	$60,000	
Cash		$60,000

b. Entries by English Bank:

1978

Allowance for doubtful accounts (or loss on restructure	$ 2,000	
Investments: Irish, Inc. CS	50,000	
Notes receivable ($110,000 - $69,000)		$41,000
Accrued interest receivable		11,000

1979, 1980, and 1981

Cash	$ 3,000	
Notes receivable		$ 3,000

Also in 1981

Cash	$60,000	
Notes receivable		$60,000

c.1.

Pre-restructure amount	$121,000	
Fair value of land transferred	55,000	
Unrecovered pre-structure amount		66,000
Total future cost flows [$60,000 + ($60,000 x .05 x 3)]		69,000
Excess of future cash flows over pre-structure amount		3,000

Therefore no gain or loss is recognized on modification of terms

Irish, Inc.—1978

Land	$ 5,000	
Gain on transfer		$ 5,000
Accrued interest payable	11,000	
Notes payable	44,000	
Land		55,000

English Bank—1978

Investments - land	$55,000	
Notes receivable		$44,000
Accrued interest rec.		11,000

2.   Since the total future cash flows after the restructure exceed the pre-restructure amount and no gain or loss is recognized, a new effective interest rate must be determined. (Computation under "c.1" above.) The difference between the annual $3,000 of stated interest per the restructure agreement and the interest based on the effective rate is a reduction of note receivable (English Bank) and notes payable (Irish, Inc.). The amount of "stated interest dollars" that are used to reduce the pre-restructure debt remaining is:

Unrecovered prestructure amount	$66,000
New face amount of note	60,000
	6,000

As a result over the remaining three years $6,000 of the $9,000 specified as interest is used to reduce the principal of the note per books.

SOLUTION GUIDE: LEASES

Problem 8   Description of Lease Accounting

a1.   Accounting for lessee's capital lease which transfers title to leased property
 Inception of lease
  Record asset and obligation
 During first year
  Apply lease payments to reduction of principal and interest expense
 Depreciate leased asset using lessee's normal depreciation policy
  Use life of asset in this case because title will pass to lessee

a2.   Accounting for lessee's operating lease
 Inception of lease
  No asset or liability recorded
 During first year
  Recognize rent expense on a straight-line basis
   Use other basis only if more representative of benfit receipt pattern (i.e., more rational)

b1.   Sales-type leases versus direct financing leases
 For both gross investment in lease is
 Minimum lease payments + unguaranteed residual value

  Minimum lease payments include guaranteed residual value but exclude executory costs
b2.   Amortization of unearned interest (lease) income for both utilizes the effective interest method
 Results in a constant rate of return per period
 Other methods of amortization acceptable if amounts obtained not materially different
b3.   Manufacturer's or dealer's profit
 Sales-type
  Profit = sales price − carrying amount
 Direct financing
  No dealer's profit
   Only income is from interest

UNOFFICIAL ANSWER: LEASES

Problem 8   Description of Lease Accounting

Part a.

1.   A lessee would account for a capital lease as an asset and an obligation at the inception of the lease. Rental payments during the year would be allocated between a reduction in the obligation and interest expense. The asset would be amortized in a manner consistent with the lessee's normal depreciation policy for owned assets, except that in some circumstances, the period of amortization would be the lease term.

2.   No asset or obligation would be recorded at the inception of the lease. Normally, rental on an operating lease would be charged to expense over the lease term as it becomes payable. If rental payments are not made on a straight-line basis, rental expense nevertheless would be recognized on a straight-line basis unless another systematic or rational basis is more representative of the time pattern in which use benefit is derived from the leased property, in which case that basis would be used.

Part b.

1.   The gross investment in the lease is the same for both a sales-type lease and a direct-financing lease. The gross investment in the lease is the minimum lease payments (net of amounts, if any, included therein for executory costs such as maintenance, taxes, and insurance to be paid by the lessor, together with any profit thereon) plus the unguaranteed residual value accruing to the benefit of the lessor.

2.   For both a sales-type lease and a direct-financing lease, the unearned interest income would be amortized to income over the lease term by use of the interest

method to produce a constant periodic rate of return on the net investment in the lease. However, other methods of income recognition may be used if the results obtained are not materially different from the interest method.

3.   In a sales-type lease, the excess of the sales price over the carrying amount of the leased equipment is considered manufacturer's or dealer's profit and would be included in income in the period when the lease transaction is recorded.

In a direct-financing lease, there is no manufacturer's or dealer's profit. The income on the lease transaction is composed solely of interest.

ANSWER OUTLINE: Leases

Problem 9   Capital Leases

a1.   Lessee entered into a capital lease
PV of minimum lease payments exceeds 90% of asset FMV

a2.   Use incremental borrowing rates (10%) to capitalize lease
Lessee does not know lessor's implicit rate

a3.   Lessee accounts affected by capital lease
Fixed asset is recorded
A corresponding liability is recorded
Classified both current and non-current
Machine costs depreciated over the life of the lease
Lease payments represent principal and interest
Interest expense is constant percentage on remaining book value of debt
Executory costs are expensed as incurred
E.g., insurance, maintenance, taxes, etc.

a4.   Lessee capital lease disclosures
Future minimum lease payments in aggregate
less
Executory costs
Interest costs
Which will equal present value of liability
Minimum lease payments for each of five succeeding years

b1.   Lessor entered into a direct financing lease
No dealer or manufacturer profit exists
PV of minimum lease payments exceeds 90% of asset FMV
Collectibility is reasonably assured

No important uncertainties exist

b2.   Record gross amount of minimum lease payments and unguaranteed residual value as lease receivable
Credit cost of machine being leased
Balancing credit is unearned interest revenue

b3.   Lessor records payments received as a reduction of the receivable
Unearned interest revenue is recognized by interest method
I.e., implicit rate times the net book value of the receivable
Implicit rate is that which discounts minimum lease payments and unguaranteed residual value to asset FMV

b4.   Lessor capital lease disclosures
Components of net investment in leases
Future minimum lease payments to be received
Unguaranteed residual values
Unearned interest revenue
Future minimum lease payments to be received
For each remaining year not to exceed 5 years

UNOFFICIAL ANSWER: LEASES

Problem 9   Capital Leases

a.

1.   Because the present value of the minimum lease payments is greater than 90 percent of the fair value of the asset at the inception of the lease, Milton should record this as a capital lease.

2.   Since the given facts state that Milton (lessee) does not have access to information that would enable determination of James's (lessor) implicit rate for this lease, Milton should determine the present value of the minimum lease payments using the incremental borrowing rate (10 percent) that Milton would have to pay for a like amount of debt obtained through normal third-party sources (bank or other direct financing).

3.   The amount recorded as an asset on Milton's books should be shown in the fixed assets section of the statement of financial position as "Fixed Assets Acquired Through Lease" or another similar title. Of course, at the same time as the asset is recorded, a corresponding liability ("Obligations Under Capital Leases") is recognized in the same

amount. This liability is classified as both current and noncurrent, with the current portion being that amount that will be paid on the principal amount during the next year. The machine acquired by the lease is matched with revenue through depreciation over the life of the lease, since ownership of the machine is not expressly conveyed to Milton in the terms of the lease at its inception. The minimum lease payments represent a payment of principal and interest at each payment date. Interest expense is computed at the rate at which the minimum lease payments were discounted and represents a fixed interest rate applied to the declining balance of the debt. Executory costs (such as insurance, maintenance, or taxes) paid by Milton are charged to an appropriate expense, accrual, or deferral account as incurred or paid.

4.   For this lease, Milton must disclose the future minimum lease payments in the aggregate and for each of the succeeding fiscal years, with a separate deduction for the total amount for imputed interest necessary to reduce the net minimum lease payments to present value of the liability (as shown on the statement of financial position).

b.

1.   Based upon the given facts, James has entered into a direct financing lease. There is no dealer or manufacturer profit included in the transaction; the discounted present value of the minimum lease payments is in excess of 90 percent of the fair value of the asset at the inception of the lease agreement; collectibility of minimum lease payments is reasonably assured; and there are no important uncertainties surrounding unreimbursible costs to be paid by the lessor.

2.   James should record the gross amounts of minimum lease payments and the unguaranteed residual value of the machine at the end of the lease as minimum lease payments receivable and remove the machine given up from the books by a credit to the applicable asset (inventory) account. The balancing amount in this entry is recorded as unearned revenue.

3.   During the life of the lease, James will record payments received as a reduction in the receivable. Unearned revenue is recognized as earned interest revenue by applying the implicit interest rate to the declining balance of a gross minimum lease payments receivable reduced by payments re-

ceived and the balance of unearned revenue. The implicit rate is the rate of interest that, when applied to the gross minimum lease payments (net of executory costs and any profit thereon) and the unguaranteed residual value of the machine at the end of the lease, will discount the sum of the payments and unguaranteed residual value to the fair value of the machine at the date of the lease agreement. This method of earnings recognition is termed the interest method of amortization of unearned revenue.

4.   James must make the following disclosures with respect to this lease:

a.   The components of the net investment in direct financing leases, which are (1) the future minimum lease payments to be received, (2) any unguaranteed residual values accruing to the benefit of the lessor, and (3) the amounts of unearned revenue.

b.   Future minimum lease payments to be received for each of the remaining fiscal years (not to exceed five) as of the date of the latest statement of financial position presented.

SOLUTION GUIDE: LEASES

Problem 10   Lessee's Capital Lease

1.   The problem requires you to find:

     A.   The present value of future lease payments.

     B.   A tax deficiency given an improper prior period's journal entry and the tax rate.

     C.   Journal entries on the books of the lessee.

2.   Note that the payments are an annuity due, i.e., the first payment is to be made at the beginning of the first year. Use an ordinary annuity for 9 years instead of 10 years and add 1 to the TVMF. Discount the annuity for years 11 through 20 back to year 10 and then take the present value of that amount back to year 1.

3.   The tax deficiency is the tax rate times the excess of claimed expenses over bona fide expenses. The bona fide expenses are depreciation, interest, tax and insurance expenses.

4. The journal entries are required for the third year which in turn requires you to determine the interest (and related principal repayment) for years 1, 2, and 3.

UNOFFICIAL ANSWER: LEASES

Problem 10   Lessee's Capital Lease

a.

Archibald Freight Company
SCHEDULE TO COMPUTE THE
DISCOUNTED PRESENT VALUE OF
TERMINAL FACILITIES AND THE
RELATED OBLIGATION TO THE LESSOR
January 1, 1978

Present value of first 10 payments:		
Immediate payment	$1,000,000	
Present value of an ordinary annuity for 9 years at 6% ($1,000,000 X 6.801692)	6,801,692	$7,801,692
Present value of last 10 payments:		
First payment of $300,000	300,000	
Present value of an ordinary annuity for 9 years at 6% ($300,000 X 6.801692)	2,040,508	
Present value of last 10 payments at January 1, 1980	2,340,508	
Discount to January 1, 1970 ($2,340,508 X .558395)		1,306,928
Discounted present value of terminal facilities and related obligation to lessor		$9,108,620

b.

Archibald Freight Company
SCHEDULE TO COMPUTE AN
ESTIMATE OF THE DEFICIENCY IN
FEDERAL INCOME TAXES
For 1978

Allowable amortization of terminal facilities:		
$10,000,000 ÷ 40 years		$ 250,000
Interest expense:		
Discounted present value	$10,000,000	
Less immediate payment	1,000,000	
Unpaid balance in 1978	9,000,000	
6% interest		540,000
Property taxes		75,000
Insurance		125,000
Total allowable expenses		$ 990,000
Rental deduction claimed		$1,200,000
Less allowable expenses		$ 990,000
Excess deductions claimed		$ 210,000
Tax deficiency (40% X $210,000)		$ 84,000

c.

Archibald Freight Company
JOURNAL ENTRIES
1980

(1)

Accrued interest payable	$ 512,400	
Leasehold obligation	487,600	
Property taxes	75,000	
Property insurance	125,000	
Cash		$1,200,000

To record lease payment

Capitalized value at January 1, 1978		10,000,000
Less immediate payment		−1,000,000
Leasehold debt outstanding for 1978		9,000,000
Lease payment on January 1, 1979	$1,000,000	
Less interest at 6% on $9,000,000	− 540,000	
Principal reduction		− 460,000
Leasehold debt outstanding for 1979		8,540,000
Lease payment on January 1, 1980	1,000,000	
Less interest at 6% on $8,540,000	−512,400	
Principal reduction		−487,600
Leasehold debt outstanding for 1980		$8,052,400

(2)

Amortization of leased properties	$ 250,000	
Buildings leased from others		250,000

To record equivalent of annual depreciation expense on leased assets ($10,000,000 ÷ 40 years).

(3)

Interest on leasehold obligation	483,144	
Accrued interest payable		483,144

To record interest accrual at 6% on outstanding debt of $8,052,400.

SOLUTION GUIDE: PENSIONS

Problem 11   Definitions

a1. Normal cost is pension cost attributable to specific years subsequent to the inception of a pension plan
   I.e., actuarially determined cost of an additional year of employee service
   To be accrued annually

a2. Past service cost represents cost attributable to employee service prior to the inception of the pension plan
   Incurred at the adoption of a plan
   Not set up as a liability unless the benefits are vested
   Expensed over future years to income
      Minimum is assumed interest on unfunded amounts
      Maximum is 10% amortization per year (straight-line)
      Independent of funding

a3. Prior service cost is attributable to years prior to a date when the plan is actuarially evaluated
   I.e., similar in nature to past service costs
      And by definition includes past service costs
   Typically due to a retroactive amendment
   Expensed as are past costs (see a2. above)

a4. Pension "interest" refers to the actual or anticipated return on amounts funded or amounts expected to be funded
   To be obtained on pension fund investment portfolio
      Includes interest, dividends, gains, losses, etc.
      Accounted for per the accrual basis
   Accrue interest on unfunded prior service costs annually

b1. Arguments in favor of accruing past service costs
  · as funded

   Past service cost may never be funded except
     as to interest
       I.e., may be indefinitely deferred
   Past service cost is an intangible not diminish-
     ing value
   Actuarial assumptions do not apply to indi-
     viduals
   Accrual may create misconception concerning
     pension accounting
   And may result in a drop in expense when
     totally amortized
     And does not extinguish the liability for
       nonaccrued and nonfunded past service
       cost
     Pension costs are expensed without regard
       to any particular period of time (and
       employee benefit)
     Other employment costs are discretionary,
       e.g., bonuses

b2. Arguments for accruing past service cost irrespective of funding

   Past service cost is an employment cost and
     should be expensed over a reasonable
     period
   Funding interest only is subjective and if
     underfunded may increase past service
     costs
   While actuarial assumptions are invalid for
     individuals, they do apply to groups of
     people
   The matching concept is a pervasive argu-
     ment
   Pension liabilities do not require immediate
     payment and thus should be done on the
     accrual basis
   Conservatism dictates expensing over a rea-
     sonable period rather than deferral

UNOFFICIAL ANSWER: PENSIONS

Problem 11   Definitions

Part a.

1. Normal cost. Normal cost represents the annual
cost assigned, under the actuarial cost method in
use, to years subsequent to the inception of a pension plan or to a particular valuation date. Depending on the actuarial method adopted, this cost may
represent (1) the present value of an annuity, to be
paid at a future date, in an amount equal to the
benefits earned by the employee(s) during the year
(unit credit) or (2) the incremental cost of an annuity in a projected amount representing the total
benefits expected to be paid to an employee or
group of employees at a future date (entry age
normal). Generally accepted accounting principles
require that normal cost be accrued annually.

2. Past service cost. Past service cost represents
pension cost assigned to years prior to the inception
of a pension plan. This cost arises when a company
chooses to recognize (at the date of the adoption of
a formal pension plan) the past service of employees
as a credit towards their eventual retirement.

   Generally accepted accounting principles provide some latitude in the accrual of past service
cost. At minimum, the interest presumed to be
earned on the unfunded past service cost must be
accrued. The minimum accrual reflects the theory
held by some actuaries that, because of the nature
of a large pool of employees covered by a pension
plan, it is highly probable that the actual amounts
representing past service cost need never be funded
in order to pay benefits as employees retire. Under
this theory it is only necessary to accrue the assumed interest earned to avoid increasing the total
amount attendant to past service cost.

   Presently the maximum accrual of past service
cost is 10 percent per year (straight-line basis) until
fully accrued. The maximum accrual was determined to prevent arbitrary and excessive write-
offs of past service cost and to recognize that the
past service cost has a finite life with respect to
the benefits provided to the company by their
incurrence. It must be stressed, however, that the
accrual of past service cost is to be accomplished
in the current and future periods (if done at all)
and not as some type of prior-period adjusting.
The accrual of past service cost is usually independent (with the exception of interest accrual
for unfunded amounts) of the actual funding of
the cost.

3. Prior service cost. Prior service cost represents
pension cost assigned, under the actuarial cost
method in use, to years prior to the date of a
particular actuarial valuation. Past service cost
(cost that represents the amount of benefits
earned by existing employees prior to the adoption
of a specific pension plan) is classified as prior
service cost, and costs attributable to prior service resulting from the amendment of an existing
pension plan are also classified as prior service
cost.

Prior service cost resulting from amendment of an existing pension plan is accounted for in the same manner as past service cost. At a minimum, the interest presumed earned on the amount of unfunded prior service cost must be accrued on an annual basis, and the maximum accrual (amortization) of prior service cost is 10 percent per year (straight-line basis). As with past service cost, prior service cost is to be accrued (if done at all) in the current and future periods and not as some type of prior-period adjustment. The accrual of prior service cost is completely independent (with the exception of interest accrual for unfunded amounts) of the actual funding of the cost.

4. Interest. In actuarial terminology, the term interest connotes the return earned or assumed to be earned on funds invested or to be invested to provide for future pension benefits. In calling the return "interest," it is recognized that, in addition to interest on debt securities, the earnings of a pension fund may include dividends on equity securities, rentals on real estate, and gains or (as offsets) losses on fund investments.

Interest earned (or assumed to be earned on unfunded prior cost) is recognized on the accrual basis.

Part b.

1. Proponents of accruing past service cost only to the extent funded list the following arguments for doing so:

- Many employers believe that past service cost will never be funded except with regard to interest. If this is true it would be improper to make accounting provision for amounts that will never be paid.

- In granting past service credits under a pension plan, an employer obtains diverse advantages of indefinite duration. Past service cost is thus in the nature of an intangible that does not diminish in value and need not be amortized (accrued).

- To require an annual provision for past service cost (in excess of payments) is to espouse the erroneous concept that pension accounting can be based on particular people at a particular time. Actuarial assumptions are not valid for individuals.

- The credit balance from accrued but not funded past service cost, if a liability, is a curious one, since it is not payable to anyone in particular.

- If the objective of accruing past service cost over a period of years is to provide a level charge to earnings, it must be considered that a sharp drop in annual pension expense may occur when the accrual (amortization) of past service cost has been completed.

- Accruing pension cost in excess of amounts funded does not effectively extinguish the liability for pensions in that the unfunded portion remains at risk as though no accrual had been made.

- Pension cost is a loading on employment cost, but without regard to the way employee benefits are measured and without regard to any particular period of time, either before or after the adoption of a pension plan. The key requirement is that the annual pension charge be a reasonable measurement of the annual amount required to balance the benefits to be paid in the future. For a relatively mature employee group, the amount of such an annuity would be approximately the same as an annual contribution of normal cost plus interest on past service cost for present employees.

- Many companies, in successful years, pay discretionary additional compensation (bonuses). Other companies have deferred profit-sharing arrangements. The cost of both bonuses and profit-sharing plans varies from year to year. Consequently, employers should have flexibility in deciding when (if at all) to charge past service cost to expense.

2. Proponents of the accrual of past service cost whether or not funded cite the following arguments in favor of their position:

- Past service cost is a cost of providing pensions for the employees initially covered and so should be charged to expense over a reasonable period following the inception of a plan.

- Funding interest alone on past service cost is subjective regarding the rate of interest the funds will earn. In fact, if the interest rate factor is too low, past service costs may grow because too little interest is accrued (funded) during a period.

· Even though actuarial assumptions are invalid for individuals, the facts concerning individuals are the raw materials for making the pension cost calculation. Since the purpose of pension cost is to estimate the cost of providing pensions for a specific group of individuals, the entire cost (including past service costs) must be considered based on the individuals that compose the group.

· The matching concept is a pervasive argument in accounting for past service cost. Matching expenses and revenues for a given period of time is essentially independent of funding the expenses. Further, a desire for levelness in charges to expense is not an adequate reason for failing to record an element of cost.

· The commitment to pay pensions to employees is long term and is not motivated by the immediate availability of earnings and cash as may be the case for bonuses and profit sharing. As such, the cost of the pension plan should be recorded in accordance with the matching and accrual concept without direct regard to earnings and availability of cash.

· The accounting concept of conservatism would appear to require that these costs, when their existence is known, be charged to earnings in a manner that does not defer a charge against earnings to a future period when a cause-and-effect relationship cannot be clearly established. If this concept were not adhered to, the effect would be to overstate earnings in the current period and understate earnings in future periods.

SOLUTION GUIDE: PENSIONS

Problem 12   Plan Calculations

1. This problem requires knowledge that actuarial gains and losses must be averaged or spread for a number of years and cannot be recognized in the period of realization (para 30 of APB 8). Also gains and losses occurring as a result of a single occurrence not related to the pension plan should be recognized separately (para 31 of APB 8).

2. The second requirement in part a involves the maximum and minimum pension charge (see para 17 of APB 8).
    Minimum
        Normal cost
        Interest on unfunded past service costs
        Provision for vested benefits
    Maximum
        Normal cost
        10% of past service cost
        10% of changes in prior service costs
        Interest equivalents on difference between provisions and amount funded

3. Pension plan disclosure requirements are outlined in para 46 of APB 8.
        Statement of who is covered by the plan
        Company's accounting and funding policy
        The cost for current period
        Excess of vested benefits over the pension fund
        Nature and effect of any other significant matters

UNOFFICIAL ANSWER: PENSIONS

Problem 12   Plan Calculations

a.   1.   The actuary's report discloses that the total of net actuarial gains for the year was recognized currently by reducing normal cost. Accepted accounting practice provides that actuarial gains and losses be given effect in the provision for pension cost in a consistent manner that reflects its long-range nature.

Those actuarial gains and losses listed by the actuary, except the one resulting from the plant closing, arise from the ordinary operation of the pension plan and the employer's business. Rather than being recognized in the year of occurrence, they should be spread over the current year and future years or recognized on the basis of an average. The spreading or averaging should be accomplished by separate adjustments of the normal cost resulting from the routine application of the method. A reasonable period for spreading of the separate adjustment is from 10 to 20 years. Alternatively, an effect similar to spreading or averaging may be obtained by applying net actuarial gains as a reduction of prior service cost (past service cost in this instance as the plan has not been amended) in a manner that reduces the annual amount equivalent to interest on, or the annual amount of amortization of, such prior service cost, and does not reduce the period of amortization.

An actuarial gain or loss arising from a single occurrence not directly related to the operation of a pension plan and not in the ordinary course of the employer's business should be recognized immediately as an adjustment of the gain or loss from the unusual occurrence. Therefore, the gain from the plant closing should be excluded from the determination of pension cost.

The actuary's report does not indicate that any consideration was given to the unrealized appreciation in the value of the fund assets. Such unrealized appreciation or depreciation should be recognized in the determination of the provision for pension cost on a rational and systematic basis that avoids giving undue weight to short-term market fluctuations. Such recognition should be given either in the actuarial assumptions or in the same manner as other kinds of ordinary actuarial gains and losses.

2. The annual provision for pension cost should be based on an accounting method that uses an acceptable actuarial cost method and results in a provision between certain minimum and maximum limitations. The method should be applied consistently from year to year.

The entry-age-normal method is an acceptable actuarial cost method. The pension cost computed under this method (after correction of the errors in computing actuarial gains) should, therefore, be compared to the limitations.

The minimum limitations is the total of (1) normal costs, (2) an amount equivalent to interest on unfunded past service cost, and (3) under certain conditions, a provision for vested benefits.

The maximum limitation is the total of (1) normal costs, (2) ten percent of past service cost (until fully amortized), (3) ten percent of the amounts of any

increases or decreases in prior service costs arising on amendments of the plan (until fully amortized), and (4) interest equivalents on the difference between provisions and amounts funded.

Some of the items entering into the computation of the limitations may, of course, be zero. For instance, the pension plan under discussion has never been amended nor has there been vesting of benefits.

b. The note to the financial statements should include at least the following information:

The company has a pension plan covering all of its employees. The total pension expense for the year was $29,015, which includes amortization of past service cost over fifteen years. The company's policy is to fund past service cost over ten years plus an amount equal to current normal cost net of actuarial gains and losses. There were no vested benefits as of June 30, 1973.

MULTIPLE CHOICE QUESTIONS

CHANGING PRICES (1–27)

1. In accordance with FASB Statement No. 33, the Consumer Price Index for All Urban Consumers is used to compute information on a
   - a. Historical cost basis.
   - b. Current cost basis.
   - c. Nominal dollar basis.
   - d. Constant dollar basis.

2. Hadley Corporation purchased a machine in 1977 when the average Consumer Price Index (CPI) was 180. The average CPI was 190 for 1978, and 200 for 1979. Hadley prepares supplementary constant dollar statements (adjusted for changing prices). Depreciation on this machine is $200,000 a year. In Hadley's supplementary constant dollar statement for 1979, the amount of depreciation expense should be stated as
   - a. $180,000
   - b. $190,000
   - c. $210,526
   - d. $222,222

3. Victor Company purchased a machine on December 31, 1977, for $100,000. The machine is being depreciated on the straight-line basis with no salvage value and a five-year life. Assume that there was a rise in current (replacement) cost of the machine of 10% during 1978, and of 10% during 1979 (based on the December 31, 1978, current cost). In a supplementary current cost statement at December 31, 1979, Victor would report accumulated depreciation for the above machine of
   - a. $42,000
   - b. $44,000
   - c. $46,200
   - d. $48,400

4. Dart Company was formed on January 1, 1978. Selected balances from the historical cost balance sheet at December 31, 1979, were as follows:

Land (purchased January 1, 1978)	$90,000
Marketable securities, non-convertible bonds (purchased July 1, 1978, and expected to be held to maturity)	50,000
Long-term debt	70,000

The average Consumer Price Index was 100 for 1978, and 110 for 1979. In a supplementary constant dollar balance sheet (adjusted for changing prices) at December 31, 1979, these selected account balances should be shown at

	Land	Marketable Securities	Long-Term Debt
a.	$90,000	$50,000	$70,000
b.	$90,000	$55,000	$77,000
c.	$99,000	$50,000	$70,000
d.	$99,000	$55,000	$77,000

5. Financial statements that are expressed assuming a stable monetary unit are   †
   - a. Constant-dollar financial statements.
   - b. Historical-dollar financial statements.
   - c. Current-value financial statements.
   - d. Fair-value financial statements.

6. Job Company purchased a machine on January 1, 1977, for $500,000. Job is depreciating the machine on a straight-line basis with no salvage and a five-year life. At December 31, 1977, the replacement cost (current value) of the machine was $410,000. On January 1, 1978, the machine was sold for $412,000. Ignoring income taxes, what amount should be shown as a result of the sale of the machine in 1978 in Job's current value statements?
   - a. $ 2,000 gain.
   - b. $ 8,000 gain.
   - c. $10,000 gain.
   - d. $12,000 gain.

7. In current cost financial statements   †
   - a. Purchasing power gains or losses are recognized on net monetary items.
   - b. Amounts are always stated in common purchasing power units of measurements.
   - c. All balance sheet items are different in amount than they would be in a historical-cost balance sheet.
   - d. Holding gains are recognized.

Items 8 and 9 are based on the following information:

In 1972, Mount Hope Inc., purchased a machine   † for $1,000. The machine has a ten-year life, and no salvage value. Mount Hope prepares supplemental constant dollar financial statements (financial statements restated for changes in the general purchasing power of the dollar), as recommended by SFAS 33. Indexes of the general price level appropriate for use in preparing those financial statements are as follows:

Year	Index (1958=100)
1972	148
1973	159
1974	175
1975	181
1976	185

8. What amount should be reflected as depreciation for this machine in Mount Hope's general price-level income statement for the year ended December 31, 1976?

    a. $100 x 181 ÷ 185.
    b. $100.
    c. $100 x 185 ÷ 181.
    d. $100 x 185 ÷ 148.

9. What amount should be reflected for this machine, before accumulated depreciation in Mount Hope's general price-level balance sheet at December 31, 1976?

    a. $1,000 x 181 ÷ 185.
    b. $1,000.
    c. $1,000 x 185 ÷ 181.
    d. $1,000 x 185 ÷ 148.

10. Constant dollar financial statements have † been a controversial issue in accounting. Which of the following arguments in favor of such financial statements is not valid?

    a.   Constant dollar financial statements use historical cost.
    b.   Constant dollar financial statements compare uniform purchasing power among various periods.
    c.   Constant dollar financial statements measure current value.
    d.   Constant dollar financial statements measure earnings in terms of a common dollar.

Items 11. and 12. are based on the following information:

The following schedule lists the following consumer price indices:

12/31/71	100
12/31/72	110
12/31/73	115
12/31/74	120
Average 1975	140

11. In December 1974, the Meetu Corporation † purchased land for $300,000. The land was held until December 1975, when it was sold for $400,000. The constant dollar statement of income for the year ended December 31, 1975, should include how much gain or loss on this sale?

    a. $20,000 loss.
    b. $20,000 general price-level loss.
    c. $50,000 gain.
    d. $100,000 gain.

12. On January 1, 1972, the Silver Company pur- † chased equipment for $300,000. The equipment was being depreciated over an estimated life of 10 years on the straight-line method, with no estimated salvage value. On December 31, 1975, the equipment was sold for $200,000. The constant dollar statement of income prepared for the year ended December 31, 1975, should include how much gain or loss from this sale?

    a. $10,600 loss.
    b. $16,000 gain.
    c. $20,000 gain.
    d. $52,000 loss.

13. An analysis of the Gallant Corporation's "Machinery and Equipment" account as of December 31, 1975, follows:

Machinery and Equipment

Acquired in December 1972	$400,000
Acquired in December 1974	100,000
Balance	$500,000

Accumulated Depreciation

On equipment acquired in December 1972	$160,000
On equipment acquired in December 1974	20,000
Balance	$180,000

A constant dollar balance sheet prepared as † of December 31, 1975 should include machinery and equipment net of accumulated depreciation of

    a. $284,848.
    b. $360,000.
    c. $398,788.
    d. $448,000.

14. Which of the following methods of reporting † attempts to eliminate the effect of the changing value of the dollar?

a. Discounted net present value of future cash flows.
b. Constant dollar.
c. Replacement value.
d. Retirement value.

15. Level, Inc., was formed on January 1, 1977, †
when common stock of $200,000 was issued for cash
of $50,000 and land valued at $150,000. Level did not
begin operations until 1978, and no transactions occurred
in 1977 except the recording of the issuance of the
common stock. If the consumer price index was 100
at December 31, 1976, and averaged 110 during 1977,
what would the purchasing power gain or loss be in
Level's 1977 constant dollar income statement?

a. $0.
b. $5,000 loss.
c. $5,000 gain.
d. $15,000 gain.

16. Index Co. was formed on January 1, 1977. †
Selected balances from the historical-dollar balance
sheet at December 31, 1977, were as follows:

Cash	$60,000
Marketable securities, stocks (purchased January 1, 1977)	70,000
Marketable securities, bonds, (purchased January 1, 1977 and held for price speculation)	80,000
Long-term receivables	90,000

If the consumer price index was 100 at December 31,
1976, and averaged 110 during 1977, these selected
accounts should be shown in a constant dollar balance
sheet at December 31, 1977, at

	Cash	Marketable Securities, Stocks	Marketable Securities, Bonds	Long-term Receivables
a.	$60,000	$70,000	$80,000	$90,000
b.	$60,000	$70,000	$80,000	$99,000
c.	$60,000	$77,000	$88,000	$90,000
d.	$60,000	$77,000	$88,000	$99,000

17. Fair Value, Inc., paid $1,200,000 in December †
1976 for certain of its inventory. In December 1977,
one-half of the inventory was sold for $1,000,000
when the current cost of the original inventory was
$1,400,000. Ignoring income taxes, what amount should
be shown as the total gain resulting from the above
facts in a current value income statement for 1977?

a. $200,000.
b. $300,000.
c. $400,000.
d. $500,000.

18. Following are four observations regarding the †
amounts reported in constant dollar financial statements. Which observation is valid?

a. The amount obtained by adjusting an asset's
cost for general price-level changes usually
approximates its current fair value.
b. The amounts adjusted for general price-
level changes are not departures from
historical cost.
c. When inventory increases and prices are
rising, last-in, first-out (LIFO) inventory
accounting has the same effect on financial
statements as amounts adjusted for general
price-level changes.
d. When inventory remains constant and prices
are rising, LIFO inventory accounting has
the same effect on financial statements as
amounts adjusted for general price-level
changes.

19. Coleman, Incorporated, purchased a machine on †
January 1, 1970, for $100,000. Coleman is depreciating
the machine on a straight-line basis with no salvage and
a ten-year life. At December 31, 1976, the current cost
of the machine was $32,000. On January 1, 1977, the
machine was sold for $35,000. Ignoring income taxes,
what amount should be shown as the gain or loss on
the sale of the machine in a current cost income statement for 1977?

a. $2,000 gain.
b. $3,000 loss.
c. $3,000 gain.
d. $5,000 gain.

20. Which of the following is not a method of
determining the current value of an asset?

a. Replacement cost.
b. Market value.
c. Restatement of cost for changes in
general price level.
d. Net present value of expected future
cash flows.

21. On December 30, 1976, Future, Incorporated, †
paid $2,000,000 for land. At December 31, 1977, the
current value of the land was $2,200,000. In January
1978, the land was sold for $2,250,000. Ignoring
income taxes, by what amount should stockholders'
equity be increased for 1977 and 1978 as a result of
the above facts in current value financial statements?

	1977	1978
a.	$ 0	$ 50,000
b.	$ 0	$250,000
c.	$200,000	$ 0
d.	$200,000	$ 50,000

22. When constant dollar balance sheets are pre- †
pared, they should be presented in terms of
  a. The general purchasing power of the dollar
     at the latest balance sheet date.
  b. The general purchasing power of the
     dollar in the base period.
  c. The average general purchasing power of
     the dollar for the latest fiscal period.
  d. The general purchasing power of the dollar
     at the time the financial statements are
     issued.

23. During a period of deflation an entity would †
have the greatest gain in general purchasing power by
holding
  a. Cash.
  b. Plant and equipment.
  c. Accounts payable.
  d. Mortgages payable.

24. In preparing constant dollar financial statements, †
monetary items consist of
  a. Cash items plus all receivables with a fixed
     maturity date.
  b. Cash, other assets expected to be converted
     into cash and current liabilities.
  c. Assets and liabilities whose amounts are
     fixed by contract or otherwise in terms of
     dollars regardless of price-level changes.
  d. Assets and liabilities which are classified as
     current on the balance sheet.

25. Gains and losses on nonmonetary assets usually †
are reported in historical-dollar financial statements
when the items are sold. Gains and losses on the sale
of nonmonetary assets should be reported in constant
dollar financial statements
  a. In the same period, but the amount will
     probably differ.
  b. In the same period and the same amount.
  c. Over the life of the nonmonetary asset.
  d. Partly over the life of the nonmonetary
     asset and the remainder when the asset
     is sold.

MAY 1981 QUESTIONS

26. Details of Monmouth Corporation's fixed
assets at December 31, 1980, are as follows:

Year acquired	Percent depreciated	Historical cost	Estimated current cost
1978	30	$50,000	$70,000
1979	20	15,000	19,000
1980	10	20,000	22,000

Monmouth calculates depreciation at 10% per annum,
using the straight-line method. A full year's depreciation is charged in the year of acquisition. There were no
disposals of fixed assets. Monmouth prepares supplementary information for inclusion in its 1980 annual
report as required by the Financial Accounting Standards Board. In Monmouth's supplementary information restated into current cost, the net current cost
(after accumulated depreciation) of the fixed assets
should be stated as
  a. $58,000.
  b. $65,000.
  c. $84,000.
  d. $91,000.

27. The following schedule lists the average consumer
price index (all urban consumers) of the indicated year:

1978	100
1979	125
1980	150

Carl Corporation's plant and equipment at December
31, 1980, are as follows:

Date acquired	Percent depreciated	Historical cost
1978	30	$30,000
1979	20	20,000
1980	10	10,000
		$60,000

Depreciation is calculated at 10% per annum, straight-
line. A full year's depreciation is charged in the year of
acquisition. There were no disposals in 1980.

What amount of depreciation expense would be
included in the income statement adjusted for general
inflation (historical cost/constant dollar accounting)?
  a. $6,000.
  b. $7,200.
  c. $7,900.
  d. $9,000.

MULTIPLE CHOICE QUESTIONS

FOREIGN CURRENCY (28–41)

28. Exchange gains and losses resulting from translating foreign currency financial statements into U.S. dollars should be included as
    a.   A deferred item in the balance sheet.
    b.   An extraordinary item in the income statement for the period in which the rate changes.
    c.   An ordinary item in the income statement for losses but deferred for gains.
    d.   An ordinary item in the income statement for the period in which the rate changes.

29. A wholly owned foreign subsidiary of Union Corporation has certain expense accounts for the year ended December 31, 1979, stated in local currency units (LCU) as follows:

	LCU
Amortization of patent (related patent was acquired January 1, 1977)	40,000
Provision for doubtful accounts	60,000
Rent	100,000

The exchange rates at various dates are as follows:

	Dollar equivalent of 1 LCU
December 31, 1979	$.20
Average for the year ended December 31, 1979	.22
January 1, 1977	.25

What total dollar amount should be included in Union's income statement to reflect the above expenses for the year ended December 31, 1979?
    a. $40,000
    b. $42,000
    c. $44,000
    d. $45,200

30. A foreign subsidiary of the Satelite Corporation has certain balance sheet accounts at December 31, 1979. Information relating to these accounts in United States dollars is as follows:

	Translated at	
	Current Rates	Historical Rates
Marketable securities carried at cost	$ 75,000	$ 85,000
Inventories carried at average cost	600,000	700,000
Refundable deposits	25,000	30,000
Patents	55,000	70,000
	$755,000	$885,000

What total should be included in Satelite's balance sheet at December 31, 1979, as a result of the above information?
    a. $770,000
    b. $780,000
    c. $870,000
    d. $880,000

31. When translating foreign currency financial statements, which of the following items would be translated using current exchange rates?
    a.   Inventories carried at cost.
    b.   Prepaid insurance.
    c.   Goodwill.
    d.   Marketable equity securities carried at current market price.

32. When translating foreign currency financial statements, which of the following items would be translated using historical exchange rates?
    a.   Notes payable.
    b.   Long-term debt.
    c.   Deferred income.
    d.   Accrued expenses payable.

33. Fore Company had a $30,000 exchange loss resulting from the translation of the accounts of its wholly owned foreign subsidiary for the year ended December 31, 1978. Fore also had a receivable from a foreign customer which was payable in the local currency of the foreign customer. On December 31, 1977, this receivable for 500,000 local currency units (LCU) was appropriately included in the accounts receivable section of Fore's balance sheet at $245,000. When the receivable was collected on February 5, 1978, the exchange rate was 2 LCU to $1. What amount should be included as an exchange gain or loss in the 1978 consolidated income statement of Fore Company and its wholly owned foreign subsidiary as a result of the above?
    a. $ 5,000 exchange gain.
    b. $20,000 exchange loss.
    c. $25,000 exchange loss.
    d. $30,000 exchange loss.

34. At what translation rates should the following balance sheet accounts in foreign statements be translated into United States dollars?

	Equipment	Accumulated Depreciation of Equipment
a.	Current	Current
b.	Current	Average for year
c.	Historical	Current
d.	Historical	Historical

35. The Marvin Company has a receivable from a foreign customer which is payable in the local currency of the foreign customer. The amount receivable for 900,000 local currency units (LCU), has been translated into $315,000 on Marvin's December 31, 1975, balance sheet. On January 15, 1976, the receivable was collected in full when the exchange rate was 3 LCU to $1. What journal entry should Marvin make to record the collection of this receivable?

		Debit	Credit
a.	Cash	$300,000	
	Accounts receivable		$300,000
b.	Cash	300,000	
	Exchange loss	15,000	
	Accounts receivable		315,000
c.	Cash	300,000	
	Deferred exchange loss	15,000	
	Accounts receivable		315,000
d.	Cash	315,000	
	Accounts receivable		315,000

36. A change in the foreign currency exchange rate between the date a transaction occurred and the date of the current financial statements would give rise to an exchange gain or loss if

a. The asset or liability being translated is carried at a price in a current purchase or sale exchange.

b. The asset or liability being translated is carried at a price in a past purchase or sale exchange.

c. The revenue or expense item relates to an asset or liability that is translated at historical rates.

d. The revenue or expense item relates to a deferred asset or liability shown on a previous statement of financial position.

37. The France Company owns a foreign subsidiary with 2,400,000 local currency units (LCU) of property, plant, and equipment before accumulated depreciation at December 31, 1978. Of this amount, 1,500,000 LCU were acquired in 1976 when the rate of exchange was 1.5 LCU to $1, and 900,000 LCU were acquired in 1977 when the rate of exchange was 1.6 LCU to $1. The rate of exchange in effect at December 31, 1978, was 1.9 LCU to $1. The weighted average of exchange rates which were in effect during 1978 was 1.8 LCU to $1. Assuming that the property, plant, and equipment are depreciated using the straight-line method over a ten-year period with no salvage value, how much depreciation expense relating to the foreign subsidiary's property, plant, and equipment should be charged in France's income statement for 1978?

a. $126,316.
b. $133,333.
c. $150,000.
d. $156,250.

38. On January 1, 1978, the Ben Company formed a foreign subsidiary. On February 15, 1978, Ben's subsidiary purchased 100,000 local currency units (LCU) of inventory. 25,000 LCU of the original inventory purchased on February 15, 1978, made up the entire inventory on December 31, 1978. The exchange rates were 2.2 LCU to $1 from January 1, 1978, to June 30, 1978, and 2 LCU to $1 from July 1, 1978, to December 31, 1978. The December 31, 1978, inventory balance for Ben's foreign subsidiary should be translated into United States dollars of

a. $10,500.
b. $11,364.
c. $11,905.
d. $12,500.

39. The year-end balance of accounts receivable on the books of a foreign subsidiary should be translated by the parent company for consolidation purposes at the

a. Historical rate.
b. Current rate.
c. Negotiated rate.
d. Spot rate.

MAY 1981 QUESTIONS

40. Certain balance sheet accounts in a foreign subsidiary of Rose Company at December 31, 1980, have been translated into United States dollars as follows:

| | Translated at | |
	Current rates	Historical rates
Accounts receivable, current	$200,000	$220,000
Accounts receivable, long-term	100,000	110,000
Prepaid insurance	50,000	55,000
Goodwill	80,000	85,000
	$430,000	$470,000

What total should be included in Rose's balance sheet at December 31, 1980, for the above items?

a. $430,000.
b. $435,000.
c. $440,000.
d. $450,000.

41. When translating foreign currency financial statements, which of the following accounts would be translated using current exchange rates?

	Property, plant, and equipment	Inventories carried at cost
a.	Yes	Yes
b.	No	No
c.	Yes	No
d.	No	Yes

PROBLEMS: CHANGING PRICES

Problem 1   Current Valuation of Assets (578, T6)

(25 to 30 minutes)

Part a.   Advocates of current value accounting propose several methods for determining the valuation of assets to approximate current values. Two of the methods proposed are replacement cost and present value of future cash flows.

Required:

Describe each of the two methods cited above and discuss the pros and cons of the various procedures used to arrive at the valuation for each method.

Part b.   The financial statements of a business entity could be prepared by using historical cost or current value as a basis. In addition, the basis could be stated in terms of unadjusted dollars or dollars restated for changes in purchasing power. The various permutations of these two separate and distinct areas are shown in the following matrix:

	Unadjusted Dollars	Dollars Restated for Changes in Purchasing Power
Historical cost	1	2
Current value	3	4

Block number 1 of the matrix represents the traditional method of accounting for transactions in accounting today, wherein the absolute (unadjusted) amount of dollars given up or received is recorded for the asset or liability obtained (relationship between resources). Amounts recorded in the method described in block number 1 reflect the original cost of the asset or liability and do not give effect to any change in value of the unit of measure (standard of comparison). This method assumes the validity of the accounting concepts of going concern and stable monetary unit. Any gain or loss (including holding and purchasing power gains or losses) resulting from the sale or satisfaction of amounts recorded under this method is deferred in its entirety until sale or satisfaction.

Required:

For each of the remaining matrix blocks (2,3 and 4) respond to the following questions. Limit your discussion to nonmonetary assets only.

• How will this method of recording assets affect the relationship between resources and the standard of comparison?

• What is the theoretic justification for using each method?

• How will each method of asset valuation affect the recognition of gain or loss during the life of the asset and ultimately from the sale or abandonment of the asset? Your response should include a discussion of the timing and magnitude of the gain or loss and conceptual reasons for any difference from the gain or loss computed using the traditional method.

Complete your discussion for each matrix block before proceeding to the discussion of the next matrix block.

Problem 2   Constant Dollar Calculations (570,Q4)   †

(40 to 50 minutes)

Skadden, Inc., a retailer, was organized during 1966. Skadden's management has decided to supplement its December 31, 1969 historical dollar financial statements with constant dollar (end of year) statements. The following general ledger trial balance (historical dollar) and additional information have been furnished:

Skadden, Inc.
TRIAL BALANCE
December 31, 1969

	Debit	Credit
Cash and receivables(net)	$ 540,000	$
Marketable securities (common stock)	400,000	
Inventory	440,000	
Equipment	650,000	
Equipment—Accumulated depreciation		164,000
Accounts payable		300,000
6% First mortgage bonds, due 1987		500,000
Common stock, $10 par		1,000,000
Retained earnings, December 31, 1968	46,000	
Sales		1,900,000
Cost of sales	1,508,000	
Depreciation	65,000	
Other operating expenses and interest	215,000	
	$3,864,000	$3,864,000

1. Monetary assets (cash and receivables) exceeded monetary liabilities (accounts payable and bonds payable) by $445,000 at December 31, 1968. The amounts of monetary items are fixed in terms of numbers of dollars regardless of changes in specific prices or in the general price level.

2. Purchases ($1,840,000 in 1969) and sales are made uniformly throughout the year.

3. Depreciation is computed on a straight-line basis, with a full year's depreciation being taken in the year of acquisition and none in the year of retirement. The depreciation rate is 10 percent and no salvage value is anticipated. Acquisitions and retirements have been made fairly evenly over each year and the retirements in 1969 consisted of assets purchased during 1967 which were scrapped. An analysis of the equipment account reveals the following:

Year	Beginning Balance	Additions	Retirements	Ending Balance
1967	—	$550,000	—	$550,000
1968	$550,000	10,000	—	560,000
1969	560,000	150,000	$60,000	650,000

4. The bonds were issued in 1967 and the marketable securities were purchased fairly evenly over 1969. Other operating expenses and interest are assumed to be incurred evenly throughout the year.

5. Assume that the Consumer Price Indices † (1958 = 100) were as follows:

Annual Average	Index	Conversion Factors (1969 4th Qtr. = 1.000)
1966	113.9	1.128
1967	116.8	1.100
1968	121.8	1.055
1969	126.7	1.014

Quarterly Averages

		Index	
1968	4th	123.5	1.040
1969	1st	124.9	1.029
	2nd	126.1	1.019
	3rd	127.3	1.009
	4th	128.5	1.000

Required:

a. Prepare a schedule to convert the Equipment account balance at December 31, 1969 from historical cost to constant dollar.

b. Prepare a schedule to analyze in historical dollars the Equipment—Accumulated Depreciation account for the year 1969.

c. Prepare a schedule to analyze in constant dollars the Equipment—Accumulated Depreciation account for the year 1969.

d. Prepare a schedule to compute Skadden, Inc.'s purchasing power gain or loss on its net holdings of monetary assets for 1969 (ignore income tax implications). The schedule should give consideration to appropriate items on or related to the balance sheet and the income statement.

Problem 3   Constant Dollar Theory (575,T7)   †

(25 to 30 minutes)

Published financial statements of United States companies are currently prepared on a stable-dollar assumption even though the general purchasing power of the dollar has declined considerably because of inflation in recent years. To account for this changing value of the dollar, many accountants suggest that financial statements should be adjusted for general price-level changes. Three independent unrelated statements regarding constant dollar financial statements follow. Each statement contains some fallacious reasoning.

Statement I

The accounting profession has not seriously considered constant dollar financial statements before because the rate of inflation usually has been so small from year-to-year that the adjustments would have been immaterial in amount. Constant dollar financial statements represent a departure from the historical-cost basis of accounting. Financial statements should be prepared from facts, not estimates.

Statement II

If financial statements were adjusted for general price-level changes, depreciation charges in the earnings statement would permit the recovery of dollars of current purchasing power and, thereby, equal the cost of new assets to replace the old ones. Constant dollar adjusted data would yield statement-of-financial-position amounts closely approximating current values. Furthermore, management can make better decisions if constant dollar financial statements are published.

Statement III

When adjusting financial data for general price-level changes, a distinction must be made between monetary and nonmonetary assets and liabilities, which, under the historical-cost basis of accounting, have been identified as "current" and "non-current." When using the historical-cost basis of accounting, no purchasing-power gain or loss is recognized in the accounting process, but when financial statements are adjusted for general price-level changes, a purchasing-power gain or loss will be recognized on monetary and nonmonetary items.

Required:

Evaluate each of the independent statements and identify the areas of fallacious reasoning in each and explain why the reasoning is incorrect. Complete your discussion of each statement before proceeding to the next statement.

Problem 4   Asset Valuation (1176,T4a)

(10 to 15 minutes)

Part a.   Valuation of assets is an important topic in accounting theory. Suggested valuation methods include the following:

> Historical cost (past purchase prices)
> Historical cost adjusted to reflect general price-level changes (constant dollar)
> Discounted cash flow (future exchange prices)
> Market price (current selling prices)
> Replacement cost (current purchase prices)

Required:

1.   Why is the valuation of assets a significant issue?

2.   Explain the basic theory underlying each of the valuation methods cited above. Do not discuss advantages and disadvantages of each method.

Problem 5   Constant Dollar and Current Cost
(Adapted from Kieso and Weygandt, Intermediate Accounting, 3rd edition, p. 1174)

(60 to 75 minutes)

Presented below is information related to Hood, Inc.

1978   Purchased land for $40,000 cash on December 31. Current cost at year end was $40,000.

1979   Held this land all year. Current cost at year end was $52,000.

1980   October 31--sold this land for $68,000. Current cost of land at date of sale is $65,000.

General price-level index:

December 31, 1978	100
December 31, 1979	110
October 31, 1980	120
December 31, 1980	120

Required:

a.   Determine the amount at which the land would be stated on a balance sheet at December 31, 1978 and 1979 under the following assumptions (end-of-year dollars):

1. Constant dollar accounting
2. Current cost accounting
3. Current cost/constant dollar accounting

b. Determine the following items (end-of-year dollars):

1. Constant dollar income for 1978, 1979, and 1980.
2. Unrealized holding gain (loss) on current cost basis for 1979.
3. Income from continuing operations on a current cost basis for 1980.
4. Realized holding gain (loss) on current cost basis in 1980.
5. The total holding gain recognized on a current cost/constant dollar basis for 1980.

c. Indicate the amount of income from continuing operations that would be reported under FASB Statement No. 33 for 1978, 1979, and 1980. Assume that the general indexes presented above also reflect the average index for the year; that is, 1978 average index equals 100; 1979 average index equals 110; 1980 average index equals 120.

Problem 6   SFAS 33 *

(25 to 30 minutes)

In 1979, SFAS 33 was issued in response to the changing price dilemma. The following questions address the issue of changing prices.

a. Marketable equity securities are presently accounted for on the lower-of-cost-or-market basis. Compare this basis with accounting for such securities on a current cost basis in regards to asset valuation and income recognition.

b. Explain briefly the theory of capital maintenance and how it relates to:
1. constant dollar accounting
2. current cost accounting

c. Describe the supplementary disclosures concerning inventory required for some companies by SFAS 33.

Prepared by John C. Borke, Northern Illinois University

PROBLEMS: FOREIGN CURRENCY

Problem 7   Foreign Currency Translation (1177,P4c)

(15 to 20 minutes)

Part c. On January 1, 1975, the Franklin Company formed a foreign subsidiary which issued all of its currently outstanding common stock on that date. Selected captions from the balance sheets, all of which are shown in local currency units (LCU), are as follows:

	December 31,	
	1976	1975
	(All amounts given in LCU)	
Accounts receivable (net of allowance for uncollectible accounts of 2,200 LCU at December 31, 1976, and 2,000 LCU at December 31, 1975)	40,000	35,000
Inventories, at cost	80,000	75,000
Property, plant and equipment (net of allowance for accumulated depreciation of 31,000 LCU at December 31, 1976, and 14,000 LCU at December 31, 1975)	163,000	150,000
Long-term debt	100,000	120,000
Common stock, authorized 10,000 shares, par value 10 LCU per share, issued and outstanding 5,000 shares at December 31, 1976, and December 31, 1975	50,000	50,000

Additional information is as follows:

· Exchange rates are as follows:

January 1, 1975—July 31, 1975	2 LCU to $1
August 1, 1975—October 31, 1975	1.8 LCU to $1
November 1, 1975—June 30, 1976	1.7 LCU to $1
July 1, 1976—December 31, 1976	1.5 LCU to $1
Average monthly rate for 1975	1.9 LCU to $1
Average monthly rate for 1976	1.6 LCU to $1

· An analysis of the accounts receivable balance is as follows:

Accounts receivable:	1976	1975
(All amounts given in LCU)		
Balance at beginning of year	37,000	—
Sales (36,000 LCU per month in 1976 and 31,000 LCU per month in 1975)	432,000	372,000
Collections	423,600	334,000
Write-offs (May 1976 and December 1975)	3,200	1,000
Balance at end of year	42,200	37,000

Allowance for uncollectible accounts:	1976	1975
(All amounts given in LCU)		
Balance at beginning of year	2,000	—
Provision for uncollectible accounts	3,400	3,000
Write-offs (May 1976 and December 1975)	3,200	1,000
Balance at end of year	2,200	2,000

· An analysis of inventories, for which the first-in, first-out (FIFO) inventory method is used, is as follows:

	1976	1975
(All amounts given in LCU)		
Inventory at beginning of year	75,000	—
Purchases (June 1976 and June 1975)	335,000	375,000
Goods available for sale	410,000	375,000
Inventory at end of year	80,000	75,000
Cost of goods sold	330,000	300,000

· On January 1, 1975, Franklin's foreign subsidiary purchased land for 24,000 LCU and plant and equipment for 140,000 LCU. On July 4, 1976, additional equipment was purchased for 30,000 LCU. Plant and equipment is being depreciated on a straight-line basis over a ten-year period with no salvage value. A full year's depreciation is taken in the year of purchase.

· On January 15, 1975, 7% bonds with a face value of 120,000 LCU were sold. These bonds mature on January 15, 1981, and interest is paid semiannually on July 15 and January 15. The first payment was made on January 15, 1976.

Required:

Prepare a schedule translating the selected captions above into United States dollars at December 31, 1976, and December 31, 1975, respectively. Show supporting computations in good form.

Problem 8   SFAS 8 Definitions (578,T3)

(20 to 25 minutes)

Part a.   The Financial Accounting Standards Board discusses certain terminology essential to both the translation of foreign currency transactions and foreign currency financial statements in its Statement No. 8. Included in the discussion is a definition of and distinction between the terms "measure" and "denominate."

Required:

Define the terms "measure" and "denominate" as discussed by the Financial Accounting Standards Board and give a brief example that demonstrates the distinction between accounts measured in a particular currency and accounts denominated in a particular currency.

Part b.   There are several methods of translating foreign currency transactions or accounts reflected in foreign currency financial statements. Among these methods are: current/noncurrent, monetary/nonmonetary, current rate, and the temporal method (the method adopted by the Financial Accounting Standards Board).

Required:

Define the temporal method of translating foreign currency financial statements. Specifically include in your answer the treatment of the following four accounts:

1.   Long-term accounts receivable.
2.   Deferred income.
3.   Inventory valued at cost.
4.   Long-term debt.

MULTIPLE CHOICE ANSWERS

CHANGING PRICES

1.	d	7.	d	13.	c	19.	c	25.	a
2.	d	8.	d	14.	b	20.	c	26.	c
3.	d	9.	d	15.	b	21.	d	27.	c
4.	c	10.	c	16.	c	22.	c		
5.	b	11.	c	17.	d	23.	a		
6.	a	12.	d	18.	b	24.	c		

EXPLANATION OF MULTIPLE CHOICE ANSWERS

1. (1180,T1,26)   (d)   In accordance with SFAS 33, the Consumer Price Index is used to compute information on a constant dollar basis. This index is used to restate financial statement elements to dollars which have the same purchasing power. Historical cost or nominal dollar information (answers a and c) requires no restatement. Information on a current cost basis (answer b) would be restated using a specific, rather than a general, price index.

2. (180,P1,17)   (d)   The requirement is the amount of depreciation expense in Hadley's supplementary constant dollar statement for 1979. The constant dollar depreciation is computed by multiplying the depreciation expense of $200,000 by the TO/FROM ratio, 200/180: ($200,000)(200/180) = $222,222.

3. (180,P1,18)   (d)   The requirement is the accumulated depreciation to be reported by Victor in a supplementary current cost statement at 12/31/79. The current cost of the machine at the end of each year is:

12/31/77		$100,000
12/31/78	($100,000)(110%)	$110,000
12/31/79	($110,000)(110%)	$121,000

Note that the 10% increase in 1979 current cost is based on 1978 current cost, not the 1977 cost. After two years of the five-year life, accumulated depreciation should be 2/5 of the current cost:

($121,000)(2/5) = $48,400

4. (580,P1,12)   (c)   The requirement is to compute the constant-dollar balances for accounts in a supplementary constant dollar balance sheet. The solutions approach is to identify which of the listed items are monetary and which are nonmonetary items. Per SFAS 33, para 18, an item is monetary if, by nature, it is already stated in current dollars. Nonmonetary items are stated in terms of past dollars and must therefore be restated when preparing constant-dollar financial statements. Only land would be adjusted for changes in the general price level. The marketable securities, non-convertible bonds and the long-term debt are already stated in terms of current dollars and therefore require no adjustment.

5. (580,T1,27)   (b)   Historical dollar financial statements assume a stable monetary unit and therefore make no adjustment for changes in the general price level, as is done with constant dollar financial statements. Fair value financial statements is a vague term which is not used. Current-value statements are not adjusted for changes in the general price level and would appear to also assume a stable monetary unit. Nonetheless, given the instructions to pick one answer, answer (b) is the best choice.

6. (1179,P1,17)   (a)   The requirement is the amount of gain on the sale of a machine on January 1, 1978 to be shown in the 1978 current value income statement. Under current value accounting, assets shall be shown at their current value in the balance sheet. Thus, the gain would be the sales price of $412,000 less the current value reported on the 12/31/77 balance sheet of $410,000. Note, no depreciation would have been recorded in 1978 as the sale took place on January 1.

7. (1179,T1,24)   (d)   In current value accounting, holding gains are recognized when asset values are revised upward to current values. As assets are revalued (debited), holding gains are credited. Answers (a) and (b) are incorrect because current value financial statements reflect asset values adjusted for specific changes in value and make no separate distinction as to changes in the purchasing power of the dollar. Answer (c) is incorrect because if the current value and the historical cost were equal, there would be no difference no matter whether historical cost or current value accounting was used.

8. (577,P1,17)   (d)   Depreciation is a nonmonetary item and thus must be adjusted into current year dollars. The $100 of historical cost depreciation ($1,000 ÷ 10 years) is converted into 1976 dollars by multiplying by the TO/FROM ratio of 185/148. When working with price indexes, always make adjustments through multiplication of the TO/FROM ratio (price level adjusting to over price level adjusting from).

9. (577,P1,18)   (d)   The machine's historical cost of $1,000 is adjusted by the same TO/FROM ratio as for the depreciation in the immediately preceding problem.

10. (577,T1,7)   (c)   Answers (a), (b) and (d) are descriptive of constant dollar statements. Since constant dollar statements only account for inflation, i.e., changes in the purchasing power of the dollar, they

usually do not measure current value. Historical costs can be converted into current values with very specific, not general, price-level indexes. There are many components of differences between historical costs and current costs, e.g., inflation, market factors, etc.

11. (1176,Q1,5) (c) Land is a nonmonetary item and therefore is adjusted by changes in the purchasing power of the dollar. The $300,000 is adjusted by the TO/FROM ratio (price-level-adjusting-to divided by price-level-adjusting-from) of 140/120. Thus, the land cost on 12-31-75 dollars is $350,000 resulting in a $50,000 gain (400—350).

12. (1176,Q1,6) (d) In 1975 dollars, the cost of the equipment was $420,000 ($300,000 x 140/100); the equipment was purchased at the beginning of 1972 which is the end of 1971. The equipment was depreciated for four of the ten-year useful life, resulting in a book value of $252,000 ($420,000 x 60%). Since the equipment was sold for $200,000, there was a $52,000 loss.

13. (1176,Q1,7) (c) The requirement is the constant dollar amount for machinery and equipment net of accumulated depreciation. The amounts presented in the problem are historical costs. Adjust the equipment purchased in 12-72 by multiplying the net historical cost of $240,000 ($400,000 minus $160,000) times the TO/FROM ratio of 140/110. Adjust the 12-74 net historical cost of $80,000 ($100,000 minus $20,000) with the TO/FROM ratio of 140/120.

1972	$240,000	x 140/110	=	$305,455
1974	$ 80,000	x 140/120	=	93,333
				$398,788

14. (1178,T1,3) (b) The requirement is the method of reporting that eliminates the effect of the changing value of the dollar. Constant dollar accounting adjusts historical cost financial statements for changes in the price level. Changes in market values are not reflected in price-level adjusted statements. Answers (a), (c), and (d) are market valuation methods which reflect more than just the changing value of the dollar.

15. (1178,P1,13) (b) The requirement is the purchasing power gain or loss for 1977. Per SFAS 33, purchasing power gains and losses arise on monetary items during changes in the general price level. Essentially a purchasing power gain or loss is computed as the difference between 1) the net monetary items on hand at the end of the year, and 2) the amount of the net monetary items as they would have been if they

were nonmonetary items. In other words, adjust all monetary items to reflect changes in purchasing power.

In this case, cash is the monetary item, and if it had been a non-monetary item it would have been restated to $55,000 ($50,000 x 110/100) at the end of the year. Since cash is a monetary item, it is only worth $50,000 and not $55,000. Thus there was a purchasing power loss of $5,000 on the cash which was held during the year. The price-level adjusted balance sheet appears below in the T-account. Both land and common stock (nonmonetary items) are adjusted upward by the 10% increase in the price level. Also the $5,000 general price-level loss is included in retained earnings.

Price Level Statement
12/31/77

Cash	$ 50,000			
Land	165,000		Stock	$220,000
			RE	(5,000)
	$215,000			$215,000

16. (578,P1,12) (c) The requirement is the constant dollar adjusted amounts to be shown at the end of 1977. Only nonmonetary items are adjusted for changes in the price level. Cash and long-term receivables are monetary items. The marketable securities are nonmonetary items (even the bonds, because they were purchased for price speculation). Accordingly, cash and long-term receivables are not adjusted. The marketable securities (both stocks and bonds) are increased by 10% as the price level increases by 10% during 1977.

17. (578,P1,13) (d) Current value income matches revenue with the current cost of the goods sold to obtain operating income. In this problem, revenue of $1,000,000 less the current cost of the inventory sold of $700,000, yields operating income of $300,000. Assuming the increase in the replacement cost of the inventory also increases current value income as a holding gain, an additional $200,000 would be added to income raising the income to $500,000.

18. (576,T1,11) (b) This question exemplifies the observation that multiple choice questions are simply a series of three true statements and one false statement or three false statements and one true statement. Note the requirement asks which observation is valid or true. Constant dollar statements are based on historical cost; the only difference is that the historical cost dollars are adjusted for changes in pur-

chasing power of the monetary unit. Answers (a), (c), and (d) are not true because historical costs adjusted for changes in purchasing power do not, and are not intended to, represent appraisal value, replacement cost, or any other measure of current value. Any correspondence between these items would be simply coincidental.

19. 1178,P1,15) (c) The requirement is the gain on the sale of a machine per current value accounting. Since the current cost of the machine was $32,000, and it was sold for $35,000, there would be a $3,000 gain. Note the sale took place on January 1, 1977, and thus no depreciation would be recorded. The depreciation under current value accounting is the decrease (increase) in the replacement cost from the beginning to the end of the year. Therefore the book value on December 31, 1976 would have to be $32,000.

20. (1178,T1,22) (c) The requirement is the method which does not determine the current value of an asset. Current values of assets are determined by a number of factors in addition to changes in the purchasing power of the dollar. Answer (c), restatement of costs for changes in the general price level, is only concerned with the changing purchasing power of the dollar and not the other factors, e.g., changes in supply and demand for the asset. Replacement cost (answer (a)), market value (answer (b)), and present value of future cash flows (answer (d)), all are "current values."

21. (579,P1,20) (d) In current value accounting, stockholders' equity is adjusted each period as a result of the assets and liabilities being recorded at current cost. During 1977, the land increased from $2,000,000 to $2,200,000 (a $200,000 increase in stockholders' equity), and in 1978 the land was sold for $2,250,000 resulting in an additional $50,000 increase in stockholders' equity.

22. (1171,Q2,18) (c) When originally on the exam, the correct answer to this question was (a), per para. 32 of APB Statement 3. However, the required balance sheet information as presented in SFAS 33 should be restated in terms of average-for-the-year dollars.

23. (1171,Q2,20) (a) During deflation it is wise to hold monetary assets, e.g., cash, rather than monetary liabilities, e.g., accounts payable. The general purchasing power of the cash increases as the price level of goods and services decreases. That is to say, as prices go down, cash will be worth more or will purchase more goods and services.

24. (1171,Q2,23) (c) Answer (c) is the definition of monetary items. Receivables and payables may be monetary items without a fixed maturity date. In addition to current liabilities, long-term liabilities are often monetary items, e.g., bonds payable. See SFAS 33.

25. (1171,Q2,25) (a) Remember that constant dollar statements are simply historical statements adjusted for changes in the price level. Thus, a gain or loss on the sale of a nonmonetary asset would be reported in constant dollar statements in the same period that they would be reported in historical statements. The amount, however, will probably be different due to adjustments in the purchasing power of the dollar.

MAY 1981 ANSWERS

26. (581,P1,1) (c) The requirement is to compute the net current cost of the fixed assets at December 31, 1980. The solutions approach is to realize that the net current cost is the estimated current cost less the percentage of the asset depreciated to date. Thus, the net current cost is computed as follows:

1978	70,000 − .30 (70,000)	=	$49,000
1979	19,000 − .20 (19,000)	=	15,200
1980	22,000 − .10 (22,000)	=	19,800
	Net current cost		$84,000

27. (581,Q1,1) (c) The requirement of this problem is to calculate depreciation expense on an income statement adjusted for general inflation using constant dollar accounting. It is necessary to calculate the amount for each asset in terms of constant dollars by multiplying the historical cost by the current year's price index over the price index that was in effect when the asset was purchased. These amounts are then used for calculating depreciation expense. The cost of each asset adjusted for inflation is:

1978	30,000 x 150/100	=	$45,000
1979	20,000 x 150/125	=	24,000
1980	10,000 x 150/150	=	10,000
	Total		$79,000

Since depreciation expense is 10% per year, straight-line, and a full year's depreciation is charged in the year of acquisition, total depreciation can be calculated by multiplying 10% by the total cost of the assets adjusted for inflation ($79,000). Depreciation expense is $7,900.

MULTIPLE CHOICE ANSWERS

FOREIGN CURRENCY

28.	d	31.	d	34.	d	37.	d	40.	c
29.	d	32.	c	35.	b	38.	b	41.	b
30.	d	33.	c	36.	a	39.	b		

EXPLANATION OF MULTIPLE CHOICE ANSWERS

(1180,T1,14)   (d)   SFAS 8, para 17, states that both exchange gains and losses should be included in net income for the period in which the rate changes. Answer (b), an extraordinary item, is incorrect because exchange gains and losses do not meet the criteria of unusual nature and infrequent occurrence.

29. (1180,P1,11)   (d)   The requirement is the dollar amount of expense to be included in Union's consolidated income statement for three of the subsidiary's expense items stated in local currency units. Patent amortization relates to a cost incurred on 1/1/77, so the exchange rate on that date (.25) should be used. The other two expenses (bad debts and rent) were incurred evenly throughout the year; the average-for-the-year rate (.22) would be used for their translation.

Amortization	(.25)	(40,000)	$10,000
Bad debts	(.22)	(60,000)	13,200
Rent	(.22)	(100,000)	22,000
			$45,200

30. (580,P1,9)   (d)   The requirement is to determine the proper (current or historical) rate to use in translating foreign account balances. The solutions approach is to apply the temporal method of translation to each of the indicated balances. Under the temporal method, the translation should change the unit of measure without changing the accounting principles. Current rates are used for translating any balances which would be reflected currently on the financial statements.

$ 85,000	Marketable securities at cost
700,000	Inventory
25,000	Refund deposit
70,000	Patents
$880,000	

31. (580,T1,31)   (d)   Assets carried in the financial statements at cost, such as answers (a), (b), and (c), are translated using the exchange rate in effect at the transaction date. Assets carried in the financial state-

ments at current market price are translated using the current exchange rate. See SFAS 8, para 7.

32. (580,T1,32)   (c)   The temporal method of translation promulgated by SFAS 8 retains the principle of measurement used by the foreign affiliates. Answers (a), (b), and (d) are reflected in foreign financial statements in current dollars and should therefore be translated at the current rate. Deferred income is a promise to perform services based on historical prices and thus would be translated using the historical exchange rate.

33. (1179,P1,9)   (c)   The requirement is the 1978 exchange gain or loss for the Fore Company and its wholly owned foreign subsidiary. The problem begins by stating that there was a $30,000 exchange loss resulting from consolidation of the foreign subsidiary. Additionally, there was a receivable from a foreign customer that was on the books at the beginning of 1978 at $245,000 (representing 500,000 LCU). When the 500,000 LCU was paid to Fore in February 1978, the exchange rate was 2 LCU to 1. Accordingly, Fore received $250,000 (500,000 LCU ÷ 2 LCU). The result was a $5,000 ($250,000 - $245,000) exchange gain on collection of the receivable. Thus, a net $25,000 exchange loss results from the $30,000 exchange loss from consolidation and the $5,000 gain from collection of the foreign receivable.

34. (1179,T1,10) (d)   The requirement is the foreign exchange rate to be used to translate equipment and accumulated depreciation into US dollars. The historical rate is used for both equipment and the related accumulated depreciation. Per para 11 of SFAS 8, monetary items in foreign statements are translated at the current rate. Per para 12 of SFAS 8, nonmonetary items carried at historical cost are to be translated at the historical rate. Accounts carried at current or future exchange prices (market values) are to be translated at the current rate. Per para 13 of SFAS 8, revenue and expense transactions are to be translated at the average rate for the year.

35. (577,P1,4)   (b)   The requirement is the journal entry to record the collection of a receivable. The receivable was $315,000 when 900,000 LCU were received at an exchange rate of 3 LCU to $1. Thus $300,000 was received to settle a $315,000 receivable resulting in a $15,000 exchange loss. See para 7 and 16 of SFAS 8 for accounting for foreign currency transactions.

36. (1178,T1,25) (a) The requirement is the type of transaction that would give rise to an exchange gain or loss if there is a change in the foreign currency exchange rate. An exchange gain or loss is recognized if an asset or liability is being translated at the current rate when there is a change in the foreign currency exchange rate. Conversely, if a historical translation rate is used, changes in the foreign current exchange rate do not affect the evaluation of assets or liabilities and will not result in an exchange gain or loss. Thus assets and liabilities carried at the same price of a current purchase or sale are being carried at the current rate and will produce exchange gains and losses if foreign currency exchange rates change. Answers (b), (c), and (d) are incorrect because assets and liabilities translated at the historical rate do not produce exchange gains or losses. See para 7 of SFAS 8.

37. (579,P1,10) (d) The requirement is the amount of depreciation expense relating to a foreign subsidiary's fixed assets for 1978. Para 7(a) of SFAS 8 requires that assets and their related nominal accounts, e.g., depreciation, be translated at the exchange rate in effect at the original transaction date (i.e., the historical rate). Since the useful life of the fixed assets is 10 years with no salvage value, depreciation will be 150,000 LCU for the equipment acquired in 1976 and 90,000 LCU for the equipment acquired in 1977. These are converted to dollars at their respective historical rates of 1.5 and 1.6 LCU.

$$\$1,500,000 \times 10\% \div 1.5 = \$100,000$$
$$\$900,000 \times 10\% \div 1.6 = \underline{56,250}$$
$$\$156,250$$

38. (579,P1,19) (b) The requirement is the year-end inventory balance of a foreign subsidiary translated into dollars. Per paras 11 and 12 of SFAS 8, nonmonetary items are translated using historical rates unless they are stated at current market values. Here, the inventory of 25,000 LCU is stated at its original cost in LCUs and would be translated at the historical rate of 2.2, which results in $11,364.

Note that the test for LCM is done after the LCUs have been translated into dollars (para 14, SFAS 8). Thus both inventory cost and market have to be converted into dollars at their historical and current rates respectively, and then compared for LCM.

39. (579,T1,2) (b) Per para 11 of SFAS 8, monetary items (cash, receivables, and payables) are translated at the current rate. Answer (a), the historical rate, is used for nonmonetary items, which are not carried at current market value. Answer (c), negotiated rate, is a nonsense term. Answer (d) the spot rate, is another name for the current exchange rate.

MAY 1981 ANSWERS

40. (581,P1,17) (c) The requirement is to compute the total dollar amount translated for the assets presented in Rose Company's balance sheet. According to SFAS 8 para 12, accounts carried in past prices shall be translated at historical rates and accounts carried in current prices shall be translated at current rates. Accounts receivable are carried in terms of current prices and, therefore, are translated at current rates. Goodwill and prepaid insurance are carried at historical prices and are translated at historical rates. Thus, the total translated dollar amount is computed as

A/R, current	$200,000
A/R, long-term	100,000
Prepaid insurance	55,000
Goodwill	85,000
	$440,000

41. (581,T1,34) (b) The requirement is which accounts would be translated using current exchange rates when translating foreign currency financial statements. Per SFAS 8, para 9, the objective of translation requires that the assets, liabilities, revenues, and expenses in foreign statements to be accounted for in the same manner as assets, liabilities, revenues, and expenses that result from foreign currency transactions of the enterprise. Accounts carried at prices in past exchanges (past prices) shall be translated at historical rates. Accounts carried at prices in current purchase or sale exchanges (current prices) or future exchanges (future prices) shall be translated at the current rate (SFAS 8, para 12). The current rate is that rate in effect at the balance sheet date and the historical rate is the rate in effect at the date a specific transaction or event occured (SFAS 8, para 30). Both property, plant, and equipment and inventories stated at cost are carried at prices in past exchanges and are thus translated at historical rates.

ANSWER OUTLINE: CHANGING PRICES

Problem 1   Current Valuation of Assets

a1.   Replacement cost method values assets at replacement cost

        Having the same production capacity

        Even though values change due to available technology, etc.

        Computation methods are subjective

            Appraisal method varies due to geographic location, purchase price, etc.

            Resale market requires comparable arm's-length transactions

            Specific price index requires such an index

            Replacement cost is not the same as market value

a2.   Present value method values assets at present value of cash flows

        Includes present value of salvage value

        Implies undue precision due to mathematical computation

        Estimates underlying computation are subject to error

            Future cash flow amounts

            Number of periods of cash flow

            Interest rate

b1.   Matrix block 2

        Retains historical cost relationships between assets

        Compares units of purchasing power rather than monetary units

        Changes asset dollar amounts in periods of inflation or deflation

            Compensates for a change in the value of the dollar

        All gain and loss is deferred until ultimate disposition

            Gains and losses are reported in current purchasing power

            Purchasing power gains and losses are eliminated

            Gain or loss is different from historical cost amount

b2.   Matrix block 3

        Asset current value relationships differ from historical cost

        No restatement due to changes in purchasing power

        Outside market forces determine asset values

        Change in current values represents "holding" gains

            Recognized currently in income statements

            Theoretically no gain or loss at disposition

        Total gain or loss is the same as historical cost

b3.   Matrix block 4

        Historical cost is simultaneously modified by current values, e.g.,

            Replacement cost

            Market value

            Net present value

            Changes in purchasing power of the dollar

        Corrects for changes in market values and purchasing power

        Annual recognition of changes in market value

            But adjusted for changes in purchasing power

            Theoretically no gain or loss at disposition

        Total gain or loss varies from historical cost

UNOFFICIAL ANSWER: CHANGING PRICES

Problem 1   Current Valuation of Assets

a1.   Replacement cost. The replacement cost method of current-value accounting (sometimes referred to as entry value) is a theoretical attempt to disclose the effect of a changing value of an asset employed by a business entity based on an estimate of the cost to replace the asset with another of essentially the same production potential at a given point in time. Specific assets change in value over a period of time due to such factors as availability, technological advances, physical deterioration, and other factors that would affect their value if they had to be replaced at a date subsequent to their acquisition.

There are several currently employed procedures for estimating replacement cost including appraisal, prices existing in a resale market, and specific price indexes (for specific assets as opposed to general price-level indexes). All of the procedures are subjective to a degree. For example, appraisals may vary for reasons of geographic location, initial purchase price, or value attributed to the asset as an integral part of a company's production process. A resale market, if one should exist, is more objective than an appraisal, but there are still some subjective assumptions regarding an arm's-length transaction, an essentially comparable asset having been traded near the valuation date, and the strength (depth) of the existing market. Specific indexes are a good method of determining the effect of changing prices on a specific asset if a specific index exists for that asset. The estimate of replacement cost computed under any of the procedures may or may not approximate the current value of the specific asset in question. The true current value of an asset is a function of future utility (cash flows) in the hands of the owner. The outside market or index may not recognize the same amount of future utility (cash flows), and, as such, the market price will be higher or lower than the replacement cost computed using one of the procedures discussed earlier.

a2.   Present value of future cash flows. The present value of future cash flows method of current-value accounting (sometimes referred to as exit value) is a theoretical attempt to disclose the effects of changing values of assets employed by a business entity based on the estimated current sales value to a third party. The present value of future cash flows method makes the assumption that the maximum market value of a specific asset to a third party is the present value of the future cash flows that will be earned or caused to be earned by the productive employment of the asset.

The procedure of computing the value of a specific asset under the present value of future cash flows assumption is to determine the present value of an ordinary annuity equal to the cash flows generated by the asset plus the present value of any residual value at the end of the asset's life. If the cash flows in the future are unequal between periods (as is usually the situation) the present value of each future cash flow in the future periods may be computed and added to the present value of any residual value of the

asset at the end of its productive life to obtain the estimate of current value. Each element of the present value computation is subjective, and an error in any element will cause the value to be misstated. If an error is made in the estimate of future cash flows, the number of periods that cash flows will continue, or the rate of interest to discount future cash flows, or any combination of the three, the resultant current value will be erroneous. Another potential area of difficulty is that, because of the mathematical method of arriving at the estimated current value, an undue degree of precision will be attributed to the resultant amount, which may be no more precise than would be derived from any other method of estimating current value.

b1.   Matrix block 2. Nonmonetary assets recorded under the method described in block 2 will retain the historical cost basis, but the standard of comparison has been changed from units of money to units of general purchasing power. This method of reflecting nonmonetary assets will cause the amount shown as an asset to differ from the traditional method in periods of inflation or deflation.

This notion is supported by the argument that the unit of measure is not a stable monetary unit, and, by stating assets in terms of a "constant dollar", the assets are stated in terms of a stable unit of measure.

All holding gains or losses not recognized during the life of the nonmonetary asset will be deferred until the ultimate disposal of the asset because the basis of the asset has not been altered during the life of the asset. This deferral of gain or loss is the same as occurs using the traditional method discussed in matrix block 1. However, the amount of gain or loss recognized upon sale or abandonment of the nonmonetary asset may be different from the amount computed using the traditional method. This difference results from the restatement of the original cost basis in terms of the constant dollar. In effect, gains or losses from the changing value of the dollar are eliminated and the gain or loss on disposal or abandonment is limited to holding gains or losses and any residual excess over or under current value stated in terms of the common dollar.

b2.   Matrix block 3. The relationship of assets recorded under the method described in block 3 has been changed from historical cost to current value, although the standard of comparison is still units of money. Under this method there is no attempt to restate the original dollars expended in terms of a "common dollar." However, it may be argued that, implicit in any current valuation method (replacement value, market value, or net present value), there is an element of current value compensating for the changing value of the dollar. This method of asset valuation does not recognize any implicit change in the unit of measure. Therefore, any difference in amounts recorded using this method and the traditional method is due to a change in the current value of the asset.

The justification for such an adjustment is based on the assumption that the value of an asset is affected by outside market factors.

The change in current value of assets throughout the life of the assets (commonly referred to as "holding" gains and losses) are recognized as gains or losses periodically during the productive life of the asset resulting in annual earnings statement recognition of holding gains or losses. Upon disposal of the asset, there theoretically will be no gain or loss because the asset is shown at current value. The sum of the holding gains or losses recognized in prior periods will comprise the total gain or loss, and any recognized gain or loss on disposal merely results in a correction of the current estimate of current value. While the timing of the gain or loss recognition under this method differs from the traditional method, the magnitude of the total gain or loss recognized will be the same under both methods. This is because the purchasing power of the dollar is assumed to remain unchanged throughout the life of the asset, and the amount of the gain or loss is computed as the difference between the dollars given up and current value of the asset (dollars received).

b3.   Matrix block 4. The relationship of assets recorded under the method described in block 4 has been changed from historic cost to current value determined by one of several methods, that is, replacement value, market value, or net present value. Further, the standard of comparison has changed in that the current value amount is restated in terms of a common dollar. For these two reasons, the amount shown for assets will differ from the amount shown using the traditional method.

This method draws its support from the justification for the methods depicted in matrix blocks 2 and 3, namely, compensating for the unstable dollar and recognition that market forces affect the value of an asset over a period of time.

Using this method of asset valuation, the earnings statement will periodically reflect holding gains or losses, but these gains or losses will be restated in terms of a common dollar. As in block 3, gains or losses will be recognized over the life of the asset due to the recognition of holding gains or losses, and at the date of sale or abandonment any remaining gain or loss recognized is merely a recognition of the error in estimating true current value. Because the current value is restated in terms of a common dollar, the total gain or loss will be different from the amount computed using the traditional method.

SOLUTION GUIDE: CHANGING PRICES

Problem 2   Constant Dollar Calculations

1.   Visualize the unofficial solution: 4 schedules. The first three concern the equipment account and the last is the purchasing power gain or loss schedule. Note that restatement is to year-end, not average-for-the-year, dollars.

2.   The $650,000 in equipment is made up of $490,000 (the retirement was from 1967 acquisitions), $10,000 and $150,000. Simply multiply these three figures by the TO/FROM ratios.

3.   Note that the TO/FROM ratios have already been divided and are called conversion factors. Use the annual average conversion factors, because the equipment has been acquired evenly over the year.

4.   Requirement (b) asks for the accumulated depreciation by year of acquisition. Remember that a whole year's depreciation is taken in the first year. For example, the accumulated depreciation on 1967 acquisitions would be 30% (3 years at 10%) of $490,000.

5.   Requirement (c) is met by multiplying the answer to requirement (b) by the same TO/FROM factors (conversion rates) used in requirement (a).

6.   Calculation of purchasing power gain or loss.

   A.   Convert net monetary items at the beginning of the year to year-end dollars. Use the fourth quarter price indexes (not annual average price indexes).

   B.   Add monetary item inflows converted to year-end dollars.

   C.   Subtract monetary item outflows converted to year-end dollars.

   D.   Compare this "as if" balance (as if monetary items are nonmonetary) to the net monetary items actually in existence at the end of the year. The difference is the gain or loss, e.g., if the actual net monetary assets are greater than the "as if" balance, a gain exists.

UNOFFICIAL ANSWER: CHANGING PRICES

Problem 2   Constant Dollar Calculations

a.

Skadden, Inc.

SCHEDULE TO ANALYZE EQUIPMENT FOR CONSTANT DOLLAR RESTATEMENT

December 31, 1969

Year Acquired	Amount (Historical)	Conversion Factor	Amount (Constant Dollar)
1967	$490,000	1.100	$539,000
1968	10,000	1.055	10,550
1969	150,000	1.014	152,100
	$650,000		$701,650

b.

Skadden, Inc.

SCHEDULE TO ANALYZE EQUIPMENT—ACCUMULATED DEPRECIATION
(Historical Dollars)

For the Year 1969

Year Assets Acquired	Balance 12/31/68	Depreciation for 1969	Retirements in 1969	Balance 12/31/69
1967	$110,000	$49,000	$12,000	$147,000
1968	1,000	1,000		2,000
1969		15,000		15,000
	$111,000	$65,000	$12,000	$164,000

c.

Skadden, Inc.

SCHEDULE TO ANALYZE EQUIPMENT—
ACCUMULATED DEPRECIATION
(Constant Dollars)

For the Year 1969

Year Assets Acquired	Conversion Factor	Balance 12/31/68	Depreciation	Retirement	Balance 12/31/69
1967	1.100	$121,000	$53,900	$13,200	$161,700
1968	1.055	1,055	1,055		2,110
1969	1.014		15,210		15,210
		$122,055	$70,165	$13,200	$179,020

d.

Skadden, Inc.

SCHEDULE TO COMPUTE PURCHASING POWER GAIN OR LOSS

For 1969

	12/31/68			12/31/69
	Historical	Conversion Factor	Restated to 12/31/69 $'s	Historical (stated in 12/31/69 $'s)
Net monetary items:				
Cash & receivables				$ 540,000
Accounts payable				(300,000)
Bonds payable				(500,000)
Net	$ 445,000	1.040	$462,800	$ (260,000)

				Restated to 12/31/69 $'s
Purchasing gain or loss				
Net monetary items—12/31/68	$ 445,000	1.040		$ 462,800
Add: Sales	1,900,000	1.014		1,926,600
	2,345,000			2,389,400
Deduct:				
Purchases	1,840,000			
Operating expenses & interest	215,000			
Purchase of marketable securities	400,000			
Acquisitions of equipment	150,000			
	2,605,000	1.014		2,641,470
Net monetary items—historical	$ (260,000)			
Net monetary items—historical —restated—12/31/69 ("as if")				(252,070)
Net monetary items—12/31/69 (actual)				(260,000)
Purchasing power loss (actual < "as if")				$ (7,930)

ANSWER OUTLINE: CHANGING PRICES

Problem 3   Constant Dollar Theory

Statement I
    Constant dollar statements are not required
        Some disclosures required by SFAS 33
    Inflation may be immaterial for one year but
      material for a series of years
    LIFO inventories, fixed assets, etc., are more
      relevant when adjusted for price-level changes
    Constant dollar statements are an extension of
      historical cost
        I.e., historical costs adjusted by the consumer
      price index
    Price indices are objectively derived

Statement II
    Constant dollar costs are unrelated to replace-
    ment costs
        Constant dollar amounts equal current value
        only by coincidence
    Historical depreciation is not concerned with
    asset replacement
        Depreciation is historical cost
        Depreciation is concerned with cost allocation,
      not replacement
    Indices are based upon average change in prices
        Current values are based upon specific asset
      prices
    Constant dollar data may improve management
    decisions

Statement III
    Current-noncurrent and monetary-nonmonetary
    are different
        Current is based on 12 months
        Or operating cycle, whichever is longer
        Monetary is cash or other fixed-dollar contract
    Purchasing power G&L only occur on monetary
    items
        Based on net monetary position
        And direction of price-level change
        Nonmonetary item restatement has no effect
      on purchasing power G&L
          Converts historical cost to current dollar
        purchasing power

UNOFFICIAL ANSWER: CHANGING PRICES

Problem 3   Constant Dollar Theory

Statement I

The accounting profession has never required that published financial statements be adjusted for general price-level changes, but it has seriously discussed, considered, and recommended such adjustments. SFAS 33 requires some constant dollar and current cost disclosures for certain companies, and both SFAS 33 and APB statement 3 recommend that general price-level adjusted financial statements should be presented as a supplement to the basic historical-dollar financial statements.

The rate of inflation may be immaterial for any given year. However, the rate has been considered material in recent years and it certainly has been material when considering a period of years. Because corporations generally publish financial statements for a series of years, the cumulative effect of constant dollar adjustments on these statements would be material. Furthermore, financial statements often contain LIFO inventories, long-lived assets, and other amounts incurred two or more years earlier that should be adjusted for general price-level changes to make the amounts more relevant and more easily understood.

Constant dollar financial statements are not a departure from, but an extension of, historical-cost financial statements. The historical-cost amounts are adjusted for changes in the general price level by use of the consumer price index. Thus, the dollar amounts contained in general price-level adjusted financial statements are historical-cost amounts adjusted for the change in the purchasing power of the dollar.

The argument for the use of facts, not estimates, should have no bearing on this discussion. Accounting is replete with estimates, such as estimates of asset lives for depreciation purposes, uncollectible accounts, income taxes expense, and many others. The average change in price levels is objectively determined (not a simple estimate) and could be used to present the facts in a more useful form.

Statement II

Constant dollar adjusted costs have no direct relationship to replacement costs. Depreciation is historical in nature and is not concerned with asset replacements; it is a process of cost allocation, not funding for asset replacements. Depreciation and constant dollar adjustments could be considered remotely related if, for example, net earnings were reduced by price-level adjustments, which in turn caused management to reduce dividends and thereby retain some assets that would otherwise have been paid out as dividends.

Constant dollar adjusted data would approximate current values only by coincidence. General price-level indexes are based on the average change in prices in the economy, not on changes in specific asset costs or industry prices. Current values are usually based on specific asset prices or asset appraisal values. These are usually a function of technology and supply and demand for these particular assets, rather than the general effect of inflation or deflation.

Management could probably make better decisions with constant dollar adjusted data than with unadjusted data, but there is a difference in purpose between internal and external reporting. Internal financial information for management decisions can be in any form that management desires. Internal financial reports are not bound by generally accepted accounting principles; they are prepared with the objective of maximum benefit to management and may be in any form or style management feels is the most useful. Thus, whether constant dollar adjusted financial statements are published or not, management should make decisions on what it believes is relevant information.

Statement III

There is a difference between classifying assets and liabilities as (1) current and noncurrent and (2) monetary and nonmonetary. Some current assets and current liabilities are monetary and some are nonmonetary, while some monetary assets and liabilities are current and some are noncurrent. The classification of an asset or liability as current is based on a period of 12 months or the operating cycle, whichever is longer. The classification of an asset or liability as monetary is based on whether it is cash or some other asset or liability whose amount is fixed by contract or otherwise in terms of numbers of dollars regardless of changes in specific prices or in the general price level.

With adjustments for general price-level changes, purchasing-power gains and losses are recognized on the holding of monetary items, but not on nonmonetary items. If monetary assets exceed monetary liabilities, the company is said to be a net monetary creditor. When the monetary assets are less than monetary liabilities, the company is said to be a net monetary debtor. The net monetary position and the amount and the direction of the change in the general price level will determine the price-level gain or loss. For example, if the company is a net monetary debtor, it will show a purchasing-power gain during an inflationary period and would show a purchasing-power loss during a deflationary period.

Restatement of nonmonetary items for changes in the general level of prices will have no effect on the amount of the purchasing-power gain or loss. It will simply cause historical-dollar amounts to be stated in current-dollar amounts of equal purchasing power.

ANSWER OUTLINE: CHANGING PRICES

Problem 4   Asset Valuation

a1.   Asset valuation affects
      Assets in balance sheet
      Timing and measurement of income

a2.   Historical cost valuation
      Acquisition cost net of depreciation
      Measured by cash exchange price
      Allocated to future periods, i.e., matching
      Gains recognized at sale
      Losses recognized when incurred
         Per conservatism, anticipate losses
   Price-level adjusted historical cost valuation
   (constant dollars)
      Reflects changes in purchasing power of $
      Is not current value measurement
      Monetary items are fixed claims
      Holding monetary items causes price-level G&L
   Discounted cash flow valuation
      Yields a current value measurement
      Based on PV of future net cash flow
      Income is stockholders' equity times discount
        rate
   Market price valuation
      Assets at current realizable sales price
      Income based on asset valuation, not transactions
      Income includes change in net asset value
   Replacement cost valuation
      Market price to replace present assets
      Approximated by appraisals
        Or specific price index adjustment
      Income in part based on asset value changes

UNOFFICIAL ANSWER: CHANGING PRICES

Problem 4   Asset Valuation

a.   1.   Valuation of assets is a significant issue because of its effect on the statement of financial position and the statement of earnings. The valuation method used affects the measurement of total assets and the timing and amount of periodic net earnings. This relationship between asset valuation and measurement of net earnings is referred to as "articulation" between these two financial statements.

2. Historical-cost valuation reports assets at their acquisition cost (net of depreciation, depletion, or amortization, if applicable) and is the total of exchange prices to obtain an asset and render it suitable for use. Such valuation is measured by the cash or cash equivalent sacrificed in exchange for the asset. There is an inherent assumption that a stable monetary unit exists.

Because acquisition cost is the vital measurement, that amount for limited life assets is allocated on a reasonable basis to future periods as expense or as a factor in the cost of goods sold (if inventory). It is, therefore, the actual past purchase price that affects the future period's measurement of net earnings under the matching concept. Because of this emphasis on matching each period's revenue and expense, the earnings statement emerges as the primary financial statement based on a transactions approach and the statement of financial position becomes partly a statement of unallocated past costs for nonmonetary assets.

Concerning allocation to the earnings statement under historical-cost valuation, gains are normally recognized in the period they are realized through sale or use. Unrealized gains are not considered. Unrealized losses, theoretically, should be treated the same as unrealized gains; nevertheless, conventional accounting practice permits recognition of some unrealized losses. This inconsistent treatment is justified under the doctrine of conservatism.

Historical cost adjusted to reflect general price-level changes (constant dollar statements) is a valuation method that uses the historical cost (previously discussed) of nonmonetary assets and applies a general price-level index to reflect changes in the standard unit of purchasing power, the dollar, so that the information reported is not biased by changes in the ability of the dollar to command goods and services. In this way, information reported in successive periods (time-series data) would be expressed in terms of a constant unit of measure. Nonmonetary assets are, therefore, stated in terms of the units of general purchasing power as of the date of the statement. These adjusted amounts do not measure any form of "current value" except by coincidence.

Monetary assets (cash, accounts receivable, etc.) are fixed claims to units of purchasing power that are the same as the units of dollars. Nonetheless, holding net monetary assets (monetary assets in excess of monetary liabilities) during a period of rising prices causes a purchasing power loss because these assets represent a fixed claim to reduced purchasing power. A purchasing power gain occurs by holding net monetary assets during periods of falling prices (or by being a net debtor in periods of rising prices). These purchasing power losses and gains would be shown on a company's earnings statement. They reflect, in part, the stewardship of management during a period of changing prices.

Discounted-cash flow valuation is one method that yields a "current-value" measurement. Under this approach, assets are reported at the present value of their expected future net cash inflows. Thus, it is considered a future exchange price. It reflects the notion that assets represent future service potential (economic benefits) and an attempt should be made to measure this potential (benefit) for reporting.

When using the discounted-cash-flow approach, net earnings would be equal to the discounted amount of stockholders' equity at the beginning of the period multiplied by the rate used to discount the future net cash flow. This reflects the amount that could be paid out to stockholders and still leave the business as "well off" at the end of the period as it was at the beginning of the period.

Market-price valuation yields a different "current-value" measurement. Under this approach, assets are reported at their present realizable sales prices at the date of the statement of financial position. These selling prices should be market selling prices of similar assets under conditions of orderly sales, rather than liquidation selling prices under conditions of forced sales. Use of current market selling prices is an indicator of present cash equivalents of the assets and reflects existing market alternatives; such use does not assume that these assets will necessarily be sold at those prices.

When using the market-price approach, net earnings would equal net assets (assets minus liabilities) at the end of the period plus capital withdrawals and dividends, less capital additions and net assets at the beginning of the period. Net earnings are, therefore, based on the valuation of the firm's assets (and liabilities) because these assets generate such earnings. Net earnings are not based on a transactions approach and, therefore, do not include arbitrary cost allocations to an accounting period.

Replacement-cost valuation yields another, and different "current-value" measurement. Under this approach, assets are reported at the market price quoted to acquire them (replacement in kind). Current replacement cost, which may be approximated by using a specific price index or by appraisals, reflects supply and demand for the specific asset(s) in question. Replacement-cost valuation can be based upon either replacement in kind or replacement of equivalent services or benefits.

When using the replacement-cost approach, net earnings include earnings computed by the transactions approach and gains or losses from holding assets (and liabilities) whose purchase prices rise or fall. The earnings statement thus contains some unrealized items (from a conventional viewpoint). Part of the traditionally determined net earnings would, under replacement-cost accounting, be reclassified as holding gains or losses. The earnings statement would show earnings from operations by deducting from current revenue the cost to replace the goods and services consumed in generating that revenue, plus holding gains or less holding losses resulting from changes in the replacement cost of the resources (and obligations) held.

SOLUTION GUIDE: CHANGING PRICES

Problem 5   Constant Dollar and Current Cost

1.   Part a requires the balance sheet amount for three reporting models.

1.1   Constant dollar balance sheet would show the historical cost of the land adjusted by the TO/FROM ratio:

$$\text{Historical cost} \times \frac{\text{price level adjusting to}}{\text{price level adjusting from}} = \text{Restated cost}$$

1.2   Current cost balance sheet would show the current cost of replacing the land.

1.3   Current cost/constant dollar balance sheet would show the same amount as current cost balance sheet because current cost is stated in terms of current purchasing power.

2.   Part b requires the computations of several income statement items.

2.1   Constant dollar income does not result until a sale has occurred; the conventional realization concept still applies.

2.2   Unrealized holding gain (loss) in a current cost system is the difference between the historical cost and current cost of assets held at year end.

2.3   Income from continuing operations is the difference between sales revenue less the current cost of inputs. Sales revenue is different from the current cost of the land because sales revenue is the amount we can sell the land for (exit value), while current cost is the amount we would pay today to acquire the land (entry value). Assets more likely to have different entry and exit values would include inventory and buildings.

2.4   Realized holding gain (loss) is the difference between the current cost and historical cost of an asset sold or consumed.

2.5   The total holding gain *recognized* on a current cost/constant dollar basis is the sum of: the holding gains and losses realized during the year, and the *change* in the unrealized holding gain or loss during the year. Only the change in unrealized items is included so as to avoid "double counting" of these gains or losses. For example, the realized holding gain ($17,000) in this problem includes the unrealized holding gain ($8,000) recognized last year. If no adjustment were made, the $8,000 would be included in both 1979 and 1980 income.

3. Part c requires the amount of income from continuing operations as required by FASB Statement No. 33 for 1978, 1979 and 1980.

3.1 Income from continuing operations must be presented on both a constant dollar basis and a current cost basis.

3.2 See 2.1 and 2.3 above for further explanations.

UNOFFICIAL ANSWER: CHANGING PRICES

Problem 5   Constant Dollar and Current Cost

Part a.

Valuation of land	Constant Dollar	Current Cost	Current Cost/ Constant Dollar
12/31/78	$40,000	$40,000	$40,000
12/31/79	44,000[a]	52,000	52,000

[a]$40,000 x 110/100 = $44,000

Part b.

1. Constant dollar income
1978	-0-
1979	-0-
1980	$20,000[a]

    [a]$40,000 x 120/100 = $48,000 constant
                          dollar basis
    $68,000 − $48,000 = $20,000 income

2.
Current cost of land	$52,000
Historical cost of land	40,000
Unrealized holding gain	$12,000

3.
Sales	$68,000
Current cost of land	65,000
Income from continuing operations (current cost)	$ 3,000

4.
Current cost of land	$65,000
Historical cost of land	40,000
Realized holding gain	$25,000

5. Realized holding gain:
Current cost of land	$65,000
Cost of land on constant dollar basis ($40,000 x 120/100)	48,000
Realized holding gain	$17,000

Unrealized holding gain:	1/1/80	10/31/80
Current cost of land	$52,000	-0-
Cost of land on constant dollar basis	44,000	-0-
Unrealized holding gain	$ 8,000	-0-
	x120/110	
Unrealized holding gain in constant dollars 10/31/80	$ 8,727	

Total holding gain recognized:

Realized holding gain	$17,000
Change in unrealized holding gains ($0-$8,727)	(8,727)
Total holding gain recognized	$ 8,273

Part c.

Income from Continuing Operations

Year	Constant Dollar	Current Cost
1978	—0—	—0—
1979	—0—	—0—
1980	$20,000[a]	$3,000[b]

[a]$40,000 X 120/100 = $48,000 constant dollar basis
   $68,000 − $48,000 = $20,000 income

[b]$68,000 − $65,000 = $3,000

ANSWER OUTLINE: CHANGING PRICES

Problem 6   SFAS 33

a.   Lower of cost or market
    Changes in market value below cost recorded
    Unrealized holding losses recognized
    Unrealized holding gains above cost ignored
  Current cost
    All changes in asset value recorded
    All changes in market value affect earnings
      Unrealized holding losses and gains

b.   Capital maintenance theory
    Capital must be maintained before income is
     recognized
    Well-offness
  Constant dollar
    Maintain purchasing power
  Current cost
    Maintain operating capacity

c.   Supplementary inventory disclosures
    Current cost stated in constant dollars
      Holding gains (net of inflation)

UNOFFICIAL ANSWER: CHANGING PRICES

Problem 6   SFAS 33

a.   Short-term investments in marketable equity securities are accounted for on a lower-of-cost-or-market basis. The asset is reported on the balance sheet at cost, unless market value falls below cost. Then the asset valuation becomes market value. Therefore unrealized holding losses (and recoveries of those losses up to cost) are recognized, while unrealized holding gains above cost are not recognized until the asset is sold.

    If accounted for on a current cost basis, the marketable equity securities would be recorded at cost when acquired. Subsequent asset valuation would be based on market value, whether above or below cost. All changes in market value would be reflected in earnings, i.e., both unrealized holding losses and gains are recognized.

b.   Capital maintenance theory holds that a company's capital must be maintained before any income can be recognized. In other words, earnings is the amount an entity can distribute to its owners and be as well off at year-end as at the beginning of the year.

    Constant dollar accounting measures well-offness in terms of purchasing power. An entity must maintain its purchasing power before income is recognized.

    Current cost accounting measures well-offness in terms of operating capacity. An entity must maintain its operating capacity before income is recognized.

c.   Two of the supplementary disclosures required for certain companies by SFAS 33 involve inventory. The current cost of inventory, restated to average-for-the-year dollars, must be presented. Also, the holding gain on inventory, net of inflation, must be reported.

SOLUTION GUIDE: FOREIGN CURRENCY

Problem 7   Foreign Currency Translation

1.   Translation of selected accounts from a foreign balance sheet into United States dollars at 12/31/76 is required. The solutions approach is to determine the proper exchange rate for each balance sheet item at December 31 of both 1975 and 1976. See para 9–15 of SFAS 8 for the general rules concerning translation of foreign financial statements. See Appendix A of SFAS 8 for further explanations and illustrations of these general rules.

1.1   Accounts receivable is a monetary item and accordingly is translated at the current rate. The allowance for bad debts is also translated at the current rate. Thus, the analysis of the accounts receivable and allowance accounts is not relevant to the solution. The current rate at the end of 1976 was 1.5 and the current rate at the end of 1975 was 1.7.

1.2   Inventories carried at cost are translated at the historical rate, and inventories carried at the current market price are translated at the current rate. In this problem, inventory is carried at FIFO cost. Since the inventories are based on FIFO, ending inventory consists of purchases of the current year. The 1976 purchases were made in June at which time the exchange rate was 1.7. The 1975 purchases were also made in June when the exchange rate was 2.0.

1.3   Property, plant, and equipment and the related accumulated depreciation are translated at the historical rate. Begin your analysis with 1975 as the balance in the fixed asset account is cumulative, i.e., the assets on hand at the end of 1975 continue to be on hand at the end of 1976. The $150,000 of net assets was all purchased when the exchange rate was 2.0 (before July 31, 1975). Thus the $150,000 of 1975 P,P&E is translated at the 2.0 exchange rate.

Note that there is no need to be concerned with the depreciation as it is to be translated at the same rate as the related fixed assets. The $150,000 of 12/31/75 fixed assets resulted from the 1975 acquisitions of 24,000 LCU and 140,000 LCU, less the 14,000 LCU of 1975 depreciation.

The 12/31/76 net fixed assets consisted of the 1975 ending balance of 150,000 LCU less another 14,000 LCU of depreciation which is to be translated at 2.0. Additionally 30,000 LCU of equipment was purchased in 1976 and 3,000 LCU thereof depreciated. The net 1976 addition is 27,000 units to be translated at 1.5 (the exchange rate of July 1976 when the 1976 acquisitions were made).

1.4 Long-term debt is a monetary item and accordingly is translated at the current rate. The current rate at the end of 1976 was 1.5 and the current rate at the end of 1975 was 1.7.

1.5 Since the ending balance of long-term debt is translated at the current rate, the information provided on additional issuances of debt is irrelevant to the solution. Common stock is a nonmonetary item and is translated at the historical rate. The stock was issued at the beginning of 1975 when the exchange rate was 2.0. Since there were no additional issuances of stock in 1976, the capital stock account is translated at the historical rate of 2.0 at both the end of 1975 and the end of 1976.

UNOFFICIAL ANSWER: FOREIGN CURRENCY

Problem 7   Foreign Currency Translation

Schedule for Problem 7 appears on following page.

ANSWER OUTLINE: FOREIGN CURRENCY

Problem 8   SFAS 8 Definitions

a. "Measure" is to quantify a unit of currency in another currency
   An exchange rate is used to make the translation
   "Denominate" means an amount is fixed in terms of a foreign currency, i.e., to be paid in the "denominated" currency
   A transaction may only be denominated in one currency

A transaction may be denominated in one currency and the denominated amount translated into another currency
   E.g., a German company with a purchase from a British company denominated in British sterling measured in German marks
A transaction may be measured and denominated in the same currency
   E.g., a German company with a purchase from another German company denominated and measured in German marks

b. Temporal method of foreign currency translation
   Cash, receivables and payables—current rate
   Nonmonetary items—historical rate
      Except items carried at market—current rate
   Revenue and expense items—average rate
      Except items related to assets and liabilities which are translated at their respective historical rates
      Long-term receivables and debt—current rate
      Inventory at cost and deferred income—historical rate

UNOFFICIAL ANSWER: FOREIGN CURRENCY

Problem 8   SFAS 8 Definitions

Part a.

The term measure, as used by the Financial Accounting Standards Board, refers to the quantification of an attribute of an item in a unit of currency other than the reporting currency. In this respect, transactions or balances reflected on a foreign financial statement are expressed in terms of U.S. dollars by applying the appropriate exchange rate to the foreign amount. This process is referred to as translation. It is possible to measure a given transaction or balance in terms of any other currency if the appropriate exchange rate is known.

An asset or liability is denominated in a foreign currency if the liability or right to receive is fixed in terms of the foreign currency, regardless of the exchange rate. When an account receivable (or payable) is created and stated in fixed amounts of the foreign currency, the entity has the right (obligation) to receive (pay) the originally stated number of units of foreign currency. A change in the exchange rate between the date of the right to receive (obligation to pay) and the date the asset (liability) is received (paid) gives rise to an exchange gain or loss. An asset or liability may only be denominated in one currency.

Schedule for Problem 7

Franklin Company's Foreign Subsidiary
**TRANSLATION OF SELECTED CAPTIONS INTO
UNITED STATES DOLLARS**
December 31, 1976 and December 31, 1975

	LCU	Translation Rate	United States Dollars
December 31, 1976			
Accounts receivable (net)	40,000 LCU	1.5 LCU to $1	$26,667
Inventories, at cost	80,000	1.7 LCU to $1	47,059
Property, plant, and equipment (net)	163,000	*Schedule 1*	86,000
Long-term debt	100,000	1.5 LCU to $1	66,667
Common stock	50,000	2 LCU to $1	25,000
December 31, 1975			
Accounts receivable (net)	35,000	1.7 LCU to $1	20,588
Inventories, at cost	75,000	2 LCU to $1	37,500
Property, plant, and equipment (net)	150,000	2 LCU to $1	75,000
Long-term debt	120,000	1.7 LCU to $1	70,588
Common stock	50,000	2 LCU to $1	25,000

Schedule 1

*Computation of Translation of Property,
Plant, and Equipment (Net) into United States
Dollars at December 31, 1976*

	LCU	Translation Rate	United States Dollars
Land purchased on January 1, 1975	24,000 LCU	2 LCU to $1	$12,000
Plant and equipment purchased on January 1, 1975:			
Original cost	140,000	2 LCU to $1	70,000
Depreciation for 1975	(14,000)	2 LCU to $1	(7,000)
Depreciation for 1976	(14,000)	2 LCU to $1	(7,000)
	112,000	2 LCU to $1	56,000
Plant and equipment purchased on July 4, 1976:			
Original cost	30,000	1.5 LCU to $1	20,000
Depreciation for 1976	(3,000)	1.5 LCU to $1	(2,000)
	27,000	1.5 LCU to $1	18,000
	163,000 LCU		$86,000

Any given transaction may be measured in one currency and denominated in another currency. An example of such a transaction would be the purchase of goods for sale by a German subsidiary of a U.S. company (measuring the transaction in German marks) from a British company payable (denominated) in pounds sterling.

A transaction may also be measured and denominated in the same foreign (with respect to a parent company) currency. An example of this type of transaction would be a British subsidiary of a U. S. company purchasing an asset from another British company. In this example the British subsidiary would measure the transaction in pounds sterling and would subsequently satisfy the debt in pounds sterling.

In the first example, a change in the exchange rate between the date of the purchase of the goods and the settlement of the debt would cause the debt to be paid at an amount different from the original balance measured in U. S. dollars at the date of the transaction. This difference arises because a fixed amount of pounds sterling must be paid in order to settle the debt regardless of the cost to obtain the pounds sterling.

In the second example, the subsidiary measures its transactions in the currency in which the debt is denominated, and so a subsequent change in the exchange rate of pounds sterling to U. S. dollars would have no effect on the amount of the debt owed.

Part b.

The temporal method generally translates assets and liabilities expressed in foreign currency in a manner that retains the accounting principles used to measure them in foreign statements and is characterized by the following:

· Cash or amounts receivable or payable that are denominated in a local foreign currency are to be translated using current rates.

· All other assets and liabilities that are not classified as above are to be translated in a manner that retains their original measurement bases. The historical rate is to be used for accounts that are carried at prices in past exchanges, and the current rate is to be used in translating accounts that are priced in current or future exchanges.

· Revenue and expense accounts are to be translated at the average exchange rate in effect during the period being reported upon. However,

revenue and expense balances related to assets and liabilities translated at historical rates are translated at the rate in existence at the time the asset or liability was attained. Examples of revenue and expense accounts to be translated at historical rates are depreciation, amortization, inventory changes in cost of goods sold, and recognition of deferred income.

The balances in long-term accounts receivable and long-term debt represent amounts receivable or payable denominated in local foreign currency and as such must be translated at the current rate of exchange.

Inventory valued at cost and deferred income each represent accounts measured in past exchanges and must be translated at historical rates.

MULTIPLE CHOICE QUESTIONS (1–34)

1. Utica Company's net accounts receivable were $250,000 at December 31, 1978, and $300,000 at December 31, 1979. Net cash sales for 1979 were $100,000. The accounts receivable turnover for 1979 was 5.0. What were Utica's total net sales for 1979?
   - a. $1,475,000
   - b. $1,500,000
   - c. $1,600,000
   - d. $2,750,000

2. Selected information for Irvington Company is as follows:

	December 31	
	1978	1979
Preferred stock, 8%, par $100, nonconvertible, noncumulative	$125,000	$125,000
Common stock	300,000	400,000
Retained earnings	75,000	185,000
Dividends paid on preferred stock for year ended	10,000	10,000
Net income for year ended	60,000	120,000

Irvington's return on common stockholders' equity, rounded to the nearest percentage point, for 1979 is
   - a. 17%
   - b. 19%
   - c. 23%
   - d. 25%

3. Selected information for 1979 for the Prince Company is as follows:

Cost of goods sold	$5,400,000
Average inventory	1,800,000
Net sales	7,200,000
Average receivables	960,000
Net income	720,000

Assuming a business year consisting of 360 days, what was the average number of days in the operating cycle for 1979?
   - a. 72
   - b. 84
   - c. 144
   - d. 168

4. Smith Company had net income for 1979 of $5,300,000 and earnings per share on common stock of $2.50. Included in the net income was $500,000

of bond interest expense related to its long-term debt. The income tax rate for 1979 was 50%. Dividends on preferred stock were $300,000. The dividend-payout ratio on common stock was 40%. What were the dividends on common stock in 1979?
   - a. $1,800,000
   - b. $1,900,000
   - c. $2,000,000
   - d. $2,120,000

5. If current assets exceed current liabilities, payments to creditors made on the last day of the month will
   - a. Decrease current ratio.
   - b. Increase current ratio.
   - c. Decrease net working capital.
   - d. Increase net working capital.

6. Which of the following ratios measures short-term solvency?
   - a. Current ratio.
   - b. Age of receivables.
   - c. Creditors' equity to total assets.
   - d. Return on investment.

7. Selected information from the accounting records of the Code Company is as follows:

Cost of goods sold for 1978	$1,200,000
Inventories at December 31, 1977	350,000
Inventories at December 31, 1978	310,000

Assuming a business year consisting of 300 days, what was the number of days' sales in average inventories for 1978?
   - a. 36.5
   - b. 77.5
   - c. 82.5
   - d. 87.5

8. Information from Life Company's balance sheet is as follows:

Current assets:

Cash	$ 4,000,000
Marketable securities	12,500,000
Accounts receivable	96,000,000
Inventories	110,500,000
Prepaid expenses	2,000,000
Total current assets	$225,000,000

Current liabilities:

.Notes payable	$ 3,000,000
Accounts payable	39,000,000
Accrued expenses	25,000,000
Income taxes payable	1,000,000
Payments due within one year on long-term debt	7,000,000
Total current liabilities	$75,000,000

What is the quick (acid-test) ratio?
- a. 1.33 to 1.
- b. 1.50 to 1.
- c. 1.65 to 1.
- d. 3.00 to 1.

9.   Delta, Inc., is a retail store operating in a state with a 5% retail sales tax. The state law provides that the retail sales tax collected during the month must be remitted to the state during the following month. If the amount collected is remitted to the state on or before the twentieth of the following month, the retailer may keep 2% of the sales tax collected. On April 10, 1979, Delta remitted $16,905 sales tax to the state tax division for March 1979 retail sales. How much of Delta's March 1979 retail sales was subject to sales tax?
- a. $331,340
- b. $331,480
- c. $338,100
- d. $345,000

10. The following common size income statements are available for Sparky Corporation for the two years ended December 31, 1975, and 1974:

	1975	1974
Sales	100%	100%
Cost of sales	55	70
Gross profit on sales	45	30
Operating expenses (including income tax expense)	20	18
Net income	25%	12%

The trend percentages for sales are as follows:

1975	130%
1974	100%

What should be the trend percentage for gross profit on sales for 1975?
- a. 58.5%.
- b. 130%.
- c. 150%.
- d. 195%.

Items 11 through 14 are based on the following instructions:

Each item describes an independent situation. For each situation, one factor is denoted X and the other factor is denoted Y. For each situation, compare the two factors to determine whether X is greater than, equal to, or less than Y.

11. Delta Corporation wrote off a $100 uncollectible account receivable against the $1,200 balance in its allowance account. Compare the current ratio before the write off (X) with the current ratio after the write off (Y).
- a. X greater than Y.
- b. X equals Y.
- c. X less than Y.
- d. Cannot be determined.

12. Kappa, Inc., neglected to amortize the premium on its bonds payable. Compare the company's net earnings without this premium amortization (X) and the company's net earnings with such amortization (Y).
- a. X greater than Y.
- b. X equals Y.
- c. X less than Y.
- d. Cannot be determined.

13. Aaron, Inc., owns 80% of the outstanding stock of Belle, Inc. Compare the consolidated net earnings of Aaron and Belle (X) and Aaron's net earnings if it does not consolidate with Belle (Y).
- a. X greater than Y.
- b. X equals Y.
- c. X less than Y.
- d. Cannot be determined.

14. Epsilon Company has a current ratio of 2 to 1. A transaction reduces the current ratio. Compare the working capital before this transaction (X) and the working capital after this transaction (Y).
- a. X greater than Y.
- b. X equals Y.
- c. X less than Y.
- d. Cannot be determined.

15. Information from Guard Company's financial statements is as follows:

	1976	1977
Current assets at December 31	$2,000,000	$2,100,000
Current liabilities at December 31	1,000,000	900,000
Stockholders' equity at December 31	2,500,000	2,700,000
Net sales for year	8,300,000	8,800,000
Cost of goods sold for year	6,200,000	6,400,000
Operating income for year	500,000	550,000

What is the current ratio at December 31, 1977?
- a. 1.20 to 1.
- b. 2.25 to 1.
- c. 2.33 to 1.
- d. 7.33 to 1.

Items 16 through 21 deal with the calculations of ratios and the determination of other factors considered important in analysis of financial statements. Prior to the occurrence of the independent events described below the corporation concerned had current and quick ratios in excess of one to one and reported a net income (as opposed to a loss) for the period just ended. Income tax effects of the events are to be ignored. The corporation had only one class of shares outstanding.

16. The effect of recording a 100% stock dividend would be to
- a. Decrease the current ratio, decrease working capital, and decrease book value per share.
- b. Leave inventory turnover unaffected, decrease working capital, and decrease book value per share.
- c. Leave working capital unaffected, decrease earnings per share, and decrease book value per share.
- d. Leave working capital unaffected, decrease earnings per share, and decrease the debt to equity ratio.

17. Recording the payment (as distinguished from the declaration) of a cash dividend whose declaration was already recorded will
- a. Increase the current ratio but have no effect on working capital.
- b. Decrease both the current ratio and working capital.
- c. Increase both the current ratio and working capital.
- d. Have no effect on the current ratio or earnings per share.

18. What would be the effect on book value per share and earnings per share if the corporation purchased its own shares in the open market at a price greater than book value per share?
- a. No effect on book value per share but increase earnings per share.
- b. Increase both book value per share and earnings per share.
- c. Decrease both book value per share and earnings per share.
- d. Decrease book value per share and increase earnings per share.

19. If the corporation were to increase the extent to which it successfully "traded on the equity" this fact would likely be manifested in a combination of facts that its
- a. Ratio of owner's equity to total assets decreased while its ratio of net income to owners' equity increased.
- b. Book value and earnings per share decreased.
- c. Working capital decreased while its current ratio increased.
- d. Asset turnover and return on sales both decreased.

20. The corporation exercises control over an affiliate in which it holds a 40% common stock interest. If its affiliate completed a fiscal year profitably but paid no dividends, how would this affect the investor corporation?
- a. Result in an increased current ratio.
- b. Result in increased earnings per share.
- c. Increase several turnover ratios.
- d. Decrease book value per share.

21. What would be the most probable cause of an increase in the rate of inventory turnover while the rate of receivables turnover decreased when compared with the prior period?
- a. Sales volume has changed markedly.
- b. Investment in inventory has decreased while investment in receivables has increased.
- c. Investment in inventory has increased while investment in receivables has decreased.
- d. The corporation has shortened the credit period for customers (tightened credit terms).

Items 22, 23, and 24 are based on the following information:

The December 31, 1975, balance sheet of Ratio, Inc., is presented below. These are the only accounts in Ratio's balance sheet. Amounts indicated by a question mark (?) can be calculated from the additional information given.

Assets:

Cash	$ 25,000
Accounts receivable (net)	?
Inventory	?
Property, plant and equipment (net)	294,000
	$432,000

Liabilities and Stockholders' Equity:

Accounts payable (trade)	?
Income taxes payable (current)	25,000
Long-term debt	?
Common stock	300,000
Retained earnings	?
	?

Additional information:

Current ratio (at year-end)	1.5 to 1
Total liabilities divided by total stockholders' equity	.8
Inventory turnover based on sales and ending inventory	15 times
Inventory turnover based on cost of goods sold and ending inventory	10.5 times
Gross margin for 1975	$315,000

22. What was Ratio's December 31, 1975, balance in trade accounts payable?
- a. $67,000.
- b. $92,000.
- c. $182,000.
- d. $207,000.

23. What was Ratio's December 31, 1975, balance in retained earnings?
- a. $60,000 deficit.
- b. $60,000.
- c. $132,000 deficit.
- d. $132,000.

24. What was Ratio's December 31, 1975, balance in the inventory account?
- a. $21,000.
- b. $30,000.
- c. $70,000.
- d. $135,000.

25. A company has a current ratio of 2 to 1. This ratio will decrease if the company
- a. Receives a 5% stock dividend on one of its marketable securities.
- b. Pays a large account payable which had been a current liability.
- c. Borrows cash on a six-month note.
- d. Sells merchandise for more than cost and records the sale using the perpetual-inventory method.

MAY 1981 QUESTIONS

Items 26 through 29 are based on the following information:

Alpha Corporation
Selected Financial Data

	As of December 31,	
	1980	1979
Cash	$ 10,000	$ 80,000
Accounts receivable (net)	50,000	150,000
Merchandise inventory	90,000	150,000
Short-term marketable securities	30,000	10,000
Land and buildings (net)	340,000	360,000
Mortgage payable (no current portion)	270,000	280,000
Accounts payable (trade)	70,000	110,000
Short-term notes payable	20,000	40,000

	Year ended December 31,	
	1980	1979
Cash sales	$1,800,000	$1,600,000
Credit sales	500,000	800,000
Cost of goods sold	1,000,000	1,400,000

26. Alpha's quick (acid test) ratio as of December 31, 1980, is
- a. 0.5 to 1.
- b. 0.7 to 1.
- c. 1.0 to 1.
- d. 2.0 to 1.

27. Alpha's receivable turnover for 1980 is
- a. 5 times.
- b. 10 times.
- c. 23 times.
- d. 46 times.

28. Alpha's merchandise inventory turnover for 1980 is
   a.   8.3 times.
   b.   10.0 times.
   c.   11.1 times.
   d.   13.3 times.

29. Alpha's current ratio at December 31, 1980, is
   a.   0.5 to 1.
   b.   0.7 to 1.
   c.   1.0 to 1.
   d.   2.0 to 1.

30. Maple Corporation's stockholders' equity at June 30, 1980, consisted of the following:

Preferred stock, 10%, $50 par value;
   liquidating value $55 per share;
   20,000 shares issued and outstanding $1,000,000
Common stock, $10 par value; 500,000
   shares authorized; 150,000 shares
   issued and outstanding   1,500,000
Retained earinings   500,000

The book value per share of common stock is
   a. $10.00.
   b. $12.67.
   c. $13.33.
   d. $17.65.

31. Pine Corporation's stockholders' equity at December 31, 1980, consisted of the following:

Cumulative preferred stock, 6%,
   $100 par value; 1,000 shares
   issued and outstanding $100,000
Common stock, $10 par value; 300,000
   shares authorized; 50,000 shares
   issued and outstanding   500,000
Retained earnings   90,000

Dividends have not been declared on the preferred stock for the years 1976 through 1980. The book value per share of common stock is
   a. $10.00.
   b. $11.20.
   c. $11.80.
   d. $14.12.

32. Financial reporting provides information about an enterprise's performance during a period when it was under the direction of a particular management
   a.   But does **not** directly provide information about that management's performance.
   b.   And directly provides information about that management's performance.
   c.   And directly provides information about both management performance and enterprise performance.

   d.   And directly provides estimates of an enterprise's earning power.

33. Which of the following is an appropriate computation for return on investment?
   a.   Income dividend by total assets.
   b.   Income divided by sales.
   c.   Sales divided by total assets.
   d.   Sales divided by stockholders' equity.

34. Which of the following accounts would be included in the calculation of the acid test (quick) ratio?

	Accounts receivable	Inventories
a.	No	No
b.	No	Yes
c.	Yes	No
d.	Yes	Yes

PROBLEMS

Problem 1   Corporation Solvency Ratios (1173,T7)

(25 to 30 minutes)

As the CPA responsible for an "opinion" audit engagement, you are requested by the client to organize the work to provide him at the earliest possible date with some key ratios based on the final figures appearing on the comparative financial statements. This information is to be used to convince creditors that the client business is solvent and to support the use of going-concern valuation procedures in the financial statements. The client wishes to save time by concentrating on only these key data.

The data requested and the computations taken from the financial statements follow:

	Last Year	This Year
Current ratio	2.0:1	2.5:1
Quick (acid test) ratio	1.2:1	.7:1
Property, plant, and equipment to owners' equity	2.3:1	2.6:1
Sales to owners' equity	2.8:1	2.5:1
Net income	Down 10%	Up 30%
Earnings per common share	$2.40	$3.12
Book value per common share	Up 8%	Up 5%

Required:

a. The client asks that you prepare a list of brief comments stating how each of these items supports the solvency and going-concern potential of his business. He wishes to use these comments to support his presentation of data to his creditors. You are to prepare the comments as requested, giving the implications and the limitations of each item separately and then the collective inference one may draw from them about the client's solvency and going-concern potential.

b. Having done as the client requested in part a., prepare a brief listing of additional ratio-analysis-type data for this client which you think his creditors are going to ask for to supplement the data provided in part a. Explain why you think the additional data will be helpful to these creditors in evaluating this client's solvency.

c. What warnings should you offer these creditors about the limitations of ratio analysis for the purpose stated here?

Problem 2   Ratio Computations (1176,P4b)
(15 to 20 minutes)

The Printing Company is listed on the New York Stock Exchange. The market value of its common stock was quoted at $10 per share at December 31, 1975, and 1974. Printing's balance sheet at December 31, 1975, and 1974, and statement of income and retained earnings for the years then ended are presented below:

Printing Company
BALANCE SHEET

	December 31,	
	1975	1974
Assets:		
Current assets:		
Cash	$ 3,500,000	$ 3,600,000
Marketable securities	13,000,000	11,000,000
Accounts receivable	105,000,000	95,000,000
Inventories	126,000,000	154,000,000
Prepaid expenses	2,500,000	2,400,000
Total current assets	250,000,000	266,000,000
Property and plant, net	311,000,000	308,000,000
Investments, at equity	2,000,000	3,000,000
Long-term receivables	14,000,000	16,000,000
Goodwill and patents, net	6,000,000	6,500,000
Other assets	7,000,000	8,500,000
Total assets	$590,000,000	$608,000,000

Liabilities and Stockholders' Equity:

Current liabilities:		
Notes payable	$ 5,000,000	$ 15,000,000
Accounts payable	38,000,000	48,000,000
Accrued expenses	24,500,000	27,000,000
Income taxes payable	1,000,000	1,000,000
Current portion of long-term debt	6,500,000	7,000,000
Total current liabilities	75,000,000	98,000,000
Long-term debt	169,000,000	180,000,000
Deferred income taxes	74,000,000	67,000,000
Other liabilities	9,000,000	8,000,000

Stockholders' equity:

Com. stk., $1 par value	10,000,000	10,000,000
5% cumulative preferred stk., par value $100 per share; $100 liqui-dating value	4,000,000	4,000,000
Additional paid-in capital	107,000,000	107,000,000
Retained earnings	142,000,000	134,000,000
Total stockholders' equity	263,000,000	255,000,000
Total liabilities and stockholders' equity	$590,000,000	$608,000,000

Printing Company
STATEMENT OF INCOME
AND RETAINED EARNINGS

	Year ended December 31,	
	1975	1974
Net sales	$600,000,000	$500,000,000
Costs and expenses:		
Cost of goods sold	490,000,000	400,000,000
S, G, & A expense	66,000,000	60,000,000
Other, net	7,000,000	6,000,000
Total costs	563,000,000	466,000,000
Income before taxes	37,000,000	34,000,000
Income taxes	16,800,000	15,800,000
Net income	20,200,000	18,200,000
Beginning retained earnings	134,000,000	126,000,000
Common stk. dividends	12,000,000	10,000,000
Preferred stk. dividends	200,000	200,000
Ending retained earnings	$142,000,000	$134,000,000

Required:

Based on the above information, compute (for the year 1975 only) the following:

1. Current (working capital) ratio.
2. Quick (acid-test) ratio.
3. Number of days' sales in average receivables, assuming a business year consisting of 300 days and all sales on account.
4. Inventory turnover.
5. Book value per share of common stock.
6. Earnings per share on common stock.
7. Price-earnings ratio on common stock.
8. Dividend-payout ratio on common stock.

Show supporting computations in good form.

MULTIPLE CHOICE ANSWERS

1.	a	8.	b	15.	c	22.	a	29.	d
2.	c	9.	d	16.	c	23.	a	30.	b
3.	d	10.	d	17.	a	24.	c	31.	b
4.	c	11.	b	18.	d	25.	c	32.	a
5.	b	12.	c	19.	a	26.	c	33.	a
6.	a	13.	b	20.	b	27.	a	34.	c
7.	c	14.	d	21.	b	28.	a		

EXPLANATION OF MULTIPLE CHOICE ANSWERS

1. (1180,P1,5)   (a)   The requirement is Utica's total net sales for 1979. The amount of cash sales ($100,000) was given, so only credit sales must be computed using the information given on accounts receivable turnover.

$$\text{A/R turnover} = \frac{\text{Credit Sales}}{\text{Average A/R}}$$

The information given can be inserted into the above equation:

$$5.0 = \frac{\text{Credit Sales}}{(250{,}000 + 300{,}000)/2}$$

Therefore, credit sales are $1,375,000. Total sales are $100,000 higher, or $1,475,000.

2. (1180,P1,7)   (c)   The requirement is Irvington's return on common stockholders' equity for 1979, which is computed by dividing net income available to common stockholders (net income less preferred dividends) by average common stockholders' equity:

$$\frac{\$120{,}000 - \$10{,}000}{(\$375{,}000 + \$585{,}000)/2} = 23\%$$

3. (580,P1,7)   (d)   The average number of days in the operating cycle is the average number of days in the inventory/cost of goods sold cycle plus the average number of days in the accounts receivable/sales cycle.

$$\frac{360 \text{ days}}{5.4 \text{ C of GS} \div 1.8 \text{ Avg. inv.}} + \frac{360 \text{ days}}{7.2 \text{ net sales} \div .96 \text{ Avg. receiv.}}$$

$$= \text{Avg. no. days sales in oper. cycle}$$

$$\left(360 \div 3\right) + \left(360 \div 7.5\right) = 168$$

4. (580,P1,13)   (c)   The dividend-payout ratio on common stock, given in this case, is obtained by dividing the dividends on common stock for the period by income available to common stockholders for the period. The solutions approach is to apply the dividend-payout ratio of 40% to income available for common stockholders.

40% ($5,300,000 net income − $300,000 pref. div.)
  = $2,000,000

5. (580,T1,1)   (b)   Payments to creditors will decrease both cash (current asset) and payables (current liability). Therefore, both answers (c) and (d) are incorrect because there is no effect on net working capital. If current assets exceed current liabilities prior to this payment, the current ratio is greater than 1. Subtracting equal amounts from both the numerator and the denominator of a fraction which is greater than 1 will increase the fraction. Note that such a payment in cases where the current ratio is less than one will decrease the ratio.

6. (580,T1,50)   (a)   Age of receivables is an activity ratio (measures how effectively assets are used). Return on investment is a profitability ratio. Both the current ratio and creditors' equity to total assets measure solvency, but the latter is geared more to long-term creditors.

7. (1179,P1,7)   (c)   The requirement is the number of days' sales in average inventories for 1978, given a business year of 300 days. The number of days' sales in average inventories is the inventory turnover ratio divided into the number of days in a year (here 300). Thus, the solutions approach is to compute the inventory turnover ratio, and then divide the inventory turnover ratio into 300 days. Inventory turnover is the average inventory divided into cost of sales. Here, the average inventory of $330,000 divided into the 1978 cost of sales of $1,200,000 is 3.64. The inventory turnover ratio of 3.64 divided into 300 business days is 82.5, which indicates that the number of days' sales in average inventories is 82.5.

8. (1179,P1,8)   (b)   The requirement is the quick (acid-test) ratio. The quick ratio is cash, net receivables, and marketable securities divided by current liabilities. The quick ratio measures the ability to pay current liabilities from cash and near cash items. Here, cash, marketable securities, and receivables total $112,500,000, and current liabilities total $75,000,000, resulting in a quick ratio of 1.5, as computed below.

Cash	$ 4,000,000
Marketable securities	12,500,000
A/R	96,000,000
	$112,500,000
	÷ 75,000,000 of CL
	= 1.50

9. (1179,Q1,11) (d) The requirement is March 1979 retail sales subject to sales tax. The problem indicates $16,905 in sales tax was paid based upon a 5% sales tax less a discount of 2% of the amount of sales tax due. The solutions approach is to determine the effective tax rate after the discount (2%) for timely payment as illustrated below. The tax rate of .049 then is divided into the $16,905 to obtain the total taxable sales of $345,000.

$$\text{Sales tax} = .05 \,(\text{sales} - .02\,(.05\text{ sales}))$$
$$\text{Sales tax} = .049 \text{ sales}$$
$$\$16,905 \div .049 = \$345,000$$

10. (1176,Q1,1) (d) The requirement is the trend percentage for gross profit in 1975. In percentage analysis of financial statements, vertical analysis presents each item in a financial statement as a percentage of some other item, e.g., sales. Note that both the 1975 and 1974 income statements are presented as percentages of sales for their respective years. These are known as common size statements. Horizontal analysis constitutes percentages reflecting the change from one period to the next period on an item by item basis, e.g., the trend percentages in this problem.

The solutions approach to this problem is to recognize that 1975 sales are 130% of 1974 sales. In the absence of other information the gross profit rate continues to be 45% resulting in a 58.5% gross profit rate in 1975 relative to the gross profit rate of 30% in 1974. Thus the gross profit and percentage for 1975 is 195%.

	1975
130%	Sales
x45%	GP rate
58.5%	GP on sales
÷30%	1974 GP on sales
195%	1975 trend %

11. (1176,T1,19) (b) The requirement is to compare the current ratio before and after the transaction. Next, explicitly note the composition of the current ratio: current assets over current liabilities. Next, note the effect of the transaction on both current assets and current liabilities. The writing off of accounts receivable against an allowance account decreases both a current asset and a contra current asset account, thus, no effect on current assets. Likewise the transaction does not affect current liabilities. Thus, the current ratio remains the same.

12. (1176,T1,20) (c) The requirement is to compare earnings without bond premium amortization (X) to earnings with bond premium amortization (Y). The entry to record bond premium amortization is to debit the premium and credit interest expense, i.e., reduce expense or increase income. Thus, the income without amortization (X) is less than income with amortization (Y).

13. (1176,T1,21) (b) Are the consolidated earnings of Aaron and Belle greater than Aaron's earnings alone? They are the same, because the equity method is applied in consolidation. The equity method is also required for unconsolidated subsidiaries (para 14, APB 18).

14. (1176,T1,22) (d) The requirement is the change in working capital resulting from a decrease in the current ratio. As illustrated below, the current ratio of 2/1 can be reduced by adding the same amount to both numerator and denominator or it can be reduced by increasing the denominator or reducing the numerator. If the same amount is added to both numerator and denominator, working capital remains the same. If the numerator is reduced or the denominator increased, working capital would decrease. Thus, we cannot determine whether working capital will remain the same or decrease.

$$\frac{2}{1} \qquad \frac{3}{2} \qquad \frac{1.5}{1}$$

15. (1178,P1,10) (c) The requirement is the current ratio at December 31, 1977. The current ratio is simply current assets over current liabilities. At the end of 1977 current assets are $2,100,000 and current liabilities are $900,000. Thus, the current ratio is $2,100,000/$900,000, or 2.33 to 1.

16. (1174,T1,4) (c) Remember in ratio analysis that you have to evaluate the numerator and the denominator as well as know whether the ratio is less than one, equal to one, or greater than one before considering the effect of some transaction on the ratio. A 100% stock dividend simply doubles the amount of stock outstanding and transfers retained earnings to paid in capital. Thus, it does not affect the current ratio or working capital nor does it affect the debt to equity ratio, because total shareholders' equity remains the same. It does decrease earnings per share and book value per share because there are more shares outstanding.

17. (1174,T1,5) (a) Payment of a dividend results in a reduction of cash and a current liability. When the dividend was declared, dividends payable, a current liability, was credited. The effect is to increase the current ratio but have no effect on working capital. Working capital remains the same because both current assets and current liabilities are decreased by the same amount, thus the difference remains constant. The current ratio increases because the current ratio was in excess of one, e.g., 4 to 3, and equal amounts are removed from the numerator and denominator, e.g., 3 to 2.

18. (1174,T1,6) (d) When a corporation purchases its own shares at a price greater than book value, the book value is decreased and the earnings per share is increased. The earnings per share increases because there are a smaller number of shares outstanding. The book value per share decreased because while the denominator, number of shares, decreased, the numerator, net assets, decreased by more than a proportionate amount.

19. (1174,T1,7) (a) Increasing leverage or trading on the equity results in more debt relative to owners' equity. If it is done successfully the income available to owners' equity should increase also. The concept does not affect return on sales, but rather return on shareholders' equity. Likewise, leverage does not affect the concept of working capital.

20. (1174,T1,8) (b) A 40% common stock interest is accounted for in an investment account which is noncurrent on the books of the investor. The investor must also use the equity method to account for the investee's earnings, i.e., accrue its share of undistributed earnings. In this question, earnings per share increase because the investee operated profitably. Instead of decreasing the book value per share, book value would be increased because of the increase in the investment account. The fact that the investment is accounted for in a noncurrent investment account precludes answers (a) and (c).

21. (1174,T1,9) (b) A solutions approach would be to jot down both ratios. The inventory turnover ratio is cost of sales over inventory, and the receivable turnover is sales over accounts receivable. Inventory turnover would decrease if the denominator inventory were increased. Receivable turnover would decrease if the denominator of accounts receivable were increased.

22. (576,P1,7) (a) This and the following two questions are a good example of the need for working some related multiple choice questions simultaneously. As noted elsewhere, you should be in the habit of studying the requirements of all related objective questions before beginning to work them. This is parallel to the suggestion that you study all of the requirements of practice problems before attempting to continue with the solutions approach. In this particular case the first step is to compute the ending inventory with the gross margin and turnover data. As illustrated below, the sales less cost of sales equals $315,000. Sales divided by the inventory is 15, and cost of sales divided by inventory is 10.5. This is solved below by determining that sales are equal to $15I$, cost of sales equal to $10.5I$, and then subtracting the CS equation from the S equation and obtaining $S - CS$ equals $4.5I$. You already know that $S - CS$ equals $315,000$, which we substitute in the next to the last equation on the right and thus determine inventory equal to 70,000.

$$S - CS = 315,000 \qquad S = 15I$$
$$\frac{S}{I} = 15 \qquad CS = 10.5I$$
$$\frac{CS}{I} = 10.5 \qquad S - CS = 4.5I$$
$$315,000 = 4.5I$$
$$I = 70,000$$

Once you have computed inventory to be 70,000, you can compute accounts receivable to be $43,000 as illustrated below. When you have the accounts receivable, you can compute total current assets to be $138,000, which is equal to 1½ times the current liability. The current liabilities consist of $25,000 of taxes payable plus accounts payable. This is solvable to determine accounts payable equal to $67,000.

$$95,000 + 294,000 + AR = 432,000$$
$$AR = 43,000$$
$$(95,000 + 43,000) = 1.5(25,000 + AP)$$
$$138,000 = 37,500 + 1.5\,AP$$
$$100,500 = 1.5\,AP$$
$$AP = 67,000$$

After you have computed payables to be $67,000, you can compute debt plus retained earnings equal to $40,000. You have also been told that the total liabilities equals 80% of the stockholders' equity, which means that the $92,000 of current ·liabilities plus debt equals 80% of $300,000 of common stock plus retained earnings. Substituting in $40,000 minus retained earnings for D, you can solve retained earnings to be a deficit $60,000, as computed below.

D + RE = 432,000 − 67,000 − 25,000 − 300,000
D + RE = 40,000 or
D = 40,000 − RE
92,000 + D = .8(300,000 + RE)
92,000 + 40,000 − RE = 240,000 + .8 RE
−108,000 = 1.8 RE
RE = −60,000

It may be advisable to pass over a problem this lengthy until later on in the exam when you find yourself with spare time. Note that these multiple choice questions are budgeted approximately three minutes each. Could you work these three problems in nine minutes?

23. (576,P1,8)   (a)   See the preceding explanation.

24. (576,P1,9)   (c)   See the preceding explanation.

25. (576,T1,12)   (c)   A. solutions approach is to begin with the ratio of current asset to current liabilities of 2:1 as illustrated below. In answer (a) the 5% stock dividend on a marketable security will not affect the numerator or denominator, because receipt of stock dividends just changes the cost per share of stock and not the overall cost of the investment in marketable securities. Answer (b) is incorrect because the payment of an account payable would reduce both the numerator and ·denominator an equal amount, e.g., would bring it to 1.5/.5, which is an increase in the current ratio. Answer (c) is correct because both the numerator and denominator would increase by an equal amount, in this case 1, bringing it to a current ratio of 1.5 rather than 2. In the last case selling merchandise for more than cost would result in an increase in current assets with no change in current liabilities. Once again the solutions approach is to jot down a revised current ratio for each answer.

$$\frac{2}{1} , \frac{2}{1} , \frac{1.5}{.5} , \frac{3}{2} , \frac{2.5}{1}$$

26. (581,Q1,15)   (c)   The requirement is to calculate the quick or acid test ratio. The acid test ratio is calculated by dividing (liquid) current assets by current liabilities. The liquid assets in this problem are all the current assets less the merchandise inventory or $90,000. The current liabilities are also $90,000, therefore, the quick (acid test) ratio is $90,000/$90,000 or 1 to 1.

27. (581,Q1,16)   (a)   The requirement is to calculate the receivable turnover. The receivable turnover is calculated by dividing the credit sales for the year by the average accounts receivable balance. The average accounts receivable balance is calculated by adding the accounts receivable balance at the beginning and end of the year together and dividing by 2: ($50,000 + $15,000) ÷ 2 = $100,000. The accounts receivable turnover is $500,000 ÷ $100,000 or 5 times.

28. (581,Q1,17)   (a)   The requirement is to calculate the inventory turnover for the year. The inventory turnover is calculated by dividing the cost of goods sold for the period by the average inventory for the period. The average inventory for the year, like the average accounts receivable, is calculated by adding the beginning inventory and the ending inventories together and divide by 2: ($150,000 + $90,000) ÷ 2 = $120,000. Inventory turnover is: $1,000,000 ÷ $120,000 = 8.33 times.

29. (581,Q1,18)   (d)   The requirement is to calculate the current ratio. The current ratio is calculated by dividing current assets by current liabilities. Since the total current assets in this problem equal $180,000 and the current liabilities equal $90,000, the current ratio is 2 to 1.

30. (581,Q1,20)   (b)   The requirement is to calculate the book value per share of common stock. The book value per share of common stock is the amount each share would receive if the company was liquidated on the basis of the amounts reported on the balance sheet. To calculate the amount of capital allocated to the common stock, the amount of capital allocated to the preferred stock must be determined first. Any residual capital, then, is allocated to common stock. The amount of capital allocated to the preferred stock holders is equal to the sum of the liquidation value of the preferred stock (if such a value exists), and any dividends in arrears if the preferred stock is cumulative. If a liquidation value is not given, the amount of paid-in capital for preferred stock is used instead. Since the liquidation value is given, the amount of capital allocated is the liquidation value per share multiplied

by the number of preferred shares outstanding or
$1,100,000 ($55 per share x 20,000 shares). The preferred stock is not cumulative, so dividends in arrears
do not enter into the computations. Therefore, the
amount of capital allocated to the common stock is
the residual amount of capital or $1,900,000
($3,000,000 − $1,100,000). To calculate the book
value per share, the capital allocated to common stock
is divided by the number of shares of common stock
outstanding. Thus, the book value per share of common
stock is $1,900,000 ÷ 150,000 shares = $12.67 per
share.

31. (581,Q2,22) (b)   The requirement is to calculate the book value per share of common stock. The
book value per share of common stock is the amount
each share would receive if the company was liquidated
based on amounts reported on the balance sheet. The
capital must be allocated first to the preferred stock,
then to the common stock. The amount allocated to
the preferred stock is equal to the paid-in capital on
the preferred stock plus any dividends in arrears. Dividends are in arrears for five years. Each year the preferred dividends amount to $6,000 (6% of $100 = $6
per share x 1,000 shares). Therefore, the total amount
of dividends in arrears is $30,000 ($6,000 x 5 years)
and the total capital allocated to preferred stock is
$130,000 ($100,000 paid-in capital + $30,000 divid-
dends in arrears). The remaining unallocated capital
is $560,000 (total capital of $690,000 less preferred
capital of $130,000) and the book value per share is
$11.20 ($560,000 ÷ 50,000 common shares outstanding).

32. (581,T1,11) (a)   The requirement is the information that is provided in financial reporting. Financial reporting provides information about an enterprise's performance during a period through the firm's
statement of financial position, results of operations,
statement of changes in financial position, and other
disclosures seen as important by investors in making a
financial decision about the firm. By reviewing these
statements and related disclosures, it may be possible
to determine how well the management of an enterprise did perform, but not on a direct basis. Management's performance can be determined indirectly by
analyzing the statements in terms of trend and ratio
percentages.

33. (581,T1,30) (a)   The requirement is the
appropriate computation for return on investment. The
return on investment is the product of two components:
net income as a percentage of sales and capital turnover
as shown below:

$$ROI = \frac{Net\ Income}{Sales} \times \frac{Sales}{Total\ Assets}$$

Through a simple algebraic manipulation, the "sales"
in both ratios cancel each other out, leaving ROI equal
to income divided by total assets. Answer (b) is incorrect because it only takes into consideration the first
component of the return on investment calculation.
Answer (c) is incorrect because it only takes into consideration the second component of the return on investment calculation. Answer (d) is incorrect because
stockholders' equity is equivalent to total assets only if
the company has incurred no liabilities (a highly
unlikely situation), and also because sales do not appear in the numerator of the ROI computation.

34. (581,T1,40) (c)   The requirement is which
accounts would be included in the calculation of the
acid test (quick) ratio. The acid test (quick) ratio is a
liquidity ratio defined as: Cash + Marketable Securities +
Accounts Receivable ÷ Current Liabilities. It eliminates
inventories and prepaid expenses from the current ratio
numerator. Thus, accounts receivable are included and
inventories are excluded from the acid test ratio.

SOLUTION GUIDE

Problem 1   Corporation Solvency Ratios

1. This question asks you to evaluate how the change in 7 ratios affects the solvency and going concern of the subject company. Also required are additional ratios relevant to the analysis and limitations of ratio analysis.

2. With all three requirements in mind, you should write out all of the ratios in the margin, e.g., current assets/current liabilities. This exercise will enable you to interrelate the ratios and provide more complete answers.

3. Write up a 2 to 3 sentence paragraph for each ratio.

4. Other ratios not listed include changes in current items other than quick assets, inventory and receivable turnover, and debt to equity.

5. The unofficial answer also contains three multiple sentence paragraphs describing the limitations of ratio analysis.

UNOFFICIAL ANSWER

Problem 1   Corporation Solvency Ratios

a. The current-ratio increase is a favorable indication as to solvency, but alone tells little about the going-concern potential of the client. From this ratio change alone, it is impossible to know the amount and direction of the changes in individual accounts, total current assets, and total current liabilities. Also unknown are the reasons for the changes.

The quick-ratio decline is an unfavorable indication as to solvency, especially when the current-ratio increase is also considered. This decline is also unfavorable to the going-concern prospects of the client because it reflects a declining cash position and raises questions as to reasons for the increases in other current assets, such as inventories.

The increase in the ratio of property, plant, and equipment to owners' equity cannot alone tell anything about either solvency or going concern prospects. There is no way to know the amount and direction of the changes in the two items. If assets increased, one

must know whether the new assets are immediately productive or need further development. A reduction in owners' equity at this point would cause much concern for the creditors of this client.

The decrease in the ratio of sales to owners' equity is in itself an unfavorable indicator because the most likely reason is a sales decline. However, this decline, which is more relevant to going-concern prospects than to solvency, is largely offset by the fact that net income has significantly increased.

The increase in net income is a favorable indicator for both solvency and going-concern prospects although much depends on the quality of receivables generated from sales and how quickly they can be converted into cash. A significant factor here may be that despite a decline in sales, the client's management has been able to reduce costs to produce this increase. Indirectly, the improved income picture may have a favorable impact on solvency and going-concern potential by enabling the client to borrow currently to meet cash requirements.

The 30% increase in earnings per common share, which is identical to the percentage increase in net income, is an indication that there has probably been no change in the number of shares of common stock outstanding. This in turn indicates that financing was not obtained through the issuance of common stock. It is not possible to reach conclusions about solvency and going-concern prospects without additional information about the nature and extent of financing.

The percentage increases in book values per common share demonstrate nothing so far as solvency and going-concern potential are concerned. It is probable that the smaller percentage increase in the current year only reflects the larger base value created in the preceding year. It is not possible to tell from these figures what the dividend policy of the client is or whether there is an increase in net assets which is capable of generating future earnings, thus making it possible to raise capital for current needs by the issue of additional common stock.

The collective implications of these data alone are that the client entity is about as

solvent and as viable as a going-concern at
the end of the current year as it was at the
beginning although there may be a need for
short-term operating cash.

b.   The creditors will probably ask for the information listed below to overcome the limitations
inherent in the ratios discussed in part a. and
to obtain more evidence to support the conclusions drawn from them.

1.   Additional ratios and other comparative
data may be requested. They are likely
to include such items as the following:

(a)   Changes in current assets other
than quick assets.
(b)   Receivables turnover, inventory turnover, and the number of days it
takes to complete the cycle from
cash to inventories to receivables
to cash.
(c)   Liabilities to owners' equity.

2.   The creditors will probably want explanations for the changes in ratios during
the current year. The client should be
prepared to respond to questions about
the age and collectibility of the receivables, the condition and salability of
the inventories, the cause of the quick-
asset position in the current year, the nature of increases in property, plant, and
equipment and their potential for providing greater sales or cost reductions in
the future, the presence of long-term
debt and the dates when it must be repaid, and the manner of controlling costs
so that a larger net income was shown
in the current year. (The comparative
financial statements themselves will answer many of these questions and will
provide insight into the client's capability
of meeting current obligations as well as
continuing profitable operations.) The
client may also be expected to provide
information about future plans and projections.

3.   The creditors may also ask for ratios and
related information for several recent years.
These data may demonstrate trends and
can be compared to data for other companies and for the industry.

c.   Although a quick evaluation of a reporting

entity can be made using only a few ratios
and comparing these with past ratios and industry statistics, the creditors should realize the
limitations of such analysis even from the best
prepared statements carrying a CPA's unqualified opinion.

A limitation on comparisons with industry
statistics or other companies within the industry
exists because material differences can be created through the use of alternative (but acceptable) accounting methods. Further, when
evaluating changes in ratios or percentages, the
evaluation should be directed to the nature of
the item being evaluated because very small
differences in ratios or percentages can represent significant changes in dollar amounts or
trends.

The creditors should evaluate conclusions
drawn from ratio analysis in the light of the
current status of, and expected changes in,
such things as general economic conditions,
the client's competitive position, the public's
demand (for the product itself, increased quality
of the product, control of noise and pollution,
etc.), and the client's specific plans.

SOLUTION GUIDE

Problem 2   Ratio Computations

1.   The solutions approach in computing financial
ratios is to specify explicitly the content of
the numerator and denominator of each ratio
and then plug in the required figures.

2.   Note that only the 1975 ratios are required.

2.1   The current ratio is current assets over current
liabilities.

2.2   The quick ratio is cash, plus receivables, plus
marketable securities over current liabilities.

2.3   Number of days of sales in average receivables
is the average accounts receivable over annual
sales divided by the number of business days.
Here the number of business days is given as
300. Here, average receivables can only be computed between the beginning and end of the
year (not monthly).

2.4   Inventory turnover is cost of sales over average inventory. Average inventory can only be
computed between the first and last of the
year.

2.5   Book value of common stock is stockholders' equity available to common stockholders . (i.e., net of a liquidation value of preferred stock) over the number of shares outstanding at the end of the year.

2.6   Earnings per share for a simple capital structure is net income less preferred dividends divided by average shares outstanding during the year.

2.7   The price-earnings ratio is the market value of common stock at year-end divided by earnings per share.

2.8   The dividend payout ratio is the dividends paid on common stock divided by the net income available to common stockholders (i.e., net income less preferred dividends).

UNOFFICIAL ANSWER

Problem 2   Ratio Computations

1. Current (working capital) ratio:

$$\frac{\text{Total current assets}}{\text{Total current liabilities}} = \frac{\$250,000,000}{\$\ 75,000,000} = \underline{3.33 \text{ to } 1}$$

2. Quick (acid-test) ratio:

$$\frac{\text{Total quick (acid-test) assets}}{\text{Total current liabilities}} = \frac{\$121,500,000}{\$\ 75,000,000} = \underline{1.62 \text{ to } 1}$$

3. Number of days' sales in average receivables:

$$\frac{\text{Average accounts receivable}}{\text{Sales on account} \div 300 \text{ business days}} = \frac{\$100,000,000}{\$\ \ 2,000,000} = \underline{50 \text{ days}}$$

4. Inventory turnover:

$$\frac{\text{Cost of goods sold}}{\text{Average inventories}} = \frac{\$490,000,000}{\$140,000,000} = \underline{3.50 \text{ to } 1}$$

5. Book value per share of common stock:

$$\frac{\text{Total stockholders' equity less liquidating value of preferred stock}}{\text{Common shares issued and outstanding at December 31, 1975}} = \frac{\$259,000,000}{10,000,000} = \underline{\$25.90}$$

6. Earnings per share on common stock:

$$\frac{\text{Net income less dividends on preferred stock}}{\text{Average common shares issued and outstanding during 1975}} = \frac{\$\ 20,000,000}{10,000,000} = \underline{\$2.00}$$

7. Price-earnings ratio on common stock:

$$\frac{\text{Market value of common stock}}{\text{Earnings per share on common stock}} = \frac{\$10.00}{\$\ 2.00} = \underline{5 \text{ to } 1}$$

8. Dividend-payout ratio on common stock:

$$\frac{\text{Dividends on common stock}}{\text{Net income less dividends on preferred stock}} = \frac{\$12,000,000}{\$20,000,000} = \underline{60\%}$$

MULTIPLE CHOICE QUESTIONS (1–13)

1. James Dixon, a partner in an accounting firm, decided to withdraw from the partnership. Dixon's share of the partnership profits and losses was 20%. Upon withdrawing from the partnership he was paid $74,000 in final settlement for his interest. The total of the partners' capital accounts before recognition of partnership goodwill prior to Dixon's withdrawal was $210,000. After his withdrawal the remaining partners' capital accounts, excluding their share of goodwill, totaled $160,000. The total agreed upon goodwill of the firm was

    a. $120,000.
    b. $140,000.
    c. $160,000.
    d. $250,000.

Items 2 and 3 are based on the following information:

Presented below is the condensed balance sheet of the partnership of Kane, Clark and Lane who share profits and losses in the ratio of 6:3:1, respectively:

Cash	$ 85,000
Other assets	415,000
	$500,000
Liabilities	$ 80,000
Kane, capital	252,000
Clark, capital	126,000
Lane, capital	42,000
	$500,000

2. The assets and liabilities on the above balance sheet are fairly valued and the partnership wishes to admit Bayer with a 25% interest in the capital and profits/losses without recording goodwill or bonus. How much should Bayer contribute in cash or other assets?

    a. $ 70,000
    b. $105,000
    c. $125,000
    d. $140,000

3. Assume that the partners agree instead to sell Bayer 20% of their respective capital and profit and loss interests for a total payment of $90,000. The payment by Bayer is to be made directly to the individual partners. The partners agree that implied goodwill is to be recorded prior to the acquisition by Bayer. What are the capital balances of Kane, Clark, and Lane, respectively, after the acquisition by Bayer?

a.	$198,000;	$ 99,000;	$33,000.
b.	$201,600;	$100,800;	$33,600.
c.	$216,000;	$108,000;	$36,000.
d.	$255,600;	$127,800;	$42,600.

4. Elton and Don are partners who share profits and losses in the ratio of 7:3, respectively. On November 5, 1978, their respective capital accounts were as follows:

Elton	$ 70,000
Don	60,000
	$130,000

On that date they agreed to admit Kravitz as a partner with a one-third interest in the capital and profits and losses upon his investment of $50,000. The new partnership will begin with a total capital of $180,000. Immediately after Kravitz's admission what are the capital balances of Elton, Don, and Kravitz, respectively?

    a. $60,000; $60,000; $60,000.
    b. $63,000; $57,000; $60,000.
    c. $63,333; $56,667; $60,000.
    d. $70,000; $60,000; $50,000.

5. On June 30, 1978, the balance sheet for the partnership of Williams, Brown and Lowe together with their respective profit and loss ratios was as follows:

Assets, at cost	$300,000
Williams, loan	$ 15,000
Williams, capital (20%)	70,000
Brown, capital (20%)	65,000
Lowe, capital (60%)	150,000
Total	$300,000

Williams has decided to retire from the partnership and by mutual agreement the assets are to be adjusted to their fair value of $360,000 at June 30, 1978. It was agreed that the partnership would pay Williams $102,000 cash for his partnership interest exclusive of his loan which is to be repaid in full. No goodwill is to be recorded in this transaction. After Williams' retirement what are the capital account balances of Brown and Lowe, respectively?

    a. $65,000 and $150,000.
    b. $72,000 and $171,000.
    c. $73,000 and $174,000.
    d. $77,000 and $186,000.

This applies to questions 6 and 7.

The following balance sheet is presented for the partnership of Davis, Wright, and Dover who share profits and losses in the ratio of 5:3:2 respectively:

Cash	$ 60,000
Other assets	540,000
	$600,000
Liabilities	$140,000
Davis, Capital	280,000
Wright, Capital	160,000
Dover, Capital	20,000
	$600,000

6. Assume that the assets and liabilities are fairly valued on the balance sheet and the partnership decided to admit Hank as a new partner with a one-fifth interest. No goodwill or bonus is to be recorded. How much should Hank contribute in cash or other assets?
   a. $120,000.
   b. $115,000.
   c. $92,000.
   d. $73,600.

7. Assume that instead of admitting a new partner, the partners decided to liquidate the partnership. If the other assets are sold for $400,000, how should the available cash be distributed to each partner?
   a. Davis, $280,000; Wright, $160,000; Dover, $20,000.
   b. Davis, $210,000; Wright, $118,000; Dover, $8,000.
   c. Davis, $206,000; Wright, $114,000; Dover, $0.
   d. Davis, $205,000; Wright, $115,000; Dover, $0.

8. Arthur Plack, a partner in the Brite Partnership, has a 30% participation in partnership profits and losses. Plack's capital account had a net decrease of $60,000 during the calendar year 1974. During 1974, Plack withdrew $130,000 (charged against his capital account) and contributed property valued at $25,000 to the partnership. What was the net income of the Brite Partnership for 1974?
   a. $150,000.
   b. $233,333.
   c. $350,000.
   d. $550,000.

9. Geller and Harden formed a partnership on January 2, 1974, and agreed to share profits 90%, 10%, respectively. Geller contributed capital of $25,000. Harden contributed no capital but has a specialized expertise and manages the firm full time. There were no withdrawals during the year. The partnership agreement provides for the following:

Capital accounts are to be credited annually with interest at 5% of beginning capital.
Harden is to be paid a salary of $1,000 a month.
Harden is to receive a bonus of 20% of income calculated before deducting his salary and interest on both capital accounts.
Bonus, interest, and Harden's salary are to be considered partnership expenses.
The partnership 1974 income statement follows:

Revenues	$96,450
Expenses (including salary, interest, and bonus)	49,700
Net income	$46,750

What is Harden's 1974 bonus?
   a. $11,688.
   b. $12,000.
   c. $15,000.
   d. $15,738.

10. Partners C and K share profits and losses equally after each has been credited in all circumstances with annual salary allowances of $15,000 and $12,000, respectively. Under this arrangement, C will benefit by $3,000 more than K in which of the following circumstances?
   a. Only if the partnership has earnings of $27,000 or more for the year.
   b. Only if the partnership does not incur a loss for the year.
   c. In all earnings or loss situations.
   d. Only if the partnership has earnings of at least $3,000 for the year.

11. Pat, Helma, and Diane are partners with capital balances of $50,000, $30,000, and $20,000, respectively. The partners share profits and losses equally. For an investment of $50,000 cash, MaryAnn is to be admitted as a partner with a one-fourth interest in capital and profits. Based on this information, the amount of MaryAnn's investment can best be justified by which of the following?

a.   MaryAnn will receive a bonus from the other partners upon her admission to the partnership.

b.   Assets of the partnership were over-valued immediately prior to MaryAnn's investment.

c.   The book value of the partnership's net assets was less than their fair value immediately prior to MaryAnn's investment.

d.   MaryAnn is apparently bringing good-will into the partnership and her capi-tal account will be credited for the appropriate amount.

12.   On March 1, 1977, Smith and Dale formed a partnership with each contributing the following assets:

	Smith	Dale
Cash	$30,000	$ 70,000
Machinery and equipment	25,000	75,000
Building	—	225,000
Furniture and fixtures	10,000	—

The building is subject to a mortgage loan of $80,000, which is to be assumed by the partnership. The partner-ship agreement provides that Smith and Dale share pro-fits and losses 30% and 70%, respectively. On March 1, 1977, the balance in Dale's capital account should be

a. $290,000.
b. $305,000.
c. $314,000.
d. $370,000.

13.   The capital accounts of the partnership of New-ton, Sharman, and Jackson on June 1, 1977, are pre-sented below with their respective profit and loss ratios:

Newton	$139,200	1/2
Sharman	208,800	1/3
Jackson	96,000	1/6
	$444,000	

On June 1, 1977, Sidney was admitted to the part-nership when he purchased, for $132,000, a propor-tionate interest from Newton and Sharman in the net assets and profits of the partnership. As a result of this transaction, Sidney acquired a one-fifth interest in the net assets and profits of the firm. Assuming that implied goodwill is not to be recorded, what is the combined gain realized by Newton and Sharman upon the sale of a portion of their interests in the partnership to Sidney?

a. $0.
b. $43,200.
c. $62,400.
d. $82,000.

PROBLEMS

Problem 1   Allocation of Partnership Income (G,J,&P)

(577,P4b)   (12 to 15 minutes)

Part b. The partnership of Gary, Jerome, and Paul was formed on January 1, 1976. The original investments were as follows:

Gary	$ 80,000
Jerome	$120,000
Paul	$180,000

According to the partnership agreement, net income or loss will be divided among the respective partners as follows:

• Salaries of $12,000 for Gary, $10,000 for Jerome, and $8,000 for Paul.

• Interest of 8% on the average capital balances during the year of Gary, Jerome, and Paul.

• Remainder divided equally.

Additional information is as follows:

• Net income of the partnership for the year ended December 31, 1976, was $70,000.

• Gary invested an additional $20,000 in the partnership on July 1, 1976.

• Paul withdrew $30,000 from the partnership on October 1, 1976.

• Gary, Jerome, and Paul made regular drawings against their shares of net income during 1976 of $10,000 each.

Required:

1.   Prepare a schedule showing the division of net income among the three partners. Show supporting computations in good form.

2.   Prepare a schedule showing each partner's capital balance at December 31, 1976. Show supporting computations in good form.

MULTIPLE CHOICE ANSWERS

1. a	4. b	7. d	10. c	13. b
2. d	5. b	8. a	11. c	
3. c	6. b	9. c	12. a	

EXPLANATION OF MULTIPLE CHOICE ANSWERS

1. (580,Q1,4) (a)   The requirement is the total agreed-upon goodwill of a firm from which a partner is withdrawing. The partner is being paid $74,000 for his interest. His capital account balance is $50,000 ($210,000 − $160,000). Thus an additional $24,000 was paid to him for his share of goodwill. The withdrawing partner shares in profits and losses at a 20% rate, so the $24,000 is 20% of total goodwill, which therefore must be $120,000.

2. (580,Q1,8) (d)   The requirement is the amount to be paid by a new partner (Bayer) for a 25% interest with no bonus or goodwill to be recorded. The current net capital of $420,000 [($252,000 + $126,000 + $42,000) or ($500,000 − $80,000)] will be 75% of the total capital after Bayer is admitted. Thus $420,000 ÷ 75% is $560,000, which will be the new partnership capital. Accordingly, Bayer will have to contribute $140,000 [($560,000 − $420,000) or (25% x $560,000)]

3. (580,Q1,9) (c)   The requirement is the capital balances of the partners after recording goodwill and selling 20% of their interest. If 20% of the partnership is worth $90,000, the entire partnership is worth $450,000. Thus, goodwill of $30,000 needs to be recorded and allocated to the old partners in their P & L ratio. The sale is recorded by crediting Bayer's account for $90,000 and debiting the old partners' accounts for one-fifth of the respective balances.

	Capital	GW	Sale	New Capital
Kane	$252,000 +	18,000 −	54,000 =	$216,000
Clark	126,000 +	9,000 −	27,000 =	108,000
Lane	42,000 +	3,000 −	9,000 =	36,000
Bayer			+ 90,000 =	90,000

4. (1179,Q1,5) (b)   The requirements are partnership balances of E, D, and K after K is admitted to a 1/3 interest in capital and profits upon investment of $50,000. Since the new partnership will have total capital of $180,000, no goodwill is to be recorded, i.e., new capital is equal to the old capital of $130,000 plus the contribution of $50,000. The solutions approach is to record the entry to admit K. K is credited with $60,000 of capital (1/3 of $180,000) and

contributes cash of $50,000. Thus, debits to the existing partners' capital accounts of $10,000 are required. Since the P&L ratio was 7:3, $7,000 is debited to E and $3,000 to D. This results in capital balances to E, D, and K of $63,000, $57,000, and $60,000, respectively.

Cash	$50,000	
E Capital	7,000	
D Capital	3,000	
K Capital		$60,000

5. (1179,Q1,6) (b)   The requirement is the capital balances of the two remaining partners after a third partner has retired. The partnership retirement agreement indicates that the assets are to be revalued to $360,000, and $102,000 in cash is to be paid to Williams for his partnership interest. The solutions approach is to prepare the journal entries to record the asset revaluation and the cash distribution as illustrated below. Note, the P&L ratios: Williams 20%, Brown 20%, and Lowe 60%. Then the revised capital balances of B and L must be computed.

Assets	$60,000	
W capital		$12,000
B capital		12,000
L capital		36,000
W capital	$82,000	
B capital	5,000	
L capital	15,000	
Cash		$102,000

B Capital	L Capital
$65,000	$150,000
+12,000	+36,000
- 5,000	- 15,000
$72,000	$171,000

6. (579,Q1,9) (b)   The requirement is the amount to be paid by a new partner (Hank) for a 1/5 interest with no bonus or goodwill to be recorded. The current net capital of $460,000 ($280,000 + $160,000 + $20,000) will be 80% of the total capital after Hank is admitted. Thus, $460,000 divided by 80% equals $575,000, which will be the new partnership capital. Accordingly, Hank will have to contribute $115,000 ($575,000 − $460,000).

7. (579,Q1,10) (d)   The requirement is how available cash should be distributed if a partnership's assets (book value of $460,000) are sold for $400,000. There would be a loss of $140,000, which would be allocated 50-30-20. The result would be an $8,000 deficit to Dover, which would be redistributed to Davis and White 5/8-3/8. The result is that the

$320,000 available for distribution to the partners would be distributed $205,000 to Davis and $115,000 to White, as the schedule below indicates. Note that there would be $460,000 total cash ($60,000 beginning cash plus $400,000 from sale of other assets and $140,000 paid to creditors).

P & L Ratio	Davis 50%	White 30%	Dover 20%
Beginning capital	280	160	20
140,000 loss	70	42	28
	210	118	(8)
Redistribution of Dover deficit	(5)	(3)	8
Cash distribution	205	115	0

8.   (575,P1,9)   (a)   The solutions approach is to construct a ledger account for Plack's investment in the partnership as is illustrated below. Given the net decrease of $60,000 during the year, a $130,000 withdrawal and a $25,000 capital contribution, the net income allocable to Plack was $45,000. Since Plack owns 30% of the partnership, the entire partnership income was $150,000.

Withdrawal		130,000
Contribution	25,000	
Net income	45,000	.30NI = $45,000
Net change	60,000	NI = $150,000

9.   (575,P1,11)   (c)   The requirement is a calculation of Harden's 1974 bonus. You are given net income after deducting salary, interest, and bonus. The bonus is 20% of income before deducting salary, interest and bonus. Thus as calculated below, you must add back the salary and interest to obtain $60,000, which is the income after the bonus. If the bonus is 20%, the income after the bonus will be 80% of the income before the bonus. The income before the bonus is $75,000 and the bonus is therefore $15,000.

NI	$46,750
Salary	12,000
Interest	1,250
	$60,000 income after bonus

60,000 = .80 NI before bonus
$75,000 = NI before bonus

10.   (575,T1,4)   (c)   Since the salary allowances are credited to the partners accounts before sharing the profits and losses, C will always benefit by $3,000. One solutions approach is to go through and distribute salary and P&L for each of the other answers (a), (b), and (d) as below. Assuming $30,000 income, $10,000 loss and $4,000 income, the P&L after salary distributions would be $3,000 of income, a $37,000 loss, and a $23,000 loss respectively. These gains or losses are allocated equally between C and K. As you can see in each case, C is $3,000 better off than K.

	30,000 inc.	10,000 loss	4,000 inc.
C salary	15,000	15,000	15,000
C P&L	1,500	(18,500)	(11,500)
	16,500	(3,500)	3,500
K salary	12,000	12,000	12,000
K P&L	1,500	(18,500)	(11,500)
	13,500	(6,500)	500

11.   (575,T1,5)   (c)   The net assets of the partnership prior to admission of MaryAnn is $100,000. If 1/4 of the partnership is worth $50,000, the partnership assets prior to the infusion of the $50,000 would appear to be worth $150,000 ($200,000 − $50,000 cash infusion). Thus answer (c), the book value of the partnership's net assets was less than their fair value prior to the admission of MaryAnn, was the correct answer. Answer (b) is incorrect as it indicates that partnership book value was greater than the fair value. Answer (a) is incorrect because if the excess of fair value over book value were accounted for as a bonus, MaryAnn would give a bonus to the other partners. If the admission were to be recorded under the bonus method (see the first journal entry below), MaryAnn's capital would be credited for $37,500 (1/4 of the $100,000 of book value plus the $50,000 cash contribution). The remaining $12,500 would be divided equally between Pat, Helma, and Diane as their P&L ratios are equal. The second entry reflects the requirements of the problem: goodwill to the new partners.

Cash	$50,000	
MaryAnn capital		$37,500
Pat capital		4,166
Helma capital		4,167
Diane capital		4,167

Cash	$50,000	
Goodwill	50,000	
MaryAnn capital		$50,000
Pat capital		16,666
Helma capital		16,667
Diane capital		16,667

Answer (d) is incorrect because if goodwill were recorded (the second journal entry) the capital accounts of the old partners would be credited. The unrecorded goodwill would be $50,000 (the difference between the book value and the fair value of the assets of $150,000).

12.   (578,Q1,10)   (a)   Dale's capital balance at the day of the partnership formation is the sum of the fair values of the assets contributed: cash of $70,000, machinery and equipment of $75,000, and building of $145,000. Note that the net value of the building contributed to the partnership is the $225,000 building less the existing mortgage of $80,000.

13.   (578,Q1,2)   (b)   The requirement is the combined gain recognized by Newton and Sharman for sale of 1/5 of the partnership to Sidney. Since the book value of 1/5 of the partnership is $88,800 ($444,000 divided by 5), the gain is $43,200 ($132,000 selling price less book value of $88,800). Note there is no need to allocate gains or losses and capital balances between Newton and Sharman, as the requirement is in terms of the combined gain.

SOLUTION GUIDE

Problem 1   Allocation of Partnership Income (G,J,&P)

1. The requirement of part b is twofold: first, a schedule showing distribution of income among partners, and second, a schedule showing each partner's capital balance.

1.1 The solutions approach is to compute the interest due to each partner; add the interest to the salary of each partner; determine whether a gain or loss after salaries and interest exists; and divide the gain or loss equally among the partners.

1.2 The interest calculation is shown below. Note that the $10,000 draw made by each partner is debited to drawing during the year, and thus does not affect the capital balance, i.e., drawings are different from partnership withdrawals.

Interest
Gary:
$ 80,000 x 8% for 6 months $3,200
$100,000 x 8% for 6 months   4,000
                                    $ 7,200

Jerome:
$120,000 x 8%   9,600

Paul:
$180,000 x 8% for 9 months $10,800
$150,000 x 8% for 3 months   3,000
                                    13,800
                                    $30,600

Salary
Gary $12,000
Jerome   10,000
Paul   8,000
                                    $30,000
        Total salary and interest $60,600
        Profit to be allocated   9,400
            Partnership "net income" $70,000

1.3 The salaries and interests total $60,600, which results in a profit of $9,400 to be divided equally among the partners.

1.4 The partners' ending balances are simply the beginning balances, plus investments, minus withdrawals, plus allocation of net income (computed above), less draws.

UNOFFICIAL ANSWER

Problem 1   Allocation of Partnership Income (G,J,&P)

b. 1. *Partnership of Gary, Jerome, and Paul*
DIVISION OF NET INCOME
For the Year Ended December 31, 1976

	Gary	Jerome	Paul	Total
Salaries	$12,000	$10,000	$ 8,000	$30,000
Interest on average capital balances *(Schedule 1)*	7,200	9,600	13,800	30,600
	19,200	19,600	21,800	60,600
Remainder divided equally	3,133	3,133	3,134	9,400
Division of net income	$22,333	$22,733	$24,934	$70,000

Schedule 1

Computation of Interest on Average Capital Balances

Gary:
$ 80,000 × 8% for 6 months $ 3,200
$100,000 × 8% for 6 months   4,000 $ 7,200

Jerome:
$120,000 × 8%   9,600

Paul:
$180,000 × 8% for 9 months   10,800
$150,000 × 8% for 3 months   3,000   13,800
                                       $30,600

b. 2. *Partnership of Gary, Jerome, and Paul*
CAPITAL BALANCES
December 31, 1976

	Gary	Jerome	Paul	Total
Balance at January 1, 1976	$ 80,000	$120,000	$180,000	$380,000
Additional investment	20,000	—	—	20,000
Withdrawal	—	—	(30,000)	(30,000)
Net income	22,333	22,733	24,934	70,000
Regular drawings	(10,000)	(10,000)	(10,000)	(30,000)
Balance at December 31, 1976	$112,333	$132,733	$164,934	$410,000

MULTIPLE CHOICE QUESTIONS (1—41)

1.   The equity method of accounting for an investment in the common stock of another company should be used when the investment
   a.   Is composed of common stock and it is the investor's intent to vote the common stock.
   b.   Ensures a source of supply such as raw materials.
   c.   Enables the investor to exercise significant influence over the investee.
   d.   Is obtained by an exchange of stock for stock.

2.   A parent corporation which uses the equity method of accounting for its investment in a 40 percent owned subsidiary, which earned $20,000 and paid $5,000 in dividends, made the following entries:

Investment in subsidiary	$8,000	
Equity in earnings of		
subsidiary		$8,000
Cash	2,000	
Dividend revenue		2,000

What effect will these entries have on the parent's statement of financial position?
   a.   Investment in subsidiary understated, retained earnings understated.
   b.   Investment in subsidiary overstated, retained earnings overstated.
   c.   Investment in subsidiary overstated, retained earnings understated.
   d.   Financial position will be fairly stated.

3.   On January 1, 1979, Barton Corporation acquired as a long-term investment for $500,000, a 30% common stock interest in Buffer Company. On that date, Buffer had net assets with a book value and current market value of $1,600,000. During 1979 Buffer reported net income of $180,000 and declared and paid cash dividends of $40,000. What is the maximum amount of income that Barton should report from this investment for 1979?
   a. $12,000
   b. $42,000
   c. $53,500
   d. $54,000

4.   The Action Corporation issued non-voting preferred stock with a fair market value of $4,000,000 in exchange for all of the outstanding common stock of Master Corporation. On the date of the exchange,

Master had tangible net assets with a book value of $2,000,000 and a fair value of $2,500,000. In addition, Action issued preferred stock valued at $400,000 to an individual as a finder's fee in arranging the transaction. As a result of this transaction, Action should record an increase in net assets of
   a. $2,000,000
   b. $2,500,000
   c. $2,900,000
   d. $4,400,000

5.   On June 30, 1979, Needle Corporation purchased for cash at $10 per share all 100,000 shares of the outstanding common stock of Thread Company. The total appraised value of identifiable assets less liabilities of Thread was $1,400,000 at June 30, 1979, including the appraised value of Thread's property, plant, and equipment (its only noncurrent asset) of $250,000. The consolidated balance sheet of Needle Corporation and its wholly owned subsidiary at June 30, 1979, should reflect
   a.   A deferred credit (negative goodwill) of $150,000.
   b.   Goodwill of $150,000.
   c.   A deferred credit (negative goodwill) of $400,000.
   d.   Goodwill of $400,000.

6.   The Troy Corporation was organized to consolidate the resources of Able Company and Baker, Inc., in a business combination appropriately accounted for by the pooling of interests method. On January 1, 1980, Troy issued 65,000 shares of its $10 par value voting stock in exchange for all of the outstanding capital stock of Able and Baker. The equity account balances of Able and Baker on this date were:

	Able	Baker	Total
Par value of common stock	$150,000	$450,000	$600,000
Additional paid-in capital	20,000	55,000	75,000
Retained earnings	110,000	210,000	320,000
	$280,000	$715,000	$995,000

What is the balance in Troy's "Additional Paid-in Capital" account immediately after the business combination?
   a. $0
   b. $ 25,000
   c. $ 75,000
   d. $395,000

7.   On January 1, 1979, Star Company paid
$1,200,000 for 40,000 shares of Comet Corporation's
common stock which represents a 25% investment in
the net assets of Comet. Star has the ability to exercise significant influence over Comet. Star received a
dividend of $3 per share from Comet in 1979. Comet
reported net income of $640,000 for the year ended
December 31, 1979. The balance in Star's balance
sheet account "Investment in Comet Corporation"
at December 31, 1979, should be
   a. $1,200,000.
   b. $1,240,000.
   c. $1,360,000.
   d. $1,480,000.

8.   On April 1, 1979, the Jack Company paid
$800,000 for all the issued and outstanding common
stock of Ann Corporation in a transaction properly
accounted for as a purchase. The recorded assets and
liabilities of Ann Corporation on April 1, 1979, follows:

Cash	$ 80,000
Inventory	240,000
Property and equipment (net of accu-	
mulated depreciation of $320,000)	480,000
Liabilities	(180,000)

On April 1, 1979, it was determined that the inventory
of Ann had a fair value of $190,000, and the property
and equipment (net) had a fair value of $560,000. What
is the amount of goodwill resulting from the business
combination?
   a. $0
   b. $ 50,000
   c. $150,000
   d. $180,000

9.   When an investor uses the equity method to account for investments in common stock, cash dividends
received by the investor from the investee should be
recorded as
   a.   Dividend income.
   b.   A deduction from the investor's share of
        the investee's profits.
   c.   A deduction from the investment account.
   d.   A deduction from the stockholders' equity
        account, dividends to stockholders.

10.   Which of the following is a potential abuse that
can arise when a business combination is accounted for
as a pooling of interests?

   a.   Assets of the investee may be overvalued
        when the price paid by the investor is allo-
        cated among specific assets.
   b.   Liabilities may be undervalued when the
        price paid by the investor is allocated to
        the specific liabilities.
   c.   An undue amount of cost may be assigned
        to goodwill, thus potentially allowing for
        an overstatement of pooled earnings.
   d.   Earnings of the pooled entity may be in-
        creased because of the combination only
        and not as a result of efficient operations.

11.   On October 1, Company X acquired for cash all
of the outstanding common stock of Company Y. Both
companies have a December 31 year end and have been
in business for many years. Consolidated net income
for the year ended December 31 should include net
income of
   a.   Company X for 3 months and Company Y
        for 3 months.
   b.   Company X for 12 months and Company
        Y for 3 months.
   c.   Company X for 12 months and Company
        Y for 12 months.
   d.   Company X for 12 months; but no income
        from Company Y until Company Y distri-
        butes a dividend.

12.   On December 1, 1978, Drew Company issued
shares of its voting common stock in exchange for
all of the voting common stock of Art Company in
a business combination appropriately accounted for
by the pooling of interests method. Net income for
each company is as follows:

	Drew	Art
12 months ended		
December 31, 1978	$2,000,000	$1,200,000
1 month ended		
December 31, 1978	220,000	115,000

During 1978 Drew paid $900,000 in dividends to its
stockholders. Art had paid $500,000 in dividends to
its stockholders in September 1978. Assuming that
the net income of Drew given above does not include
the equity in net income of Art, the consolidated net
income for the year ended December 31, 1978,
should be
   a. $ 335,000.
   b. $2,115,000.
   c. $2,700,000.
   d. $3,200,000.

13. On July 31, 1979, Light Company purchased for cash of $8,000,000, all of the outstanding common stock of Shirk Company when Shirk's balance sheet showed net assets of $6,400,000. Shirk's assets and liabilities had fair values different from the book values as follows:

	Book Value	Fair Value
Property, plant, and equipment, net	$10,000,000	$11,500,000
Other assets	1,000,000	700,000
Long-term debt	6,000,000	5,600,000

As a result of the transaction above, what amount, if any, will be shown as goodwill in the July 31, 1979, consolidated balance sheet of Light Company and its wholly-owned subsidiary, Shirk Company?

a. $0
b. $ 100,000
c. $1,200,000
d. $1,600,000

14. On January 1, 1978, Grade Company paid $300,000 for 20,000 shares of Medium Company's common stock which represents a 15% investment in Medium. Grade does not have the ability to exercise significant influence over Medium. Medium declared and paid a dividend of $1 a share to its stockholders during 1978. Medium reported net income of $260,000 for the year ended December 31, 1978. The balance in Grade's balance sheet account "Investment in Medium Company" at December 31, 1978, should be

a. $280,000.
b. $300,000.
c. $319,000.
d. $339,000.

15. Alan Company purchased the net assets of Barry Company in a business combination accounted for as a purchase. As a result, goodwill was recorded. For tax purposes this combination was considered to be a tax-free merger.

One of Barry's assets that Alan purchased was a building with an appraised value of $150,000 at the date of the business combination. This asset had a cost of $90,000 which was net of accumulated depreciation for accounting purposes. The building had an adjusted tax basis to Barry (and to Alan as a result of the merger) of $100,000. Assuming a 48% income tax rate, at what amount should Alan record this building on its books after the purchase?

a. $100,000
b. $121,200
c. $126,000
d. $150,000

16. Which of the following is the appropriate basis for valuing fixed assets acquired in a business combination accounted for as a purchase carried out by exchanging cash for common stock?

a. Fair value.
b. Book value.
c. Cost plus any excess of purchase price over book value of asset acquired.
d. Historic cost.

17. If all other conditions for consolidation are met, how should subsidiaries acquired in a business combination be shown under each of the following methods?

	Purchase	Pooling of Interests
a.	Consolidated	Not Consolidated
b.	Consolidated	Consolidated
c.	Not Consolidated	Consolidated
d.	Not Consolidated	Not Consolidated

18. Companies A and B have been operating separately for five years. Each company has a minimal amount of liabilities and a simple capital structure consisting solely of voting common stock. Company A, in exchange for 40 percent of its voting stock, acquires 80 percent of the common stock of Company B. This was a "tax free" stock for stock (type B) exchange for tax purposes. Company B assets have a total net fair market value of $800,000 and a total net book value of $580,000. The fair market value of the A stock used in the exchange was $700,000. The goodwill on this acquisition would be

a. Zero, this would be a pooling of interest.
b. $60,000.
c. $120,000.
d. $236,000.

Items 19. and 20. are based on the following information:

On December 1, 1976, Company B was merged into Company A, with Company B going out of existence. Both companies report on a calendar year basis. This business combination should have been accounted for as a pooling of interests, but it was mistakenly accounted for as a purchase.

19. As a result of this error, what was the effect upon Company A's net earnings for the year ended December 31, 1976?

     a. Overstated if B had a net loss from December 1, 1976, to December 31, 1976.

     b. Understated if B had a net loss from January 1, 1976, to November 30, 1976.

     c. Overstated if B had net earnings from December 1, 1976, to December 31, 1976.

     d. Understated if B had net earnings from January 1, 1976, to November 30, 1976.

20. What was the effect of this error upon Company A's asset valuations at December 1, 1976?

     a. Overstated under any circumstances.

     b. Understated under any circumstances.

     c. Overstated if the fair value of B's assets exceeded their book value.

     d. Understated if the fair value of B's assets exceeded their book value.

21. On January 1, 1977, the Robohn Company purchased for cash 40% of the 300,000 shares of voting common stock of the Lowell Company for $1,800,000 when 40% of the underlying equity in the net assets of Lowell was $1,400,000. Robohn amortizes goodwill over a forty-year period with a full year's amortization taken in the year of the purchase. The amortization is not deductible for income tax reporting. As a result of this transaction, Robohn has the ability to exercise significant influence over the operating and financial policies of Lowell. Lowell's net income for the year ended December 31, 1977, was $600,000. During 1977, Lowell paid $325,000 in dividends to its stockholders. The income reported by Robohn for its investment in Lowell should be

     a. $120,000.

     b. $130,000

     c. $230,000.

     d. $240,000.

22. On January 1, 1977, the Pint Corporation paid $400,000 for 10,000 shares of Quart Company's common stock which represents a 10% investment in Quart. Pint received dividends of $1.00 per share from Quart in 1977. Quart reported net income of $150,000 for the year ended December 31, 1977. The market value of Quart's common stock on December 31, 1977, was $42 per share. Ignoring income taxes, the amount reported in Pint's 1977 income statement as a result of Pint's investment in Quart was

     a. $10,000.

     b. $15,000.

     c. $30,000.

     d. $35,000.

23. Which of the following types of transactions or situations would preclude a company from accounting for a business combination as a pooling of interests?

     a. Immediately after the combination, the acquiring corporation reacquires the stock issued to effect the combination.

     b. The combined company sells assets that were acquired in the combination which represent duplicate facilities.

     c. The acquiring corporation acquires only ninety percent of the voting common stock of the other corporation in exchange for its voting common stock.

     d. The combination is effected within nine months of the initiation of the plan combination.

24. On December 31, 1977, Kim, Inc., had 2,000,000 shares of authorized $10 par value voting common stock of which 1,600,000 were issued and outstanding. On December 1, 1978, Kim issued 250,000 additional shares of its $10 par value voting common stock in exchange for all 100,000 shares of Terry Company's outstanding $20 par value voting common stock in a business combination appropriately accounted for by the pooling of interests method. The market value of Kim's voting common stock was $30 per share on the date of the business combination. What is the total consolidated common stock issued and outstanding for Kim and its subsidiary, Terry, at December 31, 1978?

     a. $17,000,000.

     b. $18,500,000.

     c. $22,500,000.

     d. $55,500,000.

25. On January 1, 1978, Harry Corporation sold equipment costing $2,000,000 with accumulated depreciation of $500,000 to Anna Corporation, its wholly-owned subsidiary, for $1,800,000. Harry was depreciating the equipment on the straight-line method over twenty years with no salvage value, which Anna continued. In consolidation at December 31, 1978, the cost and accumulated depreciation, respectively, should be

     a. $1,500,000 and $100,000.

     b. $1,800,000 and $100,000.

     c. $2,000,000 and $100,000.

     d. $2,000,000 and $600,000.

26. Which of the following transactions related to a business combination would require that the combination be accounted for as a purchase?

   a. The combination is to be completed within twelve months from the date the plan was initiated.

   b. Ninety-two percent of one company's common stock is exchanged for only common stock in the other company.

   c. The combined company is to retire a portion of the common stock exchanged to effect the combination within twelve months of the combination.

   d. The combined company will dispose of numerous fixed assets representing duplicate facilities subsequent to the combination.

27. Consolidated financial statements are prepared when a parent-subsidiary relationship exists in recognition of the accounting concept of

   a. Materiality.
   b. Entity.
   c. Objectivity.
   d. Going concern.

28. In a business combination accounted for as a purchase, how should the excess of fair value of net assets acquired over cost be treated?

   a. Amortized as a credit to income over a period not to exceed forty years.

   b. Amortized as a charge to expense over a period not to exceed forty years.

   c. Amortized directly to retained earnings over a period not to exceed forty years.

   d. Allocated as a reduction of noncurrent assets other than long-term investments in marketable securities.

29. Eltro Company acquired a 70% interest in the Samson Company in 1972. For the years ended December 31, 1973 and 1974, Samson reported net income of $80,000 and $90,000, respectively. During 1973, Samson sold merchandise to Eltro for $10,000 at a profit of $2,000. The merchandise was later resold by Eltro to outsiders for $15,000 during 1974. For consolidation purposes what is the minority interest's share of Samson's net income for 1973 and 1974, respectively?

   a. $23,400 and $27,600.
   b. $24,000 and $27,000.
   c. $24,600 and $26,400.
   d. $26,000 and $25,000.

30. Which of the following describes the amount at which a parent company should carry its unconsolidated domestic subsidiary on its separate financial statements in periods subsequent to acquisition?

   a. Original cost of the investment to the parent company.

   b. Original cost of the investment adjusted for the parent's share of the subsidiary's earnings, losses, and dividends.

   c. Current market value of the investment adjusted for dividends received.

   d. Current market value of the investment.

31. In a parent's unconsolidated financial statements, which accounts, other than cash, are affected when reflecting a subsidiary's earnings and dividends?

   a. Dividend revenue, equity in earnings of subsidiary, and retained earnings.

   b. Dividend revenue and retained earnings.

   c. Investment in subsidiary, equity in earnings of subsidiary, dividend revenue, and retained earnings.

   d. Investment in subsidiary, equity in earnings of subsidiary, and retained earnings.

32. Two calendar-year corporations combine onn July 1, 1975. The combination is properly accounted for as a pooling of interests. How should the results of operations have been reported for the year ended December 31, 1975?

   a. Combined from July 1 to December 31 and disclosed for the separate companies from January 1 to June 30.

   b. Combined from July 1 to December 31 and disclosed for the separate companies for the entire year.

   c. Combined for the entire year and disclosed for the separate companies from January 1 to June 30.

   d. Combined for the entire year and disclosed for the separate companies for the entire year.

33. In a business combination accounted for as a pooling of interests, the combined corporation's retained earnings usually equals the sum of the retained earnings of the individual combining corporations. Assuming there is no contributed capital other than capital stock at par value, which of the following describes a situation where the combined retained earnings must be increased or decreased?

a.   Increased if the par value dollar amount of the outstanding shares of the combined corporation exceeds the total capital stock of the separate combining companies.

b.   Increased if the par value dollar amount of the outstanding shares of the combined corporation is less than the total capital stock of the separate combining companies.

c.   Decreased if the par value dollar amount of the outstanding shares of the combined corporation exceeds the total capital stock of the separate combining companies.

d.   Decreased if the par value dollar amount of the outstanding shares of the combined corporation is less than the total capital stock of the separate combining companies.

The next three items relate to APB Opinions No. 17 and No. 18. Assume that any amortization of goodwill is by the straight-line method for a 40-year period. Ignore income taxes.

34.   On January 1, 1979 Investor Corporation pur- †
chased for $20,000 a 15% common stock interest in Investee Corporation whose total common stock equity had a fair and a book value of $100,000. The investment is accounted for by the cost method. If Investee's net income during 1979 is $30,000 and Investor receives dividends of $5,000 from Investee, for 1979 Investor Corporation should report income from this investment of

a. $5,000.
b. $4,875.
c. $4,500.
d. $4,375.

35.   Assume the same facts as in item 40 except that †
Investor Corporation pays $50,000 for a 40% common stock interest in Investee Corporation, accounts for the investment by the equity method and received $13,333 in dividends from Investee during 1979. For 1979 Investor Corporation should report as income from this investment the single amount of

a. $13,333.
b. $13,083.
c. $12,000.
d. $11,750.

36.   The investment described in item 41 should be †
reported as a long-term investment in Investor Corporation's balance sheet at December 31, 1979, as a single amount of

a. $63,083.
b. $50,000.
c. $48,667.
d. $48,417.

37.   Assume that Operating Corporation purchases †
a 10% common stock interest in Service Corporation for $10,000 on January 1, 1979 and an additional 20% interest for $22,000 on January 1, 1980. The balance sheets of Service Corporation, which pays no dividends, follow:

	December 31 1980	December 31 1979	January 1 1979
Cash	$130,000	$110,000	$100,000
Total assets	$130,000	$110,000	$100,000
Common stock	$100,000	$100,000	$100,000
Retained earnings	30,000	10,000	–0–
Total owners' equity	$130,000	$110,000	$100,000

During 1979 Operating Corporation carries this investment under the cost method and on January 1, 1980 adopts the equity method. For 1980 Operating Corporation should report as income from this 30% investment the single amount of

a. $9,000.
b. $7,000.
c. $6,000.
d. $5,950.

38.   The investment described in item 38 should be †
reported as a long-term investment in Operating Corporation's balance sheet at December 31, 1980 as a single amount of

a. $41,000.
b. $39,000.
c. $38,000.
d. $37,900.

MAY 1981 QUESTIONS

39.   In January 1980 Farley Corporation acquired 20% of the outstanding common stock of Davis Company for $800,000. This investment gave Farley the ability to exercise significant influence over Davis. The book

value of the acquired shares was $600,000. The excess of cost over book value was attributed to an identifiable intangible asset which was undervalued on Davis' balance sheet and which had a remaining useful life of ten years.

For the year ended December 31, 1980, Davis reported net income of $180,000 and paid cash dividends of $40,000 on its common stock. What is the proper carrying value of Farley's investment in Davis at December 31, 1980?

    a. $772,000.
    b. $780,000.
    c. $800,000.
    d. $808,000.

40.   How should long-term debt assumed in a business combination be shown under each of the following methods?

	Purchase	Pooling of interests
a.	Recorded value	Recorded value
b.	Recorded value	Fair value
c.	Fair value	Fair value
d.	Fair value	Recorded value

41.   In order to report a business combination as a pooling of interests, the minimum amount of an investee's common stock which must be acquired during the combination period in exchange for the investor's common stock is

    a.   100 percent.
    b.   90 percent.
    c.   80 percent.
    d.   51 percent.

Problem 1   Equity Method Accounting (1174,T3)

(25 to 30 minutes)

Hawkes Systems, Inc., a chemical processing company, has been operating profitably for many years. On March 1, 1974, Hawkes purchased 50,000 shares of Diversified Insurance Company stock for $2,000,000. The 50,000 shares represented 25% of Diversified's outstanding stock. Both Hawkes and Diversified operate on a fiscal year ending August 31.

For the fiscal year ended August 31, 1974, Diversified reported net income of $800,000 earned ratably throughout the year. During November, 1973, February, May, and August, 1974,, Diversified paid its regular quarterly cash dividend of $100,000.

Required:

a.   What criteria should Hawkes consider in determining whether its investment in Diversified should be classified as (1) a current asset (marketable security) or (2) a noncurrent asset (investment) in Hawkes' August 31, 1974, balance sheet? Confine your discussion to the decision criteria for determining the balance-sheet classification of the investment.

b.   Assume that the investment should be classified as a long-term investment in the noncurrent asset section of Hawkes' balance sheet. The cost of Hawkes' investment equaled its equity in the recorded values of Diversified's net assets; recorded values were not materially different from fair values (individually or collectively). For the fiscal year ended August 31, 1974, how did the net income reported and dividends paid by Diversified affect the accounts of Hawkes (including Hawkes' income tax accounts)? Indicate each account affected, whether it increased or decreased, and explain the reason for the change in the account balance (such as Cash, Investment in Diversified, etc.). Organize your answer in the following format.

Account Name	Increase or Decrease	Reason for Change in Account Balance

c.   Independent of your answers to parts a. and b. above, assume Hawkes had purchased 70% of Diversified's stock on March I, 1974.

1.   Under certain circumstances Hawkes (the parent) should not accrue income taxes on all or part of its equity in the undistributed earnings of Diversified (its subsidiary). What are these circumstances and what evidence and other considerations must be evaluated to substantiate these circumstances?

2.   What information should be disclosed in the notes to its financial statements if Hawkes does not accrue income taxes on all or part of its equity in the undistributed earnings of Diversified?

3.   Would it be appropriate to prepare consolidated financial statements for Hawkes and its subsidiary, Diversified, for the fiscal year ended August 31, 1974? Explain.

Problem 2   Business Combinations (1179,T5)

(15 to 20 minutes)

When a business combination is effected by an exchange of common stock, the transaction is accounted for as a purchase or as a pooling of interests, depending on the circumstances. The methods are not optional and each yields significantly different results as to financial position and results of operations.

Required:

Discuss the **supportive** arguments for each of the following:

a.   Purchase method.
b.   Pooling of interests method.

Do **not** discuss in your answer the rules for distinguishing between a purchase and a pooling of interests.

Problem 3   Purchase Pooling Criteria (577,T3)

(20 to 25 minutes)

Hanover Company and Case Company, both of whom have only voting common stock, are considering a merger whereby Hanover would be the surviving company. The terms of the combination provide that the transaction would be carried out by Hanover exchanging one share of its stock for two shares of Case's stock. Prior to the date of the contemplated exchange, Hanover had purchased five percent of Case's stock which it holds as an investment. Case, at the same date, owns two percent of Hanover's stock. All of the remaining outstanding stock of Case will be acquired by Hanover in this contemplated exchange. Neither of the two companies has ever had any affiliation as a subsidiary or division of any other company.

Required:

   a.   Without enumerating specific criteria, how is a determination made as to whether a business combination is accounted for as a pooling of interests or as a purchase?
   b.   Based only on the facts above discuss the specific criteria which would qualify or disqualify this business combination as being accounted for as a pooling of interests.
   c.   What additional requirements (other than those discussed in b. above) must be met in order to account for this business combination as a pooling of interests?

Problem 4   Purchase vs. Pooling Worksheet (1174,Q5) †

(40 to 50 minutes)

Blue Corporation was merged into Ace Corporation on August 31, 1974, with Blue Corporation going out of existence. Both corporations had fiscal years ending on August 31, and Ace Corporation will retain this fiscal year. The enclosed worksheet contains a balance sheet for each corporation and a combined balance sheet as of August 31,1974, immediately prior to the merger, and net income figures for each corporation for the fiscal year ended August 31, 1974. You have obtained the following addition information as of the date of the merger:

The fair value of the assets and liabilities on August 31, 1974, of Ace Corporation and Blue Corporation was as follows:

	Ace	Blue
Current assets	$ 4,950,000	$ 3,400,000
Plant & Equip. (net)	22,000,000	14,000,000
Patents	570,000	360,000
Plant rearrangement costs	150,000	40,000
Total assets	$27,670,000	$17,800,000
Liabilities	(2,650,000)	(2,100,000)
Net assets	$25,020,000	$15,700,000

Ace Corporation capitalized its fiscal year 1974 plant rearrangement costs and has always amortized them over five years beginning with the year of expenditure. All plant rearrangement costs of Ace have been appropriately capitalized and amortized for the current and preceding years. Blue Corporation incurred $50,000 of plant rearrangement costs which were expensed during the fiscal year ending August 31, 1974. Blue did not have any plant rearrangement costs in any year before 1974. Blue will adopt Ace's method of accounting for plant rearrangement costs.

Internally generated general expenses incurred because of the merger were $25,000 and are included in the current assets of Ace as a prepaid expense.

There were no intercompany transactions during the year.

Before the merger, Ace had 3,000,000 shares of common stock authorized; 1,200,000 shares issued; and 1,100,000 shares outstanding. Blue had 750,000 shares of common stock authorized, issued, and outstanding.

Required:
      (See worksheet on next page.)
   On the worksheet, prepare the balance sheet and determine the amount of net income under each of the following independent situations. Include explanations of adjustments on the worksheet. Cross-reference explanations to the adjustments. Do not prepare formal journal entries.

   a.   Ace Corporation exchanged 400,000 shares of previously unissued common stock and 100,000 shares of treasury stock for all the outstanding common stock of Blue Corporation. All the conditions for pooling-of-interests accounting enumerated in APB Opinion No. 16 ("Business Combinations") were met.

Problem 4

Ace Corporation and Blue Corporation
WORKSHEET FOR POOLING OF INTERESTS AND PURCHASE ACCOUNTING

	Ace Corporation	Blue Corporation	Combined	a. Adjustments Debit	a. Adjustments Credit	Pooling of Interests	b. Adjustments Debit	b. Adjustments Credit	Purchase
Current assets	$ 4,350,000	$ 3,000,000	$ 7,350,000						
Plant & equipment (net)	18,500,000	11,300,000	29,800,000						
Patents	450,000	200,000	650,000						
Plant rearrangement costs	150,000	—	150,000						
	$23,450,000	$14,500,000	$37,950,000						
Liabilities	$ 2,650,000	$ 2,100,000	$ 4,750,000						
Common stock $10 par value	12,000,000	—	12,000,000						
Common stock $5 par value	—	3,750,000	3,750,000						
Paid-in capital in excess of par	4,200,000	—	4,200,000						
Paid-in capital in excess of par	—	3,200,000	3,200,000						
Retained earnings	5,850,000	—	5,850,000						
Retained earnings	—	5,450,000	5,450,000						
	24,700,000	14,500,000	39,200,000						
Less treasury stock at cost, 100,000 shares	1,250,000	—	1,250,000						
	$23,450,000	$14,500,000	$37,950,000						
Net income (no extraordinary items for fiscal year ended August 31,1974	$ 2,450,000	$ 1,300,000							

b. Ace Corporation purchased the assets and assumed the liabilities of Blue Corporation by paying $3,100,000 cash and issuing debentures of $16,900,000 at face value.

Problem 5   Consolidated Balance Sheet (580,Q3)

(45 to 55 minutes)

The December 31, 1979, balance sheets of Encanto Corporation and its subsidiary, Norris Corporation, are presented below:

Assets	Encanto Corporation	Norris Corporation
Cash	$ 167,250	$101,000
Accounts receivable	178,450	72,000
Notes receivable	87,500	28,000
Dividends receivable	36,000	
Inventories	122,000	68,000
Property, plant and equipment	487,000	252,000
Accumulated depreciation	(117,000)	(64,000)
Investment in Norris Corporation	240,800	
	$1,202,000	$457,000

Liabilities and Stockholders' Equity		
Accounts payable	$ 222,000	$ 76,000
Notes payable	79,000	89,000
Dividend payable		40,000
Common stock, $10 par value:		
Encanto Corporation	400,000	
Norris Corporation		100,000
Retained earnings:		
Encanto Corporation	501,000	
Norris Corporation		152,000
	$1,202,000	$457,000

Additional information:

• Encanto initially acquired 60 percent of the outstanding common stock of Norris in 1977. This purchase resulted in no difference between cost and net assets acquired. As of December 31, 1979, the percentage owned is 90 percent. An analysis of the account "Investment in Norris Corporation" is as follows:

Date	Description	Amount
Dec. 31, 1977	Acquired 6,000 shares	$ 70,800
Dec. 31, 1978	60% of 1978 net income of $78,000	46,800
Sept. 1, 1979	Acquired 3,000 shares	92,000
Dec. 31, 1979	Subsidiary income for 1979:	67,200*
Dec. 31, 1979	90% of dividends declared	(36,000)
		$240,800

*Subsidiary income for 1979:	
60% of $96,000	$57,600
30% of 96,000 x 33-1/3%	9,600
	$67,200

Assume that Norris's net income is earned ratably during the year. Amortization of the excess of cost over the net assets acquired is to be recorded over sixty months.

• On December 15, 1979, Norris declared a cash dividend of $4 per share of common stock, payable to shareholders of January 7, 1980.

• During 1979, Encanto sold merchandise to Norris. Encanto's cost for this merchandise was $68,000, and the sale was made at 125% of cost. Norris's inventory at December 31, 1979, included merchandise purchased from Encanto at a cost to Norris of $35,000.

• In December 1978, Norris sold merchandise to Encanto for $67,000, which was at a markup of 35% over Norris's cost. On January 1, 1979, $54,000 of this merchandise remained in Encanto's inventory. This merchandise was subsequently sold by Encanto at a profit of $11,000 during 1979.

• On October 1, 1979, Encanto sold for $42,000, excess equipment to Norris. Data relating to this equipment is as follows:

Book value on Encanto's records	$36,000
Method of depreciation	Straight-line
Estimated remaining life on October 1, 1979	10 years

• Near the end of 1979, Norris reduced the balance of its intercompany account payable to Encanto to zero by transferring $8,000 to Encanto. This payment was still in transit on December 31, 1979.

Required:

Complete the consolidated balance sheet worksheet of Encanto Corporation and its subsidiary, Norris Corporation, as of December 31, 1979. Formal statements and journal entries are **not** required. Supporting computations should be in good form.

Problem 6   Consolidated Balance Sheet (1177,P3)

(40 to 50 minutes)

On June 30, 1976, Paul Corporation acquired for cash of $19 per share all of the outstanding voting common stock of Sand Corporation. Both companies continued to operate as separate entities and both companies have calendar years.

· On June 30, 1976, after closing the nominal accounts, Sand's condensed balance sheet was as follows:

Assets:

Cash	$ 700,000
Accounts receivable, net	600,000
Inventories	1,400,000
Property, plant, and equipment, net	3,300,000
Other assets	500,000
Total assets	$6,500,000

Liabilities and stockholders' equity:

Accounts payable and other current liabilities	$ 700,000
Long-term debt	2,600,000
Other liabilities	200,000
Common stock, par value $1.00 per share	1,000,000
Additional paid-in capital	400,000
Retained earnings	1,600,000
Total liabilities and stockholders' equity	$6,500,000

· On June 30, 1976, Sand's assets and liabilities that had fair values that were different than the book values were as follows:

	Fair Value
Property, plant, and equipment, net	$16,400,000
Other assets	200,000
Long-term debt	2,200,000

The differences between fair values and book values resulted in a charge or credit to depreciation or amortization for the consolidated statements for the six-month period ending December 31, 1976, as follows:

Property, plant, and equipment, net	$500,000 charge
Other assets	10,000 credit
Long-term debt	5,000 charge
	$495,000 charge

· The amount paid by Paul in excess of the fair value of the net assets of Sand is attributable to expected future earnings of Sand and will be amortized over the maximum allowable period.

· On June 30, 1976, there were no intercompany receivables or payables.

· During the six-month period ending December 31, 1976, Sand acquired merchandise from Paul at an invoice price of $500,000. The cost of the merchandise to Paul was $300,000. At December 31, 1976, one-half of the merchandise was not sold and Sand had not yet paid for any of the merchandise.

· The 1976 net income (loss) for both companies was as follows:

	Paul	Sand
January 1 to June 30	$ 250,000	$ (750,000)
July 1 to December 31	1,600,000	1,250,000

The $1,600,000 net income of Paul includes the equity in the net income of Sand.

· On December 31, 1976, after closing the nominal accounts, the condensed balance sheets for both companies were as follows:

Assets:	Paul	Sand
Cash	$ 3,500,000	$ 600,000
Accounts receivable, net	1,400,000	1,500,000
Inventories	1,000,000	2,500,000
Property, plant and equipment, net	2,000,000	3,100,000
Investment in subsidiary, at equity	20,250,000	—
Other assets	100,000	500,000
Total assets	$28,250,000	$8,200,000

Liabilities and stockholders' equity:		
Accounts payable and other current liabilities	$ 1,500,000	$1,100,000
Long-term debt	4,000,000	2,600,000
Other liabilities	750,000	250,000
Common stock, par value $1.00 per share	10,000,000	1,000,000
Additional paid-in capital	5,000,000	400,000
Retained earnings	7,000,000	2,850,000
Total liabilities and stockholders' equity	$28,250,000	$8,200,000

Required:

Prepare a condensed consolidated balance sheet of Paul Corporation and its wholly-owned subsidiary, Sand Corporation, as of December 31, 1976. Show supporting computations in good form. Ignore income tax and deferred tax considerations in your answer.

Problem 7   Consolidated Worksheet (1176,Q4) †

(50 to 60 minutes)

Presented on the enclosed work sheets are condensed financial statements for the year ended December 31, 1975, of Royal Company and its subsidiary, Butler Company:

Additional information:

• On January 3, 1973, Royal acquired from John Roth, the sole stockholder of Butler Company, for $440,000 cash, both a patent valued at $40,000 and 80% of the outstanding stock of Butler. The net book value of Butler's stock on the date of acquisition was $500,000 and the book values of the individual assets and liabilities were equal to their fair market values. Royal charged the entire $440,000 to the account "Investment in stock of Butler Company." The patent, for which no amortization has been charged, had a remaining legal life of four years as of January 3, 1973.

• On July 1, 1975, Royal reduced its investment in Butler to 75% of Butler's outstanding common stock, by selling shares for $70,000 to an unaffiliated company at a profit of $16,000. Royal recorded the proceeds as a credit to its investment account.

• For the six months ended June 30, 1975, Butler had net income of $140,000. Royal recorded 80% of this amount on its books of account prior to the time of sale.

• During 1974, Butler sold merchandise to Royal for $130,000, which was at a markup of 30% over Butler's cost. On January 1, 1975, $52,000 of this merchandise remained in Royal's inventory. This merchandise was subsequently sold by Royal in February 1975 at a profit of $8,000.

• In November 1975, Royal sold merchandise to Butler for the first time. Royal's cost for this merchandise was $80,000, and the sale was made at 120% of cost. Butler's inventory at December 31, 1975, contained merchandise that was purchased from Royal at a cost to Butler of $24,000.

• On December 31, 1975, there was a $45,000 payment-in-transit from Butler Company to Royal Company. Accounts receivable and accounts payable include intercompany receivables and payables.

• In December 1975, Butler declared and paid cash dividends of $100,000 to its stockholders.

• On December 31, 1975, Royal purchased for $58,000, 50% of the outstanding bonds issued by Butler. The bonds mature on December 31, 1979, and were originally issued at a discount. On December 31, 1975, the balance in Butler's account, "Unamortized discount on bonds payable" was $2,400. It is the intention of the management of Royal to hold these bonds until their maturity.

Required:

Complete the work sheet on the next two pages to prepare consolidated financial statements of Royal Company and its subsidiary as of December 31, 1975.

Formal statements and journal entries are not required. Ignore income taxes.

Problem 7

ROYAL AND BUTLER
WORKSHEET TO PREPARE CONSOLIDATED
STATEMENTS OF INCOME, RETAINED EARNINGS AND BALANCE SHEET

	Royal Company Dr. (Cr.)	Butler Company Dr. (Cr.)	Consolidating Totals Dr. (Cr.)	Adjustments and Eliminations Debit	Adjustments and Eliminations Credit	Minority Interest Dr. (Cr.)	Consolidated Dr. (Cr.)
INCOME STATEMENT							
Sales	$(4,000,000)	$(1,700,000)	$(5,700,000)				
Cost of Sales	2,982,000	1,015,000	3,997,000				
Operating expenses	400,000	377,200	777,200				
Dividend income	(75,000)	—	(75,000)				
Subsidiary income	(232,000)	—	(232,000)				
Interest expense	—	7,800	7,800				
Net income	$ 925,000	$ 300,000	$ 1,225,000				
RETAINED EARNINGS							
1/1/75 Retained Earnings							
Royal	$(2,100,000)		$(2,100,000)				
Butler		$ (640,000)	(640,000)				
Net income	(925,000)	(300,000)	(1,225,000)				
Dividends	170,000	100,000	270,000				
12/31/75 Retained Earnings	$(2,855,000)	$ (840,000)	$(3,695,000)				

Problem 7

BALANCE SHEET

	Royal Company Dr. (Cr.)	Butler Company Dr. (Cr.)	Consolidating Totals Dr. (Cr.)		Adjustments and Eliminations Debit	Credit	Minority Interest Dr. (Cr.)	Consolidated Dr. (Cr.)
Assets								
Cash	$ 486,000	$ 249,600	$ 735,600					
Accounts Receivable	235,000	185,000	420,000					
Inventories	475,000	355,000	830,000					
Machinery and equipment	2,231,000	530,000	2,761,000					
Investment in stock of Butler Company	954,000	—	954,000					
Investment in bonds of Butler Company	58,000	—	58,000					
	$4,439,000	$1,319,600	$5,758,600					
Liabilities and Owners' Equity								
Accounts payable	$ (384,000)	$ (62,000)	$ (446,000)					
Bonds payable	—	(120,000)	(120,000)					
Unamortized discount on bonds payable	—	2,400	2,400					
Common stock Royal Company	(1,200,000)	—	(1,200,000)					
Butler Company	—	(250,000)	(250,000)					
Contributed Capital	—	(50,000)	(50,000)					
Retained earnings (brought forward)	(2,855,000)	(840,000)	(3,695,000)					
Minority Interest								
	$(4,439,000)	$(1,319,600)	$(5,758,600)					

MULTIPLE CHOICE ANSWERS

1.	c	10.	d	19.	d	28.	d	37.	c
2.	b	11.	b	20.	c	29.	a	38.	b
3.	c	12.	d	21.	c	30.	b	39.	d
4.	d	13.	a	22.	a	31.	d	40.	d
5.	a	14.	b	23.	a	32.	c	41.	b
6.	b	15.	c	24.	b	33.	c		
7.	b	16.	a	25.	d	34.	c		
8.	c	17.	b	26.	c	35.	d		
9.	c	18.	b	27.	b	36.	d		

EXPLANATION OF MULTIPLE CHOICE ANSWERS

1. (1180,T1,19) (c) The requirement is the appropriate circumstances in which to use the "equity method." The equity method should be used in those cases where "an investor has the ability to exercise significant influence over an investee." Choices (a) and (b) indicate that such influence may be present, but are not sufficient evidence in themselves. Choice (d) is a criteria for pooling of interests accounting.

2. (1180,T1,20) (b) The requirement is the effect the two entries made by the parent company will have on the investment in subsidiary account and retained earnings. The solutions approach is to compare the journal entries made with the correct entries. The first entry made by the parent is correct; the investment account was debited and retained earnings was credited for the parent's 40% share of the subsidiary's $20,000 income. The second entry is incorrect; the investment account should have been credited instead of dividend revenue. Therefore, the investment account is overstated (should have been credited) and retained earnings is overstated (revenue should not have been recorded).

3. (1180,Q1,10) (c) The requirement is the maximum amount of income that Barton should report from its long-term investment for 1979. Barton acquired 30% of the stock of the investee so the equity method is used. The net assets of Barton had a book and market value of $1,600,000; Barton's 30% share is $480,000. Since Barton paid more than this amount for the investment, goodwill has also been purchased:

Cost of investment	$ 500,000
FMV of identifiable assets	(480,000)
Goodwill	$ 20,000

The income recognized by Barton is equal to its 30% share of the investee's income, less any goodwill amortization. To maximize income, Barton would amortize goodwill over 40 years, the maximum period permitted.

30% share of income (30%) ($180,000)	= $54,000
Goodwill amortization ($20,000/40 yrs.) =	(500)
Net income	= $53,500

Cash dividends received are ignored; when using the equity method these are credited to the investment account rather than income.

4. (1180,Q1,13) (d) The requirement is the increase in net assets to be recorded by Action as a result of acquiring all of the outstanding common stock of Master Corporation. This acquisition is a purchase because Action issued nonvoting preferred stock in exchange for all of Master's common stock. A purchase is accounted for under the basic historical cost principal; the net assets acquired are recorded at their fair value or the fair value of the stock issued, whichever is more objectively determinable. The tangible net assets acquired have a fair value of $2,500,000; the fact that the stock issued has a value of $4,000,000 indicates that intangible assets are also acquired. The total cost of acquiring the net assets is the fair value of the preferred stock ($4,000,000) plus the finders' fee of $400,000 of preferred stock.

5. (580,P1,2) (a) The situation is a business combination accounted for as a purchase where the cost of the acquired company is less than the fair market value of the identifiable assets and liabilities of Thread Company. Per APB 16, para 91, the excess of fair market value over cost ($400,000) should be used first to reduce proportionately all noncurrent assets other than long-term investments in marketable securities. Any excess remaining is a deferred credit to be amortized to income over a period not to exceed forty years (see APB 16, para 91). In this case, $250,000 of the $400,000 excess is used to eliminate the entire amount of property, plant, and equipment. Additionally, $150,000 remains as a deferred credit.

$1,000,000	Cost
1,400,000	FMV of identifiable assets and liabilities
$ 400,000	Excess of FMV over cost
250,000	Reduction of PP&E
$ 150,000	Deferred credit

6. **(580,P1,3) (b)** The requirement is to compute the balance in Troy's paid-in capital account immediately after a business combination accounted for as a pooling of interests. One solutions approach is to make an entry to record the combination on the new entity's books to reflect the $995,000 book value of the net assets. In making the entry the objective is to carry forward the maximum amount of retained earnings (see APB 16, para 53).

Net assets	$995,000	
Common stock		$650,000
Paid-in capital		?
Retained earnings		?

Paid-in capital in this case will be equal to $995,000 minus the sum of common stock ($650,000) and retained earnings ($320,000). This difference is a credit to paid-in capital of $25,000. If the sum of the par value of the common stock and retained earnings had been greater than $995,000, there would be no credit to paid-in capital and retained earnings carried forward would be reduced.

The other approach to obtain the amount of paid-in capital is to subtract from combined paid-in capital ($75,000) the difference between the par value issued for the new corporation ($650,000) and the combined par value of the constituents ($600,000).

$75,000 − ($650,000 par value issued − $600,000 combined par value) = $25,000.

7. **(580,P1,15) (b)** The requirement is to compute the balance of the "Investment in Comet Corporation" account after one year of ownership to reflect the equity method of accounting for investments. The solutions approach is to use a T-account showing earnings as an increase and dividends as a reduction in the investment account (see APB 18, para 19).

Investment in Comet

Cost	$1,200,000	$120,000 Dividend
Earnings	160,000	
Ending balance	$1,240,000	

8. **(580,Q1,18) (c)** The requirement is the amount of goodwill resulting from the purchase of the Ann Corp. Upon purchase, the acquired identifiable assets and liabilities should be assigned a portion of the cost for the company equal to their fair market value at the date of acquisition. The excess of the cost to the acquirer over the sum of the amounts assigned to individual assets and liabilities of the acquiree is goodwill (para 87 of APB 16). In this case, after adjusting inventories and property to their fair market values, the fair

values of the assets are $830,000 and the liabilities are $180,000, indicating a net book value of $650,000. Based on the $800,000 paid, there should be $150,000 of goodwill ($800,000 − $650,000).

9. **(580,T1,5) (c)** When using the equity method, an investment is recorded at cost and increased by the investor's share of the investee's earnings (recognized as income). The investment is decreased by the investor's share of losses of the investee (recognized as a loss) and dividends received from the investee. See APB 18, para 6b.

10. **(580,T1,14) (d)** The pooling of interests method of accounting for a business combination requires recording the assets and liabilities acquired at their book values. Earnings of the pooled entity may be increased as a result of the combination, not as a result of efficient operations. In addition, there will be no amortization of goodwill as may occur in purchase method acquisitions. Answers (a), (b), and (c) are incorrect because if assets and liabilities are recorded at book value in a pooling of interests, assets will not be overvalued and liabilities will not be undervalued.

11. **(580,T1,40) (b)** This acquisition was a purchase rather than a pooling of interests because the common stock of another company was acquired for cash. In an acquisition treated as a purchase, the acquirer includes net income for the acquiree only from the date of purchase (see APB 16, para 94). Note that for a pooling of interests, answer (c) would be correct. Answer (a) is a nonsense answer. Answer (d) violates the requirement of APB 16, para 94.

12. **(1179,P1,3) (d)** The requirement is the 1978 consolidated net income for two companies that combined as a pooling of interests on December 1, 1978. Per para 56 of APB 16, business combinations accounted for by the pooling of interest method should report results of operations as if the combination took place at the beginning of the year. Thus, the consolidated income would be $3,200,000 ($2,000,000 + $1,200,000). Note that the problem indicates that the surviving company (Drew) does not already include the equity in the net income of the combining company (Art). If Drew had been using the equity method, and if the $2,000,000 of Drew income already included the $1,200,000 of Art income, consolidated net income would be $2,000,000.

13. **(1179,P1,4) (a)** The requirement is the amount of goodwill arising from a business combination accounted for as a purchase. Since $8,000,000 was paid for all stock of a company with a $6,400,000 book value, the excess of cost over book value is $1,600,000. Per para 87 of APB 16, all assets and liabilities of a

company acquired under the purchase method should be recorded at their fair value. In this problem, as the table below indicates, fair market value of specific assets and liabilities exceeded book value by $1,600,000. Accordingly, the $1,600,000 excess of cost over book value will be assigned to these specific assets and liabilities, and no goodwill will result.

	Book Value	FMV	Adjustment
PP&E	$10,000,000	$11,500,000	$1,500,000 dr
Other assets	1,000,000	700,000	−300,000 cr
LT debt	6,000,000	5,600,000	400,000 dr
			$1,600,000

14. (1179,P1,13) (b) The requirement is the balance in the investment account at the end of 1978 for an investment that should be accounted for under the cost method. The cost method is appropriate per APB 18, since less than 20% of the investee is owned and the investor can not exercise significant influence over the investee. Thus the investor would record the $300,000 as an investment in stock at the time of purchase and record the $20,000 cash dividend as dividend income when received.

15. (1179,Q1,18) (c) The requirement is the amount that Alan Company should record as cost of a building that was part of net assets purchased in a business combination accounted for as a purchase. While the building had an appraised value of $150,000, its adjusted tax basis was only $100,000. Accordingly, $50,000 of depreciation ($150,000 - $100,000) will be lost relative to the purchase of a similar asset for $150,000. Thus, the valuation of the asset should be $150,000 less the $24,000 of tax benefits ($50,000 × 48%). See para 89 of APB 16.

16. (1179,T1,22) (a) In business combinations accounted for as a purchase, all identifiable assets and liabilities assumed should be recorded at their fair values per para 87 of APB 16. Answers (b) and (d) are incorrect because fair value rather than book value or historic cost is required. Answer (c) is incorrect because fixed assets are to be recorded at their fair value even if it results in an excess of fair value over purchase price.

17. (1179,T1,26) (b) The requirement is how subsidiaries acquired in purchase and pooling business combinations should be presented in the financial statements. Per para 1 of ARB 51, there is a presumption that consolidated statements are more meaningful than separate company statements. Accordingly, subsidiaries should normally be consolidated. Also see para 2-5 of ARB 51 and para 5 of APB 18.

18. (1176,T1,9) (b) Acquisition of B by A is to be accounted by the purchase method because less than 90% of B's stock is acquired by A (para 47b of APB 16). Company A acquires 80% of $800,000, or $640,000, of net fair market value for $700,000 of stock, resulting in $60,000 of goodwill (para 87 APB 16). The book value of Company B is not relevant to determine the consideration given by A or the recording of the historical cost for the amount paid for by A.

19. (577,T1,14) (d) The requirement is the effect on earnings of accounting for a business combination as a purchase instead of a pooling. First review accounting for income per purchase and per pooling. Per purchase, the income of the acquiring corporation only includes income of the acquired company after the date of acquisition (para 94, APB 16). Per pooling, income is reported as if the companies had been combined as of the beginning of the period (para 56, APB 16). In this case, the combination was accounted for as purchase instead of a pooling. Under both purchase and pooling, December earnings of B are included in A's retained earnings. Thus, the concern must be with B's operation from the beginning of 1976 through November. Thus answer (b) is incorrect because if B had a net loss in the beginning of the year and this loss was not recognized in A's retained earnings due to purchase rather than pooling accounting, A's retained earnings are overstated. Answer (d) is correct because the net earnings in the beginning of the year should have been, but were not, included in A's retained earnings.

20. (577,T1,15) (c) The requirement is the effect of recording a combination as a purchase instead of a pooling on parent's asset valuations at the date of acquisition. Note that the requirement is the effect on asset valuations, not on total asset value. Under purchase accounting, assets are recorded at their fair value; under pooling accounting, assets are recorded at their book value. Thus relative to valuation under pooling accounting, the assets will be overstated at their fair value if their fair value exceeds their book value. Remember, under pooling accounting they would have been recorded at their book value. See para 51 and 87 of APB 16.

21. (578,P1,4) (c) The requirement is the net income to be recognized by the investor, Robohn, as the result of the 40% investment in Lowell Company. The equity method is required per APB 18 since 40% of the investee is owned, and the investor can exercise significant influence over the investee. Under the equity method the investor recognizes an appropriate share of all of the investee's net income, both distributed and undistributed. This is in contrast to the cost method where only the appropriate percentage of distributed income is recognized by the investor.

Here, 40% of Lowell's reported income of $600,000 is $240,000 which must be reduced by $10,000 for the amortization of excess of cost over book value. The $1,800,000 cost of the investment was $400,000 over the $1,400,000 book value. This is to be amortized over 40 years per the problem, i.e., $10,000 per year.

22. (578,P1,11)   (a) The requirement is the investor's (Pint) income as a result of investment in the investee (Quart). Since the investor acquired only a 10% interest in the investee, the investment is carried at the lower of cost or market per SFAS 12. The only income recognized is dividends received which is $10,000. APB 18 indicates the equity method is to be used for 20%-50% investments in investees. The cost method is appropriate for investments where ownership is less than 20% of investee.

23. (578,T1,16)   (a) The requirement is the transaction which would preclude use of the pooling method in a business combination. Para 46, 47, and 48 of APB 16 specify criteria that business combinations must meet in order to be accounted for as a pooling. Answer (a), subsequent reacquisition of the stock used to initiate the combination, is prohibited per para 48a. Answer (b), selling of duplicate facilities, is permitted per para 48c. Answer (c), acquisition of only 90% of the combining company's stock, is permitted per para 47b. Answer (d), effecting the combination in 9 months is permitted per para 46a.

24. (579,P1,3)   (b) The requirement is the total consolidated common stock issued and outstanding for Kim, Inc. At the beginning of the year, Kim had 1,600,000 shares of $10 par value stock outstanding. On December 1, Kim issued 250,000 shares of its $10 par value stock in a pooling transaction. Accordingly, at year-end there are 1,850,000 shares of $10 par value stock outstanding, resulting in total consolidated common stock of $18,500,000. The answer would be the same under either the pooling or purchase method. Under the pooling method, the total value of the stock and paid-in capital credited equals the book value of the company acquired. Under the purchase method, the total value of stock and paid-in capital credited equals the fair market value of the stock issued. Note that this question, however, concerns only common stock and not paid-in capital.

25. (579,Q1,8)   (d) The requirement is the year-end consolidated balances of fixed assets and related accumulated depreciation after an intercompany sale as of the beginning of the year. The objective is to restate the accounts as if the intercompany transaction had not occurred. Since the $2,000,000 asset, which had $500,000 accumulated depreciation at January 1, was being depreciated over 20 years, the ending balances should be $2,000,000 of fixed assets and $600,000 of accumulated depreciation. On the consolidated books, depreciation expense must be adjusted since the subsidiary recorded $120,000 expense ($1,800,000 ÷ 15 remaining years), while consolidated expense would be $100,000 ($2,000,000 ÷ 20 years). The entry is:

| Accum. depr. | $20,000 | |
| Depr. exp. | | $20,000 |

Also the equipment must be debited for $200,000 to adjust the subsidiary's cost ($1,800,000) up to the parent's original cost ($2,000,000). $500,000 of accumulated depreciation must be recorded on the consolidated books to reflect the depreciation the parent had recorded. Finally, the gain on sale of $300,000 ($1,800,000 received less $1,500,000 book value) must be eliminated.

Equipment	$200,000	
Gain on Sale	300,000	
Accum. depr.		$500,000

26. (579,T1,4)   (c) The requirement is the transaction which would require a business combination to be accounted for as a purchase. Para 46, 47 and 48 of APB 16 provide criteria that must be met if a business combination is to be accounted for as a pooling. If even one of the criteria is not met, the business combination must be accounted for as a purchase. One of the criteria is to prohibit a company from agreeing to retire or reacquire all or part of the common stock issued to effect the combination. If one issues stock and at the same time agrees to reacquire it, it is the same as purchasing for cash, i.e., a purchase situation rather than a pooling situation. See para 48a of APB 16.

Answer (a) is incorrect because para 47a requires the combination to be completed within one year after the plan is initiated in order for it to be accounted for as a pooling. Answer (b) is incorrect because para 47b requires over 90 percent of the acquired company be exchanged at the date the plan is consummated in order for it to be accounted for as a pooling. Answer (d) is incorrect because para 48c permits pooling even if there is disposal of fixed assets representing duplicate facilities.

27. (579,T1,17) (b) Consolidated financial statements are based on the entity concept. Even though they are two separate companies, there is one economic entity due to the ownership of one company by the other. As a result, intercompany accounts are eliminated, and remaining accounts are combined to prepare consolidated financial statements. Answer (a) is incorrect because materiality, a basic feature of financial accounting per para 128 of APB Statement 4, is not peculiar to consolidations. Answer (c) is incorrect because objectivity, described as verifiability in para 90 of APB Statement 4, is not peculiar to consolidations. Answer (d) is incorrect because going concern is described as a basic feature of financial accounting (para 117 of APB Statement 4) and is not peculiar to consolidations.

28. (1175,P1,6) (d) APB 16, para 87, requires that all identifiable assets and liabilities obtained in a purchase business combination should be valued at their fair values at the date of acquisition. In the event that the fair value of the total net assets exceed the cost of the business combination, this excess should be allocated as a reduction of noncurrent assets other than longterm investments in marketable securities. See para 87 and 91 of APB 16. As an example, the entry below illustrates a case where $50,000 cash is paid for a company with assets having a fair value of $100,000 and liabilities of $40,000. The result would be that noncurrent assets, other than long-term investments in marketable securities, would be reduced by $10,000.

FV of assets	$100,000	
FV of liabilities		$40,000
Cash		50,000
Other noncurrent assets		10,000

29. (1175,Q1,7) (a) Without the intercompany transaction, the minority interest income from Samson in 1973 would be $24,000 (30% of $80,000). In 1974, the minority interest income would be $27,000 (30% of $90,000). On the consolidated statements in 1973 the $2,000 intercompany profit will be eliminated, because from a consolidated viewpoint an armslength transaction has not occurred with third parties. The elimination entry will be to credit inventory (which is in effect on the books of Eltro) for $2,000 and debits will be made of $1,400 to majority interest income and $600 to minority interest income. In 1974 when Eltro sells the inventory to outsiders, the

$2,000 profit has effectively been earned. In 1974 an entry will be made on the consolidated books to effectively recognize this profit and allocate it to the majority and minority interest. Thus the 1973 minority interest income will be reduced by $600 and 1974 minority interest income increased by $600.

1973	1974
24,000	27,000
− 600	+ 600
23,400	27,600

30. (1175,T1,13) (b) Para 14 of APB 18 requires parent companies to account for unconsolidated domestic subsidiaries by the equity method. The equity method results in the parent's share of the subsidiary's earnings and losses being recognized as income by the parent with a corresponding debit or credit to the investment account. As dividends are received under the equity method, cash is debited and the investment account credited. The net effect of the equity method (relative to the cost method) is that the parent's share of undistributed earnings is recognized by the parent.

31. (1175,T1,14) (d) A subsidiary's earnings and dividends are reflected in the parent's unconsolidated financial statements in the investment, subsidiary earnings, and retained earnings accounts. The key to this solution is knowledge that the parent must use the equity method to reflect the investment in the subsidiary. The investment account and subsidiary earnings accounts are affected but not a dividend revenue account. Thus answers (a), (b), and (c) are incorrect.

32. (576,T1,6) (c) When a pooling takes place in mid-year, the income statement of the pooled company should reflect pooled operations for the entire year. The rationale is that the pooled company will report on a combined basis in the future. Also required are the revenue, extraordinary items, and net income for each of the separate companies from the beginning of the period to the date of the pooling. See para 56 and 64 of APB 16. Note that this is in contrast to purchase accounting wherein the consolidated income statement only includes the parent's share of the subsidiary's income from the date of acquisition of the subsidiary. How-

ever, under purchase accounting, consolidated income as if the purchase had occurred at the beginning of the period is required on a pro forma basis in the notes to the financial statements.

33.   (576,T1,13)   (c)   In a pooling of interest, the balance sheets are simply added together. Only intercompany items such as receivables and payables are eliminated. If the legal capital (capital stock) of the surviving company exceeds or is less than the sum of the legal capitals of the combining companies, an adjustment must be made to paid-in capital and/or retained earnings. If the legal capital of the surviving company exceeds the legal capital of the combining companies, paid-in capital first and then retained earnings is debited to make up this difference. If the legal capital of the surviving company is less than the legal capitals of the combining companies, a credit is required to paid-in capital from pooling. See para 53 of APB 16.

34.   (572,Q2,17)   (c)   The excess of the investee's distribution to the investor over the investor's share of investee net income should be credited to the investment account (under both the cost and equity methods). Thus, the net credit to investment income would be $4,500. In other words, when the investee distributes more than was earned, the excess of distribution over earnings should be considered a reduction in the investment.

35.   (572,Q2,18)   (d)   In this case the investor corporation (under the equity method) would debit the investment account and credit investment income for 40% of the $30,000 earnings or $12,000. Since 40% ownership implies substantial influence, the excess of cost over book value of $10,000 should be amortized against income presumably over a 40 year period, or $250 per year. The entry for amortization would be to debit investment income and credit the investment account for $250. The net effect is $11,750. See paragraph 19B of APB 18. The excess of cost over book value is computed by multiplying 40% times the book value of the investee of $100,000. The resulting book value purchased of $40,000 is $10,000 less than the amount paid.

36.   (572,Q2,19)   (d)   The investment account at the end of the year would be the beginning of the year cost of $50,000 plus $12,000 of income less $250 of amortization, less $13,333 dividends, or $48,417.

37.   (572,Q2,20)   (c)   During 1980 the investor[†] should report 30% of the investee's earnings or $6,000. The investor adopted the equity method for the year 1980. The equity method should also be adopted retroactively for 1979 and the investment account debited and retained earnings credited for the 10% of the undistributed earnings of 1979. See paragraph 19m of APB 18.

38.   (572,Q2,21)   (b)   See the explanation to [†] above. The investment account at the end of 1980 should be the $10,000 cost as of January 1, 1979, plus the $22,000 cost as of January 1, 1980, plus $6,000 of 1980 earnings plus the retroactive adjustment for $1,000 of 1979 earnings.

MAY 1981 ANSWERS

39.   (581,Q1,4)   (d)   The requirement is the balance in the investment account at the end of the year. The solutions approach for this problem would be to prepare the journal entries for the year and then determine the ending account balance. The first entry to record the initial investment at cost.

Investment in common stock	$800,000	
Cash		$800,000

APB 18 states that ownership of 20% or more of the investee's voting stock and presence of the ability to exert significant influence indicates that the equity method should be used. When the equity method is used, the investment account is affected each year by three types of transactions. First, the investment account is increased by the investor's proportionate share of the investee's earnings.

Investment in common stock	$36,000	
Investment income		$36,000

$$36,000 = (20\%)(\$180,000)$$

Second, the investment account is decreased by all dividends received by the investor, since the investment is in effect being converted to cash.

Cash	$ 8,000	
Investment in common stock		$ 8,000

$$8,000 = (20\%)(\$40,000)$$

Finally, the excess of the cost of the investment over the book value of the investment must be amortized. The excess is attributed to an identifiable intangible asset which was undervalued on the investee's books. Therefore, this excess should be amortized over the assets remaining useful life of 10 years.

Investment income	$20,000	
Investment in common stock		$20,000

$200,000 ÷ 10 years = $20,000

This amortization is credited to the income account because income is overstated if the full value of the intangible is not amortized. Therefore, this entry corrects the amount of income from the investment. To determine the final carrying value of the investment, a "T" account should be prepared.

Investment in Common Stock

800,000	8,000	Dividends
NI 36,000	20,000	Amortization
808,000		

40. (581,T1,31) (d) The requirement is the proper value to record for long-term debt that is assumed in a business combination. Per APB 16, para 87, a company that acquires another company shall allocate the purchase price of the acquired company to the assets purchased and liabilities assumed. This allocation should be based on the relative fair market values of the individual assets and liabilities of the acquired company, at the date of acquisition. For a business combination effected as a pooling of interests, APB 16, paras 51 and 52, requires that the combined corporation record the historical cost based (recorded value) amounts of the assets and liabilities of the separate companies since the same ownership interest continues in the aquired company.

41. (581,T1,33) (b) The requirement is the minimum amount of an investee's common stock which must be acquired during the combination period in exchange for the investor's common stock in order to qualify the business' combination as a pooling of interests. Per APB 16, para 47, in order for a business combination to be accounted for as a pooling of interests, a corporation must offer and issue only common stock with rights identical to those of the majority of its outstanding voting common stock in exchange for substantially all of the voting common stock interest of another company. "Substantially all of the voting common stock" means 90 percent or more of the voting common stock of another company that is outstanding at the date the combination is consummated.

ANSWER OUTLINE

Problem 1 Equity Method Accounting

a. Primary criterion is intent of Hawkes' management
    If a marketable security: current asset
        Investment will be liquidated when needed
        Investment made from idle cash
        The investment is of a speculative nature
    If a long-term investment: noncurrent asset
        Held for dividend revenue
        Held for long-term appreciation
        For ownership control purposes
    Other factors to be considered in classifying investments
        Degree of other ownership dispersion
        Daily volume of shares traded
        Stability of market price of stock
    Base decision on evaluation of all criteria

b. The investment accounts and effect thereon are described in outline form in the Unofficial Answer below

c1. Interperiod tax allocation is not required
    If undistributed earnings will not be remitted
        Or remitted in a tax-free liquidation
    Specific plans for reinvestment required past experience

c2. Disclosures required if interperiod taxes are not accrued
    Intention to reinvest undistributed earnings permanently
        Or earnings are to be remitted in a tax-free liquidation
    The amount of undistributed earnings on which taxes are not accrued

c3. Consolidated statements are not appropriate
    Diversified and Hawke are in dissimilar industries

UNOFFICIAL ANSWER

Problem 1 Equity Method Accounting

a. The primary criterion to be considered in ascertaining the appropriate classification of the investment is the intent of Hawkes' management.

If management intends to treat the investment as a marketable security in the current-asset section of the balance sheet, its reasoning should be substantiated by one or more of the following: the invested cash is considered contingency funds, to be liquidated, whenever the need may arise; the investment was made from cash temporarily idle because of the seasonality of the business; or the holding is of a speculative nature and will be liquidated as soon as appropriate.

The investment may be held for long-term purposes indicating that it should be classified as a noncurrent asset in the investments caption because of one or more of the following reasons: the investment is held for dividend revenue; long-term appreciation of the market price of the stock is the motivating factor for holding the investment; or the investment is held for ownership-control purposes.

Although the intent of Hawkes' management is a very important criterion, other criteria should also be considered in ascertaining the appropriate asset classification of the investment. For example, the degree of ownership dispersion of the remaining outstanding shares, average daily volume of shares traded, and the stability or volatility of the market price of the stock should be considered. If the stock is closely held (not publicly traded) there may be no market or a very limited market for the stock, indicating the investment probably should be classified as a noncurrent asset. Similar arguments could be presented indicating appropriate classification of the investment as noncurrent if the stock was traded infrequently in small lots.

Of the criteria discussed above no one criterion would necessarily be determinative, and any one might have varying degrees of significance in different cases. The presence or absence of specific criteria would be cumulative in effect for ascertaining the appropriate asset classification of the investment in Hawkes' balance sheet.

b.

Account Name	Increase or Decrease	Reason for Change in Account Balance
Cash	Increase	Hawkes received $50,000 (25% of $200,000) of dividends paid by Diversified.
Investment in Diversified	Increase	The Investment account should increase by $100,000 (25% of ½ of $800,000) for Hawkes' equity in the reported earnings of Diversified and decrease by $50,000 for dividends received by Diversified, when applying the equity method of accounting for the investee company. Following the guides of APB Opinions, the equity method must be applied unless it can be demonstrated that Hawkes does not have the ability to exercise significant influence over Diversified.
Estimated income taxes payable	Increase	This liability account should increase by the amount of estimated taxes to be paid on the taxable portion of dividends received from Diversified during the accounting period.
Deferred income taxes	Increase (or decrease, depending on its prior balance)	The deferred income taxes account will be credited for an indeterminate amount because only one-half of the earnings of Diversified was paid out as dividends during the fiscal year ended August 31, 1974. The difference between the taxable portion of Hawkes' equity in Diversified's earnings and its share of the taxable portion of Diversified's dividends paid represents a timing difference for income tax purposes.
Retained earnings	Increase	Hawkes' retained earnings will increase by the amount of its equity in the reported earnings of Diversified, less applicable income taxes.
Investment revenue from investee	Increase	Hawkes' equity in Diversified's earnings of the current accounting period, since acquisition, must be included in Hawkes' earnings when accounting for the investment by the equity method.
Income taxes expense	Increase	The appropriate amount of income taxes expense should be estimated and included on Hawkes' earnings statement. The expense computation should be based on the taxable portion of Diversified's earnings recognized by Hawkes. For reporting purposes, that portion of the expense which is payable currently (based on the taxable portion of dividends received) must be disclosed separately from that portion which is deferred (based on the taxable portion of undistributed earnings).

c.   1.   The presumption that a pro rata portion of Diversified's undistributed earnings will be transferred to Hawkes may be overcome, and no income taxes should be accrued by Hawkes, if sufficient evidence shows that Diversified has invested or will invest the undistributed earnings indefinitely or that the earnings will be remitted in a tax-free liquidation.

Hawkes should have evidence of specific plans for reinvestment of Diversified's undistributed earnings which will demonstrate that remittance of the earnings will be postponed indefinitely. Experience of the companies and definite future programs of operations and remittances are examples of types of evidence required to substantiate Hawkes' representation of indefinite postponement of remittances from Diversified.

2. Hawkes should disclose, as a minimum, the following information in notes to its financial statements:

A declaration of an intention to reinvest Diversified's undistributed earnings to support the conclusion that remittance of those earnings has been indefinitely postponed, or a declaration that the undistributed earnings will be remitted in a tax-free liquidation.

The cumulative pro rata amount of Diversified's undistributed earnings on which Hawkes has not recognized income taxes.

3. The nature of Diversified Insurance Company's activities is sufficiently dissimilar to Hawkes' to preclude the preparation of consolidated financial statements. Based on all other facts given it would have been appropriate to consolidate, but because of dissimilar activities consolidated financial statements should not be published. Therefore, Hawkes should include the investment, accounted for by the equity method, in its separate financial statements.

ANSWER OUTLINE

Problem 2 Business Combinations

a.   Supportive arguments for the purchase method

One company usually acquires another
Identities of acquirer and acquiree are usually obvious
One company is usually clearly dominant and others lose control of assets and liabilities
Based on bargaining of independent parties

Parties assess current status and future prospects of individual companies
Agreed terms recognize bargained values

Business acquisitions should be accounted for by recording

1. All assets and liabilities comprising the bargained cost
2. Bargained cost of assets acquired less liabilities assumed
3. Fair value received for stock issued
4. Retained earnings from operations since acquisition
5. Expenses and net income based on bargained costs

b.   Supportive arguments for the pooling method

1. No corporate assets are disbursed
2. Net assets of issuing corporation are enlarged
3. No newly invested capital
4. No assets withdrawn, since stock is not an asset
5. Net assets and stockholder groups remain intact
6. Aggregate income not changed
7. Resources, talents, etc. combined
8. Former investment risk elements are maintained

Thus in substance, an arrangement among stockholder groups and corporations are separate from their stockholders
Pooling was developed within the historical cost system and is compatible therewith

UNOFFICIAL ANSWER

Problem 2   Business Combinations

a.   Those who support the purchase method believe that one company acquires another company in almost every business combination. The acquisition of one company by another and the identities of the acquiring and acquired companies are usually obvious. Generally, one company in a business combination is clearly the dominant and continuing entity and one or more other companies cease to control their own assets and operations because control passes to the acquiring corporation.

Proponents of purchase accounting hold that a business combination is a significant economic event that results from bargaining between independent parties. Each party bargains on the basis of an assessment of the current status and future prospects of each constituent as a separate enterprise and as a contributor to the proposed combined enterprise. The agreed terms of the combination recognize primarily the bargained values and only secondarily the constituent's recorded costs of assets and liabilities.

Those who support the purchase method of accounting for business combinations effected by issuing stock believe that an acquiring corporation accounts for the economic substance of the transaction by applying those principles and by recording

1. All assets and liabilities that compose the bargained cost of an acquired company, not merely those items previously shown in the financial statements of an acquired company.

2. The bargained costs of assets acquired less liabilities assumed, not the costs to a previous owner.

3. The fair value of the consideration received for stock issued, not the equity shown in the financial statements of an acquired company.

4. Retained earnings from the acquiring company's operations, not a fusion of its retained earnings and previous earnings of an acquired company.

5. Expenses and net income after an acquisition computed on the bargained cost of acquired assets less assumed liabilities, not on the costs to a previous owner.

b. Those who support the pooling of interests method believe that a business combination effected by issuing common stock is different from a purchase in that no corporate assets are disbursed to stockholders, and the net assets of the issuing corporation are enlarged by the net assets of the corporation whose stockholders accept common stock of the combined corporation. There is no newly invested capital nor have owners withdrawn assets from the group since the stock of a corporation is not one of its assets. Accordingly, the net assets of the constituents remain intact but combined; the stockholder groups remain intact but combined. Aggregate income is not changed since the total resources are not changed. Consequently, the historical costs and earnings of the separate corporations are appro-

priately combined. In a business combination effected by exchanging stock, groups of stockholders combine their resources, talents, and risks to form a new entity to carry on in combination the previous businesses and to continue their earnings streams. The sharing of risks by the constituent stockholder groups is an important element in a business combination effected by exchanging stock. By pooling equity interests, each group continues to maintain risk elements of its former investment, and they mutually exchange risks and benefits.

A pooling-of-interests transaction is regarded as, in substance, an arrangement among stockholder groups. A fundamental concept of entity accounting is that a corporation is separate and distinct from its stockholders.

Proponents of pooling-of-interests accounting point out that the pooling concept was developed within the boundaries of the historical-cost system and is compatible with it.

ANSWER OUTLINE

Problem 3   Purchase Pooling Criteria

a. Purchase or pooling must be used, i.e., not alternatives
    Purchase method required unless all pooling characteristics met

b. The companies are autonomous
    Have not been subsidiaries within past two years
    The companies are independent, i.e., less than 10% ownership in each other
    Substantially all of Case's common stock is exchanged
    Only voting common is being exchanged
    Substantial means greater than 90% as follows

	100%
Less 5% of Case previously held	−5%
Less 4%* per Case investment in Hanover	−4%
	91%

     * 2% investment converted to equivalent investment by Hanover (2:1 exchange ratio)

c. Additional characteristics required for pooling
1. Combination effected in a single transaction or within one year under a specified plan
2. No change in equity interests within past two years
3. Reacquisitions of common must be per systematic plan I.e., not in contemplation of combination
4. Maintenance of same relative interest by all stock holders
5. No restrictions on common stock exchanged
6. No contingent issuances

The combined corporation cannot agree or intend
1. To reacquire common issued in the combination
2. To enter into other arrangements for benefits of former stockholders
3. To dispose of a significant part of the newly combined company's assets within two years

UNOFFICIAL ANSWER

Problem 3   Purchase Pooling Criteria

a. Both the purchase method and pooling-of-interests method of reporting business combinations are in accordance with generally accepted accounting principles. However, the two methods are not interchangeable and a combination must be accounted for as a purchase unless all of the characteristics of a pooling of interests are present. In order for a business combination to be considered a pooling of interests it must have nine basic characteristics and not have entered into any of the three types of transactions that are inconsistent with a pooling of interests. If any of the characteristics are missing or any transaction that is inconsistent with a pooling of interests has taken place, the business combination must be accounted for as a purchase.

b. Because the information given is incomplete with respect to the business combination of Hanover and Case, a final determination of which accounting method must be used cannot be made. From the information given it can be determined that three of the requisite characteristics have been met for a pooling of interests business combination. The three characteristics disclosed in the facts of the question are as follows:

1. Hanover and Case are autonomous in that neither has been a subsidiary or division of another company within the preceding two years.

2. Each company is independent of the other company in that neither has an investment in the common stock of the other in excess of 10%.

3. Hanover is **exchanging** its common stock for substantially all of the common stock of Case. The Accounting Principles Board has defined "substantially" to mean 90% or greater of the outstanding common stock of the combining company (Case) at the date the plan is consummated. Hanover is to receive 100% of the outstanding common stock of Case, but for purposes of the 90% requirement this amount must be reduced by the amount of Case stock held by Hanover at the date the plan is initiated (5%). Also, the common shares of Hanover owned by Case must be converted to equivalent shares of Case using the exchange rate agreed upon by the terms of the combination and the resultant amount deducted from the amount of Case shares to be received by Hanover. The equivalent percentage of Case common stock is 4% (the 2% of Hanover stock held by Case converted at an exchange rate of one share for two shares). The sum of the two deductions is 9% which results in a 91% exchange of Case stock.

c. In addition to the information given, the following six characteristics and the absence of three types of transactions must be considered in order to make a determination as to which accounting method must be employed in accounting for this combination.

1. The combination must be effected in a single transaction or within one year under a specified plan.

2. Within the preceding two years, and between the dates that a plan of combination was initiated and consummated the equity interests of the voting common stock was not changed in contemplation of the business combination. Changes in contemplation of effecting the combination may include distributions to stockholders and additional issuances, exchanges, and retirements of securities.

3. If either of the combining companies reacquires common stock, the acquisitions must be in accordance with a systematic pattern established over the prior two years (or in accordance with the adoption of a new stock option or compensation plan if less than two years) and not in contemplation of the business combination.

4. The shareholders within each combining company maintain the same relative interest with respect to the other shareholders within the combining company.

5. The common stock of the resulting combined company conveys immediate voting rights with no restrictions upon the shareholders.

6. There are no contingencies as to the number of shares to be issued in exchange for the substantial interest of the combining company after the date the plan of combination is initiated.

Further, the combination must not contain provision for the following three transactions:

1. The combined corporation agrees directly or indirectly to retire or reacquire all or part of the common stock issued to effect the combination.

2. The combined corporation agrees to enter into other financial arrangements for the benefit of the former stockholders of one of the combining companies, such as a guaranty of loans secured by stock issued in the combination, which in effect negates the exchange of equity securities.

3. The combined corporation intends to dispose of a significant part of the assets of the combining companies within two years after the combination other than disposals in the ordinary course of business of the formerly separate companies or to eliminate duplicate facilities or excess capacity.

SOLUTION GUIDE
Alternate Solution follows the Unofficial Answer
Problem 4   Purchase vs. Pooling Worksheet

1. Ace Corporation acquires Blue Corporation at the end of the fiscal year ended August 31, 1974. You are to (1) complete worksheets and (2) determine net income under two different combination assumptions: purchase and pooling. Scan the text of the problem, studying the requirements, and review the accounts and amounts on the worksheet. Next, work through the text of the problem, paragraph by paragraph, taking notes and preparing intermediary solutions.

2.1 The first paragraph gives a general overview of the problem.

2.2 The fair value of the assets and liabilities of Blue are relevant to the purchase assumption. Under the purchase assumption the fair values rather than the book values of Blue will be recorded on the books of Ace.

2.3 If Blue Corporation had accounted for plant rearrangement costs in the same manner as Ace, Blue would have expensed $10,000 rather than $50,000 during fiscal year 1974. Blue also would have $40,000 of deferred plant rearrangement costs on the balance sheet at year-end. For the pooling assumption, the $40,000 of deferred plant rearrangement costs will have to be recorded as an asset with a corresponding credit to retained earnings. For purchase accounting the $40,000 will be recorded as an asset as indicated in 2.2 above.

2.4 The internally generated expenses incurred should not be deferred under either the pooling or purchase assumption. Under purchase accounting direct costs of acquisition of subsidiaries are considered costs of acquisition but not indirect and general expenses. They should be considered an expense of the period of acquisition. See paragraph 76 of APB 16. In pooling accounting, the expenses related to the combination are considered an expense of the period because the pooling method records neither the acquiring of assets nor the obtaining of capital. See paragraph 58 of APB 16.

2.5 The absence of intercompany transactions during the year precludes any possible elimination or adjusting entries at year-end. Note that if intercompany transactions had occurred during the year, adjustments may have been required to the combined income statement for both pooling and purchases. See paragraph 56 of APB 16 and paragraph 6 of ARB 51.

2.6 The shares outstanding and shares authorized data are redundant to the data provided in the worksheet.

3. Under the pooling assumption, the combined income for 1974 would be the sum of the reported income of both Ace and Blue. To this sum add the plant rearrangement expenditures that should have been capitalized and deduct the general expenses that were incorrectly deferred. The explanation of the pooling worksheet entries follows.

3.1 To defer $40,000 of plant rearrangement costs.

3.2 To record the expensing of indirect general expenses which were incorrectly deferred.

3.3 To record the issuance of 500,000 Ace shares for 750,000 Blue shares. This is a compound entry and consists of retiring the treasury stock to be later reissued, eliminating the par value of stock received, recording the stock issued, and making the net adjustment to paid-in capital. In pooling, the distribution of treasury stock requires it to be accounted for as retired. (See paragraph 54 of APB 16). The entry eliminates the cost of the treasury shares, eliminates Blue's paid-in capital, eliminates the par value of Blue's outstanding stock, records the additional issuance of $4,000,000 of Ace stock, and records the credit balance of the entry to Ace's paid-in capital.

4. The net income assuming a purchase combination is the parent's net income for the year less the adjustment for the erroneous deferral of $25,000 of expenses. In a similar vein, the consolidated financial statements at the time of acquisition will only reflect the retained earnings of the parent and not those of the subsidiary. The explanation of the purchase worksheet entries follows:

4.1 To adjust for the incorrect deferral of $25,000 of general and indirect expenses.

4.2 To record the payment of $3,100,000 in cash and issuance of $16,900,000 of debentures at face value as well as recording the fair market value of the assets received and $2,100,000 of liabilities assumed. Note that $4,300,000 of

goodwill or excess of cost over book value arises because $20,000,000 ($16,900,000 plus $3,100,000) was paid for $15,700,000 of net assets.

Alternative Solution

Problem 4   Purchase vs. Pooling Worksheet

The entries shown in the adjustments columns for pooling of interests in the AICPA solution above are "worksheet entries" to give effect to the pooling. The following set of entries are the "ledger entries" that would be made on Ace's books. The debit and credit amounts in these entries would be added to Ace's account balances to get the totals in the Pooling of Interests column. The purchase entries on the worksheet are also the "ledger entries" on Ace's books.

Pooling Entries

(1)	Common stock	$ 1,000,000	
	Paid-in capital in excess of par	250,000	
	Treasury stock (a)		$1,250,000
(2)	Retained earnings	$ 25,000	
	Current assets		25,000
(3)	Current assets	$ 3,000,000	
	Plant & equipment	11,300,000	
	Patents	200,000	
	Plant rearrangement costs	40,000	
	Liabilities		$2,100,000
	Common stock (a)		5,000,000
	Paid-in capital in excess of par		1,950,000
	Retained earnings		5,490,000

(a) This treatment of treasury stock is an acceptable variation. See the AICPA Unofficial Answer on the worksheet.

UNOFFICIAL ANSWER

Problem 4   Purchase vs. Pooling Worksheet

Ace Corporation and Blue Corporation
WORKSHEET FOR POOLING OF INTERESTS AND PURCHASE ACCOUNTING
August 31, 1974

	Ace Corporation	Blue Corporation	Combined	Part a. Adjustments Debit	Part a. Adjustments Credit	Pooling of Interests	Part b. Adjustments Debit	Part b. Adjustments Credit	Purchase
Current assets	$ 4,350,000	$ 3,000,000	$ 7,350,000		$ 25,000(2)	$ 7,325,000	$ 3,400,000(2)	$ 25,000(1) / 3,100,000(2)	$ 4,625,000
Plant and equipment (net)	18,500,000	11,300,000	29,800,000			29,800,000	14,000,000(2)		32,500,000
Patents	450,000	200,000	650,000			650,000	360,000(2)		810,000
Plant rearrangement costs	150,000	—	150,000	$ 40,000(1)		190,000	40,000(2)		190,000
Goodwill	—	—	—			—	4,300,000(2)		4,300,000
	$23,450,000	$14,500,000	$37,950,000			$37,965,000			$42,425,000
Liabilities	$ 2,650,000	$ 2,100,000	$ 4,750,000			$ 4,750,000		16,900,000(2) / 2,100,000(2)	$21,650,000
Common stock $10 par value	12,000,000		12,000,000		4,000,000(3)	16,000,000			12,000,000
Common stock $5 par value		3,750,000	3,750,000	3,750,000(3)					
Paid-in capital in excess of par	4,200,000		4,200,000		1,700,000(3)	5,900,000			4,200,000
Paid-in capital in excess of par		3,200,000	3,200,000	3,200,000(3)					
Retained earnings	5,850,000		5,850,000	25,000(2)		5,825,000	25,000(1)		5,825,000
Retained earnings		5,450,000	5,450,000		40,000(1)	11,315,000			
	24,700,000	14,500,000	39,200,000			37,965,000			43,675,000
Less treasury stock, at cost, 100,000 shares	1,250,000		1,250,000		1,250,000(3)			1,250,000	1,250,000
	$23,450,000	$14,500,000	$37,950,000			$37,965,000			$42,425,000
Net income (no extraordinary items) for fiscal year ended August 31, 1974	$ 2,450,000	$ 1,300,000							

Calculation of Combined Net Income

Blue net income (before adjustment)	$1,300,000	
Add market research capitalized	40,000	
Blue net income		1,340,000
Ace net income (before adjustment)	2,450,000	
Total		3,790,000
Less general expenses		25,000
Combined net income		$3,765,000

Calculation of Net Income

Ace net income	$2,450,000
Less general expenses	25,000
Net income	$2,425,000

ANSWER OUTLINE

Problem 5   Consolidated Balance Sheet

1. Problem 5 requires the completion of a consolidated <u>balance sheet</u> worksheet (which is given) with appropriate supporting schedules.

2. Since this is a balance sheet worksheet, not including the income statement accounts, all entries affecting nominal accounts will be debited or credited to Encanto's retained earnings (consolidated retained earnings). The combined account balances for Encanto and Norris are given to save time adding the individual balances.

3. The solutions approach is to analyze the balance sheets and additional information given to determine the required adjusting and eliminating entries. The detail of the investment in Norris Corporation should be analyzed for correctness. The equity pickup is correct for the mid-year purchase of an additional 30% interest in Norris. Note that Encanto is not using the full equity method of accounting for its investment in Norris. Otherwise, the investment account would reflect amortization of the "excess of cost over book value" and elimination of intercompany profits.

3.1 First, the investment account and subsidiary's stockholders' equity should be eliminated. Ninety percent of Norris' stockholders' equity will be eliminated. Two approaches exist for handling the minority interest. Either extend the balances remaining after eliminating 90% of the stockholders' equity balances to the minority interest column or eliminate 100% of the stockholders' equity and credit minority interest on the line labeled minority interest. The debit to balance the entry is the excess of cost over the book value of net assets acquired. Computation of this excess (at point of purchase) is shown below:

12/31/79 subsidiary stockholders' equity	$252,000
Less 1979 net income	(96,000)
Plus 1979 dividends	40,000
1/1/79 subsidiary stockholders' equity	$196,000
Plus 1979 net income thru Sept. 1 (2/3 x $96,000)	64,000
9/1/79 subsidiary stockholders' equity	$260,000
	x 30%
Net assets acquired (Book value)	78,000
Cost of investment	(92,000)
Excess cost over net assets acquired	$ 14,000

The information given does not indicate the nature of the $14,000. Therefore, it is necessary to assume that the fair values of the identifiable assets and liabilities are equal to their book values and that the excess is goodwill. The entry is presented below:

Common Stock (Norris)	100,000		
Retained Earnings (Norris)	152,000		
Goodwill	14,000		
Investment in Norris Corp.		240,800	
Minority Interest		25,200	

Supporting computations:

Investment Cost	$240,800
Net Assets Acquired [90% x (100,000 + 152,000)]	226,800
Goodwill	$ 14,000
Minority Interest [10% x (100,000 + 152,000)]	$ 25,200

3.2 An entry must be made to amortize the goodwill recorded in Entry 1. The goodwill must be amortized for the 4 months which have elapsed since the Sept. 1 purchase.

Retained earnings (Encanto)	933	
Goodwill		933

Supporting computations:

Goodwill	$14,000
	x 4/60
1979 amortization	$ 933

3.3 The reciprocal accounts from the declaration of dividends must be eliminated:

Dividends payable 36,000

    Dividends receivable   36,000

3.4 The unrealized profit in the ending inventory sold to Norris by Encanto must be eliminated. The remainder of the merchandise sold between affiliates in 1979 has been sold to outsiders. Therefore, no adjustment is necessary for this portion. Since the intercompany sale was "downstream," the entire amount is charged to Encanto's retained earnings (consolidated retained earnings):

Retained earnings
  (Encanto)   7,000
  Inventories   7,000

Supporting computations:

Intercompany sales not resold, at selling price	$35,000
Intercompany sales not resold at cost (÷125%)	28,000
Unrealized profit	$ 7,000

3.5 No entry need be made for the unrealized profit in the beginning inventory since those goods were sold to third parties during the year. Remember this is a balance sheet worksheet, and although cost of sales and beginning retained earnings are overstated, ending retained earnings is correctly stated. The overstatement of retained earnings (caused by the overstatement of gross profit at the end of 1978) no longer exists because the gross profit was realized in 1979.

3.6 The unrealized gain on the intercompany sale of equipment and the related depreciation expense must be eliminated:

Retained Earnings
  (Encanto)   6,000
  Property Plant and
    Equipment   6,000
Accumulated
  Depreciation   150
  Retained Earnings
    (Encanto)   150

Supporting computations:

Sale price of asset	$42,000
Book value of asset	36,000
Encanto's gain (excess cost to be depreciated by Norris)	6,000
	x 1/10
Yearly depreciation	600
	x 3/12
1979 excess depreciation	$ 150

3.7 Norris recorded the $8,000 transfer to Encanto with the following entry:

Accounts Payable   8,000
  Cash   8,000

Since the payment was still in transit at year-end Encanto should make an entry to pick up this cash.

Cash   8,000
  Accounts Receivable   8,000

UNOFFICIAL ANSWER

Problem 5　Consolidated Balance Sheet

ENCANTO CORPORATION AND SUBSIDIARY
CONSOLIDATED BALANCE SHEET WORKSHEET
DECEMBER 31, 1979

ASSETS:	ENCANTO CORPORATION	NORRIS CORPORATION	TOTAL	ADJUSTMENTS AND ELIMINATIONS DEBIT	CREDIT	MINORITY INTEREST	CONSOLIDATED
CASH	$ 167,250	$101,000	$ 268,250	8,000[7]			276,250
ACCOUNTS RECEIVABLE	178,450	72,000	250,450		8,000[7]		242,450
NOTES RECEIVABLE	87,500	28,000	115,500				115,500
DIVIDENDS RECEIVABLE	36,000		36,000		36,000[3]		
INVENTORIES	122,000	68,000	190,000		7,000[4]		183,000
PROPERTY, PLANT AND EQUIPMENT	487,000	252,000	739,000		6,000[5]		733,000
ACCUMULATED DEPRECIATION	(117,000)	(64,000)	(181,000)	150[6]			(180,850)
INVESTMENT IN NORRIS CORP.	240,800		240,800		240,800[1]		
GOODWILL				14,000[1]	933[2]		13,067
TOTAL ASSETS	$1,202,000	$457,000	$1,659,000				1,382,417

LIABILITIES AND STOCKHOLDER'S EQUITY	ENCANTO CORPORATION	NORRIS CORPORATION	TOTAL	ADJUSTMENTS AND ELIMINATIONS DEBIT	CREDIT	MINORITY INTEREST	CONSOLIDATED
ACCOUNTS PAYABLE	$ 222,000	$ 76,000	$ 298,000				298,000
NOTES PAYABLE	79,000	89,000	168,000				168,000
DIVIDENDS PAYABLE		40,000	40,000	36,000[3]			4,000
COMMON STOCK							
ENCANTO CORP.	400,000		400,000				400,000
NORRIS CORP.		100,000	100,000	100,000[1]			
RETAINED EARNINGS							
ENCANTO CORP.	501,000		501,000	7,000[4] 6,000[5] 933[2]	150[6]		487,217
NORRIS CORP.		152,000	152,000	152,000[1]			
MINORITY INTEREST					25,200[1]	25,200	25,200
TOTAL LIABILITIES AND STOCKHOLDER'S EQUITY	$1,202,000	$457,000	$1,659,000				1,382,417

Encanto Corporation and Subsidiary
ADJUSTING AND ELIMINATION ENTRIES
December 31, 1979
(Not Required)

	Debit	*Credit*
(1)		
Goodwill	$ 14,000	
Investment in Norris Corporation		$ 14,000

To reclassify excess of cost
over net assets acquired
$260,000*x30% = $78,000
30% of investment   92,000
               $14,000

(2)		
Retained earnings — Encanto Corporation	933	
Goodwill		933

To record amortization for four
months $14,000 ÷ 60 x 4

(3)		
Common Stock — Norris Corporation	90,000	
Retained earnings — Norris Corporation	136,800	
Investment in Norris Corporation		226,800

To eliminate reciprocal elements in investment and
equity accounts

(4)		
Common Stock — Norris Corporation	10,000	
Retained earnings — Norris Corporation	15,200	
Minority interest in common stock of Norris Corporation		10,000
Minority interest in retained earnings of Norris Corporation		15,200

To record minority interest's
share of common stock and
retained earnings of Norris
Corporation

(5)		
Dividends payable	36,000	
Dividends receivable		36,000

To eliminate Encanto's share
of intercompany dividends
$40,000 x 90%

(6)		
Retained earnings — Encanto Corporation	$7,000	
Inventory — Norris Corporation		$7,000

To eliminate intercompany
profit in ending inventory of Norris
Corporation $35,000 ÷ 125% =
$28,000; $35,000 — $28,000 =
$7,000 profit

(7)		
Accumulated depreciation	150	
Retained earnings — Encanto Corporation	5,850	
Property, plant, and equipment		6,000

To eliminate intercompany gain
and adjust accumulated depreciation on equipment sold by
Encanto to Norris

	Equipment	*Depreciation*
Encanto's book value	$36,000	$ 900
Selling price	42,000	1,050
Excess	($ 6,000)	($ 150)

(8)		
Cash	8,000	
Accounts receivable		8,000

To record payment in transit

*[$100,000 + ($152,000 — 96,000 + 40,000) + 2/3 x 96,000]

SOLUTION GUIDE
Alternate Solution follows the Unofficial Answer
Problem 6   Consolidated Balance sheet

1.   The requirement is a consolidated balance
      sheet as of 12/31/76 for Paul (parent) and
      Sand (subsidiary). Note that P acquired all
      of the stock of S on 6/30/76.

2.   The 12/31/76 balance sheets of P and S are
      presented. Additionally the balance sheet and
      fair value data concerning S's assets and lia-
      bilities at 6/30/76 are presented. Additional
      information is provided concerning the trans-
      actions between date of acquisition (6/30/76)
      and the date of the consolidated balance sheet
      (12/31/76).

3.   The solutions approach is to record the entries
      required on the consolidated books due to the
      acquisition on 6/30/76 and to the subsequent
      transactions. Note that the consolidated books
      are usually the worksheet consolidating the par-
      ent and subsidiary trial balances. The effect of
      these consolidating journal entries is netted with
      the combined year-end balances of P and S to
      determine the consolidated balances. Analyze
      each paragraph of additional information and
      journalize the required entries.

3.1   All the stock of S Company was acquired
      at $19 per share. The entry that was made
      on P's books was a debit to investment and
      a credit to cash for $19,000,000.

3.2   Note that $19,000,000 (1,000,000 shares at
      $19) was paid for $3,000,000 of book value
      (i.e., net assets). Thus the excess of cost over
      book value is $16,000,000.

3.3   The fair values of P,P&E, other assets, and
      long-term debt provide a basis for allocating
      the excess of cost over book value. Increase
      P,P&E from book value of $3,300,000 to its
      fair value of $16,400,000. Decrease other as-
      sets from $500,000 to $200,000. Decrease
      long-term debt from $2,600,000 to $2,200,000.
      Note that this adjustment is made as of the
      date of acquisition. In addition, excess of cost
      over book value (goodwill) should be recorded
      to bring the investment in S's account in reci-
      procity with the subsidiary's shareholders' equity
      accounts. Since $3,000,000 of book value was
      acquired for $19,000,000, a credit of $16,000,000
      is required.

a. Goodwill	$ 2,800,000	
P,P&E	13,100,000	
Long-term debt	400,000	
Other assets		$ 300,000
Investment in S		16,000,000

Due to the changes in the recorded values
of assets and liabilities on the consolidated books,
an adjustment must be made on the consolidated
books to adjust depreciation and amortization.
As given in the problem, there is a $495,000 net
increase in amortization. Since only a consolidated
year-end balance sheet is being prepared, the charge
is directly to retained earnings, i.e., there are no
nominal accounts. The entry to record the amortization is:

b. Retained earnings	$ 495,000	
Other assets	10,000	
P,P&E		$ 500,000
Long-term debt		5,000

3.4   The problem indicates that the goodwill of
      $2,800,000 (computed and recorded above) is to be
      amortized over the maximum allowable period. Per
      APB 17 the maximum allowable period is 40 years.
      Since only 6 months have passed since the acqui-
      sition, only one-half year's amortization will be
      taken (one-half of $2,800,000 ÷ 40) which is
      $35,000.

c. Retained earnings	$ 35,000	
Goodwill		$ 35,000

3.5   Since there were no intercompany receivables or
      payables at the date of acquisition there are no
      related elimination entries.

3.6   At 12/31/76, S's inventory includes $250,000 of
      merchandise purchased from P. The cost of the
      merchandise to P was $150,000. Thus there is
      $100,000 of profit reflected in P's retained earn-
      ings (S's inventory) that has not been realized
      from the consolidated point of view. According-
      ly, an entry must be made to eliminate this un-
      realized profit.

d. Retained earnings	$ 100,000	
Inventory		$ 100,000

Since none of the intercompany inventory sale of $500,000 had been paid by S to P; an intercompany payable-receivable exists. The entry to eliminate this intercompany payable-receivable is

e. A/P $ 500,000
   A/R $ 500,000

3.7 S's income of $1,250,000 from the date of the acquisition (6/30/76) to 12/31/76 is reflected in S's retained earnings. It is also reflected in P's investment in subsidiary account. The composition of the investment in subsidiary account on P's books is $19,000,000 acquisition cost plus S's $1,250,000 of income. This indicates that the $1,250,000 is also included in P's retained earnings. Since $16,000,000 has already been credited to the investment in subsidiary account, the remaining balance of $4,250,000 equals S's shareholder equity at 12/31/76 which indicates reciprocity exists between the parent's investment account and the subsidiary's shareholder equity accounts. Accordingly, the final elimination entry is:

g. Common stock $ 1,000,000
   Paid-in capital   400,000
   Retained earnings   2,850,000
     Investment in S $4,250,000

3.8 The last paragraph of additional information contains the 12/31/76 balance sheets which included information used throughout the problem.

UNOFFICIAL ANSWER

Problem 6   Consolidated Balance Sheet

Paul Corporation and Its Wholly Owned Subsidiary
**CONDENSED CONSOLIDATED
BALANCE SHEET**
December 31, 1976

Assets

Cash *(Schedule 1)*	$ 4,100,000
Accounts receivable (net) *(Schedule 2)*	2,400,000
Inventories *(Schedule 3)*	3,400,000
Property, plant, and equipment (net) *(Schedule 4)*	17,700,000
Other assets *(Schedule 5)*	310,000
Goodwill *(Schedule 6)*	2,765,000
Total assets	$30,675,000

Liabilities and stockholders' equity

Accounts payable and other current liabilities *(Schedule 7)*	$ 2,100,000
Long-term debt *(Schedule 8)*	6,205,000
Other liabilities *(Schedule 9)*	1,000,000
Common stock, par value $1.00 per share *(Schedule 10)*	10,000,000
Additional paid-in capital *(Schedule 11)*	5,000,000
Retained earnings *(Schedule 12)*	6,370,000
Total liabilities and stockholders' equity	$30,675,000

Schedule 1

Computation of Cash

Paul	$3,500,000
Sand	600,000
	$4,100,000

Schedule 2

Computation of Accounts Receivable (Net)

Paul	$1,400,000
Sand	1,500,000
	2,900,000
Intercompany balance	(500,000)
	$2,400,000

Schedule 3

Computation of Inventories

Paul	$1,000,000
Sand	2,500,000
	3,500,000
Intercompany profit ($500,000 — $300,000 $\times$ ½) *(Schedule 12)*	(100,000)
	$3,400,000

Schedule 4

Computation of Property, Plant, and Equipment (Net)

Paul	$ 2,000,000
Sand	3,100,000
	5,100,000
Excess of fair value over book value at date of acquisition (Schedule 6)	13,100,000
Depreciation thereon (Schedule 12)	(500,000)
	$17,700,000

Schedule 5

Computation of Other Assets

Paul	$100,000
Sand	500,000
	600,000
Excess of book value over fair value at date of acquisition (Schedule 6)	(300,000)
Amortization thereon (Schedule 12)	10,000
	$310,000

Schedule 6

Computation of Goodwill

Amount paid at date of acquisition (1,000,000 shares × $19)				$19,000,000
Excess of fair values over book values:				

	Fair Value	Book Value	Excess	
Property, plant, and equipment (net)	$16,400,000	$3,300,000	$13,100,000	(Schedule 4)
Other assets	200,000	500,000	(300,000)	(Schedule 5)
	16,600,000	3,800,000	12,800,000	
Long-term debt	2,200,000	2,600,000	400,000	(Schedule 8)
	$14,400,000	$1,200,000	13,200,000	

Book value of Sand ($1,000, 000 + $400,000 + $1,600,000)		3,000,000
		16,200,000
Unallocated excess of fair value over book value—goodwill		2,800,000
Amortization for six months $\left(\dfrac{\$2,800,000}{40 \text{ years}} \times \frac{1}{2} \right)$ —(Schedule 12)		35,000
		$ 2,765,000

Schedule 7

Computation of Accounts Payable and Other Current Liabilities

Paul	$1,500,000
Sand	1,100,000
	2,600,000
Intercompany balance	(500,000)
	$2,100,000

Schedule 8

Computation of Long-Term Debt

Paul	$4,000,000
Sand	2,600,000
	6,600,000
Excess of book value over fair value at date of acquisition (Schedule 6)	(400,000)
Amortization thereon (Schedule 12)	5,000
	$6,205,000

Schedule 9

Computation of Other Liabilities

Paul	$ 750,000
Sand	250,000
	$1,000,000

Schedule 10

Computation of Common Stock

Paul	$10,000,000
Sand	1,000,000
	11,000,000
Intercompany portion—Sand	(1,000,000)
	$10,000,000

Schedule 11

Computation of Additional Paid-In Capital

Paul	$5,000,000
Sand	400,000
	5,400,000
Intercompany portion—Sand	(400,000)
	$5,000,000

Schedule 12

Computation of Retained Earnings

Paul	$7,000,000
Sand	2,850,000
	9,850,000
Intercompany portion—Sand	(2,850,000)
	7,000,000
Intercompany profit—inventories (Schedule 3)	(100,000)
Depreciation—property, plant, and equipment (net) (Schedule 4)	(500,000)
Amortization—other assets (Schedule 5)	10,000
Amortization—goodwill (Schedule 6)	(35,000)
Amortization—long-term debt (Schedule 8)	(5,000)
	$6,370,000

Alternative solution appears on next page.

Alternative Solution

Problem 6   Consolidated Balance Sheet ·

A "sure fire" alternative to the above solution is to prepare a consolidated work sheet beginning with a column for the combined (Paul and Sand) balance sheet. The combined amounts are obtained by adding the given balances for both companies and writing the totals in the margin of the exam booklet.

PAUL CORPORATION AND SUBSIDIARY
Consolidated Balance Sheet
12/31/76

	Combined Totals	Adjustments Debit	Adjustments Credit	Consolidated Balance Sheet
Cash	$ 4,100,000			$ 4,100,000
Accounts receivable, net	2,900,000		$ 500,000 (e)	2,400,000
Inventories	3,500,000		100,000 (d)	3,400,000
Property, plant, & equipment, net	5,100,000	$13,100,000 (b)	500,000 (c)	17,700,000
Investment in subsidiary at equity	20,250,000		20,250,000 (a)	
Other Assets	600,000	10,000 (c)	300,000 (b)	310,000
	$36,450,000			
Excess of cost over book value		16,000,000 (a)	16,000,000 (b)	
Goodwill		2,800,000 (b)	35,000 (c)	2,765,000
				$30,675,000
Accounts payable	$ 2,600,000	500,000 (e)		$ 2,100,000
Long-term debt	6,600,000	400,000 (b)	5,000 (c)	6,205,000
Other liabilities	1,000,000			1,000,000
Common stock, par value $1 per share	11,000,000	1,000,000 (a)		10,000,000
Additional paid-in capital	5,400,000	400,000 (a)		5,000,000
Retained earnings	9,850,000	2,850,000 (a) 530,000 (c) 100,000 (d)		6,370,000
	$36,450,000	$37,690,000	$37,690,000	$30,675,000

(a) To eliminate the investment in Sand, eliminate Sand's owners equity accounts, and record the excess of cost over book value.

(b) To allocate the excess of cost over book value to specific assets and liabilities.

(c) To record depreciation and amortization of amounts allocated in (b).

(d) To eliminate intercompany inventory profits.

(e) To eliminate accounts receivable and accounts payable.

SOLUTION GUIDE

Problem 7   Consolidated Worksheet

1. The requirement is to complete the consolidated work sheet of Royal Company and its subsidiary, Butler Company, as of December 31, 1975. The income statement is required in the problem, however, if just the Balance Sheet was required, all entries to the nominal (income statement) accounts would be replaced with Retained Earnings.

2. Although not required, the solutions approach is to prepare journal entries for each item of information listed in the problem. Remember the basic steps to consolidation work sheets are first to establish reciprocity between the investment account and the subsidiary shareholder equity accounts and secondly, eliminate these accounts (here there is minority interest because of only 75% ownership at year end). The basic elimination entry is:

    Common stock
    Other paid-in capital
    Retained earnings
        Investment account

3. Since the other information in the problem usually affects the reciprocity of the investment account to subsidiary shareholder equity, one must work through each of items of additional information before being able to make the above elimination entry.

3.1 The investment in Butler Company was overstated by $40,000 (the cost of the separate patent). Thus, the investment account needs to be credited for $40,000 and patents debited. There was no goodwill in the purchase of Butler as 80% of $500,000 book value was purchased for $400,000.

    (a) Patents $40,000
            Investment in Butler $40,000

    The patent should either be expensed in the year it was purchased or amortized over its useful life of four years. See para 11c of SFAS 2. Assuming the patent has alternative future uses, e.g., sale, 1973 and 1974 amortization ($10,000 each year) should be charged to Royal retained earnings, and in 1975 amortization of $10,000 should be charged to Royal's operating expenses.

    (b) Operating Expenses $10,000
        Retained earnings—Royal   20,000
            Patents $30,000

3.2 Upon sale of 5% of Butler's outstanding common stock, only the cost of the stock should be credited to the "investment in Butler" account. Thus, the profit of $16,000 which was credited to the investment account should be taken out of the investment account and credited to gain on sale of stock.

    (c) Investment in Butler $16,000
            Gain on sale of stock $16,000

3.3 When the sale of a partial interest of a subsidiary occurs in midyear, the parent's share of income for the partial year should be recorded prior to sale as it was here. Royal has recognized a total of $232,000 of subsidiary income. The first six month's income was 80% of $140,000 or $112,000, and the second six months' income was $120,000 (subsidiary income of $300,000 minus $140,000 of which 75% is an additional $120,000).

3.4 Beginning inventory on Royal's books was overstated by $12,000 of unrealized profit ($52,000 ÷ 130% = $40,000). At the end of 1974 the adjusting entry was to credit inventory and debit Butler income. As the goods were sold in 1975, the adjusting entry is to credit cost of sales and debit Royal's beginning retained earnings and debit Butler's beginning retained earnings (minority interest) for the percentage ownership in the period of sale. Note: the adjustments required in this problem are on the consolidated books and not on either Butler's or Royal's books, i.e., the adjusting entry at the end of 1974 was not recorded on Butler's books, but rather the consolidated books.

    (d) Retained E.—Royal $9,600
         Retained E.—Butler $2,400
            Cost of Sales $12,000

3.5 Intercompany sales from Royal to Butler in 1975 must be eliminated against the cost of sales for Butler. This elimination avoids overstatement of both sales and cost of sales on the consolidated income statement. The amount of the sales was $80,000 x 1.20 = $96,000.

    (e) Sales $96,000
            Cost of sales $96,000

3.6 Butler's ending inventory is overstated by the unrealized profit in the $24,000 balance. The amount of the unrealized profit is $4,000 ($24,000 ÷ 1.2 = $20,000 cost). The eliminating entry is:

(f) Cost of sales $4,000
         Inventory $4,000

3.7 The payment in transit from Butler Company requires a debit to cash and a credit to accounts receivable.

(g) Cash $45,000
         Accounts Receivable $45,000

3.8 The Butler dividend was incorrectly recorded by Royal Company as it is included in income ($75,000). It should have been credited to the investment account rather than dividend income.

(h) Dividend Income $75,000
         Investment in Butler $75,000

3.9 From the consolidated viewpoint, a liability (on Butler's books) with a net book value of $58,800 ($60,000 face value less $1,200 unamortized discount—the $2,400 applied to $120,000 of bonds) was repurchased (by Royal) for $58,000. Thus a consolidated gain of $800 should be recognized on the consolidated books (with 25% allocation to minority interest). The investment in bonds and bonds payable should be eliminated.

(i) Bonds Payable $60,000
         Unamortized discount $ 1,200
         Bond investment—
           Butler   58,000
         Gain on retirement of bonds   800

4. After all of the adjusting and reconciling items have been taken care of, the elimination entries need to be made.

4.1 The investment account may be adjusted to its beginning of year balance by eliminating the nominal accounts (subsidiary income and intercompany dividends)

(j) Subsidiary income $225,000*
         Dividends—Butler to Royal   75,000
         Investment in Butler common   150,000
     *(75% x $300,000)

4.2 The final eliminating entry is to eliminate the investment account against the subsidiary's shareholder equity accounts

(k) Retained earnings
         1/1/75 Butler $480,000
     Capital stock—Butler   187,500
     Contributed stock—Butler   37,500
         Investment in Butler common   705,000

4.3 Minority interest in Butler's net income is calculated as follows:

a. 25% (year-end minority interest %)
     $300,000   = $75,000
b. 25% ($800—gain on bond
     retirement)   =   200
c. 20%($12,000—gross profit realized
     in 1975 from sales made by Butler
     to Royal in 1974)   =   2,400
              Total MI in 1975   = $77,600

Although $232,000 of subsidiary income was recognized on Royal's books, only $225,000 was eliminated in entry (j). The remaining $7,000 (.05 x $140,000 income for the first six months of 1975) was sold to the minority interest with the sale of the stock thereby increasing the minority interest's share of the income. On the formal consolidated income statement the $7,000 will be included with other income and the full minority interest in income will be deducted.

4.4 Minority interest in Butler is comprised of the following:

a. MI in beginning RE
     25% ($640,000) − $2,400 $157,600
   Add: MI in Butler's
     income $77,600
   Deduct: MI share of
     dividends   (25,000)   52,600
   MI in 12/31/75 R.E. of
     Butler $210,200
   MI in Butler common 25%
     (250,000)   62,500
   MI in Butler contributed
     capital 25%(50,000)   12,500
              Total Minority Interest
                at 12/31/75 $285,200

UNOFFICIAL ANSWER

Problem 7 Consolidated Work Sheet

ROYAL AND BUTLER
WORK SHEET TO PREPARE CONSOLIDATED
STATEMENTS OF INCOME, RETAINED EARNINGS AND BALANCE SHEET

INCOME STATEMENT

	Royal Company Dr. (Cr.)	Butler Company Dr. (Cr.)	Consolidating Totals Dr. (Cr.)	Adjustments and Eliminations Debit	Adjustments and Eliminations Credit	Minority Interest Dr. (Cr.)	Consolidated Dr. (Cr.)
Sales	$(4,000,000)	$(1,700,000)	$(5,700,000)				$(5,604,000)
Cost of Sales	2,982,000	1,015,000	3,977,000	(e) 96,000 (f) 4,000	(d)12,000 (e)96,000		3,893,000
Operating Expenses	400,000	377,200	777,200				787,200
Dividend Income	(75,000)	–	(75,000)	(b) 10,000			(7,000)
Subsidiary Income	(232,000)	–	(232,000)	(h) 75,000 (j)225,000			
Interest Expense	–	7,800	7,800				7,800
Gain on sale of stock					(c)16,000		(16,000)
Gain on retirement of bonds					(i) 800		(800)
Minority interest income						(77,600)	77,600
Net income	$ (925,000)	$ (300,000)	$(1,225,000)				$ (862,200)

RETAINED EARNINGS

	Royal Company Dr. (Cr.)	Butler Company Dr. (Cr.)	Consolidating Totals Dr. (Cr.)	Adjustments and Eliminations Debit	Adjustments and Eliminations Credit	Minority Interest Dr. (Cr.)	Consolidated Dr. (Cr.)
1/1/75 Retained Earnings							
Royal	$(2,100,000)		$(2,100,000)	(d) 9,600 (b) 20,000 (d) 2,400			$(2,070,400)
Butler		$ (640,000)	(640,000)	(k)480,000		(157,600)	
Net income	(925,000)	(300,000)	(1,225,000)				(862,200)
Dividends	170,000	100,000	270,000		(j) 75,000	25,000	170,000
12/31/75 Retained Earnings to Balance Sheet	$(2,855,000)	$ (840,000)	$(3,695,000)				$(2,762,600)

UNOFFICIAL ANSWER

Problem 7 Balance Sheet

	Royal Company Dr. (Cr.)	Butler Company Dr. (Cr.)	Consolidating Totals Dr. (Cr.)	Adjustments and Eliminations Debit	Adjustments and Eliminations Credit	Minority Interest Dr. (Cr.)	Consolidated Dr. (Cr.)
Assets							
Cash	$ 486,000	$ 249,600	$ 735,600	(g) 45,000			$ 780,600
Accounts receivable	235,000	185,000	420,000		(g) 45,000		375,000
Inventories	475,000	355,000	830,000		(f) 4,000		826,000
Machinery and Equipment	2,231,000	530,000	2,761,000				2,761,000
Investments in stock of Butler Company	954,000	–	954,000	(c) 16,000	(a) 40,000 (h) 75,000 (j) 150,000 (k) 705,000		
Investment in bonds of Butler Company	58,000	–	58,000		(i) 58,000		
Patents				(a) 40,000	(b) 30,000		10,000
	$ 4,439,000	$ 1,319,600	$ 5,758,600				$ 4,752,600
Liabilities and Owner's Equity							
Accounts Payable	$ (384,000)	$ (62,000)	$ (446,000)				$ (446,000)
Bonds Payable		(120,000)	(120,000)	(i) 60,000			(60,000)
Unamortized discount on bonds payable		2,400	2,400		(i) 1,200		1,200
Common stock							
Royal Company	(1,200,000)	–	(1,200,000)				(1,200,000)
Butler Company		(250,000)	(250,000)	(k) 187,500		62,500	
Contributed Capital		(50,000)	(50,000)	(k) 37,500		12,500	
Retained earnings (brought forward)	(2,855,000)	(840,000)	(3,695,000)				(2,762,600)
Minority Interest						(285,200)	(285,200)
	$(4,439,000)	$(1,319,600)	$(5,758,600)			$(285,200)	$ 4,752,600

CHAPTER FIVE
COST ACCOUNTING PROBLEMS AND SOLUTIONS

Cost questions appear with regularity on both the practice and theory sections. Review the frequency tables which follow the cost problems index. You can expect a series of multiple choice questions on both practice and theory. Additionally, expect at least one cost essay question and one cost practice problem.

Each question is coded as to month-year, section, problem number and objective question number. For example, (579,T2,27) indicates May 1979, Theory problem 2, and multiple choice question number 27. Note that P = Practice I, Q = Practice II, and T = Theory.

COST PROBLEMS INDEX

	Exam Reference	Number of Minutes	Problem Page No.	Answer Page No.
12. Budgets (Scarborough)	1178,Q4a	25-30	858	880
Sample Practice I Examination		220-270	1013	1068
Sample Practice II Examination		220-270	1025	1071

Note: See Chapter 3, Vol. I for 580,Q5

Frequency Tables of Cost Topics

The following page contains tables that indicate the frequency of cost topics on the examination since May 1977. See page 14 for a complete explanation of the table coding. Explanation of topic abbreviations appears below.

MISC	Miscellaneous
PROCESS	Process Costing
ABS-DIRECT	Absorption/Direct Costing
JOINT & BY-PROD	Joint and By-product Costing
STANDARDS & VARIANCES	Standard Cost and Variances
BUDGETING	Budgeting
RELEVANT COSTS	Relevant Costs
CAPITAL BUDGETING	Capital Budgeting
COST BEHAVIOR & BE	Cost Behavior and Breakeven
QUANT	Quantitative Methods

PRACTICE

	Misc	Process	ABS-Direct	Joint + By-Prod	Standards + Variances	Budgeting	Relevant Costs	Capital Budgeting	Cost Behavior + BE	Quant	Total
5/77		2 MC			2 MC	1 MC	½	4 MC ½	3 MC	6 MC	18 MC
11/77		2 MC	2 MC	1		1 MC	2 MC	4 MC	4 MC	6 MC	21 MC
5/78		2 MC ½	2 MC	2 MC	3 MC ½	1 MC	1 MC	3 MC	1 MC	2 MC	17 MC
11/78		2 MC ½		2 MC	3 MC	1 MC ½	2 MC	3 MC	2 MC	4 MC	19 MC
5/79		2 MC 1		2 MC	2 MC	1 MC	2 MC	5 MC	3 MC	3 MC	20 MC
11/79		2 MC		2 MC	3 MC	2 MC	2 MC	4 MC	3 MC	2 MC 1	20 MC
5/80		2 MC 1		2 MC	3 MC	1 MC	2 MC	4 MC	3 MC	3 MC	20 MC
11/80	½	2 MC ½	1 MC	2 MC	3 MC	1 MC	2 MC	4 MC	2 MC	3 MC	20 MC
5/81	2 MC	2 MC	1 MC	2 MC	4 MC 1	3 MC	1 MC	3 MC	2 MC		20 MC

THEORY

	Misc	Process	ABS-Direct	Joint + By-Prod	Standards + Variances	Budgeting	Relevant Costs	Capital Budgeting	Cost Behavior + BE	Quant	Total
5/77		1 MC		1 MC	3 MC		1 MC	1	1 MC	4 MC	11 MC
11/77	1 MC	2 MC	5 MC	2 MC	1	2 MC	1 MC	2 MC			15 MC
5/78	1 MC	2 MC	3 MC	1 MC	4 MC	2 MC		1 MC	1 MC	2 MC	17 MC
11/78	1 MC	3 MC	3 MC	1 MC	1 MC	1 MC		1 MC	1 MC 1	2 MC	14 MC
5/79	2 MC	3 MC	1 MC	2 MC	4 MC	1 MC	2 MC		2 MC	4 MC	21 MC
11/79	1 MC	1 MC	½	1 MC	½		1 MC		1 MC	4 MC	9 MC
5/80	1 MC 1	1 MC ½		1 MC	1 MC		1 MC	2 MC	1 MC	1 MC	9 MC
11/80		3 MC	1 MC	2 MC	4 MC	1 MC	1 MC	3 MC	2 MC	4 MC	21 MC
5/81	4 MC	2 MC	1 MC	2 MC	1 MC			½	½		10 MC

MULTIPLE CHOICE QUESTIONS (1—48)

1. Which of the following must be known about a production process in order to institute a direct costing system?
   a. The variable and fixed components of all costs related to production.
   b. The controllable and noncontrollable components of all costs related to production.
   c. Standard production rates and times for all elements of production.
   d. Contribution margin and breakeven point for all goods in production.

2. Relative sales value at split-off is used to
   a. Allocate separable costs.
   b. Determine relevant costs.
   c. Determine the breakeven point in sales dollars.
   d. Allocate joint costs.

3. The weighted average method of process costing differs from the first-in, first-out method of process costing in that the weighted average method
   a. Requires that ending work-in-process inventory be stated in terms of equivalent units of production.
   b. Considers the ending work-in-process inventory only partially complete.
   c. Does **not** consider the degree of completion of beginning work-in-process inventory when computing equivalent units of production.
   d. Can be used under any cost-flow assumption.

4. When using the first-in, first-out method of process costing, total equivalent units of production for a given period of time is equal to the number of units
   a. Started into process during the period, plus the number of units in work in process at the beginning of the period.
   b. In work in process at the beginning of the period, plus the number of units started during the period, plus the number of units remaining in work in process at the end of the period times the percent of work necessary to complete the items.
   c. In work in process at the beginning of the period times the percent of work necessary to complete the items, plus the number of units started during the period, less the number of units remaining in work in process at the end of the period times the per-

cent of work necessary to complete the items.
   d. Transferred out during the period, plus the number of units remaining in work in process at the end of the period times the percent of work necessary to complete the items.

5. Jonathan Company manufactures products N, P, and R from a joint process. The following information is available:

	N	P	R	Total
Units produced	6,000	?	?	12,000
Sales value at split-off	?	?	$25,000	$100,000
Joint costs	$24,000	?	?	$ 60,000
Sales value if processed further	$55,000	$45,000	$30,000	$130,000
Additional costs if processed further	$ 9,000	$ 7,000	$ 5,000	$ 21,000

Assuming that joint product costs are allocated using the relative-sales-value at split-off approach, what was the sales value at split-off for product N?
   a. $33,000
   b. $40,000
   c. $46,000
   d. $50,000

6. Sussex Corporation's production cycle starts in the Mixing Department. The following information is available for the month of April 1980:

	Units
Work-in-process, April 1 (50% complete)	40,000
Started in April	240,000
Work-in-process, April 30 (60% complete)	25,000

Materials are added in the beginning of the process in the Mixing Department. Using the weighted-average method, what are the equivalent units of production for the month of April 1980?

	Materials	Conversion
a.	240,000	250,000
b.	255,000	255,000
c.	270,000	280,000
d.	280,000	270,000

7. Ohio Corporation manufactures liquid chemicals A and B from a joint process. Joint costs are allocated on the basis of relative-sales-value at split-off. It costs $4,560 to process 500 gallons of product A and 1,000 gallons of product B to the split-off point. The sales value at split-off is $10 per gallon for product A and $14 for product B. Product B requires an additional process beyond split-off at a cost of $1 per gallon before it can be sold. What is Ohio's cost to produce 1,000 gallons of product B?

    a. $3,360
    b. $3,660
    c. $4,040
    d. $4,360

8. The Cutting Department is the first stage of Mark Company's production cycle. Conversion costs for this department were 80% complete as to the beginning work-in-process and 50% complete as to the ending work-in-process. Information as to conversion costs in the Cutting Department for January 1980 is as follows:

	Units	Conversion costs
Work-in-process at January 1, 1980	25,000	$ 22,000
Units started and costs incurred during January	135,000	$143,000
Units completed and transferred to next department during January	100,000	

Using the FIFO method, what was the conversion cost of the work-in-process in the Cutting Department at January 31, 1980?

    a. $33,000
    b. $38,100
    c. $39,000
    d. $45,000

9. Indiana Corporation began its operations on January 1, 1979, and produces a single product that sells for $9.00 per unit. Indiana uses an actual (historical) cost system. 100,000 units were produced and 90,000 units were sold in 1979. There was no work-in-process inventory at December 31, 1979.

Manufacturing costs and selling and administrative expenses for 1979 were as follows:

	Fixed costs	Variable costs
Raw materials	–	$1.75 per unit produced
Direct labor	–	1.25 per unit produced
Factory overhead	$100,000	.50 per unit produced
Selling and administrative	70,000	.60 per unit sold

What would be Indiana's operating income for 1979 using the direct-costing method?

    a. $181,000
    b. $271,000
    c. $281,000
    d. $371,000

10. Stellar Corporation manufactures products R and S from a joint process. Additional information is as follows:

	Product		
	R	S	Total
Units produced	4,000	6,000	10,000
Joint costs	$36,000	$ 54,000	$ 90,000
Sales value at split-off	?	?	?
Additional costs if processed further	$ 3,000	$ 26,000	$ 29,000
Sales value if processed further	$63,000	$126,000	$189,000
Additional margin if processed further	$12,000	?	$ 40,000

Assuming that joint costs are allocated on the basis of relative-sales-value at split-off, what was the sales value at split-off for product S?

    a. $ 72,000
    b. $ 82,000
    c. $ 98,000
    d. $100,000

11. Milton, Inc., had 8,000 units of work in process in its Department M on March 1, 1980, which were 50% complete as to conversion costs. Materials are introduced at the beginning of the process. During March 17,000 units were started, 18,000 units were completed and there were 2,000 units of normal spoilage. Milton had 5,000 units of work in process at March 31, 1980, which were 60% complete as to conversion costs. Under Milton's cost accounting system, spoiled units reduce the number of units over which total cost can

be spread. Using the weighted-average method, the equivalent units for March for conversion costs were

    a.   17,000.
    b.   19,000.
    c.   21,000.
    d.   23,000.

12.   Roy Company manufactures product X in a two-stage production cycle in Departments A and B. Materials are added at the beginning of the process in Department B. Roy uses the weighted-average method. Conversion costs for Department B were 50% complete as to the 6,000 units in the beginning work in process and 75% complete as to the 8,000 units in the ending work in process. 12,000 units were completed and transferred out of Department B during February 1980. An analysis of the costs relating to work in process (WIP) and production activity in Department B for February 1980 is as follows:

	Costs		
	Trans-ferred In	Materials	Conversion
WIP, February 1: Costs attached	$12,000	$2,500	$1,000
February activity: Costs added	29,000	5,500	5,000

The total cost per equivalent unit transferred out for February 1980 of product X, rounded to the nearest penny, was

    a. $2.75.
    b. $2.78.
    c. $2.82.
    d. $2.85.

13.   In job order costing, the basic document to accumulate the cost of each order is the

    a.   Invoice.
    b.   Purchase order.
    c.   Requisition sheet.
    d.   Job cost sheet.

14.   Maurice Company adds materials at the beginning of the process in the Forming Department, which is the first of two stages of its production cycle. Information concerning the materials used in the Forming Department in April 1979 is as follows:

	Units	Materials Costs
Work in process at April 1, 1979	12,000	$ 6,000
Units started during April	100,000	$51,120
Units completed and transferred to next department during April	88,000	

Using the weighted-average method, what was the materials cost of the work in process at April 30, 1979?

    a. $ 6,120
    b. $11,040
    c. $12,000
    d. $12,240

15.   Walton, Incorporated, had 8,000 units of work in process in Department A on October 1, 1978. These units were 60% complete as to conversion costs. Materials are added in the beginning of the process. During the month of October, 34,000 units were started and 36,000 units completed. Walton had 6,000 units of work in process on October 31, 1978. These units were 80% complete as to conversion costs. By how much did the equivalent units for the month of October using the weighted-average method exceed the equivalent units for the month of October using the first-in, first-out method?

	Materials	Conversion Costs
a.	0	3,200
b.	0	4,800
c.	8,000	3,200
d.	8,000	4,800

16.   In a process costing system that assumes that normal spoilage occurs at the end of a process, the cost attributable to normal spoilage should be assigned to

    a.   Ending work-in-process inventory.
    b.   Cost of goods manufactured and ending work-in-process inventory in the ratio of units worked on during the period to units remaining in work-in-process inventory.
    c.   Cost of goods manufactured (transferred out).
    d.   A separate loss account in order to highlight production inefficiencies.

17. Under which of the following conditions will the first-in, first-out method of process costing produce the same cost of goods manufactured amount as the weighted-average method?
   - a. When goods produced are homogenous in nature.
   - b. When there is no beginning inventory.
   - c. When there is no ending inventory.
   - d. When beginning and ending inventories are each fifty percent complete.

18. A basic tenet of direct costing is that period costs should be currently expensed. What is the basic rationale behind this procedure?
   - a. Period costs are uncontrollable and should not be charged to a specific product.
   - b. Period costs are generally immaterial in amount and the cost of assigning the amounts to specific products would outweigh the benefits.
   - c. Allocation of period costs is arbitrary at best and could lead to erroneous decisions by management.
   - d. Period costs will occur whether or not production occurs and so it is improper to allocate these costs to production and defer a current cost of doing business.

19. Information for the month of May concerning Department A, the first stage of Wit Corporation's production cycle, is as follows:

	Materials	Conversion Costs
Work in process, beginning	$ 4,000	$ 3,000
Current costs	20,000	16,000
Total costs	$24,000	$19,000
Equivalent units based on weighted-average method	100,000	95,000
Average unit costs	$ 0.24	$ 0.20
Goods completed	90,000 units	
Work in process, end	10,000 units	

Material costs are added at the beginning of the process. The ending work in process is 50% complete as to conversion costs. How would the total costs accounted for be distributed, using the weighted-average method?

	Goods Completed	Work in Process, End
a.	$39,600	$3,400
b.	$39,600	$4,400
c.	$43,000	$ 0
d.	$44,000	$3,400

20. The Wiring Department is the second stage of Flem Company's production cycle. On May 1, the beginning work in process contained 25,000 units which were 60% complete as to conversion costs. During May, 100,000 units were transferred in from the first stage of Flem's production cycle. On May 31, the ending work in process contained 20,000 units which were 80% complete as to conversion costs. Material costs are added at the end of the process. Using the weighted-average method, the equivalent units were

	Transferred-in costs	Materials	Conversion costs
a.	100,000	125,000	100,000
b.	125,000	105,000	105,000
c.	125,000	105,000	121,000
d.	125,000	125,000	121,000

21. In job order costing, payroll taxes paid by the employer for factory employees are preferably accounted for as
   - a. Direct labor.
   - b. Factory overhead.
   - c. Indirect labor.
   - d. Administrative costs.

22. Which of the following components of production are allocable as joint costs when a single manufacturing process produces several salable products?
   - a. Materials, labor, overhead.
   - b. Materials and labor only.
   - c. Labor and overhead only.
   - d. Overhead and materials only.

Items 23. and 24. are based on the following information:

Vreeland, Inc., manufactures products X, Y, and Z from a joint process. Joint product costs were $60,000. Additional information is as follows:

| | | Sales | | Sales Values and Additional Costs if Processed Further | |
Product	Units Produced	Value at Split-off	Sales Values	Additional Costs
X	6,000	$40,000	$55,000	$9,000
Y	4,000	35,000	45,000	7,000
Z	2,000	25,000	30,000	5,000

23. Assuming that joint production costs are allocated using the physical measures (units produced) approach, what were the total costs allocated to Product X?
  a. $27,000.
  b. $29,000.
  c. $33,000.
  d. $39,000.

24. Assuming that joint product costs are allocated using the relative-sales-value at split-off approach, what were the total costs allocated to Product Y?
  a. $27,000.
  b. $28,000.
  c. $28,350.
  d. $32,200.

25. Net earnings determined using full absorption costing can be reconciled to net earnings determined using direct costing by computing the difference between
  a. Inventoried fixed costs in the beginning and ending inventories and any deferred over or underapplied fixed factory overhead.
  b. Inventoried discretionary costs in the beginning and ending inventories.
  c. Gross margin (absorption costing method) and contribution margin (direct costing method).
  d. Sales as recorded under the direct costing method and sales as recorded under the absorption costing method.

26. An error was made in the computation of the percentage-of-completion of the current year's ending work-in-process inventory. The error resulted in assigning a lower percentage-of-completion to each component of the inventory than actually was the case. What is the resultant effect of this error upon:
  1. The computation of equivalent units in total?
  2. The computation of costs per equivalent unit?
  3. Costs assigned to cost of goods completed for the period?

		1	2	3
a.	Understate	overstate	overstate.
b.	Understate	understate	overstate.
c.	Overstate	understate	understate.
d.	Overstate	overstate	understate.

27. Which of the following production operations would be most likely to employ a job order system of cost accounting?
  a. Toy manufacturing.
  b. Shipbuilding.
  c. Crude oil refining.
  d. Candy manufacturing.

28. When two products are produced during a common process, what is the factor that determines whether the products are joint products or one principal product and a by-product?
  a. Potential marketability for each product.
  b. Amount of work expended in the production of each product.
  c. Relative total sales value.
  d. Management policy.

29. JV Company began its operations on January 1, 1977, and produces a single product that sells for $7.00 per unit. Standard capacity is 100,000 units per year. 100,000 units were produced and 80,000 units were sold in 1977.

Manufacturing costs and selling and administrative expenses were as follows:

	Fixed Costs	Variable Costs
Raw materials	—	$1.50 per unit produced
Direct labor	—	1.00 per unit produced
Factory overhead	$150,000	.50 per unit produced
Selling and administrative	80,000	.50 per unit sold

There were no variances from the standard variable costs. Any under- or over-applied overhead is written off directly at year end as an adjustment to cost of goods sold.

What is the net income in 1977 under direct costing?
  a. $50,000.
  b. $80,000.
  c. $90,000.
  d. $120,000.

30. What is the basic difference between direct costing and absorption costing?
    a. Direct costing always produces less taxable earnings than absorption costing.
    b. Direct costing recognizes fixed costs as a period cost and absorption costing recognizes fixed costs as a product cost.
    c. Direct costing cannot use standards, whereas standards may be used with absorption costing.
    d. Direct costing may be used only in situations where production is essentially homogeneous but absorption costing may be used under any manufacturing condition.

31. An equivalent unit of material or conversion cost is equal to
    a. The amount of material or conversion cost necessary to complete one unit of production.
    b. A unit of work-in-process inventory.
    c. The amount of material or conversion cost necessary to start a unit of production into work in process.
    d. Fifty percent of the material or conversion cost of a unit of finished goods inventory (assuming a linear production pattern).

32. If two or more products share a common process before they are separated, the joint costs should be allocated in a manner that
    a. Assigns a proportionate amount of the total cost to each product by means of a quantitative basis.
    b. Maximizes total earnings.
    c. Minimizes variations in a unit of production cost.
    d. Does not introduce an element of estimation into the process of accumulating costs for each product.

33. Which of the following would not be used in job-order costing?
    a. Standards.
    b. Averaging of direct labor and material rates.
    c. Direct costing.
    d. Factory overhead allocation based on direct labor hours applied to the job.

MAY 1981 QUESTIONS

34. During January 1981 Gable, Inc., produced 10,000 units of product F with costs as follows:

Direct materials	$40,000
Direct labor	22,000
Variable overhead	13,000
Fixed overhead	10,000
	$85,000

What is Gable's unit cost of product F for January 1981 calculated on the direct costing basis?
    a. $6.20.
    b. $7.20.
    c. $7.50.
    d. $8.50.

35. Information concerning department A of Stover Company for the month of June is as follows:

	Units	Materials costs
Work-in-process, beginning	17,000	$12,800
Started in June	82,000	69,700
Units completed	85,000	
Work-in-process, end	14,000	

All materials are added at the beginning of the process. Using the weighted-average method, the cost per equivalent unit for materials costs is
    a. $0.83.
    b. $0.85.
    c. $0.97.
    d. $1.01.

36. Department One is the first stage of Drucker Company's production cycle. The following information is available for conversion costs for the month of April:

	Units
Work-in-process, beginning (40% complete)	40,000
Started in April	320,000
Completed in April and transferred to department Two	340,000
Work-in-process, end (60% complete)	20,000

Using the FIFO method, the equivalent units for the conversion cost calculation are
    a. 320,000.
    b. 336,000.
    c. 352,000.
    d. 360,000.

37.   Stayman, Inc., manufactures products F, G, and H from a joint process.

Additional information is as follows:

| | *Product* | | | |
	F	G	H	*Total*
Units produced	8,000	4,000	2,000	14,000
Joint cost	?	?	$18,000	$120,000
Sales value at split-off	$120,000	?	?	$200,000
Additional costs if processed further	$ 14,000	$10,000	$ 6,000	$ 30,000
Sales value if processed further	$140,000	$60,000	$50,000	$250,000

Assuming that joint product costs are allocated using the relative-sales-value at split-off approach, what were the joint costs allocated to product G?

a. $28,800.
b. $30,000.
c. $34,000.
d. $51,000.

38.   Tillman Corporation uses a job-order cost system and has two production departments, M and A. Budgeted manufacturing costs for 1980 are as follows:

	Department M	Department A
Direct materials	$700,000	$100,000
Direct labor	200,000	800,000
Manufacturing overhead	600,000	400,000

The actual material and labor costs charged to Job No. 432 during 1980 were as follows:

Direct material		25,000
Direct labor:		
Department M	$ 8,000	
Department A	12,000	20,000

Tillman applies manufacturing overhead to production orders on the basis of direct-labor cost using departmental rates predetermined at the beginning of the year based on the annual budget. The total manufacturing cost associated with Job No. 432 for 1980 should be

a. $50,000.
b. $55,000.
c. $65,000.
d. $75,000.

39.   Stowe, Inc., produces two joint products, PEL and VEL. The joint production costs for March 1981 were $15,000. During March 1981 further processing costs beyond the split-off point, needed to convert the products into salable form, were $8,000 and $12,000 for 800 units of PEL and 400 units of VEL, respectively. PEL sells for $25 per unit and VEL sells for $50 per unit. Assuming that Stowe uses the net realizable value method for allocating joint product costs, what were the joint costs allocated to product PEL for March 1981?

a. $ 5,000.
b. $ 6,000.
c. $ 9,000.
d. $10,000.

40.   Janis Manufacturing Company recorded the following data pertaining to raw material X:

| | *Units* | | | |
Date	Received	Cost	Issued	On hand
1/1/80 Inventory		$1.00		400
1/8/80 Purchase	600	$1.10		1,000
1/12/80 Issued			800	200

The weighted average unit cost of raw material X at January 12, 1980, is

a. $1.00.
b. $1.05.
c. $1.06.
d. $1.10.

41.   For a manufacturing company, which of the following is an example of a period rather than a product cost?

a.   Depreciation on factory equipment.
b.   Wages of salespersons.
c.   Wages of machine operators.
d.   Insurance on factory equipment.

42.   In order to identify costs that relate to a specific product, an allocation base should be chosen that

a.   Does **not** have a cause and effect relationship.
b.   Has a cause and effect relationship.
c.   Considers variable costs but **not** fixed costs.
d.   Considers direct materials and direct labor but **not** factory overhead.

43. What is the best cost accumulation procedure to use when many batches, each differing as to product specifications, are produced?
   a. Job order.
   b. Process.
   c. Actual.
   d. Standard.

44. In the computation of manufacturing cost per equivalent unit, the weighted-average method of process costing considers
   a. Currect costs only.
   b. Current costs plus cost of beginning work in process inventory.
   c. Current costs plus cost of ending work in process inventory.
   d. Current costs less cost of beginning work in process inventory.

45. The units transferred in from the first department to the second department should be included in the computation of the equivalent units for the second department for which of the following methods of process costing?

	First-in first-out	Weighted-average
a.	Yes	Yes
b.	Yes	No
c.	No	Yes
d.	No	No

46. What factor, related to manufacturing costs, causes the difference in net earnings computed using absorption costing and net earnings computed using direct costing?
   a. Absorption costing considers all costs in the determination of net earnings, whereas direct costing considers only direct costs.
   b. Absorption costing allocates fixed costs between cost of goods sold and inventories, and direct costing considers all fixed costs to be period costs.
   c. Absorption costing "inventories" all direct costs, but direct costing considers direct cost to be period costs.
   d. Absorption costing "inventories" all fixed costs for the period in ending finished goods inventory, but direct costing expenses all fixed costs.

47. Joint costs are most frequently allocated based upon relative
   a. Profitability.
   b. Conversion costs.
   c. Prime costs.
   d. Sales value.

48. Under an acceptable method of costing by-products, inventory costs of the by-product are based on the portion of the joint production cost allocated to the by-product
   a. But any subsequent processing cost is debited to the cost of the main product.
   b. But any subsequent processing cost is debited to revenue of the main product.
   c. Plus any subsequent processing cost.
   d. Less any subsequent processing cost.

MULTIPLE CHOICE ANSWERS

1. a	12. b	23. d	34. c	45. a
2. d	13. d	24. b	35. a	46. b
3. c	14. d	25. a	36. b	47. d
4. c	15. d	26. a	37. b	48. c
5. b	16. c	27. b	38. d	
6. d	17. b	28. c	39. c	
7. d	18. d	29. a	40. c	
8. c	19. a	30. b	41. b	
9. b	20. c	31. a	42. b	
10. a	21. b	32. a	43. a	
11. c	22. a	33. b	44. b	

EXPLANATION OF MULTIPLE CHOICE ANSWERS

1. (1180,T1,31)   (a)   Direct costing considers all fixed production costs as period costs rather than product costs. Only variable production costs are product costs. Therefore, if a direct costing system is to be instituted, the variable and fixed components of all productions costs must be known.

2. (1180,T1,39)   (d)   Relative sales value at split-off is used to allocate joint costs of products produced together from one process. Common costs incurred up to the split-off point are usually allocated based on the relative sales value. Separable costs [answer (a)], is a term that is not normally used to define a category of costs. Relevant costs [answer (b)] are expected future costs that differ across alternatives. The breakeven point in sales [answer (c)] is determined by fixed expenses, variable expenses and sales.

3. (1180,T1,43)   (c)   The weighted average method of process costing differs from the FIFO method of process costing in that the weighted average method does not consider the degree of completion of beginning work-in-process inventory when computing equivalent units of production. This is true because FIFO keeps separate all costs incurred last period (beginning (WIP) and costs incurred this period. Weighted average, in effect, assumes beginning WIP costs were incurred this year; all costs are lumped together. Both FIFO and weighted average consider the ending WIP only partially complete [answer (b), requires that it be stated in terms of equivalent production [answer (a)] and are cost flow assumptions [answer (d)].

4. (1180,T1,44)   (c)   When using the FIFO method of process costing, equivalent units of production for a period includes only the work actually done that period and excludes any work done in a prior period. Therefore, the work done on beginning WIP is not included, but the percent of work necessary to complete beginning WIP is included. If the units started during the period are added, the work necessary to complete the beginning inventory, the percent of work necessary to complete ending WIP must be subtracted since that work will be done next period. In summary, equivalent units of production under FIFO includes work done this year:

1. to complete beginning WIP
2. on units started (units started less work to complete ending WIP).

Answer (a) is incorrect because total units in beginning WIP are included, instead of equivalent units to complete beginning WIP, and ending WIP is ignored. Answer (b) is incorrect also because total units in beginning WIP are included and ending WIP is added rather than subtracted. Answer (c) also includes total beginning WIP and adds rather than subtracts ending WIP.

5. (1180,P2,24)   (b)   The requirement is the sales value at split-off for product N, which results along with products P and R from a joint process. Product N was allocated $24,000 of the $60,000 joint costs (or 40%) based on relative sales value at split-off. Therefore, the sales value at split-off for product N is 40% of total sales value at split-off ($100,000), or $40,000.

6. (1180,P2,28)   (d)   The requirement is the equivalent units of production using the weighted average method. Equivalent units under the weighted average method, is equal to units completed plus equivalent units in ending work-in-process.

Beginning WIP	40,000
Units started	240,000
Units to account for	280,000
Less ending WIP	(25,000)
Units completed	255,000

Next the equivalent units of production can be computed:

	Materials	Conversion
Units completed	255,000	255,000
EU in ending WIP	25,000[1]	15,000[2]
Equivalent units	280,000	270,000

[1]Materials added at beginning of process; 100% complete

[2](25,000)(60% complete)

7. (1180,P2,32)   (d)   The requirement is Ohio's cost to produce 1,000 gallons of product B, one of two products resulting from a joint manufacturing process. The cost will include any joint cost allocated to product B, plus the additional processing cost of $1 per

gallon. The joint cost of $4,560 is allocated based on relative sales value at split-off:

	Product A	Product B	Total
Units produced	500	1,000	
Sales value at split-off/unit	$ 10	$ 14	
Total sales value at split-off	$5,000	$14,000	$19,000

The joint costs to be allocated to Product B are ($14,000/$19,000)($4,560), or $3,360. Total cost of Product B, then is $3,360 + (1,000 units)($1), or $4,360.

8. (1180,P2,33)   (c)   The requirement is the conversion cost of the ending work-in-process inventory using the FIFO method. The number of units in ending work-in-process must be computed:

Work-in-Process			
BWIP	25,000	100,000	Units completed
Units started	135,000	?	EWIP
Units to account for	160,000	160,000	Units accounted for

EWIP = 160,000 units to account for − 100,000 units completed = 60,000 units.

The next step is to compute equivalent units of production under the FIFO method:

Units completed	100,000
EU in ending WIP (60,000)(50%)	30,000
	130,000
EU in beginning WIP (25,000)(80%)	(20,000)
EU of production	110,000

Conversion cost per unit for the current period is $143,000/110,000 or $1.30 per equivalent unit. With the FIFO method, the beginning WIP is assumed to be completed during the period; therefore the ending inventory consists solely of current period costs. The cost of the ending WIP is the equivalent units in ending WIP times the conversion cost/unit of $1.30:

$$(30,000)($1.30) = $39,000$$

9. (1180,P2,37)   (b)   The requirement is Indiana's operating income using the direct-costing method. Remember, in the direct costing method only variable manufacturing costs are inventoriable; all fixed costs are assumed to be period costs. This problem is simplified by the fact that Indiana had no beginning inventory on January 1 when it began operations. The solutions approach is to construct a mini-income statement,

remembering to expense all fixed costs:

Sales (90,000 x $9)	$810,000
Variable Costs (90,000 x $4.10)	369,000
Contribution Margin	441,000
Fixed Costs	170,000
Operating Income	$271,000

10.   (580,P2,28)   (a)   The solutions approach is to subtract the total additional costs of processing and the total additional margin from the total sales value (if processed further) to yield the total sales value at split-off. The sales value at split-off for Product R is obtained in the same manner. Then the sales value at split-off for Product R is subtracted from the total sales value at split-off to yield Product S's sales value at split-off.

Total sales value at split-off
    $189,000 − ($40,000 + $29,000) = $120,000
Sales value of Product R at split-off
    $63,000 − ($12,000 + $3,000) = $48,000

Sales value of Product S at split-off $72,000

11.   (580,P2,32)   (c)   The requirement is for the number of equivalent units for conversion cost. Milton is using the weighted average process cost system. The cost of normal spoilage is spread over good units. The solutions approach is to compute the equivalent units of good work which under the weighted average method includes work from last period in the beginning inventory.

Work in Process—Dept. M			
BWIP (conv. 50%)	8,000		
Started	17,000	18,000	Completed
		2,000	Spoilage
EWIP (conv. 60%)	5,000		

Equivalent units:	
Completed and transferred	18,000
EWIP (5,000 @ 60%)	3,000
Equivalent units	21,000

12.   (580,P2,33)   (b)   Since Roy Company is using a weighted-average method, the solutions approach is to commingle the transferred-in cost, material costs and conversion costs in the beginning inventory with

their counterparts for costs added in February. The next step is to compute the equivalent units for the transferred-in, materials, and conversion elements. Finally, dividing the total costs of the beginning inventory and costs added in the period for each element by the equivalent units for the corresponding element gives the unit cost for each of the elements.

Department B

BWIP,				
(conv. 50%)	6,000	12,000	Completed &	
Transferred in			transferred	
(not needed)	?	8,000	EWIP (conv. 75%)	

Department B Product X Equivalent Units:

	Trans-ferred in	Materials	Conversion
Units comp. and transf.	12,000	12,000	12,000
EWIP (conv. 75%)	8,000	8,000	6,000
EUP	20,000	20,000	18,000

Cost per Equivalent Unit:

BWIP	$12,000	$2,500	$1,000
Costs added in Feb.	29,000	5,500	5,000
	$41,000	$8,000	$6,000
Cost per EUP	$2.05	$0.40	$0.33
		$2.78	

13. (580,T1,42) (d) The basic document used to accumulate product costs is the job cost sheet. Requisition sheets are employed to charge job cost sheets for direct materials used. Purchase orders and invoices are concerned with control over the quantity, quality, and price of materials purchased.

14. (1179,P2,33) (d) The requirement is the material cost in work-in-process at the end of April using the weighted average method of determining equivalent units of production (EUP). A T-account analysis of the Forming Department is presented below. Under the weighted average method (in contrast to FIFO), no distinction is made between goods started last period and completed this period, and goods started this period and completed this period. Accordingly, the material EUP is 112,000 units (12,000 BWIP and 100,000 added this period). The total cost of materials is $57,120 ($51,120 + $6,000). The resulting cost per EUP is $.51. The 24,000 units of material in ending work-in-process times the unit cost of $.51 is $12,240.

Forming Department

BWIP	12,000	To FG	88,000
Units added	100,000	EWIP	24,000
	112,000		112,000

$57,120 ÷ 112,000 EUP = $.51
24,000 EUP x $.51 = $12,240

15. (1178,P2,32) (d) The requirement is the excess of weighted average EUP over FIFO EUP for both material and conversion. The solutions approach is to do a T-account analysis of the manufacturing account as illustrated below. All the material is added at the beginning of the process. Beginning work-in-process of 8,000 units is 60% complete; 34,000 units are added, 36,000 are finished; and ending work-in-process of 6,000 units is 80% complete as to conversion.

The material EUP per the weighted average method is 42,000 (8,000 + 34,000). The material EUP per FIFO is 34,000, i.e., only the units added this period are included. Thus, the weighted average EUP for material exceeds that per FIFO by 8,000 EUP.

The conversion EUP per the weighted average method is 40,800 EUP which is 8,000 units in beginning work-in-process plus the 34,000 units transferred in less 1,200 EUP of work not done with respect to EWIP. The conversion EUP per FIFO is the work left to be done in BWIP of 3,200 EUP (40% of 8,000) plus the 34,000 units transferred in, less 1,200 EUP work not done in EWIP (6,000 times 20%). Thus the weighted average conversion EUP of 40,800 exceeds the FIFO conversion EUP of 36,000 by 4,800.

Manufacturing Account

BWIP	8,000	To FG	36,000
Conv.	60%		
Mat.	100%		
Trans-in	34,000	EWIP	6,000
		Conv.	80%
		Mat.	100%

	Wt. Avg.	FIFO
Materials	42,000	34,000
Conversion		
BWIP	8,000	3,200
Transferred-in	34,000	34,000
EWIP	−1,200	−1,200
	40,800	36,000

16. (1178,T1,36) (c) The requirement is how to treat normal spoilage given that it occurs at the end of the production process. As the spoilage occurs at the end of the process, it cannot be detected until the goods are finished. All spoilage relates to goods that are complete. Thus all spoilage costs should be charged to finished goods. Answers (a) and (b) are incorrect because none of the work in process has a chance to spoil until completion. Answer (d) is incorrect because normal spoilage should not be charged to a separate loss account, but rather be included as cost of finished goods.

17. 1178,T1,38) (b) The requirement is the condition which will produce the same cost of goods manufactured per FIFO as per weighted average. The difference between FIFO and weighted average is that "weighted average" averages last period's costs in beginning work-in-process with the costs incurred in the current period. FIFO keeps last period's and this period's cost separate. Thus, if there is no beginning work-in-process, FIFO and weighted average will produce the same results.

18. 1178,T1,39) (d) The requirement is the best argument for expensing period costs per direct costing. The rationale is that period costs are incurred whether or not production occurs; the act of producing does not incur period costs. Thus period costs should not be allocated to the goods produced. Answer (a) is incorrect because period costs may be controllable, i.e., the foreman may be fired. Answer (b) is incorrect because period costs may be quite substantial, especially when capital outlays and resulting depreciation are high. Answer (c) is incorrect because allocation of period costs can be done very carefully, i.e., not arbitrarily.

19. (579,P2,31) (a) The requirement is the distribution of total costs incurred between goods (finished) manufactured and ending work-in-process using the weighted average method. The problem provides the average unit cost both for materials ($.24/unit) and for conversion ($.20/unit). The solutions approach is to do a T-account analysis of the work-in-process account as illustrated below. Note that $43,000 of costs have been incurred, which must be allocated to finished goods and ending work-in-process. Since 90,000 units have been completed at $.44 ($.20 + $.24), $39,600 is allocated to finished goods. The 10,000 units in ending work-in-process are complete as to material, and at $.24 per unit are $2,400. The 10,000 units are 50% complete as

to conversion, which is $1,000 (5,000 EUP at $.20). Thus the $43,000 total cost is allocated as $39,600 to finished goods and $3,400 to ending work-in-process.

Work in Process		
		FG (90,000 @ $.44)
Material	$24,000	= $39,600
Conversion	19,000	
		EWIP (10,000)
		100% Mat @ $.24
		= $2,400
		50% Con @ $.20
		= $1,000
	$43,000	

20. (579,P2,35) (c) The requirement is the equivalent units of production for the work-in-process account in which material is added at the end of the process. The solutions approach is to prepare a T-account analysis of the Wiring Department as illustrated below. Beginning work-in-process was 60% complete as to conversion, and 100,000 units were transferred in. Thus 125,000 units must be accounted for; 20,000 were in ending work-in-process, leaving 105,000 in finished goods. The 20,000 units in ending work-in-process were 80% complete as to conversion. The transferred in EUP would be all 125,000 units using the weighted average method. The material EUP would be 105,000, because material is only added at completion. The conversion cost EUP would be 121,000 (105,000 in finished goods and 16,000 in ending work-in-process).

Wiring Department			
BWIP	25,000	FG	105,000
conv 60%			
Transf. in	100,000	EWIP	20,000
		conv 80%	
	125,000		125,000

21. (579,T1,22) (b) In job order costing, payroll taxes on factory employee wages paid by the employer are preferably accounted for as factory overhead. While payroll taxes can be directly associated with direct labor, the taxes are not incurred at a constant rate. Both state and federal employer payroll taxes are taxed up to a certain amount of annual wages and not thereafter. Thus the taxes should be accounted for as factory overhead rather than direct labor. Thus answer (a) is incorrect. Answer (c) is incorrect because indirect labor is the cost of labor that cannot be associated with specific jobs, e.g., janitorial services. Answer (d), adminis-

trative costs, is incorrect because administrative costs are concerned with costs of administration rather than of factory production employees.

22. (579,T1,31) (a) The joint costs include all the common costs, direct and indirect. Thus joint costs of several salable products would be materials, labor, and overhead incurred to produce the joint products.

23. (1177,P2,27) (d) The requirement is the total cost allocated to Product X assuming common costs are allocated based on the number of units produced. The total joint cost for X, Y, and Z is $60,000, and 12,000 total units are produced, 6,000 of which are Product X. Thus 50% (6,000/12,000) of the $60,000 are costs of Product X. Since the additional costs of processing X are $9,000, the total cost of Product X is $39,000.

24. (1177,P2,28) (b) The requirement here is the total cost allocated to Y after allocating joint costs based on relative-sales-value at split-off. Since the total sales value at split-off is $100,000, and Y's individual sales value is $35,000, Y's relative sales value is 35% (35,000/100,000). The joint costs are $60,000 and 35% (or $21,000) is allocated to Y. The $21,000 plus the $7,000 of additional Y processing costs equals a total cost for Y of $28,000.

25. (1177,T2,31) (a) The difference between absorption costing and direct costing is in the treatment of fixed overhead. Under absorption costing, fixed factory overhead is considered a product cost in contrast to a period cost per direct costing. Thus the difference in income between the methods is the difference in the fixed costs deferred. Any increase in deferred fixed costs under absorption costing relative to direct costing indicates that some of the current period's fixed overhead costs are not being expensed (which are all expensed per direct costing), i.e., the difference in direct and absorption income. Thus the income figures can be reconciled in terms of the change in deferred fixed costs: absorption income − increase in deferred fixed costs = direct costing income. Answer (b) is incorrect because discretionary costs are avoidable unlike fixed costs. Answer (c) is incorrect because contribution margin is sales less variable product costs. Fixed costs are deducted as a period cost below the contribution margin.

26. (1177,T2,34) (a) The requirement is to determine the effect of assigning a lower percentage-of-completion to ending work-in-process than was actually accomplished. The effect is to understate

equivalent units of production, because the amount of work or production that was completed was understated. Since the costs of production remain constant, the cost per equivalent unit is overstated. In turn, the costs assigned to goods completed for the period will be overstated. Note that it makes no difference whether it is a FIFO or a weighted average method, because the only difference between FIFO and weighted average is that under FIFO, the EUP already completed at the beginning of the period is subtracted from the EUP in goods completed and ending work-in-process.

27. (1177,T2,35) (b) Job order systems are used to accumulate costs of specialty manufacturing, i.e., custom jobs. Shipbuilding is much more likely to be a custom job-type operation than the manufacturing of identical units found in toy manufacturing, crude oil refining, and candy manufacturing.

28. (1177,T2,42) (c) Joint costs are common costs of two or more products with values significant to each other. When a joint product has insignificant value relative to the other products, it is called a by-product. This is an arbitrary distinction that has grown from usage. While joint costs are generally allocated based upon net realizable value, the actual net realizable value of by-products is usually credited to, i.e., reduces, overall joint costs. Thus profit is generally not reported on by-products because they are costed at net realizable value. The net realizable value of a by-product is considered to be a contra cost of joint product cost.

29. (578,P2,34) (a) The requirement is net income per direct costing. As computed below, sales are $560,000. The total variable costs (including selling and administrative) are $3.50 per unit, or $280,000. Total fixed costs are $230,000 resulting in a net income of $50,000.

Sales (80,000 at $7)	$560,000
Variable costs (80,000 at $3.50)	−280,000
Fixed costs $150,000	
_____80,000	−230,000
Net income	$ 50,000

30. (578,T2,36) (b) The basic difference between direct costing and absorption costing is the treatment of fixed factory overhead. Under direct costing, fixed factory overhead is considered a period cost, i.e., expensed in the period incurred. Absorption costing includes fixed factory overhead as a product cost, i.e., fixed factory overhead costs of inventory not

sold are deferred to future periods. The difference between the two methods is that when sales exceed production, direct costing income exceeds absorption income. Conversely, when production exceeds sales, absorption costing exceeds direct costing.

31. (578,T2,37) (a) An equivalent unit of production (EUP) is the amount of work or material required to complete one unit. EUP is used because partially complete batches of products must be converted into equivalent whole units of production for the purposes of allocating costs to goods completed during the period and EWiP and possibly spoilage.

32. (578,T2,38) (a) Common costs are allocated to two or more products based upon a systematic and rational basis. The allocation should be objective, i.e., quantitatively determined. Answers (b) and (c) are incorrect because the objective is to measure income fairly, not to maximize earnings or minimize variations therein. Answer (d) is incorrect because estimation is necessary in assigning costs to products as elsewhere in the accounting methodology.

33. (578,T2,41) (b) Direct labor and material rates would not be averaged in a job order costing system because, by definition, job order costing is used to account for manufacture of custom-type jobs. Accordingly the mix of labor and material costs would vary from job to job. Answers (a), (c), and (d) are all incorrect because standard costing, direct costing, and factory overhead allocation based on direct labor hours can be used as part of a job order costing system. That is, the peculiarity of job order accounting is cost accumulation by specific job or finished good. This requires a subsidiary ledger for the work-in-process account.

MAY 1981 ANSWERS

34. (581,P2,23) (c) The requirement is the unit cost of product F for January calculated on the direct costing basis. Under direct costing, only variable production costs (direct materials, direct labor, and variable overhead) are considered product costs. Fixed overhead is considered a period cost, and therefore, is not an inventoriable cost. Thus, the unit cost of product F is

$$\$40,000 + \$22,000 + \$13,000 = \$75,000$$

$75,000 ÷ 10,000 units = $7.50 cost per unit.

35. (581,P2,32) (a) The requirement is the cost per equivalent unit for materials costs under the weighted-average method of process costing. The solutions approach is to prepare a "T"-account analysis of department A.

Department A
(Units Only)

BWIP	17,000	Comp. & Trans.	85,000
Started	82,000	EWIP	14,000
Units to account for	99,000	Units accounted for	99,000

All units in BWIP are assumed to be started in the current period under the weighted-average method. Therefore, costs incurred this period are added to the costs in BWIP. In Department A, all materials are added at the beginning of the process. Therefore, the units in EWIP are 100% complete as to materials. The cost per equivalent unit for materials can be computed as follows:

EUP for materials:
Transferred out 85,000 + EWIP 14,000 = 99,000

Cost for materials:
BWIP $12,800 + Cost this period $69,700 = $82,500

Cost per equivalent unit:
$82,500 ÷ 99,000 EUP = $.83

36. (581,P2,33) (b) The requirement is the number of equivalent units for conversion costs for April under the FIFO process cost method. The solutions approach is to prepare a "T"-account analysis of Department One.

Department One
(Units Only)

BWIP (40% complete)	40,000	Transferred out From BWIP (40% complete)	40,000
		Started and completed (340,000 − 40,000)	300,000
Units started	320,000	EWIP (60% complete)	20,000
Units to account for	360,000	Units accounted for	360,000

Under the FIFO process cost assumption only work done in the current period is included in equivalent units of production. Thus, the equivalent units of conversion cost are the work to complete BWIP (40,000 x .60) + units started and completed (300,000) + EWIP (20,000 x .60) = 336,000.

37. (581,P2,37) (b) The requirement is to compute the joint costs allocated to product G. Note that the problem indicates that the relative-sales value at split-off is used to allocate joint costs. Product H has been allocated 15% ($18,000 ÷ $120,000) of the total joint costs. Therefore, Product H has 15% of the total sales value at split-off or $30,000 (15% x $200,000).

Since Product F has a sales value at split-off of $120,000 (given), Product G's sales value at split-off is $50,000 ($200,000 − $30,000 − $120,000). The Product G sales value just computed represents 25% (50,000 ÷ 200,000) of the total sales value at split-off. The joint costs allocated to Product G are 120,000 x 25% = $30,000.

38. (581,P2,38) (d) The requirement is to compute the total manufacturing cost associated with Job No. 432 for 1980. Total manufacturing costs include direct materials, direct labor, and manufacturing overhead. Note the problem indicates that manufacturing overhead is applied to jobs on the basis of direct labor cost. Department M's pre-determined overhead rate is 300% ($600,000 ÷ $200,000) of direct labor cost. Department A's pre-determined overhead rate is 50% (400,000 ÷ 800,000). The total manufacturing costs for Job No. 432 are

Direct Materials		$25,000
Direct Labor		
Dept. M	$ 8,000	
Dept. A	12,000	20,000
Manuf. OH		
Dept. M		
$ 8,000 x 300% =	$24,000	
Dept. A		
$12,000 x 50% =	6,000	30,000
Total Manufacturing Costs		$75,000

39. (581,P2,39) (c) The requirement is to compute the joint costs allocated to product PEL using the net realizable value method for allocating joint costs. The net realizable value is the sales price less the costs to convert the products into a salable form. The net realizable values for products PEL and VEL are

	PEL	VEL
Sales Value		
(800 x 25)	$20,000	
(400 x 50)		$20,000
Costs to convert into a salable form	8,000	12,000
Net Realizable Value	$12,000	$ 8,000

Product PEL represents 60% ($12,000 ÷ $20,000) of the total net realizable value and thus should be assigned 60% of the joint costs. Thus, the joint costs allocated to product PEL would be ($12,000 ÷ $20,000) x 15,000 = $9,000.

40. (581,Q2,35) (c) The requirement is to calculate the weighted average unit cost of raw material X at 1/12/80. The steps used to determine the weighted average cost per unit are to calculate the amount available in terms of cost and units and then divide the

number of units into the total cost. The cost of goods available is $1,060 [(400 x $1) + (600 x $1.10)] and the units available is 1,000 (600 + 400). Therefore, the weighted average cost per unit is $1,060 ÷1,000 units or $1.06 per unit.

41. (581,T1,41) (b) The requirement is to identify an example of a period cost. The wages of salespersons is considered a period cost since it does not represent any future benefit to the company. Answers (a), (c), and (d) are all properly considered product costs.

42. (581,T1,43) (b) The requirement is to indicate the characteristics of an allocation base to be used for relating costs to specific products. The allocation base chosen to relate costs to a specific product should have a cause and effect relationship. Answer (c) is incorrect since fixed production costs are allocated to specific products. Answer (d) is incorrect since factory overhead is also allocated to specific products.

43. (581,T1,44) (a) The requirement is for the best cost accumulation procedure (system) to use when many batches with differing product specifications are produced. The best cost accumulation procedure to use in this situation is job-order costing. Answer (b) is incorrect since process costing is used where there is a continuous flow of like units. Answers (c) and (d) are incorrect because they are not cost accumulation procedures (systems).

44. (581,T1,45) (b) The requirement is for the costs included in cost per equivalent unit under the weighted-average method of process costing. Under the weighted-average process cost method, current costs plus the cost of beginning inventory are taken into account in the numerator of the cost per equivalent unit computation. Answer (a) is incorrect since current costs are only considered under the FIFO process cost system.

45. (581,T1,46) (a) The requirement is for the proper treatment of transferred in costs in computing equivalent units. Units transferred into the second department should be taken into account in the equivalent units computation for the second department under both FIFO and weighted-average. They are treated the same as materials added at the beginning of a process.

46. (581,T1,47) (b) The requirement is for the difference between the treatment of manufacturing costs under absorption costing versus direct costing. Under direct costing, only the variable manufacturing costs are applied to the product. Under absorption costing, all manufacturing costs are applied to the product. Thus, it is treatment of the fixed manufacturing costs that cause the difference between absorption and direct costing, answer (b).

47. (581,T1,48) (d) The requirement is the most frequently used method of allocating joint costs. Joint costs are most frequently allocated to the joint products on the basis of relative sales value. None of the other three choices are commonly used for joint cost allocations.

48. (581,T1,49) (c) The requirement is for the treatment of subsequent processing cost incurred on by-products after joint production costs have been allocated. Under the method of by-product costing, once a portion of the joint costs are allocated to the by-product, then any subsequent processing cost must also be added to the by-product. None of the other methods are acceptable under this procedure.

MULTIPLE CHOICE QUESTIONS (1—40)

1.   A standard cost system may be used in
   a.   Either job order costing or process costing.
   b.   Job order costing but **not** process costing.
   c.   Process costing but **not** job order costing.
   d.   Neither process costing nor job order costing.

2.   The absolute minimum cost that would be possible under the best conceivable operating conditions is a description of which type of standard cost?
   a.   Currently attainable (expected).
   b.   Theoretical.
   c.   Normal.
   d.   Practical.

3.   If the actual hours worked exceed the standard hours allowed, what type of variance will occur?
   a.   Favorable labor usage (efficiency) variance.
   b.   Favorable labor rate variance.
   c.   Unfavorable labor usage (efficiency) variance.
   d.   Unfavorable labor rate variance.

4.   An unfavorable price variance occurs because of
   a.   Price increases on raw materials.
   b.   Price decreases on raw materials.
   c.   Less than anticipated levels of waste in the manufacturing process.
   d.   More than anticipated levels of waste in the manufacturing process.

5.   Sullivan Corporation's direct-labor costs for the month of March 1980 were as follows:

Standard direct-labor hours	42,000
Actual direct-labor hours	40,000
Direct-labor rate variance-favorable	$8,400
Standard direct-labor rate per hour	$6.30

What was Sullivan's total direct-labor payroll for the month of March 1980?
   a. $243,600
   b. $244,000
   c. $260,000
   d. $260,400

6.   Durable Company installs shingle roofs on residential houses. The standard material cost for a Type R house is $1,250 based on 1,000 units at a cost of $1.25 each. During April 1980, Durable installed roofs on 20 Type R houses, using 22,000 units of material at a cost of $1.20 per unit, and a total cost of $26,400. Dur-

able's material price variance for April 1980 is
   a. $1,000 favorable.
   b. $1,100 favorable.
   c. $1,400 unfavorable.
   d. $2,500 unfavorable.

7.   Information on Ripley Company's overhead costs for the January 1980 production activity is as follows:

Budgeted fixed overhead	$ 75,000
Standard fixed overhead rate per direct-labor hour	$3
Standard variable overhead rate per direct-labor hour	$6
Standard direct-labor hours allowed for actual production	24,000
Actual total overhead incurred	$220,000

Ripley has a standard absorption and flexible budgeting system, and uses the two-variance method (two-way analysis) for overhead variances. The volume (denominator) variance for January 1980 is
   a. $3,000 unfavorable.
   b. $3,000 favorable.
   c. $4,000 unfavorable.
   d. $4,000 favorable.

8.   Alden Company has a standard absorption and flexible budgeting system and uses a two-way analysis of overhead variances. Selected data for the February 1980 production activity is as follows:

Budgeted fixed factory overhead costs	$ 64,000
Actual factory overhead incurred	$230,000
Variable factory overhead rate per direct-labor hour	$5
Standard direct-labor hours	32,000
Actual direct-labor hours	33,000

The budget (controllable) variance for February 1980 is
   a. $1,000 favorable.
   b. $1,000 unfavorable.
   c. $6,000 favorable.
   d. $6,000 unfavorable.

9.   Lion Company's direct-labor costs for the month of January 1980 were as follows:

Actual direct-labor hours	20,000
Standard direct-labor hours	21,000
Direct-labor rate variance-unfavorable	$3,000
Total payroll	$126,000

What was Lion's direct-labor efficiency variance?
- a. $6,000 favorable.
- b. $6,150 favorable.
- c. $6,300 favorable.
- d. $6,450 favorable.

10. Information on Kennedy Company's direct-material costs is as follows:

Standard unit price	$3.60
Actual quantity purchased	1,600
Standard quantity allowed for actual production	1,450
Materials purchase price variance--favorable	$ 240

What was the actual purchase price per unit, rounded to the nearest penny?
- a. $3.06
- b. $3.11
- c. $3.45
- d. $3.75

11. Listed below are four names for different kinds of standards associated with a standard cost system. Which of these describes the labor costs that should be incurred under forthcoming efficient operating conditions?
- a. Ideal.
- b. Basic.
- c. Maximum-efficiency.
- d. Currently attainable.

12. A debit balance in the labor-efficiency variance indicates that
- a. Standard hours exceed actual hours.
- b. Actual hours exceed standard hours.
- c. Standard rate and standard hours exceed actual rate and actual hours.
- d. Actual rate and actual hours exceed standard rate and standard hours.

Items 13. and 14. are based on the following information:

Data on Goodman Company's direct-labor costs is given below:

Standard direct-labor hours	30,000
Actual direct-labor hours	29,000
Direct-labor usage (efficiency) variance-favorable	$ 4,000
Direct-labor rate variance-favorable	$ 5,800
Total payroll	$110,200

13. What was Goodman's actual direct-labor rate?
- a. $3.60.
- b. $3.80.
- c. $4.00.
- d. $5.80.

14. What was Goodman's standard direct-labor rate
- a. $3.54.
- b. $3.80.
- c. $4.00.
- d. $5.80.

15. Which of the following is a purpose of standard costing?
- a. Determine "breakeven" production level.
- b. Control costs.
- c. Eliminate the need for subjective decisions by management.
- d. Allocate cost with more accuracy.

16. When performing input-output variance analysis in standard costing, "standard hours allowed" is a means of measuring
- a. Standard output at standard hours.
- b. Actual output at standard hours.
- c. Standard output at actual hours.
- d. Actual output at actual hours.

Items 17. and 18. are based on the following information:

Beth Company's budgeted fixed factory overhead costs are $50,000 per month plus a variable factory overhead rate of $4 per direct labor hour. The standard direct labor hours allowed for October production were 18,000. An analysis of the factory overhead indicates that, in October, Beth had an unfavorable budget (controllable) variance of $1,000 and a favorable volume variance of $500. Beth uses a two-way analysis of overhead variances.

17. The actual factory overhead incurred in October is
- a. $121,000.
- b. $122,000.
- c. $122,500.
- d. $123,000.

18. The applied factory overhead in October is
- a. $121,000.
- b. $122,000,
- c. $122,500.
- d. $123,000.

19. If the total materials variance (actual cost of materials used compared with the standard cost of

the standard amount of materials required) for a given operation is favorable, why must this variance be further evaluated as to price and usage?

    a.   There is no need to further evaluate the total materials variance if it is favorable.

    b.   Generally accepted accounting principles require that all variances be analyzed in three stages.

    c.   All variances must appear in the annual report to equity owners for proper disclosure.

    d.   To allow management to evaluate the. efficiency of the purchasing and production functions.

20.   Matt Company uses a standard cost system. Information for raw materials for Product RBI for the month of October is as follows:

Standard unit price	$1.60
Actual purchase price per unit	$1.55
Actual quantity purchased	2,000 units
Actual quantity used	1,900 units
Standard quantity allowed for actual production	1,800 units

What is the materials purchase price variance?

    a. $90 favorable.
    b. $90 unfavorable.
    c. $100 favorable
    d. $100 unfavorable.

21.   When using full absorption costing, what costs attendant to an element of production (material, labor or overhead) are used in order to compute variances from standard amounts?

    a.   Total costs.
    b.   Variable costs.
    c.   Fixed costs.
    d.   Controllable costs.

22.   Which of the following is the most probable reason a company would experience an unfavorable labor rate variance and a favorable labor efficiency variance?

    a.   The mix of workers assigned to the particular job was heavily weighted towards the use of higher paid experienced indiduals.

    b.   The mix of workers assigned to the particular job was heavily weighted towards the use of new relatively low paid unskilled workers.

    c.   Because of the production schedule workers

from other production areas were assigned to assist this particular process.

    d.   Defective materials caused more labor to be used in order to produce a standard unit.

23.   What type of direct material variances for price and usage will arise if the actual number of pounds of materials used exceeds standard pounds allowed but actual cost was less than standard cost?

	Usage	Price
a.	Unfavorable	Favorable
b.	Favorable	Favorable
c.	Favorable	Unfavorable
d.	Unfavorable	Unfavorable

24.   How should a usage variance that is significant in amount be treated at the end of an accounting period?

    a.   Reported as a deferred charge or credit.

    b.   Allocated among work-in-process inventory, finished goods inventory, and cost of goods sold.

    c.   Charged or credited to cost of goods manufactured.

    d.   Allocated among cost of goods manufactured, finished goods inventory, and cost of goods sold.

25.   What is the normal year-end treatment of immaterial variances recognized in a cost accounting system utilizing standards?

    a.   Reclassified to deferred charges until all related production is sold.

    b.   Allocated among cost of goods manufactured and ending work-in-process inventory.

    c.   Closed to cost of goods sold in the period in which they arose.

    d.   Capitalized as a cost of ending finished goods inventory.

Items 26, 27, and 28 are based on the following information.

The following information relates to a given department of Herman Company for the fourth quarter 1974:

Actual total overhead (fixed plus variable)	$178,500
Budget formula	$110,000 plus $0.50/hr.
Total overhead application rate	$1.50/hr.
Spending variance	$8,000 unfavorable
Volume variance	$5,000 favorable

The total overhead variance is divided into three variances — spending, efficiency, and volume.

26. What were the actual hours worked in this department during the quarter?
    a.   110,000.
    b.   121,000.
    c.   137,000.
    d.   153,000.

27. What were the standard hours allowed for good output in this department during the quarter?
    a.   105,000,
    b.   106,667.
    c.   110,000.
    d.   115,000.

28. Each unit takes five hours to manufacture, and the selling price is $4.50 per unit. Based on the overhead budget formula, how many units must be sold to generate $30,000 more than total budgeted overhead costs?
    a.   27,500.
    b.   35,000.
    c.   55,000.
    d.   70,000.

29. What standard cost variance represents the difference between actual factory overhead incurred and budgeted factory overhead based on actual hours worked?
    a.   Volume variance.
    b.   Spending variance.
    c.   Efficiency variance.
    d.   Quantity variance.

30. Given below are the following notations and their respective meanings:

AH = Actual hours
SHA = Standard hours allowed for actual production
AR = Actual rate.
SR = Standard rate

Which formula represents the calculation of the labor-efficiency variance?
    a. $SR(AH-SHA)$.
    b. $AR(AH-SHA)$.
    c. $AH(AR-SR)$.
    d. $SHA(AR-SR)$.

Items 31 through 33 are based on the following information:

The data below relate to the month of April 1976 for Marilyn, Inc., which uses a standard cost system:

Actual total direct labor	$43,400
Actual hours used	14,000
Standard hrs. allowed for good output	15,000
Direct labor rate variance-debit	$ 1,400
Actual total overhead	$32,000
Budgeted fixed costs	$ 9,000
"Normal" activity in hours	12,000
Total overhead application rate per standard direct-labor hour	$2.25

Marilyn uses a two-way analysis of overhead variances: budget (controllable) and volume.

31. What was Marilyn's direct labor usage (efficiency) variance for April 1976?
    a. $3,000 favorable.
    b. $3,000 unfavorable.
    c. $3,200 favorable.
    d. $3,200 unfavorable.

32. What was Marilyn's budget (controllable) variance for April 1976?
    a. $500 favorable.
    b. $500 unfavorable.
    c. $2,250 favorable.
    d. $2,250 unfavorable.

33. What was Marilyn's volume variance for April 1976?
    a. $500 favorable.
    b. $500 unfavorable.
    c. $2,250 favorable.
    d. $2,250 unfavorable.

34. When standard costs are used in a process-costing system, how, if at all, are equivalent units involved or used in the cost report at standard?
    a.   Equivalent units are not used.
    b.   Equivalent units are computed using a "special" approach.
    c.   The actual equivalent units are multiplied by the standard cost per unit.
    d.   The standard equivalent units are multiplied by the actual cost per unit.

35. Excess direct labor wages resulting from overtime premium will be disclosed in which type of variance?
    a.   Yield.
    b.   Quantity.
    c.   Labor efficiency.
    d.   Labor rate.

36. Peters Company uses a flexible budget system and prepared the following information for 1980:

Percent of capacity	80%	90%
Direct-labor hours	24,000	27,000
Variable factory overhead	$ 48,000	$ 54,000
Fixed factory overhead	$108,000	$108,000
Total factory overhead rate per direct-labor hour	$6.50	$6.00

Peters operated at 80% of capacity during 1980, but applied factory overhead based on the 90% capacity level. Assuming that actual factory overhead was equal to the budgeted amount for the attained capacity, what is the amount of overhead variance for the year?

- a. $ 6,000 overabsorbed.
- b. $ 6,000 underabsorbed.
- c. $12,000 overabsorbed.
- d. $12,000 underabsorbed.

37. Dickey Company had total underapplied overhead of $15,000. Additional information is as follows:

Variable Overhead:

Applied based on standard direct-labor hours allowed	$42,000
Budgeted based on standard direct-labor hours	38,000

Fixed Overhead:

Applied based on standard direct-labor hours allowed	30,000
Budgeted based on standard direct-labor hours	27,000

What is the actual total overhead?

- a. $50,000.
- b. $57,000.
- c. $80,000.
- d. $87,000

38. Information on Barber Company's direct-labor costs for the month of January 1981 is as follows:

Actual direct-labor hours	34,500
Standard direct-labor hours	35,000
Total direct-labor payroll	$241,500
Direct-labor efficiency variance - favorable	$3,200

What is Barber's direct-labor rate variance?

- a. $17,250 unfavorable.
- b. $20,700 unfavorable.
- c. $21,000 unfavorable.
- d. $21,000 favorable.

39. During March 1981 Younger Company's direct-material costs for the manufacture of product T were as follows:

Actual unit purchase price	$6.50
Standard quantity allowed for actual production	2,100
Quantity purchased and used for actual production	2,300
Standard unit price	$6.25

Younger's material usage variance for March 1981 was

- a. $1,250 unfavorable.
- b. $1,250 favorable.
- c. $1,300 unfavorable.
- d. $1,300 favorable.

40. Which department is customarily held responsible for an unfavorable materials usage variance?

- a. Quality control.
- b. Purchasing.
- c. Engineering.
- d. Production.

MULTIPLE CHOICE ANSWERS

1. a	10. c	19. d	28. d	37. d
2. b	11. d	20. c	29. b	38. b
3. c	12. b	21. a	30. a	39. a
4. a	13. b	22. a	31. a	40. d
5. a	14. c	23. a	32. b	
6. b	15. b	24. b	33. c	
7. a	16. b	25. c	34. c	
8. d	17. d	26. b	35. d	
9. b	18. c	27. d	36. d	

EXPLANATION OF MULTIPLE CHOICE ANSWERS

1. (1180,T1, 38) (a) A standard cost system is used to evaluate performance by setting target costs which usually are attainable under efficient conditions. Standard cost systems may be used by any manufacturing concern, in conjunction with either job order costing or process costing.

2. (1180,T1,48) (b) There are basically two types of standard costs, currently attainable [answer (a)] and theoretical [answer (b)]. A currently attainable cost is the target cost that employees are expected to acheive under efficient conditions. A theoretical standard cost is the absolute minimum cost that would be possible under the best conceivable operating conditions. Normal [answer (c)] and practical [answer (d)] are not terms used to describe the attainability of standard costs; they are alternative bases for determining budgeted fixed cost per hour or units.

3. (1180,T1,49) (c) The requirement is the type of labor variance (rate or usage), and the direction of the variance (favorable or unfavorable), occuring when actual hours exceed standard hours. When comparing actual and standard costs, a variance is always unfavorable when actual $>$ standard, and favorable when actual $<$ standard. A rate variance deals with variations in the amount paid per hour whereas a usage (efficiency) variance deals with variations in hours worked.

4. (1180,T1,50) (a) An unfavorable price variance occurs when the price on raw materials increases. Price variances deal with changes in price [answer (a) and (b)] while waste in the manufacturing process [answer (c) and (d)] determines quantity variances. Costs which are higher than standard [answer (a) and (d)] are unfavorable, while costs lower than standard [answer (b) and (c)] are favorable.

5. (1180,P2,35) (a) The requirement is to find Sullivan's total direct-labor payroll (actual labor cost) using selected variance and standard cost data. The solutions approach is to set up a diagram for the labor

variances, and fill in any given data:

(AH)	(AR)	(AH)	(SR)	(SH)	(SR)
(40,000)	(not needed)	(40,000)	(6.30)	(42,000)	(6.30)

$8,400 F   (not needed)
RATE VARIANCE   EFFICIENCY
                          VARIANCE

To determine total direct-labor payroll, the favorable rate variance can be subtracted from the budgeted cost (actual hours times standard rate) at 40,000 hours

Budgeted Cost [(40,000($6.30)] — $8,400 favorable rate variance = $243,600.

6. (1180,P2,38) (b) The requirement is Durable's material price variance. The material price variance is the units of material used times the difference between standard and actual cost per unit:

(22,000) ($1.25 — $1.20) = $1,100.

The variance is favorable, since actual cost per unit ($1.20) was less than the standard cost per unit ($1.25).

7. (1180,P2,39) (a) The requirement is the fixed overhead volume denominator variance for January. The volume variance is the difference between fixed overhead budgeted and fixed overhead applied (standard fixed overhead rate x standard direct-labor hours allowed).

Budgeted — Applied   = Volume Variance
$75,000 — (24,000) ($3) = $3,000

Fixed overhead applied is less than budgeted; this means overhead was underapplied (an unfavorable variance).

8. (580,P2,35) (d) The budget (controllable variance) is the difference between the budget for the level of activity actually attained and the incurred overhead cost. The budget for the level of activity actually attained is the sum of the fixed costs and the variable costs at 32,000 direct-labor hours.

Actual Overhead Incurred	Flexible Budget for Good Output
$230,000	$64,000 fixed + ($5x32,000) = $224,000

$6,000 unfavorable budget (controllable) variance
Remember the budget (controllable) variance consists of both spending and efficiency factors.

9. (580,P2,39) (b) The requirement is for the direct-labor efficiency variance. Since the standard direct-labor rate per hour is not given in this situation, it is necessary to work from the actual labor cost incurred and the unfavorable direct-labor rate variance

to find the direct-labor rate. First, subtract the $3,000 unfavorable direct-labor rate variance from the actual labor cost incurred to find the $123,000 budgeted amount (standard cost of inputs) of labor cost at 20,000 hours of activity. Then divide $123,000 by 20,000 to find the standard direct-labor rate of $6.15. The $6,150 favorable labor efficiency variance is ·$6.l5 times 1,000 hours (21,000 standard hours — 20,000 actual hours).

Actual Labor Cost	Act. hrs x std. rate	Std. hrs. x std. rate
$126,000	$123,000	21,000 x $6.15 =$129,150

$3,000 unfavorable $6,150 favorable

10. (1179,P2,38) (c) The requirement is the actual purchase price per unit given a standard unit price of $3.60 and a favorable price variance of $240. Dividing the actual quantity purchased of 1,600 units into the $240 favorable variance results in a $.15 per unit favorable price variance. The actual cost per unit was $3.45 ($3.60 standard - $.15 favorable variance).

11. (1176,T2,30) (d) Currently attainable standards are those that may be incurred under efficient operating conditions. They are difficult to achieve, but possible in contrast to the ideal or maximum efficiency standards. These latter standards assume perfection by equipment and employees and generally are not attainable. Basic standards are unchanging in nature, i.e., not adjusted for changes in efficiency, cost, etc., over time, and are used to identify trends in standard costs.

12. (1176,T2,31) (b) The labor efficiency variance relates to the number of direct labor hours incurred. A debit balance indicates inefficiency or actual hours exceeded standard hours. Answer (a) describes a favorable efficiency variance. Answer (c) describes both a favorable rate variance and a favorable efficiency variance. Answer (d) describes both an unfavorable rate variance and an unfavorable efficiency variance.

13. (577,P2,32) (b) The actual direct labor rate is the actual payroll of $110,200 divided by the actual direct labor hours of 29,000 which is $3.80.

14. (577,P2,33) (c) The requirement is the standard direct labor rate. The standard direct labor rate is computed by dividing the standard payroll of

$120,000 by the standard direct labor hours of 30,000, which is $4 per hour. The standard payroll is the total payroll of $110,200 adjusted for the labor usage and labor rate variances. Since both are favorable, i.e., less was paid than standard, the $4,000 and $5,800 should be added to the total payroll of $110,200 to obtain the standard payroll of $120,000.

15. (577,T2,36) (b) A major purpose of standard costing is to institute controls over costs. Answer (a) is incorrect because cost-volume-profit analysis determines the "breakeven" production level. Answer (c) is incorrect because establishment of standard costs and interpretation of standard cost variances requires subjectivity. Answer (d) is incorrect because cost allocation does not provide additional accuracy over actual costing data; if anything, the reverse is true.

16. (577,T2, 38) (b) Standard hours allowed, as the title implies, are the standard hours permitted for a given level of production which is the actual output times standard hours. In other words, given the level of production, what are the standard hours budgeted?

17. (578,P2,30) (d) The requirement is the actual factory overhead in October. The solutions approach is to compute the budgeted factory overhead and then adjust the standard for the variances incurred to determine actual costs. The budgeted overhead for actual output is $50,000 of fixed cost plus variable overhead of $72,000 ($4 x 18,000 hrs), or total overhead of $122,000

In October there was an unfavorable budget variance of $1,000 which indicates the actual cost exceeded the budgeted cost by $1,000, or was increased to $123,000. The volume variance refers to the difference between applied fixed and budgeted fixed, but has nothing to do with <u>actual</u> fixed. It should be ignored.

18. (578,P2,31) (c) The applied factory overhead is the standard overhead of $122,000 plus the favorable volume variance of $500. Recall that volume variance is variance caused by producing a greater or lesser number of units than budgeted and thus crediting factory overhead for more or less than was budgeted. Here $500 more than was budgeted was applied to the product creating the favorable volume variance of $500.

19. (578,T2,44) (d) Total materials variance consists of cost variance and usage variance. Accordingly, analysis of the total variance into component variances will permit evaluation of the purchasing department, and analysis of the usage variance will permit evaluation of the production functions. Answer (a) is incorrect because materials variances are commonly further evaluated as to price and usage. Answer (b) is incorrect because GAAP do not require three-way analysis of variance (three-way variance includes price, usage, and price-usage). Answer (c) is incorrect because variances normally do not appear in annual reports.

20. (1178,P2,34) (c) The requirement is the material purchase price variance. Since 2,000 units were purchased at $.05 below standard cost ($1.60 − $1.55), the material purchase price variance is $100 ($2,000 x $.05).

21. (1178,T1,42) (a) When computing variances from standard amounts under absorption costing, total costs (including both variable and fixed costs) are compared with standard costs. Under direct costing, the costs relevant to an element of production are only variable costs.

22. (1178,T1,43) (a) The requirement is the situation that would produce an unfavorable labor rate variance and a favorable labor efficiency variance. Unfavorable labor rate variances will be caused by higher-paid employees. Favorable labor efficiency variances can be caused by more experienced, better trained employees. Thus higher-paid, experienced individuals would tend to produce unfavorable labor rate variances and favorable labor efficiency variances. Answer (b) is incorrect because it is just the opposite of answer (a): low-paid unskilled workers will produce favorable labor rate variances and unfavorable labor efficiency variances. Answer (c) is incorrect because workers from other areas of production will probably result in unfavorable labor efficiency variances as they are unfamiliar with the task at hand. Answer (d) is incorrect because using more labor due to defective materials to produce a standard unit results in unfavorable labor efficiency variances.

23. (579,T1,20) (a) The requirement is the usage and price variances if the actual amount of materials used exceeds standard units allowed but actual cost was less than standard cost. If actual cost is less than standard cost, the price variance will be favorable. If the actual amount used exceeds the standard amount allowed, there will be an unfavorable usage variance.

24. (579,T1,25) (b) Significant usage variances (or any other variance) should be allocated to work-in-process inventory, finished goods inventory, and cost of goods sold at year-end. If significant variances exist, the inventory and cost of goods sold figures are not stated at actual costs, i.e., they are misstated. This may be the result of faulty standards, changed conditions, etc. If the variance is favorable, inventory and cost of goods sold have been overstated. If the variance is unfavorable, inventory and cost of goods sold have been understated. An additional allocation must be made between work-in-process and finished goods inventories. Answer (d) is incorrect because cost of goods manufactured refers to the amount of goods completed in the period and transferred from the work-in-process account to the finished goods (inventory) account, i.e., it represents a flow rather than a year-end balance.

25. (579,T1,33) (c) Immaterial standard cost variances are normally taken to the income statement as part of cost of goods sold in the period in which they arise. Answers (a), (b), and (d) all indicate that the immaterial variances would be deferred, which is incorrect.

26. (575,P2,18) (b) First, note that there are three related questions on the same data. Study all of the requirements before beginning any question. Second, you should review overhead variances. Spending variance is the difference between the actual price and the standard price for items purchased. Efficiency variance is the difference between the actual input and the standard input at standard price. Fixed budget variance is the actual amount versus the budgeted amount spent. Volume variance is the difference between the budgeted fixed overhead and the amount actually applied based on the budgeted rate.

Variable Variances

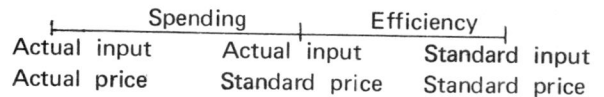

	Spending		Efficiency	
Actual input		Actual input		Standard input
Actual price		Standard price		Standard price

Fixed Variances

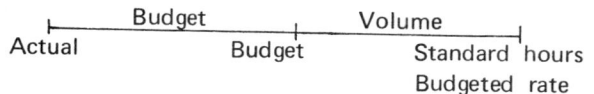

	Budget		Volume	
Actual		Budget		Standard hours
				Budgeted rate

The requirement is the actual hours worked. In this problem there was no reported fixed budget variance. Thus the fixed overhead was $110,000 and the actual variable overhead was $68,500 ($178,500 − $110,000). Take the $8,000 of unfavorable spending variance from the $68,500, and the remaining $60,500 divided by $.50 equals

121,000 actual hours worked (i.e., the budgeted variable costs divided by the variable overhead rate).

27. (575,P2,19) (d) The standard hours of good output during the quarter were 115,000. The variable overhead rate is $.50 and the total overhead rate is $1.50 making the fixed overhead application rate $1.00/hr. Not only were all of the $110,000 of fixed overhead applied but also an additional $5,000 because there was a $5,000 favorable volume variance. Recall that the volume variance is based upon standard hours at the budgeted rate.

28. (575,P2,20) (d) This is a cost-volume-profit problem. The objective is to determine how many units of sales are required to generate $30,000 more than budgeted overhead costs. Thus, the total revenue will have to equal fixed costs plus variable cost plus the profit. Total revenue would be $4.50 times the number of units sold. The fixed overhead is $110,000; the variable overhead is $2.50 (5 hrs. at $.50) times the number of units sold and the required profit is $30,000. This relationship is expressed in algebraic notation below:

$$\$4.50X = \$110,000 + \$2.50X + \$30,000$$
$$\$2.00X = \$140,000$$
$$X = 70,000$$

29. (575,T2,38) (b) The difference between actual factory overhead incurred and budgeted factory overhead is a spending variance. Answer (a), the volume variance, is the difference between the budgeted amount of fixed overhead and the actual fixed overhead applied based upon standard hours of production. The efficiency variance is the difference between the actual variable overhead incurred at standard prices and the standard input at standard prices, i.e., it is the usage variance of variable overhead. The quantity variance is the difference between actual materials used at standard and the standard materials at standard costs. See the explanation to question number 28 above for a diagram of overhead variances.

30. (1175,T1,17) (a) The labor efficiency variance is calculated by taking the standard labor rate times the difference between the actual hours incurred and the standard hours allowed for actual production. The labor rate variance is the total number of hours worked times the difference be-

tween the standard labor rate and the actual labor rate.

31. (576,P2,19) (a) The total actual labor cost $43,400, less the $1,400 of unfavorable rate variance is $42,000, which is the standard cost for the actual hours worked. Divide the $42,000 by 14,000 actual hours to get $3 per hour standard. Multiply the $3 per hour standard times the 1,000 hours of favorable variance to get a $3,000 favorable labor usage variance.

$$
\begin{aligned}
43,400 &\ \text{actual cost} \\
\underline{1,400} &\ \text{unfavorable rate} \\
42,000 &\ \text{standard for actual hours}
\end{aligned}
$$

$\div$ 14,000 actual hours = $3.00/h.rs standard
1,000 hrs. favorable X $3.00/hr. standard = $3,000 favorable usage.

32. (576,P2,20) (b) Given the budgeted fixed overhead of $9,000 and 12,000 normal hours, the fixed application rate is $.75 per hour (and the variable rate is $1.50 per hour). If the total overhead is $32,000 and fixed overhead is $9,000, $23,000 was incurred for variable overhead. Based on $1.50 variable application rate and 15,000 standard hours allowed, $22,500 of variable should have been incurred. Thus the excess of actual over standard is $500.

$$
\begin{aligned}
\$9,000 &\ \text{budgeted fixed} \\
\div 12,000 &\ \text{normal hours} \\
= \ \$.75/\text{hour} &\ \text{fixed rate and } \$1.50/\text{hour} \\
&\ \text{variable rate}
\end{aligned}
$$

$$
\begin{aligned}
\$32,000 &\ \text{total overhead} \\
\underline{-9,000} &\ \text{fixed} \\
23,000 &\ \text{variable} \\
\underline{-22,500} &\ \text{standard allowed (1.50 X 15,000} \\
&\ \text{standard hours)} \\
\hline
500 &\ \text{unfavorable}
\end{aligned}
$$

33. (576,P2,21) (c) The budgeted fixed overhead is 12,000 hours at $.75. The applied fixed overhead was 15,000 hours at $.75, thus there is a favorable volume variance of 3,000 hours at $.75.

34. (576,T2,30) (c) If standard cost systems are not used, actual costs are multiplied times the actual equivalent units. Thus when standard costs are used, standard rather than actual costs are multiplied times the actual equivalent units of work. Recall that the equivalent units calculation is made to provide a basis for allocating costs between goods completed, spoilage, and

ending work-in-process. They are called equivalent units of production because spoilage and ending work-in-process may not be 100% complete.

35. (578,T2,43) (d) Overtime premiums increase the hourly wage to employees, and accordingly result in a labor rate variance. Recall that the labor rate variance has to do with the hourly rate of pay and the labor efficiency rate is concerned with the number of hours incurred.

MAY 1981 ANSWERS

36. (581,P2,25) (d) The requirement is to compute the total overhead variance for the year. The solutions approach is to prepare a T-account analysis of the Manufacturing overhead account.

Fac. Overhead	
Actual	Applied
24,000 hrs.	24,000 hrs.
x $ 6.50	x $ 6.00
$156,000	$144,000

The total underabsorbed overhead for the year is $156,000 − $144,000 = $12,000. There is another way to approach this problem. Since the actual factory overhead was equal to the budgeted amount for the attained capacity, then the only variance occurring in the period was a fixed overhead volume denominator variance computed as follows:

$$\left(\frac{\$108,000 \text{ Budgeted Fixed Cost}}{27,000 \text{ Denominator hours}}\right) \times$$

(27,000 hrs. − 24,000 hrs.) = $12,000 unfavorable

37. (581,P2,26) (d) The requirement is to compute the actual total overhead for Dickey Company. Since the under or over-applied overhead is equal to the actual overhead minus the applied overhead, the actual overhead is computed as $42,000 variable OH applied + $30,000 fixed OH applied + $15,000 total under-applied OH = $87,000 actual total overhead. If you do not recall these relationships, prepare a schedule.

	Act	Bud.	Applied
Var. Ovhd.	?	$38,000	$42,000
Fix. Ovhd.	?	27,000	30,000
	?	$65,000	$72,000

↑——— $15,000 Underapplied ———↑

The total (variable and fixed) actual overhead is the $72,000 applied + $15,000 under-applied = $87,000. Note that the budget amounts were not needed.

38. (581,P2,27) (b) The requirement is to compute the direct-labor rate variance for Barber Company. Since the standard-direct labor rate is not given in this situation, it is necessary to work from the direct labor efficiency variance to compute the standard direct labor rate. Set up a schedule and fill in the known variables.

Actual	Budget	Applied
	34,500 hrs.	35,000 hrs.
$241,500	x Std. DL rate = (2)	x Std. DL rate (1)

├———— (3) ————┤├———— $3,200 ————┤

D.L. Rate Var.   D.L. Effic. Var.

The unknowns are keyed (1) through (3).

(1) The standard direct labor rate is equal to:

$$\frac{\$3,200}{35,000 - 34,500} = \$6.40$$

(2) The budget at 34,500 hours is

$34,500 \times \$6.40 = \$220,800$

(3) Finally, the direct labor rate variance is:

$241,500 − $220,800 = $20,700

39. (581,P2,28) (a) The requirement is to compute the material usage variance for March, 1981. The material usage variance is defined as the Std. price x (actual quantity used − standard quantity allowed). Thus, the material usage variance is computed as $6.25 x (2,300 − 2,100) = $1,250 unfavorable.

40. (581,T1,50) (d) The requirement is to identify the department customarily held responsible for an unfavorable materials usage variance. The department customarily held responsible for an unfavorable materials usage variance is the production department. Although the engineering and quality control departments may have some effect on the use of materials, they are not usually responsible for material usage variances. The purchasing department is usually responsible for material price variances.

MULTIPLE CHOICE QUESTIONS (1–65)

1. The net present value of a proposed project represents the
    a. Cash flows less the present value of the cash flows.
    b. Cash flows less the original investment.
    c. Present value of the cash flows plus the present value of the original investment less the original investment.
    d. Present value of the cash flows less the original investment.

2. Which of the following is necessary in order to calculate the pay-back period for a project?
    a. Useful life.
    b. Minimum desired rate of return.
    c. Net present value.
    d. Annual cash flow.

3. Within a relevant range, the amount of variable cost per unit
    a. Differs at each production level.
    b. Remains constant at each production level.
    c. Increases as production increases.
    d. Decreases as production increases.

4. The contribution margin ratio always increases when the
    a. Breakeven point increases.
    b. Breakeven point decreases.
    c. Variable costs as a percentage of net sales decrease.
    d. Variable costs as a percentage of net sales increase.

5. The type of costs presented to management for an equipment replacement decision should be limited to
    a. Relevant costs.
    b. Standard costs.
    c. Controllable costs.
    d. Conversion costs.

6. Jarvis, Inc., a calendar year company, purchased a new machine for $28,000 on January 1, 1980. The machine has an estimated useful life of eight years with no salvage value and is being depreciated on the straight-line basis. The accounting (book-value) rate of return is expected to be 15% on the initial increase in required investment. On the assumption of a uniform cash inflow, this investment is expected to provide annual cash flow from operations, net of income taxes, of
    a. $3,500
    b. $4,025

c. $4,200
d. $7,700

7. Energy Company is planning to spend $84,000 for a new machine which will depreciate on the straight-line basis over ten years with no salvage value. The related cash flow from operations, net of income taxes, is expected to be $10,000 a year for each of the first six years and $12,000 for each of the next four years. What is the payback period?
    a. 4.4 years.
    b. 7.6 years.
    c. 7.8 years.
    d. 8.0 years.

8. Scott, Inc., is planning to invest $120,000 in a ten-year project. Scott estimates that the annual cash inflow, net of income taxes, from this project will be $20,000. Scott's desired rate of return on investments of this type is 10%. Information on present value factors is as follows:

	At 10%	At 12%
Present value of $1 for ten periods	0.386	0.322
Present value of an annuity of $1 for ten periods	6.145	5.650

Scott's expected rate of return on this investment is
    a. Less than 10%, but more than 0%.
    b. 10%.
    c. Less than 12%, but more than 10%.
    d. 12%.

9. Hilltop Company invested $100,000 in a two-year project. Hilltop's expected rate of return was 12%. The cash flow, net of income taxes, was $40,000 for the first year. Information on present value and future value factors is as follows:

Period	Present value of $1 at 12%	Future value of $1 at 12%
1	.8929	1.1200
2	.7972	1.2544

Assuming that the rate of return was exactly 12%, what was the cash flow, net of income taxes, for the second year of the project?
    a. $51,247
    b. $60,000
    c. $64,284
    d. $80,638

10. Thomas Company sells products X, Y, and Z. Thomas sells three units of X for each unit of Z, and

two units of Y for each unit of X. The contribution margins are $1.00 per unit of X, $1.50 per unit of Y, and $3.00 per unit of Z. Fixed costs are $600,000. How many units of X would Thomas sell at the break-even point?

a. 40,000
b. 120,000
c. 360,000
d. 400,000

11. The Blade Division of Dana Company produces hardened steel blades. One-third of the Blade Division's output is sold to the Lawn Products Division of Dana; the remainder is sold to outside customers. The Blade Division's estimated sales and standard cost data for the fiscal year ending June 30, 1981, are as follows:

	Lawn Products	Outsiders
Sales	$15,000	$40,000
Variable costs	(10,000)	(20,000)
Fixed costs	(3,000)	(6,000)
Gross margin	$ 2,000	$14,000
Unit sales	10,000	20,000

The Lawn Products Division has an opportunity to purchase 10,000 identical quality blades from an outside supplier at a cost of $1.25 per unit on a continuing basis. Assume that the Blade Division cannot sell any additional products to outside customers. Should Dana allow its Lawn Products Division to purchase the blades from the outside supplier, and why?

a. Yes, because buying the blades would save Dana Company $500.
b. No, because making the blades would save Dana Company $1,500.
c. Yes, because buying the blades would save Dana Company $2,500.
d. No, because making the blades would save Dana Company $2,500.

12. Argus Company, a manufacturer of lamps, budgeted sales of 400,000 lamps at $20.00 per unit for 1980. Variable manufacturing costs were budgeted at $8.00 per unit, and fixed manufacturing costs at $5.00 per unit. A special order offering to buy 40,000 lamps for $11.50 each was received by Argus in April 1980. Argus has sufficient plant capacity to manufacture the additional quantity of lamps; however, the production would have to be done by the present work force on an overtime basis at an estimated additional cost of $1.50 per lamp. Argus will not incur any selling expenses as a result of the special order. What would be the effect

on operating income if the special order could be accepted without affecting normal sales?

a. $ 60,000 decrease.
b. $ 80,000 increase.
c. $120,000 decrease.
d. $140,000 increase.

13. The Insulation Corporation sells two products, D and W. Insulation sells these products at a rate of 2 units of D to 3 units of W. The contribution margin is $4 per unit for D and $2 per unit for W. Insulation has fixed costs of $420,000. What would be the total units sold at the breakeven point?

a. 140,000
b. 150,000
c. 168,000
d. 180,000

14. Virginia Company invested in a four-year project. Virginia's expected rate of return is 10%. Additional information on the project is as follows:

Year	Cash inflow from operations, net of income taxes	Present value of $1 at 10%
1	$4,000	.909
2	4,400	.826
3	4,800	.751
4	5,200	.683

Assuming a positive net present value of $1,000, what was the amount of the original investment?

a. $ 2,552
b. $ 4,552
c. $13,427
d. $17,400

Items 15. and 16. are based on the following information:

Plastics, Inc., is considering the purchase of a $40,000 machine which will be depreciated on a straight-line basis over an eight-year period with no salvage value. The machine is expected to generate net cash income before income taxes of $12,000 a year. Assume that the income tax rate is 50%.

15. What is the pay-back period?
a. 2.4 years.
b. 2.6 years.
c. 3.3 years.
d. 4.7 years.

16. What is the accounting (book value) rate of return on the initial increase in required investment?
a. 8.75%

b.   17.50%
c.   23.75%
d.   30.00%

17.   Day Company is a medium-sized manufacturer of lamps. During 1979 a new line called "Twilight" was made available to Day's customers. The break-even point for sales of Twilight is $400,000 with a contribution margin of 40%. Assuming that the operating profit for the Twilight line for 1979 amounted to $200,000, total sales for 1979 amounted to
    a. $600,000.
    b. $840,000.
    c. $900,000.
    d. $950,000.

18.   Moon Company sells product Q at $6 a unit. In 1980 fixed costs are expected to be $200,000 and variable costs are estimated at $4 a unit. How many units of product Q must Moon sell to generate operating income of $40,000?
    a.   50,000
    b.   60,000
    c.   100,000
    d.   120,000

19.   Roberts, Inc., purchased a machine for $240,000. The machine has a useful life of six years and no salvage value. Straight-line depreciation is to be used. The machine is expected to generate cash flow from operations, net of income taxes, of $70,000 in each of the six years. Roberts' expected rate of return is 12%. Information of present value factors is as follows:

Period	Present value of $1 at 12%	Present value of ordinary annuity of $1 at 12%
1	.893	.893
2	.797	1.690
3	.712	2.402
4	.636	3.037
5	.567	3.605
6	.507	4.111

What would be the net present value?
    a. $ 35,490
    b. $ 47,770
    c. $121,680
    d. $123,330

20.   If the fixed costs attendant to a product increase while variable costs and sales price remain constant, what will happen to (1) contribution margin and (2) breakeven point?

	Contribution margin	Breakeven point
a.	Increase	Decrease
b.	Decrease	Increase
c.	Unchanged	Increase
d.	Unchanged	Unchanged

21.   On what basis is the cost of capital derived from bonds and preferred stock measured, respectively?
    a.   Pretax rate of interest for bonds and stated annual dividend rate less the expected earnings per share for preferred stock.
    b.   Pretax rate of interest for bonds and stated annual dividend rate for preferred stock.
    c.   Aftertax rate of interest for bonds and stated annual dividend rate less the expected earnings per share for preferred stock.
    d.   Aftertax rate of interest for bonds and stated annual dividend rate for preferred stock.

22.   The Polar Company is planning to purchase a new machine for $30,000. The pay-back period is expected to be five years. The new machine is expected to produce cash flow from operations, net of income taxes, of $7,000 a year in each of the next three years and $5,500 in the fourth year. Depreciation of $5,000 a year will be charged to income for each of the five years of the payback period. What is the amount of cash flow from operations, net of taxes, that the new machine is expected to produce in the last (fifth) year of the pay-back period?
    a. $1,000
    b. $3,500
    c. $5,000
    d. $8,500

23.   The Fudge Company is planning to purchase a new machine which it will depreciate on a straight-line basis over a ten-year period with no salvage value and a full year's depreciation taken in the year of acquisition. The new machine is expected to produce cash flow from operations, net of income taxes, of $66,000 a year in each of the next ten years. The accounting (book value) rate of return on the initial investment is expected to be 12%. How much will the new machine cost?
    a. $300,000
    b. $550,000
    c. $660,000
    d. $792,000

24.   Cause Company is planning to invest in a machine with a useful life of five years and no salvage value. The machine is expected to produce cash flow from operations, net of income taxes, of $20,000 in

each of the five years. Cause's expected rate of return is 10%. Information on present value and future amount factors is as follows:

	Period				
	1	2	3	4	5
Present value of $1 at 10%	.909	.826	.751	.683	.621
Present value of annuity of $1 at 10%	.909	1.736	2.487	3.170	3.791
Future amount of $1 at 10%	1.100	1.210	1.331	1.464	1.611
Future amount of annuity of $1 at 10%	1.000	2.100	3.310	4.641	6.105

How much will the machine cost?
- a. $ 32,220
- b. $ 62,100
- c. $ 75,820
- d. $122,100

25. Heap Company invested in a two-year project. Heap's expected rate of return is 10%. The present value of $1 for one period at 10% is .909 and for two periods at 10% is .826. The machine is expected to produce cash flow from operations, net of income taxes, of $40,000 in the first year and $50,000 in the second year. How much will the project cost?
- a. $74,340
- b. $77,660
- c. $81,810
- d. $90,000

26. If the fixed costs for a product decrease and the variable costs (as a percentage of sales dollars) decrease, what will be the effect on the contribution margin ratio and the breakeven point, respectively?

	Contribution Margin Ratio	Breakeven Point
a.	Decreased	Increased
b.	Increased	Decreased
c.	Decreased	Decreased
d.	Increased	Increased

27. The Breiden Company sells rodaks for $6.00 per unit. Variable costs are $2.00 per unit. Fixed costs are $37,500. How many rodaks must be sold to realize a profit before income taxes of 15% of sales?
- a. 9,375 units.
- b. 9,740 units.
- c. 11,029 units.
- d. 12,097 units.

28. At a breakeven point of 400 units sold, the variable costs were $400 and the fixed costs were $200. What will the 401st unit sold contribute to profit before income taxes?
- a. $0.
- b. $0.50.
- c. $1.00.
- d. $1.50.

29. Maxwell Company has an opportunity to acquire a new machine to replace one of its present machines. The new machine would cost $90,000, have a five-year life, and no estimated salvage value. Variable operating costs would be $100,000 per year.

The present machine has a book value of $50,000 and a remaining life of five years. Its disposal value now is $5,000 but it would be zero after five years. Variable operating costs would be $125,000 per year.

Ignore present-value calculations and income taxes. Considering the five years in total, what would be the difference in profit before income taxes by acquiring the new machine as opposed to retaining the present one?
- a. $10,000 decrease.
- b. $15,000 decrease.
- c. $35,000 increase.
- d. $40,000 increase.

30. What capital-budgeting method assumes that funds are reinvested at the company's cost of capital?
- a. Payback.
- b. Accounting rate of return.
- c. Net present value.
- d. Time-adjusted rate of return.

31. What technique is used to deal with a range of possibilities in a capital-budgeting model?
- a. Present-value concepts.
- b. Sensitivity analysis.
- c. Markov analysis.
- d. Discounted cash flow.

32. Which of the following is a useful technique in determining the fixed and variable elements of a semi-variable expense?
   a. Linear programming.
   b. Queuing theory.
   c. Program Evaluation and Review Technique.
   d. Simple regression analysis.

Items 33., 34. and 35. are based on the following information:

Full Ton Company
FINANCIAL PROJECTION FOR PRODUCT USA
For the Year Ended December 31, 1977

Sales (100 units at $100 a unit)		$10,000
Manufacturing cost of goods sold:		
Direct labor	$1,500	
Direct materials used	1,400	
Variable factory overhead	1,000	
Fixed factory overhead	500	
Total manufacturing cost of goods sold		4,400
Gross profit		5,600
Selling expenses:		
Variable	600	
Fixed	1,000	
Administrative expenses:		
Variable	500	
Fixed	1,000	
Total selling and administrative expenses		3,100
Operating income		$ 2,500

33. How many units of Product USA would have to be sold to break even?
   a. 50.
   b. 58.
   c. 68.
   d. 75.

34. What would the operating income be if sales increase by 25%?
   a. $3,125.
   b. $3,750.
   c. $4,000.
   d. $5,000.

35. What would be the sales at the breakeven point if fixed factory overhead increases by $1,700?
   a. $6,700.
   b. $8,400.
   c. $8,666.
   d. $9,200.

36. Buck Company manufactures Part No. 1700 for use in its production cycle. The costs per unit for 5,000 units of Part No. 1700 are as follows:

Direct materials	$ 2
Direct labor	12
Variable overhead	5
Fixed overhead applied	7
	$26

Hollow Company has offered to sell Buck 5,000 units of Part No. 1700 for $27 per unit. If Buck accepts the offer, some of the facilities presently used to manufacture Part No. 1700 could be used to help with the manufacture of Part No. 1211 and thus save $40,000 in relevant costs in the manufacture of Part No. 1211, and $3 per unit of the fixed overhead applied to Part No. 1700 would be totally eliminated. By what amount would net relevant costs be increased or decreased if Buck accepts Hollow's offer?
   a. $35,000 decrease.
   b. $20,000 decrease
   c. $15,000 decrease.
   d. $5,000 increase.

37. Relay Corporation manufactures batons. Relay can manufacture 300,000 batons a year at a variable cost of $750,000 and a fixed cost of $450,000. Based on Relay's predictions, 240,000 batons will be sold at the regular price of $5.00 each. In addition, a special order was placed for 60,000 batons to be sold at a 40% discount off the regular price. By what amount would income before income taxes be increased or decreased as a result of the special order?
   a. $60,000 decrease.
   b. $30,000 increase.
   c. $36,000 increase.
   d. $180,000 increase.

38. The net present value and time-adjusted rate of return methods of decision making in capital budgeting are superior to the payback method in that they
   a. Are easier to implement.
   b. Consider the time value of money.
   c. Require less input.
   d. Reflect the effects of depreciation and income taxes.

39. Sensitivity analysis is used in capital budgeting to quantify the
   a. Amount that an assumed factor used in evaluating a project could be varied and still produce acceptable results.

b. Reaction within the marketplace to a new product.
c. Type of capital that will have to be committed to an anticipated project.
d. Relationship between the payback period and the economic lives of the assets used in a project.

40. In order for a project to be acceptable to a company using the cost of capital method of analysis, the return on invested capital must

a. At least equal the amount of cash to cover interest and principal payments for any debt obtained to finance the project.
b. Generate sufficient capital to pay for itself within the economic life of the assets committed to the project.
c. At least equal the return on invested capital currently being generated by the company.
d. Generate sufficient capital resources to justify any additional capital expenditures and reduce idle capacity within the company.

41. The weighted average cost of capital approach to decision making is not directly affected by the

a. Value of the common stock.
b. Current budget for expansion.
c. Cost of debt outstanding.
d. Proposed mix of debt, equity, and existing funds used to implement the project.

Items 42 and 43 are based on the following information:

Taylor, Inc., produces only two products, Acdom and Belnom. These account for 60% and 40% of the total sales dollars of Taylor, respectively. Variable costs (as a percentage of sales dollars) are 60% for Acdom and 85% for Belnom. Total fixed costs are $150,000. There are no other costs.

42. What is Taylor's breakeven point in sales dollars?
a. $150,000.
b. $214,286.
c. $300,000.
d. $500,000.

43. Assuming that the total fixed costs of Taylor increase by 30%, what amount of sales dollars would be necessary to generate a net income of $9,000?
a. $204,000.
b. $464,000.
c. $659,000.
d. $680,000.

44. Sant Company is planning to invest $40,000 in a machine with a useful life of five years and no salvage value. The straight-line method of depreciation will be used. Sant estimates that the annual cash inflow from operations, net of income taxes, from using this machine will be $10,000. Sant's desired rate of return on investments of this type is 10%. The present value of an ordinary annuity of $1 for five periods at 10% is 3.791. The present value of $1 for five periods at 10% is 0.621. Using the net present-value method, Sant's true rate of return on this investment is
a. 0%.
b. Less than 10%, but more than 0%.
c. 10%.
d. More than 10%.

45. Brike Company, which manufactures robes, has enough idle capacity available to accept a special order of 10,000 robes at $8 a robe. A predicted income statement for the year without this special order is as follows:

	Per Unit	Total
Sales	$12.50	$1,250,000
Manufacturing costs- variable	6,25	625,000
Manufacturing costs-fixed	1.75	175,000
Manufacturing costs-total	8.00	800,000
Gross profit	4.50	450,000
Selling expenses-variable	1.80	180,000
Selling expenses-fixed	1.45	145,000
Selling expenses-total	3.25	325,000
Operating income	$ 1.25	$ 125,000

Assuming no additional selling expenses, what would be the effect on operating income if the special order was accepted?
a. $8,000 increase.
b. $17,500 increase.
c. $32,500 decrease.
d. $40,000 increase.

46. The Bread Company is planning to purchase a new machine which it will depreciate on a straight-line basis over a ten-year period. A full year's depreciation will be taken in the year of acquisition. The machine is expected to produce cash flow from operations, net of income taxes, of $3,000 in each of the ten years. The accounting (book value) rate of return is expected to be 10% on the initial increase in required investment. The cost of the new machine will be
a. $12,000.
b. $13,500.

c. $15,000.
d. $30,000.

47.   The Seahawk Company is planning to sell 200,000 units of Product B. The fixed costs are $400,000 and the variable costs are 60% of the selling price. In order to realize a profit of $100,000, the selling price per unit would have to be
a. $3.75.
b. $4.17.
c. $5.00.
d. $6.25.

48.   Gene, Inc., invested in a machine with a useful life of six years and no salvage value. The machine was depreciated using the straight-line method and it was expected to produce annual cash inflow from operations, net of income taxes, of $2,000. The present value of an ordinary annuity of $1 for six periods at 10% is 4.355. The present value of $1 for six periods at 10% is 0.564. Assuming that Gene used a time-adjusted rate of return of 10%, what was the amount of the original investment?
a. $5,640.
b. $8,710.
c. $9,000.
d. $11,280.

49.   Bert Company has projected cost of goods sold of $2,000,000 including fixed costs of $400,000 and variable costs are expected to be 75% of net sales. What will be the projected net sales?
a. $2,133,333.
b. $2,400,000.
c. $2,666,667.
d. $3,200,000.

50.   Cooper plans to invest $2,000 at the end of each of the next ten years. Assume that Cooper will earn interest at an annual rate of 6% compounded annually. The future amount of an ordinary annuity of $1 for ten periods at 6% is 13.181. The present value of $1 for ten periods at 6% is 0.558. The present value of an ordinary annuity of $1 for ten periods at 6% is 7.360. The investment after the end of ten years would be
a. $14,720.
b. $21,200.
c. $26,362.
d. $27,478.

51.   Which of the following would cause the breakeven point to change?

a.   Sales increased.
b.   Total production decreased.
c.   Total variable costs increased as a function of higher production.
d.   Fixed costs increased due to addition to physical plant.

52.   The method of cost accounting that lends itself to breakeven analysis is
a.   Variable.
b.   Standard.
c.   Absolute.
d.   Absorption.

53.   Motor Company manufactures 10,000 units of Part M-1 for use in its production annually. The following costs are reported:

Direct materials	$ 20,000
Direct labor	55,000
Variable overhead	45,000
Fixed overhead	70,000
	$190,000

Valve Company has offered to sell Motor 10,000 units of Part M-1 for $18 per unit. If Motor accepts the offer, some of the facilities presently used to manufacture Part M-1 could be rented to a third party at an annual rental of $15,000. Additionally, $4 per unit of the fixed overhead applied to Part M-1 would be totally eliminated. Should Motor accept Valve's offer, and why?
a.   No, because it would be $5,000 cheaper to make the part.
b.   Yes, because it would be $10,000 cheaper to buy the part.
c.   No, because it would be $15,000 cheaper to make the part.
d.   Yes, because it would be $25,000 cheaper to buy the part.

54.   Light Company has 2,000 obsolete light fixtures that are carried in inventory at a manufacturing cost of $30,000. If the fixtures are reworked for $10,000, they could be sold for $18,000. Alternately, the light fixtures could be sold for $3,000 to a jobber located in a distant city. In a decision model analyzing these alternatives, the opportunity cost would be
a. $ 3,000.
b. $10,000.
c. $13,000.
d. $30,000.

55. In a make-or-buy decision,
    a. Only variable costs are relevant.
    b. Fixed costs that can be avoided in the future are relevant.
    c. Fixed costs that will continue regardless of the decision are relevant.
    d. Only conversion costs are relevant.

56. In considering a special order situation that will enable a company to make use of presently idle capacity, which of the following costs would be irrelevant?
    a. Materials.
    b. Depreciation.
    c. Direct labor.
    d. Variable overhead.

57. Which of the following cost allocation methods would be used to determine the lowest price that could be quoted for a special order that would utilize idle capacity within a production area?
    a. Job order.
    b. Process.
    c. Variable.
    d. Standard.

58. Mar Company has two decentralized divisions, X and Y. Division X has always purchased certain units from Division Y at $75 per unit. Because Division Y plans to raise the price to $100 per unit, Division X desires to purchase these units from outside suppliers for $75 per unit. Division Y's costs follow:

Y's variable costs per unit	$70
Y's annual fixed costs	$15,000
Y's annual production of these units for X	1,000 units

If Division X buys from an outside supplier, the facilities Division Y uses to manufacture these units would remain idle. What would be the result if Mar enforces a transfer price of $100 per unit between Divisions X and Y?
    a. It would be suboptimization for the company because X should buy from outside suppliers at $75 per unit.
    b. It would provide lower overall company net income than a transfer price of $75 per unit.
    c. It would provide higher overall company net income than a transfer price of $75 per unit.
    d. It would be more profitable for the company than allowing X to buy from outside suppliers at $75 per unit.

59. Tracy Corporation is planning to invest $80,000 in a three-year project. Tracy's expected rate of return is 10%. The present value of $1 at 10% for one year is .909, for two years is .826, and for three years is .751. The cash flow, net of income taxes, will be $30,000 for the first year (present value of $27,270) and $36,000 for the second year (present value of $29,736). Assuming the rate of return is exactly 10%, what will the cash flow, net of income taxes, be for the third year?
    a. $17,268.
    b. $22,000.
    c. $22,994.
    d. $30,618.

60. On January 1, 1981, Jenkins, Inc., purchased for $520,000 a new machine with a useful life of eight years and no salvage value. The machine will be depreciated using the straight-line method and it is expected to produce annual cash flow from operations, net of income taxes, of $120,000. The present value of an ordinary annuity of $1 for eight periods at 14% is 4.639. The present value of $1 for eight periods at 14% is 0.351. Assuming that Jenkins uses a time-adjusted rate of return of 14%, what is the net present value?
    a. $ 36,680.
    b. $ 94,848.
    c. $154,440.
    d. $255,145.

61. Plainfield Company manufactures part G for use in its production cycle. The cost per unit for 10,000 units of part G are as follows:

Direct materials	$ 3
Direct labor	15
Variable overhead	6
Fixed overhead	8
	$32

Verona Company has offered to sell Plainfield 10,000 units of part G for $30 per unit. If Plainfield accepts Verona's offer, the released facilities could be used to save $45,000 in relevant costs in the manufacture of part H. In addition $5 per unit of the fixed overhead applied to part G would be totally eliminated. What alternative is more desirable and by what amount is it more desirable?

	Alternative	Amount
a.	Manufacture	$10,000
b.	Manufacture	$15,000
c.	Buy	$35,000
d.	Buy	$65,000

62.   Brunswick Company is planning to purchase a new machine. The payback period will be six years. The new machine is expected to produce cash flow from operations, net of income taxes, of $3,500 a year for each of the first three years of the payback period and $2,500 a year for each of the last three years of the payback period. Depreciation of $2,000 a year will be charged to income for each of the six years of the payback period. How much will the machine cost?

    a. $ 6,000.
    b. $12,000.
    c. $18,000.
    d. $21,000.

63.   Warfield Company is planning to sell 100,000 units of product T for $12.00 a unit. The fixed costs are $280,000. In order to realize a profit of $200,000, what would the variable costs be?

    a. $480,000.
    b. $720,000.
    c. $900,000.
    d. $920,000.

64.   Sun Company's tentative budget for product H for 1981 is as follows:

Sales	$600,000
Variable manufacturing costs	360,000
Fixed costs:	
Manufacturing	90,000
Selling and administrative	110,000

Mr. Johnston, the marketing manager, proposes an aggressive advertising campaign costing an additional $50,000 and resulting in a 30% unit sales increase for product H. Assuming that Johnston's proposal is incorporated into the budget for product H, what should be the increase in the budgeted operating profit for 1981?

    a. $ 12,000.
    b. $ 22,000.
    c. $ 72,000.
    d. $130,000.

65.   Gerber Company is planning to sell 200,000 units of product O for $2.00 a unit. The contribution margin is 25%. Gerber will break even at this level of sales. What would be the fixed costs?

    a. $100,000.
    b. $160,000.
    c. $200,000.
    d. $300,000.

MULTIPLE CHOICE ANSWERS

1.	d	14.	c	27.	d	40.	c	53.	a
2.	d	15.	d	28.	b	41.	b	54.	a
3.	b	16.	a	29.	d	42.	d	55.	b
4.	c	17.	c	30.	c	43.	d	56.	b
5.	a	18.	d	31.	b	44.	b	57.	c
6.	d	19.	b	32.	d	45.	b	58.	d
7.	d	20.	c	33.	a	46.	c	59.	d
8.	c	21.	d	34.	b	47.	d	60.	a
9.	d	22.	b	35.	b	48.	b	61.	c
10.	b	23.	a	36.	c	49.	a	62.	c
11.	d	24.	c	37.	b	50.	c	63.	b
12.	b	25.	b	38.	b	51.	d	64.	b
13.	b	26.	b	39.	a	52.	a	65.	a

EXPLANATION OF MULTIPLE CHOICE ANSWERS

1. (1180,T1,32) (d) The net present value of a project represents the present value of the cash flows less the original investment. Answer (b) is incorrect because present value is not used. Answer (a) is incorrect because it is the amount of the discount on the cash flows. Answer (c) does not make sense.

2. (1180,T1,33) (d) The payback method evaluates investments on the basis of the length of time until the initial investment is returned. If annual cash flows are constant, the payback period is calculated as follows:

$$\frac{\text{Initial investment}}{\text{Annual cash flow}}$$

Answer (a) is incorrect because the payback period is not a function of useful life. Answers (b) and (c) are incorrect because the payback method ignores the time value of money.

3. (1180,T1,34) (b) Within the relevant range, the variable cost per unit is constant. Total variable cost differs at each production level [answer (a)] and increases as production increases [answer (c)]; answer (d) is incorrect because only fixed cost per unit decreases as production increases.

4. (1180,T1,35) (c) Contribution margin ratio is computed as follows:

$$\frac{\text{Contribution margin}}{\text{Sales}}$$

where contribution margin equals sales less variable expenses. Breakeven point increasing [answer (a)] or decreasing [answer (b)] does not necessarily indicate a change in contribution margin ratio; an increase or decrease in the breakeven point could be caused by an increase or decrease in fixed expenses. If variable costs as a percentage of sales increase [answer (d)], contribution margin becomes smaller. However, if variable costs decrease as a percentage of sales, contribution margin as a percentage must increase. Therefore, answer (c) is correct.

5. (1180,T1,45) (a) Relevant costs are expected future costs that differ across alternatives. When making an equipment replacement decision, management is interested in relevant costs, costs which change depending on which decision management makes. Answers (b), (c) and (d) could all be part of the total relevant costs, and could include costs which are not relevant. Limiting management to any one of these three choices would likely mean giving management only part of the relevant cost data it needs.

6. (1180,P2,21) (d) The requirement is the annual cash inflow, net of income taxes, from the investment in the new machine. Since the only information given is the initial investment of $28,000 and the fact that there is a return on this initial investment of 15%, the formula for the accounting rate of return (ARR) must be used to solve for the unknown net cash inflow.

$$\frac{\text{Net cash inflow} - \text{depreciation expense}}{\text{initial investment}} = \text{ARR}$$

Plugging the known information into the formula gives

$$\frac{\text{Net cash inflow} - \$28,000/8 \text{ years}}{\$28,000} = 15\%$$

$$\text{Net cash inflow} = (15\% \times \$28,000) + \frac{\$28,000}{8}$$

$$\text{Net cash inflow} = \underline{\$7,700}$$

7. (1180,P2,22) (d) The requirement is the payback period for a new machine where cash flows are not uniform. The payback period is the length of time needed to recover the original investment ($84,000). Remember that depreciation is ignored in the payback method. After 6 years, $60,000 [(6)($10,000)] will have been recaptured, leaving $24,000 of the original investment unrecovered. This remaining $24,000 will be recovered in 2 years ($12,000/year) making the total payback period 6 years + 2 years, or 8.0 years.

8. (1180,P2,26) (c) The requirement is the approximate expected rate of return on the investment. The initial investment of $120,000 provides a ten-year annuity of $20,000 of cash inflows net of income taxes. The solutions approach is to solve for factor implicit in the relationship between the $120,000 investment and the $20,000 net cash invlow from the investment

$$\$20,000 \times \frac{\text{Factor for ten}}{\text{periods @ i\%}} = \$120,000$$

$$\frac{\text{Factor for ten}}{\text{periods @ i\%}} = \frac{\$120,000}{\$20,000} = 6.00$$

Since the factor 6.00 falls between the factors for 10% and 12% the expected rate of return is less than 12%, but more than 10%.

9.   (1180,P2,27)   (d)   The requirement is the cash flow, net of income taxes, for the second year of the project, assuming a rate of return of exactly 12%. The unknown cash flow is an amount such that when it is discounted two periods and added to the discounted cash flow for one period ($40,000) the resulting present value is equal to the amount of the investment ($100,000).

$$\$100,000 = (.8929 \times \$40,000) + (.7972 \times \text{Year 2 net cash flow})$$

$$\text{Year 2 net cash flow} = \frac{\$100,000 - (.9 \times \$40,000)}{.8} = \$80,000$$

The closest answer is $80,638 (d).

10. (1180,P2,29)   (b)   The requirement is how many units of product X (one of three products) Thomas would sell at the breakeven point. The solutions approach is first to find the number of composite units to breakeven; a composite unit consists of the number of units of each of the three products in the mix. Since Thomas sells 3 units of X for each unit of Z and 2 units of Y for each unit of X they are selling 6 units of Y for each unit of Z; therefore a composite unit consists of 3X, 6Y, and 1Z. The total contribution margin for 1 composite unit is

$$
\begin{array}{lll}
X & (3)\ (\$1.00) = & \$\ 3 \\
Y & (6)\ (\$1.50) = & \$\ 9 \\
Z & (1)\ (\$3.00) = & \underline{\$\ 3} \\
& & \underline{\$15}
\end{array}
$$

The breakeven point in terms of units of the product mix group is:

$600,000 ÷ $15 = 40,000 composite units

Since there are three units of X in each composite unit, (40,000)(3) or 120,000 units of X are sold at breakeven.

11. (1180,P2,31)   (d)   The requirement is to determine whether or not Dana should let its Lawn Products Division purchase the blades required for production from an outside supplier. The solutions approach is to identify any differential costs between the two alternatives.

Differential Costs

	Make	Buy	Difference
Variable Costs	(10,000)		
Cost to buy			
(10,000)($1.25)		(12,500)	
	(10,000)	(12,500)	(2,500)

The cost of buying from an outside supplier is $2,500 more than making, so the Lawn Products Division should not buy the blades from the outsider. Note that fixed costs are not differential; they would be incurred under either alternative.

12. (1180,P2,34)   (b)   The requirement is the effect on operating income if the special order is accepted. Argus has sufficient unused plant capacity available; therefore, the budgeted fixed manufacturing costs per unit (lamp) can be ignored. The additional revenue per unit is $11.50, and variable costs per unit are $8.00 plus an overtime premium of $1.50 per unit. The change in operating income is (40,000 lamps) times ($11.50 − 8.00 − 1.50) or an increase of $80,000.

13.   (580,P2,21)   (b)   The requirement is for the number of total units sold at the breakeven point given a sales mix of 2 units of D and 3 units of W. The solutions approach is to divide the fixed costs by the contribution margin per composite unit. A composite unit consists of 2 units of D and 3 units of W. The number of composite units (30,000) is then multiplied by the number of units of each item in the mix to determine the number of units of that item at the breakeven point. Finally, the total number of units of D is added to the total number of units of W to come up with the total number of units.

$$\frac{\$420,000}{(2 \times \$4) + (3 \times \$2)}$$

$$\frac{\text{Fixed costs}}{\text{Contrib. per composite unit}} = \frac{\$420,000}{\$14} =$$

$$= 30,000 \text{ composite units}$$

$$
\begin{array}{lll}
D = 2 \times 30,000 = & 60,000 & \text{units} \\
W = 3 \times 30,000 & \underline{90,000} & \text{units} \\
\text{Total } = & \underline{150,000} & \text{units}
\end{array}
$$

14.   (580,P2,22)   (c)   The requirement is to find the amount of original investment given a net present value of $1,000. Recall that the net present value is equal to the present value of future cash flows from an expenditure minus the original cash outlay or investment. The solutions approach is to find the present value of the future cash flows and subtract the $1,000 net present value.

Year	Cash Flow	PV of $1 at 10%	PV Cash Inflow
1	$4,000	.909	$3,636.00
2	4,400	.826	3,634.40
3	4,800	.751	3,604.80
4	5,200	.683	3,551.60
			$14,426.80

$14,427 PV of cash inflows
 (1,000) Excess of net PV over investment
$13,427 Original investment

15. (580,P2,24) (d) In computing the payback period (with the income tax effect), it is necessary to reduce the future cash flows per year by the amount of income taxes that will be paid.

$$\text{Payback period} = \frac{\text{Investment in machine}}{\text{Annual net cash inflow}}$$

Annual net cash inflow:

Cash inflow before income taxes		$12,000
Income taxes 50% (12,000 − 5,000)		3,500
		$8,500

$$\frac{\$40,000 \text{ Investment}}{\$8,500 \text{ net cash inflow}} = 4.7 \text{ years}$$

16. (580,P2,25) (a) The accounting rate of return is equal to the after-tax income divided by the initial investment.

(Cash flow − depreciation − taxes) ÷ Investment in machine = accounting rate of return

($12,000 − 5,000 - 3,500) ÷ $40,000 = 8.75%

17. (580,P2,26) (c) The requirement is to find total sales given net income of $200,000. In cost-volume-profit analysis, total sales at the breakeven point are equal to the fixed costs plus net income divided by the contribution margin ratio (S = (FC + NI) ÷ CM%). Since net income is $0 at the breakeven point,

(FC + 0) ÷ 40% = $400,000; FC = $160,000.

Using the fixed costs to solve for total sales at a profit level of $200,000,

($160,000 + 200,000) ÷ 40% = S
S = $900,000

18. (580,P2,29) (d) The requirement is the number of units of Q that must be sold to generate an operating income of $40,000. The solutions approach is to let "x" equal the number of units sold, and to solve for "x."

NI = S − VC − FC
$40,000 = $6x − $4x − $200,000
2x = $240,000
x = 120,000 units

19. (580,P2,30) (b) The requirement is the net present value of acquiring a new machine. The solutions approach is to compare the uniform cash inflows of $70,000 for six periods with the initial outlay of $240,000. First multiply the present value factor for six periods by $70,000 (cash flow net of taxes). Then subtract the initial investment from the present value of cash inflows to find net present value.

$70,000 cash flow net of taxes x 4.111 =	$287,770
Initial investment	$240,000
Net present value	$ 47,770

20. (580,T1,47) (c) When fixed costs increase, the breakeven point will also increase because more units must be sold in order to cover the fixed costs. Contribution margin is equal to sales less variable costs. Therefore, an increase in fixed costs will have no effect on the contribution margin.

21. (580,T1,49) (d) The cost of capital is the weighted-average cost to the firm of obtaining funds. The cost of borrowing money on bonds is the after-tax interest rate since bond interest payments are deductible for tax purposes. The cost of preferred stock is generally agreed to be its annual dividend rate. Answers (a) and (b) are wrong because they refer to pretax rates of interest. Answer (c) is not a reasonable answer.

22. (1179,P2,23) (b) The requirement is the expected cash flow (net of taxes) from a machine in its fifth year. The machine will cost $30,000 and has a 5-year payback. The payback period is the number of years required to recoup the original investment. Thus, $30,000 will be returned from operating the machine in the first 5 years. The problem states that the payback (net of taxes) is $7,000 a year for the first 3 years and $5,500 in the fourth year. Thus, $26,500 is paid back in years 1 through 4. Accordingly, the payback in the 5th year is $3,500 ($30,000 - $26,500).

23. (1179,P2,24) (a) The requirement is the initial investment in a machine if it has an accounting rate of return of 12% and will generate $66,000 of net cash flow (before depreciation). The accounting rate of return is net income over the initial investment. Net income would be the net cash flow (i.e., after taxes, operating expenses, etc.) less depreciation. The solutions approach is to set up an equation to determine the cost. 12% of cost is equal to $66,000 minus depreciation (10% of cost per year). As computed below, the cost is $300,000.

.12 cost = $66,000 − .10 cost
.22 cost = 66,000
cost = $300,000

24.   (1179,P2,29) (c) The requirement is a machine's cost if the machine will generate $20,000 per year for 5 years and the expected rate of return is 10%. The $20,000 per year is an annuity of 5 payments of $20,000. The present value of this annuity is the $20,000 payment times the time value of money factor of the present value of an annuity for 5 years (3.791). Thus, the present value is $75,820 ($20,000 × 3.791).

25.   (1179,P2,30) (b) The requirement is an asset's cost given a cash flow of $40,000 in the first year and $50,000 in the second year with an expected rate of return of 10%. The solutions approach is to discount the $40,000 cash flow in year 1 and the $50,000 cash flow in year 2 back to the beginning of the first year. A time value of money factor of .909 for the first payment, and .826 for the second, yields a net present value (cost) of $77,660 (.909 × $40,000 + .826 × $50,000).

	10% PV		
Year	TVMF	Payment	PV
1	.909	$40,000	$36,360
2	.826	$50,000	$41,300

Present value (cost) of the investment $77,660

26.   (1179,T1,31) (b) The requirement is the effect on the contribution margin and the breakeven point of a decrease in fixed costs and a decrease in variable costs as a percentage of sales dollars. If the variable cost percentage of sales decreases, the contribution margin ratio will increase. The contribution margin ratio is one minus the variable cost as a percentage of sales dollars. If the fixed costs decrease, the breakeven point will also decrease because there will be a lower level of sales required to obtain the breakeven point.

27.   (1176,P2,20) (d) As above, the basic equation is sales = fixed costs + variable costs + profit. Sales equal $6.00X (X being the number of units sold). Fixed costs are $37,500 and variable costs are $2.00X. Since profit is 15% of sales, profit will be $.90 for every unit sold. Solving for X, the number of units to create a profit of 15% of sales, equals 12,097 units.

$$
\begin{aligned}
S &= FC + VC + P \\
\$6.00X &= \$37,500 + \$2.00X + \$.90X \\
\$3.10X &= \$37,500 \\
X &= 12,097
\end{aligned}
$$

28.   (1176,P2,21) (b) At the breakeven point of 400 units, there is $600 of total cost ($400 variables and $200 fixed) which equal sales. If 400 units create sales of $600, the unit selling price is $1.50. The variable cost per unit is $1.00 ($400 divided by 400). Thus, the contribution margin per unit is $.50 ($1.50 minus $1.00).

29.   (1176,P2,22) (d) Ignoring present value and tax considerations, the new machine's depreciation over its 5-year period will decrease income by $40,000 (additional cost of new machine over old machine's book value). The operating costs savings will be $25,000 per year or $125,000. Also acquisition of the new machine will result in a $45,000 loss from the sale of the old machine. The journal entry would be:

Cash	$ 5,000	
Loss on sale	45,000	
Machine (old)		$50,000

The net effect is a $40,000 increase in income over the five-year period as calculated below:

$ −40,000 additional depreciation of new machine
  −45,000 loss on sale (closed to I/S account)
 +125,000 cost savings
$ 40,000 increase in income.

30.   (1176,T2,32) (c) The payback capital budgeting method measures the length of time for the investment to return the original investment, i.e., investment divided by net annual cash flow. The accounting rate of return (also book value and unadjusted rate of return) is the increase in dollars of accounting income over the average investment (occasionally with a denominator of the entire investment). The net present value method determines the present value of the investment given a discount (profit return) rate. Alternate investments are evaluated by comparing the present values of the alternate investment projects. Presumably the project with the highest present value is the most favorable. Unfortunately, this method assumes that investment flows are reinvested at the company's cost of capital. The time adjusted rate of return method determines the discount (investment return) rate by setting the future net cash flows of an investment project equal to the amount of the required investment. In contrast to the net present value approach, the rate of return method assumes that the cash flows from the investment project can be reinvested at the rate of return obtained from the original investment project.

31.   (1176,T2,33) (b) Sensitivity analysis is an approach used to determine the effect

on the solution of a modeling process of changing input variables. For example in capital budgeting, the effect of changing the amount and length of cash inflows from the investment can be determined to indicate the sensitivity of the investment return to these changes. In this manner a range of possibilities in terms of future cash flows is considered.

Markov analysis is concerned with the movement of random processes to forecast future movements of the same variable. Present value concepts underlie discounted cash flow procedures which are common to both the net present value and time adjusted rate of return capital budgeting methods.

32. (578,T2,33) (d) Semi-variable expense consists of fixed and variable expenses. It can be separated into fixed and variable components by regression analysis. The formula is set forth below. As it indicates, total cost is equal to fixed cost plus variable cost. Regression analysis will specify b, the slope of the cost line, which represents the variable cost per unit. The intercept, a, will yield the total fixed cost. Costs at two levels of activity are required as two equations are necessary to solve for the two unknowns (a and b).

$$TC_1 = a + bx_1$$

where TC_1 = total cost at any activity level
         a = fixed cost
         b = variable cost per unit
         x_1 = level of activity in units

33. (1177,P2,29) (a) The requirement is the number of units to break even. Remember, the basic breakeven equation is sales equals fixed costs plus variable costs, as specified below. The fixed costs of $2,500 consist of $500 factory overhead, $1,000 selling expenses, and $1,000 administrative expenses. The variable costs per unit (remember, the projected income statement is based upon 100 units) consist of $15 direct labor, $14 direct materials, $10 variable overhead, $6 selling expenses, and $5 administrative expenses, which total $50. Since the selling price is $100 per unit, the variable costs are 50%. Thus, as computed below, the breakeven point is $5,000, which is 50 units at the $100/unit selling price.

$$S = FC + VC$$
$$S = \$2,500 + .5S$$
$$.5S = \$2,500$$
$$S = \$5,000 \text{ or } 50 \text{ units}$$

or

$$x = \text{units to break even}$$
$$\$100x = \$50x + \$2,500$$
$$\$50x = \$2,500$$
$$x = 50 \text{ units}$$

34. (1177,P2,30) (b) The requirement is operating income if sales increase by 25%. As specified in the formula below, net income would be sales of $12,500 (25% greater than the previous $10,000) less fixed costs of $2,500 less variable costs of $6,250. An alternative solution would be to recognize that the contribution margin (sales minus the variable cost) is 50% and thus the increase in income would be 50% of the increase in sales of $2,500.

$$NI = S - FC - VC$$
$$\$3,750 = 12,500 - \$2,500 - 6,250$$

35. (1177,P2,31) (b) The requirement is the breakeven point in total sales dollars if factory overhead increased by $1,700. This would increase the fixed costs to $4,200. Since the variable costs continue to be 50% of sales, the new breakeven point would be $8,400 as computed below. An alternative solution would be to recognize that the contribution margin continues to be 50%. Thus, an increase of $1,700 in fixed costs would require an increase in $3,400 of sales to break even (the former breakeven point was $5,000).

$$S = \$4,200 + .5S$$
$$.5S = \$4,200$$
$$S = \$8,400$$

36. (1177,P2,36) (c) The requirement is the change in cost if Buck Company buys 5,000 parts at $27 per unit from an outside party rather than manufacturing the part in house. The solutions approach is to compare the $135,000 outside purchase cost with the cost savings effected by the outside purchase. The cost savings will result in $22 per unit ($2 direct materials, $12 direct labor, $5 variable overhead, and $3 fixed overhead) or $110,000, plus the additional $40,000 savings with regard to Part No. 1211. Thus $150,000 of cost will be "saved" by spending $135,000 on the outside purchase, resulting in a $15,000 decrease in cost.

37. (1177,P2,38) (b) The requirement is the incremental income of selling 60,000 batons at $3 each ($5 per unit at a 40% discount). Since the variable cost for 300,000 batons is $750,000, the variable costs are $2.50 per unit. Thus, the contribution margin of $.50 ($3 − $2.50) times the 60,000 special-order batons equals an increase in income of $30,000.

38.   (1177,T2,37) (b)   Both the time-adjusted rate of return method and the net present value method of capital budgeting consider the time value of money. In contrast, the payback method simply measures the length of time required for the investment to return the initial capital outlay. Thus the time-adjusted rate of return and net present value method are concerned with the profitability, i.e., rate of return on investments. The payback method, measuring only the time required to return the original investment outlay, provides a measure of the risk of the investment. All three methods reflect the effects of depreciation and income taxes because they are concerned with net annual cash flows. The payback method is both easier to implement and requires less input than both the net present value and time-adjusted rate of return methods.

39.   (1177,T2,38) (a)   Sensitivity analysis generally describes the process of determining the effect of varying the inputs in an optimization model, e.g., linear programming. Thus sensitivity analysis indicates what will happen to the profitability of a project if constraints are slightly tightened, increased, etc. Sensitivity analysis would be used in capital budgeting to determine the amount that an assumed input could be varied and still produce acceptable results. Sensitivity analysis does not accomplish any of the objectives specified in answers (b), (c), and (d).

40.   (1177,T2,43) (c)   Cost of capital may be synonymous with terms such as minimum desired rate of return, cutoff rate, hurdle rate, target rate, etc. The cost of capital is an investment's rate of return that will not affect the market price of the investing company's stock. Thus, any investment project being evaluated under the cost of capital concept would have to have a greater return than other projects being used by the company, or else the value of the company's stock would be impaired. Answers (a) and (b) are incorrect because there would be no net cash flows to the investment company if the return was equal to cash outflows. Answer (d) is incorrect because the cost of capital analysis evaluates investment projects based upon their return, not upon their ability to generate capital resources for other projects.

41.   (1177,T2,44) (b)   The requirement is what does not directly affect the weighted average cost of capital approach to decision making. The weighted average cost of capital approach to decision making is to determine the proportionate share of financing to be done by different methods, e.g., debt, preferred stock, common stock, etc. Then weight the cost of each type of financing by the proportion to be thus financed to obtain a weighted average of the cost of capital for various types of financing. Answer (a), value of common stock, is necessary to compute the cost of common stock, i.e., common dividends divided by common stock value. Answer (c), cost of debt outstanding, is the cost of debt. Answer (d), the proposed mix of debt, equity, etc., is necessary to determine the weighted average of the cost of capital. Answer (b), the current budget for expansion, is a constraint upon the amount of investments to be made, but does not affect the relative ranking of desirability of investments.

42.   (1178,P2,24) (d)   The requirement is the breakeven point in sales dollars. The solutions approach is to formulate the breakeven equation as illustrated below. At breakeven, sales equals total fixed costs plus total variable costs. Fixed costs are $150,000. Variable costs for Taylor are 60% of Acdom sales (which are 60% of total sales) plus 85% of Belnom sales (which are 40% of total sales). Thus Acdom variable costs are 36% of total sales (60% VC percentage times 60% Acdom share of total sales). Belnom variable costs are 34% of total sales (85% VC percentage times 40% Belnom share of total sales).

$$\begin{aligned} \text{Sales} &= \text{FC} + \text{VC} \\ \text{Sales} &= \$150{,}000 + .60 \text{ sales } (.60) + .40 \text{ sales } (.85) \\ \text{Sales} &= \$150{,}000 + .36 \text{ sales} + .34 \text{ sales} \\ \text{Sales} &= \$150{,}000 + .70 \text{ sales} \\ .3 \text{ Sales} &= \$150{,}000 \\ \text{Sales} &= \$500{,}000 \end{aligned}$$

43.   (1178,P2,25) (d)   The requirement is the amount of sales that would be needed to generate net income of $9,000 if fixed costs increased by 30%. Fixed costs increase from $150,000 to $195,000. Variable costs are 70% of sales as explained in the previous item. The solutions approach is to set up the breakeven equation as illustrated below.

$$\begin{aligned} \text{Sales} &= \text{FC} + \text{VC} + \text{Profit} \\ \text{Sales} &= \$195{,}000 + .70 \text{ sales} + \$9{,}000 \\ .3 \text{ Sales} &= \$204{,}000 \\ \text{Sales} &= \$680{,}000 \end{aligned}$$

44.   (1178,P2,26) (b)   The requirement is the rate of return on an investment costing $40,000 and returning $10,000 a year for five years, with no salvage value.

The present value of an ordinary annuity for five periods at 10% is 3.791 as given in the problem; thus the present value of an annuity of $10,000 is $37,910. In order to earn a 10% return, one would invest $37,910 and receive $10,000 per year for five years. Since $40,000 has to be invested, the rate of return is less than 10%. The rate of return is more than 0% because $40,000 is invested, and $50,000 (both principal and interest) is received.

45. (1178,P2,29) (b) The requirement is the effect on operating income of accepting a special order of 10,000 robes at $8 a robe. The variable cost of manufacturing each robe is $6.25. The adequate idle capacity indicates there would be no increase in fixed costs. Also since this is a special order there would be no additional selling expenses, either variable or fixed. Thus the contribution of income would be $1.75 per unit ($8 − $6.25) times 10,000 robes, or $17,500.

46. (579,P2,23) (c) The requirement is the cost of a new machine if there is a 10% accounting rate of return on the initial investment. The accounting rate of return is accounting net income over book value. The book value of the new machine would be its cost. The $3,000 cash flow net of income taxes does not reflect the 10% straight-line depreciation. The solutions approach is to set up a formula in which cost is equal to $3,000 minus depreciation (which is 10% of cost) all over 10%. The numerator is the accounting income that reflects depreciation. The denominator is the capitalization rate, 10%. Solving the formula indicates that the cost of the machine is $15,000.

$$\text{cost} = \frac{\$3,000 - .10(\text{cost})}{.10}$$

.10 cost = $3,000 − .10 cost
.20 cost = $3,000
cost = $15,000

47. (579,P2,26) (d) The requirement is the selling price per unit for 200,000 units to realize a profit of $100,000. The solutions approach is to set up a break-even formula in which 200,000 units of Product B times B (selling price of each B) equals $400,000 of fixed costs plus variable costs of 60% of the selling price plus $100,000 of profits. Solving the equation, one finds B (selling price of Product B) to be $6.25.

Sales = FC + VC + Desired NI
200,000 B = $400,000 + .60 (200,000 B) + $100,000
200,000 B = $500,000 + 120,000 B
80,000 B = $500,000
B = $6.25

48. (579,P2,27) (b) The requirement is the amount of the original investment if the investment produces $2,000 a year for six years and was supposed to yield 10%. Since the TVMF of an ordinary annuity for six periods at 10% is 4.355, the present value of $2,000 for six periods is $8,710 ($2,000 x 4.355).

49. (579,P2,34) (a) The requirement is projected net sales if variable costs are 75% of net sales. Since variable costs are $1,600,000 ($2,000,000 CGS − $400,000 FC), set up an equation as illustrated below:

.75 S = $1,600,000
S = $2,133,000

50. (579,P2,40) (c) The requirement is the future value of $2,000 deposited at the end of each year for 10 years. Since the TVMF of the future value of an ordinary annuity at 6% is 13.181, the future value of the investment would be $26,362 ($2,000 x 13.181).

51. (579,T1,28) (d) The requirement is the variable which would change the break-even point. If fixed costs increase, the break-even point increases. In other words, it takes additional sales and related profits to cover the additional fixed costs. Answer (a), a change in sales, and answer (b), levels of production, are incorrect because they do not affect the break-even point. Only cost relationships affect the break-even point. Answer (c) is incorrect because total variable costs do increase with higher production. Note that answer (c) indicates that total variable costs increased, not the unit variable cost. If variable costs change as a percentage of sales dollars, the break-even point would change.

52. (579,T1,37) (a) Since break-even analysis requires a clear distinction between fixed and variable costs, variable costing, which emphasizes and isolates fixed and variable costs, lends itself to break-even analysis. Answers (b) standard costing, and (d) absorption costing, both develop unit costs that include fixed costs. Answer (c), absolute costing, is a nonsense term.

53. (580,P2,37) (a) The requirement is to evaluate an outside offer to have 10,000 units of Part M-1 made outside rather than by Motor Company. The solutions approach is to include only those costs which are incurred, if the product is manufactured internally. In addition to the variable manufacturing costs listed, it is necessary to add the opportunity cost of the rent on

the facility and to adjust the fixed cost to include only the unavoidable fixed costs.

Direct materials	$ 20,000
Direct labor	55,000
Variable overhead	45,000
Fixed overhead (unavoidable portion only)	40,000
Rent foregone	15,000
To make	$175,000
To buy	180,000
Net advantage of making vs. buying	$ 5,000

54. (580,P2,40) (a)   The requirement is the opportunity cost in a decision model analysis of two alternatives. The opportunity cost is the $3,000 for which obsolete fixtures could be sold rather than reworking them.

55. (580,T1,44) (b)   In any business decision, a cost is relevant if it is expected to be different in the future depending on which alternative is chosen. Any type of cost (fixed, variable, etc.) can be relevant as long as it fits that description. Answers (a) and (d) are incorrect because they limit relevance to certain types of costs. Answer (c) is incorrect because it describes a cost which will not differ among alternatives.

56. (579,T1,21) (b)   Note that the requirement is the cost that is not relevant in considering a special order situation. Special order situations should only consider variable costs, because the fixed costs will continue whether the special order is accepted or not. Since depreciation is a fixed cost, it is irrelevant. Answers (a), materials, (c), direct labor, and (d), variable overhead, are all variable costs, which are relevant to special order decisions.

57. (579,T1,24) (c)   The requirement is the cost allocation method that would determine the lowest price that could be quoted to use idle capacity. Variable costing considers fixed overhead to be a period cost and not a product cost, i.e., is not relevant to inventory costing. A loss equal to fixed costs would occur if no production takes place, because fixed costs will continue, so idle capacity should be used if variable costs can be covered, i.e., selling price equals or is greater than variable costs. Any additional revenue in excess of variable costs incurred would then help decrease a loss or produce income. Answers (a), job order, (b), process, and (d), standard, all describe cost allocation methods which consider fixed costs to be product costs rather than period costs.

58. (1175,P2,27) (d)   The requirement is to determine the result of enforcing an internal transfer price of $100 per unit between Divisions X and Y. Since Y's variable costs are $70 per unit, it is more profitable for the overall company to buy the units from Y than to buy them from outside suppliers, i.e., the net cash outflow is $70 when purchased from Y and $75 when purchased from outside suppliers. Overall company net income is uneffected by the level of the transfer price. The transfer price will only affect the income reported by the individual divisions X and Y. Recognize that answers (a), (b), (c), and (d) all refer to company net income rather than divisional income.

MAY 1981 ANSWERS

59. (581,P2,21) (d)   The requirement is to compute the cash flow, net of income taxes, for the third year. Assuming that the rate of return is exactly 10%, then the $80,000 investment is the present value of the 3 future cash inflows discounted at 10%. The net cash flow in year three is computed as follows:

Total Present Value	$80,000
—PV year 1 cash flow	(27,270)
—PV year 2 cash flow	(29,736)
PV year 3 cash flow	$22,994

$22,994 = .751 x year 3 cash flow

$22,994 ÷ .751 (PV of $1 year 3) = $30,618 year 3 cash flow.

60. (581,P2,22) (a)   The requirement is to compute the net present value. The question states "Jenkins uses a time-adjusted rate of return of 14%", apparently the AICPA examiners mean a "hurdle rate" of 14% because the time adjusted rate of return and the net present value methods are two distinct approaches to capital budgeting decisions. The computation of the net present value is

Annual cash flow (net of tax)		PV of ordinary annuity of $1		Present value
$120,000	x	4.639	=	556,680

Present Value	—	Initial Investment	=	Net Present Value
$556,680	—	$520,000	=	$36,680

Remember that depreciation is implicitly taken into consideration when using the time value of money factors; therefore, no adjustment for depreciation to the cash flow is necessary. Note that the effect of depreciation on income taxes is considered. However, since the $120,000 is net of income taxes, nothing needs to be done with depreciation.

61.   (581,P2,29)   (c)   The requirement is to compute the alternative (make or buy) that is most desirable and the amount by which that alternative is more desirable. The solutions approach is to list the relevant costs associated with each alternative.

Buy G		Manufacture G	
Purchase Price of G		Direct Materials:	
10,000 x $30 =	$300,000	10,000 x $ 3 =	$ 30,000
		Direct Labor:	
		10,000 x $15 =	150,000
Less cost savings		Variable OH:	
on Product H	(45,000)	10,000 x $ 6 =	60,000
		Fixed OH:	
		10,000 x $ 5*=	50,000
Total Cost	$255,000	Total Cost	$290,000

*The relevant (out of pocket) cost is the $5 cost which is avoided if part G is not manufactured.

Buying part G from Verona Company is the more desirable alternative; the net cost saving is $35,000.

62.   (581,P2,30)   (c)   The requirement is to compute the cost of the machine given the payback period and the cash flow in each year of the payback period. The payback period is the number of periods it takes to recover the initial cost of the investment. In applying the payback method where cash flows are not the same every year, it is necessary to use a cumulative approach. The cost of the machine is the total cash received in the 6 year payback period.

($3,500 x 3 yrs) + ($2,500 x 3 yrs) = $18,000 cost of machine

Depreciation is not taken into consideration in the payback computation, except as it affects income taxes which have already been determined.

63.   (581,P2,35)   (b)   The requirement is to compute variable costs. The solutions approach is to analyze the income statement equation : Sales — Variable Costs — Fixed Costs = Income. Rearranging terms gives Variable Costs = Sales — Fixed Costs — Income. Therefore, variable costs are ($100,000 x $12) — $280,000 — $200,000 = $720,000.

64.   (581,P2,36)   (b)   The requirement is to compute the increase in the budgeted operating profit for 1981 if Johnston's proposal is incorporated into the budget. The solutions approach is to compute the additional revenue and additional expenses associated with Johnston's proposal.

Additional Revenue:
$600,000 x .30 = $180,000

Additional Expenses:	
Variable $360,000 x .30 =	(108,000)
Advertising	(50,000)
Additional Profit	$ 22,000

65.   (581,P2,40)   (a)   The requirement is to compute the fixed cost given a breakeven point of 200,000 units. The breakeven point is where the contribution margin exactly equals the fixed costs. Since the contribution margin for 200,000 units is $100,000 (200,000 x $2.00 x .25), the fixed cost must be $100,000 if the 200,000 units of sales is also the company's breakeven point.

MULTIPLE CHOICE QUESTIONS (1–17)

1. A flexible budget is
    a. Appropriate for control of factory overhead but **not** for control of direct materials and direct labor.
    b. Appropriate for control of direct materials and direct labor but **not** for control of factory overhead.
    c. **Not** appropriate when costs and expenses are affected by fluctuations in volume limits.
    d. Appropriate for any level of activity.

2. Reid Company is developing a forecast of March 1980 cash receipts from credit sales. Credit sales for March 1980 are estimated to be $320,000. The accounts receivable balance at February 29, 1980, is $300,000; one-quarter of the balance represents January credit sales and the remainder is from February sales. All accounts receivable from months prior to January of 1980 have been collected or written off. Reid's history of accounts receivable collections is as follows:

In the month of sale	20%
In the first month after month of sale	50%
In the second month after month of sale	25%
Written off as uncollectible at the end of the second month after month of sale	5%

Based on the above information, Reid is forecasting March 1980 cash receipts from credit sales of
    a. $176,500
    b. $195,250
    c. $253,769
    d. $267,125

3. Anthony Company has projected cost of goods sold of $4,000,000, including fixed costs of $800,000. Variable costs are expected to be 75% of net sales. What will be the projected net sales?
    a. $4,266,667
    b. $4,800,000
    c. $5,333,333
    d. $6,400,000

4. Davis Company has budgeted its activity for April 1980. Selected data from estimated amounts are as follows:

Net income	$120,000
Increase in gross amount of trade accounts receivable during month	35,000
Decrease in accounts payable during month	25,000
Depreciation expense	65,000
Provision for income taxes	80,000
Provision for doubtful accounts receivable	45,000

On the basis of the above data, Davis has budgeted a cash increase for the month in the amount of
    a. $ 90,000.
    b. $195,000.
    c. $250,000.
    d. $300,000.

5. Terry Company is preparing its cash budget for the month of April. The following information is available concerning its inventories:

Inventories at beginning of April	$ 90,000
Estimated purchases for April	440,000
Estimated cost of goods sold for April	450,000
Estimated payments in April for purchases in March	75,000
Estimated payments in April for purchases prior to March	20,000
Estimated payments in April for purchases in April	75%

What are the estimated cash disbursements for inventories in April?
    a. $401,250
    b. $405,000
    c. $425,000
    d. $432,500

6. The Ship Company is planning to produce two products, Alt and Tude. Ship is planning to sell 100,000 units of Alt at $4 a unit and 200,000 units of Tude at $3 a unit. Variable costs are 70% of sales for Alt and 80% of sales for Tude. In order to realize a total profit of $160,000, what must the total fixed costs be?
    a. $ 80,000
    b. $ 90,000
    c. $240,000
    d. $600,000

7. Woody Company, which manufactures sneakers,

has enough idle capacity available to accept a special order of 20,000 pairs of sneakers at $6.00 a pair. The normal selling price is $10.00 a pair. Variable manufacturing costs are $4.50 a pair, and fixed manufacturing costs are $1.50 a pair. Woody will not incur any selling expenses as a result of the special order. What would the effect on operating income be if the special order could be accepted without affecting normal sales?

    a. $0.
    b. $ 30,000 increase.
    c. $ 90,000 increase.
    d. $120,000 increase.

8.   The Reno Company manufactures Part No. 498 for use in its production cycle. The cost per unit for 20,000 units of Part No. 498 are as follows:

Direct materials	$ 6
Direct labor	30
Variable overhead	12
Fixed overhead applied	16
	$64

The Tray Company has offered to sell 20,000 units of Part No. 498 to Reno for $60 per unit. Reno will make the decision to buy the part from Tray if there is a savings of $25,000 for Reno. If Reno accepts Tray's offer, $9 per unit of the fixed overhead applied would be totally eliminated. Furthermore, Reno has determined that the released facilities could be used to save relevant costs in the manufacture of Part No. 575. In order to have a savings of $25,000, the amount of relevant costs that would be saved by using the released facilities in the manufacture of Part No. 575 would have to be

    a. $ 80,000.
    b. $ 85,000.
    c. $125,000.
    d. $140,000.

9.   In deciding whether to manufacutre a part or buy it from an outside vendor, a cost that is irrelevant to the short-run decision is

    a.   Direct labor.
    b.   Variable overhead.
    c.   Fixed overhead that will be avoided if the part is bought from an outside vendor.
    d.   Fixed overhead that will continue even if the part is bought from an outside vendor.

10.   Internal reports prepared under the responsibility-accounting approach should be limited to which of the following costs?

    a.   Only variable costs of production.
    b.   Only conversion costs.

    c.   Only controllable costs.
    d.   Only costs properly allocable to the cost center under generally accepted accounting principles.

11.   Boyer Company manufactures basketballs. The forecasted income statement for the year before any special orders is as follows:

	Amount	Per Unit
Sales	$4,000,000	$10.00
Manufacturing cost of goods sold	3,200,000	8.00
Gross profit	800,000	2.00
Selling expenses	300,000	.75
Operating income	$ 500,000	$ 1.25

Fixed costs included in the above forecasted income statement are $1,200,000 in manufacturing cost of goods sold and $100,000 in selling expenses.

A special order offering to buy 50,000 basketballs for $7.50 each was made to Boyer. There will be no additional selling expenses if the special order is accepted. Assuming Boyer has sufficient capacity to manufacture 50,000 more basketballs, by what amount would operating income be increased or decreased as a result of accepting the special order?

    a. $25,000 decrease.
    b. $62,500 decrease.
    c. $100,000 increase.
    d. $125,000 increase.

12.   Which of the following items of cost would be least likely to appear in a performance report based on responsibility accounting techniques for the supervisor of an assembly line in a large manufacturing situation?

    a.   Supervisor's salary.
    b.   Materials.
    c.   Repairs and maintenance.
    d.   Direct labor.

13.   The basic difference between a master budget and a flexible budget is that a

    a.   Flexible budget considers only variable costs but a master budget considers all costs.
    b.   Flexible budget allows management latitude in meeting goals whereas a master budget is based on a fixed standard.
    c.   Master budget is for an entire production facility but a flexible budget is applicable to single departments only.

d.   Master budget is based on one specific level of production and a flexible budget can be prepared for any production level within a relevant range.

Items 14. and 15. are based on the following information:

The January 31, 1976, balance sheet of Shelpat Corporation follows:

Cash	$ 8,000
Accounts receivable (net of allowance for uncollectible accounts of $2,000)	38,000
Inventory	16,000
Property, plant and equipment (net of allowance for accumulated depreciation of $60,000)	40,000
	$102,000

Accounts payable	$ 82,500
Common stock	50,000
Retained earnings (deficit)	(30,500)
	$102,000

Additional information:
* Sales are budgeted as follows:
  February $110,000
  March $120,000

* Collections are expected to be 60% in the month of sale, 38% the next month, and 2% uncollectible.
* The gross margin is 25% of sales. Purchases each month are 75% of the next month's projected sales. The purchases are paid in full the following month.
* Other expenses for each month, paid in cash, are expected to be $16,500. Depreciation each month is $5,000.

14. What are the budgeted cash collections for February 1976?
  a. $63,800.
  b. $66,000.
  c. $101,800.
  d. $104,000.

15. What is the pro forma income (loss) before income taxes for February 1976?
  a.   ($3,700).
  b.   ($1,500).
  c. $3,800.
  d. $6,000.

MAY 1981 QUESTIONS

16. Fields Corporation projects the following transactions for 1981, its first year of operations:

Proceeds from issuance of common stock	$1,000,000
Sales on account	2,200,000
Collection of goods sold	1,800,000
Cost of goods sold	1,400,000
Disbursements for purchases of merchandise and expenses	1,200,000
Disbursements for income taxes	250,000
Disbursements for purchase of fixed assets	800,000
Depreciation on fixed assets	150,000
Proceeds from borrowings	700,000
Payments on borrowings	80,000

The projected cash balance at December 31, 1981, is
  a. $1,170,000.
  b. $1,220,000.
  c. $1,370,000.
  d. $1,820,000.

17. Mapes Corporation has estimated its activity for January 1981. Selected data from these estimated amounts are as follows:

— Sales	$1,400,000
Gross profit (based on sales)	30%
Increase in trade accounts receivable during month	$ 40,000
Change in accounts payable during month	$ 0
Increase in inventory during month	$ 20,000

— Variable selling, general and administrative expenses (S, G & A) include a charge for uncollectible accounts of 1% of sales.

— Total S, G & A is $142,000 per month plus 15% of sales.

— Depreciation expense of $80,000 per month is included in fixed S, G & A.

What are the estimated cash disbursements for January 1981?
  a. $1,238,000.
  b. $1,252,000.
  c. $1,258,000.
  d. $1,272,000.

MULTIPLE CHOICE ANSWERS

1.	d	5.	c	9.	d	13.	d	17.	c
2.	d	6.	a	10.	c	14.	d		
3.	a	7.	b	11.	d	15.	c		
4.	c	8.	b	12.	a	16.	a		

EXPLANATION OF MULTIPLE CHOICE ANSWERS

1. (1180,T1,37) (d) A flexible budget is a budget which can be adapted to any level of activity. Answers (a) and (b) are incorrect because flexible budgets are appropriate for control of all production costs, particularly when costs and expenses are affected by fluctuations in volume limits.

2. (1180,P2,23) (d) The requirement is Reid's forecast of March 1980 cash receipts from credit sales; credit sales for March will be $320,000; A/R at the end of February is $300,000, broken down as follows:

From January sales:	(¼)($300,000)	= $ 75,000
From February sales:	(¾)($300,000)	= $225,000

This problem must be read carefully; a key point is that the collection percentages given are *based on sales,* not on the A/R balance. The first step of the solutions approach is to compute January and February credit sales. January sales remaining in A/R are $75,000, but 70% of January sales have already been collected; therefore

(30%)(January sales)	= $ 75,000
January sales	= $250,000

February sales remaining in A/R are $225,000, but 20% of February sales have already been collected; therefore

(80%)(February sales)	= $225,000
February sales	= $281,250

Once the sales figures have been computed, estimated March collections can be obtained by applying the appropriate collection percentages:

Collections from	Sales	%	Cash to be collected
January sales	$250,000	25%	$ 62,500
February sales	$281,250	50%	$140,625
March sales	$320,000	20%	$ 64,000
			$267,125

3. (1180,P2,25) (a) The requirement is the projected net sales for Anthony Company. Cost of goods sold will be $4,000,000 of which $800,000 represents fixed costs; therefore, variable costs are $3,200,000.

Net sales can be computed as follows:

Variable costs	= (75%)(Net Sales)
$3,200,000	= (75%)(Net Sales)
Net Sales	= $4,266,667

4. (580,P2,23) (c) The requirement is to convert accrual net income to the cash basis. Any revenues not resulting in cash inflows this year (such as increases in accounts receivable and decreases in accounts payable) must be deducted from net income. The non-cash charges of depreciation and allowance for doubtful accounts must be added back to arrive at net income. It is necessary to assume that the provision for income taxes represents an increase in income taxes payable in order to have an answer among those shown.

Net income	$120,000
A/R increase	(35,000)
A/P decrease	(25,000)
Depreciation expense	65,000
Bad debt expense	45,000
Income tax accrual	80,000
Cash inflow	$250,000

5. (1179,P2,21) (c) The requirement is the cash disbursements for inventory in April. The problem states that $75,000 will be paid in April for purchases in March and an additional $20,000 will be paid for purchases prior to March. Additionally, April payments for purchases made in April will be 75% of April purchases. Since April purchases are estimated to be $440,000, estimated April payments will be $330,000. Accordingly, $425,000 is expected to be paid for inventories in April. Note that the beginning inventory in April and the estimated cost of of goods sold in April are extraneous data.

March purchases	$ 75,000
Pre-March purchases	20,000
75% of April	330,000
April payments	$425,000

6. (1179,P2,27) (a) The requirement is the amount of total fixed costs given the desired profit level, sales value, and variable costs. The solutions approach is to set up a formula equating profit to sales value minus variable costs minus fixed costs. As illustrated below, the profit of $160,000 is to be equal to $400,000 (100,000 units @ $4) from sales of Alt, less $280,000 for variable costs of Alt (variable costs are 70% of sales), plus $600,000 (200,000 units @ $3) from sales of Tude, less $480,000 of variable costs of Tude (variable costs are 80% of sales), minus the unknown fixed costs. Solving for fixed costs equals $80,000.

$$\$160,000 = \$400,000 - \$280,000 + \$600,000$$
$$- \$480,000 - FC$$
$$FC = \$80,000$$

7.   (1179,P2,35) (b)   The requirement is the effect of accepting a special order on operating income. The solutions approach is to multiply the contribution margin of $1.50 ($6 sales price - $4.50 variable cost) times the 20,000 pairs of sneakers to be sold, which is a $30,000 contribution to operating income. No selling expenses are incurred as a result of this special order. Also note that the $1.50 per pair fixed cost is not relevant to the decision. Acceptance of the order will not affect fixed costs and therefore should be ignored.

8.   (1179,P2,36) (b)   The problem describes a make or buy decision and requires the amount of cost savings necessary to generate an overall savings of $25,000 with a buy decision. The problem states that 20,000 units are currently produced at a variable cost of $48 per unit. Another company has offered to produce the units for $60 per unit or $1,200,000. If the unit is purchased rather than made, there will be a $9 per unit fixed cost savings, i.e., $180,000. Thus, the net cost will be $1,020,000 as calculated below. Thus, cost savings from the released facilities would be the difference between the $1,020,000 outside purchase cost less the $960,000 of present cost and $25,000 required cost savings.

Cost	
(20,000 @ $60)	$1,200,000
FC savings	
(20,000 @ $9)	(180,000)
	$1,020,000
$960,000 present cost less	
$25,000 required savings	935,000
Other cost savings	$ 85,000

9.   (1179,T1,32) (d)   In the short run, a cost which is irrelevant in deciding whether to manufacture a part in-house or to buy it from an outside vendor is fixed overhead, which cannot be saved if the part is purchased from the outside vendor. In other words, costs that will continue in either case are irrelevant to the decision. Costs that can be avoided by purchasing the part outside are relevant. For example, answer (a), direct labor, answer (b), variable overhead, and answer (c) avoidable fixed overhead, will all be avoided if the part is purchased from an outside vendor.

10.   (1178,T1,47) (c)   The requirement is the type of cost which should be emphasized in internal reports prepared under the responsibility accounting approach. The objective of responsibility accounting is to use cost data to evaluate those responsible for the activity and/or decision making in the cost center. Thus only controllable costs should be emphasized in such reports, i.e., noncontrollable costs are not relevant to responsibility accounting. Answers (a), (b), and (d) are incorrect because variable costs, conversion costs, and costs per GAAP may include noncontrollable as well as controllable costs.

11.   (579,P2,38) (d)   The requirement is the effect on profit of a special order of 50,000 basketballs at $7.50 each. The solutions approach is to compute the unit variable cost to manufacture and sell the special order. First note that the forecasted income statements are based upon 400,000 units ($4,000,000 ÷ $10). Next, the variable manufacturing cost of goods sold is $2,000,000 ($3,200,000 minus $1,200,000 of fixed costs), resulting in a variable cost of manufacturing of $5 per unit ($2,000,000 ÷ 400,000 units). The variable selling expenses are not relevant because the problem states that there will be no additional selling expenses if the special order is accepted. Thus the unit variable cost to manufacture and sell the special order is $5.00/unit, resulting in a $2.50/unit contribution margin ($7.50 - $5.00). Thus 50,000 special order units would increase net income by $125,000.

12.   (579,T1,34) (a)   The requirement is the cost which would be least likely to appear in a performance report based upon responsibility accounting techniques for supervisors. Responsibility accounting reports only assign costs to a cost center for which the cost center has control. The supervisor's salary is something that the supervisor does not have control over and therefore should not be reported in a responsibility accounting report. Answers (b), materials, (c), repairs and maintenance, and (d), direct labor, are all items of cost over which the supervisor should have control.

13.   (579,T1,38) (d)   The difference between a master budget and a flexible budget is that a master budget is usually a static budget, i.e., based on one level of performance. Flexible budgets can be prepared to forecast costs (and/or revenues) for any activity level within the relevant range. Answer (a) is incorrect because flexible budgets consider fixed as well as variable costs. Answer (b) is incorrect because the same standards and goals apply to both flexible and master budgets. The advantage of the

flexible budget is that there is a means of evaluating management in meeting goals at all levels of activity within the relevant range. Answer (c) is incorrect because flexible budgets as well as master budgets are for the entire production facility.

14. (576,P2,22) (d) Collections are 60% of the month's sales and 38% of the previous month's sales. Apparently the sales for January were $100,000, leaving $38,000 to be collected in February and $2,000 to be written off. Thus the $38,000 from January plus 60% of the February sales of $110,000 equals $104,000 ($38,000 + $66,000).

15. (576,P2,23) (c) The solutions approach is a quick tabulation in your margin as appears below. The sales are $110,000 less bad debts, cost of sales, expenses, and depreciation, giving a net income of $3,800.

Sales	$110,000
Bad debt	2,200
C of S	82,500
Exp	16,500
Dep	5,000
ST	106,200
Income	3,800

MAY 1981 ANSWERS

16. (581,P2,24) (a) The requirement is the projected cash balance at December 31, 1981, for Fields Corporation. The solutions approach is to make a "T"-account listing of cash receipts and cash disbursements as illustrated below.

Cash

Receipts:		Disbursements:	
Proceeds from C.S.	$1,000,000	Purchases of merchandise and expenses	$1,200,000
Collection of A/R	1,800,000	Income taxes	250,000
Proceeds from borrowing	700,000	Fixed Assets	800,000
		Payments on borrowings	80,000
	$3,500,000		$2,330,000
Ending balance	$1,170,000		

Note that the sales on account, cost of goods sold, and the depreciation on fixed assets do not affect cash flows.

17. (581,P2,34) (c) The requirement is to compute the estimated cash disbursements for January 1981. The solutions approach is to convert the estimated expenses from the accrual basis to the cash basis. The cash disbursements for purchases is computed as follows

CGS [$1,400,000 × (1.00 − .30)] =	$ 980,000
+ increase in inventory	20,000
cash disbursements for purchases	$1,000,000

No adjustment is necessary for accounts payable; there was no change in the beginning and ending balance. The cash disbursements for selling and general and administrative expenses can be computed as follows

Total S, G & A	
$142,000 + (.15 × $1,400,000) =	$ 352,000
− Bad debts exp. $1,400,000 × .01 =	(14,000)
− Depreciation expense	(80,000)
Cash disbursements for expenses	$ 258,000

The total cash disbursements for Mapes Corporation in January are $1,000,000 + $258,000 = $1,258,000. Note that Bad Debts Expense and Depreciation Expense are not cash outflows and must be subtracted from total S, G & A expenses to arrive at cash disbursements.

THEORY PROBLEMS

Problem 1   Process Cost Theory (1175,T6)

(25 to 30 minutes)

Presented below are four independent questions concerning a typical manufacturing company that uses a process-cost accounting system. Your response to each question should be complete, including simple examples or illustrations where appropriate.

Required:

a.   What is the rationale supporting the use of process costing instead of job-order costing for product-costing purposes?   Explain.

b.   Define equivalent production (equivalent units produced).   Explain the significance and use of equivalent production for product-costing purposes.

c.   Define normal-spoilage and abnormal-spoilage. Explain how normal-spoilage costs and abnormal-spoilage costs should be reported for management purposes.

d.   How does the first-in, first-out (FIFO) method of process costing differ from the weighted average method of process costing?   Explain.

Problem 2   Break-even Analysis (574,T7)

(25 to 30 minutes)

Cost volume earnings analysis (break-even analysis) is used to determine and express the interrelationships of different volumes of activity (sales), costs, sales prices, and sales mix to earnings. More specifically, the analysis is concerned with what will be the effect on earnings of changes in sales volume, sales prices, sales mix, and costs.

Required:

a.   Certain terms are fundamental to cost-volume-earnings analysis. Explain the meaning of each of the following terms:
   1.   Fixed costs.
   2.   Variable costs.
   3.   Relevant range.
   4.   Break-even point.
   5.   Margin of safety.
   6.   Sales mix.

b.   Several assumptions are implicit in cost-volume-earnings analysis. What are these assumptions?

c.   In a recent period Zero Company had the following experience:

Sales (10,000 units @ $200) $2,000,000

	Fixed	Variable	
Costs:			
Direct material	$ —	$ 200,000	
Direct labor	—	400,000	
Factory overhead	160,000	600,000	
Administrative Expenses	180,000	80,000	
Other expenses	200,000	120,000	
Total costs	$540,000	$1,400,000	$1,940,000

Net income $60,000

Each item below is independent.

1.   Calculate the break-even point for Zero in terms of units and sales dollars. Show your calculations.

2.   What sales volume would be required to generate a net income of $96,000? Show your calculations.

3.   What is the break-even point if management makes a decision which increases fixed costs by $18,000? Show your calculations.

Problem 3   Cost-Volume-Profit Analysis (1174,T5)

(25 to 30 minutes)

Nubo Manufacturing, Inc., is presently operating at 50% of practical capacity producing about 50,000 units annually of a patented electronic component. Nubo recently received an offer from a company in Yokohama, Japan, to purchase 30,000 components at $6.00 per unit, FOB Nubo's plant. Nubo has not previously sold components in Japan. Budgeted production costs for 50,000 and 80,000 units of output follow:

Units	50,000	80,000

Costs:

Direct material	$ 75,000	$120,000
Direct labor	75,000	120,000
Factory overhead	200,000	260,000
Total costs	$350,000	$500,000

Cost per unit	$7.00	$6.25

The sales manager thinks the order should be accepted, even if it results in a loss of $1.00 per unit, because he feels the sales may build up future markets. The production manager does not wish to have the order accepted primarily because the order would show a loss of $.25 per unit when computed on the new average unit cost. The treasurer has made a quick computation indicating that accepting the order will actually increase gross margin.

Required:

a. Explain what apparently caused the drop in cost from $7.00 per unit to $6.25 per unit when budgeted production increased from 50,000 to 80,000 units. Show supporting computations.

b. 1. Explain whether (either or both) the production manager or the treasurer is correct in his reasoning.
   2. Explain why the conclusions of the production manager and the treasurer differ.

c. Explain why each of the following may affect the decision to accept or reject the special order.

1. The likelihood of repeat sales and/or all sales to be made at $6.00 per unit.
2. Whether the sales are made to customers operating in two separate, isolated markets or whether the sales are made to customers competing in the same market.

Problem 4   Standard Costs (1177,T3)

(20 to 25 minutes)

Standards are used by many concerns to generate data relevant to the acquisition and utilization of the component cost elements in a manufacturing process. There are three basic types of standards that may be employed: 1. Fixed (basic), 2. Ideal, and 3. Attainable.

Required:

a. Define the three types of standards.
b. What do standards and related variances attempt to disclose with respect to acquisition and utilization within a manufacturing process? Limit the discussion to the two general categories: Variable costs and fixed factor overhead. Identify specific variances but do not discuss their computations.
c. How do standards relate to cost accumulation procedures?

Problem 5   Capital Budgeting   (577,T7)

(20 to 25 minutes)

Yale, president of Hotchkiss, Inc., your client, recently attended a seminar at which a speaker discussed planning and control of capital expenditures, which he referred to as "capital budgeting." Yale tells you that he is not quite sure he understands that concept.

Required:

a. Explain the nature and identify several uses of capital budgeting.
b. What are the basic differences between the payback (payout) method and the net present value method of capital budgeting? Explain.
c. Define "cost of capital."
d. Financial accounting data are not entirely suitable for use in capital budgeting. Explain.

PRACTICE PROBLEMS

Problem 6   Cost of Goods Manufactured;
            Equivalent Units of Production;
            Joint Cost Allocation (1174,P4 a & c)
            (50 to 60 minutes)

Part a. The Helper Corporation manufactures one product and accounts for costs by a job-order-cost system. You have obtained the following information for the year ended December 31, 1973, from the Corporations's books and records:

Total manufacturing cost added during 1973 (sometimes called cost to manufacture) was $1,000,000 based on actual direct material, actual direct labor, and applied factory overhead on actual direct labor dollars.

Cost of goods manufactured was $970,000 also based on actual direct material, actual direct labor, and applied factory overhead.

Factory overhead was applied to work in process at 75% of direct labor dollars. Applied factory overhead for the year was 27% of the total manufacturing cost.

Beginning work-in-process inventory, January 1, was 80% of ending work-in-process inventory, December 31,

Required:

Prepare a formal statement of cost of goods manufactured for the year ended December 31, 1973, for Helper Corporation. Use actual direct material used, actual direct labor, and applied factory overhead. Show supporting computations in good form.

Part c. The Harrison Corporation produces three products—Alpha, Beta, and Gamma. Alpha and Gamma are joint products while Beta is a by-product of Alpha. No joint cost is to be allocated to the by-product. The production processes for a given year are as follows:

In Department One, 110,000 pounds of raw material, Rho, are processed at a total cost of $120,000. After processing in Department One, 60% of the units are transferred to Department Two and 40% of the units (now Gamma) are transferred to Department Three.

In Department Two, the material is further processed at a total additional cost of $38,000. Seventy percent of the units (now Alpha) are transferred to Department Four and 30% emerge as Beta, the by-product, to be sold at $1.20 per pound. Selling expenses related to disposing of Beta are $8,100.

In Department Four, Alpha is processed at a total additional cost of $23,660. After this processing, Alpha is ready for sale at $5 per pound.

In Department Three, Gamma is processed at a total additional cost of $165,000. In this department, a normal loss of units of Gamma occurs which equals 10% of the good output of Gamma. The remaining good output of Gamma is then sold for $12 per pound.

Required:

1.   Prepare a schedule showing the allocation of the $120,000 joint cost between Alpha and Gamma using the relative sales value approach. The net realizable value of Beta should be treated as an addition to the sales value of Alpha.

2.   Independent of your answer to requirement 1, assume that $102,000 of total joint costs were appropriately allocated to Alpha. Assume also that there were 48,000 pounds of Alpha and 20,000 pounds of Beta available to sell. Prepare a statement of gross margin for Alpha using the following facts:

During the year, sales of Alpha were 80% of the pounds available for sale. There was no beginning inventory.

The net realizable value of Beta available for sale is to be deducted from the cost of producing Alpha. The ending inventory of Alpha is to be based on the net cost of production.

All other cost, selling-price, and selling-expense data are those presented in the facts under Part c.

<u>Problem 7</u>　　Alternate Production Decisions (577,Q4)

　　　(40 to 50 minutes)

This problem consists of two unrelated parts.

　　Part a. You have been engaged to assist the management of the Arcadia Corporation in arriving at certain decisions. Arcadia has its home office in Ohio and leases factory buildings in Texas, Montana and Maine, all of which produce the same product. The management of Arcadia has provided you with a projection of operations for 1977, the forthcoming year, as follows:

	Total	Texas	Montana	Maine
Sales	$4,400,000	$2,200,000	$1,400,000	$800,000
Fixed costs:				
Factory	1,100,000	560,000	280,000	260,000
Administration	350,000	210,000	110,000	30,000
Variable costs	1,450,000	665,000	425,000	360,000
Allocated home office costs	500,000	225,000	175,000	100,000
Total	3,400,000	1,660,000	900,000	750,000
Net profit from operations	$1,000,000	$ 540,000	$ 410,000	$ 50,000

The sales price per unit is $25.

　　Due to the marginal results of operations of the factory in Maine, Arcadia has decided to cease operations and sell that factory's machinery and equipment by the end of 1976. Arcadia expects that the proceeds from the sale of these assets would be greater than their book value and would cover all termination costs.

　　Arcadia, however, would like to continue serving its customers in that area if it is economically feasible and is considering one of the following three alternatives:

　　1.　Expand the operations of the Montana factory by using space presently idle. This move would result in the following changes in that factory's operations:

	Increase over factory's current operations
Sales	50%
Fixed costs:	
Factory	20%
Administration	10%

Under this proposal, variable costs would be $8 per unit sold.

　　2.　Enter into a long-term contract with a competitor who will serve that area's customers. This competitor would pay Arcadia a royalty of $4 per unit based upon an estimate of 30,000 units being sold.

　　3.　Close the Maine factory and not expand the operations of the Montana factory.

Required:

　　In order to assist the management of Arcadia Corporation in determining which alternative is more economically feasible, prepare a schedule computing Arcadia's estimated net profit from total operations that would result from each of the following methods:

　　1.　Expansion of the Montana factory.
　　2.　Negotiation of long-term contract on a royalty basis.
　　3.　Shutdown of Maine operations with no expansion at other locations.

Note:　Total home office costs of $500,000 will remain the same under each situation.

　　Part b. The management of Essen Manufacturing Company is currently evaluating a proposal to purchase a new and innovative drill press as a replacement for a less efficient piece of similar equipment which would then be sold. The cost of the equipment including delivery and installation is $175,000. If the equipment is purchased, Essen will incur costs of $5,000 in removing the present equipment and revamping service facilities. The present equipment has a book value of $100,000 and a remaining useful life of 10 years. Due to new technical improvements which have made the equipment outmoded, it presently has a resale value of only $40,000.

Additional information:

Management has provided you with the following comparative manufacturing cost tabulation:

	Present Equipment	New Equipment
Annual production-units	400,000	500,000
Annual costs:		
Labor	$30,000	$25,000
Operating costs:		
Depreciation (10% of		
asset book value)	10,000	17,500
Other	48,000	20,000
	58,000	37,500
Total	$88,000	$62,500

· Management believes that if the present equipment is not replaced now, it will have to wait 7 years before replacement is justifiable.
· Both pieces of equipment are expected to have a negligible salvage value at the end of 10 years.
· If the new equipment is purchased, the man-

agement of Essen would require a 15% return on the investment before income taxes.

The following table lists the present value of an ordinary annuity of $1 at 15%:

Period	Present Value
1	0.870
2	1.626
3	2.283
4	2.855
5	3.352
6	3.784
7	4.160
8	4.487
9	4.772
10	5.019

Required:

1.   In order to assist the management of Essen in reaching a decision on the proposal, prepare schedules showing the computation of the following:

• Net initial outlay before income taxes.
• Net present value of investment before income taxes.

2.   Would you recommend this investment, and why?

Note: Ignore any effects of net incremental cash flow from increased sales of units produced by the new machine.

Problem 8   Gross Profit, Direct Cost, Breakeven

(576,Q5)   (50 to 60 minutes)

Number 3 consists of three unrelated parts.

Part a.   You have acquired the following data for the calendar years 1974 and 1975 for Celebration, Inc.:

	1974		1975		Dollar Increase
Sales	$750,000	100%	$840,000	100%	$90,000
Cost of goods sold	495,000	66	560,000	66 $2/3$	65,000
Gross margin	$255,000	34%	$280,000	33 $1/3$%	$25,000
Unit selling price	$10		$12		

Required:

Prepare a statement in good form which analyzes the variations in sales and cost of goods sold between 1974 and 1975.

Part b. Management of Bicent Company uses the following unit costs for the one product it manufactures:

	Projected Cost per Unit
Direct material (all variable)	$30.00
Direct labor (all variable)	19.00
Manufacturing overhead:	
Variable cost	6.00
Fixed cost (based on 10,000 units per month)	5.00
Selling, general and administrative:	
Variable cost	4.00
Fixed cost (based on 10,000 units per month)	2.80

The projected selling price is $80 per unit. The fixed costs remain fixed within the relevant range of 4,000 to 16,000 units of production.

Management has also projected the following data for the month of June 1976:

	Units
Beginning inventory	2,000
Production	9,000
Available	11,000
Sales	7,500
Ending inventory	3,500

Required:

Prepare projected income statements for June 1976 for management purposes under each of the following product-costing methods:

1. Absorption costing with all variances charged to cost of goods sold each month.
2. Direct (variable) costing.

Supporting schedules calculating inventoriable production costs per unit should be presented in good form. Ignore income taxes.

Part c. Freedom, Inc., management has performed cost studies and projected the following annual costs based on 40,000 units of production and sales:

	Total Annual Costs	Percent of Variable Portion of Total Annual Costs
Direct material	$400,000	100%
Direct labor	360,000	75
Manufacturing overhead	300,000	40
S, G & A	200,000	25

Required:

1. Compute Freedom's unit selling price that will yield a projected 10% profit if sales are 40,000 units.
2. Assume that management selects a selling price of $30 per unit (40,000 units). Compute Freedom's dollar sales that will yield a projected 10% profit on sales assuming the above variable-fixed costs relationships are valid.

Problem 9   Process Costing (579,Q4)

(50 to 60 minutes)

You are engaged in the audit of the December 31, 1978, financial statements of Spirit Corporation, a manufacturer of a digital watch. You are attempting to verify the costing of the ending inventory of work in process and finished goods which were recorded on Spirit's books as follows:

	Units	Cost
Work in process (50% complete as to labor and overhead)	300,000	$ 660,960
Finished goods	200,000	$1,009,800

Materials are added to production at the beginning of the manufacturing process and overhead is applied to each product at the rate of 60% of direct labor costs. There was no finished goods inventory on January 1, 1978. A review of Spirit's inventory cost records disclosed the following information:

		Costs	
	Units	Materials	Labor
Work in process January 1, 1978 (80% complete as to labor and overhead)	200,000	$ 200,000	$ 315,000
Units started in production	1,000,000		
Material costs		$1,300,000	
Labor costs			$1,995,000
Units completed	900,000		

Required:

a. Prepare schedules as of December 31, 1978, to compute the following:

- Equivalent units of production using the weighted- average method.

- Unit costs of production of materials, labor and overhead.

- Costing of the finished goods inventory and work-in-process inventory.

b.   Prepare the necessary journal entry to correctly state the inventory of finished goods and work in process, assuming the books have not been closed. **(Ignore income tax considerations.)**

Problem 10   Standard Cost Variances (578,Q5)

(50 to 60 minutes)

Melody Corporation is a manufacturing company that produces a single product known as "Jupiter." Melody uses the first-in, first-out (FIFO) process costing method for both financial statements and internal management reporting.

In analyzing production results, standard costs are used, whereas actual costs are used for financial statement reporting. The standards, which are based upon equivalent units of production, are as follows:

Raw material per unit	1 pound at $10 per pound
Direct labor per unit	2 hours at $4 per hour
Factory overhead per unit	2 hours at $1.25 per hour

Budgeted factory overhead for standard hours allowed for April production is $30,000.

Data for the month of April 1977 are presented below:

· The beginning inventory consisted of 2,500 units which were 100% complete as to raw material and 40% complete as to direct labor and factory overhead.

· An additional 10,000 units were started during the month.

· The ending inventory consisted of 2,000 units which were 100% complete as to raw material and 40% complete as to direct labor and factory overhead.

· Costs applicable to April production are as follows:

	Actual Cost	Standard Cost
Raw material used (11,000 pounds)	$121,000	$100,000
Direct labor (25,000 hours actually worked)	105,575	82,400
Factory overhead	31,930	25,750

Required:

a.   For each element of production for April (raw material, direct labor, and factory overhead) compute the following:

1.   Equivalent units of production.
2.   Cost per equivalent unit of production at actual and at standard.

Show supporting computations in good form.

b.   Prepare a schedule analyzing for April production the following variances as either favorable or unfavorable:

1.   Total materials.
2.   Materials price.
3.   Materials usage.
4.   Total labor.
5.   Labor rate.
6.   Labor efficiency.
7.   Total factory overhead.
8.   Factory overhead volume.
9.   Factory overhead budget.

Show supporting computations in good form.

Problem 11   Process Costing and Standard Costing

(1176,Q3) (50 to 60 minutes)

Number 5 consists of two unrelated parts.

Part a.   The Dexter Production Company manufactures a single product. Its operations are a continuing process carried on in two departments—machining and finishing. In the production process, materials are added to the product in each department without increasing the number of units produced.

For the month of June, 1975, the company records indicated the following production statistics for each department:

	Machining Department	Finishing Department
Units in process, June 1, 1975	0	0
Units transferred from preceding department	0	60,000
Units started in production	80,000	0
Units completed and transferred out	60,000	50,000
Units in process, June 30, 1975*	20,000	8,000
Units spoiled in production	0	2,000

*Percent of completion of units in process at June 30, 1975:

Materials	100%	100%
Labor	50%	70%
Overhead	25%	70%

The units spoiled in production had no scrap value and were 50% complete as to material, labor, and overhead. The company's policy is to treat the cost of spoiled units in production as a separate element of cost in the department in which the spoilage occurs.

Cost records showed the following charges for the month of June:

	Machining Department	Finishing Department
Materials	$240,000	$ 88,500
Labor	140,000	141,500
Overhead	65,000	25,700

Required:

For both the machining and finishing departments, prepare in good form complete production reports for the month of June, including the following information:

1. Physical flow of units
2. Equivalent units
3. Total costs
4. Unit costs
5. Summary of total costs

Round all computations to the nearest cent.

Part b. On May 1, 1975, Bovar Company began the manufacture of a new mechanical device known as "Dandy." The company installed a standard cost system in accounting for manufacturing costs. The standard costs for a unit of "Dandy" are as follows:

Raw materials	6 lbs. at $1 per lb.	$6.00
Direct labor	1 hour at $4 per hour	4.00
Overhead	75% of direct labor costs	3.00
		$13.00

The following data were obtained from Bovar's records for the month of May:

	Units
Actual production of "Dandy"	4,000
Units sold of "Dandy"	2,500

	Debit	Credit
Sales		$50,000
Purchases (26,000 pounds)	$27,300	
Material price variance	1,300	
Material quantity variance	1,000	
Direct labor rate variance	760	
Direct labor efficiency variance		800
Manufacturing overhead total variance	500	

The amount shown above for material price variance is applicable to raw material purchased during May.

Required:

Compute each of the following items for Bovar for the month of May. Show computations in good form.

1. Standard quantity of raw materials allowed (in pounds).
2. Actual quantity of raw materials used (in pounds).
3. Standard hours allowed.
4. Actual hours worked.
5. Actual direct-labor rate.
6. Actual total overhead.

Problem 12 Budgets (1178, Q4a)

(25 to 30 minutes)

The Scarborough Corporation manufactures and sells two products, Thingone and Thingtwo. In July 1977, Scarborough's budget department gathered the following data in order to project sales and budget requirements for 1978.

1978 Projected Sales:

Product	Units	Price
Thingone	60,000	$ 70
Thingtwo	40,000	$100

1978 Inventories - in units:

Product	Expected January 1, 1978	Desired December 31, 1978
Thingone	20,000	25,000
Thingtwo	8,000	9,000

In order to produce one unit of Thingone and Thingtwo, the following raw materials are used:

Raw Material	Unit	Amount used per unit Thingone	Thingtwo
A	lbs.	4	5
B	lbs.	2	3
C	each		1

Projected data for 1978 with respect to raw materials is as follows:

Raw Material	Anticipated Purchase Price	Expected Inventories January 1, 1978	Desired Inventories December 31, 1978
A	$8	32,000 lbs.	36,000 lbs.
B	$5	29,000 lbs.	32,000 lbs.
C	$3	6,000 each	7,000 each

Projected direct labor requirements for 1978 and rates are as follows:

Product	Hours per unit	Rate per hour
Thingone	2	$3
Thingtwo	3	$4

Overhead is applied at the rate of $2 per direct labor hour.

Required:

Based upon the above projections and budget requirements for 1978 for Thingone and Thingtwo, prepare the following budgets for 1978:

a.   Sales budget (in dollars)
b.   Production budget (in units)
c.   Raw materials purchase budget (in quantities)
d.   Raw materials purchase budget (in dollars)
e.   Direct labor budget (in dollars)
f.   Budgeted finished goods inventory at December 31, 1978 (in dollars)

ANSWER OUTLINE :THEORY

Problem 1   Process Cost Theory

a. Type of manufacturing will determine cost system
   Process system for continuous mass production
   Job-order for unique goods
   The process is center of attention in continuous production
   Unit costs by cost category are possible
   Process costing is often used for
   Chemicals, food processing, oil, mining, and rubber

b. Equivalent units of production (EUP) is work completed
   Assumes whole equivalent units finished
   I.e., units completed if no BWIP or EWIP
   EUP is a denominator in ratio for assigning costs
   Numerator is amount of work in FG, EWIP, spoilage, etc.
   Often done on a unit cost basis

c. Normal spoilage is expected
   Inherent in production process
   A normal cost of production
   Abnormal spoilage is unexpected
   Not per normal efficient operating conditions
   I.e., is avoidable, controllable, etc.
   Accounted for as a loss, not production cost
   For practical reasons there may be no distinction

d. FIFO and weighted-average differ due to treatment of BWIP
   Per FIFO, BWIP is separated from current period's cost
   Finished goods are separated into
   Started this period, completed this period
   And started last period, completed this period
   Weighted average does not separate BWIP
   All costs are averaged

UNOFFICIAL ANSWER :THEORY

Problem   1   Process Cost Theory

a. The type of cost system used by a company will be determined by the type of manufacturing operations performed. A manufacturing company should use a process cost system for product costing purposes when it continuously mass produces like units; while the production of custom-made or unique goods would indicate a job-order cost system to be more appropriate.

Because there is continuous mass production of like units in a process cost system, the center of attention is the individual process (usually a department). The unit costs by cost category as well as total unit cost for each process (depart-ment) are necessary for product costing purposes.

Process costing is often used in industries such as chemicals, food processing, oil, mining, rubber and electrical appliances.

b. "Equivalent production" (equivalent units produced) is the term used to identify the number of completed units that would have been produced if all the work performed during the period had been applied to units that were begun and finished during the period. Thus, equivalent production represents the total number of units that could have been started and finished during the period, given the same effort, assuming no beginning or ending work-in-process inventories.

The work of each producing department must be expressed in terms of a common denominator; this denominator represents the total work of a department or process in terms of fully completed units. Units in process of production at the beginning and end of the period should not be counted the same as units started and completed during the period when determining the equivalent amount of production for a period. Each partially completed unit has received only part of the attention and effort that a finished unit has received and, therefore, each partially completed unit should be weighted accordingly.

The equivalent production figure computed represents the number of equivalent whole units for which materials, labor, and overhead were issued, used, or incurred during a period. The cost of each element of materials, labor, and overhead is divided by the appropriate equivalent production figure to determine the unit cost for each element. Should units be at a different stage of completion with respect to each type of cost element, then a separate equivalent production figure must be completed for that cost element.

c. Normal spoilage is the spoilage that arises under normal efficient operating conditions, i.e., it is inherent in the production process and is uncontrollable in the short run.

Abnormal spoilage is the spoilage that is not expected to arise under normal efficient operating conditions; i.e., it is not inherent in the production process and is usually considered as avoidable, or controllable, by management. Thus, by definition, the critical factor in distinguishing between normal and abnormal spoilage is the degree of controllability of units spoiled. Any spoilage that occurs during a production process functioning within the expected usual range of performance is considered to be normal spoilage. Any spoilage occurring in amounts in excess of the defined usual range is considered abnormal (controllable) spoilage.

Conceptually, the cost of normal spoilage should be included in the cost of good units produced because of its association with normal production. Likewise, cost of abnormal spoilage should be accounted for as a loss because of its abnormal (unusual) nature. The cost of abnormal spoilage should be separately identified as a loss on reports for management.

For practical reasons, there may be no distinction made between normal and abnormal spoilage in reports for management. The primary reason for not distinguishing between types of spoilage is that it is sometimes very difficult (or impossible) to distinguish between normal and abnormal spoilage. The production process may be relatively new or the process may be altered often enough to make it impractical or too costly to distinguish between normal or abnormal spoilage. Whenever possible, though, the distinction between types of spoilage should be made and accounted for as discussed in the preceding paragraphs.

d.   The primary difference between the FIFO method and the weighted-average method of process costing is in the treatment of the cost of the beginning work-in-process inventory. When applying FIFO method the cost of the beginning work-in-process inventory is kept separate from the cost of production of the current period.

When determining the FIFO cost of units completed and transferred to the next department or to finished goods, the cost of the beginning work-in-process inventory plus the cost necessary to complete the beginning work-in-process units are added together. The sum of these two cost totals is the cost assigned to the units in the beginning work-in-process inventory that are transferred out. Units started and completed during the period are assigned costs on the basis of costs incurred during the period for the equivalent units produced during that period.

In applying the FIFO method, each department is regarded as a separate accounting unit. Thus, the application of the FIFO method in practice is modified to the extent that subsequent departments usually combine all transferred-in costs into one amount, even though they could identify and separately account for the costs relating to the preceding department's beginning inventory and the costs relating to the preceding department's units started and completed during the period.

The weighted-average method of process costing is simpler to apply than the FIFO method primarily because the beginning work-in-process inventory is considered to be part of current production. In applying the weighted-average method, the beginning work-in-process inventory costs are combined with current costs even though some of the production was begun prior to the current period. When equivalent units are determined, work done on the beginning inventory in a preceding period is regarded as if it were done in the current period.

The weighted-average method is applied by adding the beginning work-in-process inventory costs to the production costs incurred during the current period. Then unit costs are determined by dividing the sum of these costs by the equivalent units produced, including the units in the department's beginning work-in-process inventory. The cost of all units transferred out of a department (process) during the period is the product of the number of units completed multiplied by the average cost to produce a unit.

UNOFFICIAL ANSWER
NOTE: Format of Unofficial Answer precludes the need
for an Answer Outline
Problem 2   Breakeven Analysis

a. 1. Fixed costs are those which remain unchanged, over short time periods at least,
regardless of changes in physical volume
(sales or production volume).

2. Variable costs are those costs that vary in
direct ratio (proportionately) to changes
in physical volume.

3. The relevant range establishes the limits
within which the volume of activity can
vary and the sales and cost relationships
remain valid. It is usually a range in
which the entity has had some recent
experience.

4. The break-even point is the level of sales
volume (assuming sales volume is equal
to production volume) where total revenues
equal total expenses and the business has
neither earnings nor a loss.

5. The margin of safety is the excess of actual
or budgeted sales over sales at the break-even
point. Expressed another way, the margin
of safety reveals the amount by which sales
could decrease before losses occur.

6. Sales mix is the composition of total sales
broken down among various products, product mix, or product lines; it is the relative
combination of the quantities of the variety
of company products that compose total
sales.

b. Assumptions which underlie cost-volume-earnings
analysis include the following:
1. Cost can be classified as either fixed or variable.

2. Variable costs change at a linear rate.

3. Fixed costs remain unchanged over the relevant range of the break-even chart.

4. Selling prices do not change as the physical
sales volume changes.

5. There is only a single product; or, if there
are multiple products, the sales mix remains
constant.

6. Productive efficiency does not change.

7. There is synchronization between sales and
production; i.e., inventories are either kept
constant or are zero.

8. Volume is the only relevant factor affecting
costs.

9. There is a relevant range of validity for all of
the other underlying assumptions and concepts.

c. Basic formula:

$$\text{Break-even sales} = \frac{\text{Fixed Costs} + \text{Earnings}}{1 - \dfrac{\text{Variable Costs}}{\text{Corresponding Sales}}}$$

1. $\dfrac{\$540{,}000 + 0}{1 - \dfrac{\$1{,}400{,}000}{\$2{,}000{,}000}} = \$1{,}800{,}000$ (9,000 units @ $200)

2. $\dfrac{\$540{,}000 + \$96{,}000}{1 - \dfrac{\$1{,}400{,}000}{\$2{,}000{,}000}} = \$2{,}120{,}000$ (10,600 units @$200)

3. $\dfrac{\$558{,}000 + 0}{1 - \dfrac{\$1{,}400{,}000}{\$2{,}000{,}000}} = \$1{,}860{,}000$ (9,300 units @ $200)

ANSWER OUTLINE

Problem 3   Cost-Volume-Profit Analysis

a. Unit cost dropped due to factory overhead averaging
With increased volume, average unit cost decreased
I.e., factory overhead contained fixed components

b1. Both the production manager and treasurer are correct
New $6.25 cost is more than $6.00 purchase price
Results in loss of $.25 per unit
Totalling $7,500 on 30,000 units
Regular sales profit increases $37,500
$.75 cost per unit decrease times 50,000 units
Net increase is $30,000 in gross profit

b2. Production manager evaluation based on unit cost
Treasurer evaluation based on marginal costs
Marginal costs are appropriate in the short run
Average costs are appropriate in the long run

c1. If offer is accepted repeat business is likely
This may establish a market price of $6.00 per unit
Which cannot be maintained in the long run
I.e., no possibility of profit from the present plant

c2. Yokohama may compete for customers of Nubo's
      regular customers
          I.e., decreasing demand to regular customers
          Reduces sales at regular price
      No effect if Yokohama operates in completely isolated
      market

UNOFFICIAL ANSWER :THEORY

Problem 3   Cost-Volume-Profit Analysis

a.   The difference in unit cost was caused by the difference in average unit cost of factory overhead. The
computations for costs per unit follow:

	Cost per Unit	
	50,000 Units of Output	80,000 Units of Output
Direct material:		
$75,000/50,000 units	$1.50	
$120,000/90,000 units		$1.50
Direct labor:		
$75,000/50,000 units	1.50	
$120,000/80,000 units		1.50
Factory overhead:		
$200,000/50,000 units	4.00	
$260,000/80,000 units		3.25
Cost per unit	$7.00	$6.25

The reason for the difference in average unit cost
of factory overhead probably was caused by some of
the overhead being fixed within the given levels of
output. In this instance the fixed component of
factory overhead may be estimated using the following reasoning.

$$\frac{\text{Change in cost } (\$260,000 - \$200,000)}{\text{Change in output } (80,000 - 50,000)} = \frac{\$60,000}{30,000}$$
$$\text{Vairable costs per unit} = \$ 2.00$$

If variable factory overhead is incurred at $2.00 per
unit, the amount of fixed costs would be computed
as follows:

$200,000 factory overhead — ($2.00 x 50,000
      units) variable overhead = $100,000 fixed
      factory overhead

or

$260,000 factory overhead—($2.00 x 80,000
      units) variable overhead = $100,000 fixed
      factory overhead.

At 50,000 units of output the fixed portion of
factory overhead is $2.00 per unit ($100,000 ÷
50,000 units). And at 80,000 units of output the
fixed portion of factory overhead is $1.25 per unit
($100,000 ÷ 80,000 units). Thus, the $.75 per unit
decrease in average unit cost apparently resulted from
spreading the fixed costs over an increased number of
units of production.

b.   1.   Both the production manager's and treasurer's
          statements are correct as given. The new
          average unit cost of $6.25 is certainly more
          than the offered purchase price of $6.00;
          thus, a $.25 per unit loss would result on
          this order. The resulting "book loss" on
          this order would be $7,500 ($.25 x 30,000
          units) as indicated by the production mana-
          ger. Not withstanding, the remaining 50,000
          units of regular sales would show an in-
          creased margin (gain) of $.75 per unit be-
          cause their average unit cost decreased
          from $7.00 to $6.25 per unit. Thus, regu-
          lar sales would show an increased profit of
          $37,500 ($.75 x 50,000 units). The net
          result would be an increase of $30,000
          in gross margin this period if the Yokohama
          company offer was accepted. Accordingly,
          the treasurer's statement is also correct be-
          cause gross margin for this period will in-
          crease if the offer is accepted.

          The treasurer's reasoning can also be il-
          lustrated by application of the marginal-
          income or contribution-margin technique.
          The extra units will generate a unit sales
          price of $6.00 and a unit variable cost of
          $5.00 ($1.50 + 1.50 + 2.00); the result is a
          $1.00 per unit contribution margin to in-
          crease gross margin. Thus, by selling the
          extra 30,000 units gross margin will increase
          by $30,000 (30,000 units x $1.00 contribu-
          tion margin per unit).

     2.   The primary reason for the difference in con-
          clusions by the production manager and the
          treasurer is in their respective methods of
          analysis. The production manager is evalu-
          ating average unit costs in comparison with
          selling price to determine the profitability
          of the special order. The treasurer is com-
          paring the difference in total costs at the

two levels of output with the difference in total revenues at the two levels of output, in effect comparing marginal cost with marginal revenue, to determine the incremental effect of gross margin. The treasurer's reasoning is appropriate for the short-run while the production manager's reasoning is inappropriate for a short-range decision but is appropriate for a long-range decision. In this instance the decision appears to be a one-time thing indicating that the treasurer's reasoning is most appropriate.

c. 1. Perhaps the most important consideration is the extent to which this short-range decision will have a long-range effect on Nubo. If the offer is rejected the chances of receiving another offer from the Yokohama Company is considerably reduced. But if the offer is accepted, a repeat order is more likely in the future.

By accepting the offer, Nubo may be inadvertently establishing a market price of $6.00 per unit for its product which cannot be maintained in the long run (average unit cost at 80,000 units is $6.25). If the customers who purchase the other 50,000 units become aware of the $6.00 units sales price charged the Yokohama firm they too may want a $6.00 unit price. If Nubo sold all 80,000 units at $6.00 each a negative gross margin of $20,000 would result, and it would have zero gross margin at 100,000 units, the practical capacity of the plant.

2. Even if the $6.00 unit selling price does not have an effect on the unit selling price to present customers, it may depress the quantity of sales of other units at the normal price. If the Yokohama firm plans to compete for the same customers as Nubo's regular customers, the ultimate effect of making the 30,000 unit sale to the Yokohama firm at $6.00 a unit may give it an unfair competitive advantage. Ultimately, a shift of customers from Nubo's regular customers to the Yokohama firm would cause a decrease in unit sales at the regular price.

If the Yokohama firm is operating in a completely isolated market from Nubo's regular customers, no undesirable effects should result from this one-time sale. An

exception to this reasoning would result if Nubo's regular customers desired to expand into this isolated market but found that they were at a competitive disadvantage because of the 30,000 unit sale made by Nubo to the Yokohama firm.

ANSWER OUTLINE : THEORY

Problem 4   Standard Costs

a. Fixed standards do not change
  May be originally ideal or attainable
  Over time, value to management decreases
  Ideal standards assume 100% capacity
  And 100% factory and labor efficiency
  Also assume minimum material, labor, etc., costs
  Attainable standards reflect factory inefficiencies
  E.g., normal spoilage
  But above-average efficiency

b. Efficiencies in acquisition of product components
  Material price variances
  Labor rate variances
  Overhead spending variances
  Efficiencies in usage of product components
  Material usage variance
  Labor efficiency variance
  Variable overhead efficiencies
  Fixed overhead variances relate budgeted amounts to standard amounts applied to product

c. Standard costs are used for cost accumulation as well as cost accounting
  Can be used in any cost accumulation framework
  Are not a mandatory component of cost accumulation

UNOFFICIAL ANSWER : THEORY

Problem 4   Standard Costs

a. A fixed or basic standard, once established, is unchanging. Such a standard may be ideal or attainable when established, but it is never altered once it has been set. Because of the obvious diminution of utility to management over a span of time, fixed standards are rarely used in manufacturing concerns.

An ideal standard is computed using utopian conditions for a given manufacturing process. Ideal standards presume that material, labor, and factory overhead items will be purchased at the minimum price in all cases. Ideal standards also are based upon the optimal usage of the material, labor, and factory overhead components at 100 percent manufacturing capacity. In reality, ideal standards cannot be met and will give rise to unfavorable variances.

Attainable standards are standards based on a high degree of efficiency, but differ from ideal standards in that they can be met or even surpassed by the employment of excellent management. Attainable standards consider that the component parts (material, labor, and factory overhead) can be purchased at a good overall price, not necessarily the lowest price at all times, but well below the expected highest price. Attainable standards also consider that (1) labor is not 100 percent efficient; (2) when material is used there will be some "normal" spoilage; and (3) a manufacturing concern cannot produce at 100 percent of theoretical capacity. Attainable standards are set above average levels of efficiency, but may be met or surpassed in efficient production situations.

b. All standards attempt to monitor costs and measure efficiency. In relation to the acquisition of goods or services related to a manufacturing situation, the variances (for example, spending variances) from standard disclose efficiencies in the "purchasing" function. With respect to the utilization of the component parts of a manufacturing process, standards and related variance reports are meant to disclose relative efficiency in the usage of the goods or services in the actual manufacturing process. For material, labor, and variable factory overhead variances, the efficiencies are measured by comparing actual operations with operations stated in standard units (dollars).

Fixed factory overhead is evaluated with reference to a budget amount that is compared to standard amounts of fixed factory overhead applied and actual amounts expended for fixed overhead items.

c. Standards are an integral part of a cost accumulation procedure (such as job order, process, direct) but do not comprise a system that could be utilized in lieu of one of the accumulation procedures mentioned above. Standards may be used within any cost accumulation procedure, but a cost accumulation procedure may be employed without the inclusion of standards.

ANSWER OUTLINE :THEORY

Problem 5   Capital Budgeting

a. Nature: long-range planning and control of expenditures
   Use: evaluating projects such as
      New products or markets
      Advertising or R&D programs

      Executive training programs
      Efficiency improvements
      Customer service programs
      Environmental programs
      Debt retirements
      Asset acquisitions

b. Difference is time value of money
   Payback method ignores time value of money
   Net present value compares present values of different projects

c. Investment rate of return not affecting value of firm
      Also cost of various sources of funds

d. Problems with accounting data for capital budgeting
      Accrual basis vs. cash flow data
      Periodic earnings vs. investment projects
      Past results vs. expected results
      Financial accounting expense may be capital budgeting capital item
      Financial accounting ignores opportunity costs
      Financial accounting may not produce differential costs

UNOFFICIAL ANSWER :THEORY

Problem 5   Capital Budgeting

a. Capital budgeting involves planning and controlling long-term expenditures. Such long-range planning generally involves a project orientation; that is, every potential long-term investment is viewed as an individual project.

Capital budgeting as opposed to short-term budgeting generally involves greater size, risk, and uncertainty because of its long-term nature. Furthermore, a capital-budgeting decision may affect other budgeting decisions. For example, the capital-budgeting decision may affect and be affected by cash budgets.

Capital budgeting may be used for evaluating the following types of projects: acquiring fixed assets; adding a product, segment, or new markets; implementing an advertising or research and development program; developing executive or employee training programs; implementing efficiency improvements, customer service programs, or environmental control programs; and extinguishing debt.

b. The basic difference between the payback (payout) method and the net present-value method of capital budgeting concerns the recognition of the time value of money. The payback method, which ignores the time value of money and all cash flows beyond the payback period for the project, is the measure of the time it will take to recover in net cash inflow the initial capital investment. Payback does not measure profitability but does measure the amount of time necessary to generate an amount of net cash inflow equal to the original cost of the asset.

The net present-value method of capital budgeting does inherently consider the time value of money. This method involves comparing the present value of all future cash inflows and outflows of a given project using some minimum desired rate of return. Future cash flows are discounted to the present value at the minimum rate, as in the cost of capital. A positive result implies that the project's rate of return exceeds this minimum rate, while a negative result indicates that the project's rate of return is less than this minimum rate. This method does not derive the project's rate of return, but merely tests the rate against a minimum rate. As with all methods of capital budgeting, the results are most often compared with alternative courses of action in an attempt to institute the plan of action that will maximize the return to the company.

c. The cost of capital concept embraces the idea that for a specific project to be acceptable to a company the expected rate of return from that project should equal or exceed the return currently being generated by the existing capital of the company. Theoretically, a project yielding the cost of capital rate will leave the "value" of the firm unchanged. Actual measurement of this rate is a complex and controversial issue. Cost of capital is essentially the cost of using various sources of funds. For debt, a stated or "reasonable" interest rate is usually sufficient. For preferred stock, there is usually a stated dividend. Common stock and retained earnings, though, usually involve no out-of-pocket costs. Here, though, there is an opportunity cost of sacrificing alternative earnings. An attempt should be made to measure such opportunity cost. Once cost figures are derived for each element of debt and equity they should be averaged to determine a company's weighted-average cost of capital.

d. Financial accounting data are not entirely suitable for use in capital budgeting for the following reasons:

1. Financial accounting uses the accrual basis. Capital-budgeting decisions generally rely on estimates of cash flows, rather than accrued earnings.

2. Financial accounting is designed to measure periodic earnings. Capital budgeting is concerned with the life of a given project. Such life seldom corresponds to usual accounting periods.

3. Financial accounting measures the results of operations of companies or segments of companies. While these "entities" sometimes correspond with a capital-budgeting project, in most cases they will not. The "entity" for financial accounting is generally composed of many intermingled capital-budgeting projects.

4. Financial accounting capitalizes expenditures in accordance with rational bases for matching such expenditures against related revenues. Sometimes, such bases are unavailable and financial accounting will not defer such expenditures. In other words, an expenditure which represents a capital-budgeting project may be an expense rather than an asset acquisition, for financial accounting purposes.

5. Financial accounting records may not necessarily be designed to produce differential costs, which are generally needed for capital budgeting.

6. Financial accounting does not recognize opportunity costs which are an important part of capital budgeting.

SOLUTION GUIDE :PRACTICE

Problem 6   Cost of Goods Manufactured;
                     Equivalent Units of Production

1. This problem consists of three separate topics: cost of goods manufactured statement; computation of equivalent units of production; and joint, by-product cost allocations.

2. The cost of goods manufactured statement is a summary of the work-in-process account.

> Beg. W.I.P.
> + Raw Materials
> + Labor
> + Overhead
> <u>   </u>
> Total Manufacturing Cost
> <u>− End. W.I.P</u>
> Cost of goods manufactured

Use T-account analysis for the work in process account.

W.I.P.

BWIP	?	C of GM	970
RM	370		
L	360	EWIP	?
O/H	270		

The O/H was 27% of $1,000,000 and is 75% of L. Labor, therefore, is $360,000 and RM is $370,000, because RM, L, and O/H equal $1,000,000. The increase in WIP of $30,000 (1,000,000 − 970,000) is 20% of EWIP. Thus EWIP is $150,000 and BWIP is $120,000.

3. Part c requires the use of the approximate relative sales value method since sales value at the split-off cannot be directly determined. The approximate sales value for a particular joint product is the difference between the selling price where it can first be determined and all separable costs of processing that particular joint product to the point where it can first be sold. For Gamma, this is simply ($480,000 - 165,000) $315,000. In Alpha, the net realizable value of Beta is added to Alpha and the separable costs in Departments 2 and 4 are deducted to approximate the sales value of $185,000 at split-off.

4. Part c (2) requires the calculation of the ending inventory of a joint product when a by-product exists. The amount of cost removed from the joint product is **equal** to the net realizable value of the by-product produced--not sold. The journal entry for the transfer is:

> By-product inventory   15,900
>   Joint product inventory   15,900

4.1 Eighty percent of the cost remaining in the joint product inventory account becomes CGS. The remaining 20% is the ending joint product inventory. The by-product inventory account will be reduced as the by-product is sold, but has no further effect on the joint product inventory.

UNOFFICIAL ANSWER :PRACTICE

Problem 6   Cost of Goods Manufactured;
                     Equivalent Units of Production;
                     Joint Cost Allocation

a.

Helper Corporation
STATEMENT OF COST OF GOODS MANUFACTURED
For the Year Ended December 31, 1973

Direct material used	$ 370,000
Direct labor	360,000
Factory overhead applied	<u>270,000</u>
Total manufacturing cost added during 1973	1,000,000
Plus beginning work-in-process inventory	<u>120,000</u>
Manufacturing costs to account for	1,120,000
Less ending work-in-process inventory	<u>150,000</u>
Cost of goods manufactured	<u>$ 970,000</u>

Supporting Computations
Factory overhead applied:
    27% x total manufacturing cost (27% x $1,000,000)
Direct labor:
    75% of direct labor equals $270,000 so direct labor was $360,000 ($270,000 ÷ 75%)
Work-in-process inventories:
    Let X = ending work-in-process inventory
        $1,000,000 + .8X − X = $970,000

$$X = \underline{\$150,000}$$
$$.8X = \underline{\$120,000}$$

Direct material used equals total manufacturing cost less direct labor and factory overhead applied ($1,000,000 − [$360,000 + $270,000]).

c. 1.

Schedules to Allocate Joint Cost Between Alpha and Gamma

Alpha

Sales value (46,200 pounds x $5)		$231,000
(19,800 pounds x $1.20)	$23,760	
Less selling expenses (Beta)	8,100	
Net realizable value (Beta)		15,660
Total sales value		246,660
Less additional costs:		
Processing (Department Two)	38,000	
Processing (Department Four)	23,660	61,660
Approximate sales value at split-off point		$185,000

Gamma

Sales value (40,000 pounds x $12)		$480,000
Less processing (Department Three)		165,000
Approximate sales value at split-off point		$315,000

	Value	Allocation Percentage	Joint Cost	Allocated Joint Cost
Alpha	$185,000	37%	$120,000	$ 44,400
Gamma	315,000	63	120,000	75,600
	$500,000	100%		$120,000

Diagram of Flow of Pounds

(Not Required)

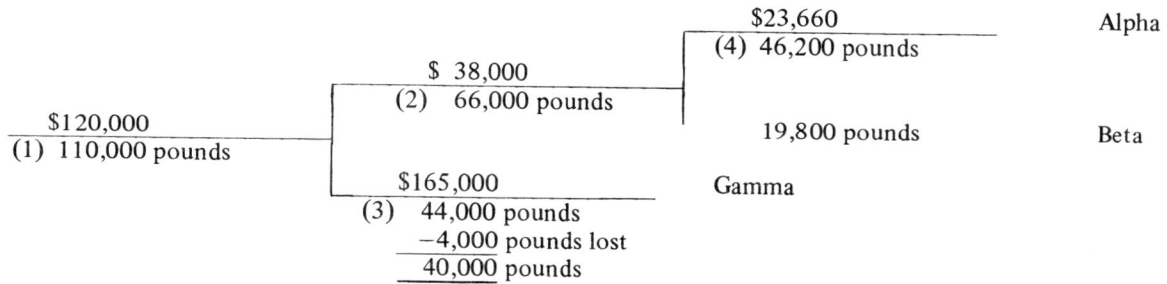

```
                                                        $23,660        Alpha
                                                        (4) 46,200 pounds
                         $ 38,000
                         (2)  66,000 pounds
                                                        19,800 pounds   Beta
  $120,000
  (1) 110,000 pounds
                         $165,000                       Gamma
                         (3)  44,000 pounds
                             −4,000 pounds lost
                              40,000 pounds
```

Computation of Pounds of Gamma Lost

(Not Required)

Let X = Good Output
44,000 − .1X = X
40,000   = X

2.

Statement of Gross Margin for Alpha

Sales (38,400 pounds x $5)		$192,000
Production costs:		
Allocated joint cost	$102,000	
Department Two	38,000	
Department Four	23,660	
Gross cost of production	163,660	
Less net realizable value of Beta	15,900	
Net cost of production	147,760	
Less ending inventory	29,552	
Cost of goods sold		118,208
Gross margin		$73,792

Net realizable value of Beta equals the revenue from Beta ($24,000) less its related selling expenses ($8,100). Ending inventory equals the net cost of production ($147,760) times 20%.

SOLUTION GUIDE:PRACTICE

Problem 7   Alternate Production Decisions

1. The requirement of part a is to compute the estimated net profit from total operations of Arcadia under three different assumptions. The solutions approach is to prepare each estimate separately, even though each of the solutions should be on the same schedule per the requirement. It should be noted that under all three alternatives, the Maine operations are going to cease. Furthermore, the problem indicates that the $100,000 of home office cost now allocated to Maine will continue to be incurred.

1.1 Expansion of the Montana factory will result in a 50% increase in sales to $2,100,000. The fixed factory costs will increase 20% to $336,000. The fixed administration costs will increase 10% to $121,000.

   The variable costs will be $672,000, $8 per unit times 84,000 units ($2,100,000 divided by $25). The $175,000 of home office costs will continue. To the resulting $796,000 of Montana profit, add the $540,000 of Texas factory profit, and subtract the $100,000 of home office overhead that was allocated to Maine.

1.2 If a competitor pays $4 for each of the estimated 30,000 units sold, $120,000 in royalties will be received. These royalties, however, will not offset the previous $50,000 of Maine profit plus the $100,000 of home office cost allocated to Maine operations. In other words, the net effect will be to decrease total income by $30,000 ($150,000 − $120,000). Thus total income will be $970,000.

1.3 If Maine operations are shut down with no alternatives, the total income will be $850,000. This is the previous total estimated profit of $1,000,000 less the estimated Maine profit of $50,000 and less the $100,000 of home office cost allocated to Maine which will continue in the future.

2. The requirement of part b is to determine the net initial outlay for some replacement equipment and the net present value of the investment, along with the recommendation as to whether or not the investment is worthwhile.

2.1 The solutions approach is to handle the three requirements (even though they are numbered as two) separately. The net initial outlay is the $175,000 equipment cost plus $5,000 of old machine removal cost less the $40,000 resale value of the old equipment. Thus, it is $140,000.

2.2 The net present value of the investment will be the excess of the present value of the annual cost savings during the next ten years over the net present outlay ($140,000 as computed just above). The annual savings will be $5,000 of labor costs plus $28,000 of other operating costs, a total of $33,000. The present value of $33,000 a year for the next ten years is $165,627 ($33,000 times 5.019). The net present value is the present value of the cost savings ($165,627) less the net initial outlay ($140,000) or $25,627.

2.3 Thus the investment should be made because in addition to the substantial net present value assuming a 15% return, there is also a 25% increase in production capacity.

UNOFFICIAL ANSWER:PRACTICE

Problem 7   Alternate Production Decisions

a. 1.   *Arcadia Corporation*
COMPUTATION OF ESTIMATED NET PROFIT FROM OPERATIONS AFTER EXPANSION OF MONTANA FACTORY

Montana factory—	
Sales	$2,100,000
Fixed costs:	
Factory	336,000
Administration	121,000
Variable costs	672,000
Allocated home office costs	175,000
Total	1,304,000
Estimated net profit from operations	796,000
Texas factory—estimated net profit from operations	540,000
Home office expense allocated to Maine factory	(100,000)
Estimated net profit from operations	$1,236,000

a. 2.   *Arcadia Corporation*
COMPUTATION OF ESTIMATED NET PROFIT
FROM OPERATIONS AFTER NEGOTIATION
OF ROYALTY CONTRACT

Estimated net profit from operations:
Texas factory	$ 540,000
Montana factory	410,000
Estimated royalties to be received	
(30,000 × $4)	120,000
	1,070,000
Less home office expense allocated	
to Maine factory	100,000
Estimated net profit from operations	$970,000

a. 3.   *Arcadia Corporation*
COMPUTATION OF ESTIMATED NET PROFIT
FROM OPERATIONS AFTER SHUTDOWN
OF MAINE FACTORY

Estimated net profit from operations:
Texas factory	$540,000
Montana factory	410,000
	950,000
Less home office expense allocated	
to Maine factory	100,000
Estimated net profit from operations	$850,000

b. 1.   *Net Initial Outlay Before*
                      Income Taxes

Cost of new equipment	$175,000
Cost of conversion	5,000
	180,000
Less resale value of present equipment	40,000
Net initial outlay	$140,000

Net Present Value of Investment
Before Income Taxes

Annual operating costs excluding depreciation:
With present equipment	$ 78,000
With new equipment	45,000
Annual cash savings before income taxes	$ 33,000
Present value of future savings	
(33,000 × 5.019)	$165,627
Net initial outlay	140,000
Net present value of investment	$ 25,627

b. 2.   The investment in new equipment should be made as
the present value of future savings is greater than the
net initial outlay.

SOLUTION GUIDE:PRACTICE

Problem 8   Gross Profit, Direct Cost, Breakeven

1.   The requirement in part a is an analysis of variance of sales and cost of goods sold from 1974 to
1975. Like cost variance the change or variation
is a function of changes in units and prices (costs).

1.1   Two way analysis of variance would be

Sales:
Volume:
5,000 units @ $10	=	$ (50,000)
Price:
70,000 units @ $2	=	140,000
Net increase		$ 90,000

Cost of Sales
Volume:
| 5,000 units @ $6.60 | = | $ (33,000) |
Price:
| 70,000 units @ $1.40 | = | 98,000 |
| Net increase | | $ 65,000 |

1.2   The unofficial solution presents three way analysis of variance. The difference is a price-volume
variance in addition to the price and volume
variances.

2.   The requirement in part b is a projected income
statement per each direct and absorption costing.

2.1   The major differences between direct and absorption costing are that (1) direct costing inventories include only variable costs and absorption costing includes fixed as well as variable costs, and
(2) on direct costing statements, variable costs
(both manufacturing and administrative) are deducted from sales to obtain the contribution
margin. Also fixed costs (both manufacturing
and administrative) are deducted from the contribution margin to arrive at net income.

2.2   In this problem unit inventory cost per direct
costing is $55 and per absorption costing is
$60. The difference of $5/unit is fixed cost.

2.3   The only twist to the problem is underapplied
overhead per absorption costing. Since only
9,000 units are being produced, only $45,000
of the $50,000 of fixed costs will be applied
in June. The unofficial answer changes this
$5,000 underapplied June overhead to the June
operating results.

3. The first requirement in part c is the selling price to produce a 10% profit. This is a breakeven type problem and should be worked from the basic breakeven formula which is

Sales = Fixed Costs + Variable Costs + Net Income
S   =   FC   +   VC   +   NI

If X is the selling price, the formula can be restated as

$$40,000 \ X = FC + VC + 10\% \ (40,000 \ X)$$

or

$$36,000 \ X = FC + VC$$

Fixed costs and variable costs equal the sum of the four annual costs in the problem (400,000 + 360,000 + 300,000 + 200,000 = $1,260,000). Thus

$$36,000 \ X = \$1,260,000$$
$$X = \$35$$

3.1 The second requirement in part c is to determine the dollar level of sales, given a $30 selling price, which will result in a 10% profit.

$$S = FC + VC + NI$$

Since NI is to equal 10% of sales, NI = .1S. Also fixed costs can be computed from the four annual costs:

0% of	$400,000 =	$ 0
25%	360,000 =	90,000
60%	300,000 =	180,000
75%	200,000 =	150,000
	Total fixed costs	$420,000

$$S = \$420,000 + VC + .1S$$

At breakeven of 40,000 units, variable costs are total costs (1,260,000) less fixed costs ($420,000) which is $840,000 or 70% of sales (once again at breakeven). Thus

$$S = \$420,000 + .7S + .1S$$
$$.2S = \$420,000$$
$$S = \$2,100,000$$

Problem 8   Gross Profit, Direct Cost, Breakeven

a.

Celebration, Inc.
STATEMENT ACCOUNTING FOR VARIATION IN SALES AND COST OF GOODS SOLD
Between the Years 1974 and 1975

Increase in net sales:	
Variation due to decrease in volume at the 1974 selling price (−5,000 x $10)	−$ 50,000
Variation due to increase in selling price at the 1974 volume (75,000 x $2)	150,000
Variation due to joint decrease in volume and increase in selling price (−5,000 x $2)	− 10,000
Increase in net sales	$ 90,000
Less increase in cost of goods sold:	
Variation due to decrease in volume at the 1974 costs (−5,000 x $6.60)	− 33,000
Variation due to increase in costs at the 1974 volume (75,000 x $1.40)	105,000
Variation due to joint decrease in volume and increase in costs (−5,000 x $1.40)	− 7,000
Increase in cost of goods sold	65,000
Increase in dollar gross margin	$ 25,000

b. 1.

Bicent Company
PROJECTED INCOME STATEMENT
For the Month of June 1976
(Absorption Costing)

Sales (7,500 units x $80)		$600,000
Beginning inventory		
(2,000 units x $60) *(Schedule 1)*	$120,000	
Production (9,000 units x $60)	540,000	
Available	660,000	
Ending inventory		
(3,500 units x $60)	210,000	
Cost of goods sold before adjustment	450,000	
Adjustment for volume variance		
(production projected as 10,000 units as "normal"; 1,000 units underapplied x $5 fixed manufacturing overhead)	5,000	
		455,000
Gross margin		145,000
Variable selling, general, and administrative (7,500 units x $4)	30,000	
Fixed selling, general, and administrative (10,000 units x $2.80)	28,000	58,000
Projected income		$ 87,000

2.

Bicent Company
PROJECTED INCOME STATEMENT
For the Month of June 1976
(Direct Costing)

Sales (7,500 units x $80)		$600,000
Beginning inventory		
(2,000 units x $55) *(Schedule 2)*	$110,000	
Production (9,000 units x $55)	495,000	
Available	605,000	
Ending inventory		
(3,500 units x $55)	192,500	
Variable cost of goods sold	412,500	
Variable selling, general, and adminis-		
trative (7,500 units x $4)	30,000	
Total variable costs		442,500
Contribution margin		157,500
Fixed manufacturing overhead		
(10,000 units x $5)	50,000	
Fixed selling, general, and adminis-		
trative (10,000 units x $2.80)	28,000	
Total fixed costs		78,000
Projected income		$ 79,500

Note *(Not Required):* The difference in the two projected income figures ($87,000 − $79,500) equals $7,500. This is accounted for as the increase in inventory (3,500 − 2,000) times the fixed manufacturing overhead application rate (1,500 units x $5). The $7,500 of fixed manufacturing overhead is included in ending inventory under absorption costing, but it is expensed under direct (variable) costing.

Schedule 1

Schedule of Inventoriable Production Costs Per Unit
(Absorption Costing)

Direct material	$30
Direct labor	19
Manufacturing overhead (variable)	6
Manufacturing overhead (fixed)	5
Total unit cost	$60

Schedule 2

Schedule of Inventoriable Production Costs Per Unit
(Direct Costing)

Direct material	$30
Direct labor	19
Manufacturing overhead (variable)	6
Total unit cost	$55

c. 1. Let X = unit selling price that will yield a projected 10% profit on sales
Total sales − total costs = projected profit
$$40,000 X - \$1,260,000 = .1 (40,000 X)$$
$$36,000 X = \$1,260,000$$
$$X = \$35 \text{ per unit}$$

2.

	Total Annual Costs	Percent of Total Annual Costs that Is Variable	Variable Costs	Fixed Costs
Direct material	$ 400,000	100%	$400,000	$ —
Direct labor	360,000	75	270,000	90,000
Manufacturing overhead	300,000	40	120,000	180,000
Selling, general, and				
administrative	200,000	25	50,000	150,000
Totals	$1,260,000		$840,000	$420,000

The variable costs are projected as 70% of sales computed as follows:
Total variable costs are $840,000 at sales of $1,200,000 (40,000 units x $30 selling price).
$$\$840,000 \div \$1,200,000 = 70\%$$
Let X = dollar sales that will yield a projected 10% profit on sales.
Total sales − variable costs − fixed costs = projected profit: $X - .7X - \$420,000 = .1X$
$$.3X - .1X = \$420,000$$
$$X = \underline{\$2,100,000 \text{ sales}}$$

SOLUTION GUIDE:PRACTICE

<u>Problem</u> 9   Process Costing

1. This problem is a process costing problem requiring equivalent units of production (weighted average method), unit costs for material, labor, overhead, and cost of ending inventories. Also, part b. requires journal entries to correct ending work-in-process and finished goods inventories.

2. The solutions approach is to analyze the work-in-process account for 1978. The left (dr) side of the account reflects the costs incurred. The costs incurred are allocated to finished goods and ending work-in-process inventories which appear as credits on the right hand side of the account.

Note: The "T accounts" for 2.1 and 2.2 follow the Solution Guide.

2.1   The total costs incurred are $5,196,000 as detailed in this "T account". Note that overhead is 60% of direct labor. The 200,000 units of beginning work-in-process are 100% complete as to material and 80% complete as to conversion costs (direct labor and overhead). During the period 1,000,000 units were started that had a material cost of $1,300,000. Also during the period $1,995,000 of direct labor and $1,197,000 of overhead were incurred.

2.2   The $5,196,000 of costs are allocated to FG and EWIP based on equivalent units of production (EUP). Compute the EUP by doing a "T account" analysis of the work-in-process account as illustrated in this "T account." Note that the "T account" contains unit data only and is a simplified version of the 2.1 "T account."

2.3   The material EUP are 1,200,000 because there are 1,200,000 units of material to assign cost (900,000 of FG and 300,000 of EWIP). Since the total cost of material is $1,500,000 ($200,000 in BWIP and $1,300,000 of material added), the unit cost is $1.25 ($1,500,000 ÷ 1,200,000).

2.1 "T Account"

Work-In-Process

BWIP (200,000 units)		FG (900,000 units)	$??
Conversion 80%		Conversion 100%	
Material 100%		Material 100%	
Material	$ 200,000		
Labor	315,000		
Overhead	189,000		
Material (1,000,000			
units added)	1,300,000		
Labor	1,995,000	EWIP (300,000 units)	$??
		Conversion 50%	
Overhead		Material 100%	
(60% of labor)	1,197,000		
	$5,196,000		$5,196,000

2.2 "T Account"

Work-In-Process (Units Only)

BWIP	200,000	FG	900,000
Conversion 80%			
Material 100%			
		EWIP	300,000
Units added	1,000,000	Conversion 50%	
	————	Material 100%	————
	1,200,000		1,200,000

Thus the material cost in FG is $1,125,000 (900,000 X $1.25), and the material cost in EWIP is $375,000 (300,000 X $1.25).

2.4   The direct labor EUP is 1,050,000 because 900,000 units were completely finished and 300,000 are only 50% complete. Thus the total direct labor cost of $2,310,000 ($315,000 in BWIP and $1,995,000 incurred this period) will be allocated 900/1,050 to FG and 150/1,050 to EWIP. Note that most cost textbooks allocate the cost by dividing 1,050,000 EUP into $2,310,000 to get a $2.20 EUP unit cost and multiply the $2.20 times 900,000 FG, EUP and 150,000 EWIP, EUP.

2.5   The overhead EUP is the same as direct labor as both are elements of "conversion." Divide the 1,050,000 EUP into overhead cost of $1,386,000 ($189,000 in BWIP plus $1,197,000 incurred this period) to obtain an overhead EUP unit cost of $1.32.

2.6   After the EUP unit costs are determined the cost of FG and EWIP can be determined, i.e., the total costs incurred, as above in 2.1, can be allocated to FG and EWIP.

FG (900,0(0 units
  at $4.77) $4,293,000
    Materi ɔl $1.25
    Direct
     labor   2.20
    Overhead   1.32
                 ─────
                 $4.77

EWIP (300,000 units)
  Material, 300,000
    at $1.25 $375,000
  Direct labor,
    150,000 at $2.20   330,000
  Overhead,
    150,000 at $1.32 198,000   903,000
                                 ─────────
                                 $5,196,000

3. Part b. requires a journal entry to correct ending inventory. Ending inventory consists of 300,000 units of work-in-process and 200,000 units of finished goods.

3.1   The books currently reflect EWIP at $660,960 while the above calculation shows the cost to be $903,000, i.e., debit work-in-process inventory for $242,040 ($903,000 − $660,960).

3.2   The books currently reflect FG at $1,009,800 while the 200,000 units priced at $4.77 (per above) should be $954,000, requiring a credit to finished goods inventory of $55,800 ($1,009,800 − $954,000). Note that there was no beginning FG inventory, i.e., the unit cost is $4.77.

3.3   Since the net adjustment is a $186,240 debit to inventory ($242,040 dr − $55,800 cr), cost of sales should be credited for $186,240.

Work-in-process $242,040
  Finished goods
    inventory $ 55,800
  Cost of sales   186,240

UNOFFICIAL ANSWER:PRACTICE

Problem 9   Process Costing

a.

Spirit Corporation
ENDING INVENTORY SCHEDULES
December 31, 1978

Equivalent Units of Production (Weighted-Average Method)

	Materials	Labor	Overhead
Units completed during year	900,000	900,000	900,000
Units on hand at December 31, 1978 (50% complete as to labor and overhead)	300,000	150,000	150,000
Equivalent units of production	1,200,000	1,050,000	1,050,000

Unit Costs of Production

	Total	Materials	Labor	Overhead
Beginning costs	$ 704,000	$ 200,000	$ 315,000	$ 189,000
Added costs	4,492,000	1,300,000	1,995,000	1,197,000
Total costs	$5,196,000	$1,500,000	$2,310,000	$1,386,000
Equivalent units of production	—	1,200,000	1,050,000	1,050,000
Unit costs of production	$ 4.77	$ 1.25	$ 2.20	$ 1.32

Costing of Inventories

	Units	Total	Finished goods	Work-in process
			Amounts	
Finished goods:				
200,000 X $4.77	200,000	$ 954,000	$ 954,000	
Work-in-process:	300,000			
Materials @ $1.25	—	375,000		$375,000
Labor @ $2.20 @ 50%	—	330,000		330,000
Overhead @ $1.32 @ 50%	—	198,000		198,000
Per costing test	500,000	1,857,000	954,000	903,000
Per books	500,000	1,670,760	1,009,800	660,960
Adjustment	—	$ 186,240	$ (55,800)	$242,040

b.

Spirit Corporation
JOURNAL ENTRY TO CORRECTLY STATE INVENTORIES
December 31, 1978

	Debit	*Credit*
Work-in-process inventory	$242,040	
Finished goods inventory		$ 55,800
Cost of sales		186,240
To adjust inventory accounts to correct cost		

SOLUTION GUIDE: PRACTICE

Problem 10   Standard Cost Variances

1. Part a requires calculation of the equivalent units of production (EUP) for material, direct labor, and factory overhead, and the cost per EUP at actual and at standard.

2. The solutions approach is a T-account analysis of the work-in-process account as illustrated below. Note that the FIFO method is to be used and beginning and ending work-in-process are 100% complete as to material, i.e., apparently material is added at the beginning of the process. Thus, the EUP for material is 10,000 (the amount added this period).

2.1 The EUP for both labor and overhead are the same as beginning and ending work-in-process and are 40% complete both as to labor and as to overhead. The EUP calculation can be done two ways. The first approach is to look at the total work that has been completed, i.e., the right side of the work-in-process account. 10,500 units have been totally completed and 40% of 2,000 have been partially completed, giving total EUP of 11,300. At the beginning of the period, however, 40% of 2,500 EUP, or 1,000 EUP, has already been completed. Thus, in this period (FIFO assumption) 10,300 have been completed.

The second approach is to look at the work that could have been completed in April, i.e., the left-hand side of the work-in-process account. Add the April input of 10,000 units to the remaining work (60%) in the 2,500 units of beginning work-in-process which totals 11,500. Subtract the amount of work

that was incomplete at the end of the period (60% of 2,000) resulting in 10,300 EUP.

Work-in-Process

BWIP 40%	2,500		
April input	10,000		
		10,500	April finished goods
		2,000	EWIP 40%
	12,500	12,500	

2.2 The actual material EUP cost is $121,000 divided by 10,000, or $12.10. At standard it is $100,000 divided by 10,000, or $10.00.

2.3 The actual direct labor EUP cost is the actual direct labor of $105,575 divided by the EUP of 10,300, or $10.25. At standard it is the standard cost of $82,400 divided by 10,300, or $8.00.

2.4 Similarly, for overhead, actual is $31,930 divided by 10,300, or $3.10, and standard is $25,750 divided by 10,300, or $2.50.

3. Part b of the problem requires variance analysis for 9 items.

3.1 The total material variance is the total actual cost less the standard cost.

3.2 The materials price variance is the difference between the actual price and the standard price times the actual quantity used. It is a useful check to note that the answers for 2 and 3 (materials price variance and materials usage variance) should equal answer 1 (total materials variance).

3.3 The materials usage variance is the difference between the actual quantity and the standard quantity at the standard cost.

3.4   The total labor variance is the difference between the total direct labor cost at actual
and at standard. It is a useful check to note
that the answers for 5 and 6 (labor rate variance and labor efficiency variance) should
equal answer 4 (total labor variance).

3.5   The labor rate variance is the difference between the actual rate and the standard rate
times actual hours worked.

3.6   The labor efficiency variance is the difference
between the actual hours worked and the standard hours worked at the standard rate.

3.7   Total factory overhead variance is the difference
between actual and standard overhead. It is a
useful check to note that the answers for 8
and 9 (factory overhead volume variance and
factory overhead budget variance) should equal
answer 7 (total factory overhead variance).

3.8   The factory overhead volume variance is the
difference between the budgeted overhead and
the standard overhead applied.

3.9   The factory overhead budget variance is the
difference between the actual overhead and
the budgeted overhead.

UNOFFICIAL ANSWER:PRACTICE

Problem 10   Standard Cost Variances

a.

Computation of Equivalent Units—Materials

	Actual units	Completed in current period (%)	Equiva-lent units
Beginning work-in-process inventory	2,500	0	0
Started and completed during the month	8,000	100	8,000
Ending work-in-process inventory	2,000	100	2,000
Total	12,500		10,000

Computation of Cost Per Equivalent Unit—Materials

Current costs ÷ equivalent units:
Actual   = $121,000 ÷ 10,000 = $12.10
Standard = $100,000 ÷ 10,000 = $10.00

Computation of Equivalent Units—Labor

	Actual units	Completed in current period (%)	Equiva-lent units
Beginning work-in-process inventory	2,500	60	1,500
Started and completed during the month	8,000	100	8,000
Ending work-in-process inventory	2,000	40	800
Total	12,500		10,300

Computation of Cost Per Equivalent Unit—Labor

Current costs ÷ equivalent units
Actual   = $105,575 ÷ 10,300 = $10.25
Standard = $ 82,400 ÷ 10,300 = $ 8.00

Computation of Equivalent Units— Combined Factory Overhead

	Actual units	Completed in current period (%)	Equiva-lent units
Beginning work-in-process inventory	2,500	60	1,500
Started and completed during the month	8,000	100	8,000
Ending work-in-process inventory	2,000	40	800
Total	12,500		10,300

Computation of Cost Per Equivalent Unit— Combined Factory Overhead

Current cost per equivalent units
Actual   = $31,930 ÷ 10,300 = $3.10
Standard = $25,750 ÷ 10,300 = $2.50

b.

1.   Total Materials Variance
Actual purchases $121,000
Standard production   100,000
                    Unfavorable $ 21,000

2.   Materials Price Variance
Actual quantity used at actual
 (11,000 lbs. x $11) $121,000
Actual quantity used at standard
 (11,000 lbs. x $10)   110,000
                    Unfavorable $ 11,000

3.   Materials Usage Variance

Actual quantity used at standard	
(11,000 lbs. @ $10)	$110,000
Standard quantity allowed	
(10,000 lbs. @ $10)	100,000
Unfavorable	$ 10,000

4.   Total Labor Variance

Actual labor cost	$105,575
Standard labor cost	82,400
Unfavorable	$ 23,175

5.   Labor Rate Variance

Actual hours worked at actual rate	
(25,000 hours)	$105,575
Actual hours worked at standard rate	
(25,000 x $4)	100,000
Unfavorable	$ 5,575

6.   Labor Efficiency Variance

Actual hours worked at standard rate	
(25,000 x $4)	$100,000
Standard hours worked at standard	
rate (20,600 x $4)	82,400
Unfavorable	$ 17,600

7.   Total Factory Overhead Variance

Actual factory overhead	$ 31,930
Factory overhead applied at standard	25,750
Unfavorable	$ 6,180

8.   Factory Overhead Volume Variance

Budgeted factory overhead	$ 30,000
Factory overhead applied at standard	25,750
Unfavorable	$ 4,250

9.   Factory Overhead Budget Variance

Actual factory overhead	$ 31,930
Budgeted factory overhead	30,000
Unfavorable	$ 1,930

SOLUTION GUIDE

Problem 11   Process Costing

The requirement for part "a" of this problem has been modified, and an alternative solution has been substituted for the AICPA unofficial answer.

1.   The requirement in part a is to prepare a cost of production report for both the machining and finishing departments.

2.   The solutions approach is to prepare a complete production report first for the machining department, then for the finishing department.

3.   The steps in the production report for the machining department are physical flow, equivalent units, total costs, unit costs, cost summary.

3.1   Physical flow is summarized in this T-account:

Machining	
Started 80,000 units	60,000 units Completed
	20,000 units End. WIP

3.2   Equivalent units are computed for materials, labor, and overhead. Ending WIP is 100%, 50%, and 25% complete for these elements respectively.

3.3   Machining costs (given) are summarized for all three elements.

3.4   The costs (3.3) are divided by equivalent units (3.2) to obtain cost per equivalent unit for all three elements.

3.5   Finally, costs are summarized for units transferred (60,000 units x Total per unit cost) and ending WIP (equivalent units for each element x Per unit cost for each element).

4.   The same five steps are used for the finishing department production report. There are two additional complications in this department: transferred-in costs and spoiled units.

4.1   Physical flow is summarized in this T-account:

Finishing	
Transferred in 60,000 units	50,000 units Completed
	2,000 units Spoiled
	8,000 units End. WIP

4.2   Equivalent units are computed for transferred-in costs, materials, labor, and overhead. Note that transferred-in costs are treated like materials added at the beginning of the process. Percentage of completion in ending WIP is 100%,100%, 70%, and 70% for the four elements respectively. Separate percentages of completion (100%, 50%, 50% and 50%) are given for units spoiled.

4.3   Finishing costs (given) are summarized for all four elements. Note that transferred-in costs in the finishing dept. = transferred-out costs from the machining dept.

4.4 The costs (4.3) are divided by equivalent units (4.2) to obtain cost per equivalent unit for all four elements.

4.5 The most complicated part of this problem is summarizing costs for the finishing dept., because the cost of spoiled goods must be considered. It is important to think thru this step carefully.

4.6 First, the cost of nonspoiled goods can be summarized for units completed (50,000 units x Total per unit cost of $10.45) and ending WIP (equivalent units for each element x Per unit cost for each element).

4.7 Finally, the cost of spoiled goods is allocated. The cost of these goods is the equivalent units spoiled x equivalent cost per unit [(2,000)($6) + (1,000)($1.50 + $2.50 + $ .45)]. This total cost ($16,450) is allocated to units completed and ending WIP based on good units in each category. Therefore, units completed are allocated 50,000/58,000, while ending WIP is allocated 8,000/58,000.

b.

1. Standard quantity of raw materials allowed:

Actual production	4,000	units
Standard raw materials per unit	x6	pounds
Standard quantity of raw materials allowed	24,000	pounds

2. Actual quantity of raw materials used:

Standard quantity	24,000	pounds
Unfavorable (debit) material quantity variance ($1,000 variance x $1 standard price per lb.)	+1,000	pounds
Actual quantity of raw materials used	25,000	pounds

3. Standard hours allowed:

Actual production	4,000	units
Standard hours per unit	x1	hour
Standard hours allowed	4,000	hours

4. Actual hours worked:

Standard hours allowed	4,000	hours
Favorable (credit) direct labor efficiency variance (800 variance ÷ $4 standard hrs. per unit)	(200)	hours
Actual hours worked	3,800	hours

5. Actual direct labor rate:

Standard direct labor rate	$4.00
Unfavorable (debit) direct labor rate variance ($760 variance ÷ 3,800 hrs. actually worked)	+ .20
Actual direct labor rate	$4.20

6. Actual total overhead:

Standard overhead (4000 units produced x $3 standard overhead rate per unit)	$12,000
Unfavorable (debit) overhead variance	500
Actual total overhead	$12,500

5. The requirement in part b is to compute six standard cost figures. The solutions approach is to calculate each amount separately.

5.1 The standard quantity of raw materials is the actual production of 4,000 units times the standard usage of 6 pounds per unit.

5.2 The actual quantity of raw materials used is the standard quantity of 24,000 lbs. (just computed above) plus the unfavorable material usage variance ($1,000 variance divided by $1.00 standard cost) of 1,000 lbs.

5.3 The standard hours of production is the actual production of 4,000 units times the standard labor usage of 1 hour.

5.4 The actual hours worked is the standard hours allowed of 4,000 less the favorable labor efficiency variance ($800 variance ÷ $4/hr.) of 200 hours.

5.5 The actual labor rate is the standard labor rate of $4 plus the unfavorable rate variance (760 ÷ 3,800 hours) of $ .20.

5.6 The actual total overhead is the standard overhead of $12,000 (4,000 units @ $3.00) plus the unfavorable overhead variance of $500.

Alternative Solution

Problem **11a**   **Process Costing**

The Dexter Products Company
MACHINING DEPARTMENT PRODUCTION COST REPORT
For the Month Ended June 30, 1976

Quantities	Physical Flow	Equivalent Units		
		Materials	Labor	Overhead
WIP, beginning	0			
Units started	80,000			
Units to account for	80,000			
Units spoiled	0	0	0	0
Units transferred	60,000	60,000	60,000	60,000
WIP, ending	20,000	20,000	10,000	5,000
Units accounted for	80,000	80,000	70,000	65,000

Costs	Totals	Materials	Labor	Overhead	Equivalent Whole Unit
WIP, beginning	0	0	0	0	
Current costs	$445,000	$240,000	$140,000	$65,000	
Total costs to account for	$445,000	$240,000	$140,000	$65,000	
Divide by equivalent units		÷80,000 =	÷70,000 =	÷65,000 =	
Cost per equivalent unit		$3	$2	$1	$6

Summary of costs:

Units transferred	$360,000		60,000 x $6
WIP, ending	85,000	20,000 x $3 + 10,000 x $2 + 5,000 x $1	
Total costs accounted for	$445,000		

The Dexter Products Company
FINISHING DEPARTMENT PRODUCTION COST REPORT
For the Month Ended June 30, 1976

Quantities	Physical Flow	Transferred-in Costs	Materials	Labor	Overhead
WIP, beginning	0				
Units transferred in	60,000				
Units to account for	60,000				
Units spoiled	2,000	2,000	1,000	1,000	1,000
Units completed	50,000	50,000	50,000	50,000	50,000
WIP, ending	8,000	8,000	8,000	5,600	5,600
Units accounted for	60,000	60,000	59,000	56,600	56,600

Costs	Totals	Transferred-in Costs	Materials	Labor	Overhead	Equivalent Whole Unit
WIP, beginning	0					
Current costs	$615,700	$360,000	$88,500	$141,500	$25,700	
Total costs to account for	$615,700	$360,000	$88,500	$141,500	$25,700	
Divided by equivalent units		÷60,000 =	÷59,000 =	÷56,600 =	÷56,600 =	
Cost per equivalent unit (EUP)		$6	$1.50	$2.50	$.45	$10.45

Summary of Costs:

Units completed[a] $536,681.03 = (50,000 x $10.45) + $\left[\$6 \left(2,000 \times \dfrac{50,000}{58,000}\right) + \$4.45 \left(1,000 \times \dfrac{50,000}{58,000}\right) \right]$

WIP, ending   78,788.97 = (8,000 x $6) + (8,000 x $1.50) + (5,600 x $2.50) + (4,600 x $.45)

$+ \left[\$6 \left(2,000 \times \dfrac{8,000}{58,000}\right) + \$4.45 \left(1,000 \times \dfrac{8,000}{58,000}\right) \right]$

Costs accounted for $615,470.00

[a] Spoilage allocated to units based on goods units

Good units = 60,000 total units − 2,000 spoiled units

Spoiled units have transferred-in costs plus materials, labor, and overhead costs

Spoilage costs = EUP cost $\left(\text{EUP quantity} \times \dfrac{\text{units transferred}}{\text{good units}} \right)$

Prepared by Professor David E. Keys, Northern Illinois Univ.

SOLUTION GUIDE :PRACTICE

Problem 12   Budgets

1.   This problem requires six budgets for 1978. The solutions approach is to prepare the budgets one at a time.

1.1   The sales budget for 1978 will be 60,000 "ones" at $70 ($4,200,000) and 40,000 "twos" at $100 ($4,000,000) which total $8,200,000.

1.2   The number of "ones" to be produced is the 60,000 units expected to be sold plus the expected increase of 5,000 units in inventory which total 65,000 units. The production budget for "twos" is the 40,000 units of projected sales plus the 1,000 expected increase in inventory which totals 41,000 units.

1.3   The raw materials purchase budget in units of material A is the 65,000 anticipated units of "ones" times four pounds (260,000 lbs.) plus the 41,000 "twos" at five pounds (205,000 lbs.) plus the anticipated inventory increase of 4,000 pounds which totals 469,000 pounds.

For material B, the 65,000 "ones" require two pounds each (130,000 lbs.); the 41,000 "twos" require three pounds each (123,000 lbs.); add the increase in inventory of 3,000 pounds for a total of 256,000 pounds.

For material C, the 41,000 "twos" will require one unit each (41,000 lbs.) plus the expected inventory increase of 1,000. The total is 42,000 units.

1.4   The raw materials purchase budget will be the anticipated purchase price times the expected usage.

	Purchase Price	Expected Usage	Extended Amounts
A	$8	469,000	$3,752,000
B	$5	256,000	$1,280,000
C	$3	42,000	$ 126,000
Total			$5,158,000

1.5   The direct labor budget for "ones" is 65,000 units at 2 hours each, which is 130,000 hours

at $3 each or $390,000. The 41,000 "twos" require 3 hours each, which is 123,000 hours at $4 each or $492,000.

1.6   Budgeted finished goods inventory cost will be "ones" inventory of 25,000 units at $52 and "twos" inventory of 9,000 units at $76.

	"Ones"	"Twos"
Material A ($8/lb)	$32	$40
Material B ($5/lb)	$10	$15
Material C ($3/unit)	–	$ 3
Direct labor	$ 6	$12
Overhead	$ 4	$ 6
Total unit costs	$52	$76
Budgeting FG Inventory	25,000 units	9,000 units
Total costs	$1,300,000	$684,000

UNOFFICIAL ANSWER :PRACTICE

Problem 12   Budgets

a.

Sales Budget
1978

	Units	Price	Total
Thingone	60,000	$ 70	$4,200,000
Thingtwo	40,000	$100	4,000,000
Projected sales			$8,200,000

b.

Production Budget (in units)
1978

	Thingone	Thingtwo
Projected sales	60,000	40,000
Desired inventories, December 31, 1978	25,000	9,000
	85,000	49,000
Less expected inventories, January 1, 1978	20,000	8,000
Production required (units)	65,000	41,000

c. Raw materials budget (in quantities)
1978

| | Raw Material | | |
	A	B	C
Thingone (65,000 units projected to be produced)	260,000	130,000	—
Thingtwo (41,000 units projected to be produced)	205,000	123,000	41,000
Production requirements	465,000	253,000	41,000
Add desired inventories, December 31, 1978	36,000	32,000	7,000
Total requirements	501,000	285,000	48,000
Less expected inventories, January 1, 1978	32,000	29,000	6,000
Purchase requirements (units)	469,000	256,000	42,000

d. Raw Materials Purchase Budget
1978

Raw material required (units)	Anticipated purchase price	Total
A—469,000	$8	$3,752,000
B—256,000	$5	$1,280,000
C— 42,000	$3	$ 126,000

e. *Direct Labor Budget*

1978

	Projected production (units)	*Hours per unit*	*Total*	*Rate*	*Total*
Thingone	65,000	2	130,000	$3	$390,000
Thingtwo	41,000	3	123,000	$4	$492,000
					$882,000

f. *Budgeted Finished Goods Inventory*

December 31, 1978

Thingone

Raw materials
A—4 pounds @ $8 $32
B—2 pounds @ $5 $10 $42
Direct labor—2 hours @ $3   6
Overhead—2 hours @ $2 per
  direct labor hour   4
                                 $52

$52 X 25,000 units = $1,300,000

Thingtwo

Raw materials
A—5 pounds @ $8 $40
B—3 pounds @ $5 $15
C—1 each @ $3 $ 3 $58
Direct labor—3 hours @ $4   12
Overhead—3 hours @ $2
  per direct labor hour   6
                                 $76

$76 X 9,000 units =   684,000

Budgeted finished goods inventory, December 31, 1978 $1,984,000

CHAPTER SIX

QUANTITATIVE PROBLEMS AND SOLUTIONS

Quantitative methods questions appear on both the practice and theory sections of the examination. Review the frequency of occurrence of quantitative problems on pages 443 and 444.

During the late Sixties and early Seventies the mechanics were emphasized (probably to encourage schools to teach the material), but this resulted in the criticism that such knowledge was not necessary for the practice of public accounting. As a result, the quantitative questions appearing on recent examinations have emphasized knowledge of the objectives, variables, and results of managerial quantitative techniques rather than mathematical calculations. Accordingly, "mechanical" math questions have been deleted from this edition. An exception is the economic order quantity (EOQ) calculation which has been required on several recent examinations (you should memorize the formula).

For the majority of questions, knowledge of when, how, and why particular optimization techniques are used is required. Do not attempt to memorize formulas, etc. Rather, try to understand the concepts underlying the technique or model. Generally the techniques provide a means of maximizing revenue (profit) or minimizing costs.

The source (month-year, section, problem number, and objective question number) appears at the beginning of the explanation of each multiple choice question. For example, (579,Q1,3) indicates May 1979, problem 1 of Practice II, and question number 3. Note that P = Practice I, Q = Practice II, and T = Theory.

MULTIPLE CHOICE QUESTIONS (1—44)

1. The estimates necessary to compute the economic order quantity are
    a. Annual usage in units, cost per order, and annual cost of carrying one unit in stock.
    b. Annual usage in units, cost per unit of inventory, and annual cost of carrying one unit in stock.
    c. Annual cost of placing orders, and annual cost of carrying one unit in stock.
    d. Cost per unit of inventory, annual cost of placing orders, and annual carrying cost.

2. The use of the graphic method as a means for solving linear programming problems
    a. Can be used when there are more than two restrictions (constraints).
    b. Is limited to situations where there are two restrictions (constraints).
    c. Is limited to situations where there is one restriction (constraint).
    d. **Cannot** be used if there are any restrictions (constraints).

3. What is the appropriate technique for defining the critical path when the completion of a total project is dependent upon the completion of various subunits at specific times to enable the work to progress?
    a. Linear programming.
    b. Multiple regression analysis.
    c. Program evaluation review technique.
    d. Queuing theory.

4. Which of the following methods can be used to determine the fixed and variable elements of a semivariable expense?
    a. Statistical scattergraph method.
    b. Linear programming.
    c. Input-output analysis.
    d. Program evaluation review technique.

5. Johnson, Inc., manufactures product X and product Y which are processed as follows:

	Type A machine	Type B machine
Product X	6 hours	4 hours
Product Y	9 hours	5 hours

The contribution margin is $12 for product X and $7 for product Y. The available time daily for processing the two products is 120 hours for machine Type A and

80 hours for machine Type B. How would the restriction (constraint) for machine Type B be expressed?
    a. $4X + 5Y$
    b. $4X + 5Y \leq 80$
    c. $6X + 9Y \leq 120$
    d. $12X + 7Y$

6. Duguid Company is considering a proposal to introduce a new product, XPL. An outside marketing consultant prepared the following payoff probability distribution describing the relative likelihood of monthly sales volume levels and related income (loss) for XPL:

Monthly sales volume	Probability	Income (loss)
3,000	0.10	$(35,000)
6,000	0.20	5,000
9,000	0.40	30,000
12,000	0.20	50,000
15,000	0.10	70,000

If Duguid decides to market XPL, the expected value of the added monthly income will be
    a. $ 24,000
    b. $ 26,500
    c. $ 30,000
    d. $120,000

7. The following information is available for Digby Company's material Y:

Annual usage in units	10,000
Working days per year	250
Normal lead time in working days	30
Maximum lead time in working days	70

Assuming that the units of material Y will be required evenly throughout the year, the order point would be
    a. 1,200
    b. 1,600
    c. 2,000
    d. 2,800

8. The following information relates to the Gerald Company:

Optimal production run	500
Average inventory in units	250
Number of production runs	10
Cost per unit produced	$5
Desired annual return on inventory investment	10%
Set up costs per production run	$10

Assuming that the units will be required evenly through-out the year, what are the total annual relevant costs using the economic-order-quantity approach?

    a. $ 225
    b. $ 350
    c. $1,350
    d. $2,625

9.   The Beauty Company produces a cosmetic pro-duct in 60 gallon batches. The basic ingredients used are material X costing $7 per gallon and material Y costing $17 per gallon. No more than 18 gallons of X can be used, and at least 15 gallons of Y must be used. How would the objective function (minimization of product cost) be expressed?

    a.   7X + 17Y
    b.   17X + 7Y
    c.   18X + 15Y
    d.   18X + 42Y

10.   The following information relates to Eagle Com-pany's material A:

Annual usage in units	7,200
Working days per year	240
Normal lead time in working days	20
Maximum lead time in working days	45

Assuming that the units of material A will be required evenly throughout the year, the safety stock and order point would be

	Safety Stock	Order Point
a.	600	750
b.	600	1,350
c.	750	600
d.	750	1,350

11.   Regression analysis is superior to other cost be-havior analysis techniques because it

    a.   Produces measures of probable error.
    b.   Examines only one variable.
    c.   Proves a cause and effect relationship.
    d.   Is not a sampling technique.

12.   Politan Company manufactures bookcases. Set up costs are $2.00. Politan manufactures 4,000 book-cases evenly throughout the year. Using the economic-order-quantity approach, the optimal production run would be 200 when the cost of carrying one bookcase in inventory for one year is

    a. $0.05.
    b. $0.10.
    c. $0.20.
    d. $0.40.

13.   Milford Company manufactures two models, medium and large. The contribution margin expected is $12 for the medium model and $20 for the large model. The medium model is processed two hours in the machining department and four hours in the polishing department. The large model is processed three hours in the machining department and six hours in the polishing department. How would the formula for determining the maximization of total contribu-tion margin be expressed?

    a.   5X + 10Y
    b.   6X + 9Y
    c.   12X + 20Y
    d.   12X (2 + 4) + 20Y (3 + 6)

14.   Simple regression analysis involves the use of
    a.   One variable.
    b.   Two variables.
    c.   Three variables.
    d.   More than three variables.

15.   Program evaluation review technique (PERT) is a system which uses
    a.   Least squares method.
    b.   Linear programming.
    c.   Economic order quantity formula.
    d.   Network analysis and critical path methods.

16.   A company manufactures two models, X and Y. Model X is processed 4 hours in the machining de-partment and 2 hours in the polishing department. Model Y is processed 9 hours in the machining depart-ment and 6 hours in the polishing department. The available time for processing the two models is 200 hours a week in the machining department and 180 hours a week in the polishing department. The contri-bution margins expected are $10 for Model X and $14 for Model Y. How would the restriction (con-straint) for the polishing department be expressed?

    a.   2X + 6Y $\leq$ 180.
    b.   6X + 15Y $\leq$ 180.
    c.   2(10X) + 6(14Y) $\leq$ 180.
    d.   10X + 14Y $\leq$ 180.

17.   Williamson Manufacturing intends to produce two products, X and Y. Product X requires six hours of time on Machine 1 and twelve hours of time on Machine 2. Product Y requires four hours of time on Machine 1 and no time on Machine 2. Both machines are available for twenty-four hours. Assuming that the objective function of the total contribution margin is

$2X + $1Y, what product mix will produce the maximum profit?

    a.   No units of Product X and 6 units of Product Y.

    b.   1 unit of Product X and 4 units of Product Y.

    c.   2 units of Product X and 3 units of Product Y.

    d.   4 units of Product X and no units of Product Y.

18. Siegal Company has correctly computed its economic order quantity as 500 units; however, management feels it would rather order in quantities of 600 units. How should Siegal's total annual purchase-order cost and total annual carrying cost for an order quantity of 600 units compare to the respective amounts for an order quantity of 500 units?

    a.   Higher purchase-order cost and higher carrying cost.

    b.   Lower purchase-order cost and lower carrying cost.

    c.   Higher purchase-order cost and lower carrying cost.

    d.   Lower purchase-order cost and higher carrying cost.

19. A scatter chart depicting the relationship between sales and salesmen's automobile expenses is set forth below:

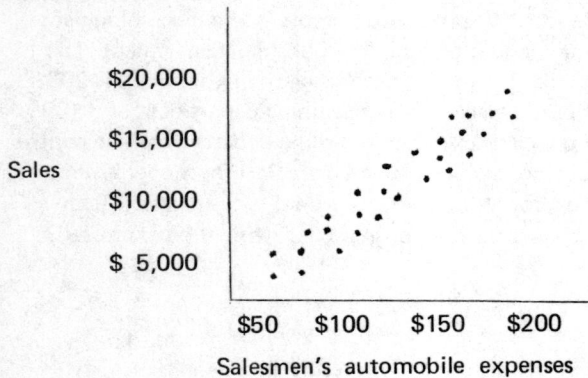

What can we deduce from the chart about the relationship between sales and salesmen's automobile expenses?

    a.   A high degree of linear correlation.

    b.   A high degree of nonlinear correlation.

    c.   No apparent correlation.

    d.   Both sales and salesmen's automobile expenses are independent variables.

20. A pay-off table (matrix) for evaluating alternative courses of action attempts to deal with

    a.   Centralization.

    b.   Uncertainty.

    c.   Goal congruence.

    d.   Motivation.

21. A Company places orders for inventory with its suppliers for a certain item for which the order size is determined in advance as

$$\text{Order Size} = \sqrt{\frac{2 \times \text{Cost to Place One Order} \times \text{Demand per Period}}{\text{Cost to Hold One Unit for One Period}}}$$

All orders are the same size. When the policy is implemented, demand per period is only one-half what was expected when order size was computed. Consequently, actual total inventory cost will be

    a.   Larger than if the expected demand per period had occurred and larger than if the actual demand per period had been used to calculate order size.

    b.   Larger than if the expected demand per period had occurred and smaller than if the actual demand per period had been used to calculate order size.

    c.   Smaller than if the expected demand per period had occurred and larger than if the actual demand per period had been used to calculate order size.

    d.   Smaller than if the expected demand per period had occurred and smaller than if the actual demand per period had been used to calculate order size.

22. The following data refer to various annual costs relating to the inventory of a single-product company:

	Cost Per Unit
Transportation-in on purchases	$.20
Storage	.12
Insurance	.10

	Total Per Year
Interest that could have been earned on alternate investment of funds	$800
Units required	10,000

What is the annual carrying cost per unit?

    a. $.22.

    b. $.30.

    c. $.42.

    d. $.50.

23.   Your client, a retail store, is interested in the relationship between sales (independent variable) and theft losses (dependent variable). Using the proper formula, you compute the coefficient of correlation as .95. What can you definitely conclude about these factors (sales and theft losses)?
   a.   An increase in sales causes an increase in theft losses.
   b.   Movement of these factors is in opposite directions.
   c.   Movement of these factors is entirely unrelated.
   d.   Movement of these factors is in the same direction.

24.   The forecast of sales for the next accounting period has been stated as $100,000 by the marketing vice-president of a merchandising company. Which of the following techniques was most likely used by the marketing vice-president in his sales forecast?
   a.   Probability analysis.
   b.   Linear programming.
   c.   Cost-volume-earnings analysis.
   d.   Program evaluation review technique (PERT).

25.   If the coefficient of correlation between two variables is zero, how might a scatter diagram of these variables appear?
   a.   Random points.
   b.   A least squares line that slopes up to the right.
   c.   A least squares line that slopes down to the right.
   d.   Under this condition, a scatter diagram could not be plotted on a graph.

26.   In a system of equations for a linear-programming model, what can be done to equalize an inequality such as $3X + 2Y \le 15$?
   a.   Nothing.
   b.   Add a slack variable.
   c.   Add a tableau.
   d.   Multiply each element by -1.

27.   What is the appropriate range for the coefficient of correlation (r)?
   a. $0 \le r \le 1$.
   b. $-1 \le r \le 1$.
   c. $-100 \le r \le 100$.
   d. $-\text{infinity} \le r \le \text{infinity}$.

28.   Your client wants your advice on which of two alternatives he should choose. One alternative is to sell an investment now for $10,000.

Another alternative is to hold the investment three days after which he can sell it for a certain selling price based on the following probabilities:

Selling Price	Probability
$ 5,000	.4
8,000	.2
12,000	.3
30,000	.1

Using probability theory, which of the following is the most reasonable statement?
   a.   Hold the investment three days because the expected value of holding exceeds the current selling price.
   b.   Hold the investment three days because of the chance of getting $30,000 for it.
   c.   Sell the investment now because the current selling price exceeds the expected value of holding.
   d.   Sell the investment now because there is a 60% chance that the selling price will fall in three days.

29.   For its economic-order-quantity model a company has a cost of placing an order equal to $10, and an annual cost of carrying one unit in stock equal to $2. If the cost of placing an order increases by 20%, and the annual cost of carrying one unit in stock increases by 25% and all other considerations remain constant, the economic order quantity will
   a.   Remain unchanged.
   b.   Decrease.
   c.   Increase.
   d.   Either increase or decrease depending on the reorder point.

30.   The Polly Company wishes to determine the amount of safety stock that it should maintain for Product D that will result in the lowest cost. The following information is available:

Stockout cost	$80 per occurrence
Carrying cost of safety stock	$2 per unit
Number of purchase orders	5 per year

The available options open to Polly are as follows:

Units of Safety Stock	Probability of Running Out of Safety Stock
10	50%
20	40%
30	30%
40	20%
50	10%
55	5%

The number of units of safety stock that will result in the lowest cost are
   a.   20.
   b.   40.
   c.   50.
   d.   55.

31. The Pauley Company plans to expand its sales force by opening several new branch offices. Pauley has $10,400,000 in capital available for new branch offices. Pauley will consider opening only two types of branches; 20-person branches (Type A) and 10-person branches (Type B). Expected initial cash outlays are $1,300,000 for a Type A branch and $670,000 for a Type B branch. Expected annual cash inflow, net of income taxes, is $92,000 for a Type A branch and $36,000 for a Type B branch. Pauley will hire no more than 200 employees for the new branch offices and will not open more than 20 branch offices. Linear programming will be used to help decide how many branch offices should be opened.

In a system of equations for a linear programming model, which of the following equations would not represent a constraint (restriction)?
   a. $A + B \leqslant 20$.
   b. $20 A + 10 B \leqslant 200$.
   c. $\$92,000\ A + \$36,000\ B \leqslant \$128,000$.
   d. $\$1,300,000\ A + \$670,000\ B \leqslant \$10,400,000$.

32. A measure of the extent to which two variables are related linearly is referred to as
   a.   Cause-effect ratio.
   b.   Coefficient of correlation.
   c.   Sensitivity analysis.
   d.   Input-output analysis.

33. When using the graphic method of solving a linear programming problem, the optimal solution will always be at
   a.   Minimum value of X.
   b.   X and Y intercept.
   c.   A corner point described by the feasible area.
   d.   Point of inception.

34. The Green Company's new process will be carried out in one department. The production process has an expected learning curve of 80%. The costs subject to the learning effect for the first batch produced by the process were $10,000. Using the simplest form of the learning function, the cumulative average cost per batch subject to the learning effect after the 16th batch has been produced may be estimated as
   a. $3,276.80.
   b. $4,096.00.
   c. $8,000.00.
   d. $10,000.00.

35. Pierce Incorporated has to manufacture 10,000 blades for its electric lawn mower division. The blades will be used evenly throughout the year. The setup cost every time a production run is made is $80, and the cost to carry a blade in inventory for the year is $.40. Pierce's objective is to produce the blades at the lowest cost possible. Assuming that each production run will be for the same number of blades, how many production runs should Pierce make?
   a.   3.
   b.   4.
   c.   5.
   d.   6.

36. The Hancock Company wishes to determine the amount of safety stock that they should maintain for Product No. 135 that will result in the lowest cost. Each stockout will cost $75 and the carrying cost of each unit of safety stock will be $1. Product No. 135 will be ordered five times a year. Which of the following will produce the lowest cost?
   a.   A safety stock of 10 units which is associated with a 40% probability of running out of stock during an order period.
   b.   A safety stock of 20 units which is associated with a 20% probability of running out of stock during an order period.
   c.   A safety stock of 40 units which is associated with a 10% probability of running out of stock during an order period.
   d.   A safety stock of 80 units which is associated with a 5% probability of running out of stock during an order period.

37.   The Hale Company manufactures products A and B, each of which requires two processes, polishing and grinding. The contribution margin is $3 for Product A and $4 for Product B. The graph below shows the maximum number of units of each product that may be processed in the two departments.

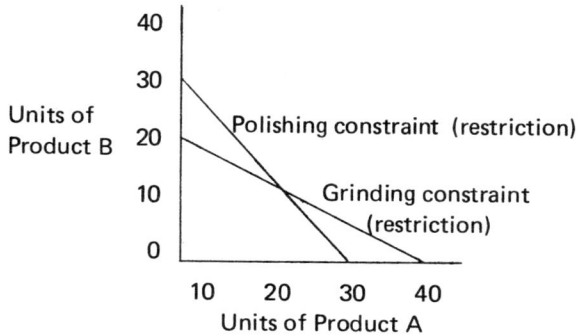

Considering the constraints (restrictions) on processing, which combination of products A and B maximizes the total contribution margin?
  a.   0 units of A and 20 units of B.
  b.   20 units of A and 10 units of B.
  c.   30 units of A and 0 units of B.
  d.   40 units of A and 0 units of B.

38. Paine Corp. wishes to determine the fixed portion of its electricity expense (a semivariable expense), as measured against direct labor hours, for the first three months of 1977. Information for the first three months of 1977 is as follows:

	Direct Labor Hours	Electricity Expense
January 1977	34,000	$610
February 1977	31,000	585
March 1977	34,000	610

What is the fixed portion of Paine's electricity expense, rounded to the nearest dollar?
  a. $283.
  b. $327.
  c. $372.
  d. $408.

39.   Which of the following is a relevant factor in the determination of an economic order quantity?
  a.   Physical plant insurance costs.
  b.   Warehouse supervisory salaries.
  c.   Variable costs of processing a purchase order.
  d.   Physical plant depreciation charges.

Items 40 through 44 are based on the following information:

A construction company has contracted to complete a new building and has asked for assistance in analyzing the project. Using the Program Evaluation Review Technique (PERT), the following network has been developed:

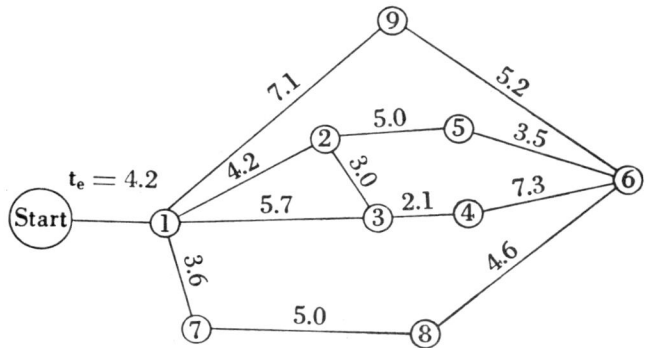

All paths from the start point to the finish point, event 6, represent activities or processes that must be completed before the entire project, the building, will be completed. The numbers above the paths or line segments represent expected completion times for the activities or processes. The expected time is based upon the commonly used, 1-4-1, three-estimate method. For example, the three-estimate method gives an estimated time of 4.2 to complete event 1.

40.   The critical path (the path requiring the greatest amount of time) is
  a.   1-2-5-6.
  b.   1-2-3-4-6.
  c.   1-3-4-6.
  d.   1-7-8-6.
  e.   1-9-6.

41.   Slack time on path 1-9-6 equals
  a.   4.3.
  b.   2.8
  c.   .9
  d.   .4
  e.   0

42.   The latest time for reaching event 6 via path 1-2-5-6 is
  a.   20.8
  b.   19.3
  c.   17.4
  d.   16.5
  e.   12.7

43. The earliest time for reaching event 6 via path
1-2-5-6 is

    a.   20.8

    b.   16.9

    c.   16.5

    d.   12.7

    e.   3.5

44. If all other paths are operating on schedule but path
segment 7-8 has an unfavorable time variance of 1.9,

    a.   The critical path will be shortened.

    b.   The critical path will be eliminated.

    c.   The critical path will be unaffected.

    d.   Another path will become the critical path.

    e.   The critical path will have an increased time
of 1.9.

PROBLEMS

Problem 1   Probability (1179,Q4)

(40 to 50 minutes)

Part a. The Wing Manufacturing Corporation produces a chemical compound, product X which deteriorates and must be discarded if it is not sold by the end of the month during which it is produced. The total variable cost of the manufactured compound, product X, is $50 per unit and its selling price is $80 per unit. Wing can purchase the same compound from a competing company at $80 per unit plus $10 freight per unit. Management has estimated that failure to fill orders would result in the loss of 80 percent of customers placing orders for the compound. Wing has manufactured and sold product X for the past 20 months. Demand for product X has been irregular and at present there is no consistent sales trend. During this period monthly sales have been as follows:

Units Sold per Month	Number of Months
8,000	5
9,000	12
10,000	3

Required:

1. Compute the probability of sales of product X of 8,000, 9,000, or 10,000 units in any month.

2. Compute what the contribution margin would be if 9,000 units of product X were ordered and either 8,000, 9,000, or 10,000 units were manufactured in that same month, (with additional units, if necessary, being purchased).

3. Compute the average monthly contribution margin that Wing can expect if 9,000 units of product X are manufactured every month and all sales orders are filled.

Part b. In the production of product X, Wing uses a primary ingredient, K-1. This ingredient is purchased from an outside supplier at a cost of $24 per unit of compound. It is estimated that there is a 70 percent chance that the supplier of K-1 may be shut down by a strike for an indefinite period. A substitute ingredient, K-2 is available at $36 per unit of compound but Wing must contact this alternative source immediately to secure sufficient quantities. A firm purchase contract for either material must now be made for production of the primary ingredient next

month. If an order were placed for K-1 and a strike occurred, Wing would be released from the contract and management would purchase the chemical compound from its competitor. Assume that 9,000 units are to be manufactured and all sales orders are to be filled.

Required:

1. Compute the monthly contribution margin from sales of 8,000, 9,000, and 10,000 units if the substitute ingredient, K-2 is ordered.

2. Prepare a schedule computing the average monthly contribution margin that Wing should expect if the primary ingredient, K-1 is ordered with the existing probability of a strike at the supplier. Assume that the expected average monthly contribution margin from manufacturing will be $130,000 using the primary ingredient, and the expected average monthly loss from purchasing product X from the competitor (in case of a strike) will be $45,000.

Problem 2   Linear Programming Graph (569,T7)

(25 to 30 minutes)

The cost accountant of the Strangren Corporation, your client, wants your opinion of a technique suggested to him by a young accounting graduate he employed as a cost analyst. The following information was furnished you for the Corporation's two products, trinkets and gadgets:

1.   Exhibit A

	Trinkets	Gadgets
Daily Capacities in Units		
Cutting Department	400	200
Finishing Department	240	320
Sales Price Per Unit	$50	$70
Variable Cost Per Unit	$30	$40

2. The daily capacities of each Department represents the maximum production for either trinkets or gadgets. However, any combination of trinkets and gadgets can be produced as long as a maximum capacity of the department is not exceeded. For example, two trinkets can be produced in the Cutting Department for each gadget not produced and three trinkets can be produced in the Finishing Department for every four gadgets not produced.

3. Material shortages prohibit the production of more than 180 gadgets per day.

4. Exhibit B is a graphic expression of simultaneous linear equations developed from the production information above.

Exhibit B
GRAPH OF PRODUCTION RELATIONSHIPS

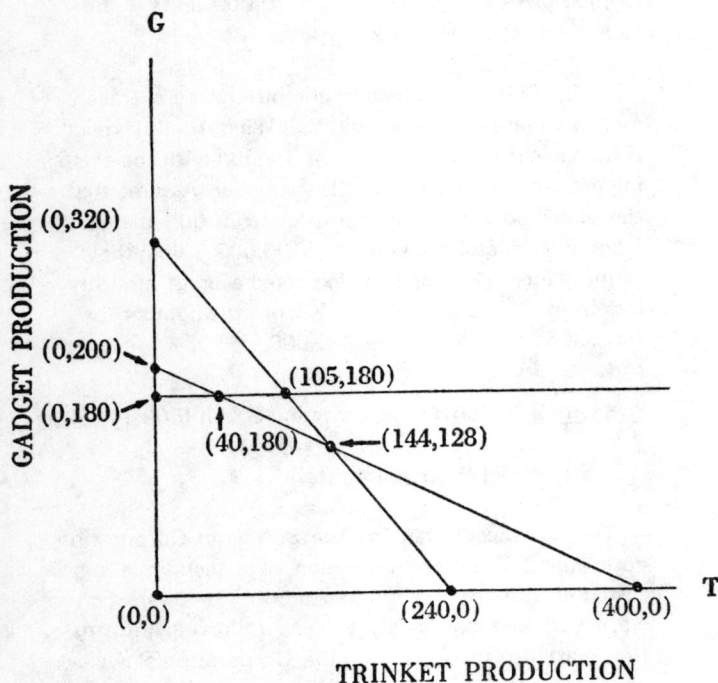

TRINKET PRODUCTION

Required:

a. For what kinds of decisions are contribution margin data (revenue in excess of variable cost) useful?

b. Comparing the information in Exhibit A with the graph in Exhibit B, identify and list the graphic location (coordinates) of the
   1. Cutting Department's capacity.
   2. Production limitation for gadgets because of the materials shortage.
   3. Area of feasible (possible) production combinations.

c. 1. Compute the contribution margin per unit for trinkets and gadgets.
   2. Compute the total contribution margin of each of the points of intersections of lines bounding the feasible (possible) production area.
   3. Identify the best production alternative.

Problem 3   Operations Research Definitions
               (1176,T6)   (15 to 20 minutes)

Part a.   Freedom, Inc., your client, is a very large corporation with branches in several major U.S. cities. Freedom has asked you, as a consultant, to be part of an advisory operations research team to the company.

Required:

What are the characteristics of the field of operations research (OR) and in what ways can you, as an accountant, contribute to this operations research team?

Part b.   One of your major clients, The Liberty Company, is planning to use several quantitative techniques to help control its operations. Liberty is seeking your advice about these techniques.

Required:

Define and discuss each of the following quantitative techniques including the assumptions and accounting data used therein:

1.   Linear programming.

2.   Economic order quantity (EOQ).

3.   Program evaluation and review technique (PERT).

4.   Regression analysis.

MULTIPLE CHOICE ANSWERS

1.	a	11.	a	21.	c	31.	c	41.	a
2.	a	12.	d	22.	b	32.	b	42.	a
3.	c	13.	c	23.	d	33.	c	43.	b
4.	a	14.	b	24.	a	34.	b	44.	c
5.	b	15.	d	25.	a	35.	c		
6.	b	16.	a	26.	b	36.	c		
7.	d	17.	c	27.	b	37.	b		
8.	a	18.	d	28.	a	38.	b		
9.	a	19.	a	29.	b	39.	c		
10.	d	20.	b	30.	d	40.	b		

EXPLANATION OF MULTIPLE CHOICE ANSWERS

1. (1180,T1,36)   (a)   The economic order quantity formula is

$$EOQ = \sqrt{\frac{2aD}{K}}$$

where a = fixed cost per order, D = annual demand on usage in units, and K = annual cost of carrying one unit in stock. Cost per unit of inventory, included in answers (b) and (d), is not necessary. Answer (c) does not include annual usage.

2. (1180,T1,41)   (a)   Linear programming is a technique used to determine optimal use of limited resources. The graphic method of linear programming can be used with any number of restraints. In solving these problems, all (restraint) constraint lines are drawn on the graph. While often only two restraints will apply, the graphic method will indicate which constraints do and do not apply.

3. (1180,T1,42)   (c)   Program evaluation review technique (PERT) is used to define the critical path when the completion of a project is dependent upon completing subunits to enable the work to progress. Linear programming [answer (a)] is a technique used to determine optimal use of limited resources. Multiple regression analysis [answer (b)] determines the functional relationship between multiple variables. Queuing theory [answer (d)] attempts to minimize the costs associated with processes that have waiting lines (queues).

4. (1180,T1,47)   (a)   Statistical scattergraph methods can be used to determine the fixed and variable elements of a semivariable expense. Linear programming [answer (b)] is a technique used to determine optimal use of limited resources. Input-output analysis [answer (c)] deals with the conversion ratio of input resources into output resources. Program evaluation review technique [answer (d)], known as PERT, is a map of the flow of work through a network of interdependent tasks.

5. (1180,P2,30)   (b)   The requirement is the constraint for the Type B machine in a linear programming problem. Type B is available for 80 hours of processing, so the time used must be less than or equal to 80. Product X requires 4 hours of machine B time and product Y requires 5 hours; the total time spent on the two products is subject to the 80 hour limit. Therefore, using X to signify units of X and Y to signify units of Y, the constraint is: $4X + 5Y \leq 80$.

6. (1180,P2,36)   (b)   The requirement is the expected value of the added monthly income if the new product is marketed. The expected value would be obtained by multiplying the possible income levels by the respective probabilities, and summing the products.

Probability	Income (Loss)	Expected Value
.10	$(35,000)	$ (3,500)
.20	5,000	1,000
.40	30,000	12,000
.20	50,000	10,000
.10	70,000	7,000
		$ 26,500

7. (1180,P2,40)   (d)   The requirement is the order point for material Y. Digby's average daily usage of the material is 10,000 units/250 days or 40 units. The order point when there is no safety stock is computed using normal lead time; however, with a proper safety stock the maximum lead time of 70 days is used. The order point is (70 days) (40 units a day) or 2800 units.

8. (580,P2,31)   (a)   The requirement is the total annual relevant costs using the EOQ model. The two elements composing this annual cost are total annual set up cost and the total annual cost of carrying the average number of units in inventory for one year.

$10 set costs per run x 10 production runs
+ 10% (250 units x $5 cost per unit produced)
= $225

9.   (580,P2,36)   (a)   The requirement is the objective function to minimize product cost. The objective function of a linear programming minimization problem consists of each of the inputs with the unit cost for each input as the coefficients.

10.   (580,P2,38)   (d)   The requirement is for the safety stock and order point. Safety stock is equal to the normal usage per day of 30 units times the difference between the maximum lead time and normal lead time, both expressed in terms of days. The order point is equal to safety stock plus the normal usage during the lead time.

Normal usage = 7,200 ÷ 240 = 30 units

Safety stock = 30 units (45 days − 20 days)
Safety stock = 750 units

Order point = (30 units x 20 days) + safety stock
Order point = 1,350 units

11.   (580,T1,46)   (a)   A major advantage of regression analysis over other cost analysis techniques is the fact that it does produce measures of probable error (such as the standard error of estimate). Another advantage is its ability to examine more than one variable, which eliminates answer (b). Regression analysis is a sampling technique (answer (d)), but does not prove cause and effect (answer (c)). It merely indicates that variables move together.

12.   (1179,P2,31)   (d)   The requirement is to determine the cost of carrying one bookcase in inventory for 1 year using the EOQ model. The economic order quantity (EOQ) is a formula based on an inventory cost function. The objective of the formula is to minimize both carrying costs and total ordering costs. The formula is:

$$EOQ = \sqrt{\frac{2aD}{k}}$$

a = fixed order cost
D = annual demand
k = unit carrying cost

This problem requires you to calculate the value of K. The solutions approach is to plug the data in the problem into the formula above, as illustrated below. Squaring both sides of the equation gives 40,000K = $16,000 or K = $.40

$$200 = \sqrt{\frac{2 \times \$2.00 \times 4,000}{K}}$$

$$40,000 = \frac{2 \times \$2.00 \times 4,000}{K}$$

40,000K = $16,000

K = $.40

13.   (1179,P2,32)   (c)   The requirement is the formula to maximize a contribution margin in a linear programming problem. The question states that the contribution margin is going to be $12 for a medium model and $20 for a large model. Accordingly, the formula to maximize the contribution margin is 12x + 20y. The data concerning the number of hours required to process each model in the machining and polishing departments are only relevant to constraint equations and are extraneous data.

14.   (1179,T1,37)   (b)   Simple regression analysis involves the use of two variables. Regression analysis determines the functional relationships between variables, e.g., the relationship of electricity costs to the level of activity. The dependent variable is the variable being explained, e.g., electricity costs. Independent variable(s) are the variable(s) that explain the change in the dependent variable, e.g., level of activity. When there is only one independent variable, the procedure is termed simple regression. When there are two or more independent variables, the procedure is known as multiple regression.

15.   (1179,T1,38)   (d)   Network analysis is the methodology to determine the shortest or longest route through a network or the maximum flow through a network. Critical path analysis is a synonym, i.e., the critical or longest path through a network. PERT (program evaluation and review technique) is a special application of network analysis that forecasts the time critical or shortest path through a network. PERT (program evaluation and review technique) is a special application of network analysis that forecasts the time required to complete a complex project by identifying those parts of the project critical to completion time. Answer (a) is incorrect because the least squares method (regression analysis) determines the functional relationship between a dependent variable and one or more independent variables. Answer (b) is incorrect because linear programming is a technique to find optimal uses for limited resources. Generally, an objective function is maximized or minimized subject to various constraints. Answer (c) is incorrect because the EOQ formula provides a method of minimizing inventory costs.

16.   (1179,T1,40)   (a)   The requirement is the constraint function for a polishing department in a linear programming problem. Linear programming models maximize or minimize an objective function subject to various constraints. Here, the polishing department has available time of 180 hours a week. Since Model X requires 2 hours of work in the polishing department, and Model Y requires 6 hours in the polishing department, 2x + 6Y ≤ 180. Answers (b), (c), and (d) are in the format of constraint functions, but do not apply to this problem

17. (1176,P2,27) (c) The objective is to produce the maximum profit given a contribution of $2.00 for each X and $1.00 for each Y produced. This objective function is subject to the constraints of only having 24 hours of machine 1 time available and 24 hours of machine 2 time available. If X requires 6 hours of machine 1 and Y requires 4 hours of machine 1, the constraint is $6X + 4Y \leq 24$. Machine 2's only constraint is X, as Y requires no machine 2 time.

Given the constraint equations below and the contribution margin, one attempts to maximize the contribution margin subject to the constraints. One approach is to evaluate each one of the four answers to determine first whether they are possible, i.e., fit within the constraints, and second to determine the amount of contribution margin they produce. This approach would find answers (a), (b) and (c) within the constraints and (c) having the maximum profit. Alternatively, one might notice that it is better to produce as many X as possible because the contribution margin for X is twice that of Y. Following this approach, one would see that only 2X are possible because of the second constraint. This would also allow 3Y to be produced.

$$6X + 4Y \leq 24$$
$$12X \qquad \leq 24$$

Cont margin = $2X + $Y

18. (1176,P2,34) (d) The economic order quantity (EOQ) model considers two costs—ordering costs and carrying costs. Ordering costs are considered to be a fixed cost for each order placed and carrying costs are based on the average level of inventory, i.e., the larger the order size, the smaller the annual order costs but the higher the carrying costs. In this case the standard order quantity is going to be raised from 500 units to 600 units. As a result, fewer orders will be placed resulting in a lower annual order cost. Conversely, a higher average inventory will be maintained, which will increase the carrying costs.

19. (577,P2,31) (a) The scatter diagram indicates salesmen's automobile expenses increase as their sales increase. The relationship appears linear, i.e., a straight line. If it were a nonlinear correlation, the relationship or the line of dots would bend, i.e., not be straight. If there were no apparent correlation, there would be no trend in the line of dots, i.e., they would be all over. Answer (d) is incorrect because it is not apparent what is causing sales and automobile expenses. Independent variables are those which explain changes in dependent variables.

cash paid for the inventory rather than the accounting valuation.

20. (577,T2,42) (b) A payoff matrix for evaluating alternative courses of action is concerned with uncertainty, e.g., alternative courses of action with different payoffs. These different alternative courses of action and payoffs generally have different probabilities that can be associated with them. Centralization concerns the delegation or lack of delegation of control and authority. Goal congruence concerns the relationship of individual participants' goals to the goals of the overall entity. Motivation concerns individual interests in achieving output, performance, etc.

21. (1175,P2,26) (c) The equation is known as the EOQ or economic order quantity. It is used to minimize the total of ordering and carrying costs of inventory. Thus, this company determines an order size that minimized the combined ordering costs and carrying costs. The requirement is to determine what actual inventory cost will be if the demand is only one-half what was expected (or used in computing the order size). Thus, the company will have to hold the inventory twice as long as expected. The effect is to increase the holding costs beyond the optimum whereas the cost to place orders will be decreased because there will be less orders. Answer (a) is incorrect because ordering costs are going to be saved, but carrying costs are going to exceed the optimum amount. Thus the inventory costs cannot be larger than if the expected demand had occurred. The actual cost would be larger than if the actual demand per period had been used to calculate the order size. Answer (b) is incorrect because the actual inventory cost will not be larger than if the expected demand per period had occurred as in answer (a). Answer (c) is correct because the total inventory cost is smaller than if the expected demand per period had occurred, because there is less order cost. It is also larger than if the actual demand per period had been used to calculate the order size, because there are more carrying costs than there would be if the actual demand per period had been used to calculate order size. Answer (d) is incorrect because the actual inventory cost is not smaller than if the actual demand had been used to calculate order size.

22. (1175,P2,29) (b) Transportation-in on purchases is not a carrying cost per unit; it is a product cost. The carrying cost of the inventory is the storage, insurance, and interest. The interest will amount to .08 per unit. Thus the carrying cost is $.12 plus $.10 plus $.08 or $.30.

23. (1175,P2,35) (d) Coefficients of correlation, or correlation coefficients, vary between -1.0 and $+1.0$. If there is perfect positive correlation, e.g., if one variable increases by 100, the other variable will increase by 100, the correlation is perfectly direct. If on the other hand, one variable increases by 100 when the other variable decreases by 100, it is a perfect indirect relationship with the correlation coefficient of minus one. If there is no relationship between variables there is said to be a zero correlation. In this particular case the correlation coefficient is .95 so there is a very strong positive relationship between sales and theft losses. Answer (d) states that movements of these factors is in the same direction which is correct. Answer (c) is incorrect because if the factors were entirely unrelated, the correlation coefficient would be zero or close to zero. Answer (b) is incorrect because it is a positive figure rather than a negative figure. Answer (a) is incorrect because correlation coefficients do not indicate causation. For example, it may be that the cause of increased theft is more people in the store, and when more people come into the store they purchase more items.

24. (1175,T1,19) (a) Probability analysis may be used to estimate future revenue or costs. A series of possible dollar outcomes can be related to a series of probabilities (the probabilities summing to 1). The expected value of each outcome is the probability of that outcome occurring times the dollar value of that outcome. The sum of all of the expected values is the expected total revenue. Linear programming is a technique to make optimal use of limited resources. An objective function describing cost or revenues is either minimized or maximized subject to two or more constraint functions. Cost-volume-earnings analysis allows determination of costs, revenues, and profits at various levels of volume. PERT (program evaluation review technique) is a model of an interrelated set of activities that must take place before a final event occurs, e.g., completion of some complex project. PERT allows the most time consuming activities to be identified and controlled.

25. (576,P2,27) (a) The scatter diagram of two variables with zero correlation would be random, i.e., there would be no correlation between the variables. If there was a positive correlation, the points would form a line from the lower left to the upper right (as one variable increased in size so would the other). If the correlation coefficient was negative, it would result in a line from the upper left to the lower right (as one variable became larger, the other would become smaller).

26. (576,P2,28) (b) Inequalities in linear programming models are equalized by adding a slack variable to obtain normal equations. If a slack variable, Z, was added to the equation in this problem to form the equation $3X + 2Y + Z = 15$, Z would be the slack variable and would be the excess of 15 over $3X + 2Y$.

27. (576,P2,29) (b) Correlation coefficients range from minus 1 to positive 1. A minus 1 indicates a perfect inverse relationship, i.e., as one variable increases in size, the other variable decreases by the same amount. A correlation coefficient of one indicates a perfect positive or direct relationship, i.e., as one variable increases, the other variable increases a like amount. If there is no correlation between the two variables, the correlation coefficient is zero. Most correlation coefficients do not approach 1 as many variables affect a single given variable rather than one variable. Thus perfect correlation, positive or negative, is rarely found, especially in the social sciences.

28. (576,P2,34) (a) The expected value is the sum of the alternative payoffs times their probability of occurrence. As computed in the table below, the expected value of the sales after three days is $10,200. Thus one should hold the investment three days, because the expected value of holding exceeds the current selling price. Answer (b) is incorrect because the expected value of the $30,000 selling price is only $3,000. Answer (c) is incorrect because the current price does not exceed the expected value of holding. Answer (d) is correct, but is not the most reasonable statement. It is correct in that there is a 60% chance that the selling price will fall (either to $5,000 or $8,000), but the best decision is still to hold, given an expected payoff of $10,200. Note that this problem does not take into account the risk of dropping down to 5,000 or $8,000. It may be that the client is risk adverse and cannot affort to drop to $5,000. In such a case the investment should be sold today rather than take a flyer at a $30,000 payoff.

5,000	.4	2,000
8,000	.2	1,600
12,000	.3	3,600
30,000	.1	3,000
		10,200

29. (576,T2,28) (b) The economic order quantity formula is as shown below. The square root of the quantity two times the fixed order costs times the demand in units for the period, all over the unit carrying costs per period. The original fixed order cost is $10 and the unit carrying cost is $2, which is shown just to the right of the general formula. The result is the square root of 10D. The change is to $12 fixed order cost and $2.50 of annual carrying cost, which is shown to the far right. The result is less than 10D. Thus, the EOQ goes from the square root of 10D to the square root of less than 10D.

$$\sqrt{\frac{2aD}{k}} \quad \sqrt{\frac{2\cdot10\cdot D}{2}} \quad \sqrt{\frac{2\cdot12\cdot d}{2.5}}$$

a = fixed order cost
D = demand per period in units
k = Unit carrying cost per period.

30. (579,P2,28) (d) The requirement is the number of units of safety stock that will result in the lowest cost. The approach is to compute the total cost for each of the 4 alternative levels of safety stock as illustrated below. The carrying cost is $2 for each unit of safety stock. The stock-out cost is the probability of running out times $80 for each of the 5 reorders. The lowest total cost of both carrying safety stock and running out is $130 [(55 units x $2/unit) + ($80 x 5% x 5 reorders)]. Thus 55 units of safety stock should be maintained.

Safety Stock	Carrying Cost	Stockout Cost/order	Stockout Cost/5 orders	Total Cost
20	$40	$32	$160	$200
40	$80	$16	$80	$160
50	$100	$8	$40	$140
55	$110	$4	$20	$130

31. (579,P2,33) (c) The requirement is an equation which is not a constraint equation. The solutions approach is to work through the data in the problem, noting each of the constraint equations. The problem begins by stating that there is a constraint of $10,400,000 to be spent; and each Type A office requires $1,300,000 and each Type B office requires $670,000, which is the constraint in answer (d). The second constraint is that there will be no more than 200 employees hired; Type A branches

require 20 persons each and Type B branches require 10 persons each, which is the constraint stipulated in answer (b). The final constraint listed is that there will not be over 20 branch offices; this is the constraint listed in answer (a). The net annual cash flow of $92,000 for Type A branches and $36,000 for Type B branches will be the objective function that the Pauley Company will attempt to maximize, not a constraint.

32. (579,T1,27) (b) The linear relationship between two variables is called a coefficient of correlation. If there is absolutely no correlation between the two variables, the coefficient of correlation is said to be zero. If there is perfect direct correlation, i.e., both variables increase by the same amount, correlation is said to be +1. If on the other hand one variable decreases by the same amount that another variable increases, the coefficient of correlation is said to be −1. Answer (a) is incorrect because, while two variables may be highly correlated, one may not necessarily cause the other, e.g., they may both be caused by a third variable. Answer (c), sensitivity analysis, is incorrect because sensitivity analysis refers to analyzing the effect of changing variables on the results of an optimization model. Answer (d), input/output analysis, is incorrect because input/output analysis shows statistically how an economy's industries interact with each other.

33. (579,T1,35) (c) The requirement is the location of the optimal solution when using the graphic method of solving a linear programming problem. Recall that programming models maximize an objective function, e.g., maximize profits or minimize costs, subject to certain constraints. On a graph this will mean being as far away as possible from the origin of the graph when maximizing and as close as possible to the origin of the graph when minimizing. In either case, the objective function must be within the constraints and thus will touch a point of interception of constraint equations (even if coinciding with a constraint).

In the example below Y_1X_2 and Y_2X_1 are constraints. Z_2 maximizes the objective function and passes through the point of interception of the constraint equations. Note Z_1 does not maximize the objective function, and Z_3 is not within the constraint equations.

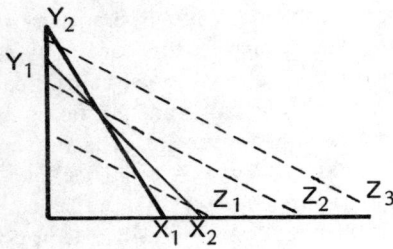

34. (1174,Q2,26) (b) An 80% learning curve indicates that the cost of a process reduced to an 80% level every time production is doubled. Thus, moving from the first batch to the second batch will result in a 20% cost savings, or the second batch will cost 80% of the first batch. The fourth batch will cost 80% of the second batch, and the eighth batch will cost 80% of the fourth batch, and the sixteenth batch will cost 80% of the eighth batch. The calculations follow below.

(1)	10,000
(2)	8,000
(4)	6,400
(8)	5,120
(16)	4,096

35. (1177,P2,26) (c) The requirement is to determine how many production runs to make given a total demand of 10,000 units. The solutions approach is to determine the economic order quantity, i.e., the optimal sized production run, and then divide the economic order quantity into total demand. See the explanation of economic order quantity just above. The economic order quantity is 2,000, as computed below. Divide the 2,000-unit economic order quantity into the annual demand of 10,000 units to find the number of production runs.

$$EOQ = \sqrt{\frac{2aD}{K}} = \sqrt{\frac{2 \cdot 80 \cdot 10,000}{.40}}$$

$$= \sqrt{160 \cdot 25,000}$$

$$= \sqrt{4,000,000}$$

$$= 2,000$$

36. (1177,P2,32) (c) The requirement is the level of safety stock that will result in the lowest total cost. Total cost consists of both the cost of carrying safety stock and the cost of being out of stock. The solutions approach is to compute the cost based on each of the four assumptions as illustrated below. The safety stock cost is simply $1 times the number of units carried as safety stock. Stock-out cost may be incurred with each of the five orders, i.e., multiply the stock-out cost by 5, as below. The cost of each stock-out is specified as a probability level

times the $75 cost. Safety stock cost plus the stock-out cost equals total cost. As is evident, the third alternative has the lowest combined safety stock cost and stock-out cost.

safety stock cost + stock-out cost = total cost

a.	$10 + 40% of $75 · 5 =	$160
b.	$20 + 20% of $75 · 5 =	95
c.	$40 + 10% of $75 · 5 =	77.50
d.	$80 + 5% of $75 · 5 =	98.75

37. (1177,P2,33) (b) The requirement is the optimum production level of Products A and B given their respective contribution margins of $3 and $4. The solution must be subject to the constraints, i.e., be within both the polishing and grinding constraints. For example, zero units of A and 20 units of B are within both constraints, but 40 units of A and zero units of B are not (the maximum number of A that can be polished is 30). The solutions approach is to first see whether each of the four answers is within both the polishing and grinding constraints, and second, to determine the level of income projection. The solutions approach is illustrated below; the maximum contribution margin possible is alternative (b).

	A	B	Total	Within Constraints
a.	$0	$80	$80	Yes
b.	$60	$40	$100	Yes
c.	$90	$0	$90	Yes
d.	$120	$0	$120	No

38. (1177,P2,37) (b) The requirement is to determine the fixed portion of the electricity expense. The solutions approach is to solve for the fixed costs with two simultaneous equations, as illustrated below. Note that 3,000 hours equals $25 of variable cost. Thus the cost for 31,000 hours will be 10 times $25 plus 1/3 of $25, or $258.33. The total cost of $585 at an operating level of 31,000 hours, less the variable cost for that level ($258.33) equals the fixed cost of $327.

$$\$610 = FC + 34,000 \, VC$$
$$\$585 = FC + 31,000 \, VC$$

Subtracting the second equation from the first equation provides

$$\$25 = 3,000 \, VC$$
$$VC = \$25 \text{ per } 3,000 \text{ hrs}$$
$$31,000 \text{ hrs} = \$258.33 \, (VC)$$
$$\$585 \text{ (sales)} - \$258.33 \, (VC) = \$326.67 \, (FC)$$

39. (578,T2,32) (c) The EOQ model minimizes variable order costs and variable inventory carrying costs. For example, incremental (variable) order costs can be reduced by fewer orders, but this increases incremental (variable) carrying costs because a larger average inventory is required.

The requirement is the cost which effects the EOQ. Since only variable costs associated with carrying inventory and purchasing are reflected in the model, the answer is variable order processing costs. Answers (a) and (d) are incorrect because physical plant insurance and depreciation cover more than just inventory carrying costs, i.e., includes insurance and depreciation on production and other facilities. They are also fixed costs. Answer (b) is incorrect because only variable, not fixed, costs are considered by the EOQ. Supervisory salaries are fixed costs.

40. (571,P5,19) (b) The expected times in the PERT network are based on the 1-4-1 three estimate method. This means that the expected time is a weighted average of the shortest time, average time, and longest time. The shortest time and longest time are weighted one and the average time is weighted 4. The critical path through each of the five alternative paths calculating the longest which is 1-2-3-4-6 which sums to 20.8.

41. (571,P5,20) (a) Slack time is the excess time over the budgeted time which will not effect the critical path time. The slack time on path 1-9-6 is determined by comparing that time with the critical path time. The expected time on 1-9-6 equals 16.5 which is 4.3 less than the critical path time of 20.8.

42. (571,P5,21) (a) The latest time for reaching event 6 is the critical path time of 20.8. By definition 20.8 is the critical path time or the greatest amount of time, therefore, no path can exceed 20.8.

43. (571,P5,22) (b) The earliest time, implying no unfavorable time variance, for reaching event 6 via 1-2-5-6 is 16.9 (the sum of the expected times).

44. (571,P5,23) (c) If 7-8 has an unfavorable time variance of 1.9, or has a time of 6.9 rather than 5.0, the path 1-7-8-6 will total 19.3 which will not affect the critical path.

SOLUTION GUIDE

Problem 1   Probability

1.   This problem consists of Part a. with 3 subparts and Part b. with 2 subparts, each of which requires various contribution margin computations and related probability analyses of levels of sales. The subparts concern the production and sale of products that become worthless if not sold in the month they are produced. The variable production cost is $50/unit and the sales price is $80/unit. The product can also be purchased from a competitor for $90/unit when sales exceed productions. This must sometimes be done so as not to lose customers.

2.   The solutions approach is to consider each of the 5 subparts (3 in Part a. and 2 in Part b.) as separate problems.

3.   Part a1. requires the probability of sales at the 8,000 unit, 9,000 unit, and 10,000 unit levels.

    3.1   Based on the past 20 (5 + 12 + 3) months, 8,000 units have been sold in 5 months or 5/20, i.e., 25% of the time. Similarly, 9,000 units were sold 12/20 or 60% of the time, and 10,000 units were sold 3/20 or 15% of the time.

4.   Part a2. requires computation of the contribution margin if 9,000 units are sold and 8,000 units, 9,000 units, and 10,000 units are produced. If 8,000 units are produced, 1,000 units will have to be purchased from the competitor at $90/unit ($80 cost + $10 freight).

    4.1   The revenue from sale of 9,000 units is $720,000 (9,000 units @ $80).

    4.2   The cost of producing 8,000 units, 9,000 units and 10,000 units (@ $50) is $400,000, $450,000, and $500,000 respectively.

    4.3   If only 8,000 units are produced, there will be an additional $90,000 of cost due to the required outside purchase of 1,000 units.

    4.4   The contribution margins are the $720,000 less the varying costs of sales figures $490,000, $450,000, and $500,000.

5.   Part a3. requires the average monthly contribution margin if 9,000 units are manufactured each month.

    5.1   The solutions approach is to compute the contribution margin for each level of sales and take the respective contribution margin times the probability of that level of sales occurring as computed in a1. above.

    5.2   The respective revenues at $80/unit are $640,000, $720,000, and $800,000.

    5.3   The respective cost of sales at $50/unit are $450,000, $450,000, and $540,000 (at the 10,000 unit level, 1,000 units have to be purchased at $90). Recall that 9,000 units are produced each period.

    5.4   Multiply the probability of sales level occurrence (25%, 60%, and 15%) times the respective contribution margins.

6.   Part b1. requires the monthly contribution margin for each level of sales assuming the component K-2 ($36/unit) is substituted for component K-1 ($24/unit) in the manufacture of product X. For this requirement, 9,000 units are manufactured at a cost of $62 ($50 plus the $12 cost increase due to the substitution of component K-2).

    6.1   Respective sales at $80/unit are $640,000, $720,000, and $800,000.

    6.2   Cost of sales (9,000 manufactured at $62) is $558,000 for each level of sales, except for 10,000 units, for which an additional $90,000 cost is incurred to purchase 1,000 units outside.

7.   Part b2. requires the average contribution margin given a 70% probability of unavailability of K-1, which requires use of the more expensive K-2. The requirement further specifies a contribution margin of $130,000 if the less expensive K-1 is used and a negative contribution margin (loss) of $45,000 if the more expensive K-2 is used.

    7.1   Since the $130,000 contribution margin will occur 30% of the time and the $45,000 loss 70% of the time, the average contribution margin is $39,000 (30% of $130,000) less $31,500 (70% of $45,000) which is $7,500.

UNOFFICIAL ANSWER

Problem 1   Probability

Part a.

1.
Wing Manufacturing Corporation
**SCHEDULE COMPUTING THE PROBABILITY
OF UNIT SALES PER MONTH
OF PRODUCT X**

Unit sales per month	Number of months	Probability
8,000	5	5/20 = 25%
9,000	12	12/20 = 60%
10,000	3	3/20 = 15%
	20	100%

2.   *Wing Manufacturing Corporation*
**SCHEDULE OF CONTRIBUTION MARGIN
FOR VARIOUS COMBINATIONS OF UNIT
SALES AND UNITS MANUFACTURED OF
PRODUCT X**

Units Manufactured (and Purchased)

Unit sales	8,000	9,000	10,000
9,000	230,000 (c)	270,000 (a)	220,000 (b)

Computation of Contribution Margin

(a) When all units manufactured are sold:

9,000 X ($80 − $50) = $270,000.

(b) Reduction per 1,000 units when more units are manufactured than are sold:

1,000 X 50 = $50,000.

$270,000 − $50,000 = $220,000

(c) Reduction per 1,000 units when units must be purchased to fill sales orders:

1,000 X (($80 + 10) − $80) = $10,000.

8,000 X ($80 − $50) − $10,000 = $230,000.

3.   *Wing Manufacturing Corporation*
**SCHEDULE COMPUTING EXPECTED
CONTRIBUTION MARGIN IF 9,000
UNITS ARE MANUFACTURED AND
ALL SALES ORDERS ARE FILLED**

Unit sales	Probability	Contribution margin	Expected value
8,000	25%	$190,000	$ 47,500
9,000	60%	270,000	162,000
10,000	15%	260,000	39,000
			$248,500

Part b.

1.   *Wing Manufacturing Corporation*
**COMPUTATION OF CONTRIBUTION
MARGIN IF 9,000 UNITS ARE MANU-
FACTURED WITH SUBSTITUTE INGRE-
DIENT K-2 AND ALL SALES ORDERS
ARE FILLED**

Sales units	Selling price	Variable cost	Marginal income
8,000 X	$80	−$558,000*	= $ 82,000
9,000 X	80	−$558,000*	= 162,000
10,000 X	80	−$558,000* + 1,000 ($90)	= 152,000

*(9,000($50 − $24 + $36))

2.   *Wing Manufacturing Corporation*
**SCHEDULE COMPUTING EXPECTED
CONTRIBUTION MARGIN WITH
PROBABILITY OF STRIKE AT SUP-
PLIER'S PLANT AND ALL SALES
ORDERS FILLED**

Expected contribution margin from manufacturing	$130,000
Probability of no strike	30%
Expected value from manufacturing	39,000
Expected marginal loss from purchasing if strike occurs	$45,000
Probability of strike	70%
Expected loss	(31,500)
Expected contribution margin	$ 7,500

SOLUTION GUIDE

Problem 2   Linear Programming Graph

1. This is a graphic (and elementary) linear programming problem. Part (a) requires a listing of uses for contribution margin data, e.g., allocation of joint costs.

2. Interpretation of the graph. Note, that only the three constraint equations are illustrated.

    A. The horizontal line from 0,180 is the gadget constraint.
    B. The 0,320 to 240,0 line is the finishing department constraint.
    C. The 0,200 to 400,0 line is the cutting department constraint.
    D. The objective function would be a series of parallel lines to a line 0,300 to 200,0, i.e., the contribution margin would be equal with sales of 300 gadgets or 200 trinkets.
    E. The area of feasible solutions is 0,0 to 40,180 to 144,128 to 240.0 (answer b3).

UNOFFICIAL ANSWER

Problem 2   Linear Programming Graph

a. Contribution margin data are useful for

    1. Identifying products which should be retained or eliminated by making it possible to determine if a product is providing at least a short-run contribution to profits through recovery of more than its variable costs.

    2. Indicating which products to emphasize and which merely to provide because they indirectly contribute to the sale of more profitable products.

    3. Comparing added costs of alternative proposals to stimulate sales volume with prospective additions to sales.

    4. Determining the number of units which must be sold in order to achieve a given profit goal.

    5. Determining the maximum allowable variable cost and minimum volume of products of a firm in an industry with firmly established selling prices.

6. Clarifying the relationship of cost, volume, and profit in pricing decisions.

7. Maximizing the total contribution to profit in product mix decisions involving a scarce resource.

b. 1. The capacity of the Cutting Department is represented graphically by the area on and beneath the line connecting points (0,200) and (400,0).

    2. The production limitation on gadgets, $G \leq 180$ units per day, is represented graphically by the area on and beneath the line connecting points (0,180), (40,180) and (105,180).

    3. The area of feasible production combinations is the area on and bounded by the polygon formed by points (0,0), (0,180), (40,180), (144,128) and (240,0).

c. 1.

COMPUTATION OF CONTRIBUTION MARGIN PER UNIT FOR TRINKETS AND GADGETS

	Trinkets	Gadgets
Sales price per unit	$50	$70
Variable cost per unit	30	40
Contribution margin per unit	$20	$30

2.

COMPUTATION OF TOTAL CONTRIBUTION MARGIN FOR EACH OF THE FEASIBLE PRODUCTION ALTERNATIVES

Trinkets			Gadgets			
$20	(0)	+	$30	(0)	=	$ 0
20	(0)	+	30	(180)	=	5,400
20	(40)	+	30	(180)	=	6,200
20	(144)	+	30	(128)	=	6,720
20	(240)	+	30	(0)	=	4,800

3. By producing 144 trinkets and 128 gadgets the Corporation will maximize its total contribution margin when its scarce resources is productive capacity. Therefore, this production alternative is best.

UNOFFICIAL ANSWER

Problem 3 . Operations Research Definitions

a.   Operations research (OR) is a collective effort of many types of talent concentrating on the application of the scientific method to the development of predictive models that describe the stable patterns of order underlying certain business operations. OR uses quantitative information to aid management in solving executive problems and is primarily a tool for planning. OR is not a unique discipline but a collection of various quantitative techniques.

OR usually involves a research team representing such various disciplines as accounting, mathematics, engineering, psychology, and statistics. This interdisciplinary approach aids in problem solving because of the additional backgrounds and dimensions introduced into the research team.

OR teams usually deal with executive problems that affect an entire company and all its interrelated departments. The concern is not so much with specific departmental problems, but with either such regularly recurring situations, as inventories or such special problems as a review of plant location.

Accountants are potentially useful members of an OR team in three major areas—problem identification, model building, and solution control. An accountant is usually in an ideal position to identify executive problems that might be solved by OR techniques because he is familiar with the overall business and the financial information system and in constant contact with all segments of a company.

OR techniques involve a quantitative presentation of data to management to aid decision making and thus are reliable only to the extent of the data used in the models. Much of this data is furnished by the accountant, for example, cost and pricing data organized by product, measurement of earnings, assets, and liabilities, and information for projections and forecasts.

To help build a model, the accountant must be able to identify and provide relevant and reliable data and to explain the various interrelationships to other OR team members. Furthermore, he must be able to analyze the data and estimate future trends.

An accountant can also provide a control on the validity of the models. Such control involves help in making the models acceptable, keeping the cost of the models within reason, and advising the rest of the OR team based on the professional experience and knowledge of that particular company.

b.   1.   Linear programming is a quantitative method for selecting an optimum plan. It is an efficient search procedure for finding the best solution to a problem containing many interacting variables. The desired objective is to maximize some function (e.g., sales, contribution margin, profits, machine utilization) or to minimize some function (e.g., costs, idle time). Determination of the optimum objective is usually subject to various constraints or restrictions on possible alternatives. These constraints describe availabilities, limitations, and relationships of resources to alternatives.

The key assumption is linearity, which prevails in two respects. First, the profit or cost associated with one unit of product or activity is assumed to be the same for all identical units. Second, resource inputs per unit of activity are assumed the same for all units. Another assumption inherent in linear programming is that all factors and relationships are deterministic.

Accounting data such as sales price, contribution margin, or cost factors would be used in determining the objective—to maximize sales, contribution margin, or earnings or to minimize cost. Accounting data would also be used to establish the constraints. Such constraints might include one or more of the following: machine capacity, labor force, quantity of output demanded, time, or capital.

Once the data are available, the linear programming model (equations) might possibly be solved graphically if no more than two variables are involved. When the model contains many variables and constraints, the solution may require the use of a computer.

2.   Economic order quantity (EOQ) is the inventory purchase order size that minimizes total annual order (setup) costs and holding (carrying) costs associated with this inventory item. The essence is to determine how much to order, not when to order. The assumptions generally characterizing EOQ models are as follows: demand is predictable and

uniform during the period; the new order arrives at a predictable time after it is placed; and all inventory-related costs are known and constant.

Accounting data would be used to provide the specific items included in the general categories of costs. For example, order costs would include costs of preparing necessary machinery, and transportation costs. Holding costs include handling, storage, insurance, interest, taxes, and obsolescence. Shortage costs include extra purchasing costs, uneconomic production runs, and disruptions of production. The most significant costs in this category are lost sales and reduced customer goodwill, but these latter costs are not part of traditional accounting records. These items are still an important part of the EOQ model.

3.   Program evaluation and review technique (PERT) is a formal, probabilistic diagram of the interrelationships of a complex time series of activities. In many business situations, there are a number of different activities that must be performed in a specified sequence in order to accomplish some project. Some of the activities may be in series (for example, market research cannot be performed before the research design is planned), whereas others may be parallel (for example, the engines for a ship can be built at the same time the hull is being constructed). For a large, complex project, the complete set of activities will usually contain a combination of series and parallel elements.

The essence of PERT is to aid a manager in planning and controlling a project. For planning purposes prior to the start of the project, the PERT technique allows a manager to calculate the expected total amount of time required to complete the entire project. The technique highlights the bottleneck activities in the project so that the manager may either allocate more resources to them or keep a careful watch on them as the project progresses. For purposes of control after the project has begun, the technique provides a way of monitoring progress and calling attention to those delays in activities that will delay the project's completion date.

Two types of information must be known or estimated for each activity in the project: first, the sequencing requirements—that is, the set of activities that must be completed prior to beginning a given activity and second, the time required for each activity. The first type of information is assumed to be readily ascertainable. The second type may be assumed to be either known or uncertain. If uncertain, the PERT model is somewhat more complex.

Accounting data would provide total costs for each activity in the project. Such costs become relevant in analyzing possible time/cost trade-offs in the PERT model. For example, an activity's required time may be shortened by adding more people to the activity thereby increasing the cost. These total cost data should be part of the accounting data.

4.   Regression analysis refers to the measurement of the average amount of change in one variable that is associated with unit increases in the amounts of one or more other variables. When only two variables are studied, it is simple regression. When more than two variables are studied, it is multiple regression. The purpose of regression analysis is to predict values of the dependent variable based on the given values of the independent variable.

Regression analysis assumes that the relationship between the dependent variable and independent variable will persist thereby validating the prediction. It also assumes that there is usually a linear relationship between the variables and that there is a reasonably uniform dispersion of points about the regression line.

Accounting data would provide the amounts for the variables needed for the analysis. For example, if management wants to predict direct-labor cost based on the size of the order, data must be accumulated about the direct-labor cost at various order sizes. Accounting data should provide the amounts needed for the variables to prepare the analysis.

CHAPTER SEVEN

GOVERNMENTAL PROBLEMS AND SOLUTIONS

Governmental or not-for-profit questions have appeared on all recent examinations. Review the frequency of occurrence of governmental and not-for-profit problems on pages 443 and 444.

In addition to municipal (governmental) accounting, recent exams have also tested the principles of accounting applicable to colleges and universities, hospitals, voluntary health and welfare organizations, and other not-for-profit organizations. The majority of governmental questions, however, have been on municipal accounting. See Chapter 12 in Volume I for discussion of each of these topics.

Each question is coded as to month-year, exam section, problem number, and objective question number. For example, (579,T2,38) indicates May 1979, theory problem 2, and question number 38. Note that P = Practice I, Q = Practice II, and T = Theory.

Several of the multiple choice questions from past examinations, or their answers, have been modified to reflect changes in law and practice since the question appeared on the exam. These problems are identified with a[t].

GOVERNMENTAL PROBLEM INDEX

	Exam Reference	Number of Minutes	Problem Page No.	Answer Page No.
63 Multiple Choice				
1. University Journal Entries (Burnsville)	1178,Q5	50-60	912	925
2. Municipality Journal Entries (Dexter)	580,Q4	45-55	913	928
3. General Fund	1179,Q5	40-50	914	932
4. Municipal vs. Financial Accounting	575,T6	25-30	915	935
5. School Journal Entries (Annaville)	576,Q3	40-50	915	936
6. Capital Projects Fund (Westgate)	1180,Q5	40-50	915	937
Sample Practice I Examination		220-270	1013	1068
Sample Practice II Examination		220-270	1025	1071
Sample Theory Examination		150-210	1059	1086

MULTIPLE CHOICE QUESTIONS (1–63)

1. One of the differences between accounting for a governmental (not-for-profit) unit and a commercial (for-profit) enterprise is that a governmental (not-for-profit) unit should
   a. **Not** record depreciation expense in any of its funds.
   b. Always establish and maintain complete self-balancing accounts for each fund.
   c. Use only the cash basis of accounting.
   d. Use only the modified accrual basis of accounting.

2. If a credit was made to the fund balance in the process of recording a budget for a governmental unit, it can be assumed that
   a. Estimated revenues exceed appropriations.
   b. Estimated expenses exceed actual revenues.
   c. Actual expenses exceed estimated expenses.
   d. Appropriations exceed estimated revenues.

3. When a capital project is financed entirely from a single bond issue, and the proceeds of the bond issue equal the par value of the bonds, the capital projects fund would record this transaction by debiting cash and crediting
   a. Bond issue proceeds.
   b. Fund balance.
   c. Appropriations.
   d. Bonds payable.

4. When fixed assets purchased from general fund revenues were received, the appropriate journal entry was made in the general fixed assets group of accounts. What account, if any, should have been debited in the general fund?
   a. No journal entry should have been made in the general fund.
   b. Expenditures.
   c. Fixed assets.
   d. Due from general fixed assets group of accounts.

5. Which of the following funds should account for the payment of interest and principal on revenue bond debt?
   a. Capital projects.
   b. Enterprise.
   c. Trust.
   d. Debt service.

6. Which of the following should be used in accounting for not-for-profit colleges and universities?
   a. Fund accounting and accrual accounting.
   b. Fund accounting but **not** accrual accounting.
   c. Accrual accounting but **not** fund accounting.
   d. Neither accrual accounting nor fund accounting.

7. A voluntary health and welfare organization received a pledge in 1979 from a donor specifying that the amount pledged be used in 1981. The donor paid the pledge in cash in 1980. The pledge should be accounted for as
   a. A deferred credit in the balance sheet at the end of 1979, and as support in 1980.
   b. A deferred credit in the balance sheet at the end of 1979 and 1980, and as support in 1981.
   c. Support in 1979.
   d. Support in 1980, and **no** deferred credit in the balance sheet at the end of 1979.

8. The accounting for special revenue funds is most similar to which type of fund?
   a. Capital projects.
   b. Enterprise.
   c. General.
   d. Special assessment.

9. The general fixed assets group of accounts would † be used for the fixed assets of the
   a. Special assessment fund.
   b. Enterprise fund.
   c. Trust fund.
   d. Intragovernmental (internal) service fund.

10. Taxes collected and held by a municipality for a † school district would be accounted for in a (an)
   a. Enterprise fund.
   b. Intragovernmental (internal) service fund.
   c. Agency fund.
   d. Special revenue fund.

11. Which of the following requires the use of the encumbrance system?
   a. Special assessment fund.
   b. Debt service fund.
   c. General fixed assets group of accounts.
   d. Enterprise fund.

12. Which of the following will increase the fund balance of a governmental unit at the end of the fiscal year?
   a. Appropriations are less than expenditures and reserve for encumbrances.
   b. Appropriations are less than expenditures and encumbrances.

c.   Appropriations are more than estimated revenues.

d.   Appropriations are more than expenditures and encumbrances.

13.   Depreciation should be recognized in the financial statements of

a.   Proprietary (for-profit) hospitals only.

b.   Both proprietary (for-profit) and not-for-profit hospitals.

c.   Both proprietary (for-profit) and not-for-profit hospitals, only when they are affiliated with a college or university.

d.   All hospitals, as a memorandum entry not affecting the statement of revenues and expenses.

14.   Repairs that have been made for a governmental unit, and for which a bill has been received, should be recorded in the General Fund as an

a.   Appropriation.

b.   Encumbrance.

c.   Expenditure.

d.   Expense.

15.   Under the modified accrual basis of accounting, which of the following taxes is usually recorded before it is received in cash?

a.   Property.

b.   Income.

c.   Gross receipts.

d.   Gift.

16.   Which fund is not an expendable fund?

a.   Capital projects.

b.   General.

c.   Special revenue.

d.   Intragovernmental service.

17.   Encumbrances would not appear in which fund?

a.   Capital projects.

b.   Special revenue.

c.   General.

d.   Enterprise.

18.   Interest expense on bonds payable should be recorded in a Debt Service Fund

a.   At the end of the fiscal period if the interest due date does not coincide with the end of the fiscal period.

b.   When bonds are issued.

c.   When legally payable.

d.   When paid.

19.   An expenditures account appears in

a.   The general fixed-assets group of accounts.

b.   The general long-term debt group of accounts.

c.   A special revenue fund.

d.   An intragovernmental service fund.

20.   Which of the following steps in the acquisition of goods and services occurs first?

a.   Appropriation.

b.   Encumbrance.

c.   Budget.

d.   Expenditure.

21.   Which of the following terms refers to an actual cost rather than an estimate?

a.   Expenditure.

b.   Appropriation.

c.   Budget.

d.   Encumbrance.

22.   How should wages that have been earned by the employees of a governmental unit, but not paid, be recorded in the General Fund?

a.   Appropriation.

b.   Encumbrance.

c.   Expenditure.

d.   Expense.

23.   "Investment in general fixed assets" accounts would appear in which fund or group of accounts?

a.   General fixed assets.

b.   Enterprise.

c.   Capital projects.

d.   General.

24.   Which of the following expenditures is normally recorded on the accrual basis in the general fund?

a.   Interest.

b.   Personal services.

c.   Inventory items.

d.   Prepaid expenses.

25.   When should revenues from interest on assessments receivable be recorded in a special assessment fund?

a.   When collected in cash.

b.   When assessed.

c.   When legally due.

d.   When the amount is known.

26. Which of the following should be accrued as revenues by the general fund of a local government?
   a. Sales taxes held by the state which will be remitted to the local government.
   b. Parking meter revenues.
   c. Sales taxes collected by merchants.
   d. Income taxes currently due.

27. An "actuarial deficiency" would appear in which fund?
   a. Agency.
   b. Trust.
   c. General.
   d. Debt service.

28. "Excess of net billings to departments over †cost" would appear in the financial statement of which fund?
   a. Internal.
   b. Enterprise.
   c. Capital projects.
   d. Special revenue.

29. Which type of fund can be either expendable or non-expendable?
   a. Debt service.
   b. Enterprise.
   c. Trust.
   d. Special revenues.

30. In the loan fund of a college or university, each of the following types of loans would be found except
   a. Student.
   b. Staff.
   c. Building.
   d. Faculty.

31. Why do voluntary health and welfare organizations, unlike some not-for-profit organizations, record and recognize depreciation of fixed assets?
   a. Fixed assets are more likely to be material in amount in a voluntary health and welfare organization than in other not-for-profit organizations.
   b. Voluntary health and welfare organizations purchase their fixed assets, and therefore have a historical cost basis from which to determine amounts to be depreciated.
   c. A fixed asset used by a voluntary health and welfare organization has alternative uses in private industry and this opportunity cost should be reflected in the organization's financial statements.
   d. Contributors look for the most efficient use of funds, and since depreciation represents

a cost of employing fixed assets, it is appropriate that a voluntary health and welfare organization reflect it as a cost of providing services.

32. Which of the following receipts is properly recorded as restricted current funds on the books of a university?
   a. Tuition.
   b. Student laboratory fees.
   c. Housing fees.
   d. Research grants.

33. Which of the following funds of a voluntary health and welfare organization does not have a counterpart fund in governmental accounting?
   a. Current unrestricted.
   b. Land, building, and equipment.
   c. Custodian.
   d. Endowment.

34. Which of the following accounts is a budgetary account in governmental accounting?
   a. Reserve for inventory of supplies.
   b. Fund balance.
   c. Appropriations.
   d. Estimated uncollectible property taxes.

35. What is the underlying reason a governmental unit uses separate funds to account for its transactions?
   a. Governmental units are so large that it would be unduly cumbersome to account for all transactions as a single unit.
   b. Because of the diverse nature of the services offered and legal provisions regarding activities of a governmental unit, it is necessary to segregate activities by functional nature.
   c. Generally accepted accounting principles require that not-for-profit entities report on a funds basis.
   d. Many activities carried on by governmental units are short-lived and their inclusion in a general set of accounts could cause undue probability of error and omission.

36. The initial transfer of cash from the general †fund in order to establish an internal service fund would require the general fund to credit cash and debit
   a. Accounts receivable—internal service fund.
   b. Transfer to internal service fund.
   c. Reserve for encumbrances.
   d. Appropriations.

37. Which of the following funds frequently does not have a fund balance?
    a. General fund.
    b. Agency fund.
    c. Special revenue fund.
    d. Capital projects fund.

38. In which of the following funds would it be †
appropriate to record depreciation of fixed assets?
    a. Capital projects.
    b. General.
    c. Internal service.
    d. Special assessment.

39. If a governmental unit established a data pro- †
cessing center to service all agencies within the unit,
the data processing center should be accounted for as
a (an)
    a. Capital projects fund.
    b. Internal service fund.
    c. Agency fund.
    d. Trust fund.

40. The "reserve for encumbrances — past year"
account represents amounts recorded by a governmental unit for
    a. Anticipated expenditures in the next year.
    b. Expenditures for which purchase orders
were made in the prior year but disbursement will be in the current year.
    c. Excess expenditures in the prior year that
will be offset against the current-year budgeted amounts.
    d. Unanticipated expenditures of the prior
year that become evident in the current
year.

41. Which of the following types of revenue would †
generally be recorded directly in the general fund of a
governmental unit?
    a. Receipts from a city-owned parking
structure.
    b. Property taxes.
    c. Interest earned on investments held for
retirement of employees.
    d. Revenues from internal service funds.

42. Recreational facilities run by a governmental
unit and financed on a user-charge basis would be
accounted for in which fund?
    a. General.
    b. Trust.
    c. Enterprise.
    d. Capital projects.

43. The City of Rover has two special-assessment
funds. In the preparation of the statement of financial position for these funds as of the end of the
fiscal year, these funds may be reported on
    a. A combined basis which shows the
total for both funds and has separate
columns to present account balances
for each fund.
    b. A consolidated basis after eliminating
the effects of interfund transactions.
    c. A separate basis, but never together
in the same statement.
    d. A consolidated basis with the general
fund after eliminating the effects of
interfund transactions.

44. When reporting for governmental units, what
type of costs should be presented in the financial
statements?
    a. Historical.
    b. Historical adjusted for price-level changes.
    c. Current appraisal.
    d. Historical and current presented in two
separate columns.

45. The Town of Newbold General Fund issued
purchase orders to vendors and suppliers of $630,000.
Which of the following entries should be made to record this transaction?

		Debit	Credit
a.	Encumbrances	$630,000	
	Reserve for en-cumbrances		$630,000
b.	Expenditures	630,000	
	Vouchers payable		630,000
c.	Expenses	630,000	
	Accounts payable		630,000
d.	Reserve for en-cumbrances	630,000	
	Encumbrances		630,000

46. The Town of Boyd Electric Utility Fund, which
is an enterprise fund, had the following:

Prepaid insurance paid in December 1976	$ 43,000
Depreciation for 1976	129,000
Provision for doubtful accounts for 1976	14,000

    What amount should be reflected in the state-
ment of revenues and expenses (income statement)
of the Town of Boyd Electric Utility Fund for the
above items?
    a. $(43,000).
    b. $0.
    c. $129,000.
    d. $143,000.

47. What type of account is used to earmark the fund balance to liquidate the contingent obligations of goods ordered but not yet received?
    a. Appropriations.
    b. Encumbrances.
    c. Obligations.
    d. Reserve for encumbrances.

48. Premiums received on general obligation bonds are generally transferred to what fund or group of accounts?
    a. Debt service.
    b. General long-term debt.
    c. General.
    d. Special revenue.

49. A statement of changes in financial position is †
prepared for which fund?
    a. Enterprise.
    b. Internal service.
    c. Special assessment.
    d. Trust.

50. A city should record depreciation as an ex-   †
pense in its
    a. General fund and enterprise fund.
    b. Internal service fund and general fixed-assets group of accounts.
    c. Enterprise fund and internal service fund.
    d. Enterprise fund and capital-projects fund.

51. Authority granted by a legislative body to make expenditures and to incur obligations during a fiscal year is the definition of an
    a. Appropriation.
    b. Authorization.
    c. Encumbrance.
    d. Expenditure.

52. An account for expenditures does not appear in which fund?
    a. Capital projects.
    b. Enterprise.
    c. Special assessment.
    d. Special revenue.

53. Part of the general obligation bond proceeds from a new issuance was used to pay for the cost of a new city hall as soon as construction was completed. The remainder of the proceeds was transferred to repay the debt. Entries are needed to record these transactions in the
    a. General fund and general long-term debt group of accounts.

b. General fund, general long-term debt group of accounts, and debt-service fund.
    c. Trust fund, debt-service fund, and general fixed-assets group of accounts.
    d. General long-term debt group of accounts, debt-service fund, general fixed-assets group of accounts, and capital-projects fund.

54. Cash secured from property tax revenue was transferred for the eventual payment of principal and interest on general obligation bonds. The bonds had been issued when land had been acquired several years ago for a city park. Upon the transfer, an entry would not be made in which of the following?
    a. Debt-service fund.
    b. General fixed-assets group of accounts.
    c. General long-term debt group of accounts.
    d. General fund.

55. Equipment in general governmental service that had been constructed ten years before by a capital-projects fund was sold. The receipts were accounted for as unrestricted revenue. Entries are necessary in the
    a. General fund and capital-projects fund.
    b. General fund and general fixed-assets group of accounts.
    c. General fund, capital-projects fund, and enterprise fund.
    d. General fund, capital-projects fund, and general fixed-assets group of accounts.

MAY 1981 QUESTIONS

56. When the estimated revenue account of a governmental unit is closed out at the end of the fiscal year, the excess of revenues over estimated revenues is
    a. Debited to fund balance.
    b. Debited to reserve for encumbrances.
    c. Credited to fund balance.
    d. Credited to reserve for encumbrances.

57. When goods which have been previously approved for purchase are received by a governmental unit but **not** yet paid for, what account is credited?
    a. Reserve for encumbrances.
    b. Vouchers payable.
    c. Expenditures.
    d. Appropriations.

58. A capital projects fund of a municipality is an example of what type of fund?
  a. Internal service (intragovernmental service).
  b. Proprietary.
  c. Fiduciary.
  d. Governmental.

59. Which of the following accounts could be included in the balance sheet of an enterprise fund?

	Reserve for encumbrances	Revenue bonds payable	Retained earnings
a.	No	No	Yes
b.	No	Yes	Yes
c.	Yes	Yes	No
d.	No	No	No

60. Which of the following accounts would be included in the combined balance sheet for the long-term debt account group?
  a. Amount to be provided for retirement of general long-term debt.
  b. Unreserved fund balance.
  c. Reserve for encumbrances.
  d. Cash.

61. Customers' meter deposits which cannot be spent for normal operating purposes would be classified as restricted cash in the balance sheet of which fund?
  a. Internal service (intragovernmental service).
  b. Trust.
  c. Agency.
  d. Enterprise.

62. For state and local governmental units, the full accrual basis of accounting should be used for what type of fund?
  a. Special revenue.
  b. General.
  c. Debt service.
  d. Internal service (intragovernmental service).

63. A gift to a voluntary not-for-profit hospital that is not restricted by the donor should be credited directly to
  a. Fund balance.
  b. Deferred revenue.
  c. Operating revenue.
  d. Nonoperating revenue.

REPEAT QUESTIONS

(581,T1,52)   Identical to item **17** above
(581,T1,54)   Identical to item **41** above

Problem 1   University Journal Entries (1178,Q5)

    (50 to 60 minutes)

Presented below is the current funds balance sheet of Burnsville University as of the end of its fiscal year ended June 30, 1977.

Burnsville University
CURRENT FUNDS BALANCE SHEET
June 30, 1977

Assets

Current Funds:		
Unrestricted:		
Cash	$210,000	
Accounts receivable-student tuition and fees, less allowance for doubtful accounts of $9,000	341,000	
State appropriations receivable	75,000	$626,000
Restricted:		
Cash	7,000	
Investments	60,000	67,000
Total current funds		$693,000

Liabilities and Fund Balances

Current Funds:		
Unrestricted:		
Accounts payable	$ 45,000	
Deferred revenues	66,000	
Fund balances	515,000	$626,000
Restricted:		
Fund balances		67,000
Total current funds		$693,000

The following transactions presented below occurred during the fiscal year ended June 30, 1978:

1.   On July 7, 1977, a gift of $100,000 was received from an alumnus. The alumnus requested that one half of the gift be used for the purchase of books for the university library and the remainder be used for the establishment of a scholarship fund. The alumnus further requested that the income generated by the scholarship fund be used annually to award a scholarship to a qualified disadvantaged student. On July 20, 1977, the board of trustees resolved that the funds of the newly established scholarship fund would be invested in savings certificates. On July 21, 1977, the savings certificates were purchased.

2.   Revenue from student tuition and fees applicable to the year ended June 30, 1978, amounted to $1,900,000. Of this amount, $66,000 was collected in the prior year and $1,686,000 was collected during the year ended June 30, 1978. In addition, at June 30, 1978, the university had received cash of $158,000 representing fees for the session beginning July 1, 1978.

3.   During the year ended June 30, 1978, the university had collected $349,000 of the outstanding accounts receivable at the beginning of the year. The balance was determined to be uncollectible and was written off against the allowance account. At June 30, 1978, the allowance account was increased by $3,000.

4.   During the year interest charges of $6,000 were earned and collected on late student fee payments.

5.   During the year the state appropriation was received. An additional unrestricted appropriation of $50,000 was made by the state, but had not been paid to the university as of June 30, 1978.

6.   An unrestricted gift of $25,000 cash was received from alumni of the university.

7.   During the year investments of $21,000 were sold for $26,000. Investment income amounting to $1,900 was received.

8.   During the year unrestricted operating expenses of $1,777,000 were recorded. At June 30, 1978, $59,000 of these expenses remained unpaid.

9.   Restricted current funds of $13,000 were spent for authorized purposes during the year.

10.   The accounts payable at June 30, 1977, were paid during the year.

11.   During the year, $7,000 interest was earned and received on the savings certificates purchased in accordance with the board of trustees resolution, as discussed in item 1.

Required:

a. Prepare journal entries to record in summary the above transactions for the year ended June 30, 1978. Each journal entry should be numbered to correspond with the transaction described above.

Your answer sheet should be organized as follows:

	Current Funds				Endowment Fund	
	Unrestricted		Restricted			
Accounts	Dr.	Cr.	Dr.	Cr.	Dr.	Cr.

b. Prepare a statement of changes in fund balances for the year ended June 30, 1978.

Problem 2 Municipality Journal Entries (580,Q4)

(45 to 55 minutes)

The Village of Dexter was recently incorporated and began financial operations on July 1, 1978, the beginning of its fiscal year.

The following transactions occurred during this first fiscal year, July 1, 1978, to June 30, 1979:

1. The village council adopted a budget for general operations during the fiscal year ending June 30, 1979. Revenues were estimated at $400,000. Legal authorizations for budgeted expenditures were $394,000.

2. Property taxes were levied in the amount of $390,000; it was estimated that 2% of this amount would prove to be uncollectible. These taxes are available as of the date of levy to finance current expenditures.

3. During the year a resident of the village donated marketable securities valued at $50,000 to the village under the terms of a trust agreement. The terms of the trust agreement stipulated that the principal amount is to be kept intact; use of revenue generated by the securities is restricted to financing college scholarships for needy students. Revenue earned and received on these marketable securities amounted to $5,500 through June 30, 1979.

4. A General Fund transfer of $5,000 was made to establish an Intragovernmental Service Fund to provide for a permanent investment in inventory.

5. The village decided to install lighting in the village park and a special assessment project was authorized to install the lighting at a cost of $75,000. The appropriation was formally recorded.

6. The assessments were levied for $72,000 with the village contributing $3,000 out of the General Fund. All assessments were collected during the year including the village's contribution.

7. A contract for $75,000 was let for the installation of the lighting. At June 30, 1979, the contract was completed but not approved. The contractor was paid all but 5 percent, which was retained to insure compliance with the terms of the contract. Encumbrances and other budgetary accounts are maintained.

8. During the year the Intragovernmental Service Fund purchased various supplies at a cost of $1,900.

9. Cash collections recorded by the General Fund during the year were as follows:

Property taxes	$386,000
Licenses and permits	7,000

10. The village council decided to build a village hall at an estimated cost of $500,000 to replace space occupied in rented facilities. The village does not record project authorizations. It was decided that general obligation bonds bearing interest at 6% would be issued. On June 30, 1979, the bonds were issued at their face value of $500,000, payable June 30, 1999.

No contracts have been signed for this project and no expenditures have been made.

11. A fire truck was purchased for $15,000 and the voucher approved and paid by the General Fund. This expenditure was previously encumbered for $15,000.

Required:

Prepare journal entries to properly record each of the above transactions in the appropriate fund(s) or group of accounts of Dexter Village for the fiscal year ended June 30, 1979. Use the following funds and groups of accounts:

- General Fund
- Capital Projects Fund
- Special Assessment Fund
- Intragovernmental Service Fund
- Trust Fund
- General Long-Term Debt Group of Accounts
- General Fixed Assets Group of Accounts

Each journal entry should be numbered to correspond with the transactions described above. Do **not** prepare closing entries for any fund.

Your answer sheet should be organized as follows:

Transaction No.	Fund or Group of Accounts	Account Title and Explanation	Amounts	
			Debit	Credit

Problem 3   General Fund (1179,Q5)

(40 to 50 minutes)

You have been engaged by the Town of Rego to examine its June 30, 1978, balance sheet. You are the first CPA to be engaged by the Town and find that acceptable methods of municipal accounting have not been employed. The Town clerk stated that the books had not been closed and presented the following pre-closing trial balance of the General Fund as at June 30, 1978:

	Debit	Credit
Cash	$150,000	
Taxes receivable — current year	59,200	
Estimated losses — current year taxes receivable		$ 18,000
Taxes receivable — prior year	8,000	
Estimated losses — prior year taxes receivable		10,200
Estimated revenues	310,000	
Appropriations		348,000
Donated land	27,000	
Expenditures — building addition constructed	50,000	
Expenditures — Serial bonds paid	16,000	
Other expenditures	280,000	
Special assessment bonds payable		100,000
Revenues		354,000
Accounts payable		26,000
Fund balance		44,000
	$900,200	$900,200

Additional information:

• The estimated losses of $18,000 for current year taxes receivable were determined to be a reasonable estimate.

• Included in the Revenues account is a credit of $27,000 representing the value of land donated by the state as a grant-in-aid for construction of a municipal park.

• The Building Addition Constructed account balance is the cost of an addition to the Town Hall building. This addition was constructed and completed in June 1978. The General Fund recorded the payment as authorized.

• The Serial Bonds Paid account reflects the annual retirement of general obligation bonds issued to finance the construction of the Town Hall. Interest payments of $7,000 for this bond issue are included in expenditures.

• Operating supplies ordered in the prior fiscal year and chargeable to that year were received, recorded and consumed in July 1977. The outstanding purchase orders for these supplies, which were not recorded in the accounts at June 30, 1977, amounted to $8,800. The vendors' invoices for these supplies totaled $9,400. Appropriations lapse one year after the end of the fiscal year for which they are made.

• Outstanding purchase orders at June 30, 1978, for operating supplies totaled $2,100. These purchase orders were not recorded on the books.

• The special assessment bonds were sold in June 1978 to finance a street paving project. No contracts have been signed for this project and no expenditures have been made.

• The balance in the Revenues account includes credits for $20,000 for a note issued to a bank to obtain cash in anticipation of tax collections and for $1,000 for the sale of scrap iron from the Town's water plant. The note was still outstanding at June 30, 1978. The operations of the water plant are accounted for in the Water Fund.

Required:

a. Prepare the formal adjusting and closing journal entries for the General Fund for the fiscal year ended June 30, 1978.

b. The foregoing information disclosed by your examination was recorded only in the General Fund even though other funds or groups of accounts were involved. Prepare the formal adjusting journal entries for any other funds or groups of accounts involved.

Problem 4   Municipal vs. Financial Accounting
(575,T6)

(25 to 30 minutes)

William Bates is executive vice-president of Mavis Industries, Inc., a publicly held industrial corporation. Bates has just been elected to the city council of Gotham City. Prior to assuming office as a city councilman, he asks you as his CPA to explain the major differences that exist in accounting and financial reporting for a large city when compared to a large industrial corporation.

Required:

a.   Describe the major differences that exist in the purpose of accounting and financial reporting and in the types of financial reports of a large city when compared to a large industrial corporation.

b.   Why are inventories often ignored in accounting for local governmental units? Explain.

c.   Under what circumstances should depreciation be recognized in accounting for local governmental units? Explain.

Problem 5   School Journal Entries   (576,Q3)

(40 to 50 minutes)

The following summary of transactions was taken from the accounts of the Annaville School District General Fund before the books had been closed for the fiscal year ended June 30, 1975:

	Post-closing Balances June 30, 1974	Pre-closing Balances June 30, 1975
Cash	$400,000	$ 700,000
Taxes receivable	150,000	170,000
Estimated uncollectible taxes	(40,000)	(70,000)
Estimated revenues	-	3,000,000
Expenditures	-	2,842,000
Expenditures—prior year	-	-
Encumbrances	-	91,000
	$510,000	$6,733,000
Vouchers payable	$ 80,000	$ 408,000
Due to other funds	210,000	142,000
Reserve for encumbrances	60,000	91,000
Fund balance	160,000	182,000
Revenues from taxes	-	2,800,000
Miscellaneous revenues	-	130,000
Appropriations	-	2,980,000
	$510,000	$6,733,000

Additional Information:

·   The estimated taxes receivable for the year ended June 30, 1975, were $2,870,000, and taxes collected during the year totaled $2,810,000.

·   An analysis of the transactions in the vouchers payable account for the year ended June 30, 1975, follows:

	Debit (Credit)
Current expenditures	$ (2,700,000)
Expenditures for prior year	(58,000)
Vouchers for payment to other funds	(210,000)
Cash payments during the year	2,640,000
Net change	$ (328,000)

·   During the year the General Fund was billed $142,000 for services performed on its behalf by other city funds.

·   On May 2, 1975, commitment documents were issued for the purchase of new textbooks at a cost of $91,000.

Required:

Based upon the data presented above, reconstruct the original detailed journal entries that were required to record all transactions for the fiscal year ended June 30, 1975, including the recording of the current year's budget. Do not prepare closing entries at June 30, 1975.

Problem 6   Capital Projects Fund (1180,Q5)

(40 to 50 minutes)

The City of Westgate's fiscal year ends on June 30. During the fiscal year ended June 30, 1979, the City authorized the construction of a new library and sale of general obligation term bonds to finance the construction of the library. The authorization imposed the following restrictions:

· Construction cost was not to exceed $5,000,000;
· Annual interest rate was not to exceed 8½%.

The City does not record project authorizations, but other budgetary accounts are maintained. The following transactions relating to the financing and construction of the library occurred during the fiscal year ended June 30, 1980:

1.   On July 1, 1979, the City issued $5,000,000 of 30 year 8% general obligation bonds for $5,100,000. The semiannual interest dates are December 31 and June 30. The premium

of $100,000 was transferred to the library
debt service fund.

2. On July 3, 1979, the library capital projects
fund invested $4,900,000 in short-term com-
mercial paper. These purchases were at face
value with no accrued interest. Interest on
cash invested by the library capital projects
fund must be transferred to the library debt
service fund. During the fiscal year ending
June 30, 1980, estimated interest to be
earned is $140,000.

3. On July 5, 1979, the City signed a contract
with F&A Construction Company to build
the library for $4,980,000.

4. On January 15, 1980, the library capital projects fund received $3,040,000, from the
maturity of short-term notes purchased on
July 3. The cost of these notes was
$3,000,000. The interest of $40,000 was
transferred to the library debt service fund.

5. On January 20, 1980, F&A Construction
Company properly billed the City
$3,000,000 for work performed on the new
library. The contract calls for 10% retention
until final inspection and acceptance of the
building. The library capital projects fund
paid F&A $2,700,000.

6. On June 30, 1980, the Library Capital Projects Fund made the proper adjusting entries
(including accrued interest receivable of
$103,000) and closing entries.

Required:

1. Prepare in good form journal entries to record the six preceding sets of facts in the Library Capital Projects Fund. List the transaction numbers (1 to 6)
and give the necessary entry or entries. Do not record
journal entries in any other Fund or Group of Accounts.

2. Prepare in good form a Balance Sheet for
the City of Westgate — Library Capital Projects Fund
as of June 30, 1980.

MULTIPLE CHOICE ANSWERS

1.	b	14.	c	27.	b	40.	b	53.	d
2.	a	15.	a	28.	a	41.	b	54.	b
3.	a	16.	d	29.	c	42.	c	55.	b
4.	b	17.	d	30.	c	43.	a	56.	c
5.	b	18.	c	31.	d	44.	a	57.	b
6.	a	19.	c	32.	d	45.	a	58.	d
7.	b	20.	c	33.	b	46.	d	59.	b
8.	c	21.	a	34.	c	47.	d	60.	a
9.	a	22.	c	35.	b	48.	a	61.	d
10.	c	23.	a	36.	b	49.	a	62.	d
11.	a	24.	b	37.	b	50.	c	63.	d
12.	d	25.	a	38.	c	51.	a		
13.	b	26.	a	39.	b	52.	b		

EXPLANATION OF MULTIPLE CHOICE ANSWERS

1. (1180,T1,51)   (b)   A major difference between governmental and commercial accounting is that governmental units maintain complete self-balancing accounts for each fund, while a commercial enterprise keeps one set of books for the entire entity. Answer (a) is incorrect because a not-for-profit entity should record depreciation expense in some funds, and answers (c) and (d) are incorrect because neither type of entity uses only the cash basis or modified accrual basis of accounting. A commercial enterprise uses accrual basis accounting, while a governmental unit uses different accounting bases for different funds, depending on the purpose of the fund.

2. (1180,T1,52)   (a)   The requirement is which relationship exists if fund balance is credited when recording a budget for a governmental unit. The solutions approach is to prepare the journal entry for recording the budget

Estimated Revenues	XXXX	
Appropriations		XXXX
Fund Balance		XXXX

If the entry results in a credit to fund balance, estimated revenues must exceed appropriations. Answer (d) is incorrect because it gives the opposite relationship, while answers (b) and (c) are incorrect because they both include an actual figure; however, only estimates are available when the above entry is made.

3. (1180,T1,56)   (a)   Capital projects funds account for the proceeds of a debt issue to be used for a capital project. When the bonds are issued, cash is debited and bond issue proceeds is credited. The fund balance account [answer (b)] is not affected until closing entries are prepared. An appropriations account [answer (c)] is not used, and bonds payable [answer (d)] are not recorded in this fund but instead are recorded in the general long term debt group of accounts.

4. (1180,T1,57)   (b)   When fixed assets are purchased from general fund revenues, an entry must also be made in the general fund since cash was expended. The debit would be to expenditures. Fixed assets [answer (c)] are never recorded in the general fund, but are recorded in the general fixed asset group and no amount is due from the general fixed assets group [answer (d)].

5. (1180,T1,58)   (b)   Payment of interest and principal on revenue bonds is made from the enterprise fund, the only fund listed in which issues of this type of bond are recorded.

6. (1180,T1,59)   (a)   Per the AICPA Audit Guide prepared for CPAs to use in examining the financial statements of colleges and universities these institutions should use fund accounting and should recognize revenues and expenditures on the accrual basis.

7. (1180,T1,60)   (b)   The requirement is to identify the proper period for recognizing support (revenue) from a pledge specifying that the amount pledged in 1979 should be used two periods later (1981). The AICPA's Audit Guide for Voluntary Health and Welfare Organizations specifies that such pledges are to be recorded as assets. The related credit is to a deferred revenue (credit) account. In this case, the asset is converted to cash when the pledge is paid in 1980 and the support (revenue) is recognized in 1981, the period which the donor specified.

8. (580,T1,51)   (c)   The special revenue fund is a special type of general fund. The general fund accounts for all transactions not accounted for in any other fund, which generally includes general revenues and expenditures for ordinary operations. The special revenue fund accounts for monies collected for a specific purpose, e.g., library taxes, motor fuel taxes, continuing federal housing grants, or gas taxes, but should not be confused with the special assessment fund. Answer (a) is incorrect because the capital project fund accounts for the proceeds of a bond issue, federal grant, etc., to be used for a capital project such as a new school or library. Answer (c) is incorrect because an enterprise fund is used to account for profit activities such as utilities. In enterprise funds, the accounting procedures are the same as those for similar private enterprises. Answer (d) is incorrect because the special assessment fund accounts for the financing of local improvements or special services for which the cost is to be borne by the beneficiary, such as curb-and-gutter projects, street lighting, etc.

9. (580,T1,52) (a) Fixed assets related to specific proprietary funds (such as enterprise funds and internal service funds) should be accounted for through those funds. The same is true for trust funds. All other fixed assets of a governmental unit are accounted for in the general fixed assets group of accounts.

10. (580,T1,53) (c) Agency funds are used to account for assets held by a governmental unit as an agent for individuals, private organizations, other governmental units, or other funds. Enterprise funds (answer (a)) are used to account for funds which are operated in a fashion similar to private business concerns. Internal service funds (answer (b)) are used to account for operations which provide goods or services for other departments. Special revenue funds (answer (d)) are used to account for proceeds that are restricted to expenditures for specified purposes, but these funds do not hold resources for another governmental unit.

11. (580,T1,54) (a) The encumbrance system is used by funds for which expenditures must be kept within authorized limits, such as a special assessment fund. It would not be used in the general fixed assets group of accounts (answer (c)) since this is an account group entity which does not make expenditures. An encumbrance system is not necessary because the expenditures (interest on long-term debt) are specifically budgeted ahead of time and overspending is not a problem. An enterprise fund (answer (d)) is a proprietary fund which utilizes the accrual basis of accounting and is similar to a private business enterprise.

12. (580,T1,56) (d) If appropriations are greater than the actual expenditures and encumbrances, this means the fund has spent less than expected. This difference will be closed to (and will increase) the fund balance. Answers (a) and (b) both state the opposite of answer (d), while answer (c) concerns only appropriations and estimated revenues, which would affect the fund balance at the beginning of the year.

13. (580,T1,60) (b) Generally accepted accounting principles are applicable to hospitals, except where they are clearly inappropriate, according to the AICPA Audit Guide. Therefore, depreciation should be recognized in the financial statements of both proprietary and not-for-profit hospitals.

14. (1179,T1,41) (c) When the general fund receives a bill for repairs, expenditures should be debited. Outflows of resources by most governmental budgetary units (funds) are termed expenditures because there is no attempt to measure profit as in the private sector. Answer (a) is incorrect because appropriations are anticipatory liabilities (expenditures) that are recorded to reflect a

budget. Answer (b) is incorrect because encumbrances are recorded to reflect future commitments to expend money. Answer (d) is incorrect because the term "expenses" implies that payments have been made to produce revenue.

15. (1179,T1,42) (a) Under the modified accrual basis, property taxes are usually recorded before they are received. The rationale is that collection of property taxes is reasonably assured (as the property can be liened and even sold for taxes). Answers (b), (c), and (d) (income taxes, gross receipts taxes, and gift taxes) are not as reasonably assured as property taxes, and therefore are not recorded as income until received.

16. (1179,T1,43) (d) The intragovernmental services fund is not an expendable fund as are the general fund, capital projects funds, and special revenue funds. The intragovernmental services fund is established to provide services to other funds. Accounting for intragovernmental services funds follows normal profit accounting except "contribution from general fund" is used in lieu of the capital stock account. Answers (a), (b), and (c) are incorrect because the capital projects, general, and special revenue funds collect monies to be spent to provide services.

17. (1179,T1,44) (d) The encumbrance account does not appear in the enterprise fund, which accounts for profit making activities such as utilities. Accounting by the enterprise fund is the same as accounting for similar private enterprises. In the capital projects, special revenue, and general funds, encumbrances is debited and reserve for encumbrances is credited when commitments are made to spend monies in the future. The balance in the appropriations account less encumbrances and expenditures is said to be the unencumbered appropriations that remain spendable.

18. (1179,T1,45) (c) Interest on bonds payable should be recorded in the debt service fund when the interest is legally payable. The debt service fund accounts for the monies used to repay debt. Thus, there is no need to accrue the interest as suggested in answer (a). Answer (b) is incorrect because there is no interest payable upon issuance of the bonds. Answer (d) is incorrect because the payable is extinguished upon payment.

19. (1179,T1,46) (c) The expenditures account appears in a special revenue fund because the special revenue fund is an expendable fund. The general fixed-assets group of accounts (answer a), general long-term debt group of accounts (answer b), and intragovernmental services fund (answer c) are not expendable funds, and accordingly do not have an expenditures account. The general fixed asset group of accounts and general long-term debt group of accounts are only self-balancing

sets of accounts to control fixed assets and long-term debt. There are no flows of funds in or out of either of these groups of accounts. Intragovernmental services funds provide service to other funds, e.g., interagency motor pools, EDP centers, etc., and accordingly matches revenue and expenses (rather than expenditures).

20. (1179,T1,47) (c) The first step in a governmental process of acquisition of goods and services is the establishment of a budget. Budgets consist of planned revenue inflows and expenditure outflows. A typical entry for a budget in which estimated revenues exceed appropriations is

    Estimated Revenues
    Appropriations
        Fund balance

Answer (a) is incorrect because appropriation is a step in the acquisition of goods and services but occurs after the budget is prepared. Answer (b) is incorrect because encumbrances are also a step in the acquisition of goods and services that occur after the budget. Encumbrances are recorded when future expenditures are committed. Answer (d) is incorrect because expenditures are the last step in the acquisition of goods and services.

21. (1179,T1,48) (a) Expenditures are made for the actual cost of acquisition of goods and services. Answer (b) is incorrect because appropriations are the formalization of the budget, which is based on estimates. Answer (c) is incorrect because the budget is the first estimate of future expenditures. Answer (d) is incorrect because encumbrances are recorded only to reflect an estimate of future expenditures.

22. (1179,T1,50) (c) Wages earned but not paid should be recorded as an expenditure in the general fund. The modified accrual basis is used in the general fund. The modified accrual basis recognizes expenses as liabilities are incurred. Revenues are recognized as they are received, except revenue is recognized as earned when receipt is certain, e.g., real estate taxes. While wages must be appropriated (answer a), they are not generally encumbered (answer b). Wages are not recorded as an expense in the general fund since the general fund is an expendable fund. In expendable funds, the emphasis is on complying with the budget rather than matching revenues and expenses or maximizing profits.

23. (1178,T1,32) (a) Investments in general fixed assets appear in the general fixed assets group of accounts. The general fixed assets group of accounts is a self-balancing list of the costs of general fixed assets. All governmental assets are accounted for in a general fixed asset fund except for assets of the internal

services and enterprise funds. Also depreciable assets held in trust are recorded in trust funds. When assets are acquired, each asset, e.g., land, building, equipment, etc., is debited in the general fixed assets account and the account "investment in general fixed assets — (fund acquiring)" is credited. When the assets are disposed of, the entry is reversed.

24. (1178,T1,33) (b) The requirement is the type of expenditure normally recorded on the accrual basis in the general fund. Personal services are expenses that are accounted for on an accrual basis, i.e., they are expensed and set up as a liability when incurred. In contrast, answers (c) and (d), inventory items and prepaid expenses, are deferrals (cash basis transaction occurs before accrual basis transactions) but are normally expensed as purchased. Answer (a) is incorrect because interest is normally expensed when paid by the general fund.

25. (1178,T1,33) (a) The special assessment fund uses the modified accrual basis for both revenues and expenses. Accordingly, only when the interest on assessments is received, should it be recorded.

26. (1178,T1,26) (a) The requirement is the item that should be accrued as revenue by the general fund. The general fund, as well as the special revenue and debt service funds, uses the modified accrual basis. The modified accrual basis recognizes expenses when they are incurred and revenues when they are received, i.e., cash basis for revenues and accrual basis for expenses. The rationale is that most governmental revenues are not assured until received, e.g., license revenues which are dependent upon persons making a decision to purchase a license. The revenue recognition rule under the modified accrual basis, however, is modified to recognize taxes when levied. When taxes are levied, they are considered collectible. The same would be true of sales taxes that have already been collected by the state which will be remitted to the local government. Answers (b), (c), and (d), parking meter revenues, sales taxes, and income taxes, are accounted for on the cash basis and not accrued.

27. (1178,T1,28) (b) An actuarial deficiency would be the amount associated with an actuarial computation where a prior actuarial estimate was insufficient. Actuarial amounts have to do with pensions which would be accounted for in a trust fund. Answer (a) is incorrect because an agency fund has to do only with short-term holdings for others, e.g., payroll taxes to be remitted to the federal government or union dues to be remitted to a union. Answers (c) and (d) are incorrect because the general and debt service funds would not administer programs in which actuarial computations are necessary.

28.   (1178,T1,29) (a) "Excess of net billings to departments over costs" would appear in the financial statements of internal service fund. The internal service fund provides services to other governmental funds. An excess of net billings to departments over cost would be the "income" figure of the fund. The objective of an internal service fund is not to create a profit, but rather to provide services at cost to other funds. Small profits or losses can be expected from time to time; these would be closed to a retained earnings account.

29.   (1178,T1,31) (c)   Trust funds are non-expendable as to principal and expendable as to income. Frequently two trust funds are established: one for principal and the other for income. Then as income is earned by the non-expendable fund, it is transferred to the expendable fund. The debt service fund (answer (a)), enterprise fund (answer (b)), and special revenues fund (answer (d)), all are exclusively expendable funds.

30.   (579,T1,42) (c) The requirement is the type of loan that would not be accounted for in a loan fund of a college or university. Loan funds typically account for loans to (a), students, (b), staff, and (d), faculty. Answer (c), building indebtedness, is usually shown as a liability in the "Investment in Plant" section of the plant fund of a college or university balance sheet.

31.   (579,T1,44) (d) Depreciation of fixed assets is recorded by voluntary health and welfare organizations because depreciation is a cost of rendering current services. Answer (a) is incorrect because fixed assets are not more likely to be material in voluntary health and welfare organizations; these organizations generally only collect and distribute funds. Answer (b) is incorrect because most not-for-profit organizations purchase their assets and would have a historical cost to determine amounts to be depreciated; i.e., this answer does not discriminate between voluntary health and welfare organizations and other not-for-profit institutions. Answer (c) is incorrect because opportunity costs should not be recorded in historical-cost-based financial statements.

32.   (579,T1,45)   (d)   The requirement is the type of receipt to be accounted for in the restricted current funds of a university. Research grants are usually made with specific restrictions as to expenditure and accordingly are accounted for in current restricted funds. Tuition, laboratory fees, and housing fees are within the general operations of a university and thus are not restricted resources, i.e., they are used to fund general operations.

33.   (579,T1,46) (b)   The land, building and equipment fund in voluntary health and welfare organizations is used to account for the net investment in fixed assets and also used to account for unexpended resources contributed specifically for the purpose of replacing land, building, and equipment. Mortgages or liabilities are also included in the fund, and depreciation is recorded on fixed assets. Thus there is no comparable fund in governmental accounting. Answer (a) is incorrect because unrestricted current funds are somewhat similar to special revenue funds in governmental accounting. Answer (c) is incorrect because custodian funds are similar to agency funds in governmental accounting. Answer (d) is incorrect because endowment funds are similar to endowment funds in governmental accounting.

34.   (579,T1,49) (c)   The requirement is a budgetary account in governmental accounting. Answer (c) is correct because appropriations is an anticipatory liability. It is only a nominal account, as it is closed to expenditures and encumbrances at the end of the year. The entry to record the budget at the beginning of the year is

Estimated revenues	$	
Appropriations		$
Fund balance		$

At the end of the year actual expenses and encumbrances are closed to appropriations with the fund balance as the balancing account. Answer (a) is incorrect because reserve for inventory of supplies is an offsetting residual account recorded when inventory is recorded. Answer (b) is incorrect because fund balance is the residual account in governmental funds. Answer (d) is incorrect because estimated uncollectible property taxes is a contra-property-taxes receivable account.

35.   (579,T1,50) (b) Governmental units use separate accounts because of the diverse nature of services and varying legal provisions and controls regarding activities of these diverse functions. Thus it is more economical and efficient to have separate types of governmental funds (entities) for these varying activities. Answer (a) is incorrect because the size of an operating entity does not preclude an adequate accounting system. Answer (c) is incorrect because GAAP do not apply to not-for-profit entities. Answer (d) is incorrect because accounting for short-lived activities would not increase the probability of errors or omissions.

36. . (1177,T2,23) (b) When the general fund transfers money to a new internal service fund, the transfer should be recorded as a transfer to internal service fund rather than as a debit to accounts receivable, reserve for encumbrances, or appropriations. Nonrecurring transfers between funds are not revenue or expense transactions.

The "reserve for encumbrances" account is not debited for cash payments. Rather the debit to "reserve for encumbrances" is part of a reversing entry wherein the "reserve for encumbrances" is debited and "encumbrances" are credited. Appropriations are only debited when they are closed at the end of the year. Appropriations are credited at the beginning of the year in the original budgetary entry. At the end of the year encumbrances and expenditures are closed against appropriations and any remaining balance is taken to the fund balance account.

37. (1177,T2,27) (b) Agency funds perform a holding operation for money, e.g., collection of union dues, employee withholding, etc. Thus the assets are usually liquid and offset entirely by liabilities rather than a fund balance. The general, special revenue, and capital projects funds all use budgetary accounts, i.e., recording appropriations, estimated revenues, etc., which result in a fund balance account.

38. (1177,T2,28) (c) Internal service funds provide services on a cost basis to other governmental funds, e.g., central data processing, motor pools, etc. Thus, in order to recoup the costs of capital assets, depreciation must be taken and computed in the service charges to other funds. In other words, the internal service fund needs to account for its costs very similarly to that of a business enterprise to be able to determine "adequate" fees for its services.

The general, special revenue, capital projects, and special assessment funds do not record fixed assets or depreciation. Fixed assets arising from expenditures by these funds are recorded in the general fixed asset group of accounts, where depreciation expense is not recognized.

39. (578,T2,29) (b) Governmental units that provide services to other governmental units are accounted for in the internal service fund. Internal service funds use accrual accounting and have accounting systems similar to for-profit organizations. The only difference is that the internal service fund attempts to price its service at cost rather than to make a profit. Answer (a) is incorrect because the capital projects fund is used to account for capital expenditures, e.g., issuance of bonds to build buildings or federal grants to construct streets.

Answers (a) and (d) are incorrect because agency and trust funds provide a fiduciary capacity, i.e., holding funds for some future use. Agency funds usually involve short-term holdings, and trust funds involve long-term holdings.

40. (578,T2,30) (b) The "reserve for encumbrances of prior years" represents amounts encumbered in prior years, but not paid in the prior year. For example, a purchase order may be submitted for a capital good, and it may be delivered and become a liability in a subsequent year. By debiting encumbrances and crediting reserve for encumbrances in the year of the ordering, the appropriations of that year may be charged with the encumbrance. The appropriations of the subsequent year will not be charged because "reserve for encumbrances of prior years" can be debited in the year the previous period's order is paid.

41. (578,T2,31) (b) Property taxes are generally recorded directly into the general fund. Receipts for a city-owned parking structure would normally be accounted for in a special revenue or enterprise fund. Interest earned on investments held for retirement of employees should be held in a trust fund. Revenues from internal services would be accounted in an internal service fund.

42. (1176,T2,38) (c) The enterprise fund is appropriate for recreational and similar facilities for which one-half or more of the finances are obtained by user charges. If more than one-half of the finances come from taxes, a special revenue fund is used. The general fund accounts for all transactions not accounted for in other funds. The trust fund accounts for assets that are going to be held on behalf of others for long periods of time, e.g., pension funds. Capital project funds account for the proceeds of bond issues, federal grants, etc., which are used to construct capital projects such as schools, libraries, etc.

43. (1176,T2,42) (a) The accounts of similar funds, e.g., special assessment, special revenue, etc., can be combined into a total column. The accounts of different types of funds can be added together on a memorandum basis only as the funds are independent entities with no right of offset. Answer (b) is incorrect because the effect of interfund transactions may not be eliminated, as the right of offset does not exist. Answer (c) is incorrect because funds may be reported on a separate basis on the same statement (but not totaled together if they are not the same type of fund). Answer (d) is incorrect as the lack of

the right of offset precludes eliminating the effects of interfund transactions.

44. (1176,T2,44) (a) At the present time all governmental reporting is in terms of historical costs without any adjustments or disclosures concerning price level changes, current appraisal amounts, etc.

45. (577,P1,15) (a) The entry to record issuance of purchase vouchers is to debit encumbrances and credit reserve for encumbrances. This is a budgetary entry which is reversed for the same amount upon payment of the invoice (after receipt of the goods or services). The entry is reversed for the same amount of dollars as originally recorded, even if the entry to record the actual expenditure is for a different amount of dollars. The entry to record the expenditure is to debit expenditures and credit the vouchers payable. The encumbering entry is made to control or hold expenditures within appropriations. Unencumbered appropriated funds available for spending are appropriations made at the beginning of the year, less expenditures and encumbrances to date.

46. (577,P1,16) (d) Enterprise funds use the same accrual accounting system and procedures as for-profit enterprises. Thus, only 1976 depreciation and 1976 bad debts expense would appear in the revenues and expenses statement. The prepaid insurance would be deferred in the statement of financial position.

47. (1175,T2,31) (d) When goods or services are ordered, appropriations are encumbered by debiting encumbrances and crediting reserve for encumbrances. If the goods and services are received in the period ordered, the foregoing entry is reversed when the expenditure is recorded. If the goods are not received in the period they are ordered, the encumbrance account is closed to the appropriations account at the end of the period (as is expenditures). The reserve for encumbrances, a real account, earmarks the fund balance to liquidate goods ordered in previous periods. Expenditures for goods ordered in previous periods are charged to the reserve for encumbrances account.

48. (1175,T2,32) (a) The proceeds of general obligation bonds are accounted for in the capital projects fund, and the debt service fund usually handles the repayment of long-term debt (except repayment of special assessment debt) and interest payments. The premiums received

on general obligation bonds are usually transferred from the capital projects fund to the debt service fund, because the premium represents an adjustment of the interest cost. If the general fund is paying the interest, the premium should be transferred to the general fund.

49. (1175,T2,34) (a) A statement of changes in financial position is prepared for the enterprise fund, because the enterprise fund accounting is very similar to private enterprise accounting.

50. (1175,T2,35) (c) Depreciation is recorded as expense in the enterprise fund and internal service fund. The enterprise fund uses GAAP and thus would depreciate its assets. The internal service fund provides services on a cost basis to other funds, e.g., central computer services, tax collector, motor pools, etc. Thus internal service funds depreciate their assets in accordance with GAAP. General funds, capital projects funds, and general fixed-asset groups of accounts do not record depreciation on their assets.

51. (1175,T2,36) (a) An appropriation is the authority granted to a governmental body to incur obligations and make expenditures. The standard budgetary entry assuming budgeted revenues are equal to appropriations is

> Estimated revenues
> Appropriations

If estimated revenues are not equal to appropriations, the entry is forced by appropriate debit or credit to "fund balance." At the year end, encumbrances and expenditures are closed to the appropriations account. Encumbrances reflect the contingent expenditures, i.e., goods and services ordered but not received, and expenditures reflect cash expenditures of the period for goods and services received. Authorizations is not generally used as an account title in governmental accounting.

52. (1175,T2,37) (b) The account "expenditures" would not be found in an enterprise fund, because the account "expenditures" does not generally appear in the accounts of profit oriented entities. Monies expended by the capital projects, special assessments, and special revenue funds are generally charged to an "expenditures" account.

53. (1175,T2,38) (d) The payment of general bond proceeds for the city hall and transfer of remaining cash to the debt service fund would be recorded in the capital projects fund. The receipt of excess cash would be recorded in the debt service fund. Relatedly, an entry must be made in the general long-term debt group of accounts to record the fact that monies have been made available to pay the debt. The entry is to debit "amounts available to repay debt" and to credit "amount required to repay debt." When the bonds were issued "amount required to repay debt" was debited and "bonds payable" credited. Also, at the completion of the project, an entry must be made in the general fixed-assets group of accounts to record the city hall. The entry is to debit "city hall" and credit "investment in fixed assets - capital projects fund."

54. (1175,T2,39) (b) The cash is transferred from the general fund to the debt-service fund. Thus an entry is required in both funds. As in the immediately preceding problem, when funds are set aside for the repayment of long-term debt, an entry is made in the general long-term debt group of accounts, debiting "amount available to repay debt" and crediting "amount required to repay debt."

55. (1175,T2,40) (b) Upon sale of fixed assets, the cash is recorded in the general fund as a debit to cash and a credit to revenue. The entry to remove the fixed assets in the general fixed-assets group of accounts is to debit "investment in fixed assets - capital projects fund" and credit "equipment". The entry would be made for the original cost as no depreciation is recorded in the general fixed-assets group of accounts.

MAY 1981 ANSWERS

56. (581,T1,51) (c) The requirement is the treatment of the excess of revenues over estimated revenues when the estimated revenue account of a governmental unit is closed at the end of the fiscal year. At the beginning of the fiscal year, a governmental unit estimates the amount of revenue it will collect during the year from various sources. The account "Estimated Revenues" is debited at the beginning of the year. When preparing closing entries, then, the amount of actual revenues over estimated revenues would be to the fund balance account.

57. (581,T1,53) (b) The requirement is the account which is credited when goods, which have been previously approved for purchase, are received by a governmental unit but not yet paid for. When goods

have been approved for purchase, an "Encumbrances" account is debited and a "Reserve for Encumbrances" account is credited for the estimated cost of the goods. As the goods are received, the following entries are recorded:

Expenditures	XXX	
Vouchers Payable		XXX
Reserve for Encumbrances	XXX	
Encumbrances		XXX

The first entry records the receipt of the goods, and the second entry reverses the original encumbrance that was set up when the goods were initially approved.

58. (581,T1,55) (d) The requirement is the fund classification for a capital projects fund. The capital projects fund is a governmental fund. The National Council on Governmental Accounting recommends the use of eight different types of funds grouped into three different types of fund entities. General funds, special revenue funds, capital projects funds, debt service funds, and special assessment funds are all grouped together as Governmental Funds. Enterprise funds and internal service funds [answer (a)] are classified as Proprietary Funds; Trust and agency funds are classified as Fiduciary Funds [answer (d)] .

59. (581,T1,56) (b) The requirement is which accounts could be included in the balance sheet of an enterprise fund. Enterprise funds are used to account for operations that are financial and operated in a manner similar to a private business, where the provision of goods or services to the general public are on a continuing basis and where all or most costs incurred are recovered from charges to users. An example of an enterprise fund is a public utility. Accounting for the operations of enterprise funds closely parallels the accounting for profit-oriented enterprises and uses the same accounts. The two accounts which closely parallel those used in profit-oriented business are revenue bonds payable (bonds which are secured by the future revenues of the fund) and retained earnings. Reserve for Encumbrances is not used in profit-oriented accounting and is also not used in enterprise funds.

60. (581,T1,57) (a) The requirement is an account that would be included in the combined balance sheet for the long-term debt account group. A governmental unit's long-term debt account group is not a fund; it is a memorandum record. Its purpose is to disclose the governmental unit's long-term liabilities which are not disclosed in one of the governmental unit's other funds. The obligations for general long-term debt are recorded in the general long-term debt account group. The amounts recorded in accounts

for general long-term debt obligations (credits) are balanced by accounts that show the amounts available and to be provided for payment of the obligations (debts).

61.   (581,T1,58)   (d)   The requirement is the fund in which customers' meter deposits, which cannot be spent for normal operating purposes, would be classified as restricted in the balance sheet. The meters are assumed to be those associated with public utilities, such as water meters or electric meters. Enterprise funds are used to account for the provision of goods or services to the general public on a continuing basis where all or most of the costs incurred are recovered from charges to users.

62.   (581,T1,59)   (d)   The requirement is to identify the type of fund for which the accrual basis of accounting should be used in governmental units. The accrual method of accounting is used by the internal service, enterprise, and nonexpendable trust funds. The modified accrual basis is used by special revenue [answer (a)], the general [answer (b)], debt service [answer (c)], capital projects, and special assessment funds.

63.   (581,T1,60)   (d)   The requirement is the account that should be credited when a voluntary not-for-profit hospital receives an unrestricted gift. According to the AICPA Industry Audit Guide, gifts that are not restricted by donors are subject to designation by the governing board; they should be reported as non-operating revenue.

SOLUTION GUIDE

Problem 1   University Journal Entries

1. Part a requires journal entries for the 11 transactions of Burnsville University. The entries are
to be recorded in the current unrestricted, current restricted, and endowment funds. Part b
requires a statement of changes in fund balances
for the year ended 6/30/78.

2. The solutions approach is to analyze each of the
11 transactions and determine the fund affected
and the appropriate journal entry. The unrestricted
current fund, as the title implies, is used for all
transactions not accounted for elsewhere, i.e.,
is similar to the general fund in municipal accounting. The current restricted fund accounts
for funds which have been externally restricted
for certain purposes. Endowment funds are trust
funds in which the principal is usually non-
expendable.

2.1 One-half of the $100,000 is to be used to pur-
chase library books, and the other half as a
scholarship fund. The $50,000 for library books
should be accounted for as a gift in the current
restricted fund. A peculiarity of university accounting is that contributions to and earnings
from restricted fund assets are usually credited
directly to the fund balance account and are
recognized as revenue when the money is expended. Therefore the current restricted fund
balance account would be credited for the
$50,000 gift for books. The remaining $50,000
contributed to a scholarship fund would be
credited to the endowment fund balance account.
When the savings certificates are purchased by
the endowment fund, debit the endowment
fund investment account and credit endowment
fund cash.

2.2 Tuition and fees are accounted for in the current unrestricted funds. The problem clearly
states that $1,900,000 should be recorded as
revenue. Since $66,000 was collected in the
prior year (debit deferred revenues) and
$1,686,000 was collected currently, $148,000
($1,900,000 − $66,000 − $1,686,000) should
be recorded as accounts receivable. Finally
the $158,000 of next year's fees collected
in advance should be recorded as deferred
revenue.

2.3 Record the $349,000 of accounts receivable
collected. Note that $350,000 of receivables

were outstanding as the $341,000 listed
in the balance sheet was net of a $9,000
allowance for doubtful accounts. Thus
$1,000 of accounts receivable must be writ-
ten off to the allowance account. At the
end of 1978 the allowance account was increased from $8,000 ($9,000 − $1,000 of
write-offs) to $11,000.

2.4 The $6,000 of interest on late student pay-
ments is revenue in the current unrestricted
fund.

2.5 The state appropriation received was the
$75,000 receivable in the current unrestricted
fund. The additional $50,000 unrestricted ap-
propriation should be reflected as appropriation revenue in the year in which the appropriation was made (note it has not yet been
paid to the university).

2.6 The unrestricted gift of $25,000 is recorded
in the current unrestricted fund as gift revenue.

2.7 The investments sold during the year were sold
by the current restricted fund as the current
unrestricted and the endowment funds did
not have investments. The $5,000 gain
($26,000 selling price less $21,000 cost) is
credited directly to the current restricted fund
balance account (remember the peculiarity
that contributions and earnings of current
restricted funds are taken to fund balance
when received and recognized as revenue
when expended). Similarly the $1,900 of
investment income is taken directly to the
fund balance account.

2.8 The $1,777,000 of operating expenses should
be recorded in the current unrestricted fund.
Since all but $59,000 of these expenses have
been paid, cash should be credited for
$1,718,000 ($1,777,000 − $59,000).

2.9 The expenditure of $13,000 by the current
restricted fund should be so recorded. Concurrently the fund balance should be reduced by
$13,000 and revenue recognized in that amount.
Again this is a peculiarity of current restricted
funds in university accounting.

2.10 The beginning accounts payable of $45,000 in
the current unrestricted fund was paid during
the year.

2.11 The $7,000 interest earned on the savings certificates in the endowment fund should be recorded in the current restricted fund, because the monies have an external restriction (by the donor). As explained above, contributions and earnings of the current restricted fund are taken to fund balance when received. They are subsequently transferred from fund balance to revenues as they are expended.

3.   Part b requires a statement of changes in fund balances for the year. The statement of changes in fund balances is a primary university financial statement as it explains the activity (inflows and outflows by type) for each fund. The solutions approach is to list the inflows and outflows for each fund to determine the net change in each fund's fund balance.

UNOFFICIAL ANSWER

Problem 1   University Journal Entries

Burnsville University
TRANSACTIONS FOR THE YEAR ENDED JUNE 30, 1978

Account	Unrestricted Debit	Unrestricted Credit	Restricted Debit	Restricted Credit	Endowment Fund Debit	Endowment Fund Credit
1. Cash			$50,000			
Fund balance				$50,000		
To record receipt of cash gift for purchase of books						
Cash					$50,000	
Endowment fund balance						$50,000
To record receipt of cash gift to establish scholarship fund						
Investment in savings certificates					50,000	
Cash						50,000
To record purchase of savings certificates						
2. Cash	$1,686,000					
Deferred revenue	66,000					
Accounts receivable—student tuition and fees	148,000					
Revenue		$1,900,000				
To record revenue on tuition and fees						
Cash	158,000					
Deferred revenue		158,000				
To record deferred revenue at June 30, 1978						
3. Cash	349,000					
Allowance for uncollectible accounts	1,000					
Accounts receivable—tuition and fees		350,000				
To record collection and write-off of accounts receivable						
Expense	3,000					
Allowance for uncollectible accounts		3,000				
To record increase in allowance account						
4. Cash	6,000					
Revenue		6,000				
To record interest earned on late student fee payments						

Burnsville University
TRANSACTIONS FOR THE YEAR ENDED JUNE 30, 1978

| | Current Funds | | | | Endowment Fund | |
| | Unrestricted | | Restricted | | | |
Account	Debit	Credit	Debit	Credit	Debit	Credit
5. Cash	$ 75,000					
State appropriation receivable	50,000					
Revenue		$ 50,000				
State appropriation receivable		75,000				
To record receipt of regular appropriation and to record additional appropriation						
6. Cash	25,000					
Revenue		25,000				
To record receipt of unrestricted gift						
7. Cash			$26,000			
Investments				$21,000		
Fund balance				5,000		
To record sale of investments						
Cash			1,900			
Fund balance				1,900		
To record income earned on investments						
8. Expenses	1,777,000					
Accounts payable		59,000				
Cash		1,718,000				
To record expenses for year						
9. Expenditures			13,000			
Cash				13,000		
To record payment of authorized expenditures						
Fund balance			13,000			
Revenue				13,000		
To record as revenue amounts expended for restricted purposes						
10. Accounts payable	45,000					
Cash		45,000				
To record payment of accounts payable at June 30, 1977						
11. Cash			7,000			
Fund balance				7,000		
To record receipt of interest income on savings certificates purchased by Endowment Fund						

Part b.

Burnsville University
STATEMENT OF CHANGES IN FUNDS BALANCES
For the year ended June 30, 1978

| | Current Funds | | Endowment Fund |
	Unrestricted	Restricted	
Revenues and other additions			
Establishment of scholarship fund			$50,000
Revenue from student tuition and fees	$1,900,000		
Revenue from additional state appropriation	50,000		
Interest income on deferred payments	6,000		
Receipt of gift for library books		$ 50,000	
Investment income		1,900	
Interest income on savings certificates		7,000	
Unrestricted gift received	25,000		
Increase in fund balance on sale of investments		5,000	
Total revenues and other additions	$1,981,000	$ 63,900	$50,000
Expenditures and other deductions			
Operating and authorized expenses	$1,777,000	$ 13,000	
Increase in provision for uncollectible accounts receivable	3,000		
Total expenditures and other deductions	$1,780,000	$ 13,000	–
Net increase (decrease)	201,000	50,900	50,000
Current funds balances, July 1, 1977	515,000	67,000	–
Current funds balances, June 30, 1978	$ 716,000	$117,900	$50,000

SOLUTION GUIDE

Problem 2   Municipality Journal Entries

1.   Problem 2 requires journal entries (excluding closing entries) necessary for 7 funds or account groups based on 11 descriptive paragraphs of information. Each paragraph describes one or two transactions, and a particular transaction may require entries in more than one fund or account group. The solution format to be used is described in the requirement.

2.   The solutions approach is to analyze each paragraph identifying in the margin the fund(s) or account group(s) affected. Be sure to glance at the list of funds and account groups given to avoid forgetting any affected funds or account groups. The next step is to make all the necessary entries.

2.1   Estimated revenues (anticipated resources) are $6,000 greater than appropriations (anticipated expenditures) resulting in a credit to fund balance.

2.2   In governmental funds expected uncollectible property taxes are treated as a reduction of revenue. Revenue can be recognized because these taxes are available (i.e., they can be used as collateral if necessary).

2.3   The $50,000 gift of securities is to be maintained in a non-expendable trust fund. The $5,500 earned on the securities is recorded as revenue.

2.4   The transfer of $5,000 to establish an intragovernmental (internal) service fund is recorded as a transfer out. Remember that transfers result from the shifting of resources between funds except for those transfers which would result in a revenue or expenditure if an outsider were involved.

The intragovernmental (internal) service fund account credited (contribution from general fund) is an equity account.

2.5   Although appropriations for special assessments are not usually recorded, this problem requires a formal entry.

2.6 The $72,000 special assessments levied are recorded as revenue, but the $3,000 contribution from the general fund is recorded as a transfer in. The next entry records receipt of all $75,000.

Entries are needed in the general fund to record the $3,000 as a transfer out and the payment of the interfund obligation created by the transfer.

An encumbrance in the amount of the contract should be recorded and reversed when the project is completed and the billing rendered, even though the project was not approved by the village. The expenditures should be recorded in the amount of $75,000 (since no other figure is given, expenditures are assumed to equal the contract price). Since 5% is to be withheld pending approval of the project, the cash payment is $71,250. Contracts payable-retained percentage is credited for 5% of $75,000. Finally, the cost of the project must be recorded in the general fixed asset group of accounts.

2.7 Credit vouchers payable or cash since the information does not indicate whether or not payment was made.

2.8 Property taxes collected exceed the net realizable value of the receivable recorded.

Taxes Receivable — current	$390,000
Estimated Amount Uncollectible	−7,800
	$382,200
Amount Collected to Date	$386,000
Excess Collected to Date	$ 3,800

Since the revenue recognized from property taxes at the date of levy was net of the estimated amount uncollectible it is necessary to reduce the allowance by $3,800 and recognize this amount as additional revenue. There is no information given to indicate what portion of the remaining $4,000 ($390,000 − $386,000) of property taxes receivable are not likely to be collected. Therefore, nothing further can be done with respect to uncollectible taxes. Licenses and permits are recognized as revenue when collected.

2.9 Only an entry to record the sale of bonds is needed in the capital projects fund. The liability for the bonds is recorded in the general long-term debt group.

2.10 Entries are needed in the general fund to remove the encumbrance. Record the expenditure and the payment of the expenditure. An alternative is to credit vouchers payable in recording the expenditure and make a separate payment entry. In the general fixed asset group, an entry is needed to record the equipment and fund source of the acquisition.

UNOFFICIAL ANSWER

Problem 2 Municipality Journal Entries

DEXTER VILAGE
TRANSACTIONS FOR THE FISCAL YEAR ENDED JUNE 30, 1979

TRANS- ACTION NO.	FUND OR GROUP OF ACCOUNTS	ACCOUNT TITLES AND EXPLANATIONS	AMOUNTS	
			DEBIT	CREDIT
1.	GENERAL FUND	ESTIMATED REVENUES APPROPRIATIONS FUND BALANCE	$400,000	$394,000 6,000
		To Record Budget		
2.	GENERAL FUND	TAXES RECEIVABLE — CURRENT REVENUES ESTIMATED UNCOLLECTABLE CURRENT TAXES	390,000	382,200 7,800
		To Record Tax Levy		
3.A	TRUST FUND	INVESTMENTS FUND PRINCIPAL BALANCE	50,000	50,000
		To Record Value of Securities Donated in Trust		

TRANS-ACTION NO.	FUND OR GROUP OF ACCOUNTS	ACCOUNT TITLES AND EXPLANATIONS	AMOUNTS	
			DEBIT	CREDIT
3.B	TRUST FUND	CASH	5,500	
		REVENUES		5,500
		To Record Revenues Earned		
4.A	GENERAL FUND	FUND BALANCE	5,000	
		CASH		5,000
		To Record Establishment of Intragovernmental Fund		
4.B	INTRAGOVERNMENTAL SERVICE FUND	CASH	5,000	
		CONTRIBUTIONS FROM GENERAL FUND		5,000
		To Record Contribution From General Fund		
5.	SPECIAL ASSESS-MENT FUND	IMPROVEMENTS AUTHORIZED (OR ESTIMATED REVENUE)	75,000	
		APPROPRIATIONS		75,000
		To Record Authorization of Assessment		
6.A	SPECIAL ASSESS-MENT FUND	ASSESSMENTS RECEIVABLE — CURRENT	72,000	
		DUE FROM GENERAL FUND	3,000	
		REVENUE — SPECIAL ASSESSMENTS LEVIED		72,000
		OPERATING TRANSFERS IN		3,000
		To Record Assessment		
6.B	SPECIAL ASSESS-MENT FUND	CASH	75,000	
		ASSESSMENT RECEIVABLE — CURRENT		72,000
		DUE FROM GENERAL FUND		3,000
		To Record Cash Received		
6.C	GENERAL FUND	OPERATING TRANSFERS OUT	3,000	
		DUE TO SPECIAL ASSESSMENT FUND		3,000
6.D	GENERAL FUND	DUE TO SPECIAL ASSESSMENT FUND	3,000	
		CASH		3,000
		To Record Cash Payment		
7.A	SPECIAL ASSESS-MENT FUND	ENCUMBRANCES	75,000	
		RESERVE FOR ENCUMBRANCES		75,000
		To Record Contract For Lighting		
7.B	SPECIAL ASSESS-MENT FUND	RESERVE FOR ENCUMBRANCES	75,000	
		EXPENDITURES	75,000	
		CASH		71,250
		CONTRACTS PAYABLE — RETAINED PERCENTAGE		3,750
		ENCUMBRANCES		75,000
		To Record Payment And Retained Percentage		
7.C	GENERAL FIXED ASSETS	IMPROVEMENTS OTHER THAN BUILDINGS	75,000	
		INVESTMENTS IN FIXED ASSETS		75,000
		To Record Improvements		
8.	INTRAGOVERNMENTAL SERVICE FUND	INVENTORY	1,900	
		CASH OR VOUCHERS PAYABLE		1,900
		To Record Purchase of Supplies		

TRANS-ACTION NO.	FUND OR GROUP OF ACCOUNTS	ACCOUNT TITLES AND EXPLANATIONS	AMOUNTS	
			DEBIT	CREDIT
9.A	GENERAL FUND	CASH	393,000	
		TAXES RECEIVABLE — CURRENT		386,000
		REVENUES		7,000
		To Record Collections		
9.B	GENERAL FUND	ESTIMATED UNCOLLECTIBLE		
		CURRENT TAXES	3,800	
		REVENUES		3,800
		To Correct Tax Revenues		
10.A	CAPITAL PROJECTS FUND	CASH	500,000	
		PROCEEDS OF GENERAL		
		OBLIGATION BONDS		500,000
		To Record Issuance of Bonds		
10.B	GENERAL LONG-TERM DEBT	AMOUNT TO BE PROVIDED FOR		
		RETIREMENT OF BONDS	500,000	
		GENERAL OBLIGATION		
		BONDS PAYABLE		500,000
		To Record Liability		
11.A	GENERAL FUND	RESERVE FOR ENCUMBRANCES	15,000	
		ENCUMBRANCES		15,000
		To Record Cancellation of Encumbrances Upon Payment For Fire Truck		
11.B	GENERAL FUND	EXPENDITURES	15,000	
		CASH		15,000
		To Record Purchase Of Fire Truck		
11.C	GENERAL FIXED ASSETS	FIRE TRUCK	15,000	
		INVESTMENT IN FIXED ASSETS		15,000
		To Record Acquisition		

SOLUTION GUIDE

Problem 3   General Fund

This problem requires (a) the journal entries to adjust and close the general fund and (b) any adjusting entries required in any other funds or groups of accounts.

The solutions approach is to analyze the pre-closing trial balance and the 8 items of additional information. General and other fund journal entries should be prepared as required. Finally, the closing entries for the general fund should be made.

1. The $18,000 allowance for uncollectible current year taxes has been recorded properly. Relatedly, the allowance for prior years' losses is $10,200, which is $2,200 greater than the related receivable. Accordingly, an adjustment should be made to reduce the allowance from $10,200 to $8,000, with the credit going to the fund balance.

2. The $27,000 which has been debited to donated land and credited to revenue should be reversed, because the entry belongs in the general fixed asset group of accounts rather than the general fund. Thus, in the general fixed asset group of accounts, land should be debited and investment in land from a state grant should be credited for $27,000.

3. The cost of an addition to the Town Hall has been charged to expenditures, which is appropriate because the general fund paid for the addition in 1978. The addition was not recorded in the general fixed asset group of accounts. The addition is to be debited and investment by the general fund credited for $50,000.

4. The $16,000 ($9,000 principal and $7,000 interest) paid on the general obligation bonds has been recorded as an expenditure in the general fund, which is correct since the general fund made the payment, and the bonds are general obligation bonds. The payment has not been reflected in the general long-term debt accounts. Debit bonds payable and credit amount to be provided.

5. In the previous year, $8,800 of encumbrances were not recorded which carried over to the current year. Accordingly, reserve for encumbrances of prior years should be credited for $8,800, and the fund balance debited for $8,800 (to correct the understatement of encumbrances of the prior period).

The expenditures associated with the prior year's encumbrances of $9,400 were charged to the current year's expenditures. Accordingly, the $9,400 should be reclassified from other expenditures to an account entitled "expenditures of the prior year".

6. The outstanding purchase orders of $2,100 at the end of fiscal 1978 should be recorded as a debit to encumbrances and a credit to reserve encumbrances for $2,100.

7. The special assessment bond proceeds should have been accounted for in a special assessment fund. Accordingly, the entry should be reversed in the general fund by debiting special assessment bonds payable and crediting a liability to the special assessment fund. In the special assessment fund, both the receivable from the general fund and the bond liability should be recorded. Also the authorization for the paving project may be recorded by debiting improvements authorized and crediting appropriations.

8. Revenues were incorrectly credited when a note was issued to obtain cash. Accordingly, revenue should be debited and tax anticipation notes payable should be credited.

Also, $1,000 received for sale of scrap by the water utility fund was recorded in the general fund's revenues. Accordingly, revenues should be debited and a liability to the utility fund should be credited for $1,000. Correspondingly, in the water utility fund, a receivable from the general fund and revenue should be recorded for $1,000.

9. The closing entries consist of reclassifying the current taxes receivable to delinquent taxes receivable, closing out all of the expenditures and encumbrances to appropriations, and closing the revenues to estimated revenues, and closing the expenditures prior years to the related reserve for encumbrances account.

Both the current year taxes receivable and the related allowance accounts should be reclassified from current to delinquent. In closing the expenses to appropriations, recall that expenses were reduced by the $9,400 of a prior year's expenditure and encumbrances of $2,100 were recognized. In closing the revenue recall that revenue was reduced by the $27,000 donation, $20,000 tax anticipation note, and $1,000 water plant scrap sale. The closing of expenditures of the prior year to the reserve encumbrances of the prior year results in a debit of $600 to the fund balance.

After preparing the general fund entries in final format, be sure to go back and record all the entries in the other funds and groups of accounts.

UNOFFICIAL ANSWER

Problem 3   General Fund

a.

Town of Rego
GENERAL FUND
Adjusting and Closing Journal Entries
July 1, 1977, to June 30, 1978

	Debit	Credit
(1)		
Estimated losses—prior year taxes receivable	$ 2,200	
Fund balance		$ 2,200
To reduce balance of estimated losses on prior year taxes receivable to amount of receivables of $8,000		
(2)		
Revenues	27,000	
Donated land		27,000
To remove accounts belonging to the general fixed assets		
(3)		
Fund balance	8,800	
Reserve for encumbrances of prior year		8,800
To record purchase orders outstanding at June 30, 1977		
(4)		
Expenditures chargeable to reserve for encumbrances of prior year	9,400	
Other expenditures		9,400
To reclassify purchases of supplies chargeable to prior year appropriations		
(5)		
Encumbrances	2,100	
Reserve for encumbrances—1977-1978		2,100
To record encumbering of appropriations for purchase orders outstanding at June 30, 1978		
(6)		
Special assessment bonds payable	$100,000	
Due to Special Assessment Fund		$100,000
To record liability to Special Assessment Fund for cash obtained from sale of Special Assessment bonds		
(7)		
Revenues	21,000	
Tax anticipation notes payable		20,000
Due to Water Utility Fund		1,000
To record tax anticipation notes payable and liability to Water Utility Fund for funds obtained from sale of scrap		
(8)		
Taxes receivable—delinquent	59,200	
Estimated losses—current year taxes receivable	18,000	
Taxes receivable—current year		59,200
Estimated losses—delinquent taxes receivable		18,000
To reclassify current taxes as delinquent		

(9)

Appropriations	348,000	
Other expenditures		270,600
Expenditures—Building addition constructed		50,000
Expenditures—Serial bonds paid		16,000
Encumbrances		2,100
Fund balance		9,300
To close out to fund balance		

(10)

Revenues	306,000	
Fund balance	4,000	
Estimated revenues		310,000
To close out to fund balance		

(11)

Reserve for encumbrances of prior year	8000	
Fund balance	600	
Expenditures chargeable to reserve for encumbrances of prior year		9,400
To close out to fund balance		

b.

Town of Rego
ADJUSTING JOURNAL ENTRIES
General Fixed Assets Group of Accounts

	Debit	Credit
(1)		
Land	$ 27,000	
Investment in general fixed assets—state grant-in-aid		$ 27,000
To record donation of land by the state		
(2)		
Structures and improvements	50,000	
Investment in general fixed assets-General Fund		50,000
To record the cost of addition to town hall		

General Bonded Debt and Interest Group of Accounts

	Debit	Credit
Bonds payable	$ 16,000	
Amount to be provided for retirement of bonds		$ 16,000
To reduce bond liability by the amount of the bonds matured		

Special Assessment Fund

	Debit	Credit
(1)		
Improvement authorized	$100,000	
Appropriations		$100,000
To record the authorization of project in the amount of $100,000		
(2)		
Due from General Fund	$100,000	
Bonds payable		$100,000
To record receivable due from General Fund for proceeds of sale of bonds		

Water Utility Fund

	Debit	Credit
Due from General Fund	$ 1,000	
Other revenues		$ 1,000
To record receivable from General Fund for cash obtained on sale of scrap		

ANSWER OUTLINE

Problem 4   Municipal vs. Financial Accounting

a.   Commercial enterprises emphasize earnings
     Governmental units emphasize budgetary control
     Governmental accounting controlled by legal provisions
         Accounts organized on the basis of independent fund
     Legal provisions take priority over GAAP
     Budgetary accounts disclosed in statements
     Commercial accounting not subject to these restrictions

Governmental units often use modified accrual method

Revenue reported when measurable and available for the financing of expenditures

Expenditures recorded essentially when incurred

Fund financial statements (Expendable funds)

Balance sheet

Statements of Revenues, Expenditures, and Changes in Fund Balance

Commercial enterprises have retained earnings instead

fund balance (and a Statement of Changes in Financial Position)

b.   Budgeting is based on outlays rather than net income

I.e., inventories are often ignored

Except in enterprise and internal service funds

Inventories are considered when preparing budgets

c.   Depreciation is computed in enterprise and internal service funds

To measure profit or efficiency

To charge users with actual cost

UNOFFICIAL ANSWER

Problem 4   Municipal vs. Financial Accounting

a.   The most significant difference in purpose between municipal accounting and commercial accounting is that commercial enterprises are operated for profit, which places much emphasis on the proper determination of periodic earnings. Governmental units are primarily concerned with providing services to their citizens at minimum cost and reporting on the stewardship of public officials with respect to public funds, which places much emphasis on budgetary controls. However, some municipal units perform commercial services that are generally secondary to their tax-financed primary services.

Another difference in accounting purpose is that municipal accounting operations are controlled by legal provisions in constitutions, charters, and regulations having the force and effect of law. Because of these legal provisions and the diversity of its governmental operations, a municipality cannot use a single, unified set of accounts

for recording and summarizing all financial transactions. If there is a conflict between legal provisions and generally accepted accounting principles applicable to governmental units, legal provisions should take precedence to the extent that the accounting system must enable the ready disclosure of compliance. However, for financial reporting purposes, generally accepted accounting principles must take precedence. Commercial enterprises usually are not controlled by charters that are as restrictive; therefore, their accounting systems are designed differently.

Legislative action may limit the use of certain tax revenues for expenditure on particular programs, the methods of tax collection, or the rates of tax assessment. Such provisions must be reflected in the accounting system and be appropriately disclosed in the municipality's financial statements as a report on the stewardship of public officials with respect to public funds.

In governmental accounting all required accounts are organized on the basis of funds, each of which is independent of the other. Each fund must be so accounted for that the identity of its resources, obligations, revenues, expenditures, and fund balance is continually maintained. These purposes are accomplished by providing a complete self-balancing set of accounts for each fund.

The basis of accounting for the reporting on governmental units is often different from that used by commercial enterprises. For example, the accrual basis of accounting is recommended for all funds except the general, special revenue, debt service fund, capital projects, special assessments, agency, and expendable trust funds. These funds should be accounted for by the modified accrual method. The modified accrual method is recommended for these funds because some of their revenue sources are difficult to measure in advance and frequently become available only a short time before cash receipt.

Generally, fair presentation of financial position and results of operations in conformity with generally accepted accounting principles requires that the financial statements of expendable funds (those that use the modified accrual basis) include a balance sheet and a statement of revenues, expenditures, and changes in fund balance. In contrast, however, a commercial enterprise would usually prepare a statement of financial position, an earnings statement, a statement of retained earnings, and a statement of changes in financial position. The statement of revenues and expenditures of the general fund and certain special revenue funds should include a comparison with a formal budget in order to conform with generally accepted accounting principles; there is no such requirement for a commercial enterprise.

b.   Inventories are often ignored in governmental accounting because of an emphasis on budgeting revenues against outlays without looking behind the outlays to determine the extent to which they represent actual usage or consumption. Put another way, there is an emphasis on the cash or fiscal aspects rather than the operational aspects. This is easy to understand when one considers that general-fund expenditures for firemen's salaries and for the purchase of a new fire truck are accounted for in the same way.

However, inventories are not wholly ignored in governmental accounting. In those funds in which accounting parallels commercial accounting practice, such as enterprise funds, inventories are taken into consideration. Similarly, in an internal service fund concerned with rendering service involving the consumption of supplies or the delivery of stores to other funds and activities, the inventories of supplies or stores are taken into consideration in computing billings to departments serviced.

Inventories can and should be taken into consideration when preparing budgets. A fund, such as a general fund, having departments that possess large inventories at year end obviously has need for smaller appropriations for the coming year than it would if those departments had zero inventories.

c.   In municipal accounting the assigning of cost of assets with lives extending over several years to accounting periods through depreciation is not followed except in enterprise funds or internal service funds. Because governmental general-obligation credit does not rest upon financial condition but upon the power to tax, valuation is not significant.

There are four reasons for computing depreciation for governmental units: (1) profit measurement for enterprise and internal service funds, (2) cost accounting for services and programs, (3) measurement of a cost to be included in the basis for reimbursements or grants, and (4) systematic amortization of cost to recognize use or obsolescence. Thus, the primary purposes of computing depreciation on fixed assets of municipalities are to charge users with their share of the cost of governmental services and to evaluate the efficiency of programs.

SOLUTION GUIDE

Problem 5   School Journal Entries

1.   The requirement is to prepare all journal entries (except closing entries) during fiscal 1975 for the school district general fund. Thus, your objective is to reconcile the beginning and ending account balances with journal entries, i.e., prepare the journal entries required to change the beginning balance of each account to the ending balance.

2.   Work through the trial balance to gain familiarity with the accounts and to note required entries. For example: it is evident that the budgetary entry at the beginning of the year was:

Estimated revenues	$3,000,000	
Appropriations		$2,980,000
Fund balance		20,000

Upon journalizing this entry you have explained the change in the estimated revenues and the approrpiations account.

3.   Work through the additional information recording required journal entries. The objective is to explain the entries in each account as is provided in the second paragraph for the vouchers payable account.

3.1   The entry to record the estimated taxes receivable is

Taxes receivable	$2,870,000	
Revenues from taxes		$2,800,000
Estimated uncollectible taxes		70,000

The entry to record the taxes collected is

Cash	$2,810,000	
Taxes receivable		$2,810,000

The increase in taxes receivable account is $20,000 ($170,000 − $150,000) rather than $60,000 ($2,870,000 − $2,810,000), because $40,000 of taxes receivable were written off.

Estimated uncollectible taxes	$ 40,000		
Taxes receivable		$ 40,000	

The entries described in these two paragraphs explain the changes in both the taxes receivable and the estimated uncollectable taxes accounts.

3.2 The data from the vouchers payable account allows you to make the following entries.

Expenditures	$2,700,000	
Vouchers payable		$2,700,000

Expenditures—prior year	58,000	
Vouchers payable		58,000

Due to other funds	210,000	
Vouchers payable		210,000

Vouchers payable	2,640,000	
Cash		2,640,000

Above entries reconcile the beginning and ending vouchers payable balance. Also suggested by the above entries are entries to record encumbrances and to reverse them for $2,700,000. Additionally, the expenditures for prior years have a zero balance, so they have been closed to fund balance.

Encumbrances	$2,700,000	
Reserve for encumbrances		$2,700,000

Reserve for encumbrances	2,700,000	
Encumbrances		2,700,000

Reserve for encumbrances	60,000	
Expenditures—prior year		58,000
Fund balance		2,000

3.3 The $142,000 is recorded in due to other funds with the debit to expenditures. At this point, the expenditures account and the due to other funds account have been reconciled.

Expenditures	142,000	
Due to other funds		142,000

3.4 Record the purchase commitment which completes the reconciliation of both the encumbrances and reserve for encumbrances accounts.

Encumbrances	91,000	
Reserve for encumbrances		91,000

4. After making all of the apparent entries from 1) working through the trial balance, and 2) analyzing the additional information, work through the trial balance once again to make sure the change in every account has been reconciled.

4.1 The only accounts not reconciled by the above entries are cash and miscellaneous which can be completed by recording the miscellaneous revenues (the general fund is on a modified accrual basis where only tax revenue is accrued; other revenues are on the cash basis).

Cash	$ 130,000	
Misc. revenue		$ 130,000

UNOFFICIAL ANSWER

Problem 5   School Journal Entries

Note: The AICPA unofficial answer consisted of a listing of the above journal entries with a brief explanation of each.

SOLUTION GUIDE

Problem 6 Capital Projects Fund

1. This problem requires journal entries for a series of capital project fund transactions and a year-end balance sheet for the fund. It is not necessary to record the transactions in any other Fund or Group of Accounts.

2. For requirement 1, the solutions approach is to analyze each transaction and prepare the journal entry or entries needed. Remember that not all of the customary budgetary accounts are used in the capital projects fund; e.g., no estimated revenue or appropriation accounts are used in the capital projects fund because a separate fund is created for each project. Proceeds from grants, bond sales, etc., are considered revenue which is closed to the fund balance at year-end. Entries are usually made to encumbrances and reserve for encumbrances when commitments are made;

the encumbrance entry is reversed when the related expenditure is recorded. At year end the expenditures and remaining encumbrances are closed to the fund balance.

2.1 The $5,100,000 proceeds from the issue of bonds is debited to cash and credited to proceeds from sale of bonds which is a revenue account. The second entry associated with transaction 1 is to make an entry reflecting the transfer of the $100,000 premium ($5,100,000 − $5,000,000) to the debt service fund from which the bonds will be retired. The debit is to operating transfers out.

2.2 The first entry associated with the second transaction is to reflect the investment in commercial paper by debiting investments and crediting cash. The AICPA solution records the $140,000 as a debit to estimated revenue and a credit to appropriations.

Authors note: In light of the generalization made in 2 above, the entry for the estimated interest of $140,000 does not appear to be necessary.

2.3 The entry needed for the third transaction is to reflect the signing of the contract with F & A Construction Co. This event is recorded by debiting encumbrances and crediting reserve for encumbrances for $4,980,000.

2.4 Two entries are needed to reflect transaction 4. The first is to record the receipt of the $3,040,000 in cash consisting of principal and interest on the commercial paper investment. Since all of the interest income must be transferred to the debt service fund, an entry is needed to reflect the transfer by debiting operating transfers out and crediting cash.

2.5 Two entries are needed to reflect transaction 5. The first entry reflects the $3,000,000 expenditure on the library, a payment of $2,700,000 and a remaining $300,000 representing the amount retained. The second entry reverses $3,000,000 of the previous encumbrance entry made in transaction 3.

2.6 The first entry needed in transaction 6 is to accrue the $103,000 of interest receivable by debiting accrued interest receivable and crediting interest revenue. A second entry is needed to record the $103,000 obligation to the debt service fund; the debit is to operating transfers out.

The last three entries are needed to close the revenue, expenditure and encumbrance accounts to the fund balance. The closing entries (one compound entry is acceptable) are made by going through all of the entries made and identifying the debits or credits to nominal accounts.

3. The second requirement is to prepare the ending Balance Sheet for the City of Westgate Library Capital Projects Fund.

3.1 The solutions approach is to simply post the transactions in the problem using "T" accounts as needed and compute the ending balances. For example

CASH		
(1) 5,100,000	(1)	100,000
	(2)	4,900,000
(4) 3,040,000	(4)	40,000
	(5)	2,700,000
		400,000 End Bal.
8,140,000		8,140,000

INVESTMENTS		
(2) 4,900,000	(4)	3,000,000
		1,900,000 End. Bal.
4,900,000		4,900,000

3.2 Finally prepare the Balance Sheet in good form.

UNOFFICIAL ANSWER

Problem 6 Capital Projects Fund

a.

City of Westgate
LIBRARY CAPITAL PROJECTS FUND
JOURNAL ENTRIES
July 1, 1979 to June 30, 1980

		Debit	Credit
1.	Cash	$5,100,000	
	Proceeds of general obligation bonds		$5,100,000
	To record issuance of bonds		
	Operating transfers out	100,000	
	Cash		100,000
	To record transfer of premium to library debt service fund		

2. Investments 4,900,000
       Cash 4,900,000
   To record purchase of
       commercial paper
   Estimated revenues 140,000
       Appropriations 140,000
   To record estimated in-
       terest on investments

3. Encumbrances 4,980,000
       Reserve for
           encumbrances 4,980,000
   To record contract price
       for the building of
       the library

4. Cash 3,040,000
       Investments 3,000,000
       Interest revenue 40,000
   To record maturing of
       commercial paper
   Operating transfers out 40,000
       Cash 40,000
   To record transfer of in-
       terest earned on
       commercial paper
       to library debt
       service fund

5. Expenditures 3,000,000
       Cash 2,700,000
       Contracts payable—
           retained percentage 300,000
   Reserve for encumbrances 3,000,000
       Encumbrances 3,000,000
   To record progress billing
       and pay contractor
       net of retained
       amount and reverse
       encumbrances.

6. Accrued interest
       receivable 103,000
       Interest revenue 103,000
   Operating transfers out 103,000
       Due to library debt
           service fund 103,000
   To record accrued interest
       receivable and related
       interfund payable
   Proceeds of general
       obligation bonds 5,100,000
   Interest revenue 143,000
       Fund balance 5,103,000
       Estimated revenues 140,000
   Appropriations 140,000
   Fund balance 3,103,000
       Expenditures 3,000,000
       Operating transfers out 243,000
   Fund balance 1,980,000
       Encumbrances 1,980,000
   To close temporary
       accounts

b.

City of Westgate
LIBRARY CAPITAL PROJECTS FUND
BALANCE SHEET
June 30, 1980

Assets
Cash	$ 400,000
Accrued interest receivable	103,000
Investments	1,900,000
Total assets	$2,403,000

Liabilities and Fund Balance
Contracts payable—	
retained percentage	$ 300,000
Due to library debt service	103,000
Total liabilities	403,000
Fund balance:	
Reserve for encumbrances	1,980,000
Unreserved	20,000
Total fund balance	2,000,000
Total liabilities and fund balance	$2,403,000

CHAPTER EIGHT
TAX PROBLEMS AND SOLUTIONS

Federal income taxation appears primarily in practice. Interperiod and intra-period tax allocation questions are presented in the "tax deferrals" section of Chapter 4, Financial Accounting. Recently, 2 of the multiple choice practice problems test federal income taxation. One generally tests individual taxation and the other tests corporate taxation. Occasionally, a section of another problem will require calculation of deferred taxes.

The month-year, exam section, problem number, and objective question are given for each question, e.g., (579,Q2,19). Note that P = Practice I, Q = Practice II, and T = Theory.

Since federal income taxation rules and regulations vary from year to year, some of the exam items have been changed so that the question, solution, and explanation reflect the current law for which you are responsible. Where those exam problems and/or solutions have been changed to reflect current law, the problems are designated by † . Past coverage indicates that the tax law in effect during the immediately preceding calendar year is tested. Thus it would appear that the 1980 tax law will be tested on both 1981 CPA examinations.

TAX PROBLEM INDEX

	Exam Reference	Number of Minutes	Problem Page No.	Answer Page No.
Individual Taxation				
73 Multiple Choice				
1. Barton and Jones	1178,P5	50-60	955	967
2. Washington and Adam	1177,P5	50-60	956	969
Transactions in Property				
24 Multiple Choice				
Partnership taxation				
26 Multiple Choice				
1. Abcoe Engineering (adapted) [a]	1168,Q1	40-50	984	988

[a]A partnership computational problem has not appeared on recent exams. This problem has been included to give exposure to an overall solutions approach in the partnership taxation area.

	Exam Reference	Number of Minutes	Problem Page No.	Answer Page No.
Corporate Taxation				
51 Multiple Choice				
1. Right and Left Corporation	579,P5	40-50	999	1007
2. Liberty Inc.	576,P3	50-60	1000	1010
Sample Practice I Examination		220-270	1013	1068
Sample Practice II Examination		220-270	1025	1071

MULTIPLE CHOICE QUESTIONS   (1—73)

1. On January 1, 1979, James Davis was awarded a post-doctorate fellowship grant of $4,500 by a tax-exempt educational organization. Davis is not a candidate for a degree and was awarded the grant to continue his research. The grant was awarded for the period March 1, 1979, through July 31, 1980.

On March 1, 1979, Davis elected to receive the full amount of the grant. What amount should be included in his gross income for 1979?

- a. $0
- b. $1,500
- c. $3,000
- d. $4,500

2. During 1979, Dennis Wilson was granted a divorce from his wife. The divorce decree stipulated that he was to pay both alimony and child support for a specified period of time. The alimony payments were considered to be periodic payments for income tax purposes. The following information was abstracted from his 1979 records:

Salary	$100,000
Interest received on bank deposit	4,000
Interest received on municipal obligations	2,000
	$106,000
Alimony paid	$ 7,200
Child support paid	9,600

What is Wilson's adjusted gross income for 1979?

- a. $ 89,200
- b. $ 96,800
- c. $ 98,800
- d. $104,000

3. The records of Paul Thorpe, a cash-basis sole proprietor, for 1979 include the following information:

Gross receipts	$60,000
Dividend income (on personal investments)	400
Cost of sales	30,000
Other operating expenses	6,000
State business taxes paid	600
Federal self-employment tax paid	1,600

What amount should Thorpe report as net earnings from self-employment for 1979?

- a. $21,800
- b. $23,400
- c. $23,800
- d. $24,000

4. Seymour Thomas named his wife, Penelope, the beneficiary of a $100,000 (face amount) insurance policy on his life. The policy provided that upon his death, the proceeds would be paid to Penelope with interest over her present life expectancy, which was calculated at 25 years. Seymour died during 1979 and Penelope received a payment of $5,200 from the insurance company. What amount should she include in her gross income for 1979?

- a. $ 200
- b. $1,200
- c. $4,200
- d. $5,200

5. For the year ended December 31, 1979, David Roth, a married taxpayer filing a joint return, reported the following:

Investment income from dividends and interest	$24,000
Long-term capital gains	25,000
Investment expenses	4,000
Interest expense on funds borrowed in 1979 to purchase investment property	70,000

What amount can Roth deduct in 1979 as investment interest expense?

- a. $20,000
- b. $30,000
- c. $45,000
- d. $70,000

6. Martin Hart, who is not an outside salesman, earned a salary of $30,000 during the current year. During the year, he was required by his employer to take several overnight business trips, and he received an expense allowance of $1,500 for travel and lodging. In the course of these trips he incurred the following expenses which were either adjustments to income or deductions from adjusted gross income.

Travel	$1,100
Lodging	500
Entertainment of customers	400

What is Hart's adjusted gross income?

- a. $28,000
- b. $29,500
- c. $29,600
- d. $29,900

7. Ray and Alice Owens elected to file a joint tax return for the current year. Their adjusted gross income was $30,000. During the year they incurred and paid the following medical and related expenses:

Medical care insurance premium ($400 each)	$ 800
Medicines prescribed by doctors	450
Doctors	1,700
Transportation to and from doctors' offices	100

In addition, they received $900 as reimbursement from their insurance company for doctor bills paid during the year. In itemizing their deductions for the current year, what amount can they report as a medical expense deduction?

     a. $ 950
     b. $1,250
     c. $2,150
     d. $3,050

8. During 1979, Anita Simms was entirely supported by her three sons Dudley, Carlton and Isidore who provided support for her in the following percentages:

Dudley	8%
Carlton	45%
Isidore	47%

Which of the brothers is entitled to claim his mother as a dependent, assuming a multiple support agreement exists?

     a.   Dudley.
     b.   Dudley or Carlton.
     c.   Carlton or Isidore.
     d.   Dudley, Carlton or Isidore.

9. Nancy and Dennis Martin are married and file a joint income tax return. Both were employed during 1979 and earned the following salaries:

Dennis	$32,000
Nancy	14,000

In order to enable Nancy to work, she incurred at-home child care expenses of $6,000 for their two-year-old daughter and four-year-old son. What is the amount of the child care credit that they can claim for 1979?

     a. $ 400
     b. $ 800
     c. $1,200
     d. $2,800

10. Alvin Pearl is a self-employed individual. During the current year, his auto, which he used 75% for business and 25% for personal use, was totally destroyed in an accident.

The auto had a fair market value of $7,200 when destroyed, which was less than the auto's adjusted basis. Pearl received only $6,000 as a recovery from his insurance company.

What amount can Pearl deduct as a casualty loss for the current year if he were to itemize his personal deductions?

     a. $1,200
     b. $ 300
     c. $ 200
     d. $0

11. In October 1979, John Dill's wife was involved in an accident while driving the family automobile. Damage to the automobile was estimated at $300. Though fully insured, Dill was fearful that his automobile insurance rates would rise as a result of the accident. He did not notify his insurance company and had the automobile repaired at his own expense. What amount can he deduct as a casualty loss on his income tax return for 1979?

     a. $0
     b. $100
     c. $200
     d. $300

12. During the current year Mike Larsen sustained a serious injury in the course of his employment. As a result of the injury sustained, he received the following payments during the year:

Workmen's compensation	$1,200
Reimbursement from his employer's accident and health plan for medical expenses paid by Larsen	900
Damages for personal injuries	4,000

The amount to be included in Larsen's gross income for the current year should be

     a. $0
     b. $ 900
     c. $4,000
     d. $6,100

13. Harold Brodsky is an electrician employed by a contracting firm. During the current year he incurred and paid the following expenses:

Use of personal auto for company business	
(reimbursed by employer for $200)	$300
Specialized work clothes	550
Union dues	600
Cost of income tax preparation	150
Preparation of will	100

If Brodsky were to itemize his personal deductions, what amount should he claim as miscellaneous deductible expenses?

    a. $1,300
    b. $1,400
    c. $1,500
    d. $1,700

14.   During 1979, William Clark was assessed a deficiency on his 1978 federal income tax return. As a result of this assessment he was required to pay $1,120 determined as follows:

Additional tax	$900
Late filing penalty	60
Negligence penalty	90
Interest	70

What portion of the $1,120 would qualify as itemized deductions for 1979?

    a. $0
    b. $ 70
    c. $150
    d. $220

15.   Grace Allen is the owner of a two-family house which contains two identical apartments. Allen lives in one apartment and rents out the other. During the current year, the rental apartment was fully occupied, and she received $4,800 in rent. During the year, she paid the following amounts:

Real estate taxes	$2,200
Painting of rental apartment	600
Annual fire insurance premium	400

For the current year depreciation for the entire house was determined to be $3,000. Allen should include in her adjusted gross income for the current year

    a.   Income of $500.
    b.   Loss of $1,000.
    c.   Loss of $1,400.
    d.   Income of $1,400.

16.   John Wolf, who is 45 years old and unmarried, contributed $600 monthly in 1979 to the support of his parents' household. The parents lived alone and their income for 1979 consisted of $1,000 from quali-

fying dividends and interest, and $3,600 from Social Security. Based on the above information, what is Wolf's filing status for 1979, and how many exemptions should he claim on his tax return?

    a.   Single and 1 exemption.
    b.   Head of household and 1 exemption.
    c.   Single and 3 exemptions.
    d.   Head of household and 3 exemptions.

17.   Jon Parks, a cash-basis taxpayer, is the owner of an apartment building containing 20 identical apartments. Parks resides in one apartment and rents out the remaining units. For 1979 the following information was available.

Gross rental income	$43,200
Fuel	5,000
Maintenance and repairs	
(rental apartments)	2,400
Advertising for vacant apartments	600
Depreciation of building	10,000

What amount should Parks report as net rental income for 1979?

    a. $25,200
    b. $25,950
    c. $26,100
    d. $35,200

18.   In 1979 Uriah Stone received the following interest payments:

    ·   Interest of $400 on refund of federal income tax for 1976.
    ·   Interest of $300 on award for personal injuries sustained in an automobile accident during 1978.
    ·   Interest of $1,500 on municipal bonds.
    ·   Interest of $1,000 on United States savings bonds (Series H).

What amount, if any, should Stone report as interest income on his 1979 tax return?

    a. $0
    b. $ 700
    c. $1,700
    d. $3,200

19.   For the year 1979 Frances Quinn had a time savings account with the Benevolent Savings Bank. The following entries appeared in her passbook for 1979.

March 30, 1979, interest credited	$150
June 29, 1979, interest credited	$160
July 25, 1979, penalty forfeiture because of a premature withdrawal	$125
September 28, 1979, interest credited	$ 80
December 28, 1979, interest credited	$ 85

The above information should be reported by Ms. Quinn on her 1979 tax return as

    a.   Interest income of $350.

    b.   Interest income of $475.

    c.   Interest income of $475 and an itemized deduction for interest expense of $125.

    d.   Interest income of $475 and a deduction of $125 in arriving at adjusted gross income.

20.   Eugene and Linda O'Brien had adjusted gross income of $30,000 in 1979. Additional information is available for 1979 as follows:

Cash contribution to church	$1,500
Tuition paid to parochial school	1,200
Contribution to a qualified charity made by a bank credit card charge on December 14, 1979. The credit card obligation was paid on January 11, 1980.	250
Cash contribution to needy family	100

What is the maximum amount of the above that they can utilize in calculating excess itemized deductions for 1979?

    a. $1,500

    b. $1,750

    c. $2,700

    d. $3,050

21.   Roger Goodfriend's adjusted gross income was $50,000 in 1979. He made the following contributions to qualified charitable organizations during the year:

    · $10,000 cash

    ·   1,000 shares of common stock of Electronics Corporation (bought in 1974 for $5,000) with a fair market value of $17,000 on the date of the contribution.

What is the maximum amount Goodfriend can claim as a deduction for charitable contributions in 1979?

    a. $15,000

    b. $21,000

    c. $22,200

    d. $25,000

22.   During 1979 Mr. and Mrs. Benson provided substantially all the support, in their own home, for their son John, age 26, and for Mrs. Benson's cousin Nancy, age 17. John had $1,100 of income for 1979, and Nancy's income was $500. The Bensons paid the following medical expenses during the year:

Medicines and drugs;	
For themselves	$400
For John	500
For Nancy	100
Doctors:	
For themselves	600
For John	900
For Nancy	200

What is the total amount of medical expenses (before application of any limitation rules) that would enter into the calculation of excess itemized deductions on the Bensons' 1979 tax return?

    a. $1,000

    b. $1,300

    c. $2,400

    d. $2,700

23.   On December 24, 1979, Otis Johnson was seriously injured in a collision while driving his car. The car, which cost Johnson $6,000 and was used solely for personal use, had an appraised value of $4,200 for trade-in purposes just before the accident. After his release from the hospital on January 25, 1980, Johnson traded in the car for a new car at an allowance of $2,200. Johnson also received a settlement of $1,500 under his collision insurance policy in February 1980. What amount can he deduct as a casualty loss on his tax return, and in which year should the deduction be taken?

    a. $400 in 1979.

    b. $400 in 1980.

    c. $500 in 1979.

    d. $500 in 1980.

24.   The following information is available for Jack and Jill Moore, who reside in Indiana, for 1979:

Adjusted gross income	$10,500
Exemptions (including 2 exemptions claimed for being over 65)	4
Social Security benefits received	$3,000

An abstract from the Optional Sales Tax Table for Indiana is presented below:

	Sales Tax	
Income	Family Size 1&2	Family Size 3&4
$10,001-$12,000	$124	$148
$12,001-$14,000	$138	$165

Assuming that the Moores elect to use the Optional Sales Tax Table, what is the maximum amount of general sales taxes that they can utilize in calculating excess itemized deductions for 1979?

   a. $124
   b. $138
   c. $148
   d. $165

25. Robert Weber resides in a state that imposes a tax on income. The following information relating to Weber's state income taxes is available:

Taxes withheld in 1979	$3,000
Refund received in 1979 of 1978 tax	300
Assessment paid in 1979 of 1977 tax	800
Paid in 1980 with 1979 tax return	200

What amount should Weber utilize as state and local income taxes in calculating excess itemized deductions for his 1979 federal income tax return?

   a. $3,200
   b. $3,500
   c. $3,700
   d. $3,800

26. Richard Brown, who retired on May 31, 1979, receives a monthly pension benefit of $700 payable for life. The first pension check was received on June 15, 1979. During his years of employment, Brown contributed $14,700 to the cost of his company's pension plan. How much of the pension amounts received may Brown exclude from taxable income for the years 1979, 1980, and 1981?

	1979	1980	1981
a.	$ 0	$ 0	$ 0
b.	$4,900	$4,900	$4,900
c.	$4,900	$8,400	$1,400
d.	$4,900	$8,400	$8,400

27. Jerry and Ann Parsell paid the following expenses during 1979:

Interest on automobile loan	$1,500
Interest on bank loan (loan proceeds were used to purchase municipal bonds)	5,000
Interest on home mortgage for period January 1 to June 29, 1979	1,800
Penalty payment for prepayment of home mortgage on June 29, 1979	1,200

What is the maximum amount that the Parsells can utilize as interest expense in calculating excess itemized deductions for 1979?

   a. $3,300
   b. $4,500
   c. $8,300
   d. $9,500

28. The following information is available for Chester Hohn and his wife Pearl for 1979:

Adjusted gross income	$25,000
Payment to an Individual Retirement Account	1,500
Total itemized deductions	7,500

Based on the above information, the Hohns should report tax table income for 1979 of

   a. $16,000.
   b. $17,500.
   c. $19,400.
   d. $20,900.

29. Jim Planter, who reached age 65 on January 1, 1980, filed a joint return for 1979 with his wife Rita, age 50. Mary, their 21-year-old daughter, was a full-time student at a college until her graduation on June 2, 1979. The daughter had $6,500 of income and provided 25% of her own support during 1979. In addition, during 1979 the Planters were the sole support for Rita's niece, who had no income. How many exemptions should the Planters claim on their 1979 tax return?

   a.   2
   b.   3
   c.   4
   d.   5

30. Mr. and Mrs. Vonce, both age 62, filed a joint return for 1978. They provided all the support for their daughter who is 19, legally blind, and who has no income. Their son, age 21 and a full-time student at a university, had $4,200 of income and provided 70% of his own support during 1978. How many exemptions should Mr. and Mrs. Vonce have claimed on their 1978 joint income tax return?

a.   2
b.   3
c.   4
d.   5

31.   Bud Ace, a self-employed carpenter, reports his income on the cash basis. During 1978 he completed a job for a customer and sent him a bill for $3,000. The customer was not satisfied with the work and indicated that he would only pay $1,500. Ace agreed to reduce the bill to $2,000 but before payment was made the customer died. Ace could not collect from the customer's estate and should treat this loss as

a.   An ordinary business deduction of $3,000.
b.   An ordinary business deduction of $2,000.
c.   A short-term capital loss of $1,500.
d.   A nondeductible loss as no income was reported.

32.   Victor and Claire Anet, residents of a separate property state, were divorced in February 1978. Specific requirements of the divorce decree and Mr. Anet's performance of those requirements follow:

· Transfer title in their personal residence to Claire as part of a lump-sum property settlement. On the day of the transfer, Victor's basis in the house was $38,000, the fair market value was $42,000, and the property was subject to a mortgage of $20,000.
· Make the mortgage payments on the twenty-year mortgage. He paid $2,500 from March 1, 1978, through December 31, 1978.
· Repay to Claire a $3,000 loan which he did on April 1, 1978.
· Pay Claire $700 per month of which $200 is designated as child support. He made ten such payments in 1978.

Assuming that Claire has no other income, her 1978 gross income should be

a. $ 7,500
b. $ 9,500
c. $12,500
d. $16,000

33.   Gilbert Quinn loaned a friend $2,000 in 1976 and it had not been repaid in 1978 when the friend died insolvent. For 1978 Quinn should account for the nonpayment of the loan as a (an)

a.   Ordinary loss.
b.   Long-term capital loss.
c.   Short-term capital loss.
d.   Deduction from adjusted gross income.

34.   John Abel, whose wife died in December 1977, filed a joint tax return for 1977. He did not remarry but continued to maintain his home in which his two dependent children lived. In the preparation of his tax return for 1978, Abel should file as a

a.   Single individual.
b.   Surviving spouse.
c.   Head of household.
d.   Married individual filing separately.

35.   Sergio Morris, age 35, single with no dependents, is a self-employed individual. For the year 1978, his business sustained a net loss from operations of $18,000. There was no net operating loss in any prior year. The following additional information was obtained from his personal records for 1978:

Interest income	$2,000
Dividend income (after exclusion)	500
Itemized deductions, including a net casualty loss of $700	4,000
Personal exemption	750

Based upon the above information, what is his net operating loss for 1978?

a. $18,000
b. $18,700
c. $20,500
d. $22,000

36.   In July 1963 Dan Farley leased a building to Robert Shelter for a period of fifteen years at a monthly rental of $1,000 with no option to renew. At that time the building had a remaining estimated useful life of twenty years.

Prior to taking possession of the building, Shelter made improvements at a cost of $18,000. These improvements had an estimated useful life of twenty years at the commencement of the lease period. The lease expired on June 30, 1978, at which point the improvements had a fair market value of $2,000. The amount that Farley, the landlord, should include in his gross income for 1978 is

a. $ 6,000
b. $ 8,000
c. $10,500
d. $18,500

37.   For the year 1979 Roberta Collins, who is divorced, reported the following items of income:

Interest income	$ 100
Wages	4,000
Earnings from self-employment	3,000

She maintains a household for herself and her 5-year-old son who qualifies as her dependent. What is the maximum earned income credit available to her for 1979?

- a. $310
- b. $362.50
- c. $400
- d. $710

38. For the year 1978 George and Mary Kay, residents of a separate property state, reported the following dividends received on their respective investments:

George

Able Corporation (a domestic publicly listed corporation)	$ 70
Garvey Corporation (a Subchapter S corporation paid out of current earnings and profits)	200

Mary

Regan Corp. (a foreign corporation)	100

If the Kays file a joint tax return for 1978 what amount should they report as dividend income after the allowable exclusion?

- a. $170
- b. $200
- c. $300
- d. $370

39. Under the provisions of ERISA, deductible contributions to a qualified retirement plan on behalf of a self-employed individual whose earned income is $20,000 are limited to

- a. $1,500
- b. $2,000
- c. $3,000
- d. $7,500

40. During 1978 Seth Parker, a self-employed individual, paid the following taxes;

Federal income tax	$5,000
State income tax	2,000
Real estate taxes on land in South America (held as an investment)	900
State sales taxes	500
Federal self-employment tax	800
State unincorporated business tax	200

What amount can Parker claim for 1978 as an itemized deduction for taxes paid?

- a. $7,500
- b. $4,400
- c. $3,600
- d. $3,400

41. During 1978 Vincent Tally gave to the municipal art museum title to his private collection of rare books that was assessed and valued at $60,000. However, he reserved the right to the collection's use and possession during his lifetime. For 1978 he reported an adjusted gross income of $100,000. Assuming that this was his only contribution during the year, and that there were no carryovers from prior years, what amount can he deduct as contributions fror 1978?

- a. $0
- b. $30,000
- c. $50,000
- d. $60,000

42. On January 1, 1978, Sandy Beech, single and a sole proprietor, purchased a new machine for $40,000 to be used in her business. The machine was estimated to have a useful life of 10 years with a salvage value of $3,000. Beech, who uses the straight-line method of depreciation, elected to record additional first-year depreciation in 1978. What is the total maximum depreciation expense that she can deduct for this machine in 1978?

- a. $ 5,800
- b. $ 7,400
- c. $ 8,000
- d. $10,360

43. On September 18, 1978, Dennis Hanes was killed in an automobile accident. In October 1978 his widow received a lump sum death benefit from his employer in the amount of $15,000. For 1978 what amount should his widow include in adjusted gross income assuming a joint tax return were filed?

- a. $0
- b. $10,000
- c. $14,000
- d. $15,000

44. Mrs. Irma Felton, by herself, maintains her home in which she and her unmarried son reside. Her son, however, does not qualify as her dependent. Mrs. Felton's husband died in 1977. What is Mrs. Felton's filing status for 1978?

- a. Single.
- b. Surviving spouse.
- c. Head of household.
- d. Married filing jointly.

45. Jack and Joan Mitchell, married taxpayers and residents of a separate property state, elect to file a joint return for 1978 during which they received the following dividends:

	Received by	
	Jack	Joan
Alert Corporation (a qualified, domestic corporation)	$400	$ 50
Canadian Mines, Inc. (a Canadian Company)		300
Eternal Life Mutual Insurance Company (dividends on life insurance policy)	200	

For 1978 what amount should the Mitchells report on their joint return as dividend income net of the allowable dividend exclusion?

- a. $550.
- b. $600.
- c. $750.
- d. $800.

46. Arthur Mends, age 19, is a full-time student at Gordon College and a candidate for a bachelor's degree. During 1978 he received the following payments:

State scholarship for ten months	$2,400
Loan from college financial aid office	1,000
Cash support from parents	2,000
Cash dividends on qualified investments	500
Cash prize awarded in contest	300
	$6,200

What is his adjusted gross income for 1978?

- a. $700.
- b. $800.
- c. $3,200.
- d. $6,200.

47. For the year 1978 Fred and Wilma Todd reported the following items of income:

	Fred	Wilma
Salary	$40,000	—
Interest income	1,000	$ 200
Cash prize won on T.V. game show	—	8,800
	$41,000	$9,000

Fred is not covered by any qualified retirement plan and he and Wilma established individual retirement accounts during the year. Assuming a joint return was filed for 1978, what is the maximum amount that they can be allowed for contributions to their individual retirement accounts?

- a. $1,500.
- b. $1,750.
- c. $6,000.
- d. $7,500.

48. James Martin received the following compensation and fringe benefits from his employer during 1978:

Salary	$50,000
Year-end bonus	10,000
Medical insurance premiums paid by employer	1,000
Allowance paid for moving expenses	5,000

What amount of the preceding payments should be included in Martin's 1978 gross income?

- a. $60,000.
- b. $61,000.
- c. $65,000.
- d. $66,000.

49. Which of the following is deductible to arrive at adjusted gross income?

- a. Unreimbursed dues to AICPA by an employee of an accounting firm.
- b. Unreimbursed union dues by an employee of a company.
- c. Medical expenses of a self-employed individual.
- d. None of the above.

50. On July 1, 1976, the original date of issue David Karp purchased for $9,520, a $10,000 ten-year bond of the Expoxy Corporation. The bond was issued for long-term financing. On January 31, 1978, he sold the bond to an unrelated party for $9,800. What amount should Karp report as a long-term capital gain from this transaction?

- a. $76.
- b. $204.
- c. $200.
- d. $280.

51. In gathering information for her income tax return for 1978, Mabel Herzog listed the following miscellaneous expenses incurred and paid for in 1978:

Hobby expenses (not engaged in for profit)	$500
Union dues	400
Employment agency fees paid in securing a new job in same profession	200
Legal fees paid in connection with a libel suit	700

What can Herzog report as allowable deductions from adjusted gross income?

    a. $600.
    b. $1,100.
    c. $1,300.
    d. $1,800.

52.   During 1978 George Burke, a salaried taxpayer, paid the following taxes which were not incurred in connection with a trade or business:

Federal income tax (withheld by employer)	$1,500
State income tax (withheld by employer)	1,000
F.I.C.A. tax (withheld by employer)	700
State sales taxes	900
Federal auto gasoline taxes	200
Federal excise tax on telephone bills	50

What taxes are allowable deductions from Burke's adjusted gross income for 1978?

    a. $4,350.
    b. $2,850.
    c. $2,550.
    d. $1,900.

53.   During 1978, Albert Mason purchased the following long-term investments at par:

$10,000 general obligation bonds of
  Tulip County (wholly tax exempt)
$10,000 debentures of Laxity Corporation

He financed these purchases by obtaining a loan from the Community Bank for $20,000. For the year 1978, he paid the following amounts as interest expense:

Community Bank	$1,600
Interest on mortgage	3,000
Interest on installment purchases	300
	$4,900

What amount can Mason deduct as interest expense in 1978?

    a. $4,900.
    b. $4,100.
    c. $3,600.
    d. $3,300.

54.   Gilda Bach is a cash basis self-employed consultant. For the year 1978 she determined that her net income from self-employment was $80,000. In reviewing her books you determine that the following items were included as business expenses in arriving at the net income of $80,000:

Salary drawn by Gilda Bach	$20,000
Estimated federal self-employment and income taxes paid	6,000
Malpractice insurance premiums	4,000
Cost of attending professional seminar	1,000

Based upon the above information, what should Gilda Back report as her net self-employment income for 1978?

    a. $91,000.
    b. $105,000.
    c. $106,000.
    d. $110,000.

55.   Phil Collins owns numerous oil leases in the Southwest. During 1978 he made several trips to inspect oil wells on the leases and to consult about future oil wells to be drilled on these sites. As a result of these overnight trips, he paid the following expenses:

Plane fares	$4,000
Hotels	1,000
Meals	800
Entertaining lessees	500

Of the $6,300 in expenses incurred, he can claim as deductible expenses

    a. $6,300.
    b. $5,800.
    c. $5,500.
    d. $5,000.

MAY 1981 QUESTIONS

56.   Phil and Joan Crawley made the following payments during 1980:

Interest on bank loan (loan proceeds were used to purchase United States savings bonds Series H)	$4,000
Interest on installment charge accounts	500
Interest on home mortgage for period April 1 to December 31, 1980	2,700
Points paid to obtain conventional mortgage loan on April 1, 1980	900

What is the maximum amount that the Crawleys can utilize as interest expense in calculating excess itemized deductions for 1980?

    a. $4,100.
    b. $7,200.
    c. $7,600.
    d. $8,100.

57.   Richard and Alice Kelley lived apart during 1980 and did not file a joint tax return for the year. Under the terms of the written separation agreement they signed on July 1, 1980, Richard was required to pay Alice $1,500 per month of which $600 was designated as child support. He made six such payments in 1980. Additionally, Richard paid Alice $1,200 per month for the first six months of 1980, no portion of which was designated as child support. Assuming that Alice has no other income, her tax return for 1980 should show gross income of

    a. $0.
    b. $ 5,400.
    c. $ 9,000.
    d. $12,600.

58.   During 1980 Howard Thomson maintained his home in which he and his sixteen-year old son resided. The son qualifies as his dependent. Thomson's wife died in 1979, for which year a joint return was appropriately filed. Thomson remarried on March 15, 1981. What is Thomson's filing status for 1980?

    a.   Single.
    b.   Head of household.
    c.   Surviving spouse.
    d.   Married filing jointly.

59.   Henry Adams, an unmarried taxpayer, received the following amounts during 1980:

Interest on savings accounts	$1,000
Interest on municipal bonds	500
Dividends on General Steel common stock	750
Dividends on life insurance policies	200

Adams should report taxable income, after exclusions, if any, from dividends and interest for 1980 in the total amount of

    a. $1,650.
    b. $1,750.
    c. $1,850.
    d. $2,150.

60.   Frank Clarke, an employee of Smithson Company, was covered under a noncontributory pension plan. Frank died on April 15, 1980, at age 64 and pursuant to the plan, his widow received monthly pension payments of $500 beginning May 1, 1980. In addition Mrs. Clarke received an employee death payment of $10,000 in May 1980. What is the total amount of the above receipts that the widow should exclude from her gross income for 1980?

    a. $ 5,000.
    b. $ 9,000.
    c. $10,000.
    d. $14,000.

61.   Benedict Atley, who is single, was out of work in the early months of 1980 and received $2,800 of unemployment benefits from his state of residence. His adjusted gross income was $22,500 for 1980 excluding the $2,800 of unemployment benefits. Assuming that Atley had no other items of income or adjustments to gross income, what amount must Atley report as adjusted gross income on his income tax return for 1980?

    a. $22,500.
    b. $23,750.
    c. $25,150.
    d. $25,300.

62.   Jim and Nancy Walton had adjusted gross income of $35,000 in 1980. During the year they paid the following medical related expenses:

Medicines and drugs	$300
Doctors	700
Health Club membership (recommended by the family doctor for general health care)	400
Medical care insurance	280

How much may the Waltons utilize as medical expenses in calculating excess itemized deductions for 1980?

    a. $330.
    b. $230.
    c. $140.
    d. $0

63.   Nelson Harris had adjusted gross income in 1980 of $60,000. During the year his personal summer home was completely destroyed by a cyclone. Pertinent data with respect to the home follows:

Cost basis	$39,000
Value before casualty	45,000
Value after casualty	3,000

Harris was partially insured for his loss and in 1980 he received a $15,000 insurance settlement. What is Harris' allowable casualty loss deduction for 1980?

    a. $23,900.
    b. $24,000.
    c. $26,900.
    d. $27,000.

64. Don and Cynthia Wallace filed a joint return for 1980 in which they reported adjusted gross income of $35,000. During 1980 they made the following contributions to qualified organizations:

Land (stated at its current fair market value)
 donated to church for new building site $22,000
Cash contributions to church   300
Cash contributions to the local community
 college   200

Assuming that the Wallaces did not elect to reduce the deductible amount of the land contribution by 40% of the property's appreciation in value, how much can they claim as a deduction for charitable contributions in 1980?

a. $10,800.
b. $11,000.
c. $17,500.
d. $22,500.

65. Dennis Cowper, age 25 and single, provided the following information for his 1980 income tax return:

Adjusted gross income $20,000
Personal exemption   1,000
Total itemized deductions   2,600

Cowper should report tax table income for 1980 of

a. $17,400.
b. $18,700.
c. $19,600.
d. $19,700.

66. Bill McDonald, a cash-basis taxpayer, is the owner of a house with two identical apartments. He resides in one apartment and rents the other apartment to a tenant under a five-year lease dated March 1, 1979, and expiring on February 29, 1984. The tenant made timely monthly rental payments of $500 for the months of January through November 1980. Rents for December 1980 and January 1981 were paid by the tenant on January 5, 1981. The following additional information for 1980 was available:

Fuel and utilities $3,600
Depreciation of building   3,000
Maintenance and repairs
 (rental apartment)   400
Insurance on building   600

What amount should McDonald report as net rental income for 1980?

a. $2,200.
b. $2,000.
c. $1,700.
d. $1,500.

67. Jon and Connie Cooke, who are filing a joint return for 1980, elect to use the Optional Sales Tax

Table which allows them to deduct general sales taxes of $400 based on their gross income and family size. During 1980 they paid general sales taxes on the following large purchases:

	General sales taxes paid
Purchase of a new car for $8,500	$510
Purchase of wearing apparel during year totaling $3,000	180

What is the maximum amount of general sales taxes that the Cookes can utilize in calculating excess itemized deductions for 1980?

a. $ 400.
b. $ 580.
c. $ 910.
d. $1,090.

68. Albert and Lois Stoner, age 66 and 64, respectively, filed a joint tax return for 1980. They provided all of the support for their blind 19-year-old son, who has no gross income. Their 23-year-old daughter, a full-time student until her graduation on June 14, 1980, earned $2,000, which was 40% of her total support during 1980. Her parents provided the remaining support. The Stoners also provided the total support of Lois' father, who is a citizen and life-long resident of Peru. How many exemptions can the Stoners claim on their 1980 income tax return?

a. 4.
b. 5.
c. 6.
d. 7.

69. Fred Harvey itemized deductions on his 1979 income tax return and his total itemized deductions exceeded the zero bracket amount by $1,000. Harvey plans to itemize deductions again in 1980 and the following information relating to his state income taxes is available:

Taxes withheld in 1980 $2,500
Refund received in 1980 of
 1979 tax   500
Assessment paid in 1980 of
 1978 tax   700

The above information should be reported by Harvey in his 1980 tax return as:

a. State and local income taxes of $2,500.
b. State and local income taxes of $2,700.
c. State and local income taxes of $3,200.
d. State and local income taxes of $3,200 and income from state and local income tax refund of $500.

70.   During 1980 Mr. and Mrs. West paid the following taxes:

Property taxes on residence	$1,800
Special assessment for installation of a sewer system in their town	1,000
State personal property tax on their automobile	600
Property taxes on land held for long-term appreciation	300

What amount can the Wests deduct as property taxes in calculating excess itemized deductions for 1980?

    a. $2,100.
    b. $2,700.
    c. $3,100.
    d. $3,700.

71.   During 1980 William and Jane Conley made the following energy-conserving component additions to their personal residence (a five-year-old house purchased by them in July 1980):

Aluminum siding (on the north side of the house)	$1,000
Insulation	750
Automatic setback thermostat	150
Used storm windows (purchased from an unrelated party)	300

Assuming that the Conleys have a tax liability of $3,000 without any other credits against their tax for 1980, what amount can they claim as a residential energy credit on their 1980 income tax return?

    a. $135.
    b. $180.
    c. $300.
    d. $330.

72.   Robert and Mary Jason, filing a joint tax return for 1980, had a tax liability of $9,000 based on their tax table income and three exemptions. Robert and Mary had earned income of $20,000 and $12,000, respectively, during 1980. In order for Mary to be gainfully employed, the Jasons incurred the following employment-related expenses for their four-year-old son John in 1980:

Payee	Amount
Union Day Care Center	$1,500
Acme Home Cleaning Service	500
Wilma Jason, babysitter (Robert Jason's mother)	1,000

Assuming that the Jasons do not claim any other credits against their tax, what is the amount of the child care tax credit they should report on their tax return for 1980?

    a. $300.
    b. $400.
    c. $500.
    d. $600.

73.   Baxter Manufacturer, Inc., a calendar-year corporation, bought the following new assets during 1980:

Property	Date bought	Date placed in service	Useful life (years)	Cost
Manuals	Jan. 2	Jan. 4	2	$ 210
Truck	April 1	June 30	3	15,000
Desk and chair	Dec. 1	Dec. 31	7	1,200

Baxter's total qualified investment in 1980 for computation of the investment credit is

    a. $2,570.
    b. $3,920.
    c. $6,200.
    d. $6,270.

REPEAT QUESTION

(581,P3,60)   Identical to item 46 above

Problem 1   Barton and Jones (1178,P5)

(50 to 60 minutes)

This problem consists of two unrelated parts.

Part a. Harold Barton is a self-employed manufacturers' representative. The following schedule of receipts and disbursements for the calendar year 1977 was prepared by his secretary from the cash book that she maintains for his business:

Cash receipts:

Commissions received	$65,100	
Rent for office sublease	5,000	
Insurance company payment	3,600	
Total cash receipts		$73,700

Cash disbursements:

Harold Barton's withdrawals	22,000	
Secretary's salary (net of taxes withheld)	8,000	
Commissions paid to outsiders	12,000	
Office rent	14,000	
Payment to Keogh retirement plan	3,000	
Automobile expenses	1,800	
Office expenses	1,160	
Country club dues and expenses	3,900	
Payroll taxes remitted:		
Taxes withheld from secretary's salary	1,262	
Employer's payroll taxes	825	
Total cash disbursements		67,947
Excess of cash receipts over cash disbursements		$ 5,753

Additional information is as follows:
· Depreciation for 1977 on fixed assets used in Barton's business was as follows:

Automobile	$1,000
Office equipment	1,600
	$2,600

· The insurance company payment was in settlement of a court suit that arose from a December 1976 automobile accident involving Mr. Barton. The payment was as follows:

Compensation for personal injuries sustained	$2,900
Repairs to automobile	700
	$3,600

Mr. Barton had paid $700 for the car repairs in 1976 and had claimed this payment as a business expense in 1976. The car involved in the accident is used 100% for business purposes.

· Of the country club dues and expenses totaling $3,900, Mr. Barton has kept records which show that 60% of the total amount was incurred in connection with his business.

· During 1977 Mr. Barton signed up to participate in a Keogh (HR—10) retirement plan. In December 1977 he made an initial contribution to the plan of $3,000 and in January 1978 made a second contribution of $1,000. His secretary was not eligible and thus not covered by the plan in 1977.

· Mr. and Mrs. Barton jointly owned 100 shares of common stock of Bramma Corporation which they acquired in 1975 for $6,900. On November 1, 1977, they sold these shares for $3,400.

· During 1977 Mr. and Mrs. Barton gave $600 to recognized charitable organizations and donated old clothes valued at $275 to a needy family in their neighborhood.

· The following taxes were paid in 1977:

Real estate (residence) taxes	$2,330
Sales taxes	770
State gasoline taxes on automobile used for personal use	102
State income tax (balance 1976)	625
State income tax (estimate 1977)	750
Federal income tax (balance 1976)	460
Federal income tax (estimate 1977)	3,750

Required:
1. Prepare a schedule to compute the adjusted gross income of Harold and Bella Barton for 1977. Prepare a supporting schedule for Harold Barton's income from self-employment. Any possible alternative treatments should be resolved in a manner that will minimize income taxes for 1977. Show supporting computations in good form.

2. Prepare a schedule to compute the total itemized deductions of Harold and Bella Barton for 1977. Any possible alternative treatments should be resolved in a manner that will minimize income taxes for 1977. Show supporting computations in good form.

Part b.   For the calendar year 1977, Agnes Jones, a widow and the mother of a four-year-old son, reported the following types of income:

Salary	$18,000
Interest income	4,000
Dividend income	
(all qualifying dividends)	600
1976 state income tax refund	700
	$23,300

An analysis of her cash expenses indicated the following:

Doctor bills	$2,400
Drugs prescribed by doctors	300
Medical insurance premiums	800
Interest paid on installment purchases	180
Real estate taxes paid (residence)	2,000
Child care expenses (paid to the Happy Day Nursery in order for Agnes to be gainfully employed)	3,600

Additional information is as follows:
  · Interest income was comprised of the following amounts:

Interest on savings deposits	$2,200
Interest on state obligations	1,800
	$4,000

· Her W-2 form for 1977 stated that $790 was withheld for state income taxes.
· Mrs. Jones included a deduction of $900 for state income taxes in her 1976 itemized deductions.

Required:
1. Prepare a schedule to compute Agnes Jones's adjusted gross income for 1977.
2. Prepare a schedule to compute Agnes Jones's total itemized deductions for 1977. Prepare a supporting schedule for Agnes Jones's deductible medical expenses.
3. Determine the amount of the child care credit that Agnes Jones can apply against her 1977 federal income tax.

Problem 2   Washington and Adam   (1177,P5)

(50 to 60 minutes)

This problem consists of two unrelated parts.

Part a.   Mr. Washington has asked you to compute the adjusted gross income for his federal income tax return for the 1976 calendar year. You have gathered the following information:

· Washington is 55 years old and single. He furnishes over one-half the total support of his widowed mother who lives with him. Washington's mother received social security benefits of $3,000 and interest income on savings accounts of $2,000 in 1976.
· On December 31, 1975, Washington retired. Washington's employer had bought retirement annuities for Washington for which Washington had contributed nothing. Retirement benefits received by Washington in 1976 were $12,000.
· Prior to his retirement, Washington had purchased for $40,000 an annuity that would pay him $300 a month starting January 1, 1976. The expected return under the annuity contract is $50,000.
· In 1976, Washington worked part time as a consultant. He earned $9,000 in fees and incurred $1,000 of various business expenses relative to his consulting work in 1976. Not included in the various business expenses given above is $200 that Washington paid to a housekeeper to watch his mother and clean the house while he was away from home on a business trip.

Washington uses his automobile in his consulting work. The automobile was used 40% in his consulting work and 60% for nonbusiness purposes. The total costs incurred in 1976 relative to this automobile were $1,850. The mileage allowance method would result in a deduction of $725. Washington did not include any automobile expenses in the various business expenses given above.
· On January 15, 1976, Washington's uncle died and Washington received $30,000 as the beneficiary under one of his uncle's insurance policies.
· Washington received dividends from domestic corporations of $500 in 1976.
· Washington had interest income in 1976 as follows:

Interest income from savings accounts	$ 300
Interest income from obligations of the United States	200
Interest income on municipal obligations	100

· Washington had capital transactions in 1976 as follows:

Gain on sale of common stock purchased in July 1974	$1,350
Loss on sale of common stock purchased in May 1975	1,150
Gain on sale of common stock purchased in April 1976 and sold in June 1976	700
Gain on sale of common stock purchased in February 1976 and sold in December 1976	200

(The alternative tax would not result in the minimization of taxable income.)

Required:

Prepare a schedule showing the adjusted gross income that should appear on Washington's federal income tax return for the 1976 calendar year. Any possible alternative treatments should be resolved in a manner that will minimize taxable income. Show supporting computations in good form.

Part b. Mr. and Mrs. Adam have asked you to compute the itemized deductions for their joint federal income tax return for the 1976 calendar year. Their adjusted gross income was $25,000. You have gathered the following information for 1976:

Medical and dental expenses:

Hospital bills for Mrs. Adam (80% of which was reimbursed by hospitalization insurance)	$2,200
Dental bills (including $1,100 for orthodontic braces for son)	1,600
Doctor bills	400
Life insurance premiums with wife as beneficiary	300
Medicine and drugs	275
Diaper service for daughter	220
Contact lenses (comparable eyeglasses would cost $50)	150
Transportation expenses in connection with medical expenses	70

Taxes:

Real estate taxes	$1,100
Employee portion of social security taxes withheld by Mr. Adam's employer	895
State income taxes withheld by Mr. Adam's employer	700
State sales taxes paid	240
State gasoline taxes	75

Interest expense:

Home mortgage	$1,400
Loan for family car	500
Debt incurred to buy municipal obligations	300
Finance charges on credit cards	100

Contributions:

Tuition paid to parochial school for son	$ 800
Art object purchased at church bazaar (fair value $500)	750
Cash contributed to church	260
Cash pledge to nonprofit college paid in January 1977	140
Fair value of used clothing contributed to church	90

Miscellaneous:

Union dues	$ 65
Fines for illegal parking	50
Registration for family car	25
Driver's license fees	10

Required:

1. Prepare a schedule showing the itemized deductions that should appear on Mr. and Mrs. Adam's joint federal income tax return for the 1976 calendar year. Any possible alternative treatments should be resolved in a manner that will minimize taxable income. Show supporting computations in good form.

2. List the items in the fact situation which were not used to determine the answer to 1. above. Explanations are not required.

MULTIPLE CHOICE ANSWERS

1.	a	16.	d	31.	d	46.	a	61.	c
2.	b	17.	b	32.	a	47.	b	62.	c
3.	b	18.	c	33.	c	48.	c	63.	a
4.	a	19.	d	34.	b	49.	d	64.	b
5.	b	20.	b	35.	b	50.	b	65.	d
6.	d	21.	d	36.	a	51.	a	66.	d
7.	a	22.	d	37.	b	52.	d	67.	c
8.	c	23.	a	38.	c	53.	b	68.	b
9.	b	24.	b	39.	c	54.	c	69.	d
10.	c	25.	d	40.	d	55.	a	70.	b
11.	a	26.	c	41.	a	56.	d	71.	a
12.	a	27.	b	42.	a	57.	b	72.	b
13.	a	28.	d	43.	b	58.	c	73.	c
14.	b	29.	d	44.	c	59.	a		
15.	d	30.	b	45.	b	60.	a		

EXPLANATION OF MULTIPLE CHOICE ANSWERS

1. (1180,Q2,21)   (a)   The requirement is to determine the amount to be included in Davis' gross income for 1979 from the fellowship grant. Scholarships and fellowships are generally excluded. But if the recipient is not a candidate for a degree, the grant must be from a government or tax-exempt organization, and the exclusion is limited to $300 times the number of months for which the grant is received (maximum of 36 months). For the 17-month period of the grant (March 1, 1979 thru July 31, 1980) up to $5,100 may be excluded, which is in excess of the amount received. Therefore, $0 is included in Davis' gross income for 1979.

2. (1180,Q2,24)   (b)   The requirement is to calculate Wilson's adjusted gross income. First, one must calculate gross income. Both the salary ($100,000) and the bank interest ($4,000) are included in gross income. The interest received on the municipal obligations is excluded from gross income. Therefore, total gross income is $104,000. The alimony payments are periodic and deductible toward adjusted gross income. The child support payments are not deductible. Therefore, the $104,000 of gross income reduced by the $7,200 of alimony results in adjusted gross income of $96,800.

3. (1180,Q2,26)   (b)   The requirement is to calculate Thorpe's net earnings from self-employment. The gross receipts of $60,000 are reduced by the cost of sales ($30,000), other operating expenses ($6,000), and state business taxes ($600). The dividend income on personal investments is not included in earnings from self-employment, and the self-employment taxes are not deductible. Thus, the computation of Thorpe's net earnings from self-employment is as follows:

Gross receipts	$60,000
Cost of sales	− 30,000
Gross Margin	$30,000
Other operating expenses	− 6,000
State business taxes paid	− 600
Net Self-Employment Earnings	$23,400

4. (1180,Q2,28)   (a)   The requirement is to determine the amount of life insurance payments to be included in a widow's gross income. Life insurance proceeds paid by reason of death are excluded from income if paid in a lump sum or in installments. If the payments are received in installments, the principal amount of the policy divided by the number of payments is excluded each year. In addition, a surviving spouse is entitled to a $1,000 per year exclusion. Therefore, only $200 of the $5,200 insurance payment is included in Penelope's gross income:

Annual installment	$5,200
Principal amount ($100,000 ÷ 25)	− 4,000
	$1,200
Surviving spouse's exclusion	− 1,000
Amount included in gross income	$ 200

5. (1180,Q2,30)   (b)   The requirement is to determine the amount deductible as investment interest expense. The deduction for investment interest is limited to $10,000 plus the amount of net investment income. Since the net investment income is $20,000 (dividends and interest of $24,000, less investment expense of $4,000), the deduction for investment interest expense is $30,000 ($20,000 + $10,000).

6. (1180,Q2,31)   (d)   The requirement is to calculate adjusted gross income. First the expense allowance of $1,500 for travel and lodging must be combined with the salary of $30,000 to arrive at gross income of $31,500. Then one must determine whether deductions are TOWARD AGI or FROM AGI. Travel and lodging expense are always deductible TOWARD AGI. Therefore, a deduction of $1,600 ($1,100 travel expense + $500 lodging expense) results in AGI of $29,900. Entertainment expenses are deductible TOWARD AGI only if reimbursed. Since the entertainment expenses of $400 were not reimbursed, they must be deducted FROM AGI.

7. (1180,Q2,32)   (a)   The $1700 paid to doctors is reduced by the $900 insurance reimbursement and the medical expense deduction is computed as follows:

Insurance Premium (½ or max. $150)		$150
Medicine and Drugs	$ 450	
Less 1% of AGI ($30,000)	(300)	
	$ 150	
Insurance Prem. in excess of $150	650	
Transportation to doctors' offices	100	
Doctors ($1,700-$900)	800	
	$1,700	
Less 3% of AGI ($30,000)	900	800
Amount Deductible		$950

Remember that 50% of medical insurance (limited to $150) is fully deductible and not subject to any percent limitation. Medicine and drugs are included in medical expense only to the extent in excess of 1% of AGI. In turn, medicine and drug expenses in excess of 1% of AGI, other medical expenses, and medical insurance premiums in excess of $150 are subject to a 3% of AGI limitation.

8. (1180,Q2,33)   (c)   The requirement is to determine which of the brothers is entitled to claim his mother as a dependent. The support test requires an individual to furnish over one-half of a dependent's support. In the event no one person provides more than 50% of the dependent's support, any individual who contributed more than 10% is entitled to claim the exemption if each other person contributing more than 10% of the support signs a written consent not to claim the exemption, i.e., multiple support agreement. Therefore, only Carlton or Isidore (who each contributed more than 10%) may claim their mother as a dependent.

9. (1180,Q2,34)   (b)   The requirement is to calculate the amount of child care credit the Martins can claim. A tax credit of 20% of the eligible child care expenses incurred to enable Nancy to work is allowed. Married couples must file a joint return, which they did. The children qualified because they are both under 15 years of age. The maximum amount of expenses that can be taken is limited to the lesser of 1) the smaller of either spouse's earned income, 2) $4,000 for two or more dependents, or, 3) the actual expenses incurred. Therefore, 20% of $4,000 ($800) is the maximum amount of child care credit available to the Martins.

10. (1180,Q2,35)   (c)   The requirement is to determine the amount of casualty loss deductible as an itemized deduction. Only personal casualty losses are deductible as itemized deductions. Since the auto was used 25% for personal use, 25% of the insurance company settlement must be subtracted from 25% of the FMV to determine the personal loss.

	Personal (25%)
FMV ($7,200)	$1800
Insurance Settlement ($6,000)	1500
Personal Casualty Loss	$ 300

Each personal casualty or theft loss is deductible only to the extent that it exceeds $100. Therefore, Alvin Pearl may deduct a personal casualty loss of $200 as an itemized deduction.

11. (1180,Q2,36)   (a)   A casualty loss must be reduced by any insurance recovery that is available. Since Dill voluntarily elects not to claim an insurance recovery, no casualty loss deduction is allowed for the damage resulting from the automobile accident.

12. (1180,Q2,37)   (a)   All three items that Larsen received as a result of his injury are excluded from gross income. Benefits received under workmen's compensation and compensation received for damages resulting from personal injury are always excluded. Amounts received from an employer's accident and health plan as reimbursement for medical expenses are excluded as long as the medical expenses were not previously deducted as itemized deductions.

13. (1180,Q2,38)   (a)   The requirement is to compute the amount of miscellaneous itemized deductions. The cost of uniforms not adapable to general use (specialized work clothes), union dues, and the cost of income tax preparation are all miscellaneous itemized deductions. The excess of auto expense over the amount of reimbursement is always deductible TOWARD AGI. The preparation of a will is personal in nature, and is not deductible. Thus, the computation of Brodsky's miscellaneous itemized deductions is as follows:

Specialized work clothes	$ 550
Union Dues	600
Cost of income tax preparation	150
	$1,300

14. (1180,Q2,39)   (b)   Of the items listed relating to the tax deficiency for 1978, only the interest is deductible. The additional federal income tax, the late filing penalty, and the negligence penalty are not deductible. Therefore, only $70 relating to the tax deficiency is deductible as an itemized deduction for 1979.

15. (1180,Q2,40) (d) The requirement is to compute Allen's net rental income or loss to be included in adjusted gross income. Since the two apartments are identical and only one is rented, one-half of all expenses common to both apartments should be deducted. The net rental income is computed as follows:

Rental Income	$4,800
Taxes (½ of $2,200)	(1,100)
Painting of rental apt.	(600)
Insurance (½ of $400)	(200)
Depreciation (½ of $3,000)	(1,500)
Net Rental Income	$1,400

The remainder of the real estate taxes ($1,100) is deductible as an itemized deduction. The balance of the insurance and the depreciation are not deductible.

16. (580,P3,41) (d) The requirement is to determine Wolf's filing status and the number of exemptions he may claim. Wolf qualifies as a "head of household" because he is unmarried and provides more than half of the cost of maintaining a household for his parents, who must also qualify as his dependents. Both his parents qualify as dependents because Wolf provides more than half of their support, and their gross income (excluding nontaxable Social Security) is less than $1,000. The problem actually states that the parents' income consisted of $1,000 from qualifying dividends and interest. Thus there must be at least $1 of dividend exclusion, which means that the gross income (not exempt from tax) is less than $1,000.

17. (580,P3,46) (b) Since Parks resides in one apartment, only 95% of the expenses relating to all apartments can be allocated to the rental units.

Gross rents		$43,200
Fuel (95% of $5,000)	$4,750	
Maintenance and repairs	2,400	
Advertising	600	
Depreciation (95% of $10,000)	9,500	(17,250)
Net rental income		$25,950

Note that maintenance and repairs and advertising were not apportioned, because the problem stated they were rental unit expenses only.

18. (580,P3,48) (c) Stone will report $1,700 of interest income. Interest on FIT refunds, personal injury awards, U.S. savings bonds, and most other sources is fully taxable. However, interest on state or municipal bonds is nontaxable.

19. (580,P3,49) (d) The requirement is to describe the reporting on Quinn's tax return of interest income and interest penalty forfeiture due to early withdrawal from a time savings account. Quinn must include in income the total gross amount of interest credited to his account, and then separately deduct the penalty forfeiture in arriving at AGI.

20. (580,P3,50) (b) Contributions to individuals and tuition paid to a parochial school are not within the statutory definition of charitable contributions and thus are not deductible. Deductible charitable contributions for individuals are limited to those actually paid or charged to a bank credit card during the taxable year regardless of when the bank is repaid. The O'Briens' deductible charitable contributions consist of the cash of $1,500, and the $250 charge to their bank credit card.

21. (580,P3,51) (d) The requirement is to compute Goodfriend's maximum charitable contribution deduction. The $10,000 cash is fully deductible, since it is only subject to the overall limitation of 50% of AGI (50% x $50,000 = $25,000). Since the contributed stock is appreciated and has been held longer than 12 months (i.e., intangible capital gain appreciated property the amount of contribution is the FMV of $17,000). The $17,000 is deductible to the extent of 30% of AGI (30% x $50,000 = $15,000). Thus, the deductible charitable contribution of $25,000 consists of $10,000 cash plus $15,000 of stock. The unused $2,000 of stock will be carried forward up to 5 years subject to the 30% limitation in future years.

22. (580,P3,53) (d) The requirement is to determine the total amount of deductible medical expenses for the Bensons before the application of any limitation rules. Deductible medical expenses include those incurred by a taxpayer, taxpayer's spouse, dependents of the taxpayer, or any person that a taxpayer could claim as a dependent except that the person had income of $1,000 or more, or filed a joint return. Thus, the Bensons may deduct medical expense incurred for themselves, for John (i.e., not a dependent only because his income is $1,000 or more), and for Nancy (i.e., a dependent of the Bensons).

23. (580,P3,54) (a) The requirement is to compute the amount of casualty loss deduction and indicate the year of deduction. Casualty losses are generally deductible only in the year in which they occur. However, where the loss is in part covered by insurance, the loss is deductible in the year in which the claim for insurance compensation is finally settled. The deductible loss must be reduced by any anticipated insurance recovery, even though payment won't be received until a later year. The amount of a personal casualty loss is the lesser of the decrease in the FMV of the

property or the adjusted basis of the property. A personal casualty loss must be reduced by a $100 exclusion and any expected insurance recovery.

Lower of basis ($6,000), or decrease in FMV ($4,200 − $2,200)	$2,000
Less expected insurance recovery	(1,500)
Less $100 per casualty	(100)
Loss deductible in year insurance claim is settled (1980)	$ 400

24. (580,P3,55) (b) The requirement is to determine the amount of deductible sales tax using the Optional Sales Tax Table provided. The estimated amount of deductible sales tax is based on (1) total available income, including nontaxable income (AGI of $10,500 plus social security of $3,000); and, (2) family size based on number of exemptions, excluding exemptions for being 65 or blind (4 − 2 = 2).

25. (580,P3,56) (d) The amount of deduction for state and local income taxes only includes amounts paid during the taxable year, i.e., withheld from salary, any estimated payments made during the taxable year, and payment during the year of a prior year's tax. Weber's deduction ($3,800) consists of the amount withheld ($3,000) and the 1977 assessment paid in 1979 ($800). The refund received of 1978 taxes is not offset against taxes paid, but may have to be included in gross income. The $200 of 1979 tax paid in 1980 will be a deduction for 1980.

26. (580,P3,57) (c) The requirement is to determine the pension (annuity) amounts excluded from income during 1979, 1980, and 1981. This is an employee annuity subject to a special rule because Brown's contribution of $14,700 will be recovered within 36 months after payments begin. Under this special rule, all amounts received are excluded from income until the employee recovers his total contribution (i.e., cost); thereafter all amounts are included in income.

	Received	Excluded	Included
1979	$4,900	$4,900	$ -0-
1980	$8,400	$8,400	$ -0-
1981	$8,400	$1,400	$7,000
		$14,700	

27. (580,P3,58) (b) Interest paid in debt incurred to purchase tax exempt obligations is nondeductible. The $1,500 interest on the auto loan, the $1,800 interest on the home mortgage, and the home mortgage prepayment penalty of $1,200 will give the Parsells a total interest deduction of $4,500.

28. (580,P3,59) (d) The requirement is to determine the "tax table income" for the Hohns who are itemizing deductions. For the Hohns, "tax table income" is their AGI ($25,000) less $4,100 of excess itemized deductions (i.e., $7,500 − ZBA of $3,400). The $1,500 payment to an IRA was already deducted in computing the Hohns' AGI.

29. (580,P3,60) (d) The requirement is to determine the number of exemptions the Planters may claim on their joint tax return. Since a taxpayer is considered to be 65 on the day before his 65th birthday, there are two exemptions for Mr. Planter, and one exemption for his spouse. In addition there is one dependency exemption for their daughter, and one dependency exemption for the niece. The dependency gross income test does not apply to their daughter since she was a full-time student for at least some part of at least 5 calendar months.

30. (1179,Q2,22) (b) The requirement is the number of exemptions claimable in 1978. Mr. and Mrs. Vonce are entitled to one exemption each. They are also entitled to one exemption for their dependent daughter since they provide over one-half of her support and she had less than $750 of income. An additional exemption for blindness is only available if the taxpayer or spouse is blind, i.e., not available for a dependent such as a daughter. No exemption is available for their son because he provided over one-half of his own support.

31. (1179,Q2,24) (d) The requirement is the deductibility of a noncollectible receivable by a cash basis taxpayer. A loss is only deductible to the extent of the basis of the property that became worthless. Accounts receivable have no basis until they are included in income. Since a cash method taxpayer does not include accounts receivable in income until payment is received, failure to collect accounts receivable results in a nondeductible loss.

32. (1179,Q2,25) (a) The requirement is the amount of gross income arising from a divorce settlement and alimony. Property settlements are treated as a division of capital and are not included in the recipient's income. To be a property settlement it must be a definite sum, and, if a series of payments, not over a period of more than 10 years. Child support is also excluded from the recipient's income. All other payments are taxable as alimony. Therefore, the transfer of title in the house is a property settlement while the mortgage payments are alimony, because they are for more than 10 years. Repayment

of a loan is merely a return of capital and not taxable. While $200 of the $700 monthly payment is excluded as child support, the remaining $500 is alimony. Thus, Claire's gross income for 1978 is $7,500.

Mortgage payments	$2,500
Alimony ($500 x 10 mos.)	5,000
	$7,500

33.   (1179,Q2,28) (c)   The requirement is the loss classification of a nonbusiness bad debt. A nonbusiness bad debt may only be deducted as a short-term capital loss. Business bad debts may be deducted as ordinary losses. Since this was a loan to a friend, it is a nonbusiness bad debt and is only deductible as a short-term capital loss.

34.   (1179,Q2,29) (b)   A surviving spouse is taxed at the same rates as taxpayers who are married filing jointly. A surviving spouse qualifies for these special rates for two years after his or her spouse's death if a dependent child lives with the surviving spouse; if the surviving spouse pays over one-half of the costs of the household; and if the surviving spouse does not marry before year-end. John Abel qualifies as a surviving spouse under these requirements.

35.   (1179,Q2,30) (b)   The requirement is the 1978 net operating loss. A net operating loss is computed with all income and loss items except that personal exemptions and nonbusiness deductions in excess of nonbusiness income are not allowed. Interest income and dividend income are considered nonbusiness income. Casualty losses are allowed in any event. Thus, the net operating loss is $18,700, as computed below:

Business loss	$(18,000)
Interest income	2,000
Dividend income	500
Itemized deductions	
(limited to nonbusiness income)	(2,500)
Net casualty loss	(700)
	$(18,700)

36.   (1179,Q2,31) (a)   The requirement is lessor's 1978 gross income. A lessor excludes from income any increase in the value of property caused by improvements made by the lessee, unless the improvements were made in lieu of rent. In this case, there is no indication that the improvements were made in lieu of rent. Therefore, Farley should only include rent in his income. In 1978, six rent payments were made: 6 x $1,000 = $6,000.

37.   (1179,Q2,32)   (b) The credit is 10% of the † first $5,000 of earned income reduced by 12.5% of the greater of earned income ($7,000) or

adjusted gross income ($7,100) in excess of $6,000.

$$\$500 - (12.5\% \times \$1,100) = \$362.50$$

38.   (1179,Q2,33) (c)   The requirement is to compute dividend income after the dividend exclusion. Each person is entitled to a $100 exclusion for dividends from domestic corporations. Dividends from Subchapter S corporations do not qualify. Therefore, George may only exclude the $70 from Able Corporation. Mary may not exclude any dividends, as hers were from a foreign corporation. On their joint return, they must report $300 ($200 from the Subchapter S corporation and $100 from the foreign corporation).

39.   (1179,Q2,34) (c)   The maximum deduction for contribution by a self-employed person to a qualified retirement plan is limited to the lesser of $7,500 or 15% of earned income. Since 15% of $20,000 ($3,000) is less than $7,500, the deduction is limited to $3,000.

40.   (1179,Q2,35) (d)   The requirement is to compute the itemized deduction for taxes. Federal income taxes are never deductible. State income taxes, real estate taxes (even if foreign), and state sales taxes are deductible as itemized deductions. Self-employment taxes are not deductible. The state unincorporated business tax is deductible as a business expense (above the line) but not as an itemized deduction (below the line). Therefore, Seth Parker may claim $3,400 as an itemized deduction.

State income taxes	$2,000
Real estate taxes	900
State sales taxes	500
	$3,400

41.   (1179,Q2,37) (a)   Vincent Tally is entitled to no deduction for contributions in 1978 because he did not give up his entire interest in the book collection. By reserving the right to use and possess the book collection for his lifetime, Vincent Tally has made a gift of a future interest. Therefore, no deduction is available. The contribution will be deductible when all his interest in the books is transferred to the art museum.

42.   (1179,Q2,39) (a)   The requirement is to compute the maximum depreciation on a new machine. Additional first-year depreciation is 20% of the cost of property, limited to $2,000 of depreciation per taxpayer. Additional first-year depreciation reduces the basis of the asset by the amount of additional first-year depreciation taken. Also, salvage value of up to 10% of the basis of personal property with a useful life of 3 years or more may be

ignored. Since Sandy Beech uses straight-line depreciation, she may deduct 10% of $38,000 ($40,000 less $2,000 additional first-year depreciation) in 1978 as straight-line depreciation. Therefore, her maximum 1978 depreciation is $5,800.

Additional first-year depreciation	$2,000
Annual depreciation	
10% ($40,000 - $2,000)	3,800
	$5,800

43. (1179,Q2,40) (b) Payments by an employer to a deceased employee's beneficiary are taxable to the extent they exceed $5,000. Therefore, the widow need only include $10,000 in her income. The first $5,000 is excluded as a death benefit.

44. (579,Q2,21) (c) Mrs. Felton qualifies as a head of household because she is both unmarried and maintains a household for her unmarried child. The unmarried child for whom she maintains a household need not qualify as her dependent in order for Mrs. Felton to claim the head-of-household status. Answer (b) is incorrect because in order for Mrs. Felton to qualify as a surviving spouse, her son must qualify as a dependent, which he does not. Although Mrs. Felton would have qualified as married filing jointly, answer (d), in 1977 (the year of her husband's death), the problem requirement is her 1978 status. Answer (a), single, is incorrect because although the widow is single, her circumstances make head of household her proper filing status.

45. (579,Q2,23) (b) Each individual filing a tax return is allowed a $100 dividend exclusion to the extent the individual has received dividends from a qualified, domestic corporation. Dividends from foreign corporations and on life insurance policies do not qualify. Up to $200 of dividend exclusion is allowed in a joint return if each spouse has dividends of $100 or more. In this case Jack is entitled to the $100 dividend exclusion from the dividends from Alert Corporation. Joan is only entitled to a $50 exclusion, because she only received $50 of dividends from a qualified, domestic corporation. Therefore the total dividend exclusion on the joint return is $150, which is netted against total dividends of $750, resulting in $600 of taxable dividends on their joint tax return. The $200 dividend on the life insurance policy from a mutual life insurance company is considered a return of premiums and excluded from income.

46. (579,Q2,24) (a) Arthur Mends' adjusted gross income is $700, consisting of $500 of dividends less a $100 dividend exclusion and a $300 prize. Scholarships awarded to candidates for a degree are excluded from income unless provided as compensation for services. Loans and cash support from parents are also excluded from income. The dividends qualify for the $100 dividend exclusion since they are from qualified investments. One must assume that qualified investments are qualified domestic corporations. Prizes are included in income unless the recipient was selected without any action on his part and if he is not required to render any additional services. Entering a contest constitutes action on the recipient's part. Therefore the prize money is included in income.

47. (579,Q2,25) (b) The Todds may contribute and deduct a total of $1,750 to their individual retirement accounts. The contribution limit when there is a nonworking spouse is the lesser of 15% of compensation or $1,750. In this case $1,750 is less than 15% of $40,000. The prize won on the TV game show does not qualify Wilma as a working spouse, nor is it compensation for purposes of computing the 15% limit.

48. (579,Q2,26) (c) James Martin's gross income is:

Salary	$50,000
Bonus	10,000
Allowance for moving expenses	5,000
	$65,000

Although the moving expense allowance must be included in income, Martin may deduct amounts spent on qualified moving expenditures. Medical insurance premiums paid by an employer are excluded from the employee's income.

49. (579,Q2,27) (d) None of the expenses listed is deductible to arrive at adjusted gross income. However, they are all deductible from adjusted gross income to arrive at taxable income, i.e., they are itemized deductions.

50. (579,Q2,28) (b) A ratable monthly portion of the original issue discount must be included in the purchaser's ordinary income each year. The amount included in income increases the purchaser's basis in the bond, so that no capital gain will be recognized if the bond is held to maturity. If the bond is sold before maturity, gain is computed as selling price less basis as adjusted by the amount of discount included in prior income. David Karp's discount was $480, which means he must include $4 per month in income. He held the bond 19 months, so $76 ($4 x 19) was included in his income and increased his basis from $9,520 to $9,596. Thus his capital gain upon sale is $9,800 minus $9,596, which is $204.

51. (579,Q2,31) (a) Hobby expenses are not deductible unless income is produced from the hobby, and then the expenses are only deductible to the extent of hobby income. Plaintiff's legal fees paid in connection with a libel suit are considered nondeductible personal expenses. However, any damages recovered are excluded from income. Union dues and employment agency fees are deductible from adjusted gross income. Therefore, Herzog may deduct $400 of union dues and $200 employment agency fees from adjusted gross income.

52. (579,Q2,33) (d) State income taxes and state sales taxes are itemized deductions for individuals. Federal income tax, FICA tax, and federal excise taxes are not deductible (the FICA and excise taxes would be deductible in a trade or business). Federal automobile gasoline taxes are not deductible. Thus Burke's allowable deductions consist of $1,000 of state income tax and $900 of state sales tax.

53. (579,Q2,35) (b) Interest expense used to purchase or finance tax-exempt income-producing property is not deductible. Since one-half of the loan from Community Bank was used to purchase the tax-exempt bonds, one-half of the interest paid to Community Bank is not deductible. Thus, Mason's interest expense deduction is $4,100.

Community Bank (limited to ½)	$ 800
Mortgage interest	3,000
Installment purchase interest	300
	$4,100

54. (579,Q2,38) (c) The requirement is Gilda's 1978 net self-employment income. The $20,000 salary drawn by Gilda is not deductible since she is not an employee. Self-employment income includes both undistributed earnings and cash drawn from the business. Also federal self-employment taxes are not deductible, just as an employee's share of FICA taxes is not deductible by the employee. Malpractice insurance premiums and professional seminar expenses are deductible. Therefore Gilda's net self-employment income is computed by adding back the non-deductible expenses to her previously computed self-employment income of $80,000.

Previously computed income	$ 80,000
Previously deducted expenses	20,000
Self-employment tax	6,000
	$106,000

55. (579,Q2,39) (a) All of the expenses are deductible providing proper substantiation and documentation have been prepared. All reasonable and necessary expenses incurred in connection with the production of income are deductible. The question states that these expenses were incurred to inspect the income-producing property and to consult about future oil wells, and thus are all deductible.

Plane fares	$4,000
Hotels	1,000
Meals	800
Entertaining lessees	500
	$6,300

MAY 1981 ANSWERS

56. (581,P3,41) (d) The requirement is to determine the amount of interest deductible in calculating excess itemized deductions. The $4,000 of interest on the bank loan is deductible since the proceeds were used to purchase U.S. Series H bonds which are taxable. The interest on installment charge accounts and the interest on the home mortgage also are deductible. "Points" are deductible as interest if they represent payment for the use of money. Points are fully deductible in the year paid if the loan was used to buy or improve a principal residence; otherwise, points are treated as interest paid in advance and are considered paid over the life of the mortgage.

57. (581,P3,42) (b) The requirement is to determine the amount of separate maintenance payments to be included in gross income. Periodic payments required by and received after a written separation agreement is executed are includible in income, except to the extent they are specifically designated as child support. Thus, ($1,500 — $600) x 6 = $5,400 is includible in income. The $1,200 per month paid for the first 6 months of 1980 are excluded from income because the payments were received prior to the signing of the written separation agreement.

58. (581,P3,44) (c) Thomson should file as a surviving spouse. A surviving spouse is taxed at the same rate as married taxpayers filing a joint return. Surviving spouse filing status is available for two taxable years after a spouse's death if--a dependent child lives

with the surviving spouse, the surviving spouse pays more than 50% of the costs of maintaining a household, and the surviving spouse does not marry before year-end.

59.   (581,P3,45)   (a)   The requirement is to determine taxable income (after exclusions) from dividends and interest for an unmarried taxpayer. The savings account of $1,000 is fully included, while the interest on the municipal bonds is fully excluded. The dividends on GM stock are included after deducting a $100 exclusion. The life insurance policy dividends are considered a reduction of the cost of insurance and not income.

60.   (581,P3,46)   (a)   The requirement is to determine the amount to be excluded from income. A beneficiary of a deceased employee may exclude up to $5,000 of death benefits received because of the employee's death. Since the pension was noncontributory, no part of the pension payments can be excluded as a recovery of cost.

61.   (581,P3,47)   (c)   The requirement is to determine AGI for a person who has received unemployment compensation. For a single taxpayer, the amount of unemployment compensation that must be included in income is limited to 50% of the excess of AGI (including unemployment compensation) over $20,000, i.e., 50% x [($22,500 + $2,800) − $20,000] = $2,650. $22,500 + $2,650 = $25,150.

62.   (581,P3,48)   (c)   The requirement is to determine the amount of medical expense deduction.

50% of insurance			$140
Medicines and drugs	$300		
Less 1% of AGI ($35,000)	350	$—0—	
Remainder of insurance		140	
Doctor		700	
		$ 840	
Less 3% of AGI ($35,000)		1,050	—0—
Amount deductible			$140

The Health Club membership for general health care is not deductible as a medical expense. Note that 50% of medical insurance (limited to $150) is not subject to exclusion.

63.   (581,P3,49)   (a)   The requirement is to compute the amount of casualty loss deduction. The deduction for a personal casualty loss is computed as the lesser of (1) the adjusted basis of property, or (2) the

decrease in FMV; reduced by any insurance recovery and $100.

Lesser of:		
Decrease in FMV ($45,000 − $3,000) =	$42,000	
Adjusted basis	$39,000	$39,000
Decreased by:		
Insurance recovery		(15,000)
$100 exclusion		(100)
Casualty loss deduction		$23,900

64.   (581,P3,50)   (b)   The requirement is to compute the Wallace's charitable contribution deduction. Since the cash gifts of $300 to church and $200 to the community college are only subject to the 50% of AGI limitation, they are fully deductible. The deduction for the gift of land is limited to 30% of AGI (30% x $35,000 = $10,500) because the land is appreciated capital gain property.

65.   (581,P3,52)   (d)   The requirement is to determine "tax table income" for Dennis Cowper, a single taxpayer. Cowper's tax table income is his AGI of $20,000 less $300 of excess itemized deductions ($2,600 − ZBA of $2,300). Note that personal exemptions are not subtracted, since they are already provided for in the tax tables.

66.   (581,P3,53)   (d)   The requirement is to compute McDonald's net rental income. Since McDonald is a cash-basis taxpayer, his rental income consists of the eleven payments received. Since he resides in one apartment, only 50% of the expenses relating to both apartments can be allocated to the rental unit.

Rents (11 x $500)	$5,500
Less:	
Fuel and utilities (50% x $3,600)	(1,800)
Depreciation (50% x $3,000)	(1,500)
Repairs to rental unit	(400)
Insurance (50% x $600)	(300)
Net rental income	$1,500

67.   (581,P3,54)   (c)   If the Optional Sales Tax Table is used, a taxpayer may add to the table amount the general sales tax paid to purchase only certain specified items including—a car, motorcycle, motor home, truck, boat, plane, mobile home, or materials used to build a home. Thus, the sales tax paid on the wearing apparel cannot be added.

Note: There is a special exception that only applies to residents of Massachusetts who may add the sales tax paid on any single item of clothing costing at least $175, in which case answer "d" would be correct.

68. (581,P3,55) (b)   The requirement is to determine the number of exemptions allowable to the Stoners. Mr. and Mrs. Stoner are entitled to one exemption each, with one additional exemption for Mr. Stoner's age. They are entitled to one exemption for their daughter since they provided over 50% of her support and she was a full-time student not subject to the $1,000 gross income test. No exemption is allowable for Mrs. Stoner's father since he was neither a U.S. citizen nor resident of U.S., Canada, or Mexico.

69. (581,P3,56) (d)   The amount of deduction for state and local taxes includes amounts withheld from salary, any estimated payments made during the year, and payment during the year of a prior year's tax. Harvey's deduction of $3,200 consists of the $2,500 withheld and the $700 of 1978 tax paid in 1980. The $500 refund of 1979 tax is not offset against taxes paid, but must be included in gross income, since its deduction in 1979 provided a tax benefit (i.e., excess itemized deductions exceeded the ZBA by more than $200).

70. (581,P3,57) (b)   The requirement is to determine the amount of property taxes deductible as excess itemized deductions. The property taxes on the residence and the land held for appreciation, together with the personal property taxes on the auto are deductible. The special assessment is not deductible, but would be added to the basis of the residence.

71. (581,P3,58) (a)   The requirement is to determine the amount of residential energy credit available to the Conleys. The credit is 15% of the first $2,000 of qualified expenditures to save energy in a personal residence. Qualifying items must be new and be expected to last 3 years. The cost of the insulation ($750) and the automatic setback thermostat ($150) qualify. The aluminum siding does not qualify. The storm windows do not qualify because they were already "used" when purchased.

72. (581,P3,59) (b)   The requirement is to determine the amount of the child care credit allowable to the Jasons. The credit is 20% of certain dependent care expenses limited to the lesser of (1) $2,000 for one qualifying individual, $4,000 for two or more; (2) taxpayer's earned income, or spouse's if smaller; or (3) actual expenses. The $1,500 paid to the Union Day Care Center qualifies, as does the $1,000 paid to Wilma Jason. Payments to relatives qualify if the relative is not a dependent of the taxpayer. Since Robert and

Mary Jason only claimed three exemptions, Wilma was not their dependent. The $500 paid to Acme Home Cleaning Service does not qualify since it is completely unrelated to the care of their child. To qualify, expenses must be at least partly for the care of a qualifying individual. Since qualifying expenses exceed $2,000, the Jason's credit is 20% x $2,000 = $400.

73. (581,Q3,59) (c)   The requirement is to determine the amount of investment qualifying for the investment tax credit. To qualify, property must be placed in service during the taxable year, and must have a useful life of at least 3 years. The manuals do not qualify because they only have a useful life of two years. Only one-third of the cost of the truck qualifies since its useful life is three years. The total cost of the desk and chair qualifies since they have a useful life of seven years. Thus, the qualified investment is:

Truck ($15,000 x 1/3) =	$5,000
Desk and Chair ($1,200 x 3/3)	1,200
Total qualified investment	$6,200

SOLUTION GUIDE

Problem 1   Barton and Jones

1. This problem consists of two unrelated parts concerning federal income taxation of individuals.

2. Part a requires a schedule of adjusted gross income for an individual with supporting schedules for self-employment income and itemized deductions. The solutions approach is to analyze each paragraph of additional information after studying the cash receipts and disbursements schedules. Notes should be made on the face of your examination indicating the tax treatment of each item including appropriate schedule.

2.1 The depreciation on automobile and office equipment is deductible as a business expense on the self-employment schedule.

2.2 The $2,900 received from the insurance company for personal injuries is excluded from income. The $700 recovered for automobile repairs is included in self-employment income, because the $700 was deducted as a business expense in 1976. If the automobile had not been used 100% for business, the recovery would have been prorated between self-employment income and personal income just as the loss would have been prorated last year.

2.3 Since only 60% of the $3,900 of country club dues and expenses was incurred in connection with the business, only $2,340 is deductible on the self-employment schedule. The remaining $1,560 of personal expenditures is not deductible.

2.4 A self-employed individual may contribute to a qualified Keogh retirement plan and may deduct up to the lesser of $7,500 or 15% of net business income. Thus net business income must be computed before determining the deductibility of the Keogh contributions. See 2.11.

2.5 The 100 shares of stock cost $6,900 and were sold for $3,400 resulting in a capital loss of $3,500. In 1977 capital losses could offset up to $2,000 of ordinary income. This is a long-term capital loss since the stock was held for over 9 months. As $2 of long-term capital loss is required to offset $1 of ordinary income,

$1,750 may be taken as a personal deduction in computing 1977 adjusted gross income. Note: in 1978 and thereafter, assets must be held for more than one year for the gain or loss to be long-term, and capital losses may offset up to $3,000 of ordinary income.

2.6 The $600 donated to recognized charitable organizations is an itemized deduction. The $275 worth of clothes donated to a needy family is not deductible, because the clothes were not donated to a recognized charitable organization.

2.7 Real estate taxes of $2,330, sales taxes of $770, state gasoline taxes of $102, and state income taxes of $1,375 are itemized deductions in 1977, the year in which paid. Federal income taxes are not deductible. Note that state gasoline taxes are no longer deductible after 1978.

2.8 After analyzing the paragraphs of additional information, review the cash receipts and disbursements to determine additional items affecting adjusted gross income. The $65,100 of commission received is self-employment income. The $5,000 office sublease income is an offset to the $14,000 of office rent.

2.9 Mr. Barton's withdrawals do not affect any schedules since he is a sole proprietor and is taxed on all of his business income. The secretary's salary of $8,000 plus the $1,262 of taxes withheld, $12,000 of commissions, $9,000 ($14,000 − $5,000) of net rent, automobile expenses of $1,800, office expenses of $1,160, and employer payroll taxes of $825 are business deductions.

2.10 Prepare the required schedules of adjusted gross income, income from self-employment, and itemized deductions in good form.

2.11 Since the net business income is $26,813, Barton may contribute and deduct up to $4,022 ($26,813 x 15%) to his Keogh plan. The contributions must be made in 1977 or in 1978 prior to the filing of his 1977 tax return in order to deduct them on his 1977 return. Thus both the $3,000 contributed in 1977 and the $1,000 contributed in January 1978 are deductible. This is a personal deduction in computing adjusted gross income.

3. Part b requires schedules of adjusted gross income, itemized deductions, medical expenses, and the child care credit. After studying the listing of income and expenses, analyze each paragraph of additional information.

3.1 The $2,200 of interest income on savings deposits is a component of adjusted gross income. The $1,800 of interest on state obligations is excluded from income.

3.2 The $790 withheld for state income taxes is an itemized deduction in 1977.

3.3 The $900 of state income taxes deducted in 1976 indicates that the $700 refund received in 1977 should be included in 1977 adjusted gross income. State income tax refunds are included in income to the extent they were previously deducted as expenses (payments).

3.4 After analyzing the paragraphs of additional information, review the listings of income and expenses for additional items affecting adjusted gross income, itemized deductions, medical expenses, and the child care credit.

3.5 Salary of $18,000 is included in adjusted gross income. Dividends of $600 less the $100 exclusion as well as the $700 state income tax refund are also included in 1977 adjusted gross income.

3.6 The medical expenses consist of three components. First, one-half of medical insurance premiums paid, limited to $150. Since $800 was paid for medical insurance, $150 is deductible. The remaining medical insurance premiums ($800 − $150) are included in the remaining medical expense computation. Second, drugs are included in the medical expense deduction to the extent they exceed 1% of adjusted gross income, i.e., $300 less 1% of gross income ($21,400) which is $86. The medical expense deduction is the resulting $86 drug expense, $650 insurance premium, and $2,400 doctor bills less 3% of AGI.

One-half of medical premiums ($150 limit)		$ 150
Drugs	$ 300	
1% AGI	−214	
	$ 86	
Balance of medical insurance premium	650	
Doctor bills	2,400	
	$3,136	
3% AGI	−642	2,494
		$2,644

3.7 The installment interest of $180 and the $2,000 of real estate taxes are also itemized deductions.

3.8 The child care expenses are not deductible but are used to determine the child care credit. A credit of 20% of child care expenses incurred to enable the taxpayer to work may be used to offset the tax liability. The maximum amount of expenses which the credit may be computed on is the lesser of taxpayer's earned income, $2,000 for 1 dependent, or actual expenses. In this case, $2,000 is less than $18,000 of salary and is less than the $3,600 of actual expenses. Therefore the credit is $400 ($2,000 x 20%).

3.9 Prepare the required schedules in good form for the grader.

UNOFFICIAL ANSWER

Problem 1   Barton and Jones

Part a.

1.   Harold and Bella Barton
COMPUTATION OF ADJUSTED GROSS INCOME
For the year ended December 31, 1977

Income from self-employment (Schedule 1)	$26,813
Long-term capital loss ($3,500 x 50%)	(1,750)
Contribution to Keogh retirement plan ($3,000 + $1,000)	(4,000)
	$21,063

Continues next page

Schedule 1

Computation of Income From Self-Employment

Gross cash receipts

Commissions received		$65,100
Reimbursement for repairs to automobile		700
		$65,800

Expenses

Secretary's salary ($8,000 + $1,262)		$ 9,262	
Commissions paid to outsiders		12,000	
Office rent, net ($14,000 − $5,000)		9,000	
Automobile expenses		1,800	
Depreciation:			
Office equipment	$1,600		
Automobile	1,000	2,600	
Office expenses		1,160	
Country club dues and expenses ($3,900 x 60%)		2,340	
Employer's payroll taxes		825	38,987
			$26,813

---

2.   Harold and Bella Barton
COMPUTATION OF TOTAL ITEMIZED DEDUCTIONS
For the year ended December 31, 1977

Contributions	$ 600
Taxes paid (Schedule 1)	4,577
	$5,177

Schedule 1

Computation of Taxes Paid

Real estate (residence) taxes	$2,330
Sales taxes	770
State gasoline taxes	102
State income tax (balance 1976)	625
State income tax (estimate 1977)	750
	$4,577

Part b.

1.   Agnes Jones
COMPUTATION OF ADJUSTED GROSS INCOME
For the year ended December 31, 1977

Salary	$18,000
Interest income	2,200
Dividend income ($600 less $100 exclusion)	500
1976 state income tax refund	700
	$21,400

2.   Agnes Jones
COMPUTATION OF TOTAL ITEMIZED DEDUCTIONS
For the year ended December 31, 1977

Medical expenses (Schedule 1)	$2,644
Interest expense	180
Real estate taxes paid	2,000
State income taxes withheld	790
	$5,614

Schedule 1

Computation of Medical Expenses

One-half of medical insurance premiums (not more than $150)		$ 150
Prescription drugs	$ 300	
1% of adjusted gross income ($21,400) x 1%)	214	
	86	
Balance of medical insurance premiums	650	
Doctor bills	2,400	
	$3,136	
3% of adjusted gross income ($21,400 x 3%)	642	
		2,494
		$2,644

3. The allowable child care credit would be limited to $400 ($2,000 limit x 20%).

SOLUTION GUIDE

Problem 2   Washington and Adam

1. This problem consists of two unrelated parts concerning federal income taxation of individuals. Work each part as an individual problem.

2. The requirement is a schedule of adjusted gross income for an individual for the 1976 calendar year. The solutions approach is to first work through each paragraph of information to analyze the effect on the adjusted gross income schedule. Notes should be made on the face of your examination booklet for later transfer to your final solution. Any supplementary schedules and supporting calculations should be made in final form on a separate sheet of paper to be attached to your final solution.

2.1 The age and marital status of the taxpayer have relatively little effect on the solution. Washington's being single will affect the dividend exclusion later in the problem. Since Washington cannot prepare a joint return with his mother, his mother's income is not relevant to the problem. While Washington's mother is a dependent (Washington furnishes over one-half of her support), the problem only requires a schedule of adjusted gross income. The $750 exemption for his mother will be deducted from adjusted gross income, i.e., not used in the computation of adjusted gross income. Note: After 1978, exemptions are increased to $1,000 each.

2.2 Since Washington has contributed nothing to produce the annual retirement benefit of $12,000, the entire benefit is taxable in 1976. Had Washington made contributions to produce the retirement benefits, the portion attributable to Washington's contributions would not be taxable when received.

2.3 Since Washington purchased an expected $50,000 of benefits for $40,000, only 20% of the benefits received are taxable. In 1976 only $720 of the $3,600 total benefits received would be taxable.

2.4 The $9,000 in consulting fees is included in gross income. The related $1,000 of business expenses are an "above-the-line" deduction, i.e., an expense in determining adjusted gross income. The $200 that Washington paid to a housekeeper is not a deduction to arrive at adjusted gross income because it is not a business expense. It would have to be deducted as an itemized deduction which probably would not be possible in this case, since there is no statement that Washington's mother was incapable of self-care. Note, in 1977 the deduction for child and dependency care expenses was changed to a credit.

Since the automobile was used 40% for the consulting work, 40% of the 1976 costs of $1,850, or $740, are deductible. The $740 deduction will be used in preference to the $725 deduction to minimize taxable income, as the problem requires. The automobile expenses are deductible to arrive at adjusted gross income because the expenses were incurred in a trade or business.

2.5 The $30,000 Washington received from his uncle's life insurance policy is not includable in gross income, nor taxable, as is true of all life insurance proceeds received in a lump sum.

2.6 Since Washington is single, he is only allowed an exclusion of $100 of dividends from domestic corporations. Thus $400 of the $500 in dividends will be taxable to Washington.

2.7 Interest income from savings accounts ($300) and U.S. obligations ($200) is taxable. The interest income on municipal obligations ($100) is not taxable as income.

2.8 Washington's long-term capital transactions consisted of a $1,350 gain on the July 1974 stock, a $1,150 loss on the May 1975 stock, and a $200 gain on the February 1976 stock. These items are netted to arrive at a $400 gain on which a 50% deduction is allowed, leaving $200 of long-term capital gain. The April 1976 stock was sold in less than six months and is therefore a short-term capital gain of $700, which is includable in gross income in full. Note that the holding period for long-term gain or loss status was increased to 9 months in 1977 and 12 months in 1978. The capital gain deduction was increased to 60% for gains after October 31, 1978.

2.9 After analyzing all of the paragraphs of information, a schedule of adjusted gross income should be prepared for the grader.

3. Part b requires a schedule of itemized deductions for an individual taxpayer in 1976. Note that there is a second requirement: a list of the items that were not deductible. The solutions approach is to work through each item on the schedule noting the extent of deductibility. Remember to mark all items that are to be included in the second requirement, i.e., those not deductible.

3.1 Medical and dental expenses: The first one-half of medical insurance premiums are deductible (limited to $150). In this case, however, there are no medical insurance premiums. The life insurance premiums do not qualify as medical insurance premiums and are not deductible.

Medicine and drugs are deductible to the extent that they exceed 1% of adjusted gross income. Since the medicine and drug expense is $275 and 1% of adjusted gross income is $250, the medicine and drugs deduction is limited to $25. This $25, doctor bills of $400, dental bills of $1,600, hospital bills of $440, contact lenses of $150, and medical transportation expenses of $70 are deductible to the extent that they exceed 3% of adjusted gross income. The total of these items is $2,685; 3% of adjusted gross income is $750; therefore, $1,935 is deductible. The diaper service is not deductible.

3.2 Real estate taxes ($1,100) are deductible; state income taxes ($700) are deductible; state sales taxes ($240) are deductible; and state gasoline taxes ($75) are deductible. These total $2,115. Social security taxes are not deductible by the employee. Note that state gasoline taxes are no longer deductible after 1978.

3.3 Interest is an itemized deduction. Interest on home mortgages ($1,400) is deductible, interest on the family car loan ($500) is deductible, and credit card finance charges ($100) are deductible. These total $2,000. Interest paid on debt to buy municipal obligations is not deductible, because the income received from the municipal obligations is not taxable.

3.4 Tuition paid to a parochial school is not deductible. It is not a contribution, but rather a payment for services. Only the excess paid for an art object over its fair market value is deductible as a charitable contribution ($750 paid less $500 FMV is $250). Cash contributed to a church ($260) is deductible. Cash pledged to a nonprofit college in 1976, but paid in 1977, is not deductible until 1977. The fair value of used clothing ($90) contributed to the church is deductible. These total $600.

3.5 Miscellaneous Deductions: Union dues are deductible as an employee expense but are an itemized deduction and may not be taken as an "above-the-line" deduction. Fines are never deductible. Registration and license fees for cars and drivers' licenses are not deductible.

3.6 After analyzing all the individual items, prepare a schedule of those which are deductible and a schedule of the items which are nondeductible.

UNOFFICIAL ANSWER

Problem 2   Washington and Adam

a.
Mr. Washington
ADJUSTED GROSS INCOME
1976 Calendar Year

Income from consulting business		$9,000
Various business expenses	$1,000	
Auto expenses ($1,850 x 40%)	740	1,740
Profit from consulting business		$7,260
Dividends from domestic corporations ($500 − $100 exclusion)		400
Interest income:		
Savings accounts	$ 300	
Obligations of the U.S.	200	
		500
Net gain from sale of capital assets (below)		900
Retirement benefits		12,000
Taxable portion of annuity income:		
Amounts received ($300 x 12 months)	3,600	
Amount excluded $\frac{\$40,000}{\$50,000}$ x $3,600	2,880	
		720
		$21,780

Computation of net gain from sale of capital assets:

Short-term capital gains and losses:		
Gain on sale of common stock purchased in April 1976 and sold in June 1976		$ 700
Long-term capital gains and losses:		
Gain on sale of common stock purchased in July 1974	$1,350	
Loss on sale of common stock purchased in May 1975	(1,150)	
Gain on sale of common stock purchased in February 1976 and sold in December 1976	200	
		400
Net gain		1,100
50% of long-term capital gains and losses		(200)
		$ 900

b.1.   Mr. and Mrs. Adam
                ITEMIZED DEDUCTIONS
                 1976 Calendar Year

Medical and dental expenses
Medicine and drugs:
   Amount paid $ 275
   1% of $25,000   250
      Amount deductible   25

Other medical and dental expenses:
   Doctor bills   400
   Dental bills   1,600
   Hospital bills ($2,200 x 20%)   440
   Contact lenses   150
   Medical transportation expenses   70

                      2,685
   3% of $25,000   750
                             $1,935

Taxes
Real estate taxes   1,100
State income taxes withheld by
  Mr. Adam's employer   700
State sales taxes paid   240
State gasoline taxes   75
                      2,115

Interest expense
Home mortgage   1,400
Loan for family car   500
Finance charges on credit cards   100
                      2,000

Contributions
Excess of purchase price over FMV
  of art object   250
Cash contributed to church   260
Fair value of used clothing con-
  tributed to church   90
                       600

Miscellaneous
Union dues   65
                    $6,715

2.   Nondeductible items

   · Life insurance premium
   · Diaper service
   · Employee portion of social security taxes
      withheld by Mr. Adam's employer
   · Debt interest to buy municipal obligations
   · Tuition paid to parochial school
   · Cash pledge to nonprofit college
   · Fines for illegal parking
   · Registration for family car
   · Driver's license fee

MULTIPLE CHOICE QUESTIONS (1—24)

1.   In 1979, Clark Corporation, not a dealer in securities, realized taxable income of $40,000 from the operation of its business. Additionally in 1979, Clark realized a long-term capital loss of $10,000 from the sale of marketable securities. Clark did not realize any other capital gains or losses since it began operations. What is the proper treatment for the $10,000 long-term capital loss in Clark's income tax returns?

    a.   Use $3,000 of the loss to reduce taxable income for 1979, and carry $7,000 of the long-term capital loss forward five years.

    b.   Use $6,000 of the loss to reduce taxable income by $3,000 for 1979, and carry $4,000 of the long-term capital loss forward five years.

    c.   Use $10,000 of the long-term capital loss to reduce taxable income by $5,000 for 1979.

    d.   Carry the $10,000 long-term capital loss forward five years, treating it as a short-term capital loss.

2.   Thayer Corporation purchased an apartment building on January 1, 1976, for $200,000. The building was depreciated on the straight-line basis. On December 31, 1979, the building was sold for $220,000, when the asset balance net of accumulated depreciation was $170,000. On its 1979 tax return, Thayer should report

    a.   Section 1231 gain of $20,000 and ordinary income of $30,000.

    b.   Section 1231 gain of $30,000 and ordinary income of $20,000.

    c.   Ordinary income of $50,000.

    d.   Section 1231 gain of $50,000.

3.   On January 5, 1979, Norman Harris purchased for $6,000, 100 shares of Campbell Corporation common stock. On July 8, 1979, he received a nontaxable stock dividend of 10 shares of Campbell Corporation $100 par value preferred stock. On that date, the market values per share of the common and preferred stock were $75 and $150, respectively. Harris's tax basis for the common stock after the receipt of the dividend is

    a. $2,000

    b. $4,500

    c. $5,000

    d. $6,000

4.   On June 8, 1979, Sam Meyer, age 62, sold for $210,000 his principal residence which had an adjusted basis of $60,000. On November 1, 1979, he purchased a new residence for $80,000. Meyer elected the exclusion of realized gain available to taxpayers over age 55.

For 1979, Meyer should recognize a gain on the sale of his residence of

    a. $0

    b. $ 30,000

    c. $ 50,000

    d. $130,000

5.   During 1979, John Bulvon had the following capital losses on security transactions:

$2,000 net short-term capital loss
$1,200 net long-term capital loss

In addition, for 1979 he reported ordinary income of $36,000. How much of this loss can Bulvon offset against ordinary income in 1979?

    a. $2,600

    b. $2720

    c. $3,000

    d. $3,200

6.   For the year 1979, Susan Otis had salary income of $19,000. In addition she reported the following capital transactions during the year:

Long-term capital gain	$7,000
Short-term capital gain	3,000
Long-term capital loss	(2,000)
Short-term capital loss	(4,000)

There were no other items includable in her gross income. What is her adjusted gross income for 1979?

    a. $19,000

    b. $20,600

    c. $21,400

    d. $23,000

7.   On January 10, 1979, Albert Hart received a gift of income-producing property having an adjusted basis of $25,000 at the time of the gift. The fair market value of the property at the date of the gift was $20,000. Hart decided to sell the property on August 1, 1979, and received $23,000 on the sale. What is the amount of the gain or loss that Hart should report for 1979?

    a. $2,000 ordinary loss.

    b. $2,000 short-term capital loss.

    c. $3,000 short-term capital gain.

    d.   No gain or loss.

8.   For the year 1979 Peter Paul had the following capital transactions:

> $3,000 net long-term capital gain
> $1,000 net short-term capital loss

What is the amount of Paul's long-term capital gain deduction for 1979?
- a. $ 600
- b. $ 800
- c. $1,200
- d. $1,800

9.   Adam King, a self-employed accountant, sold a mahogany executive desk for $1,300 on December 31, 1979. Additional information is as follows:

Original cost	$1,200
Salvage value	$ 100
Purchase date	January 1, 1975
Depreciation on the double-declining method properly deducted over the years held	$ 800
Straight-line depreciation allowable over the years held would have been	$ 550

King would recognize gain on the sale of the desk in 1979 as

	Ordinary Income	Section 1231 Treatment
a.	$100	$800
b.	$350	$550
c.	$550	$350
d.	$800	$100

10.   On December 31, 1979, Mark Corporation sold machinery for $48,000. The machinery which had been purchased on January 1, 1975, for $40,000 had an adjusted basis of $28,000 on the date of sale. For 1979 Mark should report
- a.   A section 1231 gain of $20,000.
- b.   Ordinary income of $20,000.
- c.   A section 1231 gain of $12,000 and ordinary income of $8,000.
- d.   A section 1231 gain of $8,000 and ordinary income of $12,000.

11.   For the year ended December 31, 1979, Murray Corporation, a calendar-year corporation, reported book income before income taxes of $120,000. Included in the determination of this amount were the following items:

Loss on sale of building depreciated on the straight-line method	($12,000)
Gain on sale of land used in business	7,000
Loss on sale of investments in marketable securities (long-term)	(8,000)

For the year ended December 31, 1979, Murray's taxable income was
- a. $113,000.
- b. $120,000.
- c. $125,000.
- d. $128,000.

12.   On January 1, 1977, Hubert Toast sold stock with a cost of $4,000 to his sister Melba for $3,500, its fair market value. On July 30, 1977, Melba sold the same stock for $4,100 to a friend, in a bona fide transaction. In 1977 as a result of these transactions
- a.   Neither Hubert nor Melba has a recognized gain or loss.
- b.   Hubert has a recognized loss of $500.
- c.   Melba has a recognized gain of $100.
- d.   Melba has a recognized gain of $600.

13.   In 1977, Martha received as a gift several †
shares of Good Corporation stock. The donor's basis of this stock was $2,800, and he paid gift tax of $50. On the date of the gift, the fair market value of the stock was $2,600. If Martha sells this stock in 1979 for $2,700, what amount and type of gain or loss should Martha report in her 1979 income tax return?
- a. $50 long-term capital gain.
- b. $100 long-term capital gain.
- c. $100 long-term capital loss.
- d. $150 long-term capital loss.
- e.   None of the above.

14.   On March 10, 1975, James Rogers sold 300 shares of Red Company common stock for $4,200. Rogers acquired the stock in 1972 at a cost of $5,000.

On April 4, 1975, he repurchased 300 shares of Red Company common stock for $3,600 and held them until July 18, 1975, when he sold them for $6,000.

How should Rogers report the above transactions for 1975?
- a.   A long-term capital loss of $800.
- b.   A long-term capital gain of $1,000.
- c.   A long-term capital gain of $1,600.
- d.   A long-term capital loss of $800 and a short-term capital gain of $2,400.

15. Stanley Garret purchased 1,000 shares of Pat Corporation common stock at $5 per share in 1972. On September 19, 1975, he received 1,000 stock rights entitling him to buy 250 additional shares of Pat Corporation common stock at $10 per share. On the day that the rights were issued, the fair market value of the stock was $12 per share ex-rights and that of the rights was $1 each. Garret did not exercise the rights; he let them expire on November 28, 1975.

What should be the loss that Garret can report for 1975?

    a. A long-term capital loss of $250.
    b. A short-term capital loss of $250.
    c. A long-term capital loss of $1,000.
    d. A short-term capital loss of $1,000.
    e. None of the above.

16. David Price owned machinery which he had acquired in 1972 at a cost of $100,000. During 1975, the machinery was destroyed by fire. At that time it had an adjusted basis of $86,000. The insurance proceeds awarded to Price amounted to $125,000, and he immediately acquired a similar machine for $110,000.

What should Price report as ordinary income resulting from the involuntary conversion for 1975?

    a. $14,000.
    b. $15,000.
    c. $25,000.
    d. $39,000.
    e. None of the above.

17. Jerry owns 60% of the outstanding stock of Mitch Corporation. During 1973, Jerry sold Mitch a machine for $60,000 that had an adjusted tax basis of $68,000. For tax purposes, what should Jerry report for 1973?

    a. $0 recognized loss.
    b. $8,000 ordinary loss.
    c. $8,000 Section 1231 loss.
    d. $8,000 capital loss.
    e. None of the above.

18. During 1973, Mikey Corporation exchanged an old machine used in its business for a similar new machine to be used in its business. The following chart summarizes the relevant data on the date of exchange:

	Adjusted Basis	Fair Market Value
Old Machine (to Mikey)	$4,000	$5,500
New Machine (to the seller)	$3,000	$3,500

As part of the exchange, Mikey Corporation received $2,000 cash. What is the recognized gain on this exchange, and what is the tax basis of the new machine to Mikey, respectively?

    a. $0 and $1,000.
    b. $0 and $2,000.
    c. $1,500 and $3,500.
    d. $2,000 and $4,000.

19. Murd Corporation, a domestic corporation, acquired a 90% interest in the Drum Company in 1971 for $30,000. During 1974, the stock of Drum was declared worthless. What type and amount of deduction should Murd take for 1974?

    a. Long-term capital loss of $1,000.
    b. Long-term capital loss of $15,000.
    c. Ordinary loss of $30,000.
    d. Long-term capital loss of $30,000.

20. Wonder Inc., had 1979 taxable income of † $200,000 exclusive of the following:

Gain on sale of land used in business	$25,000
Loss on sale of machinery used in business	(13,000)
Loss on sale of securities held three years	(4,000)
Loss on sale of securities held three months	(3,000)

Wonder uses the regular method for computing its federal income tax. On what amount of taxable income should this tax be computed?

    a. $200,000.
    b. $202,500.
    c. $205,000.
    d. $212,000.

21. Joseph Kurtz exchanged land that he held for four years as an investment, with a tax basis of $36,000, for similar land valued at $40,000 which was owned by Adrian Flemming. In connection with this transaction, Kurtz assumed Flemming's $10,000 mortgage and Flemming assumed Kurtz's $12,000 mortgage. As a result of this transaction Kurtz should report a long-term capital gain of

    a. $0
    b. $2,000
    c. $4,000
    d. $6,000

22. Irving Press died on December 2, 1974. In his will, he left 5,000 shares of Vichy Corporation common stock to his daughter Celia. The stock was acquired by Press in 1971 for $20,000. At the time of his death, the stock had a fair market value of $25,000. The executor of the will elected to value the stock at the date of Press's death. On January 21, 1975, the stock was distributed to Press's daughter, when the fair market value was $26,000.

What should be the basis of the stock to Press's daughter?
   a. $5,000.
   b. $20,000.
   c. $25,000.
   d. $26,000.

MAY 1981 QUESTIONS

23.   On July 1, 1980, Thomas Rich acquired certain stocks with a fair market value of $22,000 by gift from his father. The stocks had been acquired by the father on April 1, 1978, at a cost of $40,000. Thomas sold all the stocks for $28,000 on December 12, 1980. What amount should Thomas report as capital gain or loss on his 1980 tax return as a result of the above?
   a. $0.
   b. $ 2,400 gain.
   c. $ 6,000 gain.
   d. $12,000 loss.

24.   Alan Kupper had the following transactions during 1980:

   ·   Gain of $7,000 on sale of common stock purchased on June 15, 1978, and sold on April 15, 1980.

   ·   Gain of $5,000 on sale of common stock purchased on October 15, 1979, and sold on July 25, 1980.

   ·   Receipt of a $10,000 installment payment on an installment contract created in 1977 when Kupper sold for $100,000 (exclusive of 6% interest on installments) land acquired in 1975 for $20,000. The contract provides for ten equal annual principal payments of $10,000 beginning on July 1, 1977, and ending on July 1, 1986.

What is the taxable amount of Kupper's long-term capital gain for 1980?
   a. $8,000.
   b. $7,500.
   c. $6,800.
   d. $6,000.

REPEAT QUESTION

(581,Q3,45)   Identical to item **10** above

MULTIPLE CHOICE ANSWERS

1.	d	6.	b	11.	d	16.	a	21.	b
2.	d	7.	d	12.	c	17.	a	22.	c
3.	c	8.	c	13.	e	18.	c	23.	a
4.	b	9.	d	14.	c	19.	c	24.	d
5.	a	10.	d	15.	e	20.	c		

EXPLANATION OF MULTIPLE CHOICE ANSWERS

1. (1180,P3,41)   (d)   The requirement is to determine the proper treatment of Clark Corporation's $10,000 NLTCL. Capital losses of corporations are deductible only to the extent of capital gains. If there are no capital gains to offset, the loss is not currently deductible, but must be carried back 3 years and forward 5 years as a STCL to offset capital gains in other years. Since Clark Corporation has never realized any capital gains, the $10,000 LTCL is carried forward five years as a STCL.

2. (1180, P3,44)   (d)   The requirement is to determine the proper treatment of the $50,000 gain on the sale of the building, which is Sec. 1250 property. Sec. 1250 recaptures gain as ordinary income to the extent of "excess" depreciation (i.e., depreciation deducted in excess of straight-line). The total gain less any depreciation recapture is Sec. 1231 gain. Since there is no depreciation recapture (straight-line depreciation was used), the entire $50,000 gain is Sec. 1231 gain.

3. (1180,Q2,22)   (c)   The requirement is to establish Harris' tax basis of the common stock after receipt of a nontaxable preferred stock dividend. Harris' original common stock basis must be allocated between the preferred and common stock according to relative market values:

Common Stock
   Mkt. Value = $ 75 x 100 shares = $7,500
Preferred Stock
   Mkt. Value = $150 x 10 shares =   1,500
   Total Value $9,000

The ratio of the common stock to total value is 7500/9000 or 5/6. This ratio multiplied by the original common stock basis of $6,000, results in a basis for the common stock of $5,000. Note that the basis of the preferred stock is 1/6 x $6,000 = $1,000.

4. (1180,Q2,23)   (b)   Taxpayers age 55 or older may make a once in a lifetime election to exclude up to $100,000 of the gain realized on the sale of a principal residence. Deducting the excluded gain of $100,000 from the selling price of $210,000 results in an adjusted selling price of $110,000. Reinvesting $80,000

in the new residence leaves $30,000 to be recognized as gain.

5. (1180,Q2,25)   (a)   The requirement is to determine the amount of capital loss that Bulvon can offset against ordinary income in 1979. A net short-term capital loss is deducted first and reduces ordinary income dollar-for-dollar. A net long-term capital loss is then deducted, but it takes $2 of long-term capital loss to reduce ordinary income by $1. The capital loss deduction is limited to the lesser of (1) the NSTCL plus 50% of the NLTCL, (2) $3,000, or (3) taxable income reduced by the zero bracket amount. Therefore, the capital loss that Bulvon can offset against ordinary income is $2,600 ($2,000 STCL + $600 LTCL).

6. (1180,Q2,27)   (b)   Capital gains and losses must be included in computing the adjusted gross income of an individual. First the short-term capital gains and losses are netted. Then the long-term capital gains and losses are netted. The net short-term capital gain or loss and the net long-term capital gain or loss are then netted to produce a net capital gain or loss.

NSTCL	($1,000)
NLTCG	5,000
NCG	$4,000

Since the NLTCG exceeds the NSTCL, a capital gains deduction of 60% is allowed as an above the line deduction. Therefore, in addition to the salary of $19,000, one must add the remaining capital gain on $1,600 (40% x $4,000) to calculate adjusted gross income of $20,600.

7. (1180,Q2,29)   (d)   The requirement is to calculate the amount of the gain or loss that Hart is to report on the sale of property received as a gift. If property is acquired by gift, the basis for gain is the same as the donor's adjusted basis. The basis for loss is the donor's adjusted basis or FMV on date of gift, whichever is less. Because of these rules, no gain or loss is recognized when use of the basis for loss results in a gain, and use of the basis for gain results in a loss. Therefore, since the selling price of $23,000 is less than the basis for gain (the donor's adjusted basis of $25,000), but greater than the basis for loss (the FMV of $20,000 at date of gift), there is no gain or loss.

8. (580,P3,42) (c) The requirement is to compute Paul's LTCG deduction for 1979. Individual taxpayers are allowed a deduction equal to 60% of the excess of net LTCG over net STCL. Thus,

NLTCG	$3,000
NSTCL	(1,000)
	$2,000 x 60% = $1,200

9. (580,P3,43) (d) The requirement is to compute the amount and type of gain recognized to the taxpayer on the sale of his office desk. The desk is depreciable personal property, and any recognized gain on sale will be recaptured by Section 1245 as ordinary income to the extent of all depreciation deducted after 1961. Since the desk was held for more than one year, any gain not recaptured will be Section 1231 gain.

Selling price		$1,300
Cost	$1,200	
Depreciation	(800)	
Adjusted basis		400
Recognized gain		$ 900
Sec. 1245 ordinary		
income		$ 800
Sec. 1231 gain		$ 100

10. (580,Q2,23) (d) The requirement is to determine the proper reporting of recognized gain on sale of machinery. When machinery used in a business is sold, the depreciation deducted in prior years is recaptured as ordinary income to the extent of the lesser of (1) all depreciation deducted after 1961, or (2) the gain realized on the sale. In this problem, $12,000 of depreciation has been deducted and the gain is $20,000. Therefore, the lesser of the two ($12,000) is recaptured as ordinary income, and the remainder of the gain ($8,000) is Sec. 1231 gain.

11. (580,Q2,32) (d) The requirement is to determine Murray Corporation's TI given book income plus additional information. The gain on sale of land ($7,000) and loss on sale of building ($12,000) are Sec. 1231 gains and losses. The resulting Sec. 1231 net loss of $5,000 is an ordinary tax deduction which has already been deducted in computing book income of $120,000. The loss on sale of investments results in a net capital loss which is not deductible for 1979 (carry back 3 and forward 5 to offset capital gains in other years).

Book income before taxes	$120,000
Add back net capital loss	+8,000
Taxable income	$128,000

12. (578,Q2,20) (c) Losses are disallowed on sales between related parties (includes members of a family). Therefore, Hubert does not recognize the $500 loss on the sale to Melba. On the subsequent sale by Melba, the gain is recognized only to the extent it exceeds the previously disallowed loss of $500. Therefore, Melba only recognizes a gain of $100 ($600 gain less $500 previously disallowed loss).

13. (575,Q2,31) (e) There is no gain or loss to be reported. Since the sales price ($2,700) falls below the gain basis ($2,800) and above the loss basis ($2,600), there is no gain or loss. The gift tax was not added to basis because the property was not appreciated. For gifts made after December 31, 1976, the increase in basis for gift tax paid is limited to the tax attributable to the appreciation.

14. (576,Q2,16) (c) Repurchasing substantially identical stock within 30 days of the sale of stock is known as a wash sale. Losses on wash sales are disallowed. The $800 loss incurred in the wash sale ($5,000 basis less $4,200 amount realized) is disallowed. The basis of the replacement (substantially identical) stock is its cost ($3,600) plus the disallowed wash sale loss ($800). Alternatively, the basis is computed as the original $5,000 purchase price less the difference between the $4,200 original sales price and the second purchase cost of $3,600. The holding period of the replacement stock includes the holding period of the wash sale stock. The amount realized ($6,000) less the basis ($4,400) yields a long term gain of $1,600.

15. (76,Q2,18) (e) If nontaxable stock rights are received and allowed to expire, they are considered to have no basis; and thus no loss is recognized.

16. (576,Q2,26) (a) The depreciation recapture provisions apply to any disposition of tangible personal property used in a trade or business. The total gain realized on the payment of the insurance proceeds was $39,000 ($125,000 payment realized less $86,000 adjusted basis), but $14,000 ($100,000 cost less $86,000) of that gain was attributable to depreciation taken after 1961 and as such will be recaptured and constitute ordinary income.

17. (1174,P1,10) (a) No loss deductions are allowed for sales between an individual and a corporation if the individual owns more than 50% of the corporation's stock.

18. (1174,P1,8) (c) This is an exchange of like-kind property used in a business. Gain is recognized to lesser of "boot" or realized gain. The boot is $2,000 and the realized gain is $1,500 ($5,500 − $4,000). The basis of the new machine is the basis of the old machine less the boot received plus the gain recognized.

$4,000 − $2,000 + $1,500 = $3,500

19. (1175,Q2,19) (c) Worthless securities generally receive capital loss treatment. However, if the loss is incurred by a corporation on its investment in an affiliated corporation (80% or more ownership), the loss is treated as an ordinary loss.

20. (1176,Q2,24) (c) Under the regular method of corporation tax computation, net capital gain is included in taxable income on which the corporate tax is computed. Wonder has a net capital gain of $5,000 which consists of a Section 1231 gain of $12,000 ($25,000 − $13,000), a long term capital loss of $4,000, and a short term capital loss of $3,000. Therefore, the amount of taxable income under the regular method is $205,000 ($200,000 plus $5,000). The alternative method is computed by adding 28% of the net capital gain ($5,000) to the corporate tax on taxable income exclusive of the net capital gain ($200,000).

21. (1179,Q2,27) (b) The requirement is the gain to be recognized on exchange of like property subject to a mortgage. The exchange of property, held for productive use or investment, for property of a like-kind is a tax-free exchange. However, to the extent boot is received, gain is recognized. Boot is cash or other property. If property exchanged is subject to a mortgage, the mortgage is considered the receipt of boot, since the debtor is being relieved of debt. If both properties exchanged are subject to mortgages, these mortgages are netted. Since Kurtz was relieved of a $12,000 mortgage and took a $10,000 mortgage, he will recognize gain of $2,000.

22. (576,Q2,25) (c) The basis of property in the hands of a person acquiring property from a decedent is the fair market value at date of death unless the executor elects the alternate valuation date (6 months after death and the basis would be the fair market value at the alternate valuation date).

MAY 1981 ANSWERS

23. (581,P3,43) (a) The requirement is to determine the amount of gain or loss to be reported on the sale of property received as a gift. The basis for gain is the donor's adjusted basis of $40,000; the basis for loss is the FMV of $22,000 on date of gift since it is less than the donor's basis. Since the stock was sold for $28,000, there is neither a gain nor a loss.

24. (581,P3,51) (d) The requirement is to compute the taxable amount of LTCG. The $7,000 gain is a LTCG since the stock was held more than 1 year. The $5,000 gain on sale of stock held 9 months is a STCG. Since the gross profit on the installment sale of land held more than 1 year is $80,000 and the payments to be received total $100,000, $80,000/$100,000 or 80% of the $10,000 installment received in the current year is a LTCG. The taxable LTCG is:

NLTCG	$15,000
Less 60% of	
NLTCG − NSTCL	
(60% x $15,000)	(9,000)
Taxable LTCG	$ 6,000

Of course the taxpayer would also report the STCG of $5,000.

MULTIPLE CHOICE QUESTIONS (1—26)

1. For the year ended December 31, 1979, the partnership of Murray and Parker had book income of $100,000 which included the following:

Long-term capital gain (on sale of securities)	$7,000
Section 1231 loss	(3,000)
Dividends qualifying for the $100 exclusion	200
Interest paid to partners for use of capital	12,000

The partners share profits and losses equally. What amount of partnership income (excluding all partnership items which must be reported separately) should each partner report in his individual income tax return for 1979?

a. $47,900
b. $48,000
c. $50,000
d. $53,900

2. Atley had an adjusted basis of $11,000 for his interest in th Atley and Donald partnership on December 31, 1979. On this date, Atley received from the partnership, in complete liquidation of his interest, $10,000 cash and land with a basis to the partnership of $2,000 and a fair market value of $3,000. What is Atley's basis for the land distributed to him?

a. $0
b. $1,000
c. $2,000
d. $3,000

3. Clark and Lewis are partners who share profits and losses 60% and 40%, respectively. The tax basis of each partner's interest in the partnership as of December 31, 1978, was as follows:

Clark	$24,000
Lewis	$18,000

During 1979, the partnership had ordinary income of $50,000 and a long-term capital loss of $10,000 from the sale of securities. There were no distributions to the partners during 1979. What is the amount of Lewis' tax basis as of December 31, 1979?

a. $33,000
b. $34,000
c. $38,000
d. $42,000

4. In computing the taxable income of a partnership a deduction is allowed for

a. Fixed salaries paid to partners for services determined without regard to the income of the partnership.
b. The net operating loss deduction.

c. Contributions to charitable organizations.
d. Personal exemptions of the partners.

5. The partnership of Spencer and Rey realized an ordinary loss of $42,000 in 1979. Both the partnership and the two partners are on a calendar-year basis. The partners share profits and losses equally. At December 31, 1979, Rey had an adjusted basis of $18,000 for his partnership interest before taking the 1979 loss into consideration. On his individual income tax return for 1979, Rey should deduct

a. An ordinary loss of $18,000.
b. An ordinary loss of $21,000.
c. An ordinary loss of $18,000 and a capital loss of $3,000.
d. A capital loss of $21,000.

6. The partnership of Truman and Hanover realized the following items of income during the year ended December 31, 1979:

Net income from sales	$62,000
Dividends from domestic corporations	4,000
Interest on corporate bonds	3,000
Net long-term capital gains	5,000
Net short-term capital gains	1,000
Net rental income	7,000

Both the partnership and the partners are on a calendar-year basis. The total income which should be reported as ordinary income of the partnership for 1979 is

a. $72,000.
b. $75,000.
c. $76,000.
d. $82,000.

7. During 1973, Wayne sold the interest he had held for five years in the Alco Partnership for $15,000 cash. The buyer also assumed Wayne's $2,000 share of the partnership liabilities. Wayne's tax basis in the partnership was $11,000. There were no unrealized receivables or appreciated inventories involved in this transaction. What is Wayne's gain on the sale of his partnership interest in Alco?

a. $2,000 ordinary gain.
b. $2,000 long-term capital gain.
c. $4,000 long-term capital gain.
d. $6,000 long-term capital gain.

8. During 1973, Norman contributed property held more than six months to the MaryAnn Partnership for a 40% interest. The total capital after his contribution was $50,000. His tax basis in the property was $8,000, and it had a fair market value of $10,000 at the time of the contribution to the

partnership. What gain or loss should Norman report on the contribution of his property to the partnership?

    a.   No gain or loss.

    b. $2,000 long-term capital gain.

    c. $12,000 long-term capital gain.

    d. $12,000 long-term capital gain of which $10,000 is deferred.

    e.   None of the above.

9. Lewis and Clark are partners who share profits †
and losses in a ratio of 2:1, respectively. For 1979, the partnership tax return showed a net short-term capital loss of $3,000 and a net long-term capital gain of $15,000. Lewis also had a personal net short-term capital loss of $2,000. What is the net capital gain that should be included in Lewis' taxable income on his 1979 individual income tax return?

    a. $3,000.

    b. $3,500.

    c. $4,000.

    d. $6,667.

    e.   None of the above.

10. The Troika Partnership had an ordinary oper- †
ating loss of $48,000 for the current year. The partnership had assets of $58,500 and liabilities of $15,000 at the end of the year. Before allocation of the loss, partner Ashford's one-third interest had an adjusted basis of $10,000 at the end of the current year. Ashford may deduct on his income tax return as his share of the loss

    a. $14,500.

    b. $10,000.

    c. $16,000.

    d. $15,000.

    e.   None of the above.

11. Jim Cash, one of two partners, contributed business property with a basis to him of $15,000 and a fair market value of $10,000 to the partnership of which he was a member. His capital account was credited for $10,000. The property was later sold for $12,000. As a result of this transaction, Cash must report on his personal income tax return.

    a. $1,000 gain.

    b. $1,500 loss.

    c. $2,000 gain.

    d. $3,000 loss.

    e.   None of the above.

12. Howard Harper has conducted his hardware store business as a sole proprietorship for twenty-five years. On May 1, 1973, he gave a one-fourth interest in this business to his son, Lanny. After the transfer of this one-fourth interest, under what circumstances would the business be considered a partnership for federal income tax purposes?

    a.   Under no circumstances.

    b.   Only if the son is a bona fide owner of the interest which was said to have been transferred to him.

    c.   Only if the son gives his father a promissory note for the value of the interest transferred to him.

    d.   Only if the son works in the hardware store.

    e.   None of the above.

13. In January 1977 Martin and Louis formed a partnership with each contributing $75,000 cash. The partnership agreement provided that Martin would receive a guaranteed salary of $20,000 and that partnership profits and losses (computed after deducting Martin's salary) would be shared equally. For the year ended December 31, 1977, the partnership's operations resulted in a loss of $18,000 after payment of Martin's salary. The partnership had no outstanding liabilities as of December 31, 1977. What is the amount of Martin's partnership basis as of December 31, 1977?

    a. $46,000.

    b. $66,000.

    c. $76,000.

    d. $86,000.

14. The partnership of Luchen and Kup reported the following elements of net income for the year ended December 31, 1977:

Operating income	$150,000
Long-term capital gains	4,000
Dividends received on investments in domestic corporations	2,000
Net income	$156,000

Included in the determination of operating income were charitable contributions of $1,000 and deductible guaranteed payments to partners of $60,000. What is the ordinary income of the partnership for 1977?

    a. $151,000.

    b. $155,000.

    c. $211,000.

    d. $212,000.

15.   Edward owns a 70% interest in the capital and profits of the partnership of Edward and Moore. During 1977 Edward purchased a piece of surplus machinery from the partnership for $5,000. On the date of sale the machinery had an adjusted basis to the partnership of $8,000. For the year ended December 31, 1977, the partnership's net income was $50,000 after recording the loss on sale of machinery. Assuming that there were no other partnership items to be specially reported, what is Edward's distributive share of the partnership's taxable income for 1977?

    a. $35,000.
    b. $35,630.
    c. $36,470
    d. $37,100.

16.   Crater Partnership had 1979 net ordinary † income of $45,000 and a net long-term capital gain of $5,000. Mr. Abbott who has a 20% interest in the profits and losses of the partnership, had 1979 drawings of $12,500 from the partnership. The other partners withdrew $27,500 during 1979. The partnership agreement does not provide for partner salaries or bonuses. Mr. Abbott had no other capital gains or losses during 1979. By how much will Mr. Abbott's 1979 adjusted gross income increase because of his interest in Crater Partnership?

    a. $2,000.
    b. $8,000.
    c. $9,400.
    d. $10,000.

17.   On January 2, 1979, the partnership of † Evan and Jared purchased for $80,000 a new machine with an estimated useful life of ten years and a salvage value of $4,000. Evans is married and files a joint return; Jared is single. The profit and loss ratio is Evan, 60%, and Jared, 40%. Neither partner has other business interests. How much additional first-year depreciation is available to the partners for 1979?

    a. $2,000.
    b. $6,000.
    c. $8,000.
    d. $15,200.

18.   Irving Aster, Dennis Brill, and Robert Clark were partners who shared profits and losses equally. On February 28, 1973, Aster sold his interest to Phil Dexter. On March 31, 1973, Brill died, and his estate held his interest for the remainder of the year. The partnership continued to operate and for the fiscal year ending June 30, 1973, it had a profit of $45,000. Assuming that partnership income was earned on a pro rata monthly basis and that all partners were calendar year taxpayers, the distributive shares to be included in 1973 gross income should be

    a.   Aster $10,000, Brill $0, Estate of Brill $15,000, Clark, $15,000, and Dexter $5,000.
    b.   Aster $10,000, Brill $11,250, Estate of Brill $3,750, Clark $15,000, and Dexter $5,000.
    c.   Aster $0, Brill $11,250, Estate of Brill $3,750, Clark, $15,000, and Dexter $15,000.
    d.   Aster $0, Brill $0, Estate of Brill, $15,000, Clark, $15,000, and Dexter $15,000.
    e.   None of the above.

19.   Dan Paley, Fred Queenan, and Gary Rosen are partners, sharing profits and losses equally. On May 15, 1971, Paley sold land with a cost basis of $22,000 to the partnership at its fair market value of $25,000. On May 1, 1973, Queenan purchased the same land from the partnership for $31,000, its fair market value. The 1973 gain to the partners as a result of the sale to Queenan should be

    a.   Paley $4,500, Queenan $0, and Rosen $4,500.
    b.   Paley, $3,000, Queenan $0, and Rosen $3,000.
    c.   Paley $2,000, Queenan $2,000, and Rosen $2,000.
    d.   Paley $0, Queenan $3,000, and Rosen $3,000.

20.   In March 1975, Davis entered a partnership by contributing to the partnership $10,000 cash and machinery which had an adjusted basis to him of $6,000 and a fair market value of $9,000. Davis acquired the machinery in 1973 at a cost of $12,000. His capital account was credited for $20,000 which constituted one-fourth of total partnership capital, and goodwill was recorded for the difference.

What should be the tax effects to Davis of this transaction?

    a.   Long-term capital gain of $3,000.
    b.   Ordinary income of $3,000.
    c.   Long-term capital gain of $3,000; ordinary income of $1,000.
    d.   Ordinary income of $3,000; long-term capital gain of $1,000.
    e.   None of the above.

21.   On January 1, 1975, Hoover and Filmore formed a partnership with each contributing the following amounts:

Hoover	$30,000
Filmore	6,000

The partners have agreed to share profits and losses equally. During 1975, each partner withdrew $3,000; and for the year ended December 31, 1975, the partnership's operating loss was $8,000. What should be Filmore's share of the 1975 loss allowable to him, assuming the partnership had no outstanding liabilities at December 31, 1975?

    a. $1,000.
    b. $3,000.
    c. $4,000.
    d. $6,000.
    e.   None of the above.

22.   For the year ended December 31, 1976, the partnership of Bicent and Tennial reported ordinary income of $260,000, which included the following items of expenses and losses:

Salaries paid (other than to partners)	$70,000
Interest paid (other than to partners)	4,000
Real estate taxes	8,000
Contributions	2,000
Repairs	1,000
Foreign income taxes	5,000
Loss on sale of machinery held 7 years	12,000

As a result of the above items, the partnership should increase its ordinary income and report separately on its tax return

    a. $19,000.
    b. $23,000.
    c. $24,000.
    d. $74,000.

23.   The partnership of Bond and Felton has a fiscal year ending March 31. John Bond files his tax return on a calendar-year basis. The partnership paid Bond a guaranteed salary of $1,000 per month during the calendar year 1975 and $1,500 a month during the calendar year 1976. After deducting this salary the partnership realized ordinary income of $80,000 for the year ended March 31, 1976, and $90,000 for the year ended March 31, 1977. Bond's share of the profits is the salary paid him plus 40% of the ordinary income after deducting this salary. For 1976, Bond should report taxable income from the partnership of

    a. $36,500.
    b. $44,000.
    c. $45,500.
    d. $50,000.

MAY 1981 QUESTIONS

24.   The partnership of Felix and Oscar had the following items of income during the taxable year ended December 31, 1980:

Income from operations	$156,000
Tax-exempt interest income	8,000
Dividends from foreign corporations	6,000
Net rental income	12,000

What is the total ordinary income of the partnership for 1980?

    a. $170,000.
    b. $174,000.
    c. $176,000.
    d. $182,000.

25.   Charles Jordan files his income tax return on a calendar-year basis. He is the principal partner of a partnership reporting on a June 30 fiscal-year basis. Jordan's share of the partnership's ordinary income was $24,000 for the fiscal year ended June 30, 1979, and $72,000 for the fiscal year ended June 30, 1980. How much should Jordan report on his 1980 return as his share of taxable ordinary income from the partnership?

    a. $24,000.
    b. $36,000.
    c. $48,000.
    d. $72,000.

26.   Richard Wilson is a partner in the firm of Day and Wilson. His profit and loss sharing ratio is 50%. In 1978 he contributed a capital asset to the business with a basis to him of $40,000 and a fair market value of $30,000 to the partnership. His capital account was credited for $30,000. During 1980 the property was sold for $36,000. There were no other sales of capital assets in 1980. As a result of the sale, Wilson's share of the partnership's capital asset transaction is a

    a. $2,000 capital loss.
    b. $3,000 capital gain.
    c. $4,000 capital loss.
    d. $6,000 capital gain.

PROBLEMS

Problem 1   Abcoe Engineering (1168,Q1) (Adapted)

(40 to 50 minutes)

Adair, Blinker, and Coe formed a partnership on January 2, 1980 under the name of Abcoe Engineering Services. Adair contributed $10,000 in cash, Blinker contributed $5,000 in cash and securities worth $5,000 (which he had purchased for $3,000 on September 30, 1979) and Coe contributed office furniture and equipment worth $10,000. Coe had purchased the office furniture and equipment for $20,000 during 1975, depreciated it under the double-declining balance method for a 10-year life and it had an adjusted basis to him of $5,240 at the date of contribution. Each partner's capital account was credited $10,000.

The partnership agreement stipulated the three partners would receive salaries, interest would be paid on their capital accounts and any remaining net income or loss would be divided equally. The agreement also provided that for purposes of income tax reporting the first $2,000 of taxable gain from the sale of securities would be allocated to Blinker, that all depreciation on the contributed office furniture and equipment would be allocated to Adair and Blinker, and the first $4,760 of taxable gain from the sale of the office furniture and equipment would be allocated to Coe.

The following information is also available:

1.   Net income from all sources on the partnership income statement was $75,000 before allocations to the partners for salaries and interest. Salaries and interest for 1980 determined in accordance with the partnership agreement and without regard to partnertship income were:

	Salary	Interest
Adair	$18,000	$1,000
Blinker	15,000	1,100
Coe	12,000	900

2.   The securities contributed by Blinker were sold March 31, 1980 for $5,900. Dividends received on these securities before they were sold amounted to $60.

3.   On June 30, 1980 Abcoe sold for its book value of $9,500 the office furniture and equipment contributed by Coe. The same day Abcoe moved to a new building constructed at a cost of $40,000 and furnished with new furniture and equipment which cost $30,000. In the financial statements 1980 depreciation of the building was $400 (10 percent salvage, 45-year life) and 1980 depreciation of the new furniture and equipment was $1,350 (10 percent salvage, 10-year life). The partners wish to deduct the maximum depreciation allowable, including additional first-year depreciation, for income tax purposes.

Required:

a.   Prepare a schedule computing the ordinary income which should be reported by Abcoe Engineering Services in its partnership income tax return for 1980. Start your schedule with the 1980 net income for financial statement purposes of $75,000 and itemize differences which must be considered to arrive at ordinary income to be shown in the partnership income tax return. Supporting computations should be in good form.

b.   Prepare a schedule presenting each partner's distributable share of items to be reported for income tax purposes separately by each partner as a result of partnership transactions during 1980.

MULTIPLE CHOICE ANSWERS

1. a	7. d	13. b	19. c	25. d
2. b	8. a	14. a	20. e	26. a
3. b	9. e	15. d	21. b	
4. a	10. d	16. c	22. a	
5. a	11. b	17. a	23. c	
6. a	12. b	18. a	24. b	

EXPLANATION OF MULTIPLE CHOICE ANSWERS

1. (1180,P3,58) (a) The requirement is to calculate the amount of partnership ordinary income that must be reported by each partner, given book income of $100,000. All items that have special characteristics (i.e., subject to partial or full exclusion, % or dollar limitation) must be segregated and taken into account separately by each partner so that any special tax characteristics are preserved. Therefore, the long-term capital gain of $7,000, the Section 1231 loss of $3,000, and the dividends of $200 must be removed from partnership book income to arrive at ordinary income. The deduction for the interest paid to the partners for the use of capital is ordinary and does not require reconciling. The computation of ordinary income for the partnership is as follows:

Book Income		$100,000
Add: Section 1231		
Loss		3,000
		$103,000
Deduct: LTCG	$7,000	
Dividends	200	7,200
Ordinary Income		$95,800

Each partner should report one-half ($47,900) of the partnership income on his individual income tax return for 1979.

2. (1180,P3,59) (b) The requirement is to calculate the basis of the land distributed to Atley in liquidation of his interest in the Atley and Donald partnership. Since the cash distribution first reduces Atley's basis in the partnership to $1,000, Atley's basis for the land is limited to $1,000, which represents his remaining partnership basis after the cash distribution. Note that even though the FMV of the property is $3,000, Atley recognizes no gain, since gain is only recognized on a distribution if the money received exceeds basis.

3. (1180,P3,60) (b) The requirement is to determine the tax basis of Lewis' partnership interest as of December 31, 1979. Since Lewis' share of profits and losses is 40%, Lewis' December 31, 1978 basis of $18,000 is increased by $20,000 (40% of $50,000) and decreased by $4,000 (40% of $10,000) resulting in a basis of $34,000 at December 31, 1979.

4. (580,Q2,29) (a) The requirement is to determine partnership taxable income (ordinary income or loss). The net operating loss deduction and personal exemptions of partners are not applicable to partnerships. Charitable contributions are a special item and can't be netted with ordinary income. Partners' salaries (guaranteed payments) are deductible in computing partnership taxable income (ordinary income or loss).

5. (580,Q2, 30) (a) The amount of partnership loss which may be deducted by a partner is limited to the partner's basis in the partnership (at the end of the taxable year of the partnership). Rey's share of the loss is ½ of $42,000, or $21,000. Rey's loss deduction is limited to his basis of $18,000. The remaining $3,000 may be carried forward and taken as a deduction in a subsequent year in which he has basis to absorb the loss.

6. (580,Q2,31) (a) The requirement is to determine the partnership's ordinary income for 1979.

Net income from sales	$62,000
Interest on corporate bonds	3,000
Net rental income	7,000
Partnership ordinary income	$72,000

The dividends (qualifying for exclusion) and capital gains are special items which must be separately reported and not netted with ordinary income.

7. (1174,P1,14) (d)

Cash received	$15,000
Liabilities assumed	+ 2,000
Total received	$17,000
Basis	−11,000
Long term capital gain	$ 6,000

8. (1174,P1,16) (a) No gain or loss shall be recognized to a partnership or to any of its partners resulting from a contribution of property to the partnership in exchange for a partnership interest.

9. (1174,P1,12) (e) (Adapted) Net gain for Lewis' taxable income

2/3 of short-term loss (3,000)	$ (2,000)
2/3 of long-term gain (15,000)	10,000
Personal short-term loss	(2,000)
Net capital gain	$ 6,000
60% exclusion	3,600
Taxable income	$ 2,400

10.   (1176,P1,15)   (d)   The amount of partnership loss which may be deducted by a partner is limited to his basis in the partnership (at the end of the taxable year of the partnership). Ashford's share of the loss is 1/3 of $48,000, or $16,000. However, the loss is limited to his basis of $15,000. Here 1/3 of $15,000 liability was added to the $10,000 basis. The remaining $1,000 may be carried over and taken once the partner's basis has been built up. For the purpose of determining amount of loss deductible, liabilities are included in basis only if partner is personally liable for them.

11. (1172,P1,8)   (b)   Partners' ownership interests may differ for tax and capital purposes. The property Cash contributed to the partnership had a basis of $15,000 and a fair market value of $10,000. Even though his capital interest is $10,000, his tax basis is equal to the basis of the property transferred and the property retains the tax basis prior to contribution to the partnership ($15,000 in this case).

The partnership sold the property for $12,000. The basis was $15,000 thereby yielding a $3,000 loss to the partnership. An income sharing ratio is not given in the problem so you must assume the partners share equally in gains and loss. Under the equal sharing assumption, Cash would report one-half of the $3,000 loss or $1,500.

12. (1174,P1,15)   (b)   A person is recognized as a partner if he owns an interest, however acquired, in a partnership where capital is a material income producing factor.

13.   (1178,Q2,23)   (b)   Generally, a partner's basis in the partnership consists of his capital contribution plus taxable income. It is decreased by distributions by the partnership and the partner's distributed share of any partnership losses. In this case, Martin's basis in the partnership is his original contribution of $75,000 less his one-half share of the $18,000 loss. Therefore, his basis is $66,000. The guaranteed salary of $20,000 is considered as ordinary income to the partner, not a distribution of partnership capital. This is deductible as an ordinary and necessary business expense.

14. (1178,Q2,26) (a)   Partnership taxable income is computed similarly to the business income of an individual. Certain items, however, called special items, are not included in the computation of partnership taxable income but are allocated to the partners separately. Capital gains, dividends received, and charitable contributions are all examples of special items which are not included in the computation of partnership taxable income. Guaranteed payments to partners are included in the computation of taxable income of the partnership. Since the operating income of $150,000 includes a charitable contribution of $1,000, this must be added back to arrive at the taxable income of the partnership. The long-term capital gain of $4,000 and the dividends received of $2,000 should not be included in the ordinary income of the partnership.

15.   (1178,Q2,30) (d)   Generally transactions between partners and their partnership are treated as arm's-length transactions. An exception is that losses are not deductible on sales between a more than 50% partner and the partnership, or between partnerships which are more than 50% owned by the same persons. Since Edward owns more than 50% of the partnership, the $3,000 loss on the sale of the machinery to Edward will not be deductible by the partnership. This loss must be added back to the $50,000 of net income, and therefore the partnership taxable income is $53,000. Edward's 70% share of $53,000 is $37,100.

16.   (575,Q2,19)   (c)   Abbott's distributive share is 20% of $45,000 ordinary gain and 20% of $5,000 LTCG. This assumes Abbott has ample basis to absorb the $2,500 excess distribution. The LTCG is subject to a 60% capital gains deduction. Thus his adjusted gross income is increased by $9,400 ($9,000 ordinary gain plus $400 LTCG).

Note: The deduction for LTCG incurred after October 31, 1978, is increased to 60%.

17.   (1175,Q2,24)   (a) (Adapted) Additional first-year depreciation of 20% of the cost of tangible personal property may be deducted in the year of acquisition if the asset has a life of at least 6 years. The deduction is limited to $2,000 for a partnership, regardless of the number of partners or their marital status.

18.   (574,Q2,31)   (a)   Brill received nothing due to his death, but his estate is entitled to his 1/3 share ($15,000). Clark was a partner for the full period. He therefore receives his 1/3 share ($15,000). Aster was a partner for 2/3 of the year and therefore 2/3 of the 1/3 partnership income is includable by him ($10,000). Dexter must report the remaining 1/3 of the 1/3 partnership income ($5,000). The reason for the split by Aster and Dexter is due to the assumption that income was earned on a pro rata monthly basis.

19. (574,Q2,30) (c) Gains and losses are shared equally. The $6,000 gain ($31,000 - $25,000) is divided equally ($2,000 each).

20. (1176,A2,29) (e) As a general rule, no gain or loss is recognized by a partner for contribution of property to a partnership in exchange for an interest in the partnership. There are two exceptions which do not affect this problem. These two exceptions are when a partner contributes his services for a partnership interest and when property is contributed with a mortgage greater than its adjusted basis. Generally, contributed property will have the same basis to the partnership as it did to the contributing partner (here $16,000).

21. (1176,Q2,30) (b) Partnership losses deductible by partners are limited to their pro rata share (here $4,000) and also limited to the partner's basis in the partnership before reflection of the loss. Filmore began with a $6,000 basis in the partnership which was reduced to $3,000 after the withdrawal. Thus, Filmore is limited to a $3,000 loss in 1975. The excess $1,000 loss may be taken when Filmore's basis increases.

22. (1177,Q2,26) (a) Special items are items of income and expense which are not included in the computation of partnership income; they are allocated to the partners separately. Charitable contributions, foreign taxes, Section 1231 gains and losses, qualifying dividends, tax preference items, additional first-year depreciation, etc., are special items. Thus the charitable contributions of $2,000, foreign taxes of $5,000, and machinery loss of $12,000 (all of which total $19,000) are deductions that the partnership should have reported separately. Since $19,000 of expenses and losses are reported separately, the partnership would report $279,000 of operating income instead of $260,000.

23. (1177,Q2,28) (c) Both distributable shares of income and guaranteed payments are reported by partners for the year in which the end of the partnership fiscal year occurs. Note that the guaranteed payments are treated as distributions of profits. This is an exception to the normal rule of recognizing income upon cash receipt. In 1976 Bond should report 40% of the $80,000 1975-1976 income and the guaranteed salary during the partnership's fiscal year ending in 1976.

40% of $80,000	=	$32,000
9 months x $1,000	=	9,000
3 months x $1,500	=	4,500
		$45,500

MAY 1981 ANSWERS

24. (581,Q3,49) (b) The requirement is to determine the ordinary income of the partnership. Income from operations is considered ordinary income as is net rental income. Dividends from foreign corporations also are included in the partnership's ordinary income since they are not eligible for the dividend exclusion. Tax-exempt income remains tax-exempt and is excluded from the computation of ordinary income. Thus, ordinary income is:

Income from operations	$156,000
Dividends from foreign corporations	6,000
Net rental income	12,000
Partnership ordinary income	$174,000

25. (581,Q3,51) (d) The requirement is to determine the amount that Jordan should report as his share of partnership ordinary income on his 1980 tax return. Each partner reports his share of partnership income for the year within which the last day of the partnership taxable year occurs. Thus, Jordan should report $72,000 as income from the partnership on his 1980 calendar-year return.

26. (581,Q3,52) (a) The requirement is to determine Wilson's share of the partnership's capital gain/loss. The partnership's basis is the $40,000 adjusted basis Wilson had for the asset when it was contributed in 1978. Thus, the partnership's capital loss is $4,000 ($36,000 − $40,000). Since Wilson has a 50% profit and loss sharing ratio, his share of the capital loss is $2,000.

UNOFFICIAL ANSWER

Problem 1   Abcoe Engineering†

a.   ABCOE ENGINEERING SERVICES
Schedule Computing Ordinary Income to be Reported
in the 1980 Partnership Income Tax Return

Net income for 1980 from the partnership income statement		$75,000
Add:		
Excessive depreciation taken on equipment sold (1)	$ 107	
Section 1245 gain on equipment sold (4)	4,653	
TOTAL additions		4,760
		79,760
Deduct:		
Partners' salaries	$45,000	
Partners' interest	3,000	
Short-term capital gain on securities sold	900	
Dividends on securities sold	60	
Additional allowable depreciation on new building (2)	267	
Additional allowable depreciation on new equipment (3)	1,450	
TOTAL deductions		50,677
Ordinary income to be reported on the partnership income tax return		29,083

Computation of Depreciation Adjustments on Furniture and Equipment Sold and on New Building

	(1) Furniture and equipment sold	(2) New building
Tax basis	$ 5,240	$40,000
Depreciation rate (1) 150% DB		
(2) 150% DB	.15	.0333
Annual depreciation	$ 786	$ 1,333
Tax depreciation for 6 months	$ 393	$ 667
Depreciation on financial statements	$ 500	$ 400
Depreciation adjustments for tax purposes	$ 107	$ (267)

(3)
Computation of Additional Allowable Depreciation on New Furniture and Equipment

Tax basis	$30,000
20% additional first-year depreciation	2,000
Basis for depreciation	28,000
Depreciation rate	.20
Annual depreciation	$ 5,600
Tax depreciation for 6 months	$ 2,800
Depreciation on financial statements	1,350
Additional depreciation allowable for tax purposes	$ 1,450

(4)
Computation of Section 1245 Gain on Sale of Office Furniture and Equipment

Sales price		$ 9,500
Cost to Coe	$20,000	
Depreciation deduction by Coe	$14,760	
Depreciation deduction by partnership	393	
Total depreciation deductible	15,153	
Adjusted basis		4,847
Net gain allocated to Coe		$ 4,653

SOLUTION GUIDE

Problem 1   Abcoe Engineering

1. This problem consists of two related parts which require the differentiation between partnership ordinary items and special items that must be separately allocated to partners. The solution approach is to analyze each paragraph of information, making notes on the face of your examination as to the tax treatment to be accorded each item.

    1.1 Note that since the partners' contribution of property to the partnership for a capital interest is nontaxable, there is a carryover of tax basis for the contributed property in the hands of the partnership.

    1.2 On the other hand, the statement "Each partner's capital account was credited $10,000," indicates that the contributed property was recorded on the books (also reflected in financial statements) at FMV.

2. Part a requires a schedule computing partnership ordinary income, which must be arrived at by starting with financial statement income of $75,000 and itemizing differences to arrive at ordinary income for tax purposes.

    2.1 The guaranteed payments to partners for salaries and interest are deducted since they are an ordinary expense that was not subtracted in computing net income.

    2.2 $60 of dividends are subtracted because they must be separately allocated as a special item.

    2.3 The STCG on the sale of securities is a special item and must be deducted. The amount to be deducted from net income is $5,900 − $5,000 = $900.

    2.4 The maximum depreciation allowable for tax purposes must be computed and compared with the depreciation deducted on the income statement. Depreciation on the furniture and equipment ("used" tangible personal property) and on the new building (new nonresidential real property) is limited to 150% DB. Additional first-year depreciation (maximum of $2,000) and 200% DB are allowable for the new furniture and equipment.

2.5 The entire gain on the sale of the old furniture and equipment is ordinary income because of the Sec. 1245 recapture potential carried over from Coe to the partnership. Since the furniture and equipment was sold for book value (i.e., no financial statement gain or loss), all of the taxable gain must be added to net income.

3.1 Part b requires a schedule presenting each partner's distributable share of items to be separately reported for income tax purposes.

3.2 Although ordinary in nature, the depreciation and Sec. 1245 income on the equipment sold must be separately reported because they are subject to special allocations (i.e., other than general profit and loss ratio).

3.3 Note that it is the "investment in property that qualifies for investment credit" rather than an amount of credit that is reported for each partner.

b.

Schedule of Distributable Share of Items to be Reported Separately by Each Partner for 1980 Partnership Transactions

	Total	Adair	Blinker	Coe
Ordinary income	$29,083			
Depreciation of equipment sold	393			
Sec. 1245 income on sale of equipment	(4,653)			
Ordinary income subject to equal distribution	$24,823	$ 8,275	$ 8,274	$ 8,274
Guaranteed payments to partners— salaries and interest	48,000	19,000	16,100	12,900
Additional first-year depreciation	(2,000)	(667)	(667)	(666)
Dividends on securities sold	60	20	20	20
Specially allocated items:				
Short-term capital gain on sale of securities (1)	2,900	300	2,300	300
Depreciation on equipment sold	(393)	(197)	(196)	– –
Sec. 1245 income on sale of equipment	4,653	– –	– –	4,653
Investment in property that qualifies for investment credit—10-year life	30,000	10,000	10,000	10,000

(1)   Computation of Short-Term Capital Gain on Sale of Securities

Sales price	$5,900
Tax basis	3,000
Net gain	2,900
First allocation to Blinker	2,000
Balance allocated equally	$ 900

MULTIPLE CHOICE QUESTIONS (1–51)

1. Geyer, Inc., a calendar year corporation, had net income per books of $80,000 for the year 1979. For each of the years 1975-1978, Geyer's net income (loss) per books was as follows:

1975	$ 5,000
1976	15,000
1977	10,000
1978	(60,000)

Included in Geyer's gross revenues for 1978 were taxable dividends of $20,000 received from an unrelated domestic corporation. When filing its tax return for 1978 on March 10, 1979, Geyer elected to give up the three-year carryback of the loss for 1978. Geyer should report a net operating loss carryover on its tax return for 1979 of

- a. $30,000
- b. $47,000
- c. $60,000
- d. $77,000

2. On July 1, 1979, Mr. Grey formed Dover Corporation. The same date Grey paid $100,000 cash and transferred property with an adjusted basis of $50,000 to Dover in exchange for 3,000 shares of its common stock. The property had a fair market value of $85,000 on the date of the exchange. Dover had no other shares of common stock outstanding on July 1, 1979. As a result of the above transaction, Grey's basis in his stock and Dover's basis in the property, respectively, are:

- a. $150,000 and $50,000.
- b. $150,000 and $85,000.
- c. $185,000 and $50,000.
- d. $185,000 and $85,000.

3. Drury Corporation, a Subchapter S Corporation, had taxable income and current earnings and profits of $45,000 for the year ended December 31, 1979. Included in the above is $42,000 excess net long-term capital gain over net short-term capital losses. Drury paid $4,760 in capital gains taxes for 1979. Cash distributions to Mr. Hoyt, the sole shareholder, totaled $60,000 during 1979. On December 31, 1978, Drury had accumulated earnings and profits of $50,000, none of which had been previously taxed. What amount should Hoyt report on his individual income tax return for 1979 as long-term capital gain passed through from Drury?

- a. $37,240
- b. $42,000
- c. $45,000
- d. $46,760

4. Tyler Corporation had taxable income of $560,000 before deducting charitable contributions for its tax year ended December 31, 1979. The dividends received deduction was $85,000. Tyler made cash contributions of $50,000 to charitable organizations. How much can Tyler deduct as contributions for 1979?

- a. $28,000
- b. $32,250
- c. $33,000
- d. $50,000

5. During 1979 Gilbert Manufacturing Company, in need of additional factory space, exchanged 10,000 shares of its common stock with a par value of $100,000 for a building with a fair market value of $120,000. On the date of the exchange the stock had a market value of $130,000. For 1979, how much and what type of gain or loss should Gilbert report on this transaction?

- a. No gain or loss.
- b. $10,000 capital loss.
- c. $20,000 capital gain.
- d. $20,000 section 1231 gain.

6. Pursuant to a plan of reorganization adopted in 1979, Daly Corporation exchanged property with an adjusted basis of $100,000 for 1,000 shares of the common stock of Galen Corporation. The 1,000 shares of Galen common stock had a fair market value of $110,000 on the date of the exchange. As a result of this exchange, what is Daly's recognized gain and what is its basis in the Galen common stock, respectively?

- a. $0 and $100,000.
- b. $0 and $110,000.
- c. $10,000 and $100,000.
- d. $10,000 and $110,000.

7. For the year ended December 31, 1979, Canterbury Corporation had dividend income from non-affiliated domestic corporations of $50,000 and gross business income of $30,000. Business deductions for 1979 amounted to $45,000. What is Canterbury's dividends received deduction for 1979?

- a. $0
- b. $29,750
- c. $42,500
- d. $50,000

8. Wright Corporation reported $100,000 of book income before income taxes for the year ended December 31, 1979. The income statement disclosed the following information:

Christmas gifts to 40 customers at $100 each.

Dividends of $20,000 received from Morley, Ltd., a corporation not subject to United States income tax.

Insurance premiums of $15,000 on a policy insuring the life of the president of the corporation, under which Wright Corporation is the beneficiary.

What should Wright report as its taxable income for 1979?

a. $ 98,000
b. $103,000
c. $115,000
d. $118,000

9. For the year ended December 31, 1979, Marshall Corporation reported book income, before federal income taxes, of $200,000. The following items were included in the determination of income before federal income taxes:

Provision for state corporation income tax	$15,000
Interest on United States obligations	20,000
Net long-term capital loss from the sale of marketable securities	(10,000)
Interest paid on loan to purchase United States obligations	12,000

Marshall's taxable income on its 1979 federal income tax return would be

a. $192,000
b. $193,000
c. $210,000
d. $225,000

10. Chaucer Corporation reported taxable income of $350,000 on its federal income tax return for the 1979 calendar year. Selected information for 1979 is available from Chaucer's records as follows:

Interest income on municipal bonds	$20,000
Depreciation claimed on the tax return based on the double-declining-balance method	75,000
Depreciation recorded on the books based on the straight-line method	50,000
Provision for federal income tax per books	140,000

Based on the above information, Chaucer should report net income per books for 1979 in the amount of

a. $235,000
b. $255,000
c. $395,000
d. $445,000

11. Grady Corporation's book income before income taxes was $300,000 for the year 1979 after recording amortization of organization costs. Organization costs of $140,000 incurred at the organization date two years earlier are being written off over a ten-year period for financial reporting purposes, and over the minimum period for income tax purposes. Assuming that there were no other reconciling items, what is Grady's taxable income for 1979?

a. $272,000
b. $286,000
c. $300,000
d. $314,000

12. Davies Corporation (not a Subchapter S Corporation) had a deficit of $160,000 at December 31, 1978. Its net income per books was $80,000 for 1979. Cash dividends on common stock totaling $40,000 were paid in December 1979. Davies should report the distribution to its shareholders as

a. Return of capital 100%.
b. Ordinary dividends 25%; return of capital 75%.
c. Ordinary dividends 50%; return of capital 50%.
d. Ordinary dividends 100%.

13. April Corporation's book income before income taxes for 1979 was $60,000. During 1979 April paid $3,000 in cash dividends on its outstanding cumulative preferred stock and paid $4,000 as a contribution to a qualified charitable organization. For 1979 April's taxable income was

a. $54,000.
b. $60,800.
c. $60,850.
d. $61,000.

14. In determining whether a corporation is subject to the accumulated earnings tax, which of the following items is not a subtraction in arriving at accumulated taxable income?

a. Federal income tax.
b. Capital loss carryback.
c. Dividends paid deduction.
d. Accumulated earnings credit.

15. During 1979, its first year of operations, Emma Corporation had a loss from operations of $38,000 and short-term capital gains of $12,000. Included in the loss from operations was a fire loss of $7,000. Emma has a net operating loss carryover from 1979 of

    a. $19,000.
    b. $26,000.
    c. $31,000.
    d. $38,000.

16. In 1979 Nugent Corporation sold for $21,000, 1,000 shares of its own $10 par value common stock that it had reacquired in 1977. The shares were originally issued for $15 per share, and subsequently reacquired for $19 per share. For 1979 Nugent should report a long-term capital gain of

    a. $0.
    b. $ 2,000.
    c. $ 6,000.
    d. $11,000.

17. For the year ended December 31, 1979, Ginny Corporation had gross income of $180,000. Included in this amount was $48,000 of dividend income from non-affiliated domestic corporations. Its deductions for 1979 were $130,000 in business deductions and a net operating loss carryover of $4,000. What is Ginny's 1979 dividends received deduction?

    a. $39,100
    b. $40,800
    c. $42,500
    d. $48,000

18. During 1979 Ashley Corporation charged the following payments to miscellaneous expense:

    · Travel expense of $300 for the company president to offer voluntary testimony at the state capital against proposed legislation regarded as unfavorable to its business.
    · Christmas gifts to 20 customers at $75 each.
    · Contribution of $600 to local political candidate.

The maximum deduction that Ashley can claim for these payments is

    a. $ 800.
    b. $1,400.
    c. $1,800.
    d. $2,400.

19. On July 2, 1979, Milford Corporation purchased for $70,000 machinery that was installed in its factory. The machinery was estimated to have a salvage value of $4,000 and Milford elected to depreciate this machinery over eight years using the double-declining balance method of depreciation. Milford in addition elected to take additional first-year depreciation. This acquisition was the only investment in tangible personal property made during 1979. Counting the year of acquisition as one-half year, Milford should deduct depreciation on this machinery for 1979 of

    a. $10,000.
    b. $10,250.
    c. $10,500.
    d. $10,750.

20. Hastings Corporation is an accrual-basis taxpayer. For the year ended December 31, 1974, it had book income before tax of $305,000 after deducting a charitable contribution of $25,000. The contribution was authorized by the board of directors in December 1974, but it was actually paid on March 14, 1975. How should Hastings treat this charitable contribution for tax purposes to minimize its 1974 taxable income?

    a. It can do nothing for 1974, but must apply the payment to the 1975 tax year.
    b. File a proper election, claim a deduction for 1974 of $15,250, and carry the remainder over a maximum of five succeeding tax years.
    c. File a proper election, claim a deduction for 1974 of $16,500, and carry the remainder over a maximum of five succeeding tax years.
    d. File a proper election and claim a 1974 deduction of $25,000.
    e. None of the above.

21. The Guardian Corporation, not a dealer in securities, owned marketable securities that had an adjusted basis of $150,000. On June 30, 1977, when the market value of these securities rose to $180,000, Guardian distributed these securities to its shareholders. As a result of this distribution, Guardian should report

    a. No gain on the distribution
    b. Ordinary income of $30,000.
    c. A capital gain of $30,000.
    d. A capital gain of $180,000.

22. In 1977 Jonna Corporation sold some excess property for $2,500 to John Moll, an individual and one of its minority shareholders. On the date of sale the property had a fair market value of $6,000 and an adjusted basis of $4,000. Jonna must report a property distribution of

a. $1,500.
b. $2,000.
c. $2,500.
d. $3,500.

23.   The accumulated earnings tax imposed on corporations for improper accumulation of earnings in excess of reasonable needs does not apply to
a.   Closely-held corporations.
b.   Widely-held corporations.
c.   Personal holding companies.
d.   None of the above.

24.   Will Benton owned all of the stock of a corporation that has been determined to be collapsible. The basis of the stock to Benton was $25,000, and the corporation had accumulated earnings and profits of $1,000.   Benton sold his stock for $40,000. As a result of the sale Benton must report
a. $15,000 ordinary gain.
b. $1,000 ordinary income and $14,000 capital gain.
c. $14,000 capital gain.
d. $15,000 capital gain.
e.   None of the above.

25.   On October 1, 1979, Helma Corporation traded † a business automobile with an adjusted basis of $1,500 for a new automobile to be used in the business. In addition Helma paid $3,000 in cash. The new automobile has an estimated life of four years and no estimated salvage. The corporation is on a calendar year and had 1979 taxable income of $80,000. The 1979 investment tax credit allowed on this acquisition should be
a. $70.
b. $150.
c. $210.
d. $315.
e.   None of the above.

26.   Eazy Corporation's earnings and profits for 1974, its first year of operations, were $22,000. In December of 1974, it distributed to its individual stockholders, cash of $10,000 and land with a basis of $14,000 and a fair market value of $25,000 at the date of distribution.   Prior to the distribution, the stockholders' tax basis of their investment in the corporation was $76,000.

What was the stockholders' adjusted basis at the end of 1974?

a. $51,000.
b. $52,000.
c. $63,000.
d. $74,000.

Items 27 and 28 are based on the following information:

27.   The Bat Corporation, a calendar-year company, has operated as a Subchapter S corporation for the past four years. At December 31, 1973, the company had undistributed taxable income of $30,000. For the year ended December 31, 1974, it had taxable income and current earnings and profits of $145,000. During 1974, the company made four distributions in cash to its ten equal stockholders who are also on a calendar-year basis. The cash distributions to stockholders were as follows:

January 17, 1974	$15,000
March 11, 1974	20,000
June 12, 1974	25,000
October 14, 1974	30,000
	$90,000

For the calendar year 1974, what amount should be included in each stockholder's gross income from Bat?
a. $5,500.
b. $9,000.
c. $14,500.
d. $15,000.
e.   None of the above.

28.   The basis of one stockholder's stock as of January 1, 1974, was $24,000. What was the basis of his stock on October 1, 1974?
a. $21,000.
b. $32,500.
c. $33,000.
d. $38,500.
e.   None of the above.

29.   During 1979, the Alex Corporation purchased † new equipment for $600,000 that had an estimated ten-year life and qualified for the investment tax credit. The corporation's tax liability for 1979 was $50,000 before claiming an investment tax credit.
What is the maximum investment tax credit that Alex Corporation can claim for 1979?

a. $5,000
b. $37,000
c. $40,000
d. $60,000
e. None of the above.

30. For the year ended December 31, 1975, the Dab Corporation, a Subchapter S corporation, had net income per books of $60,000 which included $70,000 from operations and a $10,000 net long-term capital loss. During 1975, $30,000 was distributed to the corporation's ten equal shareholders, all of whom are calendar-year taxpayers.

For 1975, each shareholder should report as his or her share of the corporation's taxable income

a. $3,000 ordinary income.
b. $6,000 ordinary income.
c. $7,000 ordinary income.
d. $7,000 ordinary income; $1,000 net long-term capital loss.
e. None of the above.

31. The Austin Corporation was incorporated on January 1, 1976, and elected to be taxed as a Subchapter S corporation. The net income per books for 1976 was $94,000 after reflecting the following items:

Dividends from domestic corporations $4,000
Contributions to recognized charitable
    organizations   6,000

During 1976, Austin distributed $20,000 among its ten equal shareholders. What should Austin report as its taxable income for 1976?

a. $74,000.
b. $90,000.
c. $91,600.
d. $95,000.

32. During 1976, Livingston Corporation (not a Western Hemisphere Trade Corporation) donated $7,000 to recognized charitable organizations. Its taxable income for 1976, after all deductions except contributions, was $83,000. It had no capital gains or losses, but received dividend income of $20,000 from unaffiliated domestic corporations. What amount can Livingston deduct as contributions for 1976?

a. $3,150.
b. $4,150.
c. $5,000.
d. $7,000.

33. Hill Corporation and its wholly-owned subsidiary, Dale Corporation, file a consolidated return on a calendar-year basis. On March 28, 1976, Hill sold land, which it had used in its business for ten years, to Dale for $60,000. Hill's basis in the land on March 28th was $40,000. Dale held the land until June 2, 1977, whereupon it sold the property for $75,000 to an unrelated third party. What amount of income should Hill report in the consolidated return filed for 1976?

a. $0.
b. $20,000 Section 1250 gain.
c. $20,000 long-term capital gain.
d. $20,000 ordinary income.

34. Shaney Corporation repurchased its own outstanding bonds in the open market for $258,000 on May 31, 1976. The bonds were originally issued on May 5, 1974, at face value of $250,000. For its tax year ending December 31, 1976, Shaney should report

a. Neither income nor a deduction.
b. A deduction of $4,000.
c. A capital gain of $4,000.
d. A deduction of $8,000.

35. Morris Corporation, a Subchapter S corporation, had taxable income and current earnings and profits of $200,000 for its year ended December 31, 1976. It had no capital gains or losses. For the year ended December 31, 1975, it had undistributed taxable income of $30,000. During 1976 it made the following distributions to its shareholders:

February 15 $50,000 (cash)
April 15   70,000 (property)
September 15   40,000 (cash)

What should be the undistributed taxable income for the year ended December 31, 1976?

a. $40,000.
b. $70,000.
c. $110,000.
d. $140,000.

36. On December 1, 1976, Gelt Corporation distributed to its sole shareholder, as a dividend in kind, a parcel of land that was not an inventory asset. On the date of the distribution, the following data were available.

Adjusted basis of land $ 6,500
Fair market value of land   14,000
Mortgage-on land   5,000

For the year ended December 31, 1976, Gelt had earnings and profits of $30,000 without regard to the dividend distribution. By how much should the dividend distribution reduce the earnings and profits for 1976?

    a. $1,500.
    b. $6,500.
    c. $9,000.
    d. $14,000.

MAY 1981 QUESTIONS

37.   On October 1, 1980, Derek Corporation sold 4,000 shares of its $10 par value treasury stock for $60,000. These shares were acquired by Derek on January 2, 1980, for $50,000. For 1980 Derek should report

    a.   Neither income nor capital gain.
    b.   A long-term capital gain of $10,000.
    c.   A short-term capital gain of $10,000.
    d.   A long-term capital gain of $20,000.

38.   For the year ended December 31, 1980, Apollo Corporation had net income per books of $1,200,000. Included in the determination of net income were the following items:

Interest income on municipal bonds	$ 40,000
Gain on settlement of life insurance policy (death of officer)	200,000
Interest paid on loan to purchase municipal bonds	8,000
Provision for federal income tax	524,000

What should Apollo report as its taxable income for 1980?

    a. $1,492,000.
    b. $1,524,000.
    c. $1,684,000.
    d. $1,692,000.

39.   During the 1980 holiday season, Taurus Corporation gave business gifts to 34 customers. The value of the gifts, which were not of an advertising nature, was as follows:

    8 @ $10
    8 @ $25
    8 @ $50
    10 @ $100

For 1980 Taurus can deduct as a business expense

    a. $0.
    b. $ 280.
    c. $ 730.
    d. $1,680.

40.   On December 31, 1960, Homer Corporation issued $2,000,000 of fifty-year bonds for $2,600,000. On December 31, 1980, Homer issued new bonds with a face value of $3,000,000 for which it received $3,400,000 and used part of the proceeds to repurchase for $2,320,000 the bonds issued in 1960. No elections were made to adjust the basis of any property. What is the taxable income to Homer on the repurchase of the 1960 bonds?

    a. $0.
    b. $ 40,000.
    c. $280,000.
    d. $360,000.

41.   For its year ended December 31, 1980, Valor Corporation, a Subchapter S Corporation, had net income per books of $216,000 which included $180,000 from operations and a $36,000 net long-term capital gain. During 1980, $90,000 was distributed to the corporation's nine equal shareholders, all of whom are on a calendar-year basis. Each shareholder should report for 1980

    a. $10,000 ordinary income.
    b. $20,000 ordinary income.
    c. $20,000 ordinary income and $4,000 long-term capital gain.
    d. $24,000 ordinary income.

42.   Marina Corporation, a Subchapter S Corporation, had taxable income and current earnings and profits of $390,000 for the year ended December 31, 1980. There were no capital gains or losses during 1980. For the year ended December 31, 1979, Marina had undistributed taxable income of $90,000. During 1980 Marina made the following cash distributions to its ten equal shareholders:

January 31	$50,000
March 1	80,000
October 1	60,000

What is the undistributed taxable income for the year ended December 31, 1980?

    a. $200,000.
    b. $290,000.
    c. $300,000.
    d. $330,000.

43.   Norwood Corporation is an accrual-basis taxpayer. For the year ended December 31, 1980, it had book income before tax of $500,000 after deducting a charitable contribution of $100,000. The contribution was authorized by the Board of Directors in December 1980, but was not actually paid until March 1, 1981. How should Norwood treat this charitable contribution for tax purposes to minimize its 1980 taxable income?

a.   It cannot claim a deduction in 1980, but must apply the payment against 1981 income.

b.   Make an election claiming a deduction for 1980 of $25,000 and carry the remainder over a maximum of five succeeding tax years.

c.   Make an election claiming a deduction for 1980 of $30,000 and carry the remainder over a maximum of five succeeding tax years.

d.   Make an election claiming a 1980 deduction of $100,000.

44.   Pursuant to a plan of corporate reorganization adopted in 1980, Bart Smith exchanged 1,000 shares of Talbot Corporation common stock that he had purchased for $150,000, for 1,800 shares of Mark Corporation common stock having a fair market value of $172,000. As a result of this exchange, Smith's recognized gain and his basis in the Mark Corporation common stock should be

	Recognized Gain	Basis
a.	$0	$150,000
b.	$0	$172,000
c.	$22,000	$150,000
d.	$22,000	$172,000

45.   During 1980 Waner Corporation exchanged 10,000 shares of its own common stock with a par value of $10 per share for a building with a fair market value of $150,000. What should Waner report in its 1980 tax return as a result of this transaction?

a.   No gain.
b. $50,000 ordinary income.
c. $50,000 Section 1231 gain.
d. $50,000 Section 1245 gain.

46.   Robert Elk paid $100,000 for all of the issued and outstanding capital stock of Elkom Corp., a Subchapter S Corporation established in January 1978. Elkom's operating results and dividend distribution were as follows:

Date	Taxable income	Net operating loss	Dividend distribution
12/31/78		($40,000)	
9/30/79			$20,000
12/31/79	$60,000		
12/31/80	$30,000		

The basis of Elk's stock on December 31, 1980, is

a. $ 50,000.
b. $100,000.
c. $130,000.
d. $150,000.

47.   Filo, Inc., began business on July 1, 1980, and elected to file its income tax returns on a calendar-year basis. The following expenditures were incurred in organizing the corporation:

| August 1, 1980 | $300 |
| September 3, 1980 | $600 |

The maximum allowable deduction for amortization of organization expense in 1980 is

a. $60.
b. $65.
c. $81.
d. $90.

48.   Delve Co., Inc., issued $1,000,000 of 8-year convertible bonds on October 1, 1980, for $880,000. The amount of bond discount deductible on Delve's income tax return for the year ended March 31, 1981, is

a. $0.
b. $ 7,500.
c. $ 15,000.
d. $120,000.

49.   On June 30, 1980, Ral Corporation had retained earnings of $100,000. On that date, it sold a plot of land to a stockholder for $50,000. Ral had paid $40,000 for the land in 1975, and it had a fair market value of $80,000 when the stockholder bought it. The amount of dividend income taxable to the stockholder in 1980 (before the dividend exclusion) is

a. $0.
b. $10,000.
c. $20,000.
d. $30,000.

50.   Elmo Corporation had the following income and expenses for the year ended December 31, 1980:

Gross profit on sales	$150,000
Dividends from domestic taxable corporations	15,000
Salaries and wages	90,000
Interest expense	22,500
Taxes on real estate and payroll	52,500
Depreciation	15,000
Contributions	7,500

Elmo's net operating loss for 1980 is

a. $15,000.
b. $17,250.
c. $22,500.
d. $27,750.

51.   Cromwell Investors, Inc., has ten unrelated equal stockholders. For the year ended June 30, 1980, Cromwell's adjusted gross income comprised the following:

Dividends from domestic
   taxable corporations $10,000
Dividends from savings and loan
   associations on passbook
   savings accounts   1,000
Interest earned on notes
   receivable   5,000
Net rental income   3,000

The corporation paid no dividends during the taxable year. Deductible expenses totaled $4,000 for the year. Cromwell's liability for personal holding company tax for the year will be based on undistributed personal holding company income of

   a. $0.
   b. $ 3,500.
   c. $ 6,500.
   d. $15,000.

PROBLEMS

Problem 1   Right and Left Corporation   (579,P5)

(40 to 50 minutes)

This problem consists of two unrelated parts.

Part a. Left Corporation has engaged you to compute its federal taxable income for the year ended December 31, 1978. The following information was supplied by Left's bookkeeper:

Gross profit from sales	$1,500,000
Operating expenses	1,000,000
Operating income	500,000
Other expense	50,000
Income before income taxes	$ 450,000

Additional information, none of which was included above, is as follows:

On January 15, 1978, Left sold for $10,000 marketable securities that were purchased for $8,500 on January 15, 1976.

On February 15, 1978, Left sold for $8,000 marketable securities that were purchased on October 15, 1977, for $9,000.

On March 30, 1978, Left purchased 10,000 shares of its own $10 par value common stock for $210,000.

During 1978, Left received dividends from domestic corporations of $12,000 and dividends from a wholly-owned domestic subsidiary with which Left does not file a consolidated return, of $10,000.

Left has a pension plan for its employees. Left has set up an employees' trust which meets the requirements of Code Section 401. Information concerning the pension plan activities for 1978 is as follows:

Contributions to the trust by Left	$25,000
Income from the investments of the trust	7,000
Pension benefits paid to retirees	21,000

On December 20, 1978, Left distributed hams costing $400 to its employees as a Christmas bonus.

During 1978, Left made contributions to various recognized charitable organizations of $40,000 and to various indigent persons of $100.

Based on estimates of its 1978 federal income tax, Right made estimated tax payments of $430,000 in 1978.

Required:

1.   Prepare a schedule, beginning with income before income taxes of $450,000, computing the federal taxable income of Left for the 1978 calendar year. Any possible alternative treatments should be resolved in a manner that will minimize taxable income. Show supporting computations in good form.

2.   List the items in the fact situation which were not used to determine the answer to 1. above. Explanations are not required.

Part b. Right Corporation appropriately applied the normal and surtax rates to its federal income for the calendar year 1978 and arrived at $500,000. Assume that the effective combined normal and surtax rate is 50%. Additional information is as follows:

The balance due of $20,000 for the 1977 federal income tax return was paid in 1978.

Based on estimates of its 1978 federal income tax, Right made estimated tax payments of $430,000 in 1978.

Right's investment tax credit for 1978 purchases of qualified investments was $30,000. An unused investment tax credit from 1977 purchases of qualified investments was $15,000.

Right properly computed its foreign tax credit at $10,000.

Right has withheld $40,000 of Social Security taxes from employees' wages in 1978. The employer's share has already been deducted as an expense in the calculation of the total federal income tax of $500,000 above.

Required:

1.   Prepare a schedule computing Right's federal income tax due for the 1978 calendar year. Any possible alternative treatments should be resolved in a manner that will minimize income taxes.

2.   List the items in the fact situation which were not used to determine the answer to 1. above. Explanations are not required.

Problem 2   Liberty, Inc.   (576,P3)

(50 to 60 minutes)

Your client, Liberty, Inc., has asked you to compute its corporate federal taxable income for the calendar year 1975 and to prepare a schedule reconciling its book income before federal income taxes to its federal taxable income. The book income before federal income taxes for the calendar year 1975 was computed as follows:

Gross margin (sales less cost of sales)		$300,000
Operating expenses:		
Depreciation	$ 25,000	
Charitable contributions	15,000	
Amortization of goodwill	5,000	
Other deductible expenses (not enumerated elsewhere)	165,000	
Total operating expenses		210,000
Operating income		90,000
Other income (deductions):		
Interest received on state and city bonds	3,500	
Dividends received from domestic corporations	4,000	
Gains on disposals of fixed assets	22,000	
Loss on disposal of investments	(28,600)	
Total other income		900
Income before federal income taxes		$ 90,900

You have gathered the following additional information:

• The depreciation expense of $25,000 for book purposes was based on the straight-line method. Depreciation expense for federal tax purposes was properly computed as $35,500 based on an accelerated method.

• The gains on disposals of fixed assets were computed as follows:

Involuntary conversion (Machine A)	$ 2,500
Exchange (Machine B)	2,400
Condemnation of land used in business	17,100
	$22,000

Machine A had an undepreciated cost (adjusted basis) when destroyed of $9,200. Liberty used the insurance proceeds from Machine A to immediately replace it with a similar machine costing $9,700. Liberty elected the special tax provision for non-recognition of part of the gain. Any gain recognized for federal tax purposes should be considered recaptured as ordinary income. Machine B had cost $38,000 in 1971. Total accumulated depreciation through the date of exchange was $19,600. Liberty exchanged Machine B and received $7,000 cash plus a similar machine with a fair market value of $21,000.

The gain on the condemnation of the land represents condemnation proceeds in excess of adjusted basis.

• The $28,600 loss on disposal of investments represents sales of stock in other corporations all held over six months.

• In 1974 (prior year), Liberty had made a large sale of ordinary-income property qualifying for the installment method of reporting for federal tax purposes. Liberty elected to report income under the installment method for federal tax purposes but reported the entire income in 1974 for book purposes. For 1975, the taxable portion of the 1975 installment collection is $8,000.

• Liberty paid dividends of $10,200 in 1975.

Required:

a.   Beginning with gross margin, prepare a schedule computing Liberty's 1975 corporate federal taxable income. Any possible alternative treatments should be resolved in a manner that will minimize taxable income. Show supporting computations in good form.

b.   Prepare a schedule reconciling Liberty's 1975 book income before federal income taxes to its 1975 federal taxable income. The schedule should have the following format:

Book income before federal income taxes	$90,900
Adjustments:	
Add:	
Deduct:	
Federal taxable income	$_____

Show supporting computations in good form.

MULTIPLE CHOICE ANSWERS

1.	d	12.	d	23.	c	34.	d	45.	a
2.	a	13.	b	24.	a	35.	d	46.	c
3.	a	14.	b	25.	b	36.	a	47.	d
4.	b	15.	b	26.	c	37.	a	48.	b
5.	a	16.	a	27.	c	38.	a	49.	d
6.	a	17.	b	28.	a	39.	c	50.	d
7.	c	18.	a	29.	c	40.	b	51.	a
8.	d	19.	c	30.	c	41.	c		
9.	c	20.	c	31.	d	42.	b		
10.	b	21.	a	32.	c	43.	c		
11.	b	22.	d	33.	a	44.	a		

EXPLANATION OF MULTIPLE CHOICE ANSWERS

1. (1180,P3,42) (d) The requirement is to determine the amount of the NOL carryover to 1979, given a 1978 loss per books of $60,000. Since the dividends received deduction (DRD) is not reflected in the loss per books, $17,000 (i.e., 85% x $20,000) must be added to the loss per books to arrive at the amount of NOL for 1978. Since Geyer elects to give up the 3-year carryback, all $77,000 is carried forward. Note that a DRD is allowed without limitation when there is a NOL.

2. (1180,P3,43) (a) The requirement is to determine Grey's basis for his stock and Dover's basis for the property following a nontaxable transfer to a controlled corporation. Grey's basis in the stock equals the $50,000 adjusted basis of property plus the $100,000 cash transferred, a total of $150,000. Dover's basis for the property equals Grey's adjusted basis plus any gain recognized on the transfer. Since no gain was recognized by Grey, the basis of the property to Dover is $50,000.

3. (1180,P3,45) (a) The requirement is to calculate the amount of LTCG passed through to Mr. Hoyt, the sole shareholder. A sub-S corporation's NLTCG in excess of NSTCL is passed through to shareholders as LTCG after being reduced by any capital gain and minimum taxes paid. Thus, the $42,000 LTCG minus the capital gains tax of $4,760, equals $37,240, the amount to be reported as LTCG by Mr. Hoyt.

4. (1180,P3,47) (b) The requirement is to calculate Tyler Corporation's charitable contribution deduction. Since a deduction for corporate charitable contributions is limited to 5% of TI before the charitable contribution and dividends received deductions, the dividends received deduction must be added back before the 5% calculation can be made:

$560,000	Taxable Income
+ 85,000	Dividend Received Deduction
$645,000	
x 5%	Charitable Contribution Limitation
$ 32,250	Charitable Contribution Deduction

5. (1180,P3,48) (a) The requirement is to determine the amount and type of gain or loss to be reported on the exchange of stock for property. Since a corporation never recognizes gain or loss on the receipt of money or other property in exchange for its stock (including treasury stock), no gain or loss is recognized by Gilbert Mfg. Company.

6. (1180,P3,49) (a) The requirement is to determine the recognized gain and the basis in the common stock received in a reorganization. A corporate reorganization generally involves a nontaxable exchange of one corporation's stock for property or stock of another. A realized gain is recognized only if "boot" is received. Since Daly Corporation received only stock (no boot), no gain is recognized and the basis in the stock is the same as the adjusted basis of the property given up — $100,000.

7. (1180,P3,51) (c) The requirement is to calculate the amount of dividends received deduction (DRD). Dividends received from nonaffiliated domestic corporations are subject to a 85% dividends received deduction. In certain situations, this DRD is limited to 85% of taxable income before the DRD. However, the limitation does not apply if the full 85% of dividends received deduction either creates or increases a net operating loss. In this case, a deduction of 85% of the dividends received (85% x $50,000) creates a net operating loss of $7,500. Therefore, the DRD is $42,500.

8. (1180,P3,52) (d) The requirement is to calculate Wright Corporation's taxable income from book income. The Christmas gifts are only deductible to the extend of $25 each. Therefore, $3,000 ($75 x 40) must be added back to book income. Dividends from foreign corporations are not eligible for a DRD, therefore no reconciling is necessary. Life insurance premiums are not deductible if the corporation is the beneficiary. Therefore, $15,000 must be added back to book income. Thus, the computation of taxable income is as follows:

Net Income per books	$100,000
Excess deduction for gifts	+ 3,000
Life insurance premiums	+ 15,000
Taxable Income	$118,000

9. (1180,P3,53)   (c)   The requirement is to determine Marshall Corporation's taxable income, given book income of $200,000 before federal income taxes. The only reconciling item is the NLTCL of $10,000 which was deducted per books, but is not deductible in computing taxable income. Taxable income is $210,000 ($200,000 + $10,000).

10. (1180,P3,54)   (b)   The requirement is to determine Chaucer Corporation's net income per books, given taxable income. Interest income on municipal bonds is excluded from taxable income; therefore, it must be added to calculate book income. Depreciation deducted in computing taxable income exceeds depreciation per books by $25,000; therefore, it must be added back. The provision for federal income tax must be deducted to arrive at book income. Thus, the computation of book income is as follows:

Taxable Income	$350,000
Interest on municipal bonds	20,000
Excess depreciation deducted	25,000
Provision for federal income tax per books	(140,000)
Net income per books	$255,000

11. (1180,P3,55)   (b)   The requirement is to adjust Grady Corporation's book income of $300,000 to taxable income. Organization expenses may be amortized over 60 months or longer, therefore, the minimum period for income tax purposes is 60 months. Adding back the book amortization of organization costs of $14,000 ($140,000 ÷ 10 years), and then deducting the maximum amount of $28,000 ($140,000 ÷ 12/60), results in taxable income of $286,000 for the Grady Corporation.

12. (1180,P3,57)   (d)   Corporate distributions to shareholders on their stock are taxed as dividends to the extent of current and/or accumulated earnings and profits. Since Davies Corporation had current earnings of $80,000 for 1979, the dividends of $40,000 paid in December 1979 are 100% ordinary dividends.

13. (580,Q2, 22)   (b)   The requirement is to compute April Corporation's TI, given book income before taxes of $60,000. The cash dividends paid on the preferred stock are not reflected in book income, and can be eliminated from the solution because dividends paid do not affect TI either. The charitable contribution should be added back to book income, because the deduction for charitable contributions is limited to 5% of TI before the contribution deduction.

Book income	$60,000
Charitable contribution	+4,000
TI before contributions	$64,000
Correct contribution deduction (limited to 5% x $64,000)	−3,200
Taxable income	$60,800

14. (580,Q2,35)   (b)   The requirement is to determine which item would not be subtracted in arriving at accumulated taxable income for purposes of computing the accumulated earnings tax. The "capital loss carryback" would not be subtracted since it represents a reduction of earnings and profits for a different taxable year.

15. (580,Q2,36)   (b)   The requirement is to compute the amount of net operating loss carryover from 1979 for Emma Corporation. The loss from operations of $38,000 (including the $7,000 fire loss) is reduced by the STCG of $12,000 to arrive at a NOL of $26,000. Since 1979 was the first year of operations for Emma Corp., there is no carryback and all $26,000 is carried over.

16. (580,Q2,37)   (a)   The requirement is to compute the amount of gain Nugent Corporation must recognize on the sale of its treasury stock. No gain or loss is recognized on the issuance of a corporation's own stock or the sale of its treasury shares. The excess of selling price over cost is treated as an adjustment to paid-in-capital, and is not considered income for tax purposes.

17. (580,Q2,38)   (b)   The requirement is to determine Ginny Corporation's dividends received deduction for 1979. The $48,000 of dividends from unaffiliated domestic corporations is included in Ginny's income and subject to a dividends received deduction (DRD) of 85% of the dividends. A possible limitation is that the DRD can not generally exceed 85% of TI before the DRD and NOL deduction.

Gross income (including dividends)	$180,000
Less business deductions	130,000
TI before DRD and NOL deduction	$ 50,000

Since $50,000 is greater than the $48,000 of dividends included in gross income, th DRD is 85% x $48,000 = $40,800.

18. (580,Q2,39)   (a)   The requirement is to determine the deductible amount of miscellaneous expenses incurred by Ashley Corporation. The $300 travel expense is deductible because the proposed legislation was related to Ashley's business. The Christmas gifts are deductible up to $25 per customer ($25 x 20 = $500). Gifts or contributions to political parties or candidates are not deductible business expenses. The maximum deduction is $800 (i.e., $300 + $500).

19. (580,Q2,40) (c) The requirement is to determine the proper amount of depreciation deduction for Milford Corporation. Additional first-year depreciation is 20% of the cost of the asset and reduces the asset's depreciation basis by the same amount. The deduction is limited to $2,000 annually. Therefore, $2,000 of additional first-year depreciation is taken on the equipment costing $70,000 which reduces the depreciation basis to $68,000. Salvage value is ignored in computing depreciation on the double-declining-balance method (except the asset cannot be depreciated below salvage value). Given a 8-year life the DDB depreciation rate is 25% (twice straight-line rate of 12.5%).

$ 2,000 additional first-year depreciation
  8,500 DDB depreciation (25% of $68,000) x ½ yr.
$10,500 depreciation

20. (1175,Q2,31) (c) An accrual basis corporation can elect to deduct contributions authorized by its board of directors during the taxable year, if they are paid by the 15th day of the third month after the close of the taxable year. Thus:

Book income $305,000
Add back incorrect deduction   25,000
Book income before contribution deduction
  5% limit = $16,500 correct deduction $330,000

The remaining $8,500 ($25,000 — $16,500) may be carried forward for five years.

21. (1178,Q2,21) (a) Corporations generally do not recognize gains or losses on the distribution of certain property to shareholders. (Gains may be recognized on distribution of LIFO inventory, depreciable property, and property with a basis less than related liability.) Guardian Corporation would recognize no gain on the distribution of the marketable securities to its shareholders.

22. (1178,Q2,22) (d) Jonna Corporation sold property for less than fair market value to a shareholder. This is considered a bargain sale, and the excess of the fair market value ($6,000) over its selling price ($2,500) is considered a distribution to the shareholder. Therefore, Jonna Corporation must report that the shareholder received a property distribution of $3,500.

23. (1178,Q2,33) (c) Corporations are taxed (penalized) for allowing earnings and profits to accumulate to avoid taxing shareholders on distributions. This tax is called the accumulated earnings tax. It is assessed on accumulations in excess of the greater of either reasonable needs of a business, or $150,000. It applies to all corporations except personal holding companies, because personal holding companies are subject to the personal holding company tax.

24. (1172,P1,6) (a) The general rule for collapsible corporations is, any shareholder owning more than 5% of the stock of a corporation which has been determined to be collapsible, is denied capital gain treatment on either a sale of his stock or on a distribution of the corporation's assets.

The shareholder in this problem must report the full gain as ordinary income.

Sale price $40,000
Basis   −25,000
Gain $15,000

25. (1174,P1,4) (b)

Trade-in $1,500
Cash paid   3,000
Total investment $4,500
Investment credit rate   x .10
Sub total $450
For assets of useful lives
  3 to 5 years   x 1/3
Amount of credit allowable $150
  is limited to tax liability
  of corporation, or $25,000
  plus 60% of liability greater
  than $25,000, whichever is
  less.

26. (1175,Q2,18) (c) The amount of the distribution is the amount of money plus the fair market value of any property received ($10,000 plus $25,000). Distributions, to the extent of earnings and profits ($22,000), are dividends to shareholders. The portion of the distribution that is not a dividend ($13,000) is a return of capital and will reduce shareholders' basis in their stock accordingly. The $13,000 capital distribution will reduce their basis from $76,000 to $63,000.

27. (1175,Q2,26) (c) Income from a Subchapter S corporation is assigned to the shareholders of record on the last day of the corporate tax year in proportion to their stock ownership. Gross income for one shareholder would

be 1/10th of taxable income of $145,000, or $14,500. The $30,000 undistributed taxable income was included in the shareholders' 1973 gross income.

28. (1175,Q2,27) (a) The $24,000 stock basis includes $3,000 of undistributed taxable income (UTI) from 12/31/73. The UTI basis adjustment occurs because the shareholder is being taxed on income the corporation has not distributed and this is treated as an increase in stockholder's investment. When this previously taxed undistributable and taxable income is received, the stockholder's basis in stock will be reduced accordingly. If within the first 2 1/2 months of 1974 any money is distributed, it is treated as a nontaxable distribution to the extent there was undistributed taxable income as of 12/31/73. Thus 10% of the 1/17 and 3/11 distributions limited to $3,000 will be treated as a distribution which reduces the shareholder's basis by $3,000 to $21,000. The remaining 1974 distributions will not affect stock basis unless they exceed earnings and profits of the year.

29. (1176,Q2,20) (c) The investment credit is limited to the tax liability, up to $25,000 and 60% of the tax liability in excess of $25,000. In this problem the tax liability is $50,000. So the investment credit is limited to $25,000 plus 60% of the second $25,000. While the credit is 10% of the $600,000 investment, it is limited to $40,000 per the above. The excess ($20,000) is carried back three years and carried over seven years. Investment tax credits are used in the following order: to (1) carryovers, (2) current credits, and (3) carrybacks.

30. (1176,Q2,21) (c) The requirement is each shareholder's ordinary income from the Sub S Corporation. Shareholders are taxed on their pro rata share of Sub S taxable income. ($70,000 ÷ 10 = $7,000). The $10,000 LTCL cannot be netted with the income from operations because only corporate capital gains can be offset by corporate capital losses. The LTCL is not passed through to the shareholders. It may be carried over for 5 years. Although some of the current earnings were distributed and some were not, the shareholders are still taxed on the current income of the Sub S Corporation.

31. (1177,Q2,19) (d) The taxable income of a Sub-chapter S corporation is generally computed the same as the taxable income of any other corporation.

The $20,000 distributed by Austin Corporation is not relevant in computing its taxable income. Contributions are limited to 5% of taxable income before the contribution deduction. Therefore the $6,000 deducted as contributions must be added back to income ($94,000 + $6,000 = $100,000). The charitable deduction is $5,000 (5% x $100,000). The taxable income is $95,000 ($100,000 − $5,000).

32. (1177,Q2,20) (c) Charitable contributions are limited to 5% of taxable income before the charitable contributions and dividend received deductions. Here the dividend received deduction, but not the charitable contribution deduction, is reflected in the $83,000 of taxable income. Thus 85% of $20,000, or $17,000, must be added back to $83,000, equaling $100,000 which is the amount on which the 5% charitable contribution is to be taken. Taxable income is the $100,000 less the $5,000 of charitable contributions and $17,000 of dividends received deduction.

33. (1177,Q2,21) (a) Recognition of gains and losses on the sale or exchange of property or other capitalized expenditures between affiliated corporations is deferred when a consolidated return is filed. Therefore none of the $20,000 gain on sale of land to Dale Corporation (which is LTCG) will be recognized in 1976. In 1977 when the property is sold to an unrelated third party, i.e., one outside the consolidated group, a $35,000 gain will be recognized by Hill Corporation.

34. (1177,Q2,22) (d) Gains and losses are recognized on the repurchase of a corporation's bonds in the year of the repurchase. The gain or loss is determined by the relationship of the repurchase price to the net carrying value of the bonds (face value plus or minus unamortized premium or discount). In this case the bonds were issued at face value, so the loss is the amount paid to repurchase ($258,000) less the face value of the bonds ($250,000) which is $8,000 and deductible as an expense.

35. (1177,Q2,23) (d) Although current distributions of a Subchapter S corporation are generally deemed to be out of current taxable income, cash distributions during the first 2½ months of the year are considered to be made out of the prior year's undistributed taxable income (UTI). Therefore $30,000 of the February 15th distribution is 1975 UTI. The remaining $20,000 and the subsequent $40,000 cash payments are distributions of 1976

taxable income, leaving $140,000 of UTI at 12/31/76. Taxable income is not reduced by property distributions when computing UTI.

36.   (1177,Q2,31) (a)   Distributions of property to shareholders reduce earnings and profits (E&P) by the adjusted basis of the assets distributed. The reduction of E&P must be adjusted by any liabilities to which the property being distributed is subject. Therefore E & P is reduced by $1,500 ($6,500 basis of land less $5,000 mortgage).

MAY 1981 ANSWERS

37.   (581,Q3,41)   (a)   The requirement is to compute the amount of gain Derek Corporation must recognize on the sale of its treasury shares. No gain or loss is recognized on the issuance of a corporation's own stock or its treasury shares. The excess of selling price over cost is treated as an addition to paid-in-capital.

38.   (581,Q3,42)   (a)   The requirement is to compute Apollo's taxable income for 1980. None of the income/expense items listed are includible in the computation of taxable income. Taxable Income is computed as follows:

Book Income	$1,200,000
— Municipal bond interest	(40,000)
—Proceeds of life insurance	(200,000)
+ Non-deductible interest expense (to produce tax-exempt interest income)	8,000
+ Provision for federal income tax	524,000
Taxable Income	$1,492,000

39.   (581,Q3,43)   (c)   The requirement is to compute the amount of deductible expense for business gifts. The deduction for business gifts is limited to $25 per individual, not including advertising or promotional gifts costing $4 or less. Thus, the allowable deduction is computed as follows:

$$8 \times \$10 = \$ \ 80$$
$$8 \times \$25 = \ 200$$
$$8 \times \$25 = \ 200$$
$$10 \times \$25 = \ \underline{250}$$
$$\$730$$

40.   (581,Q3,44)   (b)   The requirement is to compute the taxable income to Homer Corporation resulting from the repurchase of its bonds. Ordinary income or loss is recognized on the repurchase of a corporation's own bonds determined by the difference between the repurchase price and the net carrying value of the bonds (issue price plus or minus the discount or premium amortized). In this case, the bonds were issued at a $600,000 premium which was amortized at the rate of $12,000 ($600,000 ÷ 50 years) per year. The carrying value of the bonds on December 31, 1980 is $2,600,000 − ($12,000 x 20) = $2,360,000. Since Homer retired the bonds for $2,320,000 a gain of $40,000 is recognized.

41.   (581,Q3,46)   (c)   The requirement is to determine what each shareholder in a Subchapter S corporation should report as income for 1980. A Subchapter S corporation's taxable income is taxed to shareholders whether distributed or not. If the Subchapter S corporation has an excess of NLTCG over NSTCL, it is passed thru as LTCG to shareholders. Thus, each shareholder should report $4,000 ($36,000 ÷ 9) of long-term capital gain, and $20,000 ($180,000 ÷ 9) of ordinary income.

42.   (581,Q3,47)   (b)   The requirement is to compute the undistributed taxable income of a Subchapter S corporation for 1980. Undistributed taxable income (UTI) is computed by subtracting from taxable income any cash distributions made out of current earnings and profits. The $50,000 distribution on January 31 and the first $40,000 of the March 1 distribution are distributions of the 1979 UTI of $90,000. The remaining $40,000 of the March 1 distribution and the $60,000 October 1 distribution are distributions of 1980 current earnings and profits. Thus, the 1980 UTI is computed as follows:

Taxable income for 1980	$390,000
Less cash distributions out of CEP	
March 1	(40,000)
October 1	(60,000)
UTI for 1980	$290,000

43.   (581,Q3,48)   (c)   The requirement is to determine the maximum charitable contribution deduction for 1980. An accrual-basis corporation can elect to deduct a charitable contribution paid within 2-1/2 months of the close of its taxable year if its board of directors authorize the contribution during the taxable year. Thus, the $100,000 charitable contribution is deductible in 1980, but is limited to 5% of taxable income before the charitable contribution deduction. The maximum amount deductible in 1980 is:

Book income	$500,000
+ Charitable contribution	100,000
TI before CC deduction	$600,000
	x 5%
Maximum CC deduction	$ 30,000

The remaining $70,000 can be carried over a maximum of 5 years.

44. (581,Q3,50)   (a)   The requirement is to determine the recognized gain and basis of stock received in a corporate reorganization. No gain or loss is recognized if stock is exchanged <u>solely</u> for stock in a corporation that is a party to the reorganization. Smith's basis in the Mark Corporation stock received is the same as his basic in the Talbot Corporation stock ($150,000).

45. (581,Q3,53)   (a)   The requirement is to determine the amount of gain to be recognized by a corporation on the exchange of its stock for property. A corporation recognizes no gain or loss on the receipt of money or other property in exchange for its stock (including treasury stock).

46. (581,Q3,54)   (c)   The requirement is to determine the basis of Elk's stock on December 31, 1980. A stockholder's basis in a Subchapter S corporation is decreased by his share of any net operating loss and increased by the undistributed taxable income (UTI) of any year. The UTI for 1979 was $40,000, ($60,000 − $20,000) and for 1980 was $30,000. Consequently, the basis of Elk's stock is:

Original stock basis	$100,000
− 1978 NOL	(40,000)
+ 1979 UTI	40,000
+ 1980 UTI	30,000
Stock basis 12/31/80	$130,000

47. (581,Q3,55)   (d)   The requirement is to determine the maximum deduction for amortization of organization expense for 1980. A corporation's organizational expenditures can be amortized ratably over a period of not less than 60 months, beginning with the month in which a corporation begins business. Thus, the maximum deduction for 1980 is $900 x 6/60 = $90.

48. (581,Q3,56)   (b)   The requirement is to determine the amount of bond discount deductible for the fiscal year ended March 31, 1981. Bond discount must be amortized ratably over the life of the bonds. Thus, the deduction for bond discount is $120,000 x 6/96 = $7,500.

49. (581,Q3,57)   (d)   The requirement is to determine the amount of dividend income taxable to the shareholder. If a corporation sells property to a shareholder for less than fair market value, a noncorporate distributee is considered to have received a constructive dividend to the extent of the difference between the fair market value of the property and the price paid.

Thus, the shareholder's dividend income is $80,000 − $50,000 = $30,000. Note the question states "before the dividend exclusion" which indicates that the shareholder was a noncorporate distributee.

50. (581,Q3,58)   (d)   The requirement is to determine a corporation's net operating loss. The computation is as follows:

Gross profit on sales	$150,000
Dividends from domestic taxable corps.	15,000
	$165,000
Less:	
Salaries and wages	(90,000)
Interest expense	(22,500)
Taxes on real estate and payroll	(52,500)
Depreciation	(15,000)
Loss before dividends received deduction	($ 15,000)
DRD ($15,000 x 85%)	(12,750)
Net operating loss	($ 27,750)

Note that since the charitable contributions deduction is limited to 5% of taxable income before the charitable contributions deduction and the dividends received deduction, no charitable contribution can be currently deducted. However, the full dividends received deduction can be taken since no limitation applies if it increases a net operating loss.

51. (581,Q3,60)   (a)   The requirement is to determine the undistributed personal holding company income for Cromwell Investors, Inc. Cromwell does not meet the "stock ownership test" that is required to be classified as a personal holding company. The "stock ownership test" requires that <u>more</u> than 50% of the outstanding stock must be owned directly or indirectly by five or fewer individuals. Cromwell has ten <u>equal unrelated</u> shareholders. Thus, Cromwell is not classified as a personal holding company and therefore, has no undistributed PHC income.

SOLUTION GUIDE

Problem 1   Right and Left Corporations (579,P5)

1.   This problem consists of 2 unrelated parts.

2.   Part a. requires taxable income to be computed by adjusting a preliminary taxable income figure to reflect the supplemental information given in the problem. Also supplementary information not used to adjust the preliminary taxable income figure are to be listed separately.

2.1   The solutions approach is to analyze the effects of each of the items of additional information on taxable income. Make intermediary computations of the effect of each item of information on taxable income. Note items having no effect on taxable income.

2.2   The marketable securities sold on January 15, 1978, are long-term capital assets since they were held for more than 1 year. They were purchased for $8,500 and sold for $10,000 resulting in a $1,500 long-term capital gain. Capital gains are included in the computation of taxable income even if the alternative capital gains tax is used to compute the liability.

2.3   The marketable securities sold on February 15, 1978 are short-term capital assets since they were held for less than one year. They were purchased for $9,000 and sold for $8,000 resulting in a $1,000 short-term capital loss. Corporations may only deduct capital losses to the extent of capital gains. This $1,000 loss may offset $1,000 of the $1,500 capital gain in 2.2, just above.

2.4   A corporation's purchase of its own stock for cash is not a taxable transaction. Therefore, this item will be listed as not used to determine taxable income.

2.5   The $12,000 of dividends received from a domestic corporation are subject to an 85 percent "dividends received" deduction of $10,200. The $10,000 of dividends from a wholly owned subsidiary (not part of a consolidated return) are entitled to a 100 percent deduction. However, both of these dividends must be fully included in income to compute the charitable contribution deduction limitation and thereafter the dividend deductions are taken to arrive at taxable income.

2.6   The $25,000 of contributions made by Left Corporation to its pension plan trust are deductible (assume the $25,000 is within the deduction allowed since no information on employees' salaries is given). The $7,000 of pension trust income is accumulated tax-free by the trust and has no effect on Left's taxable income. It will be listed as information not used. The pension benefits paid also has no tax effect on Left Corporation and will be listed as information not used.

2.7   The $400 worth of hams distributed to employees are deductible to Left, but the employees will not be required to include the value of the hams in their income.

2.8   Contributions to indigent persons are not deductible. Contributions must be made to qualified organizations to be deductible. Therefore, the $100 will be listed as information not used. The $40,000 of contributions are deductible subject to a limit of 5 percent of taxable income before the "dividends received" deduction discussed above in 2.5. Prior to these special deductions, taxable income is $447,100 of which 5 percent is $22,355. The remaining charitable contributions of $17,645 ($40,000 − $22,355) may be carried over for five years.

Preliminary income figure		$450,000
Add:		
Net capital gains		
Long-term gain	1,500	
Short-term loss	1,000	500
Dividends from domestic corp.		12,000
Dividends from 100% subsidiary		10,000
		472,500
Deduct:		
Pension contributions	$25,000	
Hams	400	25,400
Income before "dividend received" and charitable contributions deductions		$447,100

2.9 Prepare your final solution. Deduct the dividends received deduction of $20,200 and charitable contribution deduction of $22,355. Taxable income is $404,545 ($447,100 − $20,200 − $22,355). You should also show computations of the offsetting capital gain and loss, of the dividend received deductions, and of the charitable contributions deduction. Do not forget to list the items not affecting taxable income.

3. The requirement of part b. is to compute the income tax due by Right Corporation. Informational items "not used" are to be listed separately.

3.1 The solutions approach is to analyze the effect of each item of additional information on the preliminary tax liability of $500,000. Make intermediary computations of the effect of each item of information on the tax due. Note items not affecting the tax liability.

3.2 The balance of 1977 taxes paid in 1978 has no effect on the 1978 tax liability and should be listed as "not used."

3.3 The $430,000 of estimated tax payments made in 1978 are a deduction from the preliminary 1978 tax liability.

3.4 Both the investment tax credit for 1978 and the carryover from 1977 may be used to reduce the 1978 tax due. The carryover of $15,000 from 1977 is used first and the current credit of $30,000 is used second. The investment tax credit limitation for 1978 is $25,000 plus 50 percent of the tax liability over $25,000 which is in excess of the available $45,000 of investment credit. Note that the investment credit limit is increased after 1978 to $25,000 plus 60% in 1979, 70% in 1980, 80% in 1981, and 90% after 1981 of the tax liability over $25,000.

3.5 The foreign tax credit also may be used to reduce the amount of taxes due.

3.6 The $40,000 of social security taxes withheld from employees' wages does not affect income tax due and is listed as "not used." Right's share of FICA tax has already been deducted in computing the preliminary tax liability and is listed as "not used."

3.7 Prepare your final solution beginning with the preliminary $500,000 tax liability. The tax liability (net of credits) for 1978 is $445,000. Since $430,000 has already been paid in 1978, $15,000 is still due.

UNOFFICIAL ANSWER

Problem 1   Right and Left Corporation (579,P5)

a.

1.   *Left Corporation*
        **COMPUTATION OF FEDERAL
        TAXABLE INCOME**
        For the 1978 calendar year

Income before income taxes (per bookkeeper)		$450,000
Add:		
Net capital gains (Schedule 1)	$ 500	
Dividends from domestic corporations	12,000	
Dividends from wholly-owned domestic subsidiary	10,000	
		22,500
		472,500
Deduct:		
Contributions to pension plan trust	25,000	
Christmas bonus to employees	400	
Contributions to various recognized charitable organizations	40,000	
		65,400
Federal taxable income before special deductions and adjustments		407,100
Dividends received deduction (Schedule 2)	(20,200)	
Contributions carryover (Schedule 3)	17,645	
		(2,555)
Federal taxable income		$404,545

Schedule 1

Computation of Net Capital Gains

Long-term gain on sale of marketable securities ($10,000 − $8,500)	$1,500
Short-term loss on sale of marketable securities ($9,000 − $8,000)	(1,000)
Net capital gains	$ 500

Schedule 2

Computation of Dividends Received Deduction

Dividends received from domestic corporations ($12,000 X 85%)	$10,200
Dividends received from wholly-owned domestic subsidiary	10,000
Dividends received deduction	$20,200

Schedule 3

Computation of Contributions Carryover

Federal taxable income before special deductions and adjustments	$407,100
Contributions to various recognized charitable organizations	40,000
	$447,100
Contributions to various recognized charitable organizations	$40,000
Allowable contribution deduction ($447,100 X 5%)	22,355
Contributions carryover	$17,645

2.   Items in the fact situation that were not used to determine the answer to item 1 above are as follows:

- The purchase of 10,000 shares of its own company stock is not deductible.

- The income from the investments of the pension trust is not taxable income.

- The pension benefits paid to retirees by the pension trust are not deductible.

- The contributions to various indigent persons are not deductible.

b.

1.

Right Corporation
COMPUTATION OF FEDERAL INCOME TAX DUE
For the 1978 calendar year

Federal income tax expense		$500,000
Estimated tax payments in 1978	$430,000	
Investment tax credit for 1978	30,000	
Investment tax credit carried over from 1977	15,000	
Foreign tax credit	10,000	485,000
Federal income tax due		$ 15,000

2.   Items in the fact situation that were not used to determine the answer to item 1 above are as follows:

 • The balance due for the 1977 federal income tax return is not deducted from the 1978 federal income tax.

 • The social security taxes withheld from employees' wages in 1978 are not deductible.

 • The employer's share of social security taxes was properly deducted as an expense in the calculation of the total federal income tax of $500,000.

SOLUTION GUIDE

Problem 2   Liberty, Inc.

1.   The requirement in part a is to prepare a schedule of corporate federal taxable income.

2.   Become familiar with the income statement per books.

3.   Adjust the income statement per books for each paragraph of additional information.

3.1   Depreciation changes from $25,000 to $35,500.

3.2   Since Machine A had a book gain of $2,500 and a net book value of $9,200, $11,700 of insurance was received. The excess of proceeds received ($11,700) over cost of replacement ($9,700) is the taxable gain which is ordinary income. It is ordinary income due to depreciation recapture.

Machine B had a book value of $18,400 ($38,000 − $19,600). The amount received was $28,000 ($7,000 cash and $21,000 FMV of the new machine). For tax purposes, the gain is limited to the cash received. The basis of the new machine is $18,400 (the basis of the old machine).

The land condemnation gain ($17,100) is section 1231 which becomes long-term and is offset by the $28,600 loss on disposal of investments.

3.3   Continued from just above. The excess of the $28,600 loss over the $17,100 long-term gain is carried forward, or could be back three years, i.e., not deducted in the current year. Note, property must currently be held for more than 12 months to qualify for long-term treatment.

3.4   The $8,000 from the 1974 installment sale was recognized per books in 1974 but not for tax purposes. Thus the $8,000 should be included in 1975 income per tax return.

3.5   The dividend distribution of $10,200 is not relevant to income per books or per tax return.

4.   Review each of the thus far unaffected items in the income statement per books for possible adjustment.

4.1   The charitable contribution deduction is limited to 5% of income before special deductions and contributions (5% of $120,500 or $6,025; see schedule 3 in AICPA answer).

4.2   The goodwill amortization is not deductible for tax purposes.

4.3   The state and city bond interest is not taxable.

4.4   The dividends paid are not relevant to the solution.

5.   An 85% dividend received deduction is allowed for dividends received from domestic corporations limited to 85% of taxable income before operating loss carryforwards and carrybacks and the dividend received deduction, i.e., 85% of $4,000.

6.   Write up the income statement per tax purposes.

7.   The requirement is a reconciliation of book and taxable income.

7.1   Every item adjusted in part a above is a reconciling item. Note dividends paid required no adjustment.

UNOFFICIAL ANSWER

Problem 2   Liberty, Inc.

a.

Liberty, Inc.
COMPUTATION OF FEDERAL TAXABLE INCOME
For the Calendar Year 1975

Gross margin (sales less cost of sales)		$300,000
Dividends received from domestic corporations		4,000
Gain recognized on involuntary conversion (Machine A) (Schedule I)		2,000
Gain on exchange (Machine B) (Schedule 2)		7,000
Installment sale		8,000
Total income		321,000
Operating expenses:		
Depreciation	$ 35,500	
Charitable contributions (Schedule 3)	6,025	
Other deductible expenses	165,000	
Total operating expenses		206,525
Income before special deductions		114,475
Dividends received deduction (85% x $4,000)		3,400
Federal taxable income		$111,075

Schedule 1

Gain on Involuntary Conversion (Machine A)

Undepreciated cost (adjusted basis)	$ 9,200
Realized gain for book purposes	2,500
Insurance proceeds	11,700
Cost of replacement machine	9,700
Recognized gain (because it is lower than the realized gain)	$ 2,000

Schedule 2

Gain on Exchange (Machine B)

Original cost	$ 38,000
Accumulated depreciation	19,600
Adjusted basis	$ 18,400
Fair market value of new machine	$ 21,000
Add cash ("boot") received	7,000
Total consideration received	28,000
Adjusted basis (Machine B)	18,400
Realized gain	$ 9,600
Recognized gain (lower of the cash "boot" received or the realized gain)	$ 7,000

Schedule 3

Charitable Contributions

Total income		$321,000
Less:		
Depreciation	$ 35,500	
Other deductible expenses	165,000	200,500
Income before special deductions and charitable contributions		$120,500
Limitation on deduction for charitable contributions ($120,500 x 5%)		$ 6,025

b.

Liberty, Inc.
RECONCILIATION OF BOOK INCOME
BEFORE FEDERAL INCOME TAXES
TO FEDERAL TAXABLE INCOME
For the Calendar Year 1975

Book income before federal income taxes		$ 90,900
Add:		
Long-term capital loss in excess of long-term capital gain (Schedule 4)	$ 11,500	
Excess charitable contributions per books ($15,000–$6,025)	8,975	
Installment sale	8,000	
Amortization of goodwill	5,000	
Excess gain on exchange (Machine B) per tax return ($7,000–$2,400)	4,600	38,075
		128,975
Deduct:		
Excess depreciation per tax return ($35,500 –$25,000)	$ 10,500	
Interest received on state and city bonds	3,500	
Dividends received deduction	3,400	
Excess gain on involuntary conversion (Machine A) per books ($2,500 –$2,000)	500	17,900
Federal taxable income		$111,075

NOTE (Not Required): The dividends paid by Liberty of $10,200 are not deducted for book or federal tax purposes so they do not affect the reconciliation.

Schedule 4 (Not Required)

Long-Term Capital Loss in Excess of
Long-Term Capital Gain

The gain on the condemnation of land used in business of $17,100 is a Section 1231 gain which becomes a long-term capital gain because there are no Section 1231 losses to offset against it.

Long-term capital gain	$ 17,100
Long-term capital loss (loss on disposal of investments)	(28,600)
Net long-term capital loss	$ (11,500)

The $11,500 is not deductible by Liberty in the current year but must be carried to other years to offset capital gains.

APPENDIX A

SAMPLE CPA EXAMINATION

The following sample CPA Examination is presented to enable students to gain experience in taking a "realistic" exam. Selection of multiple choice items and problems was based on a statistical analysis of recent exams. This examination consists of five sections - Practice I and II, Auditing, Business Law and Theory.

Candidates will benefit most from this sample exam if they work each of the five parts in one sitting within the time limits allowed. Prepare your solutions as thoroughly as if you were actually taking the exam.

Unofficial answers are presented immediately following the examination.

EXAMINATION IN ACCOUNTING PRACTICE — PART I

NOTE TO CANDIDATES: Suggested time allotments are as follows:

	Estimated Minutes	
All questions are required:	Minimum	Maximum
No. 1	45	55
No. 2	45	55
No. 3	45	55
No. 4	45	55
No. 5	40	50
Total	220	270

Number 1   (Estimated time - 45 to 55 minutes)

Select the **best** answer for each of the following items relating to a **variety of financial accounting problems.**

1.   Chip Company operates in four different industries, each of which is appropriately regarded as a reportable segment. Total sales for 1978 for all the segments combined were $1,000,000. Sales for Segment No. 2 were $400,000 and traceable costs were $150,000. Total common costs for all the segments combined were $500,000. Chip allocates common costs based on the ratio of a segment's sales to total sales, an appropriate method of allocation. The operating profit presented for Segment No. 2 for 1978 should be

    a. $ 50,000
    b. $125,000
    c. $200,000
    d. $250,000

2.   An analysis of the machinery accounts of the Pending Company for 1978 is as follows:

	Machinery	Accumulated depreciation	Machinery net of accumulated depreciation
Balance at January 1, 1978	$1,000,000	$400,000	$600,000
Purchases of new machinery in 1978 for cash	500,000	——	500,000
Depreciation in 1978	——	250,000	(250,000)
Balance at December 31, 1978	$1,500,000	$650,000	$850,000

Assuming funds are defined as working capital, the information concerning Pending's machinery accounts should be shown in Pending's statement of changes in financial position for the year ended December 31, 1978, as

a.   A subtraction from net income of $250,000 and a source of funds of $500,000.

b.   An addition to net income of $250,000 and a use of funds of $500,000.

c.   A source of funds of $250,000.

d.   A use of funds of $500,000.

3.   Minor Baseball Company had a player contract with Doe that was recorded in its accounting records at $145,000. Better Baseball Company had a player contract with Smith that was recorded in its accounting records at $140,000. Minor traded Doe to Better for Smith by exchanging each player's contract. The fair value of each contract was $150,000. What amount should be shown in the accounting records after the exchange of player contracts?

	Minor	Better
a.	$140,000	$140,000
b.	$140,000	$145,000
c.	$145,000	$140,000
d.	$150,000	$150,000

Items 4 and 5 are based on the following information:

Information concerning the capital structure of the Petrock Corporation is as follows:

	December 31,	
	1975	1976
Common stock	90,000 shares	90,000 shares
Convertible pre-ferred stock	10,000 shares	10,000 shares
8% convertible bonds	$1,000,000	$1,000,000

During 1976, Petrock paid dividends of $1.00 per share on its common stock and $2.40 per share on its preferred stock. The preferred stock is convertible into 20,000 shares of common stock; but is not considered a common stock equivalent. The 8% convertible bonds are convertible into 30,000 shares of common stock and are considered common stock equivalents. The net income for the year ended December 31, 1976, was $285,000. Assume that the income tax rate was 50%.

4.   What should be the primary earnings per share for the year ended December 31, 1976, rounded to the nearest penny?

a. $2.38.

b. $2.51.

c. $2.84.

d. $3.13.

5.   What should be the fully diluted earnings per share for the year ended December 31, 1976, rounded to the nearest penny?

a. $2.15.

b. $2.32.

c. $2.61.

d. $2.74.

Items 6 and 7 are based on the following information:

On January 1, 1975, the Green Company entered into a noncancelable lease agreement with the Blatt Company for a machine which was carried on the accounting records of Green at $2,000,000. Total payments under the lease agreement which expires on December 31, 1984, agregate $3,550,800 of which $2,400,000 represents the cost of the machine to Blatt. Payments of $355,080 are due each January 1. The first payment was made on January 1, 1975 when the lease agreement was finalized. The interest rate of 10% which was stipulated in the lease agreement is considered fair and adequate compensation to Green for the use of its funds. The "interest" method of amortization is being used. Blatt expects the machine to have a ten-year life, no salvage value, and be depreciated on a straight-line basis. The lease agreement should be accounted for as a lease equivalent to a sale by Green and as a lease which is in substance a purchase by Blatt.

6.   What should be the income before income taxes derived by Green from the lease for the year ended December 31, 1975?

a. $204,492.

b. $355,080.

c. $604,492.

d. $755,080.

7.   Ignoring income taxes, what should be the expenses incurred by Blatt from this lease for the year ended December 31, 1975?

a. $204,492.

b. $355,080.

c. $444,492.

d. $595,080.

8.   Selected information from Basket Company's 1978 accounting records is as follows:

Proceeds from issuance of common stock	$8,000,000
Proceeds from issuance of preferred stock	2,000,000
Dividends on common stock	1,000,000
Dividends on preferred stock	400,000
Purchases of treasury stock	300,000
Sales of stock to officers and employees not included above	200,000

Assuming funds are defined as working capital, Basket's statement of changes in financial position for the year ended December 31, 1978, would show the following sources and uses of funds, based on the information given above

	Sources	Uses
a.	$ 9,900,000	$1,400,000
b.	$10,000,000	$1,400,000
c.	$10,000,000	$1,900,000
d.	$10,200,000	$1,700,000

9. Growing, Inc., had net income for 1977 of $10,600,000 and earnings per share on common stock of $5.00. Included in the net income was $1,000,000 of bond interest expense related to its long-term debt. The income tax rate for 1977 was 50%. Dividends on preferred stock were $600,000. The dividend-payout ratio on common stock was 40%. What were the dividends on common stock in 1977?

    a. $3,600,000.
    b. $3,800,000.
    c. $4,000,000.
    d. $4,240,000.

10. The Mann Company does not carry insurance on its office machines. On December 27, 1976, Machine A was totally destroyed by fire. The book value of Machine A, depreciated to the date of the fire, was $62,000. Disposal costs were $3,000. On January 17, 1977, prior to the issuance of the 1976 financial statements, Machine B was totally destroyed in an explosion. The book value of Machine B, depreciated to the date of the explosion, was $74,000. Disposal costs were $4,000. What is the total amount of losses that should be charged to income in 1976?

    a. $62,000.
    b. $65,000.
    c. $136,000.
    d. $143,000.

11. During 1978, Red, Incorporated, purchased $2,000,000 of inventory. The cost of goods sold for 1978 was $2,200,000, and the ending inventory at December 31, 1978, was $400,000. What was the inventory turnover for 1978?

    a. 4.0.
    b. 4.4.
    c. 5.5.
    d. 11.0.

12. Tob Corporation purchased certain machinery on January 1, 1973. At the date of acquisition, the machinery had an estimated useful life of ten years with no salvage. The machinery was being depreciated using the double-declining-balance method for both financial statement reporting and income tax reporting. On January 1, 1978, Tob changed to the straight-line method for depreciation of the machinery for financial statement reporting but not for income tax reporting. Assume that Tob can justify the change.

The accumulated depreciation from January 1, 1973, through December 31, 1977, under the double-declining-balance method was $200,000. If the straight-line method had been used, the accumulated depreciation from January 1, 1973, through December 31, 1977, would have been $140,000. Assuming that the income tax rate for the years 1973 through 1978 is 50%, the amount shown in the 1978 income statement for the cumulative effect of changing from the double-declining-balance method to the straight-line method would be

    a. $0.
    b. $30,000 credit.
    c. $60,000 credit.
    d. $60,000 debit.

13. The following condensed balance sheet is presented for the partnership of Fisher, Taylor and Simon who share profits and losses in the ratio of 6:2:2, respectively:

Cash	$ 40,000
Other assets	140,000
	$180,000
Liabilities	$ 70,000
Fisher, capital	50,000
Taylor, capital	50,000
Simon, capital	10,000
	$180,000

The assets and liabilities are fairly valued on the above balance sheet, and it was agreed to by all the partners that the partnership would be liquidated after selling the other assets. What would each of the partners receive at this time if the other assets are sold for $80,000?

	Fisher	Taylor	Simon
a.	$12,500	$37,500	$0
b.	$13,000	$37,000	$0
c.	$14,000	$38,000	$ 2,000
d.	$50,000	$50,000	$10,000

Items 14 and 15 are based on the following information:

The Nugget Company's balance sheet on December 31, 1976, is as follows:

Assets

Cash	$ 100,000
Accounts receivable	200,000
Inventories	500,000
Property, plant and equipment	900,000
	$1,700,000

Liabilities and Stockholders' Equity

Current liabilities	$ 300,000
Long-term debt	500,000
Common stock (par $1 per share)	100,000
Additional paid-in capital	200,000
Retained earnings	600,000
	$1,700,000

On December 31, 1976, the Bronc Company purchased all of the outstanding common stock of Nugget for $1,500,000 cash. On that date, the fair (market) value of Nugget's inventories was $450,000 and the fair value of Nugget's property, plant and equipment was $1,000,000. The fair values of all other assets and liabilities of Nugget were equal to their book values.

14. As a result of the acquisition of Nugget by Bronc, the consolidated balance sheet of Bronc and Nugget should reflect goodwill in the amount of
- a. $500,000.
- b. $550,000.
- c. $600,000.
- d. $650,000

15. Assuming that the balance sheet of Bronc (unconsolidated) at December 31, 1976, reflected retained earnings of $2,000,000, what amount of retained earnings should be shown in the December 31, 1976, consolidated balance sheet of Bronc and its new subsidiary, Nugget?
- a. $2,000,000.
- b. $2,600,000.
- c. $2,800,000.
- d. $3,150,000

16. The Blue Department Store uses the retail inventory method. Information relating to the computation of the inventory at December 31, 1976, is as follows:

	Cost	Retail
Inventory at January 1, 1976	$ 16,000	$ 40,000
Sales		290,000
Purchases	135,000	300,000
Freight-in	3,800	
Net markups		20,000
Net markdowns		10,000

What should be the ending inventory at cost at December 31, 1976, using the retail inventory method?
- a. $21,500.
- b. $22,500.
- c. $25,800.
- d. $27,000.

17. Tackle Company sells football helmets. In 1977 Tackle discovered a defect in the helmets which has produced lawsuits that are reasonably estimated to result in losses of $900,000. Based on its own experience and the experience of other enterprises in the business, Tackle considers it probable that additional lawsuits that are reasonably estimated to result in losses of $1,600,000 will occur even though the particular parties that will bring suit are not identifiable at this time. What amount of loss, if any, should be accrued by a charge to income in 1977?
- a. $0.
- b. $900,000.
- c. $1,600,000.
- d. $2,500,000.

18. Jenny Corporation was organized on January 1, 1978, with an authorization of 500,000 shares of common stock with a par value of $5 per share.

During 1978 the corporation had the following capital transactions:

January 5 — issued 100,000 shares @ $5 per share

April 6 — issued 50,000 shares @ $7 per share

June 8 — issued 15,000 shares @ $10 per share

July 28 — purchased 25,000 shares @ $4 per share

December 31 — sold the 25,000 shares held in treasury @ $8 per share

Jenny used the par value method to record the purchase and reissuance of the treasury shares.

What is the amount of paid-in capital in excess of par value as of December 31, 1978?

a. $175,000
b. $200,000
c. $250,000
d. $275,000

19. Donahue Corporation purchased a machine in 1976 when the general price-level index was 180. The price-level index was 190 in 1977 and 200 in 1978. The price-level indexes above are stated in terms of the 1958 base year. Donahue prepares supplemental general price-level financial statements (financial statements restated for changes in the general purchasing power of the dollar), as recommended by APB Statement No. 3. Depreciation is $100,000 a year. In Donahue's general price-level income statement for 1978, the amount of depreciation would be stated as
    a. $ 90,000.
    b. $ 95,000.
    c. $105,263.
    d. $111,111.

20. On April 30, 1979, Standard, Inc., purchased Dynamo Corporation, 10-year, 9% bonds with a face value of $120,000 for $133,600, which includes $3,600 accrued interest. The bonds mature on January 1, 1986, and pay interest on January 1 and July 1. Standard uses the straight-line method of amortization. The amount of income Standard should report for the year ended December 31, 1979, as a result of this long-term bond investment, is
    a. $6,200.
    b. $6,393.
    c. $6,533.
    d. $8,200.

Number 2   (Estimated time - 45 to 55 minutes)

Select the **best** answer for each of the following items relating to a **variety of managerial accounting and quantitative method problems.**

21. On November 1, 1977, Yankee Company had 20,000 units of work in process in Department No. 1 which were 100% complete as to material costs and 20% complete as to conversion costs. During November, 160,000 units were started in Department No. 1 and 170,000 units were completed and transferred to Department No. 2. The work in process on November 30, 1977, was 100% complete as to material costs and 40% complete as to conversion costs. By what amount would the equivalent units for conversion costs for the month of November differ if the first-in, first-out method were used instead of the weighted-average method?

a.   20,000 decrease.
b.   16,000 decrease.
c.   8,000 decrease.
d.   4,000 decrease.

22. Horn Corp. invested in a four-year project. Horn's expected rate of return is 8%. Additional information on the project is as follows:

Year	Cash inflow from operations, net of income taxes	Present Value of $1 at 8%
1	$2,000	.926
2	2,200	.857
3	2,400	.794
4	2,600	.735

Assuming a positive net present value of $500, what was the amount of the original investment?
    a. $1,411.
    b. $2,411.
    c. $7,054.
    d. $8,700.

23. Posa Co. is planning to invest $40,000 in a three-year project. Posa's expected rate of return is 10%. The present value of $1 at 10% for one year is .909, for two years is .826, and for three years is .751. The cash flow, net of income taxes, will be $15,000 for the first year (present value of $13,635) and $18,000 for the second year (present value of $14,868). Assuming the rate of return is exactly 10%, what would the cash flow, net of income taxes, be for the third year?
    a. $8,634.
    b. $11,000.
    c. $11,497.
    d.   15,309.

24. O'Connor Company manufactures Product J and Product K from a joint process. For Product J, 4,000 units were produced having a sales value at split-off of $15,000. If Product J were processed further, the additional costs would be $3,000 and the sales value would be $20,000. For Product K, 2,000 units were produced having a sales value at split-off of $10,000. If Product K were processed further, the additional costs would be $1,000 and the sales value would be $12,000. Using the relative-sales-value at split-off approach, the portion of the total joint product costs allocated to Product J was $9,000. What were the total joint product costs?
    a. $14,400.
    b. $15,000.

c. $18,400.
d. $19,000.

25. Helen Corp. manufactures products W, X, Y, and Z from a joint process. Additional information is as follows:

Product	Units Produced	Sales Value at Split-off	If Processed Further Additional Costs	If Processed Further Sales Value
W	6,000	$ 80,000	$ 7,500	$ 90,000
X	5,000	60,000	6,000	70,000
Y	4,000	40,000	4,000	50,000
Z	3,000	20,000	2,500	30,000
	18,000	$200,000	$20,000	$240,000

Assuming that total joint costs of $160,000 were allocated using the relative-sales-value at split-off approach, what were the joint costs allocated to each product?

	W	X	Y	Z
a.	$40,000	$40,000	$40,000	$40,000
b.	$53,333	$44,444	$35,556	$26,667
c.	$60,000	$46,667	$33,333	$20,000
d.	$64,000	$48,000	$32,000	$16,000

26.   Information on Overhead Company's overhead costs is as follows:

Standard applied overhead	$80,000
Budgeted overhead based on standard direct-labor hours allowed	$84,000
Budgeted overhead based on actual direct-labor hours allowed	$83,000
Actual overhead	$86,000

What is the total overhead variance?
a. $2,000 unfavorable.
b. $3,000 favorable.
c. $4,000 favorable.
d. $6,000 unfavorable.

27. Walsh, Inc., is preparing its cash budget for the month of November. The following information is available concerning its inventories:

Inventories at beginning of November	$180,000
Estimated cost of goods sold for November	900,000
Estimated inventories at end of November	160,000
Estimated payments in November for purchases prior to November	210,000
Estimated payments in November for purchases in November	80%

What are the estimated cash disbursements for inventories in November?
a. $720,000.
b. $914,000.
c. $930,000.
d. $1,042,000.

28.   Tice Company is a medium-sized manufacturer of lamps. During the year a new line called "Horolin" was made available to Tice's customers. The break-even point for sales of Horolin is $200,000 with a contribution margin of 40%. Assuming that the profit for the Horolin line during the year amounted to $100,000, total sales during the year would have amounted to
a. $300,000.
b. $420,000.
c. $450,000.
d. $475,000.

29.   Cardinal Company needs 20,000 units of a certain part to use in its production cycle. The following information is available:

Cost to Cardinal to make the part:

Direct materials	$ 4
Direct labor	16
Variable overhead	8
Fixed overhead applied	10
	$38

Cost to buy the part from the Oriole Company	$36

If Cardinal buys the part from Oriole instead of making it, Cardinal could not use the released facilities in another manufacturing activity. 60% of the fixed overhead applied will continue regardless of what decision is made.

In deciding whether to make or buy the part, the total relevant costs to make the part are
a. $560,000.
b. $640,000.
c. $720,000.
d. $760,000.

Items 30 and 31 are based on the following information:

Milligan Company manufactures two models, small and large. Each model is processed as follows:

	Machining Department	Polishing Department
Small (X)	2 hours	1 hour
Large (Y)	4 hours	3 hours

The available time for processing the two models is 100 hours a week in the Machining Department and 90 hours a week in the Polishing Department. The contribution margin expected is $5 for the small model and $7 for the large model.

30. How would the objective function (maximization of total contribution margin) be expressed?
    a.   5X + 7Y.
    b.   5X + 7Y ⩽ 190.
    c.   5X(3) + 7Y(7) ⩽ 190.
    d.   12X + 10Y.

31. How would the restriction (constraint) for the Machining Department be expressed?
    a.   2(5X) + 4(7Y) ⩽ 100.
    b.   2X + 4Y.
    c.   2X + 4Y ⩽ 100.
    d.   5X + 7Y ⩽ 100.

32. A company uses the first-in, first-out method of costing in a process-costing system. Material is added at the beginning of the process in Department A, and conversion costs are incurred uniformly throughout the process. Beginning work-in-process inventory on April 1 in Department A consisted of 50,000 units estimated to be 30% complete. During April, 150,000 units were started in Department A, and 160,000 units were completed and transferred to Department B. Ending work-in-process inventory on April 30 in Department A was estimated to be 20% complete. What were the total equivalent units in Department A for April for materials and conversion costs, respectively?
    a.   150,000 and 133,000.
    b.   150,000 and 153,000.
    c.   200,000 and 133,000.
    d.   200,000 and 153,000.

33. Lab Corp. uses a standard cost system. Direct labor information for Product CER for the month of October is as follows:

Standard rate	$6.00 per hour
Actual rate paid	$6.10 per hour
Standard hours allowed for actual production	1,500 hours
Labor efficiency variance	$600 unfavorable

What are the actual hours worked?
    a.   1,400.
    b.   1,402.
    c.   1,598.
    d.   1,600.

34. The following information is available from the Tyro Company:

Actual factory overhead	$15,000
Fixed overhead expenses, actual	$ 7,200
Fixed overhead expenses, budgeted	$ 7,000
Actual hours	3,500
Standard hours	3,800
Variable overhead rate per direct labor hour	$ 2.50

Assuming that Tyro uses a three-way analysis of overhead variances, what is the spending variance?
    a. $750 favorable.
    b. $750 unfavorable.
    c. $950 favorable.
    d. $1,500 unfavorable.

35. The Aron Company requires 40,000 units of Product Q for the year. The units will be required evenly throughout the year. It costs $60 to place an order. It costs $10 to carry a unit in inventory for the year. What is the economic order quantity?
    a.   400.
    b.   490.
    c.   600.
    d.   693.

36. Golden, Inc., has been manufacturing 5,000 units of Part 10541 which is used in the manufacture of one of its products. At this level of production, the cost per unit of manufacturing Part 10541 is as follows:

Direct materials	$ 2
Direct labor	8
Variable overhead	4
Fixed overhead applied	6
Total	$20

Brown Company has offered to sell Golden 5,000 units of Part 10541 for $19 a unit. Golden has determined that it could use the facilities presently used to manufacture Part 10541 to manufacture Product RAC and generate an operating profit of $4,000. Golden has also determined that two thirds of the fixed overhead applied will continue even if Part 10541 is purchased from Brown. To determine whether to accept Brown's offer, the net relevant costs to Golden are
    a. $70,000.
    b. $80,000.
    c. $90,000.
    d. $95,000.

37. Jarvis Co. has fixed costs of $200,000. It has two products that it can sell, Tetra and Min. Jarvis sells these products at a rate of 2 units of Tetra to 1 unit of Min. The contribution margin is $1 per unit for Tetra and $2 per unit for Min. How many units of Min would be sold at the breakeven point?

    a.   44,444.
    b.   50,000.
    c.   88,888.
    d.   100,000.

38. Dallas Corporation wishes to market a new product for $1.50 a unit. Fixed costs to manufacture this product are $100,000 for less than 500,000 units and $150,000 for 500,000 or more units. The contribution margin is 20%. How many units must be sold to realize net income from this product of $100,000?

    a.   333,333.
    b.   500,000.
    c.   666,667.
    d.   833,333.

Items 39 and 40 are based on the following information:

Flemming, Inc., is planning to acquire a new machine at a total cost of $36,000. The estimated life of the machine is six years with no salvage value. The straight-line method of depreciation will be used. Flemming estimates that the annual cash flow from operations, before income taxes, from using this machine will be $9,000. Assume that Flemming's cost of capital is 8% and the income tax rate is 40%. The present value of $1 at 8% for six years is .630. The present value of an annuity of $1 in arrears at 8% for six years is 4.623.

39. What would the payback period be?

    a.   4.0 years.
    b.   4.6 years.
    c.   5.7 years.
    d.   6.7 years.

40. What would the net present value be?

    a. $59.
    b. $5,607.
    c. $10,800.
    d. $13,140.

Number 3   (Estimated time - 45 to 55 minutes)

Select the **best** answer for each of the following items relating to **the federal income taxation of individuals.**

41. In examining the records of Bill Temple for 1979, a cash-basis sole proprietor, the following information was available:

Gross receipts	$45,000
Dividend income (on personal investments)	300
Cost of sales	22,500
Other operating expenses	4,500
State business taxes paid	450
Federal self-employment tax paid	1,400

What amount should Temple report as net earnings from self-employment for 1979?

    a. $16,150
    b. $17,550
    c. $17,850
    d. $18,000

42. Mr. and Mrs. Morris Benson were 68 years old in June of 1978 when Mr. Benson died. In filing their tax return for 1978, the maximum number of exemptions that can be taken is

    a.   1.
    b.   2.
    c.   3.
    d.   4.

43. Ben Reed purchased a personal residence for $31,000 in 1971. It had a fair market value of $56,000 on June 2, 1978, when it was damaged by a fire. The fair market value of the house after the fire was $45,000 and insurance proceeds totalled $7,000. The net amount of the casualty loss that he can claim is

    a. $ 3,900
    b. $ 4,000
    c. $ 6,900
    d. $18,000

44. Jon Parks, a cash-basis taxpayer, is the owner of an apartment building containing 20 identical apartments. Parks resides in one apartment and rents out the remaining units. For 1979 the following information was available.

Gross rental income	$43,200
Fuel	5,000
Maintenance and repairs (rental apartments)	2,400
Advertising for vacant apartments	600
Depreciation of building	10,000

What amount should Parks report as net rental income for 1979?

   a. $25,200
   b. $25,950
   c. $26,100
   d. $35,200

45. Art Hollender was divorced from his wife Diane in 1977. Under the terms of the divorce decree, he was required to make the following periodic payments each month to his former wife who retained custody of their children:

Alimony	$600
Child support	400

For 1978 his only income was his salary of $40,000, and he paid $12,000 to his former wife under the terms of the divorce decree. What is his 1978 adjusted gross income?

   a. $28,000.
   b. $32,800.
   c. $35,200.
   d. $40,000.

46. For the year 1978 Michael King reported salary and taxable interest income of $40,000. His capital asset transactions during the year were as follows:

Long-term capital gains	$2,000
Long-term capital losses	(8,000)
Short-term capital gains	1,000

For 1978 King should report adjusted gross income of

   a. $35,000.
   b. $37,500.
   c. $38,000.
   d. $39,000.

47. For the year 1979 Morgan Day had $25,000 † of ordinary income. In addition he had the following capital transactions:

$800 net long-term capital loss
$1,500 net short-term capital loss

What is the amount of Day's capital loss deduction for 1979?

   a. $1,150.
   b. $1,550.
   c. $1,900.
   d. $2,000.

48. Mrs. Grant, a widow, elected to receive the proceeds of a $50,000 face value insurance policy on the life of her deceased husband in ten annual installments of $6,800 each beginning in 1978. Of the $6,800 received in 1978, the amount subject to income tax is

   a. $ 800
   b. $1,800
   c. $5,000
   d. $6,800

49. Mark Berkson loaned a friend $1,000 in 1976 and it had not been repaid in 1978 when the friend died insolvent. For 1978 Berkson should account for the nonpayment of the loan as a

   a.   Deduction from adjusted gross income.
   b.   Long-term capital loss.
   c.   Ordinary loss.
   d.   Short-term capital loss.

50. Ruth Fleming, a widow whose husband died in 1973, maintains her home in which she and her two sons reside. Only one of her sons qualifies as her dependent. What is her filing status for 1977?

   a.   Single.
   b.   Surviving spouse.
   c.   Head of household.
   d.   Married, filing jointly.

51. In January 1977 Judy Howard was awarded a postgraduate fellowship grant of $4,800 by a tax-exempt educational organization. Ms. Howard is not a candidate for a degree and was awarded the grant to continue her research. The grant is for the period July 1, 1977, through June 30, 1979, and was paid in full on July 1, 1977. What amount should be included in her gross income for 1977?

   a. $0.
   b. $1,200.
   c. $2,400.
   d. $4,800.

52. On June 3, 1977, Leon Wren, an electrician, was injured in an accident during the course of his employment. As a result of injuries sustained, he received the following payments during 1977:

Damages for personal injuries	$8,000
Workmen's compensation	3,000
Reimbursement from his employer's accident and health plan for medical expenses paid by Wren	1,200

The amount to be included in Wren's 1977 gross income should be

   a. $0.

b. $1,200.
c. $3,000.
d. $12,200.

53.   During 1978, Albert Mason purchased the following long-term investments at par:

$10,000 general obligation bonds of
  Tulip County (wholly tax exempt)
$10,000 debentures of Laxity Corporation

He financed these purchases by obtaining a loan from the Community Bank for $20,000. For the year 1978, he paid the following amounts as interest expense:

Community Bank	$1,600
Interest on mortgage	3,000
Interest on installment purchases	300
	$4,900

What amount can Mason deduct as interest expense in 1978?
a. $4,900.
b. $4,100.
c. $3,600.
d. $3,300.

54.   During 1979 John and Mary Leonard received the following dividends on their jointly held investments:

·   Dividends of $1,400 from Dominion, Ltd., an Australian corporation.
·   Capital gain distribution of $600 from Apollo Mutual Fund.
·   Dividends of $1,000 from United Utilities Corporation, which constitutes a return of capital.
·   Dividends of $100 from Truck Company, a taxable domestic corporation.

Assuming that the Leonards file a joint return for 1979, what amount should they report as dividend income after the allowable exclusion?
a. $1,300
b. $1,400
c. $2,900
d. $3,100

55.   James Robert, a cash basis taxpayer, is a self-employed accountant. During 1977 he established a qualified defined-contribution retirement plan of which he will be the only beneficiary. In examining his records for 1977, the following information is available:

Earned income from self-employment	$40,000
Interest income	6,000
Dividend income	4,000
Net long-term capital gains	10,000
Adjusted gross income	$60,000

What is the maximum amount that Robert can deduct as a contribution to his qualified retirement plan for 1977?
a. $1,500.
b. $6,000.
c. $7,500.
d. $9,000.

56.   During 1978 Richard Jason was assessed a deficiency on his 1976 federal income tax return. As a result of this assessment he had to pay $635 determined as follows:

Additional tax	$500
Penalty	50
Interest	85
	$635

If Jason itemizes his deductions on his 1978 return, this payment of $635 will allow him to claim an allowable deduction of
a. $635.
b. $135.
c. $85.
d. $50.

57.   William and Mary Heller had adjusted gross income of $35,000 in 1979. During the year they paid the following medical expenses:

Medicines and drugs	$ 300
Doctors	1,000
Medical care insurance	700
Cost of vitamins prescribed by physician	500

What amount can the Hellers utilize as medical expenses in calculating excess itemized deductions for 1979?
a. $ 650
b. $ 950
c. $1,100
d. $1,150

58.   Stanley Brown, a self-employed individual, owned a truck driven exclusively for business use. The truck had an original cost of $4,000 and had an adjusted basis on December 31, 1976, of $1,800. On January 2, 1977, he traded it in for a new truck costing $5,000 and was given a trade-in allowance of $1,000. The new

truck will also be used exclusively for business purposes and will be depreciated with no salvage value. The basis of the new truck is

    a. $4,000.
    b. $4,200.
    c. $5,000.
    d. $5,800.

59.   Sam Peterson is a plumber employed by a major contracting firm. During 1978 he paid the following miscellaneous personal expenses:

Specialized work clothes (required by employer)	$410
Union dues	600
Preparation of will	150
Cost of income tax preparation	100
Safe deposit box rental (used only for personal effects)	20

If Peterson were to itemize his personal deductions, what amount could he claim as miscellaneous deductible expenses?

    a. $ 680
    b. $ 770
    c. $1,110
    d. $1,130

60.   On July 2, 1979, Milford Corporation purchased for $70,000 machinery that was installed in its factory. The machinery was estimated to have a salvage value of $4,000 and Milford elected to depreciate this machinery over eight years using the double-declining balance method of depreciation. Milford in addition elected to take additional first-year depreciation. This acquisition was the only investment in tangible personal property made during 1979. Counting the year of acquisition as one-half year, Milford should deduct depreciation on this machinery for 1979 of

    a. $10,000.
    b. $10,250.
    c. $10,500.
    d. $10,750.

Number 4   (Estimated time - 45 to 55 minutes)

Number 4 consists of three unrelated parts.

    Part a.   The Jackson Company manufactured a piece of equipment at a cost of $7,000,000 which it held for resale from January 1, 1976 to June 30, 1976 at a price of $8,000,000. On July 1, 1976, Jackson leased the equipment to the Crystal Company. The lease is appropriately recorded as an operating lease for accounting purposes. The lease is for a three-year

period expiring June 30, 1979. Equal monthly payments under the lease are $115,000 and are due on the first of the month. The first payment was made on July 1, 1976. The equipment is being depreciated on a straight-line basis over an eight-year period with no residual value expected.

Required:
    1.   What expense should Crystal appropriately record as a result of the above facts for the year ended December 31, 1976? Show supporting computations in good form.
    2.   What income or loss before income taxes should Jackson appropriately record as a result of the above facts for the year ended December 31, 1976? Show supporting computations in good form.

    Part b.   The Truman Company leased equipment from the Roosevelt Company on October 1, 1976. The lease is appropriately recorded as a purchase for accounting purposes for Truman and as a sale for accounting purposes for Roosevelt. The lease is for an eight-year period expiring September 30, 1984. Equal annual payments under the lease are $600,000 and are due on October 1 of each year. The first payment was made on October 1, 1976. The cost of the equipment on Roosevelt's accounting records was $3,000,000. The equipment has an estimated useful life of eight years with no residual value expected. Truman uses straight-line depreciation and takes a full year's depreciation in the year of purchase. The rate of interest contemplated by Truman and Roosevelt is 10%. The present value of an annuity of $1 in advance for eight periods at 10% is 5.868.

Required:
    1.   What expense should Truman appropriately record as a result of the above facts for the year ended December 31, 1976? Show supporting computations in good form.
    2.   What income or loss before income taxes should Roosevelt appropriately record as a result of the above facts for the year ended December 31, 1976? Show supporting computations in good form.

    Part c.   The Birch Company sells computers. On January 1, 1975, Birch entered into an installment sale contract with the Grove Company for a seven-year period expiring December 31, 1981. Equal annual payments under the installment sale are $1,000,000 and are due on January 1. The first payment was made on January 1, 1975.

Additional information is as follows:
    • The cash selling price of the computer, i.e., the amount that would be realized on an outright sale, is $5,355,000.

• The cost of sales relating to the computer is $4,284,000.

• The finance charges relating to the installment period are $1,645,000 based on a stated interest rate of 10% which is appropriate. For tax purposes, Birch appropriately uses the accrual basis for recording finance charges.

• Circumstances are such that the collection of the installment sale is reasonably assured.

• The installment sale qualifies for the installment method of reporting for tax purposes.

• Assume that the income tax rate is 40%.

Required:

1. What income (loss) before income taxes should Birch appropriately record as a result of this transaction for the year ended December 31, 1975? Show supporting computations in good form.

2. What provision for deferred income taxes, if any, should Birch appropriately record as a result of this transaction for the year ended December 31, 1975? Show supporting computations in good form.

Number 5   (Estimated time - 40 to 50 minutes)

In a special election held on May 1, 1977, the voters of the city of Nicknar approved a $10,000,000 issue of 6% general obligation bonds maturing in 1997. The proceeds of this sale will be used to help finance the construction of a new civic center. The total cost of the project was estimated at $15,000,000. The remaining $5,000,000 will be financed by an irrevocable state grant which has been awarded. A capital projects fund was established to account for this project and was designated the Civic Center Construction Fund. The formal project authorization was appropriately recorded in a memorandum entry.

The following transactions occurred during the fiscal year beginning July 1, 1977, and ending June 30, 1978:

1.   On July 1, the General Fund loaned $500,000 to the Civic Center Construction Fund for defraying engineering and other expenses.

2.   Preliminary engineering and planning costs of $320,000 were paid to Akron Engineering Company. There had been no encumbrance for this cost.

3.   On December 1st, the bonds were sold at 101. The premium on bonds was transferred to the Debt Service Fund.

4.   On March 15th, a contract for $12,000,000 was entered into with Candu Construction Company for the major part of the project.

5.   Orders were placed for materials estimated to cost $55,000.

6.   On April 1st, a partial payment of $2,500,000 was received from the State.

7.   The materials that were previously ordered were received at a cost of $51,000 and paid.

8.   On June 15, a progress billing of $2,000,000 was received from Candu Construction for work done on the project. As per the terms of the contract, the city will withhold 6% of any billing until the project is completed.

9.   The General Fund was repaid the $500,000 previously loaned.

Required:

Based upon the transactions presented above:

a.   Prepare journal entries to record the transactions in the Civic Center Construction Fund for the period July 1, 1977, through June 30, 1978, and the appropriate closing entries at June 30, 1978.

b.   Prepare a balance sheet of the Civic Center Construction Fund as of June 30, 1978.

EXAMINATION IN ACCOUNTING PRACTICE — PART II

NOTE TO CANDIDATES: Suggested time allotments are as follows:

	Estimated Minutes	
All questions are required:	Minimum	Maximum
No. 1	45	55
No. 2	45	55
No. 3	45	55
No. 4	45	55
No. 5	40	50
Total	220	270

Number 1 (Estimated time - 45 to 55 minutes)

Select the **best** answer for each of the following items relating to a **variety of financial accounting problems.**

1. Token Company sold some of its fixed assets during 1977. The original cost of the fixed assets was $750,000 and the allowance for accumulated depreciation at the date of sale was $600,000. The proceeds from the sale of the fixed assets were $210,000. Assuming funds are defined as working capital, the information concerning the sale of the fixed assets should be shown on Token's statement of changes in financial position for the year ended December 31, 1977, as
   a. A subtraction from net income of $60,000 and a source of $150,000.
   b. An addition to net income of $60,000 and a source of $150,000.
   c. A subtraction from net income of $60,000 and a source of $210,000.
   d. A source of $150,000.

2. The Hickory Company made a lump sum purchase of three pieces of machinery for $115,000 from an unaffiliated company. At the time of acquisition, Hickory paid $5,000 to determine the appraised value of the machinery. The appraisal disclosed the following values:

Machine A	$70,000
Machine B	42,000
Machine C	28,000

What cost should be assigned to machines A, B, and C, respectively?
   a. $40,000; $40,000; $40,000.
   b. $47,500; $34,500; $23,000.
   c. $60,000; $36,000; $24,000.
   d. $70,000; $42,000; $28,000.

3. During 1977, Hollin Company determined, as a result of additional information, that machinery that was previously depreciated over a seven-year life had a total estimated useful life of only five years. An accounting change was made in 1977 to reflect this additional information. If the change had been made in 1976, the allowance for accumulated depreciation would have been $2,600,000 at December 31, 1976, instead of $2,100,000. As a result of this change, 1977 depreciation expense was $200,000 greater than it would have been if the change had not been made. Assume that the direct effects of this change are limited to the effect on depreciation and the related tax provision, and that the income tax rate was 50% in both years. What should be reported in Hollin's income statement for the year ended December 31, 1977, as the cumulative effect on prior years of changing the estimated useful life of the machinery?
   a. $0.
   b. $250,000.
   c. $350,000.
   d. $500,000.

4. The Raff Company purchased a machine on January 1, 1978, for $5,500,000. The machine has an estimated useful life of ten years with no salvage. The machine is being depreciated using the sum-of-the-years digits method for income tax reporting and the straight-line method for financial statement reporting. Assuming that the income tax rate is 50%, the amount of deferred taxes charged to Raff's 1978 income statement would be
   a. $225,000.
   b. $275,000.
   c. $450,000.
   d. $550,000.

5. Fountain, Incorporated, has 5,000,000 shares of common stock outstanding on December 31, 1976. An additional 1,000,000 shares of common stock were issued on April 1, 1977, and 500,000 more on July 1, 1977. On October 1, 1977, Fountain issued 10,000, $1,000 face value, 7% convertible bonds. Each bond is convertible into 40 shares of common stock. The bonds were not considered common stock equivalents at the time of their issuance and no bonds were converted into common stock in 1977. What is the number of shares to be used in computing primary earnings per share and fully diluted earnings per share, respectively?

   a.   5,750,000 and 5,950,000.
   b.   5,750,000 and 6,150,000.
   c.   6,000,000 and 6,100,000.
   d.   6,000,000 and 6,900,000.

6. The stockholders' equity section of Sola Corporation as of December 31, 1976, was as follows:

Common stock, $20 par value, authorized 150,000 shares, issued and outstanding 100,000 shares	$2,000,000
Capital in excess of par value	400,000
Retained earnings	200,000
	$2,600,000

On March 1, 1977, Sola reacquired 10,000 shares for $240,000. The following transactions occurred in 1977 with respect to treasury stock acquired:

   June 1 — Sold 3,000 shares for $84,000.
   August 1 — Sold 2,000 shares for $42,000.
   September 1 — Retired remaining 5,000 shares.

Sola accounts for treasury stock on the cost method. As a result of these transactions

   a.   Stockholders' equity remained unchanged.
   b.   Common stock decreased $100,000 and retained earnings decreased $14,000.
   c.   Common stock decreased $100,000 and capital in excess of par decreased $14,000.
   d.   Common stock decreased $126,000.

7. The Carson Company's marketable equity securities portfolio which is appropriately included in current assets is as follows:

	Cost	Market	Unrealized Gain (Loss)
Archer, Inc.	$100,000	$100,000	$ —
Kelly Co.	200,000	150,000	(50,000)
Pelt Company	250,000	260,000	10,000
	$550,000	$510,000	$ (40,000)

Ignoring income taxes, what amount should be reported as a charge against income in Carson's 1977 income statement?

   a. $0.
   b. $10,000.
   c. $40,000.
   d. $60,000.

8. During 1979 Criterion Corporation issued at 105, two hundred $1,000 bonds due in ten years. One detachable stock purchase warrant entitling the holder to buy 20 shares of Criterion's common stock was attached to each bond. Shortly after issuance, each bond had a market value of $940, and each warrant was quoted at $60. What amount, if any, of the proceeds from the bond issuance should be recorded as part of Criterion's stockholders' equity?

   a. $0
   b. $12,000
   c. $12,600
   d. $13,404

9. On January 1, 1977, the Dan Company purchased a new machine for $4,000,000. The new machine has an estimated useful life of eight years and the salvage value was estimated to be $400,000. Depreciation was computed on the sum-of-the-years-digits method. What amount should be shown in Dan's balance sheet at December 31, 1978, net of accumulated depreciation for this machine?

   a. $2,100,000.
   b. $2,500,000.
   c. $3,150,000.
   d. $3,300,000.

10. On December 1, 1978, Chest Corporation purchased 200,000 shares representing 45% of the outstanding stock of Park Company for cash of $2,500,000. As a result of this purchase, Chest has the ability to exercise significant influence over the operating and financial policies of Park. 45% of the net income of Park amounted to $20,000 for the month of December and $350,000 for the year ended December 31, 1978. The appropriate amount of goodwill amortization to be recorded by Chest in 1978 as a result of its purchase of Park stock would be $10,000. On Janu-

ary 15, 1979, cash dividends of $0.30 per share were paid to stockholders of record on December 31, 1978. Chest's long-term investment in Park should be shown in Chest's December 31, 1978, balance sheet at

    a. $2,450,000.
    b. $2,460,000.
    c. $2,500,000.
    d. $2,510,000.

11.   The capital accounts for the partnership of Lance and Dey at October 31, 1975, are as follows:

Lance, capital	$ 80,000
Dey, capital	40,000
	$120,000

The partners share profits and losses in the ratio of 6:4, respectively.

The partnership is in desperate need of cash, and the partners agree to admit Carey as a partner with a one-third interest in the capital and profits and losses upon his investment of $30,000. Immediately after Carey's admission, what should be the capital balances of Lance, Dey, and Carey, respectively, assuming goodwill is not to be recognized?

    a. $50,000; $50,000; $50,000.
    b. $60,000; $60,000; $60,000.
    c. $66,667; $33,333; $50,000.
    d. $68,000; $32,000; $50,000.

12.   On January 1, 1977, Wilson, Inc., issued 100,000 additional shares of $10 par value voting common stock in exchange for all of Thomson Company's voting common stock in a business combination appropriately accounted for by the pooling of interests method. Net income for the year ended December 31, 1977, was $400,000 for Thomson and $1,300,000 for Wilson, exclusive of any consideration of Thomson. During 1977, Wilson paid $900,000 in dividends to its stockholders and Thomson paid $250,000 in dividends to Wilson. What should be the consolidated net income for the year ended December 31, 1977?

    a. $1,150,000.
    b. $1,450,000.
    c. $1,550,000.
    d. $1,700,000.

13.   In January 1977, Hunter, Inc., estimated that its year end bonus to executives would be $240,000 for 1977. The actual amount paid for the year end bonus for 1976 was $224,000. The estimate for 1977

is subject to year-end adjustment. What amount, if any, of expense should be reflected in Hunter's quarterly income statement for the three months ended March 31, 1977?

    a. $0.
    b. $56,000.
    c. $60,000.
    d. $240,000.

14.   The Park Company is disposing of a segment of its business. At the measurement date the net loss from the disposal is estimated to be $950,000. Included in the $950,000 are severance pay of $100,000 and employee relocation costs of $50,000, both of which are directly associated with the decision to dispose of the segment; and estimated net losses from operations from the measurement date to the expected disposal date of $200,000. Net losses from operations of $150,000 from the beginning of the year to the measurement date are not included in the estimated net loss from the disposal. Park's income statement should report a loss on discontinued operations (a separate component of income below the caption "Income From Continuing Operations") of

    a. $750,000.
    b. $850,000.
    c. $900,000.
    d. $1,100,000.

15.   The Madden Company had 600,000 shares of common stock issued and outstanding at December 31, 1977. During 1978, no additional common stock was issued. On January 1, 1978, Madden issued 400,000 shares of nonconvertible preferred stock. During 1978, Madden declared and paid $200,000 cash dividends on the common stock and $110,000 on the nonconvertible preferred stock. Net income for the year ended December 31, 1978, was $750,000. What should be Madden's 1978 earnings per common share, rounded to the nearest penny?

    a. $0.73.
    b. $0.92.
    c. $1.07.
    d. $1.25.

16.   Royal Company's net accounts receivable were $500,000 at December 31, 1977, and $600,000 at December 31, 1978. Net cash sales for 1978 were $200,000. The accounts receivable turnover for 1978 was 5.0. What were Royal's total net sales for 1978?

    a. $2,950,000.
    b. $3,000,000.
    c. $3,200,000.
    d. $5,500,000.

17.   The Park Corporation purchased factory equipment that was installed and put into service January 2, 1977, at a total cost of $32,000. Salvage value was estimated at $2,000. The equipment is being depreciated over eight years using the double-declining-balance method. For the year 1978, Park should record depreciation expense on this equipment of

    a. $5,625.
    b. $6,000.
    c. $7,500
    d. $8,000.

18.   Seed Company has a receivable from a foreign customer which is payable in the local currency of the foreign customer. On December 31, 1976, this receivable was appropriately included in the accounts receivable section of Seed's balance sheet at $450,000. When the receivable was collected on January 4, 1977, Seed converted the local currency of the foreign customer into $440,000. Seed also owns a foreign subsidiary in which exchange gains of $45,000 resulted as a consequence of translation in 1977. What amount, if any, should be included as an exchange gain or loss in Seed's 1977 consolidated income statement?

    a. $0.
    b. $10,000 exchange loss.
    c. $35,000 exchange gain.
    d. $45,000 exchange gain.

19.   Certain balance sheet accounts in a foreign subsidiary of the Brogan Company at December 31, 1977, have been transated into United States dollars as follows:

	Translated at	
	Current Rates	Historical Rates
Marketable equity securities carried at cost	$100,000	$110,000
Marketable equity securities carried at current market price	120,000	125,000
Inventories carried at cost	130,000	132,000
Inventories carried at net realizable value	80,000	84,000
	$430,000	$451,000

What amount should be shown in Brogan's balance sheet at December 31, 1977, as a result of the above information?

    a. $430,000.
    b. $436,000.
    c. $442,000.
    d. $451,000.

20.   The Lake Company sold some machinery to the View Company on January 1, 1976, for which the cash selling price was $758,200. View entered into an installment sales contract with Lake at an interest rate of 10%. The contract required payments of $200,000 a year over five years with the first payment due on December 31, 1976. What amount of interest income, if any, should be included in Lake's 1977 income statement (the second year of the contract), using the "interest method"?

    a. $0.
    b. $63,402.
    c. $75,820.
    d. $100,000.

Number 2   (Estimated time - 45 to 55 minutes)

Select the **best** answer for each of the following items relating to a **variety of financial accounting problems.**

21.   The Shamus Company was organized on January 2, 1975, and issued the following stock:
    •200,000 shares of $5 par value common stock at $12 per share (authorized 200,000 shares).
    •50,000 shares of $10 par value fully participating 4% cumulative preferred stock at $25 per share (authorized 150,000 shares).

The net income for 1975 was $420,000 and cash dividends of $72,000 were declared and paid in 1975.

What were the dividends paid on the preferred and common stock, respectively?

    a. $20,000 and $52,000.
    b. $24,000 and $48,000.
    c. $46,000 and $26,000.
    d. $72,000 and $0.

22.   On June 30, 1973, Leaf Corporation granted compensatory stock options for 10,000 shares of its $24 par value common stock to certain of its key employees. The market price of the common stock on that date was $31 per share and the option price was $28. The options are exercisable beginning January 1, 1976, providing those key employees are still in the employ of the Company at the time the options are exercised. The options expire on June 30, 1977.

On January 4, 1976, when the market price of the stock was $36 per share, all 10,000 options were exercised.

What should be the amount of compensation expense recorded by Leaf Corporation for the calendar year 1975?
a. $0.
b. $7,500.
c. $12,000.
d. $30,000.

23. The Miller Corporation was established in 1970. In 1978 it adopted a pension plan for its employees. On December 31, 1978, the past service cost was determined to be $500,000. Miller had elected to amortize past service cost over ten years and to fund past service cost over fifteen years. The past service cost of $500,000 as of December 31, 1978, should be accounted for as a charge to
a. Prior periods as a prior-period adjustment.
b. Operations in 1978.
c. Operations ratably from 1978 through 1987.
d. Operations ratably from 1978 through 1992.

24. (576,P1,15) (b) General price-level adjusted statements require adjustment of nonmonetary items for changes in the price level. Monetary items, which are essentially cash, receivables, and payables, are not adjusted. Thus the receivables, payables, and long term debt would not be adjusted. The common stock would be adjusted from $100,000 to $110,000, because it is a nonmonetary item. Note that FASB statement No. 33 requires the use of an average-for-the-year index.

25. On January 1, 1974, Hal Company purchased equipment at a cost of $31,000. The equipment was estimated to have a salvage value of $1,000 and it is being depreciated over five years under the sum-of-the-years-digits method. What should be the charge for depreciation of this equipment for the year ended December 31, 1978?
a. $1,000.
b. $2,000.
c. $3,000.
d. $6,000.

26. The owners of the Zoot Suit Clothing Store are contemplating selling the business to new interests. The cumulative earnings for the past five years amounted to $450,000 including extraordinary gains of $10,000. The annual earnings based on an average rate

of return on investment for this industry would have been $76,000. If excess earnings are to be capitalized at 10%, then implied goodwill should be
a. $120,000.
b. $140,000.
c. $440,000.
d. $450,000.

27. Information concerning the Gas Company's common stock is as follows:

	Per Share
Book value at December 31, 1977	$12,00
Quoted market value on New York Stock Exchange on December 31, 1977	9.00
Earnings for 1977	3.00
Par value	2.00
Dividend for 1977	1.00

What was the price-earnings ratio on common stock for 1977?
a. 2 to 1.
b. 2.67 to 1.
c. 3 to 1.
d. 4 to 1.

28. The balance sheet for the partnership of Lang, Monte, and Newton at April 30, 1975, follows. The partners share profits and losses in the ratio of 2:2:6, respectively.

Assets, at cost	$100,000
Lang, Loan	$ 9,000
Lang, capital	15,000
Monte, capital	31,000
Newton, capital	45,000
Total	$100,000

Lang is retiring from the partnership. By mutual agreement, the assets are to be adjusted to their fair value of $130,000 at April 30, 1975. Monte and Newton agree that the partnership will pay Lang $37,000 cash for his partnership interest, exclusive of his loan which is to be paid in full. No goodwill is to be recorded. What is the balance of Newton's capital account after Lang's retirement?
a. $51,000.
b. $53,400.
c. $59,000.
d. $63,000.

29. Jackson Corporation provides an incentive compensation plan under which its president is to receive a bonus equal to 10% of Jackson's income in excess of $100,000 before deducting income tax but after deducting the bonus. If income before income tax and the bonus is $320,000, the amount of the bonus should be
   a. $44.000.
   b. $32,000.
   c. $22,000.
   d. 20,000.

30. On January 1, 1973, Ben Corporation issued $600,000 of 5% ten-year bonds at 103. The bonds are callable at the option of Ben at 104. Ben has recorded amortization of the bond premium on the straight-line method (which was not materially different from the interest method).

   On December 31, 1977, when the fair market value of the bonds was 97, Ben repurchased $300,000 of the bonds in the open market at 97. Ben has recorded interest and amortization for 1977. Ignoring income taxes and assuming that the gain is material, Ben should report this reacquisition as
   a. A gain of $13,500.
   b. An extraordinary gain of $13,500.
   c. A gain of $21,000.
   d. An extraordinary gain of $21,000.

31. The Thoughtful Corporation adopted an employee pension plan on January 1, 1976, for all of its eligible employees. Thoughtful has agreed to make annual payments to a designated trustee at the end of each year. Data relating to the plan follow:

Normal cost	$100,000
Past-service cost on	
January 1, 1976	500,000
Funds held by trustee are expected	
to earn a 5% return.	

In accordance with APB No. 8 what is the maximum provision for pension cost that Thoughtful can record for 1976?

   a. $105,000.
   b. $125,000.
   c. $150,000.
   d. $175,000.

32. During 1978 the Henderson Company purchased the net assets of John Corporation for $800,000. On the date of the transaction, John had no long-term investments in marketable securities and had $100,000 of liabilities. The fair value of John's assets when acquired were as follows:

Current assets	$ 400,000
Noncurrent assets	600,000
	$1,000,000

How should the $100,000 difference between the fair value of the net assets acquired ($900,000) and the cost ($800,000) be accounted for by Henderson?
   a. The $100,000 difference should be credited to retained earnings.
   b. The noncurrent assets should be recorded at $500,000.
   c. The current assets should be recorded at $360,000, and the noncurrent assets should be recorded at $540,000.
   d. A deferred credit of $100,000 should be set up and then amortized to income over a period not to exceed forty years.

33. On January 1, 1975, The Jonas Company sold equipment to its wholly-owned subsidiary, Neptune Company, for $1,800,000. The equipment cost Jonas $2,000,000; accumulated depreciation at the time of sale was $500,000. Jonas was depreciating the equipment on the straight-line method over 20 years with no salvage value, a procedure which Neptune continued. On the consolidated balance sheet at December 31, 1975, the cost and accumulated depreciation, respectively, should be
   a. $1,500,000 and $600,000.
   b. $1,800,000 and $100,000.
   c. $1,800,000 and $500,000.
   d. $2,000,000 and $600,000.

34. Brad Corporation provides an allowance for its doubtful accounts receivable. At December 31, 1977, the allowance account had a credit balance of $4,000. Each month, Brad accrues bad debt expense in an amount equal to 1% of sales on account. Total sales on account during 1978 amounted to $1,000,000. During 1978 uncollectible accounts receivable totaling $16,000 were written off against the allowance account. An aging of accounts receivable at December 31, 1978, indicates that an allowance of $20,000 should be provided for doubtful accounts as of that date. Accordingly, bad debt expense previously accrued during 1978 should be increased by
   a. $26,000.
   b. $22,000.
   c. $20,000.
   d. $2,000.

35. On July 1, 1974, Gusto Corporation purchased equipment at a cost of $22,000. The equipment has an estimated salvage value of $3,000 and is being depreciated over an estimated life of eight years under the double-declining-balance method of depreciation. For the six months ended December 31, 1974, Gusto recorded one-half year's depreciation. What should be the charge for depreciation (rounded to the nearest dollar) of this equipment for the year ended December 31, 1975?

    a. $4,158

    b. $4,750.

    c. $4,813.

    d. $5,500.

36. The Robert Construction Corporation uses the percentage-of-completion method of accounting. In 1975, Robert began work on a contract it had received which provided for a contract price of $8,000,000. Other details follow:

	1975
Costs incurred during the year	$1,200,000
Estimated costs to complete as of December 31	4,800,000
Billings during the year	1,440,000
Collections during the year	1,000,000

What should be the gross profit recognized in 1975?

    a. $160,000.

    b. $240,000.

    c. $400,000.

    d. $1,600,000.

37. The Hint Corporation granted stock options for 10,000 shares of its $20 par value common stock to certain of its key employees on January 1, 1975, when the fair market value of the common stock was $35 per share. The options, which can be exercised at $38 per share, became exercisable on January 1, 1976, and expire on December 31, 1978. Those employees receiving the options must be employed by the corporation at the time the options are exercised. What amount of additional compensation should Hint record in 1975?

    a. $0.

    b. $7,500.

    c. $10,000.

    d. $30,000.

38. On January 1, 1973, Trail Co., purchased a machine (its only depreciable asset) for $150,000.

The machine has a five-year life, and no salvage value. Sum-of-the-years'-digits depreciation has been used for both financial statement reporting and income tax reporting.

Effective January 1, 1976, for financial statement reporting but not for income tax reporting, Trail decided to change to the straight-line method for depreciation of the machine. Assume that Trail can justify the change.

Trail's income before depreciation, before income taxes, and before the cumulative effect of the accounting change (if any), for the year ended December 31, 1976, is $100,000. The income tax rate for 1976, as well as for the years 1973-1975, is 50%. What amount should Trail report as net income for the year ended December 31, 1976?

    a. $20,000.

    b. $35,000.

    c. $50,000.

    d. $65,000.

39. The Swenson Company reported the following results for the two years ended December 31, 1978 and 1977 respectively:

	December 31	
	1978	1977
Income (per books before income taxes)	$1,200,000	$800,000
Taxable income	1,600,000	120,000

The disparity between book income and taxable income is attributable to timing differences. What should Swenson record as income tax expense for the year ended December 31, 1978, assuming an income tax rate of 40%?

    a. $640,000

    b. $480,000

    c. $368,000

    d. $208,000

40. In 1976 Dubious Corporation began selling a new line of products that carry a two-year warranty against defects. Based upon past experience with other products, the estimated warranty costs related to dollar sales are as follows:

First year of warranty	2%
Second year of warranty	5%

Sales and actual warranty expenditures for 1976 and 1977 are presented below:

	1976	1977
Sales	$500,000	$700,000
Actual warranty expenditures	10,000	30,000

What is the estimated warranty **liability** at the end of 1977?

    a. $39,000.
    b. $44,000.
    c. $49,000.
    d. $84,000.

Number 3   (Estimated time - 45 to 55 minutes)

Select the **best** answer for each of the following items relating to **the federal income taxation of corporations and partnerships.**

41.   The Tempest Corporation, not a dealer in securities, had accumulated earnings and profits of $75,000 at the beginning of 1979. The earnings and profits for 1979 were $25,000. On October 15, 1979, Tempest distributed to its shareholders as a dividend, marketable securities having a fair market value of $12,000. The securities had cost $7,000. As a result of the distribution, accumulated earnings and profits were

    a.   Increased by $5,000.
    b.   Decreased by $5,000.
    c.   Decreased by $7,000.
    d.   Decreased by $12,000.

42.   During the 1976 holiday season, Barmin Corporation gave business gifts to 16 customers. The value of the gifts, which were not of an advertising nature, was as follows:

$$
\begin{array}{l}
4 \ @ \ \$ \ 10 \\
4 \ @ \ \$ \ 25 \\
4 \ @ \ \$ \ 50 \\
4 \ @ \ \$100
\end{array}
$$

For 1976, Barmin can deduct as a business expense

    a. $0.
    b. $140.
    c. $340.
    d. $740.

43.   For the year ended December 31, 1976, Dormer Corporation had net income per books of $300,000. Included in the determination of net income were the following items:

Interest on income on municipal bonds	$10,000
Gain on settlement of life insurance policy (death of officer)	50,000
Interest paid on loan to purchase municipal bonds	2,000
Provision for federal income tax	131,000

What should Dormer report as its taxable income for 1976?

    a. $373,000.
    b. $381,000.
    c. $421,000.
    d. $423,000.

44.   During 1979 Lodge Corporation had net long-term capital losses of $14,000, net short-term capital gains of $6,000, gains on the sale of Section 1231 property of $3,000 and losses on the sale of Section 1245 property of $4,000. There was no capital loss carryforward from prior years. The capital gains deduction for 1979 was

    a. $0.
    b. $2,000.
    c. $3,000.
    d. $9,000.

45.   In 1977, its first year of operation, the Champion Corporation, not a dealer in securities, realized taxable income of $64,000 from the operation of its business. In addition to its regular business operations, it realized the following gains and losses from the sale of marketable securities:

Short-term capital gain	$ 5,000
Short-term capital loss	(2,000)
Long-term capital gain	6,000
Long-term capital loss	(16,000)

What is Champion's total taxable income for 1977?

    a. $57,000.
    b. $62,000.
    c. $64,000.
    d. $75,000.

46.   Logo Corporation's net income per books was $150,000 for the year 1977 after recording amortization of organization costs. Organization costs of $70,000 incurred at the organization date two years earlier are being written off over a ten-year period on the financial statements, and over the minimum period for income tax purposes. Assuming that there were no other reconciling items, what is Logo's taxable income for 1977?

    a. $136,000.
    b. $143,000.
    c. $150,000.
    d. $157,000.

47.   The Market Corporation had taxable income in 1979 of $40,000 before deducting contributions to qualified charitable organizations. During 1979 it gave $5,000 cash to a charitable organization. Market also

had a contribution carryover from 1978 of $1,000. What is Market's contribution deduction for 1979?

    a. $1,000
    b. $2,000
    c. $5,000
    d. $6,000

48. The partners of Martin, Cynthia, Libber, and Company share profits and losses in a ratio of 4:3:3 respectively. The tax basis of each partner as of December 31, 1976, was as follows:

Martin	$7,200
Cynthia	6,000
Libber	2,500

During 1976 the partnership incurred an operating loss of $15,000. The loss is not reflected in the tax basis figures shown above. As a result of this loss, Martin, Cynthia, and Libber should deduct, respectively, on their 1976 individual returns

    a. $6,000, $4,500, and $2,500.
    b. $6,000, $4,500, and $4,500.
    c. $7,000, $5,500, and $2,500.
    d. $7,100, $5,400, and $2,500.

49. The Robert Corporation, a calendar-year company, has elected Subchapter S status for the past five years. For the year ended December 31, 1979, Robert had taxable income and current earnings and profits of $185,000. At December 31, 1978, Robert had undistributed taxable income of $45,000 earned in 1978. During 1979 Robert made the following cash distributions to its ten equal shareholders who are also on a calendar-year basis:

January 29, 1979	$ 30,000
March 13, 1979	20,000
July 8, 1979	15,000
December 29, 1979	35,000
	$100,000

For the calendar year 1979, what amount should be included in each shareholder's gross income from Robert?

    a. $ 8,500
    b. $10,000
    c. $18,500
    d. $19,000

50. For the year 1979, Morris Corporation reported taxable income of $100,000 before any special deductions. Included in taxable income was dividend income of $120,000 received from unaffiliated domestic cor-

porations. What is the dividends received deduction for 1979?

    a. $0
    b. $ 17,000
    c. $ 85,000
    d. $102,000

51. The Vanity Corporation was organized and began operations in January 1979. The corporation's ten equal shareholders elected to have Vanity taxed as a Subchapter S Corporation, and such election was approved. For its year ended December 31, 1979, Vanity had taxable income and current earnings and profits of $80,000 comprised of $64,000 derived from operations and $16,000 from short-term capital gains. During 1979 it distributed $30,000 in cash to its ten shareholders. For 1979 each shareholder should include in his or her respective gross income

    a.   Ordinary income of $3,000.
    b.   Ordinary income of $3,400 and short-term capital gain of $1,600.
    c.   Ordinary income of $6,400 and short-term capital gain of $1,600.
    d.   Ordinary income of $8,000.

52. During 1977 Simon Manufacturing Corporation, in need of additional factory space, exchanged 5,000 shares of its common stock with a par value of $50,000 for a building with a fair market value of $60,000. On the date of the exchange the stock had a fair market value of $65,000. For 1977, how much and what type of gain or loss should Simon report on this transaction?

    a.   No gain or loss.
    b. $5,000 capital loss.
    c. $10,000 capital gain.
    d. $10,000 section 1231 gain.

53. For the year ended December 31, 1977, the Lewis Corporation reported net income per books of $250,000. The following items were included in the determination of net income:

State corporate income tax refunds	$ 4,000
Interest income on tax-exempt municipal securities	15,000
Loss on sale of land acquired in 1975 for investment	20,000
Interest expense on loan to purchase tax-exempt municipal securities	8,000
Provision for federal income taxes	200,000

What is the taxable income of Lewis for 1977?
- a. $270,000.
- b. $450,000.
- c. $459,000.
- d. $463,000.

54. On December 31, 1977, Topic Corporation sold machinery for $24,000. The machinery which had been purchased on January 1, 1973, for $20,000 had an adjusted basis of $14,000 on the date of sale. For 1977 Topic should report
- a. Ordinary income of $10,000.
- b. A section 1231 gain of $10,000.
- c. A section 1231 gain of $6,000 and ordinary income of $4,000.
- d. A section 1231 gain of $4,000 and ordinary income of $6,000.

55. On April 24, 1976, Fury Corporation acquired 4,000 shares of its own $5 par value stock for $40,000. Fury sold this treasury stock on June 22, 1976, for $54,000. As a result of these transactions what should Fury report for 1976?
- a. Ordinary income of $14,000.
- b. A short-term capital gain of $14,000.
- c. A long-term capital gain of $14,000.
- d. No gain or loss.

56. In order for a corporation to elect subchapter S status, the corporation should
- a. Have only individuals or corporations as its shareholders.
- b. Not have more than one class of stock.
- c. Have no more than twenty shareholders.
- d. Require that its shareholders adopt the same taxable year as itself.

57. On January 1, 1977, Dodge Corporation acquired machinery for $30,000. The machinery had an estimated useful life of ten years and salvage value was estimated at $3,000. If Dodge uses the straight-line method of depreciation, the maximum amount of depreciation that Dodge can deduct for 1977 is
- a. $4,500.
- b. $4,800.
- c. $8,100.
- d. $8,400.

58. For the year ended December 31, 1975, the partnership of Charles and Paul had book income of $75,000 which included the following:

Short-term capital loss	$(3,100)
Long-term capital gain (on sale of securities)	4,300
Section 1231 gain	1,500
Ordinary income (Section 1245 Recapture Provision)	600
Dividends qualifying for $100 exclusion	200

The partners share profits and losses equally. What should be each partner's share of partnership income (excluding all partnership items which must be accounted for separately) to be reported as taxable for 1975?
- a. $35,700.
- b. $36,050.
- c. $36,150.
- d. $37,500.
- e. None of the above.

59. In 1974, the partnership of Al, Gus, and Lew realized an ordinary loss of $90,000. The partnership and partners are on a calendar-year basis. At December 31, 1974, Lew had an adjusted basis of $30,000 for his interest in the partnership before taking the 1974 loss into consideration. Lew has a 40% interest in the profits and losses of the partnership. On his personal income tax return for 1974, what should Lew deduct relative to his partnership interest?
- a. An ordinary loss of $30,000.
- b. An ordinary loss of $36,000.
- c. An ordinary loss of $30,000 and a capital loss of $6,000.
- d. A capital loss of $36,000.
- e. None of the above.

60. During 1979 Stearn Corporation, a cash-basis corporation, paid the following education expenses for its employees:

Tuition	$10,000
Textbooks	3,000
Travel	2,000
Laboratory fees	1,000
	$16,000

The education was not required of the employees to maintain or improve their skills in their present positions. For 1979, Stearn can claim a deduction for these expenses of
- a. $0.
- b. $10,000.
- c. $11,000.
- d. $16,000.

Number 4 **(Estimated time - 45 to 55 minutes)**

Number 4 consists of two unrelated parts.

Part a. On June 30, 1978, a flash flood damaged the warehouse and factory of Padway Corporation, completely destroying the work-in-process inventory. There was no damage to either the raw materials or finished goods inventories. A physical inventory taken after the flood revealed the following valuations:

Raw materials	$ 62,000
Work-in-process	-0-
Finished goods	119,000

The inventory on January 1, 1978, consisted of the following:

Raw materials	$ 30,000
Work-in-process	100,000
Finished goods	140,000
	$270,000

A review of the books and records disclosed that the gross profit margin historically approximated 25% of sales. The sales for the first six months of 1978 were $340,000. Raw material purchases were $115,000. Direct labor costs for this period were $80,000, and manufacturing overhead has historically been applied at 50% of direct labor.

Required:
Compute the value of the work-in-process inventory lost at June 30, 1978. Show supporting computations in good form.

Part b. Lakeview Corporation is a manufacturer that uses the weighted-average process-cost method to account for costs of production. Lakeview manufactures a product that is produced in three separate departments: Molding, Assembling, and Finishing. The following information was obtained for the Assembling Department for the month of June 1980.

Work-in-process, June 1 — 2,000 units composed of the following:

	Amount	Degree of Completion
Transferred in from the Molding Department	$32,000	100%
Costs added by the Assembling Department:		
Direct materials	$20,000	100%
Direct labor	7,200	60%
Factory overhead applied	5,500	50%
	32,700	
Work-in-process, June 1	$64,700	

The following activity occurred during the month of June:

· 10,000 units were transferred in from the Molding Department at a cost of $160,000.

· $150,000 of costs were added by the Assembling Department:

Direct materials	$ 96,000
Direct labor	36,000
Factory overhead applied	18,000
	$150,000

· 8,000 units were completed and transferred to the Finishing Department.

At June 30, 4,000 units were still in work-in-process. The degree of completion of work-in-process at June 30, was as follows:

Direct materials	90%
Direct labor	70%
Factory overhead applied	35%

Required:
Prepare in good form a cost of production report for the Assembling Department for the month of June. Show supporting computations in good form. The report should include:
· Equivalent units of production;
· Total manufacturing costs;
· Cost per equivalent unit;
· Dollar amount of ending work-in-process;
· Dollar amount of inventory cost transferred out.

Number 5 (Estimated time - 40 to 50 minutes)

Number 5 consists of two unrelated parts.

Part a. On January 1, 1976, Todd Corporation made the following investments:

• Acquired for cash, 80% of the outstanding common stock of Meadow Corporation at $70 per share. The stockholders' equity of Meadow on January 1, 1976 consisted of the following:

Common stock, par value $50	$50,000
Retained earnings	20,000

• Acquired for cash, 70% of the outstanding common stock of Van Corporation at $40 per share. The stockholders' equity of Van on January 1, 1976 consisted of the following:

Common stock, par value $20	$60,000
Capital in excess of par value	20,000
Retained earnings	40,000

After these investments were made, Todd was able to exercise significant influence over the operations of both companies.

An analysis of the retained earnings of each company for 1976 is as follows:

	Todd	Meadow	Van
Balance, 1/1/76	$240,000	$20,000	$40,000
Net income (loss)	104,600	36,000	(12,000)
Cash dividends paid	(40,000)	(16,000)	(9,000)
Balance, 12/31/76	$304,600	$40,000	$19,000

Required:

1. What entries should have been made on the books of Todd during 1976 to record the following?

• Investments in subsidiaries.
• Parent's share of subsidiary income or loss.
• Subsidiary dividends received.

2. Using the "parent company theory," compute the amount of minority interest in each subsidiary's stockholders' equity at December 31, 1976.

3. What amount should be reported as consolidated retained earnings of Todd Corporation and subsidiaries as of December 31, 1976?

Note: Show all supporting computations in good form. **Ignore income taxes and deferred tax considerations in your answers.**

Part b. On December 31, 1976, Cole Company and Bond Company entered into a business combination appropriately accounted for as a pooling of interests. As a result of this combination a new company, Gold Corporation, was formed with 500,000 authorized shares of no par, $1-stated-value common stock. The management of Gold did **not** intend to retain either Cole or Bond as subsidiaries.

On December 31, 1976, Gold issued its common stock in exchange for all of the outstanding common stock of Cole and Bond as follows:

Cole: 300,000 shares of Gold common stock for all 10,000 outstanding shares of Cole's $5 par value common stock.

Bond: 200,000 shares of Gold common stock for all 4,000 outstanding shares of Bond's $10 par value common stock.

There were **no** intercompany transactions between these companies.

Presented below are condensed financial statements of Cole and Bond for the year ended December 31, 1976, prior to the pooling of interests.

Balance Sheets

	Cole Company	Bond Company
Assets:		
Current Assets	$260,000	$235,000
Property, plant and equipment (net)	410,000	320,000
Other assets	90,000	65,000
	$760,000	$620,000
Liabilities and Stockholders' Equity:		
Current liabilities	$167,000	$124,000
Long-term debt	300,000	—
Common stock	50,000	40,000
Capital in excess of par value	10,000	160,000
Retained earnings	233,000	296,000
	$760,000	$620,000

Statements of Income and Retained Earnings

	Cole Company	Bond Company
Net sales	$1,600,000	$2,200,000
Costs and expenses:		
Cost of sales	1,120,000	1,560,000
Operating and other expenses	330,000	480,000
	1,450,000	2,040,000
Net income	150,000	160,000
Retained earnings, January 1, 1976	83,000	136,000
Retained earnings, December 31, 1976	$ 233,000	$ 296,000

Cole values its inventory using the FIFO method; Bond uses the LIFO method for its inventory. Bond agreed to change its method of inventory valuation from LIFO to FIFO prior to the business combination.

Bond began operations on January 1, 1975, and data relevant to Bond's inventory are as follows:

	LIFO Method	FIFO Method
Inventory, December 31, 1975	$42,000	$62,000
Inventory, December 31, 1976	$55,000	$85,000

Required:

1.   Prepare the adjusting journal entry with the appropriate explanation and supporting calculations to be made by Bond Company on December 31, 1976, to change its inventory from LIFO cost to FIFO cost. Income taxes should **not** be considered in your solution.

2.   Prepare a schedule computing pooled retained earnings of Gold Corporation as of December 31, 1976.

3.   Prepare the December 31, 1976, journal entry on the books of Gold Corporation to record the business combination as a pooling of interests.

EXAMINATION IN AUDITING

NOTE TO CANDIDATES: Suggested time allotments are as follows:

	Estimated Minutes	
All questions are required:	*Minimum*	*Maximum*
No. 1	90	110
No. 2	15	25
No. 3	15	25
No. 4	15	25
No. 5	15	25
Total.	150	210

Number 1 (Estimated time — 90 to 110 minutes)

Select the **best** answer for each of the following items.

1. Because an expression of opinion as to certain identified items in financial statements tends to overshadow or contradict a disclaimer of opinion or adverse opinion, it is inappropriate for an auditor to issue
    a. A piecemeal opinion.
    b. An unqualified opinion.
    c. An "except for" opinion.
    d. A "subject to" opinion.

2. It is **less** likely that a disclaimer of opinion would be issued when the auditor has reservations arising from
    a. Inability to apply necessary auditing procedures.
    b. Uncertainties.
    c. Inadequate internal control.
    d. Lack of independence.

3. In connection with the study and evaluation of internal control during an examination of financial statements, the independent auditor
    a. Gives equal weight to internal accounting and administrative control.
    b. Emphasizes internal administrative control.
    c. Emphasizes the separation of duties of client personnel.
    d. Emphasizes internal accounting control.

4. For which of the following accounting changes would an auditor's report normally **not** contain a consistency qualification?
    a. A change in principle which does not result in non-comparable statements because the previous year's statements are not presented.
    b. A change to a principle required by a new FASB pronouncement.
    c. A change in principle properly reported by restating the financial statements of prior years.
    d. A change in an accounting estimate.

5. Which of the following is an invalid concept of internal control?
    a. In cases where a person is responsible for all phases of a transaction there should be a clear designation of that person's responsibility.
    b. The recorded accountability for assets should be compared with the existing assets at reasonable intervals and appropriate action should be taken if there are differences.
    c. Accounting control procedures may appropriately be applied on a test basis in some circumstances.
    d. Procedures designed to detect errors and irregularities should be performed by persons other than those who are in a position to perpetrate them.

6. A CPA who has given correct tax advice which is later affected by changes in the tax law is **required** to
    a. Notify the client upon learning of any change.
    b. Notify the client only when the CPA is actively assisting with implementing the advice or is obliged to so notify by specific agreement.
    c. Notify the Internal Revenue Service.
    d. Take no action if the client has already followed the advice unless the client asks the question again.

7. The auditor generally gives most emphasis to ratio and trend analysis in the examination of the statement of
   a. Retained earnings.
   b. Income.
   c. Financial position.
   d. Changes in financial position.

8. A well-designed system of internal control that is functioning effectively is most likely to detect an irregularity arising from
   a. The fraudulent action of several employees.
   b. The fruadulent action of an individual employee.
   c. Informal deviations from the official organization chart.
   d. Management fraud.

9. The standard bank cash confirmation form requests all of the following **except**
   a. Maturity date of a direct liability.
   b. The principal amount paid on a direct liability.
   c. Description of collateral for a direct liability.
   d. The interest rate of a direct liability.

10. An auditor's client has violated a minor requirement of its bond indenture which could result in the trustee requiring immediate payment of the principal amount due. The client refuses to seek a waiver from the bond trustee. Request for immediate payment is **not** considered likely. Under these circumstances the auditor must
    a. Require classification of bonds payable as a current liability.
    b. Contact the bond trustee directly.
    c. Disclose the situation in the auditor's report.
    d. Obtain an opinion from the company's attorney as to the likelihood of the trustee's enforcement of the requirement

11. Which of the following **best** describes a fundamental control weakness often associated with electronic data processing systems?
    a. Electronic data processing equipment is more subject to systems error than manual processing is subject to human error.
    b. Electronic data processing equipment processes and records similar transactions in a similar manner.
    c. Electronic data processing procedures for detection of invalid and unusual trans-

actions are less effective than manual control procedures.
    d. Functions that would normally be separated in a manual system are combined in the electronic data processing system.

12. In connection with an audit of financial statements by an independent CPA, the client suggests that members of the internal audit staff be utilized to minimize external audit costs. It would be **inappropriate** for the CPA to delegate which of the following tasks to the internal audit staff:
    a. Selection of accounts receivable for confirmation, based upon decision rules established by the independent CPA and with appropriate supervision by the CPA.
    b. Investigation of negative accounts receivable responses, for later review by the independent CPA.
    c. Preparation of an accounts receivable aging schedule.
    d. Determination of the adequacy of the allowance for uncollectible accounts.

13. For what minimum period should audit working papers be retained by the independent CPA?
    a. For the period during which the entity remains a client of the independent CPA.
    b. For the period during which an auditor-client relationship exists but not more than six years.
    c. For the statutory period within which legal action may be brought against the independent CPA.
    d. For as long as the CPA is in public practice.

14. The financial management of a company should take steps to see that company investment securities are protected. Which of the following is **not** a step that is designed to protect investment securities?
    a. Custody of securities should be assigned to persons who have the accounting responsibility for securities.
    b. Securities should be properly controlled physically in order to prevent unauthorized usage.
    c. Access to securities should be vested in more than one person.
    d. Securities should be registered in the name of the owner.

15. Fox, CPA, is succeeding Tyrone, CPA, on the audit engagement of Genesis Corporation. Fox plans to consult Tyrone and to review Tyrone's prior-year working papers. Fox may do so if
    a.   Tyrone and Genesis consent.
    b.   Tyrone consents.
    c.   Genesis consents.
    d.   Tyrone and Fox consent.

16. Which of the following would be an **inappropriate** addressee for an auditor's report?
    a.   The corporation whose financial statements were examined.
    b.   A third party, even if the third party is a client who engaged the auditor for examination of a non-client corporation.
    c.   The president of the corporation whose financial statements were examined.
    d.   The stockholders of the corporation whose financial statements were examined.

17. An advantage of manual processing is that human processors may note data errors and irregularities. To replace the human element of error detection associated with manual processing, a well-designed electronic data processing system should introduce
    a.   Programmed limits.
    b.   Dual circuitry.
    c.   Echo checks.
    d.   Read after write.

18. In comparison to the external auditor, an internal auditor is more likely to be concerned with
    a.   Internal administrative control.
    b.   Cost accounting procedures.
    c.   Operational auditing.
    d.   Internal accounting control.

19. Which of the following is **not** a problem associated with the use of test decks for computer-audit purposes?
    a.   Auditing through the computer is more difficult than auditing around the computer.
    b.   It is difficult to design test decks that incorporate all potential variations in transactions.
    c.   Test data may be commingled with live data causing operating problems for the client.
    d.   The program with which the test data are processed may differ from the one used in actual operations.

20. The purpose of tests for compliance is to provide reasonable assurance that the accounting control procedures are being applied as prescribed. The sampling method that is **most** useful when testing for compliance is
    a.   Judgment sampling.
    b.   Attribute sampling.
    c.   Unrestricted random sampling with replacement.
    d.   Stratified random sampling.

21. When a principal auditor decides to make reference to the examination of another auditor, the principal auditor's report should indicate clearly the division of responsibility between the portions of the financial statements covered by each auditor. In which paragraph(s) of the report should the division of responsibility be stated?
    a.   Only the opinion paragraph.
    b.   Either the scope or opinion paragraph.
    c.   Only the scope paragraph.
    d.   Both the scope and opinion paragraphs.

22. In connection with the examination of the consolidated financial statements of Mott Industries, Frazier, CPA, plans to refer to another CPA's examination of the financial statements of a subsidiary company. Under these circumstances Frazier's report must disclose
    a.   The name of the other CPA and the type of report issued by the other CPA.
    b.   The magnitude of the portion of the financial statements examined by the other CPA.
    c.   The nature of Frazier's review of the other CPA's work.
    d.   In a footnote the portions of the financial statements that were covered by the examinations of both auditors.

23. Which of the following four events may be expected to result in a consistency exception in the auditor's report?
    a.   The declining balance method of depreciation was adopted for newly acquired assets.
    b.   A revision was made in the service lives and salvage values of depreciable assets.
    c.   A mathematical error in computing the year-end LIFO inventory was corrected.
    d.   The provision for bad debts increased considerably over the previous year.

24. An auditor is planning the study and evaluation of internal control for purchasing and disbursement procedures. In planning this study and evaluation the auditor will be **least** influenced by

a. The availability of a company manual describing purchasing and disbursement procedures.

b. The scope and results of audit work by the company's internal auditor.

c. The existence within the purchasing and disbursement area of internal control strengths that offset weaknesses.

d. The strength or weakness of internal control in other areas, e.g., sales and accounts receivable.

25. In determining the type of opinion to express, an auditor assesses the nature of the reporting qualifications and the materiality of their effects. Materiality will be the primary factor considered in the choice between

a. An "except for" opinion and an adverse opinion.

b. An "except for" opinion and a "subject to" opinion.

c. An adverse opinion and a disclaimer of opinion.

d. A "subject to" opinion and a piecemeal opinion.

26. An auditor's investigation of a company's electronic data processing control procedures has disclosed the following four circumstances. Indicate which circumstance constitutes a weakness in internal control.

a. Machine operators do not have access to the complete run manual.

b. Machine operators are closely supervised by programmers.

c. Programmers do not have the authorization to operate equipment.

d. Only one generation of back-up files is stored in an off-premises location.

27. As generally conceived, the "audit committee" of a publicly held company should be made up of

a. Representatives of the major equity interests (bonds, preferred stock, common stock).

b. The audit partner, the chief financial officer, the legal counsel, and at least one outsider.

c. Representatives from the client's management, investors, suppliers, and customers.

d. Members of the board of directors who are not officers or employees.

28. Which of the following statements relating to compliance tests is most accurate?

a. Auditing procedures cannot concurrently provide both evidence of compliance with accounting control procedures and evidence required for substantive tests.

b. Compliance tests include physical observations of the proper segregation of duties which ordinarily may be limited to the normal audit period.

c. Compliance tests should be based upon proper application of an appropriate statistical sampling plan.

d. Compliance tests ordinarily should be performed as of the balance sheet date or during the period subsequent to that date.

29. Audit programs generally include procedures necessary to test actual transactions and resulting balances. These procedures are **primarily** designed to

a. Detect irregularities that result in misstated financial statements.

b. Test the adequacy of internal control.

c. Gather corroborative evidence.

d. Obtain information for informative disclosures.

30. An investor is reading the financial statements of The Sundby Corporation and observes that the statements are accompanied by an unqualified auditor's report. From this the investor may conclude that

a. Any disputes over significant accounting issues have been settled to the auditor's satisfaction.

b. The auditor is satisfied that Sundby is operationally efficient.

c. The auditor has ascertained that Sundby's financial statements have been prepared accurately.

d. Informative disclosures in the financial statements but not necessarily in the footnotes are to be regarded as reasonably adequate.

31. Transaction authorization within an organization may be either specific or general. An example of specific transaction authorization is the

a. Establishment of requirements to be met in determining a customer's credit limits.

b. Setting of automatic re-order points for material or merchandise.

c. Approval of a detailed construction budget for a warehouse.

d. Establishment of sales prices for products to be sold to any customer.

32. In connection with a review of the prepaid insurance account, which of the following procedures would generally **not** be performed by the auditor?

a. Recompute the portion of the premium that expired during the year.

b. Prepare excerpts of insurance policies for audit working papers.

c. Examine support for premium payments.

d. Confirm premium rates with an independent insurance broker.

33. Which of the following is an example of application controls in electronic data processing systems?

a. Input controls.

b. Hardware controls.

c. Documentation procedures.

d. Controls over access to equipment and data files.

34. When conducting an audit, errors that arouse suspicion of fraud should be given greater attention than other errors. This is an example of applying the criterion of

a. Reliability of evidence.

b. Materiality.

c. Relative risk.

d. Dual-purpose testing.

35. When expressing a qualified opinion, the auditor generally should include a separate explanatory paragraph describing the effects of the qualification. The requirement for a separate explanatory paragraph does **not** apply when the opinion paragraph has been modified because of

a. A change in accounting principle.

b. Inability to apply necessary auditing procedures.

c. Reclassification of an expense account.

d. Uncertainties.

36. In order to achieve effective quality control, a firm of independent auditors should establish policies and procedures for

a. Determining the minimum procedures necessary for unaudited financial statements.

b. Setting the scope of audit work.

c. Deciding whether to accept or continue a client.

d. Setting the scope of internal control study and evaluation.

37. Independent auditing can best be described as

a. A branch of accounting.

b. A discipline which attests to the results of accounting and other functional operations and data.

c. A professional activity that measures and communicates financial and business data.

d. A regulatory function that prevents the issuance of improper financial information.

38. An auditor would be **least** likely to use a generalized computer-audit program for which of the following tasks?

a. Selecting and printing accounts receivable confirmations.

b. Listing accounts receivable confirmation exceptions for examination.

c. Comparing accounts receivable subsidiary files to the general ledger.

d. Investigating exceptions to accounts receivable confirmations.

39. An independent audit aids in the communication of economic data because the audit

a. Confirms the accuracy of management's financial representations.

b. Lends credibility to the financial statements.

c.. Guarantees that financial data are fairly presented.

d. Assures the readers of financial statements that any fraudulent activity has been corrected.

40. An example of an internal control weakness is to assign to a department supervisor the responsibility for

a. Reviewing and approving time reports for subordinate employees.

b. Initiating requests for salary adjustments for subordinate employees.

c. Authorizing payroll checks for terminated employees.

d. Distributing payroll checks to subordinate employees.

41. Operating control over the check signature plate normally should be the responsibility of the

a. Secretary.

b. Chief accountant.

c. Vice-president of finance.

d. Treasurer.

42. It would be appropriate for the payroll accounting department to be responsible for which of the following functions?

a. Approval of employee time records.

b. Maintenance of records of employment, discharges, and pay increases.

c. Preparation of periodic governmental reports as to employees' earnings and withholding taxes.

d. Distribution of pay checks to employees.

43. Which of the following best describes the difference between a long-form auditor's report and the standard short-form report?

a. The long-form report may contain a more detailed description of the scope of the auditor's examination.

b. The long-form report's use permits the auditor to explain exceptions or reservations in a way that does not require an opinion qualification.

c. The auditor may make factual representations with a degree of certainty that would not be appropriate in a short-form report.

d. The long-form report's use is limited to special situations such as cash basis statements, modified accrual basis statements or not-for-profit organization statements.

44. When a company has treasury stock certificates on hand, a year-end count of the certificates by the auditor is

a. Required when the company classifies treasury stock with other assets.

b. Not required if treasury stock is a deduction from stockholders' equity.

c. Required when the company had treasury stock transactions during the year.

d. Always required.

45. The grandfather-father-son approach to providing protection for important computer files is a concept that is most often found in

a. On-line, real-time systems.

b. Punched-card systems.

c. Magnetic tape systems.

d. Magnetic drum systems.

46. An auditor performs interim work at various times throughout the year. The auditor's subsequent events work should be extended to the date of

a. A post-dated footnote.

b. The next scheduled interim visit.

c. The final billing for audit services rendered.

d. The auditor's report.

47. A CPA auditing an electric utility wishes to determine whether all customers are being billed. The CPA's best direction of test is from the

a. Meter department records to the billing (sales) register.

b. Billing (sales) register to the meter department records.

c. Accounts receivable ledger to the billing (sales) register.

d. Billing (sales) register to the accounts receivable ledger.

48. Which of the following best describes the principal advantage of the use of flowcharts in reviewing internal control?

a. Standard flowcharts are available and can be effectively used for describing most company internal operations.

b. Flowcharts aid in the understanding of the sequence and relationships of activities and documents.

c. Working papers are not complete unless they include flowcharts as well as memoranda on internal control.

d. Flowcharting is the most efficient means available for summarizing internal control.

49. The auditor learned of the following situations subsequent to the issuance of his audit report on February 6, 1976. Each is considered important to users of the financial statements. For which one does the auditor have responsibility for appropriate disclosure of the newly discovered facts?

a. A major lawsuit against the company, which was the basis for a "subject to" auditor's opinion, was settled on unfavorable terms on March 1, 1976.

b. The client undertook merger negotiations on March 16, 1976, and concluded a tentative merger agreement on April 1, 1976.

c. On February 16, 1976 a fire destroyed the principal manufacturing plant.

d. A conflict of interest situation involving credit officers and a principal company supplier was discovered on March 3, 1976.

50. The auditor interviews the plant manager. The auditor is most likely to rely upon this interview as primary support for an audit conclusion on

a. Capitalization vs. expensing policy.

b. Allocation of fixed and variable costs.

c. The necessity to record a provision for deferred maintenance costs.

d. The adequacy of the depreciation expense.

51. The securities of Donley Corporation are listed on a regional stock exchange and registered with the Securities and Exchange Commission. The management of Donley engages a CPA to perform an indepen-

dent audit of Donley's financial statements. The primary objective of this audit is to provide assurance to the
- a.   Regional stock exchange.
- b.   Investors in Donley securities.
- c.   Securities and Exchange Commission.
- d.   Board of Directors of Donley Corporation.

52.   An auditor is reviewing changes in sales for two products. Sales volume (quantity) declined 10% for product A and 2% for product B. Sales prices were increased by 25% for both products. Prior year sales were $75,000 for A and $25,000 for B. The auditor would expect this year's total sales for the two products to be approximately
- a. $112,500.
- b. $115,000.
- c. $117,000.
- d. $120,000.

53.   Florida Corporation declared a 100% stock dividend during 1975. In connection with the examination of Florida's financial statements, Florida's auditor should determine that
- a.   The additional shares issued do not exceed the number of authorized but previously unissued shares.
- b.   Stockholders received their additional shares by confirming year-end holdings with them.
- c.   The stock dividend was properly recorded at fair market value.
- d.   Florida's stockholders have authorized the issuance of 100% stock dividends.

54.   An auditor encounters the following four accounts listed among the assets of a client. The auditor most likely would take exception to the asset recognition of
- a.   Goodwill arising from appraisal.
- b.   Research and development costs to be billed to others.
- c.   Excess cost over book value of subsidiary.
- d.   Franchise fees.

55.   A CPA is most likely to refer to one or more of the three general auditing standards in determining
- a.   The nature of the CPA's report qualification.
- b.   The scope of the CPA's auditing procedures.
- c.   Requirements for the review of internal control.
- d.   Whether the CPA should undertake an audit engagement.

56.   Tennessee Company violated company policy by erroneously capitalizing the cost of painting its warehouse. The CPA examining Tennessee's financial statements would most likely learn of this error by
- a.   Discussing Tennessee's capitalization policies with its controller.
- b.   Reviewing the titles and descriptions for all construction work orders issued during the year.
- c.   Observing, during the physical inventory observation, that the warehouse has been painted.
- d.   Examining in detail a sample of construction work orders.

57.   In its electronic data processing system a company might use self-checking numbers (check digits) to enable detection of which of the following errors?
- a.   Assigning a valid identification code to the wrong customer.
- b.   Recording an invalid customer's identification charge account number.
- c.   Losing data between processing functions.
- d.   Processing data arranged in the wrong sequence.

58.   When examining a client's statement of changes in financial position, for audit evidence, an auditor will rely primarily upon
- a.   Determination of the amount of working capital at year-end.
- b.   Analysis of significant ratios of prior years as compared to the current year.
- c.   Cross-referencing to balances and transactions reviewed in connection with the examination of the other financial statements.
- d.   The guidance provided by the APB Opinion on the statement of changes in financial position.

59.   An auditor determines that a client has properly capitalized a leased asset (and corresponding lease liability) as representing, in substance, an installment purchase. As part of the auditor's procedures, the auditor should
- a.   Substantiate the cost of the property to the lessor and determine that this is the cost recorded by the client.
- b.   Evaluate the propriety of the interest rate used in discounting the future lease payments.

c. Determine that the leased property is being amortized over the life of the lease.

d. Evaluate whether the total amount of lease payments represents the fair market value of the property.

60. In connection with the study of internal control, an auditor encounters the following flowcharting symbols:

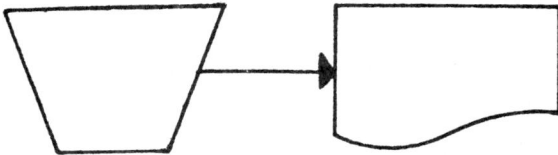

The auditor would conclude that:

a. A document has been generated by a manual operation.

b. A master file has been created by a computer operation.

c. A document has been generated by a computer operation.

d. A master file has been created by a manual operation.

Number 2 (Estimated time — 15 to 25 minutes)

Mincin, CPA, is the auditor of the Raleigh Corporation. Mincin is considering the audit work to be performed in the accounts payable area for the current year's engagement.

The prior-year's working papers show that confirmation requests were mailed to 100 of Raleigh's 1,000 suppliers. The selected suppliers were based on Mincin's sample that was designed to select accounts with large dollar balances. A substantial number of hours were spent by Raleigh and Mincin resolving relatively minor differences between the confirmation replies and Raleigh's accounting records. Alternate audit procedures were used for those suppliers who did not respond to the confirmation requests.

Required:

a. Identify the accounts payable audit objectives that Mincin must consider in determining the audit procedures to be followed.

b. Identify situations when Mincin should use accounts payable confirmations and discuss whether Mincin is required to use them.

c. Discuss why the use of large dollar balances as the basis for selecting accounts payable for confirmation might not be the most efficient approach and indicate what more efficient procedures could be followed when selecting accounts payable for confirmation.

Number 3 (Estimated time — 15 to 25 minutes)

Johnson, Inc., a closely held company, wishes to engage Norr, CPA, to examine its annual financial statements. Johnson was generally pleased with the services provided by its prior CPA, Diggs, but thought the audit work performed was too detailed and interfered excessively with Johnson's normal office routines. Norr asked Johnson to inform Diggs of the decision to change auditors but Johnson did not wish to do so.

Required:

a. List and discuss the steps Norr should follow before accepting the engagement.

b. What additional procedures should Norr perform on this first-time engagement over and beyond those Norr would perform on the Johnson engagement of the following year.

Number 4 (Estimated time — 15 to 25 minutes)

In connection with his examination of the financial statements of the Olympia Manufacturing Company, a CPA is reviewing procedures for accumulating direct labor hours. He learns that all production is by job order and that all employees are paid hourly wages, with time-and-one-half for overtime hours.

Olympia's direct labor hour input process for payroll and job-cost determination is summarized in the following flowchart:

(see flowchart on following page)

Steps A and C are performed in timekeeping, step B in the factory operating departments, step D in payroll audit and control, step E in data preparation (keypunch), and step F in computer operations.

Required:

For each input processing step A through F:

a. List the possible errors or discrepancies that may occur.

b. Cite the corresponding control procedure that should be in effect for each error or discrepancy.

Note: Your discussion of Olympia's procedures should be limited to the input process for direct labor hours, as shown in steps A through F in the flow-

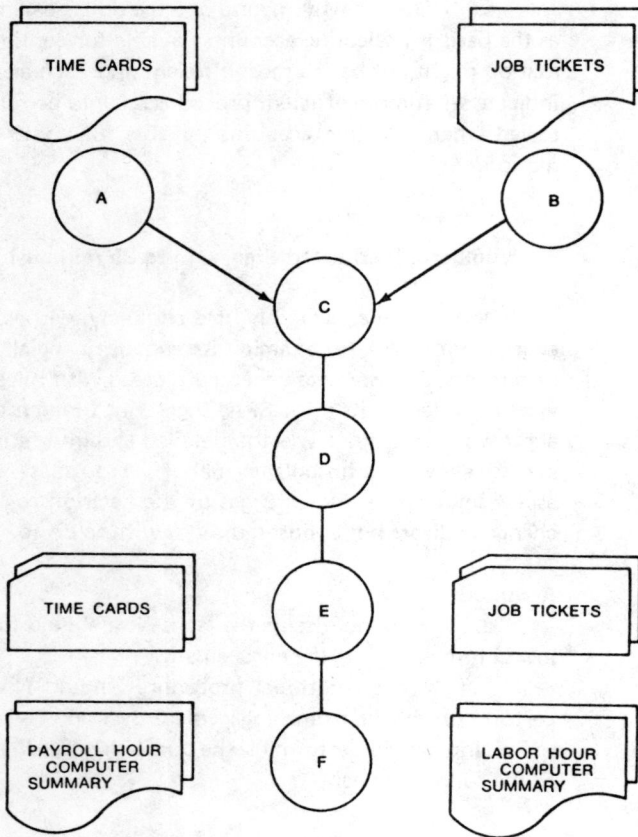

chart. **Do not discuss** personnel procedures for hiring, promotion, termination, and pay rate authorization. **In step F do not discuss** equipment, computer program, and general computer operational controls.

Organize your answer for each input-processing step as follows:

Step	Possible Errors or Discrepancies	Control Procedures

Number 5 (Estimated time — 15 to 25 minutes)

You have been asked by the board of trustees of a local church to review its accounting procedures. As a part of this review you have prepared the following comments relating to the collections made at weekly services and record-keeping for members' pledges and contributions:

The church's board of trustees has delegated responsibility for financial management and audit of the financial records to the finance committee. This group prepares the annual budget and approves major disbursements but is not involved in collections or record-keeping. No audit has been considered necessary in recent years because the same trusted employee has kept church records and served as financial secretary for 15 years.

The collection at the weekly service is taken by a team of ushers. The head usher counts the collection in the church office following each service. He then places the collection and a notation of the amount counted in the church safe. Next morning the financial secretary opens the safe and recounts the collection. He withholds about $100 to meet cash expenditures during the coming week and deposits the remainder of the collection intact. In order to facilitate the deposit, members who contribute by check are asked to draw their checks to "cash."

At their request a few members are furnished prenumbered predated envelopes in which to insert their weekly contributions. The head usher removes the cash from the envelopes to be counted with the loose cash included in the collection and discards the envelopes. No record is maintained of issuance or return of the envelopes, and the envelope system is not encouraged.

Each member is asked to prepare a contribution pledge card annually. The pledge is regarded as a moral commitment by the member to contribute a stated weekly amount. Based upon the amounts shown on the pledge cards, the financial secretary furnishes a letter to requesting members to support the tax deductibility of their contributions.

Required:

Describe the weaknesses and recommend improvements in procedures for

a.   Collections made at weekly services.

b.   Record-keeping for members' pledges and contributions.

Organize your answer sheets as follows:

Weakness	Recommended Improvement

EXAMINATION IN BUSINESS LAW
(Commercial Law)

NOTE TO CANDIDATES: Suggested time allotments are as follows:

All questions are required:	Estimated Minutes	
	Minimum	Maximum
No. 1	110	130
No. 2	15	20
No. 3	15	20
No. 4	15	20
No. 5	15	20
Total	170	210

Number 1 (Estimated time — 110 to 130 minutes)

Select the **best** answer for each of the following items.

1. Bigelow manufactures mopeds and sells them through franchised dealers who are authorized to resell them to the ultimate consumer or return them. Bigelow delivers the mopeds on consignment to these retailers. The consignment agreement clearly states that the agreement is intended to create a security interest for Bigelow in the mopeds delivered on consignment. Bigelow wishes to protect itself against the other creditors of and purchasers from the retailers who might assert rights against the mopeds. Under the circumstances, Bigelow

    a. Must file a financing statement and give notice to certain creditors in order to perfect his security interest.

    b. Will have rights against purchasers in the ordinary course of business who were aware of the fact that Bigelow had filed.

    c. Need take no further action to protect himself, since the consignment is a sale or return and title is reserved in Bigelow.

    d. Will have a perfected security interest in the mopeds upon attachment.

2. Johnson loaned money to Visual, Inc., a struggling growth company, and sought to obtain a security interest in negotiable stock certificates which are traded on a local exchange. To perfect his interest against Visual's other creditors, Johnson

    a. Need do nothing further in that his security interest was perfected upon attachment.

    b. May file or take possession of the stock certificates.

    c. Must take possession of the stock certificates.

    d. Must file and give the other creditors notice of his contemplated security interest.

3. As a secured creditor under the Uniform Commercial Code, Dawson has invariably perfected a security interest in goods which provide the underlying security for various loans. Under the circumstances, which of the following is correct?

    a. Dawson is assured that the debts will be repaid.

    b. Dawson's security interest can not be perfected by possession.

    c. Dawson is entitled to "resort to" or obtain the property even as against a trustee in bankruptcy.

    d. Dawson has a priority in bankruptcy and therefore is entitled to defeat the claims of all creditors which are asserted against the goods.

4. Migrane Financial does a wide variety of lending. It provides funds to manufacturers, middlemen, retailers, consumers, and home owners. In all instances it intends to create a security interest in the loan transactions it enters into. To which of the following will Article 9 (Secured Transactions) of the Uniform Commercial Code not apply?

    a. A second mortgage on the borrower's home.

    b. An equipment lease.

    c. The sale of accounts.

    d. Field warehousing.

5. On June 10, Central Corporation sold goods †
to Bowie Corporation for $5,000. Bowie signed a financing statement containing the names and addresses of the parties and describing the collateral. Central filed the financing statement on June 21, noting the same in its accounting books.

a. Central need not sign the financing statement to perfect its security interest in the collateral.

b. Central must file the financing statement prior to the sale if a security interest is to be perfected.

c. Central must sign the financing statement in order to perfect its security interest.

d. Central had a perfected security interest in the collateral even before the financing statement was filed.

6. Workmen's compensation laws are
a. Governed by federal regulation.
b. Applicable to all types of employment.
c. Designed to eliminate the usual defenses by the employer, such as contributory negligence, when an employee is injured.
d. Not applicable if the employee signs a waiver and consents to his noncoverage under workmen's compensation at the time he is hired.

7. Nebor Industries, Inc., manufactures toys which [†] it sells throughout the United States and Europe. Europe accounts for 25% of sales. Among its 5,000 employees in 1980 were 490 young males aged 14 and 15 who are paid at the rate of $3.50 per hour. Under the general rules of the Fair Labor Standards Act, Nebor
a. Was exempt from regulations because less than 10% of its employees were children.
b. Did not violate the law since it was paying more than the minimum wage.
c. Violated the law by employing children under 16 years of age.
d. Is exempt from regulation because more than 20% of its sales are in direct competition with foreign goods.

8. Markum was grossly negligent in the operation of a forklift. As a result he suffered permanent disability. His claim for workmen's compensation will be
a. Denied.
b. Limited to medical benefits.
c. Reduced by the percentage share attributable to his own fault.
d. Paid in full.

9. What fiduciary duty, if any, exists in an agency relationship?
a. The agent owes a fiduciary duty to third parties he deals with for and on behalf of his principal.

b. The principal owes a fiduciary duty to his agent.
c. The agent owes a fiduciary duty to his principal.
d. There is no fiduciary duty in an agency relationship.

10. Star Corporation dismissed Moon, its purchasing agent. Star published a notice in appropriate trade journals which stated: "This is to notify all parties concerned that Moon is no longer employed by Star Corporation, and the corporation assumes no further responsibility for his acts." Moon called on several of Star's suppliers with whom he had previously dealt, and when he found one who was unaware of his dismissal, he placed a substantial order for merchandise to be delivered to a warehouse in which Moon rented space. Star had rented space in the warehouse in the past when its storage facilities were crowded. Moon also called on several suppliers with whom Star had never dealt and made purchases from them on open account in the name of Star. The merchandise purchased by Moon was delivered to the warehouse. Moon then sold all the merchandise and absconded with the money. Which of the following most accurately describes the legal implications of this situation?
a. Moon had apparent authority to make contracts on Star's behalf with suppliers with whom Moon was currently dealing as Star's agent if they had no actual knowledge of his dismissal.
b. The suppliers who previously had no dealings with Star can enforce the contracts against Star if the suppliers had no actual knowledge of Moon's lack of authority.
c. Star is liable on the Moon contracts to all suppliers who had dealt with Moon in the past as Star's agent and who have not received personal notice, even though they had read the published notice.
d. Constructive notice by publication in the appropriate trade journals is an effective notice to all third parties regardless of whether they had previously dealt with Moon or read the notice.

11. Wishing to acquire a site for its factory without provoking a rise in price, Peter Corporation engaged Argus Realty Company to purchase land without disclosing Peter's name. Argus did so and signed a contract in its own name with Tyrone to purchase Tyrone's land. Under these circumstances
a. The transaction is fraudulent.
b. Argus is not personally liable on the contract.

c. Peter Corporation must formally ratify the contract if it is to hold Tyrone liable.

d. Tyrone may obtain recourse against either Peter or Argus if the contract is not performed.

12. Adams, Baker, and Carter are co-sureties on a $250,000 loan by the Wilson National Bank to Marathon Motors, Inc. Adams is a surety for the full amount of the debt; Baker's obligation is limited to $100,000; and Carter has agreed to pay $50,000 upon default. In the event of default by Marathon on the entire $250,000 loan, what is the liability of Adams, Baker, and Carter?

a. Baker is liable for the first $100,000; Carter, the next $50,000; and Adams, the balance.

b. Baker and Adams are each liable for $100,000 and Carter for $50,000.

c. If both Baker and Carter know of Adams' obligation for the full amount, then they are not liable unless Adams can not satisfy the debt.

d. Adams is liable for $156,250; Baker, $62,500; and Carter, $31,250.

13. Filbert is the surety on a loan made by Holmes to Watson. Which statement describes Filbert's legal relationship or status among the respective parties?

a. Filbert is a fiduciary insofar as Holmes is concerned.

b. As between Watson and Filbert, Filbert has the ultimate liability.

c. Filbert is not liable immediately upon default by Watson, unless the agreement so provides.

d. Upon default by Watson and payment by Filbert, Filbert is entitled to subrogation to the rights of Holmes or to obtain reimbursement from Watson.

14. Marigold, Inc., was in extreme financial difficulty. † Hargrove, one of its persistent creditors, insisted upon payment of the entire amount due on the shipments of goods to Marigold over the past four months or it would sue Marigold and obtain a judgment against it. In order to dissuade Hargrove from taking such action, Marigold persuaded Hargrove to accept its note which was secured by a second mortgage on Marigold's warehouse. Hargrove filed the mortgage on November 1, 1978, the same day that the note and mortgage were executed. On February 1, 1979, Marigold concluded that things were hopeless and filed a voluntary petition in bankruptcy. The trustee in bankruptcy is attacking the validity of the mortgage as a voidable **preference**. Which of the following is correct?

a. The mortgage is not a voidable preference since it was filed the same day it was obtained.

b. The fact that Marigold was delinquent on its payment to Hargrove establishes that Hargrove knew that Marigold was insolvent in the bankruptcy sense.

c. The antecedent indebtedness requirement necessary to establish a voidable preference has not been satisfied under the facts given.

d. The mortgage given to Hargrove was a voidable preference.

15. Your client is insolvent under the federal bankruptcy law. Under the circumstances

a. As long as the client can meet current debts or claims by its most aggressive creditors, a bankruptcy proceeding is not possible.

b. Such information, i.e., insolvency, need not be disclosed in the financial statements reported upon by your CPA firm as long as you are convinced that the problem is short lived.

c. An assignment for the benefit of creditors will constitute an act of bankruptcy.

d. Your client cannot file a voluntary petition for bankruptcy.

16. The distinction between contracts covered by the Uniform Commercial Code and contracts which are not covered by the code is

a. Basically dependent upon whether the subject matter of the contract involves the purchase or sale of goods.

b. Based upon the dollar amount of the contract.

c. Dependent upon whether the statute of frauds is involved.

d. Of relatively little or no importance to the CPA since the laws are invariably the same.

17. Keats Publishing Company shipped textbooks and other books for sale at retail to Campus Bookstore. An honest dispute arose over Campus's right to return certain books. Keats maintained that the books in question could not be returned and demanded payment of the full amount. Campus relied upon trade custom which indicated that many publishers accepted the return of such books. Campus returned the books in question and paid for the balance with a check marked "Acount Paid in Full to Date." Keats cashed the check.

Which of the following is a correct statement?

a. Keats is entitled to recover damages.

b. Keats' cashing of the check constituted an accord and satisfaction.

c. The pre-existing legal duty rule applies and Keats is entitled to full payment for all the books.

d. The custom of the industry argument would have no merit in a court of law.

18. Marco Auto Inc., made many untrue statements in the course of inducing Rockford to purchase a used auto for $3,500. The car in question turned out to have some serious faults. Which of the following untrue statements made by Marco should Rockford use in seeking recovery from Marco for breach of warranty?

a. "I refused a $3,800 offer for this very same auto from another buyer last week."

b. "This auto is one of the best autos we have for sale."

c. "At this price the auto is a real steal."

d. "I can guarantee that you will never regret this purchase."

19. If a seller repudiates his contract with a buyer for the sale of 100 radios, what recourse does the buyer have?

a. He can "cover," i.e., procure the goods elsewhere and recover the difference.

b. He must await the seller's performance for a commercially reasonable time after repudiation.

c. He can obtain specific performance by the seller.

d. He can recover punitive damages.

20. In connection with risk and expense associated with the delivery of goods to a destination under a sales contract, the term "F.O.B. place of destination" means that

a. The seller bears the risk and expense.

b. The buyer bears the risk and expense.

c. The seller bears the risk but not the expense.

d. The buyer bears the risk but not the expense.

21. On July 14, 1976, Seeley Corp. entered into a written agreement to sell to Boone Corp. 1,200 cartons of certain goods at $.40 per carton, delivery within 30 days. The agreement contained no other terms. On July 15, 1976, Boone and Seeley orally agreed to modify their July 14 agreement so that the new quantity specified was 1,500 cartons, same price and delivery terms. What is the status of this modification?

a. Enforceable.

b. Unenforceable under the statute of frauds.

c. Unenforceable for lack of consideration.

d. Unenforceable because the change is substantial.

22. The partnership of Maxim & Rose, CPAs, has been engaged by their largest client, a limited partnership, to examine the financial statements in connection with the offering of 2,000 limited-partnership interests to the public at $5,000 per subscription. Under these circumstances, which of the following is true?

a. Maxim & Rose may disclaim any liability under the federal securities acts by an unambiguous, bold-faced disclaimer of liability on its audit report.

b. Under the Securities Act of 1933, Maxim & Rose has responsibility only for the financial statements as of the close of the fiscal year in question.

c. The dollar amount in question is sufficiently small so as to provide an exemption from the Securities Act of 1933.

d. The Securities Act of 1933 requires a registration despite the fact that the client is not selling stock or another traditional "security."

23. One of the major purposes of federal security regulation is to

a. Establish the qualifications for accountants who are members of the profession.

b. Eliminate incompetent attorneys and accountants who participate in the registration of securities to be offered to the public.

c. Provide a set of uniform standards and tests for accountants, attorneys and others who practice before the Securities and Exchange Commission.

d. Provide sufficient information to the investing public who purchases securities in the marketplace.

24. Of the following securities transactions, which [†] is exempt from federal securities regulations?

a. An offering of $100,000 of corporate bonds.

b. The sales of $2,000,000 of limited partnership interest.

c. A secondary offering of stock which had been previously registered.

d. The sale of $500,000 of common stock to a single sophisticated purchaser for investment purposes.

25. Dowling is a promoter and has decided to use a limited partnership for conducting a securities investment venture. Which of the following is unnecessary in order to validly create such a limited partnership?

   a. All limited partners' capital contributions must be paid in cash.
   b. There must be a state statute which permits the creation of such a limited partnership.
   c. A limited partnership certificate must be signed and sworn to by the participants and filed in the proper office in the state.
   d. There must be one or more general partners and one or more limited partners.

26. Which of the following rights would the limited partners not have?

   a. The right to have a dissolution and winding up by court decree where such is appropriate.
   b. The right to remove a general partner by a majority vote if the limited partners determine that a general partner is not managing the partnership affairs properly.
   c. The right upon dissolution to receive their share of profits and capital contributions before any payment is made to the general partners.
   d. The right to have the partnership books kept at the principal place of business and to have access to them.

27. In the course of your audit of Harvey Fox, doing business as Harvey's Apparels, a sole proprietorship, you discovered that in the past year Fox had regularly joined with Leopold Morrison in the marketing of bathing suits and beach accessories. You are concerned whether Fox and Morrison have created a partnership relationship. Which of the following factors is the most important in ascertaining this status?

   a. The fact that a partnership agreement is not in existence.
   b. The fact that each has a separate business of his own which he operates independently.
   c. The fact that Fox and Morrison divide the net profits equally on a quarterly basis.
   d. The fact that Fox and Morrison did not intend to be partners.

28. Which of the following is a correct statement concerning the similarities of a limited partnership and a corporation?

   a. Both provide insulation from personal liability for all of the owners of the business.
   b. Both can only be created pursuant to a statute and each must file a copy of their respective certificates with the proper state authorities.
   c. Both are recognized for federal income tax purposes as taxable entities.
   d. Shareholders and limited partners may both participate in the management of the business and retain limited liability.

29. For federal income tax purposes, a partnership is

   a. A taxable entity similar to a trust or an estate.
   b. Considered to be a nontaxable entity but which must file an information return.
   c. Treated the same as an association for tax purposes.
   d. Required to pay a tax upon its profits which in turn must be assumed by its partners.

30. Lantz sold his moving and warehouse business, including all the personal and real property used therein, to Mallen Van Lines, Inc. The real property was encumbered by a duly-recorded $300,000 first mortgage upon which Lantz was personally liable. Mallen acquired the property subject to the mortgage but did not assume the mortgage. Two years later, when the outstanding mortgage was $260,000, Mallen decided to abandon the business location because it had become unprofitable and the value of the real property was less than the outstanding mortgage. Mallen moved to another location and refused to pay the installments due on the mortgage. What is the legal status of the parties in regard to the mortgage?

   a. Mallen breached its contract with Lantz when it abandoned the location and defaulted on the mortgage.
   b. Mallen took the real property free of the mortgage.
   c. If Lantz pays off the mortgage, he will be able to successfully sue Mallen because Lantz is subrogated to the mortgagee's rights against Mallen.
   d. Lantz must satisfy the mortgage debt in the event that foreclosure yields an amount less than the unpaid balance.

31. Winslow conveyed a 20-acre tract of land to his two children, George and Martha, "equally as tenants in common." What is the legal effect of this form of conveyance?
   a. George and Martha are joint owners with a right of survivorship.
   b. Each must first offer the other the right to purchase the property before he or she can sell to a third party.
   c. Neither may convey his or her interest in the property unless both join in the conveyance.
   d. Each owns an undivided interest in the whole, which he or she may dispose of by deed or by will.

32. Franklin engaged in extensive negotiations with Harlow in connection with the proposed purchase of Harlow's factory building. Which of the following must Franklin satisfy to establish a binding contract for the purchase of the property in question?
   a. Franklin must obtain an agreement signed by both parties.
   b. Franklin must obtain a formal, detailed, all-inclusive document.
   c. Franklin must pay some earnest money at the time of final agreement.
   d. Franklin must have a writing signed by Harlow which states the essential terms of the understanding.

33. An executor named in a decedent's will
   a. Can not be the principal beneficiary of the will.
   b. Must serve without compensation unless the will provides otherwise.
   c. Need not serve if he does not wish to do so.
   d. Must consent to serve, have read the will, and be present at the execution of the will.

34. Hacker is considering the creation of either a lifetime (intervivos) or testamentary (by his will) trust. In deciding what to do, which of the following statements is correct?
   a. An intervivos trust must meet the same legal requirements as one created by a will.
   b. Property transferred to a testamentary trust upon the grantor's (creator's) death is not included in the decedent's gross estate for federal tax purposes.
   c. Hacker can retain the power to revoke an intervivos trust.
   d. If the trust is an intervivos trust, the trustee must file papers in the appropriate

state office roughly similar to those required to be filed by a corporation.

35. A group of real estate dealers has decided to form a Real Estate Investment Trust (REIT) which will invest in diversified real estate holdings. A public offering of $10,000,000 of trust certificates is contemplated. Which of the following is an incorrect statement?
   a. Those investing in the venture will not be insulated from personal liability.
   b. The entity will be considered to be an "association" for tax purposes.
   c. The offering must be registered under the Securities Act of 1933.
   d. If the trust qualifies as a REIT and distributes all its income to the investors, it will not be subject to federal income tax.

36. Which of the following represents the basic distinction between a bilateral contract and a unilateral contract?
   a. Specific performance is available if the contract is unilateral whereas it is not if the contract is bilateral.
   b. There is only one promise involved if the contract is unilateral whereas there are two promises if the contract is bilateral.
   c. The statute of frauds applies to a bilateral contract but not to a unilateral contract.
   d. The rights under a bilateral contract are assignable whereas rights under a unilateral contract are not assignable.

37. Martin, a wholesale distributor, made a contract for the purchase of 10,000 gallons of gasoline from the Wilberforce Oil Company. The price was to be determined in accordance with the refinery price as of the close of business on the delivery date. Credit terms were net/30 after delivery. Under these circumstances which of the following is true?
   a. If Martin pays upon delivery, he is entitled to a 2% discount.
   b. The contract being silent on the place of delivery, Martin has the right to expect delivery at his place of business.
   c. Although the price has some degree of uncertainty, the contract is enforceable.
   d. Because the goods involved are tangible, specific performance is a remedy available to Martin.

38. Major Steel Manufacturing, Inc., signed a contract on October 2, 1978, with the Hard Coal & Coke Company for its annual supply of coal for three years commencing on June 1, 1979, at a price to be determined by taking the average monthly retail price per ton, less a ten cent per ton quantity discount. On March 15, 1979, Major discovered that it had made a bad bargain and that it could readily fulfill its requirements elsewhere at a much greater discount. Major is seeking to avoid its obligation. Which of the following is correct?

  a. The pricing term is too indefinite and uncertain hence there is no contract.

  b. Since the amount of coal required is unknown at the time of the making of the contract, the contract is too indefinite and uncertain to be valid.

  c. Major is obligated to take its normal annual coal requirements from Hard or respond in damages.

  d. There is no contract since Major could conceivably require no coal during the years in question.

39. Potter orally engaged Arthur as a salesman on April 5, 1978, for exactly one year commencing on May 1, 1978. Which of the following is correct insofar as the parties are concerned?

  a. If Arthur refuses to perform and takes another job on April 14, 1978, he will not be liable if he pleads the statute of frauds.

  b. The contract need not be in writing since its duration is exactly one year.

  c. Potter may obtain the remedy of specific performance if Arthur refuses to perform.

  d. The parol evidence rule applies.

40. Milbank undertook to stage a production of a well-known play. He wired Lucia, a famous actress, offering her the lead in the play at $2,000 per week for six weeks from the specified opening night plus $1,000 for a week of rehearsal prior to opening. The telegram also said, "offer ends in three days." Lucia wired an acceptance the same day she received it. The telegram acceptance was temporarily misplaced by the telegraph company and did not arrive until five days after its dispatch. Milbank, not hearing from Lucia, assumed she had declined and abandoned the production. Which of the following is correct if Lucia sues Milbank?

  a. The contract was automatically terminated when Milbank decided not to proceed.

  b. Lucia has entered into a valid contract and is entitled to recover damages if Milbank fails to honor it.

  c. Lucia may not take any other engagement for the period involved if she wishes to recover.

  d. Milbank is excused from any liability since his action was reasonable under the circumstances.

41. Normally, the offer initiates the process by which a contract is created. Therefore, the offer is critical insofar as satisfying basic contract law requirements. Which of the following statements is incorrect?

  a. The offer may only be expressed in words.

  b. The offer must be communicated to the other party.

  c. The offer must be certain enough to determine the liability of the parties.

  d. The offer must be accepted by the other party.

42. The parol evidence rule prohibits contradiction of a written contract through the proof of

  a. A previous oral contract.

  b. A subsequent written contract.

  c. The meaning or clarification of the contract's terms.

  d. A subsequent oral contract.

43. One of a CPA's major concerns regarding contractual questions arising in the examination of a client's financial statements is

  a. The proper court to initiate a lawsuit.

  b. The question of who has the burden of proof.

  c. Whether consideration has been provided by both parties ιo a contract.

  d. The admissibility of evidence in court.

44. An instrument is order paper when it is

  a. Payable to the order of cash on its face.

  b. Indorsed to John Smith by Marvin Frank, the payee.

  c. Payable to the order of Marvin Frank and indorsed in blank.

  d. Payable to a specified person or bearer.

45. A formal protest of dishonor must be made in order to hold the drawer or indorsers liable for all of the following foreign instruments except

  a. Drafts.

  b. Promissory notes.

  c. Trade acceptances.

  d. Checks.

46.   A holder in due course will take an instrument free from which of the following defenses?
    a.   Claims of ownership on the part of other persons.
    b.   Infancy of the maker or drawer.
    c.   Discharge in insolvency proceedings.
    d.   The forged signature of the maker or drawer.

47.   Path stole a check made out to the order of Marks. Path forged the name of Marks on the back and made the instrument payable to himself. He then negotiated the check to Harrison for cash by signing his own name on the back of the instrument in Harrison's presence. Harrison was unaware of any of the facts surrounding the theft or forged indorsement and presented the check for payment. Central County Bank, the drawee bank, paid it. Disregarding Path, which of the following will bear the loss?
    a.   The drawer of the check payable to Marks.
    b.   Central County Bank.
    c.   Marks.
    d.   Harrison.

48.   There are several legally significant differences between a negotiable instrument and a contract right and the transfer of each. Which of the following statements is correct?
    a.   A negotiable instrument is deemed prima facie to have been issued for consideration whereas a contract is not deemed prima facie to be supported by consideration.
    b.   Generally, the transferee of a negotiable instrument and the assignee of a contract right take free of most defenses.
    c.   Neither can be transferred without a signed writing or by a delivery.
    d.   The statute of frauds rules apply to both.

49.   Davidson bore a remarkable physical resemblance to Ford, one of the town's most prominent citizens. He presented himself one day at the Friendly Finance Company, represented himself as Ford, and requested a loan of $500. The manager mistakenly, but honestly, believed that Davidson was Ford. Accordingly, being anxious to please so prominent a citizen, the manager required no collateral and promptly delivered to Davidson a $500 check payable to the order of Ford. Davidson took the check and signed Ford's name to it on the back and negotiated it to Robbins, who took in the ordinary course of business (in good faith and for value). Upon learning the real facts, Friendly stopped payment on the check. Robbins now seeks recovery against Friendly. Under these circumstances, which of the following statements is correct?
    a.   Friendly could not validly stop payment on the check.
    b.   Davidson's signature of Ford's name on the check constitutes a forgery and is a real defense which is valid against Robbins.
    c.   Since both Friendly and Robbins were mistaken as to Davidson's real identity, they will share the loss equally.
    d.   Davidson's signature of Ford's name on the check is effective and Robbins will prevail against Friendly.

50.   Your client, Commercial Factors, Inc., discounted a $2,000 promissory note, payable in two years, for $1,500. It paid $500 initially and promised to pay the balance ($1,000) within 30 days. Commercial paid the balance within the 30 days, but before doing so learned that the note had been obtained originally by fraudulent misrepresentations in connection with the sale of land which induced the maker to issue the note. For what amount will Commercial qualify as a holder in due course?
    a.   None because the 25% discount is presumptive of prima facie evidence that Commercial is not a holder in due course.
    b. $500.
    c. $1,500.
    d. $2,000.

51.   Glick was the owner of a factory valued at $100,000. He procured a fire insurance policy on the building for $40,000 from Safety Insurance Company, Inc. The policy contained an 80% coinsurance clause. The property was totally destroyed by fire. How much will Glick recover from the insurance company?
    a. $20,000.
    b. $32,000.
    c. $40,000.
    d.   Glick will recover nothing because he did not meet the coinsurance requirements.

52.   DuBary and Young were business partners. They agreed that each would insure the life of the other for his own benefit (cross insurance). On the application for insurance, DuBary stated that he had never had any heart trouble when, in fact, he had suffered a mild heart attack some years before.   Young's policy on DuBary's life contained a two-year incontestability clause. Three years later, after the partnership had been dissolved but while the policy on his life was still in force, DuBary was killed when his car was struck by a car negligently driven by Peters.

The insurer has refused to pay the policy proceeds to Young, asserting that Young at the time DuBary died had no insurable interest in DuBary's life and that DuBary's misrepresentation voided the policy. Which of the following statements is correct?

    a.   The misrepresentation in the application is a bar to recovery.

    b.   If DuBary and Young were never partners, recovery will be denied.

    c.   Dissolution of the partnership eliminated any possible insurable interest and is a bar to recovery.

    d.   If the insurance company has to pay, it will be subrogated to DuBary's rights against Peters.

53. The usual fire insurance policy does not

    a.   Have to meet the insurable interest test if this requirement is waived by the parties.

    b.   Provide for subrogation of the insurer to the insured's rights upon payment of the amount of the loss covered by the policy.

    c.   Cover losses caused by the negligence of the insured's agent.

    d.   Permit assignment of the policy prior to loss without the consent of the insurer.

54. The "incontestable clause" in a life insurance policy usually provides that

    a.   The insured is covered on delivery of the policy regardless of any misstatement in the application.

    b.   If death occurs after a specified period of time, a misstatement in the application will not constitute a defense by the insurer.

    c.   Suicide of the named insured will not constitute a defense by the insurer.

    d.   Only the estate of the insured may contest the named beneficiary's rights to proceeds of the policy.

55. A corporation may not redeem its own shares when it

    a.   Is currently solvent but has been insolvent within the past five years.

    b.   Is insolvent or would be rendered insolvent if the redemption were made.

    c.   Has convertible debt that is publicly traded.

    d.   Has mortgages and other secured obligations equal to 50 percent of its stated capital.

56. The consideration for the issuance of shares by a corporation may not be paid in

    a.   Services actually performed for the corporation.

    b.   Services to be performed for the corporation.

    c.   Tangible property.

    d.   Intangible property.

57. Nicks is a troublesome chain store furniture dealer. He constantly engaged in price cutting on widely advertised name products in order to lure customers to his store so that he could sell them other products. The "big three" manufacturers agreed that Nicks could no longer sell their products unless he ceased and desisted from such practices. Nicks refused and the three manufacturers promptly cut off his supply of their branded products. Which of the following is a correct statement?

    a.   Since a businessman has the freedom to choose with whom he will deal, the conduct in question is not illegal under the antitrust laws.

    b.   If the harm to the public was minor, and the products were readily available from other appliance dealers in a market marked by free and open competition, there would be no violation of the law.

    c.   The conduct described is a joint boycott, and as such is illegal per se.

    d.   Since the conduct described was unilateral, and Nicks did not agree to stop his price cutting, the manufacturers' conduct is illegal.

58. Zebra Acquisitions, Inc., has been steadily acquiring the assets and stock of various corporations manufacturing brass. It also has been purchasing the stock of its customers and others who purchase substantial quantities of brass. It now has 8% of the brass manufacturing facilities in the United States and 22% in the tri-state area in which it is located. Which of the following claims is the United States Department of Justice likely to assert?

    a.   The relevant market in question is the entire United States.

    b.   It is illegal per se to purchase the stock of competitors.

    c.   It is illegal per se to purchase the stock of customers and other potential buyers.

    d.   The most recent acquisition substantially lessens competition in the tri-state area.

59.   Drummond Company manufactures and sells distinctive clocks. Its best selling item is a reproduction of a rare antique grandfather clock. Adams purchased 100 of the clocks from Drummond at $79.50. Much to Adam's chagrin it discovered that Young, one of its competitors, had purchased the same clock at $74.50 per clock. Adams has complained and threatened legal action. In the event the issue is litigated

    a.   Drummond will prevail if it can show it did not intend to harm Adams.

    b.   Adams has a presumption in its favor that it has been harmed by price discrimination.

    c.   Drummond will prevail if it can show that it sold the clocks at the lower price to all customers such as Young who had been doing business with it continuously for ten years or more.

    d.   Drummond will prevail if it can establish that there were several other clock companies with which Adams could deal if Adams were dissatisfied.

60.   Research Development Corporation has made a major breakthrough in the development of a super TV antenna. It has patented the product and is seeking to maximize the profit potential. In this effort, Research can legally

    a.   Require its retailer to take stipulated quantities of its other products in addition to the antennas.

    b.   Require its retailers to sell only Research's products including the antennas, and not sell similar competing products.

    c.   Sell the product to its retailers upon condition that they do not sell the antennas to the public for less than a stated price.

    d.   Sell the product at whatever price the traffic will bear even though it has a monopoly.

Number 2 (Estimated time — 15 to 20 minutes)

During the course of your year-end audit for a new client, Otis Corporation, you discover the following facts. Otis was incorporated in 1974 and is owned 94% by James T. Parker, President; 1% by his wife; and 5% by Wilbur Chumley. These three individuals were incorporators and are officers and directors of the corporation.

Otis manufactures and sells telephone equipment. In 1974, it sold approximately $350,000 of its various products almost exclusively in the state of its incorporation. In 1975, it began to branch out and sold $550,000 of its products throughout that state and $50,000 of

its products in a neighboring state. Otis expanded rapidly, and 1976 was a banner year with sales of $1,250,000 and profits of $175,000. Otis constructed a small office building on a tract of land it had purchased for expansion purposes in the neighboring state and used the top floor to establish a regional sales office and rented the balance of the building.

During the course of your audit for the year 1976, you discover that Parker commingles his personal funds with those of the corporation, keeps very few records of board and shareholder meetings, and at his convenience disregards corporate law regarding separatness of personal and corporate affairs. The corporation had 1976 sales in excess of $300,000 in the neighboring state. The corporation has not filed any papers with the Secretary of State of that state in connection with these operations.

In light of the above discoveries, it was deemed prudent to examine the original incorporation papers which were filed by Parker in 1974. The following irregularities were discovered. The powers and purposes clause states that the geographical territory in which the newly created corporation was to do business was solely the state of incorporation. Next, a certified copy of the corporate charter was not obtained and filed in the county in which the corporation's principal place of business is located, as required by state law. Additionally, Mr. Chumley and Mrs. Parker did not sign the articles of incorporation, and prior to the effective date of incorporation, a lease was taken out and a car purchased in the corporate name.

Required:

Answer the following, setting forth reasons for any conclusions stated.

Discuss the legal problems which Otis may face as a result of the above facts. **Do not consider any tax implications.**

Number 3 (Estimated time — 15 to 20 minutes)

Part a.   A CPA firm was engaged to examine the financial statements of Martin Manufacturing Corporation for the year ending December 31, 1977. The facts revealed that Martin was in need of cash to continue its operations and agreed to sell its common stock investment in a subsidiary through a private palcement. The buyers insisted that the proceeds be placed in escrow because of the possibility of a major contingent tax liability that might result from a pending government claim. The payment in escrow was completed in late November 1977. The president of Martin told the audit partner that the proceeds from the sale of the subsidiary's common stock, held in escrow, should be shown on the balance sheet as an unrestricted current account receivable. The president was of the opinion that the government's claim was groundless and that Martin needed an "uncluttered" balance sheet and a "clean" auditor's opinion to obtain additional working capital from lenders. The audit partner agreed with the president and issued an unqualified opinion on the Martin financial statements which did not refer to the contingent liability and did not properly describe the escrow arrangement.

The government's claim proved to be valid, and pursuant to the agreement with the buyers, the purchase price of the subsidiary was reduced by $450,000. This adverse development forced Martin into bankruptcy. The CPA firm is being sued for deceit (fraud) by several of Martin's unpaid creditors who extended credit in reliance upon the CPA firm's unqualified opinion on Martin's financial statements.

Required:

Answer the following, setting forth reasons for any conclusions stated.

Based on these facts, can Martin's unpaid creditors recover from the CPA firm?

Part b. A CPA firm has been named as a defendant in a class action by purchasers of the shares of stock of the Newly Corporation. The offering was a public offering of securities within the meaning of the Securities Act of 1933. The plaintiffs alleged that the firm was either negligent or fraudulent in connection with the preparation of the audited financial statements filed with the SEC. Specifically, they alleged that the CPA firm either intentionally disregarded, or failed to exercise reasonable care to discover, material facts which occurred subsequent to January 31, 1978, the date of the auditor's report. The securities were sold to the public on March 16, 1978. The plaintiffs have subpoenaed copies of the CPA firm's working papers. The CPA firm is considering refusing to relinquish the papers, asserting that they contain privileged communication between the CPA firm and its client. The CPA firm will, of course, defend on the merits irrespective of the questions regarding the working papers.

Required:

Answer the following, setting forth reasons for any conclusions stated.

1. Can the CPA firm rightfully refuse to surrender its working papers?

2. Discuss the liability of the CPA firm in respect to events which occur in the period between the date of the auditor's report and the effective date of the public offering of the securities.

Number 4 (Estimated time — 15 to 20 minutes)
Number 4 consists of 2 unrealted parts

Part a. Davidson was one of Fenner Corporation's chief stock clerks. His net weekly salary was $125. Unfortunately, he lost a substantial sum of money betting on sports events, and he owed $2,000 to the loan sharks. Under these circumstances, he decided to raise the amount of his paychecks to $725 per week. His strategem was to wait until the assistant treasurer, in whose office the paymaster check imprinting machine was located, was away from his desk. He would then go into the office and artfully strike the number 7 over the number 1 and raise the paycheck amount from $125 to $725. The checks were promptly negotiated to Smith, a holder in due course, who cashed them at his own bank, and the checks were subsequently paid by Fenner's bank, Beacon National. The fraudulent scheme was discovered within a week after Beacon returned Fenner's canceled checks for the month. By that time five weekly paychecks had been raised by Davidson and cashed by Smith. Fenner promptly notified Beacon of the fraud.

Required:

Answer the following, setting forth reasons for any conclusions stated.

1. To whom is Davidson liable?
2. What are the rights and liabilities of Fenner?
3. What are the rights and liabilities of Beacon?
4. What are the rights and liabilities of Smith?

Part b. Sill Corporation operates a retail appliance store. About a year ago, Sill borrowed $3,000 from Castle to supplement its working capital. At that time it granted to Castle a security interest in its present and future inventory pursuant to a written security agreement signed by both parties. Castle duly filed a properly executed financing statement a few days later. In the ordinary course of business, a customer purchased a $500 television set from Sill. The customer knew of the existence of Castle's security interest.

Required:

What rights does Castle have against Sill's customer? Explain.

Number 5 (Estimated time — 15 to 20 minutes)
Number 5 consists of 2 unrelated parts)

Part a. Granville Motors, Inc., wished to acquire a 4-acre tract of land owned by Bonanza Realty Developers in an industrial city. Granville did not want to waste time and money considering the suitability of the property unless assured that the plant site would be available if studies indicated that the proposed purchase would be desirable. Granville did not discuss this concern with Bonanza but proposed to Bonanza that an option be drafted granting Granville 30 days in which to purchase the plant site for $62,950. Bonanza agreed and mailed to Granville the following written option:

> For ONE DOLLAR ($1.00) and other valuable consideration, Bonanza Realty Developers hereby grants to Granville Motors, Inc., the exclusive option to purchase for SIXTY-TWO THOUSAND NINE HUN— DRED FIFTY DOLLARS ($62,950) the 4-acre tract of land known as the N.E. corner site . . . (*assume legal description included*) for THIRTY (30) days. This option is exclusive and irrevocable and will automatically expire on September 15, 1977.
>
> *Joseph T. Verona*
> Joseph T. Verona, President
> Bonanza Realty Developers

The letter containing the option was mailed on August 14, but due to a delay in the mails, did not reach Granville until August 18. Upon receipt Granville promptly engaged an expert to do a feasibility study with respect to the location and began to solicit bids on the construction of the proposed plant. Bonanza had no knowledge of these facts. Granville had no further correspondence with Bonanza after the receipt of the option, and Granville neither paid the $1.00 nor gave any other bargained for consideration.

On September 15, Jordon, Granville's President, telephoned Verona intending to accept the offer for Granville. However, before Jordon could accept, Verona stated that the property had already been sold at a higher price. The purchaser had no actual knowledge of the above facts. Jordon nevertheless accepted on Granville's behalf. The next day Jordon sent a written confirmation which stated that Granville expected performance by Bonanza, and that if Bonanza failed to perform, Granville would be forced to sue to protect . its interests. Jordon also reminded Verona that the offer was irrevocable and that substantial time, money, and effort had been expended in a feasibility study. In addition Jordon noted the adverse effect which a refusal would have on Granville's future profits in that plans had been finalized calling for the plant to be on line by April 1978 to supply the increased demand of its customers.

Required:

Answer the following, setting forth reasons for any conclusions stated.

1. Is the option legally binding on Bonanza?
2. Assuming Granville will prevail, is specific performance available to Granville?
3. Assuming Granville will prevail, what would Granville be entitled to recover if it seeks damages as a form of relief?

Part b.   The Minlow, Richard, and Jones partnership agreement is silent on whether the partners may assign or otherwise transfer all or part of their partnership interests to an outsider. Richard has assigned his partnership interest to Smith, a personal creditor, and as a result the other partners are furious. They have threatened to remove Richard as a partner, not admit Smith as a partner, and bar Smith from access to the firm's books and records.

Required:

Answer the following, setting forth reasons for any conclusions stated.

Can Minlow and Jones successfully implement their threats? Discuss the rights of Richard and Smith and the effects of the assignment on the partnership.

EXAMINATION IN ACCOUNTING THEORY

NOTE TO CANDIDATES: Suggested time allotments are as follows:

	Estimated Minutes	
All questions are required:	*Minimum*	*Maximum*
No. 1	90	110
No. 2	15	25
No. 3	15	25
No. 4	15	25
No. 5	15	25
Total	150	210

Number 1 (Estimated time —— 90 to 110 minutes)

Select the **best** answer for each of the following items relating to **a variety of issues in accounting**.

1. An accrued expense is an expense
   a. Incurred but not paid.
   b. Incurred and paid.
   c. Paid but not incurred.
   d. Not reasonably estimable.

2. The amortization of bond discount on long-term debt should be presented in a statement of changes in financial position as a (an)
   a. Addition to net income.
   b. Deduction from net income.
   c. Use of funds.
   d. Source and use of funds.

3. How should a gain from the sale of treasury stock be reflected when using the cost method of recording treasury stock transactions?
   a. As ordinary earnings shown on the earnings statement.
   b. As paid-in capital from treasury stock transactions.
   c. As an increase in the amount shown for common stock.
   d. As an extraordinary item shown on the earnings statement.

4. Abbot Co. is being sued for illness caused to local residents as a result of negligence on the company's part in permitting the local residents to be exposed to highly toxic chemicals from its plant. Abbot's lawyer states that it is probable that Abbot will lose the suit and be found liable for a judgment costing Abbot anywhere from $500,000 to $2,500,000. However, the lawyer states that the most probable cost is $1,000,000. As a result of the above facts, Abbot should accrue

   a. A loss contingency of $500,000 and disclose an additional contingency of up to $2,000,000.
   b. A loss contingency of $1,000,000 and disclose an additional contingency of up to $1,500,000.
   c. A loss contingency of $1,000,000 but not disclose any additional contingency.
   d. No loss contingency but disclose a contingency of $500,000 to $2,500,000.

5. When bad debt expense is estimated on the basis of the percentage of past actual losses from bad debts to past net credit sales, and this percentage is adjusted for anticipated conditions, the accounting concept of
   a. Matching is being followed.
   b. Matching is not being followed.
   c. Substance over form is being followed.
   d. Going concern is not being followed.

6. Which of the following requires intraperiod tax allocation?
   a. That portion of dividends reduced by the dividends received deduction by corporations under existing federal income tax law.
   b. The excess of accelerated depreciation used for tax purposes over straight-line depreciation used for financial reporting purposes.
   c. Extraordinary gains or losses as defined by the Accounting Principles Board.
   d. All differences between taxable income and financial statement earnings.

7. When a company purchases land with a building on it and immediately tears down the building so that the land can be used for the construction of a plant, the costs incurred to tear down the building should be

a. Expensed as incurred.
b. Added to the cost of the plant.
c. Added to the cost of the land.
d. Amortized over the estimated time period between the tearing down of the building and the completion of the plant.

8. Under which of the following conditions would flood damage be considered an extraordinary item for financial reporting purposes?
a. Only if floods in the geographical area are unusual in nature and occur infrequently.
b. Only if floods are normal in the geographical area but do not occur frequently.
c. Only if floods occur frequently in the geographical area but have been insured against.
d. Under any circumstance flood damage should be classified as an extraordinary item.

9. In accounting for a long-term construction-type contract using the percentage-of-completion method, the gross profit recognized during the first year would be the estimated total gross profit from the contract multiplied by the percentage of the costs incurred during the year to the
a. Total costs incurred to date.
b. Total estimated cost.
c. Unbilled portion of the contract price.
d. Total contract price.

10. Which of the following costs is not a part of the defined maximum for pension cost determination?
a. Normal cost.
b. Provision for vested benefits.
c. Interest on overfunding.
d. 10% of prior service costs.

11. Information prior to the issuance of the financial statements indicates that it is probable that, at the date of the financial statements, a liability has been incurred for obligations related to product warranties. The amount of the loss involved can be reasonably estimated. Based on the above facts, an estimated loss contingency should be
a. Accrued.
b. Disclosed but not accrued.
c. Neither accrued nor disclosed.
d. Classified as an appropriation of retained earnings.

12. In theory (disregarding any other marketplace variables) the proceeds from the sale of a bond will be equal to

a. The face amount of the bond.
b. The present value of the principal amount due at the end of the life of the bond plus the present value of the interest payments made during the life of the bond discounted at the prevailing market rate of interest.
c. The fact amount of the bond plus the present value of the interest payments made during the life of the bond discounted at the prevailing market rate of interest.
d. The sum of the face amount of the bond and the periodic interest payments.

13. A foreign exchange gain that is a consequence of translation should be
a. Included in net income in the period it occurs.
b. Deferred and amortized over a period not to exceed forty years.
c. Deferred until a subsequent year when a loss occurs and offset against that loss.
d. Included as a separate item in the equity section of the balance sheet.

14. Q, R, S, and T are partners sharing profits and losses equally. The partnership is insolvent and is to be liquidated; the status of the partnership and each partner is as follows:

	Partnership Capital Balance	Personal Assets (Exclusive of Partnership Interest)	Personal Liabilities (Exclusive of Partnership Interest)
Q	$ 15,000	$100,000	$40,000
R	$ 10,000	30,000	60,000
S	(20,000)	80,000	5,000
T	(30,000)	1,000	28,000
Total	$(25,000)		

Assuming the Uniform Partnership Act applies, the partnership creditors
a. Must first seek recovery against S because he is solvent personally and he has a negative capital balance.
b. Will not be paid in full regardless of how they proceed legally because the partnership assets are less than the partnership liabilities.
c. Will have to share R's interest in the partnership on a pro rata basis with R's personal creditors.
d. Have first claim to the partnership assets before any partner's personal creditors have rights to the partnership assets.

15. Which of the following cost items would be matched with current revenues on a basis other than association of cause and effect?
    a. Goodwill
    b. Sales commissions.
    c. Cost of goods sold.
    d. Purchases on account.

16. A company is required to disclose, usually in the footnotes to its financial statements, two main points regarding income taxes. First, it must disclose the factors causing a deferred tax expense, if any. Second, it must disclose the factors causing a difference, if any, between a tax expense figure computed at the statutory rates and its actual tax expense.

Which of the following would cause a deferred tax expense?
    a. Amortization of goodwill.
    b. Use of equity method where undistributed earnings of a 30% owned investee are related to probable future dividends.
    c. Premiums paid on insurance carried by company (beneficiary) on its officers or employees.
    d. Income taxed at capital gains rates.

17. A change in accounting entity is actually a change in accounting
    a. Principle.
    b. Estimate.
    c. Method.
    d. Concept.

18. If at the end of a period a company erroneously excluded some goods from its ending inventory and also erroneously did not record the purchase of these goods in its accounting records, these errors would cause
    a. The ending inventory, cost of goods available for sale, and retained earnings to be understated.
    b. The ending inventory, cost of goods sold, and retained earnings to be understated.
    c. No effect on net income, working capital, and retained earnings.
    d. Cost of goods available for sale, cost of goods sold, and net income to be understated.

19. The appropriate valuation of an operating lease on the statement of financial position of a lessee is
    a. Zero.
    b. The absolute sum of the lease payments.
    c. The present value of the sum of the lease payments discounted at an appropriate rate.
    d. The market value of the asset at the date of the inception of the lease.

20. A company changed its method of inventory pricing from last-in, first-out to first-in, first-out during the current year. Generally accepted accounting principles require that this change in accounting method be reported by
    a. Disclosing the reason for the change in the current year's footnotes along with pro forma effects on future earnings for the succeeding five years.
    b. Showing the cumulative effect of the change in the current year's financial statements and pro forma effects on prior year's financial statements in an appropriate footnote.
    c. Disclosing the reason for the change in the "significant accounting policies" footnote for the current year but not restating prior year financial statements.
    d. Applying retroactively the new method in restatements of prior years and appropriate footnote disclosures.

21. What are the three types of period costs that a lessee experiences with capital leases?
    a. Lease expense, interest expense, amortization expense.
    b. Interest expense, amortization expense, executory costs.
    c. Amortization expense, executory costs, lease expense.
    d. Executory costs, interest expense, lease expense.

22. When the market value of a company's current marketable equity securities portfolio is lower than its cost, the difference should be
    a. Accounted for as a liability.
    b. Disclosed and described in a footnote to the financial statements but not accounted for.
    c. Accounted for as a valuation allowance deducted from the asset to which it relates.
    d. Accounted for separately in the shareholders' equity section of the balance sheet.

23. In a business combination what is the appropriate method of accounting for an excess of fair value assigned to net assets over the cost paid for them?
    a. Record as negative goodwill.
    b. Record as additional paid-in capital from combination on the books of the combined company.
    c. Proportionately reduce values assigned to nonmonetary assets and record any remaining excess as a deferred credit.

d.   Proportionately reduce values assigned to noncurrent assets and record any remaining excess as a deferred credit.

24.   In addition to a statement of financial position, earnings statement, retained earnings statement, and statement of changes in financial position, a complete set of financial statements must include
   a.   Adequate disclosure of accounting policies.
   b.   An auditor's opinion.
   c.   A ten-year summary of operations.
   d.   Historical "common size" financial summaries.

25.   Which of the following is the appropriate basis for valuing fixed assets acquired in a business combination accounted for as a purchase carried out by exchanging cash for common stock?
   a.   Historic cost.
   b.   Book value.
   c.   Cost plus any excess of purchase price over book value of asset acquired.
   d.   Fair value.

26.   Gilbert Corporation issued a 40% stock split-up of its common stock which had a par value of $10 before and after the split-up. At what amount should retained earnings be capitalized for the additional shares issued?
   a.   There should be no capitalization of retained earnings.
   b.   Par value.
   c.   Market value on the declaration date.
   d.   Market value on the payment date.

27.   When translating an amount for fixed assets shown on the statement of financial position of a foreign subsidiary, the appropriate rate of translation is the
   a.   Current exchange rate.
   b.   Average exchange rate for the current year.
   c.   Historical exchange rate.
   d.   Average exchange rate over the life of each fixed asset.

28.   The sale of a depreciable asset resulting in a loss, indicates that the proceeds from the sale were
   a.   Less than current market value.
   b.   Greater than cost.
   c.   Greater than book value.
   d.   Less than book value.

29.   A parent corporation which uses the equity method of accounting for its investment in a 40% owned subsidiary, which earned $20,000 and paid

$5,000 in dividends, made the following entries:

Investment in subsidiary	$8,000	
Equity in earnings of subsidiary		$8,000
Cash	2,000	
Dividend revenue		2,000

What effect will these entries have on the parent's statement of financial position?

   a.   Financial position will be fairly stated.
   b.   Investment in subsidiary overstated, retained earnings understated.
   c.   Investment in subsidiary understated, retained earnings understated.
   d.   Investment in subsidiary overstated, retained earnings overstated.

30.   The terminal funding method and pay-as-you-go method of accounting for pension plans are not generally accepted accounting methods because
   a.   They do not require the funding of past service costs.
   b.   They are not actuarially sound.
   c.   They do not recognize pension costs prior to the retirement of employees.
   d.   They are not acceptable methods for federal income tax purposes.

31.   The concept of objectivity is complied with when an accounting transaction occurs that
   a.   Involves an arm's-length transaction between two independent interests.
   b.   Furthers the objectives of the company.
   c.   Is promptly recorded in a fixed amount of dollars.
   d.   Allocates revenues or expense items in a rational and systematic manner.

32.   Which of the following principles best describes the current method of accounting for research and development costs?
   a.   Immediate recognition as an expense.
   b.   Associating cause and effect.
   c.   Systematic and rational allocation.
   d.   Income tax minimization.

33.   An increase in inventory balance would be reported in a statement of changes in financial position as a
   a.   Use of working capital.
   b.   Source of working capital.
   c.   Source of cash.
   d.   Use of cash.

34. A true process costing system could make use of each of the following except
    a. Standards.
    b. Individual lots.
    c. Variable costing.
    d. Responsibility accounting.

35. Joint costs are most frequently allocated based upon relative
    a. Profitability.
    b. Conversion costs.
    c. Sales value.
    d. Prime costs.

36. In analyzing factory overhead variances, the volume variance is the difference between the
    a. Amount shown in the flexible budget and the amount shown in the master budget.
    b. Master budget application rate and the flexible budget application rate multiplied by actual hours worked.
    c. Budget allowance based on standard hours allowed for actual production for the period and the amount applied during the period.
    d. Actual amount spent for overhead items during the period and the amount applied during the period.

37. Which of the following characteristics applies to process costing but not to job-order costing?
    a. Identifiable batches of production.
    b. Equivalent units of production.
    c. Averaging process.
    d. Use of standard costs.

38. Which of the following quantitative methods will separate a semi-variable cost into its fixed and variable components with the highest degree of precision under all circumstances?
    a. High-low method.
    b. Simplex method.
    c. Least squares method.
    d. Scattergraph method.

39. If the fixed costs attendant to a product increase while variable costs and sales price remain constant what will happen to (1) contribution margin and (2) break-even point?

	Contribution margin	Breakeven point
a.	Unchanged	increase
b.	Unchanged	unchanged
c.	Increase	decrease
d.	Decrease	increase

40. Spoilage occurring during a manufacturing process can be considered normal or abnormal. The proper accounting for each of these costs is

	Normal	Abnormal
a.	Product	Period
b.	Product	Product
c.	Period	Product
d.	Period	Period

41. Why is direct costing not in accordance with generally accepted accounting principles?
    a. Fixed manufacturing costs are assumed to be period costs.
    b. Direct costing procedures are not well known in industry.
    c. Net earnings are always overstated when using direct costing procedures.
    d. Direct costing ignores the concept of lower of cost or market when valuing inventory.

42. The quantitative analysis tool whose primary objective is to define a critical path is
    a. Linear programming.
    b. Queuing theory.
    c. Program evaluation and review technique.
    d. Multiple regression analysis.

43. To obtain the break-even point stated in terms of dollars of sales, total fixed costs are divided by which of the following?
    a. Variable cost per unit.
    b. (Sales price per unit — variable cost per unit) ÷ sales price per unit.
    c. Fixed cost per unit.
    d. Variable cost per unit ÷ sales price per unit.

44. The minimum return that a project must earn for a company in order to leave the value of the company unchanged is the
    a. Current borrowing rate.
    b. Discount rate.
    c. Cost of capital.
    d. Capitalization rate.

45. A useful tool in financial statement analysis is termed "common size financial statements." What does this tool enable the financial analyst to do?
    a. Evaluate financial statements of companies within a given industry of the approximate same value.
    b. Determine which companies in a similar industry are at approximately the same stage of development.

c. Compare the mix of assets, liabilities, capital, revenue, and expenses within a company over a period of time or between companies within a given industry without respect to relative size.

d. Ascertain the relative potential of companies of similar size in different industries.

46. A company buys a certain part for its manufacturing process. In order to determine the optimum size of a normal purchase order, the formula for the economic order quantity (EOQ) is used. In addition to the annual demand, what other information is necessary to complete the formula?

a. Cost of placing an order, and annual cost of carrying a unit in stock.

b. Cost of the part, and annual cost of carrying a unit in stock.

c. Cost of placing an order.

d. Cost of the part.

47. Which type of cost is a vital part of decision making but omitted from conventional accounting records?

a. Out-of-pocket cost.

b. Sunk cost.

c. Opportunity cost.

d. Direct cost.

48. A company manufactures two joint products at a joint cost of $1,000. These products can be sold when split off or when further processed at an additional cost and sold as higher quality items. The decision to sell at split-off or further process should be based on the

a. Assumption that the $1,000 joint cost is irrelevant.

b. Allocation of the $1,000 joint cost using the relative sales-value approach.

c. Assumption that the $1,000 joint cost must be allocated using a physical-measure approach.

d. Allocation of the $1,000 joint cost using any equitable and rational allocation basis.

49. Which of the following quantitative techniques is used to determine the fixed and variable elements of a semivariable cost?

a. Queuing theory.

b. Linear programming.

c. Simplex method.

d. Least squares.

50. How is a labor rate variance computed?

a. The difference between standard and actual rate multiplied by standard hours.

b. The difference between standard and actual hours multiplied by actual rate.

c. The difference between standard and actual rate multiplied by actual hours.

d. The difference between standard and actual rate.

51. When the budget of a governmental unit is adopted and the estimated revenues exceed the appropriations, the excess is

a. Debited to reserve for encumbrances.

b. Credited to reserve for encumbrances.

c. Debited to fund balance.

d. Credited to fund balance.

52. Which of the following funds should use the modi- †
fied accrual basis of accounting?

a. Capital projects.

b. Intragovernmental (internal) service.

c. Special revenue.

d. Trust.

53. What is not a major concern of governmental units?

a. Budgets.

b. Funds.

c. Legal requirements.

d. Consolidated statements.

54. A reason for a voluntary health and welfare organization to adopt fund accounting is that

a. Restrictions have been placed on certain of its assets by donors.

b. It provides more than one type of program service.

c. Fixed assets are significant.

d. Donated services are significant.

55. When a truck is received by a governmental unit, it should be recorded in the General Fund as a (an)

a. Appropriation.

b. Encumbrance.

c. Expenditure.

d. Fixed asset.

56. Within a governmental unit, three funds that are accounted for in a manner similar to a for-profit entity are

a. General, Debt Service, Special Assessment.

b. Special Assessment, Enterprise, Intragovernmental Service.

c. Intragovernmental Service, Enterprise, General.

d. Enterprise, General, Debt Service.

57. What is the recommended method of accounting to be used by colleges and universities?
    a. Cash.
    b. Modified cash.
    c. Restricted accrual.
    d. Accrual.

58. Under the modified accrual method of accounting used by a local governmental unit, which of the following would be a revenue susceptible to accrual?
    a. Income taxes.
    b. Business licenses.
    c. Property taxes.
    d. Sales taxes.

59. The accounting for special revenue funds is most similar to which type of fund?
    a. Capital projects.
    b. General.
    c. Enterprise.
    d. Special assessment.

60. Which governmental fund would account for fixed assets in a manner similar to a "for-profit" organization?
    a Enterprise.
    b. Capital projects.
    c. General fixed asset group of accounts.
    d. General.

Number 2 (Estimated time - 15 to 25 minutes)

Number 2 consists of two unrelated parts.

Part a. Cost for inventory purposes should be determined by the inventory cost flow method most clearly reflecting periodic income.

Required:
1. Describe the fundamental cost flow assumptions of the average cost, FIFO, and LIFO inventory cost flow methods.
2. Discuss the reasons for using LIFO in an inflationary economy.
3. Where there is evidence that the utility of goods, in their disposal in the ordinary course of business, will be less than cost, what is the proper accounting treatment and under what concept is that treatment justified?

Part b. Pension plans have developed in an environment characterized by a complex interaction of social concepts, legal considerations, actuarial techniques, income tax laws, and accounting practices. APB Opinion No. 8 delineates acceptable accounting practices for the cost of pension plans.

Required:

1. The following terms are relevant to accounting for the cost of pension plans. Define or explain briefly each of the following:
    a. Normal cost.
    b. Past service cost.
    c. Prior service cost.
    d. Funded plan.
    e. Vested benefits.
    f. Actuarial gains and losses.
    g. Interest.
2. Identify the disclosures required in financial statements regarding a company's pension plan.

Number 3 (Estimated time - 15 to 25 minutes)

Number 3 consists of two unrelated parts.

Part a. Incurring long-term debt with an arrangement whereby lenders receive an option to buy common stock during all or portion of the time the debt is outstanding is a frequently used corporate financing practice. In some situations the result is achieved through the issuance of convertible bonds; in others the debt instruments and the warrants to buy stock are separate.

Required:

a. 1. Describe the differences that exist in current accounting for original proceeds of the issuance of convertible bonds and of debt instruments with separate warrants to purchase common stock.

    2. Discuss the underlying rationale for the differences described in a.1. above.

    3. Summarize the arguments which have been presented for the alternative accounting treatment.

Part b. Capital stock is an important area of a corporation's equity section. Generally the term "capital stock" embraces common and preferred stock issued by a corporation.

Required:
1. What are the basic rights inherent in ownership of common stock, and how are they exercised?
2. What is preferred stock? Discuss the various preferences afforded preferred stock.

Number 4   (Estimated time - 15 to 25 minutes)

The following is the complete set of financial statements prepared by Oberlin Corporation:

Oberlin Corporation
STATEMENT OF EARNINGS AND RETAINED EARNINGS
For the Fiscal Year Ended August 31, 1976

Sales		$3,500,000
Less returns and allowances		35,000
Net sales		3,465,000
Less cost of goods sold		1,039,000
Gross margin		2,426,000
Less:		
Selling expenses	$1,000,000	
General and administrative expenses (Note 1)	1,079,000	2,079,000
Operating earnings		347,000
Add other revenue:		
Purchase discounts	10,000	
Gain on increased value of investments in real estate	100,000	
Gain on sale of treasury stock	200,000	
Correction of error in last year's statement	90,000	400,000
Ordinary earnings		747,000
Add extraordinary item — gain on sale of fixed asset		53,000
Earnings before income tax		800,000
Less income tax expense		380,000
Net earnings		420,000
Add beginning retained earnings		2,750,000
		3,170,000
Less:		
Dividends (12% stock dividend declared but not yet issued)		120,000
Contingent liability (Note 4)		300,000
Ending unappropriated retained earnings		$2,750,000

Oberlin Corporation
STATEMENT OF FINANCIAL POSITION
August 31, 1976

Assets

Current Assets

Cash	$ 80,000	
Accounts receivable, net	110,000	
Inventory	130,000	
Total current assets		$ 320,000

Other Assets

Land and building, net	4,000,000	
Investments in real estate (current value)	1,508,000	
Investment in Gray, Inc., at at cost (Note 2)	160,000	
Goodwill (Note 3)	250,000	
Discount on bonds payable	42,000	
Total other assets		5,960,000
Total assets		$6,280,000

Liabilities and Stockholders Equity

Current Liabilities

Accounts payable	$ 140,000	
Income taxes payable	320,000	
Stock dividend payable	120,000	
Total current liabilities		$ 580,000

Other Liabilities

Due to Grant, Inc. (Note 4)	300,000	
Liability under employee pension plan	450,000	
Bonds payable (including portion due within one year)	1,000,000	
Deferred taxes	58,000	
Total other liabilities		1,808,000
Total liabilities		2,388,000

Stockholders' Equity

Common stock	1,000,000	
Paid-in capital in excess of par	142,000	
Unappropriated retained earnings	2,750,000	
Total stockholders' equity		3,892,000
Total liabilities and stockholders' equity		$6,280,000

Footnotes to the Financial Statements

1. Depreciation expense is included in general and administrative expenses. During the fiscal year, the Company changed from the straight-line method of depreciation to the sum-of-the-years'-digits method.

2. The company owns 40% of the outstanding stock of Gray, Inc. Because the ownership is less than 50%, consolidated financial statements with Gray cannot be presented.

3. As per federal income tax laws, goodwill is not amortized. The goodwill was "acquired" in 1973.

4. The amount due to Grant, Inc., is contingent upon the outcome of a lawsuit which is currently pending. The amount of loss, if any, is not expected to exceed $300,000.

Required:

Identify and explain the deficiencies in the presentation of Oberlin's financial statements. There are no arithmetical errors in the statements. Organize your answer as follows:

a. Deficiencies in the statement of earnings and retained earnings.

b. Deficiencies in the statement of financial position.

c. General comments.

If an item appears on both statements, identify the deficiencies for each statement separately.

Number 5   (Estimated time - 15 to 25 minutes)

Number 5 consists of two unrelated parts.

Part a.   Although direct costing is not a current generally accepted method of costing inventory for external reporting, it is useful for internal pruposes.

Required:
1. Describe the difference between direct costing and the current generally accepted method of costing inventory for external reporting.

2. Describe how a direct costing structure facilitates calculation of the contribution margin and the breakeven point.

Part b.   An important part of managerial accounting is the analysis of the types of costs that a business entity can incur. These types of costs are generally classified as variable, fixed, and semivariable.

Required:
With respect to a semivariable cost
1. Define and discuss the idenifying characteristics of a semivariable cost.

2. Discuss the three basic methods employed to "break down" a semivariable cost into its component parts.

ANSWERS TO SAMPLE EXAMINATION
ACCOUNTING PRACTICE — PART I

Answer 1		**Answer 2**		**Answer 3**	
1. a	11. b	21. d	31. c	41. b	51. a
2. b	12. b	22. c	32. b	42. d	52. a
3. c	13. a	23. d	33. d	43. a	53. b
4. b	14. b	24. b	34. a	44. b	54. b
5. b	15. a	25. d	35. d	45. b	55. b
6. c	16. c	26. d	36. b	46. b	56. c
7. c	17. d	27. b	37. b	47. c	57. c
8. d	18. d	28. c	38. d	48. a	58. d
9. c	19. d	29. b	39. b	49. d	59. c
10. b	20. a	30. a	40. a	50. c	60. c

Answer 4

Part a.

a. 1.

Crystal Company
COMPUTATION OF EXPENSE
ON OPERATING LEASE
For the Year Ended December 31, 1976

Rental expense ($115,000 x 6 months) $690,000

2.

Jackson Company
COMPUTATION OF INCOME BEFORE
INCOME TAXES ON OPERATING LEASE
For the Year Ended December 31, 1976

Rental income ($115,000 x 6 months)	$690,000
Depreciation	
($7,000,000 ÷8 years x 6 months)	437,500
	$252,500

Part b.

b. 1.

Truman Company
COMPUTATION OF EXPENSE
ON LEASE RECORDED AS A PURCHASE
For the Year Ended December 31, 1976

Depreciation ($3,520,800	
(Schedule 1) ÷8)	$440,100
Interest expense *(Schedule 2)*	73,020
	$513,120

2.

Roosevelt Company
COMPUTATION OF INCOME BEFORE
INCOME TAXES ON LEASE
RECORDED AS A SALE
For the Year Ended December 31, 1976

Profit on sale:		
Sales price *(Scheduel 1)*	$3,520,800	
Cost of equipment	3,000,000	
		$520,800
Interest income *Schedule 2)*		73,020
		$593,820

Schedule 1

Computation of Purchase Price of Equipment

Equal annual payment	$ 600,000
Present value of an annuity of $1 in	
advance for 8 periods at 10%	x 5.868
	$3,520,800

Schedule 2

Computation of Interest Expense

Purchase price of equipment	$3,520,800
Payment made on October 1, 1976	600,000
	2,920,800
Interest rate	10%
Interest expense (October 1, 1976 to	
October 1, 1977)	292,080
Interest expense applicable to	
1976 (3 months)	25%
	$ 73,020

Part c.

c. 1.

Birch Company
**COMPUTATION OF INCOME BEFORE
INCOME TAXES ON
INSTALLMENT SALE CONTRACT**
For the Year Ended December 31, 1975

Sales	$5,355,000
Cost of sales	4,284,000
Gross profit	1,071,000
Interest income *(Schedule 1)*	435,500
Income before income taxes	$1,506,500

Schedule 1

*Computation of Interest Income on
Installment Sale Contract*

Cash selling price (sales)	$5,355,000
Payment made on January 1, 1975	(1,000,000)
	4,355,000
Interest rate	10%
	$ 435,500

2.

Birch Company
**COMPUTATION OF PROVISION FOR
DEFERRED INCOME TAXES ON
INSTALLMENT SALE CONTRACT**
For the Year Ended December 31, 1975

Gross profit for accounting purposes		$1,071,000
Gross profit for tax purposes:		
Payment made on January 1, 1975	$1,000,000	
Gross profit percentage ($1,071,000 ÷ $5,355,000)	20%	
		200,000
Timing difference		871,000
Income tax rate		40%
Provision for deferred income taxes		$ 348,400

Answer 5

a.

City of Nicknar
CIVIC CENTER CONSTRUCTION FUND
Journal Entries
July 1, 1977 to June 30, 1978

	Debit	*Credit*
(1)		
Cash	$ 500,000	
Due to General Fund		$ 500,000
To record loan received from General Fund		
(2)		
Expenditures	320,000	
Cash		320,000
To record unencumbered expenses		
(3)		
Due from state government	5,000,000	
Revenues		5,000,000
To record grant due from state government		
(4)		
Cash	10,100,000	
Premium on bonds		100,000
Bond Issue Proceeds		10,000,000
To record sale of bonds		
(5)		
Premium on bonds	100,000	
Cash		100,000
To record transfer of bond premium		
(6)		
Encumbrances	12,000,000	
Reserve for encumbrances		12,000,000
To record encumbrance for contract let		
(7)		
Encumbrances	55,000	
Reserve for encumbrances		55,000
To record encumbrance for materials ordered		

(8)		
Cash	2,500,000	
Due from state government		2,500,000
To record receipt of grant		

(9)		
Reserve for encumbrances	55,000	
Expenditures	51,000	
Encumbrances		55,000
Cash		51,000
To record receipt of materials ordered and payment		

(10)		
Reserve for encumbrances	2,000,000	
Encumbrances		2,000,000
To reverse, in part, entry setting up encumbrance for contract with Candu Construction Company		

(11)		
Expenditures	2,000,000	
Contracts payable		1,880,000
Contracts payable— retained percentage		120,000
To record expenditures to date on construction contract		

(12)		
Due to General Fund	500,000	
Cash		500,000
To record repayment of loan to General Fund		

(13)		
Fund balance	12,371,000	
Encumbrances		10,000,000
Expenditures		2,371,000
To close out to fund balance		

(14)		
Bond Issue Proceeds	10,000,000	
Revenues	5,000,000	
Fund Balance		15,000,000

b.

City of Nicknar
CIVIC CENTER CONSTRUCTION FUND
BALANCE SHEET
June 30, 1978

Assets

Cash	$12,129,000
Due from state government	2,500,000
Total assets	$14,629,000

Liabilities and fund balance

Liabilities:		
Contracts payable		$1,880,000
Contracts payable — retained percentage		120,000
Total liabilities		2,000,000
Fund balance:		
Reserve for encumbrances	$10,000,000	
Fund balance — unreserved	2,629,000	
Total fund balance		12,629,000
Total liabilities and fund balance		$14,629,000

ANSWERS TO SAMPLE EXAMINATION

ACCOUNTING PRACTICE — PART II

	Answer 1			Answer 2				Answer 3	
1. c		11. d		21. b	31. c			41. c	51. d
2. c		12. d		22. b	32. b			42. c	52. a
3. a		13. c		23. c	33. d			43. a	53. d
4. a		14. d		24. b	34. b			44. a	54. d
5. c		15. c		25. b	35. c			45. c	55. d
6. c		16. a		26. a	36. c			46. b	56. b
7. c		17. b		27. c	37. a			47. b	57. b
8. c		18. c		28. a	38. c			48. a	58. b
9. b		19. c		29. d	39. b			49. c	59. a
10. a		20. b		30. b	40. b			50. d	60. d

Answer 4

Part a.

Padway Corporation
COMPUTATION OF VALUE OF
WORK-IN-PROCESS INVENTORY LOST
June 30, 1978

Sales		$340,000
Less gross profit (25%)		85,000
		255,000
Add finished goods, June 30, 1978		119,000
Goods available for sale		374,000
Less finished goods, January 1, 1978		140,000
Goods manufactured and completed		$234,000
Raw materials, January 1, 1978		$ 30,000
Purchases		115,000
Total available		145,000
Raw materials, June 30, 1978		62,000
		83,000
Labor	$ 80,000	
Overhead	40,000	
Work-in-process, January 1, 1978	100,000	220,000
Cost of production		303,000
Less cost of goods completed		234,000
Work-in-process inventory lost		$ 69,000

Part b.

Lakeview Corporation Assembling Department
COSTS OF PRODUCTION REPORT
For the Month Ended June 30, 1980

Description	Total	Transferred In	Direct Materials	Direct Labor	Factory Overhead
Physical units to be accounted for:					
a. Beginning inventory	2,000				
b. Transferred in	10,000				
Units to be accounted for	12,000				
Equivalent units of production:					
c. Transferred out	8,000	8,000	8,000	8,000	8,000
d. Ending inventory*	4,000	4,000	3,600	2,800	1,400
e. Equivalent units	12,000	12,000	11,600	10,800	9,400

*4,000 x percentage of completion.

Description	Total	Transferred In	Direct Materials	Direct Labor	Factory Overhead
Total Manufacturing Costs:					
f. Beginning inventory	$ 64,700	$ 32,000	$ 20,000	$ 7,200	$ 5,500
g. Current - June	310,000	160,000	96,000	36,000	18,000
h. Total manufacturing costs	$374,700	$192,000	$116,000	$43,200	$23,500
Cost per equivalent unit*	$32.50	$16.00	$10.00	$4.00	$2.50

i. = (h ÷ e)
   *Total manufacturing costs ÷ equivalent units.

Description	Total	Transferred In	Direct Materials	Direct Labor	Factory Overhead
Allocation of total costs:					
Amount of ending work-in-process (d. x i.)	$114,700	$ 64,000	$ 36,000	$11,200	$ 3,500
Amount transferred out*	260,000	128,000	80,000	32,000	20,000
Total cost (c. x i.)	$374,700	$192,000	$116,000	$43,200	$23,500

*8,000 x equivalent unit cost.

Answer 5

Part a.

	Debit	Credit

1.   **Investments in subsidiaries**
Investment in common stock of Meadow Corporation — $56,000
Investment in common stock of Van Corporation — 84,000
   Cash — — $140,000
To record acquisition of investments in
Meadow: 800 shares ($50,000 ÷ $50 = 1,000 shares
           x 80%) @ $70 per share
Van: 2,100 shares ($60,000 ÷ $20 = 3,000 shares
        x 70%) @ $40 per share

Parent's share of subsidiary income or loss
Investment in common stock of Meadow Corporation — 28,800
Equity in subsidiary loss — 8,400
   Investment in common stock of Van Corporation — — 8,400
   Equity in subsidiary income — — 28,800
To record parent's share of subsidiaries' income or (loss)
Meadow: $36,000 x 80% = $28,800
Van: ($12,000) x 70% = ($8,400)

Subsidiaries dividends received
Cash — 19,100
   Investment in common stock of Meadow Corporation — — 12,800
   Investment in common stock of Van Corporation — — 6,300
To record dividends received from subsidiaries
Meadow: $16,000 x 80% = $12,800
Van: $9,000 x 70% = $6,300

2.   **Meadow Corporation**

Common stock	$50,000
Retained earnings, December 31, 1976	40,000
	$90,000
Minority interest ($90,000 x 20%)	$18,000

Van Corporation

Common stock	$60,000
Capital in excess of par value	20,000
Retained earnings, December 31, 1976	19,000
	$99,000
Minority interest ($99,000 x 30%)	$29,700

3.   *Computation of Consolidated Retained Earnings*

at December 31, 1976

Todd Corporation:		
Retained earnings, January 1, 1976		$240,000
Net income from operations—1976		104,600
		344,600
Less: Dividends paid—1976		(40,000)
		304,600
Equity in earnings or (loss) of subsidiaries:		
*Meadow Corporation		28,800
*Van Corporation		(8,400)
Consolidated retained earnings		$325,000

Author's Note: Since the facts given in this problem are silent as to whether the "cost" or "equity" method was used for the two investments in subsidiaries, an alternative solution is to not include the $28,800 and the ($8,400) under the assemption that the "equity" method was used in which case they would have been picked up in the net income, $104,600.

Part b.

b. 1.
On the books of Bond Company at
    December 31, 1976:

Current assets (inventory)	$30,000	
Cost of sales		$10,000
Retained earnings		20,000

To record change in inventory costing method
from LIFO to FIFO as follows:

Increase in ending inventory	$30,000
Increase in opening inventory	20,000
Decrease in cost of sales	$10,000

2.

Gold Corporation
**COMPUTATION OF POOLED
RETAINED EARNINGS**
As of December 31, 1976

Retained earnings of Cole Company, December 31, 1976			$233,000
Retained earnings of Bond Company, December 31, 1976			296,000
			529,000
Add effect on retained earnings of change in inventory costing method			30,000
			559,000
Less excess of stated value of new stock over paid-in capital prior to merger:			
Common stock issued by Gold Corporation in exchange for common stock of Cole and Bond		$500,000	
Less paid-in capital prior to merger:			
Cole Company:			
Common stock	$ 50,000		
Capital contributed in excess of par value	10,000		
	60,000		
Bond Company:			
Common stock	40,000		
Capital contributed in excess of par value	160,000		
	200,000	260,000	240,000
Pooled retained earnings, December 31, 1976			$319,000

3.

On the books of Gold Corporation at
December 31, 1976:

Current assets	$525,000*	
Property, plant, and equipment	730,000	
Other assets	155,000	
Current liabilities		$291,000
Long-term debt		300,000
Common stock		500,000
Retained earnings		319,000

To record the combination of Cole Company
and Bond Company as a pooling of interests.

_____

Current assets of Cole and Bond plus $30,000 inventory adjustment.

ANSWERS TO SAMPLE EXAMINATION
AUDITING

Answer 1

1. a	11. d	21. d	31. c	41. d	51. b
2. b	12. d	22. b	32. d	42. c	52. b
3. d	13. c	23. a	33. a	43. a	53. a
4. d	14. a	24. d	34. c	44. d	54. a
5. a	15. a	25. a	35. a	45. c	55. d
6. d	16. c	26. b	36. c	46. d	56. b
7. b	17. a	27. d	37. b	47. a	57. b
8. b	18. c	28. b	38. d	48. b	58. c
9. b	19. a	29. c	39. b	49. d	59. b
10. c	20. b	30. a	40. d	50. c	60. a

Answer 2

a. The accounts payable audit procedures should be directed toward searching for proper inclusion of all accounts payable and ascertaining that recorded amounts are reasonably stated because the primary audit purpose is to reveal any possible material understatements.

The principal objectives of the accounts payable examination are

(1) To determine adequacy of internal control for processing and payment of invoices.
(2) To prove that amounts shown on the balance sheet are in agreement with supporting accounting records.
(3) To determine that liabilities existing at the balance sheet date have been recorded.

b. Mincin is not required to use accounts payable confirmation procedures. Unlike accounts receivable, accounts payable require no opinions as to valuation. The auditor is required to obtain direct confirmation of accounts receivable, since the primary audit test is for possible material overstatements and generally the client has available only internal documents such as sales invoices. For accounts payable the auditor can examine external evidence such as vendor invoices and vendor statements which substantiate the accounts payable balance. Although not required, the accounts payable confirmation is often used. The auditor might consider such use when

(1) Internal accounting controls are weak.
(2) The company is in a "tight" cash position and bill-paying is slow.

(3) Physical inventories exceed general ledger inventory balances by significant amounts.
(4) Certain vendors do not send statements.
(5) Vendor accounts are pledged by assets.
(6) Vendor accounts include unusual transactions.

c. A selection technique using the large dollar balances of accounts is generally used when the primary audit objective is to test for overstatements (e.g., accounts receivable audit work). Accounts with zero balances or relatively small balances would not be subjected to selection under such an approach. When auditing accounts payable the auditor is primarily concerned with the possibility of unrecorded payables or understatement of recorded payables. Selection of accounts with relatively small or no balances for confirmation is the more efficient direction of testing since understatements are more likely to be detected when examining such accounts.

When selecting accounts payable for confirmation, the following procedures should be followed:

(1) Analyze the accounts payable population and stratify it into accounts with large balances, accounts with small balances, accounts with zero balances, etc.
(2) Use a sampling technique that selects items based on ciiteria other than the dollar amount of the items (e.g., select based on terminal digits, select every n^{th} item based on predetermined interval, etc.).
(3) Design a statistical sampling plan that will place more emphasis on selecting accounts with zero balances or relatively small balances,

particularly when the client has had substantial transactions with such vendors during the year.

(4) Select prior-year vendors who are no longer used.

(5) Select new vendors used in the subsequent period.

(6) Select vendors that do not provide periodic statements.

(7) Select accounts reflecting unusual transactions during the year.

(8) Select accounts secured by pledged assets.

Answer 3

a. The procedures that Norr should follow prior to accepting the engagement include the following:

(1) Norr should explain to Johnson the need to inquire of Diggs and should request permission to make such inquiries.

(2) Norr should request that Johnson authorize Diggs to respond fully to all of Norr's inquiries since Diggs would be prohibited from disclosing confidential information obtained in the course of his professional engagement with Johnson.

(3) Norr should advise Diggs of Johnson's decision to change auditors. Norr would be in violation of the AICPA Code of Professional Ethics if he did not advise Diggs of Johnson's decision. In addition, advising Diggs would be a good business judgment as well as an act of professional courtesy.

(4) Norr should make reasonable inquiries of Diggs regarding matters that will aid in deciding whether to accept the engagement. (Norr's inquiries should include questions regarding facts which might bear on the integrity of management, disagreements with management as to accounting principles, auditing procedures or other significant matters, and Diggs' understanding of the reason(s) for the change of auditors).

(5) Norr should weigh all the information received from Diggs. If Diggs does not respond fully to Norr's questions, Norr should consider the implications of the limited response in deciding whether to accept the engagement.

(6) After weighing all information received from Diggs, Norr should inform Johnson that a first-time audit is more time-consuming than a recurring audit because the new auditor is generally unfamiliar with the client's operations and does not have the benefit of past knowledge of company affairs to use as a guide.

(7) A discussion with Johnson of the estimated required audit time and fee arrangement should be coordinated with a clear explanation of the purpose and scope of the audit. Any work that can be done by client personnel should also be discussed so that excess audit time might be eliminated and proposed report deadlines can be reasonably met.

(8) To satisfy Norr's quality control objectives, Norr should use procedures such as reviewing the financial statements of Johnson; inquiring of third parties such as Johnson's banks, legal counsel, investment bankers, and others in the business community as to Johnson's reputation and evaluating his ability to serve Johnson properly with reference to industry expertise, size of engagement, and available staff.

(9) If Norr has no reservations, after all significant factors have been considered, discussed, and agreed to, Norr should accept the engagement and confirm the understanding in an engagement letter.

b. Norr's procedures on this first-time audit should include the following:

(1) Norr should review the workpapers of Diggs to obtain information that will help plan the audit work.

(2) Norr should make arrangements as early as possible for the initial meeting with "key" company personnel who will be contacted throughout the engagement.

(3) Since basic information about the company is not readily available to Norr on this first-time audit, information of a general nature should be obtained as early in the planning stage as possible. (Such information should include company history, nature of the business, credit policies, financing methods, sales methods and terms, seasonal business patterns, products, services, plant locations, internal procedures, accounting policies, tax status, etc. Client procedures manuals and manuals of accounts should be read to obtain such information.)

(4) Norr should immediately start obtaining the data needed to create a permanent working paper file. (The file should include items such as articles of incorporation, minutes, internal audit reports, deeds of trust, pension agreements, loan agreements, leases, important contracts, and other pertinent data.)

(5)   Norr must determine the scope of work necessary to verify the opening balances. Such balances must be reviewed to determine whether they are stated on a basis comparable with those of the period under review. If Norr cannot verify the opening balances, Norr should consider disclaiming an opinion on the earnings statement and statement of changes in financial position.

(6)   The composition of all important accounts should be reviewed. Norr should limit his examination of prior period accounts to a review or survey of such accounts, without a detailed examination, unless the results of Norr's survey and analyses indicate the need for further investigation of accounting methods in the prior years.

(7)   Norr must consider whether the financial statements are prepared using generally accepted accounting principles that were consistently applied. If, after performing necessary audit procedures, Norr cannot be satisfied as to consistency, considerations must be given to qualifying the auditor's report as to consistency.

(8)   Norr should use professional judgment to determine the extent of reliance that should be placed on the work of Diggs. The scope of Norr's work may be reduced as a result of Norr's consultation with Diggs and a review of the prior-year workpapers of Diggs.

Answer 4

Step	Possible Errors or Discrepancies	Control Procedures
A	1. Time may be improperly reported by employees.	1. (a) Timekeeping for payroll hours should be an independent function. (b) Time clocks should be used under the observation of timekeeping. (c) Strict rules should be enforced requiring each employee to punch his own time card. (d) Timekeeping should make periodic floor checks of employees on duty.
	2. Payroll may be padded by timekeeper.	2. (a) Employees should be paid directly by paymaster. (b) Personnel department should advise payroll audit and control and the computer department of new hires and terminations.
	3. Employees may work unauthorized overtime hours.	3. A procedure for authorization of overtime should be devised, and timekeeping should determine that required authorizations are made.
B	4. Employees may not work effectively during the hours reported to timekeeping. Also, they may disguise inefficiencies by spreading excess hours to other jobs.	4. (a) Employees should report hours by job, preferably by use of a time clock. (b) Supervisor should review and approve job tickets, and timekeeping should check to see that these approvals are made. (The effectiveness of this system depends upon the supervisor's ability to evaluate the time spent on particular jobs and his conscientious review of the job tickets.) (c) Employees should be instructed to assign actual hours to jobs. Either the supervisor or timekeeping should enforce this policy.
	5. Overtime work on a job may not be authorized, and the job may not be charged at the premium overtime rate.	5. Timekeeping should check required authorizations and appropriately note hours that should be charged at the premium rate.
C	6. Job tickets and time cards may not be in balance.	6. Absolute balancing may be impractical or unnecessary for cost accumulation, allocation, or control; reasonable difference limits should be established by appropriate authority. Assuring that differences fall within established limits can be accomplished by: (a) Having timekeeper balance hours per time card with hours per job tickets and resolve differences; or, (b) Programming computer to zero balance total hours on job tickets with total hours on time card by employee. Differences which exceed established limits would be printed out as exceptions for follow-up by payroll audit and control and/or timekeeper.

Step	Possible Errors or Discrepancies	Control Procedures

D	7. Time cards and job tickets may be lost in transit from timekeeping to payroll audit and control.	7. (a) Timekeeping should promptly forward time cards and job tickets accompanied by a transmittal slip denoting the number of employees for which time is being reported. Payroll audit and control should reconcile the number of employees reported with the master-payroll record, considering employees on vacation, illness, etc. (b) To assure that all cards have been accounted for, timekeeping can prepare a hash total of employee numbers for both time cards and job tickets. These totals can be included in the transmittal slip described under (a) above.
	8. Payroll audit and control may total hours incorrectly in preparing the control total for the batch transmittal form.	8. If this is a frequent error, payroll audit and control should recompute all control totals. If it is an infrequent occurrence, it can be handled as an exception printout from the computer.
E	9. Time cards and job tickets may be lost in transit from payroll audit and control to data preparation.	9. Payroll audit and control should batch time cards and related job tickets. A consecutively numbered transmittal sheet should accompany each batch and contain a control total, such as total hours. This control total should be compared to total shown by keypunch machine.
	10. Keypunch operator may transcribe data incorrectly.	10. Keypunching should be verified by another operator. Errors also will be detected through use of batch controls.
	11. The employee identification number may have been recorded or carried forward improperly.	11. Employee identification numbers should contain a self-checking digit and the computer should be programmed to test the validity of each employee's number.
F	12. Time cards and job tickets may be lost in transit from data preparation to the computer.	12. Supplementing the programmed computer checks, payroll audit and control should check the computer output hours against its input log.
	13. Errors detected by programmed computer controls may not be reentered in the system.	13. Payroll audit and control should maintain an error log.

Answer 5

		Weakness	*Recommended Improvement*
a.	1.	Financial secretary exercises too much control over collections.	To extent possible, financial secretary's responsibilities should be confined to record-keeping.
	2.	Finance committee is not exercising its assigned responsibility for collections.	Finance committee should assume a more active supervisory role.
	3.	The auditing function has been assigned to the finance committee, which also has responsibility for the administration of the cash function. Moreover, the finance committee has not performed the auditing function.	An audit committee should be appointed to perform periodic auditing procedures or engage outside auditors.

4. The head usher has sole access to cash during the period of the count. One person should not be left alone with the cash until the amount has been recorded or control established in some other way.

The number of counters should be increased to at least two, and cash should remain under joint surveillance until counted and recorded so that any discrepancy will be brought to attention.

5. The collection is vulnerable to robbery while it is being counted and from the church safe prior to its deposit in the bank.

The collection should be deposited in the bank's night depository immediately after the count. Physical safeguards, such as locking and bolting the door during the period of the count, should be instituted. Vulnerability to robbery will also be reduced by increasing the number of counters.

6. The head usher's count lacks usefulness from a control standpoint because he surrenders custody of both the cash and the record of the count.

The financial secretary should receive a copy of the collection report for posting to the financial records. The head usher should maintain a copy of the report for use by the audit committee.

7. Contributions are not deposited intact. There is no assurance that amounts withheld by the financial secretary for expenditures will be properly accounted for.

Contributions should be deposited intact. If it is considered necessary for the financial secretary to make cash expenditures, he should be provided with a cash working fund. The fund should be replenished by check based upon a properly approved reimbursement request and satisfactory support.

8. Members are asked to draw checks to "cash," thus making the checks completely negotiable and vulnerable to misappropriation.

Members should be asked to make checks payable to the church. At the time of the count, ushers should stamp the church's restrictive endorsement (For Deposit Only) on the back of the check.

9. No mention is made of bonding.

Key employees and members involved in receiving and disbursing cash should be bonded.

10. Written instructions for handling cash collections apparently have not been prepared.

Particularly because much of the work involved in cash collections is performed by unpaid, untrained church members, often on a short term basis, detailed written instructions should be prepared.

b. 1. The envelope system has not been encouraged. Control features which it could provide have been ignored.

The envelope system should be encouraged. Ushers should indicate on the outside of each envelope the amount contributed. Envelope contributions should be reported separately and supported by the empty collection envelopes. Prenumbered envelopes will permit ready identification of the donor by authorized persons without general loss of confidentiality.

2. The church maintains no permanent record of amounts pledged and contributed. These records are needed to (1) provide valid support for tax deductibility, (2) permit better planning for fund drives and (3) provide a basis for direct confirmation of amounts contributed.

A members' contribution record should be prepared by the financial secretary from the pledge cards and collection envelopes.

3. No investigation is made of differences between the amounts pledged and contributed.

All members should be furnished with periodic written advice of the amounts pledged and contributed. If properly handled by the audit committee, this procedure can be combined with direct confirmation of the amount contributed. Not only will control be better, but members more likely will fulfill their pledges.

ANSWERS TO SAMPLE EXAMINATION
BUSINESS LAW

Answer 1

1. a	11. d	21. b	31. d	41. a	51. c
2. c	12. d	22. d	32. d	42. a	52. b
3. c	13. d	23. d	33. c	43. c	53. d
4. a	14. d	24. c	34. c	44. b	54. b
5. a	15. c	25. a	35. a	45. b	55. b
6. c	16. a	26. b	36. b	46. a	56. b
7. c	17. b	27. c	37. c	47. d	57. c
8. d	18. a	28. b	38. c	48. a	58. d
9. c	19. a	29. b	39. a	49. d	59. b
10. a	20. a	30. d	40. b	50. b	60. d

Answer 2

The facts pose the following legal problems.

(1) Is there a valid corporate entity? There are two two separate aspects of this problem. First, the incorporation was irregular. Second, there is a question whether the corporation is a mere sham.

It is possible that the irregularities in the original incorporation procedures would be of sufficient gravity to result in a finding that Otis was neither a corporation *de jure* nor *de facto*. This issue would not arise unless Otis encountered financial difficulty and it became necessary for a party to try to impose personal liability against Parker or others associated with him, such as directors, owners, and managers of Otis. When deciding the problem of *de jure, de facto,* or *no corporation,* the key legal factor that often is not clearly articulated by the courts is the question of deciding on what basis the plaintiff dealt with the corporation. Obviously, from a practical standpoint, all of the irregularities should be remedied by the corporation's attorney. Any existing contracts which were made prior to incorporation should be adopted by or re-executed in the corporate name.

By and large, courts are reluctant to disregard the corporate entity. This is so because the very purpose of incorporation is to permit the avoidance of personal liability. However, Parker has treated the corporation as his alter ego and has ignored its existence; consequently, a court may not respect the corporate entity in view of the fact that Parker himself has not. Certainly

the commingling of funds and near total disregard for the formalities required by law would create problems for the corporation and Mr. Parker.

(2) What is the effect of doing business in the neighboring state without having first qualified to do business in that state?

The volume of business, the frequency of contact, and, most important, the fact that it has established a facility in the neighboring state is conclusive evidence that Otis is doing business in that state. Under the circumstances, Otis was obligated to file the appropriate papers necessary to qualify for doing business in the neighboring state. Failure to do so can have serious legal consequences. Although the law varies from jurisdiction, the corporation may be subject to fines, penalties, or injunction proceedings to prohibit its carrying on business in the state. Furthermore, the corporation may be denied the right of access to the courts of the neighboring state. This has the effect of making its contracts legally unenforceable.

(3) What is the effect of doing business outside the state of incorporation, where the corporate charter is narrowly drafted and does not permit engaging in business outside of that state?

This question has not been adjudicated frequently by the courts in recent times. Current practice is to draft purposes and powers clauses in such a manner that virtually anything can be done at any time and anywhere by the corporation. Consequently, the charter under which Otis is operating, in this fact situation, raises the question of *ultra vires.* Currently the courts by and large take a practical and sensible view of the matter. Although the contracts made in the neighboring state exceed the corporate purposes and powers as stated in the charter they are a *fait accompli;* therefore, they should be recognized as valid except in extraordinary circumstances which would not appear to be present in the facts given. From a practical standpoint, it is obvious that the corporate charter should be amended immediately to permit the corporation to do busness anywhere and everywhere.

Answer 3

Part a.

Yes. The CPA firm is guilty of a common law *deceit,* commonly referred to as "fraud." The CPA firm was associated with fianancial statements that were not in conformity with generally accepted accounting principles because of the failure to disclose the restriction on the cash received, as well as the contingent liability. This association constitutes the commission of an actionable tort (deceit) upon the creditors. The fact there was no privity of contract between the creditors and the accountants is immaterial in relation to an action based on deceit. Where *deceit* is involved, the defense of lack of privity is not available. Deceit is an intentional tort, and those who engage in it must bear the burden of their wrongdoing, even though they may not have intended harm to those affected.

The common law elements of deceit in general are—

1. A false representation of a material fact made by the defendant.
2. Knowledge of belief of falsity, technically described as "scienter."
3. An intent that the plaintiff rely upon the false representation.
4. Justifiable reliance on the false representation.
5. Damage as a result of the reliance.

Clearly, the elements of deceit are present. The only element that needs further elaboration is the "scienter" requirement. About the only defense available to the CPA firm would be that it honestly believed that the government's claim was groundless based upon the president's statement. However, even if this were true, the CPA firm did not have a sufficient basis to express an unqualified opinion that the financial statements were fairly presented. The law includes not only representations made with actual knowledge or belief of falsity but also those made with a reckless disregard for the truth. The fact that the CPA firm did not intend to harm anyone is irrelevant. The CPA firm must be considered liable in light of its training, qualifications, and

responsibility and its duty to those who would read, and might act upon, financial statements with which the firm is associated.

Part b.

1. No. Neither federal nor common law recognizes the validity of the privilege rule insofar as accountants are concerned. Furthermore, even where the privilege rule is applicable, it can only be claimed by the client. Only a limited number of jurisdictions recognize the rule, and these jurisdictions have by statute overridden the common law rule which does not consider such communications to be within the privilege rule. The privilege rule applies principally to the attorney-client and doctor-patient relationships.

2. The Securities Act of 1933 requires a review by the auditor who reported on the financial statements accompanying the registration statement of events in the period between the date of the auditor's report and the date of the public sale of the securities. The auditors must show that they made a reasonable investigation, had a reasonable basis for their belief, and they did believe the financial statements were true as of the time the registration statement became effective. The auditor defendants have the burden of proving that the requisite standard was met. Therefore, unless the auditors can satisfy the foregoing tests, they will be liable.

Answer 4

Part a.

1. The embezzler, Davidson, is liable to whichever party bears the ultimate loss.

2. Fenner Corporation would normally be able to recover $600 per check from Beacon National because it has a real defense (material alteration), which is valid even against a holder in due course. However, Beacon National has a possible defense of contributory negligence by Fenner on the basis that Fenner did not exercise proper safeguards to prevent improper use of the check-imprinting machine. The Uniform Commercial Code provides that any person who by his negligence substantially contributes to a material alteration of the instrument is precluded from asserting the alteration against a holder in due course or against a drawee or other payor who pays the instrument in good faith and in accordance with the reasonable commercial standards of the drawee's or payor's business. In any event, Fenner is still liable to the extent of the original amount of $125 per check.

3.   Normally, Beacon National must credit Fenner's account for the overpayments. It in turn has an action against the parties endorsing the instruments based upon a breach of their warranty that there were no material alterations. However, as discussed above, the possible defense of contributory negligence would be equally applicable here.

4.   Smith, as a holder in due course, has the same rights and liabilities as Beacon National as they are given above.

Part b.

None. The Uniform Commercial Code provides that a retail customer in the ordinary course of business takes free of a security interest created by his seller even though the security interest is perfected and even though the buyer knows of its existence. A buyer in the ordinary course of business is, generally, a person who, in good faith and without knowledge that the sale to him is in violation of the ownership rights or security interest of a third party in the goods, buys goods from someone in the business of selling them.

By duly filing a financing statement, Castle perfects its security interest in then-existing as well as after-acquired inventory. Even though Castle held a perfected security interest in Sill's inventory, the customer who purchased the television set from Sill in the ordinary course of business took the property free of Castle's security interest.

Answer 5

Part a.

1.   The option is not legally binding on Bonanza. The issue is whether the option fails for want of legal consideration. The option involved here must meet the necessary common law requirements to establish a legally enforceable contract. Since land is the subject matter of the option, it is tested under the common law rules as contrasted with the more liberal Uniform Commercial Code rule on options. The main pitfall is the lack of consideration. Despite the facts that the promise was written and was signed by the offeror, and that it recited consideration, and manifested a clear intent that it be irrevocable for 30 days, it is not legally binding. It is not supported by actual consideration and, therefore, fails to meet the requirements necessary to establish a valid contract under common law principles.

Neither the signed written offer, nor the expenditures made by Granville constitute consideration. With respect to the feasibility study, the parties did not bargain for the performance of such acts and expenditures by Granville in exchange for the promise contained in the option. The facts indicate that Bonanza had no knowledge that Granville was incurring the expense of a feasibility study prior to reaching a decision whether to exercise the option.

Although the courts generally are receptive to a formal satisfaction of the consideration requirement by the actual payment of $1.00 or some other bargained for token consideration, they do not accept fictional statements of receipt of consideration. If the option were valid, the acceptance would of course be timely even if made orally on September 15, provided the fact of acceptance could be established. One need not use the same means of communication in order to have a valid acceptance, provided it is received prior to the termination of the offer.

2.   No. Although specific performance generally is not available as a remedy for breach of contract, there is a notable exception with respect to contracts for the sale of real property. Real property is deemed to be unique, and therefore, specific performance usually is available. However, when there has been a subsequent sale to a good faith third-party purchaser, the courts will let the title rest where they find it. Thus, Granville would fail unless the third party had actual or constructive notice of the option granted by Bonanza to Granville. If this option agreement had been recorded, the third party would be deemed to have constructive notice.

3.   Granville would be limited to recovery of the typical contract measure of damages, that is, the difference between the fair market value and the contract price at the date the contract was to be performed. The sale at the higher price to the third party will have strong evidentiary value as to the fair market value. Recovery for the expenditures made it possible but not probable unless these facts were known to the seller and thus was within the contemplation of the parties at the time the contract was made. Such does not appear to be the case. This would also apply to the lost future profits. In addition, the lost future profits are at best speculative and would appear to be unattainable as damages.

Part b.

Unless there is an express prohibition against the assignment of a partner's partnership interest stated in the partnership agreement, it is assignable. This rule applies whether all or part of the partnership interest is assigned. Probably the most common situation in which a partner assigns his partnership interest is in connection with collateralizing a personal loan. Therefore, barring an express prohibition or a clause requiring the consent of the other partners, Richard may assign his interest.

As a result of the above assignment, Richard remains a partner. Although Richard has assigned his partnership interest he still remains a partner and rerains all of the rights, privileges, perquisites, duties, and liabilities he formerly had vis-a-vis the partnership and his fellow partners. The assignee (Smith) has only the right to Richard's share of the profits in the event of a default. He would succeed to Richard's rights, in whole or in part, upon the dissolution and winding up of the partnership or upon its bankruptcy. Smith does not, however, succeed to Richard's right to access to the partnership's books and records.

ANSWERS TO SAMPLE EXAMINATION
ACCOUNTING THEORY

Answer 1

1. a	11. b	21. d	31. c	41. b	51. a
2. b	12. b	22. c	32. d	42. d	52. a
3. c	13. a	23. d	33. b	43. a	53. b
4. b	14. b	24. b	34. a	44. b	54. b
5. b	15. a	25. d	35. d	45. b	55. b
6. c	16. c	26. d	36. b	46. b	56. c
7. c	17. d	27. b	37. b	47. c	57. c
8. d	18. d	28. c	38. d	48. a	58. d
9. c	19. d	29. b	39. b	49. d	59. c
10. b	20. a	30. a	40. a	50. c	60. c

Answer 2

Part a.

1.   The average cost method is based on the assumption that the average costs of the goods in the beginning inventory and the goods purchased during the period should be used for both the inventory and the cost of goods sold.

The FIFO (first-in, first-out) method is based on the assumption that the first goods purchased are the first sold. As a result, the inventory is at the most recent purchase prices, while cost of goods sold is at older purchase prices.

The LIFO (last-in, first-out) method is based on the assumption that the latest goods purchased are the first sold. As a result, the inventory is at the oldest purchase prices, while cost of goods sold is at more recent purchase prices.

2.   In an inflationary economy, LIFO provides a better matching of current costs with current revenue because cost of goods sold is at more recent purchase prices. Net cash inflow is generally increased because taxable income is generally decreased, resulting in payment of lower income taxes.

3.   Where there is evidence that the utility of goods to be disposed of in the ordinary course of business will be less than cost, the difference should be recognized as a loss in the current period, and the inventory should be stated at market value in the financial statements. In accordance with the concept of conservatism, inventory should be valued at the lower of cost or market.

Part b.

a.   1.   a.   Normal cost is the annual accrual-basis pension cost assigned, under the actuarial cost method in use, to each year subsequent to the inception of a pension plan. It represents the service credit currently earned by employees during the current year.

b.   Past service is the pension cost assigned, under the actuarial cost method in use, to years before the inception of a pension plan. It represents the service credits earned by employees before the pension plan was established by the company. The company may choose to recognize these retroactive service credits when determining potential benefits for each employee under the pension plan.

c.   Prior service cost is the pension cost assigned under the actuarial cost method in use, to years prior to the valuation date. For example, if a company amends its existing pension plan by substantially increasing benefits, it may desire granting retroactive service credit to employees for prior services. Prior service cost includes any remaining past service cost associated with those years.

d. A funded (pension) plan is one under which an employer makes periodic payments to a funding agency, which is an independent third party outside of the company. The funding agency, as trustee, accumulates the assets under the plan and pays the benefits as they become due to each recipient. Under a funded plan, the control of the funds rests with the trustee outside of the company.

e. Vested benefits are benefits that are not contingent on the employee's continuance in the service of the employer. In some plans, the payment of the benefits will begin only when the employee reaches the normal retirement date; in other plans, the payment of the benefits will begin when the employee retires (which may be before or after the normal retirement date). The actuarially computed value of vested benefits represents the present value, at the date of determination, of the sum of (1) the benefits expected to become payable to former employees who have retired, or who have terminated service with vested rights, at the date of determination, and (2) the benefits, based on service rendered prior to the date of determination and expected to become payable at future dates to present employees (taking into account the probable time that employees will retire) at the vesting percentages applicable at the date of determination. The determination of vested benefits is not affected by other conditions, such as inadequacy of the pension fund, which may prevent the employee from receiving the vested benefits.

f. Actuarial gains and losses are the effects on actuarially calculated pension costs of deviations between actual experience and the actuarial assumptions used, or changes in actuarial assumptions concerning future events. Actuarial gains and losses may have to be recognized annually to reflect deviations between actual experience and assumptions. They may be recognized periodically (less frequently) to reflect revisions in underlying assumptions. Accounting for such gains and losses generally involves spreading them over the current year and future years or recognizing them on the basis of an average.

g. Interest is the return earned or to be earned on funds invested or to be invested to provide for future pension benefits. Interest, as so designated, includes the return on debt securities, equity securities, real estate, and realized and unrealized gains or losses on fund investments.

2. Pension plans are of sufficient importance to an understanding of financial position and results of operations that the following disclosures should be made in financial statements or their notes:

(a) A statement that such plans exist, identifying or describing the employee groups covered.

(b) A statement of the company's accounting and funding policies.

(c) The provision for pension cost for the period.

(d) The excess, if any, of the actuarially computed value of vested benefits over the total of the pension fund and any statement-of-financial-position pension accruals, less any pension prepayments or deferred charges.

(e) Nature and effect of significant matters affecting comparability for all periods presented, such as changes in accounting methods (actuarial cost method, amortization of past and prior service cost, treatment of actuarial gains and losses, etc.), changes in circumstances (actuarial assumptions, etc.), or adoption or amendment of a plan.

Answer 3

Part a.

a.　1.　When the debt instrument and the option to acquire common stock are inseparable, as in the case of convertible bonds, the entire proceeds of the bond issue should be allocated to the debt and the related premium or discount accounts.

　　　When the debt and the warrants are separable, the proceeds of their sale should be allocated between them. The basis of allocation is their relative fair values. As a practical matter, these relative values are usually determined by reference to the price at which the respective instruments are traded in the open market. Thus, if the debt alone would bring six times as much as would the stock purchase warrants, if sold separately, one-seventh of the total proceeds should be apportioned to the warrants and six-sevenths to the debt securities. That portion of the proceeds assigned to the warrants should be accounted for as paid-in capital. The result may be that the debt is issued at a reduced premium or at a discount.

　　2.　In the case of convertible debt there are two principal reasons why all the proceeds should be ascribed to the debt. First, the option is inseparable from the debt. The investor in such securities has two mutually exclusive choices: He may be a creditor and later receive cash for his security; or, he may give up his right as a creditor and become a stockholder. There is no way to retain one right while selling the other. Second, the valuation of the conversion option presents practical problems. For example, in the absence of separate transferability, no separate market values are established and the only values which could be assigned to each would be subjective.

　　　Separability of the debt and the warrants and the establishment of a market value for each results in an objective basis for allocating proceeds to the two different equities—creditors' and stockholders'—involved.

3.　Arguments have been advanced that accounting for convertible debt should be the same as for debt issued with detachable stock purchase warrants. Convertible debt has features of debt and stockholders' equity, and separate recognition should be given to those characteristics at the time of issuance. Difficulties encountered in separating the relative values of the features are not insurmountable and, in any case, should not result in a solution which ignores the problem. In effect, the company is selling a debt instrument and a call on its stock. Coexistence of the two features in one instrument is no reason why each cannot receive its proper accounting recognition. The practical difficulties of estimation of the relative values may be overcome with reliable professional advice. Allocation is a well recognized accounting technique and could be applied in this case once reliable estimates of the relative values are known. If the convertible feature was added in order to sell the security at an acceptable price, the value of the convertible option is obviously material and recognition is essential. The question of whether or not the purchaser will exercise his option is not relevant to reflecting the separate elements at the time of issuance.

Part b.

1.　There are four basic rights inherent in ownership of common stock. The first right is that common shareholders may participate in the actual management of the corporation through participation and voting at the corporate stockholders meeting. Second, a common shareholder has the right to share in the profits of the corporation through dividends declared by the board of directors (elected by the common shareholders) of the corporation. Third, a common shareholder has a pro rata right to the residual assets of the corporation if it liquidates. Finally, common shareholders have the right to maintain their interest (percent of ownership) in the corporation if additional common shares are issued by the corporation, by being given the opportunity to purchase a proportionate number of shares of the new offering. This last is most commonly referred to as a "preemptive right."

2.   Preferred stock is a form of capital stock that is afforded special privileges not normally afforded common shareholders in return for giving up one or more rights normally conveyed to common shareholders. The most common right given up by preferred shareholders is the right to participate in management (voting rights), and, in return, the corporation grants one or more preferences to the preferred shareholder. The most common preferences granted to preferred shareholders are these:

   a.   Dividends may be paid to common shareholders only after dividends have been paid to preferred shareholders.

   b.   Claim ahead of common shareholders to residual assets (after creditors have been paid) in the case of corporate liquidation.

   c.   Although the board of directors is under no obligation to declare dividends in any particular year, preferred shareholders may be granted a cumulative provision stating that any dividends not paid in a particular year must be paid in subsequent years before common shareholders may be paid any dividend.

   d.   Preferred shareholders may be granted a participation clause that allows them to receive additional dividends beyond their normal dividend if common shareholders receive dividends of greater percentage than preferred shareholders. This participation may be on a one-to-one basis (fully participating); common shareholders may be allowed to exceed the rate paid to preferred shareholders by a defined amount before preferred shareholders begin to participate; or, the participation clause may have a maximum rate of participation to which preferred shareholders are entitled.

   e.   Preferred shareholders may have the right to convert their preferred shares to common shares at a set future price no matter what the current market price of the common stock is.

   f.   Preferred shareholders may also agree to have their stock callable by the corporation at a higher price than when the stock was originally issued. This item is generally coupled with another preference item to make the issue appear attractive to the market.

Answer 4

a.   Deficiencies in the Statement of Earnings and Retained Earnings

Purchase discounts—These should preferably be shown as a reduction of purchases in the cost-of-goods-sold computation. While some accountants treat purchase discounts as financing revenue, most accountants would argue that a company theoretically **cann**ot generate revenue by purchasing goods.

Gain on increased value of investments in real estate—This is an unrealized gain that does not appropriately belong on a corporation's earnings statement.

Gain on sale of treasury stock—This is not part of an earnings statement, but it should be treated as an increase to a paid-in capital account.

Correction of error in last year's statement—This should be treated as a prior-period adjustment; it should be added, net of applicable income tax effect, as an adjustment to the beginning retained earnings.

Gain on sale of fixed asset—Two possible deficiencies are identified. First this type of gain is not an extraordinary item because it does not meet the conditions of being unusual and infrequent; it should be shown among the ordinary items. Second, assuming an item is properly classified as an extraordinary item, it should be shown net of the applicable income tax effect as per requirements of intraperiod tax allocation.

Income tax expense—One can logically assume that there were timing differences during the fiscal year necessitating the use of interperiod tax allocation procedures. Under this condition, the components of income tax expense relating to amounts currently payable and to tax effects of timing differences should be separately disclosed per disclosure requirements of Accounting Principles Board opinions.

Depreciation expense (Note 1)—Oberlin changed its method of depreciation. Such a change should be accounted for as a change in accounting principle requiring the following steps:

        The cumulative effect of the change on the beginning retained earnings should be included in net earnings of the period of the change. This cumulative effect should be shown separately between earnings before extraordinary items and net earnings.

- The effect of adopting the new accounting principle on earnings before extraordinary items and on net earnings (and related per-share amounts) of the period of the change should be disclosed.

Equity method—The investment in Gray should be accounted for under the equity method. Oberlin's earnings should reflect its share of Gray's earnings for the year because the ownership exceeds 20%, per APB Opinion 18.

Earnings per share—These amounts must be shown on the face of the earnings statement. They have been omitted from Oberlin's statement. Because there is a simple capital structure in this situation, only a single series (primary) or earnings-per-share figures are required rather than a series of figures for primary and fully diluted earnings per share.

b. Deficiencies in the Statement of Financial Position

Accounts receivable, net—The allowance for doubtful accounts should be shown either parenthetically or as a contra-asset account for disclosure.

Inventory—the basis for valuation of the inventory needs to be disclosed.

Land and Building, net—Two deficiencies are identified. First, land and building accounts should be shown separately because land is not depreciable. Second, the accumulated depreciation on the building must be disclosed.

Investments in real estate (current value)— Assets are appropriately valued at historical cost with the current value indicated parenthetically or in a footnote if management so desires.

Investment in Gray, Inc.—This should be reported based on the equity method rather than the cost method because the ownership exceeds 20%, per APB Opinion 18.

Goodwill—This should be amortized as an expense each period for financial accounting purposes in accordance with APB Opinion 17.

Discount on bonds payable—This should be a contra-liability account rather than an asset because the discount is a valuation adjustment of the liability.

Stock dividend payable—This should be classified as part of stockholders' equity rather than as a liability because it does not involve a distribution of corporate assets.

Due to Grant, Inc.—This is a possible loss contingency but does not meet the conditions of Statement of Financial Accounting Standards Board No. 5 that requires accrual by a charge to earnings. Therefore the contingency should be disclosed in a footnote, or management may appropriate a portion of retained earnings, as it did. Such appropriation, however, should be included in the stockholders' equity section and not shown as a liability.

Liability under employee pension plan—A footnote should be added disclosing facts about the plan, the funding policies, and the annual provision for pension cost. Apparently such cost is included in the general and administrative expenses on the earnings statement.

Bonds payable (including portion due within one year)—The interest rate and maturity date should be disclosed. The portion due within one year should be reclassified as a current liability so that working capital will not be distorted.

Common stock—The number of shares authorized, issued, and outstanding, and the par (or stated) value should be disclosed.

c. General Comments

Statement of changes in financial position— Oberlin Corporation should also prepare a statement of changes in financial position, including a summary of changes in each element of working capital or cash depending on which approach is more appropriate. Such a statement of changes in financial position is required if the corporation issues an earnings statement and a statement of financial position because it discloses certain information not readily attainable from these other statements.

Supporting schedules—Oberlin could prepare schedules showing the composition of cost of goods sold, selling expenses, and general administrative expenses. The schedules could be attached to the earnings statement for better disclosure.

Accounting policies—A corporation is required to disclose its accounting policies, e.g., inventory method. This is usually done as a footnote.

Answer 5

Part a.

1.   Under direct costing, only variable manufactoring costs are included in inventory; whereas, under absorption costing (the current generally accepted method of costing inventory for external reporting), all manufacturing costs, both variable and fixed, are included in inventory.

2.   Direct costing charges the product with only those manufacturing costs that vary directly with volume. In order to do this, a direct-costing structure must separate variable (product) costs and fixed (period) costs. As a result, a direct-costing structure facilitates calculation of the contribution margin and breakeven point because sales less variable costs equals the contribution margin, and the contribution margin, as a percentage of sales divided into fixed costs, equals the breakeven point.

Part b.

1.   A semivariable cost is a cost that reacts to a change in activity, but not with the direct relationship that a true variable cost exhibits. A semivariable cost is made up of two components: a variable cost and a fixed cost. Therefore (within a relevant range), there is an element of a semivariable cost that does respond in direct proportion to a change in the activity factor, but there is also an element of cost that remains unchanged in relation to the activity factor.

2.   The managerial accountant analyzes a semivariable cost by separating the cost into its variable and fixed components. Three basic methods can be used to separate these components.

The first is the *"scattergraph" method,* by which a graph is drawn with semivarable cost amounts on the vertical *y* axis and activity on the horizonal *x* axis. The accountant then plots various values of the semivariable cost at different activity levels and attempts to draw a straight line through the points that will approximate the trend shown by the greatest number of plotted points. The point at which this line intersects the *y* axis is approximately the fixed-cost element of the semivariable cost. The variable component is determined by subtracting the fixed element from the total cost.

The second method is the *high-low method,* which analyzes the change in the semivariable cost at two different activity levels. Since the only change in the cost is brought about by the variable element of the cost, the difference in amounts of the cost divided by the change in activity level will give the variable cost per unit of change in the activity level. At any given activity level, the variable component of the cost is computed by multiplying the activity level by the variable cost per unit of activity. The fixed component is then computed by subtraction. It must be noted that because the high-low method uses only two data points, it may not yield answers that are as accurate as those derived when a larger number of points are considered as in the other two methods.

The third method of breaking out the variable and fixed components of a semivariable cost is called the *"least-squares" method* or *"simple regression" analysis.* This method analyzes the difference between the mean activity and mean amounts of the total cost as compared to the actual values for activity and amounts and mathematically computes a line drawn through a set of plotted points such that the sum of the squared deviations of each actual plotted point from the point directly above or below it on the regression line is at a minimum. The computation is as follows. For each known value of the total cost, the difference between the actual activity and average activity is squared; the results of this operation are then added together. Simultaneously, for each known value of the total cost, the difference between the actual cost and average cost for all known values is multiplied by the difference between actual activity level and average activity level at that cost; the results of this operation are then added together. Finally, the summed results of the squared activity differences are divided into the summed results of the differences for activity times difference from mean cost to yield the variable factor per unit of activity. The fixed-cost component can be computed by subtraction after computing total variable cost at a given activity level.

The fixed-cost component can also be computed by substituting the variable cost factor and mean total cost and activity factors into the general equation for a straight line; $y = a + bx$. In this equation y equals average total cost, a equals the fixed-cost element, b equals the variable cost factor, and x equals the average activity level.

There must be a high level of correlation between the activity base and the cost for any of the three methods to be reliable. Correlation can be computed mathematically.

Appendix B: Notebook - Notecards

NOTEBOOK ARRANGEMENT

Although Volumes I and II of CPA EXAMINATION REVIEW are so constructed that they may be used independently, most students will find it desirable to work with the corresponding parts of Volumes I and II. Experience has shown that most students, particularly those participating in a program where these volumes are appropriate, and perhaps the primary text, make up a notebook combining the related sections from the two volumes.

We would recommend that you set up one or more two or three ring binders, with tabs for each major topical heading and in turn combine the topical headings in related sections as displayed below.

As you cover each area of study remove the pertinent pages from Volume I at the perforation and transfer them to your notebook. Follow this with the problems and solutions from Volume II for that area. Snip off the top right-hand corner of the pages containing the problems to distinguish them from the pages containing the outlines and study guides.

Suggested Dividers

AUDITING: Audit Ethics, Internal Control, Audit Evidence, Audit Reports, Statistical Sampling, Auditing EDP and SASs.

BUSINESS LAW: Accountant's Legal Liability, Contracts, Sales, Agency, Suretyship, Negotiable Instruments, Secured Transactions, Partnerships, Corporations, Federal Securities Law, Antitrust, Bankruptcy, Employer-Employee Relations, Property, Insurance, and Trusts and Estates.

ACCOUNTING PRACTICE AND THEORY: Miscellaneous, Financial Statements, Accounting Changes, Working Capital, Inventory, Fixed Assets, Tax Allocation, Stockholder Equity, Present Value Applications, Inflation Accounting, Ratio Analysis, Partnerships, Consolidations, ARB/ABP/FASB Pronouncements, Cost Accounting, Quantitative Methods, Governmental and Non-Profit Accounting, and Taxes.

NOTECARDS

Use index cards to record formulas, definitions, etc. which you want to commit to memory. Keep the cards handy for fast reference and for capitalizing on spare time. Following are some suggested notecard items and on the next two pages are actual notecards which have been reproduced.

> Auditing
> > Formula for determining sample size
> > GAAS
>
> Business Law
> > Elements of a contract
> > Acts of bankruptcy
>
> Accounting Practice and Theory
> > Capital lease criteria
> > Corporate tax rate structure
> > Formula for EOQ

Sample Note Cards

Future Amount of Ordinary Annuity

```
0      1      2      3      4      5

     1.00   1.00   1.00   1.00   1.00
                                  ↓
                               →  ?
```

$n = 5$ Payments of Rents
$n-1 = 4$ interest periods

Retail Inventory

	include Bi	exclude Bi
mkup + mkdwn	AVE COST	FIFO COST
mkups only	Conventional AVE L-C-M	FIFO L-C-M

SYD - Depreciation

$$\frac{\text{useful life Remaining}}{\text{sum of Yrs to depr.}} \times \binom{\text{cost-}}{\text{Salvage}}$$

$$\frac{n\,(n+1)}{2}$$

Consolidations

PRIMARY PURPOSE OF CONSOLIDATED F/S IS to PRESENT FOR BENEFIT OF SHAREHOLDERS, CR of PARENT, the ni and B/S of a Parent and' its SuB- "SUBSTANCE OVER FORM."

LIMITATIONS OF CONSOLIDATING —
• SUB INFO NOT DISCLOSED
• DIVERSIFALATION ELEMENTS HIDDEN
• LOOSE INFO AS YOU AGGREGATE

L.T. Contracts - % of Completion

Income Earned to date =

$$\frac{\text{Cost to Date}}{\text{Est. TOTAL Cost}} \times \begin{array}{c}\text{ESTIMATED INCOME}\\ \text{OVER LIFE OF}\\ \text{CONTRACT}\end{array}$$

INCOME EARNED this Year =
(Income earned to Date — Income earned in Previous Years)

Funds

GOVERNMENTAL
• General
• SPECIAL REVENUE
• CAPITAL PROJECTS
• DEBT SERVICE
• SPECIAL ASSESSMENT

PROPRIETARY
• INTERNAL SERVICE
• ENTERPRISE

FUDUCIARY
• TRUST & AGENCY

NONFUND
• GENERAL FIXED ASSET GROUP
• GENERAL LONG TERM DEBT GR.

Prepared by Kevin Williams,
Former student at
Northern Illinois University

Prepared by Margaret Monat,
Student at
Northern Illinois University

SAMPLE NOTE CARDS

DEDUCTIONS FOR ADJUSTED GROSS INCOME

- TRADE/BUSINESS
- RENT/ROYALTY
- ALIMONY
- CAPITAL LOSS/NET OPERATING LOSS
- LTCG (60%)
- EMPLOYEE EXPENSES
- MOVING
- BUSINESS CASUALTY

4 METHODS OF AGENCY

1) BY AGREEMENT (no Consideration Needed)
2) BY LAW
3) BY ESTOPPEL - Actions of "P"
4) RATIFICATION
    need • Agent Rep PRINCIPAL
         • PRINCIPAL EXISTS
         • "P" HAS Knowledge of ALL Material FACTS

NEGOTIABLE INSTRUMENT

- IN WRITING
- SEMI PERMEABLE MOVABLE FORM
- SIGNED BY APPROPRIATE PERSON
- UNCONDITIONAL PROMISE TO PAY SUM CERTAIN IN MONEY
- WORDS OF NEGOTIABILITY
- NO 2nd PROMISE (collateral-ok)
- PAYABLE ON DEMAND OR AT DEFINITE DATE

ASSUMPTIONS OF ECONOMIC ORDER QUANTITY

- Constant Usage
- Price Constant
- No Quantity Discount
- ORDER AND CARRYING COSTS Linear
- ENTIRE QUANTITY RECEIVED AT ONE TIME
- NO LIMIT ON STORAGE SPACE

$$EOQ = \sqrt{\frac{2AD}{C}}$$

A = order
D = DEMAND
C = CARRY

PURPOSE OF STUDY & EVALUATION OF INTERNAL CONTROL

1) TO ESTABLISH A BASIS FOR RELIANCE thereon IN Determining the nature, extent & TIMING OF AUDIT TESTS

2) SECONDARY IS TO PROVIDE SUGGESTIONS CONCERNING IMPROVEMENTS IN I/C

The 2 dimensions →
    Accounting Control
    Administrative "

INFLATION ACCOUNTING

General Price Level - adresses the Question of the standard that should be used to compare diverse Resources

Current Value Accy - addresses the Question of the relationship between the resource and the standard

Prepared by Margaret Monat,
Student at
Northern Illinois University

ACCOUNTING TEXTBOOKS FROM JOHN WILEY AND SONS

Beford, Perry and Wyatt: ADVANCED ACCOUNTING, 4th

Buckley, Buckley and Plank: SEC ACCOUNTING

Burch and Sardinas: COMPUTER CONTROL AND AUDIT

Burch, Strater, and Grudnikski: INFORMATION SYSTEMS: THEORY AND PRACTICE, 2nd

Copeland and Dascher: FINANCIAL ACCOUNTING

Copeland and Dascher: MANAGERIAL ACCOUNTING, 2nd

DeCoster, Ramanathan, and Sundem: ACCOUNTING FOR MANAGERIAL DECISION MAKING, 2nd

DeCoster and Schafer: MANAGEMENT ACCOUNTING: A DECISION EMPHASIS, 3rd

Gleim and Delaney: CPA REVIEW Volume I OUTLINES AND STUDY GUIDE

Gleim and Delaney: CPA REVIEW Volume II PROBLEMS AND SOLUTIONS

Gross and Jablonsky: PRINCIPLES OF ACCOUNTING AND FINANCIAL REPORTING FOR NONPROFIT ORGANIZATIONS

Guy: STATISTICAL SAMPLING IN AUDITING

Haried, Imdieke and Smith: ADVANCED ACCOUNTING, 2nd

Kieso and Weygandt: INTERMEDIATE ACCOUNTING, 3rd

Loeb: ETHICS IN THE ACCOUNTING PROFESSION

McCullers and Schroeder: ACCOUNTING THEORY, 2nd

Mock and Grove: MEASUREMENT, ACCOUNTING, AND ORGANIZATIONAL INFORMATION

Moscove and Simkin: ACCOUNTING INFORMATION SYSTEMS

Ramanathan: MANAGEMENT AND CONTROL IN NONPROFIT ORGANIZATIONS, TEXT AND CASES

Sardinas, Burch and Asebrook: EDP AUDITING: A PRIMER

Stenzel: APPROACHING THE CPA EXAMINATION: A PERSONAL GUIDE TO EXAMINATION PREPARATION

Taylor and Glezen: AUDITING, 2nd

Taylor and Glezen: CASE STUDY IN AUDITING

Wilkinson: ACCOUNTING INFORMATION SYSTEMS